Civic Ideals

The Institution for Social and Policy Studies at Yale University
The Yale ISPS Series

Civic Ideals

Conflicting Visions of Citizenship in U.S. History

Rogers M. Smith

Yale University Press   New Haven and London

Printed in the United States of America
by Book Crafters, Chelsea, Michigan.

Library of Congress Cataloging-in-Publication
Data
Smith, Rogers M., 1953–
Civic ideals : conflicting visions of citizenship in
U.S. history / Rogers M. Smith.
p. cm. (The Yale ISPS Series)
Includes bibliographical references and index.
ISBN 0-300-06989-8 (cloth: alk. paper)
0-300-07877-3 (pbk.: alk. paper)
1. Citizenship—United States—History.
2. Discrimination—Law and legislation—United
States—History. 3. Minorities—Legal status,
laws, etc.—United States—History. 4. United
States—Race relations. I. Title.
KF4700.S63 1997
323.6'0973—dc21 96-54880
CIP

A catalogue record for this book is available
from the British Library.

The paper in this book meets the guidelines
for permanence and durability of the Committee
on Production Guidelines for Book Longevity
of the Council on Library Resources.
10 9 8 7 6 5 4 3 2

For Virginia
in every way

Contents

Acknowledgments

In the long course of working on this project I have accumulated more obligations than I can recount, much less repay. My greatest intellectual debt is to Adolph Reed, Jr., whose searingly honest understanding of race in America informs the analysis throughout. I owe scarcely less to Ian Shapiro, who read multiple drafts with alacrity and acuity and probed the arguments in innumerable discussions. My wife, Mary Summers, came on the scene part way through the project and then contributed immeasurably to its content and style. Stephen Skowronek's many suggestions were extraordinarily useful, and constructively critical commentary from Bruce Ackerman and David Mayhew also compelled me to make many improvements. Charles E. Lindblom convened a memorable dinner in which Ira Katznelson persuaded me to modify my views, if not as much as he wants. Shelley Burtt, Cathy Cohen, Robert Dahl, Martin Gilens, Donald Green, Joseph Hamburger, Victoria Hattam, Robert Lane, David Lumsdaine, David Plotke, George Shulman, Steven Smith, Norma Thompson, Alex Wendt, and many other Yale colleagues and students, past and present, have all usefully discussed chapters or related essays with me. Members of a graduate seminar in 1992 that waded through a dense early version of the manuscript deserve special thanks, as do my co-authors on related writings, Peter Schuck and Michael Barzelay. William Antholis, Fred Bartol, Eileen Bresnahan, Peter Berkowitz, Robert Devigne, Miriam Feldblum, Mark Graber, Rogan Kersh, Kris Kobach, Andrew Koppelman, Kevin O'Leary, Dean Robinson, Laura Scalia, Jeannie Sclafani Rhee, and Barry Shain are former students whose related writings have shaped my thinking, and Shain's reading of seven draft chapters was especially valuable. Comments from discussants and audiences at many conference and seminar presentations of aspects of this project also aided greatly, as did those of anonymous readers and Eric Foner, an exceptionally helpful reader who lifted the veil. Many other colleagues in other Yale departments and at other institutions also greatly merit thanks, especially Benjamin Barber, Joseph Carens,

Nancy Cott, Emily Gill, Robert Johnston, Linda Kerber, James Kloppenberg, Micaela di Leonardo, Stephen Macedo, Suzanne Marilley, Anthony Marx, Eileen McDonagh, Nancy Rosenblum, Alexander Saxton, Marion Smiley, Deborah Klang Smith, Dan Tichenor, John Wallach, Frederick Whelan, Bernard Yack, Iris Young, and Richard Zinman. A full list would overwhelm the patience of my gracious Yale editor, John Covell, who gets thanks, too.

My thesis supervisor, Judith Shklar, was almost as attentive to this project as she was to my dissertation, especially when she began writing her own book, *American Citizenship*. I regard it as my greatest professional achievement that Dita wrote there in her acknowledgments and in a note that I actually changed her mind on some points (whether or not I really did). Our last conversation before her untimely death came when she called to approve what became both the first chapter of this book and a fittingly controversial *American Political Science Review* article. Finally, a long line of hard-working research assistants deserve much gratitude, including Kim Dettelbach, Amy Glickman, Corey Robin, Jill LePore, Mia Levine, Hillary Greene, David Hughes, Keith Whittington, Dean Robinson, Greg Lumelsky, and above all Rogan Kersh. Marilyn Cassella, Pam O'Donnell, and Rita Santoroski provided secretarial assistance. Noreen O'Connor was a superb copyeditor. The Rockefeller Foundation and various internal Yale funds provided financial assistance, including the Social Science Research Fund, the Whitney Griswold Fund, and the Institute of Social Policy Studies Program on Race, Inequality, and Politics.

The early work on this book coincided with a sad period in my personal life. In that time as always, I received wonderful support from my parents, Henry Dale and Betty Smith, my brothers, Dale, Christopher, and Andrew Smith, and their families. Everything that I know to be good in American life and my own life I have always found in these great people. Just as important were my longtime friends Gary Handwerk, Kevin Nelson, and Chas Blythe, along with the ubiquitous Professors Reed and Shapiro. Meeting Mary Summers improved my personal life even more dramatically than it did the book, and the subsequent arrivals of Caroline and Reed have made book-writing harder and all else more enjoyable. But it was their older sister, Virginia Sole-Smith, who most shared the difficult years with me; and as I promised her long ago, this book is dedicated to her. I wish that in all that time the book had become half as terrific as she has always been. She and her spirited siblings can be counted on to assure the world that responsibility for its shortcomings must be assigned not to any of the aforementioned, but solely to their incorrigibly disorderly and fashion-challenged father.

Introduction

Today, Martin Luther King, Jr.'s dream of an integrated nation seems not only remote but undesirable to many black and white Americans. Proposals for immigration restriction abound, and controversies rage over the lines that should be drawn between aliens and citizens. American cities crackle with explosive tensions among Latinos, Korean-Americans, West Indians, Asian Indians, Jews, and many other groups, not just "blacks" and "whites"; and disputes over multiculturalism, hate speech, and so-called femi-Nazis reverberate throughout the land.[1] In these times little justification may be needed for a study of American citizenship laws that pays special attention to issues of race, ethnicity, and gender. The relevance of the central thesis of this book now seems all too plain. In the ensuing pages, I show that through most of U.S. history, lawmakers pervasively and unapologetically structured U.S. citizenship in terms of illiberal and undemocratic racial, ethnic, and gender hierarchies, for reasons rooted in basic, enduring imperatives of political life.

Despite its currency, this work began more than a decade ago as a very different project. The idea came as I was completing a study in which I used changing constitutional doctrines to challenge political scientist Louis Hartz's famous claim in 1955 that American thought has always been dominated by a liberal political ideology resembling the thought of the seventeenth-century English philosopher John Locke. I contended that the Lockean liberalism admittedly visible in early America contained internal problems that had repeatedly driven leaders to graft onto it elements of quite different political outlooks, making a none too satisfying patchwork out of America's constitutional law. I concluded by advancing what I hoped was a more coherent version of American liberal constitutionalism. But as I finished, I grew interested in two more basic challenges to received understandings of the United States as a Lockean liberal society.[2]

One was an historical argument stemming from the works of Bernard Bailyn, Gordon Wood, John Pocock, and others. They claimed that the United States had been shaped by traditions of republicanism that were not reducible to, and in some respects opposed, Lockean liberalism. The other was a normative critique put forth by communitarian political theorists like Michael Sandel and Alasdair MacIntyre. They thought that modern America was indeed dominated by an individualistic liberal philosophy, but they contended that this philosophy was incoherent and unsatisfying, given the socially constituted character of human beings. Sandel and MacIntyre also argued that republican traditions provided better bases for an attractive American public philosophy. Though both these revisionist schools made some exaggerated claims, they raise crucial issues that American liberals like myself have to face.[3]

It occurred to me that these historical and normative arguments could be assessed through a study of American citizenship laws—the statutes and judicial rulings that have defined what American citizenship was and who was eligible to possess it. If the United States was a product of visions of a privatized, atomistic liberal society and a more communitarian, participatory republican one, these different perspectives should surface and clash in legislative and judicial efforts to define legal membership in the American political community. I hoped that patterns of citizenship laws might thus prove to be rough but useful empirical indicators of how liberal or republican American political culture really had been during different periods. I also believed that the history of how Americans had officially defined the meaning of their citizenship would be a good starting point for normative arguments addressing the liberal-communitarian debate. I envisioned a relatively short book offering a broad overview of the patterns visible in major American citizenship statutes and judicial rulings and some normative reflections based on the lessons of past American experience.

This book is not that book. Very quickly I concluded that although many liberal and republican elements were visible, much of the history of America's citizenship laws did not fit with liberalism as Hartz described it or republicanism as Pocock described it. Furthermore, the communitarian features of these laws were not ones that many modern communitarian theorists would embrace. Rather than stressing protection of individual rights for all in liberal fashion, or participation in common civic institutions in republican fashion, American law had long been shot through with forms of second-class citizenship, denying personal liberties and opportunities for political participation to most of the adult population on the basis of race, ethnicity, gender, and even religion. There were elements in liberal and republican thinking, particularly the republican stress on a homogeneous and martial citizenry, that Americans used to justify some of these forms of civic inequality. But many of the restrictions on immigration, naturalization, and equal citizenship seemed to express views of American civic identity that did not feature either individual rights or membership in a republic. They manifested passionate beliefs that America was by rights a white nation, a Protestant nation, a nation in which true Americans were native-born men with Anglo-Saxon ancestors.

Such beliefs had appeared only marginally in the courses and books on American political thought that I had been exposed to; but they were familiar to me nonetheless. A year before the Supreme Court's 1954 decision in *Brown v. Board of Education,* I was born into a white Anglo-Saxon Protestant family in legally segregated Spartanburg, South Carolina, once the home region of John C. Calhoun. I then grew up in Springfield, Illinois, the adult home of Abraham Lincoln. In those years the civil rights movement spurred bitter antagonisms in the South that I frequently visited. Hence painful arguments about the proper racial and religious character of America were a vivid part of my youth. I also knew well that sincere if horribly wrong beliefs in racial and gender inequality and Protestant superiority were common not only among my genteel Southern relatives but also among the pillars of my Northern church and community. Many good people defended inegalitarian principles of social ordering far more stubbornly than any doctrines of universal human rights or republican government. Probably because of this background, the evidence of American citizenship laws soon led me to conclude, against much of my education, that intellectual and political traditions conceiving of America in inegalitarian racial, patriarchal, and religious terms had long been as much a part of American life as the liberal and republican doctrines that scholars stressed.

Those inegalitarian terms encompass some very different ideological systems, to be sure; but in the U.S., beliefs in white Anglo-Saxon Protestant male superiority notoriously tend to cluster together, and I saw at least one element they had in common. Against liberal and democratic republican views describing citizenship as a human creation that ought to rest on the consent of all involved, these positions all assigned political identities—including full citizenship with eligibility for voting rights and the highest political offices—on the basis of such ascribed characteristics as race, gender, and the usually unaltered nationality and religion into which people were born.[4] According to such outlooks, these traits assigned people to places in hereditary hierarchical orders that citizenship laws should reflect. Thus I rested my book, and other early writings drawn from the research for it, on a framework that added what I first called ethnocultural, and then inegalitarian ascriptive traditions of Americanism to the liberal and republican strands that other scholars featured.[5] In place of the common portrait of America as the preeminent liberal democratic republic, with a political culture characterized by conflicts between the beneficiaries of liberal property rights and the democratic masses, I began to work out a more apparently irrational picture. In it, to be sure, political conflicts stemming from tensions inherent in capitalist market institutions and in liberal democratic values abounded. But many Americans also defined their core political identities in terms of their race, gender, religion, ethnicity, and culture. They warred passionately and often successfully against every force and faction that threatened to give the U.S. citizenry a different cast. The reasons for those passions, moreover, lay within the divided heart of American civic identity, in ways that time has altered but never destroyed.

Initially, few other scholars took my alternative framework to heart.[6] Even close colleagues who read the bulk of the book manuscript I had completed after five years expressed deep reservations about my argument. It became clear that I was proposing a more basic reinterpretation of American political culture than I had realized, one that could not be briefly sketched. It needed to be elaborated, argued for, and documented in detail.

Hence, about six years ago I undertook a new phase of research. Taking advantage of the expanded availability of legal sources via electronic services like Lexis-Nexis and Westlaw, I sought with the help of research assistants to examine all the federal statutes and all the federal district, circuit, and Supreme Court decisions from 1798 to 1912 pertaining to fourteen dimensions of U.S. citizenship laws. Those dimensions seemed to me to encompass everything relevant for judging how far American citizenship had been officially defined in accord with Hartzian liberal, Pocockian republican, or my inegalitarian ascriptive Americanist principles.[7] One of those issues—the granting of federal jurisdiction on the basis of the diverse state citizenship of the parties—encompasses virtually all federal lower court decisions in the early part of U.S. history, and others, such as the civic status of African-Americans and women, are quite open-ended. Hence I cannot assert that we have canvassed every relevant case. We have, however, surveyed more than 2,500 in relatively systematic fashion, along with hundreds of statutes and secondary sources. I am therefore confident that this work rests on more comprehensive evidence than any competing view.

I concluded that the evidence relevant to my claims was so massive that I could no longer hope to survey the whole history of American citizenship laws in one volume. There also were good reasons to go from the nation's origins to where the present book ends, with the Progressive Era. Developments in American citizenship laws from Reconstruction through the Progressive years seemed disturbingly parallel to what was happening in the U.S. while I was writing. The egalitarian reform spirit of the civil rights movement and the 1960s gave way to more conservative political and intellectual trends during the 1980s and 1990s, and I thought I saw why. I began arguing in the late 1980s that we should expect new intellectual as well as political defenses of racial, ethnic, and gender inequalities to resurge in our own time in reaction to the liberalizing changes of the 1960s, just as occurred in reaction to Reconstruction during the Gilded Age and Progressive Era. Those claims, which again initially met with skepticism, have been all too abundantly borne out by the appearance in recent years of best-selling books arguing for the intellectual inferiority of blacks and Latinos and the desirability of immigration policies aimed at keeping the U.S. predominantly white.[8] The strong resemblance of these books to prominent turn-of-the-century predecessors made it appropriate to end for now with the emergence of the latter.[9] Thus the current work seeks to provide crucial material for reflection on some of the most pressing civic problems in America's present as well as its past.

But if issues of ascriptive inequality have thus proven far more central to this book than first anticipated, it remains an effort to canvass all the major disputes over U.S. citizenship visible in American law during the years it reviews. Americans have, for example, long struggled over whether state or national citizenship is or should be primary. Many thought that question was settled by the Civil War or the New Deal, but it has resurfaced in recent political and legal debates.[10] These federalism conflicts, like the far less pivotal but often intense debates over denial of national voting rights to citizens in the District of Columbia, have at times been shaped heavily by stances toward racial equality, but they are not reducible to them. Hence I give them and other such citizenship issues separate attention.

Critics of my articles that have preceded this book have argued that my framework assigns too much of the responsibility for the ills of American life to the nation's ascriptive traditions, wrongly exonerating liberal values and institutions from any share in promoting unjust inequalities. It is true that I regard the more egalitarian versions of America's liberal republican traditions as primary contributors to the most inspiring reform eras in U.S. history, even though I stress that liberalizing and democratizing changes have often created the conditions for the resurgence of inegalitarian ideologies and institutions. I also, however, see liberal principles as constitutive of one of the most striking and unjust features of America's civic past: during most of the nineteenth century, federal courts provided assistance to powerful business corporations in myriad ways via the legal fiction that they were citizens for the purposes of federal jurisdiction, even as those same courts often refused even to hear, much less to aid, women and African-American citizens. That story, often embedded in a mass of technical diversity jurisdiction cases, is a dramatic symbol of how American civic life has in a staggering variety of ways been designed to further "liberal" corporate economic interests, usually controlled by white men, rather than the interests and aspirations of all.

To lay the groundwork for these arguments, in the first chapter I critique accounts of American political culture inspired by Louis Hartz and Alexis de Tocqueville, which stress its liberal democratic features at the expense of its inegalitarian ascriptive ones. I advance instead a multiple traditions view of America, supported by a theory of the crafting of civic identities that leads us to expect this sort of complexity. This multiple traditions thesis holds that American political actors have always promoted civic ideologies that blend liberal, democratic republican, and inegalitarian ascriptive elements in various combinations designed to be politically popular. American citizenship laws have always emerged as none too coherent compromises among the distinct mixes of civic conceptions advanced by the more powerful actors in different eras.

My underlying theory of citizenship laws presents them as responses crafted by political elites to meet two basic political imperatives that scholars often slight. First, aspirants to power require a population to lead that imagines itself to be a "people"; and, second, they need a people that imagines itself in ways that make leadership by those aspirants appropriate. These needs drive political leaders to offer civic ideologies, or myths of civic identity, that foster the requisite sense of peoplehood, and to support citizenship laws that express those ideologies symbolically while legally incorporating and empowering the leaders' likely constituents. For these political tasks, liberal and democratic political ideologies offer some great advantages, especially their promises of prosperity and political and personal freedom for all citizens. Most liberal democratic positions are, however, less effective than ascriptive views of civic identity in fostering beliefs that a certain group is a distinctive and especially worthy "people." That is why virtually all successful American political actors have not been pure liberals, democratic republicans, or ascriptive Americanists, but have instead combined politically potent elements of all three views.[11]

In chapters 2 through 12 I examine American citizenship laws from the colonial era through the Progressive years, showing that the patterns visible therein are better accounted for by this multiple traditions analysis than by more standard Tocquevillian accounts. The argument follows a historical institutional approach.[12] The starting point in each chapter is the preexisting array of laws of political membership and the main traditions of political discourse about civic identity that political actors have used to justify or oppose those laws. I then explore how those actors sought to protect or alter various citizenship arrangements in light of changing political conditions, and how they used the political traditions available to them as the raw materials out of which they synthesized distinctive civic ideologies that were likely to attract support and further their causes.

I then discuss the roles that these rival civic ideologies, usually advanced by leaders of major parties but sometimes by other actors like abolitionists and nonpartisan reformers, played in the prominent political conflicts of each era. I note how these conflicts prompted certain leaders to reformulate their civic visions in important ways that often became institutionalized. Finally, I describe the overall pattern in American citizenship laws that emerged from the conflicts of each particular era. These patterns never conform fully to the desires of any particular actors, but they do reflect the balance of power among the system's participants, and they structure the terrain and content of later conflicts.

The book is organized by the periods when a distinct pattern in civic rules prevailed despite ongoing struggles, until those battles reached turning points and inaugurated different basic civic patterns. The divisions conform broadly to the periodization suggested by scholars of realignments in the nation's party system, because leaders of powerful parties usually structure citizenship laws in ways that express their political ideologies and interests. But sometimes significant shifts in the civic vision of the dominant party can occur without its losing power: most notably, the Radical Republicans during Reconstruction worked dramatic transformations in American citizenship laws that contrasted sharply with the policies of the Gilded Age Republicans who followed, even though the Republican party continued to win most national elections all the while.[13]

To establish the arguments that were used to justify various civic measures, I focus especially on judicial decisions, because they present official, systematic efforts to connect citizenship policies with the regime's basic principles. Congressional debates are the secondary focus because they often do the same, but only views that are written into law become legally binding.[14] I have chosen to examine these sources thoroughly rather than to survey a wider variety of evidence more superficially. This choice means that, despite the magnitude of the evidence assembled here, I do not pretend to have captured all the ways Americans have conceived of their citizenship, especially those Americans who have been denied opportunities to become lawmakers or judges. This is admittedly a top-down view of American political life, albeit one that tries to be unusually attentive to how those at the top perceive and respond to pressures from below.

I believe it worthwhile to focus on how American officials have legally defined American citizenship because their actions have literally constituted the American civic community, and their rationales have for that reason expressed politically important elements in American thought. I also believe that it would be seriously misleading to write as if the views of those who were ineligible to hold political office shaped American citizenship laws as much as the views of those who did possess such prerogatives. Large portions of the population were for long stretches of time literally not seen or heard in the halls of power in America. Those exclusions mattered precisely because they severely limited the capacities of large numbers of Americans to shape their collective civic fates through the exercise of potent political agency. It remains true that there is much more to the story of what American identity has meant to millions of people and how it has been shaped than I encompass here; but the history of elite struggles is complex and significant enough to merit detailed consideration.

Although I have sought to write an accessible historical narrative of these periods, the argument also aims to show in suitably social scientific fashion that the evidence of citizenship laws, comprehensively examined, falsifies a set of specific Tocquevillian and Hartzian claims about American political culture and instead is consistent with multiple traditions contentions. Each chapter implicitly treats both modern Tocquevillian and multiple traditions accounts as offering civic ideology as their independent variables and the citizenship laws of that era as their dependent variables.

The logic of the rival Tocquevillian and multiple traditions hypotheses, which I then test against the historical evidence, is as follows. If Tocquevillian accounts are right, the civic ideologies invoked in congressional debates, statutes, and judicial opinions should be variants along a spectrum of liberal democratic outlooks, some more liberal, individualistic, and property-oriented, some more democratic, public-spirited, and community-oriented. Conflicts affecting the dependent variables (citizenship laws) should occur chiefly between those benefiting from liberal rights, especially property rights, and majorities suffering from them. The latter should invoke democratic principles to argue against massive inequalities, without going so far as to challenge the notion of private property altogether. These basic battles—rich liberals versus poorer democrats—should map onto the party system fairly readily, with Federalists, Whigs, and Republicans taking the former position, and Jeffersonian, Jacksonian, and postbellum Democrats the latter. Citizenship laws should move in more democratic directions primarily when the latter parties are in power; but once they so move, the American cultural impulse toward democratic equality should not permit them to be reversed. There should also be conflicts between those benefiting from preliberal institutions, such as slavery, and virtually everyone else; but the defenders of preliberal arrangements will be transparently motivated by self-interest, and they will, sooner or later, lose. After they lose they will have no way to restore legitimacy to anything like their discredited old orders. Hence the trajectory of American citizenship laws should be firmly toward full realization of liberal democratic principles.

In contrast, a multiple traditions approach leads us to expect that the major political parties and actors will offer varying civic conceptions blending liberal, republican, and ascriptive elements in different combinations, and that important conflicts will occur over all these contrasting elements. Jeffersonians, Jacksonians, and postwar Democrats will be parties of not only agrarian democratic republicanism but also white supremacy. Federalists, Whigs, and Republicans will champion not only governmental promotion of economic growth and protection of vested "free labor" property rights, but also Anglo-Saxon Protestant cultural supremacy, advanced by such policies as immigration restrictions and assimilative systems of civic education. Contests over egalitarian, consensual versus inegalitarian, ascriptive arrangements will not be secondary to the conflicts between more democratic and more liberal factions, but sometimes even more important. Liberalizing and democratizing civic reforms will not come steadily and almost automatically, but only when economic, political, and military factors create overwhelming pressures for change. Defenders of ascriptive inegalitarian arrangements will not lack for arguments recognized as intellectually respectable and principled; they will not always lose political struggles; and when they lose they will have opportunities to design new systems of ascriptive inequality recapturing some desired features of older ones, such as overall white supremacy. Indeed, the very success of liberalizing and democratizing reforms is likely to unsettle many, creating constituencies for rebuilding ascriptive inequalities in new forms. The overall pattern will be one of fluctuation between more consensual and egalitarian and more ascriptive and inegalitarian arrangements, with the long-term trends being products of contingent politics more than inexorable cultural necessities.

If readers agree that the evidence overwhelmingly supports these multiple traditions claims, the book's main aim will be achieved. Yet this project originated with concerns about modern America's political direction; and in the last chapter I have felt impelled to draw some normative lessons. I contend that not only explanatory analyses of citizenship laws but also normative arguments about civic identity must begin with the basic political imperatives outlined in the theory of the construction of civic identities advanced here. The starting point should be awareness that political elites must find ways to persuade the people they aspire to govern that they are a "people" if effective governance is to be achieved. The failure of liberal democratic civic ideologies to indicate why any group of human beings should think of themselves as a distinct or special people is a great political liability in this regard. Liberal democratic principles as Tocquevillian scholars have understood them instead challenge many traditional claims supporting such conceptions of peoplehood as irrationally hostile to universal equal human rights. They are often thought to point instead to a cosmopolitan world order in which memberships in particular political communities would have little or no importance.

However appealing such a cosmopolitan vision may be, and it appeals to me, advocates of liberal democratic principles still cannot safely be blind to the fact that for the foreseeable future, politicians proposing a just, democratic regime to govern all the world's people as one are not likely to compete for power successfully against those offering more particularist political visions. The feasibility and benefits of such a world order are at best highly speculative. Not unreasonably, populations who share various traits are far more likely to believe claims that they will fare best by supporting leaders who promise to serve them as a distinct people above all others.

The history recounted here demonstrates how powerful the latter sorts of appeals are, even in a nation with the concededly strong liberal democratic traditions that the U.S. possesses. Hence modern advocates of liberal democracy need to think hard about how these political imperatives of contested state-building can be addressed without ultimately sacrificing key liberal values. Yet contemporary liberal democratic thinkers have failed to say much on these points. The greatest empirically oriented contemporary theorist of liberal democratic regimes, Robert Dahl, argues honestly but not too helpfully that the answers cannot come "from within democratic theory" itself. The greatest normatively oriented contemporary philosopher of liberal democracy, John Rawls, instead inexcusably evades the whole issue by theorizing only in regard to a hypothetical closed society whose members "enter it only by birth and leave it only by death." Such a society could not exist in the modern world, and it would be neither liberal nor democratic in its membership policies if it did.[15] Thus liberal democratic traditions as practiced in the United States and as articulated by the best contemporary thinkers remain in some ways ill-equipped to combat the politically potent illiberal strains in American civic life and in political life generally. In light of the inability of liberal democratic precepts even to affirm why Americans should be Americans, it is not surprising that many U.S. citizens remain unpersuaded that conforming more fully with egalitarian liberal democratic ideals, instead of adhering to other long-held values, is good or right.

My argument, however, is not that egalitarian liberal values must lose politically or that they deserve to lose. Their political and moral attractions are real and great, and heightened awareness of the historical potency of ascriptive Americanist civic ideals only underscores, in my view, the signal contributions of liberal and democratic reforms to American life. Such awareness does, however, help us appreciate how difficult those changes have been, and it can aid us in thinking about how they may be properly maintained and extended in the present and future, if we wish to do so.

Liberal democrats need to find ways to affirm the genuine value that particular political communities have for efforts to realize desirable goals in the world as it is constituted now, but they must do so without denying the dangers of these memberships. The greatest threats come from profound political and psychological tendencies to treat such communities as natural, in ways that seem to legitimate both oppressive internal hierarchies and harsh injustices toward outsiders. Hence all efforts to mythologize nations or peoples as somehow "prepolitical," as families or primordial kinship groups, must be rejected. At the same time, states and nations are too necessary for meeting human needs to be simply denounced as unmitigated evils.

The answer, I suggest, is to recognize political communities as entities that are, from a moral point of view, weightier members of the same species as political parties. As the theory of civic identities proposed here suggests, such communities are ineradicably political human creations, crafted to govern and assist some people more than others. They are capable of performing vital human services, and, indeed, efforts to do without them have thus far been failures. Still, they are likely to behave in unduly partisan ways. In light of the good that they do, we may rightly value them highly and feel great loyalty toward them; but in light of their dangerous tendencies, we should understand them to be imperfect human instruments and not take them as the proper objects of our full trust or ultimate allegiance.

Despite those essential qualifications, liberal democratic positions that conceive of political communities in the ways I propose can, I believe, legitimately capture some of the engaging features of ascriptive Americanism and other myths glorifying allegedly transcendent national identities. U.S. citizens, and people who embrace membership in other political communities, can and should see their citizenships as forms of participation in enormously important collective historical enterprises that in fact do transcend their individual lives in time and space. These are or should be, however, enterprises whose meanings citizens can help determine, even as the character and fate of their political communities in turn shape the meanings possible in their personal lives. Hence people can legitimately believe that their civic memberships represent identities with great, enduring significance that extends beyond themselves, while also seeing those civic identities as genuinely their own, as communities to which they belong and which by rights belong to them.

Yet if American citizens, in particular, are to believe today that their political community should seek to sustain and further the realization of egalitarian liberal democratic values, and if the U.S. is genuinely to do so, more work is needed. Partisans of those values must show persuasively how, under current conditions, concrete liberalizing and democratizing changes can enrich human lives and promote well-founded senses of civic and personal worth. In making that case, less attention should be paid to the philosophical fairness of abstract principles and to the epistemological and conceptual foundations of liberalism. Much more attention should be given to the shared historical experiences of American civic life, to the practical contributions of liberal democratic ideals and institutions to rendering that life more rewarding for most Americans, and to specific policies and institutions that might better realize liberal democratic ideals in ways that would generate actual goods for many more people. And in such advocacy, at times American liberals also must recognize they cannot please everyone and must fight for controversial causes.

That sense of the modern tasks of liberal democratic state-building requires liberal egalitarians in the U.S. and elsewhere to give up conceiving of good governments as bloodless neutral umpires of private activities and preexisting rights. Rather, such states must be thought of as historically shaped collective enterprises created by different groups of people to craft richer and freer lives first for themselves, but ultimately for all, in their special circumstances and to the best of their capacities. National regimes carrying forward those efforts should be seen as deserving of their citizens' loyalties insofar as they do this work better than any feasible alternative, but not farther. This view of liberal democratic polities does not, it must be admitted, describe what the U.S. has always been. It is rather what the U.S. might become, if its citizens choose to make it so.

These normative contentions represent quite different notions of the American state and American civic identity and purpose than those fostered by Tocquevillian accounts of America as the world's preeminent liberal democracy. Admittedly, those standard accounts have at times supported warranted civic pride and admirable reforms in the United States. But too often they have allowed many Americans to feel complacent about their nation's continuing shortcomings, even as they have led others like Louis Hartz to despair of the prospects for meaningful change. I believe that the alternative views advanced here can do a better job of supporting both qualified but genuine senses of civic loyalty and zeal for constructive reforms. I am confident that these positions are, in any case, better informed by the realities of the nation's past than their alternatives have been, and I believe that those realities are the surest guides for reflection on America's present and future. But as the reception of an argument is quite properly among the most democratic of processes, all this is for readers to judge.

1

The Hidden Lessons of American Citizenship Laws

Once, subjectship to the political ruler under whom one was born was believed to be natural—sanctioned by divine will and rationally discoverable natural law. Persons who acquired allegiance to a new ruler were therefore said to be "naturalized." Today, notions that political allegiances and memberships are natural in this sense seem absurd. Political societies are seen as artifices whose human creators are perhaps guided, surely limited, but ultimately not determined in their course by nature. The modern view was influentially announced in the Declaration of Independence, which stated that governments were "instituted among men, deriving their just powers from the consent of the governed," and that they were subject to popular alteration whenever they became destructive of their proper ends. Yet most people still acquire American citizenship, implying allegiance to the United States government, not by their consent but through an accident of birth, as in feudal England. Those who acquire it by consent at a later age are still said to be "naturalized" via the Immigration and Naturalization Service—a term that few find absurd.[1]

It is striking that Americans structure access to their civic identity via terminology and institutions that harken back to political systems their Revolution was meant to overthrow. It is all the more striking that this fact has generally gone unremarked in a country often alleged to be haunted by the question of its own identity. The puzzling survival of the term *naturalization* is, however, only one tip of a huge iceberg of anomalies and contradictions that lurk below the surface of American citizenship laws.

In common parlance, to say that someone is an American citizen often simply means that the person is legally recognized as having American nationality and is eligible to carry a U.S. passport. At times, American courts and executive officials have endorsed that view. But the term *citizenship* has always carried more demanding connotations that courts and other American political leaders have often also endorsed. The word *citizen* derives from the ancient Greek and Roman city-states, and, as Aristotle famously argued, in its strict sense it originally referred only to those men who had some share in the political life of their polis, not to all who lived there.[2] Among adults in these city-states, slaves, resident aliens, and women were not true citizens. The Americans who revolted against England called themselves "citizens" to emphasize that they were no longer subjects of the British crown, and that they were creating modern self-governing republics that recognized the equal rights of man. From early on, those causes led American judges and legislators to proclaim on occasion that all American citizens were equal.

But, in fact, so many Americans through so much of U.S. history have not possessed equal political rights that courts and executive officials have struggled to decide who was truly a citizen. They have responded at various times by legally dividing Americans into a bewildering range of categories, including not just birthright and naturalized citizens and state and U.S. citizens but also nonvoting citizens, "jurisdictional" citizens, "commercial" citizens, citizens subject to incarceration or deportation without due process owing to their race, denizens, U.S. nationals, and even colonial subjects. American citizenship, in short, has always been an intellectually puzzling, legally confused, and politically charged and contested status.

This book stresses the last characteristics. It provides a political explanation for these complexities and contradictions and uses that account to guide reflection on American citizenship's moral significance. I believe that those puzzles cannot be accounted for by the views of American political culture and citizenship that have become conventional in post–World War II America, and I do not think that those views are adequate normative guides. They are, however, so deeply entrenched that it is best to begin by carefully considering their leading expositions to see how and why they go astray.

The Misleading Orthodoxy on American Civic Identity

What does it mean to be an American citizen? A widely quoted passage by historian Philip Gleason expresses the leading answer. Historically, to be an American, "a person did not have to be of any particular national, linguistic, religious, or ethnic background. All he had to do was to commit himself to the political ideology centered on the abstract ideals of liberty, equality, and republicanism. Thus the universalist ideological character of American nationality meant that it was open to anyone who willed to become an American." Gleason quickly adds that "universalism had its limits from the beginning, because it did not include either blacks or Indians, and in time other racial and cultural groups were regarded as falling outside the range of American nationality." Thus there was "a latent predisposition toward an ethnically defined concept of nationality." But this "exclusiveness ran contrary to the logic of the defining principles, and the official commitment to those principles has worked historically to overcome exclusions and to make the practical boundaries of American identity more congruent with its theoretical universalism."[3]

On this view, then, Americans have always officially defined full membership in the American civic community in terms of readiness to embrace egalitarian, liberal, republican political principles. Most people have probably supported those principles in part due to their religious convictions, and, historically, dissenting Protestantism has seemed especially to incline people to embrace liberalism and republicanism. But even so, these political tenets have no specific religious presuppositions and can be shared by people of widely differing faiths. Due to their broad appeal, these precepts have progressively delegitimated and eliminated all the logically inconsistent, illiberal, and undemocratic exclusions that lingered on the margins of American society for a time. This is an account endorsed by prestigious writers and politicians throughout U.S. history, and it remains popular today.[4]

This standard view captures important truths. But a quick overview of American citizenship laws demonstrates that it fails to give due weight to inegalitarian legal provisions that have shaped the participants and the substance of American politics throughout history. The problem is not just that, as many scholars now argue, feudal institutions survived longer in America than these accounts acknowledge. Although that is true, feudalism did not include chattel slavery, race-based immigration and naturalization restrictions, ineligibility of women and the foreign-born for the highest political offices, segregation, or many of the other forms of civic hierarchy I will describe. Hence those hierarchies cannot be merely forms of "belated feudalism."[5] But they have been pervasive indeed: when restrictions on voting rights, naturalization, and immigration are taken into account, it turns out that for over 80 percent of U.S. history, American laws declared most people in the world legally ineligible to become full U.S citizens solely because of their race, original nationality, or gender. For at least two-thirds of American history, the majority of the domestic adult population was also ineligible for full citizenship for the same reasons.[6] Those racial, ethnic, and gender restrictions were blatant, not "latent." For these people, citizenship rules gave no weight to how liberal, republican, or faithful to other American values their political beliefs might be.

Nor is it true that these exclusions were all present at the outset of the nation as vestiges of prerevolutionary institutions, but then were steadily eliminated. American civic history has been far more serpentine, and major liberalizing changes have come more rarely and at far higher costs than many celebratory accounts reveal. Overall, there have been three great eras of democratizing American civic reforms: the Revolution and Confederation years, the Civil War and Reconstruction epoch, and the civil rights era of the 1950s and 1960s. It is a sign of how strong resistance to realizing liberal democratic ideals has been that during all these periods Americans fought great wars against opponents hostile to such ideals, first the British monarchy, then the Southern slavocracy, then the totalitarian regimes of Hitler and Stalin in World War II and the Cold War years. Only when those circumstances made fuller pursuit of egalitarian liberal republican principles politically advantageous—indeed, necessary for national elites—did Americans create state and national democratic republics, free slaves, end Jim Crow, and expand women's rights.[7]

Even then, many of the achievements of those eras proved short-lived. In the ensuing chapters we will see that, for example, many African-Americans were conceded to be U.S. citizens, with voting rights, in states as far south as North Carolina in the 1820s; but most had lost the vote by 1857, when the Supreme Court ruled that none were legally U.S. citizens after all. African-Americans regained citizenship and the franchise by the hundreds of thousands in the 1870s and retained the vote for more than two decades. But most lost their voting rights again by 1905, not to regain them until after 1965. Similarly, women could retain a national citizenship independent of their husbands prior to 1855. But from that point on, foreign women who married Americans were automatically naturalized, and from 1907 until 1931, Congress clarified that even native-born American women could be expatriated by marriage to a racially "inappropriate" foreigner. The independence of the Native American tribes was also more fully acknowledged in 1790 than it would be sixty years later. All persons of European ancestry, moreover, were U.S. citizens if they were born in a U.S. territory up until the Spanish-American War. Thereafter, even European-descended natives of the new "unincorporated" territories of Puerto Rico, the Philippines, and Guam were U.S. nationals but not citizens. The residents of Puerto Rico and Guam remain in some respects second-class citizens today. The U.S. had no racial or ethnic restrictions on immigration until 1882, and it did not adopt a permanent system of national origins quotas in order to preserve the existing ethnic makeup of the American citizenry until 1924. Federal bans on immigrants guilty of "immoral" conduct also originated in the late nineteenth century, and their application to homosexuals appears to be a largely twentieth-century phenomenon. Until the 1920s, southern and eastern Europeans could immigrate and be naturalized without limit. From then until 1965, their numbers were limited explicitly because lawmakers now viewed them, too, as "lower races."

Although such facts are hardly unknown, they have been ignored, minimized, or dismissed in several major interpretations of American civic identity that have massively influenced modern scholarship, especially Alexis de Tocqueville's classic *Democracy in America* (1840), and two books of the American mid-twentieth century that explicitly follow Tocqueville, Gunnar Myrdal's *American Dilemma* and Louis Hartz's *Liberal Tradition in America*.[8] Many of the arguments of these works have become so familiar they will seem like natural truths to most readers; but close scrutiny of the original texts shows them to be deficient in important respects.

All these Tocquevillian accounts falter because they center on relationships among a minority of Americans—white men, largely of northern European ancestry—analyzed in terms of categories derived from the hierarchy of political and economic status such men held in Europe: monarchs and aristocrats, financial and commercial burghers, farmers, industrial and rural laborers, indigents. Because most European observers and most white American men regarded these categories as politically basic, it is understandable that from America's inception they thought that the most striking fact about the new nation was the absence of one specific type of fixed, ascriptive hierarchy. There was no hereditary monarchy or nobility native to British America itself, and the Revolution rejected both the authority of the British king and aristocracy and the creation of any new American substitutes. Those genuinely momentous features of American political life made the United States appear remarkably egalitarian in comparison to Europe.

But the relative egalitarianism that prevailed among white men (at first, moderately propertied white men) was surrounded by an array of fixed, ascriptive hierarchies, all largely unchallenged by the leading American revolutionaries. Men thought themselves naturally suited to rule over women, within both the family and the polity. White northern Europeans thought themselves superior, culturally and probably biologically, to Africans, Native American Indians, and all other races and civilizations. Although religious appeals were used to support every competing position in American politics, as they have been ever since, many British Americans treated religion as an inherited condition and regarded Protestants (or some subset thereof) as created by God to be morally and politically, as well as theologically, superior to Catholics, Jews, Muslims, and others. They also punished homosexual acts as crimes that could result in loss of civic privileges. Taken together, nonwhite, nonmale, non-Christian, nonheterosexual peoples have always comprised the vast majority of the world's population, and they have always added up to far more than a majority of the inhabitants of the territorial

United States as well. Yet their places and roles in American society have never been captured by the categories analysts stress in characterizing American politics. They have instead been "lower races," "savages" and "unassimilables," slaves and servants, aliens and denizens, "unnatural" criminals and second-class citizens, wives and mothers.

These statuses have been generated by ideological and institutional traditions of political identity that steadfastly resist the efforts of Tocquevillian analysts to reduce them to varieties of liberalism or democratic republicanism. In contradiction to liberal democratic dictates, they do not define civic status by consent or by universal rights. Instead, they provide elaborate, principled arguments for giving legal expression to people's ascribed place in various hereditary, inegalitarian cultural and biological orders, valorized as natural, divinely approved, and just. That is why a multiple traditions approach to American political culture is necessary.

More than many of his successors, Tocqueville did ultimately discuss the nonwhite and female populations that surrounded and supported his main American protagonists. His analysis nonetheless remained framed by the absence of a European-style aristocracy in the U.S. He began *Democracy in America* by calling attention to the "immense influence" of one "basic fact" that was the "creative element" from which "each particular fact" and the "whole course" of American society derived: the equality of conditions. This fact mattered because Tocqueville saw a "democratic revolution" occurring in Europe, breaking down the power of nobles and kings. In the U.S., this revolution seemed "almost to have reached its natural limits." Thus, by studying America, Tocqueville could draw lessons for France and Europe.[9]

America was so well advanced in this democratic revolution, Tocqueville argued, because several elements had conspired to produce its egalitarian "point of departure." The vast stretches of land "inhabited only by wandering tribes who had not thought of exploiting" the soil made it possible for Europeans to spread out and make their fortune. In Europe most lands were locked up in large hereditary estates. Settlers came chiefly from England, where they had unusual "acquaintance with notions of rights and principles of true liberty," reinforced in New England especially by "democratic and republican" Protestant beliefs. They also came without any "idea of any superiority of some over others," because few great lords moved to the colonies, and the large landowners who did lacked aristocratic privileges. Instead, a "middle-class and democratic freedom" flourished. This mix of comparatively equal and open economic and social conditions and an ideological legacy conducive to democratic republicanism and personal liberties made America the ideal laboratory to study a society that from the start was free, egalitarian, and democratic in theory and practice.[10]

The influence of Tocqueville's insights on American scholarship was magnified by Myrdal and Hartz, though in ways that compounded his deficiencies. Each stressed one aspect of Tocqueville's account of America's starting point, for different reasons. Myrdal's 1944 study of American race relations was driven by his passionate antipathy toward racial hierarchies. Like many participants in the civil rights movement, Myrdal strove to persuade Americans that those institutions violated their deepest values. Thus in describing American life he emphasized the ideals of Enlightenment "humanistic liberalism." Elaborated by revolutionary leaders to define and justify their cause, these beliefs became, in Myrdal's view, the tenets of the "American Creed" that Americans saw as the "essential meaning" of their struggle for independence. It thus served as the "cement" of the nation, written into the documents comprising "the highest law of the land." This democratic creed proclaimed the moral equality of all individuals and their inalienable rights to freedom, justice, and a fair opportunity. It denounced, Myrdal insisted, "differences made on account of 'race, creed or color.'"[11]

Because Myrdal's subject was the "Negro problem," he knew that Americans' fidelity to such beliefs was questionable. His celebrated explanation for this inconsistency was that the creed represented "valuations preserved on the general plane," which Americans knew to be "morally higher" than their discriminatory values. Those were merely expressions of "interests," "jealousies," "prejudices"— "impulses" known to be "irrational" even by many who harbored them. Americans defended racial discrimination only "in terms of tradition, expediency, or utility." And they often gave up those defenses: this "equalitarian creed" and "national ethos" inspired the reforms that defined the course of American civic development. American conflicts also stemmed from internal tensions between creedal values of equality and liberty; but, with evident approval, Myrdal saw egalitarian values as having largely "triumphed." Refusals to follow egalitarian ideals in racial matters were now, he thought, typical only of "poor and uneducated white" people in "isolated and backward rural" areas of "the deep south." Thus Myrdal offered hope that this inequality, too, would soon be overcome.[12]

If Myrdal's wish to provide a legitimating heritage for racial equality led him to stress Tocqueville's argument that early Americans held egalitarian ideals, Louis Hartz in 1955 had different concerns. He was appalled by the frenzied successes of McCarthyism and by the general tendency of Americans to dismiss socialist critiques of American life. But Hartz believed that those phenomena went deeper than the level of conscious ideas, so he emphasized Tocqueville's account of America's relatively egalitarian and free economic and social conditions. Americans' lack of feudal institutions, classes, and traditions and their lived experiences of "atomistic social freedom" made the U.S. a "liberal society." Hartz viewed the presence of "the liberal idea" in America as important, but he did not think that intellectual awareness of a specific ideological heritage made Americans liberals. Most were "instinctive," even "irrational" Lockeans. Rather, it was chiefly their material conditions that led Americans to favor liberal beliefs in individual rights, "petit-bourgeois" democracy, and Horatio Alger myths of social and economic mobility. More than Myrdal or Tocqueville, Hartz bemoaned the "fixed, dogmatic" character of this liberalism born "of a liberal way of life," seeing it as a tyranny of unanimity that went far beyond mere tyranny of the majority. In particular, the absence of any real sense of class and the widespread regard of middle-class values as natural supported the McCarthyite antisocialist policies in domestic and foreign affairs which Hartz despised.[13]

Hartz saw conflicts in American history, but they were in his view all conflicts within liberal boundaries, between majority rule and individual or minority rights and, specifically, between democracy and capitalist property rights. Slavery (not true feudalism) had also had to be eliminated. But to Hartz these conflicts were never as problematic as the stifling consensus from which they stemmed, "the secret root" of all that was most distinctive and fundamental about America and its history.[14]

Thus Tocqueville, Myrdal, and Hartz differed mildly in their accounts of why American political culture was so liberal democratic, more significantly in their motivations for writing and in their judgments of the culture's desirability. Many analysts have since advanced similar interpretations out of the same range of motivations, thereby reinforcing beliefs that American values have always been as these great writers described. Yet all three wrote during periods when the nation was denying most persons access to full citizenship on racial, ethnic, or gender grounds. Their ability to stress the democratic nature of American values despite these facts is vivid testimony to how their comparative baseline of European class politics led them to minimize other types of ascriptive inequality. But each of them did take some notice of America's exclusionary practices, again in influential ways.

Race, Ethnicity, Gender, and Tocquevillian Analyses

Tocqueville dealt with these topics most perceptively. Despite some misleading passages in his early chapters, he did not claim to have written an account of American political identity in toto. In the last chapter of the first volume of *Democracy in America,* he said that he had finished his main task, "to describe democracy." But he noted that there were "other things in America besides an immense and complete democracy," which were "like tangents to my subject, being American, but not democratic." Those things were the position of the "Indians and the Negroes . . . within" (not outside) "the democratic nation."[15]

Thus Tocqueville distinguished being democratic from being American, though he still let readers believe that the U.S. was democratic, apart from these exceptions. He also did not believe that this racial "aristocracy founded on visible and indelible signs" would ever "vanish." He thought it more likely that the "Indian race" would resist becoming "civilized," so that it was "doomed." Tocqueville dryly underscored the inhumanity of American policies toward the tribes, but he insisted that, whatever those policies might be, as "the Europeans" filled the continent, Indians would "cease to exist."[16]

Tocqueville believed that blacks posed, in contrast, "the most formidable evil threatening" the nation's future. He was not optimistic that they would ever be included in America's democracy, either, but it was not easy to imagine them fading away. Anticipating Myrdal, Tocqueville treated racism as mere prejudice, ignoring the burgeoning scientific racism in Jacksonian America. But he correctly saw racism as prevalent throughout the nation, even though most blacks lived in slavery in the South. That institution was in Tocqueville's view uneconomic, as well as repulsive to Northern Christian and Enlightenment values, so its survival was improbable. Yet should it be eliminated, Tocqueville foresaw only deepening white repugnance toward blacks. Doubting that the "white and black races will ever be brought anywhere to live on a footing of equality," yet dubious of colonization efforts, he bleakly concluded that massive violence between American blacks and whites was "more or less distant but inevitable."[17] Thus Tocqueville did not see nonwhites as members of America's democracy, nor did he think that they would become so. Instead, he anticipated prejudice-driven genocides.

In his first volume, devoted chiefly to U.S. political institutions, Tocqueville said nothing about women and their lack of equal political rights. That omission reinforced the sweeping quality of his initial descriptions of American equality. But he did consider women in what for him was their proper place, his second volume, chiefly concerned with American civil society. There Tocqueville defended their status as an aspect of democratic equality, rather than an exception to it.

He felt compelled to do so, as he argued that "democracy destroys or modifies those various inequalities which are in origin social," including relations such as master-servant and father-son. Tocqueville saw a corollary tendency to make women "more nearly equal to men." He argued, however, that American democracy was not attempting what he presented as the mistake of making men and women "creatures who are, not equal only, but actually similar." Because nature had "created such great differences between the physical and moral constitution of men and women," Americans traced "clearly distinct spheres of action for the two sexes," which both were "required" to keep. To do otherwise, they thought, "degrades" both sexes.[18]

All this allegedly meant many benefits for American women. Men saw them as competent to have major domestic responsibilities. Women were taught to think for themselves, and their husbands respected their judgment. They were also free from a sexual double standard: male seducers, Tocqueville claimed, were as "much dishonored" as their female victims. Women were also protected, and not even those in poor families had to undertake "rough laborer's work" or "hard physical exertion." But men remained the family heads, just as they alone had voting rights and other formal political powers. Tocqueville contended that American women themselves embraced these strictures; or at least "the best of them" did, and "the others keep quiet."[19]

These claims are familiar themes of views of women's proper role as being in the domestic sphere, though Tocqueville's statement of them provided influential reinforcement. And it is true that all societies must take account of the different reproductive roles of women and men, far more clearly than they need give weight to differences in skin color or ethnicity. Tocqueville's benign portrayal of the condition of American women was highly romanticized, and his indications that a social system of separate spheres is the best response to sexual differences are rightly no longer so widely shared. Still, no consensus exists on better answers.[20]

Even so, Tocqueville's arguments plainly did not establish that women were the civic equals of men. In their different ways, women and men could have "equal worth." It may be true that American arrangements were more beneficial to women than European ones. But the law did not treat women either as rulers in their homes or as capable of exercising the core power of self-governing citizens, the franchise. They could not occupy most governmental and professional offices, and even making speeches on political issues was difficult for them. When Tocqueville suggested that these political inequalities, and women's "social inferiority" more broadly, prevented a jumbling of "nature's works," he was endorsing a slightly modified ascriptive hierarchy that denied American women full democratic citizenship.[21]

By frequently writing in unqualified terms about America's supposedly egalitarian conditions, by relegating blacks and Native Americans to the status of tangents in a final chapter, by neglecting the rising intellectual respectability of racism, and by ignoring women entirely while discussing political institutions (and then implying that their unequal domestic status was natural), Tocqueville did much harm. He made it easy for readers to conclude that the dynamics of democracy, sparked by a setting of initial equality, simply were the story of America. The less comprehensive analyses of Myrdal and Hartz intensified all these failings.

Both were thunderingly silent on the subject of women, much less homosexuals, who had become explicit targets of discrimination in American citizenship laws by the times they wrote. The thorough scholarship on race undergirding Myrdal's work, however, led him to undermine gradually many of his opening assertions about what defines American political culture. He first made it seem that only blacks were outside the American Creed, chiefly in the South, and owing to what most knew to be irrational biases. Yet as his work proceeded, readers could discover that through much of U.S. history, right up to the 1940s, many Americans imputed racial inferiority to "lower classes of whites" and "non Anglo-Saxon immigrants" as well as blacks.[22]

Nor were those beliefs merely matters of bigoted ignorance; they were supported by the "long hegemony" of the "biological sciences and medicine, firmly entrenched" in American universities. Indeed, "scientific and popular writings with a strong racialistic bias" had "exploded in a cascade" in the years around World War I, feeding thereafter into immigration restriction. Myrdal contended that "a handful of social and biological scientists" had in the twentieth century "gradually" compelled "informed people," but not the "ordinary man," to give up "some of the most blatant" of racist biological beliefs. Thus, far from being primarily prejudices of uneducated rural Southerners, hierarchical racial theories, as Myrdal showed, have had great prestige through most of American history. He eventually conceded that as "political ideologies go," white supremacy should "not be denied high qualities of structural logic and consistency." And although he insisted that matters were better in the North, he admitted that, as a result of these beliefs, "the North has kept much segregation and discrimination." Far from being an exceptional or marginal phenomenon, moreover, the nation's racial ordering, Myrdal acknowledged, affected virtually all aspects of American life.[23]

Myrdal did offer one answer to how academic doctrines of racial inequality squared with his claim that only liberal and democratic values received "higher" intellectual defenses in America. He contended that the American Creed's very dominance "calls forth" dogmas of racial inequality to legitimate what are at root prejudices. And he insisted that the philosophical bases for such racism were the same Enlightenment outlooks that spawned liberalism. Americans favored scientific accounts of biological differences to explain their hierarchies because these accounts comported with Enlightenment rationalism.[24]

Myrdal was surely right that embracing liberal egalitarian ideals can create pressures to legitimate or transform racial hierarchies—pressures Americans have sometimes met by using liberal arguments for inegalitarian ends. But appeals to modern science are not enough to show that an illiberal doctrine shares the philosophical roots of the American Creed. If so, then Hitler's Germany and Stalin's Russia must also be held to be grounded in the bedrock Enlightenment liberalism that is supposed to make America exceptional. More crucially, it is simply not true that all major defenses of racial inequality in the United States rested on Enlightenment rationalism. American racial justifications also drew on other traditional beliefs that were at least as intellectually influential, a point Myrdal again conceded.[25] Racist readings of the Bible were immensely important. Only slightly less so were doctrines of historical and cultural identity spawned by the romantics' rebellion against Enlightenment views of human nature and reason.[26] If the use of religious and romantic themes to oppose egalitarianism is not illiberal, then writers like Carlyle and Nietzsche should also be placed in the boundless liberal fold.

Unlike Myrdal, Louis Hartz claimed to treat America comprehensively, and thus his failure to discuss women, especially, is even more discreditable. Hartz did, however, address racist and nativist ideologies briefly in *The Liberal Tradition*, and more fully in his 1964 book, *The Founding of New Societies*. His efforts to fit ascriptive outlooks into his liberal framework are in some ways more tortured than Myrdal's, but, again, many followed suit.

In his earlier work, Hartz largely ignored Native Americans, Chinese and Japanese immigrants, and most aspects of racial discrimination. He dealt with race chiefly in terms of defenses for slavery in the antebellum South, and even in this regard he slighted theorists of racial differences. Instead, Hartz stressed the states' rights constitutionalism of John C. Calhoun and the effort to give a paternalistic, feudal defense of slavery advanced by Southern journalist George Fitzhugh in the 1850s. Hartz also exaggerated Fitzhugh's importance, presenting Fitzhugh not only as a "romantic nationalist," which is correct enough, but as the leading expression of romantic nationalism in America. That claim reflects Hartz's effort to minimize those same elements in mainstream Whig thought, where the illiberal role they often played was probably more important than Fitzhugh's writings. Hartz stressed Fitzhugh's romanticism because it offered an "organic" and ascriptively hierarchical view of society that justified slavery without appealing chiefly to racial inequality. Though Fitzhugh made such racial appeals, he also argued that slavery was good in any human society, however ethnically homogeneous. Many other proslavery paternalists, as well as all antifeudal white supremacists, instead stressed the scientific and religious doctrines of inferior races that pervaded antebellum America. By emphasizing Fitzhugh's nonracial arguments, Hartz illegitimately deprecated the significance of overtly racist positions.[27]

Yet Hartz could not ignore scientific racism entirely, and initially he did not flinch from its illiberal character. He conceded that defenders of racism like Alabama physician Josiah Nott forged in the 1840s "one of the most vicious and antiliberal doctrines of modern times," one existing "curiously enough, on a plane that was alien to liberalism and feudalism alike." But Hartz did not pause to explore this curiosity, so unaccounted for by his theory. Instead, he suggested that these "alien" doctrines (pioneered by Thomas Jefferson) were necessary if slaveholders were to limit their feudalism and "keep democracy for the whites." Hartz thought that this desire showed their commitment to democracy, but it provides as much evidence for Southern whites' insistence on preserving racial hierarchy, against the dictates of Hartz's liberal American values. Hartz therefore also tried to write off these ideologies, saying that they resulted only in "confusion" because of their conflicts with Fitzhugh's position. They all were just part of "the madhouse of Southern thought before the Civil War," not of lasting influence. But soon, Hartz had to concede briefly that a "theory of racial supremacy," specifically "Anglo-Saxon superiority," contributed to late nineteenth-century American imperialism and renewed subjugation of blacks. Once more Hartz recognized these outlooks as "basically alien to the national liberal spirit." But he asserted that for this reason they, too, had limited impact, amounting only to "the prejudice of loose elements" amid "the massive and uniform democratic faith" by which a "liberal community . . . lives."[28]

The battle for civil rights in the 1960s, and the scholarship that accompanied it, eventually made it hard for Hartz to dismiss American racist thought so offhandedly. In 1964, he made a different argument. If we "go beneath the surface of the racial attitudes," he maintained, "we will soon encounter" what his liberal society hypothesis insisted must be there: the "familiar figures" of liberal thinkers like "Suarez and Locke." Hartz stated that because their "European ideologies" and "social categories" did not "know race," "battles break out" among the adherents of such ideologies "over their application to race." Nonetheless, those adherents kept "seeking to apply the ideologies," and in America's "liberal fragment" society, the only European ideology left for Americans to apply was liberalism. The problems of justifying racial hierarchies in liberal terms were, Hartz admitted, very great. If blacks were considered human at all, he thought that liberalism demanded that they "receive full equality." Hartz therefore claimed that Americans could oppose black equality only by consigning blacks to the status of "property" or an "inhuman species," not an inferior human species. He admitted that after the Civil War, "the spirit of separatism continued" and the "South won the battle of Reconstruction." But he took refuge in the ways the civil rights movement, almost a century later, was starting to displace that spirit.[29]

Hartz also took notice of Indians for the first time, predictably stressing the (very real) influence of the Lockean argument that they had not mixed their labor with American soil enough to be able to claim it. He again treated the role of racial ideologies with silence. And, overall, Native Americans did not seem important to him. Only the fate of blacks amounted to a "major imperfection that marred the American liberal" society, having been "one of the central conscious preoccupations of our history."[30]

Hartz's mature answer, then, was much like Myrdal's: contrary to what he had said in 1955, American defenses of racial inequality had a liberal philosophical base after all. And on liberal premises, Americans could only justify racial inequalities by denying the humanity of blacks.

Although such compulsions were certainly present, this response is transparently inadequate. It fails first because it cannot explain why, even after the abolition of slavery and constitutional recognition of the humanity of blacks, Americans created new systems of racial inequality affecting not only blacks but all nonwhite peoples and maintained them through much of the twentieth century. Hartz only grudgingly admitted this occurrence, without providing any reasons for it. His failure in that regard reflected the second and deeper failure of his whole analysis. If "European ideologies" such as liberalism did not "know" race, where did the category of race come from that they had to take into account? Why was this "unknown" classification a "central conscious preoccupation" throughout U.S. history? The answer is that the category has been articulated by influential intellectual traditions of racial hierarchy, many inarguably nonliberal. Most originated in Europe but were greatly elaborated at many points in American history in order to justify massive deviations in American citizenship laws from what Hartz claimed to be the defining beliefs of American political culture.

The Tocqueville-Hartz Thesis Today

On this rereading, the works of Tocqueville, Myrdal, and Hartz may seem dated, if still forceful in some respects. Yet much scholarship today perpetuates the misleading features of these views of American political culture, for reasons similar to the ones motivating the original accounts. Some find it convenient to deem America the preeminent liberal democracy so that they can compare aristocracy and democracy, as Tocqueville did. Some feel they must insist that America's core values have always been democratic and egalitarian if they are to legitimate further reforms, as Myrdal did. And many scholars on the left continue to argue, as Hartz did, that America's core problem is a hegemonic liberalism that masks many kinds of exploitation, though now racial and gender inequalities are often stressed, rather than merely capitalist ones.[31]

The scholars who share Tocqueville's preoccupations with what is lost and gained in the transition from European-style aristocracy to democratic egalitarianism often dwell on only part of his richly ambivalent assessment. Some writers contrast allegedly liberal and democratic America to ancient Greece and

Rome and medieval Europe chiefly because they wish to criticize egalitarian tendencies in America. The most publicized such author is the political theorist Allan Bloom, whose views derived heavily from Leo Strauss.[32]

Many more writers, however, have used contrasts with old Europe to highlight what they see as strengths of liberal democratic America's exceptionalism. For example, in 1981 political scientist Samuel Huntington offered a book-length Tocquevillian analysis of American politics that expressed fears about the practicality of living up to liberal democratic ideals, but was, on balance, clearly celebratory. Huntington held that "creedal passions" have moved Americans ever closer to the not fully attainable realization of their principles, and that because of those ideals, any increase in American "power or influence" anywhere in the world generally resulted in "the promotion of liberty and human rights."[33] The leading study of American citizenship laws, by historian James Kettner, is structured in similarly reassuring terms.[34]

The writers who retain Tocquevillian premises out of the same spirit as Gunnar Myrdal are, in contrast, not defenders of the American status quo. They believe, however, that the cause of human equality is best served by reading egalitarian principles as America's true principles, while treating the massive inequalities in American life as products of prejudice, not rival principles. In the early 1990s, for example, political philosopher Michael Walzer repeatedly endorsed Gleason's formulation in appraising the meaning of being American, finding democratic commitments to be the culture's core values and adding that with "severe but episodic exceptions," tolerance has been the American "cultural norm."[35] He reached that conclusion, however, only by setting aside blacks and minimizing women's longtime second-class citizenship, among other omissions. A similar effort to construe the nation's "egalitarian strand" as its most authentic, so that inegalitarian measures represent "hypocrisy," structures the most acclaimed recent constitutional analysis of citizenship, by legal scholar Kenneth Karst.[36]

The many other analysts who sustain Tocquevillian frameworks for Hartzian reasons do not celebrate American liberalism or urge return to older aristocratic virtues, and they doubt that a more egalitarian society can be built by appealing to Americans' "core" values. Instead, they see a hegemonic liberal ideology buttressing an inegalitarian capitalist system as the source of American hostility to socialism and a wide range of other egalitarian movements. For political scientists Ira Katznelson and Walter Dean Burnham, it remains true that the "direction, ideological claims, and relative chances of success" of the politics of class in the United States, and the dynamics of its party conflicts, have their "secret root" in the liberal national character that Hartz discerned.[37] Like-minded scholars, including the cultural analyst Sacvan Bercovitch, add to such arguments a focus on the Protestant strains in America that Hartz neglected. Many other analysts follow J. G. A. Pocock in stressing civic republican strains in American thought, generally portrayed as attractive alternatives to liberal hegemony that were eventually eclipsed. These emendations do not, however, basically alter modern Tocquevillian stories in which liberal democratic principles and practices, with their internal tensions, ultimately dominate American life.[38]

Before and especially after Hartz, other scholars have devoted far more attention to America's vast record of racial, ethnic, and gender inequalities than he did. But perhaps because of the hold Marxism has had on the imagination of modern intellectuals and reformers, explanations of these inegalitarian systems have often been structured in parallel with Hartz's liberal hegemony explanation for the absence of socialism.[39] Scholars frequently deny the claims of liberals like myself that white supremacy and patriarchy are logically inconsistent with consensual liberal democratic principles, so that the links observable in American practice need to be explained in social psychological and political terms. Rather, these inequalities are held to be inherent in the liberal ideas as well as liberal social and economic institutions that are still said to form the core of American life, driving yet masking all forms of exploitation within it.[40]

Derrick Bell's casebook on racism in American law, for example, accepts Myrdal's claim that the American Creed has been violated by white Americans not because of any rival "values and morals" but out of "White Self-Interest." Bell departs from Myrdal's optimism, however, because he accepts "contemporary Marxist accounts" and kindred analyses that argue for the enduring "functional utility of racism within a capitalist economy," despite its violation of American ideals. Hence Bell suggests, with political scientist Jennifer Hochschild, that racial problems reflect a "fundamental problem of reconciling liberalism with democracy," a tension between the self-interested desires of the white democratic majority to preserve their privileges and principled liberal commitments to universal rights.[41] Treating America's problems as a clash of selfishness justified by appeals to democracy versus liberal principles actually minimizes the racism that Bell has been accused of exaggerating. Racism appears only as white self-interest, just as in Hartz, not as one of America's constitutive, fundamental ideological components.[42]

African-American historian Barbara Fields makes this claim about racism explicitly. She denies that racist and sexist ideologies have been serious intellectual and political rivals to liberal principles in America. Instead, they are merely "an inconsistent afterthought" in the American mind, each tacked on to explain the anomalous status of a minority exploited in somewhat distinctive ways within an essentially liberal capitalist system. Yet on her neo-Marxist view, American liberalism and democratic ideals are equally ideological mystifications justifying economic exploitation. Thus it is not clear why we must consider ideologies of racial and sexual hierarchy mere afterthoughts, while liberal democratic ideologies remain basic to American political culture. Again, American laws denied full citizenship on these ascriptive grounds not just to a minority, but to much more than half the American population through most of U.S. history—far longer than they maintained class discriminations, which have also been abundant.[43]

Ironically, a similar Hartzian variation structures many leading works addressing the biggest issue he ignored. A large number of feminists argue that, instead of or in addition to blinding Americans to the illegitimacy of existing class inequalities, liberal hegemony in America has been the root of gender inequalities. Political theorist Carol Pateman has argued most influentially, against other feminists, that liberal capitalism and patriarchy are not merely "intertwined" yet "relatively autonomous" intellectual, economic, and political systems. Instead, she insists that liberal theory has always had a patriarchal structure that is essential to it. She agrees with Tocqueville that the subordinate status of American women has been not only consistent with, but expressive of, liberal democratic principles. Yet Pateman acknowledges that the premise of classical liberal contract theory—that all people are "naturally free and equal"—is potentially "subversive of all authority relations, including conjugal relations." She contends, correctly, that early liberal theorists like John Locke responded by asserting that women were not naturally equal to men.

But, as Pateman also observes, these writers were "extremely vague" on what capacities women lacked that were relevant to moral and political equality. Indeed, they sometimes conceded that women had sufficient capacities to enter contracts with men as equals. Pateman provides undeniable evidence that liberal writers endorsed conventional beliefs in natural sexual inequality; but, far from showing that liberalism logically required those beliefs, her evidence suggests that theorists like Locke did not really reconcile their inherited patriarchal beliefs with implications of their more novel, distinctively liberal arguments which they were not prepared to accept.[44] Hence it makes sense to view liberalism and the patriarchal institutions Americans derived from feudalism, and later recast as forms of the "republican motherhood" or "domestic citizenship" that Tocqueville described, as two intertwined but relatively autonomous systems of ideas and practices that contract theorists and many Americans have often inconsistently endorsed.[45]

The evidence that follows supports this view, first advanced by the feminist scholars that Pateman criticizes. Similarly, as Marxism has receded in its political power and intellectual influence, some analysts have begun to assert that racism, like patriarchy, merits independent status as a "central ideological underpinning of American society" that often conflicts with American liberalism in theory and practice.[46] Indeed, even some Marxian scholars, black and white, have begun to argue that, in the words of philosopher Charles Mills, "the normative moral and political theories, and the juridical rules, which assign moral standing to, and codify the legal status of, the inhabitants of this society, cannot be understood in terms of an abstract liberalism, even a flawed one." They must instead be seen as outcomes of a "peculiar hybrid system," a "white-supremacist liberalism" in which both components are equally constitutive.[47] But many left scholars remained concerned that such a move may exonerate American liberalism, so they cling to more Hartzian formulations like those of Pateman and Bell.[48] We instead need an alternative account that gives full weight to America's pervasive ideologies of ascriptive inequality, as well as to liberalism and democratic republicanism, and explains why each has been centrally constitutive of American life. That is the task of this book.

A Fresh Start: Toward a Theory of Civic Identities

To improve upon Tocquevillian accounts, we must do more than return to the nation's colonial point of departure and observe that it contained ideologies and institutions of ascriptive hierarchy that writers have for various reasons minimized. Because the liberal republican elements in American life that these accounts stress were undoubtedly present, we must also consider whether they were likely to be as corrosive of inequalities as Tocquevillian analysts expect. To suggest why movement toward full democracy might not be quite so inexorable, we need to abandon the rather arbitrary baseline of the European class system for a more basic initial question: How and why do people come to construct civic identities? The answer should tell much about the forms of civic identity that are likely to prove most satisfactory and enduring.[49]

In this section I sketch a theory of how civic identities are created and sustained. It suggests why the politics of citizenship laws are likely to generate sets of rules filled with anomalies, even contradictions: such laws usually result from compromises among rival views of civic identity that are themselves filled with understandable internal tensions. The account also indicates why, despite their elite origins, citizenship provisions reveal much about whole political cultures, while shaping their politics in basic ways. Most important, it suggests why we should expect American citizenship laws, like the laws of most societies, to express ideologies beyond the liberal and democratic traditions whose power Tocquevillian analysts have well explained.

Citizenship laws—laws designating the criteria for membership in a political community and the key prerogatives that constitute membership—are among the most fundamental of political creations. They distribute power, assign status, and define political purposes. They create the most recognized political identity of the individuals they embrace, one displayed on passports scrutinized at every contested border. They also assign negative identities to the "aliens" they fence out. The attention people give to national citizenship reflects the hard-boiled reality that governments are more likely to use their powers to aid those who are their citizens than those who are not. But citizenship defines political identity even more deeply than this crucial signaling of which guns are likely to be arrayed on a person's behalf. Citizenship laws also literally constitute—they create with legal words—a collective civic identity. They proclaim the existence of a political "people" and designate who those persons are as a people, in ways that often become integral to individuals' senses of personal identity as well.

Citizenship laws are so basic that it is easy to overlook them, just as in sports we usually watch the game and take its rules for granted. And politicians, like athletes, are often happy to let those rules stand so they can get on with trying to win. But like the rules defining who gets to be a player, citizenship laws are first and foremost an institutionalized response to one of the most elemental necessities for organizing and conducting an associated enterprise, in this case a political society. Before all else, associations need members. Would-be political leaders need a people to lead, a collection of persons that generally understand themselves and are understood by others as forming one political society. Once a people exists, aspiring leaders then need to convince its membership—by force, logic, or rhetoric—that they will best serve that people's interests and ideals. But this second necessity is greatly shaped by the response to the first: a leader's quest for support is heavily defined by who the members of the leader's people are and what they hope to get out of their political community.[50]

Potential leaders now live in a world with many established peoples and well-defined national boundaries that can at times be taken for granted, as fully as the location of foul territory in a stadium. But here the sports analogy runs out. Games are rarely won by redrawing their constitutive rules while play is under way. Frequently, however, political struggles can be won by altering existing civic boundaries in ways that add or strengthen friends and expel or weaken foes. Hence, contestation over laws defining membership is ongoing in most societies. Sometimes these disputes take place quietly, at the margins of major political conflicts, while most civic rules are left intact because they do not disturb the leading political forces. But at other times, especially when old regimes are being toppled and people are building new ones, battles over membership take center stage, as they have in many parts of the former Soviet bloc.[51] Yet even when they are not venues of great struggles, citizenship laws are essential but potentially incendiary institutions that mirror and shape politics in obvious and subtle ways.

Their importance and volatility stem from the fact that the fundamental task of fostering a "people" is today a difficult challenge in most societies.[52] Almost every state contains many people whose political history, religious or political beliefs, ethnicity, language, or other traits give them reason to decide that their primary political identity and allegiance is to some group other than that defined by the regime governing the territory in which they reside. All modern political boundaries are products of long periods of struggle which have left members of losing sides still living in regimes they can potentially be mobilized to oppose. Even an old nation-state like Great Britain has Irish, Scottish, and Welsh nationalist movements of fluctuating intensity. France has strong traditions of rural localism and conflicts over the "Frenchness" of North African immigrants and their descendants, as well as over the nation's relationship to the European Community. The U.S. has native tribes that have never accepted the national government's claim of sovereignty, black and Chicano nationalists, citizens who believe that their religious memberships outweigh their national allegiance, and many others who at least sometimes do not feel that they are first and foremost Americans. Globally, there may be an indigenous people untouched by the governance of any distant metropol or imperial power, but there are probably none over whom such authority has never been asserted. In a world long shaped by clashing empires and nationalist separatist movements of a sort that are now resurgent, most governments have good reason to fear challenges to their authority over some or all of "their" territories and peoples.

As in all politics, force is one way to meet these challenges, to define who belongs to a people and who does not, especially when a society is first formed but also thereafter. But it is a political truism that few societies can long be kept together, much less effectively governed, by force alone. Most aspirants to power wish to govern people who are genuinely persuaded of these two crucial points: first, that they are one people, and, second, that they are a people well served by following those leaders. Then the tasks of ruling become much simpler.

Thus political leaders need compelling stories to convince their constituents of these things. As the very allegiance of a society's members is at stake, those stories should ideally be so persuasive that the existence of a shared national identity seems to the populace an unshakable truth. Leaders are therefore likely to invoke any and all preexisting senses of common identity they can that will also support their own rule, such as widely shared languages, ancestries, cultural customs, religion, suitable doctrines of "natural" group identity, and histories of oppression (as either conquered or conquerors). Leaders will also point out tangible benefits that people are likely to gain by acting as one society under their governance, such as greater economic resources and growth, heightened military defense against internal and external aggressors, and greater opportunities for members of that society to gain influential political positions.

One crucial further point about the behavior of civic leaders may be harder to accept. As Plato suggested long ago, the stories of civic identity fostered by political elites are virtually always false or at least highly dubious in important respects. To be sure, because these stories are meant to inspire as deep and enduring an allegiance as possible, leaders have an incentive to make them true descriptions of the people's common characteristics and the benefits of embracing a common civic identity. But they have only an incentive, not a categorical imperative; there are powerful countervailing factors. Because no community or leadership is simply natural, and because their members' diverse histories, interests, and perceptions may move many current or desired members of a society to give allegiance to challengers to its incumbent regime, leaders usually foster loyalty by playing as many psychological chords as possible. They worry less about whether their various appeals are true, or whether they fit together logically, than about whether they work politically. They thus simultaneously appeal to lofty rational moralities and thinly veiled greed and lust for power. But most have found irreplaceable the engaging, reassuring, inspiring, often intoxicating charm provided by colorful civic myths.

By *myth* I mean, to cite the *American Heritage Thesaurus,* "a traditional story or tale dealing with ancestors, heroes, supernatural events, etc., that has no proven factual basis but attempts to explain beliefs, practices, or natural phenomena." A *civic myth* is a myth used to explain why persons form a people, usually indicating how a political community originated, who is eligible for membership, who is not and why, and what the community's values and aims are. By invoking these definitions instead of the many other meanings of the term *myth,* I admittedly wish to highlight the unpalatable fact that stories buttressing civic loyalties virtually always contain elements that are not literally true. But these definitions also suggest, correctly, that factual elements may well be present in myths, and especially that they may contain accounts of the meaning of their social and natural worlds that people rightly find convincing. People's interests and ideals may in fact be well served by life in the stable societies that civic myths can support.[53]

Indeed, the reasons for embracing memberships defined in civic myths may seem strong enough not to need fictional embroidery. But as James Madison argued, so long as there is no "nation of philosophers," the "most rational government will not find it a superfluous advantage to have the prejudices of the community on its side." Civic myths inspiring faith that memberships are preordained and blessed can especially foster prejudices that may do more than "enlightened reason" to instill "reverence" for the laws constituting their society.[54] That advantage is not easily foregone.

Why might people find partly fictional civic myths so attractive? A reasonable guess is that most people want to believe that a membership as important as that of their political society is an intrinsically right and good one. It takes no high-powered psychology to observe that people also have considerable capacity to believe what they want, including great improbabilities that are intermingled with undeniable truths. And the leaders who propagate civic myths often merge their longings for power into narratives of meaningful civic membership that include elements that they genuinely value, such as a shared religion, ethnicity, language, history, or political ideology. Thus it should be no surprise that the propagators of civic myths are sometimes their truest believers. Their belief then strengthens their power to persuade others.

These points suggest that civic myths have great, perhaps indispensable value. On reflection they may contain much wisdom, enabling people to live together fruitfully and stably, while prompting them to realize the values expressed in their myths in ways that may enrich the lives of all citizens. Civic myths may be "noble lies." But this salutary role is only a possibility, not an inevitability. Civic myths may also cloak the exploitation of citizens by their leaders, demonize innocent outsiders, and foster invidious inequalities among the members of a regime. They may be ugly, ignoble lies.

And they are often likely to be so, just because a populace's acceptance of a civic myth normally aids the power of some leaders against their domestic and foreign opponents, who all offer competing narratives to justify their causes. In the resulting conflicts, political leaders are strongly tempted to exploit harsh implications of their own civic myths to vilify scapegoats outside the society or rivals within it.

Similarly, once in office, political leaders are likely to strengthen their causes by creating policies and institutions that damage their enemies, including citizenship laws defining membership and distributing powers in biased ways. We should not expect citizenship laws to be constantly rewritten in favor of the incumbents' faction, however, precisely because people's citizenships are established institutions to which most are both tangibly and symbolically attached. Officeholders can ill afford to reconstruct citizenship laws in ways that drive out people who are useful national resources, even if they are not political allies; nor can leaders be cavalier about disrupting widely accepted rules that promote a sense of common identity, even if those rules are otherwise not consistent with their party's interests or ideologies. (We will see that such considerations explain the persistence of birthright citizenship and the term *naturalization* in American law.) And for both tangible and symbolic reasons, a party in power may admit economically and symbolically valuable immigrants even if a lot of them are likely to vote for its opponents. It may also feel compelled to lock out applicants who could be valuable if their entry would undermine doctrines of ethnically or religiously based national identity that the party's leaders have advanced. These sorts of tensions can be eased in a variety of ways, but they must be recurrently confronted.

Citizenship laws thus emerge from a variety of often conflicting political imperatives: to maintain arrangements that support a useful sense of civic identity, to include political friends and exclude foes, to add persons who can help promote the regime's prosperity and power, to reinforce narratives of civic identity that foster allegiance to the regime and its current leaders. If, as in most modern pluralist societies, no group or set of leaders has enough power to have its way on every issue, then citizenship laws will also usually be products of compromises among factions and the always partly false civic myths they favor. It would thus be astonishing if the citizenship laws of even a stable, well-established society were an ideologically unified, internally coherent, and intrinsically plausible whole. They are instead likely to be full of anomalies and to satisfy almost no one completely, even though they have enough support to prevail. They are also likely sites of further contests over membership and civic identity that will frequently manifest some of a political society's most vital political cleavages. And most contestants are likely to deploy civic ideologies that contain "naturalizing" ascriptive elements, though some will feature them far more than others.[55]

These considerations suggest, then, why American citizenship laws should also be expected to display deep inconsistencies. They indicate as well why citizenship laws form a more useful map of a society's political culture than may first appear. They are crafted by elites, but elites acting in relation to pressures—sometimes violent, sometimes economic, sometimes political and ideological—exerted by a wide range of constituent and rival groups inside and outside the country. Such groups are, to be sure, often treated as pawns in the struggles of elite power seekers. But pawns often threaten kings, and sometimes take them.

American Civic Myths

With these general observations in mind, let us turn to the question of the civic ideologies that we are likely to find in America's historical circumstances. Tocquevillian analysts have been right to argue that the absence of a European-style aristocracy, the material circumstances initially limiting gross inequalities among European immigrants, and the usefulness of principles of liberal individual rights and democratic republicanism in America's Revolution all made these traditions central resources for the creation of an American civic community. Many features of liberalism and democratic republicanism have since offered continuing advantages as conceptions of a people's civic identity. Liberal doctrines of individual rights have repeatedly advanced effective claims for personal independence from many repressive structures. They have also supported institutions that provide the rule of law and much domestic tolerance and tranquillity; and they legitimate market systems that generate economic growth. The tremendous appeal of the promise that a liberal society will be a free, peaceful, diverse yet tolerant, and prosperous community should be apparent. Similarly, the conception of society as a democratic republic offers the prospect of political self-governance and of membership in a community of mutually supportive citizens. Again, there are clear attractions in a civic life that is expressive of one's personal dignity, responsive to one's concerns, and shared with sturdy, loyal peers.

Yet whatever their true benefits, even liberalism and republicanism have gained part of their appeal from mythical components. The liberalism of the Declaration of Independence includes the unproved but sanctifying claim that men have individual rights "endowed by their Creator." Both liberal and republican traditions also often invoke stories of social compacts created in a state of nature that represent quasi-religious political creation myths, easily adapted to confer legitimacy on American constitutions. The claim of popular sovereignty—taken to imply that the people as a whole ever do engage or ever have engaged in extensive public deliberation on an egalitarian basis in order to resolve directly any concrete issues of public life—is also a myth or "fiction," as Edmund Morgan has argued.[56] Political decisionmaking is in reality almost always more a matter of elite bargaining than popular deliberation. Insofar as there is such deliberation, most people do not participate in it, those that do differ greatly in their resources, and it rarely determines actual policy outcomes. These features of political life seem unavoidable, and they have characterized the United States throughout its history. Thus even the liberal and republican traditions stressed in standard accounts of American political culture are themselves not simply rationalist political doctrines but also civic myths, much more than those accounts generally acknowledge.

Yet if America was not born equal but instead has had extensive hierarchies justified by illiberal, undemocratic traditions of ascriptive Americanism, we must next ask whether these ideologies and institutions might also have attractions persisting after the founding era. After all, these traditions express what now seem to many to be clear falsehoods, far more than liberalism or republicanism. The answer proposed here is that ideologies of ascriptive Americanism have always done some of the work that civic myths do more effectively than liberalism or democratic republicanism, despite the mythical components that those traditions also possess.

For both liberalism and republicanism, in theory and in practice, place great strains on citizens. Liberal notions of natural rights as expounded in the Declaration of Independence and writings of philosophers like Locke make a prima facie case that all those capable of developing powers of rational self-guidance should be treated as bearers of fairly robust individual rights. Legal systems that automatically subordinate women, blacks, Native Americans, homosexuals, and non-Christians are then presumptively invalid. Even preference for one's countrymen over aliens is suspect if it involves infringements of basic human rights. That is a major reason why the logic of Enlightenment liberalism points away from particular national memberships and toward more inclusive, if not cosmopolitan political arrangements. Democratic republican conceptions of civic identity that stress political participation and community service more easily support devotion to one's country, but they can also have strongly egalitarian implications, suggesting that all ought to possess meaningful civic responsibilities. At a minimum, they militate against the claims of private religious, familial, and cultural groups, as well as personal conscientious choices, to trump duties to contribute to common civic endeavors. But many Americans have instead professed to feel more deeply obliged to such groups than to democratic public life; and they have accordingly wished to maintain white supremacy, to preserve old gender roles, to uphold Protestantism in public life, and in other ways to resist many egalitarian demands in liberal and democratic ideologies. Hence they have been attracted to civic visions that are less threatening than rigorously liberal democratic ones.

Furthermore, the requirements that liberal and democratic republican ideologies set for individuals to gain a secure sense of personal worth are dauntingly high. Liberal morals demand that individuals show themselves to be industrious, rational, and self-reliant, usually via economic productivity. In times of economic distress, especially, many Americans have found it hard to meet those standards; and the workings of markets mean that they will always do so unequally. Democratic republicanism denies the title of "virtuous" to those unwilling or unable to undertake extensive political participation and sacrifices for the public good, despite the pressures of a competitive market economy. Neither doctrine offers much reassurance that even most hardworking individuals will ultimately avoid being eclipsed by their own mortality. Good liberal individuals may be recalled by their families and businesses, a few republican heroes will be celebrated by the republics they helped maintain, but most will soon be lost to human memory.

Frequently, moreover, both philosophical and political proponents of liberal democratic causes have not made much effort to envision and promote alternative arrangements that might cushion the shocks of the quite sweeping changes they have sought. Many reformers called for the end of slavery, equal rights for women, and broader tolerance for all religions largely by decrying the evils of the status quo, not by painting a promising future that could quiet fears. Hence their positions seemed as threatening as advocacy of same-sex marriage appears to many believers in traditional families today.

Finally, and probably most important, in their pure, unalloyed forms, liberal and democratic republican political ideals have offered few reasons why Americans should see themselves as a distinct people, apart from others. In the context of opposition to British monarchy and Southern slavery, to be sure, the causes of personal liberty and anti-aristocratic republicanism could rally support for the U.S. government during the Revolution and Civil War. But the defenders of those causes argued positively for political institutions that they believed could and should be embraced by any people, not especially by Americans. If, as Thomas Paine argued, the cause of America was "the cause of all mankind," then there were good reasons for every country to establish republican governments and to protect inalienable rights; but there was no special reason to be a U.S. citizen rather than a citizen of any other similarly free land.[57] As we shall see, however, not even Paine thought it safe to suggest to Americans that their civic identities were so optional; most U.S. citizens seem to have wished to hear that their peoplehood was more deeply rooted, and of more intrinsic importance, than liberal republican doctrines have ever indicated.

It is thus unsurprising that many Americans have been attracted to ascriptive civic myths assuring them that, regardless of their personal achievements or economic status, their inborn characteristics make them part of a special community, the United States of America, which is, thanks to some combination of nature, history, and God, distinctively and permanently worthy. Those assurances have helped millions of Americans to feel proud and confident about who they are and about their futures, both as individuals and as a national community. Men who have hoped to lead the United States have clearly had an interest in having citizens imbued with such inspiriting patriotism. And, more broadly, people sitting atop the prevailing social arrangements in America have also had obvious reasons to find such claims convincing. But these stories have often helped many in less powerful positions to feel part of a larger, more enduring whole of intrinsic worth that will still flourish after they have perished, so that they will not have lived in vain. And many forms of ascriptive Americanism include religious elements that imply that all who display patriotic devotion will gain eternal life. From the Revolution on, many American preachers have affirmed that brave citizens who sacrificed for their country would surely be rewarded by the divine Providence that had reserved a special mission for the United States.[58]

Because inegalitarian ascriptive Americanist accounts of the nation's civic identity thus can make being American seem natural, providentially favored, and a sign of superior worth in ways that liberal and democratic republican ideologies do not, few American political actors have neglected to invoke some version of this sort of compelling civic myth. Various political parties and factions have certainly mixed liberal, republican, and ascriptive conceptions in quite different ways as they have sought to gain political leverage against their opponents. Almost all political leaders have, however, relied on congenial aspects of all three traditions in order to persuade people to think of themselves as patriotic Americans, and to think of American patriotism in ways that served the leaders' causes.

The basic imperatives of state-building outlined here thus account for why American politics displays clashes not simply between advocates of more liberal and more democratic versions of liberal democracy, along with some battles against unprincipled defenders of pre-liberal arrangements, as in Hartzian accounts. Perhaps less than in some nations, but still pervasively, U.S. history displays struggles between opposing parties and movements that all also build support by endorsing various ascriptive themes. It is true that some major partisan conflicts have nonetheless centered on clashes between liberal property rights and democratic ideologies, as when Populists called for public control of credit in the late nineteenth century. But often the most wrenching clashes have turned on ascriptive ideologies and institutions, as when Republicans opposed black enslavement, when women's groups opposed female disfranchisement, when Great Society Democrats opposed segregation, and when black nationalists today oppose integration. Analysts lose both explanatory and predictive power when they try to view all such disputes as wars between liberalism and democratic republicanism. The story of American civic development is in some ways more disturbing, but also more comprehensible, when our vision encompasses America's illiberal, undemocratic traditions as well.

2

Fierce New World
The Colonial Sources
of American Citizenship

In 1606, King James I of England chartered the Virginia Company, authorizing it to establish the first English settlement in the New World. The same year, Robert Calvin was born in Scotland, under the rule of King James VI of Scotland, who had become James I of England in 1603. James's union of the two thrones raised new questions about the political identity of baby Calvin and of all the king's Scottish and English subjects, just as the settling of Virginia would raise questions about the political identities of the members of that partly old, partly new community.

For the next 170 years, lawmakers and jurists in London would give those questions essentially the same answers. They would follow the lead of the greatest legal mind of his day, Sir Edward Coke, who in 1608 used a controversy over young Robert's inheritance rights to define the political status of all born in the realms of the monarch who sat on the English throne. Despite growing qualms, most educated North American colonists would continue to accept the rules that Coke and his fellow jurists laid down to decide *Calvin's Case* as binding statements of their political identities and duties right up to the eve of the American Revolution. But those rules were from the outset a strange yet murkily compelling mass of legalistic mythmaking, better designed to serve King James and Sir Edward than most of James's subjects, especially the American colonists.

Confronted with a problem endemic in modern state-building—the task of asserting a measure of common governance over otherwise distinct societies—the judges that Coke led crafted a remarkable response.[1] Ironically, they met their new challenge by reemphasizing older feudal conceptions of status and obligation, rejecting the sixteenth-century currents moving western Europe toward more territorially and ethnically defined senses of nationality. Feudal traditions enabled them to appeal beyond national laws to nature and God to insist on unalterable, perpetual allegiance from all those born under the protection of their monarch, whether they were in England, Scotland, or Jamestown.

In later years, the royal judges' handiwork may well have satisfied Robert Calvin, whom they enabled to inherit English lands. But many Virginians and other members of England's North American colonies would eventually come to feel enchained, not empowered, by those rules. To the eve of the Revolution, many colonists remained stirred by the filial image of grateful subjectship that Coke's report of the case painted. Many decided, however, that its precepts worked against their material interests and denied them their due political powers. Perhaps most important, its doctrines failed to recognize, much less honor, what British Americans came to see as their true character as a people. For by then, they had myths of their own.

In this chapter I begin by analyzing the conception of political identity articulated in *Calvin's Case* against the historic backdrop of the construction of the British nation-state. Britain's rise was a key part of the reordering of the world into systems of nation-states that has shaped the development of the United States up to the present. I then survey the experiences of the North American British colonists from 1607 to the verge of revolution, indicating how and why they grew restive about the political identity thus crafted.

This analysis challenges the traditional Tocquevillian views discussed in chapter 1 in two ways. First, instead of picturing colonial Americans as people characterized by considerable cultural homogeneity and relative equality, the account here stresses the racial and ethnic diversity and conflicts within the British American colonies, and the clashes between those colonies and the surrounding tribes and rival Spanish and French colonies. Second, these disputes show that the British colonists' growing unhappiness with English rule reflected more than the admittedly important economic grievances and the frustrations over lack of political representation that conventional accounts stress. The colonists' struggles led them to forge political unity and to defend coercive policies by giving more prominence to religious, cultural, and racial understandings of their identity than Coke had done, and more than their imperial governors wished them to do. These senses of identity became the bases for new doctrines of who Americans were that increasingly pointed to independence.

The Legacy of English Subjectship

The Rise of Nation-States. Though challenges to its predominance abound, no form of political community is more widely favored today than the nation-state, conceived as a relatively large-scale, centralized political system governing a population whose members by and large believe that they form a distinct people, because of language, ethnicity, religion, culture, ideology, propaganda, or some other factor. Most official doctrines of national identity present those identities as ancient, deeply rooted, as natural to people as their grandfathers or their skin color. Yet it is an academic commonplace that these are myths, and that nation-states and nationalism—the claim that each people should be ruled by fellow nationals and in that sense be self-determining—are mostly late modern phenomena.

Relatively few self-governing nation-states emerged in Europe prior to the eighteenth century, including France, Spain, Holland, and, most pertinently, England. Only in the nineteenth century did nationalism become politically central throughout the West. Western nations then built empires that ruled much of the world well into the twentieth century. But with the dismantling of the European empires after World War II, and since the demise of the Soviet Union, attempts to build nation-states have become global. In this modern history the United States holds a special place. As the first major colony of an imperial nation-state to gain independence, America has origins that display with rare clarity vestiges of the feudalism it repudiated, the imperialism that generated it, and the new world of nation-states and mystical nationalisms that followed.[2]

There is much scholarly furor over the question of how the original nation-states of Europe arose, but we must glide quickly over those controversies. Few dispute that medieval Europe exhibited relatively little in the way of clearly nationalist political or legal structures. People were officially bound together instead by hierarchical, overlapping religious and dynastic systems that provided sharply defined roles and duties, often across linguistically and geographically diverse populations. Governing bodies identified both masses and elites in terms of their kinship and vassal relationships and their religious memberships more than nationalities. Marriages and fealty oaths could render persons who were physically distant more a political unit than neighboring nobles who owed allegiance to rival lords. Legally, people were peasants, gentlemen, barons, burghers, laity, or clerics first, and Englishmen, Belgians, or Germans second or third if, at all.[3]

But from roughly A.D. 1200 on, various factors—including intellectual, economic, and political restlessness with the relatively static and repressive medieval Christian world; expansion of overseas trade and increases in popular mobility;

growth in market agriculture and in the geographic range, intensity, and complexity of market interactions generally; and accompanying elite conflicts—all led some rulers to seek more unified and centralized governance in the form of the more absolutist monarchical "old" European nation-states. Many political sociologists analyze these developments in terms of the ascendancy of royal patrimonial authority over pure feudalism. This description captures part of what England's Tudor monarchs did as they vigorously enhanced royal power in the sixteenth century.[4] But the Tudors did not simply ground their claims to govern on images of the king as the father of all fathers, whose rule was sanctioned by myths of natural patriarchy and divine right. They also minimized feudal ties of allegiance in favor of a new sense of English national identity, buttressed by their nationalized Church of England, reinforced by such cultural works as the plays of Shakespeare.

Most famously, in *Henry V*, written in 1599, late in the Tudor era, Shakespeare showed his "patriot king" Henry inspiring men of all ranks to fight for England against the French at Agincourt by promising: "he today who sheds his blood with me / Shall be my brother. Be he ne'er so vile, / This day shall gentle his condition; / And gentlemen in England now abed / Shall think themselves accurs'd they were not here / And hold their manhoods cheap whiles any speaks / That fought with us upon Saint Crispin's day."[5] This passage offers an image of political membership in which men of all conditions can win nationwide honor and the fraternal devotion of their king if they have the "manhood" to war for England against hateful foreigners. Feudal status will matter less than the acclaim garnered by service to crown and country. Thus the flames of national and royal allegiance were fanned by the roars of the crowds around Elizabethan stages.

But when Elizabeth's Stuart cousin James ascended to the English throne in 1603, he found this new English nationalism far less serviceable. He was as hungry for absolute power as any Tudor and would try to be even more lordly toward parliament. But he was, after all, a Scottish king, and few Englishmen thought of him or his countrymen as their brothers. Indeed, he had acceded by right of blood but in violation of a parliamentary statute limiting succession to the (by then generally unpopular) Suffolk line. James soon found, moreover, that parliament was seeking to exploit his relative ignorance of English law to claim powers for itself at the expense of royal departments and courts such as the chancery.[6] It also refused to accept the recommendation of a royal commission that all those born in either Scotland or England should now be viewed as "mutually naturalized in both." Hence the new king needed to assert his unified authority over both England and Scotland, and over parliament. His royal judges similarly wished to assert the power of royal courts through both realms and against parliament's claims to define English law, and the combative Coke had still other fish to fry.

On behalf of his bench, and to some extent for parliament as well, he aimed to assert legal limits to James's claims of absolute power, even as he otherwise assisted the king. *Calvin's Case* was brought to permit the judiciary to address these multiple political dilemmas.[7]

The Case of Robert Calvin. Technically, *Calvin's Case* concerned a dispute over whether young Robert could inherit lands in England as an English subject or whether he was an alien, ineligible to inherit under English law. For a long time that law had remained feudal in having no real conception of the nation and no fixed distinction between Englishmen and others. But with the rise of royal power and incipient English nationalism, by the seventeenth century officials drew sharper legal demarcations between the subjects of the English king and aliens. The crucial contrasts centered on the capacity to possess land, which was reserved to the king's subjects. In theory the king owned the entire realm, and he firmly insisted that anyone with rights to part of it had to bear allegiance to him. The right to possess land was crucial, because in England's agrarian society, land-holding was the literal and symbolic key to virtually all else—wealth, social position, political power.[8] Hence, it was understandable that the law defined the "English" essentially as those persons who possessed or had the right to possess the lands of England, rather than simply the longtime inhabitants of those lands.[9]

To say that the Scot Robert Calvin had such rights, however, would run counter to more popular territorial and ethnic definitions of who was truly English. It would also confer the rights of an Englishman upon a subject governed by the Scottish, not the English parliament; hence the latter's opposition to Calvin's claim. Nonetheless, Coke's much-cited report for the Court of the Exchequer-Chamber supplied the basic answer that James wanted. Calvin did have the same right to inherit English lands as subjects born in England. The ruling moved Scotland and England closer to the political unification that would not be formally complete until the Act of Union created Great Britain with one united parliament in 1707. To defend his king's prerogatives, Coke denigrated both territorial definitions of political identity and the parliamentary law. He also managed, however, to admonish the king that judicially discovered law was beyond even royal control.[10]

For the chief justice, the status of "subjectship" did not depend ultimately on English, Scottish, or any man-made "municipal law." He argued that the "law of nature" must "direct this case." Coke held that law to be "part of the laws of England," but he stressed that it was also "before any judicial or municipal law in the world." It was "immutable and cannot be changed."[11]

On Coke's account, nature dictated personalistic, feudal conceptions of political identity, as matters of relationships of governance and allegiance among higher and lower ranked individuals, lords and vassals. Coke stressed that allegiance went to the person of one's lord, not simply to his office and certainly not to any territorial entity, *not* to "England it self, taking it for the continent thereof." Coke also minimized the importance of the volitional element in these relationships, represented by feudalistic oaths of allegiance. He described such oaths as the source of "legal obedience," part of an "order and form" for ties of subjectship prescribed by "the municipal laws of the realm." But he appeared to regard such legal obedience as simply a means to give formal recognition to the "natural allegiance" of persons, which remained fundamental.[12]

Nature generated this basic, nonconsensual obligation as an expression of a person's divinely assigned place in the natural human hierarchy. Birth into a certain rank under the jurisdiction of a particular monarch was a divine sign of where a person's nature fit him or her to stand. People's allegiance to their monarchs was also natural, because it was natural to be indebted to the one whose power protected them in their helpless infancy and childhood. Allegiance was, then, "an incident inseparable to every subject, for as soon as he is born he oweth by birthright ligeance and obedience to his Sovereign."[13]

Because allegiance was owed for protection, moreover, Coke thought that it went to the sovereign in his natural as well as his political capacity, as a physical person as well as a legal entity. The legal status of sovereign was necessary to provide a natural person with the power and right to afford protection, but it was the natural person, not the legal status, who did the actual protecting. Hence the person became the object of a perpetual obligation. Because James the person, as well as James the king, was the recipient of Robert Calvin's natural allegiance, it did not matter whether Calvin had been born in James's Scottish or English realm. To be sure, as a Scotsman Calvin would be represented to his sovereign through the Scottish, not the English parliament. But he was still a natural-born subject of James; he thus could not be an alien to the community of allegiance James headed. Indeed, he would not have been an alien even if he had been born under James's protection overseas, for again it was protection, not the mere "climate nor the soil," that fixed allegiance. Whether or not Calvin was English, then, he was entitled to inherit in England as a natural subject of its king.[14]

Coke's emphasis on the natural and divine sources of subjectship had a further king-pleasing corollary that Coke underlined repeatedly. As God's will and natural law were perfect, eternal, and immutable, one's natural subjectship was unalterable by anyone short of God Himself.[15] A sovereign might prove hopelessly weak or corrupt and be exiled by his own people or conquered by a stronger lord. A subject might unsuccessfully try to unseat his king, forfeiting his life via treason. He might move to a distant land and swear allegiance to its sovereign, or pledge obedience to a successful usurper of his original monarch's throne in return for the protection that the new sovereign provided. But under all these circumstances, the subject would still retain a valid obligation to the natural person who was his sovereign at birth, regardless of how powerless or distant that person might become or of any new allegiances the subject incurred. And a sovereign always had an (essentially unenforceable) duty to safeguard his subject. Even if the subject were a traitor, he had a right to his king's protection against lawless violence up to the moment when the duly authorized executioner's blade fell.

The manner in which Coke's reasoning appealed beyond English law to universalistic natural law, explicitly deprecating territorial and nationalistic conceptions of allegiance along the way, may seem surprising. As J. G. A. Pocock has argued, Coke was the archetypal common lawyer who thought that English law was "purely English" and all the better for that. Through most of his career Coke also relied on the judiciary's superior knowledge of the "artificial reason" of the law to defend extensive judicial power.[16] The appeal to nature in *Calvin's Case* doubtless expressed genuine faith in a Christian Aristotelian view of the entire cosmic order. Coke, indeed, cited Aristotle while maintaining that the universe was governed by a "moral law, called also the law of nature," made by God and infused into all human hearts at creation.[17]

But however deep his natural law beliefs, Coke's reasoning here also shrewdly served to strengthen rather than limit the power of English judges. The law of nature was, after all, to be defined by judges, as part of English law; and Coke reminded all that no man, not even the king, was wiser than the law the judges announced. The fact that the decision rested on natural law, moreover, rhetorically placed it beyond both parliamentary and royal alteration.[18] And, on the merits, it permitted Coke to reach the results James wanted. The king had to support it.

Coke was not able to reach those results, however, without some uncomfortable anomalies in his theory of subjectship. The most glaring was a fact that Coke mentioned only in passing in *Calvin's Case.* Although each person was born the perpetual subject of some sovereign, presumably in accordance with God's will and natural indebtedness, English law rather impiously permitted aliens to be "naturalized" into full subjectship, with landholding and political rights equal to native-born Englishmen.[19] Such naturalization was logically inconsistent with the deference to divine ordering that justified perpetual allegiance by English-born subjects, but the advantages of some naturalizations were too good to be passed up.

The Tudors had accepted that such naturalizations had to be granted by the sovereign king-in-parliament, although the king could by himself confer denizenship (an intermediate status that ordinarily provided all the rights of subjectship except inheritance and eligibility to sit in parliament). That was an issue on which Coke regularly sided with parliament against royal absolutism. He agreed that the consent of the existing subjects, expressed through their parliamentary representatives, was necessary for an alien to gain full rights of hereditary transmission, as those rights might preclude the current subjects' claims. In the British king's various realms, naturalized subjects were treated by the parliaments that had naturalized them as fully equal to native-born subjects. But this equal status was acknowledged to be a "fiction of law" that gained its legitimacy not from nature but from the consent of the king and the subjects concerned. It followed that there remained a distinction between natural and naturalized subjects: an alien who had been naturalized only by the Scottish parliament was, unlike Calvin, still an alien in England.[20]

In *Calvin's Case,* Coke simply ignored the question of whether it was right to "naturalize" persons who were born subjects of other sovereigns. Later judges followed suit, and they also embraced the other difficulties posed by his reasoning. The fact that allegiance went not only to the natural person of the king but also to the crown he wore at the time of a subject's birth meant that English law could still treat Scottish subjects born before James took the English throne as aliens to England. James had not, after all, worn the crown of England then. On the other hand, the fact that allegiance went not only to the crown but also to the natural person of the king meant that his subjects would still owe him allegiance even if he should be conquered or deposed. They might also, however, have acquired allegiance to his successor. Finally, the fact that a sovereign's protection at birth compelled allegiance meant that a child born in England to alien parents would normally be both a natural subject of the English king, who provided him immediate assistance, and a subject of his parents' sovereign, who formally continued to protect the family while it was abroad.[21] These multiple allegiances clearly could conflict.

In regard to naturalization, that problem might have been avoided if Coke had permitted birthright allegiances to be subsequently ended, at least by mutual consent of sovereign and subject, which might be taken as indicating God's assent. The other sources of conflicting allegiances might have been resolved if Coke had held that allegiance was owed only to the crown, regardless of the head upon which it rested, or if he had argued that allegiance was owed only to the sovereign of one's parents, rather than the ruler of any place in which they happened to be sojourning at the time of one's birth.

Coke's refusal to make such moves was reasonably true to his professed premises: some natural person was actually preserving the peace in the lands where a subject was born, presumably in accordance with God's will, and that circumstance created a duty of subjectship that was an unalterable natural fact. Yet Coke's positions flow even more readily from the assumption that he wished to provide his king with a legal community of allegiance that was as unified, extensive, and enduring as possible, while retaining for royal judges the power to define the relevant law. Coke clearly preferred a legal theory that gave James numerous permanent subjects, albeit some with multiple allegiances, over theories that would deny the king allegiance in various cases. This preference is visible both in Coke's use of natural law to bind all of James's subjects to him fully and forever, heedless of any other allegiances they might acquire, and in the chief justice's tacit acceptance of naturalization, which seems an illicit usurpation of a divine prerogative on his premises. The other approaches noted above would suggest that even those born after James's accession, like Calvin, were subjects only of the Scottish, not the English crown. That result would have hampered the drive to create a united monarchical state. Coke's endorsement of a parliamentary role in naturalization, on the other hand, preserved both a legislative limit to unilateral royal authority and the judiciary's role in defining such limits. At bottom, then, not only the perceived dictates of natural law but also practical concerns of state-building and political power generated the decision in *Calvin's Case*.

The Stuart kings subsequently faced more and more opposition to their policies and their claims to power, so that the seventeenth century became England's "century of revolution." In the course of those struggles the various foes of royal absolutism and champions of representative government sometimes wrote in yet more universalistic terms than Coke, arguing in the manner of John Locke that governments were constrained by principles of universal natural rights and by the terms of an original social contract.[22] But other opponents of Stuart tyranny offered the sorts of nationalistic appeals that neither Coke nor Locke featured. Many relied on a burgeoning myth built from common law and Protestant traditions: the English were a people with a special capacity and destiny for political and religious liberty.

When resisting royal power, common lawyers like Coke frequently asserted that English liberties were inherited unchanged from the ancient constitution of their sturdy Anglo-Saxon ancestors.[23] Protestant divines often claimed that God had chosen the English to uphold true and free religious beliefs against slavish Catholicism. John Milton's *Areopagitica*, attacking royal censorship in 1644, sounded that theme clearly. Milton called the "Lords and Commons of England" to consider "what Nation is whereof ye are," one capable of everything "the highest human capacity can soar to." England was most blessed by the "favour and the love of heav'n," indicated by that fact that it was the "Nation chos'n before any other" to proclaim the Reformation (for which it received insufficient credit). It was God's manner to show Himself "first to his English-men" and to protect their "mansion house of liberty." Milton's later writings reveal that he actually attached little importance to native lands or English nationality; but his linkage of the latter to love of liberty was well calculated to gain support for his cause.[24]

Similarly, though James Harrington's elaborate 1656 defense of republicanism, *Oceana,* did not rely on the myth of restoring ancient Anglo-Saxon liberty as other radicals like the Levellers did, he did not hesitate to suggest that the English were especially capable of liberty and, indeed, had a divine mission to carry the cause of political freedom forward. Later in the seventeenth century and throughout the eighteenth, neo-Harringtonians would blend the common lawyers' claims for the antiquity of English liberties with Protestant assertions of God's favor and Harrington's depiction of a free commonwealth, claiming that the ancient Anglo-Saxon constitution had actually been a kind of republic. Hence affinities for political liberty came with English blood due to nature, history, and divine providence.[25]

Those more ethnic, religious, and cultural conceptions of English identity would become leading ingredients in American politics, along with the Enlightenment liberalism of Locke and the civic republicanism of Harrington. But despite the success of the Glorious Revolution of 1688 in strengthening parliamentary power and religious toleration, and despite the subsequent role of wars with Catholic powers in strengthening a sense of common Protestant British identity, none of these views had much impact on the legal doctrines of subjectship announced by Coke. Throughout the seventeenth and eighteenth centuries, in British courts political allegiance was still largely not a matter of choice or contract, not a matter of positive law, not a matter of territorial, ethnic, or national identifications, and not something subjects of the English king could abandon. Though in the eighteenth century Catholics were subjected to a range of legal discriminations in political rights and educational and economic opportunities, reflecting a sense that they were "potential traitors, as un-British," those born under British protection were subjects owing perpetual allegiance nonetheless.[26] These Cokean doctrines continued on the whole to work well for imperial authorities in London, and most American colonists strongly affirmed their royal allegiances at least through the mid-eighteenth century. Yet from the 1760s on, many circumstances led them to think that their political identities should involve choice, positive law, territoriality, ethnicity, and, ultimately, independent nationality.

The Colonial Pattern: Contested "Wilderness"

The rulers of the first European nation-states built them in part by uniting their countrymen in pursuit of profitable overseas ventures. That aim meant that the colonies they planted in the New World were supposed to benefit their homelands, whatever else they might do. Many accounts of the British American colonies stress how over time colonists felt hampered by their increasing subjection to trade regulations and taxes designed to advance the domestic and foreign policy goals of the imperial authorities in London, at the cost of colonial self-sufficiency and growth. The more ambitious among the colonial elites also came to feel frustrated because they had chances to rise to leadership only in colonial government, not the British parliament. They longed for greater opportunities to govern themselves. But more recent scholarship stresses that the British Americans also had other concerns that mounted through the colonial era. For despite what they often told themselves, they were not cohesive communities arriving in virgin wilderness to advance religion, civilization, and their own prosperity.

That image must be drastically altered by recognizing that from the very start, British Americans lived on lands that were temptingly expansive but always intensely contested, especially in the middle colonies. The New World was a further arena of struggle among the great powers of Europe, especially Spain and France, as well as Britain. It was also a populated continent, with cultivated fields and well-traveled forests that supported a multitude of native tribes. The British colonists then complicated things further. They sought to support themselves and produce for the home market by importing large numbers of European indentured servants and enslaved Africans. All those circumstances, along with growing resentments against their imperial governors, spawned conflicts that impelled colonial elites to craft senses of common identity incorporating religious, ethnic, and racial components that went beyond and eventually against their identity as English subjects. These "proto-nationalist" conceptions, to use Eric Hobsbawm's term, would only be refined into particular versions of American civic identity during the revolutionary struggle.[27] But the tensions to which they responded were already evident in many of the less-discussed grievances in the Declaration of Independence. Seen through the lenses of the politics of state-building, those complaints reveal the colonists' intense desires to gain more power to define who would and would not be Americans.

The disgruntled colonists' nation-building efforts were aided by the spread of commercial printing in market systems. The resulting popular gazettes and pamphlets helped create, in Benedict Anderson's phrase, a sense of "imagined community" among fellow English speakers and readers who shared political and economic interests, as British colonists throughout North America did. Though London tried to direct both trade and communication back through it, the colonists soon became aware that the very specialization among the colonies that made them dependent on the home market might also be a basis for economic interdependency and political cooperation.[28]

The fact that they shared interests defined by their common colonial status and communicated them in a language they shared with their imperial rulers also meant, however, that the colonists continued to define their communities geographically and culturally in terms derived heavily from Britain. The notion that they possessed a distinct national identity emerged more slowly and was expressed less prominently than their economic and representational grievances. Nonetheless, it arose from some of their most intense fears and ambitions and most passionate dissatisfactions with British rule.[29] Many of those issues centered on citizenship questions, on who would be full members of the colonial communities and who would instead be subjugated, expelled, or killed.

To see what the task of constructing an American national identity entailed requires a clear sense of just how much diversity there always was in the North America of which the English colonists were an anxious but aggressive part. When the Virginia Company established Jamestown in 1607, they entered a half-continent inhabited by a population whose size is a matter of intense scholarly debate. But whatever the precise numbers, there were many well-established, agriculturally productive, and politically sophisticated native communities, though most were struggling to overcome the devastating diseases brought by earlier European arrivals.[30] The Native Americans were broadly divided into three cultural groups containing numerous tribes—the Algonquians, including the Penobscot, Wampanoag, Pequot, and Narragansett in New England and the Delaware and Powhatan Confederacy farther south; the confederated Iroquois nations—the Cayuga, Mohawk, Oneida, Onondaga, and Seneca tribes—in modern-day New York and Pennsylvania, to which the Tuscarora were allied after 1720, and to which the Cherokees of the South were related; and the other Southeast tribes—Muskhogeans, Apalachees, Chickasaws, Choctaws, Creeks, Natchez, and Seminoles. Most pursued semisedentary ways of life that included skilled farming and crafts as well as hunting and fishing.

Thereafter North America rapidly received other, predominantly English settlers, reaching thirteen British colonies by 1732.[31] The British settlements also contained, however, immigrants from many other European nations. The Dutch West India Company founded New Netherland in 1623, giving it up to the English who rechristened it New-York in 1664, but not until it had accepted a kaleidoscope of newcomers, including Danes, Norwegians, and Dutch Jews leaving Brazil after the Portuguese seized it in 1652. A Swedish joint-stock company initiated Delaware in 1638, though it succumbed to the Dutch in 1655 and then was ceded to England. From early on, many German and French as well as Scottish and Irish immigrants came into all the English colonies as indentured servants, a class that comprised more than half the European immigrants to the colonies south of New England prior to the Revolution.

Waves of religious and political refugees also arrived: French Huguenots and German Mennonites, as well as English, Irish, and Welsh Quakers in the 1680s; German Protestants from the Palatinate and Swiss Mennonites in the first decades of the eighteenth century. Most of these settled in New York and especially in the tolerant Pennsylvania colony of Quaker William Penn. In the eighteenth century, the colonies also received a steady flow of free German immigrants, who would total 10 percent of the North American population by 1775. Sizable Scotch-Irish Protestant emigration began with Irish droughts between 1715 and 1720 and continued thereafter.

Finally and momentously, the Dutch and English began bringing blacks from Africa by the 1620s, perhaps initially as indentured servants. In the 1660s legal codes started to define for blacks throughout the colonies the formal status of chattel slavery, though some blacks were nonetheless recognized to be free. Although no precise estimates of the numbers of blacks brought to the British American colonies in the seventeenth and eighteenth centuries exist, in 1750 there were more than 235,000 blacks in the thirteen colonies, which had white populations totaling around 1 million. Most blacks lived in the South Atlantic colonies, where virtually all were slaves.[32]

Outside these colonies, moreover, were the rival European settlements, as well as an even broader range of native tribes. The English had been preceded in the New World by the Portuguese, French, Dutch, and especially the Spanish. By the early seventeenth century Spain had already supplied some 90,000 colonists, located mostly in Peru and Mexico, but also in the North American southwest, Florida, and various points up the Atlantic coast to the Chesapeake Bay. The Spanish even had a foothold in Newfoundland, where they contested the French, who largely confined themselves to the Canadian coastal and river territories that Spain for the most part eschewed. France was also less willing to permit economic and military adventurers to advance in its name with very little regulation, and its restrictions meant that only 27,000 French moved to Canada between 1608 and 1760, 10,000 along the St. Lawrence River.[33] New Netherland and the Spanish and French colonies inevitably leaked inhabitants into British America.[34]

That diversity within their bounds affected the English colonies less, however, than their conflicts with the rival colonies of the two great Catholic powers, France and Spain. Vividly aware of the presence of these enemies as well as recalcitrant tribes, British imperial officials always regarded their American colonies as "in some sense frontier garrison settlements." But because their colonies were separated by large tracts of tribal lands, the Europeans in North America engaged in direct combat only occasionally. Instead, they competed via efforts to gain support among the Native American tribes, occasionally using tribal warriors as their surrogates or allies in war. Sometimes the Europeans won native loyalties by exploiting tribal animosities. But the Iroquois and the Creeks, in particular, proved equally adept in playing the imperial powers against each other for as long as possible.[35]

On the whole, it was the English who gained during these years, both in Europe and in North America. In the 1680s, having consolidated their hold on the St. Lawrence River Valley, the French began exploring and establishing forts along the Illinois and Mississippi rivers, reaching down to the Gulf of Mexico. Their hope was to enclose the English settlements from the north and west. The French advances helped spark armed hostilities beginning in 1689, which were known as King William's War or, in its European phase, the War of the League of Augsburg. It ended inconclusively with the Treaty of Ryswick in 1697. The Spanish also tried to drive the English away from Spanish Florida in 1702, an effort that formed part of Queen Anne's War, during which both the Spanish and French opposed England. The Spaniards' Florida campaign failed, however, and the British mounted a devastating counterattack in 1704. Meanwhile, the French met with setbacks in Europe, leading to the war's termination with the Peace of Utrecht, agreed to by the three empires in 1713. That treaty gave the British the following: Nova Scotia, Newfoundland, and the Hudson Bay; alleged sovereignty over the Iroquois; trading rights with western tribes previously exclusively allied with France; and a monopoly on the slave trade with Spanish America. But the French and British each continued to build forts and trading posts and to seek other strategic edges.

In this tense climate, the European War of the Austrian Succession in 1744 triggered another inconclusive American conflict, pitting Spain and France against Britain from 1745 to 1748. Then, from 1754 to 1763, what is variously called the French and Indian War, in its European phase the Seven Years' War, or, most aptly, the Great War for Empire, proved to be "the most dramatically successful war the British ever fought," in Linda Colley's words, with British victory ratified by the 1763 Peace of Paris.[36] Britain gained Canada from France and Florida from Spain. Spain received New Orleans and Louisiana from France.

The British immediately confronted new disturbances, however, because many of the tribes formerly allied with the French denied that France had any right to cede their lands: they had been allies, not conquered subjects. An Ottawa chief, Pontiac, led a confederacy of these angry western tribes in an unsuccessful struggle to drive the English out of the Ohio Valley. The vicious combat included gifts of contaminated blankets from British commander Lord Jeffrey Amherst to spread smallpox among the tribes again. To try to end such troublesome resistance, the British authorities issued the landmark Proclamation Act of 1763. It created four new governments for Granada in the West Indies, East Florida, West Florida, and Canada, and it reserved the region between the Alleghenies and the Mississippi from Florida to 50 degrees north latitude (about 475 miles north of Toronto) for the use of the tribes. The colonists were ordered to remain east of a Proclamation Line drawn along the crest of the Alleghenies. This restriction, culminating a long history of British restraints on colonial expansionism, was fiercely denounced by the colonists. Britain lacked a state apparatus sufficiently strong to enforce the line, and its efforts to do so only helped accelerate the rising tensions that moved the colonists from their imperial service during the Seven Years' War to their Declaration of Independence in 1776. Thus British colonial history was a story of endlessly impending and active warfare with rival European powers and diverse tribes, and disputes between the colonists and the home government, as well as a tale of European expansion and colonial growth.[37]

Ethnic Diversity and Naturalization. Those struggles transformed what their British subjectship meant to many American colonists. In one area, naturalization, most colonists defined their political identity more expansively than parliament wished. The tasks of trying to build up fragile new communities in conflict with the native tribes and by means of African subjugation often made the colonies more than willing to accept other Europeans as full members. Hence the Declaration would complain of King George: "He has endeavored to prevent the population of these states; for that purpose obstructing the laws for naturalization of foreigners, refusing to pass others to encourage their migrations hither, & raising the conditions of new appropriations of land."[38]

The British authorities' general opposition to easy naturalization throughout the colonial period is traceable to their chronic warfare with rival European powers, especially the great Catholic powers of France and Spain, along with their struggles with religious dissenters at home. They feared an influx into England of religious and political dissidents who would seek to share in Britain's increasing success while exacerbating its internal divisions and perhaps adding foreign sympathizers. British home officials were more willing to accept Europeans as British subjects in the young colonies; but they were never as eager to do so as the colonists. Moreover, the British government generally recognized such Europeans as subjects only within the colonies. In Great Britain and Ireland they were still aliens.[39] But the officials in London had little reason to fear encroachments from Native Americans or Africans. Consequently, they recurrently favored policies that officially regarded members of friendly tribes, and even free Africans, as loyal "overseas" British subjects almost like the colonists themselves. The 1763 Proclamation Act was the culmination of that pattern.

The British American colonists differed sharply on all these counts. They generally welcomed all Europeans except Catholics, who were theologically disdained by many and politically mistrusted by even more, due to Britain's chronic conflicts with the Catholic nations and longstanding suspicions of papal power. But the colonists were far more bitter at the suggestion that Native Americans and free Africans might also be British subjects, a bitterness increasingly expressed in racial senses of their own identity. To flourish, most British colonists felt that they had to dispel the tribes and enslave Africans. Any suggestion of political equality was therefore anathema to them. Instead, they needed myths of their own superiority.

They found suitable ones, not in the doctrines of *Calvin's Case* (which were not Calvinist enough) but in the claims for the religious and cultural superiority of Englishmen made by English Protestant leaders, neo-Harringtonians, and the more Anglophilic common lawyers. New Englanders, especially, stressed their senses of themselves as God's chosen people among all Englishmen, destined to build John Winthrop's "city on a hill." Throughout the colonies, notions of the supremacy of Anglo-Saxon civilization, to be brought to further heights in America, also served their ends well, though they were sometimes recast as "European" civilization to be more inclusive. Thus, as imperial and colonial leaders each sought naturalization policies serving their own interests, they clashed repeatedly over who should be included and increasingly over what being a British subject really meant.[40]

In 1609, at the outset of the colonial period, parliament codified its reluctance to permit easy naturalization in a statute that denied naturalization to all non-Protestants, as well as all those unwilling to take an oath of allegiance. In several navigation and trade acts commencing in 1651, aliens were also prohibited from participating in shipping and trade between England and the colonies; and owing to increasing regulations, more and more colonial trade had to be routed through Britain. Europeans seeking to gain British subjectship for purposes of trade or immigration to the colonies were, moreover, often thwarted by parliament's procedures, which provided only for slow, expensive individual legislative naturalizations. And as Britain's empire grew, bringing with it both new riches and new conflicts, parliament, the Lords of Trade, and other London imperial councilors repeatedly rejected colonial efforts to extend naturalization generously or, especially, to treat naturalized subjects as political equals of "natural" Englishmen.[41]

The colonists began those efforts almost as soon as they landed in North America, and they pursued them persistently. Colonial charters, such as those of Virginia and Maryland, granted colonial officials powers to admit "Strangers and Aliens" and bestow property rights upon them. Local officials often read those provisions as licensing them to grant denizenship, even naturalized subjectship, to Europeans. For a time North and South Carolina performed such admissions by enrollment, accepting any who swore their loyalty before county officials. Colonial legislatures and governors also both naturalized and endenized European aliens during the seventeenth century, sometimes authorizing naturalization of whole groups by statute, and sometimes explicitly granting the newly naturalized full political rights. The colonists' eagerness to naturalize was further evident in a few colonial naturalizations of children born in Virginia and Maryland to parents from the European continent. Those acts also showed, however, the colonists' sense that English subjectship really did involve an ethnic or national identity: under Coke's reasoning, those children should already have been natural-born subjects of the king.[42]

Through much of the century, parliament remained silent on these colonial practices. And British monarchs, whose zeal for empire-building tended to exceed parliament's, sometimes shared the colonists' willingness to incorporate Europeans into colonial subjectship.[43] Gradually, however, London imperial officials began to check colonial liberality. They favored the system adopted by Virginia in 1680, which centered naturalization in the royal governor, an appointee more easily controlled from Britain than local assemblies. Furthermore, supported by the judiciary, the Lords of Trade began to insist in the 1680s and 1690s that colonial naturalizations and denizations were legal fictions, binding only in the colony that conferred them and granting no rights to engage in the colonial trade, much less rights of subjectship in the home country. In 1700, an order-in-council made this position settled British law, while also restricting colonial powers of denization so stringently as to eliminate them. That order was followed by another in 1705 annulling a Pennsylvania statute granting group naturalizations. The home officials then terminated all group naturalizations in the colonies.[44]

Colonial opposition to these restrictions, along with other imperial considerations, did win a major concession from the British government in 1740. Parliament passed a general enabling act that allowed aliens who had resided in the colonies for seven or more years to become English subjects without the special act of parliament normally required. Persons naturalized under this statute could hold political office in any colony, though not in Great Britain or Ireland. They also still had to prove their Protestantism (requirements modified in the cases of Quakers and Jews, but not ever-suspect Catholics).[45] Hence, despite these reforms, British subjectship remained a status that was not easily acquired by those not born to it, and was not acquired at all if the individual was too religiously or politically unfaithful to British orthodoxies.

The relative liberality of the bill was briefly extended further due to the exigencies of warfare with the French and their allied tribes. In 1756, parliament permitted the king to commission foreigners as officers and engineers in colonial regiments to lead local European-born recruits; and in 1761 it granted approval for admission of these alien soldiers to subjectship, so long as they were Protestant and swore allegiance. Like those naturalized under the 1740 act, these persons were also allowed to hold political office in all the colonies. But as conflicts between the home officials and the colonists began to mount, especially after

1763, London again began to restrict these naturalizations. The home officials were all the more concerned to do so because from the end of the Seven Years' War until the outbreak of the Revolution the colonies received a much larger influx of immigrants than ever before, more than 220,000. Parliament toyed with cutting off emigration entirely, and it did restrict land sales to newcomers. Finally, in 1773 colonial governors were instructed not to assent to any more special naturalizations. That final restraint triggered the complaint included in the Declaration.[46]

The colonists' receptivity to newcomers should not be overstated. From 1670, colonial leaders protested against the English practice of dumping convicted felons into North America. And when upper-class Protestant English colonists found their control even potentially threatened, their local officials sometimes endorsed restrictive measures to protect the political hierarchies and cultural identities of their communities. Thus Virginia banned Catholics from political office in the 1640s; Massachusetts banished all priests in 1647; and even in Maryland, where half the colonies' Catholics lived, Protestants became the majority and in 1654 revoked a Toleration Act passed in 1649 for the Catholics' protection. Up to 1689, NewYork, Pennsylvania, Virginia, and Maryland had statutes or practices that permitted Catholic naturalizations, but after the Protestant settlement in England of 1689 that policy ended. A long history of anti-Catholic measures ensued. By the end of the century, restrictions on Catholic worship were nearly universal in the colonies, remaining relatively light only in Rhode Island and Pennsylvania. After the French and Indian War, moreover, several colonies imposed extra taxes on Catholics and subjected them to surveillance and disarmament. It is thus understandable that the 1774 Quebec Act, granting Quebec Catholics religious liberty and expanding Quebec to the Ohio River, was perceived as another provocation by the colonists to the south and east.[47]

Less frequently but portentously, various colonies sometimes also denied full membership to all or some non-Catholic Europeans. New England was the most exclusionary. In the second half of the seventeenth century, Massachusetts and New Hampshire limited "freeman" status, then tantamount to subjectship, to Englishmen, while Connecticut and Rhode Island required special methods of approval for any "foriner, Dutch, French, or of any other nation" seeking to be admitted as a freeman. In the 1740s, heretofore tolerant Pennsylvania went through a period of intense controversy over the alleged unassimilability of its German Palatine settlers, with Ben Franklin one of the anti-German critics. The Germans soon proved willing, however, to embrace "the famous English liberty" that assimilation offered to them. Colonial suffrage restrictions also revealed ethnocentric elements, with nonwhites excluded virtually everywhere and non-English immigrants often ineligible also. Indeed, Jefferson's draft of the Declaration included a passage complaining that the British were sending over "not only souldiers of our common blood, but Scotch & foreign mercenaries to invade and destroy us," a remarkably narrow definition of colonial "common blood."[48] The Continental Congress deleted that passage, no doubt with the approval of its Scottish members.

The colonists also maintained English class hierarchies in legislating the political rights of even their British members. The "one outstanding and universal requirement" for suffrage was some type of landed property qualification, which disfranchised servants and laborers. Colonial America thus remained in many ways a medieval political world, with power structures defined by titles to estates more than commitments to self-governance.[49]

As the eighteenth century progressed, some colonies, particularly the more populated ones, began to relax these strictures to ensure the support of lower-class Englishmen. They permitted personal property as well as real property to meet suffrage requirements, a pattern that the revolution would somewhat accelerate. By 1776, however, only five of the thirteen rebelling colonies had made even this modest change.[50] A variety of other colonial laws indicated that the "proper" electorate ought not go much beyond free, white, Protestant adult native, English-born, or naturalized male property owners. Virginia was the most openly exclusionary; its 1762 statute specifically denied the suffrage to free blacks, mulattos, Native Americans, women, minors, and all non-Protestants, with Catholics expressly banned. Other religious tests and property qualifications of varying stringency were present throughout the colonies. In all these ways the colonists made clear that although they saw themselves as British subjects, only British subjects with certain ethnic, religious, and class traits were entitled to exercise political privileges.[51]

But just as the imperatives of colony-building led to lessened suffrage restrictions, limitations on full membership for non-British Europeans were not always rigorously enforced. The need for new settlers was felt to be too great for discouraging rules to maintain enduring support. Occasionally, colonial authorities even tolerated political participation by aliens, though they also tended to sustain doctrines limiting alien land rights, which could in turn disqualify aliens from full political privileges.[52]

When they turned from fellow Europeans to consideration of Native Americans and Africans, moreover, the colonists insisted almost unanimously on protecting the British cultural content of their identity by denying these groups political membership more emphatically than Coke's theory had done or British home officials wished to do. The British colonists' antipathies to these "others" also exceeded those of the Spanish and Portuguese colonists to the south. The southern European imperial powers subjugated Native Americans and Africans, to be sure, but they also assimilated them into their new societies as slaves, concubines, or fully accepted spouses. In their colonies, even bondage sometimes led to the gradual acceptance of slave descendants as genuine community members. In contrast, in regard to both native peoples and blacks, questions of gradual assimilation via social intermixing, marriage, or formal naturalization were almost never on the agenda of the British colonists. Their only concern was whether these groups should be permanently incorporated into British America as slaves or simply dispelled or killed. Most chose expulsion for the Native American tribes, permanent slavery for blacks.[53]

Historians have advanced many reasons for this pattern: the allegedly greater cultural and ideological insularity of Northern European Protestants versus Spanish and Portuguese Catholics; the pervasive disdain of the English, in particular, toward all other peoples they encountered; the fact that the British colonists encountered less populous tribes, making their elimination more plausible; the comparatively greater number and variety of British settlers, which lessened their need to rely on outsiders for skilled labor or oversight positions, for fellow soldiers, or for wives—for anything beyond manual labor. In any case, in their effort to distinguish themselves from these groups, the colonists crafted their community identities more restrictively than British law formally required, often thereby exacerbating their disputes with the home government. These ascriptive, inegalitarian conceptions of their political identity were also reflected in the status they accorded women. I shall consider each of those excluded or subordinated groups in turn.[54]

Native Americans

English–Native American relations were peaceful for a brief moment, often romanticized in later years by whites recalling the first Thanksgiving. But the English colonists' refusal to contemplate extensive intermingling with the tribes, the tribes' own resistance to the limited English efforts to assimilate them, and the colonists' insistence on acquiring more and more tribal land all made warfare inevitable. Through those brutal conflicts the English colonists would come to forge an ever-stronger sense of themselves as a culturally and biologically superior people, intended by God to displant hateful inferiors. Because British imperial strategies were sometimes served by policies according the tribes more respect than those engaged in death struggles with them could tolerate, parliamentary policies toward Native Americans also became a grievance in the Declaration of Independence, which denounced British endeavors "to bring on the inhabitants of our frontiers, the merciless Indian savages, whose known rule of warfare is an undistinguished destruction of all ages, sexes, and conditions."[55]

War between the colonists and natives came quickly. After a catastrophic assault on Virginia whites by the Powhatan Confederacy in 1622, the colonists there successfully pursued a policy of massive retaliation verging on annihilation. They claimed that they could now "by right of War" destroy their enemies and take over "their cultivated places." In 1637 Massachusetts colonists, aided by Narragansett warriors, killed more than 500 Pequots and enslaved the rest. Six years later, those colonists were instead allied with the Mohegans against the Narragansetts, mounting a threat that forced land cessions by the tribe. Virginians faced a second uprising, by the Chesapeakes, in 1646, signing a treaty two years later that guaranteed those tribes extensive territory north of the York River. Then, in 1675–76, the Wampanoag leader Metacom, called King Philip by the English, instigated a war to forestall further advances by the New England Puritan colonies. His offensive failed in 1676, doomed by food shortages and disease as much as colonial military successes. Though it took time for the colonists to recover towns lost in the war, Metacom's defeat and death proved the last gasp of armed resistance by the New England coastal tribes. Most were thereafter confined to one of four villages, while a few hundred others became servants or tenant farmers in the English colonies. Statutes denying former tribesmen rights to testify in colonial courts, imposing curfews, restricting travel, and requiring observance of Christian practices then multiplied in the region where Native American rights had previously been most advanced.[56]

In the wake of these conflicts, colonial authorities came to divide Native Americans into three classes: "foreign" or "independent" Indians, who belonged to unconquered tribes on the outskirts of the colonies; "plantation" or "reservation" Indians, who belonged to tribes that had been effectively engulfed by white settlements and had allegedly acknowledged subjection to the crown in return for relative local autonomy; and individuals who had been more or less completely absorbed into the white populace, though subject to special discriminatory laws.[57]

The second of these classes was a chronic source of difficulty between the colonists and both the Native Americans and the British home authorities. The very nature of their status was ambiguous. The British generally still preferred to deal with these tribes via treaty, thereby implying that the tribes were fully independent nations like those of Europe. Yet the language of the treaties usually suggested that the tribes were under British protection—subjects, not sovereign aliens. Because of this ambiguity, when tribes claimed a fully independent status that the crown did not acknowledge, some local officials in the colonies were occasionally sympathetic.

Much more typically, however, local and imperial attitudes differed because colonial Americans were far more hostile to the tribes than London's imperial officials. The king's ministers wished to assert, consistent with Coke's premises, that those Native Americans who had signed treaties avowing allegiance were members of subject conquered nations, like the Irish. Hence they were members of the royal community of allegiance in a manner not wholly unlike the colonists themselves. The resentment with which the colonists greeted this assertion is unsurprising, as it compared their own status with that of the Native Americans and, more significantly, limited their right to treat the Native Americans as alien enemies who could be destroyed at will. Because of their longstanding conflicts with the tribes, the colonists often spoke of the Native Americans as "not civil, not Christian, perhaps not quite human in the way that white Christian Europeans were" well before they had elaborated a similar view of blacks.[58]

Virginian gentry like the young Thomas Jefferson sometimes magnanimously viewed Native Americans as ignorant heathens who might be the equals of whites with proper education, but many others increasingly viewed the demonic savagery they assigned to tribesmen as inherent, thereby construing Native Americans as an inferior, hostile race. Using Locke's view that property rights originated only with rational productive labor, they also persistently portrayed the tribes as too primitive and nomadic to have any true title to their lands, even though for years the English colonists were not able to farm as fruitfully. In fervently religious New England, especially, colonists also assured themselves that the Native Americans' vulnerability to smallpox and other European diseases was a sign that God was "making room" in these lands for Christian Englishmen to occupy them with "cleared . . . title." No doubt reliance on that justification for rejoicing in death increased their psychological need to see themselves as a divinely chosen people.[59]

Bacon's Rebellion in Virginia during 1676 arose in part out of colonial anger over the comparative tolerance shown by the royal governor, Sir William Berkeley, to Native Americans, as well as from class resentments of poorer colonists toward the governing elites. Settlers arriving after the 1648 agreement with the Chesapeakes, particularly indentured servants who had served their time, thought that the lands north of the York River should be opened up to them. When a dispute between whites and Doeg and Susquehannock tribesmen led to bloodshed that the Virginia government ignored, the Susquehannocks began a series of attacks on Maryland and Virginia settlements, prompting brutal reprisals in the spring of 1676. Nathaniel Bacon was a leader of those counterassaults, which he soon extended to attacks on friendly tribes who held coveted lands. Then in May, Berkeley refused to support those incursions. Bacon moved into rebellion, attacking various tribes and Berkeley's supporters alike. On October 26, 1676, Bacon died of fever and his rebellion succumbed with him; but the Susquehannocks were severely damaged, and the pattern of tensions between colonial land aspirations and imperial policies of restraint, as well as the failure of royal authorities to hold back the colonists, were established.[60]

More wars followed. In 1711, the Tuscaroras of North Carolina, a village-dwelling tribe that had suffered raids by tribes allied with Carolina slave traders as well as by German and Swiss immigrants, led similarly aggrieved local tribes in attacks on English and German colonists. The thinly populated North Carolinian settlements received help from South Carolina, whose slave traders mobilized their Native American allies and crushed the Tuscaroras the following year. One of the Carolinians' allied tribes, the Yamasees, then revolted in 1715 in response to white slave-trading of their women and children. They were joined by the Creeks, whom the French encouraged to provide assistance. But the Carolina whites won the military support of their trading partners among the Cherokees, and within two years they had crushed the attacking tribes and enslaved many. By their success in pursuing this divide-and-conquer policy, the still relatively few European settlers managed to overwhelm resisting coastal tribes in the south as in the north.[61]

Faced with the British colonists' ongoing advances via diplomacy and force, it is unsurprising that most of the tribes to the west sided with the French in the Seven Years' War. Their opposition was only exacerbated by most local officials' open hatred of virtually all Native Americans. Hence early on in the war British imperial authorities, who hoped to gain neutrals if not allies among the tribes, tried to displace these officials by centralizing control over Native American affairs in new imperial officers. Superintendents of Indian Affairs for the north and south were appointed in 1755 and 1756. The London Board of Trade also tried to direct all purchases of Native American lands. These British efforts at more conciliatory, imperially directed tribal policies culminated after the war's end in the 1763 Proclamation that so outraged the colonists. It did not, however, curb their expansionism: Virginia's Governor Dunmore launched a war with the Shawnees in 1774 that prompted imperial authorities to impose various inflammatory new measures, including the Quebec Act.[62]

The war and the unenforceable Proclamation settled few of the issues concerning the legal status of the affected tribes. It was clear, however, that the tribes' longstanding efforts to play the various European powers against each other had come to an end. Henceforth, they would primarily confront the British colonists and British imperial officials. Yet it remained ambiguous whether the British home authorities, the colonists, and the tribes themselves viewed the tribes' status as conquered British subjects, voluntary subjects, semi-independent "protected" nations, or as truly independent nations joined with the British empire only via certain treaty agreements. Positions varied with the shifting interests of the parties involved; but the basic dynamic was for the British colonists to find any rationale available to assert their right as a people to lands that had long belonged to others.

Their fierce denunciation of the "merciless Indian savages" expressed how deep their racial and cultural hostility had become by the time of the Declaration. Very few were willing to accord the tribes the status of independent sovereign nations, nor could many colonists contemplate welcoming as equals any Native Americans who might wish to become fellow subjects or citizens. Yet even within the colonies, there were more respectful countercurrents. Many colonists found much to admire in the freedom, relative equality, and spirit of cooperation that characterized the political life of numerous tribes, such as the Iroquois nations.[63] The question of the Native Americans' appropriate political identity was not clearly answered during the colonial era. After the Revolution, the issue of whether they could possess a status like those of independent European nations or American whites would become a major dilemma for a new nation that sometimes proclaimed that all who were not aliens had rights to be self-governing citizens.[64]

African-Americans

There was one population whose status was so controversial that the portion of Jefferson's draft listing their presence as a grievance was omitted from the Declaration: African-Americans. They were too essential as slaves for many colonists to countenance criticism of their presence or to consider accepting them as equals. While the Europeans initially provided only an international extension of an internal African slave trade—and the Dutch were the leading traders and masters of African slaves in North America during the mid-seventeenth century—the English entered into the trade vigorously from 1663 onward and came to dominate it by the mid-eighteenth century. In their initial entry as indentured servants, blacks in North America apparently could become freemen and property owners after their time was served, like European servants. But soon the English began regarding Africans with a contempt exceeding the hostility they showed toward all outsider groups. Special restrictions were imposed on blacks that expanded into an extraordinary variety of legal burdens during the last decades of the seventeenth century. The most important of these was legal recognition of hereditary lifetime bondage itself. After Virginia pioneered the legal codification of chattel slavery in 1661 and Maryland followed suit in 1663, it quickly became almost the exclusive status of blacks in the southern regions and the dominant one in the middle and northern colonies. In terms of the categories of English law, this black chattel slavery amounted to a new kind of subjectship— a subjectship to an individual master so complete that American legal authorities strove, never quite successfully, to ignore the slaves' humanity and to view them simply as property.[65]

As Barbara Fields has argued, the colonial gentry targeted Africans for such full subjugation because these subordinates could not claim even the minimal legal protections that English servants had won for themselves. The colonists also did not need to fear discouraging African immigration. But still slavery had to be justified, a task that prompted the colonists to elaborate the doctrines of racial inequality that they had begun to devise to defend taking Native American lands. By increasingly making African descent or dark skin color a basis for legal restrictions, they established by positive law a racially defined gulf in the status of human beings so vast that in 1772, the highest common law court in England disavowed it. In the famous case of *Somerset v. Stewart,* Lord Mansfield, Chief Justice of the King's Bench, decreed absolute slavery to be so "odious" that it could exist only by positive law—and hence that while it did exist in America, it had no legitimate place in England. Blackstone took the same view: blacks were free in England and protected by law. Those pronouncements heartened some in the colonies, but to many more they provided new examples of English disregard for the colonists' interests. Yet even in American law, the impossibility and immorality of treating fellow humans as things led the administrators of the colonial slave laws into agonizingly tortuous paths that many scholars have sensitively explored. The essential point here is that by legislating black chattel slavery, Americans went beyond any explicit provisions in English law and gave legal expression to an increasingly racialized sense of their identity so powerful that the very humanity of these outsiders was denied.[66]

But not all African-Americans were slaves. During the eighteenth century, some of the colonies found slavery to be economically infeasible, and by midcentury some Quaker leaders like Philadelphia's Anthony Benezet began to call for abolition, using arguments that merged over time with the rhetoric of the growing agitations for freedom in the colonies generally. As a result, some masters freed their slaves, and a relatively small number of slaves were able to earn enough to purchase their freedom.[67] The status of these free blacks was even more problematic than that of the assimilated Native Americans, for they dwelt alongside the explosive institution of black slavery. By the late eighteenth century, virtually all black freemen had been born in the colonial realms of the English king. On the premises of *Calvin's Case,* they were natural-born British subjects. Indeed, few legal authorities directly disputed this, though in some southern colonies all blacks were legally presumed to be slaves until they proved otherwise.[68]

But most colonists were not prepared to recognize free blacks as equal fellow subjects. Instead, as the black population increased, the white colonists repeatedly expressed fear that free blacks would inspire slave insurrections, directly or by example. To forestall such threats, all the colonies elaborated restrictive codes. Ordinarily slaves were prevented from moving freely or congregating without passes or other forms of special permission, provisions enforced by white patrol forces. As early as 1668, the Virginia Assembly added that free blacks "ought not in all respects to be admitted to a full fruition of the exemptions and immunities of the English," an attitude all the colonies shared. Even so, one record indicates that "mulattos and Negroes were polled" in a 1701 assembly election in South Carolina, and they sometimes fought in local militia. But by the early eighteenth century free blacks were widely denied rights to hold office, to vote, to testify against whites, to assemble, and to serve in the militia; and the colonies almost universally banned interracial sexual relations (again, unlike the Spaniards and Portuguese).[69]

Because free blacks were generally recognized to be subjects, however, the centrality of property rights to British subjectship seems to have worked in their favor: in contrast to the treatment of aliens, the property rights of free blacks were less often circumscribed than their political powers. Restrictions were mildest in New England and tended to be greatest in the southern colonies, which sometimes did refuse to recognize any property rights for blacks. The pattern was, however, a shifting and checkered one, generally reflecting the relative size of the local black population and the incidence of recent anti-slavery unrest. Nonetheless, throughout the colonies popular attitudes always, and legal doctrines generally, distinguished blacks as well as Native Americans from subjects of European descent. Regardless of birth within the king's allegiance, only the "lovely White," in Ben Franklin's phrase, were seen by most colonists as natural British subjects.[70]

The fears about black uprisings expressed in these repressive laws were certainly not ill-founded: blacks acted repeatedly to resist their oppression. Although no really large-scale revolts took place, some New York City blacks did burn a building and kill nine whites who tried to quell the blaze in 1712; and in 1713, 1722, 1730, and especially 1739–41, slave uprisings or conspiracies occurred in Virginia, South Carolina, New Jersey, and New York. In each case whites reacted with exceedingly violent punitive measures. In 1712, twenty-five New York slaves, including women and Native American slaves, were hanged, burned, or broken on a wheel. The assembly then adopted a harsh slave code like those in the south, and neighboring colonies soon followed suit. In 1740 and 1741, New York imprisoned one hundred and fifty allegedly conspiratorial slaves and twenty-five whites, tortured and hanged eighteen slaves and four whites, burned thirteen slaves at the stake, and transported seventy others to the West Indies. Aided by Native American allies, South Carolina's militia crushed the approximately one hundred slaves who seized arms, killed several whites, and fled in 1740, and it went on to elaborate its already severe black codes. Carolinians and Virginians were, moreover, reluctant to supply militia during the Seven Years' War because they would not then be able to "keep these Slaves in proper Subjection," as Virginia's governor indicated. It is likely that such white vigilance and repressive violence combined to help prevent any massive slave uprisings.[71]

Colonial authorities were also concerned about possible revolutionary alliances between black laborers and white indentured servants, anxieties triggered in part by Nathaniel Bacon's offer of liberty to any slaves who would join his Virginia rebellion of 1676. At least eighty blacks appear to have responded to this promise. Subsequently, the colonies met the threat of such partnerships by improving the status of poor whites and by sharpening racial distinctions in the law. Early in the eighteenth century, for example, Virginia required masters of white indentured servants to give the servants food, money, and a gun at the completion of their service, and its assembly also sharply reduced the poll tax. Edmund Morgan has persuasively suggested that these measures represent actions similar to those that Immanuel Wallerstein attributes to local elites who respond to the impact of foreign capitalist economies by fostering nationalism. These policies of assistance to the white servant class were in Morgan's view also efforts to foster a sense of ethnic community in order to forestall class conflicts. Morgan's argument is supported throughout Anglo-America by the panoply of legal devices that colonial officials adopted in the early eighteenth century restricting not only the entitlements of black freemen but also opportunities to liberate slaves via individual manumissions: freed blacks were better situated than slaves to make common cause with whites who had also recently risen from servitude.[72]

British imperial officials, again, were somewhat more willing to treat blacks, as well as Native Americans, as subjects like any others. They favored, for example, efforts to convert and baptize both groups, giving them the appropriate religious outlook for English subjectship. Predictably, perhaps, New Englanders often agreed. But farther south, many colonists opposed black baptisms on the ground that they fostered claims to spiritual equality and legal independence. Just such notions were spread by Virginia slaves influenced by missionary activity in the 1730s and the Great Awakening of the 1740s. Only when leading white Protestant ministers clearly affirmed the position of state law—that baptism gave no claims to emancipation—did this opposition fade. It is likely, however, that many blacks espoused the Christian message of humility around whites, but its affirmations of their dignity among themselves.[73]

There were some, perhaps many, among the British colonists who endorsed those affirmations to some degree; if not sufficiently to embrace blacks as equals, at least strongly enough to abhor their enslavement. Though the Quakers were relatively lonely spokesmen for rapid abolition during the colonial era, even slaveholding Virginia gentry leaders like Thomas Jefferson could see how slavery violated the Enlightenment and Christian principles of human rights they otherwise espoused. Thus Jefferson included in his draft of the Declaration the accusation that King George was waging "cruel war against human nature itself, violating it's most sacred rights of life and liberty in the persons of a distant people who never offended him, captivating & carrying them into slavery. . . . [H]e is now exciting those very people to rise in arms among us, and to purchase that liberty of which he has deprived them, by murdering the people on whom he also obtruded them." But enough of the most powerful among his countrymen thought black slavery either right or expedient to exclude this statement from the final document, just as they condemned the anti-slavery rhetoric of *Somerset v. Stewart*. Many remained outraged by Lord Dunmore's 1775 proclamation freeing all "Negroes" and "indented servants" who would fight for the British against the rebellious colonists. While Americans agonized over the institution the slave trade had nurtured, and most resented imperial interference with it, most (including the slaveowning Jefferson) were not prepared to challenge the propriety of their "peculiar" civic hierarchy.[74]

Women

Of the status of female colonists, there is much less to be said. There are no grievances concerning women in the Declaration of Independence. The fact that they are not mentioned at all reflects the agreement between colonial leaders and home officials that ordinarily women had no proper place in the public realm and only a subordinate one in the home. Little had changed in this regard from the early colonial era, when John Cotton argued that God thought it "good for the Wife to acknowledg all power and authority to the Husband, and for the Husband to acknowledg honour" but neither power nor authority "to the Wife." It is true that, when Anne Hutchinson dared to lead religious meetings in her home in the 1630s, Cotton nonetheless tried to moderate her critics. More typical, however, were the responses of Governor John Winthrop, his fellow judges, and the Massachusetts general assembly, who joined in condemning Hutchinson's behavior as not "fitting for your sex," as well as heretical. Few women challenged these notions of their proper place very openly or strongly. When Anne Bradstreet ventured to publish her poetry in 1650, for example, she conceded to those who would say "my hand a needle better fits" that "Men can do best, and women know it well. Preeminence in all and each is yours; Yet grant some small acknowledgment of ours."[75] The prevalence of such views in British America meant that for the entire colonial period there are no organized political movements, no major legal or extralegal conflicts, no important new statutes affecting the political status of women.

Historians dispute whether social and economic conditions nonetheless made practice depart sharply from law and custom in some parts of the colonial era, creating a "golden age" of relative female independence. But few deny that in regard to her formal legal status, the colonial woman's place was still governed by the English common law of coverture. In Blackstone's late eighteenth-century view, that law made daughters the property of their fathers and completely absorbed the legal identity of the married woman, the *feme covert*, into that of her husband. Married women were thus subjects not only of the crown but of their spouses, leaving them without any meaningful civic rights of their own.

From early in the colonial era, American courts with equity powers did hold, contrary to Blackstone, that women could sometimes hold separate estates; but only a tiny percentage of married women actually did so. In addition, the unmarried adult woman, the *feme sole*, did have an independent legal personality, and in the colonial era sometimes could even vote. But again, this appearance of relative equality is misleading. Although the number of single women grew during the colonial era, it probably reached only 10–15 percent of the female population, and few single women ever exercised their rights of franchise. The political subordination of women to men was thus largely accepted as part of the customary British way of life. The new proto-nationalist political identity that British Americans were forming still largely presumed men's continuing legal right to govern women both in state institutions and in the home.[76]

It is possible, moreover, that male desires to control women were enhanced by the increased emphasis on the racial and ethnic conceptions of their identity that British Americans formed to defend their subjugation of Native Americans and African slaves. If superior blood was part of the colonists' claim to the land and labor of others, then the policing of perceived biological boundaries by preventing interracial sexual relations was essential. It is true, however, that white men often permitted themselves and forced on women the interracial couplings that they formally forswore by law. Their political desires to sustain claims of racial purity and superiority thus never wholly governed their conduct. At most they added another motive for the maintenance of systems of male domination that were usually given scriptural defenses. But the language of emergent ascriptive Americanism, defining identity in terms of natural traits and divine ordering, was a convenient idiom to express all these claims of supremacy, and during the colonial era and thereafter they often appeared in mutually reinforcing rhetorical combinations. God, nature, and custom all supported the rule of white men over people of color and women.[77]

Yet despite the colonists' perpetuation of legal doctrines defining women's "natural" subordinated status, inherited views of women did undergo some modifications during the colonial era. Although the dominant strains of Protestantism still regarded women as unfit for political or religious office, they overrode notions in some medieval thought that depicted women as innately inclined to be wanton temptresses. American Protestants instead portrayed mothers as natural custodians of Christian morality and governesses of the household and children. In practice, colonial women often assumed more equal responsibilities for both home and work due to the demanding conditions of frontier life. In the relatively few urban, commercial areas, single women could be declared "*femc sole* traders," entitled to sue, conduct businesses, enter into contracts, sell real property, and be attorneys-in-fact, though not law. The slightly broader rights that women had in colonial customs than in English law reflected the economic realities of life in the thinly populated colonies. It may have contributed to the greater willingness to recognize women as equals in some sense that Tocqueville would note; but there is little evidence that it fundamentally altered the inferior status held to be appropriate to a female British subject, in the colonies as in the home countries. As the colonies became more settled, most if not all the early departures from that status were undone. While the colonies' population increases were accompanied by growing numbers of single women, with theoretically greater legal rights than married women, most of these *femes soles* found it very hard to provide for themselves in the colonial men's world. Few had property or training that permitted them to compete economically, and few men would assist them in doing so. These impoverished unmarried women and widows were hardly well situated to crusade for women's rights.[78]

On many subjects, then, the views of the colonists changed little from those of their fellow Englishmen. They were still at bottom loyal subjects of the British mixed monarchy; the place of women colonists was largely that prescribed in Britain by common law, religious leaders, and custom; only propertied classes could rule. In some ways, however, the colonial period led British Americans to think of their political identity more expansively than the home authorities did. Non-Catholic European aliens struck most as suitable, indeed, badly needed fellow subjects. But in still other ways, colonial ideas became more overtly exclusive. To be a British American meant, in colonial law as well as belief, that one held a station naturally placed above native tribesmen and blacks, whose rights could never be equal, indeed, whose very humanity was dubious. This ethnocentric sensibility, felt by the colonists to be inadequately honored by imperial officials, was an important if ugly factor in moving these colonists toward revolution and nation-building. In interaction with their other, more emphasized causes, it would profoundly shape their understanding of what that new nation should become.

3

Forging a Revolutionary People
1763–1776

Although their conflicts with the French, Spanish, Native Americans, and blacks sharpened the British American colonists' sense of their distinctive collective identity, they did so largely by making the colonists more militantly British. If they further defined who they were, most probably still turned to their religious or colonial memberships, not to being "American." Yet after 1763 especially, many leading British American colonists decided, often with shock and pain, that their British identity was the root of their greatest problems. Far from being the wellspring of their military security, economic prosperity, personal and political rights, and spiritual destiny, their British subjectship instead seemed to make them vulnerable puppets in Britain's imperial maneuvering with the tribes and rival European powers, and shackled field hands of England's economy—producing, buying, and selling only as its governors dictated. They felt treated far more like subjects by conquest than by mutual obligation—forbidden to speak as equals in the hostile parliament and royal councils that decided their laws, fettered in their choice of where and with whom to live, unable even to close their doors to the armed enforcers of their rulers' distant decrees. Those who had a strong sense of religious mission felt that it was being betrayed by their ties to what seemed an increasingly corrupt British ruling class.

But the colonies were feeble, underpopulated communities, apparently hopelessly overmatched against Britain's imperial might. How could leaders gain British redress of their growing grievances or rally the colonists to resistance? The men who headed the Revolution—mostly educated, affluent, American-born, and young—could not be too particular about means. They sought to win support by invoking every discourse of political legitimation they could, in ways that shifted with the course of their struggles.[1]

Aggrieved colonists first appealed to their constitutional rights as Englishmen.[2] That failing, they went on to define their cause heavily in terms of the Enlightenment claims of universal natural rights and the ideals of civic republicanism that had long aided English challenges to abusive monarchs, as most Tocquevillian scholars stress.[3] But from the start the American leaders also blended their evocations of all those principles with ascriptive ethnic and cultural notions of their own common identity. Beginning with political and religious views of themselves as bearers of what even other Europeans called "the famous English liberty," they increasingly argued that Americans were in fact a superior new breed, with qualities that made them not only properly independent but quite possibly mankind's "redeemer nation." The result was a complex conception of American nationality within which all the colonists' most valued traditions seemed for a time miraculously to cohere. As Edmund Morgan has argued, American nationality was thus the child more than the parent of the Revolution. But as John Murrin has added, this child was fragile and often much less beloved by the colonists than their local, religious, or imperial attachments.[4]

The Immediate Provocations

As the burdens of ruling an ever larger empire swelled and the colonies grew in numbers and resources, royal officials and parliamentary leaders asserted more control over their possessions. The motifs worked out in over one hundred years of English opposition writings made it natural for colonists to portray many of those measures as shocking invasions of personal and economic freedoms, violating the doctrines of individual rights we now call "liberal," and as taxation without representation, contrary to republican values. For example, the infamous general search warrants or writs of assistance, which enabled British soldiers to search colonial houses for illegal goods virtually at will, violated liberties that the colonists thought were guaranteed them by English constitutional and natural law. The economic regulatory acts of 1764 and 1765, the Townshend Acts of 1767, the 1773 conferral of a tea monopoly on the British East India Company, and the 1774 Coercive Acts pushed both liberal and republican alarm buttons. These measures raised customs duties, added new commodity taxes, banned colonial paper money, mandated the purchase of stamps for most circulating documents, and suspended Massachusetts's charter and replaced its officials after the Boston Tea Party, while compelling colonists to quarter the British troops who enforced these hated measures.[5]

Yet it is striking that this period of mounting agitation began with the 1763

Proclamation Act, curbing colonial efforts to displace native tribes, and culminated with the 1774 Quebec Act, giving protection to Catholics, and with final rejection of all colonial powers to grant special naturalizations accompanied by threats to suspend British emigration. Only then did the colonists convene the first Continental Congress. That timing suggests that the colonists were driven to revolution by what they saw as profound threats to their capacities to craft the ethnic, cultural, and religious content of their collective identities, as well as their more analyzed economic, libertarian, and representational concerns.[6]

It is probably impossible to resolve questions about how far revolutionary leaders were driven by principled political convictions, anxieties about maintaining and extending colonial racial hierarchies, economic motivations, cultural divergences from Britain, paranoia traceable to inherited religious and republican fears of corruption, or more purely personal grievances and ambitions. It is even harder to judge what most impelled the colonists who supported those leaders. The main themes of the colonial protests do, however, correspond well to elements stressed in recent accounts of modern nationalism and nation-states. The American revolutionaries were local elites of the sort these analysts describe, chafing at imperial limits on their economic and political opportunities, eager to govern the territories that the empire had defined as theirs. Gordon Wood has long argued that these emotions best explain the revolutionary leadership. He maintains that beneath "all the specific constitutional grievances against British authority" lay an embittering "sense of political and social deprivation," a "spirit of resentment" over English hereditary privileges, especially the crown's ability to control all positions of power and prestige.

That resentment gained fuel from the colonial elite's fears that British policies might not always support their efforts to assert control over Native Americans, blacks, and poor whites.[7] It therefore makes sense that these elites, like later nation-builders, strove hard to gain adherents by nationalist appeals, arguing as Richard Bland did in 1766 that "the People of the Colonies" were no longer simply English but rather "a distinct People." And though the American Revolution was less centered on ethnic or cultural nationalism than others, these appeals were more prominent than standard accounts stressing American exceptionalism admit.[8]

Ascriptive Identity and Revolutionary Americanism

What was the character of this "distinct People"? Bernard Bailyn and most other leading analysts of the revolutionary era recognize that the colonists believed from the start that "they, as Britishers, shared in a unique inheritance of liberty." That heritage had many dimensions. Most religious-minded Americans thought, as Milton and Harrington had suggested, that being English meant sharing in the divine mission of Anglo-Saxon peoples to bring about some sort of Protestant millennium, overcoming Papist (Roman, French, and Spanish) spiritual tyranny and securing the freedom to practice "true religion." The colonists also assumed, like Coke and seventeenth-century English opposition writers, that Britain's legal traditions were uniquely protective of political, religious, and personal liberties. Many further presumed the correctness of the cultural stereotype of English people as naturally unruly, liberty-loving, and stubbornly resistant to authority. They wholeheartedly embraced the now long familiar myth that, in Edmund Morgan's words, all Englishmen were proud descendants of a "golden age of Anglo-Saxon purity and freedom," and they believed that they had special capacities for liberty that were culturally and providentially, if not biologically, definitive of their race.[9]

In this vein, James Otis declaimed in 1764 that "liberty was better understood, and more fully enjoyed by our ancestors, before the coming in of the first Norman tyrants than ever after, 'till it was found necessary, for the salvation of the kingdom, to combat the arbitrary and wicked proceedings of the Stuarts." Ten years later, in his influential pamphlet "A Summary View of the Rights of British Americans," Thomas Jefferson relied on the colonists' "Saxon ancestors" even more elaborately to defend their right to free government and unrestricted trade. He insisted that the ancient Saxon constitution, restored by the Glorious Revolution of 1688, regarded the monarch not as the bearer of divine right or the owner of all lands but simply as "the chief officer of the people." Feudal and absolutist notions of governance and landholding were illegitimate Norman imports that Americans had sometimes erroneously indulged. Early Americans had been "farmers, not lawyers." But as Saxon descendants, Americans were legally entitled to claim "absolute dominion" of their lands and to govern themselves through their own parliaments, along with their officer, the king. Reginald Horsman has detailed how this "myth of Anglo-Saxon England" and its liberty-loving people pervaded many other revolutionary writings.[10]

To be sure, the colonists' claims about their libertarian Anglo-Saxon race were often useful simply for reinforcing their appeals to the personal freedoms Enlightenment liberals celebrated and the powers of political self-governance republican writers defended. Nonetheless, their Saxon mythology did imply a connection between a people's unique cultural traits and their shared ancestry, and it was often used to distinguish British Americans biologically as well as culturally from Native Americans and African-Americans, whom they disdained as savages. When James Otis instead asserted, consistent with Coke, that all "colonists, black and white, born here, are free born British subjects," John Adams was one of many who "shuddered."[11]

And from early on, colonial leaders were quick to suggest that in their passions for liberty British Americans were, in Gordon Wood's words, "more English than the English," a view many European observers endorsed. As colonial elites began trying to fire up their neighbors to resist the British, that theme became ever more pronounced. The Puritans had already envisioned America as a haven for Protestant religious dissenters, and Enlightenment writers had occasionally praised America as a pristine virgin land where a better, freer society could be built. In 1763 Boston preachers had suggested that success in the French and Indian War was a divine sign that America was in fact the New Israel, destined to be raised to "this highth of greatness and dominion, to be the refuge and asylum of Truth and Liberty: by its influence and example to free the western world from Error and Superstition; and to fix on this extensive Continent, what will be its *peculiar* glory, the universal establishment of Civil Freedom and true Religion." In 1765 John Adams turned this presumptuous view to the support of colonial grievances against Britain, solemnly assuring his fellow colonists that the "settlement of America" was "the opening of a grand scene and design in Providence for the illumination of the ignorant and the emancipation of the slavish part of mankind all over the earth." The colonists' complaints against British treatment of them as "slaves" were part of this righteous cause.[12]

At that point, however, Adams still sought reconciliation, and so he said that the "spirit of liberty" was "as ardent as ever among the body" of the English nation, "though a few individuals may be corrupted." Bland was more gloomy, fearing that in England "the Gangrene has taken too deep Hold to be eradicated in these Days of Venality." John Dickinson, too, thought that the "people of Great-Britain" had been "artfully excited" by conniving conspirators to the point where they were "blinded by the passions," lost to the cause of freedom. By 1775, writing under the name Novanglus, Adams agreed that "luxury, effeminacy and venality" had arrived at "such a shocking pitch" of "corruption" in England that vice had become "incurable, and a necessary instrument of government." Proclamations that the "People of England were depraved, the parliament venal, and the ministry corrupt" were "most melancholy truths."[13]

The revolutionaries could therefore assert what they badly needed to assert: that British Americans were now the *sole* bearers of the providentially favored Anglo-Saxon mission to build a realm of enlightenment and spiritual and political liberty. Symbolic of this new sense of American identity was the spread of "St. Tammany" societies after the formation of the first one at Philadelphia in 1772. These centers of incipient patriot activity took as their symbol the Delaware chief Tamenend, who was thought to have thwarted a Jesuit conspiracy to tyrannize the New World. His name thus gave apt expression to the groups' anti-Catholic and anti-foreign, as well as anti-English outlook, and their conviction that America, not Europe, was where human capacities for liberty would reach their height. But the societies also clearly believed that Anglo-Saxon or at least northern European stock and Protestantism were both necessary for that result. Though they symbolically laid claim to Tamenend's virtues, they presented only themselves, not the still "brutish" and "savage" tribes, as "native Americans" destined to pioneer new frontiers of freedom.[14]

Analysts of the Revolution often slight how this conception of Americans as a distinct people, chosen to serve the Protestant God's emancipating purposes, forms a major if rather disingenuous theme of Tom Paine's massively influential 1776 pamphlet, "Common Sense." Though Paine was surely an Enlightenment liberal and a passionate republican, and though he was at best a deist for whom no revelatory text was truly authoritative, he knew how powerfully many North American colonists identified with the Israel of the Old Testament. He therefore explained that it was the ancient Jews, rather than the British, who had originally had a republican constitution, only to have it perverted into a monarchy, incurring divine disapproval. They, not the arrogant English, were the ancient republican "Chosen People" who were in the deepest spiritual sense the colonists' forebears. And Paine claimed to see in the location of America and the timing of its "discovery" the "design of Heaven." The "Almighty graciously meant to open a sanctuary to the persecuted" Protestants of Europe. Clearly, Paine grasped the enormous value of persuading religious Americans that the revolutionaries were on a mission from God.[15]

Paine's work also, however, reflected the fact that the new sense of nationality the revolutionaries were crafting contained significantly different strands—one more parochial, one more cosmopolitan. The two strains were not sharply differentiated then, but they would later diverge widely. The predominant contention was the more parochial claim that Americans were an essentially Anglo-Saxon people, specially chosen by the Protestant God to carry forth the torch of freedom that was the emblem of their race. On this view of American nationality, persons of different ethnic, religious, or racial origins were presumptively outsiders.

But a few writers and leaders, often foreign-born ones like Paine, Hector St. John Crèvecoeur, and James Wilson, along with some natives like Rhode Island's Silas Downer, assigned the new American nationality a somewhat more cosmopolitan meaning. Building on the patterns established by the colonies' generous naturalization policies, they insisted that America was an "asylum nation" descended from all the countries of Europe, "melted into a new race of men," in Crèvecoeur's words. As writers like Stephen Hopkins and Samuel Adams noted, the 1740 naturalization law indicated that foreigners granted British subjectship in the colonies possessed "all the rights of natural born subjects of Great Britain," at least while they remained in those colonies (though Adams's ethnic biases may be evident in his remark that "even" naturalized foreigners could claim such rights). Americans, then, were not simply English or Anglo-Saxon.[16]

The cosmopolitan character of this conception should not be exaggerated: Downer, Crèvecoeur, and Paine agreed that, in Paine's words, Christian "Europe and not England is the parent country of America." They did so knowing full well that nonwhite non-Europeans with different faiths resided in North America in large numbers. Paine noted that "tens of thousands" of Americans were eager to expel the "hellish power" of Britain because it had "stirred up the Indians and the Negroes to destroy us," a policy he denounced as treacherous to "them" as well as to "us." Only the most radical egalitarians among the colonists, like Otis and at times Benjamin Rush and Joel Barlow, were willing to contemplate abandoning these broader racial and religious restrictions in favor of more universal doctrines of the rights of man. Indeed, though writers like Paine and Crèvecoeur suggested that Americans intermixed the best of Europe, and though the British Americans claimed to have absorbed what was best about Native Americans as well, most saw these admixtures as creating a nationality that Winthrop Jordan described as "modified Englishmen."[17]

Virtually all the pamphleteers also presumed without discussion the continuation of male political supremacy. Even Paine, the radical critic of patriarchal defenses of monarchy, repeatedly referred only to "men" as exercisers of political rights. He said that Americans claimed "brotherhood with every European Christian" and disparaged those unwilling to resist Britain as "unmanly," while mentioning in passing that gender distinctions were rooted in "nature." These passages show that Paine had no thought of changing the status of women. He saw the political community as male.[18]

Similarly, when in March 1776 Abigail Adams sent her now-famous letter to John turning the revolutionaries' arguments about "Representation" to the cause of gender equity, she received a patronizing reply. Abigail urged her husband to "Remember the Ladies" in building an independent nation by limiting the power of "Naturally Tyrannical" husbands over their wives, replacing subjectship with friendship. John wrote back that he could not "but laugh." The revolutionaries were being accused of inspiring disobedience among "Indians" and "Negroes," but hers was the first suggestion of female discontent he had heard. He insisted that "Masculine" domination was "little more than Theory," and that if men gave up "the Name of Masters," they would be fully subjected to "the Despotism of the Peticoat." Though expressed jocularly, his opposition to the loss of male legal prerogatives was real. Two months later, he wrote James Sullivan more bluntly that "nature" had made women "fittest for domestic cares," not "the great businesses of life," the "hardy enterprises of war," or "the arduous cares of state."[19]

Although even proponents of the more cosmopolitan view of American identity, which later writers have exaggerated into a "national legend," thus accepted gender hierarchies, they usually contended that it was not chiefly ancestry that created the Americans' special character. To Crèvecoeur, this "new man, the American," was a product of the unique material and social circumstances of the New World, which seemed providentially shaped to "metamorphize" newcomers into industrious, independent, egalitarian free men who loved liberty and were capable of practicing it. Thus this position moved at least some Americans toward conceptions of national identity that did not refer to ethnicity, religion, or national origins at all.[20]

Neither the more narrowly ascriptive nor more cosmopolitan conception of American nationality fully served the revolutionaries' purposes, however. The narrower, Anglo-Saxon-centered view left out too many colonial inhabitants whose support colonial elites desperately needed, and it promoted connection to England as easily as rebellion. Loyalists regularly appealed to the ties of kinship many colonists felt with the English. In comparison, the notions of Americans as "Christian Europeans" put forth by Paine and Crèvecoeur must have seemed strange and questionable to many of the predominantly English-descended colonists, and so it could hardly be their central rallying cry. These circumstances probably explain why the American revolutionaries did not rely on nationalism as heavily as those in other lands would later do. Furthermore, many American leaders were optimistic about the nation's capacity to assimilate individuals of non-English (albeit European) origins. Thus they stressed liberal and republican appeals, invoked both versions of their new Americanism, and muted the exclusionary implications of their revised Anglo-Saxon myth despite its emotionally potent appeal. Even so, they did not fail to assure British American men that they had a special, divinely favored character which justified their rule over non-Europeans and women and augured success for their national Revolution.[21]

Liberalism and Revolutionary Americanism

As Coke's reasoning in *Calvin's Case* showed, it was always possible to assert that English law embodied an even more fundamental natural law, which Locke and others redefined in more liberal terms in the seventeenth and eighteenth centuries. When imperial lawyers called attention to the numerous precedents for parliamentary legislation over the colonies—along with colonial charter provisions recognizing British sovereignty—and the reality of virtual representation even in Britain, many colonists were persuaded of their legal duty to obey. Those who were not felt impelled to move beyond positive law to England's natural law traditions. Because even religious and racial discourses had often contended that

English liberties accorded with the principles of true human nature (though most of the world's peoples were too slavish to realize this), shifting from "rights of Englishmen" to the "rights of man" rarely seemed jarring. But, in fact, restrictive notions of Americans as specially chosen Anglo-Saxons, improved perhaps by some European admixtures, were in deep tension with moral doctrines of universal and equal human rights.[22]

After his extensive appeals to Americans' "Saxon" rights in his 1774 "Summary View" pamphlet, Jefferson (like many other revolutionary writers) went on to contend that the liberties of colonists and ancestors alike should also be traced to nature and to its God. A year later, one of the foreign-born architects of the new American nation, Alexander Hamilton, made the break from dependence on English traditions even more dramatic. The "sacred rights of mankind," he argued, were "not to be rummaged for among old parchments or musty records. They are written, as with a sunbeam, in the whole volume of human nature, by the hand of divinity itself, and can never be erased or obscured by mortal power." In "Common Sense," appeals to the Saxons vanished, and reliance on the immutable "natural rights of all mankind" to oppose not only imperial policies but also the monarchical and aristocratic elements of the English constitution itself became complete.[23]

Because invoking natural rights and liberties in these ways had long been known as a very English thing to do, it is easy to minimize how the colonists here were blending conceptions of their national identity that were politically complementary but philosophically dissonant. The emphasis on their specifically Anglo-Saxon character violated several strains in Enlightenment rationalist political theory. The most influential of such writers in the American colonies was the man Voltaire called "Father of the Enlightenment," John Locke.[24] In Locke's attacks on all forms of absolutism, including Stuart monarchical power and seventeenth-century intellectual orthodoxies, the Anglo-Saxon myth and the concepts of race and natural political communities had no place.

Instead of "races," Locke focused on individuals; and though he recognized differences in cultural attainments, he traced these differences to contrasting systems of socialization and education, not to differences in natural rational capacities. Locke insisted that the "natural Endowments" of "savage *Americans*" fell "in no way short" of "those of the most flourishing and polite Nations," and he dismissed as childish the notion that "*a Negro is not a Man.*" Unlike many of his contemporaries, he never suggested that history or nature made descent from Anglo-Saxon stock, rather than educated reason, a prerequisite for exercising basic liberties.[25]

Locke also explicitly repudiated the claim that men were born natural subjects of any sovereign or political community, thus rejecting Coke's feudal view of the cosmos as divinely ordered into natural hierarchies. With the major exception of the family, to Locke the human order of ranks appeared to be entirely conventional, a matter of human creation. And though persons were born subject to the natural authority of their parents, even that tutelage was bounded and temporary, a necessary means to prepare children for the equal, independent status that reason, nature, and Christianity showed to be proper for all mature, rational beings.[26]

Locke, in fact, carried this insistence on the artificial character of political communities to a more radical extreme than any government, including the United States, has ever been willing to accept. He expressly denied that citizenship could be determined by birth within a certain territory or under a particular government. Instead, "a *Child is born a subject of no Country and Government. He is under his Father's Tuition and Authority, till he comes to Age of Discretion; and then he is a Free-man, at liberty what Government he will put himself under; what body politick he will unite himself to.*" Apart from patriarchal rule over wives and children, which Locke endorsed only in weakened form, no type of political membership or subjectship was in any sense natural.[27]

Because men were born free, without birthright citizenship in any political community, Locke argued, they could only acquire such a membership through human choices—the choice of the individual to join some civil society and obey its government, and the choice of the existing members of that society to accept him. Thus Locke reached his view that governments ought to originate in social compacts among free individuals, a position that Paine would dramatize by asking his readers to imagine sturdy free and equal men in a state of nature sitting around a tree to create a state and "deliberate on public matters." Though Locke sometimes wrote in a similarly poetic fashion, he held that membership in most existing political societies was founded only on tacit consent, usually expressed by a person's willingness to accept his inheritance under laws that gave that power only to that society's subjects or citizens. Locke assumed also that, if given the choice, most people would decide to live in a society to which they had vital ties, most often the land of their birth, though sometimes the homeland of their parents, or of their linguistic, religious, or ethnic group. But Locke did not stress this point, for he presented such attachments simply as things to which people might want to give weight in deciding which polity to join. Those ties did not make their political memberships in any sense "natural."[28]

In accordance with this insistence that political identities were matters of human artifice and choice, Locke argued that they could be changed, individually and collectively, notwithstanding Coke's doctrine of perpetual allegiance. Individuals whose subjectship had originated only in tacit consent, usually via their acceptance of an inheritance, could sell their land and go elsewhere, thereby expatriating themselves from their original political community.[29] Locke's consensualism represented the clearest challenge to Coke's view of political membership in Anglo-American law, and it greatly influenced European thought more generally. The eighteenth-century Swiss international law writers Jean-Jacques Burlamaqui and Emmerich de Vattel, whom the revolutionaries also often cited, built on Locke to argue for even broader expatriation rights. They agreed that citizens had obligations based on their past engagements within and with a polity, so that they should not depart when needed in war, or when they had unsettled public debts of a criminal or financial nature. But ordinarily, citizens could seek expatriation whenever they wished. If no pressing needs intervened, governments should concur. If a government violated their basic liberties, the citizens' rights of expatriation became "absolute."[30]

As that last point suggests, the Lockean emphasis on the artificial nature of political membership did not mean that Enlightenment rationalists saw political life as lacking natural standards entirely; and those standards also supported collective rights to overturn sovereigns on some occasions. Reasoning on men's God-given natural freedom led, Locke believed, to the conclusion that all persons had certain divinely authorized natural rights and duties, which governments were created to uphold and advance. No government could depart from those purposes and remain legitimate. If via "a long train of Abuses" a government proved that it intended to overstep the bounds of its authority—failing to exercise its legislative power in a representative fashion and for the public welfare, and instead infringing on rights of its subjects—then the government, not the people, had broken the mythical but implicit social contract. Hence it could legitimately be replaced. If a portion of the people could obtain just government only by withdrawing from their fellow subjects, this step, too, was justified.[31]

These conceptions of the nature of political membership had already been merged to some extent with Coke's doctrines in English legal and political thought by the time of the pre-revolutionary debates. Blackstone had departed from Coke's insistence that natural allegiances were immutable and perpetual to hold that a subject's allegiance could be dissolved by the "concurrence" of the subject and parliament. He found this more consensualist view of membership so consonant with parliamentary sovereignty and with real political practices as to be irresistible. Blackstone firmly rejected, however, Locke's defense of a right to rebel.[32]

Even so, the British government and loyalists in America invoked liberal mythology to defend their cause, just as the revolutionaries did. British officials argued that, because legitimate governments were supposedly created after the formation of a political society via a social contract, a people could alter that government without eroding any member's obligation to continue to obey the judgment of the community as a whole. The actions by which the British had re-formed their constitution to give primacy to the king-in-parliament in Britain, not the king alone or the king and any other assembly, had taken place without any dissolution of the British political community. Those actions were therefore fully binding on all members of the community, British Americans included. Par-liament also seemed the logical embodiment of the "supream" legislative power that Locke expected to be assigned to representative assemblies. Though the British used other arguments for parliamentary authority, these often proved ser-viceable. Indeed, in 1775 the loyalist Joseph Galloway cited Locke at length on be-half of legislative supremacy and the Americans' obligations to the majority of the civil society they had joined, either explicitly or by accepting land. Galloway did because Locke had "been often heretofore relied on by the American advo-cates."[33]

Yet Locke supplied the revolutionaries with more potent ammunition. The colonists were accustomed by their longtime advocacy of easy naturalizations to stress the consensual origins of political membership, and they passionately de-sired to deny British claims that they were perpetual subjects. Thus early on Richard Bland cited Locke and Vattel to proclaim: "Men in a State of Nature are absolutely free and independent of one another as to sovereign Jurisdiction," be-coming members of "a Society" only "by their own consent." Jefferson's Declara-tion of Independence began by invoking similar Lockean premises, announcing that, according to the "laws of nature and of nature's God," just governments are "instituted" among men via the "consent of the governed" in order to secure their inalienable rights of life, liberty, and the pursuit of happiness. Then it went on to show that British policies were textbook examples of Locke's "long train of abuses" justifying rebellions. They had not only failed to secure basic rights but had massively violated them via denials of representation and economic and per-sonal liberties. Jefferson listed all those grievances before going on to the racial and religious threats to the British Americans' supremacy noted earlier.[34]

But though Lockean liberal views of political membership as originating in consent, not nature, helped legitimate the revolutionaries' cause, they left many questions unanswered; and some answers they implied were hard to accept. The universalist, egalitarian claims of inalienable rights with which the Declaration began rested uncomfortably with the denunciation of Indian "savages" and the silence on women and African-American slavery that followed, however smoothly the rhetoric flowed for those who regarded racial and gender hierar-chies as natural. Nor was there much room for the myth of superior English or Saxon blood that the revolutionaries exploited in other writings and that Jeffer-son's original draft invoked in passing. The contradictions between the consen-sual, egalitarian principles that the colonists were trumpeting and their older ascriptive beliefs and practices did not go unnoticed in the revolutionary era, which saw serious antislavery efforts led by Quakers and even faint stirrings on behalf of gender equality by elite women like Abigail Adams. The focus on the fierce struggle against Britain, however, muted those issues for the time being.[35]

In the years after 1776, American leaders would have to address these issues. Rather than undertaking yet more sweeping changes, many would turn various themes in Enlightenment thought to support for ascriptive racial, gender, ethnic, and religious hierarchies.[36] None, however, ever really reconciled the morally egalitarian universalism of the Declaration of Independence with the inegalitarian ascriptive components of the new nation. Their claims of massive racial and gender inferiority rested on dubious evidence, given the great differences in education and opportunities that existed. Enlightenment claims of entitlement to basic rights for all people who were minimally rational thus still indicted both governmental and private conduct that denied people such liberties.[37] More extensive resources for defending existing hierarchies, as well as for designing new political institutions, would be found in the accounts of republicanism made by English opposition writers and also many Enlightenment thinkers; but in America, republican views, too, often had a disturbingly egalitarian ring.

Republicanism and Revolutionary Americanism

If asked in late 1776, most American revolutionaries would surely have first described their cause not as liberalism or Americanism but independence and republicanism. Though the elements suggested by the first two labels were vitally important to them, their struggle against those whom most colonists regarded as kinsmen led them to feature their opposition to the British monarchy and unrepresentative parliament. Republicanism became in America the key term announcing one's allegiance to "popular" government founded on consent and to the Revolution, as opposed to aristocracy and monarchy founded on natural allegiance and the mixed British constitution.

But in Western political history this "ism" had many meanings, making republican slogans adaptable to many purposes. Republics could be egalitarian or hierarchical, isolationist or imperialistic, libertarian or totalitarian. As Gordon Wood has described, the English-speaking world "confused and blended" monarchy and republicanism, holding both sets of values "side by side," just as Americans would hold liberal, republican, and ascriptive values. Thus even colonists with republican leanings long felt that they could proclaim the mixed British Constitution "the best that ever existed among men," as Stephen Hopkins said. This blending also meant, however, that most people thought it appropriate to judge British governments by "republican standards" of liberty, the common good, and resistance to corruption.[38] The revolutionaries made great use of that advantage.

Although Harrington himself had recognized the traditional Anglo-Saxon constitution as feudal, many revolutionaries followed neo-Harringtonians like Gordon and Trenchard and depicted it as a republic. Thus in their alarums they were able to blend the narrative of their providentially favored Anglo-Saxon identity fairly seamlessly with the well-established republican scenario of corruption. All such free, self-governing regimes could be perverted into despotisms via conspiratorial elite factions who used financial regulations enforced by a standing army to enrich themselves at public expense. The British imperial officials were doing just that, thereby not only violating republican principles but also betraying their divinely bestowed racial mission. As revolutionary pamphleteers gave themselves classical republican pseudonyms and invoked this scenario of corruption against Britain over and over, they simultaneously elaborated their myths of hereditary Anglo-Saxon liberties and Protestant millennialism without any sense of disjuncture. And just as their polemical reliance on human rights over British legal rights led them to espouse rationalist liberalism without fully recognizing the threats it posed to their sense of inborn superiority, so the angry colonial leaders increasingly rejected the nonpopular aspects of the British Constitution in favor of majoritarian republicanism, without fully grasping how far-reaching its egalitarian dimensions could be.[39]

Again, this was a dynamic that reached its apex in the master pamphleteer who touched so many chords in American ideology, Tom Paine. Whereas even Jefferson in "A Summary View" was still beseeching the king on behalf of his loyal "subjects in British America," who sought only "fraternal love" throughout the empire, Paine's "Common Sense" was the first American pamphlet to denounce openly all but the "Republican" part of the British Constitution, the Commons. Paine particularly assaulted the "ridiculous" institution of monarchy, claiming that all its inherent flaws were now revealed through the presence on the throne of the "Royal Brute of Great Britain." The form of governance that men in a state of nature would choose to create—a republican assembly—was the ultimate standard for political legitimacy. Although a number of the colonial gentry class retained grave reservations about popular republics that would be aggravated under the Articles of Confederation, by the end of the Revolution it was almost universally accepted that the new governments in America had to have a basically majoritarian republican form. Virtually all who stayed believed that Americans should never again be subjects instead of citizens.[40]

But to make republican citizenship work, the most ardent American republicans thought that they had to create a whole "new world," a special sort of social order and way of life. A successful republic required citizens to be profoundly socialized into certain beliefs, aspirations, and character traits. Men must be converted into "republican machines," in Benjamin Rush's phrase, able and willing to place the good of their country above their own self-interest. As Boston's pseudonymous Preceptor exhorted in 1772, republicanism presented the fundamental "duties" of man's "social state" as "*love of our country, resignation and obedience to the laws, public spirit, love of liberty, sacrifice of life and all to the public, and the like.*" Achieving civic institutions and forms of social life that promoted republican virtue in all, expressed through actions in public life that aimed at advancing the common good, was no easy task. As heirs of the Calvinist legacy that preached man's inherent moral weakness, many of the revolutionary generation doubted whether Americans could hope to sustain such austere civic virtue. But amidst the intoxicating unity bred by the common revolutionary cause, these doubts were muted, and Americans dared hope that they could find ways to prove that men were indeed capable of republican self-governance.[41]

The extensive literature on republicanism seemed a treasure trove of such ways. First and most encompassing, analysts of republicanism like Montesquieu agreed that viable republics needed considerable homogeneity in their civic bodies along many social dimensions. Similarity in ethnicity, gender, economic status, and cultural traditions all seemed necessary to foster the sense of a "common interest" among civic brethren that issued in an unqualified "love of country." Harrington had especially stressed limiting economic inequalities among citizens, though eighteenth-century discussions of commercial republics and many American revolutionaries did so less frequently.

Second, republics had to have a relatively small number of citizens, bound to other peoples, if at all, via either a loose confederation or imperial domination. Meaningful participation in self-governance became more difficult as regimes grew more extensive, more complex, and less accessible to the comprehension or political action of individual citizens. Homogeneity also became harder to preserve. And, finally, given the power of religious faiths in human life, it was particularly important that the dominant forms of religiosity in a state reinforced republicanism, as Protestantism was thought to do, rather than undermine it, as many believed Catholicism did.

These beliefs authorized the new American republicans to exclude aliens as well as home-grown undesirable "others" from full civic membership, as the predominantly Protestant Anglophone male citizenry saw fit. But this accommodation between republicanism and ascriptive Americanist beliefs in a special national identity was logically far from perfect. In their most rigorous articulations by writers like Harrington, Rousseau, and (on some readings) Machiavelli, republican doctrines did not privilege any one "people" as intrinsically best suited for popular self-governance. Republicanism based membership on consent, not ascriptive traits, and it counseled homogeneity largely as a tactic to breed the harmony of sentiments and ideas that helped republics thrive. Preceptor's pamphlet made explicit republicanism's espousal of a political system rather than any ascriptive identity by arguing that "*love of our country* does not import an attachment to any particular soil, climate, or spot of earth . . . but it imports an affection to that *moral system*, or *community* which is governed by the same laws and magistrates . . . and all united upon the bottom of a common interest." Because most Americans tried to join their republicanism not only with ascriptive civic myths but also with Enlightenment doctrines of personal liberties and human equality, this instrumental endorsement of homogeneity was not always sufficient to ease the tensions between their liberal, egalitarian precepts and their embrace of many traditional civic hierarchies.[42]

On the whole, however, the need to promote love of country and civic virtue within small popular republics made American elites comfortable about majoritarian expulsions and restrictions on full civic membership for aliens, nonwhites, and women. Maintaining a Christian, Anglo-Saxon, male-dominated citizenry seemed appropriate if Americans were to fulfill their mission to create a spiritual city on a hill, a bastion of Christian virtue and freedom, as well as a model republic. It helped, too, that republicanism, Anglo-Saxonism, and Christian morality overlapped in their calls for sacrifice, even though they differed in the human realms and endeavors with which they were most concerned. Hence, as Gordon Wood notes, "religion and republicanism" came to "work hand in hand" in striving for a new America of both civic and religious virtue—a "Christian Sparta," in Samuel Adams's words.[43]

The more optimistic American republicans argued that, fortunately, the American people already possessed many unifying qualities: a largely English-descended populace; far greater social and economic equality than in Europe; dedication to the common good sparked by revolutionary endeavors; and a pervasive Protestantism, usually tempered by a measure of tolerance for minority Christian and Jewish sects. The revolutionaries believed, however, that innovations were needed to preserve those advantages, including not only popular governments but also support for a yeoman agrarian economy, republican iconography and civic celebrations, educational systems fostering virtue, egalitarian republican manners, and thriving state religions. Thus in 1776 leading Virginians strove to alter codes governing "inheritance, landowning, education, religion, administration," and the legal system in ways they believed would foster egalitarian republicanism. Several states also considered sumptuary laws to curb corrupting luxuries. Many of these reform proposals were not adopted, but efforts to create a social order conducive to republican citizenship, often by maintaining homogeneity, became a recurring part of American life.[44]

Republican themes also served other purposes. Many republican theorists had long accepted that a small republic could rule large numbers of noncitizens as slaves, as Sparta did. Southerners relied on those authorities when building up their slave "republics." Some republican treatises had followed Machiavelli in further advocating an imperial policy through which small martial republics would rule conquered rivals. But Montesquieu and Vattel suggested instead that modern republics might establish defensive confederations with other republican regimes, meeting their military needs without establishing potentially corrupting empires. Though some American revolutionaries happily contemplated an empire of their own, many took these latter works as textbooks for revolutionary experiment in confederation and their later creation, their experiment of constitutional federalism.[45]

Thus republicanism not only provided additional rationales for maintaining systems of ascriptive hierarchy. It also argued for a high degree of decentralization, to make state citizenship more fundamental than national citizenship in the new American political order. That legacy would shape American political development, including struggles over ascriptive inequalities, far into the nation's future.

In sum, from 1776 on, revolutionary leaders were actively promoting conceptions of true Americans as, first, the bearers of a new, unique, and precious ascriptive identity; second, the rational social contractors creating governments dedicated to securing individual rights imagined by Lockean liberals; and, third, public-spirited republican citizens, spurred by concerns for political liberty and the common good. Despite their contradictions, there was as yet little sense of conflict among these conceptions. The colonists' Anglo-Saxon heritage was presented as bestowing a special awareness of men's natural liberties and also unique capacities for self-governance—traits reinforced by America's environment. American men thus considered themselves naturally suited to take up the banner of the Enlightenment cause of human rights; and that cause seemed to demand their exercise of a Lockean right of revolution, their establishment of a separate American national identity, and their creation of popular republics. But despite these apparently mutually reinforcing features, it remained true that this new sense of Americanism was, as Linda Colley has said of Britishness, something "superimposed over an array of internal differences."[46] As the former colonists began the tasks of nation-building in earnest, the differences in the experiences, interests, and ideas of many of those now labeled "Americans" soon threatened to unravel the happy combination of their political traditions forged in their Revolution.

4

Citizens of Small Republics
The Confederation Era 1776–1789

From the standpoint of citizenship laws, it is ironic that the Confederation era is rarely celebrated in conventional depictions of America's allegedly steady progress toward fuller realization of its "core" liberal democratic ideals. Instead, this period is often portrayed as a false start that had to be corrected via the Constitution.[1] Yet if commitments to egalitarian liberal republican ideals are or should be the heart of American identity, the years from 1776 to 1787 ought to stand as one of the greatest eras of American civic reform. In striking contrast to most of the periods examined in this book, there were no major new inegalitarian ascriptive civic provisions during these years. Instead, citizenship laws were rewritten to make American institutions more inclusive, more democratic, more protective of civil liberties, and less supportive of racial, religious, and ethnic hierarchies than they had been before the war. Americans strove generally to fulfill the principles of their Revolution by creating a league of egalitarian small republics, not a dangerously centralized nation. The new northern republics also began the First Emancipation, eliminating slavery in half the nation and expanding the rights of free blacks. The Confederation Congress's diplomats sometimes treated the unconquered tribes with the respect shown independent nations, and northwestern Native Americans were offered membership in the new United States. States also altered inheritance laws and franchise qualifications to lessen the legal reinforcement of economic class structures.

The needs of revolutionary leaders to win support for their dangerous war undeniably formed the immediate cause of the Americans' advocacy of comparatively radical versions of the rights of man and republicanism. The same needs even pushed the British in the same direction: in 1775, short of manpower, Lord Dunmore promised African-Americans freedom in exchange for military service. Rhode Island's assembly eventually responded with a similar promise in 1778.[2] Leaders who resort to such tactics then usually face pressures to live up to them; many Americans were in any case genuinely persuaded that they should do so.

Thus, after their triumph in the war, Rhode Island along with the other northern states did legislate emancipation. Even the states of the upper South lightened restrictions on slaves and free blacks, a tribute in part to the American nation-builders' passionate belief in the principles for which they had risked their lives.[3] It is also clear, however, that these efforts were heavily shaped and constrained by economic and political forces. Emancipation was able to succeed in the North largely because northern economies were not much reliant on slavery, and steadfastly antislavery religious groups like the Quakers happened to be concentrated there. Even so, change came slowly and bred backlash. The respect the Confederation government displayed toward the tribes was also more a matter of avoiding costly quarrels than of principle. And the weakening of class inequalities in the new state republics played a major role in spurring the countermovements that produced the Constitution.

Indeed, the most important lesson of the Confederation may be the routine denigration it receives today (long matched by similar dismissals of Reconstruction, and now echoed in criticisms of the civil rights and Great Society reforms of the 1960s). Though extreme political crises like wars may lead Americans to stress the inclusive, democratic strains in their political culture over traditional hierarchies, liberalizing and democratizing reforms usually spawn counter-efforts to rebuild systems of inequality. Those efforts have frequently been so successful that what seemed like egalitarian changes later came to be portrayed as destructive nonsense.

The full story of the Confederation era, then, includes more than the ways American leaders culminated their Revolution by constructing a league of democratized and liberalized small republics. As in later reform eras, this is also a story of some continuing ascriptive hierarchies and growing opposition to egalitarian republicanism. Many Continental Congressmen, national military leaders, and colonial financial elites had reservations about the new state governments from the outset. By 1787 many states had already revised them, and leading figures were fighting for a new, more nationalistic constitution.

The growing division between supporters and critics of the state regimes became fundamental to American politics. It represented, to be sure, a quarrel between elites who were all republicans, all defenders of liberal natural rights, and all loyal Americans supportive of many American ascriptive systems. But the advocates of state power were most firmly in the small-republic tradition, concerned above all to preserve popular and localist control of potentially corrupt elites. The proponents of elite-guided national governance tended to stress liberal goals of securing productive property relations, sound currency, and expanding commerce, as well as more nationalistic visions of American glory. As popular enthusiasm for revolutionary reform faded, neither group was much concerned to challenge further inequalities that ensconced white Christian men in leadership positions and left blacks, women, Native Americans, and the indigent as subjects of one sort or another, and not true citizens. Consequently, the burst of egalitarian republicanism with which the Confederation began soon gave way to conflicts between state-centered and nationalistic elites, in ways that would dominate American citizenship struggles for many years. Challenges to the nation's most constitutive denials of egalitarian, liberal republican civic principles would be relegated to sideshows.

The Context of Struggle

The state-centeredness of American political life from 1776 to 1789 must be stressed because the era includes some of the most momentous collective acts in the nation's history. Operating through the extralegal Continental Congress, the revolutionaries launched their war for independence by calling on the states to form new governments in May 1776, issuing the Declaration in July, forming a national army in October. The Articles of Confederation were then proposed, though not ratified, in 1777. But none of these were unambiguously national acts. Despite the revolutionaries' exhortations, only one-third of the British colonists actively supported their cause. One-fifth or more opposed it. About one-quarter of those, 80,000 to 100,000 British loyalists left. Some returned to England, but by far the greater part moved to Canada. Many other Americans living on small rural farms saw the revolutionary quarrels as irrelevant disputes between imperial officials and colonial elites, though calls for their military service soon brought the conflict home.[4]

Nor was the reconstruction of the colonial governments a national enterprise. The colonies had already begun their recrafting before Congress's call; they did so under their own direction, and by and large they created regimes that were models of state-centered, democratic republican views. By the end of 1776, eight colonies had formed new republican constitutions, and Rhode Island and Connecticut had altered their otherwise republican (though far from democratic) charters to eliminate references to royal authority. Georgia and New York adopted new constitutions the following year, as did Vermont. Massachusetts reinstituted its abrogated 1725 charter and began a labored process of constitution-making that culminated with John Adams's handiwork in 1780. It was in these self-created state republics, not in the Continental or Confederation congresses, that most American self-governing was done.[5]

The Declaration of Independence itself was a product of the representatives of the "United states," not of Americans as individuals. That fact has often been read to suggest that the revolutionaries accepted the political supremacy of state communities over individuals, in republican fashion. Although different interpretations are plausible, the reality of state resistance to assertions of national authority cannot be denied.[6] For example, by October 1776 the revolutionaries had been engaged in armed conflict with British forces for more than a year, and George Washington had been pleading with Congress to form a national army for some time. Congress agreed reluctantly, because many preferred to wage war using the state militias. National naval forces remained minimal, so Washington had to rely on the states' erratic willingness to provide support in order to gain troops and supplies. After the war, the national army was largely dismantled.

As for the Articles of Confederation, their ratification was delayed until 1781 because of Maryland's and New Jersey's insistence that all states, especially Virginia, cede the Confederation Congress authority over most of the lands west of the 1763 Proclamation Line.[7] Even some Virginians like Jefferson and Richard Henry Lee agreed, though not out of nationalism. They believed that a single republic could not flourish in the vast territory their state would have to govern if it expanded westward. Finally, all the states ceded their land claims and Maryland ratified the Articles in 1781. Americans then had an official national government with extensive territories. But the whole controversy, like the conduct of the war, only underlined the ideological power of small-state republicanism and the political power of the states.

As would often be the case, international factors as much as domestic actions determined the fate of the revolutionaries' efforts to create a new country. Eager to recover from their defeats of 1763, the French recognized the United States and allied with it against Britain in 1778. Spain and Holland then renewed warfare against the British as allies of France, though not of the United States. France provided the Americans with a navy in 1780, and they began to win victories. Britain also faced mounting tensions with Russia, Denmark, and Sweden in the early 1780s. When Washington used French forces and the Continental Army to compel Lord Cornwallis to surrender at Yorktown in 1781, the British decided that the colonies were not worth the costs.

The Americans gained formal independence via the Peace of Paris in 1783, but they were internationally seen as something like the Czech regime after World War II, far more a dependent beneficiary of a superpower's triumph than an equal member of the family of nations. Indeed, the American ambassadors—Ben Franklin, John Jay, and John Adams—were instructed by Congress to demand only independence, while obeying France on all other matters. The envoys proved more enterprising. They negotiated on their own to gain boundaries that stretched from Canada to the north, west to the Mississippi, and south to Florida, which the U.S. had to return to Spain in a separate treaty. But even after the peace, America's national existence was still more a project than reality.[8]

To carry out that project, Americans adopted a wide range of civically constitutive acts, from the state constitutions to the Articles to the Northwest Ordinance of 1787, along with laws and treaties affecting British loyalists, blacks, Native Americans, and aliens seeking citizenship. Though state-centered republicanism was most prominent, the overall effect of these measures was to institutionalize elements of all the partly reinforcing, partly conflicting civic conceptions in American culture. Thus few of the basic questions about American political identity were resolved. The Confederation's legal and political frameworks nonetheless had enduring consequences. They can best be perceived by first mapping out the new nation's republicanism and then detailing the liberal and ascriptive elements that Americans mixed into their multiply constituted civic institutions.

Republicanism in the Nation and the States

Republicanism at the National Level. The clearest proofs of the dominance of state-centered republicanism in the nation's new citizenships were the laws and structure of the Confederation itself. The most overt expressions of popular republicanism in the Articles were prohibitions in Article VI against the bestowing of any titles of nobility by the states or the "united states," and against the holding of national or state offices by anyone possessing a foreign title. There would be no aristocracy or monarchy in America's civic body. But the impact on the Confederation of republican fears about a strong national government, even a popular one, were almost as great.

The Articles of Confederation did not purport to create more than a "firm league of friendship" for purposes of "defence, the security of their Liberties, and their mutual and general welfare" (Art. III). The newly acquired "sovereignty, freedom, and independence" of the separate state republics were left intact, save for those powers "expressly delegated to the United States" (Art. II). These powers included authority to borrow money and to request arms and funds from the states, and exclusive or ultimate power to regulate the currency and weights and measures, establish a postal service, settle admiralty cases, and manage relations among the states, with foreign nations, and with the independent Indian tribes

(Arts. VI, IX). But structurally, the Confederation Congress was an instrument of the states, not their regulator. Each state cast one vote (Art. V). Although many decisions were to be made by simple majority, nine votes were required for most important functions, including treaties, wars, money matters, and additions to Congress's powers (Arts. IX, X). Taxes could still be levied only by the states (Art. VIII), and military forces were to be raised and many officers appointed by the states (Arts. VII, IX). Congress also had no authority to regulate commerce. And though Congress could appoint officials to carry out certain functions, and Article IX provided for temporary judges to decide disputes between states or citizens of different states, there was no national chief executive or permanent judiciary.[9] Thus, despite proclamations of the Congress's exclusive or ultimate authority in certain areas (Art. XIII), in practice state compliance with Confederation measures was voluntary. At the most basic level—control over money and arms—the new "perpetual union" remained an alliance of still-sovereign smaller republics.[10]

State-centered republicanism was visible even in congressional acts concerned with loyalty oaths, treason, naturalization, and requirements of native birth for officeholding, which might seem vehicles for defining national citizenship and giving it legal primacy. In 1775, Washington obtained apparent authorization from the Continental Congress to require oaths of loyalty to Congress and its military leaders from militia troops, and then from suspected British sympathizers in Rhode Island and Long Island. But in March 1776, New York's congressional delegation offered a temporarily successful resolution to leave loyalty oaths to the states. On June 24, 1776, Congress resolved that "all persons abiding within any of the United Colonies, and deriving protection from the laws of the same, owe allegiance to the said laws, and are members of such colony," whereas "all persons passing through, visiting, or make [sic] a temporary stay in any of the said colonies, being entitled to the protection of the laws during the time of such passage, visitation or temporary stay, owe, during the same time, allegiance thereto." Thus the aid of any such persons to Britain made them "guilty of treason against such colony."[11]

That resolution and later ones advised the colonial legislatures to punish such traitors, along with counterfeiters; and the states soon passed seemingly innumerable treason and loyalty oath statutes. After July 4 they often took a willingness to endorse the Declaration of Independence as the key test. Though Congress did not itself impose such oaths, in 1777 it did authorize Washington to conduct some ill-administered loyalty testing in New Jersey. Thereafter it authorized tests only for army or congressionally appointed civil officials. The Articles of Confederation did not require any loyalty oaths, though Article IV guaranteed that a person charged with treason "in any state" would be delivered to that state if subsequently found "in any of the united states." After the Peace of Paris, in which national officials agreed to forgive British loyalists, loyalty testing became largely a thing of the past.

The coercive imposition of these loyalty oaths was hard for the revolutionaries to justify in terms of the consensual conceptions of political membership for which they were allegedly fighting, as we shall see. But in regard to the issue of state versus national citizenship, the key point was that all these "national" measures still centered citizenship, loyalty, and treason at the state level. Although the June 1776 congressional resolution was a national act defining political membership, it indicated that each colonial resident was a member of one colony, not of the "United Colonies." Congress then simply urged the new state governments to punish treason, just as it largely left loyalty testing to the states. The Continental and Confederation congresses also did not naturalize aliens. They only passed resolutions instructing the states to naturalize various groups, and in 1788 Congress urged the states not to permit the transportation of convicts to America. It did confine employment in the U.S. foreign service to native-born citizens, but that status was widely thought of as state citizenship. The more generous policies toward British loyalists proposed by national officials after the Peace of 1783 also required voluntary state compliance. Hence all these citizenry-defining acts fit with republican views that American loyalties should be chiefly on the state level.[12]

The centrality of state citizenship was only slightly less pronounced in the major national effort to define America's future citizenry during the Confederation—the Northwest Ordinance of 1787. A modification of Jefferson's Ordinance of 1784 (which had never gone into effect), it provided for both republican self-governance within the new states and their eventual membership in a confederation that would remain a partnership of equally sovereign republics. Once a territory had acquired 5,000 "male inhabitants of full age," it was entitled to elect a general assembly of representatives serving two-year terms. Such an assembly was the key institution of a popular republic, and though the territorial legislature was also to include a five-member legislative council appointed for five-year terms by the Congress, the Congress chose from nominees selected by the elected assembly delegates. The second article of the ordinance indicated that these assemblies were to be relatively democratic: they were to be maintain a "proportionate representation" of the people, a policy not followed in the existing states, where representation by geographical districts was common.

In time, the inhabitants could form states that would be admitted to the Confederation on full equality with the existing sovereign states. Hence the new regimes would have as much power in relation to the Congress that authorized them as the original state republics. The Confederation's subordinate, instrumental character would not be altered even by this nationally directed expansion in the members of the United States.

Other provisions also implied the influence of republican notions of citizenship, though not necessarily state-centered ones. Republican beliefs in the political value of religiosity and virtue were echoed in the stipulation of the ordinance's third article that because religion, morality, and knowledge were necessary to good government and human happiness, education that included religious instruction "shall forever be encouraged." The ordinance also banned the aristocratic institution of primogeniture, thus curbing concentrations of hereditary lands. But the republics that the ordinance contemplated were far from egalitarian: their citizenry would have pronounced class and gender hierarchies. Electors had to own at least 50 acres of land and representatives at least 200 acres—steep requirements even for the thinly populated northwest. And again, only male inhabitants counted in representation. It is unclear whether these provisions flowed from common-law notions of the importance of landowning and masculinity for political membership, from republican concerns to make sure that citizens were self-supporting, manly farmers, or from other rationales. But they ensured that the new republics' leading citizens would be male property owners. Some support for viewing these strictures chiefly as products of republicanism came in the ordinance's fifth article, which made explicit that all new state governments had to "be republican, and in conformity to the principles contained in these Articles." Although some parts of the ordinance pointed in nationalistic and liberal directions, as discussed below, overall those principles suggested that even Congress conceded the power of states to place the interests and identities of their small republics above citizenship in the confederated nation.[13]

Republicanism at the State Level. In 1776, then, the state constitutional conventions and legislatures were understood to be the key arenas in which the republican civic lives of Americans would be conducted. Perhaps the most remarkable aspect of these new state governments was the extent to which they seemed radically democratic to many American political leaders. Democracy did not mean, however, that the franchise was universally distributed or that government was intensely participatory. The term referred chiefly to the fact that a popularly elected legislature possessed virtually all of each state's powers. In many other respects, the states displayed inegalitarian features. Yet in the early glow of independence, leaders designed state institutions that strove to empower ordinary citizens more fully than would ever be true in the U.S. again.[14]

The great sensitivity of public opinion to unrepublican inequalities in these years was dramatized by the furor over the Order of the Cincinnati, founded in

1783 by General Henry Knox and other Continental Line officers and intended to have hereditary membership. Quickly attacked as an incipient "Military Nobility" and repudiated by George Washington, the short-lived society became a symbol of the continuing threat of antirepublican elements. The attendant insistence on purely popular assemblies was so strong that elites who worried about legislative excesses had to struggle to establish relatively separate executive and judicial bodies and to oppose unicameral legislatures. John Adams's *Thoughts on Government* (1776) led the campaign against government by democratic assemblies alone during the crucial period of state constitution-making. Adams contended that such assemblies lacked the secrecy and dispatch to carry out executive functions effectively, as well as the legal skills to exercise the judicial power. Hence a separate executive and judiciary were desirable. Adams especially advocated bicameral legislatures. He insisted that, despite the fate of the Cincinnati, "aristocrats"—defined as those who could control more than one vote—would arise in any regime. By establishing an upper house or council, preferably elected by the lower, such talented potential corrupters of the public weal could be utilized but also watched.[15]

Arguments like Adams's had an impact. All the states forming constitutions in 1776 (except Pennsylvania) established an upper house; and by the end of the 1780s every state, even the once radically democratic Pennsylvanians, had come around. All the state constitutions, moreover, endorsed a separation of powers, though initially those separations were mostly theoretical. In the wake of the Americans' rage against King George, opposition to strong executives was so great that most governors were hemmed in by senates or legislative councils, short terms, legislative election, bans on reelection, and lack of veto powers. Pennsylvania's radicals created an even less effectual vetoless plural executive. Similarly, the states limited judicial tenures or subjected judges to extensive legislative controls.[16]

In true republican fashion, the states also retained control of their own civil militias after the war's end. Defense would be provided by local citizen-soldiers, not a mercenary national standing army. Congress maintained only a few confederation forces to protect against hostile tribes and British garrisons in the Northwest, and these were supplied by state militias.

Five states also retained established churches as bulwarks of public morals, while others imposed religious requirements for office. But American political traditions conflicted on the topic of state religions, and James Madison and Jefferson strongly urged the liberal view that these religious institutions divided republics more than they unified or edified them. They succeeded in winning fairly complete disestablishment of the Anglican church in Virginia, and much of the south followed suit. The Confederation regimes also generally abandoned religious tests and proof of "moral character" as requirements for the franchise that identified men as full republican citizens.[17]

As noted above, states' power to define citizenship was also maintained through their control of the process of naturalization. The different ways the states chose to regulate access to citizenship created a plethora of standards that left unclear just who were naturalized citizens, especially when persons moved from one state to another. The most frequent requirements included an oath of allegiance to the state government, a disavowal of foreign allegiances, evidence of good moral character, and a period of residency before political privileges were bestowed.[18] Unlike most states, Maryland continued to insist on the profession of Christianity. The southern states explicitly limited naturalization to whites.

In his *Notes on the State of Virginia,* published in 1787 after circulating privately for several years, Jefferson feared that American republicanism, a blend of "the freest principles of the English constitution, with others derived from natural right and reason," might suffer from "emigrants" raised under "absolute monarchies." He agreed that if they came "of themselves," they were "entitled to all the rights of citizenship"; but he thought that America's government would remain more "homogeneous, more peaceable, more durable" if immigrants were not encouraged. No moves to ban immigration followed, but Americans often gave similar rationales for residency requirements, oaths of allegiance, and moral and racial restrictions on naturalization. All seemed necessary to ensure the uniformity and quality that republican citizenship demanded. Plainly, these regulations also reflected white Americans' sense of their special racial and cultural identity and their desire to maintain certain ascriptive features as constituents of citizenship.[19]

Liberalism in the Nation and the States

National Liberal Elements. Despite the predominance of state-centered republicanism in these years, Americans also included liberal and ascriptive features in their first constitutive laws. At the national level, the Articles of Confederation tried to promote a prosperous commercial economy, giving a liberal cast to American civil life. Though the Confederation's powers to regulate the currency, weights and measures, communications, and supralocal disputes were limited, they were aimed at helping trade flow freely among the states and at protecting American commerce against hostile foreign laws. The Confederation's assumption of all revolutionary congressional debts (Art. XII) and its policy of recognizing property rights of British subjects were also meant to stabilize the economy and reassure investors, in accord with liberal economic precepts. Robert Morris, Congress's energetic superintendent of finance, even won formal state support for an impost duty and taxes to meet war debts. But state collection was sporadic, and his campaign for stronger revenue powers failed, leading many financial elites to conclude that the Confederation could not serve their interests adequately.[20]

The Confederation's Article IV contained perhaps the most significant provision from nationalistic and liberal perspectives, positions that were quickly becoming regularly aligned. The "privileges and immunities" clause established a kind of national or at least interstate citizenship, with a content that was liberal in its relative inclusiveness and its guarantees of individual rights, along with its legitimation of class inequalities. The "free inhabitants" of each state—"paupers, vagabonds, and fugitives from justice" excepted—were to receive "all privileges and immunities of free citizens in the several states," and the people of each state were to be allowed to enter, leave, and trade within the other states freely. The language of the clause was exceedingly clumsy; it seemed to render free *inhabitants* of one state actual *citizens* of the others. But it was meant as a "comity clause" that would allow a full citizen of any state to be treated equally with the citizens of any other state he should enter, thereby creating a measure of national civic community as well as freer trade. The clause's exceptions indicated, however, that full membership in this community was not available to the indigent or to slaves, in accordance with the class hierarchies of the North and South. Even so, Congress decisively defeated a South Carolina motion to limit the clause's guarantees to whites. In this era of the First Emancipation, many Northerners rejected official denials of citizenship to free blacks as inconsistent with the egalitarianism of the Declaration. The privileges and immunities clause thus represented a country-wide shield for the rights of free, propertied nonwhites, making it a tentative but recognizable expression of liberal and nationalistic precepts.[21]

Only when Congress had acquired control of the northwestern lands that lay outside any of the original colonies, however, did it create something that resembled national citizenship in law. In 1783, Congress in effect created the category of United States citizenship independent of state citizenship, and defined that category relatively inclusively, when it authorized its commissioners to promise its protection and privileges to Native American and French inhabitants of the northwest territories who would pledge allegiance to the United States—not, this time, to any particular state. The subsequent Northwest Ordinance has often been said to reveal the founders' true civic vision, as they were legislating with less constraint from existing arrangements. And it is sometimes held to show that, regardless of state practices, U.S. citizenship was originally conceived as membership in an inclusive republic that conformed to enlightened views of human rights.

There is something to this argument, though the ordinance can be explained in terms of nation-building imperatives as much as liberal ideology, and though it remained a disputed question whether the territorial inhabitants were really citizens or "subjects" of the national government. The ordinance's intimations of a national civic identity nonetheless had some impact on the existing states. State courts cited Article IV, the existence of the articles generally, and other congressional measures to compel their governments to recognize actions affecting citizenship taken by other states.[22] And there were undeniably liberal elements in the ordinance's blueprint for new republics. Its first section stated that they were to be based on "fundamental principles of civil and religious liberty." Those principles were said to be permanently enshrined by the creation of the ordinance as a consensually based, constitutive "compact" between the existing states and the "people and States" of the territories, forever "unalterable, unless by common consent." Hence the ordinance's liberal republican consensualism was plain.

In keeping with Congress's desire to populate the territories, the first section also provided political rights to all those who had resided two or more years in their districts, as well as to newly arrived citizens of any established state. Thus the ordinance naturalized long-term alien inhabitants as U.S. territorial citizens, without any explicit discriminatory qualifications. French inhabitants, Catholics, the irreligious, free blacks, and individual Native Americans all could claim this new kind of national citizenship. Furthermore, the ordinance contained a miniature Bill of Rights, guaranteeing religious toleration in the first article, and legal rights of habeas corpus, trial by jury, freedom from cruel and unusual punishment, just compensation, and protection against impairments of contracts and deprivations violating the law of the land (the precursor of due process clauses) in the second article.

Those were all precepts endorsed by more liberal accounts of English constitutionalism, natural law, and republicanism. The insistence that rights be codified in written constitutional documents was chiefly a product of American experience, but it fit well with liberal desires to provide secure bulwarks for individual freedoms against governmental oppression. But Americans were, of course, accustomed to seeing such liberties as universal in principle and yet also as traditional English rights. When the ordinance made Anglo-American common law enforceable in the new territories, they knew that this action was far from culturally neutral. It signaled that the French Catholic and Native American territorial populations could have access to U.S. citizenship, but that they would have to conform to the central legal traditions of the nation's Anglo-Saxon heritage. The ethnocentrism of most American leaders was such that this requirement seemed little different from saying that outsiders had to become rational and civilized.

Even so, in its first section the ordinance promised to respect the property "laws and customs" of all existing French and Canadian inhabitants who had previously "professed themselves citizens of Virginia." The third article promised the "utmost good faith" toward "the Indians, their lands and property," which were never to "be taken from them without their consent; and in their property, rights and liberty" they were never to be "invaded or disturbed, unless in just and lawful wars authorized by Congress." Although these liberal civic sentiments were undercut in practice, their official statement nonetheless enhanced their authority. The fourth article protected national economic development by banning state taxes or other forms of interference with congressional land policies, by protecting nonresident land proprietors from higher taxes than residents, and by guaranteeing that the Mississippi and St. Lawrence rivers would remain "common highways, and forever free," available to all territorial inhabitants, U.S., and state citizens.

Most important, the famous sixth article banned slavery and involuntary servitude in the territories, though it also guaranteed the return of fugitive slaves. This step represented a great departure from the oppressive racial policies that had long prevailed in America. No doubt this and other humane, egalitarian features of the ordinance partly reflected the national officials' concerns to encourage commercial growth, immigration, and consequent new federal revenues in the territories, none of which slavery assisted. Possibly, too, Southerners saw this antislavery policy as consistent with national acceptance of slavery in the nation's southwestern territories, an acceptance Congress soon confirmed. Nonetheless, these official actions, taken when legislating for areas without so many entrenched economic and political hierarchies, institutionalized features legitimating what we now define as egalitarian liberal ideals of republican citizenship.[23]

State Liberal Elements. The liberal strains in American thought were similarly visible in the states' fondness for written constitutions with bills of rights that summarized Lockean principles of individual rights, social compacts, and separated powers. They, too, blended such general principles with procedural rights drawn from English legal traditions and saw all these measures as simultaneously expressive of Enlightenment doctrines of the rights of man and the libertarian heritage specific to Anglo-Saxon peoples.[24] State constitution-makers also rejected the direct civic assemblies of Athens and Rome in favor of representative bodies. And though some argued, like Paine, that representation was merely a necessary device in larger republics, and that representatives should mirror the populace as precisely as possible, different rationales also surfaced. Jefferson and others thought of representation as a device to ensure that the "natural aristocracy," in practice the most academically talented along with the richest, would do the governing, not the popular rabble. Such concerns were shared by some, like Hamilton, who admired much in the aristocratic British Constitution, and others, like Madison, who thought that such representation was truer to the ideals of deliberative republicanism than "mob" democracy. But though representation had many defenses, commentators today usually count these systems as steps toward more liberal forms of republicanism, because they impeded direct majoritarian decisionmaking and bolstered the power of propertied, educated elites.[25]

The states also began transforming property qualifications for the franchise and officeholding in ways that moved toward what are now viewed as liberal positions. Republicans like James Harrington had always preached that corruption could be avoided only if citizens were not economically dependent on others, usually through ownership of their own self-supporting, fee-simple farms. By 1776 many white male citizens had such real property, though they frequently supported it only with the wageless labor of their wives and slaves. Thus although most white men could vote, that amounted to only about one in six American inhabitants.[26]

Even though real property qualifications disfranchised comparatively few white men, state leaders increasingly replaced them with personal property or taxpaying requirements. The changes partly reflected the rise of commercial economies in which men might have money but not land; but few men were as yet in that situation, so the new property tests are better seen as signs of Americans' eagerness to become a more commercial society. Defenders of the new tests argued that they marked voters as proven contributors to the public weal and sufficiently propertied to act responsibly on financial issues, even if they did not provide republican proofs of economic self-sufficiency.[27] For the many Americans excited by liberal visions of commercial prosperity, those warrants sufficed. Indeed, at times Americans described property as "an interest in its own right," rather than a precondition for independent republican citizens. That interest might legitimately be protected by confining political power to the propertied, whatever their form of property, and by designing representation to reflect in part the holdings of various districts and classes. Again such notions of representation express more the economic concerns we now associate with liberalism than traditional agrarian republican ideals.[28]

As changes like these occurred in the 1780s, tensions between Americans' communal, agrarian republican values and individualistic, commercial, liberal conceptions of their civic identity became more visible. Various leading Americans became more critical of the state constitutions of 1776, no doubt in part, as Merrill Jensen argued, because these elites felt that their dominance was threatened by the legislatures they could not always control. Those fears intensified with popular agitations for debtor relief during the economically troubled mid-

1780s. Jefferson was, of course, an ardent advocate of agrarian republicanism who thought that the "cultivators of the earth" were not only the "most independent and virtuous citizens" but the true "chosen people of God," if any were. He denounced urban "work-shops" and "mobs" as "sores" on the body politic. But even he criticized the "elective despotism" of unbridled popular assemblies in his *Notes*; and with Adams's 1780 Massachusetts constitution as a partial model, many elites urged stricter separations of powers, direct rather than legislative election of chief executives, and limited veto powers for those executives. Many leaders also urged a more independent judicial role. When local reforms proved inadequate in their eyes, they sought change at the national level in the form of a new Constitution.[29]

But it is vital for understanding American civic identity to recognize that not even these disgruntled elites tried to restore the old English class system or mixed constitutions. Instead, they strove only to restructure American republicanism to make it more restrained by elite deliberations and by institutional protections for personal liberties and property rights. They worked not against republicanism but for nationalism and liberalism. The basic elements of the revolution in American political identity remained intact. Those elements continued to include ascriptive features that were neither democratic nor liberal.

Ascriptive Americanism in the Nation and the States

Even as Pennsylvanians created the most radical of the new state republics, they defended it as a return to the "Genuine Principles" of the "golden Anglo-Saxon age" before 1066.[30] Such consciousness of themselves as bearers of a superior cultural or racial heritage remained vivid as Congress and the states dealt with various groups they saw as below the circle of full members of the civic body— British loyalists, blacks, Native Americans, and women. In their policies toward all these groups Americans continued to elaborate doctrines of "natural," immutable political status that fit poorly with their liberal republican consensualism. Their employment of these ascriptive myths had obvious value in preserving the supremacy of the white, propertied, European-descended but largely native-born male gentry who were the chief architects of the new governments. But their persistence suggests that they contributed to a sense of the intrinsic meaningfulness of their new national identity for many ordinary Americans as well.

I will examine the ascriptive aspects of American citizenship laws during the Confederation by considering each "outsider" group in turn. Most of the measures discussed were adopted in the states, though they were often buttressed by national support. But the more difficult tasks of building support at the national level, over populations of great diversity and mild nationalist sensibilities, meant that national elites found inclusive and tolerant principles to be serviceable more frequently than state leaders did.

Natural Allegiance and British Loyalists. The first example of ascriptive definitions of American civic identity in this era underlines how elites often maintain older understandings of membership that serve their purposes, even if these traditions contradict their other principles. As noted above, the Continental Congress encouraged the very willing states to brand British loyalists as traitors in 1776. The revolutionaries' motives for doing so are plain: their cause was risky and dangerous, and its opponents had to be dealt with severely. But in terms of the consensus views of government they were trumpeting, it was hard for revolutionary leaders to justify punishing loyalists as traitors. They invoked the Lockean argument that, because the king had broken the social contract, the majority in each colony had the power to decide what to do next, a power binding on the minority of their members who supported the old regime. Those who refused to profess loyalty to the government created by the majority might then be deemed traitors. But that argument required a more formal majoritarian decision to rebel than any colony ever undertook. Thus it denied loyalists their right to decide that the Americans, not the king, had violated the compact, or that their paramount membership was in British society. On consensual premises, the revolutionaries could perhaps justify requiring loyalty oaths precisely as a means to register consent to their new governments. Then they might legitimately view loyalists as enemies whose allegiances put the two groups into a state of war. But to designate loyalists not as enemies but as traitors involved rejecting their rights of political choice in a way that could not be reconciled with liberal republican principles. And, in fact, in dealing with loyalist "traitors" the revolutionaries often abandoned consensualist discourses. Frequently they claimed that their governments were the automatic successors to the sovereignty and obedience the king had commanded, in just the way one of Coke's bearers of the crown could be replaced by another. Thus their treason laws perpetuated the feudal view that birth under a sovereign made one a natural member of that sovereign's community of allegiance.

Although American officials would wrestle with the difficulties of preserving that doctrine in a liberal republic for years to come, during the Confederation era some began to suggest that the revolution did involve a period when all inhabitants of the colonies had a "right of election" to join either the revolutionary or the British cause. A pioneering decision in this regard was *Respublica v. Chapman*. There Samuel Chapman, who had left Pennsylvania in 1776 to join the British Legion, contended that the "doctrine of perpetual allegiance to be found in the books, applies only to established and settled governments; not to the case of withdrawing from an old government, and erecting a distinct one. Then every member of the community has a right of election, to resort to which he pleases; and even after the new system is formed, he is entitled to express his dissent; and, dissenting from a majority, to return with impunity into another country." The jury decided that a 1777 Pennsylvania act appeared to allow such a "period of election," and found Chapman not guilty of treason.[31]

Some states defined this period of election by statute, some by judicial decision, some never did so clearly, and its origin and duration were timed differently; but most provided some such recognition. Yet because the states generally treated this right of election as resulting only from the anarchic conditions of the Revolution, they did not go so far as Locke's view that no political membership was natural. After the war, those born in American states were still viewed as natural birthright citizens. But the period of election doctrine did ease the tension between the revolutionary cause and their treason statutes, which in any case they did not much enforce.[32]

Blacks. Americans did enforce black chattel slavery, a fact that makes the genuine liberalizing reforms in the status of African-Americans during this period less fundamental than the continuation of the harshest system of ascriptive inequality imaginable. The reforms were largely confined to the North and the upper South; even there, they never approached genuine civic equality, and they proved largely a false dawn.

Indeed, scholars have rightly argued that the turn of white Americans toward egalitarian republicanism during these years was aided in some ways by their exploitation of a black lower caste, and whites' fervent insistence on their own rights may well have been fueled by their vivid awareness of the horrors of the slavery. Yet the progress that was made in ending slavery in the North and improving the status of free blacks suggests that, at least under favorable conditions, Christian and rationalist notions of human rights could assist significant challenges to existing inequalities.[33] The libertarian agitations leading up to the Revolution included a resurgence of local and state antislavery organizations, especially Quaker groups centered in Philadelphia, who became the mainstays of a powerful postwar manumission and abolitionist movement. The war also advanced black interests in other ways. Slaves exploited its upheavals and ran away in large numbers, at times joining the British forces, sometimes simply escaping bondage. In response, albeit reluctantly, many states recruited both free blacks and slaves into their regiments, eventually offering freedom to the latter, as Rhode Island did. These experiences added to the white antislavery agitations and sparked petitions for abolition among blacks.[34]

In the North, the answers to these demands came in the 1780s and 1790s in the form of direct legislation providing for gradual emancipation and, in Massachusetts, through judicial interpretation of the guarantees of freedom in the 1780 constitution.[35] The Northern abolitionist statutes usually ended slavery for all blacks born after certain dates, and laws prescribing manumission practices then sped the institution's demise. The various religious and economic reform groups that contributed to these victories also helped win the antislavery provisions of the Northwest Ordinance, thus creating a band of formally free states and territories running from the northeast coast through the nation's northwestern borders.

Further south, Virginia also provided freedom to all black revolutionary veterans and passed a statute in 1782 permitting manumission, a step all other Southern states except for North Carolina had taken by 1790. In the 1780s, Virginia, the Carolinas, and Maryland also followed the lead of the North by banning or heavily taxing the slave trade. But Southern manumissions were not so great as to threaten slavery as an institution, and the limitations on the slave trade were probably motivated by fears of slave insurrections as much as egalitarian sentiments. In any case, the trade survived. The slave population doubled during the Confederation years due to continued importation and natural increase. And although some Southern whites showed ambivalence about the institution, most remained insistent on its perpetuation. Consequently, as slavery died in the North, it grew only more entrenched in the south.

Even so, during the initial stages of First Emancipation the defenders of slavery were, in Larry Tise's words, "unusually silent." Tise goes so far as to argue that the "proslavery tradition . . . seemed dead," though it would soon revive with a vengeance. And though no major proslavery tracts appeared, newspaper writers, ministers, and Southern politicians continued to suggest that the scriptures authorized slavery, that it worked to convert slaves to Christianity and therefore to uplift them, and that it was in any case a necessary evil, a form of property that the South could not yet eliminate.[36]

Even if few Americans were prepared to challenge egalitarian revolutionary ideology by defending slavery as a positive good, most continued to espouse doctrines of white supremacy. In a telling display of the bitter blends of racism and liberalism that have run so deeply in American thought, it was Thomas Jefferson who provided the most intellectually prestigious statement of inherent black inferiority, even as he strongly condemned slavery. His *Notes* castigated that institution as a "great political and moral evil" meriting divine punishment, and he hoped for "a complete emancipation of human nature." But Jefferson thought that ex-slaves would then have to be "colonized," for living with whites would end in "extermination of one or the other race." That gloomy prognosis was based partly on white "prejudices" and black resentments, but also on "real distinctions" in the races that were "fixed in nature." In sharp contrast to his defense of the capacities of Indians, Jefferson drew on racist folklore and his own observations to provide the cornerstone statement of American scientific racism. Blacks were, he suggested, short-sighted creatures, "inferior" in "reason" and "imagination" to whites, "more tolerant of heat, and less so of cold," requiring less sleep, emitting a "very strong and disagreeable odour," and dominated by strong but transient passions. Their men preferred sex with white women over black ones, just as black women were sought after by the "Oran-ootan." Jefferson admitted that conditions were harsh for American blacks and that the mental and physical differences he had observed and heard reported might be traceable to those factors. He called for further work in "natural history" to settle that issue. But Jefferson thought that he knew how those studies would come out. He compared blacks unfavorably both to Indians and to allegedly more mistreated Greek and Roman slaves. He also cited the "improvement" in the bodies and minds of offspring resulting from "their mixture with the whites" to justify his "suspicion" that black "inferiority is not the effect merely of their condition of life." From the disinterested standpoint of "philosophy," he thought it advisable to "keep those in the department of man as distinct as nature has formed them." That purely philosophic position happened to serve the interests of all those who benefited from Virginia's white supremacist laws, like Jefferson himself. In his hands, Enlightenment rationalism opposed black civic equality even as it condemned slavery.[37]

Others were more optimistic. Princeton president Samuel Stanhope Smith published his *Essay on the Causes of the Variety of Complexion and Figure in the Human Species* in 1787, arguing that physical and mental differences in the races resulted from differences in the climates and "habits of society" where they resided. Those influences, he thought, were hereditary. Smith, a Presbyterian minister, was deeply concerned to show that natural philosophy did not contradict the Genesis account of the original unity of mankind, something of less moment to Jefferson. But even Smith's Christian universalist view of humanity and his environmentalist explanation of racial differences were not free of hierarchical notions. He assumed that as all men lived under civilized conditions they gradually gained the superior physical and mental features of whites (though he acknowledged that skin color was slowest to change). His blend of Christian and Enlightenment egalitarianism with profound belief in the inferiority of the traits blacks displayed characterized even the most inclusive views of the day.[38]

The civic status of free blacks was accordingly mixed. The new or revised constitutions of New Hampshire, Vermont, Connecticut, Rhode Island, New York, and Massachusetts did not explicitly ban free blacks from voting. New Jersey's hastily written 1776 constitution permitted both blacks and women to vote, and there is some evidence that they actually did. Even in North Carolina, Maryland, Kentucky, and Tennessee, propertied free blacks could vote, and they possessed rights to a jury trial and to have witnesses and counsel. After 1783, however, Maryland denied full civic equality to recently manumitted blacks, granting them only property rights. And in the lower South, free blacks were generally subjected to disabilities as extensive as in colonial days. Petitions to modify harsh colonial legislation, such as South Carolina's Negro Act of 1740, were ignored.[39]

In practice, emancipated blacks also were everywhere still limited in their economic opportunities. Sometimes they were captured and reenslaved, albeit illegally. Thus, despite some real progress, emerging scientific and religious ideologies of racial inferiority, the legal status accorded slavery in the South, and ongoing discriminations against free blacks nationally meant that, taken as a whole, America's laws and its ideals of civic membership still displayed a severely inegalitarian ascriptive racial structure.[40]

Native Americans. In dealing with the native tribes, the new American governments often claimed to be complying with their egalitarian revolutionary principles; but their conduct remained explicable only in ascriptive terms. Especially at the national level, officials continued the British practice of employing treaties to settle affairs with the tribes, suggesting that their relations were conducted on a basis of mutual consent between sovereign nations. Repeatedly they promised respect for Native American rights. But the "consent" gained via treaties was often a thin disguise for concessions won by coercion. Even when it was not, both state and national leaders often treated Native Americans as conquered peoples, and their actions expressed illiberal views of what that status implied. The mass of white Americans were intensely conscious of the cultural gulf between themselves and the tribes, and they also coveted tribal lands both individually and as a society. Rather than recognizing Native Americans either as members of independent nations or as fellow citizens, they disparaged "the animals vulgarly called Indians" in order to justify their expansionism.[41]

The anti-Native American feelings among the colonists that had caused so many conflicts with both the tribes and British authorities during the prerevolutionary years were further inflamed during the war itself. Owing to the past protection they had received from Britain and their conviction of its superior power, most tribes sided with the British. Congress tried to modify this tribal loyalism, perceiving it as a serious strategic threat. Initially it urged the tribes to stay neutral, and eventually it tried to gain assistance in its military efforts, though the British did so more successfully. To win allegiants, the Congress was sometimes willing to treat Native Americans as potential citizens: a 1778 treaty with the

Delawares contemplated the admission of a Native American state into the Confederation.[42]

But Congress was also promising land in lieu of immediate payment to its soldiers, promises that could be met only at the tribes' expense.[43] It was, moreover, quite limited in its power to curb hostile state actions. Article IX of the Articles of Confederation gave to Congress "the sole and exclusive right and power of . . . regulating the trade and managing all affairs with the Indians, not members of any of the States, provided that the legislative right of any State, within its own limits be not infringed or violated." The qualifying phrases—concessions to state sovereignty—permitted New York, North Carolina, Georgia, and other states to purchase or seize Native American lands in violation of congressional policies.[44]

The loyalist tribes expected their British allies to protect their lands in negotiating the 1783 Paris Peace treaty. Its articles, however, contained protection only for the property of British subjects generally, without any explicit provisions defending tribal interests. Furthermore, the treaty ceded various lands under British dominion to the United States, especially the disputed territories west of the 1763 Proclamation Line. Those cessions allowed the U.S. to claim sovereignty over all tribes who owed allegiance to Britain (and in principle it preempted most state claims to western tribal lands, though in practice it did not). And if the tribes claimed only to have been independent allies of Britain, the treaty denied them any protection at all. Because the U.S. claimed to have defeated all who had opposed the revolutionary cause, the tribes allied with Britain were subject to its will as conqueror.[45]

The U.S. government left the position of most Native Americans relatively undefined, however, because many tribes possessed ample power to resist its policies, and they could still get some aid from Spain and Britain. Furthermore, even if the U.S. viewed the Native Americans as conquered peoples, its nonascriptive political principles limited the claims it could assert over them. Whereas Coke had treated conquered peoples, like the Irish, as subject to the unbridled authority of the sovereign who had vanquished them, Locke insisted that legitimate government could originate only in consent and that the valid powers of even just conquerors were bounded. A conqueror had a "purely Despotical" title based on "bare Force" to dominion over the lives of those who had wrongly warred against him, and he had a right to some of their property for reparations. But that right extended only to an annual crop or two, and it did not include dominion over their wives or children. Thus it did not support the permanent claims to the lands and allegiance of Native Americans that the new American governments wished to assert.

Many international law writers, especially Vattel, defined the rights of conquest more broadly than Locke, but even Vattel presented these doctrines as concessions to the "voluntary laws of nations" rather than as expressions of "rigid justice." And though Vattel said that a conquered people might be put "in a state of slavery" for "some time" if their "idocility" could be corrected in no other way, he still repudiated the "monstrous principle" of Coke and Hugo Grotius—that a conqueror had an "absolute" power to do "as he pleases" with those he has subdued. When "the danger is over," Vattel insisted, the conqueror should make them equal citizens, and throughout he should adopt "the mildest means" necessary to ensure his security and correct injustices. U.S. officials often professed to be adopting such generous measures and to be preparing the "uncivilized" Native Americans for full citizenship. But in fact their promises of liberal treatment proved as thin as their claims to have conquered the western tribes in a just war.[46]

Despite the studied ambiguity in U.S. documents on the status of Native Americans, government officials showed that they thought they were dealing with inferior peoples who should be subject to their sovereign authority. The United States repeatedly attempted to designate who would negotiate for the tribes; it insisted on treaties written in English; it employed deception and coercion; and, despite promises of aid, the basic thrust of its efforts was to extinguish, not respect, tribal property claims. The states, moreover, often still treated the tribes as foreign belligerents or the objects of negotiations or, more usually, further conquest.[47]

The U.S. attitude toward the tribes was ratified in the precedent-setting Fort Stanwix Treaty of 1784. Until that time, Congress had been slow to seek new treaties because of unresolved disputes over the terms under which Virginia would cede its western land claims. Pennsylvania moved to negotiate a treaty with the Iroquois in the state on its own, prompting Congress to act preemptively. In the resulting Fort Stanwix Treaty, representatives of the powerful Six Nations confederation acknowledged U.S. sovereignty and relinquished their claims to various lands. On paper, this arrangement appeared consistent with the revolutionaries' consensual premises. The tribes were supposedly being treated as a confederation of nations that were voluntarily giving up ultimate sovereignty in exchange for the partial autonomy of dependency status. Vattel argued explicitly that governments of sovereign but weak peoples could choose to place themselves under the protection of a more powerful state via treaty in this way, without relinquishing all claims to sovereignty. To a greater degree than many scholars recognize, from this point forward the U.S. often officially regarded the tribes in just such Vattelian terms, as voluntarily "dependent" nations.[48]

The Fort Stanwix Treaty, however, was a product not of consent but of duress imposed by federal troops. The federal commissioners informed the Iroquois that they were "a subdued people" who had to accept the terms the U.S. offered.

Hence the treaty was considered invalid by most Native Americans, who instead recognized only an accompanying purchase of lands by Pennsylvania on terms that were truly mutually satisfactory.

When the tribes proved still able to resist white aggression, Confederation Secretary of War Henry Knox began to push for more genuinely liberal policies of peaceful dealing and land purchases. In the Treaty of Hopewell in 1786, Congress promised the Cherokees the right to be represented by a delegate in Congress. And the Third Article of the Northwest Ordinance made stirring promises of the "utmost good faith" toward that region's Indians. But the ordinance also expressly permitted Congress to pass laws "founded in justice and humanity" that would be binding upon those tribes (as well as permitting further "just and lawful" wars against them). Its preamble also provided for making available lands to which "indian titles shall have been extinguished." These provisions expressed the ethnocentric side of Knox's policy: the belief that over the next half century the tribes should be converted to Christianity and assimilated into the white community, losing their distinct territorial and political existences. The provisions for extinguishing tribal land titles also formed part of policies that encouraged a white land rush, creating conditions that would make the survival of Native American autonomy impossible.[49]

The land rush in the Northwest and encroachments elsewhere showed that even the tribes' legal status as conquered national protectorates remained largely fictional. After the Fort Stanwix Treaty, New York and other states still dealt with various tribes with little regard for the Confederation. In 1786, Congress passed a new ordinance reasserting its preeminence in Indian affairs; but Georgia ignored it later that year, signing a treaty with a few would-be tribal representatives in order to claim large chunks of Creek land. These conflicts contributed to the calls for a stronger national government that led to the Constitution.[50]

In fairness, it would have been hard for either national or state officials to reconcile the Confederation's commitment to republicanism with the traditional structures of tribal authority, which the tribes wished to preserve. Hence a policy of mutual assimilation seemed impossible. The white community's felt imperatives toward economic growth, the propagation of its culture, and accompanying territorial expansion were also enormously difficult to resist, so policies of respectful coexistence also seemed utopian. Nevertheless, those aims clearly expressed and were defended by white Americans' sense of ascriptive superiority over the aboriginal "savages." That belief in their own rightful supremacy overrode the restraints the liberal, consensual strain in their principles implied.[51]

Again, Jefferson's view is revealing. He devoted much attention in his *Notes* to arguing that if "the circumstances of their situation" were taken into account, it was clear that Native Americans were "formed in mind as well as in body, on the same module with the 'Homo sapiens Europeaeus.'" He also had much praise for the consensual, deliberative character of tribal political life. But it was clear throughout that he wished most of all to refute the claims of French philosophes like Buffon and Raynal that North American conditions made animals and men inferior to European ones. He asserted instead that "human nature is the same on every side of the Atlantic" and also suggested that Americans were as capable of genius as Europeans and more self-reliant and freedom-loving. But, conscious of white desires to subordinate African-Americans and to displace the tribes, Jefferson also stressed that this universalistic talk was not meant to deny "that there are varieties in the race of man, distinguished by their powers both of body and mind." He continued to speak of the aboriginal peoples as "savages" who must be raised to the level of whites or driven out. As with the St. Tammany societies, his main point in praising Native Americans was to defend native Americans.[52]

Women. Rhetorically, revolutionaries were always more willing to grant women a kind of "equality" than they were either blacks or Native Americans. But, ironically, as they provided some benefits to blacks and at least promised some to Native Americans, they actually moved women further away from full citizenship. After the revolution, the new governments adhered more rigorously to Blackstone's view that both natural and common law required the identity of a married woman to be entirely subsumed in her husband's. This legal reassertion of ascriptive feudal views of women's natural place was possible largely because most late eighteenth-century proponents of liberal and republican principles refused to challenge gender inequalities. Instead, they offered new arguments for them. As Linda Kerber has shown, the most elaborate defenses came from the champions of republicanism.[53]

One particularly pertinent manifestation of the increased enforcement of coverture was the way the revolutionary governments treated married women's national allegiances. A colonial woman who actively worked against the Revolution could be prosecuted as a traitor. A woman who simply followed her husband back to Britain, however, was held to have exercised no choice of her own during the period of election. He had chosen for her; she had done her marital duty. Hence she had not committed treason. Thus most treason statutes extended their embodiment of naturalistic ascriptive conceptions to include the subordination of women.[54]

The new state constitutions also generally restricted the franchise to men, beginning with New York's express provision to that effect in 1777. The voting rights exercised by some property-holding single women during the colonial era were lost everywhere but in New Jersey, where they would not last beyond the first decade of the new century.[55]

Explaining why liberal and republican notions of consensus membership and civic equality did not improve the legal status assigned women is controversial. Much in those traditions logically demanded gender reforms. For example, though Locke "granted" that male rule over women had "some foundation in nature" because men were "stronger and abler," he presented marriage, like political society, as a voluntary compact between equals. He also assigned mothers and fathers equal authority over their children and claimed for wives more independent property rights than English law conferred; and he suggested that young girls be educated similarly to young boys. Yet he made little of these mild moves toward gender equality, once condescendingly remarking that he had "more admired than considered" the female sex.[56] It is not obvious why he and revolutionaries like Paine were so insensitive to the plain case their principles made for female equality.

As I have noted, many scholars respond by arguing that liberalism's premises have always quietly but inextricably demanded the subjugation of women in both the family and politics.[57] There can indeed be no denying that men espousing liberalism overwhelmingly supported forms of patriarchy from the Enlightenment until, at best, the 1960s. That fact does not, however, prove that misogyny has been logically inherent in, as opposed to merely intertwined with, liberal notions of human rights. In any case, people's principles and actions can be contradictory when it suits their immediate purposes. Even scholars who see liberalism as integrally patriarchal recognize that the liberal rhetoric of natural rights has repeatedly been a valuable political instrument for women seeking gender equality, whether or not it has been used consistently.[58] Gender reforms did not, however, serve the revolutionaries' purposes. As John Adams's reply to Abigail indicated, most American leaders felt that they were demanding much of their supporters by asking them to reject Britain, their king, and many of their customary political beliefs in favor of frail, experimental new republics. It is not so surprising that the Americans, like Locke, callously refused to look much beyond the Revolution in which they were engaged.

Furthermore, their human rights beliefs were thoroughly intermixed with republican views that usually gave positive endorsements to the exclusion of women from full citizenship. There were exceptions, such as Condorcet, but most analysts of republics denied that women could be citizens in the same sense as men. Republican citizenship, after all, was identified with the material self-reliance and martial virtue that combated political corruption and foreign domination. Custom and law made women economically dependent on their husbands, and if that status did not originate in their natural physical or intellectual inferiority, their limited military capacities were thought to justify it. The very words *public* and *virtue* derived from Latin terms signifying manhood. The revolutionaries' rhetoric continually linked effeminacy with those ultimate republican evils, corruption and ignorance. It was hard for them to conceive that women might have the qualities that public-spirited, virtuous republican citizenship demanded.

Yet their doctrines of universal rights and Christianity implied that women were in some sense the moral equals of men. Men also did not wish to deny that women were in some sense fellow citizens of their new republics. In a liberal republic, it seemed, women thus had to be both equal and not equal citizens. Kerber has best explored how the American male revolutionaries justified leaving "intact" the basically feudal law of "baron et feme" (lord and woman), even as they were asserting their right to overthrow their own political lords. Although they maintained feudal legal doctrines, they dramatically reformulated the rationale for those rules by "politicizing women's traditional roles" in terms of republican ideology. Wifely functions now were not the labors of "subjects" but rather the duties of "republican motherhood." As "republican mothers," women were indeed citizens and moral equals, as egalitarian liberal republicanism required. They were, however, a different kind of citizen who remained sharply unequal in legally recognized powers, in politics, and in the family. Women might sew, cook, or raise money for the revolutionary cause, and sometimes even issue broadsides on behalf of republican political principles. But they were not to vote or fight. Their function was a domestic one, the rearing of sons who would be virtuous republican citizens and daughters who would raise such sons. When liberal republicans like Jefferson claimed women's "natural equality" and their "rights" were recognized in civilized America, they meant only that such republican mothers were as politically and morally valuable as men, not that women should have equal political, legal, or economic rights. If women should "mix promiscuously in gatherings of men," Jefferson wrote, the result would be "depravation of morals" for all concerned. Hence women must always be excluded from public deliberations and offices.[59]

The revolutionaries had ample authority in European Enlightenment and English Whig writings for the propriety of this republican conception of women's place. Even Montesquieu, who thought that women had more freedom in republics than in Eastern despotisms, expected the greater "family" of the republican community to preserve subordinate female status. He praised the "admirable institution" of the republican Samnites, who allowed the young men most distinguished by virtue and service to the community to choose their wives from among the eligible women. The custom dramatized the republican esteem for civic virtue; but only men could choose. Rousseau described the authentic "female citizen" as one who thanks the city's gods for a military victory in which all her sons have been slain. He then made clear that, because of their different natures, only men could be full citizens, while women's contributions, as a general rule, could only be wifely and maternal.

Rousseau's *Emile* played a prominent role in popularizing similar notions in England after its publication in 1762, but the extent of Rousseau's influence on the elite of the revolutionary generation is questionable. His views on these issues were, however, cited in other works known to be widely read in America, such as Lord Henry Home of Kames's *Sketches of the History of Men*. Kames argued that "man, as a protector, is directed by nature to govern: the woman, conscious of inferiority, is disposed to obey." Each man was thus master of his house and its political representative. His wife and children were "connected" with "their country through him only." But Kames insisted that in civilized societies women had an equal, reciprocal governance with their husbands, for "he governs by law: she by persuasion."[60]

These views were sometimes echoed by women themselves, either sincerely or tactically. Even Abigail Adams did not think it worthwhile at this juncture to press much for the right to vote. Women usually became involved in public life under the Confederation only when they deferentially petitioned the new governments to be allowed to join a husband in exile, or to win the release of an imprisoned male relative. More directly political petitions were in any case ignored. Rather than respond, most men preferred to use the new republicanism to consign women even more explicitly to a domestic sphere for which they were held to be fitted by nature as well as tradition and policy. Yet, as Kerber notes, the new republican motherhood was an "unstable" ideological position. Its immediate conservative impact could not entirely obscure the fact that, in comparison to subjectship, this new role was "a substantial step in the direction of a liberal individualism that recognized the political potential of women."[61]

Overall, then, the revolutionary and Confederation eras gave rise to new institutions of American citizenship that attempted to flesh out their ideals of republican self-rule and individual rights. The revolutionaries' accomplishments in these regards should not be underestimated. More popularly elected governments were created. Hereditary aristocracy was so discredited that it vanished as a political alternative. And the revolutionary appeals to human rights not only challenged British rule but also supported more humane policies toward blacks and Native Americans.

The disparities in American conceptions of their new political identity also became manifest, however. Beliefs that American citizens had to share a certain ascriptive identity, especially if they were to be fit to participate in republican government, continued to limit the impact of egalitarian principles. Furthermore, American leaders from the various regions were already quite conscious that they differed considerably in how far they thought the institution of black slavery could be reconciled with liberal and republican precepts. They also knew that these differences could threaten the maintenance of any form of shared civic identity. And, most crucially at this juncture, the American leaders most shaped by the national military experiences of the Revolution, as well as those whose economic interests were most endangered by the fluctuating and apparently increasingly populist policies of some of the state governments, came to believe that the republican emphasis on state sovereignty was threatening the Revolution's success. If the nation's commercial future was to be ensured against threats from foreign powers and from domestic debtors, a less popularly elected, more powerful, and in certain ways more liberal national government seemed required. Thus the advocates of the forms of the republican state citizenship created during these years were confronted by proposals to foster a new and preeminent national citizenship via the Constitution.

5

The Constitution and the Quest for National Citizenship

Nothing is more revealing about the Constitution's relationship to American political identity than the original document's failure to say much about citizenship. Its great motivating aim, to "form a more perfect Union," compelled its framers to be silent or ambiguous on many crucial but controversial issues of civic statuses. The 1787 text mentioned citizenship three times as a requirement for federal offices, though only the elective ones. It gave Congress the power to establish a uniform rule of naturalization. It also referred to citizenship in assigning jurisdiction to the federal courts, and in a "privilege and immunities clause" derived from the Articles of Confederation.[1] Otherwise, citizenship was not expressly addressed. The Constitution more often spoke of persons, though it always used masculine pronouns. It frequently referred discreetly to slavery. Twice it spoke of "Indians."[2] But the Constitution did not define or describe citizenship, discuss criteria for inclusion or exclusion, or address the sensitive relationship between state and national citizenship. Even treason was defined only as "levying War" against the United States, or "adhering to their Enemies," by a "Person." The Constitution did not say that one must be a citizen to be a traitor—or a justice of the U.S. Supreme Court.[3]

The constitutional lawyer Alexander Bickel therefore rhapsodized that "the concept of citizenship plays only the most minimal role in the American constitutional scheme. . . . The original Constitution presented the edifying picture of a government that bestowed rights on people and persons, and held itself out as bound by certain standards of conduct in its relations with people and persons, not with some legal construct called citizen." Bickel, a brilliant Jewish immigrant, celebrated this "idyllic state of affairs." But, in truth, the Constitution said little about citizenship owing to the status's pivotal, not minimal, importance. Issues of state versus national identity and slavery, especially, were so explosive that the framers avoided raising them whenever possible and left them largely unresolved. They dared clash openly only over the less volatile issue of restrictions on access to national office for the foreign-born, and there more ascriptive views prevailed. The civic conflicts thus left unsettled would profoundly shape the course of the new nation. And despite America's receptivity to brilliant immigrants, the Constitution's silences long permitted ascriptive denials of rights not explicitly protected by its provisions.[4]

The Roots of Ambiguity

Because most American elites agreed with state policies that limited full citizenship to propertied white men, the civic issues that divided them pivoted on whether popular sovereignty and citizenship would be primarily located in the states or the nation, and on the equally basic question of whether the regime would permit slavery. Those clashes were inextricably intertwined with conflicts between traditional republican and liberal conceptions of political identity. The Articles of Confederation had established a union of liberal republics in which state-centered republicanism predominated but slavery was confined to the south. The Constitution replaced it with a union embodying a more nation-centered and liberal republicanism. But the political price of that change included preserving many state powers and providing slaveholders new national guarantees.

Barring a recession in 1786–87, the Confederation period was overall an era of rapid economic growth. Nonetheless, its structural problems made the Confederation Congress ineffective in important regards. It was incapable of commanding state compliance with its fund-raising, diplomatic, and military endeavors, often unable even to gather a quorum after 1783. Some state legislatures, moreover, gave large landholders, financiers, and commercial elites real cause for alarm by experimenting with inflationary paper money, interfering in court cases involving land titles and contracts, and providing massive debtor relief. Even the economic successes of the Confederation disturbed the more aristocratic-minded gentry. They feared the collapse of public virtue via a pervasive pursuit of gain. Many were also appalled by how the new states seemed dominated by scheming, untrustworthy "new men."

Consequently, these segments of the nation's elites believed that the Confederation was a failure, jeopardizing the whole revolutionary endeavor. They initiated the Philadelphia Convention. Congress only endorsed amending the Articles in order to give the national legislature more authority over interstate and foreign commerce, where its weakness had made it virtually unable to negotiate treaties with European nations or native tribes. But while commercial interests formed a vital unifying concern, delegates arrived with a shared sense that yet more far-reaching changes were in order.[5]

By analyzing the convention's votes and debates, Calvin Jillson has shown that the delegates were divided philosophically between supporters of an extended national republic, who tended to come from the Middle Atlantic states, and adherents of traditional small republics, who came primarily from upper New England and the deep South. Proponents of a new nation-centered republicanism like James Madison and Alexander Hamilton also favored commercial expansion and relatively inclusive conceptions of American civic identity, though they cared far more about the former. They qualify as "liberals" in that they minimized direct participation in self-governance in favor of enhanced national peace and prosperity, to be guaranteed by an elite-guided, unified foreign policy, uniform commercial regulations, and both civil and military protection of certain individual liberties. They favored rights which would encourage the exercise of men's economic and intellectual capacities, thereby improving the nation's material conditions and elevating its civilization. Their liberal nationalist vision implied the primacy of national citizenship.

They had allies on at least some issues in every region, for all the regional political cultures mixed liberal, republican, and inegalitarian ascriptive features in their thinking, albeit in conflicting combinations that forced compromises. Despite its localism, New England was more receptive to commerce and more egalitarian than the slaveholding South. The southerners were, however, less obsessed with religious conformity. Less ideological cleavages also intervened, including positions like that of New Jersey's William Paterson, who did not object to new national powers so much as the domination of smaller states by larger ones. Thus both the politics of the convention and its handiwork were complex, not expressive of any single, coherent conception of the new nation. Agreement was nonetheless possible because the convention as a whole centered on the more nationalistic end of a political spectrum that extended to the highly localistic views of many state, town, and rural elites who opposed the Constitution.[6]

The most extreme adherents of localism, like Patrick Henry, refused even to participate in the convention. Those who came generally shared certain background experiences that fostered more nationalistic perspectives. Some were born abroad, and thus did not have such strong affective ties to particular states (Alexander Hamilton and James Wilson). Others had been educated in Europe, somewhat eroding their provincialism (John Dickinson, even South Carolina's John Rutledge). Probably the most powerful factor, shaping men like Washington and Madison, was service as officers in the Continental Army or as members of Congress. Those experiences made many talented young men vividly aware of the many needs that nation-building might meet, while also giving larger compass to their ambitions.[7]

Their Anti-Federalist opponents were more diverse, but most cast themselves as valiant men of the people combating privileged, wealthy elites. Yet many possessed wealth and local status that exceeded that of most nationalists, in part because they were generally older. Even more typically, many were, in Forrest McDonald's words, "state-centered men with local interests and loyalties," leaders at lower political and social levels who lacked the desire or the resources to compete for national posts, and who feared the loss of their prerogatives. They tended to be less educated and more parochial, often because they lived in regions with less access by road, ship, or post to the wider world. But if they were parochial, they were also representative: most American men were so uninvolved in larger affairs that three-quarters of the adult male population did not vote in the elections for the state conventions that ratified the Constitution—a low turnout that probably aided the nationalist cause.[8]

And though their outlooks reflected their circumstances and interests, the Anti-Federalists could deploy many principled and popular liberal republican arguments. They yielded little to the nationalists in their doubts about the reliability of public virtue, their concern for stability, and their attachment to property rights. Though many favored primarily agrarian republics over primarily commercial ones, the more moderate opponents and supporters of the Constitution were not far apart on those issues. But Anti-Federalists saw all the evils and corruptions to which governments were prone as more likely to occur if republican state citizenship gave way to a less engaged membership in a vast national polity ruled, inevitably, by a distant few. Hence they favored, at most, more collective power to negotiate commercial treaties and limit state protectionism, but not any alteration of the basic sovereignty of the states.[9]

The nationalists who predominated at Philadelphia confronted these views constantly, because all knew of their popular power, because few delegates were entirely free of them, and because some, like the Maryland maverick Luther Martin and New York's John Lansing, vociferously advocated them. All these concerns compelled the Constitution's framers to adopt several great and many small compromises, especially between centralists and decentralists, large and small states, and opponents and advocates of slavery.[10] Because questions of the nature and locus of American citizenship affected all these issues, it is not surprising that the delegates also compromised on citizenship matters. Indeed, if the extension of citizenship to the lower classes was the central problem of state-building in nineteenth-century Western Europe, the clash between state and national citizenship and interlocked conflicts over racial hierarchies in a consensual republic would prove to be the central problems of nineteenth-century American state-building. In discussing how the Constitution frames those problems, I will also note how citizenship issues were discussed at the convention and in the *Federalist Papers,* recognizing that its authors desired a more truly national and liberal republic than the one they were so skillfully marketing.

Naturalization. The Constitution proclaims itself the creation of "We the People of the United States," words that suggest a national political community and one not necessarily confined to citizens. Yet it was written and ratified by representatives selected by the people as citizens of the several states. Hence the ambiguity over whether the nation or the states constituted the primary form of political community in America was there from the start.

The one power over citizenship directly granted to Congress—the naturalization power in Article I, section 8—provides an equally good example of how the Constitution remained unclear on the basic locus of citizenship. Again, the process of naturalization, though not the term, is consistent with the consensual view of civic membership common to both liberalism and republicanism; yet the term, though not its American meaning, originates with ascriptive common-law views. In itself, then, the naturalization power reveals little about the notions of citizenship that the Constitution embodies.

The power was assigned to Congress because, as Madison argued in the *Federalist,* the "dissimilarity in the rules of naturalization" resulting from disparate state actions "has long been remarked as a fault in our system." With the aid of the Confederation's poorly worded privileges and immunities clause, "obnoxious" aliens could gain citizenship in one state requiring recognition in all states, even when they were banned from some. Hamilton contended in *Federalist #32,* as Charles Pinckney had at the convention, that the congressional power to "establish a uniform rule" must thus "necessarily be exclusive; because if each State had power to prescribe a DISTINCT RULE, there could not be a UNIFORM RULE."[11]

But in its final form the Constitution did not *expressly* give Congress an exclusive power over naturalization. The states arguably still possessed concurrent jurisdiction to naturalize, so long as they did not violate any congressional criteria. In keeping with convention references to admissions of undesirable foreigners, Roger Sherman later argued that the national power was meant only to prevent "improper" state naturalizations, not to permit foreigners to "be received on easier terms" than some states wanted. On this view, sufficient uniformity could be achieved through congressional laws setting minimal guidelines for state naturalizations, leaving further criteria to the states. That position would mean that the states retained much power to decide who would become American citizens. Hence the Constitution's language left open the question of how far authority to determine which aliens would become citizens had been shifted from the states to the nation.

Even so, the Constitution did give shape to U.S. civic identity. Its main thrust was to make Americans citizens of a large, commercial, national republic. That type of nation was such a startling innovation that the Philadelphia delegates and the *Federalist* devoted much energy to defining and defending it, in ways now familiar yet still perhaps not wholly persuasive.

The Constitution's National Republican Citizenship

In introducing the Virginia Plan for a new government at the convention, Edmund Randolph said that its "basis" must be "the republican principle," and the framers' commitment to republicanism is evident enough in the text of their handiwork. The reality of that commitment was nonetheless challenged by state-centered patriots like Patrick Henry, and it has been disputed since by those who find the Constitution insufficiently democratic. Yet if republicanism means popular government, then the Constitution qualifies. It establishes a government in which all official positions and powers are derived, however indirectly, from popular choices. Article I, section 9, also prohibits the United States from granting any titles of nobility, or permitting its officeholders to hold titles or offices bestowed by any king, prince, or foreign state, a provision Hamilton called "the cornerstone of republican government." Article I, section 10, adds that the states may not bestow titles of nobility, and Article IV, section 4, requires the United States to "guarantee to every State in the Union a republican form of government." But the nature of republican government is not defined beyond repudiation of monarchy and aristocracy, and the Constitution's form reveals that much traditional republican thought was also being repudiated by its enactment.[12]

Plainly, it is not popular government so much as the commitment to small republics, and thus to the preeminence of the states, that is sharply modified if not rejected by the constitutional system. To be sure, the small states won representation as equal units in the Senate and made that feature permanently immune to amendment in Article V, the only explicit constraint on future popular sovereignty that the Constitution contains. The states also retained all governmental powers not granted to the new federal institutions. Hence the question of their ultimate sovereignty was left unresolved, rather than settled in the negative. But there were many features that pointed almost irresistibly to the primacy of national political authority and identity, from the "necessary and proper" clause of Article I, section 8, to the designation of the national courts as referees of the federal system in Article III, section 2, to the "supremacy" clause of Article VI.[13] Even the popular nature of the system was suspect, because under the Constitution's arrangements the people never directly participate in any nonelectoral national decision. From the standpoint of the republican notions of small size and democratic governance enshrined in the Confederation and repeatedly invoked by the Anti-Federalists, these features meant that the Constitution was not genuinely republican.

Consequently, it was perhaps the central task of the Constitution's proponents, including the authors of the *Federalist,* to defend the republican character of the new system. "Publius" acknowledged, as the framers at Philadelphia had, that the public would not support anything other than republicanism, that the "fundamental principles of the Revolution" demanded it, and that, if republics were not strictly required by rational principles, it was nonetheless "honorable" to "rest all our political experiments on the capacity of mankind for self-government." The *Federalist Papers* succeeded in making a plausible case for the Constitution's republican character, but only by proposing a different conception of republicanism than the more traditional ones espoused by its critics.

Most famously, in #10 Madison redefined the very concept, contending that only in a "pure democracy" did "a society consisting of a small number of citizens" assemble and administer the government "in person." A "republic" included a "scheme of representation," which the *Federalist* regularly presented as the great key to overcoming various ills of the Confederation, especially tyranny by an illiberal majority "faction." Through representation a greater variety of interests could be encompassed in a regime, which might serve to check each other. And potentially factious popular rule would be "filtered" by the "total exclusion" of any direct popular participation in policymaking, a feature Madison praised, and by the progressively less direct connection between popular choices and federal officeholders, ranging from the two-year House, to the six-year, legislatively selected Senate, to the President chosen by the electoral college, to the appointive federal justices who served for life. Clearly, while political participation in the new regime was possible for virtually any man, significant participation would be confined to a relative few, contrary to more democratic strains of republicanism.[14]

How, then, to answer traditional republican fears that a large republic will fall under the sway of a corrupt scheming elite? In *Federalist* #2, John Jay tried to do so by using ascriptive conceptions of American identity. He invoked the myth of America as a divinely favored people, and he also made the extravagant claim that the new nation already possessed the homogeneity needed to make republics work. "Providence," he wrote, "has been pleased to give this one connected country to one united people—a people descended from the same ancestors, speaking the same language, professing the same religion, attached to the same principles of government, very similar in their manners and customs, and who, by their joint counsels, arms, and efforts, fighting side by side throughout a long and bloody war, have nobly established their general liberty and independence." America and Americans, Jay contended, "seem to have been made for each other," and "providence" surely intended that "an inheritance so proper and convenient for a band of brethren" should "never be split into . . . alien sovereignties."[15]

As many have noted, this passage is all the more striking because Jay came from cosmopolitan New York City and had no English ancestors, being three-eighths French and five-eighths Dutch. Like Paine's "Common Sense," it is an audacious attempt to deploy every strand in American political culture to defeat deeply entrenched beliefs, here the idea that the U.S. could remain free only as a league of small republics. In liberal republican language, Jay reminds Americans that their national "liberty and independence" had been won by their own joint efforts, by virtuous public service and common consent. But he also tells them that it is God's will that they be one people, and that their shared hereditary and cultural traits make them one by nature and tradition.

The passage was plainly contrived to counter republican fears of heterogeneity by asserting a mythical unity. It is an early example of an alliance between republican concerns for homogeneity and ascriptive Americanism that would have a long future. But it is too simple to dismiss it as insincere. Though he exaggerated in #2, Jay apparently truly believed that most Americans shared or should share traits tied to nativity that set them apart from others. In some early drafts at the convention, the new commander in chief was not required to be a citizen. Jay wrote to George Washington on July 25, 1787, suggesting that "to provide a strong check to the admission of Foreigners into the administration of our national Government," that post should not be held by any "but a natural born citizen." That requirement later surfaced in the Constitution, without recorded debate. Even if Americans did not all have common ancestry, then, Jay thought that the fact of American birth suggested a natural political identity and allegiance that should not only be recognized but required for the new nation's leading office.[16]

Both at the convention and in the *Federalist,* such ascriptive mythologizing of American identity occurred only rarely, yet always in regard to the most crucial issues. For example, George Mason invoked providential regard for America negatively by raising the threat of divine punishment for slavery as a reason to empower the general government to prevent its increase. And though the Constitution gave considerable protection to slavery, Madison still claimed divine sanction for the new system in *Federalist* #37, writing that it was "impossible for the man of pious reflection not to perceive in it a finger of that Almighty hand which has been so frequently and signally extended to our relief in the critical stages of the revolution." He also appealed, like Jay, to both the "kindred blood" and the "mingled blood" of "American citizens" to answer the charge that America was too large to be a republic. And in #63, Madison appealed to the law of "nature's God" to answer the "very delicate" question of how the Confederation could legitimately be altered without the unanimity it explicitly required.[17]

Because the framers sought to compromise many divisive issues by permitting certain kinds of diversity, and because "Publius" frequently contended that diversity would give a large republic advantages over small, homogeneous ones, such reliance on claims of shared religious and ancestral identities and beliefs were infrequent. But those arguments were used on the most vital issues, and they were given a prominence that suggests that they were seen as unusually potent. Later they provided founding authority for ascriptive views of American identity on which elites could and would draw.

The Constitution's Liberal Nationalism

Although its advocates sometimes defended the Constitution's new republicanism via ascriptive arguments, its major innovations reflected the liberal concerns that motivated much of the dissatisfaction with the Confederation as well as the desires for a stronger national government. Charles Beard's charge that the founders were merely defending their own immediate economic interests does not map so well onto the voting behavior of those who supported and opposed the Constitution, but no one, certainly not the framers themselves, has ever denied that one basic aim of the Constitution was to make certain individual economic and civil rights more secure.[18]

Property and Personal Rights. Most of the Constitution's new powers directly or indirectly promoted a national commercial system, free of protectionist state measures, secured lives and property against foreign or domestic violations, and spurred growth further by promoting communications, a stable national currency, and new enterprises and inventions. Article I, section 8, not only gave Congress regulatory authority over commerce with foreign nations, the Indian tribes, and among the states, it also included powers to tax and spend, to borrow and coin money, and to legislate generally in regard to the currency, bankruptcies, and piracy. In several ways, sections 9 and 10 directed the new government to prevent economic favoritism by and toward any state or states, thereby encouraging free trade among them. Section 8 empowered Congress to provide for a postal system and patents, thus assisting not only commerce but also the "Progress of Science and useful Arts." A proposal for a national university nonetheless failed.

Article II created a chief executive who was empowered not only to command the armed forces, conduct foreign relations, and appoint executive officers with the advice and consent of the Senate, but to recommend measures that "he shall judge necessary and expedient" (Art. II, secs. 2, 3). These provisions enabled the President to provide the "energy" that Hamilton argued was needed for government to provide for "the protection of property" and "the security of liberty." Article III created a national judiciary with broad jurisdiction and life tenure for judges "to guard the Constitution and the rights of individuals," to use Hamilton's words once again. Its powers were only weakly compromised by the decision to leave it to Congress to decide what part of the federal judicial power, if any, would be invested in lower federal courts. In sum, typically liberal measures and institutions to promote the typically liberal goals of civil peace, security for property rights and individual liberties, free domestic markets, commercial prosperity, and intellectual progress pervaded the document.[19]

Prominent also were concerns to limit government, which most framers still understood as both expressions of natural rights and the special legacy of British legal traditions. They included the provision of Article I, section 9, for the traditional English legal right of habeas corpus and bans on congressional bills of attainder and ex post facto laws. Section 10 extended those prohibitions to the states, along with a distinctively liberal stricture against impairing the obligations of contracts.[20] Article III, section 3's requirements for treason defined the crime very narrowly and included the quite protective procedural requirements that convictions be based only on the testimony of two witnesses to an overt act, or on a confession in open court. The section also indicated that a traitor's descendants were not to be punished in turn. Those guarantees were clearly aimed at preventing the illiberal treason prosecutions that the revolutionary governments had authorized, even if those who could be traitors were still not restricted to citizens. *Federalist* #63 explained that "new-fangled and artificial treasons" were the "great engines" of "malignity" wielded by the "violent factions" that were the "natural offspring of free government," so that in a republic these checks were especially needed.[21]

And with certain important exceptions, Bickel was right: the Constitution did speak of persons, not men, whites, or even citizens, when describing those under its jurisdiction and eligible for many of its privileges. The convention abandoned early language which would have based representation in part on numbers of "white and other free citizens and inhabitants." All references to color were dropped. That change might be read liberally, as a refusal to give rhetorical emphasis to "white" citizens, though it is at least as likely that it reflected southern objections to the implication that nonwhites could be citizens.[22] More strikingly, though federal elected officials must all be citizens, a proposal that citizenship be required of federal judges did not make it into the final text. Aliens (and even nonlawyers) were thus permitted to construe officially the fundamental prerogatives of persons and citizens—a cosmopolitan position indeed.[23]

The framers also went well beyond England's partial tolerance of dissenting sects to forego any nationally established church. Article VI ringingly concludes that "no religious Test shall ever be required as a Qualification to any Office or public Trust under the United States."[24] Nonetheless, the Constitution quietly assumes a predominantly Christian nation. In Article 1, section 9, Article V, and Article VII, it employs the Christian dating system, referring to the "Year of Our Lord" 1787 in Article VII. Article 1, section 7, excepts Sundays from the ten days the President has to return bills to Congress, thus treating it as a day of rest in Christian fashion.

More important, the Constitution left the surviving state religious establishments untouched. Any national action on religion would surely have preempted at least some of these. Hence here, too, an apparently liberal national policy can be interpreted as a recognition of the primacy of republican state institutions within a Christian nation. The incontrovertible fact is, once again, the Constitution's ambiguity on a basic issue of civic identity, in a way that won support but did not resolve fundamental conflicts.

Liberal National Citizenship. In other respects the Constitution quietly went further than the Articles of Confederation toward fostering the evolution of a national community of citizens, liberally defined. Section I of Article IV requires each state to give "Full Faith and Credit" to the acts and proceedings of "every other State" and gives Congress power to legislate toward that end. Thus the clause gives the national government a mandate to promote—indeed, to require—basic forms of cooperation among the states. Article IV, section 2, presents the Constitution's modified privileges and immunities clause. It is much simpler than its predecessor, holding only that "the Citizens of each State shall be entitled to all Privileges and Immunities of Citizens in the several States."

In *Federalist* #80, Hamilton argued that this clause was so crucial to national community as to be the very "basis of the Union." He used it, in turn, to explicate Article III, section 2's grant of jurisdiction when "one State or its citizens are opposed to another State or its citizens" (the "diversity of citizenship" jurisdiction clause). Hamilton called this jurisdiction "necessary" to "secure the full effect" of "so fundamental" a provision as the privileges and immunities clause "against all evasion and subterfuge." And he made it clear that he saw the threat of "subterfuge" coming from the "local attachments" of state judiciaries. The federal judiciary, in contrast, would "never be likely to feel any bias inauspicious to the principles on which it is founded"—would, in short, predictably lean toward national views. Hence Hamilton plainly saw the Article III "diversity" clause and especially the Article IV "privileges and immunities" clause as important means by which the national government could combat any parochial, balkanizing tendencies in the states. In this he was in some ways prescient: his arguments would later be cited by the federal courts to support expansive readings of their jurisdiction, often in ways that assisted corporations (a result Hamilton would surely have approved).[25]

Yet the privileges and immunities clause that Hamilton stressed never came to play so central a role in fostering national unity as he expected. Its rather cryptic brevity would prove a source of frustrating ambiguity. It is not self-evident whether the provision is merely a "comity clause," insisting that each state treat recently arrived citizens of other states as it would its own, or whether it suggests that there are certain substantive privileges and immunities that all states must honor, or whether it has any of several other possible meanings—nor is it clear from where or by whom those privileges and immunities are to be derived or defined. These uncertainties left ample room for proponents of state-centered constitutional views to interpret the clause in ways that did not threaten their principles or interests.

For many, those interests included slavery, an institution they knew to be at risk if it coexisted with free black citizens. Hence southerners especially regularly opposed the expansive, nationally unifying readings of the clause that Hamilton anticipated. They did not wish out-of-state blacks to be able to come and claim extensive privileges and immunities within their borders. Rather than tamper with the volatile issue of slavery, many courts eventually interpreted the clause in the narrowest ways.[26]

The clause did, however, eliminate the Confederation article's exception of "paupers, vagabonds, and fugitives from justice" from its ambit, and it did not make any overt distinctions among citizens, white or black, native or naturalized, male or female, rich or poor. The potential of Article IV to promote a more genuine national community among both states and individuals was therefore quite real. But here as elsewhere, the framers drew back from plainly denying the states extensive power to define citizenship and its prerogatives as they wished.

The termination of the Confederation's explicit denial of protection to paupers and vagabonds had a liberalizing counterpart within the convention itself. A resolution to specify requirements of "landed property" for officials in all three branches of the new government ultimately failed. Rufus King thought that "the monied interest" should not thus be excluded from federal officeholding. Conversely, John Dickinson felt that the requirement reflected an unrepublican "veneration for wealth" instead of "poverty and virtue." Gouverneur Morris and Madison preferred to confine such restrictions to the electors rather than the elected, and that meant, once more, that the states would be free to decide whether to have any sort of property qualification or not. Ben Franklin invoked the myth of the old Anglo-Saxon republic, praising what he claimed was the "antient" British practice of letting all freemen vote.[27] They carried the day; so the Constitution did not impose class requirements for full citizenship, but it also did not ban them.

Here, as throughout the document generally, national citizenship thus appears to be conceived preeminently in liberal terms; but it is far from clear that national citizenship is preeminent for American civic identity or political life. At the convention, only the Pennsylvania nationalist James Wilson addressed the relationship of state and national citizenship at any length, and though he did so to suggest that the national legislature be elected by individual citizens, not states, he did not go so far as to assert full-fledged national supremacy. Instead, he said that every man would "possess a double character, that of a Citizen of the United States and that of a Citizen of an individual state," and should be represented as appropriate for each role. He also suggested gently that men would not feel themselves particularly "complimented" by the "epithet" of their state citizenship or "degraded by being called a citizen of the United States." But after some early debates in which a few delegates incautiously hoped that the states might eventually be eliminated, most nationalists strove to enhance national powers and liberal rights without explicitly derogating state citizenship.[28]

Nationalism and the Federal District. The Constitution did, however, strive to protect the new national government by authorizing what many came to see as a diminution of local citizenship in Article I, section 8. It authorized Congress to exercise "exclusive Legislation in all Cases whatsoever" over a district that might be ceded by the states to serve as the seat of government. The provision was adopted without much recorded discussion, but scholars have long seen it as prompted by the experience of the Confederation Congress in Philadelphia in 1783. Pennsylvania veterans demanding back payments marched on the assembled lawmakers, who locked their doors for safety. Many Pennsylvanians sympathized with the soldiers more than the fledgling national legislature, and neither city nor state officials responded to Congress's requests for assistance.[29]

It thus seemed that if the new, controversial national government was to be safe from indifferent or actively hostile local and state officials, it needed exclusive power over its surrounding territory. Little attention was given to what such power implied for the political rights of the district's residents, but Madison circumspectly addressed the issue while endorsing the district as an "indispensable necessity" in *Federalist #43.* He suggested that the compact with the state or states ceding territory would provide "for the rights and the consent of the citizens" living therein, and that they would have a "municipal legislature for local purposes." That phrasing indicated an awareness that they might very well not be entrusted with representation in the Congress that would ultimately govern them. Madison implied that denial of representation would be needed to keep the locals' influence over Congress from being excessive, and that this denial could be reconciled with consensual principles by the fact that they "will have had their voice" in the adoption of the system by which they would be governed. These arguments laid the groundwork for what many came to see as second-class citizenship, or even subjectship, for district inhabitants, governed by an assembly they did not elect. It is a relatively small but telling example of how the tasks of nation-building sometimes trumped more notions of equal republican citizenship.[30]

The Constitution and Ascriptive Citizenship

The new nation's major denials of civic equality were, however, of a different order. Although the Constitution's treatment of citizenship reveals most clearly the need to compromise between nationalistic liberal and state-centered republican conceptions of the status, ascriptive notions also remain discernible in the text as well as the convention debates and the *Federalist Papers*. Though rarely defended at length, these ascriptive views nonetheless were made more symbolically legitimate and practically constitutive by their expression in the Constitution and in its most famous commentary.

Electoral Requirements. The most direct examples of such notions are the requirements in Article I, sections 2 and 3 for representatives and senators to have been citizens for at least seven and nine years, respectively, and the rule in Article II, section 1 that the President be a "natural born Citizen, or a Citizen of the United States" when the Constitution was adopted. The convention's Committee on Detail was more generous to naturalized citizens, recommending requirements of only three and four years' citizenship for representatives and senators and mere citizenship for the chief executive. But delegates including George Mason, Gouverneur Morris, and Charles Pinckney successfully argued for longer periods, though Morris did not get the fourteen years he proposed for Senate eligibility.

Their arguments expressed concern in part that representatives possess adequate "local knowledge," including knowledge of republican principles and practices. More prominent, however, were fears that "foreigners"—as naturalized citizens were revealingly described—would prove to be biased in favor of the political ideas and interests of their nations of origin, if not actual "tools" of foreign conspiracies. The delegates were quite conscious that they were quarreling over more nativistic and more cosmopolitan views of American identity. Morris disdainfully announced that he did not wish to see in public councils any of "those philosophical gentlemen, those Citizens of the World" who renounced all "wholesome prejudices" in favor of their own country. He was wary of anyone who could turn his back on his homeland, and though willing to let foreigners "worship at the same altar" as native Americans, he "did not choose to make Priests of them" (especially, no doubt, the Catholics).

Mason indicated that his doubts about the loyalties of those from elsewhere were such that if many foreign-born persons (including some at the convention) had not done worthy service during the revolution, he would have favored restricting the Senate to natives. Elbridge Gerry similarly hoped that eligibility in the House might be confined to natives in the future. South Carolina's John Rutledge feared some people closer to home. He wished residency requirements to apply to the state from which an officeholder was elected, rather than residence anywhere in the United States. Pennsylvania's George Read argued successfully that this proposal was inconsistent with "the idea that we were one people."

Madison criticized all these restrictions as giving a "tincture of illiberality" to the Constitution. Like Paine and Crèvecoeur, he wanted American identity to be open to all "foreigners of merit and republican principles." West Indies-born Alexander Hamilton proposed that mere citizenship suffice for federal office, to Madison's approval.[31] Scottish-born James Wilson was most passionate against the "mortification" of "galling" discriminations aimed at foreigners, which he said he had suffered. Both Ben Franklin and Edmund Randolph viewed receptivity to aliens as required by America's revolutionary principles and its historical practices.

But Roger Sherman argued that even existing state-naturalized citizens should not be exempted from the longer waiting periods the delegates adopted for congressional offices, because state policies should not bind the new nation. In the wake of these debates, committees added the requirement that the President be a "natural born citizen" as Jay had suggested. The delegates did exempt those who were already U.S. citizens from this most stringent requirement.

Although the more cosmopolitan conception of American nationality defended by Madison and Hamilton was thus emphatically rejected, Publius dutifully if briefly recited the arguments of the supporters of the Senate restrictions. Madison still stressed in regard to the House, however, that despite "these reasonable limitations," the door to these offices was "open to merit of every description, whether native or adoptive, whether young or old, and without regard to poverty or wealth, or to any particular profession of religious faith." This misleading passage was clearly an effort to give the text a liberal spin. It ignored many state suffrage restrictions that the Constitution made applicable to federal elections. In writing the papers on the presidency, Hamilton was silent on the natural-born requirement he had opposed. And though Jay said that the convention gave "very particular attention" to the qualifications for the presidency, he did not mention the ascriptive criterion he had suggested.[32]

Hence on this topic the *Federalist* is not a reliable guide. There was a stronger sense at the convention that full political rights should be reserved to those whose loyalties could be trusted due to native birth or extensive domestic residence. That belief in the power of place of birth and inhabitancy to shape one's sense of political identity and allegiance, however psychologically plausible, effectively linked full citizenship to a person's position in an external physical order, not simply to political consent. Thus these requirements expressed emerging nativist outlooks more than republican or liberal ones.

The undebated provision that the President be "natural born" was, however, again ambiguous. As Madison observed in 1789, there were two conceptions of citizenship by birth available to the framers. Birth derived its "force" as a "criterion of allegiance . . . sometimes from place," as in the common-law tradition of *jus soli* expounded by Coke and Blackstone, and "sometimes from parentage," from birth to one or more citizens, a position known as the *jus sanguinis* and endorsed by Vattel and Burlamaqui. Although these international law writers based membership on "mutual consent," they developed a non-Lockean view supporting birthright citizenship, perhaps out of concern about the impracticality of Locke's insistence that children were not members of any political community. They tried to obtain the advantages of older naturalistic views of membership by arguing that children should be treated as provisional members of their parents' society, who were guaranteed the option of full membership at maturity if they so chose. The Swiss writers traced this guarantee to hypothetical consent, arguing that parents "are supposed to have stipulated" that their children have this option as a condition of their own membership. Burlamaqui stated that children could thus gain citizenship "in the place of their parentage, or in their native country"—unclear phrasing that might suggest both citizens and resident aliens obtained this option for their children. Vattel said that children of resident aliens should be guaranteed only the status of their parents.[33]

In the eighteenth century, most writers saw this international law view of birthright citizenship, the *jus sanguinis,* as more consistent with consensual principles than Coke's feudal view of *jus soli.* But in keeping with the nativistic tone of the debate over these clauses, and not with the Constitution's predominant liberal republicanism, it was almost certainly the common-law criterion of place of birth that the delegates meant to install in Article II, as Madison later asserted.[34] It thus perpetuated the older view of "natural" civic membership in a way that conformed to xenophobic sentiments.

Women. In regard to the nation's ascriptively defined political subordinates—women, Native Americans, and blacks—the Constitution was again largely silent or ambiguous, so that it disrupted the status quo as little as possible. Of women it said nothing directly. It did, however, use masculine pronouns thirty times in describing U.S. Representatives, Senators, the Vice-President, and the President.[35] Later these pronouns would be used to argue on the floor of Congress and in state courts that the Constitution denied federal office-holding to women.[36] To be sure, no federal court ever confirmed that position. Among other things, this claim confronted the difficulty that a masculine pronoun is also employed in Article IV, section 2, requiring states to extradite fugitives charged with treason, felonies, or other crimes, a provision no one wished to confine to men. And the Constitution's preferred nouns were invariably gender-neutral, referring to a "persons," "members," or "parties," never "men." Those usages might in the abstract have been taken to permit women various political rights.

The salient fact, however, was that the Constitution left intact the state constitutions that denied women the franchise and other legal and political privileges. Hence their status was unaltered. Neither the convention delegates nor Publius commented on that circumstance. But, like the Constitution itself, they recurrently assumed that citizens should be as masculine as possible, a "band of brethren" displaying "manly spirit." Apart from references to royalty, the *Federalist* mentioned individual "females" only to describe the baneful political consequences in Europe of their "bigotry . . . petulancies" and "cabals." The papers referred to women categorically just once, in a discussion of statutory interpretation that used the example of a statute expanding married women's rights of conveying property. The illustration is revealing of the founding mindset: such expansions of women's economic rights would, indeed, be the main form of legal liberalization of women's status that American male elites found acceptable for the next century.[37]

Native Americans. In two places the Constitution did explicitly recognize "Indians" as a separate category of persons, ethnoculturally defined, though again with a terseness that could be interpreted in various ways.[38] The only certain point was that large numbers of Indians would be treated as outside, though not necessarily independent of, the American political community. Article I, section 2, called for the apportionment of federal representatives and direct taxes according to the "Numbers" in each state, to be determined by adding to the "whole Number of Free Persons, including those bound to Service for a Term of Years, and excluding Indians not taxed, three fifths of all other Persons." These "Indians not taxed" provisions went essentially undiscussed.[39] Their language suggested that Indians who were taxed, in addition to indentured servants, did count for purposes of assigning representation as well as taxes. Although that indicated that some Native Americans could be regarded as part of the civic community, it did not guarantee that they, any more than servants, would be able to vote. And the clauses clearly contemplated the existence of many free Indians who would not count as part of the new nation at all.

As noted previously, Article I, section 8, gave Congress power to "regulate Commerce" with the Indian tribes, as well as with foreign nations and among the states. Thus it appeared that "Indians not taxed" were to be dealt with as members of separate societies, but societies that were neither American states nor fully "foreign nations." Although the ambiguity that had existed in Anglo–Native American relations since before the Proclamation of 1763 was not directly resolved by these words, the basic implication remained unchanged. The most plausible interpretation was that the Constitution viewed the majority of Native Americans as members of tribes that were effectively dependent nations. Whether this was definitively so and just what it meant would not be answered in any detail, however, until the 1830s. In itself, the Constitution's terse language permitted the tribes to be distinguished from "foreign nations" on some other ground than their alleged dependence.

Unlike the Articles of Confederation, moreover, the Constitution did not assert for Congress any exclusive authority to deal with any part of the Native American population. But Article I, section 10, did prohibit the states from entering into treaties, while Article II, section 2, gave the President the power to make treaties with the advice and consent of the Senate. In view of the longstanding practice of putting negotiations with Native Americans in treaty form, it was readily arguable that these provisions, along with Article I, section 8, effectively retained for the new federal government the exclusive right to deal with the tribes that the Confederation Congress had unsuccessfully claimed. The *Federalist* suggested that national control of relations with the tribes was wisest in order to keep the peace, protect Americans against Indian "ravages and depredations," and promote trade.[40] Yet the Constitution's vagueness again left it open to the states to claim power to legislate for Native Americans dwelling within what the states asserted or desired to be their boundaries. Thus the states would continue to claim autonomy in this area as well. Overall, then, the Constitution did suggest that Native Americans could be members of the United States political community, and that the federal government would play the lead in dealing with unconquered tribes, by treaty. But Native Americans were marked out as a group distinct from citizens in general, belonging to ill-defined but clearly lesser classes. They were not guaranteed opportunities for citizenship, yet neither were they recognized to be members of fully independent nations. In all these respects, the Constitution left Native Americans much where they were under the Articles of Confederation.

Blacks. The Constitution's treatment of blacks was more complex. Many matters relating to slavery could not be ignored, but the issue threatened to prevent both the document's creation and its ratification. Hence again the framers sought compromise via silence and ambiguity. The Constitution could be interpreted as placing ultimate authority over slaves with either the nation or the states, and as either sanctioning slavery in perpetuity or contemplating its eventual abolition, with equal citizenship for free blacks.

As many scholars have noted, the framers often adopted awkward circumlocutions to avoid referring to slavery directly because more explicit language was "not pleasing to some people." As Luther Martin bitterly contended, many no doubt saw the word as "odious" in a Constitution professing to secure the blessings of liberty. Almost from the outset leading delegates tried to finesse the explosive issue through guaranteeing southern whites extra representation in Congress by counting their slaves as three-fifths of a person. But that did not protect slavery enough for South Carolinians Charles Pinckney and Pierce Butler, who accused "some gentlemen" of having a "very good mind" to take "their negroes" from them "within or without doors." Antislavery delegates did object to the "indirect encouragement to the slave trade" the three-fifths clause gave, and to the "incoherence" of treating slaves as partly persons, partly property. Eventually they launched all-out attacks on the "infernal" slave trade as well as the "domestic slavery" that violated the "sacred laws of humanity." James Wilson also noted that it gave "disgust" to Pennsylvanians for whites to be blended with blacks in assigning representatives, and George Mason complained that slavery not only discouraged "arts and manufactures" but also prevented "the immigration of whites, who really enrich and strengthen a Country." That array of arguments reveals well how even antislavery positions were often motivated not by egalitarianism but by contempt for blacks.[41]

Pinckney replied that slavery was "justified by the example of all the world."[42] Rutledge defended slavery not as a matter of right but in *realpolitik* terms, insisting that "religion and humanity had nothing to do with the question" and that "interest alone was the governing principle with nations." They both made clear that the deep south would not be part of any antislavery union. Consequently, Madison fretted frequently that slavery was the one great issue that could tear the convention apart. Pragmatic northerners like Oliver Ellsworth said that, though slavery "considered in a moral light" ought to be abolished everywhere, in the future the increase of "poor laborers" would render slavery "useless," and insurrections could be forestalled by "kind treatment." Hence the convention need not "intermeddle" with the institution.

Eventually the Carolinians agreed to permit the national government to regulate commerce and navigation in return for compromises on slavery. The three-fifths clause did enhance the congressional representation of slave states. The call in Article I, sections 2 and 9, for direct taxes to be apportioned in accordance with the three-fifths clause strove to prevent Congress from encouraging emancipation by imposing a head tax on slaves. Section 9 prevented Congress from banning the importation of "Persons," meaning slaves, prior to 1808, and Article V prohibited any amendments intended to affect either this ban or the one on differently apportioned taxation before that year. Article IV, section 2, the "fugitive slave" clause, prevented states from emancipating those held in "Service or Labour" in other states who should escape into their jurisdictions, as some northern states did under the Confederation. Such fugitive slaves had to be returned upon the claim of their masters. Article I, section 8, and Article IV, section 4, also gave the federal government responsibility to assist in preventing violence in the states, powers inspired by fears of slave uprisings as well as debtor insurrections like Shays's rebellion.[43]

These provisions strengthened slavery by giving slaveholders special representation and a guarantee of the return of fugitive slaves that they had not previously had. Only the indication that Congress could ban slavery after 1808, the formal possibility of imposing a head tax on slaves, and the refusal to recognize the institution by name stood as elements that could be used to give the document an antislavery reading, as James Wilson did in the Pennsylvania ratification debates. The *Federalist* termed the slave trade a "barbarism" imposed on "unfortunate Africans" and presented slavery as a matter of positive law that deprived "Negroes" of their "rights." But Madison indicated there and in the Virginia ratifying debates that accepting it was necessary to avoid what he took to be the "worse" evil of national dismemberment. That moral judgment is still disputed. Whatever the role of the Constitution in making possible a nation that would end slavery, its immediate impact was to give the institution greater, though still ambiguous, security.[44]

The Bill of Rights

The Constitution's acceptance of slavery created some opposition to it in the north, but predictably the threat the new system posed to republican state sovereignty engendered the fiercest controversy during the ratification process. The renowned result was a further compromise: the Constitution was adopted only with the understanding that a Bill of Rights would be added. Under Madison's leadership, the initial Congress fulfilled this commitment by proposing to the nation the Constitution's first ten amendments. Thus, when it was adopted, the Bill of Rights represented above all a reassertion of states' rights republicanism, and hence a diminution of the importance of national citizenship. It imposed a range of further limits on the new government while stressing state prerogatives. Indeed, several provisions are classic expressions of traditional republican concerns to preserve local self-governance, specifically: the Second Amendment's guarantee of the right to bear arms in order to sustain "well regulated" state militia; the Fifth Amendment's right to grand jury indictment; the Sixth and Seventh Amendments' guarantees of local juries in criminal and civil trials; and the Tenth Amendment's reservation to the states or to the people of all powers not delegated to the United States or prohibited to the states.[45]

Whereas the Bill of Rights was a republican-inspired set of limits on the national government, and though much of it could be seen as carrying forth the heritage of common-law liberties, most of its strictures reinforced the liberal cast of national citizenship. The amendments invariably referred to the rights of persons, not citizens. Individual rights of speech, press, religious exercise, assembly, and petition were protected by the First Amendment in strikingly absolutist terms. The Third through the Sixth Amendments set limits on the conduct of the federal government in the course of its military and police functions that embodied not only common-law guarantees but also the lessons of American resistance to burdensome English practices. More broadly, they concretely articulated the Constitution's aim of securing personal liberty.

This liberalism was particularly evident in the Fifth Amendment, which guaranteed that "life, liberty and property" could not be taken from "persons" without "due process of law." That rephrasing of the traditional "law of the land" guarantees dating back to Magna Carta articulated both the Lockean trinity of basic rights and the liberal concern for rule of law. The Fifth Amendment also guaranteed just compensation for takings of private property for public use, again suggesting a liberal economic outlook. Particularly notable was the Ninth Amendment, indicating that the enumeration in the Constitution of certain rights should not be taken as a denial that the people also possessed other, unnamed rights. That guarantee was a reasonably direct expression of Enlightenment beliefs in the existence of human rights that did not depend on positive law for their legitimacy. Thus the Bill of Rights satisfied a number of particular concerns while on balance preserving the Constitution's pervasive ambiguity. Though its thrust was to set limits to the federal government on behalf of the states and localities, its content could also be construed as indicating that American citizenship was fundamentally dedicated to individual rights, and hence liberal.

Consequently, the Constitution as amended still altered the much more republican Articles of Confederation in a nationalistic, liberal direction. But its challenges to both the reality and the ideal of state civic primacy were muted and qualified; and, largely via silence, it also permitted the various ascriptive civic hierarchies that American law already contained to continue. With the addition of this new national system onto the modified but still quite republican state constitutions created during the Confederation years, the essential institutional structure that would govern American citizenship up to the Civil War was established. Yet the fundamental questions concerning American citizenship were far from settled. Renewed contests over American civic identity began almost immediately.

6

Attempting National Liberal Citizenship
The Federalist Years 1789–1801

Amid one of the most rapidly repudiated Supreme Court decisions in history, *Chisholm v. Georgia* (1793), Associate Justice James Wilson digressed to complain about the spreading custom of offering toasts to "the United States." He chided, "This is not politically correct." Because such toasts were meant to praise "the first great object in the Union," they should be given to the "People of the United States." Wilson wished to stress, in good republican fashion, that the people, not their government, were sovereign. But he also wanted to insist that Americans were one people who had created their national government as an act of collective sovereignty, rather than seeing that government as the work of the sovereign states, as he feared too many Americans did.[1] Like the *Chisholm* ruling itself, Wilson's digression thus reflected the great concern of the Federalists to meet the political imperatives of leadership by fostering a sense of American national identity conducive to their aims and governance.

Few scholars would deny that assertion. Even so, many have tended to underestimate how necessary this task was for the Federalists, and how their ultimate defeat by the Jeffersonian Republicans was intimately tied to their inability to accomplish it. For example, in their magisterial study of the Federalist era, Stanley Elkins and Eric McKitrick fail to mention the *Chisholm* decision at all. They also give little attention to many other controversies over citizenship rules that sparked considerable anti-Federalist agitation in the Jeffersonian press. Hence they have trouble making sense of the Alien and Sedition Acts, even though they perceive those measures as having played a major role in discrediting the Federalists.[2]

In contrast, I will emphasize here how struggles over citizenship laws formed a major dimension of Federalist and Jeffersonian conflict that intensified throughout the 1790s, a dimension that explains many otherwise puzzling Federalist statutes and judicial rulings. I will also argue that these battles did not only center on the clashes between national and state allegiances that concerned Wilson in *Chisholm,* important as those were. They involved intense disputes over contrasting ascriptive notions of American identity that the Federalists and Jeffersonians blended into their different versions of liberal and republican ideals. The Federalists became the party of national power and commerce, but also the champions of almost unalterable hereditary allegiances and nativism. The Jeffersonians became the party of state power and agrarian republicanism, but also, in a bitter irony, the defenders both of citizenship based on mutual consent and of aggressive civic racism. Both partisan positions were the results of comprehensible political calculations as well as sincere principles, though in the end the Jeffersonians pursued their vision with greater electoral success.

Like the ardently nationalistic Wilson, most members of George Washington's first administration were keenly aware that they had to establish concrete policies, institutions, and customs and traditions that would give flesh and form to the new extended republic. Early on, officials in all three branches tended to erupt into high-flown disquisitions on first principles of republican citizenship in order to settle issues ranging from import duties to expatriation to how a republican chief executive should dress (plainly but with dignity; basic black preferred). Their intensity came from their acute awareness that their novel regime faced severe challenges from every direction. Many American citizens had to be persuaded that the new government was any good at all, much less the proper object of their highest loyalty. Communal attachments were overwhelmingly local, extending at most to state or regional (as well as denominational) identities. Most state and local officials were likely to resist all assertions of new national authority. The European powers could be expected to be oblivious to American interests or to deride and bully the colonial upstarts. The regime's success also seemed to require displacing many native tribes and exploiting slaves. Those groups would struggle against white domination whenever they could, in ways that challenged the physical security and the moral legitimacy of the new nation.[3]

Most significantly, the new national leadership was divided among itself. At the outset, the government was largely staffed by the more nationalistic and liberal-minded Federalists who had won adoption of the Constitution, including Hamilton and Washington himself. And in that first blush of elite unity, they were joined by Secretary of State Thomas Jefferson and their floor leader in the House,

James Madison. These Virginian friends' revolutionary experiences had left them indelibly attached to the national cause, even though Jefferson opposed Hamilton's stress on rapid commercial growth aided by national actions, and Madison was closer to Jefferson on those issues than to his recent co-author. Like so many ex-colonial nation-builders, all the new American leaders shared a desire to show their British former governors, and indeed all the haughty Europeans, that Americans could create a previously undreamed of enlightened republic.[4] But soon, their deep differences over what sort of nation they were creating broke out into clashes between hostile Hamiltonian Federalist and Jeffersonian Republican camps.

Their mounting conflicts particularly drove segments of these competing elites to define their legal conceptions of American citizenship in ever more sharply opposed terms. Initially, the differences were not severe. Prominent figures in both camps endorsed liberal republican notions of consensual membership, though some Federalists stressed the value of native birth. Most leaders expressed hope for peaceful assimilation of the tribes and the eventual demise of slavery, though few championed racial equality. The Federalist vision of a great commercial republic involved a stress on the primacy of a common national identity and expansive national powers, blended with eagerness to gain immigrant workers for the eastern cities and a relatively passive policy toward the unconquered western tribes. Conversely, the Jeffersonian Republican vision of a westward-expanding, much more state-centered agrarian republic always sanctioned slavery and conquest of the tribes, often by alleging their racial inferiority. But Republicans quickly realized that immigrants often felt more affinity for the partisans of small farmers and democratization than for mercantile and financial elites. Hence they reversed course on immigration, abandoning the qualms Jefferson had expressed during the 1780s.[5] And just as the need for immigrants kept most Federalists from displaying aversions to the foreign-born, so Southern and western Federalists quickly persuaded most of their Northern allies to stifle all hints of antislavery measures and to downplay opposition to white settlers encroaching on Indian lands. Hence, though the nascent parties differed over policies concerning blacks, Native Americans, and immigrants, as well as economic policies and national powers, at first all seemed compromisable.

But in a nation where the voters were overwhelmingly white men with primarily local allegiances, the Federalists' reservations about slavery and westward expansion and their advocacy of national powers aroused suspicion from the start. As their economic and foreign policies spurred Jeffersonian opposition, Federalists increasingly came to believe that they could not afford to be so tolerant of disloyalty to the national regime by citizens or so welcoming to potentially subversive immigrants. Thus Federalist officials in all three branches increasingly rejected their more cosmopolitan and consensual notions of national identity for restrictive ones, launching what John Higham calls the "first great wave" of American nativism.[6] By enacting statutes and judicial rules defining political identities and allegiances heavily in terms of birthplace, they hoped both to compel obedience to the new nation and to curb the influx of foreign-born Jeffersonian voters.

Correspondingly, the Jeffersonian Republicans came to champion policies encouraging immigration, including expansive expatriation, naturalization, and voting rights. Hence they became more and more the party of consensually based democratic citizenship, the party of "the people"—though only for whites. In the 1800 election, the Jeffersonian blend of the country's liberal, republican, and racially ascriptive civic traditions proved most politically potent; but the Federalist era left a vital residue of nationalistic institutions as constitutive features of American civic life.

The Federalists' Liberal National Republic

The citizenship laws of the age of Federalism formed part of a broader context of institution-building through which the first two administrations tried to set the direction of national life. As at the Constitutional convention, various forms of ascriptive inequality, particularly slavery, went largely unchallenged or were even reinforced as part of the price of winning support for economic policies, at home and abroad, favoring commerce, manufacturing, and rapid development. Others, including a predilection toward nativism and maintenance of the political subordination of women, ran deep in Federalist thought. Nonetheless, on all fronts the Federalists initially stressed policies designed to create a distinctively liberal national republic. The results of their efforts reveal how fervently many Americans have wanted to maintain ascriptive hierarchies along with some measure of democratic liberalism, because most of the more liberal features of the Federalists' program proved to be massive political liabilities. Yet when they resorted to nativism to recoup, they only permitted the Jeffersonians to drape a mantle of egalitarian inclusiveness around their vote-getting support for racially exploitative policies.

Economic Policy. The centerpiece of the first administration's attempts to shape a new national society was Treasury Secretary Hamilton's economic program. By funding the war debts, creating a national bank, generating income, and aiding infant industries via bounties and a tariff, and promoting manufacturing and commerce in other ways, Hamilton hoped to foster the kind of bustling, productive, large-scale commercial polity that we identify today with liberal civic life and that many see as quintessentially American. These actions aimed not so much at stockpiling wealth in national coffers (as in traditional mercantilism) as at promoting both economic development and loyalty to the national government. Hamilton's measures were meant to attract commercial and financial elites to buy national securities and start new enterprises, thus enriching and being enriched by the new regime. The holders of federal bonds issued to pay war debts would have a vested interest in seeing their great public debtor flourish. So would those whose businesses relied on federal trade protections. The U.S. government would in many ways be linked to the wealthy leaders of the nation's more dynamic economic forces, reinforcing socioeconomic and political hierarchies that Hamilton thought beneficial.[7]

As he spelled out in his 1791 *Report on Manufactures,* through this sort of economy Hamilton sought to create a new, more liberal American character, dominated by the "spirit of enterprise" instead of the often "careless" and "remiss" work habits all too prevalent among farmers. This "new energy" would be encouraged by the spread of "different kinds of industry," for among this new variety of occupations "each individual" could "find his proper element" to labor with fullest "vigour." Hamilton's Americans were to be vigorous indeed. The new exertions he contemplated included the undertaking of "extra employment" by "industrious" workers, who would add extra jobs during their leisure time. He also advocated increased employment of "women and Children" in manufacturing. The growth of such industries would then encourage "emigration from abroad," which would in turn increase "the useful and productive labour of the country." Thus Hamilton envisioned a fast-growing nation in which immigrants, women, children, and men of all ranks would be embraced as equals—though largely as equal resources for "augmenting the fund of national Industry." Slavery, which Hamilton despised, had no proper part in such an economy, though Hamilton otherwise displayed little concern for the conditions of workers. The modern identification of citizenship in a liberal market society with absorption in relentlessly competitive work and money-making well describes his aims.[8]

Although Hamilton was unable to get all his proposals enacted and several were later discontinued, the country still moved in most of the directions he charted. His efforts reinforced broader economic and social forces working toward those ends, and they established in the national government financial initiatives and institutions that would forever be linked to views tying American citizenship to the protection and enjoyment of property rights and the pursuit of rational economic self-interest. Even many of the "small republics" (the states) adopted measures to promote economic development akin to those Hamilton pioneered on the nation level. At the same time, however, his efforts to aid economic elites via expansively defined national powers seemed unfair and unconstitutional to many voters, and they triggered deeply entrenched fears about the financial conspiracies of despotic centralized governments.[9] The more the Federalists became liberal nationalist Hamiltonians, the more a great part of the electorate became receptive to state-centered Jeffersonian Republicanism.

African-American Slavery. Because the Federalist vision of America had little place for the nation's most illiberal institution, black chattel slavery, in some ways the new administration proved willing to work against its growth. But even these mild expressions of antislavery sentiment hurt the Federalists politically, and so they also offered major concessions to slaveholders, unsuccessfully striving for damage control. On the more liberal side of the ledger, the new government reenacted the antislavery, ethnically inclusive Northwest Ordinance with only slight modifications, and it rejected later efforts to open the Northwest to slavery. Federal officials also made only perfunctory demands that Britain pay reparations for slaves taken from Americans during the war. Eventually Hamilton and John Jay dropped that demand, among others, in negotiating the unpopular Jay Treaty with Britain in 1794, sparking charges of betrayal by slave-owning Jeffersonians. Congress also banned exports of slaves in 1794, with little debate.[10]

At the same time, some political actors sought racially egalitarian reforms at other levels. State abolitionist movements continued to push for emancipation throughout the land, inspired by Quaker religious appeals, egalitarian revolutionary ideology, and the skillful deployment of these arguments by Northern free blacks like Absalom Jones, pastor of the African Episcopal Church of Philadelphia. Many state courts, even in the South, strove to construe slave-related laws and procedural issues *in favorem libertatis* during the 1790s, promoting emancipation whenever possible. And Southern manumissions occurred often enough to help the free black population grow three times as fast as the white and slave segments under the Federalists.[11]

In most regards, however, Federalist leaders either refused to confront slavery or actively supported it. In the first Congress, Pennsylvania Quakers submitted an antislavery petition, soon reinforced by another from the state's Society for Promoting the Abolition of Slavery and signed by the society's president, Ben Franklin. A clamor ensued, with Southern delegates warning that any steps toward emancipation would produce civil war. Georgian and South Carolinian representatives cited biblical references and the examples of the ancient republics to defend slavery's religious and republican rectitude. South Carolina's William Smith read Jefferson's discussion of blacks in his *Notes on the State of Virginia* into the record, claiming it proved that "negroes were by nature an inferior race of beings," below "even . . . the Indians." He added that Quakers might want emancipation for Negroes, but none of them ever married one. Some Northern congressmen responded by attacking the immorality of "traffic in human flesh," but Madison and other Washington allies strove to drop the subject. No one holding real power was willing to risk Southern wrath on the issue. By 1798, Southerners won a resolution stating that such petitions were matters for strictly "judicial cognizance."[12]

The only question thus became how much the federal government would aid the slaveholders. From 1789 on, Governor Arthur St. Clair of the Northwest Territory interpreted the ordinance's ban on slavery as applying only prospectively. Existing property rights in slaves must, he insisted, be respected, a dubious reading of Congress's action which it tacitly accepted.[13] Under pressure from the Southern states, particularly North Carolina, Congress also organized the Southern territories—first the Southwest Territory, which became Kentucky and Tennessee, then the Mississippi Territory, which became Mississippi and Alabama—under provisions similar to those governing the Northwest, except that slavery was allowed. Kentucky was then admitted as a slave state in 1792, Tennessee in 1796. Though Kentucky came in with an "egalitarian" constitution guaranteeing universal male suffrage, its 1799 constitution excluded blacks, mulattos, and Native Americans from the vote. Congress also sanctioned slavery in the District of Columbia; and in 1792, it passed a Militia Act which called for the enrollment of all "free, able-bodied, white male" citizens. It was unclear whether this provision prohibited blacks from serving or merely required whites to enroll. But, fearful of arming blacks, most states, including all the Northern ones, went on to ban blacks in their own militia laws.[14]

The greatest support the national government gave to slavery was the Fugitive Slave Act of 1793, passed with little recorded debate and a one-sided vote (48–7 in the House). Don Fehrenbacher has argued that there was no clear constitutional mandate for any such congressional enforcement of the constitutional requirement to "deliver up" fugitive slaves. The matter might have been left to the courts, or to the semi-sovereign states themselves, as so much else was. But Congress chose to act, in ways that Northern state officials found offensively dismissive of their legal systems. Slaveowners were authorized to enter other slave states, seize their alleged fugitive slaves, and to obtain from a local magistrate a certificate entitling them to take the alleged slave home, once they had provided proof of ownership. To the slaveholders' great benefit, the law thus abrogated virtually all the normal canons of legal due process, including habeas corpus, trial by jury, assistance of counsel, protection against self-incrimination, and time limitations on vulnerability to arrest. On balance, both by silent consent and active legislation, Congress did much to perpetuate slavery in these years and virtually nothing to move blacks toward freedom or citizenship. Federalist concerns to ensure support for the new nation by placating the slave states, fears raised by the Haitian blacks' rebellion in 1791, and the religious and scientific arguments that slavery's defenders mounted easily trumped religious and rationalist arguments for equal human rights. Yet Northern Federalists still managed only to alienate antislavery forces while failing to end Southern suspicions that they would move against the institution if they could.[15]

Native Americans. On the surface, the Federalists' policies toward the native tribes went further toward complying with what one of their chief architects, Secretary of War Henry Knox, termed "liberal justice." In reality, however, they were similarly conflicted, and their apparent liberality only made them even more of a political liability. Though Washington himself displayed genuinely humanitarian sentiments in this regard, his policies were in part due to necessity. It was still hard to dictate to the tribes instead of negotiating with them. General St. Clair's forces were badly beaten in the Northwest by Shawnees and others in 1791, and federal forces achieved substantial control over those territories only in 1794. The victories that year subdued the Ohio Indian Confederation and the Cherokees and led to the Jay-Grenville (or Greeneville) Treaty, wherein the southwest quarter of the territory (much of present-day Ohio) was ceded to the U.S. for a minor payment.[16]

The continuing power of the tribes was one reason that the U.S. dealt with them by treaty, instead of pressing its postrevolutionary claims that the tribes had been conquered and legislating directly over them. Arguing that those claims should be waived, Knox always referred to the tribes as "foreign nations." Federal treaties supposedly were consensual agreements with these sovereign foreigners. The leaders of the infant national government were undoubtedly attracted to this course by the fact that if the tribes were foreign nations, the Constitution clearly required that they be dealt with by the United States exercising its exclusive treaty powers, not by the states. Washington's men were well aware of the crippling inability of the Confederation Congress to constrain state actions toward the tribes, and they knew that, apart from the treaty clause, their constitutional title to exclusive conduct of Native American affairs was ambiguous. Even with his government's augmented military powers, Washington despaired of its inability to "restrain Land Jobbers, and the Incroachment of Settlers, upon the Indian Territory." Thus it seemed strategic to secure constitutional sanction for federal predominance by treating the tribes as nations.[17]

Those strategic judgments, however, may not have properly weighed the full political costs of these policies. As with slavery, the Federalist policy of relative passivity toward Native Americans fueled opposition to the national regime, both among Americans seeking to expand at the expense of the tribes and among supporters of state power. Complaints that the federal government was holding back settler "Incroachment" were underlying grievances in the Whiskey Rebellion of 1794, when Washington had to call out militia against angry western Pennsylvanians.

Knox and Secretary of State Jefferson tried to make their ultimate loyalty to the interests of white citizens and the states clear by claiming for the U.S. government and the states a "right of preemption." Although official statements of this doctrine contained ambiguities that prompted later litigation, its basic meaning was clear.[18] American officials conceded that the tribes had property rights in the lands they occupied, but those rights were essentially limited to occupancy. The American government, state or national, within whose limits a tribe resided had a preemptive right to purchase any lands the tribe might wish to sell and to veto sales to others. There would soon be heated disputes over whether the states had ceded all their preemptive powers to the federal government; but localists and nationalists, Jeffersonians and Federalists alike, agreed that the U.S. government should prevent Europeans, at least, from acquiring Native American lands without its approval. The premise of Federalist policy was still that most Native American claims in the east would be "extinguished" via governmental purchases at the convenience of the U.S. government alone.[19]

In 1790, the Congress passed the first of a series of Intercourse Acts that explicitly required federal approval for Indian land transfers and stipulated that all persons wishing to trade with the tribes must obtain a federal license. Traders were thereby compelled to abide by national regulations. These acts were motivated in part by desires to curb the perennial problem of exploitative white traders and settlers. But the assertion of such preemptive regulatory rights confirmed the implication in the Constitution: the U.S. did not really regard the tribes as independent nations. Instead, it still assumed a vague measure of special authority over them that looked like a claim to ultimate sovereignty. Hence the government treated the tribes as subordinate parts of the new nation in some ill-specified sense.[20]

These policies did make clear, however, that tribal members were not to be treated simply as conquered subjects who could be legislated upon by state or nation without their agreement. Their lands, moreover, were to be purchased, not confiscated, as more militant state officials longed to do. Knox supported this measure of respect for tribal property claims by attributing to them the Lockean natural rights of man.[21] Although the tribes' status was still not precisely defined, and they certainly were not equals, a qualified liberalism was thus genuinely evident in the administration's Indian policies, however much it might trace to desires to strengthen national authority versus state officials. But because the new government was in reality too weak to constrain state and private behavior effectively, in the end this national liberalism only mildly softened the basic imperialism of American whites toward the tribes. It also infuriated Jeffersonian proponents of white expansion and states' rights, cutting further into the Federalists' popularity.

Women. The Federalists neither made nor considered any major changes in the laws governing the civic status of women. Some Federalist leaders, however, continued the ideological task of working out how to fit women into the nation's new egalitarian liberal republican notions of citizenship with at least superficial coherence. The most notable such effort came in James Wilson's 1792 *Lectures on Law,* which presented the comprehensive philosophy of the founding generations' best legal scholar. But even though Wilson tried hard to defend female citizenship as different but equal, his arguments were inconsistent, precisely because neither he nor any other (male) Federalist was willing to contemplate reform of women's subordinate civic status. Instead, Federalists ended up accusing Jeffersonians of radically egalitarian views on women's political rights, even though in fact neither party championed that cause.

Wilson's passionate national republicanism, visible throughout the *Lectures* as much as in his *Chisholm* opinion, was heavily influenced by the Scottish Enlightenment thought in which he was educated. He was also a fervent Protestant and a liberal who ultimately emphasized private pursuits over public ones. And though he gave it liberal republican readings, he revered the common law as a means for injecting a restraining concern for tradition in popular governments. His traditionalism, his privatism, and his Protestantism are all visible in his comments on women, even as he sought to make his position compatible with more egalitarian versions of republicanism. To do so, he blended liberal, republican, and older ascriptive doctrines into a textbook account of the "domestic sphere" of "republican mothers."[22]

All this came as an apparent aside to the ladies at the start of one lecture. Wilson's tone was casual and condescending, but his arguments revealed the great difficulties of his task. His egalitarianism spoke when Wilson assured women that, contrary to traditional views of female inferiority, they were "neither less honest, nor less virtuous, nor less wise" than men. Why, then, should they not participate in politics? Wilson first appealed to a strongly privatistic version of liberalism's instrumental view of states, arguing that "publick government and public law" were made not for themselves but "for something better," for "domestick society." And he argued that women formed the "better part" of such society—that is, if they did not acquire "masculine" traits through public pursuits. Here Wilson moved to ascriptive, religious naturalism joined with republicanism. Women should develop their unique qualities, bestowed by nature and its Creator, so that they might "embellish" and "exalt" social life by their "beauty," "virtue," and "affection." Their proper political role, again, was to form their daughters for similar service, and to refine their sons' virtues, adding to male spiritedness the civility and concern for others that republican citizenship required.[23]

Later in his lectures, Wilson endorsed more Lockean doctrines upholding education for women and treating marriage as a civil contract. Yet he also defended the coverture status imposed by the common law, not in terms of women's natural capacities so much as through a privatistic liberal appeal to the importance of limiting public interference in home life. Wilson said the law ought, like a "benevolent neighbor," to assume "all to be well" with husband and wife, so that they had a total identity of interests. It must not intrude on their matrimonial privacy unless this presumption proved so flagrantly untrue that "the peace and safety of society" were endangered.[24]

Rhetorically, then, Wilson recognized female equality, including an equal entitlement to basic human rights, and he attributed to women a vital role in republican government. They were said to be of at least equal worth but distinctive abilities, so that they contributed most by shaping future citizens in their proper domestic sphere, a sphere actually higher than that of government. But Wilson's synthesis was far from seamless. The contribution of "republican mothers" was too indirect for women truly to be equal citizens. And while some strains in liberal thought might support deferring to the private arrangements of husband and wife, it was hard to find good reasons why the male must always be the sole public representative of their united identity. That step rested on embracing the inegalitarian ascriptive beliefs about the destiny of women embodied in common law and religious traditions. But because Wilson's view of women's place seemed on the surface to satisfy Enlightenment egalitarianism, traditional ascriptive outlooks, and the republican insistence on social roles consistent with a virtuous, homogeneous citizenry all at once, it is not surprising that this position proved dominant in the new but still ascriptive American liberal republic.

There were countercurrents, but they were very weak. A few voices spoke for broadening the education of women: Benjamin Rush thought more study of history, biography, and geography appropriate if they were to be effective republican mothers. In the 1790s, Judith Sargent Murray of Massachusetts published essays arguing for the "equality of the sexes" in regard to their mental and spiritual capacities. She insisted that women would appear less inferior with more adequate education, and she was gratified to see some slight increase in the number of female academies, though they were more finishing schools than training grounds for equal citizens. Murray did not, however, proselytize for equal political rights.

The most radical argument for female equality during these years came from

England and built even more extensively on Enlightenment liberal commitments to human reason and human rights. In 1792 Mary Wollstonecraft, a London writer who moved in radical Enlightenment philosophical circles, criticized Rousseau's arguments for denying women equal citizenship and called for greater female independence, including equal, coeducational schooling, in her *Vindication of the Rights of Woman*. Though she did not entirely reject claims for women's special maternal duties or for male superiority in certain physical respects, Wollstonecraft did argue that all professions, as well as political representation, should be open to women. She rested much of her case on the duties of citizenship, claiming that if men would but "snap our chains, and be content with rational fellowship instead of slavish obedience, they would find us more observant daughters, more affectionate sisters, more faithful wives, more reasonable mothers—in a word, better citizens." Often described as the founding work of the modern women's movement, her book was soon reprinted in a Republican periodical in America. It quickly won criticism from Federalist traditionalists, and leading Jeffersonians never embraced it, but its assaults on excessive absorption in fashion, sentimentality, and useless feminine refinements accorded with anti-aristocratic American sensibilities to which Republicans were appealing. But with the aid of the controversial 1798 memoir of her by her husband, William Godwin, Wollstonecraft's views soon came to be linked to French revolutionary excesses and promiscuity. Because Federalists were trying to tar the Jeffersonians with those profligacies, the Republican press ceased favoring Wollstonecraft, and her writings did not then spark any major reform efforts in the U.S.[25]

Although Federalist policies on the national economy, slavery, relations with the tribes, and even women all became grist for partisan conflicts during these years, the greatest political battles over how national identity should be shaped in law came on three other fronts. First were Federalist legislative and judicial efforts to declare the legal primacy of national over state citizenship—measures that regularly inflamed Jeffersonians espousing state-centric republican views. Second were Federalist judicial rulings insisting on near-perpetual allegiance to the nation, in conflict with the revolutionary doctrines of consensual membership that Jeffersonian critics trumpeted in reply. Third were the Federalists' mounting legislative attempts to deny full political privileges to immigrant Jeffersonians.

On all three fronts Federalists increasingly expressed a sense of American national identity with powerful nativist elements. Yet that development, too, was ironic: even though Federalists like Jay had longstanding nativist sentiments, initially not only Hamilton, but virtually all the Federalist architects of the new national order believed that it had to be built by attracting European immigrants. This necessity led them to stress the more inclusive, cosmopolitan conception of

American identity of Paine and Crèvecoeur, holding that America's special role in promoting freedom would be advanced by providing opportunities for all European newcomers. Thus it was easy for the nation's officers to adopt what they referred to as the "liberal" policy of open immigration. Washington himself had long called for America to be an "asylum" for the "oppressed and persecuted of all Nations and Religions," a view that gave higher moral purpose to Hamiltonian arguments for the economic benefits of adding laborers.[26] The resulting absence of direct national limits on immigration (excepting the eventual ban on the slave trade) survived largely intact until after the Civil War, establishing a tradition that has always played a major part in American civic debates.[27] From the mid-1790s on, however, these same Federalists provided some of the seminal texts of the rival restrictionist tradition that has often since prevailed. In this and other ways, the political wars of the 1790s ensured that potent elements of states' rights republicanism and ascriptive Americanism would be built into American citizenship laws along with nationalistic liberal features.

State-Centered Jeffersonian Republicanism and National Citizenship

Although nationalist-minded Federalists maintained a strong hold on Congress and the Cabinet through the late 1790s, Jeffersonian defenders of state prerogatives usually could compel concessions in nationalizing and liberalizing laws.[28] Thus many of the most controversial actions on citizenship came from Federalists in the judiciary, interpreting statutory and constitutional provisions nationalistically. The constitutional text offered the federal judiciary some tempting bases for expanding both its own power and the rights of national citizenship. Article III, section 2 (the diversity of citizenship clause), extended the federal judicial power to cases "between a State and Citizens of another State" and between "citizens of different States." Article IV, section 2, granted the citizens of "each state" all the "privileges and immunities of citizens in the several States." The diversity clause gave the federal courts opportunities to assert and expand the primacy of national membership, and their own definitions of civic rights, by allowing national judges to rule whenever citizens were involved in interstate conflicts. The terse language of the privileges and immunities clause offered federal jurists an even more open-ended vehicle for giving national content to the rights of the "citizens of the several states." But efforts to read both provisions broadly ran afoul of the power of state-centered republican beliefs.

Federal Jurisdiction and Citizenship. Even choices to create lower federal courts and grant them any diversity jurisdiction were controversial in the first Congress, where proposals to ban both actions by constitutional amendment were introduced. Congress nonetheless adopted a version of Senate Bill 1, the landmark Judiciary Act of 1789. It was written largely by the Connecticut Federalist Oliver Ellsworth, who had also been a chief author of the judiciary article in the Constitution and who would follow John Jay as Chief Justice of the Supreme Court. Unsurprisingly, it mapped out broad national powers; but here as elsewhere, Federalists also made important concessions to champions of state prerogatives.

The Judiciary Act did not give the federal courts anything like the full range of powers Article III permitted them. Most notably, it denied lower federal courts jurisdiction over federal questions, which thus could be decided nationally only as matters of original Supreme Court jurisdiction or on appeal from the states. As a result, almost all the business of the lower federal courts up to the Civil War would come under "diversity of citizenship" jurisdiction. And even though that jurisdiction seemed necessary to prevent state courts from discriminating against out-of-state citizens, it, too, was limited. Civil diversity cases had to involve amounts greater than $500. More important, one of the parties had to be a citizen in the state in which the suit was brought, and the states retained concurrent jurisdiction over such disputes, though if a plaintiff in a state case was a resident of that state, the defendant had the important new power to "remove" the case to the presumably more impartial federal courts. Most significantly, federal courts had to apply state laws in "trials at common law." Thus litigants could not bring suit in a federal court far from the state whose political interests their cases might implicate, nor did the federal courts have much power to craft distinct national common law rules. These features meant that the state republics would not be excessively subordinated to the national courts.[29]

The Supreme Court nevertheless appealed to the centrality of national membership to read its diversity jurisdiction expansively in *Chisholm v. Georgia*, creating a national furor. Alexander Chisholm, a South Carolinian, sued the state of Georgia for payment of a war debt owed to an estate of which he was executor. Georgia denied that the Supreme Court had jurisdiction. It insisted that the words of Article III, section 2, granting jurisdiction in controversies "between a State and Citizens of another State," had never been intended to override a sovereign state's venerable common-law right not to be sued without its consent. Indeed, Georgia claimed that the case was such an affront to its sovereignty that it refused even to appear before the Supreme Court, thereby alienating the justices.

Georgia's claim was quite strong. True, the broad phrasing of Article III did not mention the exception the state asserted, and that absence had been both criticized and defended in ratifying debates. Two members of the Committee on Detail, Edmund Randolph and James Wilson, urged ratification while arguing for the ability of the states to be sued. But in Virginia, Madison had asserted that Article III was not meant to end traditional sovereign immunity. Even Hamilton argued in *Federalist* #81 that to read the Constitution as altering this prerogative would be "forced and unwarrantable."[30]

Yet with Wilson on the bench and Edmund Randolph representing Chisholm as a private client (though Randolph was also the U.S. Attorney General), the Supreme Court ruled that Chisholm could indeed sue Georgia, with only Justice James Iredell of North Carolina in dissent. Iredell argued that the Judiciary Act's indication that the Court should apply state common-law doctrines meant that it could not take jurisdiction here, for he thought that those doctrines did not under these circumstances authorize the particular writ Chisholm sought.[31] But the other justices stressed the absence of any overt recognition of state immunity in the Constitution and the clear vulnerability of the states to suits from other states. Chief Justice Jay as well as Wilson grandly insisted that the true issue was the worth of national membership.

Wilson was glad of the occasion to drive that point home. Calling the case "of uncommon magnitude," he contended that it rested on the "radical" question, "do the people of the United States form a Nation?" Wilson rejected as "degrading" the "feudal" conception that governments were sovereign and could refuse to be sued if they chose. Instead, in a real nation, the "body of the people" held "supreme power." In that spirit, the ancient "Saxon government" could be sued by all comers, Wilson asserted, citing Coke. And he argued that the republican state governments of the U.S., built on this Saxon tradition, should be suable as well.[32] Thus Wilson blended the Saxon myth of American ethnicity, Tudor notions of nationhood, and the national republican doctrine that the American people formed one popular sovereign to assert a nationally enforceable citizenship right limiting state sovereignty.

Jay's brief opinion carried forth his *Federalist* argument that, even prior to the Declaration of Independence, Americans were one people "already united for general purposes." He dismissed the allegedly sovereign early state governments and the Articles of Confederation as mere "temporary arrangements." Jay also claimed, with the same casual disregard for facts that he displayed in *Federalist* #2, that American citizens were all "as to civil rights perfectly equal." Because all free citizens could sue all other citizens, Jay maintained, some citizens of one state should be able to sue all citizens of another state, as represented by their state government. To hold otherwise would be to violate equal justice for all, for "the few against the many, as well as the many against the few."[33]

Jay's insistence on the importance of the rights of the "few" in question—public creditors—was true both to Hamiltonian economic precepts and to the Federalists' political base among wealthy elites. By the same token, it was in every way anathema to most of the believers in republican state sovereignty. Georgia refused to comply with the decision. It was widely attacked in the states as fostering "a general consolidation of these confederated republics." In January 1794, opponents introduced the Eleventh Amendment in Congress, aiming to undo *Chisholm*. The Senate quickly approved it 23–2, the House, 81–9. Even most Federalists seemed not to favor such a direct, confrontational assertion of the supremacy of national citizenship and national courts over state prerogatives. State ratifications came almost as fast. The requisite number was reached by February 1795, though presidential certification of ratification did not come until 1798.[34]

The battle reenergized those advocating state-centered republicanism and seemed to give the more nationalistic justices pause. Subsequently, the Marshall Court would try to compel states to honor their debts through broad readings of the contract clause. But after the dramatic failure of the Court in *Chisholm*, federal judges did not use the theoretical primacy of national citizenship to elaborate broad and novel readings of either federal diversity jurisdiction or Article IV privileges and immunities.[35]

The Supreme Court instead treated most diversity of citizenship cases in narrow technical terms.[36] Only rarely during these years did it touch on the larger diversity issues that might have produced confrontations with basic questions of political membership.[37] The Court's technical approach mattered less than it might have, however, because these cases defined citizenship only for jurisdictional purposes. Someone who could legitimately claim a state's citizenship under the Supreme Court's jurisdictional rules did not need to be regarded by that state or by the federal courts as its citizen in other contexts. Hence, these cases also provide evidence of how multifaceted and apparently contradictory legal definitions of citizenship already were. From the nation's outset and throughout its history, Americans have been able to be state citizens for some purposes and not for others.

Privileges and Immunities of Citizenship. Despite Hamilton's great expectations for the privileges and immunities clause, during these Federalist years the Supreme Court did not find any occasion to define its meaning very fully. That fact may indicate how few litigants had any strong sense that national citizenship implied prerogatives that the states could not violate. State courts provided the few constructions of the clause that appeared, and they usually treated it as a comity clause, like its Confederation predecessor.[38] The one extended federal judicial discussion of citizenship rights came in the Pennsylvania circuit decision *Van Horne's Lessee v. Dorrance* (1795). But there even Circuit Justice Paterson defined the relevant rights via interpretation of the Pennsylvania constitution, not the U.S. Constitution. That approach suggested that the privileges and immunities of citizenship were primarily matters of state, not national membership and authority.[39]

Ascriptive Citizenship and Federalist Nation-Building

Leading historical accounts of the conflicts between Federalists and Jeffersonian Republicans rightly stress their differing constituencies, their clashing economic visions, and their conflicts on foreign policy, including the identification of the Republicans with France and the Federalists with England. Some note without emphasis that the two camps also struggled over judicial decisions and proposed laws governing expatriation and naturalization. Most recognize that a climactic feature of these battles was the passage of the Alien and Sedition Acts and a new Naturalization Act in 1798, all designed to prevent immigrants from gaining citizenship and to silence and deport dissidents. Many scholars, however, present the Federalists' swelling nativism as a rather foolhardy outgrowth of their Anglophilia that only helped propel the Jeffersonians to victory. Elkins and McKitrick present the laws as irrational creations of "Federalist bedlamites." Yet they acknowledge that the leading advocate of the 1798 Naturalization Act, Harrison Gray Otis, was no extremist but rather a "'moderate' Adams supporter."[40]

Though irremediably counterproductive, the Federalists' expatriation and naturalization rulings and laws are comprehensible if one focuses on how their political struggle pushed Federalists and Republicans to advocate increasingly divergent views of American citizenship. For reasons high and low, out of their genuine commitment to the primacy of a national republic, their real belief in the superiority of the native American variant of northern European Christian civilization, and their desire to command allegiance to the government they dominated, during the 1790s the Federalists in Congress and on federal benches moved toward the position foreshadowed by Jay in *Federalist* #2. They maintained that American citizenship was rightfully as much a matter of birth, heritage, and natural allegiance as of choice, and that certain sorts of "blood" were more truly American than others. The nativistic laws of 1798 were only the final sour fruit of this trend toward more naturalistic, restrictive Federalist conceptions of citizenship. Conversely, both principle and partisan advantage fueled the rising Jeffersonian assault on these Federalist doctrines as "feudal" and unrepublican, in violation of the Revolution's principles of liberty and enlightenment. The key point for historical understanding is to see how the Federalists' turn to ascriptive conceptions initially gave them many legal tools to reinforce their hold on power. It also expressed a vision of common identity that many found wise and inspiring. Thus it seemed both prudent and right, even if it proved instead to offer the party short-term gains at severe long-term political costs.

Birthright Citizenship. An illuminating prelude to these developments occurred almost as the first congressmen were taking their seats. Dr. David Ramsay of

South Carolina petitioned the new House not to accept one of South Carolina's elected representatives, William Smith, the same man who would invoke Jefferson to defend slavery. Ramsay claimed that Smith had not been a naturalized citizen of the United States for the requisite seven years, if indeed he was a citizen at all. Smith, born in Charleston, had been sent to study in Europe in 1770 at age twelve and did not return to the U.S. until 1782, missing the entire Revolution. In his petition, which Ramsay also published as a pamphlet on the ways American citizenship could be acquired, he maintained that citizenship was something more than mere inhabitancy. It involved a share of "the common sovereignty," including "the right of voting at elections," which was why "Negroes are inhabitants, but not citizens." Blending Blackstone and Locke, Ramsay said that such a share of sovereignty could be acquired in five ways: by being a party to the original declaration of independence; by taking an oath to a revolutionary state government; by tacitly consenting to remain in the states as they achieved independence; by being born in such a state after it attained independence; or by formal naturalization. Smith had done none of these things. His absence meant that he had neither explicitly nor tacitly consented to the Revolution. He had been born in South Carolina prior to its independence. And, on return, he had never been formally naturalized.[41]

Smith responded in Congress that he and other young men had been effectively authorized by the revolutionary South Carolina legislature to continue their studies abroad and that many of his actions showed that he had always chosen to be an American citizen, a fact his fellow South Carolinians had often affirmed by electing him to office. But Madison, speaking on Smith's behalf, took a less consensual though also un-Cokean view. He contended that people acquired allegiances at birth primarily to the society in which they were born, and only secondarily to the sovereign it happened to have established. When the society replaced that sovereign, its members continued to owe allegiance to it by "ties of nature," and they all had to obey the new sovereign the society designated. Smith was thus "bound by the decision" of the revolutionary states, "with respect to the question of independence and change of Government," so that it would have been treason for him to have sided with Britain. Others sharply criticized Madison's view because it implied that even American-born children of Loyalists could claim U.S. citizenship. They preferred to say that the Revolution had created a state of nature, with children owing allegiance only to their parents. Congress seated Smith without resolving that debate.[42]

Ramsay, Smith, and the critics of Madison all accepted that though children always owed their parents allegiance and might ordinarily owe allegiance to the society in which they were born, the Revolution had created a situation in which individuals had to choose their political membership. But Madison took the more ascriptive view that birthright citizenship created ongoing duties to one's society, even if its people changed governments without one's own participation or choice. Though he called the issue "a question of right, unmixed with the question of expediency," Madison was probably influenced in this ascriptive direction by desires to end this minor controversy and get on with business, to affirm the duty of allegiance both to the states and to the United States, and to define American citizenship inclusively. The concern to require allegiance, however, would later prompt ascriptive Federalist doctrines that Madison rejected once he moved into opposition.[43]

Expatriation and Natural Allegiance. Federalists and Jeffersonians began to clash over citizenship in regard to rights of expatriation. Though logically implied by consensual views of membership, such rights were also convenient vehicles for disavowing duties to the new national regime. Amid the international conflicts of the 1790s, many Americans engaged in lucrative overseas trading and privateering, particularly in partnership with France. They often wished to drop their links to the weak, officially neutral but tacitly pro-British U.S. government. As the authority of their administration was at stake, Federalist congressmen especially urged restricting such expatriations, and Federalist judges turned away from the consensualism of Locke and the Declaration to the modified ascriptive views of Blackstone. The Jeffersonian press responded with polemical outrage.

The impetus to support some sort of expatriation right came not only from Americans' revolutionary legacies, Blackstone's common-law doctrine that British subjects could be expatriated with parliamentary approval, and international law, but also from the need for new loyal citizens to aid state-building. Specifying expatriation rights and procedures proved controversial, however, because it was hard to deny Americans rights that the U.S. claimed on behalf of incoming foreigners. Some high Federalists like Theodore Sedgwick were far more concerned to hold on to the native born than to accept newcomers. They spoke longingly of the advantages of perpetual allegiance and were attracted to Madison's view that there were permanent obligations at birth to one's society, if not its sovereign.

Such men thought that Americans could not be expatriated without specific legislative approval, as in Blackstone, and should then never be readmitted to citizenship. More argued, like William Vans Murray, that American consensual principles compelled the assumption of legislative approval when a citizen indicated his intent to expatriate himself through a variety of legal acts, especially permanent emigration. Yet few agreed on what acts did or did not count. For example, Murray complained that Virginia's statute, drafted by Jefferson in 1779, wrongly permitted men to expatriate themselves without leaving the country.

Congress discussed expatriation provisions in 1794 and especially in 1797, when concerns about Americans violating neutrality by joining "foreign ships of war" were at their height. But divisions over the scope of federal versus state responsibility, judicial versus legislative authority, and the extent of any birthright allegiance were all too great for any agreement to be reached.[44]

While Secretary of State, Jefferson continued his longtime defense of expatriation as a natural individual right. He insisted, however, that neither treason nor any other criminal act could be construed as a permissible indication of intent to relinquish citizenship. This stipulation soon produced confusion, because certain acts undertaken at sea or abroad, such as violations of neutrality, were criminal only if the individual remained a citizen. In keeping with his more state-oriented republicanism, Jefferson also believed that a state expatriation act, such as the one he had drafted for Virginia, terminated federal citizenship as well. Few of his successors as Secretary of State upheld him on this point, but most did endorse his general defense of expatriation rights. They were frequently intent on criticizing the demeaning British practice of impressing Americans into the royal navy, which the British defended by claiming that Americans born under the British crown still owed the king perpetual allegiance. Executive branch officers thus usually supported expatriation during the Federalist years.[45]

The judiciary, however, found itself considering cases involving none too patriotic Americans, not British highhandedness, and Federalist judges thus were much less warm toward broad expatriation rights. Many tried increasingly to restrict the right without ever denying it completely. In 1793, the Pennsylvania Circuit Court considered *Henfield's Case,* involving an American, Gideon Henfield, who had joined a French privateer and been made "prize-master" in charge of a captured English vessel.[46] President Washington had then declared the U.S. neutral between France and England, and Henfield was accused of violating that proclamation. He responded in part that he had no obligation to honor it because he had relinquished his citizenship abroad. The report of the case provides Chief Justice Jay's general charge upon the impaneling of the grand jury as well as the charge concerning the *Henfield* case offered by Circuit Justice Wilson. Again these two centralizing Federalists used the new national republicanism to defend the claims of the national polity; but now they did so against unqualified consensual membership and against the use of those rights to justify service to radical France.

Jay insisted that it was part of every individual's "contract with society" to abide by "the will of the people" as expressed in law. The "common good and the welfare of the community" depended on enforcing the contractual "rights of society and of one another." Hence individuals could not escape the (national) social contract at will. Wilson expounded at more length on how the Enlightenment's "spirit of liberty" animated the American system so that it might uphold "the dignity of man." But he, too, stressed that both states and individuals had "duties" to provide for human preservation and general happiness. Although men did have a "natural right of emigration," that right could be exercised only by acts consistent with their civic duties. And Wilson implied that, even though the U.S. was not at war nor had Henfield been liable for any crime when he left America, he still had general civic obligations that he had not rightfully relinquished. Those obligations required conformity to American foreign policy.

Even though Jefferson later endorsed Wilson's line of argument, it was a contorted effort to preserve consensual doctrines and a right of expatriation while severely constraining them in the name of broad, open-ended civic duties. And despite these charges clearly aimed at prompting conviction, the jury acquitted Henfield, accepting that he had not known of the declaration of neutrality.[47] The case thus not only showed Jay and Wilson struggling to define consensual national allegiances that could not easily be altered; it also revealed the jury's lack of zeal for enforcing duties to the new nation. Many Jeffersonians similarly began to suspect that these doctrines of national duties were instruments for Federalists to compel allegiances that they could not inspire.

In later cases Federalist judges displayed even greater wariness about expatriation rights and moved toward ever more binding conceptions of national allegiance. In *Talbot v. Janson* (1795), the Supreme Court rejected claims of expatriation made by two natives of Virginia who had commanded a French privateer illegally fitted out in the U.S.[48] The justices affirmed a lower court ruling that rights of expatriation did not include any right to injure the country of one's "native allegiance."[49] The appellants' brief insisted at length that such a stress on perpetual allegiance corresponded to the "servitude" of feudal subjectship, whereas citizenship was the result of a "compact" and could be freely "relinquished." Even the appellee brief conceded that on American principles "birth gives no property in the man."[50] Though all justices professed to accept these consensual views to some degree, they ruled that the appellants' acts, including their illegal ones, could not be construed as amounting to "reasonable" expatriation procedures.

Most interesting are the opinions of Justices William Paterson, the former New Jersey convention delegate, and North Carolina's Iredell. Paterson focused on the illegalities of the appellants' conduct and called for a federal statute on expatriation to forestall such claims in the future. He also argued, like William Vans Murray and contrary to Jefferson, that even if appellant Ballard had complied with Virginia's expatriation statute, he had relieved himself only of state, not U.S. citizenship. As Ballard had not left the country and acquired another national citizenship, recognition of his alleged national expatriation would in Paterson's view render him a denationalized "citizen of the world," a status the justice dismissed as "a creature of the imagination." Paterson's call for federal legislation, his refusal to subordinate national citizenship to state citizenship, and his denial of the possibility of full denationalization all suggest that even this erstwhile champion of the small states saw a need to assert the claims of national political membership against the states, other nations, and a dangerously rootless cosmopolitanism.[51]

Iredell ringingly invoked the Lockean view that birth on "a particular spot" did not mean a man should "be compelled to continue in a society" to which he was thus "accidentally attached, when he can better his situation elsewhere." Even so, the Southern Federalist justice had become more receptive to national claims than he was in *Chisholm*. Though expatriation was a "reasonable and moral right," it was not a "natural right" that could be exercised at will. It was constrained by "principles of patriotism and public good" which ought "in a Republic" to win over "private inclination." Men could accept foreign naturalization and acquire dual allegiances, but they did not thereby dislodge all the obligations a citizen "owes to his own country."[52]

In their concern to preserve national authority against the potentially anarchical implications of pure consensualism, all these justices turned chiefly to assertions of republican civic obligations, now directed to the national community. Some arch-Federalists found this insufficient. As fears of French radicalism mounted, such men revived the more traditional defenses for claims of national membership, despite their clash with consensualism: the naturalistic doctrines of English common law. While sitting on Connecticut's Circuit Court in 1799, Chief Justice Ellsworth considered *Williams' Case*, which involved yet another American sailing on a French ship that warred with Britain.[53] But Isaac Williams had formally renounced his U.S. citizenship and been naturalized in France in 1792, residing on French territory thereafter. In the absence of any congressional specification of correct procedures, his actions might well have been deemed sufficient for expatriation.

Yet Ellsworth, asserting that "the common law of the country remains the same as it was before the Revolution," rejected Williams's claim. American citizenship, like British subjectship, could only be dissolved with the "consent or default of the community." That had not been explicitly granted, nor could it ever reasonably be inferred, because the new nation had "no inhabitants to spare." If Williams had acquired dual allegiance by his own act, that "folly" was "his own." It did not alter his American obligations.[54]

Thus, instead of straining to read the social contract as imposing consensually based national duties, Ellsworth flatly reasserted Blackstone's ascriptive view of obligations unalterably incurred at birth. That reversion to unrepublican common-law doctrine did not go unnoticed. Though Madison had suggested a similar view to seat William Smith, now the Jeffersonian press denounced the decision as abrogating a "natural right" through appeal to an "obsolete . . . feudal" principle. Ellsworth's alleged "birth-duty of allegiance" was "a fraud upon infancy" that fastened the "chains of slavery" on innocent children. The Republicans' polemics were exaggerated, as Ellsworth had not gone all the way back to the perpetual allegiance of Coke, but the decision was an attempt to assert *almost* unshakable claims of national identity. *Williams* thus exemplifies how notions of American civic membership contradictory to liberal republican consensualism could be invoked to combat threats perceived by the governing elites. Here, arch-Federalist judges thought that broad rights of expatriation were too dangerous to the nation they headed, so they abandoned consensualism and defined membership in older ascriptive terms. But doing so after a well-publicized series of expatriation decisions that moved steadily away from membership by consent, especially when invoked to help France, was again impolitic. The ruling gave new vividness to Jeffersonian portraits of Federalists as unrepublican, Anglophilic Tories.

Naturalization and Territorial "Subjectship." The Federalists gave Republicans even more ammunition by other controversial ascriptive features that they built into national citizenship laws, especially restrictions on naturalization. Anxieties about easy naturalization rose after the French Revolution fed into international warfare in 1792, and after Toussaint L'Ouverture's black and mulatto rebellion in Haiti. The U.S. became a haven for diverse European refugees, who prompted alarm in virtually all segments of the nation's ruling elites. Federalists feared an influx of radical French Jacobins. Jeffersonians worried about the arrival of escaping aristocrats. They therefore agreed at times on naturalization restrictions, but increasingly the topic turned into a political football, with the Federalists on the offensive.

In the first Congress, naturalization restrictions were not yet controversial. Though the new representatives left immigration and permanent residence open to all, they agreed that citizenship should not be. The first naturalization act in 1790 provided citizenship to any "free white person" who resided in the U.S. for two years and for one year in the state in which the person sought admission. Applicants also had to prove their "good character" and take an oath to "support the Constitution of the United States." Children were included in their parents' naturalization, and foreign-born children of citizens were to be citizens if their fathers had once resided in the U.S.[55]

In these and later naturalization debates, congressmen regularly weighed the benefits of new population against the dangers to republican citizenship and institutions that immigrants might bring. But perhaps most revealing were the matters they did not discuss. The racial and patriarchal features of naturalization bills never received any recorded consideration. Perhaps the propriety of sustaining both these ascriptive civic hierarchies was so widely accepted that none was required. Perhaps the racial issue was judged too controversial to be debated openly. At any rate, the promotion of racial homogeneity and patriarchally defined membership became an integral part of naturalization policies suitable for "republican government."

The first Congress did debate whether the nation's view of itself as an "asylum" for all, including "Jews and Roman Catholics," should be altered in light of the risk that the "foreign-born" might lack sufficient knowledge and attachment to the U.S. and its free institutions. High Federalists like Sedgwick, who wished to confine citizenship and office as much as possible to the native-born, took over Jefferson's argument that those born to "monarchical and aristocratical governments" might lack a proper "zest for pure republicanism." Jeffersonians, in contrast, no longer worried about good sturdy European farmers and mechanics and instead decried the emigration of foreign "merchants" and their financiers who would be "leeches" in America. These differences could be resolved, however, through compromise. Most agreed that the best remedies were residency requirements: time spent in America would foster informed loyalty toward it.[56]

In other respects, more traditional conceptions of citizenship were visible in these debates. Despite the increasing identification of republican citizenship with political rights rather than real property rights (as in Ramsay's pamphlet), landholding as well as officeholding were still discussed as the most important rights at stake in conferring citizenship. Little notice was taken of the suffrage. A number of congressmen also accepted that the states would continue to exercise considerable regulatory authority over the rights of both aliens and citizens, including naturalization into U.S. citizenship.[57] The judges of the Pennsylvania Circuit Court, including even the nationalistic Wilson, agreed in 1792. In *Collet v. Collet*, that bench ruled that states could exercise a "concurrent authority" over naturalization so long as they did not "contravene" national legislation by conferring citizenship in a "too narrow," insufficiently "liberal" fashion. Hence ascriptive and republican concerns for civic homogeneity and for state powers again joined to shape doctrines that made American citizenship less open and less nationalistic.[58]

The increasingly partisan character of citizenship disputes became apparent in 1794, when the Federalist-controlled Senate refused to seat Albert Gallatin, the Geneva-born Jeffersonian. The Federalists claimed that he had not fully complied with state naturalization laws. Compelled to bear the burden of proof, Gallatin noted that the Declaration had made British barriers to naturalization one of its "principal" complaints, and that "encouraging population" was the wisest American policy. He also argued that his "active part" in the Revolution made him "a citizen according to the great laws of reason and of nature," at least as much as the absent William Smith. But he could not claim specific compliance with state laws, and with the northeastern Federalists set against him, Gallatin was unseated by a 14–12 vote.[59]

The incident strengthened Republican beliefs that the Federalists were conniving to use citizenship laws to deny their opponents access to office. They were suspicious when men like Sedgwick went on later in 1794 to argue for greatly extending residency requirements for naturalization, if the nation did not confine officeholding to natives. Sedgwick maintained that Americans were more "wise and virtuous" and "better qualified" for republican government than any people on earth; but they were so as a result of their "early education," and he doubted that "republican character" could be formed any way "but by early education." Hence all adult foreigners were a risk. They should not be encouraged to come merely for "accumulation of commercial capital," certainly not when Europe was in Jacobinite upheaval.

Jeffersonians resented all the Federalist talk of Jacobin threats but equally feared foreign aristocrats and merchants. Thus most accepted some lengthening of residency requirements. William Giles of Virginia also wished to compel newcomers to profess their "attachment to the Republican form of government" and to renounce all hereditary titles and claims to nobility. Federalists derided the "Republican" requirement as too vague, and they exploded when Jeffersonians demanded a roll-call vote on requiring the renunciation of titles. They saw the vote as a device to portray Federalists as the party of aristocracy. Samuel Dexter of Massachusetts tried to turn the tables on the Republicans by proposing that new arrivals be required to free their slaves. That motion raised the temperature in the House even higher. In the end, Congress extended the residency requirement to five years, required that applicants file a declaration of intent three years before naturalization, and added the demand for renunciation of all hereditary titles of nobility. The intense debate showed how strongly the nation was becoming polarized between parties with clashing views of what it meant to be an American citizen.[60]

By a 13–11 vote, with northeastern Federalists again prevailing, Congress also added that aliens were to be naturalized on these conditions "and not otherwise." Many Jeffersonians saw that phrase as imperiously rescinding permission for state naturalizations, at least those claiming to grant federal citizenship. And because the requirements pertained to processes making a person "a citizen of the United States, or any of them," any naturalizations purporting merely to confer state citizenship could not be done on easier terms.[61] Congress further buttressed federal control of naturalization by giving federal territorial courts the power to grant foreigners citizenship in their jurisdictions.[62] Thus Federalists simultane-

ously acted to render American citizenship more native-centered and more nationally directed. Both these changes ran counter to Jeffersonian principles and
political prospects.

The Northwest Territory's Governor St. Clair also outraged Republicans in the
mid-1790s by arguing that not only did the Northwest Ordinance fail to confer
full citizenship on the French inhabitants of the territories; even the Anglo-
American state citizens who moved there "ceased to be citizens of the United
States, and became their subjects." St. Clair was disturbed that so many of the inhabitants were "indigent and ignorant" men who he thought were unprepared
for full citizenship, especially as they were likely to vote Republican. Jeffersonians denounced St. Clair as "a British nabob" with "princely ideas" that "no man
with the blood of an American in his bosom can contemplate with pleasure"—
criticisms that neatly blended republican and anti-British ascriptive themes. The
Washington administration did not endorse St. Clair's position, but the controversy over it added to Federalist unpopularity.[63]

The political warfare became all-out when the Federalists enacted the Naturalization, Alien Friends, Alien Enemies, and Sedition Acts in 1798 as part of stri-
dently nativist efforts to censor, disfranchise, and deport immigrant Jeffersonians. Voting along sharply partisan lines, Congress first extended the residence
requirement for naturalization to a draconian fourteen years. Robert Harper of
South Carolina went further to suggest that only the native-born should be citizens, and Harrison Gray Otis of Massachusetts proposed that federal offices, at
least, be limited to natives. Otis was concerned that the "wild Irish," whom the
English had long depicted as a drunken, Popishly enslaved lower race, would
overrun his home state and more. The Republicans successfully argued that Otis's
proposal would create a second-class citizenship in violation of the Constitution.
Although second-class citizenship for free blacks, women, and assimilated Native Americans already existed, tiers among white men were less tolerable.[64]

Next, on the crest of the anti-French xenophobia churned up by the XYZ affair in France, the Federalists squeaked through the Alien Friends Act, which
passed 46–40 in the House. It made all "dangerous" aliens in the U.S. subject to
arbitrary arrest and deportation in peace and war, even if the U.S. was not officially an enemy of their homeland. The act expired in 1800 and no one was deported under it; but in the interim the Jeffersonians denounced it as tyrannical,
almost as much as they did the Sedition Act, which applied to citizens and foreigners alike. Congress also enacted the less controversial Alien Enemies Act, giving the President special wartime powers to control aliens from countries the U.S.
was opposing. The Republicans worked to ensure that this law could not apply
to citizens, but most supported it.[65]

In the course of advocating these measures in the late 1790s, many Federalists finally turned their backs on their earlier view of the U.S. as an "asylum" nation and spread harsh denigrations of not only the Irish and the French but the foreign-born in general. Even Washington had retreated from his earlier cosmopolitanism. By the time of his Farewell Address in 1797, he had become deeply concerned that the growing national absorption in the pursuit of "mammon" and in partisan conflicts threatened national unity. He spent much of the speech persuading Americans, whether citizens "by birth or choice," that they should exalt their national identity over local ones. Like Jay in the *Federalist,* Washington tried to convince Americans that they had "the same religion, manners, beliefs, and political principles," with but "slight shades of difference." And he urged them to cultivate their religiosity as a check on their divisive economic and political ambitions. He never spoke against rising Federalist nativism. Hamilton also now stated that though foreigners were desirable as workers, they could prove a "Grecian horse" if they were admitted to citizenship too quickly. And more extreme Federalists spoke as if American "freedom" was not, after all, a universal principle of natural right, but rather a special feature of native white Americans' unique traditions, education, and inbred character.[66]

The Federalists' nativistic stances on expatriation, naturalization, and alien rights angered many voters and made Republicans out of some, such as the German-Americans of Pennsylvania, who had previously been fairly content with Federalist governance. Although the Supreme Court steered clear of considering the Sedition Act (the measure that most upset such immigrants), even a moderate Federalist like Justice Iredell felt compelled to defend it in the notorious treason trial of the German-American rebel John Fries. Iredell admitted that during the Constitution's ratification he had denied that Congress would have such powers, but he now saw that view as dangerously "erroneous." Many Americans instead saw greater danger in all these Federalist laws and trials.[67]

Furthermore, the Jeffersonians had succeeded in preserving enough loopholes in the statutes so that they still found ways for large numbers of recent immigrants to vote against the Federalists in 1800. That immigrant vote was an important factor in the Jeffersonian victory, which was relatively close in the electoral college. Perhaps if the Federalist laws had been harsher yet, they might have held on to power. Now scholars tend to regard the Federalists' moves toward more ascriptive conceptions of Americanism as last-ditch efforts to combat trends that would have overwhelmed them anyway, but that judgment is speculative and was much less widely shared then.[68] What is clear is that the Federalists were openly stressing restrictive, naturalistic views of American identity that many had long quietly favored, because their more cosmopolitan, consensual positions seemed to help their political foes.

Yet even if many Federalists had recognized these acts as desperate and probably futile measures, they might well have undertaken them; for their program was ill-suited to win elections. Because in reality they favored helping financial and commercial elites, slowing the rapid displacement of the native tribes, and discouraging slavery, they were on the more liberal but less popular side of most of the issues that mattered to the great majority of white American men. Most citizens' lives, moreover, were centered on local communities, usually small, agrarian towns whose important policies were set by local elites, and in which fairly strong and traditional communitarian and religious sensibilities survived. The fact that small-community republican and traditionalist ascriptive civic visions described reasonably well the everyday life of most American men was perhaps the major reason why the Federalists were right to see their task of advancing liberal national republicanism as so difficult. Resort to a nativistic, restrictive Americanism that justified imprisonments, disfranchisements, and deportations of at least some of their foes was one of the few options available.

Yet most Americans did embrace the Federalist vision of a rapidly growing commercial society that could generate exciting new economic opportunities, and some Hamiltonian institutions, like the Bank and the funded debt, played their desired role in promoting those ends. The Federalists' Americanism also provided leaders with a patriotic discourse that celebrated a stirring vision of a national republic with great powers, a dynamic market economy, and a national identity centered on the traits of Anglophone, native-born white men. Up to our own time, many Americans would find that discourse a valuable if morally controversial resource in as yet unended struggles to strengthen the nation and define what it should become.[69]

7

Toward a Commercial Nation of White Yeoman Republics
The Jeffersonian Era, 1801–1829

Jefferson won the presidency in 1800; Jeffersonian Republicans won control of Congress; and candidates claiming to be Jefferson's heirs would win every presidential election for the next forty years. Only the federal courts, led by John Marshall, retained much leverage to champion Federalist nationalism, and they succeeded most on points that the Jeffersonians least disputed. Hence the nation's citizenship laws increasingly reflected Jeffersonian views of American nationality, tempered by a few compromises with Federalist principles that did not threaten the dominant coalition.

Yet the Democratic Republicans still faced severe problems in crafting the sort of new nation they envisioned. For Jefferson himself, that vision was clear enough, if hardly tension-free. As in his *Notes*, the goal remained a great but state-centric union of smallish agrarian republics, populated by self-supporting, educated white yeomen, joined and governed by the mutual consent of all those capable of and dedicated to free republican citizenship. Such citizens would choose to be led by enlightened, college-trained, Unitarian-minded members of mankind's "natural aristocracy," like Jefferson himself. To realize that vision, citizenship for white men had to be made more fully consensual, by easing naturalization and expatriation and expanding the franchise. Public education needed to be established; the rationalization of religion needed to proceed. Agricultural methods had to become more scientific. But many Americans had little taste for Jefferson's highly cerebral Enlightenment views of schooling, farming, religion, and leadership, which created problems that would eventually help generate the age of Jackson. Beyond its meritocratic elitism, moreover, Jeffersonianism faced practical difficulties as a guiding philosophy for a still-fragile new nation. Those difficulties often compelled Jeffersonian office-holders to temper their state-centered republicanism with elements of Federalist nationalism.

In office, Jefferson himself soon recognized that to be militarily and economically secure in a world of rich, combative great powers, the U.S. had to have manufacturing and the cities it spawned, however much he disliked them. It also required the thriving national and international commercial trade he both relished and feared. And, at times, it needed arms. He and his successors thus frequently felt pressured to sustain or expand Federalist measures like the Bank of the United States, high tariffs, internal improvements, and a national military in order to give the nation the strength it required.[1] But whenever they complied with those pressures, they contaminated the republic in their own eyes and alienated many supporters.

Hence, for Jefferson, acceptance of urbanism and industry in the east made it imperative that the U.S. expand its "empire of liberty" westward, increasing the domain of yeoman farmers. To do so again required wielding national powers expansively, as in the Louisiana Purchase, the Indian wars, and the negotiations with Spain that regained Florida under James Monroe in 1819. Jefferson and his successors shelved their anxieties about centralized power and did what seemed necessary in these matters, trying peaceful means but proving willing to resort to force.[2] Even if they had not been so inclined, masses of white traders, land speculators, and settlers, including many slaveholders, were pushing west anyway. The national government still had no way to stop this private expansionism, the states still supported it, and most of this vanguard of the "empire of liberty" were Jeffersonian constituents whose wishes could not be lightly disregarded.[3]

Thus, even as Jeffersonians strove to transform citizenship doctrines in the more consensual, democratic directions that had helped defeat the Federalists, they felt compelled to justify faster displacement of the native tribes and continued enslavement of African-Americans, very much against the consent of those peoples. In response, legislators and courts of the era proved impressively inventive in explaining how consensual premises actually justified the "dependent nation" status assigned to the tribes and the alleged ineligibility of even free blacks for full U.S. citizenship. In discussing their most brutally coercive policies, leaders of the Jeffersonian era often still managed to preserve the rhetoric of membership and self-governance by consent of the citizenry, if not of all the governed.

That fact may suggest that Hartzians are right, after all: most Americans have always treated liberal republican consensualism as the core of their political beliefs. Both the consensual form and the acquisitive substance of these Jeffersonian policies can be explained in terms of the institutions and "ethos of democratic liberalism," which here involved a "liberal agrarianism" making its peace with urban capitalism. Hartz and his successors have indeed argued that during these years Americans were propelled by the economic necessities and dreams of liberal market systems to seek new resources and opportunities westward, as they used slave labor to produce profitably for the international market. To assuage their liberal consciences, white Americans then began elaborating superficially plausible consensual defenses of their civic inequalities, buttressed by pseudo-scientific Enlightenment and Protestant religious doctrines of racial and cultural superiority. In so doing they tacked white supremacist qualifications onto a basically Lockean understanding of American political identity.[4]

There is much truth in such accounts. Jeffersonians' efforts to develop consensual defenses for their most illiberal policies provide undeniably strong evidence of the importance of both liberal and republican values in America. Yet these interpretations underestimate the degree to which Americans recognized the tensions between doctrines of human rights and their ascriptive policies, recognized that their ends might be pursued through measures more consistent with universalistic liberalism, and nonetheless felt *justified* in rejecting such liberalism. It is true that rights-respecting measures were less appealing and slower and less certain in furthering the goals of white Americans than ascriptive coercion. But regardless of their efficacy, many did not, in fact, believe that liberal policies were morally required. Their invocations of consent rested on deeper commitments to ascriptive notions of who was capable of consent, and hence who America's true citizens were and who could join their number.

The presence in the nation's political culture of well-established arguments for the divine mission of the American people, the superiority of Anglo-Saxon civilization, patriarchal rule in the family and polity, and white racial supremacy all not only permitted white American Christian men of the Jeffersonian age to be proud, rather than apologetic, about their exclusive possession of full citizenship. As much or more than the Declaration of Independence, those notions defined the meaning of the American nation whose interests had to be advanced. They made acceptance of the equality of those who did not share these traits seem a betrayal of shared values, not a fulfillment of liberal justice. Although white Americans did feel compelled to explain their superior status in ways that accorded with all their principles, including government by consent, at key moments they invoked their ascriptive Americanist conceptions as much as their commitments to consensualism. Those moments occurred more and more frequently as Jeffersonians extended the domain of white supremacy. Thus, overall, the Jeffersonians strengthened not only the legitimacy of state-centered, republican citizenship based on "popular" consent, but also racially hierarchical, ascriptive conceptions of American national identity.

Extensions of Consensual Citizenship

The Jeffersonians' zeal to make American citizenship laws more consensual on a remarkably wide variety of fronts was impressive. They repealed nativistic naturalization measures. They fought, without full success, for broader expatriation rights, including expansive views of the "period of election" during the Revolution. Most worked to lessen property restrictions on the franchise. Some tried to justify the subordinate status of free African-Americans, slaves, Native Americans, and women in consensual terms. Many also sought to locate consensual citizenship primarily in the states, but both the surviving power of Federalist judges and their own political imperatives as national leaders limited how far they could go in that direction. By surveying these issues, we can see the broad-ranging consensualist civic thrust of the Jeffersonian era.

Naturalization. The Jeffersonians moved quickly to ensure their electoral support from immigrants and vindicate their claims to be the party of consensual citizenship by introducing naturalization reforms, overturning the nativist measures of the Adams years. In 1802 Congress reduced residency requirements to five years in the U.S., with one year in the state of application, and with a "declaration of intent" still needed three years prior to naturalization. Applicants also still had to swear to uphold the principles of the Constitution and to renounce any foreign allegiances. Without debate, Jeffersonians maintained paternalistic principles through provisions that wives and children would automatically gain citizenship when husbands or fathers were naturalized (though ambiguity remained concerning children born abroad prior to such naturalizations). All immigrants had to register with official authorities, and alien enemies were still banned from naturalization. By and large, these provisions governed naturalization for the rest of the nineteenth century. That same term, Congress also stripped Northwest Territory Governor Arthur St. Clair of most of his powers, making his ongoing opposition to citizenship for territorial inhabitants and rapid statehood unimportant.[5]

Immigration and the Slave Trade. The federal government took no major actions to encourage or restrain the influx of new immigrants during these years. But as a great wave of newcomers began to reach American shores after the War of 1812, Congress became concerned about the unhealthy, overcrowded conditions of the ships carrying them. Hence in 1819 it passed the first in what became a series of "passenger" or "steerage" laws, requiring steamship lines to provide adequate space, food, and water for passengers and requiring records of all arriving immigrants. Thus an essentially liberal, open immigration stance was maintained.[6]

This liberalism was reinforced by the congressional ban on the international

slave trade passed in 1807. Because this action came after South Carolina had restored slave trading in 1804, reversing the pattern of the late Confederation years,
it was not trivial. But it partly reflected fears of black insurrection sparked by the
Gabriel Prosser Rebellion in Virginia in 1800 and the establishment of the black
republic of Haiti in 1804. Many concluded from these events that increases in the
slave population would mean an uprising to establish a black republic in the
United States. In the end, Congress's action did not greatly allay those anxieties,
nor did it much effect the viability of domestic slavery. Even the foreign slave traffic continued, illegally. Still, the ban had great symbolic importance. Free blacks
rejoiced over its passage, and opponents of slavery could argue that the nation
was carrying out the aim of many framers to set the institution on the path to extinction.[7]

Expatriation. Rights of expatriation were much debated during the Jeffersonian
years, but their legal status remained unresolved. Several factors kept the issue
alive: disputes over native-born Americans doing business overseas, especially
with the French, despite American trade restrictions; Britain's ongoing efforts to
impress English-born sailors who had been naturalized and had joined the
American navy; and, later, controversies involving Americans captaining ships
on behalf of South American countries striving to create independent republics.
Executive officials and courts often viewed these issues as distinct types of expatriation questions, and they differed on the answers. Espousals of broad expatriation rights came most often from Jeffersonian executive officers, who found it
diplomatically useful to denounce British claims of perpetual allegiance as
despotic. At the same time, they also offered Britain various (rejected) compromises that would have limited the rights of naturalized citizens to serve on American ships.

   In part, those offers reflected the lack of unified American opposition to
British policies. Like many of their counterparts on the bench, Federalist politicians and pamphleteers argued in favor of honoring the common-law doctrine
of native allegiance. Although the U.S. could legitimately naturalize English subjects, those naturalized were not identical to native-born citizens. England could
reassert authority over them should they venture back into its waters. The partisan debate over this issue reached a new peak after the War of 1812, when Republicans and Federalists assaulted each others' expatriation views in a lively
pamphlet war. A Louisiana Jeffersonian named Thomas Robertson sought to
have Congress prescribe the means of exercising the "natural, and inalienable"
right of expatriation, to the distress of Federalists. The matter was tabled, but in
1818 Robertson proposed permitting citizens to expatriate themselves in federal
district courts. The bill's supporters hoped that it would prevent Americans fight-

ing for revolutionary South American republics from being declared pirates under a U.S. treaty with Spain.

But many Jeffersonians refused to concede the national government unilateral power over expatriation; a Delaware Federalist, Louis McLane, went further. Pursuing the turn to state-centered constitutionalism that some Federalists made after Jeffersonian control of the national councils seemed unbreakable, he contended that only state citizenship was a "natural relation" stemming from birth. U.S. citizenship was a mere "civil relation" created by a compact among the states, so that a federal expatriation power dissolving state citizenship was unconstitutional. Though partly disarmed by this fusion of Federalist naturalism with their own state-centric theories, Jeffersonians denounced McLane's echo of the "old feudal doctrine of perpetual allegiance" and saw partisan motives behind it. But enough were opposed to national authority over the "natural right" of expatriation to defeat Robertson's bill narrowly, the last effort to define expatriation until 1868.[8]

Expansion of the Suffrage. In keeping with the Jeffersonian espousal of decentralized, comparatively democratic republicanism, the federal government during these years was pulled along by a state-initiated reform movement—the broadening of the franchise. At least in terms of the property restrictions, Americans succeeded in democratizing the hierarchical republicanism that had prevailed in fact, if not always in rhetoric, since the Revolution. Though massive political inequalities persisted, in regard to traditional class structures it became more appropriate as well as more common to transform a term many founders had used pejoratively into praise, by speaking glowingly of "democracy in America."

The pattern of development was already evident during the Confederation and Federalist years. Real property requirements for the vote typically gave way to taxpaying and other, more easily met alternatives, and finally universal white manhood suffrage followed. In most of New England, blacks also received the vote, but their trivial numbers in this region rendered this "expansion" more formal than real. By the mid-1820s, the progressive relaxation of voting restrictions was well advanced.

The many reasons for the reforms cannot be separated from the overall Jeffersonian enterprise of building a more consensually based republic, but, unlike in Europe, specific efforts by national elites to win supporters for national elections or for nation-building enterprises were not major factors in these largely state-level changes. Partisan conflicts within the states did play a large role, especially in the North, where the Federalists represented the entrenched upper crust. But though Republicans were most often allied with democratization, in Jefferson's own Virginia and in other middle and Southern states they often represented older, wealthy planter families wary of franchise changes. Hence, nation-wide, advocates and opponents of a wider franchise could be found in both parties. In addition to partisan jockeying, technical difficulties of property qualifications in rapidly changing economies, repeated experiences of their fraudulent manipulation, and a growing recognition that they had little practical effect unless they were set far higher than was politically feasible, all contributed to the demise of such franchise restrictions. Veterans also argued effectively that they should be allowed to vote if propertied ex-Tories could. All these circumstances reinforced the credibility of democratic ideas treating all restrictions on the vote for adult white males as suspect.[9]

Although most of the changes came in the states, from early on the federal government found itself similarly propelled when dealing with the territories. The high freehold requirement for the franchise established in the Northwest Ordinance and succeeding territorial acts (fifty acres), it was soon proved, disqualifed all but an embarrassingly tiny number of the new inhabitants. In Mississippi, only 236 men could vote out of 4,444 in 1804. In Illinois, the figure was also between 200 and 300. Consequently, Congress progressively weakened these requirements, adopting taxpaying or simple residency requirements.[10] And from the admission of Tennessee with an easily met freehold requirement in 1796 through 1821, Congress accepted eight states into the Union, five with full adult white male suffrage and the others with liberal taxpaying qualifications. Unlike New England, efforts to enfranchise African-Americans in the territories failed. Whites feared attracting free blacks to the new regions. Territorial laws thus implied that, as a Michigan man put it, only blacks and Native Americans were excluded from the "great" (and patriarchal) "North American family."[11]

Within the existing states, Maryland—long dominated by a few leading families—was the first to reform its highly restrictive suffrage, beginning in the late Federalist years. In 1797 Michael Taney, a sometime Federalist (and father of Jackson's Chief Justice, Roger B. Taney), introduced an act for universal manhood suffrage. The indirectly selected Maryland senate, whose members were more united by their elite origins than party affiliations, rejected the bill, precipitating battles in which members of both parties assaulted the senate. In the end, the senators accepted universal white male suffrage to forestall reforms in their own inegalitarian selection system.[12] Other Southern states had similar struggles. By 1810, Virginia and North Carolina were the only ones not to have moved to either taxpaying requirements or universal white male suffrage. Surprisingly, Tennessee and North Carolina still permitted blacks to vote if they qualified.[13]

In the old North, the loosening of voting requirements came with more intense partisan struggles. In New England, Federalists usually held the seats of privilege and opposed change. The unpopularity in the region of the Republicans' embargo and 1812 war helped to discredit the Republican suffrage reform movements of the same period. By 1817, however, Republicans had gained sufficient power in Connecticut to institute a written, secret ballot—another reform widely enacted during this era—and to prompt the adoption of a somewhat more democratic new constitution in 1819.[14] Maine separated from Massachusetts and then received statehood that same year with a constitution that foreshadowed many state provisions to come. It rejected property tests entirely, but it excluded persons under guardianship (minors and the insane), paupers, and temporarily resident sailors, soldiers, marines, and students from voting. Unlike many other states, Maine's convention did not disfranchise persons convicted of an "infamous crime" (which presumably included unconventional sexual acts), and it also rejected an effort to exclude free blacks. But the delegates felt no need to ban Native Americans from voting, because they, unlike blacks, were thought not to be part of the polity.[15]

Massachusetts then held a convention that proposed somewhat liberalized suffrage laws, over the pessimistic objections of convention chair John Adams. The Commonwealth moved only to taxpaying, as well as age, residence, and citizenship requirements. The following year, New Yorkers struggled momentously over suffrage in their constitutional convention, with Federalists, led by Chancellor James Kent, defending the old order. Republicans attacked real property qualifications as feudal "Norman" holdovers. Federalist conservatives raised nativist fears about the dangers of granting the vote to "tumultuous" Irish and German immigrants, as in the late Adams years. In New York, that argument still proved politically potent. Free blacks, on the other hand, had long voted in New York if they could meet the state's property requirements. Though very few did, they had generally voted Federalist. Many Republicans consequently urged that they be excluded, against the opposition of Federalists like Kent. All these suffrage issues became further embroiled in the struggles of the Clintonian and "Bucktail" Van Buren Republican factions, in ways that made some expansion of the franchise for whites politically unavoidable. Taxpaying and military service requirements were made sufficient for voting in 1821, although free blacks had to own $250 worth of property on which they paid taxes, usually a prohibitive requirement. (In 1825, in New York City some sixteen blacks voted out of a black population of nearly 13,000.) Then in 1826, another amendment provided universal white male suffrage, retaining the property standards for blacks.[16]

Virginia, the home of what might be termed the "high Jeffersonians," resisted all change until 1829. Then it held a constitutional convention that included such stellar figures as James Madison, James Monroe, John Marshall, and Edmund Randolph—none of whom trusted the recently triumphant, less genteel and def-

erential Jacksonian Democrats, and none of whom favored sweeping suffrage reforms. The prestige of these gentry statesmen was such that they were not greatly
challenged.

But a major incentive for change came from a different source, repeating a
colonial pattern. Mounting racial tensions, which erupted in Nat Turner's Rebellion the following year, led some Virginians to defend a more democratic suffrage as a means of creating greater unity among whites and thus greater security
for slavery. One state senator revived the specter of the Haitian revolution and
called for a broader franchise to give "all white men . . . a direct interest" in the
government. Unenfranchised whites serving on "white patrols" made the same
demand. Thus the Virginia convention adopted complex leaseholding and
homeowning alternatives to a more attainable real property requirement. Even
so, observers estimated that only about eight thousand had been made eligible
by these reforms, leaving almost one-third of white men over the age of twenty-
one disfranchised. Virginia, then, remained a pioneer of politically crafted racial
solidarity as a means to preserve slavery, but otherwise was a hold-out against
suffrage expansion. In most other states, the age of Jackson dawned with near-
universal suffrage for adult white men nearing reality.[17]

Consensualist Defenses of Subordination

In other regards, the consensualist rhetoric of the Jeffersonian years served not
to promote democratization but only to defend partial or full denials of citizenship to groups that white male Americans felt entitled to rule. For many Americans, governing whole classes of people without their consent was not hypocriti-
cal, but only because they believed in ascriptive notions of American identity that
circumscribed the range of consensual membership.

Consensualism and District of Columbia Citizenship. Perhaps the mildest, though
still hotly disputed, deviation from equal U.S. citizenship enacted in this era was
the denial of the federal franchise to residents of the new District of Columbia.
Until 1800 Maryland and Virginia still governed the areas they had ceded for
the federal district, and citizens there voted in both state and national elections.
The act organizing the district's government passed by the first Jeffersonian-
controlled Congress provided for federal rule without giving district residents
the vote in federal elections or any direct congressional representation. Though
Madison had anticipated as much in the *Federalist,* both congressional debates
and district resident meetings showed that many regarded these denials as inconsistent with full citizenship. Virginia's John Randolph fumed in the House
that the district was being placed "in the situation of a conquered country." John

Smilie of Pennsylvania complained that its residents were being "reduced" from citizens "to the state of subjects."

Defenders of exclusive federal governance relied chiefly on consensualist arguments. South Carolina's Robert Harper contended that the arrangement rested on the consent of the American people as a whole. The Constitution had bestowed exclusive power over the federal district on Congress in order to protect the "dignity and independence of the Government of the Union" from possibly hostile state actions. His fellow South Carolinian John Rutledge noted that most district residents also seemed to endorse the arrangement, for many had supported a petition urging federal assumption of jurisdiction. Historians agree that this consensual justification for the diminished political rights of district citizens was plausible. Few thought that preservation of their federal votes were worth the loss of economic benefits the nation's capital would bring. Hence the defenders of federal control prevailed. But the debate heated up periodically thereafter, as it has to the present day.[18]

Consensualism and Ascriptive Hierarchies: African-Americans. In keeping with the Declaration of Independence's doctrine of human equality, many in the Jeffersonian era continued to argue that Native Americans and African-Americans were inferior only because of environmental factors, as Samuel Stanhope Smith had long contended. But the views of Smith, an increasingly controversial Federalist, were by no means uncontested. In 1810 he felt compelled to publish an expanded version of his 1787 argument that included replies to several noted authorities: Lord Kames's view that the races had different origins; an English surgeon, Charles White, who contended that anatomy showed mankind was divided into permanent higher and lower racial "gradations"; and a New York professor of anatomy, James Augustine Smith, who had published a lecture attacking Smith's essay on similar grounds. White relied in part on Jefferson's denigration of blacks in his *Notes,* so Smith had to address that argument as well. In a political climate favoring racial exploitation, Smith plainly felt that the intellectual tide was starting to turn against his environmentalism. Even those who agreed with him generally believed that racial "inferiority" would disappear very slowly.[19]

Hence American leaders often spoke as if equal citizenship was imaginable for Native Americans, though at some distant date. Like Jefferson, many thought, in contrast, that the scars of slavery were too deep for blacks and whites ever to live together. Distinguished leaders of both parties, including Henry Clay and John Randolph, joined in founding the American Colonization Society in 1817, seeing African-American removal as the only humane option.

This bleak and condescending "humanitarianism" did little to resist the powerful economic and political imperatives that were driving increasingly harsh policies toward the "lower races." A vicious dialectic unfolded in which fears of blacks led to harsher restrictions; those restrictions inspired both black and white resistance; and that resistance in turn prompted further elaboration and hardening of racism and racist laws. Assertions of the irrevocable inferiority of blacks and Native Americans by political leaders as well as intellectuals, North and South, became more and more common. Though many Jeffersonians still tried to assert that the nation's racial hierarchies were somehow consistent with equal rights and government by consent, some admitted that this was not so and argued that it need not be.[20]

From the standpoint of their immediate material interests, it is not surprising that under the Virginia Republican dynasty the federal government repeatedly reinforced the subjugation of all blacks, as its leaders were slaveholders who represented a like-minded constituency. In addition to regularly accepting into the union both slave states and states denying free blacks the vote, Congress also banned blacks from being postal carriers in 1810, again partly because of fears that they would assist rebellious conspiracies. Congress maintained the Fugitive Slave Act and permitted slavery and the slave trade in the District of Columbia, whose unfinished Capitol was being constructed by slave labor.[21] And in 1820 it authorized the district's citizens to elect white municipal officials and to adopt a viciously restrictive municipal code for free blacks as well as slaves, as discussed below.[22]

The most direct federal confrontation with the question of black citizenship came, however, in the debates over the admission of Missouri to statehood, which led to the Compromise of 1820. That compromise involved extending the existing north-south division in regard to slavery by permitting Missouri to enter as a slave state, and allowing the territory to the south of it to include slavery, while banning the institution in the northern portions of the Louisiana Purchase. But this agreement was threatened in December 1820 owing to a clause in the proposed Missouri constitution that barred free blacks and mulattos from entering the state. Many congressmen argued that this provision violated Article IV's privileges and immunities clause. Free black citizens, they maintained, would be denied a privilege of entry granted all other citizens. Defenders of the restriction replied that free blacks were not citizens within the meaning of the clause.

Here a signal irony occurred. Proponents of black citizenship, chiefly antislavery Northern Federalists, made several arguments. The central one was a typical Federalist appeal to the ascriptive common-law notion that native birth conferred a natural political membership. Some of the Federalists seemed to advance the more consensual version of birthright citizenship developed by Vattel, basing native membership on parentage. Rep. Joseph Hemphill of Pennsylvania argued, "If being a native, and free born, and of parents belonging to no other nation or tribe, does not constitute a citizen in this country, I am at a loss to know in what manner citizenship is acquired by birth." His mention of parentage, his rejection of the "feudal" view of birthright citizenship as "slavish," and his description of citizenship as "in the nature of a compact, expressly or tacitly made," all suggest that Hemphill had the international law position in mind. But he was not explicit, and most supporters of black citizenship instead simply endorsed the common-law view, in which only place of birth mattered, making native-born free blacks citizens. Many stressed, too, that national unity would be shattered if comity toward persons regarded as citizens in their home states were not upheld.[23]

With defenders of free blacks using ascriptive and nationalistic views of citizenship, opponents of black citizenship were again able to present themselves as somehow the champions of consensual membership against the feudal common-law understanding of birthright citizenship. They could not, of course, claim that the consenters to the subordinate status of African-Americans included blacks themselves. Instead, they argued that native birth alone did not confer citizenship. The consent of the existing citizenry was needed to create new citizens. Hence, only birth into a class of persons that current citizens had given rights sufficient for citizenship counted. Southern spokesmen offered varying accounts of what rights sufficed, but they all insisted that the legal discriminations to which free blacks were subject, even in the North, left them short of the required status.

Southerners deemed the ineligibility of blacks for naturalization under the 1790 law the most decisive indication that Americans had not consented to African-American citizenship. Jeffersonian Congressman Alexander Smyth and maverick Federalist Rep. Louis McLane also each cited Vattel's view that children follow the status of their fathers as a condition of the fathers' own consent to membership. They then claimed that all past and present black fathers were noncitizens ineligible for naturalization. Hence all free black children born in the U.S. must share that condition.

McLane also made it clear, as he had in the earlier expatriation debates, that his consensualism was undergirded by ascriptive beliefs in natural, unequal political statuses. He argued that, though he abhorred slavery, the nation knew there was not "any possibility" that the "weaker caste" of blacks could "assimilate" with whites, any more than "oil with water." Not just positive law but also "reason" and "nature" had "drawn a line of discrimination which can never be effaced." America was at core and would always be a "white community," in which even free blacks must belong to an "inferior order." These contentions presented racial inequalities as intrinsic, not environmental, and rejected any prospect for blacks to gain equal rights.

Because the invocations of Vattelian *jus sanguinis* views pointed the debate toward the status of the parents of contemporary free blacks, Charles Pinckney added a further line of argument that would be elaborated in *Dred Scott*. Falsely claiming to have been the author of the Article IV privileges and immunities clause, Pinckney contended (also incorrectly) that no blacks had been citizens anywhere in the U.S. at the time of the Constitution's ratification. Though some might subsequently have been treated as citizens of certain states, Pinckney added, none had since acquired U.S. citizenship. In keeping with titularly consensualist views of citizenship, that status was confined to the descendants of the original (white) parties to the Constitution and of those later admitted to citizenship via treaty or naturalization.[24]

In the end, Congress blurred the issue by voting to admit Missouri on the condition that its controversial clause not "be construed to authorize the passage of any law . . . by which any citizen . . . shall be excluded from the enjoyment of any of the privileges and immunities to which such citizen is entitled under the constitution of the United States." If blacks were not citizens, of course, this proviso offered them no protection whatsoever. And when Missouri subsequently restricted and then entirely banned the admission of free blacks, Congress silently acquiesced.[25]

Though the Supreme Court did not rule on black citizenship during these years, Monroe's Attorney General William Wirt did address the issue in 1821 when interpreting federal laws that limited the command of vessels engaged in the coastal trade to citizens. He advised a Norfolk official that Virginia's blacks could not qualify under these regulations, because they were denied voting, officeholding, and other prerogatives and so did not enjoy "the full and equal privileges of white citizens in the State of their residence." Wirt therefore saw the Constitution's privileges and immunities clause as a bar to regarding Virginia's blacks as citizens. If they were, then on a Virginia black's "removal into another State, he acquires all the immunities and privileges of a citizen of that other State [such as voting], although he possessed none of them in the State of his nativity: a consequence which certainly could not have been in the contemplation of the convention."[26]

Wirt's argument favored state-centered, consensual, participatory republican views of U.S. citizenship in three ways. It made the status dependent on rights granted at the state level; it insisted that grants of full political privileges were required for genuine citizenship; and it added that though blacks might owe a certain natural allegiance to their states in return for the "protection" they received, citizenship could be acquired by noncitizens only by an oath of allegiance, which blacks could not take. Wirt did not address the reverse question of whether free blacks residing in states where they did possess equal privileges to white citizens could claim U.S. citizenship. If so, his comity approach to the privileges and immunities clause might have required him to hold that such blacks were entitled to full civic privileges in Virginia or any other state they might enter. It is likely that Wirt would have resisted that conclusion, but his opinion did not preclude it. The point may well have seemed moot, as blacks did not enjoy perfect equality anywhere in the country.[27]

The federal courts occasionally did give blacks some support during this era, though not always intentionally. In 1823 Justice William Johnson, sitting on circuit for his home state of South Carolina, struck down that state's law requiring free black seamen to be incarcerated if they came ashore while their ships were in Carolina ports. In his opinion he fumed, but not about the mistreatment of blacks. Far more nationalistic than most Jeffersonian Carolinians, Johnson raged that the state's arrest of a black British seaman infringed federal authority over foreign commerce, violated a treaty with Britain, and threatened to make the Union "a mere rope of sand."[28] The year before, Justice Joseph Story had strongly denounced the slave trade as an immoral violation of the law of nature and of nations, so that a slave ship could be seized as a pirate vessel. But Chief Justice Marshall then ruled that when the trade was sanctioned by another nation's positive law, American courts must uphold those laws in any context where deference to foreign law was the norm. Even as they recognized the incompatibility of slavery with doctrines of natural rights to which Americans allegedly subscribed, then, the federal courts undertook no significant challenges to repressive racial legislation.[29]

In both Southern and Northern states, such legislation proliferated. White Americans remained haunted by the specter of the rebellion which spawned the Haitian black republic, the second independent new nation in the hemisphere. The U.S. refused to recognize that government until 1862, and from 1806 to 1809 the Jeffersonians imposed an embargo on trade with Haiti, over the protests of Northern commercial interests. But the West Indies were still a source of free black refugees, to the alarm of whites in the Southern states and territories, who made ineffectual attempts to prohibit their entry.[30]

White fears were reinforced not only by Prosser's 1800 Virginia insurrection and Denmark Vesey's unsuccessful conspiracy in Charleston in 1822, but more generally by the rapid increase in the number of free blacks during these years. Immigration, manumission, the addition of Louisiana with its distinctive traditions (including a large, relatively well-off free black caste), along with natural increase, all made free blacks by far the fastest growing segment of the Southern population by 1810. The response in both the upper and lower South was to end most vestiges of the brief dawn of greater equality for free blacks during the Confederation era. Southerners imposed new restrictions on manumission and often required freed slaves to leave their states. Slaves were also prevented from hiring themselves out for extra work in order to buy their freedom. Denial of the vote to free blacks was made explicit throughout the South except North Carolina and Tennessee. Incoming free blacks were discouraged by requirements that they post bonds, or by outright prohibitions. The upper South generally adopted the North Carolina system of registering free blacks. North Carolina itself compelled them to wear shoulder patches reading "free." Vagrancy laws permitted unemployed blacks to be coerced into virtual servitude. The rights of free blacks to obtain jury trials, testify in courts, and obtain counsel were generally explicitly denied, and special brutal criminal penalties for blacks were enacted. Blacks were also refused access to many trades and commercial licenses. Some public institutions, including prisons, began to segregate. Others, including the relatively few schools and libraries that existed, adopted whites-only rules. In sum, the condition of free blacks deteriorated along almost every dimension.[31]

In the North, matters were only a little better. There blacks had more freedom to express their grievances, but not much more success in having them remedied. Several of the Northwest Ordinance states banned black immigration in the manner that caused controversy in Missouri. Others set prohibitive bond requirements as guarantees of good behavior. These laws were not vigorously enforced, but they could be used by whites to harass blacks at will. Free blacks like Philadelphia's James Forten, a revolutionary war veteran, fought successfully against the adoption of such laws in the northeast, denying claims of black inferiority and insisting that blacks were entitled to the equal rights proclaimed in the Declaration and protected by the Constitution. But, as noted above, apart from Massachusetts, New Hampshire, Vermont, and Maine, blacks were largely denied the vote above the Mason-Dixon line, too. And, as in Virginia, at times the expansion of the franchise in the North succeeded only when explicit exclusions of blacks were also adopted. The Northwest states often restricted blacks' procedural rights as well, in a manner parallel to the Southern restraints; and segregated institutions, though products of custom more often than law, spread there, too. Beginning in the 1820s, blacks were also often denied access to trades and crafts because these were increasingly monopolized by white European immigrants.[32]

After the rise of these restrictions and the Missouri debates, state courts started to consider whether free blacks could be termed citizens at all. In particular, the question of whether the privileges and immunities clause required slave states to recognize Northern free blacks as citizens, at least within the meaning of that clause, proved unavoidable. Initially, Southern courts did not differ greatly from Northern ones on this issue. Courts throughout the country were reluctant to declare free blacks wholly nonmembers of the polity or to recognize them as full citizens. For example, while granting a privileges and immunities claim in 1820, Judge Benjamin Mills of Kentucky stated rather tentatively: "Free people of colour in all the states are, it is believed, quasi citizens, or at least denizens. Although none of the states may allow them the privileges of office, and suffrage, yet, all other civil and conventional rights are secured to them." At least they were in some states, and comity required Kentucky to honor at least those rights.[33] Similarly, another Kentucky judge argued the same year that although free blacks were not full parties to the social compact, "they are certainly, in some manner, parties," entitled to at least minimal protection.[34] The judge could not overlook the obvious point that on consensualist accounts of membership, free blacks had to be in some sense participants in the social contract if the governments allegedly thus created were to govern them legitimately at all.

But two years later, perhaps affected by the Missouri debates, the Kentucky Court of Appeals reached a different answer in *Amy (a woman of colour) v. Smith.* Here Mills found himself in dissent. Amy contended that she was not William Smith's slave, having been born in Pennsylvania under its gradual emancipation act, albeit to a slave whom Smith claimed he owned. The privileges and immunities clause, she maintained, required Kentucky to treat her like any other Pennsylvanian citizen.

The Kentucky court, however, ruled that despite her birth in Pennsylvania, Amy was not a citizen there. Acknowledging the common-law rule that place of birth determined subjectship, the court insisted that it took "something more to make a citizen." As the Southern congressmen had contended in the Missouri debates, one had to be born into a class endowed with "rights and privileges" sufficient for citizenship. These rights had to include eligibility, if not possession, of all the rights of the "highest class of society." As blacks were "almost everywhere" not entitled to such rights, they could not claim citizenship under the privileges and immunities clause.

Acknowledging that white women were deemed citizens, yet were also not eligible for the political rights of the "highest class," the court claimed that they shared the status of the adult males on whom they were dependent. As a defense of the court's ruling on the status of dependent blacks, which the court held Amy to be, this theory failed badly. It implied that they, like wives, should share the citizenship of their masters. Perhaps aware of this, the court then added that even if Amy were a citizen of Pennsylvania, she was being treated by Kentucky in just the way the state treated its own blacks. Hence the privileges and immunities clause still had not been violated.[35]

That argument did not really respond to Amy's demand to be treated like a white Pennsylvania citizen visiting Kentucky. It instead assigned her to a category of "Kentucky blacks and out-of-state blacks visiting Kentucky," who were all deprived of most rights. Amy's racial classification was thus treated as more fundamental than her Pennsylvanian citizenship, without justification. Overall, then, the court failed to find any coherent way to defend its denial of privilege and immunities protection to Amy. Similarly hemmed in by the logic of citizenship doctrines, Southern courts thereafter sometimes still granted genuine comity. But such instances were few; most treated racial and gender hierarchies as more controlling. It was all the easier to do so because Southerners were right in claiming that the North usually did not grant free blacks or women many more rights, even when it called them "citizens."

Consensualism and Ascriptive Hierarchies: Native Americans. If anxieties raised by the increase in the number of free blacks largely account for the discriminatory measures taken toward them, the desires of white Americans to expand westward largely explain Republican policies toward Native Americans. The basic aim of Jefferson and his successors was to concentrate the tribes and persuade them to exchange their homes for federal lands farther west. There the government promised to help them prosper by turning to farming and eventually gaining citizenship. Jefferson promised that "we shall all be Americans . . . your blood will run in our veins and will spread with us over this great continent."[36] All this was supposed to come about through consensual agreements with the tribes, who would come to appreciate the chance to share in American Christian civilization.

That scenario shows that the Jeffersonians well understood the pacific policy implications of principles of consensualism and respect for human rights. But though some Cherokees, in particular, did move to Arkansas, exhortation produced little change, and white Americans grew impatient. The repeatedly announced policy of relocating and "civilizing" the tribes also reinforced public officials' and citizens' belief that Native Americans were incompetent cultural inferiors, whose legal claims against white encroachments were being indulged, not recognized as true rights. Regardless of tribal wishes, the "policy of the United States was based on an assumption that white settlement should advance and the Indians withdraw."[37]

That process had already begun under Adams, who was less willing than Washington to restrain the invasions of frontier whites on Native American territories. It became standard policy under Jefferson.[38] In promising to extend citizenship eventually to all who wished it, Jefferson was probably sincere and, by his own ethnocentric lights, benign. But he was none too scrupulous: he encouraged government traders to lure the tribes into debt so that they might feel they had to cede their lands. Later, he grew embittered by tribal interest in Aaron Burr's conspiratorial plans, and many Republicans resented the renewed assistance Native Americans gave the British in the War of 1812. Still, President Monroe's inclinations were no less humane than those of Jefferson's finer moments. With Monroe's support, in 1819 Congress passed an act for the "civilization" of the Indian tribes via the dispersal of $10,000 annually to benevolent societies that would provide schools and agricultural training. This effort was supplemented by federal school funds promised in various treaties. Though not what the tribes wanted, these measures were more pacific than genocidal warfare. Yet the decisive element of the Republicans' policies remained the belief that Native American land claims extended only to occupancy, and only until the government could find some way to hold that those rights had been extinguished.[39]

It is revealing that while Washington had addressed tribal chiefs as "brothers," Jefferson, Madison, and Monroe reverted to the British practice of referring to them as "red children." They did not take Native American aspirations to equal, respectful treatment seriously. In 1801, parts of the Northwest Territory were set aside as an Indian Territory governed by William Henry Harrison, but the U.S. immediately commenced a series of treaties (fifteen in the next four years) that whittled away the tribes' holdings. After the Louisiana Purchase, pressures grew to move the southern tribes westward, by coercion if necessary. Although the Republican national administrations did not adopt this policy, they did obtain southern tribal lands via numerous treaties, often signed by the tribes facing aggression from settlers or the states. The acquisitiveness of white Georgians, for example, undoubtedly helped convince many Cherokees that Arkansas would be more desirable. Other Native Americans, however, responded to this progressive diminution of tribal lands with armed resistance. The increasingly superior attitude of the United States toward the tribes reflected the fact that it was increasingly able to prevail in these struggles. The most publicized instances were Harrison's victories at Tippecanoe in 1811 and the Battle of the Thames in 1813, and later Andrew Jackson's repeated assaults on Creeks, Seminoles, and Cherokees.[40]

Throughout these years there was no set answer as to how far the alleged American right of preemption reflected U.S. sovereignty over the tribes, or whether such authority as did exist resided in the states, the national government, or some combination of both. Like the first administration, the Marshall Court displayed some solicitude for Native American rights, as well as national prerogatives, but it spoke hesitantly and equivocally. In *Fletcher v. Peck* (1810), the Court considered Georgia's claim to lands that adjacent tribes had granted to an individual. The state's attorneys argued that the tribes had been conquered and held their land only at the sufferance of their conquerors, which could be withdrawn at any time. Georgia's lawyers did not clearly identify whether the U.S. or Georgia could exercise the powers of the tribes' "conqueror," merely insisting that the Native Americans were left with no right to alienate their lands at will. Marshall answered tentatively that the tribes' claims to occupancy, if not absolute ownership, were to be respected until "legitimately extinguished"; yet under some unspecified circumstances, a state might seize the land. Justice Johnson, in dissent, insisted more liberally that the tribes west of Georgia, at least, retained a "limited sovereignty" and were "absolute proprietors of their soil." (Other tribes, he indicated, had "totally extinguished their national fire" and subjected themselves to state law, whereas some had agreed by treaty to "hold their national existence at the will of the state within which they reside.") But the most Georgia could ever have claimed was a right of preemption over any land sales, and this right, Johnson maintained, the state had ceded to the United States via the Constitution.[41]

Johnson's view was more consistent with both the preceding treaty history and more liberal versions of the rights of conquest; but it was less politically potent.[42] In 1817 and 1819, the Monroe administration expressed a similar spirit when it tried to win Senate ratification of treaties that granted land to the tribes in fee simple. That policy would have recognized the tribes as legal equals and made any further acquisition of their land a matter of more genuinely consensual transactions. But the treaties were rejected on explicitly hierarchical grounds. They were said to jeopardize the federal "guardianship" over Native American affairs to which the U.S. was entitled and which the tribes supposedly needed.

Occasionally, treaties did bestow such absolute land rights, and the promise of citizenship, on individual Native Americans; in 1820 the Choctaw tribe was granted land that was supposed to remain inviolate until its members were prepared to become citizens. That prospect was held out even though Native Americans were otherwise ineligible for citizenship under federal naturalization laws. These promises were, however, usually no more than devices to win support for the treaties from a few influential tribal leaders. In the end they provided no real security for Native American lands, no real recognition of tribal rights, and no progress toward citizenship for most tribal members on either a consensual or a nonconsensual basis.[43]

Perhaps due to these treaties, the precise citizenship status of Native Americans became a legal issue at this time, in ways that were to be of great significance for American citizenship laws generally. After all, on the common-law, *jus soli* understanding of birthright membership, no one had a better claim as native-born Americans than Native Americans. If the U.S. held ultimate fee in their lands, then they were born in the U.S. If the U.S. exercised guardianship over them, and if, as Coke and Blackstone had held, membership and allegiance hinged on protection at birth, the logically inescapable implication was that their very dependence rendered Native Americans members of the U.S. political community. And if they were not, then apparently they were members of sovereign independent nations, with whom Jeffersonians should deal only through peaceful, consensual treaties. Yet clearly few whites were willing to embrace those conclusions. How then, was the status of tribal members to be defined and defended?

In *Jackson v. Goodell* (1822), New York Chief Justice Ambrose Spencer reluctantly decided that, given the claims of sovereignty made by American governments, the citizenship of Native Americans could not be denied. New York had long claimed authority and imposed regulations on the tribes within its borders, even against the express will of Congress, and it was not willing to stop. Spencer believed that its assertions of sovereign power implied that Native Americans were the American equivalent of common-law subjects. Citing Blackstone, he noted that Indians were "born in allegiance to the government of the state," and held that "we must conclude, that they are citizens." Spencer knew of "no halfway" position on the matter.[44]

New York's greatest jurist, the high Federalist Chancellor James Kent, found one. Like the Jeffersonians arguing against free blacks' citizenship, he perceived that here, too, ascriptive hierarchies might be buttressed by consensualist arguments. Kent therefore abandoned the common-law view of membership that he and most other Federalists upheld in other contexts. He turned instead to the modified Lockean consensual doctrines of the Swiss public writers, especially Vattel. Reversing Spencer on appeal in *Goodell v. Jackson* (1823), Kent cited Vattel to define the tribes as "dependent" peoples who had, owing to their weakness, voluntarily *chosen* to place themselves "under the protection" of the U.S. They were thus "restrained of their sovereignty in certain respects," but they retained enough to be considered independent states, whose native-born inhabitants were not subjects or citizens of the larger power on which they were dependent.[45] Thus in Kent's skilled hands Lockean voluntarism justified the political subordination of Native Americans.

Eventually, Marshall's Supreme Court endorsed Kent's approach, though the issue remained clouded for a time. In the same year that Kent wrote, the Court decided *Johnson v. McIntosh*, which considered the claims of the U.S. and its beneficiary, one McIntosh, to lands purported to have been granted to others by the Peankeshaw and Illinois tribes during colonial days. Counsel for McIntosh blended liberal and inegalitarian ascriptive arguments in a way different from Kent's. Relying on the familiar Lockean argument that only those who labored productively upon it had a right to land, McIntosh's lawyer maintained that the Native Americans' hunting and gathering proved them to be an "inferior race of people." Hence they had never been recognized by European powers as having any territorial claims whatsoever.[46]

Marshall's opinion was much less extreme, but he upheld McIntosh's title. With rare honesty, he dismissed the argument that Native Americans had no title because they were merely hunters as factually incorrect, as the Peankeshaws and others did also farm. The Chief Justice focused instead on the view of the rights of conquest expressed in the past practices of the European powers and the U.S. He openly doubted whether those practices conformed to the principles of "natural right" that "ought to regulate" conquest in general; but he thought them too entrenched in "the law of the land" to be overturned. He concluded that, whereas Native Americans had a right of possession or occupancy, ultimate dominion over their lands, its alienation, and extinguishment of their titles all rested with the conqueror.[47]

At this point, Marshall viewed the tribes as conquered and acknowledged that he was departing from his general adherence to Lockean notions of natural rights and consensual membership; but he seemed not to see any other course open to him. Kent's opinion showed how courts could claim a superficially consensual route to results that would be basically similar. But even Kent's false attribution of Vattelian consent to the tribes implied greater limits to white powers over them than conquest doctrines did. Perhaps that is why the Chief Justice adopted it in the famous Cherokee cases of the 1830s.

Consensualism and Ascriptive Hierarchies: Women. Whereas the condition of blacks and Native Americans worsened during this era, the legal status of women remained stable. In relation to gender, national jurists and lawmakers still played negligible roles. The relatively few Americans who addressed the political status of women continued to do so in terms of "republican motherhood." That was, after all, again a way of rhetorically presenting a disempowered status as the product of the choices of all involved, as well as being in accord with nature. When the federal courts specified women's legal status, however, they typically endorsed common-law views of women as subjects of men rather than as "different but equal" republican citizens.

For example, in *Kempe's Lessee v. Kennedy* (1809), the lessee of Grace Kempe, who had married a British loyalist and gone to England during the Revolution, challenged a New Jersey law confiscating the land of inhabitants of other states who were guilty of aiding America's enemies. He contended that this law should not apply to Kempe's lands because she was a *feme covert*. As such, her departure represented not aid to the enemy, but simply allegiance to her husband. That was an obligation ranking among "the most important duties of social and domestic life" that he did not think the law had meant to override. Furthermore, as a *feme covert* Kempe was not in his view even an "inhabitant of a state." Her husband was the inhabitant—so again the law could not be applied to her. Although the Supreme Court decided against Kempe's lessee on jurisdictional grounds, Marshall indicated some sympathy to his views on the merits. Clearly, if a married woman's status was thus so subordinate to her husband that she could not even be deemed an inhabitant of a political community in her own right, she possessed in the law's eyes no meaningfully independent republican citizenship.[48]

Americans did begin educating girls more extensively during this era, accounting for much of the increased school enrollment of the period. The education of girls was designed, however, essentially for the domestic duties of "republican motherhood." American writers like Hannah Mather Crocker, who published *Observations on the Real Rights of Women* in 1818, were influenced by Judith Sargent Murray's and Mary Wollstonecraft's demands for women's education and by the individualistic, rights-oriented legacy of radical Enlightenment thought. But though Crocker agreed that women could benefit from a more broad-ranging curriculum, she still believed it "morally wrong, and physically imprudent" for women to pursue abstract studies like metaphysics or public careers like law.

Some went further: Emma Hart Willard fought to teach the natural sciences as well as domestic sciences in several northeastern female academies. And another exponent of the most radical currents of the Scottish Enlightenment, the renowned Frances Wright, traveled several times from Scotland to America in the 1820s, eventually settling to become one of the leaders of the American free thought movement. With Robert Dale Owen, she edited the *New Harmony Gazette,* the journal of his socialist utopia in Indiana, and later the *Free Enquirer* in New York. But she was best known as the first prominent female lecturer in the United States. Her *Course of Popular Lectures,* published in 1829, called for common schools with equal education for young women, and she also spoke out for the gradual abolition of all slavery. Like Wollstonecraft, however, she was mocked as a free-love advocate and atheist, and her ideas began to bear fruit only in the Jacksonian years.[49]

The Ongoing Conflicts over State versus National Citizenship

Faced with the task of governing a still-fledgling nation effectively while maintaining a commitment to state-centered republicanism, Jeffersonians often found themselves internally divided between more and less nationalistic factions. The federal courts generally remained inclined to assert nationalism when they could; but they were chary of interfering with strongly defended state claims and with racial hierarchies. Hence, despite the Jeffersonian hegemony, conflicts over the primacy of state and national citizenship continued unresolved.

Privileges and Immunities. Overall, the ascendancy of state-centered Jeffersonianism helped perpetuate relatively narrow judicial interpretations of the rights inherent in United States citizenship. Article IV's privileges and immunities clause arguably offered the Federalist-dominated judiciary a promising route to define various liberties, especially economic ones, as vital to national citizenship and hence immune against interference by the normally republican state legislatures. The Marshall Court sometimes used the contract clause for similar purposes, but the federal judiciary still did not elaborate any broad doctrines on the rights of national membership per se. Judges continued to endorse many interpretations grounded on claims of states' rights.

As in the 1790s, litigation invoking the privileges and immunities clause was rare. Hence much of the discussion of this guarantee still took place in the state courts. With reasonably solid historic and textual support, most state judges still defined the guarantee essentially as a "comity" or proto–equal protection clause. In the words of New York's James Kent, it meant "only that citizens of other states should have equal rights with our own citizens" should they enter New York. "Their persons and property must, in all respects, be equally subject to our own law."[50] Many courts held that the clause did not do even this much: only the more basic of a state's civic privileges and immunities had to be accorded to citizens of other states. Some discriminations between residents and visitors were still permissible.[51]

That interpretation was essentially sustained by the federal courts. In *Costin v. Washington* (1821), the D.C. Circuit Court upheld a virulently racist by-law of the district's charter. The by-law prevented free blacks from residing in the district unless they obtained a license by proving their moral character and their means of support, and by entering into a twenty-dollar bond with a "respectable" white man to provide surety for their families' good conduct. William Costin, a highly respected mulatto messenger for the Bank of Washington (and said to be related to Martha Washington), refused to obtain the bond and appealed to the Circuit Court. There the Federalist Chief Judge William Cranch (Abigail Adams's nephew) read these requirements as applicable only prospectively. Cranch assumed that Congress would not have imposed these burdens on previously resident free blacks without saying so more unequivocally. But he also held that the charter's provisions were reasonable measures to protect public security against the problems raised by incoming free blacks. Cranch dismissed the argument that the restrictions constrained incoming blacks who were citizens in other states, and thus violated the privileges and immunities clause. He claimed that they were to be treated in the same way as free blacks resident in the district, with the exception of those already resident when the charter was passed. As a state could deny its free blacks the vote, so the district could deny its free black residents liberties that other residents possessed.[52]

Reflection on this convoluted argument reveals that Cranch showed only that incoming free blacks who were citizens in other states would in the future be treated the same as incoming free blacks who were not, not that they would be treated the same as the district's existing free black inhabitants like Costin. The latter would continue to be exempt from the charter's special impositions. As with the Kentucky court in *Amy v. Smith*, Cranch's tortured logic made sense only if one assumed that the racial identity of incoming free blacks defined the class that had to be treated similarly, not their possession or lack of state citizenship. Thus, despite his solicitude for the district's existing black residents, on balance Cranch, too, treated race as legally more basic than citizenship. The result again was to deny meaningful protection for civic privileges and immunities against contrary state or local actions.

The most influential federal court statement concerning the privileges and immunities clause came two years later from the pen of Federalist Justice Bushrod Washington, the first President's nephew, who specialized in both Article III and IV citizenship issues. Sitting on circuit in *Corfield v. Coryell*, Washington ruled on a New Jersey law that permitted citizens of the state, but not outsiders, to mine oyster beds in the state's waters. In response to the question of whether this discrimination violated the privileges and immunities of citizens of other states, Washington defined those rights in influential phrases. They were rights "which are, in their nature, fundamental; which belong, of right, to the citizens of all free governments," and he gave as examples: "Protection by the government; the enjoyment of life and liberty, with the right to acquire and possess property of every kind, and to pursue and obtain happiness and safety; subject nevertheless to such restraints as the government may justly prescribe for the general good of the whole."[53] This language has often been interpreted as meaning that there are certain fundamental natural rights which all state governments must respect and secure.[54] But Washington upheld the New Jersey law in question; the point of his stress on fundamental rights was chiefly to indicate that access to oysters was not a basic right. And although he undoubtedly thought that basic rights expressed natural justice, his indication that states could regulate even such rights again appears to leave little room for federal relief should they be greatly attenuated by state legislatures.

It may seem puzzling that Federalist judges so closely tied to the first two administrations should have perpetuated comity clause interpretations, rather than use Article IV to defend what they took to be crucial national and personal rights against state interference, as Hamilton had hoped. No doubt the shadow of the *Chisholm* experience still loomed large in an inhospitable political climate. Perhaps the comity clause, in contrast to the contract clause, was too open-ended to appear safe. It is most likely, however, that the Missouri debates had made judges aware of how broad readings of the privileges and immunities clause might be used to aid free blacks, in a manner that was politically explosive. Hence federal judicial deference to state authority in this area may well have been another effort to accommodate racial hierarchies.[55]

Civic Education. If on some fronts Jeffersonians had to make concessions to nationalism, in one area, even Jefferson's ideas involved too much invasion of local and individual interests to gain support from his constituents. From early on, he and others often insisted that education was vital to the flourishing of republicanism in the new nation. Education came to be so identified with preparation for citizenship that noncitizens were often denied it. But despite much discussion, the national and state governments did virtually nothing to establish schools until the 1830s. "Public" education, a term that more often referred to schools open to the public than to schools created by governments, remained a local matter during this era.[56]

In 1779, in the 1790s, and again in 1817 Jefferson ardently advocated an elaborate three-tiered plan for a state-administered educational system in Virginia. Benjamin Rush made a similar proposal in Pennsylvania, and both Republicans and Federalists repeatedly suggested a national university. There were predictable differences in their objectives. More egalitarian Republicans hoped to enhance personal capacities for political participation and intellectual progress, whereas more aristocratic Republicans and most Federalists stressed fostering social obedience, and sometimes the integration of all citizens into a new, common national culture. But all agreed that the basic purpose of education should be to form the sort of moral character—reasonable, self-controlled, imbued with a sense of personal and civic duties—needed for a republican citizenry to be truly virtuous, or at least less vulnerable to dissension and corruption. In addition, the dominance of Bible-reading Protestantism in American life gave literacy a high value. Consequently, from the Northwest Ordinance through the early state constitutions, public documents often proclaimed the importance of education. Over time the federal government made available to the states increasing sums of money from the sale of federal lands within their borders, often indicating that these funds should be devoted to public education.[57]

Yet the proposals for national and state civic education during this period were essentially failures. It is perhaps emblematic of the way historical circumstances favored certain values of the founding elites over others that, though they avoided establishing a national church, and Hamilton managed to create his national bank, the calls for a unifying national university issued at various times by Washington, Jefferson, Madison, John Quincy Adams, and others all came to naught. Furthermore, Jefferson's agrarian constituents repeatedly disappointed him by opposing the increased taxation, the partial increase in state authority, and the attendance requirements his plans involved. Similar proposals outside Virginia fared little better.

Hence, from the nation's founding through 1830, most of the education of America's rural and village populations (over 90 percent of the nation's total) took place in locally created and run district schools, funded by tuition, property taxes, and occasional state aid. These schools seemed adequate to the bulk of the population's limited educational objectives, and with the spread of Noah Webster's nationalistic texts, they did help foster a common culture. But they were often as much day-care facilities as schools, subject to seasonal overcrowding or poor attendance, sometimes characterized by a stifling focus on memorization and by harsh discipline. Even so, as new transportation and communication systems expanded national markets during the early nineteenth century, literacy became more highly valued, and enrollments increased. About 60 percent of New York's school-age population was enrolled in 1825.[58]

In the nation's few cities, fears about the growing numbers of urban poor, especially when immigration increased after 1812, led to efforts to create new city schools as well. Unlike England, where many members of the upper classes viewed education for the masses as dangerous, Americans almost unanimously believed that education would help foster desirable moral habits, a shared culture, and a sense of trust among all social strata. A number cited Locke's educational theories, which emphasized the malleability of children's minds and the importance of inculcating practices of self-restraint. For many school advocates, the goal of social control that these notions served was already more central than facilitating economic mobility or political participation.

Even so, owing to this widespread enthusiasm for education, schooling was provided fairly widely through private voluntary organizations, aided by occasional public funding. Religious groups, secular Free School or Public School Societies, tradesmen's mutual aid associations, ethnic groups, societies to aid free blacks, among others, all established their own schools, relying on relatively low tuition fees and private donors for their support. Thus concerns about reaching the minimal educational levels and cultural unity necessary for republican citizenship were more or less satisfied during these years, but not through state, much less national, governmental actions.[59]

Jeffersonian Compromises with Federalist Nationalist Liberalism

Though the Federalists' continuing dominance of the judiciary, particularly the Supreme Court, did not much restrain Jeffersonian policies, federal judges did shape some less politically salient legal doctrines in ways that proved to be important. American citizenship laws as a whole thus visibly remained products of the conflicting partisan visions built out of the nation's multiple civic traditions, not Jeffersonian Republicanism alone.

Naturalization and Federalist Nationalism. The rump Federalists manning the national courts also generally construed the naturalization issues of this era in consensual terms, but they occasionally seized opportunities to assert the primacy of national over state membership. And sometimes they still used ascriptive naturalistic conceptions to bolster national obligations, as high Federalist judges had done in the late 1790s. In *Chirac v. Chirac* (1817), Marshall definitively ruled that Congress's power over naturalization into U.S. citizenship excluded state naturalizations, as Hamilton had argued and as the 1795 naturalization act implied. The decision came at a point when more nationalistic versions of Jeffersonian Republicanism were in vogue, and it did not endanger any key Jeffersonian political interests, so it prompted little criticism. Marshall did not directly consider a more sensitive issue, suggested in one brief: whether states could still confer their own citizenship, thought not U.S. citizenship, on foreigners.[60] Like privileges and immunities litigation, that topic was bound up with the scope of state powers over entry by free blacks and immigrants. Few states would abandon claims to such discretionary powers lightly. Some subsequent federal and state court opinions nonetheless appeared to deny the states this authority; but the question was not definitively addressed at the federal level, and it later became a sore point in *Dred Scott.* National governance of access to national citizenship was, however, now firmly established, the renewed ascendancy of state-centered republicanism notwithstanding.[61]

In 1824, Marshall tried to strengthen national citizenship another way. In a widely cited bit of dicta, he argued that Congress's naturalization authority was limited in certain ways. Congress could set the rules governing acquisition of citizenship by the foreign-born, but it could not regulate the prerogatives of that status once acquired. Like the Republicans in 1798, and against more nativistic Federalists, Marshall insisted that naturalized citizens were to be "distinguishable in nothing" from native citizens, "except so far as the constitution makes the distinction" (as in eligibility for federal offices).

Despite its focus on congressional limits, Marshall's reading strengthened national citizenship by giving a constitutional assurance that those admitted to it would possess virtually all its rights and privileges—providing protection against state as well as federal efforts to create second-class citizens. More broadly, he indicated that membership based on choice would not be treated as less genuine than membership stemming from natural origins.[62] Marshall's establishment of this point by way of dicta in an unrelated case typifies the ways he often tried to entrench his constitutional views quietly in the face of a hostile political climate.[63]

Yet Marshall did not reject ascriptive doctrines entirely, especially when they served his nationalistic purposes. For both expansionist Jeffersonians and nationalistic Federalists, it was particularly easy to eschew consensualism when dealing with noncitizens. Both state and federal courts did so by holding that Congress could naturalize persons unilaterally, through admission of territories to statehood.[64] (They thereby rejected St. Clair's claim that territorial inhabitants were not U.S. citizens.) In 1828 Marshall carried those rulings a step further, in a way that again buttressed national citizenship. But here he did so by taking national authority beyond the scope allowed by his usual consensual premises.

In *American Insurance Co. v. Canter,* the Chief Justice held that whenever the U.S. acquired a territory, whether "by conquest or by treaty," that act transferred sovereignty and hence the allegiance of the territorial inhabitants. They automatically became U.S. citizens, though not state citizens, like it or not.[65] Marshall thus rejected Locke's views that conquest did not automatically transform the allegiances of all in the conquered territories, but rather gave "despotical" power only over those who had actively warred against the conqueror, and that "consent" that had been "extorted by Force" was not valid.[66] Marshall's position, which recalled Coke's premises more than principles of government by consent, was surely influenced by the country's parallel desire to assert unrestrained U.S. sovereignty over the lands of tribes who were seen either as conquered or as peoples who had given consent only under pain of military force.[67]

Expatriation and Federalist Ascriptive Nationalism. If Jeffersonian executive officials were inclined to uphold expatriation rights, the courts leaned the other way, though far from unequivocally. State judicial views ranged from the Virginia Court of Appeals' defense of expatriation as one of the "inherent rights of man" which could not be surrendered, to the Massachusetts Supreme Court's support of the common-law rule that "no subject can expatriate himself."[68] Most courts acknowledged a right of choice of nationality during the revolution, an issue that remained pressing during the early Jeffersonian years. But few denied all state claims to the involuntary allegiance of those they governed. Even Virginia's great Jeffersonian jurist Spencer Roane ruled that persons prosecuted as traitors during the revolution had legally been made unwilling "citizens" through an "implied compact" of submission to the state officials arresting them. Roane left little doubt, however, that this was membership by conquest, not true consent, and that it fit ill with republicanism. He also treated Virginia-born loyalists who had escaped to England not as citizens or traitors but simply as aliens.[69]

The federal courts, including the Supreme Court, generally remained hostile toward broad expatriation rights. Some indicated that persons who were minors during the revolution had a right to choose their political membership when they reached maturity; but most federal judges treated this choice as a special option made available by the revolutionary "right of election," not one possessed by all children at all times, as Locke had claimed.[70] The Supreme Court avoided settling the issue definitively.

In *Murray v. The Schooner Charming Betsy* (1804), Marshall did carve out a commercial exception to common-law conceptions of allegiance, at mild cost to Federalist mercantilism.[71] Jared Shattuck, a native-born American who had lived for years on the Danish Caribbean island of St. Thomas and had sworn allegiance to the Danish crown, had his title to his ship challenged upon its recapture by a previous owner, Alexander Murray. Murray claimed that Shattuck was trading with France in violation of the embargo imposed by the Federalists' Intercourse Act of 1800. Marshall's opinion for the court avoided the question of whether Shattuck's oath to the Danish king had "absolutely" divested himself of his birthright American citizenship. Marshall claimed that earlier cases showed that an American citizen living abroad could assume the "commercial privileges attached to his domicil"—the commercial rights a subject of that regime would possess, including exemption from U.S. trade restrictions. Such an American might not, however, be an expatriate for other purposes.

Marshall's position, surprising if viewed strictly in partisan terms, seems traceable to sympathy for a property holder who had done all he could to expatriate himself in the absence of an American expatriation statute.[72] Yet overall, the decision did not represent a clear choice of consensual conceptions rather than naturalistic ones. Instead, it underlined how, when the justices perceived conflicting imperatives, they were willing to respond simply by multiplying citizenship statuses. Shattuck could be a Danish subject trading with France for commercial purposes, while remaining an American citizen as far as many other obligations were concerned.

With various minor refinements, this "commercial membership" doctrine proved useful for resolving many prize cases, especially after the War of 1812.[73] But the Court often stressed that no general expatriation right was thereby endorsed.[74] Justice Washington particularly insisted that the doctrine did not mean that the Court had abandoned the common-law view of expatriation or acknowledged a right for a citizen to "throw off his allegiance to his country" without "some law authorizing him to do so."[75] And when state laws did not authorize a "period of election," the Supreme Court did not supply it.[76]

Its most restrictive treatment of expatriation came in the case of the *Santissima Trinidad* (1822), which presented circumstances like those prompting Rep. Robertson's 1818 expatriation bill. A native-born U.S. citizen, James Chaytor, had captured a Spanish ship while captaining an Argentinean one. He claimed that he had previously expatriated himself, so that U.S. laws barring his action did not apply. On behalf of the ship owners, Daniel Webster urged the Court to adhere to the common-law rule that expatriation could occur only with the nation's consent, rejecting both the "slavish principle of perpetual allegiance" and the "fanciful novelty of a man being authorized to change his country and allegiance at his own will and pleasure." Justice Story's opinion did not settle the question, but he leaned toward Webster's view. Story held that if expatriation could occur at all, it required removal of one's domicile out of the country, and Chaytor, who now styled himself "Don Diego Chaytor," had always officially lived in Baltimore.[77] Thus, despite much espousal of expatriation rights during this era, Federalist judges adhering to notions of natural membership still prevented their full recognition.

Diversity Jurisdiction, Nationalism, and the Rise of the Corporation. For the most part, the Marshall Court continued to treat Article III, section 2 diversity cases as narrow technical issues. Most cases focused on requirements for records and averments, Bushrod Washington's specialty.[78] The ascendancy of state-centered Jeffersonianism and *Chisholm*'s repudiation probably forestalled any other course. Yet occasionally Marshall's liberal nationalism peeked through even here. Like Hamilton, he often stressed how federal jurisdiction helped check "local prejudices"; and he contended that U.S. citizenship automatically carried with it citizenship in the state where the citizen resided.[79] But Marshall did not try to use this jurisdictional clause to usurp state decision-making in any major way.[80]

Marshall did expand the Court's diversity jurisdiction in one key respect, by permitting corporations to sue under the clause in *Bank of the U. S. v. Deveaux* and *Hope Ins. Co. v. Boardman,* both in 1809.[81] But his holding was narrow, for the issue caused him difficulty. Given his Federalist desire to protect the economic rights of individuals against legislative encroachments, Marshall did not wish to treat corporations simply as artificial legal creatures made by popular legislatures. He preferred to look to the natural persons who comprised the corporation and to derive its rights from their more inviolable ones. Yet if corporate rights were to be defended against hostile locales, access to federal courts seemed essential. And because corporations were neither states nor aliens, the Constitution's language seemed to require them to be citizens to gain diversity jurisdiction. To so hold would, however, accord corporations a significant measure of independent legal personality.[82]

In the *Deveaux* case, Marshall relied on an earlier noncorporate precedent to hold that persons sharing a joint interest could be sued under diversity jurisdiction only if all "the persons concerned" were suitably qualified individually.[83] First, he asserted firmly that a corporation, that "invisible, intangible, and artificial being, that mere legal entity . . . is certainly not a citizen; and, consequently, cannot sue or be sued in the courts of the United States"; but he added, "unless the rights of the members in this respect, can be exercised in their corporate name." And he argued that the latter must be so, at least when all the members of the corporation had differing citizenship from the opposing party. Marshall observed that "the constitution itself" either apprehended dangers of biased state decisions or viewed with great "indulgence" such apprehensions on the part of litigants, including members of corporations. Hence granting jurisdiction to those members to sue via their corporate name fell within the "spirit and terms" of Article III, section 2. Marshall added that such corporate rights had gone unchallenged until corporate critics had resorted to "metaphysical and abstruse reasoning."[84]

The dependence of the corporation's right to sue on appropriate citizenship for *all* its members was a significant limitation.[85] It would become even more serious as corporations grew from local entities to multistate businesses with far-flung, fast-changing shareholders of many citizenships. Even so, the *Deveaux* rule appreciably advanced Marshall's Hamiltonian vision by helping federal courts to adjudicate and often protect corporate rights.[86] It was perhaps the most important of the several victories Marshall won during these years for Federalist notions of national citizenship rights and values.

The Reality of Rising Ascriptive Americanism

Thus some elements of Federalist naturalism and Hamiltonian economic nationalism survived, even under the long rule of the Jeffersonians and the state centric, consensualist, agrarian republican policies they favored. Hartzian accounts of American political development do not, however, have to strain much to accommodate either such relatively minor feudal survivals or more nationalist economic liberalism. What they fail to explain adequately in this era are the ways that legal developments strengthened rather than weakened the nation's ascriptive hierarchies of race and gender.

Those developments did not come because Americans could not conceive of alternative paths. Harshly inegalitarian policies toward women, African-Americans, Native Americans, and immigrants were criticized as violations of revolutionary human rights ideology and Christian charity. Even ascriptive common-law doctrines provided arguments for inclusion that made some judges decide that free blacks and Native Americans must be citizens. Those positions increasingly lost out, however. As dependence on slavery, fears of free blacks, and desires for tribal lands mounted during the Jeffersonian years, the trend of the time was toward harsher regulation of all African-Americans, slaves and free, and more deceptive, exploitative policies toward the surviving tribes. Those measures could not be defended in terms of principles of basic human moral equality, qualified only by alterable environmental differences that temporarily prevented the extension of consensual citizenship to all adults governed by the U.S. Even as legislators and courts tried to wrap consensual cloaks around these policies, time and time again the gaping holes in their arguments allowed their ascriptive commitments to show through. Thus, as efforts to entrench racial hierarchies grew, many American leaders began making their beliefs in inherent, unalterable racial hierarchies more explicit.

Jefferson's *Notes* provided only the most prestigious authority for such widely shared ideas. Many Americans believed, as the Indian-fighting General Andrew Jackson argued, that the tribes "must necessarily yield" to a "superior race," because they had "neither the intelligence, the industry, the moral habits, nor the desire of improvement" for civilization. Even border state Federalists like Louis McLane adapted naturalistic doctrines to argue that the U.S. was and must always be a nation made up of "States composed of a white population." His example shows again how the availability of multiple traditions of civic identity provided resources political actors could deploy in new ways. McLane's fusion of Federalist naturalism with racism and states' rights pioneered the pattern of the Jacksonian era.[87] It would be closely followed in *Dred Scott* by Jackson's Chief Justice, another mid-Atlantic man with Federalist roots, Roger B. Taney.

During the Jeffersonian era, then, citizenship laws were recast in state-centric, consensualist terms without fully repudiating Hamiltonian nationalism; simultaneously, American ascriptive traditions were greatly elaborated. The citizenship policies that resulted mattered enormously for American political development. Without them, the roles of Jackson and Taney would probably have been quite different, if they had come to power at all. The democratization of the franchise and the restoration of easy naturalization for white immigrants played important parts in providing Jacksonian voters. Decisions to set consensualist and human rights concerns aside and pursue expansion at the expense of the native tribes, by force if necessary, aided Jackson's personal rise to prominence during the Jeffersonian years. And though it is hard to speculate on the consequences of female enfranchisement, the political and economic interests of voting Americans would clearly have been dramatically different if free blacks had been treated as equal citizens, and if the federal government had opposed and not aided slavery's spread during these years. Instead, the Jeffersonians succeeded in shaping an America in which full political membership and power was increasingly held by men willing to praise both democracy and white supremacy more unequivocally than any of their predecessors, ultimately including the Jeffersonian leaders themselves.

8

High Noon of the White Republic
The Age of Jackson, 1829–1856

The Age of Jackson has special significance in debates over American political identity. Jacksonian America was the America that Tocqueville visited in 1831–32. It was also Louis Hartz's focus, discussed in nearly half the chapters of his 1955 book. If ever an era in U.S. history fit Tocquevillian and Hartzian accounts, this should be it.[1]

Intriguingly, in his 1837 Farewell Address, Andrew Jackson gave his own reading of the nation as it entered the middle of the era now named for him. He worried about states' rights extremism and nationalist economic machinations; but still, the outgoing President boasted, the country was "flourishing beyond any former example" in history. The Constitution was "no longer a doubtful experiment." If Americans were but "true to yourselves," Jackson promised, nothing could impede their "march to the highest point of national prosperity." This was especially so because through "the paternal care of the General Government," the "Indian tribes" that had retarded the safety, comfort, and improvement of "our citizens" were now removed "beyond the reach of injury or oppression." With that "ill-fated race" out of the way, Americans could be true to themselves with undreamed-of success.[2]

Modern Tocquevillian analysts have seconded Jackson's celebration of his time as the era when America was able to become its true self virtually unimpeded. Samuel Huntington contends that during these years the "American dream and American reality came close to joining hands," more so "than at any other time in American history," at least "outside the South." Hartz saw this as the crucial period in which America's central political figure emerged: the "great new democratic hybrid unknown in any other land," the

American farmer-laborer democrat who in his heart dreamed of becoming a capitalist. In Hartz's stylization, the politics of the day saw the seemingly endless triumph of this "strange new democratic giant" over wealthy interests, until Whigs at last realized, especially in their reincarnation as Republicans, that this giant could be seduced by a rhetorically democratic politics based on Horatio Alger's myth promising capitalist success for all.

Yet while he mocked the Whigs' earlier "stupidity," Hartz failed to explain how they regularly managed to attract almost half the vote in nearly every part of the country until they succumbed to the slavery issue.[3] Nor did Hartz notice the ascriptive view embedded in Jackson's claim that American citizens could be "true to themselves" only with the removal of at least one "ill-fated race." Thus Hartz gave little hint of what citizenship debates show to be the main development in legal and political conceptions of American civic identity during these years. Both major parties gave unprecedented prominence to partly overlapping, partly opposed inegalitarian ascriptive versions of Americanism, blended in with their different mixes of liberal republican principles.

More emphatically than the Jeffersonians, Jacksonian Democrats presented America as a state-centric, commercial, *white* republic, and they now defended that claim chiefly in terms of racial superiority rather than strained doctrines of consent. More fervently than the Federalists, the Whigs presented the purpose of America as the advancement of Protestant Anglo-American civilization via a prosperous, progressive national republic, a patriotic vision that helped compensate for the party's otherwise antipopulist platform. Many Jacksonians resented the Whigs' smug claims to be the party of piety and their efforts to impose cultural uniformity. They denounced Whig policies as incompatible with American traditions of freedom, including separation of church and state and local control. But many Whigs, in turn, justly accused the Jacksonians of seeking ever more national support for the greatest of all violations of liberty, black chattel slavery, and for imperialist wars on the tribes and in Mexico. Thus each party used the more liberal and democratic elements in its outlook to denounce the ascriptive positions advanced by the other, as Hartzians would expect. But each probably gained at least as much support as it lost from its advocacy of ascriptive inequalities; and, on balance, the laws that resulted strengthened illiberal hierarchies.

For despite the differences in their responses to the electorate's growing diversity and divisions, both parties agreed that white Christian male dominance must prevail. They were, however, divided with each other and among themselves on the proper ways to preserve that dominance. Those clashes meant that neither party succeeded in forging a vision of American nationality that could hold the country together. The Jacksonians did have more electoral success, and after 1850 the Whigs fell apart. But by then, both parties were losing ground to a range of more ideologically extreme third parties and social movements, some championing slavery in all states, some espousing nativism, some urging more racial and gender equality in the name of God and the Declaration of Independence. Seeking to stifle that fragmentation, Chief Justice Roger Taney tried to write Jacksonian racism into the nation's laws via his 1857 *Dred Scott* ruling—that no black could be a U.S. citizen "within the meaning of the Constitution."[4] Though hardly the fulfillment of the "American dream" as modern scholars describe it, that decision briefly fulfilled the actual dreams of most Democrats, who wanted a nation unequivocally committed to slavery, white supremacy, and states' rights. But it inflamed opposition that soon turned into a massively destructive national conflagration. If ever an era fit a "multiple traditions" account in which racist, nativist, and patriarchal views structured American political development and conflicts as fully as liberal republican ones, this is it.

Before making that case, let me acknowledge that Hartzian scholars bent on salvaging his gist have paid insightful attention in the past two decades to the glorifications of slavery and Indian removal by Jacksonians, the nativism of the Whigs, and the patriarchalism of both. Michael Rogin's *Fathers and Children: Andrew Jackson and the Subjugation of the American Indian* (1975) pioneered the way by portraying Jacksonian America as a time of rapidly expanding liberal markets increasingly open to new entrants. He depicted Jackson as playing the role of national father, combating obstacles to this "market freedom" posed "at home" by old Federalist and Jeffersonian gentry privileges and "in the west" by the surviving tribes. Thus "the Bank War, Texas, and Manifest Destiny" were "at the center of the Jacksonian agenda." Not all of these planks prompted an invocation of racist views. Jacksonians justified the dismantling of Hamiltonian aids to economic elites by appealing to a democratic republican insistence on states' rights and on special privileges for none, especially not financial and corporate interests. But, Rogin contended, the central tasks of Indian removal and maintenance of slavery had to be defended by portraying Native Americans and African-Americans as, at best, primitive "children" in need of the government's fatherly benevolence. In this manner, Rogin alleged, "Jackson's negative, laissez-faire, paternal state made the logical marriage of paternal authority to liberal egalitarianism."[5]

Some have similarly treated Whig nativism as a logical correlate of imperialistic liberalism. But other scholars have followed Eric Foner and agreed that the rising nativist Americanism of this era, culminating in the briefly potent Know-Nothing movement, was distinct from liberal "free labor" ideology, which advocated open markets and property rights for anyone who worked productively. Many have nonetheless shoehorned nativism into conventional interpretive frames by contending, as Michael Walzer does, that the restrictionists of the 1850s were "above all republican," most passionate about preserving the civic homogeneity that republics require.[6]

These accounts rightly suggest that westward expansion was spurred by market forces interdependent with the slave labor cotton economy, and that liberal democratic policies encouraging rapid commercial growth, social mobility, broader political enfranchisement, and largely open immigration all bred anxieties about republican government and the preservation of traditional social orders. They are also correct in noting that advocates of liberal policies often had little useful to say about the problems they generated. And they are right that champions of ascriptive inequalities employed many liberal and republican themes, from property rights to scientific naturalism to the need to preserve civic virtue and states' rights, in order to legitimate their repressive solutions to such problems. But it is still wrong to conclude that liberal republican principles and policies motivated and justified all the inegalitarian outcomes of the era.

Intertwined with their liberal democratic arrangements, Americans throughout the land, not simply in the South, still had extensive institutions and ideological traditions supporting white supremacy and slavery, Protestant hegemony, patriarchy, and Anglo-Saxon predominance. These interests and commitments best explain why American elites did not pursue market growth strictly through consensually negotiated contracts and treaties with the tribes and with Mexicans, through recognition of property and voting rights for all who worked productively, through the extension of free labor systems, and through secular schooling, which instilled needed economic and political skills on an equal basis. These policies all had advocates during this era, and they were all more consistent with liberal republican principles than those America followed. But leaders advancing such liberal policies faced a severe political problem: they could not claim that these measures would fully satisfy those who wanted tribal lands, Protestant hegemony, black slave labor, and female subordination.

Because this fact was so clear, both parties, but especially the Jacksonians, rallied support in part through ideologies that instead openly glorified illiberal ends and means. More than ever, Jacksonian officials used racial and gender categories to define property and civic rights and pursued territorial expansion and economic growth through deceptive and coercive means. Their tactics included broken treaties, military conquest, near-genocidal forced removals, and ever-deepening systems of involuntary servitude. To justify all this, they crafted much more grandiose ascriptive doctrines, still mixing in whatever rationales they could from liberal republican traditions. The ties binding liberal, republican, paternalist, racist, and nativist doctrines that resulted were real, but not chiefly "logical." These were shotgun marriages made for political, economic, and psychological convenience.[7] When the marriages failed, the shotguns fired.

The Rival Civic Ideologies

The Jacksonian Democrats. A classic example of multiple traditions, the party of the blunt, raw Jackson was more openly racist, but also more radically libertarian and more militantly republican than any in U.S. history. The fearsome general stormed into the White House in 1828 on a crusade to restore the virtuous "Old Republic" that he believed had fallen into corruption under the lax James Monroe, the conniving John Quincy Adams, and Nicholas Biddle's insidious Second Bank. Jackson and his heirs, Martin Van Buren and James K. Polk, eventually succeeded in killing the bank and placing national funds in an independent treasury system, lowering the protective tariff, seizing vast new western territories, and loosening federal restraints on the opening up of western lands by private parties, ending all vestiges of a national internal improvements program, removing most eastern tribes, and otherwise leaving governance to the states, localities, or no one at all.[8]

Scholars are right to call this state-centered, rhetorically populist program a democratic version of civic republicanism. In reality as well as in Jacksonian anti-elitist rhetoric, the now largely enfranchised white male American masses were active republican citizens during these years. They entertained themselves at grand revival-style political rallies, marched in parades, listened excitedly to incredibly long speeches, and voted in percentages rarely approached since then. Participation in presidential elections went from 29 percent of white adult males in 1824 to a stunning 80.2 percent in 1840, among the highest ever. Even so, to analyze these years solely through the prism of scholars' "republican revival" is dangerously incomplete.[9]

The Jacksonians did not, after all, restore the mythical Old Republic. Instead, they meshed their republican sentiments with more ardent commitments to the growing commercial, cash crop economy, minimizing older, static Jeffersonian ideals of agrarian self-sufficiency. Most were also far more willing than Jefferson to accept white urban mechanics and laborers as fellow producers.[10] And despite their fears of elite privileges and growing corporate power, they launched a new wave of state and local efforts to promote economic growth, granting public funds and powers to canals, mills, and railroads and adopting easy incorporation laws so that many more might have a chance to rise in the world. Their coalition joined new entrepreneurs to large and small farmers, along with poorer immigrant groups and religious minorities in the South, the west, and the cities.[11]

But in doing so, Jacksonian Democrats had to wrestle with tensions between their notions of republican virtue and the cheerful self-seeking of what Marvin Meyers evokes as the "age of Dodge and Bragg." They also had to harmonize their opposition to centralized government with their need to foster unity as the country burgeoned rapidly, economically and territorially, and absorbed increasing numbers of immigrants. From 1840 to 1860 the U.S. received 4.3 million people, with the immigrant share of the total population peaking in the mid-1850s at levels as high as any in U.S. history. Most of the newcomers were natural Jacksonian voters, especially the later, poorer, and more Catholic Irish and German arrivals, driven by crop failures and land squeezes. By 1860, the Catholic church was one of the largest denominations in a still heavily Protestant country. To aid these constituents, Democratic politicians strove to separate government from the powerful Protestant churches, even defending Sunday mail deliveries, though such measures disturbed many Protestant Democrats. One such, the artist and inventor Samuel F. B. Morse, became a seminal spokesman for the anti-Catholic nativism that siphoned off some Democrats along with many Whigs into a series of third parties. Most momentously, Jacksonian leaders had to curry the support of rich slaveholders in the South, where Jacksonianism was strongest, along with poor farmers and laborers throughout the country. Forging these disparate elements into a cohesive national party, especially while espousing a state-centric ideology, was no small order.[12]

In many respects the Jacksonians did not fill the bill, even though they dominated national politics for thirty years. Jackson himself made the presidency a great unifying national institution. When opposition to the high protective tariff and to abolitionist stirrings culminated in South Carolina's efforts to nullify the "tariff of abominations" in 1831–32, Jackson rejected such a denial of national authority.[13] But he then worked for the lower tariff that South Carolina sought, and Jacksonians generally sustained popular unity by assaulting such special privileges and fighting for new lands.[14]

But once Jackson had slain the Monster Bank, the heroes that these policies produced tended to be Whig generals, not Democratic Presidents; so Jackson's successors had trouble maintaining the office as the unifying center of national life. Martin Van Buren and others instead stressed that the new system of mass political parties that the democratized franchise had spawned could preserve the moderate but responsive national government the framers wanted. But as Jacksonian leadership devolved much governance from the federal level, it largely fell to the heads of local and state parties to build coalitions. They often did so simply by servicing economic and ethnic groups in return for dollars and votes. The result was what Major Wilson has termed a "brokered state" with logrolling, pork barrel politics, limited leadership, and weak national integration.[15]

To many, such a political rule was corrupt and ineffectual. Under Roger Taney, the Supreme Court tried to give more principled Jacksonian resolutions to the basic issues of the day. Through doctrines of dual federalism, the Court strove to preserve the state and national governmental roles the founders had designed, but without the tilt in favor of national authority and national citizenship that Marshall had installed whenever politics permitted. The Court was now inclined toward state sovereignty and state citizenship, at least when states could be trusted not to harm Jacksonian interests.[16] But neither as constitutional theory nor as political practice could these doctrines hold together the party Jackson had built, much less unify the nation. Dual federalism hardly offered a reassuring, inspiring, or commanding vision of civic identity to Americans made anxious or ambitious by economic change and the clash between free and slave labor systems, rendered isolated or aggressive by territorial expansion, and stirred to alarm or excitement by the diversity that immigration brought.

Many Americans thus sought to establish boundaries and stability for this fluid, volatile society through other means, especially their ascriptive civic myths. The old Jeffersonian device of claiming that subordinate status somehow rested on consent was being obviously belied by struggles over slavery, tribal removal, and women in politics. It seemed necessary to assert openly that America was a great "white republic" in which many could be governed without their consent.[17]

In aid of that claim, new intellectual defenses of inegalitarian ascriptive systems sprouted rapidly from old roots.[18] Cultivating them posed special challenges to the Jacksonians, however. They were the party of Jefferson, who had declared all men equal in basic rights, and the party of democracy. They needed strong arguments to deny others the equal rights they vociferously invoked for themselves. Many found the answer in more elaborate scientific accounts of white superiority, which made bans on political rights for "lower" races seem progressive. It was wonderfully helpful that Jefferson himself had pioneered scientific "proofs" of black inferiority in his Notes. Particularly as abolitionist sentiments grew during the 1840s, white supremacist writers followed Jefferson's lead with accelerating zeal.

The self-dubbed "American school of ethnography" was launched by Samuel George Morton's Crania Americana in 1839. It drew on the world's largest collection of skulls to assert a physical basis for racial differences and, especially, the intellectual inferiority of Native Americans. Morton's work was extended by the prolific Josiah Nott, a prominent, well-educated physician in Mobile, Alabama. Nott, who privately referred to his scholarly endeavors as "niggerology," chiefly desired to justify slavery. He allied himself with John C. Calhoun and then, along with the flamboyant popularizer George R. Gliddon, persuaded the leading naturalist of the day, Louis Agassiz of Harvard, to join in a massive work, Types of Mankind, in 1854. The Bell Curve of its day, it was quickly recognized as the American school of ethnology's magnum opus. It went through seven printings in the next year, startling sales for a bulky, expensive, scientific book.[19]

Though not incompetent for its day, as science the book was weak. Nott strug-

gled, as all scientific racists have done, with the inherent unworkability of biological racial categories. He had to concede that the intermingling of peoples
made "all classifications of the races of men heretofore proposed," including his
own, "entirely arbitrary." Yet in flat contradiction to that reality, he still insisted
that races were fixed, unchanging, "as indelibly permanent" as stone carvings.
Nott was also sure that the "Caucasian races" had "been assigned, in all ages, the
largest brains and the most powerful intellects" and made humanity's "rulers." It
was their providential destiny "to conquer and hold every foot of the globe" where
climate permitted. They had the "mission of extending and perfecting civilization."[20]

References to the New York physician John Van Evrie and lawyer
William Van Amringe also added popular works supporting the new biological
defenses of traditional hierarchies. Both went to the extreme of claiming that
blacks belonged to a "different and inferior species." Both also linked the advocates of black equality and equal political rights for women, who were often the
same. The Northern ascriptivists charged all these reformers with urging an
equality among "those created unlike" which was "an outrage on nature." Virtually all types of periodicals spread discussion of these scientific racist and patriarchal ideas. The Jacksonian *Democratic Review* treated them as established; and
though the *American Whig Review* was less favorable, other Whig journals termed
the new racist ethnology the "science of the age."[21]

References to the American school's ethnological themes soon populated the
rhetoric of Jacksonian leaders. By 1855, when a Free-Soil Whig, Francis Gillette
of Connecticut, argued in the Senate that natural law and the "national declaration" proclaimed "the exact equality of all men in natural rights," regardless of
"physical differences," color, or creed, even Northern antislavery Democrats like
John Pettit of Indiana could be condescendingly dismissive. Invoking recent
studies professing to show that the races were "distinct in their organization, the
volume and amount of intellect, of mind, of brain," Pettit called the Jeffersonian
notion that men were "physically, mentally, or morally" equal "a self-
evident lie."[22]

The American school was most controversial not for its racism but for the
challenge to the Genesis story embedded in its claims for the separate creation of
the races. That fact has permitted writers like Eugene Genovese and Barbara
Fields to stay on Hartz's trail by minimizing the importance of scientific racist
doctrines.[23] They stress instead Southerners' reliance on religion, states' rights
republicanism, and particularly the seigneurial or patriarchal defenses of slavery
advanced by George Fitzhugh. All these elements were certainly present, and the
several justifications of racial hierarchy could conflict. Fitzhugh disavowed Nott's
Types of Mankind because of its biblical heresy and its neglect of the goodness of

slavery for the white man's "dependent brethren." He disliked what Alexander Saxton has called the "hard" racism of Nott and others who portrayed blacks and the tribes as violent, rapacious monsters.

But these differences notwithstanding, as always many simply blended all these rationales for racial hierarchy. Though the American school rejected biblical literalism, its adherents lauded religious defenses of slavery, presenting their work as only additional evidence of God's inegalitarian intentions. Conversely, though Fitzhugh argued that civilization flourished best in societies based on well-tended slave labor, black or white, he also relied on "soft" racist assertions of black inferiority. In his first book, *Sociology for the South* (1854), Fitzhugh called the "negro" a "grown up child" and said that not even the "maddest abolitionist" would deny that the "negro race is inferior to the white race." All knew that "the Anglo-Saxons of America are the only people in the world fitted for freedom." And even as Calhoun evoked the specter of majoritarian tyranny to defend the South's interests in his *Disquisition on Government*, he decried the "dangerous error" of supposing that "all people are equally entitled to liberty." To bestow freedom on "a people too ignorant, degraded and vicious to be capable either of appreciating or enjoying it" ignored "all-wise Providence." All knew who Calhoun had in mind.[24] Far from being marginal, then, throughout the scientific, religious, mock-feudal, and states' rights defenses of slavery, assertions of innate black inferiority formed the common thread.[25]

In the 1840s, as the obstacle to western expansion increasingly became not merely recalcitrant tribes but land rich Mexico, Jacksonian leaders like Polk's militant Secretary of the Treasury Robert J. Walker and Secretary of State James Buchanan propagated narrower versions of this racial ideology. They assigned true supremacy not just to whites but to northern Europeans, often lumped together as Anglo-Saxons.[26] Van Evrie and others quickly provided "scientific" confirmation that unlike the "Anglo-American," whose "high instinct of superiority" had led him to reject "all admixture with the aboriginals," Spanish conquerors had bred "wretched hybrids and mongrels" who were "in many respects actually inferior to the inferior race itself." God's design for the Anglo-American race included its Manifest Destiny to rule over the west and more, displacing all such degenerate, despotic, Jesuitical Spanish influences.[27] Even Rep. William Brown of Indiana, a true agrarian republican who lauded sturdy independent western farmers against the "corruption" of "the great cities and manufacturing districts," defended expansion primarily in these racial terms. He predicted that the "Anglo-Saxon race, like a mighty flood," was destined to cover not only "all Mexico" but all of South America down to "Patagonia's snow-invested wilds," creating "republics" whose "destinies will be guided by Anglo-Saxon hands."

For many Southern Jacksonians like Walker, moreover, the motives for acquiring Texas and other Mexican lands included strengthening slavery. The nation could not suffer territory to its west to "fall into the hands of the semi-barbarous hordes of Mexico," made up of "every poisonous compound of blood and color," Walker argued. Those shocking primitives were "now openly engaged in the crusade of abolition" and "prepared in peace, to stimulate the servile population to revolt and massacre." The west needed to be secured to make the world safe for slavocracy.[28]

When the Treaty of Guadalupe Hidalgo ended the war in 1848 by adding more than one million square acres to U.S. territory, halving Mexico in the process, that goal seemed to be achieved magnificently. Yet despite the popularity of that success and its racist justifications, Jacksonian ideologues could not escape wholly from the contradictions of both affirming and repudiating Jefferson's Declaration and equal political and economic rights for all. It was hard to see amid those dissonances where the Jacksonians' hearts really lay. That was one reason why many Americans were attracted to the Whigs' seemingly more coherent vision of the nation's moral meaning.

Whigs and Know-Nothings. The Whigs had to make moral and patriotic appeals because they could not credibly claim to be furthering the immediate economic or political interests of much of the electorate. Their homeland was the old northeast and the interests and values of established middle- and upper-class commercial, financial, manufacturing, and professional groups. For a time, however, they were a truly national party, principally founded by Kentucky's Henry Clay. He stressed neo-Hamiltonian economic policies that promised to benefit all, but through initially aiding economic elites. The Whigs supported the National Bank, a nationally directed credit system, and industrial growth spurred by protective tariffs. To evade constitutional challenges, Clay also initiated dispersing federal funds to states, local governments, and private actors who would build railroads, canals, and highways. Whigs offered similar schemes for a wide range of other "internal improvements," including public education at all levels, rehabilitative prisons, and mental hospitals.

For economic and cultural reasons, most Whigs opposed rapid westward growth aided by cheap public land policies and aggressive militarism, and they grew ever more anxious about immigration. They wanted a prosperous Anglo-Saxon Protestant society, relatively free of Hispanic, French, and Irish Catholics, Native Americans, and Africans. Hence many attacked Jacksonian wars of conquest against the native tribes and Mexicans as imprudent and immoral. Some called those wars of aggression inhumane and unchristian. Others worried, often in virulently racist terms, that they would compel the nation to try to incorporate an "incongruous mass of Spaniards, Indians, and mongrel Mexicans."

Similarly, many decried the horrors of slavery, but most also favored governmental aid to the bipartisan American Colonization Society, which sought to persuade the nation's free blacks to move far, far away.[29]

For the Whigs, those positions represented support for true religion, civilization, and progress combined with humanity toward others. And though the Whigs, unlike the old Federalists, officially accepted the new era of mass democratic politics, many of them clearly did not relish it. They seemed more concerned to lecture than to aid the common man. Hence Jacksonians found it easy to portray the Whigs as conniving to use a corrupt central government to benefit the greedy rich—just the sort of tyranny that Americans had hated since the nation's inception.

In response, the Whigs presented their positions in terms that blended piety with fervid patriotism. They christened their policies the American System and sketched providential histories assigning religious purpose to the American union and their program. And though they often opposed the nation's wars, they ran the resulting military heroes for President. Their patriotic appeals could not entirely blunt the economic and cultural bristles stirred by various Whig policies. But they did present a coherent, compelling set of symbols that made it easier to believe Whig promises and to feel proud to be American.[30]

To construct their stirring nationalist narratives, many Whigs drew not so much on scientific racism as on European romanticism and their own Puritan traditions. Leading Whig orators like Daniel Webster traced the nation's birth far more to the Pilgrim landing than to the Revolution or the Constitution, and they identified its meaning more with the Protestant millennialist vision of the redeemer nation than with the advancement of property rights, though they heartily defended such rights. And although many insisted, like Webster, that "Bacon and Locke," along with "Shakespeare and Milton," were parts of the unique heritage the colonists had bequeathed to their descendants, conservative Whigs like Rufus Choate discarded Locke's individualistic versions of the state of nature and the social contract to venerate the religious nationalism of Edmund Burke.[31]

This Burkean and romantic emphasis on the unique, historically shaped character and destinies of different peoples allowed Whigs to make specific ethnic and religious traits intrinsic to "Americanism" without having to repudiate Enlightenment doctrines of human rights and racial environmentalism, or Christian humanitarianism. Though America's dominant bloodlines, culture, and religion were God's chosen ones, Americans could and generously would lift many less favored peoples up to their level over time.[32] Many might eventually become capable of government by consent. Thus Webster could, on the one hand, profess to support freedom without regard to "complexion, white or brown"; on the other, he could aver that, "under the providence of God," Englishmen had been formed for "the great work of introducing English civilization, English law, and, what is more than all, Anglo-Saxon blood, into the wilderness of North America" so as to create "the great republic of the world." That formulation left hope for all to gain republican liberty, and hence gave the Whigs their own more inclusive claim to be the party of government by consent. At the same time, Anglo-Saxon blood was clearly a very great plus if people were actually to be self-governing. Hence it seemed natural to be concerned that such blood remain predominant in America. These Whig sanctifications of American identity, conceived as having a specific religious and ethnic center, were as vital a part of U.S. culture as the democratic tropes of their opponents.[33]

The Whigs got great help in propagating their Protestant Americanism from the popularity of many nineteenth-century British and German romantic historians and novelists.[34] These writers' conceptions of national cultural identities, which treated Enlightenment political principles as a precious but particular Anglo-American heritage, were defended among academics by scholars like the German-American political scientist Francis Lieber, expounded to a broader intellectual public by English writers like the mystical poet Samuel Coleridge and the savagely polemical essayist Thomas Carlyle, and conveyed to the American public at large by the enormously popular Saxon-glorifying novelist Sir Walter Scott. The appeal of these histories and novels was augmented by the fact that many romantic writers in both Germany and England linked Tacitus' portrait of freedom-loving ancient Germanic tribes with the mythical "old Anglo-Saxon constitution" of England, just as some American revolutionaries had done. To Americans, these views of world history not only proved the Anglo-Saxon race's innate propensities for civil and religious liberty but also confirmed America's mission to be history's leading exemplar of freedom.[35] Such romantic patriotism provided impressive costuming for the Whig American System. Good schools, good work habits, and good roads would inculcate good Saxon-like morals, producing not only prosperity but the advance of Christianity and republicanism.[36]

This reliance on romanticized notions of Anglo-Saxonism only reinforced, however, near-instinctive Whig beliefs that these advances had to be primarily for and by northern European-descended Americans. Hence Clay presented congressional funding for the Colonization Society as an integral part of completing the American System. American self-governance was for whites; African-Americans were to be self-governing in Liberia. Furthermore, only a few male Whigs were willing to endorse the new female activism that emerged during these years. The young Lincoln suggested equal voting rights for women, and New York Governor William Seward championed equal educational opportunities for the sexes, but neither did so strenuously. Most mainstream leaders in both parties endorsed Tocquevillian views of the desirability of sexual "equality" within distinct spheres, with men retaining legal power to govern in the home, the market, and the political arena.[37] These ascriptive elements in Whiggery certainly did not hurt the party electorally.

But even in regard to their patriotic vision, the Whigs proved to be more severely divided internally than the Jacksonians. It was hard to assert the manifest destiny for greatness of white Anglo-Saxon America while opposing the wars through which the Jacksonians sought to fulfill that destiny, however uneconomic, destructive, and immoral many Whigs thought them to be. Even more important, Northern Whigs were almost all free labor supporters, though many were not actively antislavery. The leading Southern Whigs were large slaveowners. Hence Clay and Webster attempted endless compromises: accepting slavery in the South, promoting colonization, yet professing personal opposition to slavery and seeking to prevent its expansion. That approach did not placate the antislavery "Conscience Whigs" led by William Seward or the proslavery Southern Whigs like Georgia's Alexander Stephens. When Seward's faction denied the nomination for the presidency to Whig incumbent Millard Fillmore in 1852, the resulting desertions of proslavery Whigs and the disastrous defeat of the eventual nominee, Mexican war hero Winfield Scott, spelled the party's end.[38]

Electorally, however, the Whigs gave way in the late 1840s and early 1850s not so much to antislavery third parties like the Free-Soil and Liberty parties as to new nativist factions. The northeastern elites and old-stock middle class that formed the Whigs' core were unable to curb their fears as the new immigration become more massive, more Catholic, and heavily concentrated in their own region. Anti-Catholic agitators continuously publicized the ways that Popes Gregory XVI and Pius IX had denounced republican institutions, including the "detested LIBERTY OF THE PRESS," and that "most pestilential error," the "dangerous" and "absurd" doctrine of "liberty of conscience." In 1850, New York's pugnacious Archbishop John Hughes also promised to convert every American to Catholicism and urged Protestants who didn't like that idea to "pack up as quickly as they can and go." Paranoid as nativist fears of Catholic conspiracies were, the clash between Catholic beliefs and liberal republican ideology was real.[39]

Samuel Morse's newspaper essays and pamphlets in the mid-1830s laid out all the themes of anti-Catholic nativism up to the Civil War. Morse cited the argument of Friedrich Schlegel, the German romanticist who had converted to Catholicism and served in the Austrian cabinet, that "*Protestantism* favors *Republicanism*," whereas "*Popery*" supports "*Monarchical* power." Morse especially indicted the Jesuit St. Leopold Foundation in Vienna. Funded by the Austrian emperor but created in response to requests for aid from German Catholics in the American west, the society was in Morse's view plotting the overthrow of Protestant, republican America via its assistance to the immigration of Catholics who were unfit for citizenship.

If Morse had stopped there, he might be thought to have been purely a devotee of republican government, concerned only to exclude those whose beliefs led them to oppose it. But Morse went on to insist that "Providence" had allowed only some to be "native Americans," and that such men had by "RIGHT OF BIRTH" a "paramount claim" to civil and political rights over any foreigner who made America "*the country of his choice*," no matter "how well fitted for office, or how infallibly honest." Morse was at least as concerned to maintain the political privileges of the providentially chosen native-born as he was to confine citizenship to those willing and able to live by republican principles. A share in American governance was the "peculiar birthright" of native citizens, and, Morse added, nothing in the Declaration's proclamation of rights implied that anyone born outside the U.S. had any claim to admission into the native-born "large family, separated from all others," that comprised the American nation. He proposed that no foreigner should henceforth "*ever be allowed the right of suffrage*."[40]

Alongside Morse's pamphlets, Maria Monk published her notorious 1836 "biography," *Awful Disclosures of the Hotel Dieu Nunnery*. This classic example of anti-Catholic soft pornography was the nation's best-selling book until the publication in 1852 of Harriet Beecher Stowe's great work of romantic antislavery paternalism, *Uncle Tom's Cabin*—a fact that attests to the centrality of nativism and racism as well as the control of sexuality in antebellum American culture. Monk's lurid lies about the abuse of girls by priests and nuns were swiftly imitated in a flow of other convent "exposés" that fed American anti-Catholicism and sexual fantasies for decades to come.

Not all nativism was cast in anti-Catholic terms. The 2.5 million Irish who came to America from 1815 through 1855, especially during the Great Famine, from 1845 to 1854, continued to be denigrated by many Anglo-descended native Americans in racial as well as religious and republican language. The Irish were "savages," like "negroes, Indians, Mexicans," and indeed were sometimes called "Irish niggers." They responded with a pattern that many subsequent immigrant groups would emulate. They became great champions of white supremacy, thus claiming solidarity with white Americans and justifying exclusion of blacks from jobs the Irish were seeking to occupy. Blacks recognized the tactic, one saying that the immigrant Irish soon learned "it is popular to give Jim a whack." But it made the Irish all the more natural constituents of the proslavery, white labor Jacksonians.[41]

Though anti-Irish, Morse himself was a rabidly proslavery Jacksonian who scorned the egalitarianism of the Declaration and favored secession during the

Civil War. He unsuccessfully ran for mayor of New York on the Native American Democratic Association ticket and later for Congress, again as a Democrat. But his party affiliations were unusual: he and other anti-Irish, anti-Catholic nativists won votes largely from Whigs. Influential Whig preachers like Harriet Beecher Stowe's father, Lyman Beecher, endorsed Morse's fears that Catholic immigration, probably spurred in part by conspiracies, endangered the future of the republic. Beecher's widely read *Plea for the West* disavowed discrimination against native-born or naturalized Catholics, but it urged "immediate and energetic" governmental regulation of "the influx and the conditions of naturalization" for the "*preservation of our liberty and national prosperity.*" His words were potent indeed. Preaching in Boston in 1834, Beecher cited the Ursuline Convent in Charlestown as a Catholic institution that indoctrinated Protestant children. A mob burned it to ashes the next day.[42]

The Whigs had to decide to what extent to embrace this fevered nativism. But here, as on slavery and war issues, they were divided. From Morse's campaigns in the 1830s, through the successes in the 1840s of the American Republican or Native American party, to the spectacular rise of the Know-Nothings in the 1850s, nativist parties fared best when they had tacit or explicit Whig support. Many politicians like Millard Fillmore had feet in both camps. Yet some Whigs like Lincoln and Seward firmly rejected nativism. Lincoln repeatedly worried that Americans would soon read the Declaration as saying "all men are created equal, except negroes and foreigners and Catholics." Even many attracted to nativist parties were drawn as much by the groups' willingness to oppose slavery and urge temperance as they were by anti-immigrant proposals.[43]

Nonetheless, the depth of nativist commitments among the Know-Nothings, rival nativist groups, and many Whigs should not be minimized. They sought to lengthen the time prior to naturalization to a daunting twenty-one years, and they revived the repressive Federalist proposal to ban office-holding by the foreign-born entirely, creating another ascriptively defined lower class of citizens. Their core theme—"Americans must rule America"—was far too prominently trumpeted to be secondary to their appeal. As the Whigs crumbled in the early 1850s, that appeal was staggering. In 1854, Know-Nothing support was crucial to the election of mayors in Salem, Massachusetts, Boston, Philadelphia, and San Francisco, numerous offices in Beecher's Cincinnati, governors in Massachusetts, Pennsylvania, and Maine, nine of eleven congressmen in Indiana, eleven congressmen from New York, most of the Pennsylvania delegation, and all of the Massachusetts delegation along with all but three of more than four hundred seats in the state assembly. In all, nativists gained at least forty-eight congressional seats along with numerous other offices. Further victories in 1855 made it appear as if the Know-Nothings might soon be the nation's dominant party.[44]

The Know-Nothings were, however, no more agreed on the divisive issue of slavery than the Whigs. Even when parties within states were unified, they were often united in opposing directions: for example, antislavery in Massachusetts and proslavery in Texas. Hence the Know-Nothings had no hope of becoming a successful national party, a fact confirmed by Fillmore's failure as their presidential candidate in 1856. They quickly gave way to a group composed chiefly of Conscience Whigs and Free-Soil Democrats and explicitly devoted to opposing the expansion of slavery: the new Republican party.[45]

The Republicans' rise indicates that many Americans were not satisfied to respond to the changes and challenges of the antebellum era through heightened legal assertions of ascriptive inequalities. For diverse economic, political, and moral reasons, many voters grew increasingly receptive to further liberalizing measures, especially in the North. The reforms favored by abolitionists, women's rights champions, and supporters of Native American rights were too radical to find much expression in the two leading parties, but their agitations increasingly shaped the politics of the day. Their more egalitarian ideological blends of American political traditions, the relationship of those ideologies to the civic vision of the Lincoln Republicans, and their role in the decisive political drama of the late Jacksonian era—the conflict over slavery—will be described in the next chapter. But their rising challenges to traditional American hierarchies should be borne in mind here. They loomed as the great alternatives to the vision of America as a white man's republic that Jacksonian officials instead chose to enact.[46]

The Structure of Jacksonian Citizenship

The Jacksonians' efforts to write their view of America into citizenship laws were tireless and broad-ranging. Despite their nearly equal electoral support, the Whigs managed to modify the new civic patterns only at the margins, even with the aid of the aging Federalists on the Supreme Court. Given Jacksonian priorities, it is unsurprising that many major conflicts over civic status occurred at the state level. By the time of the Whig party's creation, its leaders had already largely lost one of the most important struggles, over universal white manhood suffrage. Those who still wished to could prevent neither its final full establishment nor the emergence of expanded racial restrictions reflecting Jacksonian, not Whig, versions of ascriptive Americanism. The Whigs had more success in shaping the other major state civic innovation of this era, the creation of Protestant-dominated public schools in the North and west. But at the national level, the Jacksonians swept the table, maintaining open immigration, curbing judicial suggestions of the primacy of national over state citizenship, and repelling claims of Native Americans, women, and African-Americans to equal political rights.[47]

The rest of this chapter sketches the pattern of citizenship rules that resulted, with the exception of the issue of African-American citizenship. The forces involved in that most polarizing question are discussed in chapter 9.

The Suffrage. The Jacksonian sense of American civic identity was fully revealed in the era's franchise laws. Though in 1828 fourteen states still had property or taxpayer requirements for voting, by 1860 only South Carolina still retained a version of the restrictions that had long built class hierarchies into American voting laws. Change came in the name of egalitarian republican conceptions of citizenship. In the 1850s, these notions so dominated that, as Chilton Williamson wrote, "it became a vote-getting issue for politicians who attacked their opponents for having been critical of or opposed to manhood suffrage at any time in their careers." Western state leaders, primarily Jacksonians, also extended their party's liberality toward immigrants by granting voting rights to aliens who had legally declared their intent to become citizens.[48] Yet once wealth restrictions that had disfranchised most free blacks and assimilated Native Americans were abandoned, Jacksonian racism made it imperative to make such ascriptive disqualifications explicit. And as women began to voice their demands for the franchise more widely, Democratic officials almost universally rejected them.[49]

Each state produced its own mix of suffrage qualifications, and little would be gained by reciting the details.[50] Congress acted only in regard to the District of Columbia, and there it proceeded slowly. Like the Jeffersonians, Jacksonians in Washington showed no great zeal to expand the political powers of local residents, though they did comply with local demands by returning the town of Alexandria and nearly one-third of the district's land to Virginia in 1846. That action restored white Alexandrians to full voting rights and, not incidentally, strengthened the power of slaveholders in the Virginia Assembly. But no one started a new campaign to give D.C. residents federal voting rights, and universal white manhood suffrage for municipal elections came only with a new district charter in 1848. By then such a franchise seemed automatic.[51]

The last great defense of the colonial era's propertied hierarchies had come in 1842, when the Rhode Island government tried to suppress Thomas Dorr's urban-centered rebellion of the disfranchised. The state was still governed under its 1663 crown charter, with high real property requirements that limited power to a "closed corporation" of wealthy gentry families. Dorr and his supporters set up a rival democratic government in what had become an industrial state with a large, unpropertied, discontented wage-labor force. The legislature declared the Dorrites' acts treasonous, but state leaders adopted a new constitution the next year that gave the vote to all native-born citizens who paid one dollar in taxes or did military service. The charter thus enacted a nativist restriction. It also allowed

African-Americans to vote, a measure that blacks pressed for and white Whigs supported, over the protests of their supposedly more democratic, but also white supremacist Jacksonian opponents.[52]

In *Luther v. Borden* (1849), Roger Taney's Supreme Court considered which of the two state constitutions and governments that resulted—the existing regime's reformed arrangements or Dorr's insurgent forces—was truly "republican" within the meaning of the Article IV, section 4 guarantee to each state of a "republican form of government." The court refused to choose. It called the issue a "political question," properly decided by the elected branches of the federal government and by the people of Rhode Island. Because by the time of the decision, Congress, the executive branch, and most Rhode Island citizens had long recognized the reformed regime that the ruling groups created in 1843, this holding underlined Dorr's defeat. Even though Rhode Island had expanded the franchise more on Whiggish than Democratic lines, the Court's opinion embodied a Jacksonian dual federalist approach. It affirmed the extensive power of elected officials, and especially the authority of each state, to define the structure of republican citizenship. Throughout the country, many applauded the Court's refusal to concede the superior republican legitimacy of the government that Dorr's people had created "out of doors." But public opinion also largely approved the broadened franchise his struggles produced. Politicians concluded that the tide had turned irresistibly in favor of universal white manhood suffrage.[53]

In reaction to the ending of all but the most easily met financial requirements and the rise of declarant alien voting in the west, nativists in Congress urged new restrictions on the franchise, including a proposal first introduced in 1844 that the vote not be granted until two years after naturalization. That idea ignored traditional state prerogatives to define voting qualifications; but, simultaneously, many nativists complained that state conferrals of the right to vote on aliens violated the Constitution's assignment of naturalization to Congress. They made no headway at the federal level. After the Know-Nothings' victories in 1855, however, Connecticut added an English literacy test designed to eliminate foreign-born voters. Massachusetts Republicans and Know-Nothings adopted a similar measure in 1857. Two years later the state added the previously proposed voting requirement of two years' residence after naturalization. Nationally, however, it still became easier, not harder, for white immigrants to gain the franchise during these years.[54]

The abandonment of virtually all real property and taxpaying qualifications led even Jacksonian-dominated states to make explicit various other exclusions that those requirements formerly achieved. Some rules reflected desires to protect state autonomy against outsiders. Residency requirements, normally for one

year, became almost universal. Fourteen states also explicitly banned some combination of the insane, idiots, and persons under guardianship as incompetent
to vote, even if white and male. Fifteen excluded paupers and inmates of public
institutions, generally including almshouses and poor farms as well as mental
asylums and penitentiaries. Those provisions restored an element of class hierarchy to voting privileges, but only the most severely impoverished were disfranchised. Nineteen states permanently disfranchised those convicted of various crimes, including "penitentiary offenses," bribery, perjury, forgery, larceny,
and dueling. Though these laws made no ethnic distinctions, many of their most
vocal proponents were nativists who thought that immigrants were so dispro-
portionate a percentage of the poor, insane, and criminal that these "neutral" exclusions would suffice to remove them from the rolls. Though the Irish and German immigrants who came driven by hunger did provide many of America's
poor and imprisoned, these measures still did not produce massive immigrant
disfranchisement.[55]

The only successful new exclusionary efforts were the ones Jacksonians supported, aimed at denying the vote to free blacks, mulattos, and often Native Americans. As new states were formed and the older states held constitutional conventions during these years, the status of these groups was hotly contested, with
the champions of racial minorities almost always losing. None of the new western states granted blacks the vote, and often even assimilated Native Americans
were disfranchised as nonwhites (though Minnesota banned only "uncivilized
Indians"). Oregon added Chinese immigrants to the list of the racially excluded.
Tennessee formally took the franchise away from propertied free blacks in 1834,
North Carolina did so in 1835, and Pennsylvania in 1838. New Yorkers repeat
edly defeated referenda that would have lessened the prohibitive property requirements that black voters had to meet, although they also refused to abolish
black voting completely. By the Civil War, blacks had some form of franchise in
only six states (Maine, Vermont, New Hampshire, Massachusetts, Rhode Island,
and, formally, New York). The low number of eligible blacks, combined with social pressures, still prevented them from being a major political presence even in
these areas.[56]

Like citizenship laws generally, this pattern of enfranchising alien whites and
disfranchising native free blacks and Indians was a symptom, but also a cause, of
the racially articulated views of American identity that American public law increasingly expressed and legitimated during this period. If property restrictions
on the vote could somehow have survived, the Whigs would have fared better. If
free blacks and assimilated Native Americans had voted, and if tribal Native
Americans had been recognized as having true rights of self-government, many
other civic policies that were hostile toward them would have been harder to

achieve. As it was, voting laws made it clear that the Americans who "merited" political power were white men.

Civic Education. The voting developments made past realities only more official, however. In contrast, the era's great departure from earlier patterns of citizenship laws was the firm establishment in the North and midwest of one key institution long advocated by many American republican theorists and political leaders of various stripes. Public elementary schools proliferated rapidly after decades of popular resistance. By 1850, 50.4 percent of American whites between the ages of five and nineteen were enrolled in schools. That level placed the U.S. among the world's leaders in ratio of students to the total population. The chief contributor to expanding school attendance was the spread after 1830 of "common schools" supported by public taxation.[57] Congress again followed rather than led these changes. It approved a provision in the 1848 District of Columbia charter that provided a one-dollar poll tax for school support, thereby enabling the city to operate tuition-free schools for white children, male and female. Before this tax, blacks attended private segregated schools in greater percentages than whites attended the public schools. Even with the tax, white enrollments in D.C. schools lagged far behind most Northern cities, for the capital reflected the South's resistance to publicly provided education.[58] Nonetheless, the new schools elsewhere set a pattern that would become thoroughly entrenched in America through the late twentieth century.

Common schools could not have grown so rapidly without support from both Democrats and Whigs. But they were always politically controversial, and today scholars are equally divided over their causes and aims. Public education was defended in terms of Enlightenment goals of elevating human minds and Protestant desires for biblical literacy, but those aspirations had always been present in America and cannot alone account for the spread of common schools at this time. Structural changes in the nation's territory, transportation systems, and economy strengthened the case for public schooling. A self-sufficient Jeffersonian yeoman farmer might manage without reading or arithmetical skills, but Jacksonian commercial farmers, who purchased and sold goods via written agreements and the exchange of money and sometimes traveled to distant markets, could not. The greater availability of news, journals, and books further enhanced the attractions of literacy. But the often impassioned politics of education involved more than such predictable responses to altered structural conditions.[59]

Many scholars attribute to the school reformers the more political purposes of buttressing class, cultural, and religious hierarchies, with good reason.[60] Employers wanted urban laborers and factory workers to be properly socialized, if not enlightened, by the schools. Middle-class Protestants thought that the country was being threatened by the lower-class Catholics, who needed to be taught "American" values. Yet rhetorically, the central theme of a wide variety of public school defenders remained the same in these and many years to come. Public education was to be republican civic education.

As Jefferson and Rush had unsuccessfully argued, public schools were required to endow citizens with the qualities required to participate well in republican institutions. In 1862, the superintendent of public instruction in Illinois summarized the winning case for public schools by stressing that "The chief end is to make GOOD CITIZENS. Not to make precocious scholars . . . not to impart the secret of acquiring wealth . . . not to qualify directly for professional success . . . but simply to make good citizens." Horace Mann, the nation's preeminent educational reformer, expressed the harsh side of this argument, warning that if America's "republican institutions" did not "confer upon that people unexampled wisdom and rectitude" along with powers of self-governance, "we shall perish." Immigrant children especially had to be "liberalized, Americanized" into "intelligent, virtuous, patriotic American citizens," as a Boston School Committee member said.[61]

Though the language of preparation for republican citizenship remained central to defenses of public schools throughout the era, the subtexts of that rhetoric, and its chief promulgators, shifted dramatically. At first, public education was promoted most strenuously by Democratic labor spokesmen, who resented the special economic and political opportunities that privately educated elites enjoyed. They assailed those privileges as similar to special corporate charters: they were "aristocratic" supports for artificial inequalities, inconsistent with republican ideals. From the late 1820s through the mid-1830s, Jacksonian leaders of workingmen's associations, including Stephen Simpson in Pennsylvania and Frederick Robinson in Massachusetts, railed against resistance to common schools. Robinson proclaimed equal public education "the first, the great reform" needed to achieve "our emancipation from the power of aristocracy."[62]

But circumstances changed. After the Panic of 1837 brought hard times, bread-and-butter economic issues came to preoccupy the labor movement, which also fell prey to factious disputes. Many poorer workers viewed school attendance as a needless financial burden on their families. Although organized labor, which largely represented better-paid skilled workers, never opposed public education, it often ceased to be its prime supporter. Leadership of the cause passed instead to middle- and upper-middle-class reformers, whose heavy reliance on the rhetoric of republican citizenship partly shielded inegalitarian and narrowly assimilative aims.[63]

Carl Kaestle notes that most of these middle-class reformers, like Mann and Connecticut's Henry Barnard, were "native-born Anglo-American Protestants," usually Whigs. They shared patriotic beliefs in the superior worth of American institutions and peoples, but also anxieties about the erosion of harmony and morality that urbanization and immigration might bring. For them, "republican" education meant chiefly moral education with specific religious and political content. They wished not so much to provide economic and political opportunities for all as to ensure that children learned habits and values that would lead them to use those opportunities in the ways that higher-class Protestants thought wise. They believed that public schools could shape all those capable of proper character development—which generally did not include nonwhites—into believers in industry, thrift, property rights, law-abidingness, familial duties, and suitable religious tenets. This education would provide a common background that might help "obliterate factious distinctions in society," Mann promised, without any catastrophic social leveling or erosion of middle-class Protestant standards.

Most upper-class public school advocates thought that such moral perspectives required daily reference to the Protestant Bible in all classrooms. Most working-class school supporters instead favored keeping religion out of them, and many strongly opposed requiring the King James Bible.[64] School reformers also called for more centralized town and state administrative systems, thereby challenging longstanding Democratic commitments to local control. Some Democrats protested what they called a "Prussian" system of centralized schooling to the point of opposing public schools altogether.

Southerners also charged that public school teachers were instruments to forge a uniform national culture resting on hostile "Northern" values, which indeed they often were. Hence, except in North Carolina, Southern elites attended private academies rather than common schools, and most Southerners received only spotty education from itinerant teachers. Catholics and even some of the less conventional Protestant sects, finding public school religious training either hostile or insufficient, created their own parochial schools. For a time, New York's Catholics, who had obtained city funds like other denominational schools prior to the establishment of the state school system, fought fiercely against their subsequent exclusion and the proliferation of a Protestant public curriculum. They obtained the endorsement of the antinativist Governor Seward, and the Maclay Act of 1842 created decentralized district boards of education that gave Catholic neighborhoods more control over their schools. But the act was met by bloody riots; and increasingly New York's Catholics decided to build their own parochial schools with their own funds. That decision was abetted by the yet more severe Philadelphia Bible riots in 1844, when thirty died and hundreds were wounded as Protestants and Catholics battled over the version of the scriptures that would be used in public schools. In the same state, however, German Protestants who wanted schools that taught their brand of Lutheranism in their native language continued to operate about one hundred of their own institutions through 1850, despite the inroads of the public school crusade. Their counterparts in Wisconsin also managed to maintain instruction in German within the public system, but bilingualism was ended in law, though not in practice, in 1852, as arguments for assimilative education gained power.[65]

If Catholics were fenced out by school reformers, women received perhaps too much attention. The educators' native Protestant ideology embraced and elaborated the notion that women properly belonged to a "domestic sphere" —so that although they needed rudimentary education in common elementary schools, their further instruction was to be directed toward domestic skills, such as household management. Male reformers like Horace Mann were joined by many female educators in endorsing this view. The most prominent was Lyman Beecher's elder daughter, Catharine, founder of home economics both in her *Treatise on Domestic Economy* (1841) and in her Hartford Female Seminary. She contended that, compared to domestic training, the "intellectual culture" of girls should "be made altogether secondary in importance." Mann and Beecher also stressed, however, that special traits of women made them ideal as elementary school teachers in the few years between the end of their own schooling and marriage. Those traits included a maternal image that was soothing to young children and a willingness to accept low wages. Hence the feminization of teaching began.[66]

The story of education for blacks and Native Americans during these years is grim but not a void. In the 1830s Louisiana, Georgia, Virginia, Alabama, and the Carolinas responded to slave unrest and the rise of abolitionism by making it illegal to teach slaves to read. Free blacks, in the North and South, had only somewhat greater educational opportunities. Nonetheless, African-American churches and schools continued to teach Southern blacks secretly; even some slaves became literate (about 5 percent, according to W. E. B. Du Bois).[67] Literacy rates were higher among free blacks, reaching 80 percent among the relatively well-off free blacks of New Orleans, who were excluded from white public schools but established a private system of their own that survived until more repressive laws were passed in the 1850s.

In the northeast, black churches and white religious groups, abolitionists, and philanthropists established charity schools for free black children. Most of these were eventually absorbed by the new public school systems and operated as underfunded, segregated institutions when they were not abolished. But the fight that blacks and some whites waged against this discrimination was far from a complete failure. Indeed, in 1855 the Massachusetts legislature mandated integrated public education (over the opposition of the Boston School Committee). Some colleges in the northeast and midwest also accepted blacks.[68] Truly equal education was, however, something whites were unprepared to accept, much less promote. As blacks' voting rights were of little potency in northeastern politics and nonexistent elsewhere, the arguments defending education for republican citizenship could be held largely irrelevant to them. Thus most public school advocates paid little attention to blacks' needs.

Education did play a significant if fluctuating role in governmental policies toward Native Americans. With removal substantially completed in the late Jacksonian era, reformers lobbied for new aid to missionary societies to run schools offering literacy and religious and vocational training on the new reservations. The tribes, however, often resisted these efforts as culturally imperialistic, and they were not massive. Even so, by 1848 there were sixteen manual labor schools and more than fifty other schools educating some 2,700 students.[69]

Thomas Jefferson and the early Jacksonians would probably have viewed the extensive common schooling in America at the end of the 1850s as a victory for democratic republican ideas of equal opportunities for all. Yet Carl Kaestle is right to argue that the ideology of the more elite reformers who won the movement's chief victories centered on the three values of Protestantism, republicanism, and capitalism—a nice formula for the blend of ascriptive, republican, and liberal elements that typified Whig civic ideology.[70] The fact that this is the only significant area in which new citizenship laws and institutions were tilted more in a Whig than a Jacksonian direction may well suggest that the revisionist historians have been right to say that civic education was structured to socialize workers into the ways of the factory and wage labor market systems, institutions that both Jacksonian and Whig leaders generally supported. The overall impact of the schools was genuinely to expand educational opportunities for whites, in line with Jacksonian aims, but the schools also embodied hierarchical structures of opportunities that sent a message of America's meaning embodying the ascriptive views of Whigs and Jacksonians alike.

Dual Federalist Citizenship Rights and the Emergent Corporation. Although voting and public schools were state-level policies that structured national citizenship in ways too basic to ignore, they were not deeply affected by U.S. citizenship statutes and judicial rulings. At the federal level, the Jacksonian story was one of minimizing the importance of national as opposed to state citizenship, along with yet more explicit recognition of gender and racial restrictions on full civic membership. The federal courts played a large role in these developments, especially in regard to Bill of Rights protections, Article IV civic privileges and immunities, and their own jurisdiction under the Article III diversity of citizenship clause. Once Roger Taney became Chief Justice, they did so in ways that chiefly expressed Jacksonian values.

Indeed, in *Barron v. Baltimore* (1833), even John Marshall rejected the notion that at least some provisions of the Bill of Rights might be enforceable against the states as rights of national citizenship. The claim was admittedly audacious, yet the context was unusually auspicious. The City of Baltimore had diverted some streams while constructing streets, thereby dumping so much mud at Barron's wharf that it became unusable. Barron claimed that his property had been taken for public use without compensation, in violation of the Fifth Amendment. The Amendment's protection of private property against governmental takings was dear to Marshall's heart.[71] Its provisions also do not specify which levels of government are required to provide "just compensation." Nor was it unthinkable to find it applicable to the states: a Jacksonian appointee to the Court, Henry Baldwin of Pennsylvania, had not long before suggested that the guarantee was so essential to legitimate government that it might be enforceable versus state actions even if the Constitution did not explicitly say so.[72]

Marshall's opinion nonetheless appealed to the "history of the day" to rule that all the Amendments in the Bill of Rights were meant to restrict only the federal government. Thus no federal right had been violated, and the Court lacked jurisdiction.[73] Marshall might have said that it was equally part of the Constitution's history that the national government was created to check state violations of at least some economic rights. The broader political climate of the time, however, must have worked against any temptation he felt to read the Bill of Rights so broadly. The decision came on the heels of the nullification crisis, and the justices may have feared that an activist decision would give ammunition to the opponents of the national government when the President had just stood up for national authority. Furthermore, Jackson's reaction to the decision earlier that year opposing Cherokee removal (*Worcester v. Georgia*) showed that executive enforcement of strongly antistate decisions was unlikely. The issue of the applicability of the Bill of Rights to the states would not be seriously reconsidered until after the Civil War.[74]

It was still possible, however, to interpret the Article IV privileges and immunities clause as a shield for rights of national citizenship, and the Court had many chances to do so. Free blacks often complained that their privileges and immunities were violated by discriminatory state legislation. Precisely for that reason, however, federal courts had long shied away from potentially incendiary "P and I" claims, even in nonracial contexts. Most adjudication of those claims remained at the state level. The Supreme Court said virtually nothing, and lower federal courts provided no clear pattern in defining the clause beyond ritual invocations of the opaque holding in *Corfield v. Coryell*.[75] The result was that the privileges and immunities clause's meaning remained as undeveloped as during the Jeffersonian years.

In general, the same pattern prevailed in Jacksonian decisions governing access to federal courts under the Article III diversity of citizenship clause.[76] In some respects, the Taney Court made access to the federal judiciary easier than the Marshall Court had done.[77] It was more willing to infer different state citizenships without direct averments by litigants. But once it found jurisdiction, the Taney Court often deferred on the merits to state laws and precedents. That mix of assertiveness and restraint was typical of its dual federalism, designed to give states great leeway while reserving federal power over matters crucial to Jacksonians.[78]

Yet in one vital regard, the Supreme Court under Taney defined diversity of citizenship access in a way that went beyond the Marshall rulings, underlining the great if conflicted receptivity of Jacksonians to the expanding capitalist economy.[79] Over impassioned dissents from some Southerners, the Court upheld the claims of those increasingly potent economic and political entities—limited liability corporations—to sue in federal courts as quasi-state citizens. Though some businesses regarded this development as a mixed blessing, most knew that such federal access significantly limited their vulnerability to hostile state laws.

And in the Jacksonian era particularly, corporations needed that protection. The years from 1830 to 1860 formed the heart of a major transformation in the nation's economic and legal systems: efforts to launch private business corporations, which had still been relatively novel in 1800, grew by the tens of thousands. Corporations thus became the main engines of American economic and often political life by the late nineteenth century. State and federal lawmakers struggled to define suitable doctrines to create and regulate these entities, producing rapidly changing rules; for many Jacksonian leaders, this explosive increase in corporate businesses was hard to resist, yet hard to swallow. On the one hand, the corporate form was proving enormously useful for efficient, centralized management and for attracting new investors, especially when corporations received grants of limited liability. On the other, those grants amounted to favors to the rich that sometimes fostered exploitative monopolies—exactly what Jacksonians most feared and despised. Hence, as Lawrence Friedman has argued, "no issue was more persistent" in these years than "the issue of public control over corporations."[80]

For some purists like Democratic lawyer Theodore Sedgwick, Jr., in 1835, the matter was simple. To any mind cast in a "republican mold," every corporate grant was "directly in the teeth of the doctrine of equal rights, for it gives to one set of men the exercise of powers which the main body can never enjoy." In the *New York Evening Post*, Jacksonian editor William Leggett was more pungent: the corporate owner was a "chartered libertine that pretends to be manacled only that he more safely pick our pockets and lord it over our rights." Most Jacksonians, however, took the more moderate position of David Henshaw: except for banks and other money-traders, business corporations were "generally beneficial" if "judiciously granted and suitably regulated." They were, after all, driving desirable technological innovations and economic growth. The proper tack was to encourage them, but to make their privileges less "special," according to Henshaw, via the passage of general incorporation laws. These acts made standardized incorporations routine and widely available by the 1880s.[81]

But as legislators wrestled their way to that position, fierce courtroom battles over corporate powers boiled through a long series of cases. The issue of access to the federal courts for state-chartered corporations under the diversity clause was particularly contentious, because all knew that with such access, federal judges would sometimes overrule state legislatures' efforts to regulate their own creations. Still, if the upshot was to aid the good work of Henshaw's "generally beneficial" corporations, many Jacksonian judges favored federal jurisdiction.

A large problem loomed, however. Diversity jurisdiction extended only to citizens. Granting federal access thus seemed to require courts to treat corporations themselves, and not their members, as bearers of Article III "citizenship." Many Jacksonians remained shocked at the notion that those tools of wealthy elites might be legally recognized as citizens. Would business corporations acquire legal standing equal to that of the common man, to go along with economic resources that vastly exceeded his?[82]

Despite those anxieties, the Taney Court sided with the corporations.[83] In 1844, Justice James Wayne, a Georgia Democrat but a corporate enthusiast, wrote the key decision, *Louisville Railroad Co. v. Letson*.[84] The case was politically propitious because here jurisdiction worked against the corporation. The South Carolina-chartered Louisville Railroad appealed a decision in favor of Thomas Letson, a New York citizen who had sued it for breach of a contract relating to road construction. The company claimed that the federal courts lacked jurisdiction because its stockholders were not all citizens of any one state to which it could be assigned citizenship, as *Strawbridge v. Curtiss* and *Bank of U.S. v. Deveaux* seemed to require. Wayne said that those precedents were being taken "too far." A corporation "created by a state and only suable there, though it may have members out of the state, seems to us to be a person, though an artificial one, inhabiting and belonging to that state, and therefore entitled, for the purpose of suing and being sued, to be deemed a citizen of that state," quite "as much as a natural person."[85] Perhaps because here federal jurisdiction hurt the corporation's interests, there were no dissents (though an ill Taney did not participate). Corporate citizenship thus seemed firmly established, at least for jurisdictional purposes.[86]

The apparent consensus in *Letson* did not long endure. In *Rundle v. Delaware and Raritan Canal Co.* (1852), Justices John Catron and Peter Daniel dissented sharply when the Court took jurisdiction. Catron, a Tennessee Democrat, insisted that he had concurred in *Letson* only because he thought that the citizenship of a corporation's officers—its president and directors—and not its "constantly changing stockholders" should be decisive for jurisdictional purposes. The officers must, he maintained, all possess citizenship in the state where the corporation was chartered and sued, as the Louisville Railroad's officers had. Justice Daniel, a Van Buren appointee from Virginia, took the more extreme view that a citizen must be "a natural person," possessing "social and political rights, and sustaining, social, political, and moral obligations," not a "mere creature of the mind" like a corporation. He attacked *Letson* head on, arguing that if a corporation were a citizen for one purpose, it must be a citizen for all purposes; it must even be eligible to be President of the United States! Daniel maintained that there was no place under the Constitution for "quasi" citizens such as *Letson* created.[87]

Most politicians were too attracted by what corporations had to offer, generally or personally, to support Catron and Daniel. The dissenters did not relent, however.[88] Their passionate protests persuaded their brethren to concede in *Marshall v. Baltimore and Ohio Railroad Co.* (1853) that it was "metaphysically true in a certain sense" that corporations could not be citizens. The Court then ruled, however, that henceforth all of a corporation's members would simply be presumed as a matter of law to be citizens of the state where it had its "necessary habitat." Thus de facto corporate citizenship and federal diversity jurisdiction over many corporate cases were preserved. Daniel fumed that this "vortex of federal incroachment" was placing "the people of the States and their governments under an habitual subserviency to federal power."[89]

Daniels believed that his fears were confirmed when the Court ignored the shades of the Monster Bank and instead sided with the spirit of Dodge and Bragg in *Dodge v. Woolsey* (1855). In the first Supreme Court case involving a stockholder's challenge to his own corporation, John Woolsey of Connecticut sued tax collector George Dodge and the Commercial Branch Bank of Cleveland, Ohio, in which Woolsey held thirty shares. Dodge and the bank had paid a state tax that Woolsey thought to be in violation of the bank's state charter, and therefore void under the Constitution's contract clause. The bank officers agreed, but they doubted that the Ohio courts would. Hence Woolsey sued his own bank to get them all into a friendly federal court under diversity jurisdiction.

Justice Wayne rewarded their efforts by upholding federal jurisdiction and the bank's contract clause claim against the state tax. He expounded at length on how the Constitution was supreme over the states, and how federal diversity jurisdiction was essential to "make the people think and feel" that their interests "were protected by the strictest justice, administered in courts independent of all local control or connected with the subject-matter" of disputes involving state laws.[90] When corporate interests were at stake, the Taney Court could thus sound surprisingly like John Marshall defending the Bank of the United States. Appalled by those echoes, recently appointed Justice John Campbell of Alabama raged against all such aid to the powerful and often "evil" corporate "caste"; but to no avail.[91]

Though driven by Southern fears of the great corporate motors of the northern free labor economy, and of federal assistance to that economic system over slavery, the arguments of Campbell, Catron, and Daniels did expose what proved to be real problems in corporate diversity citizenship. As corporations became increasingly multistate entities, their "habitats" became unclear, and their opportunities for manipulative legal forum-shopping grew. Most of the justices thought that these dangers were outweighed by the promise of economic expansion and perhaps by their own desires to preserve judicial power to decide major issues. In any case, corporations might have come to dominate the nation's economy, gaining massive political influence as they did during the mid-nineteenth century, without this diversity citizenship. Nonetheless, this legal assistance facilitated their spread. Hence, even as Jacksonian courts minimized national citizenship generally and tightened so many ascriptive restrictions on full citizenship, they contrived legal fictions to bestow a valuable form of national citizenship on that "artificial being," the corporation.[92]

Immigration and Naturalization. Unlike these important but somewhat obscure battles over corporate citizenship, struggles over immigration and naturalization were dramatically visible features of the Jacksonian era. Time and time again, the Democrats succeeded at the national level in stemming nativist tides and maintaining the open immigration and easy naturalization policies that produced so many Jacksonian voters. Indeed, Democrats rolled out new welcome mats whenever they could. In 1834, Congress established a precedent for generosity toward refugees by granting land in Illinois and Michigan to Polish exiles at low prices. In 1847, 1848, and 1849 under James K. Polk and in 1855 under James Buchanan, Congress passed new acts to improve unhealthy conditions for Atlantic and Pacific ship passengers (although these laws were rarely enforced for Chinese labor transports).[93] Democratic legislators also repelled all efforts to extend the time of residency prior to naturalization, and the courts routinized naturalization doctrines in ways that sheltered naturalizations from legal challenges.[94]

Yet as immigration swelled and nativist parties gained popularity, sustaining generous policies became harder. Congressmen began expressing concern about foreign governments sending convicts and paupers to the U.S.; although they conducted immigration investigations and urged diplomatic protests, no formal congressional actions ensued. Efforts at regulation had more power in the north-eastern seedbeds of nativism. Since colonial times, the states of New York and Massachusetts, whose ports received the most immigrants, had required ship captains to report new arrivals and to supply bonds for any who might become public charges. Those regulations were elaborated and strengthened as immigration increased fivefold during the Jacksonian years, with over two-thirds of the more than 2.8 million that arrived during the 1850s landing at the port of New York. But like the new voting restrictions in many states—indeed, like the literacy test adopted in Massachusetts and Connecticut—the registration and bonding statutes were officially aimed at problems posed by paupers, lunatics, the diseased, criminals, and other classes widely thought undesirable, not at foreigners per se. Many who supported such laws did so more out of concern for the public treasury and health than nativist motives. In New York, even many supporters of immigration viewed a state tax to provide medical services for newcomers as an aid, not a liability.

But the new requirements accompanied rising nativist agitation, and politicians openly allied with nativists always championed these measures most vociferously. In California and Texas during the 1850s, moreover, bipartisan coalitions of Anglo-Americans joined in passing laws that were openly hostile to Mexican and Chinese immigrants, restricting job opportunities and imposing special taxes. California required three dollars a month from every foreign miner who was not seeking citizenship, knowing full well that the Chinese were racially ineligible to do so. In the late 1850s and early 1860s, the state also taxed ship owners who imported Chinese immigrants, then tried to ban such immigration explicitly, and then imposed a Chinese Police Tax to make immigrant labor uneconomical. In light of the *Passenger Cases* of 1849, however (in which the Supreme Court produced eight opinions and a 5–4 vote that overturned state taxes on immigrants but established no clear doctrine), the state supreme court invalidated all of those laws.[95]

Because nativists tried to discourage immigration and to regulate the voting rights of naturalized citizens at both the state and national levels, they reopened profoundly divisive questions of whether the states or the federal government had ultimate authority over who could claim state and national citizenship rights. The Jacksonian-dominated Supreme Court found those questions hard to answer. As the state laws discouraged immigration, Jacksonians could be expected to oppose them, and ultimately the Taney Court did. But many Democrats, including Taney himself, wanted to uphold the states' authority over citizenship and migration across their borders in order to preserve their control over free blacks and slaves. Hence the new state immigration acts splintered the Court and weakened Taney's own authority.

On the merits Taney rarely wavered. Keeping state prerogatives to ban free blacks centrally in view, he always upheld state immigration laws. He also carried the court with him in the first major immigration case, *Mayor of New York v. Miln*, in his initial 1837 term.[96] But Taney lost his majority and all semblance of judicial unity in the *Passenger Cases* of 1849.[97]

In *Miln*, the court reviewed New York's 1824 law requiring captains to report on their passengers to help identify paupers. Virtually all the litigants' and justices' discussion focused on commerce power issues. But given existing federal laws governing slave importations and fugitive slaves, state laws that demanded bonds from entering free blacks or banned them outright, and Justice Johnson's 1823 opinion striking down South Carolina's black seamen law on commerce power grounds, questions of slavery and the movement of free blacks loomed large in the background. Writing for the Court, Virginian Justice Philip Barbour upheld state authority by denying that the act was a regulation of commerce at all.[98] He saw it as an exercise of the state's "police power," its broad authority to provide for the health, safety, welfare and morals of its people. This argument typified the Jacksonian jurists' efforts to give the ill-defined doctrine of state police powers new prominence, thereby defending state sovereignty. Barbour also provided a device to limit federal regulation of free black travelers by asserting that passengers were not articles of commerce. Taney concurred happily with this use of state-centered republicanism to uphold state powers over immigrants and, implicitly, out-of-state free blacks as well.[99]

But from the standpoint of Jacksonian politics, the anti-immigrant *Miln* result was anomalous. It did not survive the bitterly debated *Passenger Cases*. They considered the New York law that taxed passengers from foreign ports in order to finance a marine hospital and a Massachusetts law that required a fee of all alien passengers except lunatic, indigent, or infirm persons, for whom a $1,000 bond had to be supplied. Of the five justices who found the laws unconstitutional, all relied on preemptive federal powers over commerce, but three also gave some explicit attention to citizenship issues.[100] More by fiat than argument, Justice Wayne, the friend of corporations and commerce, here reassured his fellow Southerners that state powers to prevent the entry of slaves and free blacks were not impugned by striking down these anticommercial laws.[101] Ironically, the anticorporate, antiblack Justice Catron reached the same result by eloquently invoking the receptivity to poor immigrants, at least "all free white persons," embodied in federal laws and expressive of "the spirit of the Declaration of Independence." He found these state actions repugnant to those traditions. Justice John McKinley of Kentucky was yet more nationalistic. He argued that the mention of "migration" as well as "Importation" in the "slave trade" clause of Article 1, section 9 meant that Congress had preemptive authority over both immigration and commerce in slaves.[102] Together the opinions expressed Jacksonian approval of liberal national immigration policies, even at the expense of state authority; but most of the justices explicitly excepted blacks from this endorsement of civic openness.

Taney dissented harshly.[103] He insisted that state sovereignty must include the ability to expel "objectionable persons," and he thought that the states' concerns about aliens swelling the public rolls of paupers, patients, and prisoners were well-founded. If they could expel such persons, moreover, they could stop them from entering. Taney read Congress's Article I power over migration and importation of persons as applying only to the slave trade. He also argued that naturalization powers had to be exclusively national (to prevent one state from naturalizing persons unacceptable to other states, including, no doubt, free blacks). Permission to enter, in contrast, could and should be shared by both levels of government.[104] Thus for Taney, "dual federalism" included federal acquiescence in state membership restrictions, even those favored by nativist Whigs. Taney lost, and subsequently states generally confined themselves to obtaining information from immigrants. Yet the fact that these anti-immigrant measures almost survived at the hands of this wholly Democratic bench shows how nativism and racism fomented divisions in Jacksonian ranks.

Birthright Citizenship and Expatriation. Like their Jeffersonian predecessors, American authorities during the Jacksonian era often gave rhetorical support to wholly consensual conceptions of citizenship while finding it politically difficult to challenge birthright citizenship or define expatriation rights too broadly. The Democrats' solicitude for their immigrant supporters led some Jacksonians, James Buchanan in particular, to insist with new vigor that naturalization extinguished all obligations to the country of a person's birth. In contrast, the traditionalist organicism of Whigs like Daniel Webster argued for continued adherence to Blackstone's common-law rule that birthright memberships and obligations could be modified only by the mutual consent of subjects and sovereigns. Hence, whenever a naturalized citizen returned to his native land, he was still subject to its government.[105] Few Americans approved that policy, but it made for pacific diplomacy with Britain. And faced with more serious challenges from anti-immigrant legislators, the Democrats gave low priority to fighting the more "feudal" rules of birthright membership that courts still often followed.

In the late Marshall years, Justice Story made the most relevant of the Supreme Court's few statements on these issues. He gave more weight to the common-law view of membership than to consensual positions, but he avoided reaching any politically unpopular conclusions. In two 1830 cases, *Inglis v. Trustees of Sailor's Snug Harbor* and *Shanks v. DuPont,* the Court considered whether dependents who had left the U.S. during the revolutionary era could assert all the property rights of U.S. citizens.[106] Inglis was born in New York not long before his loyalist father moved to Nova Scotia rather than accept the new state government. Mrs. Shanks was a South Carolina native who had married a British officer and moved to England in 1782. In each case the justices unanimously held that common-law doctrines of membership ordinarily applied in America. The majority reasserted, however, that the U.S. and Britain had agreed in the Treaty of 1783 to recognize the Revolution as a special "period of election," and both Inglis and Shanks were held to have chosen British subjectship. Thus, despite the Court's rhetorical endorsements of more ascriptive common-law doctrines of membership, no one was prevented from choosing a nationality, nor did the Court uphold any unpopular claims to property by British loyalists.[107]

Even this mild concession to consensualism was too much for the nationalistic Justice Johnson, who dissented in both cases. He complained that the Court "gave too much weight to natural law and the suggestions of reason and justice" instead of "the principles of political and positive law." Talk of a "social compact" and inalienable rights to change membership was but "a popular and flattering theory." In fact the common law governed. It left no room for a "period of election."[108] Though the majority disagreed with that point, no one disputed the primacy of common-law notions of political membership providing only attenuated expatriation rights.

The Taney Court made no definitive statement on expatriation, but it upheld a similar period of election in applying the Treaty of Guadalupe Hidalgo. Article VIII gave Mexican citizens in ceded territories one year to reject U.S. citizenship publicly; otherwise, they were deemed to have elected it. The article also guaranteed their property rights whatever their choice.[109] Lower federal courts interpreted the treaty as providing only another narrow exception to general common-law rules defining membership largely in ascriptive terms. One circuit judge held, for example, that Mexico had no power to set the terms for electing nationality in the case of a native-born Englishman who had been naturalized into Mexican citizenship. As his land of "natural allegiance," England still had more authority over him than the government to which he owed "mere voluntary or statutory allegiance."[110]

Some state courts agreed with this emphasis on the common law's naturalism, but others still viewed the Revolution as expressing a commitment to consensual conceptions, especially to a right of expatriation.[111] The pattern of state decisions probably correlates with the judges' adherence to Democratic and Whig outlooks on citizenship generally rather than any particular political interests at stake in most cases, which were usually minor and often ambiguous.[112] In any event, questions about birthright obligations and rights of expatriation still lacked definitive legal answers, though most judges leaned toward more conservative common-law doctrines.[113]

Buchanan, however, made the opposing position a personal trademark. While he was Secretary of State in 1848, Britain claimed authority over returning Irish-born persons who were naturalized U.S. citizens. Buchanan then won the hearts of Irish immigrants by his sharp instructions to the American minister in London. U.S. policy, he wrote, was to "resist the British doctrine of perpetual allegiance, and maintain the American principle that British native-born subjects, after they have been naturalized under our laws, are . . . as much American citizens, and entitled to the same degree of protection, as though they had been born in the United States." As President, Buchanan and his Attorney General, Jeremiah Black, again attacked British conscription of a returning native who had become a naturalized U.S. citizen, saying that expatriation was "a natural right of every free man" which in no way depended on "the consent of the natural sovereign." These stances contrasted with the tendency of Whig Secretaries of State to imitate Webster, defer to British feelings, and recognize duties of returning naturalized citizens to their original governments.[114]

Black's predecessor as Attorney General, Caleb Cushing, confirmed in 1856 that Democrats had another reason for rejecting common-law views of birthright citizenship. They did not wish to accept that blacks or Native Americans "born in the United States" were citizens.[115] As in the Missouri Compromise debates, here the Jacksonians' consensualist posture served racially exclusionary purposes, even as it allowed them to champion the cause of immigrants. They did not, however, press these issues so far as to challenge in any major way the continuing hold of common-law membership doctrines on most American judges.

Rights of Women. In regard to women, the relatively placid surface of Jacksonian citizenship laws concealed turbulence below. The face of the law showed minor changes that fit well with general Jacksonian treatments of civic identity. Women acquired some additional economic rights that assisted the elaboration of both free market and slave economies; but the few explicit changes made in their civic status brought them even more in line with the limiting doctrines of republican motherhood, buttressed now by stronger biologically based claims for the propriety of their political subordination. Though few judges or major party politicians disputed that status, profound challenges arose from the growing numbers of participants in the nation's first significant women's movement, headed by Elizabeth Cady Stanton, Susan B. Anthony, and others. The more radical reformers had less success, however, than spokeswomen for improving the condition of women in ways more consistent with traditional domestic and political roles, like Catharine Beecher. The arguments between these female leaders defined issues that have since persisted in American life.

In their views, these women, as with American men, blended Enlightenment liberal, republican, religious, and cultural, and biologistic ascriptive themes in different combinations. Among the more radical female activists, the egalitarian, individual rights-oriented rhetoric of the Declaration of Independence was most prominent, along with unconventional but impassioned religious sentiments. In many respects, the leading female reformers of the antebellum years worked out what they called the "liberal principles of republicanism" and human rights more consistently than Locke or any early American had done.[116] They did so largely because the Christian and liberal languages of equal human rights, however limited the scope of those rights and however qualified by implicit commitments to existing social forms, were nonetheless natural vehicles for their protests. For most Americans, they touched what Lincoln would call "mystic chords of memory" of the Puritan founding and the revolutionary cause. They also stated ideals that many believed to be both especially central to America and supported by God, nature, and reason. Many recognized that, despite their narrow historical applications, these principles were often stated in universal terms that could be used to claim rights for virtually all oppressed groups. It was only necessary to discredit the arguments used to justify exceptions to those rights in order to assert that all women, like black men, were entitled to them.

The seeds of the intellectual and political quests to make these challenges were sown when, with the sponsorship of William Lloyd Garrison and other abolitionist leaders, women began to form female antislavery societies in the 1830s. By the end of the decade, there were some 112 of these groups, present in every Northern state. An initial national conference, the Antislavery Convention of American Women, met in New York in 1837. The American Anti-Slavery Association also hired two female lecturers from South Carolina, Sarah and Angelina Grimké, the first women since Frances Wright to become prominent public speakers on political issues. Angelina called "the Anti-Slavery cause" the "high school of morals in our land," where "*human rights* are more fully investigated, and better understood and taught, than in any other." When the Massachusetts Congregationalist clergy attacked the Grimké sisters for their public involvements, they began writing and speaking in defense of women's rights, invoking the natural rights egalitarianism of the Enlightenment as extended to women by Mary Wollstonecraft, as well as their own biblical readings. Angelina argued that rights stemmed from "moral nature," not a person's "physical constitution." Thus she dismissed doctrines that spoke of "masculine and feminine virtues" and rights (instead of "human rights") as both unreasonable and "anti-christian."[117]

Stanton, Anthony, Lucy Stone, Lucretia Mott, and other women's rights lead ers all also began their activism in the American Anti-Slavery Association and other antislavery groups. Garrison, in turn, began defending women's rights. But when other antislavery activists objected to combining the causes, Stanton and Mott organized the 1848 convention that launched their own movement. Their Seneca Falls Declaration of Sentiments exemplifies how they synthesized ideological elements in ways that gave liberal rights claims greatest prominence, but with reverberations of republican motherhood, Protestantism, and ascriptive and class concerns all audible.

It proclaimed that "all men and women are created equal" and "endowed by their Creator with certain inalienable rights," including the "inalienable right to the elective franchise." It culminated in the demand that women "have immediate admission to all the rights and privileges which belong to them as citizens of the United States," the franchise included. In so arguing, they merged a republican stress on the franchise as the badge of full citizenship with the Enlightenment's "inalienable rights" in a fashion long common among American democrats. But their declaration's insistence that women were entitled to a fully "equal station" in the republic was novel. These relatively well-off, white Protestant women also played on class and ethnic allegiances by complaining that American men had withheld from women "rights which are given to the most ignorant and degraded men—both natives and foreigners." But overall, their tone, like the Grimkés' a decade earlier, stressed the "equality of human rights" that resulted from "the identity of the race in capabilities and responsibilities."[118]

Although the vote remained the centerpiece of egalitarian women's activism for decades, many movement leaders had much broader reform visions. Stanton called for more egalitarian property, marriage, and divorce laws, more equal family roles, and even reformed Christian beliefs. For other female leaders, all this went too far. Catharine Beecher was happy to envision an age when "land-monopolies" and "abuse of capital" would cease due to "the guidance of Christianity." But even in this utopia, she expected women to be "wives, mothers, and housekeepers," performing the "labor appropriate to their sex," given their "physical conformation," character, and habits. Men would still control both arms and wealth and command the obedience of their wives. She urged that all women be better educated for their "highest vocation," the "*training of the human mind in the years of infancy and childhood,*" whether in public schools or in their homes. But otherwise, women did not need the vote or any other reform to influence laws and society in "*an acceptable manner.*" Beecher's stress that biology and the Bible taught what was "acceptable" for women reflected the general Jacksonian trends concerning women's place and defenses of subordinate status.[119]

Even so, Jacksonian efforts to foster population and growth in frontier regions produced state laws that expanded the rights of women in limited ways. Other circumstances produced some national judicial decisions that, objectively, also expanded women's rights. But these developments did not involve any acceptance of female political equality, and they were accompanied by others that firmly rejected that notion.

From 1839 on, many states passed Married Women's Property Acts of various sorts that incrementally expanded the powers of women to inherit, own, and transfer property independently of their husbands. By 1850, seventeen states had passed such statutes. Conservative judges sometimes tried to void or limit the reforms to protect vested economic rights, but those efforts were defeated by Jacksonian claims to expansive state police powers. These laws gave women some of the economic rights that both Democrats and Whigs held to be basic for white men, and they were supported in part by egalitarian feminist activists. Most scholars describe them, however, as uncontroversial adjustments to fast-changing economic conditions. Westward expansion and economic growth created family separations and sharp rises in market transactions. Hence Americans sought more clarity in family property titles and greater ease in exchanging property when men were absent. These conditions also abetted mild continuing movements toward more liberal divorce laws.[120]

Some scholars contend further that insofar as these reforms had noneconomic motives, they did not express egalitarian sentiments so much as paternalistic efforts to provide women with resources sheltered against debts incurred by their husbands or fathers. The first Married Women's Property Act, passed in Mississippi in 1839, principally secured women's rights over slaves. Hence it maintained racial inequality more than it advanced gender equality. Although the later laws covered less "peculiar" property holdings, none established full female parity in economic matters. Most of the litigation of such provisions, moreover, did not present claims by women to independence from their husbands. They were defenses by couples against creditors.[121] Thus, although these acts had liberalizing effects, they did not reveal any major ideological shift toward egalitarian gender views. Even so, leaders like Stanton and Anthony cited them as helping to inspire their activism.[122]

In some contexts, the courts recognized women as having a different civic status from their husbands, tempering coverture's eclipse of female political identity. But when they did so, judges usually still exhibited inegalitarian beliefs. Again, when Justice Story in *Shanks v. DuPont* held that a native-born American woman did not automatically change her nationality by marrying an alien, he relied on the common law's doctrines of birthright allegiance and limited expatriation rights. Mrs. Shanks had been entitled to change nationalities during the period of election, and her marriage and emigration signaled her choice. But otherwise, she could not have altered her citizenship through marriage, any more than foreign women could be naturalized by marrying an American citizen. In Story's view, this acceptance of a woman's independent nationality on ascriptive premises did not jeopardize recognition of all the other "incapacities of feme coverts, provided by the common law." And under U.S. statutory law, a foreign woman *was* automatically naturalized when her foreign-born husband gained U.S. citizenship.[123]

Related ambiguities surround one of the few other antebellum Supreme Court cases that touched on female citizenship. In *Barber v. Barber* (1858), the Court permitted a mistreated wife who had been granted a divorce *a mensa et thoro* (a status in which the couple lived separately while remaining legally man and wife) to sue her husband for alimony in federal courts, as they resided in separate states. As with diversity jurisdiction for corporations, this federal access implied that she held a distinct state citizenship from her husband, at least for jurisdictional purposes. That implication seemed anomalous, because in regard to state as well as national citizenship, married women ordinarily derived their status from their husbands. The Court dealt with this problem by stressing that women would be placed "upon a very unequal footing," without relief in cases of interstate desertion, were they to be denied this access to federal courts. The decision might be read as a nod to women's demands for recognition as civic equals, or as paternalistic concern for women's welfare; its tone bespeaks more the latter.[124]

Nonetheless, the Court's most ardent states' rights Southerners, Justices Daniel and Campbell and Chief Justice Taney, still found the decision too egalitarian and too nationalistic. Daniel's dissent cited Blackstone and Kent on behalf of the common-law view that marriage made man and woman into "one person," the husband, so that the wife was not "a citizen at all, or a person *sui juris*." Further, Daniel insisted that only "the particular communities of which . . . families form parts," not the federal government, should be permitted to regulate "the domestic relations of society," again linking states' rights republican and inegalitarian ascriptive views, here in the context of gender, not racial hierarchies.[125] Daniel's failure to carry a majority means that, even with all its ambiguity, this minor case is the closest the Court came to a liberal egalitarian view of the status of women during the antebellum years.

As many scholars have noted, the Jacksonian era instead saw the further entrenchment of beliefs that women were especially suited for the domestic sphere, concerned primarily with child-rearing, housekeeping and hygiene, and religiously based personal morality. Hence it is not surprising that in 1855 Congress passed a new Naturalization Act that automatically naturalized all women who married U.S. citizens, though only if the women "might lawfully be naturalized under the existing laws." That qualification was added "to prevent the citizenship of negro, Indian or Chinese women." The law did not specify whether American women who had married aliens lost their citizenship, and the issue would not be definitively answered until 1907. The lack of specificity probably reflects the fact that the provision was tacked onto an act mainly concerned with another goal.[126] It provided that all children born overseas to fathers who were U.S. citizens would be deemed citizens, if the fathers had ever resided in the United States. True to the law's pervasive patriarchalism, Congress rejected a version that would have granted citizenship to children of mothers who were citizens.

This automatic naturalization of formerly alien *femes covert,* imposed whether they wished it or not, received a revealing defense. A supporter in the House indicated that the provision involved little cost to anyone, because "women possess no political rights," and so lost nothing by a change of citizenship. Furthermore, the measure might lead a wife to do a better job for her husband in "the instilling of proper principles in his children." Wives would, in other words, be better republican mothers if they were officially citizens, denied any power to participate politically themselves, but charged with the civic duty to convey political morality to children. This "reform," undoing the legal recognition of women's partly independent political status granted in *Shanks,* indicates that although various liberalizations in the legal status of women occurred during these years, traditional ascriptive views of women's place remained powerful and found some new legal expressions, as with other American hierarchical systems.[127]

The Evolution of Native American Policies. Apart from blacks, the Jacksonians' rejection of liberal consensual notions in favor of racist views was most emphatic in regard to Native Americans. That fact was dramatized when, after much vacillation, John Marshall denied Georgia's sovereignty over the Cherokees in 1832. When Jackson sided with Georgia, later courts ignored Marshall's ruling and analyzed Native American issues in explicitly racial as well as state-centric terms. The basic doctrine that resulted, here as elsewhere during the age of Jackson, was that only white men ruled in America.

Even in their most liberal moments, the nation's governors had never contemplated whites living together with unreconstructed Native American tribes as part of one diverse, pluralistic society. The only possibilities American elites ever perceived were assimilation of the natives to Anglo-American civilization or else their expulsion or destruction. By the late 1820s, even those officials who had most hoped to educate the eastern tribes were concluding that schooling was often failing, and that in any case white encroachments could not be forestalled. Thus Jackson succeeded in winning passage of the 1830 Indian Removal Act, providing funds, lands, and authority to move tribes in the North and South to western territories. The act was "just" and "humane," in the tribes' best interests, Jackson asserted. And as he had previously argued, if any "partial evil" were involved, it was permitted by providence as a means to replace "a country covered with forests and ranged by a few thousand savages" with an "extensive Republic . . . filled with all the blessings of liberty, civilization and religion."[128]

Many religious leaders and Whigs were unconvinced, denouncing the removal measures as a betrayal of past humanitarian policies. Nonetheless, in 1834 Congress provided a reorganized Indian office headed by a Commissioner for Indian Affairs to carry out this work. By 1840, most eastern Indians, including the five Civilized Tribes of the South and many smaller Northern tribes, had been moved west, often through force and fraud. The Northern tribes received no counterpart to the southwestern Indian Territory. For a time in the North many small reservations were offered in exchange for removal, but the government came to disfavor these few pockets of tribal land.[129]

Despite the frequent deceptions perpetrated by land purchasers and government treaty-makers, the cruel coercion and outright warfare, and the brutal suffering in transit that accompanied those removals, many whites truly believed that in the west the tribes would flourish. By that whites meant that Native Americans would become Christian farmers and artisans, perhaps eventually joining the Union as a confederated Indian state. Even Jackson himself described this as a possibility. Hopes ran highest in the reform-minded 1840s, though Native Americans were not made the object of a specific movement like temperance, revivalism, abolitionism, and women's rights. In 1849, the Bureau of Indian Affairs was transferred from the War Department to the new Interior Department, indicating that the tribes now posed the challenge of development, not conquest. The government's new aid to missionary societies for tribal education was intended in the same spirit.[130]

The tribes were, however, diverse in their customs and aspirations. Some were interested in Christianity, agriculture, and other forms of manual labor. Most despised such assimilation.[131] Even though promises of full political equality in the form of citizenship were occasionally part of the treaty arrangements by which tribes were persuaded to remove, only 3,072 Native Americans had gained citizenship via such means as late as 1887. In trying to determine their place and way of life in their new environs, moreover, the various relocated tribes struggled among themselves and with indigenous western tribes resentful of intruders. And, very quickly, the additions of Texas, New Mexico, California, and the Pacific northwest, gold rushes in California and Colorado, and the construction of western railroads diminished to near oblivion the lands that whites were willing to leave the tribes.

Hence, soon after relocating, the tribes once more faced invading white

settlers protected by federal troops as well as internecine strife over their shrinking holdings. By the 1850s, the tasks of Interior's Indian Bureau had again become far more the acquisition of land and other resources from the tribes rather
than any assistance. For a time, the government tried to maintain large Indian
territories to the south and north of the lines of travel across the Great Plains,
but white expansionism was too great. In 1854 alone, tribes relocated west of
Missouri and Arkansas relinquished 18 million acres of the land promised to
them in perpetuity. As in parts of the old northwest, the federal government then
carved out much smaller reservations that could not realistically support traditional forms of tribal life.[132]

The Judicial Pattern. These legislative and executive actions had a massive impact
on the tribes, and they delivered a grim political message to courts. Efforts by nationalist judges to oppose state claims and western removal in favor of Whiggish
hopes of "civilizing" the tribes in the east would fail, and they would endanger judicial authority.[133] The key battles came when Jackson's election in 1828 and the
discovery of gold on some Cherokee lands in 1829 prompted the Georgia legislature to claim ownership of Cherokee territories within the state's borders and
pass a legal code for their governance. The Georgians had long complained that
the federal government had never "extinguished" Native American claims within
the state, as it had promised to do in 1802. Instead, President Monroe had indicated in 1824 that Indian land titles were not invalidated by the 1802 agreement.
Federal officials had also encouraged the Cherokees in the great progress toward
literacy and successful farming that they had achieved. Those very accomplishments made the Cherokees' voluntary removal less likely. The state decided that
it must assert its sovereignty on behalf of the white settlers who were rushing to
occupy tribal lands.[134]

    The passage of the Removal Bill signaled to the Georgians that their cause had
presidential backing, but it also prompted legal resistance by the Cherokees.[135]
In *Cherokee Nation v. Georgia* (1832), the tribe sued as a "foreign state" to invalidate Georgia's assertions of authority over it, insisting that it must be dealt with
by federal treaty. Marshall hedged, ruling that the Court lacked jurisdiction because the tribe was not a "foreign nation" within the meaning of Article III, section 2. Its status was a "peculiar" one. Though it was indeed in some sense a nation, it was not fully so. As past treaties confirmed, it was a "domestic, dependent
nation," a "ward" in a "state of pupilage" to its protective "guardian," the U.S. government. Marshall cited Vattel in regard to this dependent status but said little on
whether it was based on conquest or consent, leaving ambiguities that satisfied
no one.

    The Court's reticence probably reflects the fact that stressing conquest could have supported Georgia's claims, whereas Vattel's consensualism could be used to argue that the tribe remained sufficiently sovereign to be a foreign state. The first result was unpalatable to Marshall, the second impolitic. Even so, Kent's fellow New Yorker, Justice Smith Thompson, sharply defended the tribe's substantial sovereignty in a widely noted dissent.[136] He now insisted that because Indians were not citizens, "they must be aliens or foreigners," retaining meaningful sovereign independence despite their tributary status.[137] Georgians seethed at these suggestions.

Their anger exploded when Marshall finally spelled out the status of the tribes the following year in *Worcester v. Georgia.* The landmark case involved the prosecution of two Vermont missionaries, Samuel Worcester and Elizur Butler, who refused to leave the Cherokee territory as mandated by Georgia's new laws. Their out-of-state citizenship solved jurisdictional problems, and here Marshall ruled the Georgia laws invalid. He reviewed the whole history of European and American relations with the tribes, giving liberal nationalistic readings of every point.

Marshall first dismissed the longstanding doctrine that European "discovery" had given title to Native American soil. "Discovery" of an occupied land by outsiders, Marshall stated, could not have "annulled the pre-existing rights of its ancient possessors." He then argued that the right of preemption, so often cited as evidence of U.S. sovereignty over the tribes, originally represented simply an agreement among the European powers as to who could purchase Native American lands, should the tribes be willing to sell. That agreement affected only the European parties to it, not "the rights of those already in possession." (In this he described the historical reality correctly, but not what European invaders had claimed.) Similarly, crown grants of land had asserted "a title against Europeans only, and were considered a blank paper so far as the rights of the natives were concerned." Marshall then minimized the significance of Native American professions of dependence and subjectship in treaties with Britain, often taken as evidence of their conquered status. He observed that the tribes were not "well acquainted with the exact meaning of words" and probably made such statements only to facilitate useful agreements, without intending to give up their "actual independence" and "right to self government."[138]

Marshall stressed instead that most U.S. treaties had in fact dealt with the tribes via the "language of equality." He deprecated the nation's occasional pretensions to superior status as rhetorical efforts to impress the Native Americans with U.S. power vis-à-vis Britain. Marshall did not even insist on the nation's "ultimate fee" in tribal lands, as his own previous decisions had done. He stressed instead that the authority the U.S. gained via the Cherokee treaties, in particular, stemmed from voluntary agreements made "between nation and nation, by mutual consent." The tribes were indeed like Vattel's dependent "tributary" or "feudatory" states, who had voluntarily agreed to give up a portion of their sovereignty in return for protection by a stronger power. Thus they maintained "self government and sovereign and independent authority" in all other respects. Their domestic laws could not be overridden without their direct consent or the authorization of the treaties to which they agreed, both factors absent in *Worcester*. They certainly could not be overridden by a state. Without bothering to review the claims for state authority in detail, Marshall held sweepingly that the treaties, the U.S. Constitution, and congressional laws collectively indicated that "all intercourse" with all the Native American tribes "shall be carried on exclusively by the government of the union."[139]

This opinion was truly extraordinary. Marshall had shifted from defining the tribes' status in terms of illiberal rights of conquest to Vattelian consensual premises, and he rejected all state regulation of Native American affairs or acquisition of tribal lands. He even moderated U.S. claims to ultimate sovereignty while promising that national power would be used to protect the tribes against state and private encroachments. These points were vulnerable to charges that they minimized past legal claims by European nations and the states, however spurious. And even in principle, Marshall's position still left the tribes dependent on, and thus arguably subject to, the dominion of the United States, though they were not American nationals.[140] Nonetheless, Marshall made a strong liberal case on which later courts could build.

In the short term, however, the decision proved a defeat for the Cherokees as well as Marshall. Jackson did not enforce the ruling, compelling the Cherokees ultimately to accept expulsion.[141] Shortly after *Worcester*, two federal circuit courts simply ignored it. They also engaged in astonishingly activist negations of federal laws favorable to Native Americans. Most scholars have neglected these decisions, but they are stunning evidence of how rapid and total the rejection of Marshall's ruling was.

The most striking assault on federal claims over Indians residing within the limits of existing states came in *United States v. Bailey*, an 1834 decision of the U.S. Circuit Court for Tennessee. Like *Worcester*, this case concerned Cherokee lands, but the unsigned *Bailey* opinion did not refer to Marshall's ruling, and it contradicted his nationalistic reasoning. The circuit court ruled partly unconstitutional an 1817 act of Congress that punished any crimes committed by any persons on Indian lands that would have been crimes in places where the U.S. government had sole jurisdiction. (Bailey had murdered another white man on Cherokee lands in Tennessee.) The court had no solicitude for Cherokee tribal rights: it agreed that the U.S. could exercise general police powers over tribes in federal territories. The case was "wholly different," however, when it involved "Indian territory within the limits of any state." There, Congress had no general legislative authority, nor did the Cherokee treaty confer it. Congress could exercise only its constitutional power to regulate commerce with the Indian tribes on these lands. Insofar as this act went beyond commercial matters, it was void. The court did not rule on whether states could exercise police powers over tribal lands within their borders, but it noted that New York and Georgia had long done so over their own citizens when on those lands. In any case, the U.S. government had no such jurisdiction.[142]

This sharply antinationalistic opinion, which boldly struck down important aspects of a congressional statute, had great potential significance for both federal and state powers over Native Americans and also for the boundaries of the federal commerce power. Its rejection of the liberal views and assertions of exclusive national authority that Marshall had advanced in *Worcester* must have been intended. But perhaps because the tribes were being removed in any case, the case did not generate great controversy.[143]

An 1835 opinion of the Ohio Circuit Court, *United States v. Cisna*, next wrestled with the spheres of federal and state Indian jurisdiction, and it limited federal authority in an even more unusual way. Cisna had stolen a horse from a "friendly Indian" on the reservation of the Wyandott tribe in Ohio, a tiny twelve-mile square plot that had become thoroughly intertwined with the surrounding communities and transportation routes. An 1802 congressional statute provided for punishment of any person entering such a reservation and committing a crime against a friendly Indian. The court nonetheless saw as open the "delicate" question of whether federal or state authorities had jurisdiction here. It thought that some formal "concurrent" legislative action on the matter was desirable; but it also noted, as the Tennessee circuit court had done, that New York and Georgia had regulated such matters in the past. It feared undue intrusion on state prerogatives if it upheld this statute. The law had been intended, the court said, to apply to tribes remote from any white settlement. Federal enforcement of it in relation to the Wyandotts had largely ceased, and intervention now, when they were so intimate a part of Ohio's society, would invade state prerogatives far more than had been expected. Hence the court declared that the originally constitutional statute was now "inoperative by force of circumstances."[144] The notion that changed circumstances might render a previously valid law a dead letter is controversial today.[145] It was a remarkable measure of judicial activism then, and it directly opposed the thrust toward national protections in *Worcester v. Georgia.*[146]

Four years later, with Taney and three other Jacksonians from Southern and border states added to the bench, the Supreme Court began writing Jacksonian doctrines of Native American status into constitutional law in *Clark v. Smith.* William Clark was heir to lands granted to George Rogers Clark by Kentucky in 1795. The grant was subject to the extinction of Chickasaw occupancy rights, achieved by treaty in 1818. Smith, a rival claimant to the lands, challenged Kentucky's right to alienate tribal lands prospectively in this way, and he had a strong case. If any American government could transfer the "ultimate fee" to these tribal lands—a proposition that *Worcester* could be used to challenge—it appeared to be the U.S. government, not Kentucky. Justice Catron nonetheless found Clark's title to be wholly unproblematic. He held that the "ultimate fee [encumbered with the Indian right of occupancy] was in the crown previous to the Revolution, and in the state of the Union afterwards, and subject to grant."[147] Catron's provocative assertion that the states, not the United States, acquired ultimate fee came without discussion or qualification. Thus while the Court still recognized tribal occupancy rights, here it affirmed that the states could otherwise regulate Native American affairs.

The Taney Court's most cited statement on authority over Native Americans was *United States v. Rogers* (1846), written by Taney himself. The case did not involve any conflict of state and national powers. It concerned the murder of one white by another in the western Cherokee territory, adjacent to Arkansas but not within any state's borders. Hence only national and tribal authority were in question: William Rogers claimed that both he and the man he killed, Jacob Nicholson, had become Cherokees, and that only the tribe had jurisdiction over his crime. Taney rejected Rogers's contention in language that asserted American sovereignty over the tribes more emphatically than Marshall had done. The Chief Justice denied that any tribes were ever acknowledged as "independent nations" or as "owners of the territories they respectively occupied." If tribal land was in U.S. territory, not a state, Congress could "punish any offence committed there" by "a white man or an Indian."

Taney also took an explicitly racial view of the 1834 Intercourse Act, which denied the federal government power over crimes committed "by one Indian against the person or property of another Indian." He insisted that it exempted only those belonging to the "race" or "family" of Indians, not merely "members of a tribe." Although Rogers may have become for certain purposes Cherokee, he was "still a white man," and so subject to federal punishment.[148] Thus being an Indian was officially a matter of "race," not consensual political membership. Because Taney also carefully left room for state governance over the tribes, little of the national and liberal principles suggested by *Worcester v. Georgia* remained.[149]

Hostile racial attitudes were also evident in *United States v. Ritchie* (1854). There the Court grudgingly acknowledged that a land title derived from a Mexican grant to a Californian Indian prior to the Treaty of Guadalupe Hidalgo was valid under that treaty because Indians had been citizens of Mexico. Gratuitously, Justice Samuel Nelson cast doubt on whether the treaty's guarantee of U.S. citizenship to all Mexican residents who did not elect to retain their former nationality really meant that all New Mexican and California Indians were now full and equal American citizens. Though Mexico may have granted citizenship to Indians because "considerable advancement had been made in civilizing and christianizing the race," he stated, "their degraded condition . . . and ignorance" meant that "the privileges extended to them in the administration of the government must have been limited, and they still, doubtless, required its foster care and protection." Thus, despite the explicit treaty provisions, the Court argued against full citizenship for Native Americans, a result pleasing to all good Jacksonians.[150]

Sometimes, to be sure, this stress on the "pupilage" or "ward" status of the tribes could prompt judicial protection of them against individual white aggression.[151] The Taney Court rarely, however, carried this guardianship so far as to protect the tribes against the states. In *New York ex rel. Cutler v. Dibble* (1858), it did not have to choose. There the Court upheld a New York statute that restrained white settlers by making it unlawful for anyone but an Indian to settle on tribal lands. The Court's stress was on state powers more than tribal interests, however. Justice Grier wrote that notwithstanding "the peculiar relation which these Indian nations hold to the Government of the United States, the State of New York had the power of a sovereign over their persons and property, so far as it was necessary to preserve the peace of the commonwealth," which included preventing trespasses. The state's police power for this end was "absolute and has never been surrendered," despite claims to the contrary over the past seventy years.[152]

In so holding, the Court was indeed consistent with many earlier practices of state regulation, practices made questionable by the reasoning in *Worcester*. By regularly emphasizing the nation's sovereign guardianship outside state limits and state regulatory powers within them, and by casting doubts even on the potency of the Native American citizenship recognized in the Treaty of Guadalupe Hidalgo, the Taney Court left most national and state policies toward Native Americans constitutionally unencumbered, while affirming powers in the states that Marshall's doctrines denied. These rulings of the Taney Court in regard to Native Americans and all the other "outsider" groups in America lead to the inescapable conclusion that inegalitarian racial and gender conceptions were more directly and pervasively endorsed in law during the years of the Jacksonian "American Dream" than ever before. Enlightenment liberal arguments, blended with reformist religiosity, provided the chief terms of opposition offered against them. But that opposition only led many Americans to dismiss the moral authority of liberal measures; and, perversely, liberal economic policies and democratic political reforms helped generate the conditions under which ascriptive arguments had great appeal. Nowhere was this dynamic more apparent than in regard to the greatest ascriptive hierarchy in America, white supremacy over African-Americans.

9

Dred Scott Unchained
The Bloody Birth of the Free Labor Republic, 1857–1866

The year 1852 was momentous. Harriet Beecher Stowe published *Uncle Tom's Cabin,* the African-American polymath Martin Delany published his pioneering work on the condition of blacks in America, the Whigs suffered shattering electoral defeat, and the former slave Frederick Douglass spoke to a largely white audience at a Fourth of July celebration in his adopted hometown of Rochester, New York. "Americans!" he expostulated,

> your republican politics, not less than your republican religion, are flagrantly inconsistent. You boast of your love of liberty, your superior civilization, and your pure christianity, while the whole political power of the nation, as embodied in the two great political parties, is solemnly pledged to support and perpetuate the enslavement of three millions of your countrymen. . . . You discourse eloquently on the dignity of labor; yet, you sustain a system which, in its very essence, casts a stigma upon labor . . . you notoriously hate, (and glory in your hatred,) all men whose skins are not colored like your own. You declare, before the world . . . that you "*hold these truths to be self evident, that all men are created equal*" . . . and yet, you hold securely in bondage . . . *a seventh part* of the inhabitants of your country.

Slavery, Douglass warned, "is the antagonistic force in your government, the only thing that seriously disturbs and endangers your *Union*. . . . It fetters your progress; it is the enemy of improvement, the deadly foe of education; . . . it is a curse to the earth that supports it; and yet, you cling to it . . . you consent to be the mere *tools* and *body-guards* of the tyrants of Virginia and Carolina . . . *for the love of God, tear away,* and fling from you the hideous monster!"[1]

With these words Douglass bared all the searing dilemmas that neither Democrats nor Whigs could resolve. Those dilemmas were not just matters of white America's failure to live up to its professed principles. Better than Tocqueville, Douglass knew that the nation had traditions that permitted whites to "glory" in their alleged racial superiority, and that both parties were "solemnly pledged" to protect slavery where it existed, even if some Democrats and many Whigs opposed its expansion. Yet like Tocqueville, Douglass also knew that many white consciences could be pierced by arguing that those traditions violated other American traditions, especially Christianity and the principles of the Declaration. If their assertions of moral equality included blacks, then slavery, not the Bank, stood revealed as the monster that had always most endangered the Union. And Douglass knew that many Americans who were not idealists could be moved by condemnations of slavery as economically inefficient, a burden on agricultural, commercial, and industrial progress, a hindrance to the pride in productive labor and thirst for education needed for Americans to flourish, and a source of power for regional leaders who put their own selfish interests ahead of the nation. Though America's ideological, political, and material contexts provided ample materials for the Jacksonians to craft an America more explicitly dedicated to white supremacy and slavery, they also provided the motives and means to mount profound challenges to those principles and practices.

The fact that advocates of two sharply opposed visions of American life each had potent weapons at their command produced in the years after Douglass's speech bitterly intense contestation that went first one way, then the other. Five years after he spoke, the Supreme Court indicated that no black man could be an American citizen and that slaveholding was a constitutional right. Ten years after he spoke, the President indicated his intent to set all the slaves in the South free. The challenges to Jacksonian ascriptive institutions began chiefly with people at the fringes of the American political spectrum, including former slaves like Douglass, women like his fellow Rochester resident, Susan B. Anthony, and radical religious abolitionists like William Lloyd Garrison. But as Douglass's speech showed, these figures articulated not just moral but also economic and political grievances that many powerful "mainstream" figures shared. The white reformers, male and female, also often had familial, denominational, or social ties to members of elite political, economic, and religious circles, especially in the northeast, and they helped bring African-Americans like Douglass to more general attention. As the major parties proved unable to contemplate the major transformations needed to address the concerns raised by radicals but increasingly shared by a broader range of Americans, these "outside" positions moved into the big house of American political life.

As they did, that mansion became more and more a "house divided," in Lincoln's phrase; and the divisions were not just between antislavery and proslavery whites. Rising out of their below-stairs quarters, Americans like Douglass who were often not even acknowledged as candidates for citizenship demanded to be heard in the nation's governing chambers. Though few could be deaf to the rising clamor of those voices, even many of the most sympathetic white listeners found it hard to believe that they issued from minds equal to their own. Others sought to compel silence by any means necessary, including new laws that strove to force free blacks and slaves ever deeper into the cellars of American life. As those efforts finally stirred raging battles, the whites and blacks who sided with freedom began to build a new national republic in which all would have rights to enjoy the fruits of their labors, and everyone who so willed could be an American citizen. Attachments to racial inequality did not die, even among reformers; but in rhetoric and law, egalitarian liberal republican precepts became more central than ever.

Those outcomes did not, however, result from any Hartzian liberal hegemony. They were the far from inevitable products of an angry dialectic involving the increased respectability granted to theories of racial inferiority after 1830, and the rise of more egalitarian reform movements—above all, antislavery—during the same period. The course of events that led to freedom and black citizenship was more obviously the result of advantages in resources, arms, political and military skill, and luck than enduring "liberal" popular sentiments. The Great Emancipator was elected President in a race in which over 60 percent of the electorate supported candidates who did not want the federal government to oppose slavery in any way. Emancipation then came only as a product of an immense fratricidal war in which more American lives were lost than in all other American wars before and since added together.[2]

Yet even though neither ideology nor anything else predetermined the outcomes, these struggles and civic transformations are not intelligible without understanding the content and appeal of the ideas that leaders deployed. In this chapter I first examine the ideologies of various antislavery forces. Then I detail how Jacksonian officials spurred conflicts with those forces by expanding the legal subjugation of blacks, just as they were siding with ascriptive views in other ways. That process culminated in the masterwork of Jacksonian racist constitutionalism, Roger B. Taney's *Dred Scott* opinion. Finally, I show how, in a climate dominated by slavery, a new minority party was able to gain power and begin to build a new free labor republic.

Keys for Dred Scott's Chains: The Ideologies of Liberty

Though many Democrats and nativists professed to regret the spread of the "peculiar institution," during the Jacksonian age the swords of antislavery were most often wielded by reformist Whigs, and even more by the Liberty, then Free-Soil parties, and finally by the Republicans. Outside and often opposed to political parties, the Garrisonian abolitionists and their allies in the burgeoning women's movement condemned slavery yet more fiercely. Free blacks not only worked with white abolitionists but also had their own organizations and leaders who resisted the condescending paternalism of many friendly whites even as they aided them in their joint cause. And recurringly, slaves rose up violently against their bondage, individually and sometimes collectively, in ways that dramatized the dangers of the slave system to all.

Historians debate the motives of the various white antislavery forces: how much their positions can be traced to concerns to protect Northern capitalism; how much they reflected fears of more massive black uprisings and desires to get rid of blacks via colonization; how much of their effective leadership came from black or white antislavery activists; how much they formed part of more sweeping domestic and international reform movements; how far they were moved by genuine moral abhorrence of slavery, even real commitments to the moral equality of all races; how much their moral stances were religious, or traceable to more rationalistic Enlightenment views.

Without attempting to resolve all those issues, a focus on the nation's multiple traditions of civic ideology highlights most sharply how reformers, white and black, blended the more egalitarian and libertarian strains in Christianity, Enlightenment rights doctrines, and republicanism to forge outlooks that were in many ways more internally coherent than Jacksonian or Whig thought, though still not free from deep tensions. They did a better job of meshing their universalistic assertions of human rights with their particular cultural commitments and public policies, even if tempered beliefs in racial differences and the superiority of Christianity and Anglo-American civilization and male dominance all still had force for them.

The ways they combined these beliefs varied. For the Garrisonian abolitionists, most scholars concur, allegiance to God was foremost. Many had begun as humane colonizationists, including Garrison himself. But moved by black protests against that scheme at a convention of African-American leaders in Philadelphia in 1831, Garrison began championing the rights of blacks to live freely in America in the newspaper he founded shortly thereafter, the *Liberator*. In 1844, Garrison's American Anti-Slavery Society decided to urge more radically that "the existing national compact should be instantly dissolved" because, as a conscious compromise that incorporated "the slave system into the government," the Constitution was "null and void before God, from the first hour of its inception." To defend this course, the Garrisonians invoked the Declaration of Independence, but with special stress on the fact that men had rights "endowed BY THEIR CREATOR." They then derogated the Constitution as "anti-christian" as well as "anti-republican." And when they urged separation from the slaveholders "to clear our skirts of innocent blood" and "to obey God and vindicate the Gospel" of "Christ our leader," they suggested that salving their religious consciences, rather than the advancing republicanism or even extending liberty to slaves, was their primary goal.[3] Even so, that religiosity issued in commitments to eventual achievement of egalitarian republics with human rights respected for all which appear genuine enough, even if they did not wholly overcome notions of racial differences.

For other antislavery activists, doctrines of equal republican citizenship and, especially, universal individual rights occupied the primary rhetorical position, with religious views more subordinate. Appalled by the complicity of so many religious leaders in slavery and persuaded that the Garrisonians' calls for dissolution of the Union played into the slaveholders' hands, Douglass privately questioned organized religion entirely and publicly gave it only conventional, platitudinous recognition. He preferred to appeal more to "common sense and common justice" as these were understood in Enlightenment rationalist traditions, and he insisted that all Americans were entitled to interpret the Constitution "in favour of justice and liberty." He saw these values as defined by the principles of the Declaration, which should guide interpretation of the Constitution. There was no reason to construe that charter's compromises and ambiguities in ways hostile to blacks.[4]

In his 1852 book, Martin Delany affirmed the divine origin of Christian principles and even suggested that the much-vaunted plan of Providence to make America an asylum nation might also signify the destiny of blacks to flourish in the Americas as a whole. He said more forcefully, however, that he "had rather be a Heathen *freeman,* than a Christian *slave.*" Delany also decried America's violation of its principles of "republican equality," and he insisted that, despite the discriminations imposed on them, African-Americans had every claim to be full American citizens.[5] Like antislavery spokesmen in the Missouri Compromise debates, Delany rested that claim in part on common-law notions of "birthright citizenship" giving "natural claims upon the country" and "natural rights." But he argued more elaborately that "politically considered," citizenship rested on having made "contributions and investments in the country," which African-Americans had done abundantly. This argument represented an appeal not so much to liberal republican consensualism as to a sort of Lockean labor theory of civic value and an old argument for property qualifications—that those who owned a country should run it. For Delany, civic ownership came not just from possessing property but from contributing civically beneficial labor. Those who had "made the greatest investments" of their productive industry in a country could be counted on to be most interested in its well-being, and so they deserved "the most sacred rights of the country." This was a distinctive liberal argument for black citizenship that had much logic and moral force.[6]

Delany's view was, however, ahead of the times. The first white antislavery electoral organization, the Liberty Party, included advocates of both the more purely religious and the more secular, constitutionalist antislavery outlooks, represented by Garrison and Douglass, respectively. It was founded in 1839 by religious abolitionists in New York. After 1841, however, it took much of its direction from Ohio's Salmon Chase, originally an antislavery Democrat who voted Whig in 1840 but then sought a more firmly antislavery political home. Chase's own opposition to slavery was also deeply religious, but he thought it politically unfeasible to advocate total abolition. He instead favored the complete divorce of the federal government from any protection for slavery, an only mildly less radical stance. In the platforms he wrote for the Liberty and Free-Soil parties, and in his own legal practice as Ohio's "attorney general for runaway negroes," Chase advanced this policy in ways that made him a chief architect of antislavery constitutionalism. Chase admitted that the founders had left slavery untouched in the states, but he insisted that they despised it and gave it no place in the national constitutional order, a belief expressed in the slogan "slavery local, freedom national." Hence Congress could not authorize slavery in the territories, or even pass a fugitive slave law. Once outside the slave states, blacks were free. Because the eastern members of the Liberty party still wanted to call for slavery's abolition even in the South, and because the party had little success at the polls, in 1848 Chase helped form the Free-Soil party on a platform stressing federal nonenforcement of slavery. It fared no better electorally, but it perpetuated the arguments that slavery was opposed to the principles of the Declaration and was constitutionally protected, if anywhere, only in the old Southern states.[7]

Though there was thus no single antislavery ideology, and though religious impulses probably drove most antislavery activists, their most public common touchstone always was the Declaration of Independence. It was invoked on the first page of the first issue of Garrison's *Liberator*, and recurrently cited in the antislavery constitutional arguments of the Liberty and Free-Soil partisans. It was the model for the American Anti-Slavery Society's 1833 Declaration of

Sentiment, just as for the Declaration of Sentiments of the 1848 women's rights convention. For many others it was, as Lincoln said, the "sheet-anchor of American republicanism." It seems fair to conclude that antislavery outlooks collectively most stressed religious and Enlightenment human rights themes, which were then used to justify egalitarian views of republican citizenship and the Constitution.[8] That ideological package fit together more easily than either the Jacksonians' blend of states' rights republicanism, economic laissez-faire, and white supremacy or the Whigs' nationalist republicanism, Hamiltonian economics, and religiously defined nativism.

Most white antislavery leaders, however, still held patronizing attitudes toward blacks. As Delany grimly observed, even white abolitionists he regarded as true allies "presumed to *think* for, dictate to, and *know* better what suited color people, than they know for themselves." Nowhere was this more clear than in the antebellum period's leading best-seller, *Uncle Tom's Cabin.* Inspired by revulsion at the 1850 Fugitive Slave Act, Harriet Beecher Stowe created a heartrending depiction of black suffering and white degradation that fed the growing sense of moral outrage in the North and the belief that a true antislavery party was needed. Yet Stowe did not question the reality of racial differences. She presented blacks not as true equals so much as "an affectionate, magnanimous race," better suited than whites for gentle Christian morals, but unable to compete with the "hard and dominant Anglo-Saxon race" to which "has been intrusted the destinies of the world, during its pioneer period." Though she insisted on the "equal rights" of African-Americans to American citizenship, Stowe favored educating blacks and then sending them to Liberia. Like most religious abolitionists and white antislavery politicians, she found it hard to give up all notions of the special providential role and "commanding" traits of Anglo-Saxon Americans.[9]

Nonetheless, her novel's potent religious and humanitarian appeals helped create a climate in which the vacillations of the Whigs and Know-Nothings on slavery, especially on the expansion of the "slave power," proved fatal at the polls. Then old Whigs, antislavery Democrats, and Liberty and Free-Soil party veterans, including black leaders like Douglass, coalesced into the new Republicans. In terms of scholarly debates today, that name is ironic: the new party was bound together more by ideals of free labor drawn from what are now considered "liberal" sources than from republican ideals of active citizenship. In the dramatic Lincoln-Douglas Senate debates of 1858, Democrat Stephen Douglas claimed the republican mantle of "popular sovereignty" for his view that every territory could vote slavery "up or down." But in keeping with the Jacksonians' racial Americanism, Douglas also insisted that the decision should be made by white men alone, because "this government of ours . . . was made by the white man, for the benefit of the white man, to be administered by white men." Each "inferior race" should receive only the rights that white men thought proper, and "equality they never should have."

As many critics have noted, Lincoln in reply was careful not to present himself as an advocate of full social and political equality for blacks, a position he admitted to be intolerable to the feelings of "the great mass of white people," whether those feelings were "well or ill-founded." And unlike his rejection of nativism, Lincoln never fully disavowed popular ascriptive beliefs in racial differences, though he always refused to label them just. But in classically liberal fashion, Lincoln did reject the notion that republican government included unlimited power of the white majority over the individual rights of blacks, especially property rights. He insisted that in regard to "all the natural rights enumerated in the Declaration of Independence," and especially "the right to eat the bread . . . which his own hand earns," the black man "*is my equal . . . and the equal of every living man.*" On other occasions Lincoln even made that claim on behalf of the "black woman." These basic rights might have to be extended to blacks gradually where slavery now existed, Lincoln conceded, but slavery could not be established in the territories without violating "moral and abstract right!" Lincoln also thought slavery abhorrent to God, and the religious element in his sense of the nation's troubles grew more pronounced as those troubles, and his own responsibilities for meeting them, became almost overwhelming in the 1860s. But prior to the war, Lincoln and most Republicans spoke of the right of free labor more often in economic and rationalistic moral terms likely to attract Democrats rather than in the religious language common among Whigs.[10]

Yet despite this "liberal" emphasis on individual natural rights, the new party's "republican" name was apt. The Republicans did build on ideas of equal republican citizenship, initially by objecting to the special privileges of slaveholders, finally by coming to endorse equal citizenship rights for blacks.[11] That last commitment was, however, never very firm in most white Republicans' hearts. Many opposed slavery because it brought blacks into the nation, not because it denied them equal rights. As Eric Foner and others have described, the Republicans were most united on Lincoln's quasi-Lockean claim that all people were entitled to the right of free labor, the right to own for use or sale the fruits of their own work. With liberal economic traditions, Republicans believed that this right encouraged productive human activity; that such labor was the chief source of economic value; that it disciplined and elevated the laborer, fostering virtuous character and personal independence even as it produced an abundance that would benefit others; and that governmental policies, including property rights, should be designed to encourage such labor. Not only moral repugnance at slavery, but also the market economy of the North, were thought to follow.[12]

Campaigning in New Haven in 1860, Lincoln showed how this ideology could be used to forge a coalition of Jacksonian free laborers and Whig employers alike, united as Hartz rightly said by an Algeresque promise that all would have a real chance for upward mobility. Lincoln applauded a labor system "*under which laborers can strike*" and "quit" at will, and he hoped that "it might prevail everywhere," even as he also opposed any law that would "prevent a man from getting rich." Lincoln maintained that it was "best for all to leave each man free to acquire property" and "better his condition," including black men. In that way a man could "hope to be a hired laborer this year and the next, work for himself afterward, and finally to hire men to work for him!" Through this "ceaseless round" the system of "free society" would produce more prosperity and progress for more of humanity than any other.[13] Men like George Fitzhugh were wrong to claim that the slave labor system was more productive and humane, and men like Josiah Nott were wrong to insist that blacks were incapable of free labor, whatever their other limitations.

These beliefs meant that, like the Jacksonians, Republicans favored an economy with many "middling" producers and entrepreneurs, only adding that blacks might be among them. Yet whereas they heaped rhetorical praise on self-employed yeoman producers, most Republicans were not so laissez-faire nor so fearful of governmentally bestowed economic privileges as many Jacksonians had been. They believed, with the Federalists and Whigs, in national governmental measures to foster new productive enterprises, from internal improvements to education to publicly supported banking and protective tariffs that could make small manufacturers into large ones. They were, in David Greenstone's term, "reform liberals" concerned to use governmental institutions to assist citizens' self-development—economic, intellectual, and moral. Most Republicans were persuaded, too, that although the decentralized structure of American government was generally beneficial, it had too greatly hampered national efforts to promote free labor in many ways, including limitations on actions to advance commerce and inhibit slavery.

Yet most Republicans had equally given up all high Federalist and Whig notions of openly limiting political influence to propertied elites. They also generally did not offend the former antislavery Democrats among them by stressing native birth and specifically Protestant religiosity in the manner of the Know-Nothings and many Whigs. Thus they were very much entitled to call themselves "republican," and fairly egalitarian republicans at that. But they still retained Madison's concern that direct popular governance could endanger personal rights to liberty and the fruits of rational labor, as well as political rights. For both reasons they remained republicans in Madison's special sense, advocates of indirect, representative popular self-governance in an extensive national and liberal republic.[14]

As this summary indicates, there were important intellectual and political tensions in Republican positions: granted that blacks could labor productively, were the uneducated masses of blacks really ready to be political equals to whites? In any case, would most whites ever accept them as such? How much claim did blacks have to the wealth that their labor had produced under the coercive direction of Southern whites, or to the lands upon which their labors had been done? If redistribution were called for, would it be politically sustainable, especially given the coercion that would inevitably be required? Were free labor values really fulfilled when a market economy and governmental aid generated powerful corporations, or were such entities—was perhaps wage labor itself—a threat to the maintenance of an economy of self-reliant free labor producers? What forms of governmental assistance generated greater productivity, rather than providing corrupting special privileges? What counted as rational, productive labor anyway? Should the work of business managers, lawyers, bankers, and stock-traders qualify? What would be a better balance of state and national policy-making?

All those issues, however, would not become vexing until the postwar years. From the Republican party's founding after the 1852 Whig debacle to the outbreak of the Civil War, opposition to the expansion of slavery was its great unifying theme, albeit one not suited to unify the country. During the early 1860s, unhindered by opposition from seceded Southern Democrats, the Republican-dominated Congresses passed a flood of legislation expressing the positions most shared, a version of the Whigs' American System modified to reflect the divergent elements in the new party's membership and outlook. Then the Republicans forcibly achieved the constitutional capstone of the free labor agenda, the Thirteenth Amendment banning all forms of involuntary servitude, though not many other forms of legal and political inequality for blacks. Only at that point did they confront the further, still divisive issue of equal black citizenship.

Those statutory and constitutional changes, and many more that followed during Reconstruction, gave the nation's laws a more decidedly liberal cast than ever before. In fact, they seemed to express a more egalitarian and nationalistic liberal republicanism than most Americans were prepared to embrace. Both the politics of combating extreme white supremacist, states' rights positions and the mechanics of displacing the legal embodiments of those views propelled Republican lawmakers to give prominence to the language of their radical wing beyond what most were ready to put into practice. Sweeping measures seemed necessary to transform the vast legal structure the Jacksonians had begun building with the first stirrings of abolitionism and slave revolt, the myriad rules denying virtually all rights to slaves and national citizenship to free blacks. During the antebellum years it was not hard to see, as Lincoln did, a body of law moving toward a goal it never quite reached: the declaration that not only was the U.S. a white man's nation, but black chattel slavery was constitutionally protected throughout the land. That was the legal prison in which Roger Taney tried to lock Dred Scott and his people forever. It was what had to be broken open by new laws hammered home by Union arms.[15]

Blacks and Jacksonian Law: Hardening State Restraints

During the Jacksonian years, increasingly harsh state restrictions were imposed on all blacks, slave and free, throughout the nation, although the particulars varied with region. The South, which held 4 million slaves by 1860, also confronted a free black population that nearly doubled from 1820 to 1860, reaching about 260,000, largely as a result of natural increase and immigration from the West Indies.[16] Though the great majority of Southern whites did not own slaves, and less than 6 percent owned large numbers, even nonslaveowning whites generally did not want blacks to be free to compete with them for jobs and status. As John Catron noted while still Tennessee's Chief Justice, the free blacks living alongside slavery were officially seen as "a very dangerous and most objectionable population," due to fears that they would "excite rebellion among the slaves."[17] Those fears were far from imaginary. Repeatedly Southern whites had to suppress slave revolts, from Nat Turner's much decried 1831 rebellion in Southampton, Virginia, in which sixty whites died, to lesser uprisings in Alabama, Louisiana, Mississippi, and North Carolina over the next two decades. Southern white leaders blamed this unrest on the rise of Northern abolitionism. Some banned distribution or possession of writings like Garrison's *Liberator,* and most strove to ensure that federal laws supported their institution. They also took strong measures against blacks themselves.[18]

The main instruments of constraint were the elaborate, brutal Black Codes imposing special restraints and punishments on both free blacks and slaves. Some state courts added racist "common law" doctrines that punished offenses like black "insolence" that were not banned by statute.[19] On paper, the codes did provide blacks some personal protections against white abuses, but bans on testimony by blacks against whites made these protections meaningless. The other restrictions on free blacks that mounted in the South after 1830 could be detailed at great length. Some Southern states had previously accorded mulattos more rights than "pure" African-Americans, but white leaders came to regard that policy as too dangerous. They imposed new restraints on all who had one drop of "black blood." Free blacks were generally forbidden from assembling for political and even benevolent purposes, and by 1835 they were also barred from entering most Southern as well as some Northern states. Often they could not reenter after leaving for any extended period, and some states restricted mobility via curfews as well. With the exception of Louisiana, Southern law also presumed blacks to be slaves unless they could prove otherwise. Free blacks usually had to be able to produce a registration paper, pass, certificate of freedom, evidence of a white "guardian," or proof of means of support at all times. Freed slaves were generally required to leave the state, sometimes the country; and by the 1850s, manumission had been banned in all the slave states except Arkansas, Delaware, and Missouri. Black preachers were also outlawed in many places between 1830 and 1835, though slaves often had to attend services led by white preachers, who counseled humble submission. Detailed municipal regulations added to the burdens imposed by state black codes and guardianship laws. Hence in the South the institutions of law and religion combined, on balance, to deepen black subjugation.[20]

These new regulations were often not enforced, but their threat was always present. Free blacks were also still generally entitled to own and dispose of property, the right that was hardest to deny to free men for anyone at all attached to liberal republican principles. As Justice Lewis of Pennsylvania wrote in 1853, "it would be a mockery" to tell an emancipated slave "he is a 'free man,' if he be not allowed the necessary means of sustaining life," including the "right to the fruits of his industry."[21] If they were judged not to be "industrious," however, even free blacks could be compelled to "hire out" under near-slavery conditions. They were also often denied outright other economic liberties, including rights to purchase on credit, to buy or sell certain commodities, and to work in certain trades, or else they were forced to pay special taxes or licensing fees in order to do so. When white laborers and craftsmen failed to have blacks legally excluded from particular occupations, they frequently achieved the same result via private discrimination. By the late 1850s, the condition of Southern free blacks was so severe that Louisiana and Florida passed laws encouraging them to choose white guardians for their own protection.[22]

In 1860 about 225,000 free blacks lived in the North. Because they were effectively excluded from the franchise in all but the five New England states, over 90 percent of these blacks could not vote, and they could be jurors only in Massachusetts. A mix of other public and private discriminations also limited their economic and educational opportunities and confined them to residential ghettos in many cities. Efforts at change were often met by race riots, as in Philadelphia in 1834 and Cincinnati in 1841. Some Northern opinionmakers like the popular New York writer James K. Paulding attacked the abolitionists as "traitors to the whiteskin" who were probably driven by "ungovernable passions, perverted into an unnatural state by their own indulgence." Those attitudes were not propitious for the status of Northern free blacks.

Even so, northeastern blacks could still assemble with relatively few restrictions and speak out for redress of their grievances. Black churches, in particular, served as vehicles for a wide range of social and political activities. And in centers of abolitionism like Boston, blacks did win small victories in obtaining more equal educational and employment opportunities. They faced worse conditions in the old Northwest Ordinance and the later western states, which all resisted free black immigration with varying degrees of success. Here, as in the slave states, free blacks generally could not testify against whites and were otherwise more legally disabled than in the east. Consequently, blacks remained a relatively small percentage of the population in the midwest during these years. In 1830 there were 16,000 blacks in Ohio, Indiana, Illinois, and Michigan, even fewer farther west, and the heightening restrictions meant that these numbers rose slowly.[23]

State Courts and Black Citizenship. As their legal privileges deteriorated, the question of citizenship for free blacks became increasingly acute. Southern and Northern courts began to diverge more sharply on the subject. Yet for all American judges, the common law's stress on birthright membership and allegiance, along with political concerns to impose legal obligations on blacks, militated against complete denials of free black citizenship. Liberal notions of property rights to the products of one's labors, again reinforced by practical concerns, also made it difficult for courts to deny free blacks basic economic rights. But neither region was prepared to grant them genuinely equal citizenship. Northern courts generally acknowledged black citizenship formally while rejecting democratic notions of the political privileges inherent in that status. Southern courts tended to deny black citizenship altogether. To do so, many continued to invoke strained consensual notions, but more began adding appeals to the Jacksonian ascriptive doctrines upholding all-white citizenship.

Cases debating these issues, including *Crandall v. State of Connecticut* (1834), often won nationwide attention.[24] There, lawyers for a Quaker schoolteacher, Prudence Crandall, argued that she could legally operate a school for out-of-state black children that she had founded with Garrison's aid after authorities forbade her to teach integrated classes. In 1833, Connecticut had responded by banning such schools in order to prevent "the increase of this population." Crandall's attorneys argued that the law violated the children's rights as out-of-state citizens under the privileges and immunities clause. In the initial trial, prosecutor Andrew Judson, a champion of colonization, denied that even native-born free blacks were citizens, an issue the court viewed as "undecided" by precedents. Judson disputed at length the common-law view that place of birth determined citizenship. He stressed the analogy of the Indians, who "were literally natives of our soil; they were born here, and yet they are not citizens." Sitting as trial judge, Judson's fellow colonizationist, Connecticut Chief Justice David Daggett, agreed, announcing, "I am bound, by my duty, to say, they are not citizens," and ruling against Crandall.[25]

The state Supreme Court of Errors reversed Daggett on a strained technicality, disingenuously professing to be unclear as to whether Crandall's school had a license that exempted it from the ban. The court evaded the incendiary issue of citizenship.[26] But the attorneys' briefs focused on that topic, and their arguments received wide publicity. By and large, they echoed the positions advanced in the Missouri Compromise debates. Crandall's lawyers used the common-law "doctrine of natural allegiance, a tie created by birth" to contend that if the state wished to claim that "allegiance is due from our coloured population," it must acknowledge that it owed "the correlative . . . protection and equal laws." That correlative implied citizenship; a free black should not be "*a citizen to obey, and an alien to demand protection.*" Nor could free blacks be assigned some "intermediate status." The absence of voting privileges did not prove that free blacks were not full citizens, because "females and minors" were citizens despite their disfranchisement. The Indian analogy was also misleading. Most Indians owed allegiance to their tribes, unlike free blacks. And while the status of those Indians who did not was unclear, they were sometimes thought to be citizens.[27]

The attorneys for the state answered that this position threatened to "destroy the government itself and this American nation," giving it over to "the African race." They argued that here state sovereignty trumped the privileges and immunities clause, and they denied black citizenship vehemently. No one, they averred, had imagined blacks to be citizens at the time of the Constitution's adoption, so blacks were not parties to the original compact. And they particularly stressed that the "very foundation of a republican government" was "the right of suffrage," an "immunity" inseparable from citizenship, at least for adult men. As blacks did not possess it, they could not be viewed as genuine citizens.[28]

The argumentative battle lines rehearsed in *Crandall* continued to structure the debate over black citizenship in the ensuing years, which still meant that neither side presented citizenship in purely liberal republican terms. Most Northern courts took the route sketched by Crandall's attorneys, relying on common-law notions of birthright citizenship and rejecting democratic identifications of citizenship with political self-governance.[29] They thus accepted that blacks had citizenship but that citizenship had multiple classes, with only the most fortunate or worthy receiving full political privileges.[30] Most influentially, Massachusetts Chief Justice Lemuel Shaw held in *Roberts v. City of Boston* (1849) that, although blacks were "equal before the law," this meant only that they were "equally entitled to the paternal consideration and protection of the law" for whatever rights had been legally assigned them. Hence a public policy of school segregation did not violate their "equal" rights. Although Boston reformers then banned segregation legislatively, Shaw's opinion was long cited in support of both black citizenship and the "separate but equal" doctrine.[31]

Predictably, Southern courts instead adhered closely to the state's position in *Crandall*, using consensualist arguments about the parties to the original social contract and the importance of the vote to citizenship in order to justify racial exclusions. By and large, they remained willing to grant free blacks certain basic economic rights, and in the early 1830s some Southern judges were still prepared to agree that blacks were "citizens" for certain purposes, while stressing that this status did not imply "political rights and privileges."[32] But contrary currents soon swamped those rulings. Writing in 1834 as Tennessee blacks were losing the vote, Chief Justice Catron acknowledged that state-sanctioned manumission could amount to adopting "a new member with all the privileges and duties of citizenship." But he noted that Tennessee in fact was "ejecting" manumitted slaves, and he endorsed this policy, holding that for the black man "to be politically free, to be the peer and equal of the white man, to enjoy the offices, trusts and privileges our institutions confer on the white man, is hopeless now and ever." Hence he recognized the inheritance rights of slaves freed by a will only on condition that they quickly emigrate to Liberia.[33]

Judges in North Carolina, the other slave state still permitting free black voting, gave credence to black citizenship for somewhat longer.[34] But in 1844, the Carolina high court held that their limited rights meant that free blacks could not "be considered as citizens, in the largest sense of the term, or, if they are, they occupy such a position in society" that the legislature could rightfully enact laws "peculiar to them."[35] In 1850, they were described as a "third class" that could be discriminated against at will.[36]

As hostile to free blacks as they became, Tennessee and North Carolina remained unusually solicitous of black rights among Southern states.[37] More typical was Arkansas judge Edward Cross, who in 1846 appealed to doctrines of inherent racial inferiority, denials of black participation in the "original compact," and a racist religiosity to repudiate black citizenship. Cross dismissed the claim of John Pendleton, a free black, that Arkansas' demand of a $500 bond from emigrating free blacks violated the privileges and immunities clause. Free blacks were not citizens "within the meaning of the clause." They possessed at best "a kind of quasi citizenship," because the Constitution "was the work of the white race." And necessarily so, for the two races, "differing as they do in complexion, habits, conformation and intellectual endowment, could not nor ever will live together upon terms of social or political equality. A higher than human power has so ordered it, and a greater than human agency must change the decree."[38]

The Georgia legislature passed a resolution in 1842 unanimously resolving that free blacks were not U.S. citizens, and Georgia courts subsequently took their absence of political rights as evidence that they were instead in "a state of pupilage."[39] Yet that term rarely implied any effort to improve blacks; rather, as Georgia's Judge Joseph Lumpkin indicated in 1853, such "pupilage" was expected to be "perpetual." Lumpkin relied on the doctrine popularized by Louisiana physician Samuel Cartwright that black degradation reflected the Biblical curse imposed on them as "the descendants of Ham." He contended that "the thriftless African" was so ineradicably lacking in the "energy and skill" of the white population as to forever bar black citizenship.[40] Even after *Dred Scott,* many Southern courts were willing to defend some property and procedural rights for free blacks, but from roughly 1840 on, citizenship was no longer a viable claim.[41]

Federal Views on Black Citizenship. The Supreme Court remained silent on black citizenship up to *Dred Scott;* but other federal officials occasionally took some stance on the matter. The nation's Attorneys General usually adhered to Wirt's 1821 view that blacks could not be citizens under the privileges and immunities clause so long as they lacked full political privileges. Using the ascriptive reasoning of the common law, in 1843 Attorney General Hugh Legare did endorse the occasional state court designations of free blacks as "denizens" in order to permit blacks to apply for public lands.[42] But in 1856, Attorney General Caleb Cushing rejected Legare's position, arguing that to acquire such land, aliens or denizens must have declared their intent to become naturalized citizens, which blacks were ineligible to do. Cushing also argued that to obtain protection under the privileges and immunities clause, a person must be entitled to a kind of national "citizenship in all the States," a status determined by "the General Government," as well as state citizenship. He did not believe that the federal government accorded any blacks recognition as such citizens. Taney used these arguments to supplement his own in *Dred Scott.*[43]

Secretaries of State fluctuated even more in their willingness to give free blacks passports certifying American citizenship. Some were granted; one was denied in 1839 to a Philadelphia black on the ground that Pennsylvania's denial of the suffrage meant that its blacks were not citizens, a position that implied, again, that U.S. citizenship depended on full citizenship rights in one's home state. From 1847 on, the express policy was to give blacks special certificates, not regular passports. Yet a passport was issued as late as 1854.[44]

The Federal Government and Slavery. Federal judges and other federal officials found it much harder to avoid taking stances on complex issues involving the preservation and extension of slavery. They had to rule on controversies arising from the illegal but continuing international slave trade, the domestic interstate commerce in slaves, and, most momentously, on the issues of slavery in the federal territories and the status of blacks who moved between free and slave states, especially fugitive slaves. Though no decisions were more bound up with the fate of American citizenship, these massively discussed cases rarely considered citizenship directly. Here I will note only the chief developments and the ways they threatened to enshrine racially ascriptive Jacksonian notions of civic identity permanently.

Despite recurrent calls by Presidents for additional resources, through the Jacksonian era Congress failed to take measures necessary to enforce seriously the 1808 ban on international slave trading.[45] For years the U.S. was the only major maritime power that refused to sign a treaty of "reciprocal search and seizure" with Britain to render enforcement more effective. Finally, in 1842 a Whig-led Congress consented to grant the British search rights, and it established an African Squadron to suppress the trade. But Congress gave the squadron few ships and little encouragement: the navy instructed its members that the U.S. did "not regard the success of their efforts" as the country's "paramount interest, nor . . . paramount duty," not an electrifying exhortation.[46] As part of the Compromise of 1850, Congress did end the slave trade in the District of Columbia. But, on the whole, it did little to stop the ongoing marketing of blacks.[47]

When it came to the still-legal domestic slave trade, the Supreme Court had great difficulty achieving a united view, just as it did on the related issues of state control over immigration, interstate commerce, and free blacks. The upshot of its most important ruling, *Groves v. Slaughter* (1841), was that the states could regulate the slave trade as they wished, a states' rights result acceptable to both usually nationalistic but antislavery Northerners and proslavery Southerners. At issue was a Mississippi constitutional prohibition on the importation of slaves "as merchandise, or for sale." The motivations for the ban were multiple, but they converged on the state government's desire to keep the simmering system of slavery under its direct control as much as possible. Even so, the legislature did not enact an enforcing statute. As counsels for the slave-trader, Henry Clay and Daniel Webster argued that the ban unconstitutionally infringed exclusive congressional authority over the slave trade, a position that would have upheld national economic powers and permitted their use for or against slavery, in typical Whig fashion.

That view found no takers. Justice Smith Thompson's majority opinion held that the court could not enforce the ban in the absence of an implementing statute, so he did not officially rule on the prohibition's constitutional validity.[48] Most of the justices nonetheless indicated approval of this type of restriction. Justice Story, joined by Kentucky's McKinley, voted in dissent to uphold the Mississippi prohibition even without an enforcement act. John McLean, an antislavery Ohio Democrat who, like Salmon Chase, would eventually turn Republican, thought that such a statute was needed. But he agreed that states could ban the slave trade, while stressing that this conclusion did not mean that they could regulate interstate commerce. Taney took the sweeping states' rights view that the subject of the slave trade was "exclusively reserved to the states," outside all national power. Henry Baldwin added the even more radically proslavery claim that the privileges and immunities clause actually protected slaveholders who carried their slaves through free states.[49] The only clear winner was state power over slavery.

Similarly, the Court dealt with the thorny issue of the status of blacks who had lived in free and slave states essentially by deferring to the laws of the state in which they were resident. It therefore usually declared that it lacked any jurisdiction over such cases.[50] In a District of Columbia case in 1844, where federal jurisdiction could not be denied, the Court's deference to local law within one of the district's two counties had the effect of sustaining a black man's freedom.[51] But in *Strader v. Graham* (1851), Taney wrote for the Court upholding the slave status in Kentucky of Kentucky blacks who had traveled into free Ohio, indicating that the Court would honor each state's determination of the condition of blacks "domiciled within its territory."[52] Slave states had nothing to fear on these counts from national courts.[53]

Neither Congress nor the federal courts, however, could refer crucial slavery questions to the states entirely. The linked issues of fugitive slaves and of slavery in the territories raised the fundamental problem of whether slavery would be protected and extended by federal law or constrained in ways that might foster its demise. The fugitive slave issue became pressing first. In 1820 and 1826 Pennsylvania had passed widely imitated "personal liberty" laws, laying down procedural restrictions on how blacks who were claimed to be fugitives could be recaptured, and levying penalties for illegal seizures.[54] Previously, slaveowners had exercised an almost unlimited "right of recaption" via self-help, and many protested the advent of new Northern restrictions on that right. A fragmented Supreme Court inflamed the issue further by striking down the 1826 statute as an unconstitutional obstruction of the 1793 Fugitive Slave Law in *Prigg v. Pennsylvania* (1842). Justice Story's plurality opinion held that the Fugitive Slave Law was a valid implementation of the Constitution's fugitive slave clause, and that the power to regulate slave recoveries was "exclusive in Congress." Regulations like Pennsylvania's were invalid because otherwise incompatible state regulations might multiply.[55]

Story added that though states could not regulate restorations to particular owners, they could arrest and remove runaway slaves as an exercise of their police powers. That was not enough for some slavery advocates. While saying that he concurred "altogether" with Story's opinion, Justice Wayne laid greater stress on the obligations of all states to honor slaveowners' titles. Chief Justice Taney's concurrence insisted, against Story, that the states did have the right and indeed the duty to take actions that would specifically assist masters in recovering their slaves. The fiery proslavery Justice Daniel agreed, maintaining that enforcement would fail if limited to the "inconsiderable number of federal officers."[56]

Perhaps disingenuously, Story suggested to some that he had aimed to create such failure, making the decision a "triumph of freedom." Unpersuaded abolitionists assailed *Prigg* for stopping Northern states from granting blacks procedural shields against unscrupulous slave catchers, who often seized any person vaguely resembling the fugitive allegedly being sought. The ruling certainly did not end such violent, fraudulent "recaptions." Beginning with Massachusetts in 1843, however, various Northern states took advantage of *Prigg* to pass new noncooperative personal liberty laws. These statutes prevented state officers from arresting persons claimed to be fugitive slaves, and state judges from accepting jurisdiction in such cases. Pennsylvania's 1847 law went further. It prohibited state cooperation with slave catchers and added new penalties for seizing free blacks. It also allowed judges to use habeas corpus to review such seizures. Slaveholders were outraged.[57]

Antislavery forces also mounted new legal challenges to the Fugitive Slave Act itself, and here Southerners could take satisfaction in their support by the federal judiciary. In the famous *Van Zandt* litigation, Salmon Chase, joined by William Seward, took to the Supreme Court the claim that the Constitution, properly construed in light of natural rights and the Declaration of Independence, gave no recognition to slavery as any other than a state institution. Hence national enforcement of slavery via the 1793 Fugitive Slave Act had always been unconstitutional. But even Justice McLean felt that these arguments required courts to look too far beyond enacted law, and in 1847 the Supreme Court again upheld the Fugitive Slave Act emphatically.[58]

These developments formed one root of the Compromise of 1850. The other was the issue of slavery in the territories, made pressing by the massive territorial acquisitions resulting from the Mexican-American war.[59] As that conflict commenced in 1846, Pennsylvania Democratic Congressman David Wilmot introduced his controversial Proviso that tried to ban slavery in any territories the war might produce, in order, he stated, to protect the interests of "free white" laborers. Though one-term Whig Congressman Abraham Lincoln voted for the proviso "at least forty times," the refusal of most Whigs to endorse it helped prompt the formation of the Free-Soil party in 1848. Southerners feared that the proviso's success might mean a permanent shift in the national balance of power to nonslave states. Slaveholders would then always feel vulnerable to hostile legislation. Hence when California applied for admission as a free state in 1849, Southerners began talk of secession.[60]

To forestall that danger, Henry Clay introduced his complex Compromise resolutions in 1850. As enacted, these bills provided for: the admission of California as a free state; the organization of the other Mexican acquisitions, divided into the New Mexico and Utah territories, without reference to slavery, leaving the issue to "popular sovereignty" in those territories; resolution of disputed boundaries between New Mexico and Texas; abolition of the slave trade, but not slavery, in the District of Columbia; and adoption of a horrifically Kafkaesque Fugitive Slave Act.

The new law created district court-appointed federal commissioners who received exclusive authority to decide fugitive slave cases. But courts in slave states could issue certificates verifying the claims of their slaveholders, and the federal commissioners had to accept these as unimpeachable evidence that the claimant was legitimately in pursuit of a runaway slave. The commissioners were to appoint marshals to recover such runaways, and those marshals could require bystanders to give them assistance. Shockingly, the commissioners earned twice as much for deciding to return a "fugitive" as for decisions on the black person's behalf, and both marshals and their deputies received financial penalties if they failed to execute their commissioners' mandates. Alleged fugitives also could not testify in their own cause.

The 1850 bill thus virtually nailed the procedural scales down on the side of the slaveholders, provoking scathing criticisms from antislavery representatives. But with the support of Clay, Webster, and Stephen Douglas, it and the other parts of the Compromise were enacted. This Fugitive Slave Act rendered the federal government, and through its compulsion the Northern populace, more actively supportive of slavery via recapture of runaways than ever before. Along with the refusal to enact any version of the Wilmot Proviso, it made the Compromise a victory for slave forces.[61]

Nonetheless, the Compromise failed to resolve the two main issues that had precipitated it—recaption of fugitive slaves and slavery in the territories. In the last years of the 1850s, the Taney Court tried to settle them both. The 1850 Fugitive Slave Act had galvanized black and white antislavery activists into myriad forms of resistance that were met by harsh federal countermeasures, a dramatic story that included many much-publicized struggles in state and federal district courts. Although these cases involved citizenship only peripherally, they were an important contributing factor to the heightening of tensions over the slavery issue. The most striking development came in 1854, when the Wisconsin Supreme Court declared the 1850 Fugitive Slave Act invalid on the grounds that the Constitution gave no power over slavery, as Chase had argued in *Van Zandt*. The act was also said to violate rights to trial by jury and due process. When the United States sought review by the U.S. Supreme Court, the Wisconsin court refused to cooperate, making a states' rights argument on behalf of its power to regulate fugitive rendition. A unanimous Court decided the issue with few fireworks in *Abelman v. Booth* (1859), two years after *Dred Scott*. Taney's brief opinion took the constitutionality of the Fugitive Slave Act for granted and strongly asserted national judicial supremacy over all federal questions. Taney thereby showed that when slavery interests and preservation of his court's power so dictated, he could be as protective of national authority as Marshall.[62]

While the initial Wisconsin decision was being handed down, the next important development on the question of slavery in the territories came in the form of Stephen Douglas's 1854 Kansas-Nebraska Act. It provided for the organization of territorial governments in those two regions preparatory to statehood, and it permitted them to decide on slavery for themselves, "subject only to the Constitution of the United States." That element of popular sovereignty was seen as a repeal of the line between slavery and freedom drawn by the Missouri Compromise, and it precipitated bitter Northern opposition as well as the violent struggles over a new constitution that spawned the gory nickname, "Bleeding Kansas." With the territorial question at the center of national attention, the Supreme Court heard *Dred Scott*.[63]

The Constitutional Chains of Dred Scott

Jacksonian conceptions of American civic identity here reached their constitutional high water mark. The nature of American citizenship became the legal focal point for the nation's increasingly unbearable conflicts over the kind of political economy that would prevail as the nation expanded westward, over the primacy of state or national power on a whole range of issues, and especially over whether America would be officially defined as a white man's nation rather than a union dedicated to human moral equality and individual rights. Chief Justice Roger Taney gave definitive Jacksonian answers to these and most of the related questions about citizenship that had long festered: the meaning of Article III diversity of citizenship jurisdiction, Article IV privileges and immunities, state and national naturalization powers, territorial citizenship, and the civic status of women and Native Americans, as well as blacks.

Beginning in 1846, Dred Scott sued in both the state and federal courts in Missouri, the slave state in which he resided, to win recognition as a free man, a citizen of Missouri, and a citizen of the United States. Born a slave, probably in Virginia, Scott claimed to have become free either when his owner, U.S. Army surgeon John Emerson, took him in 1833 from Missouri to reside for over two years at a fort in the free state of Illinois, or when Emerson next took him for four years to another fort in the Wisconsin part of the Louisiana Purchase, made free federal territory by the 1820 Missouri Compromise.[64] Scott's return to Missouri in 1846 after further travels made him a Missouri resident, but it could not, he contended, legally revive or reattach his servitude. Comity and the state's own precedents required Missouri to recognize his emancipation. In keeping with the standard form for such freedom suits, Scott pleaded that his putative owners had instead subjected him to assault and imprisonment as if he were yet a slave.[65]

Scott first sued John Emerson's widow, Irene Emerson, who claimed ownership over him by inheritance, in the state courts. He lost in 1852. Using the conflict-of-laws approach endorsed by Joseph Story's treatise on the subject and by Taney in *Strader v. Graham,* the Missouri Supreme Court found that the state's judiciary had discretion to decide whether to honor laws of other jurisdictions. The Court concluded that, given the growing antislavery climate of the North, it was imprudent to honor out-of-state laws of emancipation, despite several contrary Missouri precedents. Scott's lawyers did not try to appeal this decision to the federal courts.[66]

Instead, in 1853 Scott initiated a new suit in the U.S. Circuit Court for Missouri. His opponent was now Irene Emerson's brother, John Sanford, who had allegedly bought Scott in 1852 or 1853. Sanford was now a citizen of New York, though he often visited St. Louis for business and family reasons. And Scott now claimed that, as an emancipated native-born black residing in Missouri, he was a Missouri citizen, entitled to sue New Yorker Sanford in the federal courts under the diversity of citizenship clause. The circuit court granted jurisdiction, but it found Scott to be a slave. Following the *Strader v. Graham* rule that decided a black's status by the laws of his state of residence as well as *Scott v. Emerson*'s ruling on Missouri law, District Judge Robert Wells instructed the jury that the law was with Sanford, and they so decided.[67] Technically, if Scott were a slave, he should not have been able to sue in the first place; but the court did not bother to withdraw its grant of jurisdiction. That grant was potentially momentous, as it could have served as precedent for blacks seized under the 1850 Fugitive Slave Act to escape hearings under the special commissioners it had set up. Instead they might have sued for release in federal courts.[68]

That possibility may well have concerned Taney when the Supreme Court took the case on appeal. He devoted nearly half his opinion to whether jurisdiction had been properly granted. The issue was central, because everyone agreed that if Dred Scott were still a slave, he could not sue as a citizen of Missouri. In the end, the majority so ruled, citing *Strader v. Graham* and deferring to Missouri law. The result was eminently defensible in light of existing doctrines on slavery and conflict of laws, and if the justices had left it at that, the case would have been only an obscure footnote to *Strader.*

But ignoring a dozen opportunities to decide the case more narrowly, Taney pumped the jurisdictional issue up into the much broader question of whether any blacks, slave or free, could ever be regarded as state or U.S. citizens "within the meaning of the Constitution of the United States."[69] After denying that they could, Taney went on to consider whether Scott's Northern residences had made him free, an issue he again posed expansively by asking whether Congress had power to ban slavery in some territories. Once more his answer was no.

Though legally Taney had no need to make those incendiary broader assertions, he clearly wanted to block off every possible legal route for recognizing either constitutional citizenship for blacks or federal power to ban slavery.[70] To get all that on the table, Taney grandly termed the power to sue in federal courts one of the basic "privileges" of constitutional citizenship, even though it was also possessed by aliens and corporations. He thereafter treated the case as if it concerned a claim to citizenship under the broadly worded privileges and immunities clause rather than the narrow diversity clause. Taney was thus able to confront his readers with a fear long harbored by Southern whites. If blacks were citizens in any state according to the privileges and immunities clause, and those blacks then visited other states, then the clause would compel those states to treat them as possessed of all the privileges and immunities they granted to their white citizens.[71]

Various opinions of U.S. Attorneys General and state courts had laid out many ways to circumvent such an explosive holding, generally by defining the privileges of visiting blacks in terms of rights that other blacks had in their old or new states, not those that white citizens possessed anywhere. Taney ended up endorsing that general ascriptive approach. His waving of the specter of black civic equality thus seems designed chiefly to enable him to rule that blacks were not and could not be U.S. citizens in any sense.

Taney began working toward that end by expanding earlier suggestions that there were two types of state citizens: those who were only state citizens and not U.S. citizens, and those who held both citizenships. Blacks could be the former, he grudgingly conceded, but not the latter. And only the latter, Taney held, could claim the protection of the privileges and immunities clause. That view nicely combined a Jacksonian stress on the importance of state citizenship with a full negation of the constitutional claims of blacks.[72]

Why could blacks not be U.S. citizens? There were at least three routes to that status: birth on U.S. soil, birth to an American father, and naturalization. Confirming the difficulty of crafting coherent citizenship rules that accomplish all one's partisan purposes, Taney had to modify slightly some of his Jacksonian positions on other issues in order to close off all those routes to blacks; but he conceded as little as possible.

As he had previously, Taney maintained nationalistically that federal power over naturalization into U.S. citizenship was exclusive, against early nineteenth-century views that had claimed concurrent authority for the states. The federal naturalization laws unequivocally denied blacks access to U.S. citizenship, and Taney did not want to leave any room for Northern states to claim that their grants to blacks of their own state citizenship resulted in national citizenship for those blacks. Here, he was able to achieve his aim while adhering to precedents; and though the doctrine that states could grant state citizenship, and the federal government could grant U.S. citizenship, had less tilt to state power than Taney often sought, it was readily defensible as a logical result of dual federalism.[73]

At the same time, Taney made a much more important contribution to the exclusion of blacks from U.S. citizenship by reading the federal naturalization power narrowly in one critical regard. Taney contended that Congress could make citizens only of "persons born in a foreign country, under a foreign government." It had no power to naturalize "any one born in the United States, who from birth or parentage, by the laws of the country, belongs to an inferior and subordinate class." Taney was right to assert that the common law traditionally presented naturalization as applying to the foreign-born, but it had done so because all native-born persons were viewed as already subjects or, later, citizens. If such status was denied to blacks, it was more logical to place them among aliens, eligible for naturalization, than in the limbo Taney created. He did concede that Congress could naturalize any foreign-born person, "of any color"; but apparently slaves did not count as such "persons," because he soon added, without explanation, that Congress could not naturalize even blacks "imported into" the United States.[74]

Useful as it was to shut out blacks, this extraordinary view of the naturalization power compelled Taney to backtrack from his Jacksonian ascriptivism in another regard. In *United States v. Rogers* Taney had denied that the native tribes were recognized by the U.S. as "independent nations" or "owners of the territories" they occupied. But if so, then they were all born on U.S. soil, like blacks. They, too, should not qualify as "foreign-born" persons eligible for naturalization.[75] Yet some of them had undeniably been naturalized by various treaties. Ensnared in this contradiction, Taney reversed himself on the status of the tribes. Now the "Indian race" was indeed "a free and independent people," and though many had dwelt in territories to which "the white race claimed the ultimate right of dominion," whites always admitted that they had no right to those territories "until the tribe or nation consented to cede it." Treaties were negotiated with them "as foreigners not living under our Government." Hence Indians could, "like the subjects of any other foreign Government, be naturalized by the authority of Congress."[76] In this one aspect, then, Taney quietly departed from the main thrust of Jacksonian thought and his own rulings. He preferred to elevate the status of the tribes to "foreign Governments," to be dealt with by consensual agreements, rather than concede that Congress might naturalize native-born blacks.[77]

Next Taney had to defeat the possibilities that birth on U.S. soil or to American parents made blacks U.S. citizens, especially since some blacks were born within states that recognized them as state citizens. In response, Taney advanced a federal version of the line developed by Southern courts to deny state citizenship. Such birth did indeed mean that blacks owed "allegiance" to both the state and federal governments, but it made U.S. citizens only of persons born into a class that possessed a sufficient array of rights under federal law to qualify as citizens. Taney did not specify that array very fully; but he insisted that a person's class should at least be eligible for naturalization into U.S. citizenship, and he had shown to his own satisfaction that no native-born blacks were or ever could be under the existing Constitution.[78]

What, then, of the other form of birthright U.S. citizenship, birth to parents who were U.S. citizens? Taney denied that any blacks could meet that description, either. Because in his view neither the states nor the Congress had granted federal citizenship to any blacks since the founding, claims of U.S. citizenship by descent would have to be traced back to ancestors who had been state citizens and then U.S. citizens upon the adoption of the Constitution. But Taney, disingenuously writing as if he thought public opinion in the founding period sadly more benighted than in his own, contended that no blacks had been thought of as state or U.S. citizens during that era. Most blacks were slaves, and free blacks were lumped together with slaves. Therefore, he claimed, neither the Declaration of Independence nor the Constitution could have possibly meant to include blacks in their proclamations of rights.[79]

Taney supported his erroneous pretension that blacks were nowhere state citizens at the founding largely through indirect evidence, including state antimiscegenation statutes, requirements for militia to be all white, restraints on blacks' rights to travel, and a few later state court decisions, especially *Crandall v. State of Connecticut*. He denied that any state could have regarded blacks as citizens when they were "stigmatized" by these restrictions. The dissent by Justice Benjamin Curtis of Massachusetts, the only professed Whig ever to sit on the Supreme Court, provided irrefutable evidence that several states had indeed explicitly viewed blacks as citizens, despite their legal disadvantages. If all state citizens became U.S. citizens with the Constitution's ratification (or sooner), then these blacks were included. Taney agreed, after all, that in his own day some Northern states granted citizenship to their free blacks even while subjecting them to similar legal restraints. But Taney still insisted that the earlier disabilities meant that the Constitution had been made by whites alone. Thus only their (purebred) descendants or those they naturalized were U.S. citizens.[80]

By choosing to address the broad question of whether any blacks could be viewed as constitutional citizens, Taney provided a rationale for his rather incontestable result that was far more clearly false than any of several alternative routes he might have taken. But through his tortuous forced march, Taney reached his goal: there was no route short of constitutional amendment—not birth in the U.S., not birth to citizen parents, not state or national naturalization—via which native blacks could gain U.S. citizenship.

His arguments that the legal disabilities of black state citizens disqualified them from privileges and immunities clause protection caused him further problems, however. Taney had to clarify the status of native-born white women and minors, who as state citizens were denied the franchise and many economic rights in ways comparable to free blacks. Were they similarly citizens of a lower order that could not claim privileges and immunities clause protection? If they could claim it, did that mean that every state had to give incoming women and children all the rights they gave white men? McLean pushed this analogy in dissent, so Taney could not ignore it.[81] He answered that, unlike blacks, women and minors *were* U.S citizens as well as state citizens, entitled to privileges and immunities clause protection. Such women and children were, Taney said, "part of the political family" of those "who form the sovereignty." Blacks were outside the "family."[82] This reliance on familial imagery underscored Taney's Jacksonian willingness to define civic statuses in terms of "natural" ascribed status, and it was rhetorically shrewd. Most white men could be expected to be repelled by the idea that black men were family members.[83]

But Taney's difficulties were not over. He still had to find a way to deny that out-of-state women and children citizens could claim all the rights of adult white male state citizens via the privileges and immunities clause. He responded with the very tactic he had earlier eschewed as a device to limit the claims of black state citizens. Taney now explicitly agreed that the clause permitted a state to give to out-of-state citizens with certain ascriptive traits only those rights it gave to its own citizens with similar traits. Thus, if women should ever be allowed to vote in one state, they would not be allowed to vote in any new state to which they moved if it extended the franchise only to male citizens. That view was not controversial, but it did underscore Taney's Jacksonian deference to both state sovereignty and ascriptive definitions of civic status. It also showed that his worries about free blacks claiming privileges and immunities protection had been a fright tactic.[84]

Taney was still not done. Wishing to shelter slavery against federal interference, he proceeded to correct "errors" in the lower court's treatment of Dred Scott's residence in a free state and territory. Taney used that topic to deny all congressional authority to ban slavery in the territories. (State authority to end slavery was not directly challenged, though critics like Lincoln thought that Taney

carefully reserved the issue for another day.) Here his argument was equally convoluted, but as it did not directly pertain to citizenship, its details are much less
relevant.

In essence, Taney asserted that the Northwest Ordinance, with its ban on slavery, had been a compact among the sovereign states, not an exercise of congressional power; that the clause in Article IV, Section 3, granting Congress regulatory power over "the Territory . . . of the United States" applied only to territory
held when the nation was founded, although Congress could exercise general
governmental powers over later territorial acquisitions as a result of its power to
admit new states; and that, even so, Congress could not ban slavery in any territory, because it was empowered only to defend property rights affirmed in the
Constitution, as Taney contended that slavery had been. Thus the Missouri Compromise, though not the Northwest Ordinance, was invalid; and so residence in
the Wisconsin territory had not made Scott free. He also had no claim from residence in Illinois, Taney ruled, because there the Northwest Ordinance had been
displaced by state law, and because *Strader v. Graham* indicated that Missouri had
no obligation in any case to honor an emancipation granted by another state.
Scott was thus not free in Missouri, and Congress could not make him or anyone
else free.[85]

The dissents by McLean and Curtis did not add up to a full-fledged rival portrait of liberal nationalistic Whig or Republican civic conceptions. In fact, as matters of positive law, their arguments for Dred Scott's Missouri citizenship were
weak. Both justices followed Taney by ignoring all distinctions between diversity
and privileges and immunities citizenship claims. Justice McLean's opinion rehearsed the tenets of antislavery constitutionalism, as developed by his fellow
Ohioans Salmon Chase and Joshua Giddings, in competent fashion. Justice Curtis's dissent more richly explored citizenship issues, but it gave little solid aid to
Dred Scott or most African-Americans.

McLean contended that slavery was strictly a "state institution," that many free
blacks had held citizenship at the Constitution's enactment, that various sorts of
"colored" persons had been naturalized by later treaties, and that "the leading
men, South as well as North," of the founding era had believed that slavery would
"gradually decline" to extinction. He then defended congressional power over
slavery in the territories, citing John Marshall, and he attributed the Northwest
Ordinance to this congressional power. Most important, McLean argued that the
Supreme Court was not required to honor the Missouri court's ruling in *Scott v.
Emerson* because that decision had been an inappropriate departure from the
settled policy of the state embodied in common law. Using the religious language
so central to the antislavery cause, McLean then insisted that even a slave "bears
the impress of his Maker and is amenable to the laws of God and man; and he is

destined to an endless existence." Yet how his possession of an immortal soul might legally qualify a man for Missouri citizenship, McLean did not make clear.[86]

Curtis argued, with most Northern judges and against Taney, that citizenship according to place of birth, not descent, was the basic American rule. He also thought that the Constitution implied that any native-born state citizen was also a U.S. citizen, though he could appeal only to the absence of any contrary stipulation. If Scott had become a free citizen of Illinois, then he could claim diversity and privileges and immunities clause protection as a U.S. citizen as well.[87]

But Curtis went on to make that conclusion more difficult; for, unlike McLean, he did not believe that *all* native-born free persons were automatically state citizens. He thought that the states retained the authority to say which native-born persons should be state citizens, and hence U.S. citizens. Congress's naturalization power, moreover, did extend only to the foreign-born. Thus if a state regarded its native-born free blacks as noncitizens, the U.S. government must also treat them as such.[88] The decisive question then became: what state's judgment of Scott's status was authoritative?

Before answering, Curtis argued inclusively that all those who were accorded state citizenship by any state were U.S. citizens with privileges and immunities clause protection, whether or not they possessed the franchise or any other particular right. States could, however, also impose on out-of-state citizens all the "qualifications" of full privileges they imposed on in-state citizens with similar traits, as Taney and others had argued. The clause only forbade states from denying out-of-state citizens the basic rights of "mere naked citizenship" that they provided to all their own citizens.[89]

If Dred Scott were somehow a citizen, that claim still seemed to protect his jurisdictional rights; but Curtis then added more concessions that were virtually fatal to Scott's case. Tacitly accepting a version of Taney's distinction between "only" state citizens and state-and-U.S. citizens, Curtis indicated that though a free state might permit the emancipation of out-of-state blacks and give them state citizenship rights, the U.S. Constitution "does not recognise such citizens." It "does not . . . permit one State to take persons born on the soil of another State, and, contrary to the laws and policy of the State where they were born, make them its citizens, and so citizens of the United States." Curtis quickly added that the United States could naturalize blacks if it so chose and that it had done so, but he did not retract his earlier indication that the U.S. could naturalize only foreign-born blacks.[90] Thus, according to Curtis, neither residence in a free territory nor residence in a free state could make Scott a U.S. citizen, unless he had been born in a state that recognized free black citizenship, which he probably had not.

Curtis was able to avoid that result only by relying on technicalities. Exploiting the fact that the plea to deny Scott's citizenship had been severely deficient in relevant facts, he claimed that the Court could not go beyond the record provided to decide whether Scott was a citizen. In light of its inadequacy, Curtis contended, Scott should be given the benefit of the doubt.[91]

Curtis's opinion was strong on the broad questions of whether free blacks could anywhere be U.S. citizens and whether Congress could ban slavery in the territories, but his general views on citizenship really implied that Dred Scott was not one. By refusing Congress the power to naturalize native-born blacks, and by agreeing with Taney that there might be blacks who were treated as state citizens in their state of residence but who were not citizens "within the meaning of the Constitution" because they were not born citizens, Curtis left not only Scott but most of the nation's blacks ineligible for U.S. citizenship. McLean implied a more inclusive approach but did not confront the legal issues his assertions raised. Thus the dissents offered little hope that Taney's Jacksonian Democratic view of citizenship, particularly black citizenship, could be rebutted via judicial adoption of the views that lost in *Dred Scott.* New statutory and constitutional legislation would be required for more nationalistic, more inclusive, and more egalitarian conceptions of citizenship to become American law.[92] But making those changes would be enormously difficult: Lincoln made opposition to the principles of *Dred Scott* as well as "popular sovereignty" over slavery in the territories the centerpiece of his Senate campaign against Douglas, and he barely won the popular vote, while losing in the legislature. If that was the result in the free state of Illinois, it is likely that, at least in the absence of blacks and women voting, a national poll would have shown that a majority of Americans approved of the *Dred Scott* decision and its racist vision of American citizenship.

The New Birth of Freedom

Even so, after Lincoln won the presidency in 1860, Southern states began to secede, concluding that hostile antislavery forces had at last captured the national government. Southern beliefs that this drastic step was necessary may have been unwarranted. After all, despite being the only antislavery candidate in a four-man race, Lincoln received less than 40 percent of the popular vote, the least of any elected President before or since. Far from endorsing Lincoln's liberal readings of the Declaration and the Constitution, a large majority of the electorate apparently still preferred to see slavery unopposed. In both the House and the Senate of the newly elected 37th Congress, Republicans held less than half the seats that would have been occupied had the South remained in the Union, though they would still have been the largest single party. Of the votes going to the two leading parties in House races, Democrats received 48 percent nationally, 45 percent in the North and west, not fatal deficits. But Lincoln received 180 of 303 electoral college votes and swept the North, losing only New Jersey. To a lesser degree, Republicans also dominated Northern congressional state delegations. Southerners saw that pattern as too threatening.[93]

Within three months of Lincoln's election, seven Southern states elected conventions that endorsed secession, formed the Confederacy, drafted a constitution, and established a government. If the extent of Northern commitment to antislavery was at best unclear, the overwhelming desire of these Southerners to preserve slavery and white supremacy as central political principles is unquestionable. They complained that a "Black Republican" party "founded on the single sentiment . . . of hatred of African slavery" now controlled the national government, and the grievances against the North recited in the first of their conventions, in rabid South Carolina, all involved perceived opposition to slavery. Drawing on their familiar alliance of civic arguments, the Southerners labeled this opposition both unrepublican and unnatural. Slavery made possible comparative equality among free white citizens and so it made republicanism feasible. Moreover, the inferiority of the black race made slavery its "natural and normal condition." Their states' rights republicanism, their beliefs in white supremacy, and their quasi-liberal claim that their property rights were endangered affirmed to Southerners that they had a constitutional as well as a moral right to revolution. Although Alexander Stephens, now Vice President of the Confederacy, asserted rightly that their new government was "founded upon exactly the opposite idea" from the "assumption of the equality of the races" stated in the Declaration, its constitutional premises were in fact very much the ones Taney had delineated in *Dred Scott*.[94]

Lincoln's first inaugural, delivered after the secessions had begun, was not a call to arms against slavery. He repeated his frequent denials of any constitutional authority to interfere with slavery in the states; he affirmed the constitutional obligation for fugitive slaves to be returned; and he said he had no objection to a proposed Thirteenth Amendment that would make constitutional protection for slavery in the existing states explicit. Lincoln hedged, however, on who should see that fugitive slaves were returned, and he called attention to the need to respect the privileges and immunities clause. He also stated plainly that the "only substantial dispute" dividing the nation was whether slavery "is wrong, and ought not be extended," and gave no indication that he would soften on that point.[95] He then moved firmly to accept war rather than either secession or union on the South's terms. Though Lincoln was profoundly dedicated to keeping the nation intact, he was willing to do so only on a basis of resistance to the spread of slavery.

Secession and war then created two circumstances that enabled Lincoln's Republicans to work more far-sweeping transformations than would otherwise have been imaginable. They produced a long-lasting, agonizingly intense military emergency in which drastic executive and legislative measures seemed necessary. They also left the Republicans in Congress with only a small remnant of Northern Democrats to resist their initiatives. It was those special conditions—expressive of irrepressible ideological conflict, not consensus or liberal hegemony—that enabled the Republicans to erect new, more inclusive statutory and constitutional scaffolding for American civic identity, including specific reforms in citizenship laws as well as a wide range of nationalizing, liberalizing domestic programs. Those bitterly contested transformations were the work of a party that was only the largest minority faction in a fragmented nation, and one that retained power only by military force, at times veering close to defeat.

The Republicans thus could not credibly present their work as the fruits of any liberal republican consensus, however much they might be contributing to its realization in the future. In order to justify their coercive actions and expand their limited support, they therefore increasingly blended their stress on free labor with the organic, nationalistic republicanism of their Whig predecessors and, especially, the sense of America's providential duties and destinies espoused in different ways by Whigs and Garrisonians alike. It was at the end of his first inaugural, as he tried to persuade Southerners to return to the Union, that Lincoln made one of his most famous rhetorical contributions to romantic nationalist conceptions of America, calling the "mystic chords of memory" that would be "touched" by the "better angels of our nature" the music that would "swell the chorus of the Union." This language blended romantic mysticism and religious metaphors into marvelous political poetry. Thereafter, his religious invocations became less and less metaphorical. As for Tom Paine and the revolutionaries, so for Lincoln and the Republicans; the task of winning support for a difficult cause in a divided, dangerous time led to appeals that went beyond prosaic economic concerns to a vision of national identity expressive of higher, divinely favored purposes.[96]

Religious Republican Nationalism. There was much to justify, including near-dictatorial governmental measures and, very soon, bloodshed of staggering proportions. After South Carolinians fired on Fort Sumter on April 12, 1861, Lincoln blockaded the ports of seceded states, mustered state militias into federal service, instituted martial law and suspended the writ of habeas corpus in designated areas, and permitted soldiers to arrest allegedly disloyal civilians under a program initially headed by the zealous Secretary of State William Seward. He proved none too scrupulous about protecting the rights of potential enemies: eventually 18,000 were jailed, most without ordinary due process. Virtually all received quick releases, but only after they took loyalty oaths, a device that proliferated at both the state and national levels (and in the Confederacy as well) during the fratricidal conflict. About the same time, in 1862, Congress passed a militia act that allowed the national government to enroll men in militia units that it called up, by conscription if necessary. That law was followed by a national conscription act in March 1863, which permitted men with wealth to escape personal service via paying a $300 commutation fee or hiring a substitute. That law sparked riots in a number of Northern cities, including the infamous New York City draft riot of July 12–16, 1863, the worst in the nation's history. The rioters were predominantly Irish, working-class, proslavery whites who attacked black businesses and orphanages, the offices of Republican newspapers, some Protestant churches and wealthy individuals, and large numbers of blacks, killing more than one hundred people. Army troops had to restore order.

Yet hated (and inefficient) as it was, conscription was needed, because lives were being lost at a record pace, far faster than volunteers for the slaughter could be found. James McPherson notes that more than twice as many lives were lost in one day at Antietam in 1862 than fell in combat during the 1812, Mexican, and Spanish-American wars combined. To ensure that the national government would retain the power to compel such sacrifices, in 1863 Congress enacted a Habeas Corpus Act that legitimated Lincoln's earlier suspensions, authorized further ones, and provided for removals from state to federal courts in cases involving national officers. Collectively, these vast executive and military powers forcibly asserted the primacy of national authority and national citizenship over state sovereignty and citizenship; but they also raised serious constitutional questions about the limits of executive authority, national power, and the security of personal liberties.[97]

Many of those issues go beyond my concerns here.[98] From the standpoint of legal definitions of American citizenship, the oath laws were most significant, because they compelled citizens to affirm supreme loyalty to the national Constitution as opposed to the states. Both the content of that affirmation and its compulsory character were (and remain) controversial. In August 1861, the federal government adopted a statute requiring loyalty oaths of all federal civil and military officers, a rule strengthened the next year to include an attestation of past loyalty (the ironclad test oath). Another act compelled federal jurors to swear their loyalty, and over the next three years Congress extended the ironclad oath requirement to almost everyone doing business with the federal government (including even congressmen). The military demanded similar oaths from defecting rebels and virtually all participants in public life, indeed sometimes all residents in Union-occupied areas. Lincoln himself made taking milder loyalty oaths, usually requiring only professions of future loyalty, the crucial element of his "10 percent" Reconstruction plan in 1863. Although that plan was soon displaced, the various subsequent Reconstruction governments all required loyalty oaths that worked to disfranchise most Confederate officeholders and military leaders. Even Andrew Johnson's 1865 Amnesty Proclamation required an oath of all former rebels while denying amnesty altogether to those who had held public office in the South during the war. Nonseceding border states imposed their own oaths on voters and state and local officials. When the former rebel states rewrote their constitutions during the late 1860s, however, most weakened their oath requirements to mere repudiation of the doctrines of the Confederacy, not denial of any service under it, or they abandoned such oaths altogether. The Amnesty Act, passed on May 22, 1872, removed most remaining disabilities arising from past support of the rebel cause.[99]

With some wrenching, America's Enlightenment traditions of respecting individual liberties could perhaps be made to accord with, even to justify, these measures. Lincoln's contentions that the Constitution must be interpreted as adequate to fulfill its purposes, and that it was right to violate some of its provisions to save the whole, indicated how governmental commitments to expanding personal liberty for all in the long run might justify severe temporary restrictions under emergency wartime conditions. But these arguments were quite disputable, because on Lincoln's own view, a government that ceased to secure personal liberties did not deserve to exist, and a government based on consent should not ordinarily coerce large numbers of citizens into professing their allegiance and fighting to save the regime. Reconciling these justifications with Enlightenment liberal emphases on consensualism and individual rights principally rested on insistences that these stringent steps were necessary and would be short-lived. Those guarantees grew less persuasive as the war dragged on.

Hence the wartime measures, including the loyalty oaths and the draft, were more easily defended via a demanding version of the Burkean nationalist republicanism elaborated by many Whigs, which made both direct consent and protection of many individual rights less central to governmental legitimacy. To it Republicans added the intense religiosity of the antislavery crusades, which could be used to argue that violence was needed to advance the cause of human liberty, as John Brown had testified in more than words at Harpers Ferry in 1859. The "Battle Hymn of the Republic" blended Christianity and republicanism in stirring fashion by urging, "As He died to make men holy, let us die to make men free," so "His truth" would go marching on.[100]

Harold Hyman notes that Northern leaders used this blend of religious and republican nationalism explicitly to minimize claims of personal liberties, emphasizing that "the need for loyalty transcended individual rights." Seward frequently took the position that "No one of us ought to object when called upon to reaffirm his devotion to the Union, however unconditionally." But no American politician has ever remotely approached so awesome a defense of sacrifice as Lincoln made in his haunting second inaugural. After four years of a conflict far longer and vastly more destructive than anyone's worst nightmare, the Union citizenry in 1865 was beginning to anticipate the war's end at last. But with the sternness of an Old Testament prophet, Lincoln warned, "If God wills that it continue until all the wealth piled by the bondsman's two hundred and fifty years of unrequited toil shall be sunk, and until every drop of blood drawn with the lash shall be paid by another drawn with the sword, as was said three thousand years ago, so still it must be said, 'The judgments of the Lord are true and righteous altogether.'"[101]

Although the religious, romantic nationalism the Republicans relied on to justify their harsh policies (perhaps above all to themselves) was far removed from conventional legalisms, by and large the Supreme Court avoided reviewing these coercive measures.[102] The conscription acts never came to the highest bench. A closely divided Court did check national and state powers to compel loyalty to the national republic in 1866, but the restrictions were fairly limited in scope and effect. In *Ex Parte Garland* and *Cummings v. Missouri,* a bare majority of five declared that Congress could not require the Court to compel attorneys admitted to its bar to take the ironclad oath, and Missouri could not force teachers and trustees of church property to take an even more severe oath.[103] The judicial coalitions were intriguing. In both cases Justice Field, an antislavery Democrat from California appointed by Lincoln, wrote for the Court. His opinions rejected the oath requirements as bills of attainder and ex post facto punishments; but, typically, this future architect of laissez-faire constitutionalism was most concerned that liberties to pursue vocations like law and teaching were being infringed.[104] He was joined by Jacksonian holdovers Wayne, Nelson, Grier, and Clifford, who were probably more interested in disavowing the all-encompassing obligations to the Republican-dominated nation that the oaths professed.

The dissenting defenders of the oaths were led by Iowa Republican Samuel Miller, in an opinion appended to *Garland.* That case caused him difficulties, because despite his ardent Republicanism he was a champion of state prerogatives, a stance that did not help to sustain a federal oath requirement. Miller did so by relying not on religious nationalism but on a mixture of republican and strikingly ascriptive rhetorics of patriotic duty. He stressed that it was essential to demand "true and loyal" fidelity to the government from all those granted the "privilege" of practicing law, as the "history of the Anglo-Saxon race" showed lawyers to be powerful forces for good and ill. Miller then argued at length that these measures, which effectively disqualified former Confederates, should not be deemed punishment. They were not so, Miller said, any more than the restriction of the presidency to the native-born was a punishment of the naturalized, or the restriction of the franchise to whites a punishment of blacks. Thus his arguments for governmental claims of loyalty and the nature of punishment, which many scholars have found persuasive, were undergirded by reminders that America was basically a country of native-born Anglo-Saxons in which various sorts of ascriptive political exclusions were simply "natural."[105]

Overall, these decisions voiding oath requirements had limited impact. As long as Congress wished, it continued to include such requirements in its postwar programs. What Harold Hyman termed the "era of the oath" ended only when Reconstruction came to a close. Yet the political forces that led to that ending were already visible in the test oath cases. Although Field's opinions challenged the oaths in terms of liberal economic rights enforced by the national judiciary, the votes he won from Jacksonians instead reflected the enduring aversions to national power, rooted in state-centered republicanism and augmented by ascriptive restrictiveness. The fact that those same themes echoed in Miller's dissent was a harbinger of their resurgent triumphs in the next decade.[106]

The National Economy. If the Republicans felt forced to undertake the coercive military measures that pressed to the limits of liberal republican legitimacy and beyond, they eagerly exploited their opportunity to pass a dazzling array of domestic developmental laws embodying their vision of a national free labor republic. Agriculture, industry, land ownership, finance, transportation, education, and culture all received new, Republican legal frameworks. The task of financing the war provided the initial occasion for these innovations. In 1861 Congress enacted the greatly increased Morrill Tariff, which inaugurated two generations of protectionist federal aid to domestic manufacturing, and then added the nation's first (and short-lived) income tax.[107] In February 1862 the first national paper currency was created—the greenback—via the Legal Tender Act, which in turn required a new Bureau of Printing and Engraving. Later that year, Congress adopted a vast array of sales and license taxes, administered by a Bureau of Internal Revenue. Even so, it felt compelled to accept a skyrocketing national debt which reached nearly half the total gross national product by 1865.

Also in 1862, Congress adopted the Homestead Act, making vast public lands in the west available virtually for free. It created the Department of Agriculture partly to assist in those lands' productive, "scientific" development. It passed the Morrill Land Grant College Act, realizing the old dream of a national role in promoting higher education in a form acceptable to the party's formerly Democratic agrarian and labor elements, by fostering state colleges specifically dedicated to "agriculture and the mechanic arts." Via the Pacific Railroad Act, it provided the first of the nation's major land grants and financial aid packages for the construction of a transcontinental railroad (followed by two other large grants in successive years). It also initiated a generous system of pensions for veterans and an ever-lengthening list of their dependents (entitlements which swelled to one-third of the nation's budget by the end of the century). These measures and its emancipatory legislation meant that "the 37th Congress did more than any other in history to change the course of national life," in James McPherson's judgment.[108]

Yet much more was to come. In 1863 Congress passed the landmark National Banking Act, a Whiggish reform that Lincoln had long favored, and it created the Office of Comptroller of the Currency. The Banking Act quickly fostered a system of more than 1,600 banks, dominated by larger urban institutions, which obtained new federal charters and the right to issue national bank notes without the stifling tax imposed on state-chartered banks. In return, these new national banks had to purchase specified amounts of federal bonds. The same year Congress instituted the National Academy of Sciences, originally to facilitate technological developments that might assist the war effort, though it became a vehicle for encouraging scientific endeavors more broadly. In 1864 Congress made efforts to attract European laborers to the nation's expanding industries, military and nonmilitary, via the Contract Labor Act and a new Office of Immigration. After the Civil War, Congress passed a Mining Claims Act in 1866, opening the public domain to mining, completed the major railroad land grants, and added a Department of Education in 1867 to foster common schools to "harmonize" the recently discordant nation.[109]

The impact of most of these measures can be disputed—the new federal bureaus were small; the alleged benefits of the high tariffs are still debated; the greenbacks and most of the taxes, including the income tax, did not endure; importation of contract labor was not large-scale; land speculators and railroads exploited the Homestead Act for their own ends; the new national banking system, designed to win support from formerly Democratic Republicans, was still far from a central bank; war pensions did not beget a welfare state; the land grant colleges were basically state institutions, not the truly national (and nationalizing) university long favored by Federalists and Whigs; the Department of Education was downgraded to a bureau in the Interior Department in 1869 and largely limited to data-gathering.[110] Yet, like Hamilton's initiatives, these acts established precedents for national action even when they did not last. They also generated some national institutions, including transportation, educational, and banking and currency systems, that did endure, promoting a more expansive national market and a national culture more conducive to liberal nationalistic civic ideals.

Black Citizenship. The most important civic transformations wrought by the wartime Republicans came, however, in pursuit of the ultimate free labor objective: the elimination of chattel slavery. At first, the Republicans adhered to their professed position of respecting the rights of slaveholders in the existing states. Slaves captured in early military encounters with Southern forces were treated not as "freedmen" but as "contraband of war." Indeed, initially some were returned to their owners. But the enormous loss of lives soon fired Northern anger at the South and heightened support to end the slave system that was increasingly seen both as a source of Southern military strength and as proof of the enemy's perfidy. In August 1861, following the stunning Union defeat at Bull Run and urged on by radical Republican Congressman Thaddeus Stevens, Congress cited its powers to punish treason to justify its first Confiscation Act. The law authorized federal seizures of the property of those who had been employed directly by the Confederate armed forces, thereby ending their control over their slaves. More and more slaves then bolted for the North—half a million by the war's end. The new status of those slaves was unclear, but public opinion soon began to support more extreme measures.

In March 1862 Congress ordered Union armies not to return any fugitive blacks, even to loyal slaveholders. That month, it also passed a resolution urged by Lincoln promising financial aid to states that would undertake gradual abolition. In April Congress ended slavery in the District of Columbia, with $300 compensation per slave, and in June it prohibited slavery in the federal territories. The District then repealed its Black Codes and authorized public schools for black children, albeit on an underfunded, segregated basis. At the same time the administration recognized the black republics of Liberia and Haiti and signed a treaty with Britain, at last permitting British officers to search American merchant ships and end the outlawed international slave trade. In July Congress added a somewhat ambiguous second Confiscation Act that took the property of five classes of persons convicted of treason or shown to support the rebellion, though these confiscations were to revert eventually to the rebels' heirs. Their slaves were to be free forever, though the act also endorsed colonization. Finally, the law authorized enrolling blacks into Union forces, as some officers had already done. By the end of the war, blacks received equal pay with whites, though the pioneer black regiment, the 54th Massachusetts, had to refuse their unequal pay for a year in order to get equity. In all some 186,000 blacks served as soldiers, and more than one-third lost their lives. Many more blacks worked in supporting roles. Lincoln said that the war could not have been won without them.

But in 1862, the President still thought it appropriate to work on colonization schemes, chiefly to Central America and Haiti. On September 22 he issued a preliminary Emancipation Proclamation, indicating that all slaves in rebel states would be free as of January 1, 1863, and offering loyal states financial aid for abolition and colonization. When January 1 came, Lincoln declared the proclamation in effect and authorized the military to recruit black soldiers in large numbers. Congress endorsed the proclamation in December 1863, and required West Virginia to abolish slavery to join the Union that year. In June 1864, it repealed its fugitive slave laws. By then, the North's determination to eradicate slavery throughout the land had become integral to its cause. And as border and Northern-occupied slave states began repealing their slave laws by statute or state constitutional amendments, this great abolitionist aim moved close to success.[111]

The Freedmen Question. The issue then became the civic status of the newly freed slaves and, indeed, all blacks. Colonization quickly proved wholly impractical economically and politically. Few countries in Central America or Africa would give up productive resources to American blacks. Few African-Americans wanted to leave the only country known to them and, usually, to their parents and grandparents. Thus Congress repealed its earlier endorsement of colonization in 1864.[112] American blacks would continue to live with American whites, but on what basis?

In November 1862, Attorney General Edward Bates had advanced a much-noted claim that free native-born blacks were citizens of the United States, though he admitted that the law was quite unclear on the whole question of citizenship. Bates reached his conclusion via long-familiar ascriptive reasoning. He went wholeheartedly with the common-law view that citizenship was conferred normally by place of nativity, and sometimes by naturalization laws that could affect only the foreign-born. Bates explicitly denied that citizenship "is ever hereditary," rejecting the more liberal international law view of birthright citizenship by descent. He also denied that citizenship had any special relationship to "republican forms of government," asserting that "English subjects are as truly citizens as we are." Bates further contended, equally controversially but without any argument, that "every citizen of a State is, necessarily, a citizen of the United States," while "every citizen of the United States is a citizen of the particular State in which he is domiciled," and that all citizens "are, politically and legally, equal," without any intermediate statuses such as denizenship.

He did not address, however, whether slaves either were citizens or became so upon their emancipation; nor was his defense of equal citizenship as sweeping as it seemed. Like Coke, Bates thought that citizenship involved only mutual obligations of allegiance and protection. It did not entail equal political rights, certainly not eligibility for all offices or the franchise. Those were privileges, and Bates did not think that all citizens had equal privileges. He used the example of a "free, white, natural-born female infant" as someone who was "certainly a citizen," but not entitled to the full privileges of adult male white citizens. Even more than earlier exponents of common-law arguments for black citizenship, then, Bates explicitly disavowed both the liberal and republican character of American citizenship, making it not much more than subjectship. He also accepted the near-universal regulations that rendered free blacks (and women) de facto second-class citizens, whatever he might say. Still, in context his was an unusually inclusive view. Many whites believed that it granted blacks too much.[113]

Though influential, Bates's opinion was but one source of arguments concerning the status of blacks. Frederick Douglass cited Bates to support black citizenship during the war, but he urged above all that black men fight in the Union army: "Let him get an eagle on his button, and a musket on his shoulder, and bullets in his pocket, and there is no power on the earth . . . which can deny that he has earned the right of citizenship in the United States." Black military service did prove a powerful argument for black citizenship, but the decisive struggles to gain full legal status still had to be waged in Reconstruction debates. Congressional radicals like Stevens saw Reconstruction as an opportunity to "revolutionize Southern institutions, habits, and manners," displacing entirely the old planter class, in part by recognizing black citizenship and enfranchising blacks, in part by confiscating planter lands and redistributing them to the blacks who had worked them. Moderate Republicans, including Lincoln, believed that the old Southern leadership included many ex-Whigs who would support Republican policies if they were treated favorably. The Republicans accepted black citizenship but were less eager to gain the vote for blacks. They also opposed sweeping redistributive measures, although not programs allowing blacks to buy public lands on easy terms. Most Northern leaders also supported the military's policy of employing freed blacks strictly in the South. Despite severe labor shortages in the midwest, Northern white racism politically foreclosed removal measures that otherwise made both economic and strategic sense.[114]

In December 1863 Lincoln proposed his "10 percent" reconstruction plan— that pardoned persons who took an oath of allegiance to the U.S. and its antislavery laws, restored to them all rights "except as to slaves," and permitted them to form a government in their state when their numbers reached 10 percent of the state's voters in 1860. Lincoln cited the requirement in Article IV, section 4, that the United States guarantee every state a "Republican Form of Government" as his constitutional authority for these measures. Both Congress and the President thereafter relied on that guarantee as their basic justification for Reconstruction, producing many references to republican governance, but not much new consensus on what republicanism required.

Because only Confederate officeholders and high-ranking soldiers were excluded from participation in the new government by Lincoln's proposal, and because Lincoln also privately endorsed systems of apprenticeship for freed blacks, radicals charged that his plan would preserve much of the old political hierarchy, replacing slavery simply with landless, disfranchised black peonage. Lincoln nonetheless ordered the military governors he had appointed in 1862 for occupied territories in Tennessee, Louisiana, and Arkansas to implement this blueprint, hoping that it might produce divisions in the enemy. He indicated, however, that he was willing to consider different Reconstruction measures, and he agreed that Congress could decide whether to seat the representatives of these governments. Congress refused, because Radical Republicans doubted their commitment to full black civic equality.[115]

The Thirteenth Amendment. In other respects, the differences between these Radicals and the Lincoln administration were neither polarizing nor paralyzing. Radical Republicans began proposing antislavery amendments in 1863, and after Lincoln also urged one early in 1865, Congress passed the Thirteenth Amendment. It banned slavery definitively, omitting compensation as inappropriate after such a costly and bitter war. (In any case, by then most slaves had already been freed.) Democrats denounced the proposal as exceeding the scope of the amending power, alleging that it would "revolutionize the whole Government" by establishing that the federal government could be given power over the most internal affairs of states. Republicans answered that the amendment would instead fulfill the spirit of the Constitution, as defined by the Declaration of Independence. Southern sympathizers then complained that the amendment was illicitly ratified by reconstruction state governments, acting without full congressional recognition and under coercive orders from Lincoln's successor, Andrew Johnson. Criticism faded, however, when state ratifications went well beyond the three-fourths required. When the amendment was declared adopted on December 18, 1865, Republicans celebrated so mightily that the House had to be adjourned.[116]

The most controversial question raised by the Thirteenth Amendment was how much it authorized beyond abolition. It first declared that neither "slavery nor involuntary servitude . . . shall exist within the United States." A then-novel second section explicitly granted Congress the "power to enforce this article."[117] Radicals in 1866, and Jacobus ten Broek in 1965, argued that this congressional power must go beyond mere abolition of slavery, which the first section seemed to do by itself. Debate still rages over whether section 2 was originally thought to authorize only narrow implementing legislation, such as specifying appropriate remedies and penalties, or whether it was a mandate for sweeping congressional action to secure full black civil and political equality. A point against the broader reading is that Congress rejected more radical language proposed by Senator

Charles Sumner. His text ran: "All persons are equal before the law, so that no person can hold another as a slave," and it gave Congress all "necessary and proper" enforcement powers. Senator Jacob Howard complained that Sumner's phrasing derived from the constitution of the French Revolution. Howard preferred "the good old Anglo-Saxon language" of the Northwest Ordinance. Thus Howard used a Whiggish ethnic appeal to justify a lesser commitment to racial equality. Even so, Sumner still claimed that the amendment allowed Congress to enfranchise blacks if it deemed that necessary to secure their freedom, despite the riders South Carolina and Alabama had added to their ratification acts insisting that the amendment conferred no such power. In reality, neither the amendment's text nor the 38th Congress's debates made it clear whether the amendment even conferred citizenship on freedmen.[118]

The amendment was nonetheless a monumental step toward a more fully liberal law of American political membership, disavowing a status that on free labor premises ought never to have existed. Its ratification triggered a volley of new legislative initiatives aimed at defining the status of blacks more precisely, in the states and at the national level. Those initiatives cut sharply different ways. In 1865, the federal government created the Freedmen's Bureau, and along with some Northern states it also passed laws expanding black civil rights.[119] That same year, Mississippi and South Carolina pioneered the enactment of new Black Codes that were almost as oppressive as slavery. Those countercurrents left Lincoln's successor, Andrew Johnson, in a pivotal position to influence which pattern would prevail. As the nation moved beyond the end of slavery to the question of equal black citizenship, the federal government was thus divided once more between Radical Republicans in Congress and an antislavery but white supremacist former Democrat in the White House. Not even the most radical hour in American history, postwar Reconstruction, would be a time of liberal democratic consensus.

Native Americans. Though the spirit of radical reform that boiled up out of the fires of war created unprecedented support for improving the condition of African-American men, at no point did it extend easily to the other main subordinates in the American civic hierarchy: Native Americans and women. Indeed, if blacks and, to a lesser degree, women earned greater favor among Northern white men by their wartime efforts, many Native Americans embittered them by siding with the Confederacy. None outraged Northerners more than the tribes of the southwest, particularly the relocated Five Civilized Nations. Despite the long if checkered history of federal efforts to restrain hostile state policies in Georgia, Florida, and the Carolinas, these tribes all chose to ally themselves with the South. To some extent this decision was virtually unavoidable given the strength of nearby Confederate forces. Tribes in Oklahoma and Arkansas, in particular, faced Texan troops to the south and west and a range of Confederate state forces to the east. These tribes were also economically dependent on the Confederacy, and its agents offered them attractive (albeit deceptive) terms. But many in the Civilized Nations had another reason for giving their support freely: even after the disruptions caused by their removal, they, too, owned significant numbers of slaves. The Choctaws and Chickasaws especially displayed zeal for "our Southern friends," with whom they shared "social and domestic institutions." When hostilities commenced, most Cherokees reluctantly joined them, though some fought with the North against their own tribesmen. Soon, the slaveowning Southern tribes were not the Union's only Native American opponents. Resentful of countless U.S. treaty violations, tribes throughout the northwest and west also took advantage of the Union's focus on the Confederacy to assault white settlers.

Unsurprisingly, then, Lincoln's Native American policy was largely a matter of bringing rebellious tribes back into submission. The commissioner of Indian affairs, William Dole, also advanced the reservation system more strenuously, seeking to concentrate and isolate troublesome Indians as far away from most whites as possible. Although that strategy was not carried very far during the war itself, Union power did quickly subdue most Native American resistance on every front. Even so, one Cherokee leader, Stand Watie, refused to surrender longer than any other Southern commander. But when the tribes' Confederate allies proved of little assistance, they were compelled to sign new treaties with the federal government relinquishing even more of their lands and autonomy. Union victories in the northwest soon followed, often as a result of tactics of shocking brutality. Most notorious was the Sand Creek massacre of 1864. In response to a sneak attack, Cheyenne chiefs raised a white flag and stood with arms crossed in a peace gesture. Union soldiers proceeded to kill 150 Cheyenne without warning. After the war, outrage over such abuses would trigger a reform era of paternalistic politics toward the tribes, but the new measures would still express the values and interests of whites far more than those of the native peoples.[120]

Women. The Civil War era was more mixed for women. Agitation for women's rights was sharply curtailed by military concerns; but the political status of women was nonetheless subtly enhanced through their contributions to the war effort, extending the small gains begun during the antislavery campaigns of the 1850s. Just before the war, female activists in the North helped gain support for more laws allowing married women to control their earnings. New York enacted one in 1860. After a wartime hiatus, these expansions of women's economic rights resumed, albeit still more out of concerns for market efficiency, as well as male protectiveness, than from acceptance of equal civic status for women.

Between 1861 and 1866, wartime preoccupations also compelled the suspension of the now-annual series of woman's rights conventions. Catharine Beecher's more conservative American Woman's Educational Association disbanded in 1862 as well, although Beecher herself continued to advocate domestically oriented female education. More radical women activists in the North instead devoted themselves wholeheartedly to antislavery and the Union cause. Susan B. Anthony and Elizabeth Cady Stanton founded the Woman's National Loyal League to work for abolition, gathering 400,000 signatures in favor of the Thirteenth Amendment and building organizational networks in the process. Others, including Dorothea Dix, Elizabeth Blackwell, and the U.S. Sanitary Commission, as well as Clara Barton and the Red Cross, organized medical assistance and supplies for Union efforts. Many, like Josephine Griffin and the National Freedmen's Relief Association, helped establish schools and hospitals in occupied areas for both blacks and whites, as noted above. Southern women assisted the Confederate armies. On the home front, the summons of so many men to fight opened up 100,000 factory jobs for women, as well as public and private clerical positions, farm work, normal schools, and teaching posts. These experiences raised many women's expectations for their futures in peacetime. Thus as the war ended, women's rights activists joined in the surging tide of Reconstruction reforms, hopeful that it would carry them as well as the freedmen to the golden shores of enfranchisement and full citizenship.[121]

The waves of reform they had helped swell were powerful mixtures of egalitarian religious, free labor, and republic civic sentiments that generated a period of liberalizing civic reforms unmatched in the nation's history. Yet once the special wartime conditions ceased, and once the overriding purpose of reform was not combating Southern aristocrats and slavery but instead accepting equal citizenship for blacks and possibly women, the political landscape shifted. All those who had ideological, psychological, and material reasons to defend traditional forms of ascriptive hierarchy found themselves again in strong positions to shape American civic life. Though a glorious era of liberal victories still emerged, it would prove hard-fought and short-lived.

10

The America That "Never Was"
The Radical Hour, 1866–1876

To forge a new Union without slavery, Republicans emancipated and empowered blacks, first with arms, then with citizenship and civil rights, and finally with the franchise. Their dramatic efforts produced three constitutional amendments and six major federal statutes that comprised the most extensive restructuring of American citizenship laws in the nation's history, apart from the adoption of the Constitution itself. And the legal foundations of this restructuring were far more consistent than those of the heavily compromised Constitution: though not wholly unalloyed, the Thirteenth, Fourteenth, and Fifteenth Amendments, the Civil Rights Acts of 1866, 1870, 1871, and 1875, the Expatriation Act of 1868, and the Naturalization Act of 1870 all proclaimed egalitarian, nationalistic liberal republican principles to a degree that was unimaginably radical for most Republicans in 1860. The laws did not prevent the building of new systems of racial injustice in the United States, but they did establish a new framework for civic arguments that could not easily be ignored. In accounts stressing the liberal democratic character of America's "true" civic ideals, these reforms are rightly prominent.

Yet authors of those accounts face the grave task of explaining the swift eclipse of Radical Congressional Reconstruction, already well under way in the early 1870s, though its final repudiation did not come until the 1890s. That eclipse contrasts to the ongoing success of Reconstruction's Republican sponsors. From 1864 to 1912, the party of Lincoln gained popular majorities in nine of twelve presidential elections and won ten. It controlled the Senate for forty-four of those forty-eight years and the House for thirty, with the Democrats in full control of Congress for only four years. Once

Lincoln appointed Salmon Chase to replace the deceased Taney as Chief Justice in 1864, Republican appointees also remained in the majority on the Supreme Court through 1937. From 1872 to 1888, years in which the Court struck its most lethal blows against Reconstruction statutes, only the nominally Democratic Justice Stephen Field broke its all-Republican ranks.[1] If Reconstruction is seen as triumphantly correcting the one great exception to a hegemonic liberal democratic creed, then its collapse despite its sponsoring party's hold on power seems inexplicable.

Louis Hartz tersely acknowledged Reconstruction's failures but offered no real reason for them, preferring to stress the Republicans' electoral successes and liberal capitalist policies, in keeping with his neglect of racial inequalities. Later scholars have, however, found authority for a Hartz-like explanation in a great work which does not ignore race: W. E. B. Du Bois's *Black Reconstruction in America*. In this masterpiece of Marxian historical analysis, Du Bois wrote much that attributed Reconstruction's demise to the shortcomings of "liberalism" and the "American Assumption" that in a capitalist market system all could flourish. Only Thaddeus Stevens and a few other radicals, Du Bois argued, saw that Reconstruction required the use of "force" to "change the basis of property and redistribute income" in the South. The great majority of Union supporters could not "bring themselves to countenance" such redistribution because of their liberal attachments to property rights and opposition to labor radicalism. For most white laborers and many in the petty bourgeoisie, these beliefs represented counterproductive delusions, Du Bois thought. They expressed only the interests of leading industrialists and financiers. Although those high capitalists supported black political rights when it seemed strategic, they feared economic radicalism and disorder, and so they soon made their peace with large Southern landowners at the expense of blacks. Following Eric Foner, who cites Du Bois's example, much scholarship has cast this argument in terms of the contradictions and inegalitarianism of the Republicans' free labor ideology, usually described as a form of republicanism that was "liberal" in its commitments to capitalist market property rights.[2]

Du Bois recognized throughout his book, however, that not only could "national industry . . . get its way easier by alliance with Southern landholders than by sustaining Southern workers," but also that "after the momentary exaltation of war, the nation did not want Negroes to have civil rights." That racist aversion divided labor and facilitated the capitalist-planter alliance Du Bois saw as prevailing. Even so, he contended that, although black rights were often opposed in the name of "racial . . . animosity," it was the "determination of land and capital to restrict the political power of labor" that was the "fundamental" reason for Reconstruction's failings. Yet he also argued that "the color problem" was "the

Blindspot of American political and social development" which prevented "logical" alliances, "black and white, North and South," in support of "industrial democracy." He considered it "the key," as well, to the career of Andrew Johnson, the man who slammed shut Reconstruction's largest window of opportunity for black economic progress.[3]

Any plausible account of Reconstruction must give weight to all the factors Du Bois identified: Northern capitalist and Southern planter desires for a stable economy untainted by labor radicalism, white labor fears of black competition, ideological beliefs in private property and the adequacy of market systems for all, as well as the reinvigorated racist doctrines he described.[4] But like Hartz, though to a far lesser degree, Du Bois, owing to his socialism, judged too dogmatically that the "real underlying industrial causes" of resistance to Reconstruction were only "obscured" by "race hatred." His example has strengthened later scholars in the same conclusion. If we view the evidence through a multiple traditions approach instead of a narrower capital-versus-labor frame, white commitments to racial hierarchy emerge as even more pivotal than capitalism in explaining the end of America's radical hour.

To be sure, the racist doctrines and practices that had been so thoroughly reinforced by the policies and public intellectuals of the Jacksonian era were for a time submerged by the egalitarian religious and moral principles that came to define the war's mission for many Northerners. But overcoming entrenched hierarchies proved a dauntingly complex and costly task, and new theories of racial evolution also began elevating the intellectual credibility of scientific racism to new heights, especially after 1870. This racism, old and new, mass and elite, proved most crucial to Reconstruction's demise, and it was his unwillingness to break from his class and region's especially potent heritage of prejudice that most accounted for Andrew Johnson's fateful obstructionism. The broader resurgence of notions of racial superiority in the postwar American political and intellectual climate gave value to the "psychological wage" of white supremacy, a "wage" that Du Bois correctly invoked to explain alliances of rich and poor that fly in the face of both Marxian and liberal notions of economic self-interest.[5]

In the postwar era, both parties continued to blend liberal, republican, and ascriptive elements in ideological combinations designed to assist partisan nation-building; and in order to understand the fate of egalitarian reforms, it is vital to recognize that the Democratic mix continued to have many advantages over the Republican mosaic, especially as presented by radical Republicans. That fact is obscured by the undeniable reality that the Democrats bore very heavy burdens. They had defended the discredited causes of slavery and secession. Yet their enduring tenets of white male supremacy, states' rights, and no special privileges for any groups all retained great popular appeal even at their lowest ebb, in the mid-

1860s. Republican ranks contained many former antislavery Democrats who still endorsed these three positions. But most Republicans were former Whigs who usually favored only the first—white supremacy—and they were joined uneasily by egalitarian white radicals and new black voters, who challenged all three. Without antislavery to unite them, it was hard during the postwar years to find planks that could appeal to all of this coalition, much less the general electorate.

Even so, the Republicans had great assets. With their successful leadership during the war and their redefinition of its aims in terms of stirring moral and religious purposes, they were well positioned in its aftermath to win support by wielding the Whigs' old weapon, patriotism. For a time, with the populace profoundly stirred by the triumph of the sanctified cause of human liberty and the ensuing martyrdom of the Great Emancipator, many leading Republicans thought it both right and strategic to use their power to build the great new legal systems of racial equality that are Reconstruction's enduring achievements. Without those dramatic violent events, combined with the genuine depth and breadth of American beliefs in liberal republican free labor principles, Reconstruction could not have occurred. But soon, many white Americans felt threatened by the radical changes those laws entailed. And as the new evolutionary theories refreshed the legitimacy of racist beliefs that had been partly discredited by the war's moral fervor, and states' rights republicanism, racism's old ally, also gained new credibility because of the massive national coercions Reconstruction involved, finally not even the bloody flag could sustain political support for radical reforms. From the early 1870s on, prominent Republicans began turning away from the now-scorned cause of genuine racial justice. By the mid-1890s, the legal pillars of equality they had erected with so much hope and pain became imposing but empty monuments to an abandoned dream.

The Stages of Reconstruction

The Reconstruction era in which all this occurred involved at least four stages. The first, "preliminary" stage was from 1862 to 1865, as Lincoln adopted tentative plans for reconstituting recaptured states, in tense but not antagonistic dialogue with congressional radicals. At his death, the radicals had reason to believe that Lincoln was moving in their direction, and the political climate produced by the combination of Lee's surrender and Lincoln's assassination then provided the best chance for truly sweeping changes in the defeated and demoralized South. But in the second, "obstructed" stage of Reconstruction, from late May 1865 through 1867, Andrew Johnson mulishly opposed the radicals' efforts and imposed his own reactionary policies. Congressional radicals then wrested national control from Johnson's hands, creating the third stage of "Radical

Congressional" Reconstruction; but they did so in a political context made much less favorable by Johnson, who had both removed racial egalitarians from key offices and renewed the hopes of white Southerners to maintain their privileges. Congressional Reconstruction, from 1867 through 1876, was thus less radical than it had once promised to be, particularly in regard to land redistribution, but it still was strongly committed to black political rights. That dedication eroded through the early 1870s, however. It was never a central party commitment after the infamous bargain of 1877 that led to the election of President Rutherford B. Hayes at the price of ending military occupation of the South. But as recent scholarship has shown, Reconstruction cannot be said to have ended then. During a fourth, "remnant" stage, many Republicans still were trying to secure their hold on power with black votes, a strategy that required protecting at least some black political rights. Only after more struggles in the 1890s did Republicans acquiesce in the disfranchisement of blacks, abandoning a political alliance that once promised to build a more truly egalitarian nation.[6]

In assessing Reconstruction civic reforms, the balance sheet cannot be limited to blacks alone. Central as their role was, Reconstruction always involved efforts to reconstitute American citizenship more generally in ways that had broadly parallel effects on a wide range of groups and citizenship issues. In most areas, including legislative and judicial rules governing expatriation, naturalization, immigration, diversity of citizenship jurisdiction, and civic privileges and immunities, prevailing laws initially were reshaped by the nationalizing, liberalizing, and egalitarian thrust of Reconstruction reforms, just as rules governing African-Americans were. But in virtually all these areas, opposition soon arose that undercut these changes after 1876.

There were two partial exceptions to this pattern: women and Native Americans. Neither shared much in the reform spirit of the late 1860s. In the case of women, the close antebellum alliance between advocates of equal rights for blacks and for women shattered by 1867 on the shoals of the antagonisms that both causes stirred. That break-up most hurt women's rights, which made few further advances until the twentieth century. And because Native Americans had largely sided with the South, and some continued to engage in armed resistance, they were not objects of much solicitude during Reconstruction's height. But then, in a bitter irony, many reformers who had faltered in the task of making yeoman farmers and full American citizens out of African-Americans, most of whom ardently desired this status, went on in the 1870s to try harder to make yeoman farmers and at least second-class citizens out of Native Americans, who fiercely resisted the same changes. These efforts also failed. Only the citizenship of white men and the quasi-citizenship of corporations remained intact as Reconstruction closed.

Race, Gender, and the Intellectual Context of Reconstruction

Scholars have sometimes understated the role of racism during these years because they have not given due weight to the broader climate of thinking on race, in Europe as well as America, during Reconstruction. Intellectual changes were stirring that would eventually transform American civic ideologies more than ever before, or since. The scientific racism of the American school of ethnology that came to intellectual predominance as a slavery defense during the Jacksonian years persisted, and it was regularly invoked by Democratic politicians and racist writers to oppose Reconstruction. In 1868, John Van Evrie republished his lengthy defense of white supremacy, prefaced with a denunciation of Reconstruction, and he distributed the English ethnologist James Hunt's lecture endorsing Samuel George Morton's claims for black inferiority.[7] These scientific racist doctrines were not answered on the same intellectual plane for another generation. Instead, the defenses of egalitarianism that the Republicans made were almost entirely moral and religious, not scientific. Though they insisted that blacks were endowed by the creator with moral equality in terms of basic rights, not even the most radical white Republicans really tried to refute claims for the intellectual, emotional, and biological inferiority of blacks. Many instead conceded such inferiority, only urging that it did not justify denials of the rights in the Declaration of Independence. Most other reformers maintained that the question of black inferiority must await the results of experience under conditions of equal opportunity.

But if antislavery advocates were silent on the scientific issues of racial inequality, others were not. The main intellectual task of the 1860s—indeed, of the second half of the nineteenth century—was coping with the staggering concept of evolution, including the evolution of humanity. Accepting nature's evolutionary character required proponents of Enlightenment liberal, civic republican, and ascriptive Americanist views to engage in major philosophic reconstructions of their positions, a process that shaped American politics for generations to come. Initially, however, the primary effect was to strengthen ascriptive outlooks. By the mid-1870s, the revivification of theories of racial hierarchy was bolstering the official retreat from radical political reconstruction and also new policies hostile to Chinese immigrants, even as it justified renewed paternalism toward the native tribes and undercut the much weaker efforts to liberalize the status of women.

Charles Darwin was the most prestigious proponent of evolutionary doctrines, but Herbert Spencer was perhaps more politically influential. Both explicitly drew a conclusion that was devastating for the egalitarianism of Reconstruction: though the scientific racists were wrong about polygenesis, they were right that racial inequalities were real and largely ineradicable. Darwin's *Origin of Species* (1859) did not discuss human evolution, but it kindled so much debate that it made "'anthropology' in the broad sense . . . the central intellectual problem of the 1860s." In America, that "problem" inevitably centered on the questions of the status of blacks as well as women.[8]

After a decade's debate by others, in which many drew racially hierarchical conclusions, Darwin addressed the issues himself in his *Descent of Man*, published in 1870 just as Americans ratified the Fifteenth Amendment giving blacks the vote. His observations were speculative and inconclusive, but they, too, most favored defenses of racial and gender inequality. Darwin cited Nott and Gliddon's *Types of Mankind* four times, only once respectfully disagreeing, and he also relied on the extensive studies of American soldiers during the Civil War, many conducted on scientific racist premises. Though he stated that there were "numerous points of mental similarity between the most distinct races of man," Darwin used these sources to argue that there was "no doubt that the various races, when carefully compared and measured, differ much from each other," and that their "mental characteristics are likewise very distinct; chiefly as it would appear in their emotional, but partly in their intellectual faculties." To be sure, Darwin often supported racial minorities and women, holding their precise potential to be unclear, and favoring education and opportunities so that the best equipped individuals could achieve all they proved capable of doing. Even so, this long-awaited work placed his great authority firmly on the side of racial and gender differences, as well as the superiority of "civilized nations" to "barbarians."[9]

Herbert Spencer was one of several writers who put forth evolution as a universal principle of physical development before Darwin's work appeared. Spencer's version emphasized the doctrine of the French zoologist Jean-Baptiste Lamarck that acquired characteristics could be inherited, rather than Darwin's account of natural selection among random variations. Many Americans embraced Lamarckianism, and evolutionary ideas also drew on the ideas of human historical and cultural development put forth by Hegel before the Civil War and elaborated by German historians and philosophers after it. Hence it is wrong to equate the impact of the idea of evolution with Darwin's influence. But in many ways, the different evolutionary theories were mutually reinforcing. Darwin was also Lamarckian in part, seeing some evolutionary role for inheritance of acquired traits. Such Lamarckianism also served as a vital linchpin between cultural and biological notions of evolution. It explained how differences originating in varying social as well as physical environments could become biologically transmissible traits. Thus "higher" cultures produced people who were "better" than those of "lower" ones.[10]

The massive statistics compiled during the Civil War strongly buttressed the scientific credibility of these claims, and most Anglo-American analysts of race, anthropology, and evolution for the rest of the century relied on them. Aided by funding from insurance companies, the private U.S. Sanitary Commission compiled extensive information on soldiers, "contraband" blacks, and various comparison groups, as did the army's Provost Marshal-General's Bureau. The studies included physical measurements and many photographs of more than 22,000 subjects, classified according to the ethnologists' categories of "higher" and "lower" races. The data provided grist for both hereditarian and environmentalist views of the determinants of human traits, thus aiding both sides in the still-raging polygenesis-versus-monogenesis debate. But regardless of that issue, most analysts claimed to find empirical support for the physical and mental superiority of whites. The indefatigable Josiah Nott argued in 1866 that this was what counted. If the races were perhaps "not distinct species," evolution moved so slowly that for all practical purposes they should nonetheless be regarded as "permanent varieties" of mankind, hierarchically ranked. Similarly, California physician Arthur B. Stout opposed Chinese immigration in 1862 on racial grounds, relying in part on Nott's writings. In 1870, Stout switched to using Darwin as the foundation of the same case without missing a bigoted beat. In his 1874 *Study of Sociology*, as well as other writings, Herbert Spencer added his own evolution-based affirmation of these inegalitarian positions. However races originated, he regularly insisted, modern science gave "abundant proofs that subjection to different modes of life, produces in the course of ages permanent bodily and mental differences" in the races.[11]

Here, as so often, these claims of racial inequality were intertwined with arguments for gender hierarchies. White women, to be sure, were never so bitterly denounced as hopelessly inferior as all blacks were. Opponents of full gender equality still rhapsodized endlessly about the genteel virtues of their wives and daughters. Scientific racists like Van Evrie and Van Amringe often claimed that the superior treatment of women was one of the hallmarks of more advanced races. Early in his career Herbert Spencer went further, not only frequently celebrating the improved status of women as the hallmark of "civilized" as opposed to "savage" societies, as Jefferson did, but also advocating equal rights for women. Yet Spencer still found it hard to fathom that women expected to play more than a complementary domestic role to men, being so obviously biologically suited for lives centered around reproduction. In his view, civilized life actually tended to widen the gap between male and female capacities, making women, like all more advanced forms of life, increasingly suited only to their more specialized roles.

Many male scientists had more extreme attitudes. Motivated by theoretical commitments, concern for their own professional hegemony, or both, male scholars of human development frequently identified the traits, growth processes, and mental abilities of women with those of racial minorities during these years. As Nancy Stepan has shown, for these scientists, "lower races represented the 'female' type of human species, and females the 'lower race' of gender." Cynthia Russett thus argues that in their accounts "the issues of race and sex were intimately related—not two separate problems but two aspects of the same problem." Analysts claimed that the Civil War measurements and some other studies (along with much flimsy anecdotal authority) showed just why women as well as the "inferior races" were so lowly. Smaller brain size continued to be a favorite explanation, but it was reinforced by a new, erroneous, but prevalent allegation. Although nonwhite races and women developed "normally" as children, various scientists claimed that around puberty, their cranial sutures closed and cut off brain growth, unlike the pattern in white men. Hence in all women and in colored men, the impulsive emotionality that puberty kindled was said not to be checked by expanding ratiocinative powers. That left them both childlike and dangerously passionate (especially around each other). Darwin himself legitimized this linkage, writing that many of the defining qualities of women "are characteristics of the lower races, therefore of a past and lower state of civilization." Hence, although they were rarely so vituperative about women as about the "colored races," late nineteenth-century scientists were in the forefront of renewed arguments for sharply limiting women's educational and professional advancement. The leading work attacking equal education for women, Edward Clarke's *Sex in Education* (1873), was written by a Harvard Medical School professor who cited both Darwin and Spencer.[12]

There was one vital distinction in evolutionary scientists' treatment of women and "lower" races. Although some favored paternalistic programs of improvement for racial minorities, many expected that all such efforts would go for naught. They believed that the multifaceted competition with whites in which emancipated blacks had to engage would mean their extinction in the near or not-so-near future. Darwin made that prediction explicitly in *Descent of Man.* And although some favored humanitarian efforts to forestall this development, to most it seemed futile to try to stay the inevitable consequences of the natural struggle. A policy of neglect that was not expected to be benign was the only reasonable course of action. The rising intellectual prestige of these inegalitarian racial views in the late 1860s and early 1870s militated strongly against efforts to help blacks adjust to freedom. In contrast, though few scientists predicted gender equality, none imagined women's demise.[13]

Most evolutionists also affirmed the dangers of the possibility that most inflamed opposition to people of color: miscegenation. The pejorative term was used as the title of an anonymous pamphlet written by Democratic journalists

David Goodman Croly (father of centrist progressive thinker Herbert Croly) and George Wakeman in 1863. Purporting to be a Radical Republican document, it asserted the superiority of mixed races and claimed that such intermarriage was the Republicans' goal. The uproar it engendered led the War Department's Freedmen's Inquiry Commission to argue in 1864 that "mixed" races were inferior to "pure" ones. Most postwar scientists and evolutionary theorists agreed. Spencer maintained that interbreeding among the European "races" could have positive consequences. But white pairings with blacks, Chinese, Japanese, and other more "distant" races would produce only stunted, backward offspring. These scientific endorsements of sexual separation of the races greatly reinforced the views of those who insisted that even if the political rights of blacks had to be increased, social segregation should be enforced.[14] Evolutionists like Spencer also frequently supported claims that the Anglo-Saxon race was uniquely equipped for political freedom by its heritage from ancient Teutonic tribes. That argument was increasingly bolstered by scholars inspired by Sir Henry Maine's insistence on the historically shaped character of the institutions of each "race" or "people" in his *Ancient Law* (1861). Evolutionary biology thus not only strengthened scientific racism and folk scientific claims of racial and gender inequality; its reinforcement of romantic historicism became a significant resource for advocates of inegalitarian citizenship policies.[15]

Reconstruction and the Battle over Republicanism

A final backdrop to Reconstruction was the continuing power of states' rights republican views among two groups essential to Republican success: antislavery Democrats and, especially, constitutional lawyers. The battle between more nationalistic and more state-centric versions of republicanism had, of course, a long history, tracing back through the Federalists and Jeffersonians and the Whigs and Jacksonian Democrats. States' rights republicanism had always been bound up with the efforts of laissez-faire advocates to resist national economic management, and it was particularly tied to defenses of black subordination. During Reconstruction those alliances became even firmer. Such republicanism was, however, always more than purely a surrogate for either of those positions. The state powers thus defended were often used for economic regulations, contrary to laissez-faire. And even sincere proponents of African-American freedom like Salmon Chase, the architect of antislavery constitutionalism, resisted sweepingly nationalistic views of republican governance as potentially dictatorial.

For nearly a generation, moreover, the nationalist constitutional views of Whigs like Webster and Clay had been losing to the state-tilted dual federalism of the Jacksonians, so that a large body of constitutional law had been built up on the latter premises. As Michael Les Benedict and others have shown in the past two decades, many lawyers and judges felt reluctant to sweep aside those precedents, even when they were not wholehearted advocates of laissez-faire versions of free labor ideology or white supremacy. Their constitutional positions thus often made them reluctant allies of the latter position. Effective Reconstruction required massive exertions of national power that could not help but trigger the fears of centralized, unrepublican despotism that traced back to the nation's birth.[16]

Led in this, as in so much else, by Charles Sumner, congressional radicals tried to still those fears by employing the republican guarantee clause as their constitutional license for the Union's coercive military and Reconstruction measures. But in order to do so, they had to elaborate quite a different sense of what republicanism demanded. Generally, moderate as well as Radical Republicans identified a republican government with conformity to the Enlightenment guarantees of rights and liberties in the Declaration of Independence. Such conformity meant at least the end of slavery and roughly equal economic rights for blacks. For Sumner, republicanism also meant full political and civil equality for all races. Few of his colleagues were willing to follow him quite that far, partly because they feared embracing such unvarnished radicalism, partly because his legal arguments, though learned and creative, tended to be too loose and sweeping to be fully convincing. Sumner's fullest exposition of the guarantee clause came, moreover, in a speech against the proposed Fourteenth Amendment as insufficiently protective of equal rights and "complete" citizenship for blacks.[17] Though most Republicans rejected that uncompromising stance, many still agreed that the guarantee clause provided a mandate for virtual federal omnipotence, empowering the President, and especially Congress, to transform the states as much as necessary to realize egalitarian republican principles.[18]

Anti-Reconstruction forces were initially taken aback by the radicals' identification of the guarantee clause with these strikingly liberal and nationalistic definitions of republicanism, so sharply opposed to the state-centered as well as racist views that republican rhetoric had long served. But that heritage enabled the Democrats to rally quickly and to insist that the constitutional meaning of republican government had to be defined almost entirely by reference to institutional forms in the states, preferably those existing in 1787. They also stressed that nothing was more unrepublican than centralized tyranny and the enfranchisement of those unfit for republican citizenship, both of which they saw as integral to Radical Reconstruction. These themes appear frequently in the congressional speeches of Confederate-leaning "Copperhead" Northern democrats and white Southerners and in the veto messages and State of the Union addresses that Andrew Johnson used to oppose most forms of assistance to freed blacks. A "republican form of government" was not "guaranteed to the states," he repeatedly insisted, by "stripping whole States of their liberties" and reducing them to "military dependencies."[19]

Even after Salmon Chase became Chief Justice, many on the Supreme Court found these familiar Jacksonian versions of states' rights republicanism more constitutionally plausible in many respects. The Taney Court precedent of *Luther v. Borden* provided them with a convenient avenue for avoiding taking a clear position on what constitutional republicanism involved, as it held that the Constitution assigned that question largely to other officials. Thus in *Texas v. White* (1869), the Court cited *Luther* to uphold both national executive and legislative actions affecting the rebel state of Texas. Like the Jacksonian he had in some respects always remained, Chase stressed that "the power to carry into effect the clause of guaranty is primarily a legislative power, and resides in Congress," and that "a discretion in the choice of means is necessarily allowed."[20] Hence the Court would accept provisionally what the President did in the clause's name, and it would then approve whatever permanent measures, large or small, Congress said that republicanism required. On its face and to a considerable degree in effect, that ruling permitted radical congressional measures to carry the day; but it did so while refusing to give radical views constitutional status. Thus, when public opposition to the costs and aims of Reconstruction prompted Republicans to accept new racial injustices by the Southern states, the Court continued to defer. The republican guarantee clause that Sumner had tried to make the source of a constitutional mandate for radical Reconstruction became by the mid-1870s a "dead letter," in William Wiecek's judgment.[21] By then, the Court itself was using states' rights arguments to resist Reconstruction laws and racial and gender equality.

In this chapter I first discuss legislation, then court decisions, in order to convey the import of the judiciary's attachment to states' rights. Broadly, the Supreme Court and Congress were in step during these years, with support for egalitarian, nationalistic measures in the late 1860s giving way to various retreats from radicalism by the mid-1870s. But the Court significantly shaped those retreats by reading the recently enacted Reconstruction statutes and amendments narrowly, often building on states' rights and inegalitarian ascriptive conceptions rather than free labor precepts in order to do so. Hence the Court frequently developed doctrines that were deeply opposed to the spirit of what Congress had done, though not necessarily so distant from what many congressmen were thinking by the time the justices acted. Both branches also dealt with an extraordinarily dense mass of citizenship issues in these years. To keep their distinct roles clear, I will here first discuss all of the major Reconstruction legislative initiatives that aimed, at least at first, at more equal citizenship for all. Then I will discuss the separate evolution of judicial rulemaking on these various civic fronts.

Battles for Equal Citizenship: The Freedmen's Bureau

Yet even bearing in mind the renewed power of racist and states' rights republican traditions, along with liberal aversions to economic radicalism, the stages of Reconstruction appear more the result of contingent political struggles than any inevitable outcome. Never one to romanticize white humanitarianism, W. E. B. Du Bois contended that for "a brief period" in the late 1860s and early 1870s, "the majority of thinking Americans of the North believed in the equal manhood of Negroes. They acted accordingly with a thoroughness and clean-cut decision that no age which does not share that faith can in the slightest comprehend." In so believing, white Americans were not totally transformed. They instead chose to embrace more fully than ever their political and religious traditions of human moral equality and to reject many of their logically inconsistent ascriptive hierarchical notions (though even Du Bois, like most Reconstruction radicals, continually expressed otherwise inclusive traditions in terms of the rights of "manhood"). If racism and fears of centralized despotism were being reinforced during these years, egalitarian commitments were also enormously strengthened by their increasing identification as the war's great moral purpose, their attendant glorification in the popular songs and stories the war produced, and their initial strategic value for consolidating the North's triumphs with black support.[22]

One measure of the fervor of the period was congressional passage of a denationalization provision on March 3, 1865, the same day that Congress created the Freedmen's Bureau. It added to the penalties for desertion the stipulation that military deserters "shall be deemed and taken to have voluntarily relinquished and forfeited their rights of citizenship and their rights to become citizens." This penalty, which remained on the nation's statute books until the U.S. Supreme Court invalidated it in 1958, could find some justification in liberal republican consensualism. If citizenship rested on a sort of civic contract, presumably it could be forfeited if the citizen broke the contract's terms. But it was in tension with the nation's liberal tradition of protecting individuals from the asymmetries introduced by the enormous powers of the republic the hypothetical "social contract" created.[23] Even so, amid the militant patriotism stirred by the war, state courts sustained the measure with little debate. They regarded it as "highly penal," however, and insisted that denationalization could result only if full due process, in the form of a court-martial proceeding, had been completed.[24]

Given this aroused, even vindictive Northern mood, the fate of Reconstruction may have turned on the fact that Andrew Johnson succeeded to office when Lincoln was assassinated five days after Lee's surrender. At that point, prospects for change were at their peak. To be sure, the Lincoln administration had not much exercised its authorization to confiscate rebel lands, and congressional radicals like Sumner and Stevens had found Lincoln's initial reconstruction plans too indulgent toward Southern whites. But Lincoln had stressed that he was not wedded to those specifics, and throughout his career he often moved to more radical positions as soon as he thought it politically feasible to do so. Indeed, it was Lincoln's endorsement of voting rights for literate blacks and black veterans in a speech on April 11 that drove John Wilkes Booth to shoot the President three days later. Lincoln's stance, Booth fumed, meant "nigger citizenship."[25] Lincoln's martyrdom heightened the charged emotions surrounding Union victory just when morale among defeated white Southerners was at a low ebb. An egalitarian new President might then have been able to push through sweeping changes.[26]

How sweeping is a matter of dispute. Many of the claims that American liberal ideology prevented truly radical Reconstruction measures turn on the failure of the federal government to make farmland available to the freedmen, to fulfill the hopes for "forty acres and a mule" during this period. That failure was indeed crucial, because without this basis for economic independence and advancement, not even the voting rights they acquired protected blacks from exploitation and domination. Du Bois traced this "disaster" chiefly to America's liberalism, which allegedly did not recognize that "economic power underlies politics" and so would not "countenance" redistribution of property in the form of land and tools to blacks, and many scholars since have essentially agreed. Thus Eric Foner has suggested that "the constraints of the free labor ideology" inhibited "efforts to provide an economic underpinning for blacks' new freedom"; George Fredrickson has contended that "the dominant *laissez-faire* ideology" placed "a priori limitations" on measures to aid blacks; Claude Oubre has traced Reconstruction's failings to "the economic concepts of the time"; and Herman Belz has argued that "the individualistic, self-help ethic of laissez-faire capitalism precluded" more extensive reforms.[27]

A general liberal ideological opposition to property redistribution did exist in 1865 and thereafter, but it probably was not as pivotal as these quotations imply. The key steps preventing redistribution often violated free labor precepts and were justified instead in racial or states' rights terms. Since Locke, after all, much liberal economic thought had insisted that valid property rights originated only in rational, productive labor, and that national governments could structure property relations to see that such labor was encouraged. Those views had challenged the property rights of landed aristocrats in England, and it was easier intellectually to challenge the claims of largely idle slaveowners on behalf of those who worked their fields. Perhaps the planters had some liberal claim to the fruits of labor they had rationally organized, but not much. They had used immoral coercion, and blacks did not only the physical labor but even much of the supervision. Thus, as Du Bois wrote, "by every analogy in history, when they were emancipated the land ought to have belonged in large part to the workers."[28]

Indeed, far from finding redistribution unthinkable, in 1864 Andrew Johnson had insisted that the rebel leaders' treason alone meant that their "great plantations" should be "seized and divided into small farms, and sold to honest, industrious men," though he did not mean blacks. The year before, one of the three members of the War Department's Freedmen's Inquiry Commission, James McKaye, explicitly urged confiscation and redistribution of planters' lands for freedmen.[29] Consonant with Lockean concepts, African-Americans repeatedly argued during this period that they were seeking title to property they had earned as a matter of right: as a Tennessee freedman said, "We made what our Masters had." In January 1865, a group of blacks led by a carpenter-minister, Garrison Frazier, urged Secretary of War Edwin Stanton to support land for blacks so that they could "reap the fruit of our own labor." Stanton's actions that year suggest that he was persuaded. Four days after the meeting, General William Sherman issued Special Field Order 15, granting South Carolina's Sea Islands and part of the state's coastal lands to blacks, at least temporarily, thus providing a precedent for redistribution. Stanton ordered General Rufus Saxton, who would soon become a leading Freedmen's Bureau official, to enforce the order. Saxton meant the redistributions to be permanent.[30]

Most important, the act establishing the Bureau of Refugees, Freedmen, and Abandoned Lands (the Freedmen's Bureau), inspired by the report of the Inquiry Commission and passed on March 3, 1865, specifically provided aid to blacks in gaining land. It was only a temporary, one-year measure to help emancipated blacks adjust to their new circumstances, without a budget of its own. But it inherited jurisdiction over confiscated and abandoned lands from the Treasury Department and over a large force of former slaves from the War Department, and its efforts proved extraordinarily broad-ranging. The Freedmen's Bureau was entitled to make confiscated and abandoned Southern lands available to free blacks, who could work them and purchase them with their profits at low prices within three years. Without specific authorization, the bureau also undertook to promote black education, provide aid for the destitute and medically needy, pressure state governments to treat blacks fairly, adjudicate some disputes in its own courts, and, above all, to integrate blacks into a new free labor economic system in the South.

The bureau's strange combination of huge tasks with a brief life span and limited resources reflected a compromise among the ideological and political currents in Congress, as states' rights, laissez-faire, and white supremacist concerns all checked the powerful commitments many congressmen felt to help the freedmen. As a result, the bureau's fate depended on how it was administered. It was headed by the "Christian General," Oliver Otis Howard, whose assistant commissioners included men like the pro-redistribution Saxton overseeing South Carolina, Georgia, and Florida, the likeminded preacher Thomas Conway in Louisiana, and the radical abolitionist General Edgar Gregory in Texas, along with some more conservative figures. Though none of these men approached Thaddeus Stevens's economic radicalism, many were strongly determined to protect blacks against exploitation, preferably by placing them on their own land. As William McFeely notes, however, Howard was "a good general but only when he served a great one," and his assistants depended on him. In the political climate of 1865, a great egalitarian president might have found these men invaluable in working out sustainable ways to provide blacks with the resources they needed; but President Johnson was instead their greatest enemy.[31]

Some scholars have stressed that, in any case, getting land sufficient for the four million freed blacks was a major problem, as the wartime Confiscation Acts had not been much enforced. The bureau thus could lay claim only to some 850,000 acres of abandoned, captured, or confiscated Southern lands, when extending the policy of Special Order 15 to all blacks would take some 40 million acres. The South did contain 46 million acres of federally owned land, but much of it was swampland or coastal beaches without farming potential that had long gone unpurchased, even at giveaway prices. Yet like the barriers posed to redistribution by liberal ideology, the problems of land supply should not be exaggerated. From 1862 through 1871, the federal government granted 120 million acres of land to the railroads and conferred another 105 million acres on western homesteaders and the Morrill Act land grant colleges. More than 67 million acres were given the railroads during the three years of the Freedmen's Bureau's existence, when redistribution to blacks was supposedly paralyzed by a laissez-faire ethic.

It is true that much of that land was to the west and north of the soil with which blacks had mixed their labor. But few of the eventual recipients had earned Lockean titles to those lands, either. They merely promised to labor on them in ways that would serve the public good. Many blacks were much more willing to move to those regions and work them productively than the local white inhabitants were to welcome them, though it is true that many blacks would have needed help getting west. Yet if the nation's goal really was a self-supporting, racially egalitarian yeoman citizenry, few measures could have served this end more effectively. It was not, then, lack of land, nor liberal nor states' rights opposition to federal land provision per se, that kept freed blacks from obtaining their forty acres.[32]

Andrew Johnson had, moreover, many political incentives to support radical Reconstruction measures. He was despised by the Southern plantation elite he had denounced throughout his career. And as the heir of Lincoln and commander-in-chief of a victorious army he was at first enormously popular in the North, the recipient of staunch support from both the moderate and radical Republicans who dominated Congress. In these circumstances he had little apparent reason to divide the North and his new party by picking fights with Congress. Service to their causes might well have made him a popular long-time President. Indeed, when Johnson first assumed office, his private conversations gave hope to some radicals, particularly Sumner, that he would side with them more fully than Lincoln had done.[33]

But on May 9, 1865, Johnson recognized a reconstructed Virginia government that congressional radicals rejected; and on May 29, the President stunned them by granting amnesty to all but the most prominent and the most wealthy Confederates, and promising that their confiscated lands would be restored. Even the rebel leaders could seek personal presidential pardons, a move well designed for Johnson to convert old foes into allies. By implication, the Amnesty Proclamation abrogated the provisions in the Freedmen's Bureau Act giving the agency control over confiscated lands. Through the summer of 1865, Howard, Saxton, and other bureau officials, supported by Stanton and Attorney General James Speed, tried to assert the bureau's ongoing authority and redistributive mission. But Johnson countermanded their orders and began replacing bureau officials whom he viewed as too zealous for black rights. Conway lost his Louisiana post in September; South Carolina blacks had their new lands forcibly repossessed; Saxton was replaced in January 1866; and by then Howard had been cowed into placating Southern planters. Blacks thereafter lost lands assigned them in Virginia, North Carolina, Louisiana, Mississippi—everywhere they had been able to settle during the war.[34]

Defeated white Southerners gained new hope from Johnson's support and undertook new forms of resistance to black rights in ways that made the tasks of Reconstruction infinitely harder thereafter. They began to engage in the clandestine acts of brutal antiblack and anti-Yankee violence that soon grew into various secret terrorist societies, especially the first Ku Klux Klan. In late 1865, Southern elites also began recreating formal legal caste systems via their new Black Codes. These were efforts, initiated by Mississippi and South Carolina, to constrain the legal rights of the freedmen in many regards, but especially their economic opportunities. Mississippi forbade blacks from renting land and required them to have proof of employment, to sign annual labor contracts without rights to strike, and not to leave jobs once contracted or risk punishment for vagrancy and "insolence." Thus blacks could not pursue opportunities in western or Northern markets, regardless of their pay or working conditions. South Carolina heavily taxed all typical black occupations other than farmer or servant and required blacks to sign annual contracts. When bureau officials and Northern opinion-makers attacked these laws, other Southern states enacted racially neutral va-grancy, contract labor, and compulsory apprenticeship laws. The explicitly black economic codes were short-lived. But in practice these new "neutral" laws were applied simply to confine blacks. And in many other respects, including the im-position of special head taxes, criminal punishments, restrictions on weaponry, and denials of political or juridical representation and access to education, Southern states passed racially discriminatory laws with the Johnson adminis-tration's tacit or express approval.[35]

Freedmen's Bureau agents sometimes checked procedurally unfair and phys-ically brutal punishments imposed by such laws, but their role was limited be-cause their own policies often aimed at similar goals of black contractual em-ployment. Though the better bureau agents argued strenuously that the spread of coerced contract labor was "utterly foreign to free institutions," many other federal officials were unable to accept that blacks would labor as readily as whites if properly rewarded. Hence, they aided Southern and military efforts to compel all blacks to sign the hated forced contracts. As Eric Foner concedes, far from manifesting liberal ideology, this coercive system "violated the principles of free labor," as did the unfair treatment that Southern courts accorded blacks when they resisted. But the compulsory contract system satisfied the desires of North-ern capitalists as well as Southern planters to revive the Southern economy through ongoing exploitation of cheap black labor.[36]

That strategy not only displayed a lack of genuine commitment to free labor precepts; it expressed more virulently racist white beliefs in black inferiority. Only such racial hostility explains why so many whites, even many bureau offi-cials, believed that economic stability required subjecting blacks to labor systems resembling the slavery they otherwise condemned as immoral and inefficient. They believed that blacks were too lazy or too stupid to work productively in a true free labor system. As Du Bois argued, whites clung to that belief in face of contrary evidence, because many were dependent on the "psychological wage" of being part of the socially recognized "master race." That racism also explains the massive, often violent hostility that greeted black efforts to acquire land in the South or to exercise any of their new rights as civic equals. It similarly explains the resistance of Northern and western whites to the idea that blacks might relo-cate in their regions.

And perhaps most crucially, racism best explains Johnson's self-destructive political choices. It is true that, during a period of flux, Johnson was not mad to believe that he could put together a coalition of antiblack poor whites and Southern planters and defeat the Radicals; but only his deep hatred of black equality explains why he wanted to do so. Johnson's racism, veiled in his early presidential messages, became increasingly open as he made himself the champion of white supremacists against congressional radicals. In his third annual message in December 1867 he declaimed that "negroes have shown less capacity for government than any other race of people. . . . They have shown a constant tendency to relapse into barbarism." The "great difference between the two races in physical, mental and moral characteristics" meant that if "the inferior obtains the ascendancy," it would make "half of our country" a "wilderness."[37] This was not the voice of free labor or states' rights. This was pure racism, and it was, indeed, the key to Johnson's actions.

The Southern Homestead Act. Radical efforts to provide blacks with land persisted despite Johnson's opposition. In 1866, Congress passed Senate Bill 60, making the Freedmen's Bureau permanent and national and also authorizing the government to purchase farmlands for resale to homesteading blacks on manageable terms. Johnson vetoed it, and an override effort failed by a mere two votes. The bureau's life was extended for two years in July by a bill that survived another Johnson veto, but it did not contain the same land provisions. Congress did, however, enact Indiana Representative George Julian's 1866 Southern Homestead Act, which set aside 46.4 million acres in Arkansas, Alabama, Florida, Kentucky, and Mississippi for use by freedmen and loyal white refugees until January 1, 1867. For that period, only actual settlers could be accepted, to forestall speculators, and these new yeoman farmers then could acquire titles at minimal cost. Women, however, could acquire land only if unmarried. Johnson signed the bill, which was neither confined to freedmen nor well designed to assist them, in June 1866.

The barriers to freedmen's efforts to take advantages of this act were numerous. Many blacks tied down by unyielding labor contracts could not leave to become settlers, and others who tried met many forms of white opposition, including Klan attacks. After August 20, 1866, when Johnson proclaimed peace and ended martial authority in the South, army and bureau officials who wished to combat white resubjugation of blacks felt deprived of authority to do so. Furthermore, after 1867 the new Homestead Act permitted any Southern white to gain land merely by taking a loyalty oath. By the time that many blacks were free to occupy the lands, productive farmlands were largely gone. With its promise betrayed, the act was repealed in 1876 so that Southern public lands could be made available to timber and mining companies.[38]

But if racism was pivotal in defeating land redistribution and contractual freedom, liberals and free labor liberalism cannot be wholly exonerated. Here again, rapid compliance to liberal precepts involved massive changes in the existing social order. Even many of those relatively sympathetic to blacks were bound to experience such changes as disquieting and potentially dangerous. The Radical Republicans often simply promised that all would work out well if blacks were given their free labor rights, without doing much to address specific concerns or to give bureau agents guidance on the sorts of social worlds they should be trying to foster in place of those being destroyed. This failure of liberal advocates to anticipate fully, much less address adequately, the pitfalls of the uncharted social territory they were opening up meant that even well-intended bureau agents and Southern whites tended to recoil from the upheaval that Radical Reconstruction required. Only keeping former slaves close to their old plantations and locked into reliable production arrangements seemed safe. As Eric Foner argued, this inability "to conceive of blacks as anything but plantation laborers doomed" efforts to establish a Southern free labor industrial economy, and it was disastrous for blacks.[39]

The 1866 Civil Rights Act. The enactment of the vicious Black Codes cost Johnson's state governments much of their Northern support and led to the most significant legislative session in U.S. history from the standpoint of citizenship and civil rights, the 39th Congress of 1866–67. Though the Southern Homestead Act proved disappointing, that Congress extended the bureau's existence, passed the Civil Rights Act of 1866, and sent the Fourteenth Amendment to the states for approval. Collectively, these measures overturned the entire structure of antebellum state-centered, all-white citizenship delineated by Taney in *Dred Scott.* What replaced it was, however, ambiguous. The new laws clearly guaranteed basic free labor rights for all men regardless of race. But the views of the 39th Congress on citizenship remain matters of intense disputes.[40]

Amid various extremes, William E. Nelson has defined a plausible intermediate position. He sees the congressional Republicans as consciously concerned to end state discrimination in regard to "civil," not "political" or, as Michael McConnell has stressed, "social" rights. But many Republicans conceived of those civil rights expansively; and though they thought that these laws would prompt the states to secure them, they also suggested some ill-defined increased federal role should the states falter. So although most did not anticipate or desire any dramatic shift in the federal system toward national regulation, their vague measures, which had to be made specific by the courts, could plausibly be interpreted as justifying such a transformation when states failed to secure rights for all. Those ambiguities have meant that these measures long served as interpretive arenas for struggles among distinct conceptions of citizenship and civic rights that their language alone cannot resolve.[41]

Even so, they plainly worked some basic transformations. The major architects of these acts, like Lyman Trumbull in the Senate and John Bingham in the House, agreed with Attorney General Edward Bates that native-born blacks were already U.S. citizens, either by the fact of birth "upon the soil" of the nation, or by native birth in combination with the emancipation provided by the Thirteenth Amendment. Iowa's James Wilson, the House manager of the civil rights bill, cited Bates and Blackstone to support this claim and denounced Locke's view that "a child is born a citizen of no country" as an "absurd doctrine" favored by Democrats in order to use "the negro as a football for partisan games." Like Senator Lot Morrill of Maine, most Republicans described the "essential elements" of citizenship in Cokean terms: a person owed "allegiance to the country of his birth, and that country owes him protection."[42]

Yet the Republicans did not adhere strictly to Coke. Trumbull admitted that, though he wanted to define citizenship solely in terms of birthright allegiances, the logic of that approach went further than he desired. The offspring of "temporarily resident" parents such as foreign ministers did receive protection at birth and so did owe "a sort of allegiance," as did all native-born Indians. Occupying armies also might produce children on titularly American soil. The common law, again, dealt with ambassador's children via the legal fiction that they resided on their homeland's soil, and the children of enemy armies could be excluded on Coke's premises because they did not receive the U.S. government's protection. But Indians remained a thornier case, because most Republicans refused to disavow ultimate American sovereignty over the tribes or to make them citizens.

A further problem was that Coke's position did not define very fully what rights "protection" entailed. Some Republicans like Bingham grandly asserted "the absolute equality of all citizens of the United States politically and civilly," claiming that every citizen was entitled to "all . . . the privileges of citizens of the United States in every State." Most Republicans, however, did not believe that those rights included "political rights," such as the vote, nor did most think that they should outlaw all forms of discrimination even in regard to civil rights, such as distinctions between men and women, adults and children. Wilson indicated that he did not expect all citizens to sit on juries, or children of all races to attend the same schools.[43]

In the end, the Civil Rights Act "declared to be citizens of the United States" all "persons born in the United States," but with the proviso that they must not be "subject to any foreign power," and with the exclusion of "Indians not taxed." It also specified certain economic and juridical rights, including free labor rights to contract and hold property, as ones that all citizens must have, a list that could be read as exhaustive.[44] And, expanding on the 1863 Habeas Corpus Act, the bill greatly increased the jurisdiction of the federal courts, allowing them to punish violators of section 1 directly, to take appeals from the state courts' rulings on such rights, and to remove litigation from the state courts. All federal law officers, including Freedmen's Bureau agents and court-appointed commissioners, could initiate actions against violators.[45] Thus, native-born blacks were clearly designated nationally protected citizens; but they were not so clearly made equal citizens.

Although the Republicans said that their citizenship legislation was merely declaratory of existing law, they had to answer Democratic challenges asserting that blacks were not citizens and that Congress had no power to make them so, or to protect their civil rights against other individuals or the states. The conservative position was that *Dred Scott* stood unreversed, and that Congress could alter it only by constitutional amendment. Senator Garrett Davis of Kentucky insisted, like Taney, that "none of the inferior races" were U.S. citizens at the time of the Constitution's enactment, and none had been made so since. He held that the naturalization powers of Congress reached only those born on foreign soil, and he added that Congress could constitutionally naturalize only Europeans, because the nation was "a closed white corporation." Not even the amendment power could be used to change that, because it was a power "simply to amend; it is not a power to revolutionize."

Democratic House leader Andrew Rogers of New Jersey did not go so far, but he dismissed the Republican case for birthright citizenship by arguing that "the common law is not in force under the Constitution of the United States." Democratic Senator Reverdy Johnson of Maryland played both sides of the issue, but eventually cited Justice Curtis's dissent in *Dred Scott* to argue that nativity conferred U.S. citizenship only on those who were born citizens under the law of the state of their birth. And Senator James Guthrie of Kentucky offered a plainly disingenuous consensualist objection to the 1866 act, saying that the bill would make blacks citizens "without their consent," as they would not be asked to take an oath. While acknowledging that the Thirteenth Amendment had freed blacks, Democrats denied that it had made them citizens or that it gave Congress power to regulate directly civil rights which had traditionally been in the states' domain, as the Civil Rights Act seemed to do.[46]

The Republicans answered that the naturalization power could indeed extend to those born on U.S. soil, citing the examples of Indians and minor children born of temporarily resident ambassadors. Ohio Representative Samuel Shellabarger added that no oath was necessary from native-born blacks, as they owed no allegiance elsewhere, and their continuing residence was sufficient indication of their consent to citizenship. Many Republicans, moreover, were happy to claim the second section of the Thirteenth Amendment as sufficient authorization for their protection of the rights listed in the Civil Rights Act. Some derived further authority from the Article IV privileges and immunities clause. But on all these points they thought that the Fourteenth Amendment could lay to rest any constitutional doubts.[47]

The Fourteenth Amendment. Thus the Fourteenth Amendment was in part an effort to constitutionalize the views of citizenship the Republicans had laid out in discussing the Civil Rights Act. Based on a bill sponsored by the Ohio moderate John Bingham and considered after the extensive debates on the Civil Rights Act, the momentous civic provisions of the Fourteenth Amendment's section 1 received limited discussion.[48] Yet the citizenship clause in section 1 made four changes in the clause that began the Civil Rights Act. It added those who had been "naturalized" to those "born . . . in the United States" in defining the citizenry. It changed the qualifying phrase "and not subject to any foreign power" to "and subject to the jurisdiction" of the United States. It dropped the phrase "excluding Indians not taxed." It also added that such citizens were not only citizens of the United States but "of the State wherein they reside."[49]

The first change gave constitutional support to the status of naturalized citizens, and the last made national citizenship primary by preventing states from denying their own citizenship to any resident U.S. citizens. Though this wording did not eliminate the nativist constitutional clauses that gave recently naturalized citizens fewer political opportunities than the American-born, it did underline the equality of new and old citizens in regard to other civic rights. The clause also did not explicitly deny the states power to confer their own citizenship on aliens, a power all the opinions in *Dred Scott* had explicitly endorsed. It nonetheless implied that the statuses were not meant to be separated, as the courts eventually ruled.[50]

The substitution of the jurisdiction requirement for foreign subjection and the omission of the "Indians not taxed" exclusion were both new efforts to fit the Native American tribes into a doctrine of birthright citizenship. Lyman Trumbull—aided by Jacob Howard, who drafted the clause—acknowledged that the Republicans were still struggling with the fact that Cokean notions of allegiance did not seem to leave room for denying citizenship to unassimilated tribal Indians. Because that denial had long been defended in American jurisprudence by appealing to international law conceptions of consensually based membership, Peter Schuck and I have argued that the jurisdiction requirement should be read as an admittedly awkward effort to synthesize Cokean and consensual views of citizenship.[51]

The sources of that awkwardness are clear. The amendment's framers wanted the administrative advantages of a *jus soli* rule; they wanted to include the nation's blacks in citizenship, yet they did not want to include most tribal members.

The jurisdiction clause was meant to signal the tribes' special status as persons who were not fully subject to the U.S. because they had another primary political allegiance. The wording did not, however, really do the job. It only said not "subject" to U.S. jurisdiction, and most federal officials had long regarded the tribes as instances of Vattel's "dependent nations," who *were* in decisive regards subject to U.S. sovereignty in return for its protection or at least forbearance.[52] Hence the tribespeople were still persons born in the U.S. and subject to its jurisdiction—birthright citizens as the clause was phrased, birthright citizens under the common-law rule of *jus soli* its authors seemed to be writing into the Constitution. The clause's proponents, Trumbull and Howard, made some effort to avoid this problem by stressing that the clause implicitly required "full and complete" jurisdiction. Insofar as they clarified what that meant, however, they identified it with a lack of any divided political allegiance. Yet Trumbull also said that the clause did include the children of resident Chinese aliens, who also owed allegiance to another government.[53]

The framers' root problem was that they were trying to have it both ways on two levels. First, they wished to claim a limited but ultimate (and therefore not truly limited) sovereignty over the tribes, while denying that the tribes were members of the American political community, as Vattel's consensual version of birthright citizenship seemed to permit them to do. But second, they wanted to grant citizenship securely to blacks by endorsing the common law's more purely ascriptive doctrine of citizenship based on place of birth. On that view, Native American citizenship could not logically be denied. Simply cobbling the jurisdiction phrase onto birthplace citizenship did not resolve these differences between the consensualist and ascriptive conceptions of citizenship that the framers were invoking.

As a result, their citizenship clause cannot be interpreted to make it fully coherent. Schuck and I have suggested interpreting the jurisdiction proviso as rendering the citizenship clause closer to the consensual notions of membership expressed in the international law writers than to common-law ascriptive concepts. We urged reading the clause as guaranteeing citizenship by birth to children born of parents legally admitted to permanent residence in the U.S. political community. Doing so produces the main results most framers endorsed: constitutional inclusion for blacks and permanent resident aliens like the Chinese, but no such inclusion for the tribes.[54]

Many have objected to our argument, and some of the objections have force.[55] Our reading still leaves the amendment an uneasy compromise between ascriptive and consensual citizenship conceptions. Other compromises may be more plausible or attractive.[56] But all such readings are problematic; and so the clause stands as troubling testimony to the ways Americans have mixed inconsistent views, expressing both inclusive and exclusionary motives, in their most basic legal definitions of citizenship.

Even in regard to black citizenship, there were ambiguities. The amendment clearly covered all native-born blacks. No congressman discussed the status of foreign-born blacks, many of whom probably had been illegally brought to the U.S. as slaves after 1808, and all of whom were still ineligible for naturalization. The illegally imported slaves were most problematic: because they were neither "born . . . in the United States" nor "naturalized" in any conventional way, it is hard to see how the amendment might have made them citizens. The courts never confronted that issue. Prompted by pleas from resident alien blacks, in 1867 Charles Sumner did call for amending the naturalization laws to make blacks eligible for citizenship, and Congress finally did so in 1870. But anti-Chinese sentiments led to the rejection of Sumner's proposal that the word "white" simply be eliminated from the naturalization statutes.[57] Instead, eligibility was extended to "aliens of African nativity and persons of African descent" as well as "whites."[58] Yet because the debates discussed only the status of legal black immigrants, not the presumably much larger population of illegally imported former slaves, their position in relation to U.S. citizenship remained unnoticed and unresolved.[59]

Section 2 of the amendment gave the federal government a never-exercised tool for aiding black citizenship in the states. It required a proportionate reduction in the congressional representation of any state that denied the suffrage to "male inhabitants" who were twenty-one years old and U.S. citizens, unless they had been guilty of rebellion or some other crime. As this provision bore most harshly on Southern states that refused the vote to their black populations, it was bitterly contested in Congress. Another aspect of the amendment prompted angry grumbles about violated property rights: Section 5 stated that neither the United States nor any state would pay compensation "for the loss or emancipation of any slave," declaring all such "debts, obligations and claims" to be "illegal and void." Compensation, a policy that had seemed progressive a few years before, now seemed an immoral concession to slaveholders.[60]

The conservatives opposed to the Civil Rights Act and the Fourteenth Amendment still relied on states' rights republican and ascriptive Americanist arguments. They tirelessly invoked the specter of a federal "consolidation of power" into "one imperial despotism."[61] And they relied on overt denunciations of blacks as an "inferior race" to argue that citizenship should be confined to whites, a view for which they claimed "divine" and "ethnological" support.[62] The Republicans replied by defending black equality in regard to basic rights, but they were even less clear than in their Civil Rights Act debates about just what those entailed. Most explicitly denied that the amendment conferred the right to vote, but otherwise they displayed a range of views on the scope of section 1. Some implied that it required states to extend whatever rights they provided to blacks as well as whites. Some suggested instead that it protected various substantive rights against invasion. Those in the latter camp differed, however, on what those rights were. They also left unclear whether such rights were protected against direct state invasions, against both state invasions and state failures to protect the rights against private individuals, or, most sweepingly, against state invasions, state failures, and infringements by private individuals as well.[63]

When responding to Democratic charges of national despotism, Republicans usually stressed more limited views of the amendment's consequences, indicating that it would justify action only against noncomplying states, and that the need for such actions would soon cease. But the wide-ranging debates over the amendment and the Civil Rights Act produced ample quotations for most of the positions in the quarrels over their scope and meaning that continue today. Even Herman Belz, who sees the amendment aimed essentially at voiding explicitly discriminatory state laws like the Black Codes, agrees that "for purposes of advocacy at constitutional law it is possible to argue a sovereign national power over civil rights."[64] Given the ambiguities of the legal texts and the legislative records, the official answers to these questions had to be provided by implementing legislation and interpreting judicial decisions. Their answers have changed dramatically over time.

There was one issue, however, on which the courts had substantial guidance: the applicability of the Fourteenth Amendment to women. In 1866, the Eleventh National Woman's Rights Convention, in combination with members of the American Anti-Slavery Society, transformed itself into the American Equal Rights Association, seeking to "bury the woman in the citizen," as the new organization's constitution stated. It was soon clear, however, that opposition to equal female citizenship remained widespread. Despite a petition drive begun by Elizabeth Cady Stanton and Susan B. Anthony in 1865, the Fourteenth Amendment condoned exclusion of women from the suffrage. The decision to penalize only denials of votes to male inhabitants made the Constitution appear to embrace female disfranchisement openly for the first time. Similarly, in 1867 the nation's leading reform journalist, Horace Greeley, persuaded a New York constitutional convention to endorse suffrage for blacks but not women. Shortly thereafter, Kansas considered separate constitutional reforms that would have extended the vote to black men and all women. Without expressing opposition, such abolition leaders as Frederick Douglass and Wendell Phillips refused to work for women's suffrage there, fearing that it would jeopardize support for black enfranchisement. It was, they insisted, the "Negro's hour." As a result, an infuriated Susan B. Anthony accepted the aid of a wealthy, ambitious, and rabidly antiblack Democrat, George Francis Train, in an ugly Kansas campaign in which both campaigns for franchise extension lost.[65]

But even as the coalition of advocates of black and female rights began to come unstuck, congressional anger over President Johnson's obstructionism was peaking. Early in 1867 Republicans gave the vote to blacks in the District of Columbia and the territories, overriding local white opposition and a Johnson veto, and also shelving the President's proposal to give the district representation in Congress. In March Congress passed a Military Reconstruction Act (over Johnson's veto) that established military rule over the Southern state governments, commencing Congressional Reconstruction. Army officers were to see that each state convened a new constitutional convention, elected by black as well as white male voters but not including past rebels, to craft constitutions that would establish similarly broad franchises. The new legislatures then had to ratify the Fourteenth Amendment, after which they would gain congressional recognition. Broadly those steps were implemented; but Johnson was still entitled to oversee the army officers, and his efforts, along with the Southern white resistance he helped inspire, ensured that many state officers kept their jobs and invented additional ways to keep blacks from voting. Congress added amending bills to overcome presidential and state efforts to undermine the act, but the number of soldiers and Freedmen's Bureau agents it placed in the South remained too small to ensure real compliance.[66]

The Burlingame Treaty and the 1868 Expatriation Act. Even so, on other fronts the reform spirit of Congressional Reconstruction produced civic measures that were significantly, if rarely unequivocally, liberal and egalitarian. The west coast was already embroiled in mounting hostility to the Chinese immigrant laborers who had begun arriving in the 1850s. Initially that opposition created pressures to ban the coolie trade, a position that antislavery champions like Charles Sumner could endorse (though most Chinese immigrant laborers were not actually coolies). Thus Congress passed such laws in 1862 and again in 1869; but by then virulently anti-Chinese westerners like California Congressman James A. Johnson were openly advocating those restrictions and more as a way to prevent the entry of Asian "inferior races." Whites labeled the Chinese as "barbarians" like the Indians and as only slightly above blacks. But even though in 1868 Congress quietly repealed the 1864 law that sought to attract immigrant labor, it also ratified the Burlingame Treaty with China. Partly in response to heavy lobbying by the affluent Chinese Six Companies in San Francisco, and to the dismay of many western Sinophobes, that treaty granted Chinese nationals unrestricted immigration to America, though not access to naturalization, in return for China receiving "most favored nation" commercial privileges. Ironically, some Southerners supported the measure because they hoped that competition from Chinese coolie labor would put blacks "in their place" and create a new system of racial servitude.[67]

The final major piece of civic legislation passed in 1868 expressed even more unqualifiedly liberal, consensual views of citizenship. During the war the U.S. government did not push foreign governments to recognize the legitimacy of U.S. naturalizations of aliens, because it was busy drafting native-born Americans who sometimes claimed to have acquired a foreign nationality. But in 1866 and 1868, the issue of international recognition of expatriation rights excited many Americans again. Irish-born naturalized Americans engaged in political agitation in Ireland were repeatedly arrested there and charged with treason. In response, on July 27 Congress enacted the 1868 Expatriation Act, which is still in effect today. It declared expatriation to be "a natural and inherent right of all people, indispensable to the enjoyment of the rights of life, liberty, and the pursuit of happiness." The act guaranteed that all naturalized American citizens would receive the same protection as native-born citizens. If foreign governments deprived such citizens of their liberty, the President was to use all means short of war to procure their release.[68]

In affirming the right of expatriation, in terming it a natural right (perhaps the only use of that term in U.S. statutes), and in linking it to the Declaration of Independence's trinity of rights, the statute gave clear expression to the liberal conceptions of civic membership. The last vestiges of the common-law doctrine of perpetual allegiance were disavowed. The U.S. went on to negotiate a series of naturalization treaties, first with Germany in 1868, then with many other European and Latin American nations, including Great Britain in 1870, that provided for mutual recognition of each nation's naturalization processes.

Because the 1868 act was aimed at prompting other nations to honor America's naturalizations, it did not explicitly indicate that U.S. citizens, too, could expatriate themselves. But these naturalization treaties were acknowledgments of that right, and in 1873 the U.S. Attorney General agreed that Americans also possessed this "natural and inherent right of all people." The act also did not stipulate what procedures amounted to expatriation, an issue that had to be worked out via State Department policies and, eventually, further legislation.[69] But the controversies dating back to the Revolution over whether American citizenship included a general right of expatriation, not merely a right of election under special conditions, were now settled.

The Fifteenth Amendment and Other Reconstruction Laws. By 1868, the Republicans had found, however, that their electoral successes against Johnson's hostile campaigning in 1866, which had emboldened them early in 1867, were not repeated in that year's state elections. White opposition to black voting appeared to cost them support in the North, although black voters helped secure Republican victories in the South. Kansas, Minnesota, and Ohio again rejected black suffrage in referenda. Indeed, only in Iowa and Minnesota would Northern referenda voters eventually support black enfranchisement.[70] In 1868, though the Republicans regained the presidency behind their war hero Ulysses S. Grant, Democrats made new gains in the South and among Northern white voters tiring of the difficult struggles to win black rights in the South. The Republicans responded in 1869 by trying to preserve their Southern base, shore up their support in closely divided border states, and perhaps expand their Northern electorate through extending the franchise to blacks nationally via the Fifteenth Amendment.[71]

The amendment was far from a truly radical measure. It only prevented the federal government and the states from abridging citizens' voting rights "on account of race, color, or previous condition of servitude." Thus it did not confer any right to vote per se; and though it banned racial requirements, it left the states power to enact many other restrictions, including property qualifications and exclusions from office holding, that could negate the formal political rights of blacks and many other citizens as well. Like the Fourteenth Amendment, however, the Fifteenth included a second clause granting Congress "power to enforce this amendment by appropriate legislation," and there were again many views of what sorts of measures this power included. Republicans still reassured critics that extensive federal encroachments on the states would not be required.

The need for these assurances makes it doubtful whether enough political support could have been found to ratify a more sweeping guarantee. True, ratification via the state legislatures, rather than special conventions or popular referenda, meant that the Republicans could count on their elected officials' partisan loyalties to provide more support than white voters might have done. (Democrats therefore attacked the ratification procedures as unrepresentative.) But even so, ratification was hard-fought. Supported in the South due to the black enfranchisement that Congress had already required, and as a condition of congressional recognition for Virginia, Mississippi, Georgia, and Texas, the amendment was rejected in the border states of Maryland, Kentucky, Tennessee, and (initially) Delaware. It succeeded only with major struggles in several midwestern and Northern states. It was also initially defeated in California and Oregon, largely due to fears of Chinese voting. Hence its narrow scope may have been politically shrewd; and despite its limits, the amendment was another major step toward a more inclusive and democratic nation that had but recently seemed utopian.[72]

Even so, the amendment understandably deepened the anger of Stanton, Anthony, and others toward the Republicans. They stressed that the Fifteenth had grown out of a proposal by Anna Dickinson in 1866 for an equal suffrage guarantee encompassing both women and blacks. The consequent controversies over the unwillingness of the Republicans and male abolitionists to support female suffrage strongly, and the willingness of both Stanton and Anthony to ally with outspoken racists, led to the shattering of the young Equal Rights Association and the formation of two competing women's suffrage groups. Stanton and Anthony formed the more radical National Woman Suffrage Association, with only women as officers, two days after the Equal Rights Association convention came apart in May 1869. Lucy Stone, Julia Ward Howe, Henry Blackwell, and others in the New England Woman Suffrage Association, which had preceded the NWSA by six months and favored continuing alliance with abolitionists and Republicans, formed the opposing American Woman Suffrage Association in November.[73]

The organizations' rivalry was intense, though some of the national leaders retained close contacts, and many state suffrage associations affiliated with both. Beyond their common goal of winning female suffrage, there were important differences. The AWSA was concerned almost exclusively with the suffrage, and it laid more stress on promoting change at the state level. The NWSA advocated far more broad-ranging reforms, encompassing changes in religious as well as political and legal doctrines and challenges to a range of marital, familial, and workplace arrangements. It attempted to ally with labor unions and other reform groups, and it chiefly sought to gain the suffrage at the national level, via constitutional interpretation or constitutional reform.[74]

The differences were partly traceable to worries of AWSA leaders about taking positions that would embarrass the Republicans in national politics and harm their efforts to assist blacks. But they also expressed ideological contrasts: the AWSA leaders were less willing to challenge women's ascribed social roles across the spectrum. They were more inclined to advance "domestic feminist" arguments holding that traditional female virtues would make women good voters. Somewhat more often, Stanton and Anthony's NWSA perpetuated the prewar stress on equal rights based on a common humanity, and their positions on social issues sought fundamental restructuring to realize meaningful gender equality in many areas of life.

Yet this contrast, although real, must not be overdrawn. In important ways, the NWSA's egalitarianism was more circumscribed, as the AWSA's Republican alliance involved more continuing solicitude for black rights. In contrast, the quarrels over Kansas and the Fifteenth Amendment prompted Stanton, and to a lesser degree Anthony, to set their claims for educated, native-born white women like themselves in opposition to those of immigrants, as well as newly freed blacks and other ethnic outsiders. The cynically racist statements that resulted formed a dissonant coda to the soaring hymns to equal human rights that had climaxed their abolitionist speeches. Thus Stanton stated in 1869: "American women of wealth, education, virtue and refinement, if you do not wish the lower orders of Chinese, Africans, Germans and Irish, with their low ideas of womanhood to make laws for you and your daughters . . . awake to the danger of your present position" and demand the vote.[75]

The prestige of evolutionary theories of racial hierarchy made such appeals easier. Radicals also, however, used the argument that evolution had fostered essentially different natures in men and women to claim woman's intrinsic superiority. Meanwhile, more conservative reformers like Catharine Beecher, still busily preaching female pursuit of domestic excellence, invoked such notions of difference to oppose direct female political involvement, including the suffrage with its allegedly corrosive effect on female uniqueness. Finally, the nation's first ordained female minister, Antoinette Brown Blackwell, deployed Spencer and Darwin to argue for a more unified future in which each sex would acquire the virtues, not the faults, of the other. But only a diminishing minority in her AWSA, as well as the NWSA, believed in that vision of progress. Instead, emphasis on naturally generated differences treated as irrevocable became more the order of the day.[76]

It was not necessary to stress what the sexes had in common, however, in order to favor female suffrage. During these years women succeeded in getting the vote in two western territories—Wyoming in 1869 and Utah in 1870. These gains were traceable less to receptivity toward women's emancipation than to the old western habit of using broad grants of the franchise to encourage population growth, as well as the desire of Mormon men in Utah to use their wives' votes to combat the influence of new non-Mormon arrivals. Women in several states also won eligibility for elective school offices and could vote in school board elections.[77]

Yet neither these localized successes nor women's accompanying litigative struggles for equal rights, discussed below, warmed a political climate that had become increasingly chilly toward equal rights. The cause of female equality was not aided by the lurid 1871 Beecher-Tilton sex scandal, which reinforced the identification of women's rights with sexual licentiousness.[78] The cause of racial equality was also on the defensive. Even as the Fifteenth Amendment was ratified, the aroused South continued to fight all expansions in black rights both publicly and privately, through legal machinations and the Klan's violence. Congress at first responded vigorously with several Enforcement Acts. The most important, passed on May 31, 1870, strove to implement the Fifteenth Amendment by setting penalties for state officials who denied persons the vote on racial grounds, for private persons who hampered state officials in such duties, and for private persons who directly prevented or intimidated, or conspired to prevent or intimidate, persons from voting. More generally, it reenacted the protections of the 1866 Civil Rights Act under the Fourteenth and Fifteenth Amendments.

Further major enforcement laws—the National Elections Act passed in July 1870 and a follow-up bill adopted in February 1871—set up a system of national supervision of congressional elections to curb racial discriminations therein. And in April 1871, Congress passed the landmark Ku Klux Klan Act, providing federal punishments not only for state authorized denials of constitutional rights but also for private conspiracies to prevent the state from protecting such rights equally for all, among other provisions. Representative Shellabarger had wished to punish private violators of constitutional rights directly, arguing that a state's failure to punish these offenders amounted to state denial of equal protection guaranteed to all citizens by the Fourteenth Amendment. But others argued that such failure justified only action against state officials, or at most against private persons interfering with state officials. Hence the complex compromise language of the statute.[79]

The violence that those acts tried to curb was not confined to white black relations. The 1870 civil rights law also banned state taxes imposed on immigrants from some countries and not others, another concession won by Chinese merchants to curb discriminatory measures in California. But anti-immigrant forces were gathering strength on both coasts, and as labor competition grew they found it easy to arouse racial animosities against the Chinese. In 1871, twenty-two Chinese were lynched in Los Angeles, and various western states continued to pass laws designed to discourage Asian immigration and deny basic rights to Chinese immigrants who were already present. Northeastern states also adopted new measures to curb the entry of unwanted immigrants; and western congressional representatives made their demands for national restrictions on Chinese and Japanese immigration more vociferous. Politicians of all stripes took notice. In 1867 the Republican nominee for governor of California exhorted voters that "the same God created both Europeans" and "our Asiatic brethren," and in 1870 a Nevada Republican Senator, William Stewart, denounced "mob violence" and "wicked" local laws aimed at "injustice . . . toward the Chinese." But soon thereafter, electoral pressures led the California GOP to announce that it was "inflexibly opposed" to Chinese immigration, and the national party moved toward that position. Stewart then joined those denouncing Sumner's proposals for colorblind naturalization, complaining that the Chinese were "pagans," "monarchists," and not of "our own race." Southern Democrats quickly sought to build a new South-west coalition of white supremacists, rendering Republican support for racial equality ever more politically perilous.[80]

Native Americans

The winds of Reconstruction swirled patterns in the federal policies governing Native Americans that differed on the surface but had deeper similarities. The tribes were possibly the greatest sufferers from resurgent ascriptive inegalitarianism during the postwar years; yet it was in this area that Americanist policies came most elaborately clothed as humanitarian reforms.[81] Indians not sufficiently assimilated to be taxed were not only denied most of the benefits of the 1866 Civil Rights Act and the Fourteenth and Fifteenth Amendments, including birthright citizenship. Under President Grant, the U.S. also adopted the most pervasive and deliberate effort to destroy native cultures it had yet undertaken.

The dismal spectacle of ongoing warfare between the tribes and Union armies during and after the Civil War persuaded reformers and Indian-haters alike by 1868 that the old system of treaty agreements administered by Indian agents, often patronage appointments, was failing. The tribes, they agreed, did not deserve to be treated as separate peoples and trading partners. That system invited their exploitation and violence. Those most fervently anti-Indian, especially in the west, saw no hope of progress and favored a policy of extermination. Religious reformers instead argued to Grant that if the tribes could be kept separate from all whites except missionaries, eventually they might be ready to be American citizens. The reformers were helped by Grant's abhorrence of the corrupt Indian agents he had seen during service on the frontier and by his apparent acceptance of the myth that William Penn and the Quakers had managed relations with Indians peacefully. The Indian-haters, on the other hand, appealed to Grant's longstanding conviction that problems sometimes had to be settled by military actions.

The result was that, in his 1869 inaugural, the new President promised to pursue policies that would "civilize" Native Americans and lead to their "ultimate" citizenship. Grant then fired all existing Indian agents and initiated his extraordinary Peace Policy. The tribes were even more fully confined to remote reservations (intensifying Lincoln's policy) and governed by new Indian agents chosen for Grant by the Quakers and, later, other Christian denominations. This shift represented the most extensive state and church interlocking at the federal level in the nation's history. Grant's policy was applauded by many former abolitionists, and it seemed gentle in comparison to governance by brutal soldiers or avaricious traders. At bottom, however, it expressed what the judicious Jesuit historian Francis Paul Prucha has termed "ethnocentrism of frightening intensity." Consonant with burgeoning Darwinist views, the policy's architects assumed that Indians who proved sufficiently fit must assimilate to the superior race, and those who did not must perish. The Peace Policy effectively made repudiation of native religions and ways of life, and acceptance of middle-class American Christianity with its attendant customs, official prerequisites for admission to U.S. citizenship.[82]

The new agents administered greatly expanded federal funds for missions and schools aimed at these ends. The Office of Indian Affairs spent $3.7 million in 1869, twice the previous year's expenditure. Grant also created a Board of Indian Commissioners, staffed by wealthy Protestants, to oversee the program along with the Department of Interior's commissioner of Indian affairs. To that post he appointed his staff brigadier general, Ely Parker (or Hasanoanda), an educated full-blooded Seneca. Parker's appointment was, however, at least equally a concession to those who wanted to keep Indian affairs under military control; he was not reluctant to impose order on unassimilated tribes. Initially, Grant also assigned nearly seventy Indian agent posts to military officers, available in surplus with the war's end. But in 1870, a Congress seeking to limit executive and military power banned such military appointments, and Grant permitted other denominations to fill the posts, including Catholics but not Mormons or Jews.[83]

The Peace Policy quickly met with difficulties. Parker and the Board of Commissioners struggled for primacy. Parker was forced out in 1871, but the entire membership of the Board resigned in 1874 when they could not win permission to remove Indian affairs from the Interior Department, which they saw as hopelessly corrupt. Many denominations, moreover, did not really wish to assume the duties assigned them and performed them in lackluster fashion. They nonetheless squabbled fiercely over regions of influence. Most important, the tribes continued to resent the reservation system bitterly, as well as the massive hostility toward their cultures that suffused the policy, bringing their religions, forms of work, languages, foods, marriages, gender roles, ceremonies, recreations, and forms of dress under assault. The tribes' responsive outbursts of violence, such as war with the Modoc Indians in California in 1872–73, strengthened the voices of the policy's critics. Some wanted more tolerance of native cultures. More favored genocide.

Meanwhile, the House sought more control over Indian affairs. Many voters were upset about the manner in which the Interior Department could acquire tribal lands and dispose of them, often to rich railroad magnates or land speculators, without the lands ever officially becoming part of the public domain, available for homesteading. These controversies generated legal disputes over land titles that involved the judiciary, as noted below; but members of the House thought that they should control both these lands and the public officers who administered them. Expansion of the House's power was thus the immediate motive for legislation in 1871 that repealed the treaty system, which had given most of the control over Indian policies to the executive branch and the Senate. That step represented a historic rejection of the notion that the tribes were even "dependent" nations, though the legislators presented it as a logical exercise of powers they had long held. It meant that henceforth Indians would be individually subject to U.S. legislative authority and compelled either to be "made white men" or to face governance as subject persons, confined to isolated reservations that, according to Wilcomb Washburn, "frequently took on the character" of concentration camps.[84] To be sure, in many instances Congress still did not legislate directly over the tribes; but now agreements with them had to be approved by Congress as a whole as well as the President. The law was expressive, moreover, of widely shared official sentiments that the pretensions of Indians to meaningful political and cultural autonomy should no longer be indulged.

Accordingly, in 1875, Congress enacted further incentives to assimilate by making the benefits of the 1862 Homestead Act available to Indians if they would leave their tribes and settle on public lands. To insure that they would commit to farming, they were not allowed to sell the land for five years. Life on the reservation was also made even less attractive. All Indian males between the ages of eighteen and forty-five who continued to receive annuities and supplies promised by past treaties were now required to labor "at a reasonable rate" to get those usually meager benefits. As a result of these measures, many Native Americans found, in Robert Keller's words, "that the alternative to submission was death, and that submission often meant working and starving."[85]

With the end of the Grant administration, support for his reliance on religious denominations faded, replaced by patronage as usual. But the Peace Policy's efforts to compel tribal children to learn in U.S. schools that denigrated native cultures, to end legal recognition of tribal identities, and to foster farming on individually owned lands held in fee simple all persisted, with allegiance to American nationality now more emphasized than Christianity. Thus in many respects the Peace Policy pioneered the heightened Americanist views that would be expressed in many U.S. civic policies during the late nineteenth century.[86]

Civic Education

The nationalistic liberal republicanism that reigned during the war and early Reconstruction fueled remarkable educational progress throughout the nation, designed to equip many more Americans for citizenship. But the new schools still reflected only mildly attenuated versions of American inegalitarian racial, gender, and religious traditions. And here, too, many inclusive reforms succumbed with Reconstruction's fall.

After the 1862 Morrill Act made the U.S. the first nation to provide massive support for higher education, Congress added ex-Confederate states to the act in

1866 and made an additional 13 million acres of federal land available. Republicans also revived the old dream of a national university. Resistance from the private colleges, led by Charles Eliot, president of Harvard, defeated the idea yet again, but Congress did charter Howard University for blacks in 1867. President Grant even proposed a constitutional amendment in 1875 guaranteeing a free education to all Americans.[87]

The Morrill Act, moreover, had major results. The colleges it fostered, along with private foundings of denominational colleges, teacher training institutes, women's colleges, and various institutions of higher learning for blacks, transformed the U.S. into a "land of colleges" by 1875. The public colleges culminated what was becoming an increasingly comprehensive system of public education, ascending from new kindergartens through elementary and high schools to the college level in relatively orderly fashion (though most high schools were as yet private). States began consolidating these systems under centralized county superintendents and state boards of education. Public educational expenditures rose from just under $20 million in 1860 to almost $62 million by 1870, when they constituted roughly two-thirds of all educational expenditures.[88] School enrollments rose, reaching over 61 percent for whites between the ages of five and nineteen by 1870, with a majority in publicly funded schools.

In many parts of the South, ravages of war instead led to actual reductions in the numbers of schools, teachers, and pupils in 1870, compared to 1850. But those losses were combated and, by the early 1870s, more than offset in some areas by Civil War and Reconstruction efforts to expand public education in the South, especially for blacks. Throughout these years, whenever Republicans and Union forces came to power, as either occupying forces or reconstituted state governments, they established or expanded free, tax-supported public school systems (often along with roads, hospitals, asylums, penitentiaries, health and legal services, and poverty relief programs, among other measures). Accompanying those efforts, and frequently preceding them, a number of private agencies set up schools: abolitionist-founded Freedmen's Aid societies, eventually united in the American Freedmen's Union Commission (AFUC); the American Missionary Association (AMA) and other evangelical groups; and self-help efforts by such black churches as the African Methodist Episcopal and other black groups. Often federal officials and private agencies worked cooperatively. AMA teachers followed the Union armies, teaching in "contraband" camps and setting up schools in recaptured areas. Eventually the Freedmen's Bureau gave funds to it and other groups to establish and staff almost 3,000 schools, teaching 150,000 pupils. The AMA in turn lobbied for and assisted expansion of public schools after 1865.

The result, for a time, was extraordinarily rapid expansion in Southern schooling (except during Johnson's obstructionism). For example, the proportion of school-age whites in South Carolina schools rose from 12 percent in 1869 to 50 percent in 1875, blacks from 8 to 41 percent, with more than one thousand black teachers. In Mississippi, the 1876 figures were 48 percent for whites and 45 percent for blacks, and enrollments in Florida and Texas were similar. In the District of Columbia in the late 1860s, more blacks attended public schools than whites, largely due to white residents' refusal to pay for public schooling. Similar white sentiments in border states that were less subjected to Northern domination slowed the spread of schools there.[89]

Increases in educational opportunities for women were also impressive, though controversial. Elementary education was now almost entirely coeducational; indeed, records show more female elementary students than males in 1872. Secondary education for women also became more common. This educational access had "special meaning" for women, Catherine Clinton argues, because it was "their privilege as citizens in the new republic."[90] The new public colleges also officially admitted both sexes on an equal basis, although in fact women were often channeled into teacher preparatory programs, whereas only men received broad-based educations. That pattern was also true of coeducational private colleges; and leaders eastern elite private institutions often encouraged the creation of women's colleges, such as Vassar in 1865 and Radcliffe in 1874, instead of opening their own doors. Even so, with education both more extensive and inclusive, Americans achieved relatively high literacy rates and sustained more newspapers and libraries than any other nation.[91]

In making America the world's public education leader, political figures and educators in all regions continued to treat public education as preeminently intended to shape citizens, to plant "genuine republicanism." That conception meant, however, that during this era the new schools sparked conflicts that displayed the full range of existing positions on the federal distribution of powers and on the ideological, racial, and cultural characteristics the American citizenry should possess. U.S. Education Commissioner John Eaton echoed many educators when he wrote in 1874 that unless public schools "elevated and harmonized" the citizenry—especially poor, ignorant blacks and whites in the South, as well as immigrants—the "existence of a republic" would be an "impossibility."[92]

But Democrats contended that this valid republican concern did not justify national imposition of "the Prussian system of compulsory education." Rather, republicanism meant local choice and control over educational systems. Catholics added denunciations of all efforts to force "the New England Evangelical type" on the nation. Hence Grant's amendment, like the national university idea, failed. And, as opposition to Reconstruction's initiatives grew, these educational reforms suffered significant reverses. First came the reduction of the Education Department to an information-collecting and hortatory Bureau within the Interior Department in 1869. Then, in the mid-1870s, some Northern states began decentralizing authority and slowing school expenditures. In the South, from the start many whites ferociously opposed Northern teachers and all efforts to educate blacks, regularly subjecting white teachers to harassment and black teachers and students to Klan-led violence. The evangelical AMA also quarreled with the AFUC, Catholics, and other advocates of a less militantly sectarian education. Army officers and civilian officials sometimes failed to deliver on promised aid to private educators, at times insisting on subjecting freed blacks to labor contracts instead of educating them. And even though many white educators championed racial equality in principle, they often shrank from recognizing it in practice, opposing integration and assigning subordinate statuses to black teachers and organizations. Men also wanted female teachers to be more subordinate than they sometimes were. As a result, despite real gains, in the early 1870s the majority of white children in Southern and border states were still not attending public schools, and a larger majority of blacks were not getting much regular schooling at all.[93]

The question of school integration was especially vexed. The AMA and the AFUC were both officially committed to integrated, egalitarian schools, the Reconstruction state constitutions of Louisiana and South Carolina required them, and all the Southern states' new constitutions permitted them. Louisiana did integrate schools in New Orleans in the early 1870s, although the rural parishes remained segregated. South Carolina even integrated its university in Columbia. But both victories came only with great struggle and proved short-lived. Many blacks were most concerned to establish schools, integrated or not, so white opposition to integration generally prevailed. That was, after all, also the pattern in the North.[94]

And even whites who supported integration often advanced condescending romantic racialist views, describing blacks as limited by past brutal treatment and denials of opportunity, but as possessing childlike "poetic" and "emotional qualities" rather than the "prosaic . . . intellectual" skills of whites (as the New England Freeman's Aid Society expressed it in 1865). At best, such doctrines justified an education extending the Americanist paideia, uplifting blacks as much as possible to "Yankee" traits of rationality, industry, thrift, orderliness, and other Protestant virtues. The New England society in fact boasted that it could "make a New England of the whole South." But because even these philanthropical Northerners had low regard for blacks' current capacities; they could turn against egalitarian reforms when change proved difficult; and the hurdles presented by Reconstruction were immense. All these reservations about truly equal education for blacks produced General Samuel Chapman Armstrong's influential advocacy of segregated, vocational black education for blacks. Charged with superintending Freedmen's Bureau programs in Hampton, Virginia, Armstrong founded the much-imitated Hampton Institute with AMA assistance in 1868 to promote black education for industrial labor, character-building, and economic self-help, but explicitly not the advancement of black intellectual or political equality.[95]

With the forces supporting education thus divided, as Southern Democrats succeeded in "redeeming" the Reconstruction governments in the 1870s, they were able legally to segregate their schools, cut funding (especially for black schools), and eliminate state school boards. Sometimes they dismantled the new Yankee-dominated public schools entirely. The border states led the way, with Tennessee repealing its state educational law in 1869, and Maryland closing many schools in 1871. Tennessee then had only 29 percent of its children in schools by 1872. Mississippi and Alabama abolished statewide school taxes in the late 1870s, leaving financing up to local communities; Texas charged fees. Florida abandoned its uncompleted Agricultural College in 1877, leaving the state without any institution of higher education. Louisiana so neglected its schools that white illiteracy actually rose during the 1880s.

Private assistance fared no better. As early as 1869, the overwhelmed and faction-ridden AFUC disbanded. Black schooling then flagged in the nation's capital and elsewhere. By the late 1870s, surviving private groups like the AMA had retreated from commitments to racial equality in favor of doctrines of racial inferiority, alliances with white Southerners, and repressive paternalistic treatment of blacks. Like other postwar intellectuals, educators increasingly stressed doctrines of social evolution which suggested that it was unwise to extend opportunities beyond vocational training to blacks.[96]

The decline of Reconstruction did not, however, mean the complete overturning of the educational achievements of the era. Though much battered, egalitarian national educational initiatives, Southern public schooling, and schooling for blacks and women all survived. The U.S. public school system gave more citizens more opportunities than most other countries at the time. Though it reproduced traditions of ascriptive inequality, it still gave many Americans weapons they could use against its injustices.

The Rise and Fall of the District of Columbia Territory

Amid these broader national transformations, District of Columbia residents renewed efforts to revise the district's political status in order to expand their political rights. In 1871, Congress created a new district territorial government that included a popularly elected lower house along with a presidentially appointed governor, upper chamber, and board of public works. The territory was represented in Congress by an elected nonvoting delegate who sat on the House District Committee. Efforts by Congressman George Julian to get women's suffrage in the new territory, and by Charles Sumner to include a civil rights clause, failed. Even so, territorial status appeared a step to greater political empowerment for district inhabitants. But when Grant's all-Republican appointees, including Frederick Douglass and several other blacks, undertook expensive new building projects, opposition grew.

By 1874 the costs of hasty construction had mounted disturbingly. Congressional and D.C. whites blamed the territory's black officials—though Grant's corrupt, incompetent white cronies were most at fault—and Congress declared territorial government a failure. After several sessions of indecision, in 1878 Congress created a new permanent governing board. Three presidentially appointed commissioners were given full power to run the district, and the U.S. government funded half the city's expenses, the rest coming from local taxpayers. This system alleviated great financial burdens and lasted ninety years, but it left district residents more disfranchised than ever.[97]

The 1875 Civil Rights, Immigration, and Jurisdiction and Removal Acts

Though the tide was going out, Congressional Reconstruction was not over in the mid-1870s. Despite Democratic victories and renewed violence in 1874, Republicans motivated by both hard-nosed political strategy and high-minded esteem for the recently deceased Charles Sumner passed one last enforcement bill, the Civil Rights Act of 1875. Although the final version jettisoned a ban on segregated schools that Sumner had treasured, the act guaranteed equal access for all, banning discrimination in places of public accommodation (including inns, streetcars, theaters, and restaurants). The act's supporters described such establishments as sufficiently "public" in character to be within Congress's enforcement power under the Fourteenth Amendment. The law also banned racial discrimination in federal and state juries and gave federal courts exclusive jurisdiction over its provisions.[98]

Thus the act displayed continuing official opposition to racial caste systems. But, in reality, that opposition was weakening. Chinese immigrants, who did not have the potential voting power of blacks, were left even more vulnerable to the new racism. When anti-union employers transplanted Chinese laborers to North Adams, Massachusetts, Belleville, New Jersey, and Beaver Falls, Pennsylvania, in 1869 and 1870, labor groups predictably complained. The accompanying stories also provoked more widespread anxieties about the dangers of allegedly unassimilable, dirty, disease-carrying, culturally and biologically unsuitable Chinese immigrants. Even long-time abolitionists like Wendell Phillips thought the Chinese too different, albeit not necessarily inferior, to be admitted into the country in large numbers.

Thus the anti-Chinese western representatives finally won a qualified but clear initial victory in the Immigration Act of 1875—the first federal law restricting immigration in the nation's history. Prompted also by President Grant's 1874 message about the evils of the coolie trade and immigrant prostitutes, the 1875 act banned the importation of the following: Oriental persons "without their free and voluntary consent," coolie labor, of women "for the purposes of prostitution," and any persons who had made service agreements "for lewd or immoral purposes." Though it was then true that many of the comparatively few Chinese female immigrants were prostitutes, because many Chinese men sought only to make their fortune and return home, in practice the statute prevented those who wanted to bring their wives over permanently from doing so.[99] Enactment of this law, known to be prompted by anti-Chinese feelings, signaled that in regard to immigration, as with blacks, the liberal national legislative and judicial initiatives of the Civil War era were ending.

Even so, Republican hopes of building strong national institutions under their control, including a powerful national judiciary, remained high. The fact that the Judiciary Act of 1789 gave state courts concurrent jurisdiction over most federal cases, while leaving few avenues of appeal, had hampered national initiatives throughout the war and Reconstruction. Thus the 1863 Habeas Corpus Act proved to be but the first of a series of Removal Acts, which were passed in 1866, 1867, 1868, and 1871. These laws steadily expanded the types of defendants entitled to remove cases from state to federal courts prior to final state determinations of federal questions. Though motivated by skepticism about Southern justice, the acts eventually applied throughout the country and altered the relationship of national to state courts, and of national to state citizenship and political power, more generally. In 1869, Congress also provided circuit judges for each circuit, making the circuit work of the Supreme Court justices more manageable.

The "capstone" of this "trend of expanding federal judicial authority," according to William Wiecek, was the Jurisdiction and Removal Act of March 3, 1875, passed on the tenth anniversary of the creation of the Freedmen's Bureau. Unlike the 1875 Civil Rights Act, the Removal Act was no watered-down version of a more liberal and nationalistic initiative. Instead, it at last gave national courts general federal question jurisdiction, it gave the circuit courts more complete jurisdiction of diversity and alienage civil suits, and it permitted plaintiffs as well as defendants to remove state diversity cases, along with federal question cases, to federal courts. Concerns about state legislation that was hostile to railroads as well as to blacks prompted the act's sweeping breadth. It was not, however, purely a pro-business bill. Aware that, after *Dodge v. Woolsey,* corporations sometimes urged out-of-state stockholders to sue them for the companies' own purposes, the act's authors provided for terminating suits if they were judged to be collusive. Those jurisdictional decisions rested, however, with the federal courts themselves. For the first time in history those courts possessed original and removal jurisdiction as broad as the bounds of Article III.[100]

The Federal Judiciary and Civil Rights Protection

That expansion of judicial power came, however, only after the courts had signaled that their support or even tolerance of radical Reconstruction measures would be limited. The Supreme Court was largely either supportive or silent toward Congressional Reconstruction up to 1873, but then it embarked on an increasingly anti-radical course defended by states' rights and ascriptive reasoning. Up to that point, the Grant administration had implemented civil rights laws vigorously, greatly diminishing the power of the Klan. But after Grant's reelection in 1872, during which members of the more laissez-faire Liberal Republican movement left the party in anger over the Klan Act and the continuing federal role in the South, his will for intervention started to wane. The fact that the Court had begun to endorse constitutional challenges to Reconstruction reinforced this shift, which would become complete after the 1876 election.[101]

The First Phase: Judicial Support for Reconstruction. The federal judiciary's initial readings of the Civil War statutes and amendments were expansive.[102] In the Kentucky circuit court case of *United States v. Rhodes* (1866), Justice Noah Swayne upheld the 1866 Civil Rights Act as an exercise of congressional enforcement power under the Thirteenth Amendment. When white vigilantes robbed and assaulted a black Kentucky woman, Nancy Talbot, U.S. Attorney Benjamin Bristow tried the case in a U.S. district court because Kentucky state law prevented blacks from testifying. After the jury found the defendants guilty, their lawyers asked Swayne to arrest the judgment. They claimed that the 1866 act gave no grounds for trying the case in the federal court, because the criminal prosecution involved only the state and the defendants and did not sufficiently affect Talbot; and, in any event, the act exceeded the authority provided by the Thirteenth Amendment. Swayne, whose son was a Freedmen's Bureau official, responded that the act "clearly" intended to grant blacks a federal forum whenever discriminatory state procedures meant that their rights would not be protected by state courts.[103] Furthermore, Kentucky's denial of the right to give evidence protected by Section 1 of the act gave the federal courts jurisdiction.[104]

Swayne went on to argue that the Thirteenth Amendment's enforcement clause, added out of "abundant caution," gave ample power for Congress to choose means for ensuring that slavery was truly abolished. Hence it validated the 1866 act. But because Swayne focused on the need to combat various kinds of "legislative oppression" that threatened to "restore" slavery, it was unclear whether he saw the act as aimed at state violations or as authorizing direct federal action against private infringements of every right it specified.[105]

Even so, this ruling invigorated federal efforts to protect black rights in the courts of the United States.[106] It was reinforced by a brief but emphatic opinion of Chief Justice Chase, sitting on circuit in Maryland in 1867, in which he struck down an "apprenticeship" arrangement resembling slavery.[107] Other decisions also implied extensive judicial support for the changes that Congress had wrought.[108]

In particular, newly appointed Justice Joseph Bradley, sitting on circuit along with Judge William Woods in Louisiana, read the Fourteenth Amendment and the 1866 Civil Rights Act in broad free labor terms when deciding one of the controversies that would reach the Supreme Court as the *Slaughter-House Cases* of 1873.[109] The Louisiana Reconstruction government had incorporated the Crescent City Slaughter-House Company and granted it exclusive rights for twenty-five years to provide a facility for slaughtering cattle near New Orleans. Self-employed butchers had to pay a fee to work at the facility. Although the growth in cattle processing had led to regulation of abattoirs elsewhere, many Louisianans thought that the legislators were rewarding a bribe-mongering Northern syndicate, so they bitterly resented the company.[110]

Although Bradley professed himself originally inclined to view both the amendment and the civil rights bill as simply guaranteeing blacks the same rights as white citizens, on reflection he decided that in guaranteeing all citizens the privileges and immunities of U.S. citizenship, the amenders had done much more. They had given the federal government additional means to protect certain fundamental rights that were meant to be "absolute." None stood higher among these rights than "the sacred right of labor." The right to pursue noninjurious employments did not preclude "police power" laws ensuring that practitioners were qualified, that their numbers did not exceed the level that the common weal would bear, and other reasonable regulations. But this monopolistic charter struck Bradley as simply a means of increasing the profits of a favored few by limiting the economic opportunities of others. He held that jurisdictional rules required the butchers to wait until the highest state court had decided and then appeal to the U.S. Supreme Court; but he made it clear that he thought their claims were sound, and his conclusion received wide publicity.[111]

In 1871, Judge Woods, after correspondence with Bradley, went further.[112] In

United States v. Hall, he argued that the Fourteenth Amendment's privileges and immunities clause must include all rights expressly secured in the Constitution, against either the federal or the state governments. He included the freedoms of speech and assembly among such rights. Even more strikingly, Woods contended that the enforcement powers given Congress by the Fourteenth Amendment extended to "insufficient" as well as overtly discriminatory state laws, because denials of equal protection included "inaction as well as action." And, finding it "unseemly" for Congress to "interfere directly with state enactments," Woods held that if a state should fail to protect rights that the amendment aimed to secure, the "only appropriate" course for Congress was "that which will operate directly on offenders and offenses, and protect the rights" concerned. He therefore sustained an indictment of private actors for conspiring to prevent blacks from exercising their free speech rights.[113] Other judges interpreted federal civil rights guarantees more narrowly in other 1871 cases, but the doctrinal base for broad readings was well laid.[114]

Other National Citizenship Rights. This early judicial willingness to uphold Reconstruction protection of black rights was accompanied by some extraordinary activism on behalf of rights of national citizenship generally, even when those rights were not explicit in any written law. Most notable were two opinions of Justice Samuel Miller. In 1867, while enthusiasm for national protection of personal rights was still high, Miller wrote for the Court in *Crandall v. Nevada,* striking down a state head tax on all persons leaving the state by any form of hired transportation. Miller invalidated the law on the basis of a novel "right to interstate travel" that he found implicit in the Constitution's structure of national citizenship. A largely self-trained lawyer who characteristically stressed what he took to be the reason or principle of laws over form and precedent, Miller did not rely on the Article IV privileges and immunities clause or any other particular provision. Instead, he contended that this national civic right to be immune from burdensome state legislation was discernible precisely like the national immunity from hostile state taxation identified by Marshall in *McCulloch v. Maryland.* The Court's Democratic holdover, Justice Clifford, found this sort of implied right of national citizenship dangerously nebulous. He argued that the result should be presented as a protection of interstate commerce.[115]

But even Clifford joined a yet more striking Miller opinion for the Court that has long been ignored both by the Court and constitutional scholars. In *Yates v. Milwaukee* (1870), the Supreme Court struck down a Milwaukee ordinance that declared an existing wharf a public nuisance because it extended beyond a dock line that the city had just established. As the wharf did not obstruct navigation, Miller wrote, the city's action was arbitrary. For the Court to uphold such an act would "place every house, every business, and all the property of the city, at the uncontrolled will of the temporary local authorities." He insisted the wharf owner's property could be taken for the public good only if some evidence that it was "injurious to the public" appeared on the record, and if "due compensation" were provided. Though the holding sounds very much like an unprecedented application of Fifth Amendment just compensation requirements to the states, Miller again eschewed any textual basis for it. He instead described it as an application of common law as construed by federal judges, overriding the common-law doctrines of Wisconsin judges. The decision was later cited to uphold judicial powers to protect economic privileges and immunities secured by the Fourteenth Amendment against arbitrary state laws, as well as for economic due process rights.[116]

Miller's activism in these cases on behalf of nonexplicit and common-law rights is especially intriguing, because he would soon be the chief architect of narrow readings of explicit textual provisions for national citizenship rights.[117] Other justices achieved results expressing a similar expansive spirit at this time, but they usually relied on the commerce power or the Article IV privileges and immunities clause.[118] In any case, this early Reconstruction judicial activism on behalf of implied, common-law, and explicit rights of citizenship was not to endure.

By 1877, the Court under Chief Justice Morrison Waite, an Ohio Republican appointed by Grant in 1874, was retreating from the expansive protection against uncompensated regulatory takings it had defined in *Yates*. In *Railroad Co. v. Richmond,* Waite wrote upholding the power of cities to regulate all property within their bounds without recompense unless they violated specific contractual provisions. *Yates* went undiscussed.[119] Later cases involving state laws that placed out-of-state citizens at a disadvantage usually relied on the commerce clause rather than on Article IV civic privileges and immunities, leaving these rights of citizenship fairly undeveloped.[120]

The Second Phase: Supreme Court Resistance to Egalitarian Nationalism. That backing off from expansive readings of Article IV, federal common-law protections, and implicit rights of citizenship formed part of the path the Supreme Court set from 1873 on, when cases involving the Reconstruction civil rights laws and amendments began to reach it. Although the more expansive lower court readings of those measures greatly aided federal efforts to destroy the Ku Klux Klan and secure the rights of African-Americans, in 1873 a bare majority of the Court strained to read constitutional protections of citizenship and personal rights in appallingly narrow ways.[121]

First, in *Blyew et al. v. United States* (1873), the Court reversed the position taken by Justice Swayne in *United States v. Rhodes,* with Swayne and Bradley in dissent.[122] The case involved a murder of a black woman, Lucy Armstrong, and Kentucky law prevented black witnesses from testifying against the white defendants. But here, Justice William Strong wrote that only "the government and the persons indicted" were parties to a criminal prosecution. Victims had no special concern beyond those common to all citizens (and Lucy Armstrong was "beyond" all mundane cares anyway). Strong's reasoning was affected by traditional federalism worries: he indicated his fear that to give the federal courts jurisdiction whenever a black might testify would make them open to every civil and criminal cause. But, as Bradley noted, the Court's position ignored the law's "liberal objects," particularly the protection of black victims of white crimes, whose right to have such crimes punished was thwarted by hostile state evidentiary laws. Thus, beyond states' rights precepts, white obliviousness to black interests was also visible.[123]

Weeks later, Strong also joined the four other justices who severely contracted the protections provided by the postwar amendments in the famous *Slaughter-House Cases*.[124] That decision, combining the *Live-Stock* case with two related suits, was all the more significant because it limited federal power to intervene even against what were inarguably state actions. In part the case turned on the genuinely debatable question of whether the Crescent City Company's charter was an unreasonable burden on the liberties of New Orleans butchers. They could, after all, continue to ply their trade upon payment of a relatively modest, state-regulated fee. Justice Miller and four colleagues did not regard the measure as a serious interference with the butchers' free labor rights. Justices Field, Bradley, Swayne, and Chief Justice Chase did, finding it reasonable to require slaughterhouses to locate out of town, but not to grant any exclusive privileges.[125] That issue was far from trivial, but it could have been decided either way without greatly altering the potential scope of the amendment.[126]

But Miller went on to deny that the question had to be addressed, for he denied that the postwar amendments protected the sorts of rights the butchers claimed.[127] The case centered on the privileges and immunities clause, for which Miller advanced a largely novel interpretation designed to maintain the importance of the states, and state citizenship, in the federal system.[128] He first noted that the citizenship clause that began the Fourteenth Amendment referred to both U.S. citizenship and state citizenship. Next, he assumed, without argument, that those two statuses had to be entirely "distinct." Miller then emphasized, incontrovertibly, that the Fourteenth Amendment's privileges and immunities clause referred to U.S. citizenship; and he asserted, far more controversially, that the Article IV privileges and immunities clause referred exclusively to rights of state citizenship, augmented only by the proviso that states grant the most basic among such rights to visiting out-of-state citizens. On those premises, Miller invoked Justice Bushrod Washington's opinion in *Corfield v. Coryell* defining Article IV privileges as those "which are fundamental" in order to hold that rights of state citizenship included "nearly every civil right for the establishment and protection of which organized government is instituted."[129] And because state citizenship alone included such basic rights, they could not be privileges and immunities of national citizenship protected by the Fourteenth Amendment. It referred only to rights stemming *exclusively* from possession of U.S citizenship, not rights also traceable to state citizenship or personhood. Thus it was confined to rights such as the federal government's protection when abroad, on the high seas, in U.S. waters, or while traveling to and petitioning the U.S. government, along with other privileges deriving solely from possession of national citizenship.

As the dissenters showed, Miller's extraordinarily narrow view of the prerogatives of U.S. citizenship rested on shaky ground. Even Taney's dual federalism had portrayed Article IV protections as stemming from *both* U.S. and state citizenship. And while Taney and most other antebellum judges had, like Miller, interpreted Article IV as a comity clause, their reading did not mean that the rights states had to provide for out-of-state citizens were *exclusively* rights of state citizenship. Washington's *Coryell* opinion had, after all, held that they were privileges belonging to citizens of "all free governments." Bradley and Swayne, in dissent, spelled out the obvious conclusion: certain rights belonged to *both* U.S. and state citizenship. American citizenship then added other rights stemming from its national character, whereas state citizenship conferred rights "local in their character." And, as Field noted, even prior to the Fourteenth Amendment, Miller and the Court had protected implied rights derived from national membership and the national character of the federal government. If this was all the amendment did, "it was a vain and idle enactment, which accomplished nothing, and most unnecessarily excited Congress and the people on its passage."[130]

Miller admitted that his peculiar doctrine of citizenship was motivated by fears about the "consequences" of taking a different tack. His concerns did not reflect free labor ideology; he was opposing its implications. Rather, like Strong in *Blyew,* Miller worried about legitimating national powers that might "radically" alter the federal system, "fetter and degrade the state governments," making them subject to Congress and to a Supreme Court that would be "a perpetual censor" on all state laws. Miller's fervent language suggests real anxieties about centralized despotism born of state-centered republicanism. After elaborating those fears, Miller briefly dispensed with the butchers' due process and equal protection claims, holding that the first had never been applied to anything like the regulations here, and that equal protection was chiefly a guarantee for blacks.[131]

As the Court's opinion had the effect of sustaining a Reconstruction measure, did not directly involve black rights, and repeatedly trumpeted the aim of the amendments to protect blacks, it was not initially much opposed by Republican and radical politicians and editorial writers. But it revealed growing reservations about the great draining struggles required by an ongoing federal role of policing the states' treatment of basic civic rights. Its doctrines soon provided a legitimating framework for Republican desires to back off from the liberal nationalizing initiatives of the 1860s.[132] Although the slim majority of five included one Democratic holdover, Nathan Clifford, and David Davis (who would become a Democrat), Miller, Strong, and Ward Hunt were all solid Republicans. Their narrow reading of their party's enactments is another instance of how even political bearers of egalitarian liberal principles found their implications so disruptive that they faltered in their pursuit. Despite their pro-black rhetoric, in 1873 the majority had to know that the ruling's stress on states' powers might also mean deference to efforts to preserve or rebuild the old racial status quo.

Against Miller's reassertion of states' rights republicanism, the four dissenters supported more plausible nationalistic free labor readings of the amendments' content, blending Jacksonian aversion to special economic privileges with Whig concern for national power to promote growth, as Republicans did generally.[133] They contended that the Fourteenth Amendment, particularly the privileges and immunities clause, made all the basic rights common to U.S. citizenship, state citizenship, indeed citizenship in any free government enforceable by the federal government against the states. Although a few rights had already been given that status in the Constitution, including protection against contractual infringements and ex post facto laws, most had not. With some exaggeration, Bradley and Swayne argued that the amenders had quite deliberately taken the fateful step of expanding national power in this regard. Bradley added, like the congressional Republicans, that the increase in national power would not be so great, because the states would be compliant and the courts would soon define civic privileges well enough to forestall extensive litigation. But the dissenters indicated that the nation must accept the consequences of the amendments, whatever they proved to be.[134]

As to the content of these privileges and immunities, both Field and Bradley stressed, above all, "the right of free labor, one of the most sacred and imprescriptible rights of man." Field cited Adam Smith and the French economist Turgot to claim that "equality of right among citizens in the pursuit of the ordinary avocations of life" was the "distinguishing privilege of citizens of the United States" and "the fundamental idea upon which our institutions rest." Bradley agreed that among U.S. civic rights, indeed among human rights, "none is more essential and fundamental than the right to follow such profession or employment as each one may choose, subject only to uniform regulations equally applicable to all."[135] The last, Jacksonian point was crucial: economic pursuits could be regulated, but the law must treat all practitioners the same. Short of compelling necessity, grants of exclusive privilege were "onerous" and "indefensible." Arbitrarily depriving all but a few of such liberty and the property it represented violated not only the privileges and immunities clause, but also the due process and equal protection guarantees.[136]

Though one could debate the extent of the burden on free labor rights here, the dissenters were undeniably closer than Miller to the "free labor" principles animating the Civil War amendments. The majority preference for dual federalist values, however, heralded the future. The Grant administration was halting new prosecutions under the Enforcement Acts and granting pardons for many past offenses even as the Court was preparing its decision. When the Klan's renewed terrorism prompted more vigorous federal enforcement measures in 1874, the courts adopted further restrictive readings of federal civil rights powers under the 1870 and 1871 Enforcement Acts.[137] Bradley indicated in an 1874 letter that he now shared Miller's worries about letting Congress "legislate on all subjects of legislation whatever," thus "establishing a duplicate system of government and law for all purposes." That April, his circuit opinion in *United States v. Cruikshank* contrived several new distinctions to limit the scope of the postwar amendments.[138]

The case arose from the bloodiest incident of Reconstruction. When the 1872 Louisiana election results were widely disputed, blacks in Grant Parish fortified the courthouse and the town of Colfax against Klan veterans who laid siege. After three weeks the whites broke through and slaughtered almost three hundred blacks, including more than fifty surrendering under a white flag. Federal officials indicted nearly one hundred whites under the May 31, 1870, Enforcement Act for conspiring to deprive two African-Americans, Levi Nelson and Alexander Tillman, of many constitutional rights, including rights of assembly and due process, the right to vote, and the right to bear arms. At the end of lengthy trials which resulted in but three convictions, Bradley (against Woods' objections) sustained a motion to arrest the judgments, finding that the indictments (and by implication, sections 6 and 7 of the Enforcement Act) could not be justified in terms of Congress's constitutional powers.[139]

Bradley contended first that, although the Thirteenth Amendment gave Congress power to move against private actions that went beyond direct imposition of chattel slavery (such as expulsions of blacks from leased land), it could do so only when such action was shown to be motivated by hostility to the injured person's "race, color, or previous condition of servitude." Only then was the injury the kind of perpetuation of slavery's harms that the amendment aimed to end. The Fifteenth Amendment, in turn, gave Congress the power to punish state actions abridging the right to vote, but only if they stemmed from such motives. It also authorized federal measures to protect the right to vote against racially driven private infringements, if the state failed to provide remedies.

As for the Fourteenth Amendment's privileges and immunities clause, Bradley now thought it necessary to distinguish among the rights it included, as some lower courts had done. Certain rights, Bradley indicated, were created by the Constitution alone, in the manner of the Fifteenth Amendment's limited voting guarantees. Congress and the federal courts could act directly on private violators to make sure that these rights were effectively secured. Some other rights were birthright civic and natural rights that the Constitution did not create but only recognized, usually via language describing the rights as limits on state or federal action. These rights could be congressionally and judicially protected only against state or federal violations. Hence, if sections 6 and 7 of the 1870 Enforcement Act were interpreted to reach private violations of all rights mentioned in the Constitution, as they appeared to do, they would go too far.[140] Bradley saw Fourteenth Amendment due process rights of liberty and property as rights of his second type, protected only against state actions. No state complicity was alleged in *Cruikshank*. Freedom of assembly, explicitly protected in the First Amendment only against Congressional action, was also a right of the second sort. Indictments against private conspiracies to restrict it could not be sustained, either. According to Bradley, the Second Amendment was aimed only at governmental infringements of the right to bear arms, so it, too, was irrelevant to the case. As for the protections of life and liberty originally contained in the 1866 Civil Rights Act, they stemmed from the Thirteenth Amendment. As such, they were protected against private conspiracies only if the violations were "on account of" the victims' "race, color, or previous condition of servitude." Bradley somehow found racial motives not shown in the Colfax massacre. Saying that the other counts had the same flaws or were too vague and general, he dismissed them all.[141]

These distinctions displayed more creativity than craftsmanship. But Bradley's confinement of the Thirteenth and Fifteenth Amendments to protection only against racially motivated private infringements, and his virtual restriction of Fourteenth Amendment privileges and immunities to protection against state violations, inspired other narrowing judicial decisions.[142] Those rulings, in turn, help explain why the enforcement efforts provoked by the renewed Klan violence of 1874 again faded by late 1875. At that point, only a changed Supreme Court stance could have reinvigorated prosecutorial will.[143]

Instead, the Court continued the erosion of Reconstruction by upholding Bradley's stance in *Cruikshank* and adding another major restrictive decision, *United States v. Reese*, in 1876. In both cases, Chief Justice Waite's opinions for the

Court were redolent of the Northern Republican retreat from continued civil rights struggles.[144] In *Cruikshank,* Waite offered a mini-treatise on citizenship that was both liberal and republican, endorsing notions of citizenship as based on consent, involving political rights, and dedicated to securing both individual and collective rights and the general welfare, especially the principle of the "equality of the rights of citizens" that was a basic "principle of republicanism."[145] But, citing *Slaughter-House,* he stressed that Americans had created a dual system of state and national citizenship to achieve these ends, and he interpreted that system exactly as Bradley had done in his circuit opinion. In America all nondelegated residual sovereignty was left to the states, including all power to protect rights that were not derived solely from the Constitution (unless the Constitution explicitly reassigned such power). The right of assembly for all purposes except petitioning Congress was a right of this type, pre-constitutional, subject only to state protection. So was the right to bear arms, when defended against anyone but Congress. Even more so were rights of life and personal liberty, "natural rights of man" that it was the states' "very highest duty" to secure. The Fourteenth Amendment, moreover, sheltered such rights only against active "arbitrary exercises" of state power. Waite did not explicitly deny the amendment's potency in cases of state inaction against private discrimination, but his failure to discuss this possibility eclipsed it. Waite also agreed that the indictments did not sufficiently allege that rights were to be violated because of the victims' race, as Thirteenth and Fifteenth Amendment powers exercised in the 1866 Civil Rights Act and the 1870 Enforcement Act required. These arguments took care of all but two indictments. Waite, like Bradley, found those too vague.[146]

In *United States v. Reese,* Waite considered a dispute over whether the Fifteenth Amendment-based provisions of the 1870 Enforcement Act permitted an indictment of two Kentucky municipal election inspectors who had refused to receive or count the vote of a black citizen, William Garner. Acknowledging that the Fifteenth Amendment created a constitutional right for otherwise qualified voters not to be excluded on the basis of race, color, or previous condition of servitude, the Chief Justice voided sections 3 and 4 of the Enforcement Act because they were not explicitly confined to infringements of voting rights based on those reasons. The qualifying reasons were listed in the first two sections of the act, but Waite refused to find them implicit in the next two. Hence Congress had as yet failed to enforce the amendment by "appropriate legislation." Though the statutory flaw Waite stressed could easily have been remedied, his obvious quest to escape rigorous enforcement of black rights was all too reflective of Congress's mood and much public sentiment. No such remedy was enacted.[147]

Cruikshank and *Reese* were, to be sure, not the end of the Court's major nineteenth-century rulings on black civil rights. A number of other issues, including the validity of the era's final monument, the 1875 Civil Rights Act, remained to be settled. But these cases mark the end of the radical hour in American citizenship policies. The later issues would almost always be settled in ways hostile to full black citizenship, informed by the revived state-centered federalism endorsed in *Slaughter-House* and *Cruikshank,* and by the pro-racist intellectual climate of the late nineteenth century. Racial egalitarianism was not wholly effaced: in law, equal black citizenship had been officially achieved, and in politics, many Republicans still sought black votes. But these decisions made it clear, undoubtedly to the satisfaction of a majority of white Americans, that government officials would not really attempt the daunting task of altering social reality to conform to liberal egalitarian precepts.

The Judiciary and Women's Citizenship

The courts also confronted women's rights claims during the Reconstruction era, and though women similarly fared best early on, judges soon proved even less receptive to their interests. In the late 1860s, many federal courts were willing to grant exceptions to the traditional doctrine that a woman's domicile was the same as her husband's, thus allowing a woman to sue in federal courts as a citizen of another state if she did not live in the same state as her husband. Federal judges also construed laws as allowing women to inherit or own land in their own names, even when the statutes did not so indicate.

Thus in *Bennett v. Bennett* (1867), Oregon District Judge Matthew Deady admitted that the "general rule" was that women were "in law . . . incapable of acquiring a different domicil" from their husbands, but he insisted that "when the reason of the law ceases the law ceases with it." Sanford Bennett had left his wife, Susan, and taken their daughter, Anna, to Oregon, prior to their being divorced. Deady decided that when a marriage had effectively ceased, the fiction of a common domicile should not bar access to the federal judiciary.[148] Similarly, in *Cheever v. Wilson* (1869), Justice Swayne wrote for the U.S. Supreme Court that the rule was "that she may acquire a separate domicil whenever it is necessary or proper that she should do so" in the case of Annie Jane Cheever, who successfully claimed independent status on the basis of a divorce recognized in Indiana but not in the District of Columbia.[149] In *Silver v. Ladd* (1868), the Court strained to read an 1850 congressional act as permitting a widow to settle on and claim territorial lands, even though its language expressly referred only to men.[150] Justice Field then firmly enforced the claims of all wives and female descendants under the act in the Supreme Court case of *Davenport v. Lamb* (1871).[151]

Because these decisions came during the phase of Reconstruction when the courts were reading the rights of blacks fairly expansively, they might be interpreted as reflecting the influence of accompanying claims for women's independence and vocational rights. But that inference is almost surely unwarranted. The domicile rulings simply followed the precedent set in *Barber v. Barber* in 1858.[152] The real property decisions fit perfectly with the protective but inegalitarian attitudes toward women visible in much of the support for Married Women's Property Acts, and their rhetoric is quite similar. In *Silver v. Ladd,* for example, Justice Miller stressed the need to give "the unprotected female" at least those economic rights extended to "a married woman, who has the care and protection of a husband."[153] That same year, in *Kelly v. Owen,* Justice Field held that the 1855 Naturalization Act, which declared that all women eligible for naturalization were automatically naturalized if their husbands were U.S. citizens, conferred citizenship even on women whose husbands gained American citizenship after their marriage.[154] Field was right about the law's intent, but his easy acceptance of its patriarchal subordination of wives' political status to that of their husbands displays no doubts about the legitimacy of hierarchical gender status.

Even so, and despite the failure of female suffrage advocates to gain recognition in the postwar amendments, the faint prospects for legislated reforms led them to adopt the key tactic comprising their "New Departure." Women began voting. Then they contended in court that the recent amendments logically implied that women had the vote. With only a little squirming, the courts rebuffed them.

Francis Minor, a St. Louis lawyer and husband of Virginia Minor, the president of Missouri's woman suffrage group, first advanced arguments that the Fourteenth Amendment had enfranchised women in 1869. Francis Minor contended that the amendment confirmed that women were U.S. citizens, and so they were entitled to all civic privileges and immunities as well as equal protection. He assumed that the vote was a privilege of citizenship that could not be bestowed unequally. Two years later the radical journalist Victoria Woodhull made similar arguments as the first woman to testify before Congress. Invoking the revolutionary slogan of "no taxation without representation" and the Fifteenth and Fourteenth Amendments, Woodhull insisted that because the Constitution did not specifically exclude women from the suffrage, the broad terms of the postwar amendments must include them. Her much-publicized testimony was endorsed by the NWSA. It advised women to register and vote, or sue if they were not allowed to do so.[155]

A wave of efforts by women to vote ensued, compelling the Supreme Court to address the issue. The best-known cases involved Susan B. Anthony and Virginia Minor in 1872. They evoked rulings that brought the New Departure to an abrupt halt. These cases form some of the clearest examples in the nation's history of clashes between egalitarian liberal principles that demanded changes in existing social, economic, and political hierarchies, and the desires of governors who found those implications too threatening and who invoked state-centered republican and ascriptive arguments to rationalize their rejection.[156]

The first of these dramas of American citizenship was *Bradwell v. State of Illinois*, heard in January 1872 but held back so that it could be rendered immediately after Justice Miller's momentous decision in the *Slaughter-House Cases* of 1873. The Court thereby signaled sharply that not only would the postwar amendments be read narrowly; they would specifically not be read as embracing the equal rights views of female reformers.

AWSA activist Myra Bradwell, editor of the *Chicago Legal News* and wife of a Cook County judge, had sued because the Illinois Bar Association and the Illinois Supreme Court refused to license her to practice law, even though she had passed the requisite examination. Senator Matthew Carpenter, the Wisconsin Republican who was the attorney for the Reconstruction-fostered monopoly in the *Slaughter-House Cases*, here made arguments not unlike his rival in that case, John Campbell. Carpenter denied that the postwar amendments had given women the vote, although he indicated that that result was not "at all to be dreaded." But he insisted that the Fourteenth Amendment did protect the privileges and immunities of all U.S. citizens, including women.

Carpenter had also been one of the attorneys who successfully challenged test oaths as improper burdens on teachers' and lawyers' vocational rights in *Cummings v. Missouri* and *Ex parte Garland*. Here he drew on those victories, quoting Justice Field's dictum in *Cummings* that the "theory upon which our political institutions rest is, that all men have certain inalienable rights—that among these are life, liberty, and the pursuit of happiness, and that in the pursuit of happiness, all avocations, all honors, all positions, are alike open to every one, and that in the protection of these rights all are equal before the law." Carpenter used the *Garland* case to show that being an attorney was such an "avocation," and thus a right or "privilege and immunity" of U.S. citizenship. He insisted that women were both persons and citizens within the meaning of the amendment, which must be read as opening "to every citizen of the United States, male or female, black or white, married or single, the honorable professions as well as the service employments of life." Bradwell was clearly qualified, save for her sex. Carpenter suggested that gender should perhaps be a concern for clients, but not for courts defining basic civic rights.[157]

Carpenter's arguments presented a very reasonable free labor reading of the Fourteenth Amendment and the Constitution, supported by some recent precedents and built squarely upon property-centered liberal republican traditions. The extension of these rights to women was controversial, but his analogy of their claims to those of the free blacks who were the amendment's central concerns was both logically powerful and familiar. Legislatures and courts were already expanding various economic rights for women, although admittedly not in ways that threatened to provide them with equal professional status. Carpenter's contentions were also not answered by any opposing counsel. Instead of contesting the case, Illinois was busy changing its law to permit women to obtain legal licenses. The state did so, and Bradwell gained honorary membership in the state bar in 1872.

The case was thus effectively moot when the Court handed down its verdict. But the justices still used it to deliver a resounding repudiation of claims for new civil rights protection for women under the Fourteenth Amendment. Justice Miller, who had dissented from Field's position in *Cummings* and *Garland,* wrote for the majority and used a state-centered republican view of the Constitution to deny Bradwell's assertion of her economic rights in precisely the same way he denied the *Slaughter-House* butchers' claims. The right to practice law was not a privilege and immunity of U.S. citizenship, only state citizenship. The state could confer the privilege as it wished.[158]

That result should not have come so easily for Bradley, Field, and Swayne, the advocates of strong protection for vocational rights against such assertions of state-centered republicanism in their *Slaughter-House* dissents and elsewhere.[159] If they had been pure, consistent free labor liberal republicans, they would have dissented again.

Instead, Bradley wrote a concurrence, joined by Field and Swayne, that rejected Miller's state-centered views but actually went further in affirming his result. Bradley argued, in effect, that no state should allow a woman to become a lawyer, through a now-notorious elaboration of ascriptive "separate spheres" ideology. According to Bradley, "nature herself," along with "the divine ordinance," indicated "the domestic sphere as that which properly belongs to the domain and functions of womanhood." Man should be "woman's protector and defender." Neither the "recent modifications" in women's status wrought by the new property laws nor the fact that some women did not marry could alter the "general constitution of things," which designated woman's "paramount destiny" to be the fulfillment of the "noble and benign offices of wife and mother." This was "the law of the Creator," and the Constitution permitted the state's police powers to enact it. Chief Justice Chase was the sole dissenter in the case, and he did so silently.[160]

Even though it was only a concurrence, Bradley's opinion represented the most elaborate and authoritative endorsement of separate spheres ideology in American law up to that time. It is possible that Miller and his majority preferred to stress state-centered republicanism rather than to endorse traditional hierarchies explicitly in Bradley's fashion. It is more likely that the Miller group agreed with Bradley but wished to underline their denial of broad national powers under the Fourteenth Amendment. In any event, the decision sent a clear signal that, through the resurgent alliance of state-centric republican and inegalitarian ascriptive views, public policies restricting women to traditional roles would be upheld. Although the courts would support protective measures for women, even judicial proponents of economic liberalism would not take it so far as to disturb men's general ascendancy. The intellectual and political climate permitted judges instead to treat naturalist and religious doctrines of inherent gender differences as legal truths.

Similarly, in June 1873, Susan B. Anthony was tried for voting illegally in a case heard by Justice Ward Hunt, presiding over his first circuit criminal case after being appointed by Grant to the U.S. Supreme Court. After hearing arguments stressing that the privileges and immunities protected by the Fourteenth Amendment, as well as the Fifteenth Amendment, should be construed to encompass female suffrage, Hunt instructed the jury that as a matter of law, voting was a privilege of state citizenship, citing the recent *Slaughter-House* and *Bradwell* decisions for support. As Anthony therefore had no right to vote, Hunt believed that there was nothing for the jury to decide. He directed it to issue a verdict of guilty, ordered that verdict recorded, and released the jurors without permitting them to speak. Anthony refused to pay her $100 fine, but Hunt did not order her incarcerated, thus preventing her from appealing to the Supreme Court via habeas corpus. Though the case received much publicity and Hunt was widely criticized in Congress and in the press for his peremptory conduct, its legal history was over.[161]

Because of Hunt's tactic, it was Virginia Minor's case, not Anthony's, which provided the occasion for the Supreme Court to close the door on claims for an implied constitutional right of female suffrage in 1874. For all its significance, *Minor v. Happersett* was predictable. The newly appointed Chief Justice Waite made the Court unanimous in its denial of claims for female rights under the postwar amendments, and he wrote the opinion in the case. Waite acknowledged that women were citizens under the Fourteenth Amendment, and so he felt compelled to separate U.S. citizenship and republican citizenship firmly from possession of the franchise. Though not novel, that holding at this juncture proved an influential rejection of more participatory views of republican citizenship, here cast in terms of both privileges and immunities and guarantee clause arguments. Republican citizenship meant, Waite said, "membership of a nation and nothing more." And he agreed with congressional Democrats that the legal bounds of republicanism were to be gleaned from the practices of the founding states, leaving the suffrage largely to state discretion. Waite did grant the case "importance," and he seemed uncomfortable at the manner in which his deference to states' rights resulted in support for arrangements that might be "wrong" and work "hardship." But the Court was firmly committed to the course Miller set in *Slaughter-House* and *Bradwell*. The last shred of hope that Reconstruction might be the era in which women achieved full citizenship thus disintegrated. Time would show that the limited view of citizenship that Waite endorsed could sustain renewed racial and ethnic restraints as well, as Susan B. Anthony warned.[162]

The Judiciary and Immigration

In other regards, however, the Supreme Court signaled its support for national power, sometimes under circumstances that supported more racially egalitarian citizenship laws. In 1876 it sided with a series of state judicial decisions enforcing national immigration policies and the Burlingame Treaty against anti-immigration state laws from both coasts.[163] First, in *Henderson v. Mayor of New York*, the Court invalidated a New York regulation that imposed a $1.50 head tax for every alien passenger brought into the city's port. The money went to the city's Commission on Emigration as an immigrant welfare fund, so it was far less hostile to newcomers than the west coast anti-Chinese laws. But, burying the many ambiguities left by the *Passenger Cases*, Justice Miller here took a strongly nationalistic view, holding that immigration regulations were commerce regulations, not police power measures, because immigrants bring "the labor we need to till our soil, build our railroads, and develop the latent resources of the country." He added that immigration's "national," indeed "international" character required a "uniform system" of laws, so that the whole subject should be regarded as exclusively "confided to Congress by the Constitution."[164] No justice dissented. With slavery dead, no one perceived this affirmation of national power as endangering any truly crucial state prerogatives. Immediately thereafter, the Court added *Chy Lung v. Freeman*, confirming the invalidity of a California system for demanding bonds for immigrants that Field had struck down on circuit. Miller ruled that the powers that the state was trying to exercise belonged to Congress and that the law also went far beyond any necessary state measures for self-defense.[165]

Diversity Jurisdiction and Corporations

The availability of the federal courts to corporations under the diversity of citizenship clause was heavily litigated during Reconstruction, but the Court's position did not much waver. It remained committed to the *Letson* rule, under which a corporation was presumptively treated as a citizen of the state in which it was created for purposes of diversity jurisdiction.[166] Questions did arise when corporations were chartered by more than one state, potentially permitting corporations to claim or avoid federal jurisdiction by asserting citizenship in one or another locale. Generally the federal courts still decided these claims in favor of their own jurisdiction, giving corporations significant dimensions of national citizenship without the title. But beyond concerns for their own authority, the courts seem to have been prompted as much by desires to permit ordinary citizens to sue corporations as to assist corporate operations.[167]

Judicial intent to safeguard federal jurisdiction was, however, most persistent. In *Insurance Co. v. Morse* (1874), the Supreme Court invalidated a Wisconsin statute that banned out-of-state fire insurance companies unless they agreed not to remove their legal disputes from Wisconsin state courts to the federal courts. Hunt wrote for the Court that Wisconsin's statute effectively negated a federally bestowed right; hence, it exceeded constitutional state regulatory powers.[168] The ruling was an early example of the doctrine of "unconstitutional conditions," which bans legislative provisos on state-conferred benefits that burden the exercise of constitutional rights. The Court was, however, more concerned with its formal jurisdiction than with the substantive corporate right of access. Two years later, it permitted Wisconsin to revoke the license of a corporation that had chosen to exercise its right of removal, even though Bradley, Swayne, and Miller, in dissent, argued cogently that this result negated the right as fully as in *Morse*.[169]

And though the federal courts maintained the *Letson* presumption of corporate citizenship for jurisdictional purposes, they still refused to treat corporations as citizens within the meaning of the Constitution's privileges and immunities clauses. In *Paul v. Virginia* (1869), even Justice Field refused to grant corporations Article IV recognition, partly because it would too greatly enhance their power at the expense of the states.[170] Here Field endorsed a comity interpretation of the Article IV clause, holding that it guaranteed to citizens of each state those privileges and immunities granted by other states to their citizens which formed the basic rights of their state citizenship. The clause did so, he indicated, as a means of constituting "the citizens of the United States" as one people.[171] But that end was not served, he wrote, by treating corporations as Article IV citizens. To do so in a time when "the wealth and business of the country are to a great extent controlled" by corporations that could incorporate anywhere would be disastrous. In time, "the principal business of every State would, in fact, be controlled by corporations created by other States," who would thus be largely immune from local regulation. Field believed that the privileges of state-chartered corporations must be viewed as "special privileges," not as general rights of state citizenship that must be extended to nonresident corporations.[172] Overall, then, the Court maintained access to the federal judiciary for corporations under the diversity clause; but it did so more to preserve national authority over the scope of basic rights and corporate claims than to enhance corporate power.[173]

The Judiciary and Native Americans

The courts played only a peripheral, permissive role in the main policy developments toward the native tribes. They never considered any challenge to the Grant Peace Policy's violation of bans on religious establishment and religious tests for office-holders. It is likely that the Supreme Court would have denied that these restrictions applied when dealing with Native Americans. Although the federal courts favored national over state authority in relation to the tribes in a manner closer to Taney's reasoning in *Dred Scott* than to most state-centered Jacksonian rulings, they still showed little desire to protect the tribes against the federal government.

For example, Justice Miller found for the Court in *United States v. Holliday* (1865) that the commerce power permitted the U.S. to ban sales of liquor to any Indian under the authority of an Indian agent, even if the sale took place off the reservation, on state lands.[174] In 1866, the Court voided efforts by Kansas and New York to tax tribal lands held under federal treaties. So long as the U.S. recognized tribes not as citizens but as "distinct" dependent peoples, Justice Davis wrote, they were "to be governed exclusively by the government of the Union" and immune to state taxation. The Court also confirmed that ambiguous treaties should be construed to the tribes' benefit.[175] Judicial support for federal power, however, often overrode that promise. Justice Swayne wrote in the *Cherokee Tobacco* case (1870) that it was "not difficult" to decide that Congress could tax tobacco grown on Cherokee land, notwithstanding any earlier treaties. Quite simply, an act of Congress could supersede a treaty.[176]

The federal courts did not, however, display any zeal on behalf of their own jurisdiction.[177] In *Karrahoo v. Adams* (1870), the circuit court for Kansas disavowed jurisdiction over a case brought by a member of the Wyandot nation who claimed she was a "foreign citizen or subject" entitled by Article III, section 2, to sue state citizens in federal courts. Citing Marshall's language in the *Cherokee Nation* case, Judge Dillon affirmed that Indians were not truly "foreign citizens or subjects." Although he agreed that this made their status "very peculiar," it prevented them from challenging states or their citizens in federal courts. Dillon showed no interest in using Marshall's greater stress on tribal independence in *Worcester v. Georgia* to make the federal courts more available to adjudicate Native American interests.[178]

The baleful consequences of that reluctance is evident when *Karrahoo* is compared with an Oregon district court decision of 1871, *McKay v. Campbell*. At issue was whether William McKay, born of a British father and a Chinook mother at Fort George in Oregon when Britain and the U.S. were disputing title over that territory, was a native-born U.S. citizen guaranteed the vote under the 1870 Enforcement Act. District Judge Deady ruled that though the U.S. later carried its claim to the soil in question, Fort George was at the time of his birth under the control of the British Hudson Bay Company for which McKay's father worked. Hence Britain, not the U.S., had exercised the actual power and protection that commanded birthright allegiance.

The judge then expressed doubt over whether McKay inherited the political identity of his British father or his Chinook mother. Following the common law, instead of the special "one drop of blood" rule lawmakers usually favored in regard to persons of African descent, Deady leaned toward the patriarchal position, which again made McKay British. But Deady held that if instead the fort's soil was American and McKay was Chinook, he would then be a member of an "independent political community," not a person born subject to the jurisdiction of the United States. Thus there was no way McKay could claim citizenship or the vote, although Deady admitted that Oregon often allowed such "persons of mixed blood" to do so.[179]

Although minor, McKay v. Campbell is revealing in several respects. It shows the ongoing hold of ascriptive common-law views of membership, which assigned civic status first on the basis of protection at birth and next patriarchally. But it also shows how the federal courts, like the Reconstruction Congress, tried to make the status of the tribes as "peculiar" and as vulnerable as possible. When tribal members claimed judicial protection, they were insufficiently "foreign" to gain access. When they claimed the vote on the strength of their native status, they were once again members of "independent political communities." Through such maneuvers the federal courts generally found ways to sustain the land rights and governmental powers the elected branches of the national government recognized the tribes as possessing, but only insofar and in such ways as the national government recognized them, whatever the tribes' wishes.[180]

The Court's deference in this era was well summed up in United States v. Forty-Three Gallons of Whiskey (1876), affirming U.S. power to punish whites who sold liquor to Chippewas even when the sales took place on state lands. The Court ruled that this was an appropriate commercial implementation of a policy aimed at keeping Native Americans as "separate, subordinate, and dependent" federal wards. Justice Davis's opinion for the Court acknowledged in passing that it "may be" that federal policies "on the subject of Indian affairs has, in some particulars, justly provoked criticism"; but the justices clearly felt that any challenges to those policies should be made through electoral, not judicial processes.[181] This deference meant judicial acquiescence in the high-minded but ethnocentric Americanism of Grant's Peace Policy.

That policy, titularly aimed at making all Native Americans eligible for full republican U.S. citizenship, fit the pattern visible throughout rulings governing black citizenship, immigration, birthright citizenship, expatriation, naturalization, female citizenship, civic education, national civic privileges, and corporate rights during these years. Greater civic inclusion was promised and sometimes pursued, but it had to come on terms highly protective of the world that Protestant white men had made, or not at all.[182]

The multiple traditions in American life are visible not only in this complex, contested Reconstruction history, but also in the sharply divergent ways in which it has since been viewed. For years Reconstruction's egalitarianism was widely portrayed as a disastrous error. Then in the 1960s more scholars began daring to call the period a time of noble aims and achievements. Since the late 1970s, many have revived W. E. B. Du Bois's argument that the nation's liberalism, especially, prevented the reforms of this era from going far enough. A multiple traditions perspective suggests instead that it was politically and intellectually reinvigorated white racism—and attachments to ascriptive hierarchies more generally—that played the most decisive role in stirring the largely successful opposition to these changes. Even so, much in the Reconstruction laws did fit the pictures that Myrdal, Hartz, and others would paint of the "true" American liberal democratic character, and the greatest reforms of the era, passed on the crest of war fervor, remained on the nation's lawbooks thereafter as enduring resources for efforts to achieve racial justice. But because of the strength and appeal of its ascriptive traditions, the U.S. still remained the nation that Langston Hughes would speak of when he urged his fellow citizens to "let America be America again, the land that never has been yet." The land that had not yet been was a truly equitable nation. Even in its most radical hour, Hughes knew that America "never was America to me."[183]

11

The Gilded Age of Ascriptive Americanism, 1876–1898

For Louis Hartz, the Gilded Age unfolded under "the golden banner of Horatio Alger." The democratic capitalist dream of a "pot of American gold" for every plucky lad seduced so many of the potential foes of Big Business, Hartz argued, that the champions of Hamiltonian Whiggery, now termed Americanism, reached their Promised Land at last. Few writers today would define Gilded Age Americanism by ignoring issues of race, ethnicity, and gender as massively as Hartz did, but many still share his focus. Morton Keller, like most influential historians and political scientists writing on this era, terms the "confrontation with industrialism," especially the problems of building a regulatory state in the context of growing corporate power and ongoing sectional divisions, the "major theme" of public life in these years. In these accounts, struggles between capital and labor loom large. Conflicts over race, religion, and gender tend to be secondary.[1]

For many purposes, this focus on industrial capitalism is appropriate. But from the standpoint of American citizenship laws, seeing the Gilded Age as a response to industrialism and as the triumph of Algerism relegates the main story to the background. That story is the mounting repudiation of Reconstruction egalitarianism and inclusiveness in favor of an extraordinarily broad political, intellectual, and legal embrace of renewed ascriptive hierarchies. Though some Republicans continued to champion the rights of racial minorities, and though some farm and labor groups accorded greater respect to blacks and women, at the national level new liberalizing and democratizing civic reforms, even reforms overtly benefiting corporate citizenship, were few and far between. Instead, reinforced by favorable intellectual and international trends and the responses of anti-Reconstruction white voters, both parties increasingly featured their ascriptive views of American identity. Hence legislators often agreed on new legal systems of racial and ethnic subordination and exclusion.[2]

As a result, the era of Alger and Carnegie was equally the era of Chinese exclusion, the antitribal Dawes Act, stagnation in the women's suffrage campaign, the rise of Jim Crow segregation and disfranchisement, the emergence of the literacy test and other proposals to curb non-Nordic immigration, resurgent anti-Catholicism, and finally the racially justified imposition of colonial rule over Latinos and Asians via the Spanish-American War. It was, in short, the era of the militant WASP, whose concerns to protect and enhance his cultural hegemony were vastly more pronounced in citizenship laws than efforts to aid capitalism. Even Alger's most famous hero, "Ragged Dick" Hunter, was a brave Anglo-Saxon who triumphed over a cowardly Irish bully, Micky Maguire. The Harvard-educated Alger described Maguire as the "despotic" leader of a "gang of young ruffians" who, with "a trifle more education" would have been a corrupt ward politician and "a terror to respectable voters," like so many Boston Irish.[3]

To be sure, all these civic developments were intimately bound up with the efforts of unions and employers to gain advantages in their struggles, with the concerns of corporate leaders and many other Americans to achieve stability conducive to economic growth, and with the desires of American business and political elites to advance their interests in a world increasingly shaped by Western economic expansion and imperialism. These were years when educators like Nicholas Murray Butler celebrated the "limited liability corporation" as "the greatest single discovery of modern times," while others deplored the development of a corporate-dominated economy in which, by 1890, 1 percent of the U.S. population controlled more wealth than the remaining 99 percent.[4] Yet central as those economic concerns were, no simple economic explanation of the era's citizenship laws can work. The new ascriptive legal systems won support among many segments of the population whose material interests were not well served by them, and arguably were severely harmed. In view of the full panoply of civic changes in the Gilded Age, rather than celebrating naked capitalism, many Americans anxiously rejected the prospect of a fully liberal free labor society, with equal rights and opportunities for all races, religions, and genders. Such a society endangered too much that they valued. Hence leaders in both parties found that they could best gain support by responding to the fears and hopes of this era in a different way. They promised to guard Americans against the new dangers from within and without via policies of restriction, exclusion, and mandatory assimilation; and they defended all these measures by appeal to newly elaborated ascriptive civic myths, some harsher, yet for many more compelling, than ever before.

Civic Ideologies in the Gilded Age: The New Americanism

In 1885, in the midst of what Mark Twain dubbed "the Gilded Age," the Rev. Josiah Strong proclaimed that Americans were living through the "pivot" of their national history.[5] And indeed, the years from the end of Reconstruction to the Spanish-American War were ones of extraordinary economic, demographic, political, legal, and intellectual change in American life.[6] The nation crossed the watershed between a largely agrarian society of small family farms and a new manufacturing society of large corporations and masses of workers. The era's amazing industrial growth and scientific innovations strengthened Americans' Enlightenment faith in science. But the severe new economic inequalities and hardships that accompanied this growth violated the old liberal promise that technologically progressive commercial economies would improve the welfare of all. Growth also spawned huge, unruly cities headquartering powerful financial, manufacturing, and transportation corporations on a scale that made the agrarian, localistic vision of many Jeffersonians and Jacksonians seem quaint. The arrival of millions of new immigrants—many poor, ill-educated, not speaking English, unfamiliar with the nation's political institutions or heavily Protestant culture—also threatened the civic homogeneity long prized in republican thought and in ascriptive versions of Americanism. The still-growing numbers of Chinese in California especially compounded the anxieties that many Americans felt about governance that pursued the racially egalitarian republicanism of the Civil War years. Yet older forms of ascriptive inegalitarianism endorsing slavery were no longer viable. The pressures imposed by European powers building empires in Africa and Asia as their older colonies in North and South America won independence also made both the isolationism of America's state-centered republican traditions and the pacific commercial internationalism long favored by its more nationalistic leaders seem ineffectual. In sum, Enlightenment liberalism, agrarian localistic and more commercial nationalistic versions of republicanism, and aspects of ascriptive Americanism all seemed endangered or inadequate.[7]

Americans were also still coming to terms with the challenges to their traditions posed by the idea of evolution in its many biological and cultural variants. More and more, evolution made old notions of unchanging individual natural rights seem like reassuring fairy tales. The hard truth seemed to be that all individuals and groups were engaged in a bitter struggle to survive amid an unfriendly nature. In that struggle there were no certain guides: the conduct that would produce success, and the species and subspecies achieving it, had changed over time and could again. All standards for conduct seemed relative to shifting conditions. And in a universe constituted by the fluctuating play of physical forces, human thriving could seem a meaningless and temporary accident, not the fulfillment of providence. The once eternal verities of the benefits of a market economy, republican institutions, the American way of life, even the Protestant faith in a hard but benevolent God that was at the core of so many tales of Americans as a chosen people, all had to be reconsidered. To the most thoughtful Americans, confronting evolution required rethinking America's civic traditions and institutions and the human condition itself from the ground up, a task that drove Henry Adams to despair. Even less reflective people knew that momentous issues had to be confronted.[8]

Understandably, most Americans tried to do so while preserving as much as possible of what they cherished in their thought and practices. Up until the Progressive Era, few politicians in either major party favored radical transformations in the institutions through which they held their power. Reform ideas that gained some political potency, like civil service and the paper money policies of the Greenbackers, generally had most support outside professional political circles. They were enacted only if they provided strategic aid to one party or the other, as civil service did for Republicans by promising to limit Democratic patronage systems. The Democrats remained the party of states' rights and laissez-faire, blended with genially corrupt public assistance at state and local levels for both immigrants able to provide votes and businesses able to provide dollars. Only when threatened with displacement by Populists and Socialists did the Democrats come to endorse a more regulatory, redistributive state after the mid-1890s. The Republicans remained dedicated to promotion of economic growth via governmental aid to big businesses, retreating toward laissez-faire only as hostile regulatory movements gained power. With the barest lip service to equal rights, Democrats also still trumpeted their belief in America as a white Christian nation. Though Republicans were more divided, most insisted that whoever might be included as Americans, the Protestant and Anglo-Saxon character of the national culture had to be not just preserved but enhanced. Hence conflicting blends of republican political ideas, liberal economic ideas, and Americanist cultural ideas all continued to dominate the major parties' ideologies.[9]

Those combinations were, however, not responsive to the suffering and anxiety that many Americans were experiencing. Thus political movements arose outside the main parties. They included the Populists, who used grass-roots democratic activism among poor farmers to break from agrarian laissez-faire traditions and call for national ownership of the railroads and a democratically controlled system of credit (named the "sub-treasury" system in Jacksonian fashion, but far more radical). Many Populists also endorsed Henry George's "single tax," meant to end profits from land ownership. A variety of industrial workers' unions and Socialist organizations pursued laws curbing employer abuses, along with direct collective action to defend their interests in the workplace. Middle-class reformers increasingly forged independent, nonpartisan organizations to combat what they saw as the corruption of the major parties and powerful corporations while also opposing more extreme socialistic solutions. They responded enthusiastically to Edward Bellamy's charming vision of a future America united into one great corporate trust in *Looking Backward*, an 1888 best-seller that inspired reformist "New Nation" societies throughout the land. African-Americans, women, and others denied civic equality also continued to speak out for their interests in ways that ranged from conservative gradualism to angry radicalism.

Yet truly new civic visions did not emerge. Most reformers still invoked the Reconstruction languages of liberal individual rights and equal republican citizenship. Among farmers and workers' organizations, traditional republican aims of making producers self-reliant, not dependent on creditors or wage-paying employers, remained prominent. Middle- and upper-class reformers of all races and genders spoke most often in the vernaculars of Enlightenment science and Christian virtue. Few interracial coalitions were attempted by any movement; fewer were achieved. Real acceptance of gender equality was also rare. Hence, even among radical extraparty movements, continuing devotion to all the main themes of American civic thought remained evident.[10]

Across the spectrum, however, from laissez-faire enthusiasts and white supremacists through Socialists and black separatists, leading writers accepted evolution in ways that permanently altered how they understood even the features of American life they endorsed. Herbert Spencer had, of course, argued that evolution implied support for free markets and had opposed many traditional forms of governmental intervention and aid. In his 1883 classic, *What the Social Classes Owe to Each Other*, Spencer's American follower William Graham Sumner showed that such a position involved rejecting older notions of individualism and natural rights in basic ways.

To be sure, few cherished property rights more than Sumner, and he still saw them originating, as Locke did, in the labor that wrested value out of a flinty nature. But where Locke portrayed rightfully earned forms of property as the fulfillment of a divine mandate for rational human industry, for Sumner they were only goods gained in compliance with the brutal necessities that the human race faced if it wanted to survive. And racial survival, more than individual flourishing in this life or salvation in the next, dominated Sumner's thought. His was an individualism that really rested on a new sense of collectivism, on the belief that humanity was an organism whose survival could paradoxically be best promoted through individuals seeking their own survival. The industrial market system properly relied on spurring individuals via competitive pressures, the only reliable goad to productivity. But it did so ultimately as "a great social cooperation," an automatic set of "machinery," indeed "organs," that enabled the "whole human race" to prosper in its "combined assault on Nature." To preserve one's self was thus not purely self-interest but also one's primary "social duty" to the race. Both individualism and property rights were ultimately not so much divine absolutes as tough-minded instruments in the human species' battle for supremacy—laws of the cosmic jungle. In this jungle, unsentimental science was man's greatest weapon; but that weapon revealed its own limits. No scheme of man-made regulation could benefit the race as much as arrangements rewarding rather than curbing the voracious personal acquisitiveness that was crucial to survival.[11]

Thus Sumner, like Spencer, effectively refounded free market economics on a basis that recognized evolutionary science, humanity's often antagonistic but organic interdependency, the relativism of all particular survival strategies amid the unchanging need to struggle, and, especially, the likelihood of vast inequalities that involved the rightful elimination of the unfit instead of enhanced conditions for all. Individuals who failed to care for themselves should be left to "the process of decline and dissolution" by which nature "removes things that have survived their usefulness." Similarly, within humanity, those "races" that failed to develop "energy enough for a new advance" should be left to "permanent barbarism." Only women, on Sumner's account, merited governmental protection against the tendency of more powerful men to "dishonor" them and exploit them economically, presumably because the race could not survive without healthy mothers.[12]

To appreciate the different economic strains in American legal thought during these years, it is important to recognize that views like Sumner's gave renewed intellectual ammunition not only to corporate defenders of the nation's vast new economic inequalities, but also to old Democratic champions of laissez-faire. Sumner was almost as intensely critical of Whiggish efforts to give business "plutocrats" special aid via public "jobbery," such as internal improvements and high tariffs, as he was of Socialists. Like the Jacksonians, Sumner thought of democratic republican government chiefly as the abolition of feudal hierarchies in favor of free but "loose" systems in which all were to have equal chances without any special privileges guaranteeing success. But his republicanism was shorn of the agrarian promise of self-sufficiency for all, in favor of an industrial competition that served only the fit, as well as the race as a whole. And in contrast to the Jacksonians, for whom democracy meant an abolition of property qualifications, Sumner's republicanism labeled paupers unfit for the franchise, because they might vote for public charity. His evolutionary perspective also moved his defense of the aspects of liberal, republican, and Americanist positions he defended to a new terrain. Though Sumner had been a minister, and though others would fit his principles to Christian doctrines, he argued in secular, naturalistic terms, foregoing any claims of divine providence for U.S. citizens or anyone else.[13]

In these regards he differed from what is perhaps the most representative work of the late nineteenth century, Reverend Strong's *Our Country,* published by the American Home Missionary Society in 1885. Strong is rightly remembered as the leading voice of resurgent American nativism during these years. But he was also an architect of the liberal Social Gospel movement, a prototype of the "ministers of reform" that Robert Crunden has identified as the protagonists of progressivism. Strong's book canvassed the ways in which Americans were responding to their turbulent age, displaying sympathy with a wide range of views and the mixture of excited hope and anxious fears that drove many to social activism. *Our Country* makes clear why even reformers deeply attached to liberal republicanism and willing to embrace many of the era's changes still felt impelled to espouse illiberal doctrines upholding the Protestant, Anglo-Saxon supremacy that they thought America needed.[14]

Our Country began by celebrating the economic and scientific progress and the immense promise of the Western world, particularly the United States. Strong praised even more the modern "great ideas" of "individual liberty," which had not only spurred material growth but also abolished slavery, and of "honor to womanhood," which had lifted women above the level of property. He similarly commended the "enhanced valuation of life" in modern societies and, with Tocqueville, perceived an irreversible trend toward "popular government," at least among "the races of Europe." All this praise was well within the frame of American liberal republicanism. Indeed, Strong seemed more optimistic than the Reconstruction Radicals at their zenith.

But Strong also had fears for his country. Many of these were cast in terms of dangers to personal liberty and republican self-governance. His chapter on the perils of immigration was dominated by classical republican concerns about the need for a virtuous, homogeneous citizenry to make popular self-governance work. Strong proclaimed that free republican institutions required that "the average citizen" remain above a "dead-line of ignorance and vice," for "intelligence and virtue are as essential to the life of a republic as are a brain and heart to the life of man." Though a "strong centralized government" like imperial Rome could "control heterogeneous populations," local self-government demanded "close relations between man and man, a measure of sympathy, and, to a certain extent, community of ideas." Poor, ill-educated foreigners were sources of crime and civic incompetence. And though Strong stressed the dangers of immigration for Protestant supremacy in America, he initially cast this concern, too, in terms of republican citizenship. The Catholic "allegiance demanded by the Pope" of too many immigrants was "wholly inconsistent with republican institutions" and with "good citizenship." It was also hostile to freedoms of conscience and expression, and to the proper roles of church and state in "republican and Protestant America." Strong did not treat these concerns as simple anti-Catholicism: Mormonism, with its "American pope," was also dangerous.[15]

Strong echoed early liberals like Locke in insisting that modern commerce enabled a "thousand civilized men" to thrive "where a hundred savages starved" in the past, and he cited Spencer against socialist threats to these liberal achievements. But he was not sanguine like Spencer and Sumner about the competitiveness, spiraling inequalities, and mass suffering visible in America's new industrial age. He followed the reform economist and Christian Socialist Richard Ely, a founder of the American Economic Association, in condemning the International Workingman's Association for fomenting violence and, especially, opposing religion. But Strong indicated that the more moderate Socialist Labor Party advocated "much that is reasonable," given what he saw as the tendency of "our present industrial system" to "separate classes more widely, and to render them hereditary," conditions that were "unrepublican and dangerous." He accepted that Christian populist and socialist critics like Henry George and the muckraker Henry Demarest Lloyd were right to see the current labor system as causing workers to "degenerate" and as spawning "over-production" and "an unemployed class." It also created heartless monopolies and a capitalist class that threatened to become a new aristocracy. These conditions amounted, Strong charged, to "a modern and republican feudalism" that was "a despotism vastly more oppressive" than that against which the colonists had rebelled.

Strong in fact seemed to object to socialism only when it was antireligious. After he gained fame, he championed urban reform efforts to aid the working classes, in sharp contrast to Spencer and Sumner. Though he was fully aware of their arguments, Strong's Christianity inclined him toward what Eric Goldman called "reform Darwinism," accepting evolution but hopeful that human intelligence could guide society to more widely beneficial results than the "industrial system" otherwise produced. In so doing Strong, Ely, and other liberal Protestants like Washington Gladden blended Spencerian evolutionism with the early liberal economic promise of enhanced prosperity for all, refusing to accept that the industrial horrors of their day were natural and right.[16] Thus they generated for the first time an economic liberalism that called strongly for governmental measures aimed not merely at promoting growth but at directly redressing brutal inequalities and grinding poverty.

But though he was an important architect of the liberal evangelicalism that would be a central strain in progressivism, Strong's opposition to Catholicism, Mormonism, and atheistic socialism all showed that beneath his attachment to liberal economic promises and the welfare of republican institutions lay a deeper concern. He feared above all that America's character and destiny as the chosen people of the Protestant God were in danger. These anxieties led him to espouse virulent doctrines of Anglo-Saxon racial supremacy in a chapter that jars alongside the humanely universalistic rhetoric of much of the book. He echoed the themes of the new Teutonic school of historians and political scientists centered at Johns Hopkins under Herbert Baxter Adams and at Columbia under John Burgess. These scholars were influenced by the historicism of the German universities that trained so many new American Ph.D.s and by the antebellum romanticism that had kept the Anglo-Saxon myth alive. They busily traced the "Teutonic germs" of Americans' unique capacities for civil and political liberty. Their work seemed to Strong and others to reinforce Darwin's and Spencer's praise for the qualities produced in America by natural selection.[17]

Strong similarly proclaimed that the "Anglo-Saxon branch" of "the great German family" had in its blood a special affinity for liberty and reform Christianity. As a result, he thought that the "mighty Anglo-Saxon race," now centered in America, was "divinely commissioned" to lead in the elevation of the human race. Strong also invoked the Civil War medical statistics to show that native Americans of Anglo-Saxon descent were the most fit of all racial types. And in the Anglo-Saxon's "instinct or genius for colonizing" Strong saw signs that Americans were being divinely prepared to spread their race over the earth, "down upon Mexico, down upon Central and South America, out upon the islands of the sea, over upon Africa and beyond." Anglo-Saxon Americans would assimilate "feebler and more abject races" if possible, burying them if not, in "*the final competition of races.*" But Americans had to cease their dangerously polluting immigration policies; they had above all to preserve their Protestant character, if this destiny were to be fulfilled.[18]

Strong's view was simultaneously on the side of exclusion of "inferior races" from citizenship and imperial domination of them, hallmarks of late Gilded Age policy. And it was espoused by a religious leader who applauded the end of slavery, the elevation of women, industrial and scientific progress, and efforts to assist the new urban masses. Strong said nothing about African-Americans, probably because he still felt allegiance to the egalitarian cause of the Civil War. But his assertions of Anglo-Saxon supremacy left him, like many other Northern reformers, with little room to object to those who would deny full citizenship to blacks or any other domestic "lower race." The many intellectual, political, economic, and social problems that seemed to him resolvable by a renewed commitment to Anglo-Saxon Protestant Americanism required abandoning the old cause of racial equality. In so moving Strong was blazing a path that many liberal Protestants and later progressives would follow.

Many leaders of the new academic professions quickly echoed Strong's arguments. Economist Francis A. Walker, president of the Massachusetts Institute of Technology, said in his presidential address to the fourth annual meeting of the American Economic Association in 1890 that immigration was extending dangerously to "great stagnant pools of population which no current of intellectual or moral activity has stirred for ages," people at "the very lowest stage of human degradation" who belonged to "races" that would not "for generations develop that capability of responding to the opportunities and incitements of their new life" which republican citizenship required.[19] Anthropologist Daniel G. Brinton, in his presidential address to the American Association for the Advancement of Science in 1895, similarly argued that, even though all persons were unique individuals, each of the "races" and "each ethnic group" had its own "special powers and special limitations." Races were not "equally endowed." The "black, the brown, and red races" had a "peculiar mental temperament which has become hereditary" that disqualified them for "modern enlightenment" and left them "recreant to the codes of civilization, and therefore technically criminal." It was time, Brinton urged, to revise doctrines in political economy as well as existing legislation "on lines which the new science dictates." Revisions should take as their "only sure foundations" the "peculiarities" of races, nations, and tribes, "not a priori notions of the rights of man" endorsed in "older philosophies" still invoked by poorly informed "social reformers."[20] Few political scientists, sociologists, doctors, or other experts disagreed.

Just as Strong's calls for restriction were attuned to the rising intellectual positions of his day, his liberal Protestantism was also more allied than divided from the conservative evangelicalism of revivalists like Dwight L. Moody and Ira Sankey. They were believers in biblical literalism who were forerunners of twentieth-century fundamentalism. Though the positions would soon diverge, with liberal Social Gospel advocates like Strong espousing forms of social activism that fundamentalists rejected, they had no quarrel over the importance of Protestant supremacy to America's fulfillment. Hence Strong's Americanism had appeal across the Protestant spectrum. It obviously was less attractive to the growing number of Catholic and Jewish Americans.[21]

Among "reform Darwinists," there were also those further left, like the autodidact Lester Ward, who helped organize the U.S. Geological Survey and later became the first president of the American Sociological Association.[22] Ward did not share Strong's insistence on Anglo-Saxon domination. He was a product of the most egalitarian strains in the nation's political traditions, a crusader who idolized Lincoln and refused to abandon the most extravagant hopes of Radical Republicanism. His *Dynamic Sociology*, first published in 1883 but most influential after a second edition in 1896, argued against Spencer and for the possibility of human direction of evolution for the good of all mankind, especially under the guidance of the benign experts produced from the new professions of social science. It also denied all intrinsic racial, gender, and class differences in intellectual potential. Ward's emphasis on practical reform, his faith in social science expertise, his belief in the possibility for uplifting all mankind directly, would all provide inspiration for left progressives in years to come. But few of Ward's countrymen were so sure that a better future could be assured by egalitarian social scientific direction. In light of science's bitter evolutionary teachings and the dislocations wrought by immigration and industrialization, Strong's Americanism seemed a safer bet.[23]

The Legal Scaffolding of the New Americanism: Immigration

Accordingly, American citizenship policies during this era were dominated by the massive new immigration from Europe and Asia and the nation's response of heightening restrictions. Only the subsequent and interlinked construction of Jim Crow laws approached immigration in importance.

Three main developments in immigration law reconfigured citizenship laws in this era. First was the adoption and repeated strengthening of more restrictive federal immigration laws. They excluded applicants due to moral, political, and economic concerns, but desires to prevent "inferior races" from acquiring U.S. citizenship were strikingly prominent. Second, the Supreme Court adopted a new understanding of federal power to exclude immigrants, moving from reliance on the commerce clause, which presented immigration as an economic issue, to reliance on the implicit but inherent sovereign powers of the national government. That argument echoed the new historicist emphasis on the organic nation in ways hospitable to racial conceptions of "true" American identity. Third was a recurring pattern of initial judicial resistance followed by increasing deference to executive decisions on immigration made by new national administrative agents. For years, many judges tried to uphold liberal procedural principles, as well as their own powers, in ways that limited racist immigration policies. Over time, however, the courts, led by the Supreme Court, became compliant.

Although the chief civic innovations of these years expressed narrow Americanist views, they did not yet efface the dominant liberal character of U.S. immigration policy. Immigration remained virtually unrestricted until 1882. Generally applicable restrictions came only in the 1890s, and even then most who tried to come succeeded. During the Gilded Age the U.S. accepted just under 10 million immigrants, an unprecedented influx. Over half came in the 1880s, with immigration falling in the depression-ridden 1890s and reaching new heights again in the early 1900s. Even so, the U.S. was not becoming much more "a nation of immigrants." From 1870 on, the proportion of the population that was foreign-born never exceeded 14.7 percent. In 1860 it had been 13.2 percent. But in absolute terms, the numbers of new arrivals vastly exceeded what any established nation had ever undergone.[24]

This era began the now-traditional tales of the American immigrant experience, the anxious arrivals at the new federal immigration stations on Ellis or Angel islands, the difficult struggles to find decent work and habitation in a New York or San Francisco bursting with unmanaged growth, the success, in many cases, in building prosperous and productive lives in the new country. For many citizens, old as well as new, the opportunities provided to all those who, otherwise so diverse, shared a dream of bettering themselves represented the true meaning of Americanism. They railed against the bigotry of all proposed restrictions, insisting on the ideal of a liberal nation in a way that later generations would celebrate. Yet though a comparatively generous immigration policy remained in place, its proponents were losing most of their battles against the rising exclusionary impulses that would prevail for over half of the next century. Many who succeeded in coming during these years did so in spite of, not because of, the immigration laws that Congress favored.

Immigration Legislation. In all four Congresses from 1875 through 1882, both houses gave immigration much attention. Midwesterners and some easterners still wished to encourage and protect European immigrants. After the Supreme Court struck down state regulation of immigration in 1876, many argued that the federal government must assume the load. Attention focused on the perceived problems of the growing Chinese immigration, including the "threat" of Chinese citizenship. After the completion of the transcontinental railroad, many more Chinese laborers sought factory jobs held by whites, igniting explosions of race hatred.

Political leaders could not ignore those feelings and most chose to appeal to them. In 1876 the Democratic party platform called for action to "prevent further importation or immigration of the Mongolian race." Republicans urged that the issue be investigated.[25] Congressional resolutions and reports argued that the Chinese were unassimilable in ways that made them poor potential citizens and also unfair competition for American laborers. Both the ethnocultural and economic dimensions of the opposition must have mattered, for support for Chinese restriction was staggering, greatly exceeding that given to any purely pro-labor measure in the nation's history. In a California referendum, voters cast 154,638 ballots against Chinese immigration, 883 in favor, in 1879; Nevada voted 17,259 versus immigration, 183 for, in 1880.[26] Both party platforms then demanded restriction of Chinese immigration, the Republicans more weakly. Later in 1880 outgoing President Rutherford B. Hayes concluded a treaty with China permitting the U.S. to limit or suspend, but not prohibit, immigration of Chinese laborers. In 1882, Congress and President Chester A. Arthur, successor to the recently slain James Garfield, agreed on three major immigration bills.

The first bill updated old laws assuring that immigrant ships were adequately spacious, ventilated, healthy, and safe. The second, the Immigration Act of 1882, was a major step toward full federal control of immigration. The law was to be administered by state officials, but they were now directed by the Treasury Secretary. The act also imposed a fifty-cent head tax on immigration, and it denied entry to persons likely to become public charges, such as convicts, "lunatics," and "idiots." Immigrants who became public charges due to causes existing prior to their arrival, including paupers, persons convicted of nonpolitical crimes, and those suffering from "mental alienation," could all be deported, with the cost charged to the tax-supplied immigrant fund.

The final law was the Chinese Exclusion Act, passed on the crest of a flood of petitions from all parts of the United States. It banned immigration of Chinese laborers for ten years (because a permanent ban would have violated Hayes's treaty with China). It also authorized identification certificates for Chinese laborers already legally in the U.S. and deportation of Chinese illegally present, and it explicitly banned Chinese naturalizations. In signing it, Arthur averred that the "experiment of blending" the "habits and mutual race idiosyncracies" of Chinese laborers with Americans had proven "unwise, impolitic, and injurious to both nations." Thus the doors closed on both state-regulated immigration and race-blind, largely nonexclusionary immigration policies.[27]

The transfer of authority over immigration to the federal level was formally another defeat for states' rights republicanism. Yet in reality, it was a victory for policies that most states favored but had been judicially barred from enacting. It was also a major defeat for racial liberalism. The congressional debates over Chinese exclusion provide a rich survey of the Gilded Age elite's civic conceptions. They show that exclusionist congressmen redefined or even decried the nation's liberal traditions in favor of grim but popular Americanist stances, defended via evolutionary theories as well as economic and republican concerns.

The opponents of exclusion, led by Massachusetts Republican Senator George Hoar, skillfully deployed all the arguments in the nation's liberal legacies to urge nonracial immigration policies. They also invoked inclusive views of what republican government and America's Christian civilization meant. The centerpiece of Hoar's presentation was an appeal to the natural rights in the Declaration of Independence, which he held to include rights to seek better opportunities in new lands on an equal footing with all others. The "doctrine that free institutions are a monopoly of the favored races," he insisted, was a canard "of quite recent origin." Hoar admitted that racial prejudices had left "hideous and ineradicable stains on our history" but said the nation had at least been free of immigration restraints based on race and occupation. He pointed out that many had condemned blacks as racially unfit for citizenship and that experience had proven otherwise. Hoar also expressed confidence that the Chinese would assimilate adequately if they were freed from discriminatory state laws that now enchained them in menial trades and ghetto existences. He was convinced that the American economy was providing plenty of work for all, so that American laborers need not fear competitors. Hence, in his view, the nation's faith in rights of free labor remained wise.[28]

The most passionate articulation of this liberal sense of America's meaning came from Tennessee Republican William Moore, who protested:

> The establishment of such a precedent by the United States, the recognized champion of human rights—the nation of all others in the world whose chief pride and glory it has been to truly boast of being known and recognized everywhere as the home of the free, the asylum of the oppressed, the land where all men, of all climes, all colors, all conditions, all nationalities, are welcome to come and go at will, controlled only by, and amenable only to, wise and beneficent laws applying equally and alike to the people of every class—is one that does so much violence to my own sense of justice that I cannot, under any stress of evident passion, consent to aid in establishing it.[29]

Supporters of exclusion answered every point. Several used evolutionary theories and argued in racial terms. California Senator John Miller claimed that over "thousands of years," the "dreary struggle for existence" had led to the "survival" of Chinese workmen who were in some ways "fittest" because they were "automatic engines of flesh and blood." Hence they could thrive on low wages and in poor conditions, outdoing American labor, even though they were sources of degradation for the higher, free, "Anglo-Saxon" American and so were unfit for citizenship. Delaware Senator Thomas Bayard conceded that all people were "children of the same Great Father," but he insisted that the "centuries" which shaped men differently amounted to "God's arguments" for their separation. California Representative Romualdo Pacheco took the gloves off, saying of "the Chinaman":

> By the laws of heredity the habits of his ancestors live in his character and are incorporated into his blood and brain. . . . Family ties and obligations and the sweets of home life are

naught to him. The long course of training which has gone on for so many generations has made of the Chinaman a lithe, sinewy creature, with muscles like iron, and almost devoid of nerves and sensibilities. His ancestors have also bequeathed to him the most hideous immoralities. They are as natural to him as the yellow hue of his skin, and are so shocking and horrible that their character cannot even be hinted.[30]

The exclusionists were unmoved by paeans to the American tradition of open immigration. Most enfolded the vision of America as an asylum nation in racial theory, contending that the U.S. had only been and should only be "the asylum of the oppressed" for "European nations." Even though other immigrants had not been forbidden, naturalization had always been racially restricted, and those of "yellow hue" remained ineligible. Exclusionists also cited as precedent the nation's long history of efforts to expel the tribes and to assign blacks inferior status. Lincoln himself, they said, had believed in superior races and opposed treating blacks equally in all respects.

The repeated invocation of the Declaration of Independence met with several responses. Some restrictionists acknowledged its authority and conceded that it justified rights of expatriation; but, they argued with some force, it implied nothing about rights of entry. Others insisted that the Declaration, too, referred only to the rights of white men. Some were bolder yet, openly dismissing the Declaration's notions of equality as "sentimentalist," reflecting a "speculative and Utopian" theory that was absurd "in practice." Missouri Congressman Aylett Buckner called "the assertion in the Declaration of Independence that all men are created equal" a "principle absolutely false" when applied to American conditions at any time in history.[31]

The nation's "right and power" of self-preservation entitled it to exclude any who would harm it, the anti-Chinese leaders asserted. Many stressed that they were most concerned to prevent the Chinese from becoming citizens. In answer to Hoar's comparison with black citizenship, a few asserted that blacks were better than the Chinese—more gentle, less competitive, American-reared, and Christian. Senator Henry Teller of Colorado also denied that blacks had been made equal in law even after formal citizenship had been granted. Others, like Mississippi Senator James George, hinted that the time might come when black citizenship would be reconsidered (in, he hoped, the "calm" and "philosophic" manner that Chinese exclusionists were displaying). Buckner remained the most daring, asserting that the Civil War amendments were "logical and inevitable" results of the Declaration's principle of equality; but its falsehood meant that they should be repudiated and blacks sent "back" to Africa.[32]

Despite all the talk of race, it is likely that for many exclusionists, especially Democrats, concerns to protect native white laborers were paramount. Employers did indeed hire sojourning Chinese immigrants who accepted wages and working conditions that Americans resisted, and companies deliberately used them to erode labor solidarity. Scholars now debate how harmful these tactics were to American workers, economically and politically. But for some leaders then, like Representative John Sherwin of Illinois, the evidence seemed plain enough to justify exclusion to protect American workers, without denying the equal humanity of the Chinese. Sherwin saw neither "republican government" nor the "Christian religion" as endangered by these immigrants, only control of "our own workshops."[33]

Yet many exclusionists saw more at stake. Some Northerners, including Vermont Senator George Edmunds and Wisconsin Representative George Hazelton, presented the major threat precisely as the survival of "republican institutions." Republics required "a homogeneous population," not what Ohio Representative Alden McClure called an "ethnological animal show." Others, like Nevada's George Cassidy, held primary the survival of American civilization and Christianity, topics he distinguished from racial purity. But most who spoke of civilization and religion did not differentiate these cultural traits from racial ones. Delaware Senator Eli Saulsbury said that he did not object to Chinese immigration "upon the ground that they enter into competition with labor." He was opposed to how "it introduces a distinct race of people with a different civilization . . . wholly incapable of assimilation with our people."[34]

But whatever the precise mix of economic motives, republican concerns, and racial objectives among the exclusionists, even those who spoke chiefly for labor almost always chose to do so only on behalf of native white male workers. Thus ascriptive conceptions were powerful throughout the opposition to the Chinese. The economic arguments did add vital support that racial and republican justifications could not gain. Most who stressed the latter concerns wished to ban all Chinese. Lacking support to do so in 1882, they settled for the suspension of admitting laborers, which passed by lopsided margins. Anti-Chinese leaders then began working toward total exclusion.[35]

In part they did so in response to the federal courts. Many judges tried to interpret this and later acts to render them consistent with U.S. treaties and due process rights. In so doing, they often let in Chinese laborers whom executive officials, and the white public, wanted to repel, prompting overriding legislation. Congress also kept adding new measures out of fear that these laws were not working, partly because of concerted Chinese resistance, partly because the government lacked adequate administrative capacities to enforce them.

Hence in 1884, Congress amended the Exclusion Act to clarify that it encompassed all Chinese people, not just those arriving directly from China. The new law also required all alleged nonlaborers to present identification certificates from the Chinese government affirming their economic status, voiding judicial rulings that had accepted alternative evidence. Prior to the election of 1888, in response to widespread charges that immigrants were using false certificates of residence to gain entry, Congress suspended Chinese labor immigration for twenty years, made new certificates harder to obtain, limited their validity to one year, and required a U.S. consular representative, not the Chinese government, to affirm that incoming Chinese were nonlaborers. The suspension provisions were, however, conditional on China accepting a new treaty. China refused. In anger, Congress then stopped the issuing of identity certificates and voided the 20,000 or so that had already been supplied. These steps violated the existing treaties with China as well as the expectations of many Chinese residents traveling abroad, confident that their certificates guaranteed their right to return.

In 1892, the Geary Act renewed the exclusion policy for another ten years and authorized a new registration system for all Chinese residents, who would now receive certificates of residence from the local collector of internal revenue if they registered within one year after passage of the act. Reflecting the widespread conviction that the Chinese were natural liars, and the very real Chinese efforts to circumvent these policies, all Chinese people were required to have at least one "white" witness swear to their veracity. Led by San Francisco's resourceful Six Companies, the Chinese in California boycotted this registration system, expecting that the courts would strike it down. When these hopes were dashed in 1893, Congress extended registration for six months and softened the witness rule, permitting two non-Chinese witnesses to suffice. Most Chinese then registered.

From 1885 on, Congress also moved against non-Chinese immigration. It banned all contract labor, due to pressures from anti-Catholic nativist groups and the erroneous belief that undesirable immigration was made possible only by companies prepaying the fares of laborers who would sign contracts. This act, too, proved hard to enforce, despite strengthening amendments in 1887 and 1888. But agitation about all immigrants kept rising, especially as alien radicals were repeatedly blamed for violent confrontations between workers and police forces aiding employers, as in the infamous Chicago Haymarket riot of 1886.

Thus in 1891 Congress passed a major new immigration act, applicable to all but Chinese immigrants, designed to reinforce existing laws and to extend the list of excludables. It added persons suffering from certain diseases, polygamists, and immigrants who had received financial assistance, along with idiots, insane persons, paupers, persons convicted of a felony or an "infamous crime . . . involving moral turpitude." It also made all who entered illegally, or who became public charges after arrival, deportable for one year. Decisions of immigration inspectors could be appealed to the Treasury Secretary but not the courts. Immigrant shippers had to carry back at their own cost all passengers the U.S. inspectors rejected. The law also created a superintendent of immigration in the Treasury and gave federal officials direct responsibility for screening new arrivals. One result was the opening of the Ellis Island station in 1892, through which 80 percent of American immigrants would pass during the next two decades (even though only steerage, not cabin passengers had to disembark there). Congress then kept tinkering with the immigration laws, passing measures aimed at making existing acts tougher and more enforceable in 1893, 1894 (when the head tax on immigrants was raised to one dollar), and 1895. But none of these measures slowed immigration sharply. Though the Chinese were rejected at much higher rates, ranging from 5 to 34 percent annually, overall the nation turned away just over 1 percent of those arriving at U.S. ports.[36]

The most popular proposal to curb immigration significantly was the literacy test championed by Henry Cabot Lodge, first in the House and then the Senate, and by his allies in the Immigration Restriction League, a group originating among Harvard graduates who were influential in academic, political, and business circles.[37] On the surface, such tests addressed intellectual qualifications, not race. Persons were to pass reading tests, usually lines from the Constitution, in English or their own language. These tests were more workable than most of the exclusionary criteria then in use, and they were not so offensive to liberal sensibilities.

But, as Lodge acknowledged openly, the true aim of his literacy test was to weed out "inferior" races. In 1896, Lodge stated that committee research showed that the test would most affect the races "most alien to the great body of the people of the United States," including "the Italian, Russians, Poles, Hungarians, Greeks, and Asiatics" (including Jews). English speakers, Germans, Scandinavians, and the French would be affected "very lightly or not at all." Lodge, a former Harvard faculty member whose study of Anglo-Saxon law won him a then-novel doctorate in political science and history, elaborated the "vital" teachings of "modern history" and "modern science" on race. He summarized evolutionary theories about how racial characteristics were indelibly acquired through thousands of years, drawing heavily on the French social psychologist Gustave Le Bon; and he invoked Thomas Carlyle to reprise the standard Americanist history of the nation's noble Teutonic roots. Lodge also stressed that, despite the apparent focus of the literacy test on intellectual abilities, the real difference between races, and the true source of the need for exclusion, was "something deeper and more fundamental than anything which concerns the intellect." What made a race was "above all, moral characteristics, the slow growth and accumulation of centuries of toil and conflict." Its history gave to each race "an indestructible stock of ideas, traditions, sentiments, modes of thought" as "an unconscious inheritance" that was the "soul of a race." The fact that literacy worked to exclude undesirables thus was fortuitous, because education could not alter this racial "soul." Upon it "argument has no effect." Races were guided "across the centuries" by moral qualities in which they could only "blindly believe."

Lodge then warned that the moral qualities of a superior race could be lost if "a lower race mixes with a higher in sufficient numbers." At stake in that mixing was not republican "forms of government" so much as "the mental and moral qualities which make what we call our race." Twice he pointed to the threat to "the quality of our race and citizenship" if current immigration continued. Just as the nation had "closed the door upon the coming of the Chinese," it must fence out all lower races.[38]

In reply to this thundering orchestration of racist themes, Senator Charles Gibson of Maryland dismissed the "dread of race deterioration" as a "monster conjured from the realm of fantasy and without reality." He argued that the nation would benefit more from uneducated "healthful toilers" determined to rise by their own labor than it would from the "filthy anarchists" and "communist and socialist" elements who would pass a literacy test. The "ultimate perfection of the human race" would be better advanced by giving "recognition of the right of every man to be treated as a man."[39]

Then and for years to come, Gibson's side had fewer votes. Lodge's literacy test passed in 1896 but was vetoed by outgoing President Grover Cleveland, a member of the party of immigrants, an opponent of national bureaucracies, and a Chief Executive concerned about the problems that immigration restrictions posed for relations with other nations. But Congress would continue to support the literacy test throughout the ensuing Progressive years.

Immigration and the Judiciary. Set against the accelerating flood of restrictive laws, many judicial decisions on immigration during this period appear as brave, lonely islands of humanitarianism amid a sea of hostility. As many of the federal judges involved expressly opposed Chinese immigration, and all faced great political pressures to stem it, it is striking that they so often checked the new racist initiatives. That fact is strong evidence of the power of legal traditions and the value of written constitutional strictures. But though they argued for humane statutory interpretations and insisted on some recognition of due process and equal protection, few judges denied that citizenship could be denied or limited on racial grounds. And as hostility grew toward the "new" European arrivals as well as Chinese immigrants, judges acquiesced in arbitrary treatment of those "races."[40]

Quarrels between the lower federal courts and immigration officials began almost before the ink on the 1882 Chinese Exclusion Act was dry. The San Francisco customs collector refused entry to the first Chinese man to arrive after the act passed, even though Ah Sing, an American resident since 1876, was returning aboard a U.S. ship on which he served as a cabin waiter and never went ashore. Thus he had no way to acquire an identification certificate and had technically never left U.S. jurisdiction. Thereafter, inundated by such draconian enforcement cases, Circuit Justice Stephen Field and several district court judges insisted that the U.S. should admit Ah Sing and all others who, being at sea or abroad, were unable to obtain certificates. These judges often stressed their sympathy with the law's aims. They enforced it whenever it was clearly applicable, and they sustained exclusion of those who were "racially" Chinese, not just Chinese subjects. But they argued that failure to implement the act in "reasonable and just" ways would bring its policy into disrepute.[41]

After the California press and citizenry vehemently criticized these rulings, Congress mandated harsher enforcement in 1884. The judges strove to comply. They refused to overlook minor defects in documentation and at times separated families. The local judges remained unwilling to require certificates when it had been physically impossible for applicants to obtain them; but Field now endorsed even this.[42] Even so, he upheld the birthright citizenship status of all Chinese born within U.S. jurisdiction, as well as broad expatriation rights. And he ruled that citizens, regardless of race, did not need certificates.[43]

On December 8, 1884, the U.S. Supreme Court made its initial statements on the new immigration laws in *Chew Heong v. United States* and the *Head Money Cases*. Justice John Marshall Harlan wrote in the first, overturning Field's cruel ruling that even a resident Chinese laborer who had left the U.S. in 1880, before any certificates existed, could not return without one. Harlan construed the exclusion acts in light of U.S.-China treaty agreements that guaranteed passage to laborers resident prior to 1882, and he held that Congress had not meant to impose conditions "impossible of performance." Field dissented angrily, storming that Congress could violate treaties if it pleased. While disavowing "race prejudices," he contended that, because "the Chinese cannot assimilate with our people" yet threatened to come in "vast hordes" that would "degrade labor," absolute exclusion was reasonable.[44] But the more generous stance of the western judges was for the moment sustained.

In the *Head Money Cases*, the Court upheld the 1882 Immigration Act and tax, with Justice Samuel Miller resting exclusive federal authority over immigration firmly on the commerce clause power over intercourse with foreign nations. That textually plausible basis suggested that immigration regulation was primarily an economic matter, intended to protect the nation's prosperity, not its racial composition, in keeping with the Republican party's economic liberalism.[45] These decisions strengthened the western judges in their resolve to enforce immigration laws fairly and to protect their prerogatives, especially their habeas corpus jurisdiction.[46] But the rulings also reinforced beliefs that the courts were enemies of exclusion. Thus Congress made its 1888 ban on reentry so unequivocal that the lower court judges felt unable to soften it, a stance unanimously affirmed by the Supreme Court in the *Chinese Exclusion Case*.[47]

Despite the unanimity, the verdict was by no means self-evident or inescapable. The 1888 law was vicious. The Chinese laborer involved in the case, Chae Chan Ping, had lived in California from 1875 to 1887, when he left for China with the return certificate required by the 1884 amendment to the 1882 act. He arrived back in California one week after Congress adopted the 1888 act, only to be told that his certificate was now invalid and his reentry illegal. His attorneys termed this a restraint of his liberty, "the birthright and inalienable possession of all men, as men," without due process. It also violated a right vested in him by U.S. treaties and the first exclusionary statutes. Those laws, his attorneys contended, created a contract with the Chinese who obtained certificates that the government could not constitutionally abrogate. These arguments expressed prestigious liberal traditions of procedural and economic rights that had been reinforced by the free labor ideology of the postwar constitutional amendments. The same traditions would soon be sculpted by the Supreme Court into the antiregulatory jurisprudence of economic substantive due process that reigned, with interruptions, through the early New Deal. Here, these liberal principles also voiced demands of common decency and fairness.[48]

But Field, so often the champion of economic liberties and contractual rights, rejected them here for a stonefaced Supreme Court. Reviewing the history of Sino-American relations and Chinese immigration, he reiterated his longstanding positions that "differences of race," the unwillingness or inability of the Chinese "to assimilate with our people," and the threat of "vast hordes" overrunning the nation all justified exclusion. Like the anti-Chinese forces in Congress, Field rested restriction not on the commerce clause but on the "sovereign powers" that the United States possessed as a nation, which could only be limited by "the consent of the nation itself." It was "the highest duty" of a nation to preserve its independence and security. That duty could not be "the subject of barter or contract." If it required abrogating treaties or previous laws, so be it. Field then slipped in an exception for violations of transferable property rights, which could be and must be honored, presumably via compensation. But rights which were "personal and untransferable," such as reentry and residence, could not limit sovereign powers.[49]

Field's rhetoric transferred the whole subject of immigration from the realm of commercial powers aimed at economic welfare to a realm of inherent national powers for organic self-preservation, against threats not just to "material interests" but to "morals," "civilization," and "race."[50] This was the realm of Americanism, expounded in the conventional tropes of late nineteenth-century discourse on race and nationality. Field's commitment to liberal economic doctrines, so dominant in his opinions elsewhere, did not vanish here, as his solicitude for property rights indicated. But this decision and many similar ones supply strong evidence that for many federal judges, doctrines of human liberties, even economic liberties, were confined within an ascriptive frame that granted full rights only to superior races and nations. Congress had already sanctioned such views via the Chinese Exclusion Act. In this post-Reconstruction era, the Court treated these burgeoning Americanist precepts, not the wizened liberalism of the postwar amendments, as authoritative.

Several other Supreme Court decisions bolstering exclusionary powers followed. In 1891 Field upheld racist dismissals of Chinese testimony claiming native-born citizenship, despite his nephew Justice David Brewer's pointed dissent. The following year Justice Horace Gray cited Field's "sovereignty" reasoning to uphold the 1891 Immigration Act, although shortly thereafter the Court permitted resident Chinese merchants to return from temporary trips without certificates from the government of China.[51] Given these high court rulings, lower courts could do little to check exclusions. Yet some tried, refusing to enforce unratified provisions of the 1888 act, upholding the rights of Chinese sailors who never left U.S. ships, protectively if paternalistically granting women and children the status of their merchant husbands and fathers.[52]

The provisions in the 1892 Geary Act—which presumed all Chinese to be deportable aliens unless they proved otherwise and cut off judicial review of immigration decisions—also seemed questionable to some lower courts.[53] In *Fong Yue Ting v. United States*, however, Justice Gray once again stressed the nation's sovereign powers in order to uphold the act. He did not believe that any Chinese were denied due process or equal protection by the adverse presumptions the statute required, which could be overcome only by obtaining certification of legal status with the aid of a white witness. If they were neither citizens nor legal residents, Gray reasoned, Chinese people had no right to be in the country. Deportation thus was not a criminal punishment but merely a means to restore the civil status quo. Hence, he continued, in immigration hearings the procedures appropriate to a criminal trial need not apply. The fact that only the Chinese had to prove their citizenship or legal status in these ways was not decisive. Congress could choose to treat Chinese immigration as a special problem.[54]

Justice Brewer dissented at length, joined by Chief Justice Melville Fuller, an Illinois Democrat appointed by Grover Cleveland in 1888, and, surprisingly, by his aging uncle, Justice Field. All stressed with some passion the liberties and procedural rights of persons, not citizens. As yet no one made much of the fact that some U.S. citizens were now facing threatening requirements that others did not, simply because of their race. Brewer disputed the focus on "powers inherent in sovereignty" that Field had introduced, calling it "indefinite and dangerous" and sarcastically terming authority for "the expulsion of a race" something "within the inherent powers of a despotism." Insisting that "deportation is punishment," a penalty for unlawful presence, he argued that it could not be constitutionally ordered without a trial involving normal procedural protections. Field's dissent reiterated his views on sovereignty, but he argued that, as persons possessing "our common humanity," Chinese were entitled to procedural protections instead of "brutality" and "cruelty."[55]

Despite its wild implausibility, the *Fong Yue Ting* decision's refusal to treat deportation as punishment proved enduring.[56] At times judges tried to moderate U.S. policies by ruling that imprisonment at hard labor for uncertified Chinese persons certainly was punishment, even if deportation was not; by rejecting exclusions based on flimsy technicalities; and by insisting on judicial review of claims of citizenship.[57] A Court with several new members briefly gave some support to these more generous rulings, agreeing in 1896 that hard labor could not be imposed without a trial, and in 1900 that wives of Chinese merchants did not need certificates from China, but the justices also refused to overturn the more restrictive precedents.[58] All the lower courts concurred that birth within the U.S. made citizens of the children of Chinese aliens. The Supreme Court agreed in *United States v. Wong Kim Ark* in 1898 (see chapter 12).[59] But those modestly inclusive decisions as the Progressive Era dawned did not alter the basic shift toward immigration restriction and inegalitarian civic ideals.

Naturalization

The restrictive Americanist ideologies of the Gilded Age also strengthened racial, ideological, and gender constraints in the nation's naturalization laws. In doing so, the federal government increased its practical as well as formal control over naturalization, as it did with immigration.[60] The huge growth in the number and variety of immigrants made it especially pressing to clarify just who were "white persons" eligible for naturalization.

Lower federal courts struggled with that question extensively but inconclusively during the Gilded Age. Early on, both executive officials and judges seemed confident that issues of racial identity could be settled by appeals to common sense, supplemented in borderline cases by reference to ethnological works. Yet clear, plausible definitions of race proved elusive. The judges began asking for more legislative guidance, and Immigration and Naturalization Service officials urged increasingly contrived answers. These difficulties make the artificial character of the category *race* dramatically clear. Yet these cases did not prompt any great doubts about whether racial identities were as natural as the nation's governors maintained. And here, as in immigration, the courts only raised a few paper-thin barriers against the march toward exclusion.

That pattern was set in the first case considering the eligibility of a native Chinese person for naturalization, *In re Ah Yup*, in 1878. There California circuit judge Sawyer admitted that the category of "white person" was "very indefinite"; but he thought that the words had "a well settled meaning in common popular speech" and literature. He had no doubt that these sources justified excluding the "Mongolian or yellow race." *Webster's Dictionary's* reliance on the racial classifications of Blumenbach, Buffon, Linnaeus, and Cuvier, and the Senate's rejection of Charles Sumner's efforts to strike the word *white* from the naturalization laws in 1870, provided Sawyer with two additional sorts of authority. His assured opinion was often followed thereafter.[61] Even so, the controversy prompted Congress to adopt its explicit 1882 ban on Chinese naturalization.[62] That ban was significant, for, unlike the immigration restraints, it applied to all Chinese, not just laborers. Hence it made decisive the racial, as opposed to the class requirement for full citizenship.

Given the climate of heightening hostility toward immigrants, it is not surprising that in 1897, a federal district court in Texas considered whether a Mexican was racially eligible for naturalization. Still, the issue might have been thought settled by the mass naturalization of Mexicans under the Treaty of Guadalupe Hidalgo. Judge Maxey thought so, for he disavowed reliance on "ethnological writers," whom he admitted would "probably not" classify the applicant, Rodriguez, as white. Instead, he appealed to various past collective naturalizations of Mexicans as proof of U.S. policy, and he invoked the "spirit and intent" of American naturalization and expatriation laws. They aimed to bestow the right of citizenship "freely and with a liberality unknown in the old world."[63] Though Maxey's conferral of citizenship here prevailed, his rhetoric expressed a fading ethos in an age of new racial exclusions.

The other prominent concern of the new immigration laws—to keep radical leftists out of America—was also manifest in this area. Many naturalizing judges became more vigilant on behalf of the requirement that applicants display "attachment to the principles" of the U.S. Constitution. In an 1891 Texas case, for example, a judge denied naturalization to a German applicant who expressed belief in the doctrines of the socialist Johann Most. Although, in liberal fashion, Judge Paschal conceded Richard Sauer's right to hold and express such beliefs, he termed them "un-American, impracticable, and dangerous in the extreme," and adequate grounds to refuse citizenship. Along with Americanism, liberal republican precepts provided arguments on behalf of these restrictions because they presented allegiance to proper political ideals as the core requirement for membership. But they could also have been used to challenge demands for ideological conformity, because the clash of political opinions had long been seen as an engine of effective democratic self-governance. Those Americans with the resources to litigate, however, seemed to feel that the system had all the clashes it needed. Hence these ideological restrictions did not face powerful legal challenges.[64]

The Nadir of African-American Citizenship

The general fate of black citizenship in these years is well-known, even if many shrink from recognizing the magnitude of the horrors committed.[65] State and national legislators, executives, and judges completed the retreat from protection of black civic rights begun in the early 1870s. Through the early 1890s, many congressional Republicans still professed commitment to the cause of the freedmen, publicized abuses, and opposed Democratic efforts to weaken Reconstruction statutes, sometimes in alliance ("fusion") with Populists. But their will for enforcement continued to decline, especially as they decided that they could retain national control while losing the South; Democrats gained substantial repeals of Reconstruction reforms by making concessions on other matters, such as the tariff. The federal judiciary often abetted these trends by ruling that national officials had no power to combat discrimination by private businesses or even the violence of private white groups.[66]

Even so, private discriminations did not occur often enough to suit the Redeemer governments in the Southern states.[67] Southern leaders began calling on Northerners to permit the New South to settle its race problem via pacifying, tutelary systems of segregation and disfranchisement, as *Atlanta Constitution* editor Henry Grady urged in a widely reprinted 1886 speech. Thus, beginning around 1890 and with a surge around 1900, Southern and border states began legally codifying seemingly innumerable forms of Jim Crow segregation, disfranchising mechanisms, and practices excluding blacks from juries. As early as 1879, some 40,000 blacks from Deep South states moved to the midwest, especially Kansas, in an exodus from the rising tide of renewed Southern white bondage, but to no avail. Jim Crow flew there, too. Driving these developments were palpable white desires not merely to separate from blacks but also to limit or utterly prohibit their access to political, juridical, and economic power, as well as reputable social statuses. A few whites may have believed that they were creating a separate civic status for blacks that either was equal or on its way to being so. But most knew that they were making blacks second-class citizens at best, and many anticipated that under those conditions blacks would leave or, more probably, perish. The motivations of whites to impose these suffocating systems undoubtedly often stemmed from partisan and class concerns to prevent poor blacks from allying with white Populists, as C. Vann Woodward suggested. But as Woodward also noted, Jim Crow's broad appeal for whites of all parties and classes suggests that most whites believed that their increasingly turbulent world could best be shaped into a meaningful, workable new order only if white superiority were reinforced by law.[68]

It is especially clear that the strictures on political rights during these years aimed at exclusion, not separate-but-equal segregation. Blacks were not to serve on any juries or vote in any elections. For many, economic, educational, and marital segregation also had exclusionary aims. Blacks were not to attend the "best" schools or marry into the "best" families. Segregation also sharply limited the capacities of all blacks (and some willing whites) to buy and sell freely in burgeoning national markets. Racist defenses of these laws always lurked not far beneath the surface deference to equality.

Thus Louis Hartz had hold of part of the truth when he argued that American liberalism required all people either to be accepted as equals or to be excluded as subhuman. Many white Americans who rejected racial equality did hope instead for total exclusion of nonwhites, even as federal laws compelled them to pretend that they were treating blacks equally. Nonetheless, the prevailing doctrines of racial inferiority permitted whites to live comfortably with what resulted after subordinated blacks did not leave or die off: a vast set of legal, economic, and social institutions that treated blacks as just what Hartz thought a liberal society could not tolerate—second-class citizens, permanent but lower-grade Americans. When these bleak developments are seen in the context of all the changes in the nation's civic statuses during these years, moreover, second-class black citizenship looks in no way exceptional. It was instead the cornerstone of a general legal elaboration of ascriptive hierarchies.

Miscegenation and School Segregation. To be sure, in some respects Jim Crow laws only formalized deeply entrenched systems of racial separation and hierarchy. That was especially true of the two areas where segregation went largely unchallenged: marriage and education. In considering state anti-miscegenation laws, the lower federal courts found it easy to apply *Slaughter-House* and hold that marriage was a state matter, and that in any case these laws treated blacks and whites equally. One district judge in Virginia even read the Fifteenth Amendment as implying that, apart from voting, states could abridge any civic privilege on the basis of race. A more troubling issue was whether states forbidding interracial marriages had to honor weddings performed in jurisdictions where they were legal, as the Article IV comity clause seemed to require. The courts held that, as this course would allow out-of-staters privileges denied to in-state citizens, such recognition was not mandatory. And against claims that these laws interfered with sacred contractual liberties, the courts responded, here as elsewhere in the law, that marriages were not just contracts. They were social institutions vital to morals and civilization.[69]

The U.S. Supreme Court dealt with the topic only in an opinion by Field sustaining an Alabama law that punished interracial adulterers more severely than intraracial ones. Because black and white violators were punished identically under both statutes, Field found no equal protection violation. He did not address any other issues, including whether the higher penalties for interracial philandering were part of a system of white supremacy.[70] But the case contributed to that system significantly; it was often cited as proving the legitimacy of antimiscegenation and other segregation laws.

In regard to education, segregationists regularly invoked the opinion of Massachusetts' prestigious Chief Justice Lemuel Shaw in *Roberts v. Boston* (1849), holding that separate but equal schools met state constitutional requirements.[71] Hence federal courts found it easy to follow a pattern that would prove true of segregation generally. Officially, blacks could not be excluded from public schools, and their segregated schools had to be roughly equal to those for whites; but schools that were in fact terribly unequal, and some failures to provide schools altogether, often escaped correction.[72]

Transport. Transportation was the chief arena of segregation litigation. In 1877 the law governing the area appeared twofold.[73] The common law of common carriers treated transport companies as quasi-public businesses, legally required to provide services to all paying customers, with only "reasonable exceptions" for the disorderly, diseased, and other undesirables. The 1875 Civil Rights Act also banned racial discrimination by all such enterprises and all other places of "public accommodation." Discrimination certainly included denials of service because of the customer's race. It arguably included even "separate but equal" services.

Courts did not need the 1875 act to reach outright refusals to serve blacks. Interpreting common-law standards in light of the changes wrought by the Civil War, state and federal judges generally held that these refusals were unreasonable and illegal.[74] Although business owners could and did claim an economic liberty to transact with whomever they wished, denials based on race were now deemed to prevent blacks from having meaningful economic rights, rendering the whole system less peaceful and productive. Those were good grounds for regulation.

But by 1877, many courts had also indicated that it was reasonable for common carriers to offer separate facilities to whites and blacks. The Supreme Court's first important statement on the issue came that year in *Hall v. DeCuir*. In 1869, the Reconstruction Louisiana government had banned racial discrimination on common carriers, and the Louisiana courts had held that the provision prohibited separate accommodations for whites and blacks. Hence Josephine DeCuir sued successfully when she was denied access to a steamboat cabin set aside for white passengers. But the Supreme Court reversed the ruling, finding that the statute burdened interstate commerce, which could not flourish if each state were allowed to adopt different rules in regard to white and black passengers. Chief Justice Morrison Waite wrote as if Congress had passed no relevant legislation, paying no heed to the 1875 Civil Rights Act. He indicated that in the absence of congressional action, the common law prevailed, and he took it to permit racial segregation. Such practices were not mandatory; but in Waite's view they did not deny important opportunities to blacks, and might foster public peace, so they fell within the discretion granted even businesses with special public significance. Rhetorically, then, Waite's opinion gave weight to liberal concerns for economic freedoms and republican concerns for public tranquillity. It ignored how business discriminations contributed to a system of racial subordination destructive of those values.

Justice Clifford, the last Buchanan appointee, concurred and suggested that segregation was desirable. He cited an influential Pennsylvania case, *West Chester & Philadelphia Railroad Co. v. Miles* (1867), to support the wisdom of seating passengers so as to "prevent contacts and collisions arising from natural or well-known customary repugnancies which are likely to breed disturbances, where white and colored persons are huddled together without their consent."[75] Equality did not "mean identity." Otherwise, single men would be allowed in ladies' cabins, contrary to "the nature of things."

Clifford's comparison was an early but not uncommon example of how legal justifications for racial segregation relied on the analogy of the "separate sphere" constructed for women, alleged to be an equal sphere, rather than on explicit doctrines of racial inferiority, such as those invoked on behalf of Chinese exclusion. But the analogy did not go far. If the separation of women from men could be presented as a chivalrous effort of gentlemen to protect ladies, the separation of blacks from whites was plainly driven by white contempt for blacks. Clifford saw that distaste as "natural" and a good ground for segregation. He still insisted that blacks were entitled to equal accommodations, which he thought DeCuir had been offered.[76]

Clifford's insistence on substantial equality of accommodations was not purely lip service. Here, as in the area of Chinese exclusion, liberal egalitarian principles enshrined in law continued to display some weight in judicial deliberations, even if they were only minor obstacles to racism. After *DeCuir* blacks often won cases when they could show that they had been denied service or offered grossly unequal quarters on common carriers, even though they lost when they simply protested the fact of segregation.[77]

The lower courts also began to explore the question of whether the 1875 Civil Rights Act provided relief for victims of racial discrimination. But following the Supreme Court's lead in decisions like *Slaughter-House* and *Cruikshank*, they generally held that the states retained authority over intrastate transportation companies, whereas the Fourteenth Amendment allowed Congress to legislate only against state discriminatory actions. Insofar as the 1875 act tried to make local companies subject to prosecution in federal courts for their racial policies, it was unconstitutional.[78] In 1883, deciding five disputes as the momentous *Civil Rights Cases*, the Supreme Court agreed.[79]

The cases concerned denials of services to blacks seeking entry to an inn, a hotel, the better seats in a theater and opera house, and a railroad ladies' car reserved for whites. Justice Bradley's opinion for the Court might be read as a triumph of pro-business economic ideology, as owners were allowed to discriminate if they so chose, subject at most to state constraints. But his chief argument was now like Miller's in *Slaughter-House:* if Congress could directly regulate the conduct of intrastate businesses, it would "take the place of the State legislatures" and "supersede" them. The Fourteenth Amendment's guarantees prohibited only biased "state action," not private discrimination.[80]

Though this argument sounded most explicitly in the tradition of states' rights republicanism, its racist underpinnings were not completely concealed. They showed through at the opinion's close, in an argument much commentary neglects. There Bradley brusquely dismissed claims that economic discriminations were "badges and incidents" of slavery in violation of the Thirteenth Amendment. Bradley noted that state statutory and common-law rules compelled all innkeepers and common carriers to serve all unobjectionable persons. He did not comment on the fact that those rules had usually been construed to permit "separate but equal" accommodations. Instead, he noted that prior to the abolition of slavery, "thousands of free colored people" had been subjected to "discriminations on account of race or color," denying them access to places of public accommodation. Because their status was clearly distinct from that of slaves, these discriminations against free blacks could not, Bradley thought, be deemed "badges or incidents" of slavery, then or in 1883.

Those discriminations had, however, been justified via the same beliefs in black inferiority that slavery's defenders deployed, and much of the impetus for the discriminations came in from the stigmas accompanying slavery. Treating those discriminations as separate from slavery was glaringly false, and it served to minimize their evil dramatically. Though Bradley conceded that many such discriminations might have been constitutionally invalidated by the other post-war amendments, the bulk of his opinion claimed the Fourteenth Amendment had no such implications. The upshot was to suggest that when racial discrimination fell short of chattel slavery or violation of a few basic rights, it was not only constitutional but uncontroversial.

Bradley ended by insisting that there had to "be a stage in the progress" of the black man "when he takes the rank of mere citizen, and ceases to be a special favorite of the laws, and when his rights as a citizen, or a man, are to be protected in the ordinary modes by which other men's rights are protected." Despite the visibly gathering storms of oppressive forces that loomed over American blacks, Bradley felt that they had reached that high plain of equality. His ruling made federal withdrawal from protection of black rights undeniable.[81]

Off the Court, Frederick Douglass responded with one of his last great denunciations of white injustice. On the Court, Justice Harlan argued, alone but in impassioned detail, that the Thirteenth Amendment authorized Congress to act against all racially motivated infringements of the "civil freedom" of blacks, and that the Fourteenth, along with the "principle of republicanism" and the very concept of "American citizenship," all required "equality of civil rights among citizens of every race in the same State." The Fourteenth conferred both U.S. and state citizenship on blacks, a "distinctly affirmative" action, further specified by the privilege and immunities, due process, and equal protection clauses. It also gave Congress power to protect that citizenship and those rights against individual, corporate, and state violators. Harlan also contended that "railroad corporations, keepers of inns, and managers of places of public amusement" were in any case state "agents," because they were state-licensed and regulated. Hence even Bradley's demand for state action was met. And Harlan maintained that the 1875 act, viewed as an exercise of the commerce power, must at least apply to the interstate railroad involved in one case. As for Bradley's claim that blacks must cease to be the special favorites of the law, Harlan insisted that the 1875 law was needed to "compel a recognition of the legal right of the black race" to "take the rank of mere citizens."[82]

Harlan wrote as if blacks had simply been denied service in all these cases and did not address the validity of separate but equal service. Although Bradley's opinion denied the federal government power to reach even outright refusals of black customers, he did so in part by claiming that state laws would correct such denials if they were unreasonable. He did so fully aware that those laws had been interpreted to permit segregated service. Thus the decision made clear only that the federal government had the duty to punish state racial discrimination, whereas the states had the duty to punish gross racial discriminations by common carriers and places of public accommodation. The constitutional status of segregation was not addressed, although Bradley appeared to align the Court with doctrines favoring it.

The issue was settled thirteen years later in *Plessy v. Ferguson* (1896). In the interim the lower federal courts adhered closely to the Supreme Court's positions, voiding actions brought under the 1875 Civil Rights Act, finding separate but equal facilities to be reasonable, but awarding damages when blacks were not offered even roughly equal services on interstate trains and ships.[83] A few federal judges expressed their disapproval of racial prejudice; one called the hostility of whites to blacks "unreasonable and foolish," and another suggested that color prejudice was most characteristic of those whites who "have little to be proud of in the way of birth, lineage, or achievement."[84] They nonetheless agreed that because many whites felt that way, common carriers could minimize friction by establishing separate but equal accommodations.

In *Louisville, New Orleans, and Texas Railway Co. v. Mississippi* (1890), the Supreme Court gave an important signal in favor of segregation when it ruled that a Mississippi segregation statute, construed as affecting only intrastate railroad traffic, was consistent with the federal commerce clause.[85] Justice Brewer distinguished *Hall v. DeCuir* on the ground that the Louisiana steamboat law had required burdensome relocations of interstate passengers in transit through the state. Here the law professed to concern only commerce within Mississippi, and Brewer ruled only on the requirement that additional cars be attached to trains, if necessary, so that each race could have its own car in Mississippi. He found that burden minor. Brewer professed not to have to address whether black passengers traveling interstate could be required to leave their car and move into the coach newly added for blacks. Harlan and Bradley dissented, insisting that interstate passengers would often be forced to change cars by the law, so that the mandatory segregation law here burdened interstate commerce just as much as the mandatory integration statute judged excessive in *DeCuir*.[86]

It was indeed hard to see how this pro-segregation law encumbered interstate commerce less than the anti-segregation Louisiana one.[87] Lower courts reconciled the cases by treating the Mississippi ruling as upholding segregation of passengers on journeys wholly within a state's borders.[88] Whether or not a state could impose segregation on interstate passengers remained unclear. And as the Mississippi case did not involve any Thirteenth or Fourteenth Amendment arguments, their impact on segregation also remained open.

Justice Henry Billings Brown's opinion in *Plessy* answered the latter questions, though not the issue of interstate passengers.[89] A Louisiana law required "equal but separate" accommodations on all railroads operating within the state except streetcars, either by providing separate coaches or by partitioning coaches. Homer Plessy's lawyers attacked the statute on Thirteenth and Fourteenth Amendment grounds. Brown cited the *Civil Rights Cases* to give the Thirteenth Amendment claims short shrift. He focused on the argument that the law violated equal protection, an issue that he thought turned, as in common law, on whether the regulation was reasonable. Brown denied that the law of its own force harmed blacks by casting them as inferiors, and he, too, thought it reasonable for legislatures to minimize the risks arising from racial hostilities by separating blacks and whites. Echoing arguments familiar from the sociological theories of the day, Brown insisted that "social prejudices" and "racial instincts" could never "be overcome by legislation." Attempts to do so would "only result in accentuating the difficulties" of race relations.[90]

This assumption of instinctive racial aversions is significant. Brown was a Massachusetts Republican, a sometime supporter of state economic regulation, and a participant in the American Social Science Association; but as such he was also a consumer of the new scholarship on race. Those views undergird his *Plessy* opinion.[91] Brown's reasoning cannot be attributed either to a liberal ideology protective of economic rights, which he did not consistently endorse, or to the influence of powerful corporations. Although in some other cases businesses had felt it economically necessary to conform to the prejudices of their white customers, the Louisiana railroads had not supported this law and did not wish to enforce it. Providing extra cars was expensive, so they were concerned that segregation would cost them more than it gained.[92] They saw the statute as a limit, not an aid, to their economic freedom.

Similarly, the line Brown drew between laws properly aimed at promoting political and civil equality and laws vainly seeking to promote social equality is often said to reflect liberalism's public-private distinction. That argument, too, fails in this context. The Louisiana law *replaced* a system in which racial mixing was unregulated with a system in which some forms of private association were publicly banned. It is true that the desires of whites not to associate with blacks on trains might have been thwarted if railroad cars had been open to all. The precedents showed, however, that when railroads believed that most of their customers wanted segregation, the companies complied of their own accord. The fact that many railroads did not wish to do so shows that the demand for segregated facilities was sometimes not so overwhelming. Under those circumstances, nothing in liberal doctrines of economic rights or protection of private choices suggested that the desires of whites who wished to avoid blacks should be given the force of law.

Like most of the other major citizenship decisions of this era, then, *Plessy* must be read as resting not on the laissez-faire strain in social Darwinism, but on its much more powerful racial component.[93] Brown treated "racial instincts," including racial antagonisms, as natural—to be altered, if at all, by long processes of social evolution that no legislation could beneficially influence. These "instincts" made it reasonable for states to impose segregation instead of merely acting to still racial hostilities should they break out. The fact that Brown spoke more of the futility of attacking social inequality by law than he did about how this law had been enacted by Louisiana's elected officials also suggests that he was not simply bowing to the authority of the popular majority. *Plessy* rested on the racial strains in American political culture much more than its liberal or republican elements.

As such, Brown's ruling faced the same problem that the courts were confronting in naturalization cases: someone had to decide who was white and who was not. This was tricky in *Plessy*, since Homer Plessy was seven-eighths "white" and did not appear to be black. But as all states were supposed to treat all citizens equally, Brown thought the question of who was white for purposes of segregation could safely be left "to be determined under the laws of each state." Hence, even though he felt that laws were "powerless" to "abolish distinctions based upon physical differences," Brown accepted that state laws might assign American citizens to different "races" as they traveled through the states.[94]

Harlan's dissent did not fail to note that, far from treating private choices as inviolable, both the managers of the railroad and many individual passengers were not being "allowed to exercise any discretion" under the statute. It thus denied not only "that equality of rights which pertains to citizenship" but also citizens' "personal freedom." Nor would Harlan accept the fiction that the law invaded both races' liberties equally; that was a "thin disguise." All knew that the legislature had aimed to compel blacks "to keep to themselves" as part of an effort to keep whites the "dominant race," constituting "a superior class of citizens." State segregation was not "equal" but "a badge of servitude," imposed in violation of the postwar amendments and of the constitutional guarantee of republican government on which Reconstruction had been based. In chillingly prophetic words, Harlan predicted that the Court's ruling would foster more and more vicious segregation, generating more racial conflict. Indeed, from 1900 through the 1930s, Jim Crow would spread rapidly, like a virulent cancer. As C. Vann Woodward noted, in Southern courtrooms Christian blacks and whites sometimes could not even swear on the same Bible.[95]

Juries. The Supreme Court's main rulings on statutes and policies excluding blacks from jury service largely preceded the major decisions on segregation in transportation, although disputes over the racial composition of juries continue to this day. The litigation was less extensive here than with railroads because the justices' early rulings seemed to spell out clearly what limits the Fourteenth Amendment and its implementing legislation set on state efforts to keep blacks off juries. Those rulings appeared to give teeth to equal protection guarantees, but they left loopholes that permitted the South to deny justice systematically to black citizens.

That acquiescence could have been avoided. In 1878, district judge Alexander Rives courageously held that when a state court impaneled an all-white jury for a black defendant, its action could not "be imputed to chance" but "must be taken as the result of design in derogation of his right to a fair jury for his trial." Standards of fairness had to fulfill "equal protection," and Rives believed that such protection required racially mixed juries. Perhaps with Andrew Johnson's constituency in mind, Rives suggested that blacks might not have needed mixed juries if they "were to be tried by former slaveholders, once allied to them by interest, affection, and sympathy"; but he thought that blacks were greatly at risk when placed in the hands of "white men who never knew or felt these ties."[96] It seemed that there were not enough paternalistic old slaveowners for blacks to be safe with all-white Virginian juries.

The following year, the Supreme Court reversed Rives in the centerpiece of a famous trilogy of jury cases that largely still governs race and jury selection. The best known, *Strauder v. West Virginia*, was the briefest, clearest, and most liberal opinion of the three. An 1873 West Virginia law limited jury service to "white male persons" twenty-one years of age or older, state officials excepted. Justice William Strong, while stating that slavery had left blacks "mere children" needing the protection of "a wise government," found this refusal to permit blacks on juries a patent violation of equal protection. (In an influential incidental comment, he observed that confining "selection to males" was unproblematic.)[97] The decision parallels the many holdings that denials of transport services to blacks were illegal. Nonetheless, Justices Field and Clifford dissented, for reasons that Field laid out in *Ex parte Virginia*.[98]

That companion case involved a Virginia county court judge, J. D. Coles, who was in charge of culling names of voters qualified to be jurors and placing them in a jury box for selection. The record showed that Coles never picked names of blacks. For Justice Strong and the majority, Coles's conduct was a racially discriminatory action by a state agent in violation of the 1875 Civil Rights Act, and thus was equivalent to the law struck down in *Strauder*.[99]

Field, in dissent, objected to the charge to the grand jury by the district judge, because Rives had instructed the jury to presume that failures to appoint blacks were based on race. To refute this, Field indicated, Coles would have had to show that there were no qualified blacks in the county. Field found this burden so unfair that he said it was difficult to discuss "in the language of moderation." He therefore offered no explanation of why it was so grotesque. In later jury cases he readily assumed instead that no qualified blacks could be found.[100]

Field's main argument was against the constitutionality of the 1875 act as applied to the selection of jurors in state courts. He discoursed at length on how the national government was confined to general matters, not local concerns. He insisted that the recent amendments had not been intended to shift "the fundamental theory" of the American "dual system" of government, and he expressed anxieties about fostering "degrading dependence" of the states on the central government. All that sounded like Miller in *Slaughter-House*, not Field's own nationalistic dissent. He also insisted that Coles had been engaged in a discretionary, and hence unreviewable, judicial function. And in his most powerful argument, Field contended that equal protection did not mean that blacks had to serve on a jury that tried a black person, because it did not mean that resident aliens, women, children, or the aged had to be represented on juries when individuals from these groups were tried. Being a juror was, Field thought, not an "absolute and personal" civil right—it was a matter of state discretion. The district judge's view implied, Field claimed, that blacks should only be tried by all-black juries and judges, a reductio ad absurdum that has often been repeated.[101]

Field's defeat meant that the Court had clearly rejected any jury selection process acknowledged to exclude blacks simply on the basis of their race. But in the third of these cases, *Virginia v. Rives*, the justices severely undercut the other rulings.[102] With Field and Clifford now concurring with Strong, the Court reversed Rives's ruling in *Ex parte Reynolds*. Virginia's state attorneys had argued that Rives had no cause to remove the *Reynolds* case into his federal court, because Virginia law did not deny blacks the right to serve on juries. The all-white jury in *Reynolds* had been legitimately drawn from the names in the jury box. How that box came to be so stuffed with white names was not at issue; the question was whether the federal court could take over the case from the state courts.

Strong answered no. Once a state trial had begun, it had to be completed and appealed through the state appellate system. Only then might the case go to the U.S. Supreme Court, if an equal protection violation stood uncorrected.[103] If it were true that the officer who put the names in a jury box refused to include blacks, presumably the state courts would "redress the wrong." In a crucial passage, Strong also indicated that a jury selected impartially might well be all-white. There was no equal protection right to a mixed jury, only to one chosen without racial discrimination. Thus Strong put the burden of proof where Field wanted it. Alone, the exclusion of blacks from a jury, or all juries, did not justify an inference of racial discrimination. Conscious bias must be shown. In *Ex parte Virginia*, Coles had not denied that his aims were racist. Without such concessions, racial intent could not be assumed. And if Virginia's higher courts found no discrimination in the selection of an all-white jury, the Supreme Court would probably be able to do little on review. The upshot was that unconfessed racial discrimination would probably go uncorrected.[104]

That stance rewarded hypocrisy, as later cases confirmed, even though Harlan began to speak for the Court in jury cases, and he did not readily indulge legal fictions of racial equality. In *Neal v. Delaware* (1880), he affirmed that the absence of an explicit ban on jury service by blacks in Delaware's laws deprived a black defendant of one possible ground for removal into federal court. But Harlan took seriously the part of the *Rives* ruling which held that state failures to correct equal protection violations were subject to review. He noted that the state had not contested an affidavit contending that discrimination explained why no black had ever served on any Delaware jury. Harlan dismissed the Delaware court's "violent presumption" that this pattern arose because most blacks were "utterly disqualified" by lack of "intelligence, experience, or moral integrity" for jury service. In the absence of a better defense against charged discrimination, federal review was warranted. In dissent, Chief Justice Waite and Justice Field contended that a mere pattern of exclusion combined with an assertion of its racial motivation should not suffice to find an equal protection violation. Field added that the Delaware court's bigoted presumptions about blacks did plausibly justify the state's all-white juries.[105]

In *Bush v. Kentucky* (1882), Harlan found for a black defendant with Field, Waite, and Gray in dissent. Harlan reiterated the *Rives* ruling that an all-white jury might be legitimately selected, as equal protection required only a jury chosen without discrimination. But he noted that Kentucky had in 1873 and 1877 reenacted requirements that jurors be white, repealing them only after the state Court of Appeals voided them in 1880. Hence Harlan presumed that the jury in the case had been unconstitutionally chosen. Despite those laws, the dissenters refused to believe that *Strauder*'s strictures against racial discrimination in juror selection had been ignored.[106]

These cases only confirmed that a state should not be so foolish as to admit its exclusions were race-based. Although that constraint shows some impact for the amendments' racial egalitarianism, it was not a serious barrier to official enforcement of white racism. Consistent with the *Rives* framework, the Supreme Court subsequently refused to hear black complaints about all-white juries if they were not first properly raised at trial and then appealed through the state court system. Harlan still often wrote for the Court in these cases, and when states denied that their all-white juries were the result of deliberate racial exclusions, even he generally found that blacks had not proven otherwise. The Court usually ignored as grounds for bias statements by state legislatures and courts describing blacks as inferior if those beliefs were not codified in the state constitution or laws. And it dismissed complaints that state courts had not issued subpoenas enabling blacks to acquire evidence that might supply needed proof. It did sustain blacks when state courts refused to hear their evidence.[107] But those rulings were of limited benefit, because its main civil rights enforcement decisions, as applied by lower courts, prevented federal punishment of private actors who stopped blacks from testifying.[108] The Court's claim that nondiscriminatory processes might produce all-white juries rang hollow when it willfully ignored pervasive practices aimed at blocking meaningful black participation in criminal justice decisions. The result was that, by 1900, blacks had disappeared from Southern juries.[109]

Disfranchisement. No developments exemplified the retreat from racial equality, nor contributed so much to black disempowerment, as did the successful efforts to disfranchise black men during the 1890s and early 1900s. (Voting by black women was not remotely on the agenda.) And nowhere was the hypocrisy engendered by the postwar amendments more evident. Because of the Fifteenth Amendment, blacks could not be denied the vote by explicit racial criteria. Yet lawmakers frequently admitted, indeed boasted, that such measures as complex registration rules, literacy and property tests, poll taxes, white primaries, and grandfather clauses were designed to produce an electorate confined to a white race that declared itself supreme. Courts refused to admit this reality, with the Supreme Court resorting to ever more farcical reasoning in order to evade the facts. Meanwhile, blacks began to vanish from the formal democratic process.[110]

State and local governments did most of this work, but the policies of national legislators were vital to their success. In 1890, Henry Cabot Lodge and George Hoar tried to carry on the seminal cause of the Grand Old Party by introducing a Federal Elections Bill, dubbed by Democrats a new "Force Bill." It sought to supply federal supervision of registration and voting in national elections whenever one hundred citizens in a state petitioned for it. The bill narrowly failed; but Democrats made attacks on it a premiere issue in their successful 1892 campaign, and they followed suit in 1894 with their repeals of several still operative sections of the 1870 and 1871 civil rights laws regulating elections and franchise offenses. Little more than the formal declaration of a right to vote remained.[111]

Even before these repeals, the federal courts addressed state disfranchisements guided chiefly by the restrictive precedents of *Cruikshank* and *Reese.* They indicated that the federal government could act only against racially motivated violations of voting rights, and they supported claims that Congress could reach only infringements by state actors, although Bradley's lower court opinion in *Cruikshank* had been ambiguous on that issue. Even in the North, federal courts generally accepted these stifling restraints.[112]

But that approach was far from inevitable, as shown by the one Supreme Court decision markedly favorable to black voting rights in this era, *Ex parte Yarbrough* (1884).[113] There the unpredictable Justice Miller read congressional powers to protect voting rights broadly as he sustained the conviction of Jasper Yarbrough and seven other Georgia white men for conspiracy and assault against a black man, Berry Saunders, who was thus denied his right to vote. Typically, Miller's opinion was grounded not in any constitutional clause but in republican political theory, and it was rich with old republican rhetoric. He contended that all republics faced two "great natural and historical enemies" of their lifeline, free elections: "open violence and insidious corruption." Therefore, the American republic had to have implied powers to protect elections against subversion, whether it came from private actors or the states. Miller declared it "a waste of time to seek for specific sources" of federal authority to pass such laws. The power inhered in "political sovereignty." But after noting Congress's Article I, section 4, powers to regulate the time, place, and manner of federal elections, he contended that the Fifteenth Amendment had conferred on blacks a right to vote whenever the only ground of denial was race, "and Congress has the power to protect and enforce that right."[114] As with congressional Republicans, the Waite Court's commitments to protect the franchise of blacks against white violence remained significantly stronger than concerns for other black rights.

But even more than *Strauder*, *Yarbrough* was a beacon of hope that would be extinguished by a series of dismally dishonest Supreme Court decisions. They began after Cleveland appointed Fuller Chief Justice and spread after the 1890 Elections Bill failed. Lower courts began deferring to state restrictions of voting rights, an approach Fuller reinforced for the Court in 1892.[115] South Carolina circuit judge Goff did hold high the Reconstruction banner of equal rights in *Mills v. Green* (1895) by striking down an array of "vexatious" state registration requirements adopted in 1882. Goff noted that the state had "virtually admitted" with a "candor that was as frank as it was amazing" that its rules aimed at removing "the greatest number of the ballots of the citizens of African descent" while interfering "with as few as possible of those of the white race." Goff found Fourteenth and Fifteenth Amendment violations.[116]

But the Circuit Court of Appeals reversed in an opinion by Fuller, sitting as circuit judge. Whether afflicted by moral myopia, hypocrisy, or partisan or racial loyalties, the Chief Justice saw no "discrimination on account of race, color, or previous condition of servitude." Fuller also contended that the courts could not extend equity relief because only a political right, as opposed to a civil or property right, was alleged to be infringed.[117] When the case reached the Supreme Court, the justices adopted a different evasionary tactic. Noting that the election in which Mills had been trying to vote had been held already, the Court claimed no relief could be provided.[118] A pattern of abjuring honest scrutiny of blatantly racist obstacles to black voting had begun. It would only deepen during the ensuing Progressive Era.

Private Discrimination and Peonage. The Supreme Court played an even more decisive role when it repudiated other protective rulings. In the landmark case of *United States v. Harris* (1882), an apparently chastened Justice William Woods abandoned his strong support for black rights as a circuit court judge. Here he refused to concede any congressional power to reach private actors who had seized, assaulted, and in one case murdered black suspects in the custody of a Tennessee deputy sheriff. With less argument than Bradley would provide in the *Civil Rights Cases,* Woods found no state action involved, and hence no federal power under the Fourteenth or Fifteenth Amendments or the Article IV privileges and immunities clause. He also thought that the conspiracy provisions of the 1871 Enforcement Act went beyond conspiracies aimed at imposing involuntary servitude, so they exceeded congressional power under the Thirteenth Amendment.[119] Thereafter it, too, played no real role in protecting African-Americans against hostile Gilded Age civic ideals.

The Trajectory of Women's Rights Reform

Rather than simply revealing the era's spirit of exclusion, the evolution of women's political status during the late nineteenth century displays the ways in which Americans have blended dissonant civic conceptions. In some respects women began to make real progress toward full citizenship. More states granted at least limited suffrage to females. Women became ever more actively involved in civic reform efforts via women's clubs and, especially, the Women's Christian Temperance Union. Many joined farm and labor struggles, occasionally as at least titular equals to men.

But in all these efforts, most female activists rode the tide of the times by minimizing the equal rights discourses of Reconstruction in favor of views endorsing distinct social and political roles for women, defended in both religious and evolutionary terms. Many also embraced broader doctrines of Anglo-Saxon Christian middle-class supremacy. Frances Willard's WCTU slogan, "For God, Home, and Native Land," expresses succinctly this reliance on religion, nativism, and an enlarged but basically domestic role for women to advocate female enfranchisement and other causes. The slow rise of women's suffrage was, moreover, accompanied by rulings governing marriage, property, naturalization, and civil rights for women that reinforced legal support for the traditional patriarchal family, with females' citizenship derived from husbands and fathers. Thus, despite some progress toward voting rights, claims for female civic equality stayed narrowly confined within notions of naturally based social orders. The prevailing ideological blend, accepted by both parties, endowed the female sphere with more rights than most preceding versions. It was heavily tilted toward ascriptive Americanism even so.

The National Woman Suffrage Association and the American Woman Suffrage Association continued their distinct efforts at national and state suffrage reform up to 1890, with minor successes; but they were tarred by their ongoing quarrels. Leadership shifted after 1876 to a variety of more respectable women's clubs and, especially, the Women's Christian Temperance Union. By 1890, when the declining NWSA and AWSA merged to form the National American Woman Suffrage Association, their combined membership was only 13,000. The General Federation of Women's Clubs, formed two years later, claimed 20,000. In contrast, the WCTU then had 150,000 dues-paying adult members in more than 5,000 locals, with another 50,000 members belonging to its juvenile societies.[120]

Although temperance was the WCTU's raison d'être, under Frances Willard it came to champion women's suffrage and a startling variety of other reforms. Prisons, prostitutes, health care, kindergartens, day care, maternal and vocational education, and the conditions of working women all had WCTU departments. Willard began pushing more conservative WCTU leaders to work intensively for the suffrage in 1876, and it became a centerpiece of her long WCTU presidency from 1879 to 1898. Ruth Bordin and Suzanne Marilley have suggested that, for Willard, "winning the vote and sustaining organized political action" were more important than prohibition itself. But like many of the younger women activists, Willard distanced herself from what she called the suffrage movement's "clamor for 'rights.'" She instead defended a broadened political role for women in terms of female "duties" to "children" and "country." Her "civic maternalism" urged expanded protection for women, children, and virtue in the American home, not gender equality.[121]

Willard's reform vision was a perfect example of the ongoing appeal of ascriptive Americanist ideologies in the face of, and in part because of, the liberalizing legal, political, and economic innovations of the Civil War years. Its religious and patriotic resonances were more stirring and less threatening to many people than the old equal rights slogans. Like temperance itself, Willard's protectionism provided an apparently concrete and constructive response to the disruptive impact of the war, Reconstruction, and late nineteenth-century immigration, urbanization, and industrialization. Those changes produced many more middle-class, educated women with some leisure and sense of vocation for organized action. They also led to the proliferation of saloons and a heightening of drinking rates, slums, poverty, and crime. Thus by the 1880s it seemed more necessary than ever to shield women, children, and the body politic from the ravages of drunken men, especially non-WASP working-class men; and many women felt more able to do so. Willard promised to fight the saloons and the era's other social ills through enfranchising women, though she softened the fears of middle-class WASP men about that change through her use of religious nativist slogans.[122]

Her Americanist rhetoric did not prevent Willard from trying to include virtually all women in WCTU activities, albeit not in equal roles. She led the WCTU into ecumenical activities, informally allied it with the Knights of Labor, created a Department of Colored Work, and started programs for Native Americans, working women, and immigrants. African-American women generally belonged only to segregated WCTU units, however, and few working-class or immigrant women held leadership posts. Because Willard and her organizers also brought Southern white women into a national reform movement for the first time, they felt compelled to abandon any strong push for racial equality, in society at large or within the WCTU. As nativism grew in power in the 1890s, moreover, the organization, and Willard herself, grew more exclusionary. In 1897 she urged Congress to prohibit all further influx of "the scum of the Old World." That was strong language, and doubtless Willard did share the growing biases against blacks and immigrants to some degree. But though her ideological mix—including some acceptance of separate spheres and republican motherhood, but also expanded rights for all women—was on balance less liberal than the short-lived Equal Rights Association, it was more liberal than the WCTU rank and file. After Willard's death the WCTU became more sternly nativist and racist than she ever was.[123]

During the late nineteenth century, women's clubs, white and black, also grew. The white groups fostered women's organizational and leadership abilities and often supported community reforms, despite their focus on social and literary activities and their attachment to traditional gender roles. But the General Federation of Women's Clubs, initiated by Jane Cunningham Croly, excluded blacks entirely and refused to endorse women's suffrage until 1914. It did support legislative efforts to assist children and working mothers and create civil service systems. The National Congress of Mothers favored expanded female education, if only to prepare women for "educated motherhood." The National Federation of Afro-American Women, formed in 1895, worked for the vote for all women. Its membership and resources were much more limited than those of white clubs, however, and its efforts to foster interracial alliances received cool responses.[124]

Few of the women who helped work the nation's farms and the increasing numbers working in manufacturing and service industries in its cities participated in clubs or even suffrage groups. But they, too, began to join organized political efforts during the late 1900s. The Grange was probably the first major American organization to extend membership equally to women, who participated in a wide variety of programs to aid farm families. In 1885 the Grangers declared the "equality of the two sexes" to be a "fundamental" principle and urged that women receive the suffrage and equal citizenship. Around the same time, the Knights of Labor organized "women's assemblies" alongside, though not integrated with, associations of male workers in various trades. Neither the Grangers nor the Knights endured as mass movements, however. And although the Populists included highly active female members, they rarely held high offices. Later labor unions like the American Federation of Labor professed concern for women's problems, but made gender equality a low priority. Many male workers saw women as competition and advocated hard-line separate spheres positions to block their access to jobs outside the home.[125]

Of all these groups, and despite their difficulties, the NWSA as well as the AWSA were most focused on winning women the vote. Their chief difference was whether suffrage should be sought nationally (the NWSA strategy) or state by state (the AWSA tactic). Until 1875 Susan B. Anthony and the NWSA still claimed that women already possessed the vote under the Constitution. Abandoning that tack in 1878, Anthony's friend, California Senator A. A. Sargent, introduced the Anthony amendment, which would eventually be ratified unchanged as the Nineteenth Amendment. It was submitted to almost every Congress after 1878, and in 1882 both houses appointed Select Committees on Woman Suffrage and reported the amendment to the floor, an action repeated up to 1893.

The most pitched debate came in 1887; but throughout, the arguments took familiar forms. In 1886 Senator Henry Blair insisted, in Enlightenment liberal terms, that the vote was an "individual right," to be exercised by all competent persons, not by the alleged head of a family unit. He maintained that women were clearly competent to vote, for they equally with men possessed souls, which had "no sex" but were all of "inherent independence, equality, and dignity." Pro-suffrage advocates also used ascriptive inegalitarian arguments, however: Mary Stewart of Delaware, for example, complained that the "white men of this country" had "thrown out upon us, the women, a race inferior" that possessed the ballot. The opponents of female suffrage endlessly reiterated the doctrine of the separate "sphere of the males and females," claiming that the sexes were naturally endowed by "the Creator" for different roles. Their view prevailed: the amendment failed, 34–16, with twenty-six absent. In fact, Congress took the vote away from women in Utah that term via the Edmunds-Tucker Act, which also strengthened bans on polygamy.[126] The association of female enfranchisement with Mormon sexual practices reinforced fears that suffrage was part of a vicious current threatening the family and Christian civilization. After those defeats, enthusiasm for the Anthony amendment ebbed. After 1895 Congress did not report it out of committee again until 1913.[127]

In 1890, opponents of female suffrage did discover one fresh argument while debating whether Wyoming should be admitted to the Union with female suffrage in its state constitution. Citing a Washington state case, *Bloomer v. Todd,* Senator Morgan contended that Wyoming was trying to make women eligible for federal office-holding in violation of the federal Constitution. That document's exclusive use of masculine pronouns in reference to federal elective offices indicated, he argued, that the framers meant these posts for men. Congress admitted Wyoming but remained adverse to female voting.[128]

Only a bit more success greeted efforts to obtain female suffrage at the state level, often pursued by NWSA locals as well as AWSA ones (and many locals affiliated with both). Of more than four hundred campaigns to hold state referenda, only seventeen got the issue on state ballots, only two in eastern states (Rhode Island and New Hampshire). And only two referenda campaigns succeeded, Colorado in 1893 and Idaho in 1896. Utah did restore female suffrage in the constitution it carried into statehood in 1896, after Wyoming's inclusion with female voting. But demoralizing failures in South Dakota in 1890, Kansas in 1894, and California in 1896 caused state-by-state efforts to flag in the late 1890s.[129]

The federal judiciary reinforced these trends. They weeded out all vestiges of the common-law view that a woman's national citizenship was determined by birth and so might vary from her husband's, in favor of complete subordination of her civic identity to his. Sometimes judges would grant different *state* citizenship for diversity clause purposes in cases of marital separations. But in doing so, they usually made it plain that they were being manly protectors of women, not recognizing female independence.[130]

In regard to wives' national citizenship, the courts responded to the ambiguities left by the 1855 naturalization act in overwhelmingly patriarchal fashion: judges assigned women the citizenship of their husbands.[131] Just when anti-immigrant sentiments began to gain power, *Leonard v. Grant,* an 1880 Oregon circuit case decided by Judge Deady, reinforced that policy. Mrs. D. G. Leonard (the records do not include her first name or maiden name) had been born Swiss. She later married Leonard, a native-born U.S. citizen, who died in 1878. In 1880, Mrs. Leonard sought to get into federal court under diversity jurisdiction in order to sue the Oregon administrator of her husband's estate for certain monies. She contended that Leonard's death had ended her American citizenship, gained exclusively via marriage, and that she was once again Swiss. Deady disagreed. He found in the law no evidence of such "contingent" citizenship; and he insisted that when Mrs. Leonard married, she was "presumed to assent" to permanent

U.S. citizenship. Deady added, with evident distaste for the practices of many naturalizing courts, that Mrs. Leonard was "as well qualified" for the status as "the thousands of poor, ignorant, and unknown aliens who are yearly admitted to citizenship, in the larger centers of foreign population, by the local courts of practically their own creation."[132]

And though the 1855 law had not specified that American women lost their citizenship by marrying foreigners, a Michigan circuit court judge ruled in 1883 that they did. He observed that "legislation upon the subject of naturalization is constantly advancing towards the idea that the husband, as the head of the family, is to be considered its political representative, at least for the purposes of citizenship, and that the wife and minor children owe their allegiance to the same sovereign power."[133]

The Supreme Court also continued to uphold discriminations in women's civic privileges. It noted that women could properly be denied jury service.[134] It permitted the Virginia courts to rule that the term *person* in a law defining qualifications for the bar did not include women.[135] It also upheld the 1887 act outlawing female suffrage in Utah.[136] The justices did not give these cases much discussion. The second-class civic status of women was clear to them.[137]

One countervailing force was at work. For the Gilded Age judges most devoted to property rights, like Stephen Field, economic concerns sometimes dictated deviations from strict female coverture. Most judges, moreover, continued to follow the legislative lead toward greater recognition of independent property rights for married women, though some did so more readily than others.[138] Yet although they mixed their conceptions of gender with economic precepts in different ways, as a whole federal judges defined the status of women in even sharper patriarchal terms during these years. Wives could purchase land only with their husbands' consent; they lacked power of attorney; they could not legally be "settlers" on federal lands; and they could not testify against their husbands, whatever violence their husbands had done to them.[139] As with women's groups, the main judicial splits were only between adherents of more narrow and more expansive views of traditional gender roles. Even more than in regard to the "lower races," the Court had no strong proponents of women's equal rights, economic or otherwise.[140]

Native Americans

Legislative Developments. In apparent contrast to this pattern of declining commitments to civic equality, several factors conspired to produce policies extending citizenship to Native Americans fairly rapidly during the Gilded Age. The difference was, however, largely illusionary. Even reformers who felt well disposed toward Native Americans chiefly aimed to further Christianity and American economic interests.[141]

Somewhat ironically, their "benign" reforms were challenged by the evolutionary views expounded in Hubert Howe Bancroft's Spencerian *Native Races of the Pacific States* (1874) and Lewis Henry Morgan's massively influential *Ancient Society* (1877), and by Morgan's great admirer, John Wesley Powell, named the first director of the nation's new Bureau of Ethnology in 1879. These social evolutionists thought that environmental forces shaped people more than heredity (though Morgan accepted that cultural advances fostered larger brains). Hence they ardently believed that all humanity could progress. At times Powell even joined with reform Darwinists like his close friend Lester Ward in holding that government could accelerate human evolution by promoting Native American economic development. But the main thrust of these evolutionists was caution: a people must progress on its own through unalterable stages toward civilization. The tribes should thus be left to develop on their reserved common lands. Perhaps the government could help them build industries and trades; but perhaps it should instead cut off all annuities and other aid, so that the hard purifying forces of evolutionary struggle could work. Bancroft, Morgan, and Powell suggested that the tribes should not be expected to "jump ethnical periods" it had taken whites eons to traverse. In the 1870s, officials like Francis Walker, briefly the Commissioner of Indian Affairs, agreed. Walker was later Census Director as well as the man Brian Dippie and others have dubbed the "philosopher of immigration restriction." He was also a "natural-born segregationist" who thought reservations best for a lesser race that would assimilate very slowly, if at all.[142]

But despite these anxious messages, the direction of Gilded Age policy was set by new religious reformers, including the Boston Indian Citizenship Committee (founded 1879), the Women's National Indian Association (1879), and the Indian Rights Association (1882). They and others became participants in the famed annual Lake Mohonk Conference of the Friends of the Indian that shaped national measures from 1883 through the early twentieth century. Their activities were triggered by the army's efforts to keep Chief Standing Bear and his fellow Poncas from returning from the southwestern Indian Territory to their home farms. A federal district court judge ruled against the army in *Standing Bear v. Crook* (1879).[143] Standing Bear then went on a lecture tour that inspired the new groups and journalist Helen Hunt Jackson. She wrote the fast-selling *A Century of Dishonor*, denouncing U.S. treaty violations, and began assaulting the "despotic" reservation system.[144]

Even so, the reformers' goals were much like those of Grant's Peace Policy: to Christianize Indians and prepare them for citizenship. Most believed that the reservations had become sinkholes of backwardness that added only corruption and dependency to retrograde Native American ways.[145] The solution instead was a more rigorously transformative education, preferably in boarding schools modeled on the Carlisle Indian School, founded in 1879. Then experiences of owning and working individual farms would be sufficient to achieve the "extermination of the Indian as an Indian," as Indian Commissioner William Jones later put it. From 1880 on, reformers lobbied for legislation directly governing Indians as individuals, assimilative education, the assignment of reservation lands to individual Indians, and conferral of citizenship upon them. The Major Crimes Act of 1885 was a severe blow to tribal self-government, giving federal courts direct jurisdiction over seven serious crimes. The Dawes Act of 1887 was, however, the reformers' crowning success. It authorized the President to allot reservation lands in severalty, that is, to individual resident Indians, in acreage shares like those of the U.S. Homestead Acts. Of the 138 million acres then held by the tribes, the formula left more than 80 million acres as "surplus" lands, available to whites.[146]

That availability was crucial. Although the religious reformers were the most outspoken advocates of allotment, the policy owed much to the support of railroads, mining companies, white settlers, and agrarian activists whose main concern was to acquire tribal lands. Many religious leaders were, moreover, just as certain as businessmen that more tribal lands should be made available for white use. Supporters of allotment regularly listed this as one of its goals. Texas Senator Richard Coke argued in 1880 that "whites cannot be restrained from intrusion upon these large reservations," so it was time to recognize "the logic of events." Interior Secretary Carl Schurz promised that allotment would indeed "open to settlement by white men" the "large tracts of land" that were "not used by the Indians." The government also worked assiduously throughout these years to win seven other major land cessions that opened up even more territory to whites than did the Dawes Act.[147]

Allotment was opposed from several directions. The better endowed tribes, including New York's Senecas and the Five Civilized Tribes in the southwest, recognized it as part of what Father Prucha terms a "flood" of "Protestantism and Americanism" that aimed at washing away their traditional cultural identities, economies, and resources. Some westerners like Colorado Senator Henry Teller insisted that the tribes neither wanted to be citizen farmers nor were prepared to be. These protests had some impact on the final shape of the bill.

Section 6 of the act did make Native Americans citizens upon receipt of their allotments, and it gave citizenship to "every Indian" born within the U.S. who had already separated from his tribe and "adopted the habits of civilized life." But against the advice of William Graham Sumner, reformers accepted that newly "emancipated" Native Americans might be vulnerable to white exploitation. Unlike Morgan and Powell, Sumner thought Native Americans should immediately be made full citizens. Typically, he also said they should get no special treatment. The Dawes Act instead prevented even the new "allotment citizens" from selling or giving away their lands for twenty-five years. It also freed them from having to pay taxes on their allotments. Yet even as the "friends of the Indian" perpetuated a wardship status that belied the full citizenship that they claimed to bestow, they surrendered what should have been a crucial requirement for respecting Native American interests—that allotment and citizenship come only with a tribe's consent. Instead, both could be imposed at the President's discretion.[148] The Civilized Tribes gained exemption from the Dawes Act, but they merely delayed a similar fate. Only the New York Indians, aided by an unpopular right of preemption to their lands held by the Ogden Land Company, escaped repeated tries to allot their properties.[149]

Altogether, the Dawes Act and other federally induced concessions reduced Native American lands from 155,632,312 acres in 1881 to less than half that amount, 77,865,373 acres, by 1900. In laws passed in 1891 and 1894, Congress made it easy for Native Americans to lease out their allotments for ever longer periods. That policy was more consistent with the full citizenship that few Native Americans wanted, and also with the rapid exploitation that many whites sought. Because many of these tribesmen had little motivation or skill to become farmers and whites offered seemingly attractive lease terms, from one-third to three-fourths of the lands on various former reservations ended up leased within a few years. Leasing then often proved a way station to land alienation. Thus the basic effects of the Dawes Act were to destroy traditional Native American ways of life and to transfer most of the tribes' resources to whites.[150]

Judicial Rulings. Although numerous and complex, on balance the judicial decisions governing Native Americans deeply underscored that pattern. Prior to the Dawes Act, most federal judges, and finally the Supreme Court justices, firmly denied that unnaturalized tribesmen were birthright citizens or that they could be naturalized without specific congressional authorization. Courts regarded Native American citizenship as an ultimate but still long-term goal. Most notably, in *Ex parte Crow Dog* (1883), the Supreme Court refused to interpret an 1877 congressional statute which specified that Indians were "subject to the laws of the United States" as authorizing federal courts to adjudicate Native American crimes directly, displacing tribal jurisdiction over offenses committed by one member against another.[151] Consistent with Grant's Peace Policy, Justice Stanley Matthews thought that the government's aim was to civilize the tribes first as communities, on reservations, not as individual citizens. That goal meant that the nation's "wards" must learn the art of "self-government." Congress thus could not have wished to displace tribal courts with those of "superiors of a different race."[152]

The debates over the Fourteenth Amendment had shown, moreover, that exclusion of unassimilated Native Americans was the chief exception to the nation's policy of birthright citizenship. Not surprisingly, the courts continued so to rule. In 1876, an Oneida Indian born and resident in New York was indicted for voting in a congressional election. The federal district judge upheld his right to vote, but only because his tribe had ended its "tribal integrity" prior to the Fourteenth Amendment, and New York had taxed the former tribesmen as citizens. Hence they had been extended citizenship by the 1866 Civil Rights Act and the Fourteenth Amendment. Native Americans then still in tribal relations had to be naturalized by further congressional action.[153] And in the minds of at least some judges, race, not simply tribal membership, was central to denials or grants of birthright citizenship. Descent from whites or blacks was sufficient to make citizens even of those living in tribes, so long as they had not been formally admitted therein; and though a black man so naturalized might be recognized as a tribal member, he was still "not an Indian."[154]

The Supreme Court affirmed these birthright citizenship doctrines in *Elk v. Wilkins* (1884), which concerned another assimilated would-be voter. Justice Gray noted that U.S. policy had "tended more and more towards the education and civilization of the Indians, and fitting them to be citizens." Nonetheless, the question of whether any Indian had become "so far advanced" as to "be let out of the state of pupilage" was "a question to be decided by the nation whose wards they are . . . and not by each Indian for himself." Like the framers of the Fourteenth Amendment, the justices reasoned that because tribal members were not born "completely subject" to U.S. jurisdiction, "owing them direct and immediate allegiance," they did not meet the amendment's requirements for birthright citizenship. But the justices went no further than their predecessors in explaining why ultimate allegiance was insufficient to confer membership. They simply held that the choice of the U.S. to assert only this inferior, dependent status was paramount. Though individual Native Americans might come to live in apparent full allegiance to the U.S., it had not naturalized them, and no one could "become a citizen of a nation without its consent."[155]

Justices Harlan and Woods dissented. They argued that the 1866 Civil Rights Act had aimed to naturalize any Indian who became assimilated enough to be taxed, a policy that the Fourteenth Amendment had elaborated to encompass all those who left their tribes and became subject to the full jurisdiction of the U.S. government. By denying citizenship to those no longer belonging to tribes, the majority's approach perversely produced "a despised and rejected class of persons, with no nationality whatever." Surely, Harlan and Woods argued, it made more sense to read the Fourteenth Amendment as expressing the nation's consent to membership for those who assimilated, whenever they assimilated.[156]

Both sides thus recognized that the jurisdiction requirement in the Fourteenth Amendment added a consensual component to birthright citizenship. Both knew that its framers had nonetheless failed to address the question of Native Americans who might leave their tribes after its enactment, as John Elk had done. And both tried to construe the amendment in light of the policy that it could most plausibly be held to represent. But while Harlan and Woods focused on the ultimate aim of absorbing "civilized" Native Americans as Americans, the majority sided with the ample precedents indicating that the U.S. should never be presumed to have accepted Native Americans as members unless it did so explicitly. That is a conclusion that may well have been true to the framers' outlooks. It was also one that gave great weight to the disdain for Native Americans that had long shaped U.S. policy.[157]

Crow Dog and *Elk v. Wilkins* prompted antireservation reformers first to partially displace tribal courts with federal jurisdiction via the Major Crimes Act, and then to propose grants of citizenship. They could no longer hope that individuals would simply win recognition as citizens as they assimilated, and that tribal courts would thereby be displaced, as a few federal judges had suggested.[158] But whenever Congress did make Native Americans citizens by treaty, statute, or allotment, questions still remained about what this status implied for their rights and for the authority of surviving tribal governments, the states, and the federal government. Much in American law suggested that naturalized Native Americans should be treated just like other state citizens, governed in most matters by the state in which they resided. But that conclusion ran against the interests of tribal leaders, the federal Indian bureaucracy, and the fading concerns of national courts and legislators to maintain their authority over Native Americans vis-à-vis the states.[159]

The result was a mass of further litigation over the comparative powers and rights of individuals, tribes, the states, Congress, the Indian Bureau, and federal courts. Some basic patterns are discernible. During the Gilded Age, the federal courts regularly held that Congress could exercise ultimate sovereign power over Indian lands, tribes, and individual Native Americans whenever it wished.[160] By asserting guardianship over its "wards," the federal government could prevail over claims of individual rights, tribal rights, and states' rights. In *United States v. Kagama* (1886), for example, the Supreme Court had no trouble sustaining the Major Crimes Act, even though it blunted *Crow Dog*.[161] But once the government permitted lands to be sold and individuals to become citizens, the courts were reluctant to hold that these lands and citizens were legally distinguishable from others.[162]

In particular, many courts at first leaned toward the view that the citizenship and land titles conferred by the Dawes Act sharply limited or terminated the federal government's special powers over allotment recipients. In *Ross v. Eells* (1893), for example, a circuit court in Washington State ruled that an Indian agent could not prevent Puyallup Indians who had received allotments from permitting railroad construction on their lands.[163] Soon, however, dissatisfactions with those consequences began to appear, on benches as well as off. The *Ross* decision was reversed by the circuit court of appeals in *Eells v. Ross* (1894), holding that the Dawes Act, "which confers citizenship, clearly does not emancipate the Indians from all control, or abolish the reservations." Abolition, to be sure, was the "ultimate hope," but, the judges cautioned, "it will not be soonest realized by attributing fanciful qualities to the Indians, or by supposing that their nature can be changed by legislative enactment."[164] The Supreme Court refused to reverse that ruling, leaving its embrace of the "natural" subordinate status of Native American citizens intact.

Civic Education during the Gilded Age: The Spencerian Backdrop

Just as few adults living in America or seeking to do so failed to feel the impact of the dramatic transformations in American civic ideals during the Gilded Age, so too were those developments mirrored in the educational institutions that sought to prepare children for America's future. Civic education was also heavily shaped by the evolutionary outlook of Herbert Spencer and kindred American evolutionists, though again that influence took many forms. Spencer's *Education*, an essay collection published in the U.S. in 1860, became a touchstone for American educational debates through the end of the century. To promote the survival of the fittest, Spencer insisted, schooling should give priority to forms of knowledge conducive to self-preservation. The focus should be on skills needed for the maintenance of "health" and "the gaining of a livelihood." Such knowledge was best provided by a curriculum stressing applied forms of mathematical and scientific studies. Courses in ancient languages, art, music, and the history of battles and kings primarily assisted refined "leisure" and so should be given the lowest priority. As far as Spencer was concerned, then, most traditional education, aristocratically centered on belles lettres, neglected "the plant for the sake of the flower." But, predictably, Spencer also dismissed reformers' notions "that an ideal humanity might be forthwith produced by a perfect system of education." Like other schemes of governmental improvement, such transformative schooling required "a degree of intelligence, of goodness, of self-control, possessed by no one." Edu-

cators should instead focus on the attainable goal of providing the long nurtur-
ing in means of self-preservation required by highly evolved forms of life.[165]

The Mixed Pattern of Educational Expansion. Spencer's endorsement of a more
utilitarian education jibed well with concerns shared by employers, workers, immigrants, and government officials to fit most of the fast-growing, increasingly
diverse population into some productive role in the emerging industrial order.
The expansion first of manual training as an aspect of a liberal arts curriculum,
and then of vocational education to prepare less scholarly students directly for
work, therefore became central themes of these years. Congress accordingly expanded the agricultural and mechanical college system in 1890 via the "Second
Morrill Act." Vocational training would remain the chief aim of all major federal
education bills for years to come.[166]

   Though reform Republicans half-heartedly tried through the late nineteenth
century also to extend federal aid to elementary and secondary schools, only vocationally oriented measures came close to passage. Centrally controlled, compulsory public schools continued to be feared by Southerners who saw them as
barriers to "redemption," by Catholics and ethnic immigrants who resented imposition of an Anglo-Saxon Protestant *paideia* on their communities, and by
many Democrats who remained committed to general policies of decentralization or laissez-faire, rather than "Prussian autocracy" in education. Those constituencies represented too formidable a coalition to overcome at the federal
level; and though proponents of compulsory schools still gained ground in the
states, where promises of local accountability were more plausible, such laws
would not become universal until 1918.

   Even so, below the federal level, the chief educational story of these years was
the remarkable ongoing expansion and professionalization of American public
education, which kept the U.S. system in the forefront of the world. The nation
went from 9.8 million children in public schools in 1880, 9.7 million of them
kindergarten through eighth grade, to 15.5 million in 1900, almost 15 million in
K–8. Urban school systems popularized the K–8 structure as well as public high
schools, which exceeded the enrollments of private secondary schools in the
1880s and almost doubled in enrollment every decade thereafter up to 1930. They
began, however, with a very low attendance base; only about 2 percent of seven-
teen-year-olds graduated from public or private high schools in 1870. By 1900
the figure still was only 6.4 percent. In contrast, at the elementary and secondary
level, by 1900 over 90 percent of white children received some elementary education, and public schools enrolled over 90 percent of those receiving schooling.
Though poor nonwhites fared the worst, most children of all backgrounds
achieved literacy, basic arithmetical skills, and some of the socialization that ed-

ucators tried to provide. Enrollments also grew in institutions of higher education, from 116,000 in 1880 to 238,000 in 1900. But here private school enrollments probably exceeded public ones, with the greatest growth coming in medical, nursing, and teaching schools, as well as the rapidly proliferating small private colleges, often denominational and coeducational.[167]

The surge in public school growth, funded by substantial increases in taxpayer dollars, reflected broad popular support for education despite quarrels over how it should be structured. It was particularly a victory for the emerging class of professional educators, whom scholars concede to be the most successful of the many interests vying to shape American education during these years.[168] Most of the new educational leaders were reform Darwinists, consciously or unconsciously, accepting the reality of evolutionary processes but believing that they could be shaped by human intelligence to the betterment of all, especially through education. Some, especially the proponents of the newly professionalizing social sciences, were directly influenced by Lester Ward's arguments that the greatest panacea for "the perfectionment of the social state" was "the increase and diffusion of knowledge among men," a process that could not, however, "be trusted to take care of itself." Most other champions of public education professed some version of the Social Gospel, the belief that it was the religious duty of Americans to spread enlightenment to all citizens, if not all mankind. Although even liberal Protestants varied greatly in their willingness to support racial, ethnic, and gender equality, they shared common ground in their general commitments to social action and to many specific reforms, and they found allies for their social efforts in other faiths. Many of their educational endeavors centered on organizational offshoots of churches, but they shaped the thinking of reformers who were reconstructing American public education and provided leadership in gaining popular support for the expansion of public schooling.[169]

From 1870 to the turn of the century, the leading figure in these efforts was the longtime St. Louis School Superintendent William Torrey Harris, who went on to serve as U.S. Commissioner of Education from 1889 to 1906. Harris, a protégé of the New England transcendentalist Bronson Alcott, became a devout Hegelian, a founder of the St. Louis Philosophical Society, and the influential editor of its *Journal of Speculative Philosophy*. His Hegelianism made Harris comfortable with notions of evolution and of its constructive social direction. It led him particularly to stress rationally structured institutions as the chief vehicle of social progress, in conscious imitation of the Prussia that Democrats decried. Harris popularized kindergartens as an introduction to the sort of unified, graded elementary, secondary, and, in principle, higher education systems that American cities increasingly strove to create. And Harris agreed with his great predecessor, Horace Mann, as well as his greater successor, John Dewey, that public education should aim not just at imparting economic skills but, above all, at preparing all citizens for "participation in civilized life." His biographer suggests that Harris's primary educational goal was to train good citizens and thereby "safeguard democracy, freedom, and individuality," which Harris saw as "the essence of Americanism." Harris resisted the growing emphasis on manual and then vocational training as too narrow for this goal, so that most federal vocational education laws came after his tenure at the federal Bureau of Education had ended.

Instead, Harris advocated a broad liberal arts education for white men and women of all classes. He insisted, however, on all students learning orderly discipline as well as the cognitive skills he thought necessary in a complex industrial society. He also accepted segregated, vocationally oriented schooling for blacks. Harris's policies thus provide ammunition for scholars who see public schooling as essentially aimed at social control. Yet he did much to foster the spread of public school systems and to sustain the view that they were central to enlightened citizenship for all Americans.[170]

This mixed legacy is confirmed by the ascriptive features built into the structures of schooling created during these years. Even as American public education grew generally, progress in creating new public schools for blacks essentially ended after 1877. The South, where 90 percent of the black population still lived, was divided between those who thought that schooling for blacks was unnecessary and incendiary and those who believed that agricultural and mechanical vocational education could turn blacks into a better labor force. Such private philanthrophic societies still working for educational reform as the American Missionary Association, the Southern Education Association, and the General Education Association, all increasingly fell in with the latter, Hampton-Tuskegee model of purely industrial education for blacks. Southern white Populists pushed for public schools for their children, but often powerful planter interests complied by diverting funds from Reconstruction-era segregated black schools to poorer white students. Aided by mounting black disfranchisements, white supremacists thus succeeded in increasing the disparity in funding between white and black schools in every Southern state as the Gilded Age closed. They also ended money for transportation to many black schools. Advocates of truly universal education that would prepare blacks for higher things were marginalized.

As a result, though the numbers of black school-age children rose by 25 percent from 1880 to 1900, the percentage attending public schools declined to an average of 36 percent for children aged five to fourteen. Black enrollment in secondary schools, previously almost nonexistent, did rise during these years but remained paltry. At best, Southern cities had only one black high school, regardless of the number of black residents. Many sizable Southern cities and most rural re-

gions had no high schools for blacks. Black colleges and professional schools enrolled tiny numbers of students, less than 4,000 throughout the South in 1900,
and only a handful of private liberal arts colleges really offered blacks higher education. The public land grant colleges primarily provided vocational training at
secondary or even elementary school levels. Yet blacks still thirsted for education:
the schooling that did take place lowered the illiteracy rate from 95 percent of
blacks in 1860 to 30 percent by 1900. By then blacks had begun to move to the urban North, with somewhat more accessible schooling, and new if embattled efforts to improve black education began in the South.[171]

The situation in regard to education of Asian-Americans was comparable. San
Franciscans and other Californians tried to expel the Chinese from public
schools entirely in the early 1880s. Then, when California courts held that the native-born Chinese were legally entitled to receive schooling, segregated institutions were created, despite Chinese resistance. These schools, like schools for
blacks, received far less funding than white ones. They were never viewed as
adequate by those they were supposed to serve.[172]

In contrast to the treatment accorded blacks and Asian Americans, and in
variance with its general neglect of education, the federal government plowed
dollars into Native American schooling during the Gilded Age. But these federal
policies reflected similar views of Native Americans as members of a "lower race"
that might some day assimilate, but only if they received strictly vocational education for a long time. The U.S. government supported Native American education energetically because schooling formed part of its Dawes policy of breaking
up the tribes so that most of their common lands would become available to
whites.

Government schools were also inadvertent beneficiaries of Protestant efforts
to displace Catholic Indian schools. Though federal officials laid Grant's Peace
Policy to rest in the early 1880s, federal funding for Indian schooling continued
to rise, going from $20,000 in 1870 to almost $3 million by 1900. Catholics, who
created their own Bureau of Catholic Indian Missions in 1879, managed through
strenuous efforts under President Cleveland to obtain more than $400,000 of
these funds annually by 1889. But matters changed quickly under President Harrison's Commissioner of Indian Affairs, Thomas Jefferson Morgan, a Baptist
minister with a record of anti-Catholicism. His Bureau of Indian Affairs largely
acceded to a new demand of Protestant reformers: public funds should go to
schools run directly by the government, with, of course, a predominantly Protestant cast to their curriculum, rather than to either Protestant or Catholic mission
schools. When Cleveland returned to office in 1893, he chose not to fight further
on behalf of the Catholic schools. Morgan also tried to conform the new government schools to Harris's educational views, creating a graded system that cul-

minated in fully assimilative off-reservation vocational schooling of the Carlisle variety. By 1900, two-thirds of the government school students attended more fully assimilative boarding schools, with just under one-half of those in off-reservation schools, though even the off-reservation institutions labeled colleges rarely offered education even at a secondary school level. Such government schools had more than doubled in number, to 307, from the late 1870s to 1900, and their students had increased sevenfold, to 21,000, though an equal number of school-age Indian children were not enrolled in any school. Missionary schools were by then enrolling fewer than 2,000 students, and though Catholics managed to fund those schools for a time, their role was no longer important.[173]

The story of women's civic education is similar though less extreme. Proponents of the new systems of professionalized education generally envisioned a corps of largely female teachers led by male principals and administrators, and women came to dominate teaching during the Gilded Age, amounting to over 70 percent of all teachers by 1900. The task of training them led to the proliferation of normal schools, coeducational programs in newer private colleges and the land grant institutions, and such sister colleges as Barnard and Pembroke for established universities like Columbia and Brown. To prepare for these institutions, all through the Gilded Age more girls than boys graduated from public high schools, which were largely coeducational, except in the South. The heavy involvement of women in public education as teachers and students helped make school elections one of the first areas where women gained the vote.

But opposition to female teachers rose as their numbers mounted and they became more of a threat to traditional notions of women's place. Female teachers continued to be paid much less than men in similar positions, and prevailing norms also insisted that women forego marriage if they pursued a career. To do so, however, meant receiving criticism for failing to fulfill a woman's obligations to the furthering of the species. Apart from teacher training, much of the education women received was simply preparation for female responsibilities like cooking, made more "scientific" via the new discipline of "domestic economy" or home economics. The land grant colleges in particular made women second-class institutional citizens, largely confined to teacher preparatory and home economics courses by restrictions on their access to standard liberal arts classes. Some coeducational private colleges like Antioch and Oberlin and many of the new women's colleges like Radcliffe and Smith afforded women wider opportunities, but they were significantly less well funded than their all-male counterparts like Harvard and Yale. Professional education was similarly restricted by gender: nursing schools for women proliferated during these years, whereas medical schools remained largely male preserves. Defenders of such differentiated education—men and women alike—spoke often of the separate civic spheres of female and male citizens. They were reinforced by influential Spencerian evolutionists like Edward Clarke and Harvard president Charles Eliot, along with psychologists like Stanley Hall, who all argued that women were biologically ill-equipped for anything else. Traditionalist religious leaders confirmed that women ought to receive a different education to prepare them for their divinely imposed reproductive duties.[174] Thus, though more inclusive visions competed to set the agenda, Gilded Age Americans drew ascriptive hierarchies in their blueprints for "modern" schools.

The Legacies of Reconstruction's Liberal Nationalism

In light of all these changes, it is less surprising that this era of bursting industrial capitalism saw so few new liberal citizenship policies. The Reconstruction amendments, particularly the Fourteenth's equal protection clause, did serve as a basis for some vital judicial checks on subjugating legislation. And as agrarian and labor unrest mounted during the 1890s, courts began to draw on Spencerian economic views and surviving Jacksonian opposition to special privileges to turn the due process clause and other provisions into powerful nullifiers of pro-labor and pro-consumer regulatory efforts. Those national elites, at least, were determined to preserve a regime that was more favorable to market capitalism than radical egalitarianism. But judicial legitimations of civic hierarchies overwhelmed the few inclusive equal protection decisions; and even economic rulings favoring business did not formally enhance corporate citizenship.

Rights of National Citizenship: Article III Jurisdiction. On issues of national versus state power, the Republican party's predominance at the national level and the Democrats' domination of many states reinforced each party's ideological traditions and resulted in predictable conflicts. The Republicans in Congress and on federal benches remained committed to broad federal power over disputes between citizens of different states via the Article III diversity of citizenship clause, particularly in the case of corporate litigants. Their electoral successes meant that, in this area, the Civil War era's new liberal nationalistic legal structures largely survived, with the exception of some major statutory reductions in federal powers to enforce civil rights laws after the Democrats regained the White House in 1887 and 1893.[175] Yet partisan clashes on these issues were less severe than elsewhere. Even Democratic federal judges did not resist expansions of their own authority as much as they opposed new rights for African-Americans and women. Even many Republican judges displayed only qualified zeal for their new powers. That diffidence in part reflects the ongoing power of anticentralizing dual federalist legal traditions, as well as resistance to the ways expanded jurisdiction embroiled judges in the mounting contradictions between the recent constitutional promises of equal protection and the rebuilding of racial hierarchies. Even so, the new laws defining federal jurisdiction compelled judges to face fresh questions concerning the criteria for state citizenship and the conditions under which diversity of citizenship entitled litigants to remove cases to the federal courts.[176] During the nation's great industrial expansion, the controversies raising those questions usually involved corporations.

Indeed, the many new corporate enterprises in late nineteenth-century America engaged in an elaborate rondolé with state and federal legislatures and courts. More than ever, the companies sought to use the diversity of citizenship clause, among other means, to give themselves maximum flexibility in jurisdiction shopping and minimum vulnerability to regulation. Few litigants could afford to follow corporations into often distant federal courts or to hire counsel who could navigate the seas of state and federal rules as well as corporate lawyers could. Federal rules, shaped by the better endowed corporate bar, also were comparatively favorable to corporate interests. Though state legislatures passed incorporation laws designed to attract businesses, or at least to have them incorporate locally, they also sought to gain greater control over these increasingly powerful economic entities. One way they did so was by trying to curb their access to federal courts. The national judges sought to protect corporations against what they saw as unfair and inefficient state measures, though many also tried to limit the ability of businesses to manipulate the judicial system. Those imperatives often conflicted.[177] As a result, though federal rulings in this area were hardly anticorporate or antinationalist, they were less tilted toward business and national judicial power than many portrayals of this era of laissez-faire constitutionalism suggest. Though many federal courts felt especially compelled to protect corporations during the strife-ridden 1890s, the decidedly mixed pattern of diversity rulings overall reveals the great opposition to liberalizing, nationalizing changes during this era. The complexity of diversity issues, federal judges' stake in their own authority, and the influence of corporations should have made adherence to full-blown liberal nationalism easy here. Yet courts often held back.[178]

The Supreme Court justices, and most lower federal judges, proclaimed repeatedly that they had no wish to read the postwar amendments as vastly expanding federal judicial powers.[179] But the Gilded Age Court still accepted that the laws culminating in the 1875 Jurisdiction and Removal Act, which gave the federal courts federal question as well as diversity jurisdiction, had worked "radical changes" in the powers of litigants to take cases from state to federal courts prior to completion of state proceedings.[180] Congress had mandated that in order to protect newly guaranteed federal rights on a uniform basis nationally, all citizens, including corporate "citizens," could now jettison state courts for federal ones in many circumstances.[181] The structure was in place, then, for the federal courts to guide American civic development more than ever before.

And from the 1880s on, corporations began using diversity jurisdiction to remove more and more cases to the federal courts. Opposing litigants responded with many tactics to try to maintain state jurisdiction.[182] Most of these struggles did not center on questions of corporate citizenship, but they usually presumed it, and so corporations won reaffirmations of their citizenship for diversity purposes throughout these years.[183] In some ways, however, federal judges refused to protect corporations against states.[184] Perhaps most important, in *Hawes v. Oakland* (1882) and other cases of the 1880s, the pioneer of judicial retreat from Reconstruction, Justice Miller, led the Court in denouncing collusive stockholder suits that allowed corporations to evade "natural" state forums for federal ones. Though the Court sustained the *Dodge v. Woolsey* ruling that stockholder suits were permissible in genuine conflicts, it formulated Equity Rule 94, which defined and banned collusive suits.[185] Federal courts also resisted expansion of their jurisdiction in other ways.[186]

But the Supreme Court gave confusing answers to some questions about corporate citizenship that were crucial for defining the scope of federal judicial power. Under what circumstances, if ever, did corporations acquire multiple state citizenships when they did business or were formally incorporated in more than one state? If corporations had multiple state citizenships, it was not clear whether states could insist that all corporations doing business within their borders were their citizens, unable to remove cases to federal courts, or whether the corporations could invoke one of their other state citizenships when they wished to escape a state's tribunals. If the first situation prevailed, corporations might be denied federal access, but the second allowed companies to forum-shop at will. Neither outcome seemed desirable.[187]

The Court struggled to find a consistent course. In *Lehigh Manufacturing v. Kelly* (1895), Justice Harlan wrote that a corporation could not gain federal jurisdiction by creating a new corporation elsewhere with a different state citizenship and transferring disputed property to it.[188] The Court then held in *St. Louis and San Francisco Railway Co. v. James* (1896), that a Missouri citizen could not gain federal jurisdiction by suing a corporation first chartered in Missouri, then later in Arkansas, as an Arkansas citizen.[189]

The Court's results showed a desire to confine citizenship to a company's state of first incorporation. That position prevented states from claiming that all corporations operating in their limits were their citizens, and it also prevented corporations from choosing among several state citizenships as their interests dictated. Thus it is not true that, as Edward Purcell claims, the *James* ruling gave corporations "the greatest possible access to the national courts"; but it did give them very wide removal powers. As corporations were citizens only of their original states, they could take citizens of other states in which they did large amounts of business into federal court at will.[190]

But while the *James* decision enabled corporations to gain extensive federal access via diversity jurisdiction, the justices embraced a narrowing of their jurisdiction by upholding the Democrats' various reductions in removal rights. Like the removal provisions in the 1866 Civil Rights Act, the 1867 removal law, as revised in 1874, permitted persons eligible for diversity jurisdiction to remove cases begun in state courts if they alleged local prejudice against them. That policy was designed to help both blacks and white Northerners faced with hostile Southern state courts. But the jurisdiction acts passed under President Cleveland in 1887–88 included what Oregon district judge Matthew Deady termed "confederate" provisions. Prompted by Democratic opposition to federal interference with state regulation of both blacks and corporations, they required more evidence than a simple allegation to show local prejudice, and they also allowed only defendants to remove cases.[191] The Supreme Court decided that actual proof of local prejudice was now required, and that motions for removal had to be made early in the proceedings. The fact that the issues had implications for black rights probably made results that were hostile to federal jurisdiction easier to reach.[192] On the whole, federal courts were more receptive when corporations claimed "local prejudice" under the 1867 act than when blacks sought removals under the 1866 Civil Rights Act, but the Supreme Court was still less supportive than corporations wished.[193]

Outside that context, one of the most highly charged issues concerning jurisdiction was how far states could act to inhibit corporate removals. Here the Court clearly if not unequivocally sided with the corporations. Because of the Court's inconsistent treatment of the issue in the earlier *Morse* and *Doyle* cases, states continued to pass laws designed to prevent out-of-state corporations from exercising their diversity removal rights.[194] In 1886, for example, Iowa required "foreign" (including out-of-state American) corporations to obtain permits to do business in the state that would be revoked if they removed any cases to federal court. In *Barron v. Burnside* (1887), the Supreme Court overturned the statute for infringing on a federally guaranteed privilege. Thus overall, Reconstruction's jurisdictional initiatives fared well enough in this era so that by its end, "corporations had most of the legal standing that attached to national citizenship," as Morton Keller has noted.[195] Yet even corporate citizens had not wholly escaped the corrosive winds blowing through the civic laws of the Gilded Age.

Privileges and Immunities under Article IV, Section 2. Federal judges attended to the two privileges and immunities clauses in the Constitution much less than to diversity jurisdiction, but here, too, the order of the day was maintenance without expansion of national protections. In Article IV, section 2, cases, judges continued to strike down state laws that overtly discriminated against citizens of other states; but what was now almost universally viewed as the comity clause underwent no real growth.[196] There were contexts, to be sure, where the Court still found the nationalizing aims of the Article IV guarantee compelling. As Justice Field observed, that clause could not have had "a more fitting application" than in *Williams v. Bruffy* (1877). There the commonwealth of Virginia argued that it did not have to pay a Pennsylvanian a debt owed by an estate it had sequestered during the Civil War, because Virginia had then been part of an independent nation, free from duties of comity. Field gave that claim short shrift. The U.S. had never conceded the Confederacy's legal existence and was hardly about to do so in 1877.[197]

In other cases that turned on blatant violations of equal treatment for citizens of other states, federal courts upheld the requirements of Article IV, section 2, with similar firmness.[198] But, on the whole, activism on behalf of equality in civic privileges and immunities was rare during the late nineteenth century.[199] In most cases that offered alternative grounds of decision, such as the commerce or equal protection clauses, courts placed less reliance on Article IV.[200] During an era of litigation dominated by corporations, the fact that the Supreme Court continued to hold that corporations could not be citizens within the meaning of the clause undoubtedly contributed to its reduced emphasis.[201]

Privileges and Immunities under the Fourteenth Amendment. The Constitution's newer privileges and immunities clause was rarely invoked during the Gilded Age except in the company of due process and equal protection claims; and despite objections by Field and Harlan, the Supreme Court regularly relied on Miller's reasoning in *Slaughter-House* to dismiss most of these invocations. The very robustness of American traditions of natural rights, common-law rights, and rights of state citizenship independent of U.S. citizenship evacuated most of the Fourteenth Amendment clause's potential content. The judiciary's rising concern in the 1880s to protect nonexplicit economic rights, especially corporate rights, did not alter that pattern. These were rights defined as prerogatives of persons, not citizens, thereby enabling corporations to claim them; and they were held to originate in common and natural law, not U.S. citizenship. Hence the due process and equal protection clauses were their natural Fourteenth Amendment vehicles, and the privileges and immunities proviso became a useless appendage to its section 1 partners.[202]

Occasionally, as in the *Stockton Laundry Case* (1886), a federal court stressed that a law (here one banning all public laundries) denied a liberty that was a Fourteenth Amendment privilege and immunity, as well as a right sheltered by due process and equal protection.[203] But before and after this case, the limited assistance courts provided to Chinese immigrants came chiefly under the equal protection clause and due process procedural guarantees. Later, most judges would protect such economic liberties solely via substantive due process.[204]

Judicial receptivity to the privileges and immunities clause was not enhanced by its prominence in litigation seeking to protect the liquor trade against state prohibitions, despite Justice Field's ruling in favor of such bans in *Bartemeyer v. Iowa* (1873). As Field's example indicates, even judges inclined to protect economic liberties against state police powers rarely assisted commerce in alcohol. None agreed that it was a basic right of U.S. citizenship.[205] The Court was also unreceptive to most other efforts to add to the narrow list of national citizenship privileges that Miller provided in *Slaughter-House*.[206]

One dramatic effort to invigorate the clause came as a result of the death sentences that Illinois imposed on eight members of the International Working Peoples' Association (IWPA) for their alleged participation in the Haymarket Square bombing. The explosion killed seven policemen and wounded about seventy others who were trying to break up an IWPA rally protesting vicious police strikebreaking tactics. Determined to get convictions, Illinois police, prosecutors, and the trial judge ran roughshod over normal procedural guarantees; but the Court's precedents made all those rights matters of state regulation. Attorney J. Randolph Tucker boldly tried to reinterpret the precedents from *Slaughter-House* on in order to contend that the privileges and immunities clause protected against the states any constitutional right that was not specifically directed only against the federal government and that was one of the "fundamental rights—common law rights—of man." Like Campbell's *Slaughter-House* brief, his argument required accepting that Fourteenth Amendment privileges included all prerogatives basic to U.S. citizenship, common law, and human rights as well. With Chief Justice Waite writing in *Spies v. Illinois* (1887), the Court dismissed these arguments as not involved in the "determination of the case as it appears on the face of the record."[207]

His choice to avoid rather than reject Tucker's claims seems to have given new life to the dispute over the scope of the clause.[208] First Field, then Harlan recurringly argued for reading section 1 of the Fourteenth Amendment, particularly the privileges and immunities clause, as "incorporating" most of the Bill of Rights, especially its criminal justice procedures.[209] Although they kept what Tucker had termed a "liberal" view of the clause alive, they never prevailed. The content of the privileges and immunities of U.S. citizenship remained severed from doctrines of basic rights, in contrast to the spirit of the postwar amendments, but in keeping with resurgent states' rights views.

National Voting Rights of White Men

The retreat from national protection of civil rights generally during this era, along with opposition to black and female voting rights, dominated Gilded Age legislation and litigation pertaining to the franchise.[210] Though the U.S. remained the nation in the world closest to universal white manhood suffrage, the resulting actions had some restrictive impact on the voting rights even of these citizens.

Congress's major actions affecting voting rights during these years were its refusal to strengthen voting rights enforcement under the Republicans in 1890 and its repeal of major Reconstruction voting rights enforcement mechanisms under the Democrats in 1894. That repeal helped Southern lawmakers disfranchise many poor white Populists as well as blacks. Courts litigated many resulting voting rights controversies, broadly following their pattern on civil rights topics generally: early activism gave way to deference to the states by the late 1890s. But here, the basic legal frame permitting state discriminations had been set before the end of Reconstruction by *Minor v. Happersett* and *United States v. Reese.* They made it clear that the Court did not view the Constitution as conferring any right to vote per se. It only set specific limits on state prerogatives to distribute the franchise as they wished.

Those cases had, however, not settled the question of what powers were implied by the grant of authority to Congress to make or alter regulations governing the "time, place and manner" of elections for House and Senate members (Art. I, sec. 4). In the late 1870s, federal courts proved willing to use both Article I and the Fifteenth Amendment to sustain fairly vigorous enforcement of voting laws, at least as applied to white participation in congressional elections. Up until 1890, most federal decisions involving voting rights treated the issues as judicially cognizable, and many afforded relief. For example, in 1878 Circuit Judge Woods ruled in the spirit of his early support for Reconstruction that Article I, section 4, provided a right to vote in congressional elections to anyone eligible to vote in a state legislative election. He concluded that Congress had the power to protect that right against hostile conspiracies via the 1870 Voting Rights Enforcement Act.[211] The next year, the Supreme Court agreed. In *Ex parte Siebold,* Justice Bradley sustained the constitutionality of that law as applied to a case of ballot-box stuffing in Baltimore. He rejected Maryland's "transcendental view of state sovereignty" in favor of a "fair and obvious" reading of the Constitution as granting state and nation "concurrent" powers over federal elections.[212] Dissenting in *Siebold* and *Ex parte Clarke,* Justice Field sounded the states' rights themes he sometimes favored during this period, when his presidential hopes were at their highest. Here he claimed that because eligibility to vote in congressional elections depended on state laws governing state elections, vote fraud violated state, not national law; and the federal government could not compel a state officer to enforce state laws. Granting state officers that power was a dangerous advance "toward the conversion of our Federal system into a consolidated and centralized government."[213]

The importance of the majority's contrary rulings in *Siebold* and *Clarke* should not be overstated. The justices agreed unanimously and tersely the next year, in 1879, that federal voting rights statutes did not permit the federal judiciary to overturn the result of a state election, even if blacks had unlawfully been intimidated not to vote. But especially when white voters were involved, the courts regularly gave force to congressional laws protecting the franchise, and at least entertained arguments about constitutional limits on the conduct of state elections, until after the failure of the Republicans' 1890 elections bill.[214] Then decisions hostile to federal power over voting multiplied.

Already in 1890, the Supreme Court agreed that elected members of the presidential and vice presidential electoral college were state, not national officials. Thus fraud in their election was outside the scope of federal authority, despite their role in choosing the nation's top executives.[215] It was true that the Constitution explicitly gave Congress only power to determine the time and day of choosing such electors, not the place and manner, as in the case of congressional elections. Yet holding that the presidential electors were federal officers would not have been far-fetched. But the Court under Fuller was bent on a different course.[216] Collectively, its precedents formed a sturdy fence against federal challenges to all but state regulation of congressional elections. Then the 1894 enforcement repeals further sapped judicial authority and resolve to protect the vote of any citizen against hostile state measures.

Thus poor white voters suffered from the inegalitarian political trends they all too often embraced. To be sure, in some national institutions, and among some reformers like Lester Ward, the potential for liberalizing, egalitarian reforms remained visibly alive through the Gilded Age. But the new evolutionary world views and the politics of crafting a national identity that could appeal to both the anxieties and the ambitions of the Protestant native-born white American males, who remained the majority of voters, all favored the rebuilding of innumerable ascriptive hierarchical civic laws and institutions during this time of change. With these in place, the nation's wealth and power grew rapidly, but highly unequally. For African-American, Native American, Chinese-American, and most other immigrant men, and all women, the prospect that American citizenship would be structured in ways true to egalitarian liberal republican principles increasingly seemed a fiction more extravagant than any Algeresque rags-to-riches fantasy.

12

Progressivism and the New American Empire, 1898–1912

Though scholars dispute what progressivism was, few deny that both major parties and American politics generally changed during the first two decades of the twentieth century in ways that comprise a distinct Progressive Era. The impact of the range of political, social, and intellectual movements that may be termed *progressivism* is proven by the 1912 election.[1] In it a Progressive third-party candidate, Theodore Roosevelt, ran against Democrat Woodrow Wilson, who espoused a less nationalistic version of progressivism, and against Roosevelt's former protégé, Republican William Howard Taft, a conservative who still supported many of Roosevelt's reforms. Though he was by then reviled by followers of the other two, even Taft falls in a lineage that deserves to be termed "right progressivism." Conversely, the surprisingly successful Socialist candidate that year, Eugene V. Debs, had long shared many positions with left progressives, though he remained more radical. After Wilson won, he set about implementing his version of progressivism until World War I interrupted and modified those efforts, sharpening their nationalistic and anti-socialist elements in ways that would have an enduring impact on American citizenship in the twentieth century.[2]

Important as those later developments were, by 1912 all the main reformulations of American civic ideologies that would compete in the rest of the twentieth century were already visible. They confirm beyond question the persistent, often resurgent appeal of inegalitarian ascriptive civic ideologies, along with egalitarian liberal and republican themes, in American politics. Hence it is in 1912 that this historical survey will close. This point is admittedly a bit arbitrary, for the Progressive years represented only the deepening and broadening of trends already visible in the Gilded Age, and the most important formulations of, particularly, left progressive thought on citizenship were still to come. Trying to adhere to precise boundaries in this survey is futile, and I will not hesitate to refer to later developments to complete the picture. But by 1912, American political thinkers had already woven together many inherited strands into significantly new views of U.S. civic identity that have since largely defined the spectrum of national thought. I will argue that, from the perspective of U.S. citizenship laws, the Progressive Era should be seen as a period of triumph for centrist versions of progressivism, a triumph that would last largely intact through the 1950s. Then modern descendants of the left progressive views of thinkers like John Dewey, Horace Kallen, W. E. B. Du Bois, and Charlotte Perkins Gilman came to the fore, championed by the civil rights and women's movements and the Great Society.

The civic visions that instead prevailed for over half a century, advanced by centrist progressives like Theodore Roosevelt and the political writer he most praised, Herbert Croly, were far less inclusive. They held that the U.S. should be a modern democratically and scientifically guided nation that was also culturally ordered, unified, and civilized due to the predominance of northern European elements in its populace and customs. Thus structured and guided, centrist progressives promised, Americans could do more than cope with a rapidly changing world: they would lead it. After the anxieties and strife of the Gilded Age, that positive message was so exciting a vision of national identity that both major parties tried to offer it.[3]

The appropriate starting point for the Progressive period is thus the Spanish-American War. If the exclusionary civic policies of the Gilded Age reflected desperate efforts to limit the transformations wrought by immigration, urbanization, industrialization, and Reconstruction, the war instead reflected the exuberant new confidence of progressives like Colonel Roosevelt. They believed that the U.S. had abundant technological and cultural capacities to order the future, at home and abroad. The Republicans' defenses of colonial rule over their new subjects made it clear, however, that this future included racial hierarchies. GOP leaders relinquished almost entirely their old opposition to the racist ideologies of their Democratic opponents, even as Democrats found that they could sustain voter appeal only by showing that, they, too, had leaders who were mastering instead of resisting the forces of change. Hence it is fitting that in 1912, the Republicans' split caused Roosevelt to lose to a man who was a founding father of the nation's new faith in scientific guidance and expert management, but who was also a Southern Democrat concerned to extend Jim Crow.[4] As much as Roosevelt's platform, that mix defined centrist progressivism.

The Varieties of Progressive Ideology

Though progressivism can be painted in many ways, some features are widely accepted. The bulk of the thinkers and activists now commonly labeled progressive tended to be products of suburban or small-town, steadfastly Protestant, moderately prosperous families, inspired by Lincoln's liberal Republicanism to believe in the nobility of moral initiatives in public life, but buffeted by the wrenching changes of the late nineteenth century. They sought to comprehend, to purify, and above all to direct their rapidly transforming world by building a range of new organizations and professions, from scientific corporate managers and public administrators to scientific lawyers, economists, political scientists, sociologists, social psychologists, and social workers, as well as theologically liberal social gospel reformers. Most professed beliefs in empirical scientific expertise, experimentation, efficiency via rational organization, evolution, pragmatically defined values, and the fundamental reality of human interdependence. They thought that these beliefs supported ultimate democratic control of government and values of honesty, community service, and virtuous personal self-realization. The outlooks of the masses were less converted to scientific pragmatism than those of many leaders, and so in some ways the gulf between American elite and mass beliefs present since the Revolution deepened severely. But because elites from right to left often shared these new progressive perspectives, that gulf did not as yet find a strong political voice.[5]

Even so, this elite convergence did not mean an end to right, left, and center divisions in American politics. Progressive tenets were deployed on behalf of many economic policies, from aid to huge, allegedly efficient corporations and trusts, to strict laissez-faire, to governmental regulations, even to some public ownership, aimed at protecting workers, consumers, and the environment. Progressives also argued for locating power everywhere from local neighborhoods to centralized national institutions, even transnational bodies, and they supplied defenses for clashing programs of heightened democratic participation, strong executives, and the creation of nonpartisan, independent expert regulators. That is why not only the two Roosevelts and Wilson, but also Taft, and later Herbert Hoover, shared many elements of progressivism. Influenced by Herbert Spencer and William Graham Sumner (whom Taft credited with most "stimulating my mental activities" at Yale), such "right progressives" embraced the refounding of economic individualism on new evolutionary and pragmatic grounds and esteemed not only market forces but also scientific management and even some voluntary "cooperative" coordination among governmental and private actors.[6] The views of American citizenship that emerged during these years could be spun out in similar variety. But on many citizenship issues, there were powerful tendencies for Americans to fall into two main camps, with one far larger than the other.[7]

That larger camp, which I am terming *centrist progressivism*, represented the views of people whom scholars have labeled "organizational," "administrative," or "social control" progressives. They strove to bring economic, political, and moral order to their turbulent world by adopting many modern innovations while trying to sustain the finest cultural verities of the past. Despite some differences in their ultimate civic visions, members of this camp increasingly agreed on the importance of cultural homogeneity, the dangers of immigration, the improvidence of black enfranchisement, the propriety of Anglo Saxon racial domination, and the maintenance of some basic distinctions in the domestic and civic responsibilities of men and women, even as they sincerely professed themselves to be committed to democracy and human rights. Roosevelt was right to regard Herbert Croly as the most important centrist progressive thinker. More fully than anyone else, Croly worked through the foundational arguments for progressive civic policies of social control, including the propriety of American imperialism. Other progressives provided defenses of hierarchical and exclusionary domestic citizenship policies. On these ascriptive issues, right progressives like Taft were one with centrists like Roosevelt. Taft's condescending tutelary reign over the Philippines as Roosevelt's appointed governor perfectly suited his President's advocacy of rule by the "English-speaking races." They parted company on how far legislatures and courts should service corporate interests, with Taft (even) more pro-business. Centrists like Roosevelt and Wilson, in turn, differed in their degree of attachment to national versus state or local governance, and on the forms of governmental aid to corporations, consumers and, workers. Still, the agreements between Roosevelt's New Nationalism and Wilson's New Freedom were more obvious than their differences.[8]

The greatest figure among left progressives, advancing a new conception of American citizenship that was at once both more truly democratic and more cosmopolitan, was John Dewey. Yet even Dewey was often embarrassingly reticent on issues of race, ethnicity, and to some degree gender. Thus the possibilities for left progressive civic conceptions were most fully worked through, albeit in contrasting ways, by writers like Horace Kallen, Randolph Bourne, W. E. B. Du Bois, and Charlotte Gilman. But though their different civic ideals would become so influential in America that for many they now define progressivism, they are a minor part of the story here. None came close to prevailing during the Progressive years.

Centrist Progressivism: Croly and Nationalist Democratic Citizenship. Herbert Croly's 1909 classic, *The Promise of American Life*, never found a mass audience, but its elite impact was remarkable. It helped define the meaning of Roosevelt's New Nationalist progressivism for Roosevelt himself. It did so, despite Croly's genuine attraction to an extraordinarily rich conception of democracy, because his immediate message accorded with the young Walter Lippmann's demand that elite leaders replace "drift" with "mastery." Croly's book was a self-conscious effort to reconstruct American political thought in ways that could capture the best in the nation's Hamiltonian and Jeffersonian traditions while also confronting modern political and intellectual changes. As such, it required reconceiving the liberal, republican, and ascriptive elements in American thought and life.

For Croly, Jeffersonian republicanism contributed a commitment to democracy that deserved recognition as the central American value and purpose; but the Jeffersonians and Jacksonians had been wrong about nearly everything else. The scale and complexity of modern life instead vindicated a variant of Hamilton's liberal economic nationalism. Government must attempt to build community and prosperity at the national level, especially by assisting large-scale, more efficient forms of economic organization—big business and big labor unions. As the addition of unions to this prescription indicated, Croly thought it unconscionably undemocratic for government to aid business interests alone or to make a fetish of property rights. Government also had to be much more than the neutral referee urged by advocates of laissez-faire and "chaotic individualism" like William Graham Sumner and the Jacksonians. It had to play favorites; and it had to be as severe as Sumner toward those who did not serve the national interest. The small businessman was to be allowed to "drown." The nonunion laborer was to be weeded out for the benefit of the economy's "fruit- and flower-bearing plants."[9]

By evoking a Bellamyesque world in which big government, big business, and big labor would order American life efficiently, Croly stirred anxieties even in his own mind about the role that would remain for democratic citizens. He promised that progressive reforms creating a more nationalized democratic citizenship would lead to the realization of "genuine individuality" stemming from personal "distinction" in "the efficient performance of special work." Such fulfillment would come to all, within a "higher level of associated life" approaching human "brotherhood."[10]

But Croly acknowledged and indeed insisted that such individual realization came only through work, and work structured by the regulatory authorities of the larger society in light of the broader community's needs. Personal fulfillment to Croly was only secondarily something spiritual, aesthetic, passionate, or pleasurable. Chiefly it meant an individual's coming to hold a "definite and serviceable position in his surrounding society" in which he would do "special work adapted" to his abilities, but structured and regulated "by the community, and nothing less than the whole community." To provide such work, society should create "a national structure" with "innumerable special niches, adapted to all degrees and kinds of individual development." All people could then find a "particular but essential function" that provided them with "individual fulfillment" as they served their nation.[11]

This corporatist vision of American citizenship resembled a Puritan view of personal realization within one's officially designated vocation, and nationalist republicanism's doctrines of obedient allegiance to central governmental authorities, more than it did liberal privatistic individualism or localistic participatory republicanism. Its apparent potential for coercion was not allayed, moreover, by Croly's often vague rhetoric of democratic purpose. What assurance did an individual have that she really would be fulfilled by work within her niche, and in what sense could a society that weeded out those who did not fit its large-scale, centrally regulated organizations be termed "democratic"? To modern ears, some of Croly's views suggest fascism as much as democracy. Similar doubts were expressed in his own day.

Croly tried to answer such concerns in his more radical 1914 work, *Progressive Democracy*. There he drew on the social psychology of Charles Cooley to argue that the individual, "merely in the sense of a man who inhabits a certain body and possesses a certain continuity of organic sensations, is largely an illusion." The formation of human bodies and minds was "essentially social," so that, Croly claimed, an individual "has no meaning apart from the society in which his individuality has been formed."[12] It was therefore logically impossible for people to achieve fulfillment except by playing their proper roles in their society's realization of its larger purposes.

Croly also assured his readers that those roles included the "incessant and relentless" social criticism required by the inadequacies of current arrangements, along with some measure of obedience. Yet he still presented his progressive democratic citizens as "willing prisoners" to the dictates of allegedly more competent but admittedly dangerous national leaders who would "mold their followers after their own likeness." To reduce the dangers of such leaders, Croly also urged the importance of preserving diverse "smaller societies" within the nation. But these, too, had to "be fitted" into the social "whole," acceding to its "permanent interests and needs."[13] He also promised that in his America, all institutions would become ever more democratic, allowing all to help shape lives that each would find fulfilling. Otherwise, Croly conceded, progressive democracy would be "a snare and an illusion."[14]

But the point at which popular political education would be advanced enough to permit everyone, not just leaders, to participate in shaping the regulations through which the nation defined people's "niches" seemed distant in Croly's writings. And though he was clear on some immediate reforms, the concrete institutions and practices of his democratic utopia—in which people would finally realize "the mystical unity of human nature" along with diverse individual realization—remained so uncertain that Croly was hard-pressed to say why it should define the national purpose.

At times, he responded in good pragmatic fashion that this purpose simply was dominant among U.S. traditions and that it fit with American industrial, political, and social developments, as well as the desires of the American people. He promised that democratic nationalism was thus technically and politically best suited to produce national prosperity. But Croly also buttressed his case through claims, reminiscent of Strong's Protestant Americanism, that the progress he envisioned was part of "the march of Christian civilization." And, like Strong, Croly argued that, claims of "abstract individual rights" notwithstanding, this march should be carried on through colonial expansion. Those peoples who lacked "an accumulated national tradition" were not capable of self-governance. This was "the condition of the majority of Asiatic and African peoples." They required some "preliminary process of tutelage" like Western imperial rule if they were to be capable of "genuine national advance" in the future.[15]

Croly appeared to believe that such progress might come for all peoples, and he did not endorse the cognate arguments for subjecting African-Americans and Native Americans to extended "tutelage" within the U.S. He decried quests for excessive internal "homogeneity" and "uniformity," contending that a nation "gains enormously from a wide variety of individual differences." Many niches can then be well filled. But Croly dismissed cosmopolitan ideals of a "universal nation." A people must be "effectively united by national habits, traditions, and purposes," and any "destruction or weakening of nationalities" in favor of some "ideal bond" would only destroy social order.[16] These arguments, and his endorsement of imperial rule over Asians and Africans, may well have made his grand narrative of American democratic realization more persuasive to many of his fellow citizens. These tenets also, however, left ample room for others to contend that such hierarchical tutelary governance was needed at home as well as abroad. Hence Croly's vision of nationalized, democratized U.S. citizenship authorized an America designed along highly unequal, ascriptive lines.

Though he opposed imperialism, the Wisconsin labor historian and progressive reformer John R. Commons, a product of the Hopkins "Teutonic" school, applied similar reasoning to support immigration restrictions. In a 1903 article, "Races and Democracy," he affirmed that the Declaration of Independence should not be given a "literal interpretation." It was "futile" to extend citizenship and the franchise to people unfit for them. Commons said that the "fearful collapse of the experiment" of black enfranchisement had been "inevitable," and he thought that immigration of non-Anglo-Saxons equally mistaken. Races were "the fundamental division of mankind," established "in the very blood and physical constitution," and alterable only by "the slow processes of the centuries." Even changes in religion, governments, work, language, and education might not improve the lower races' "physical, mental, and moral capacities and incapacities," so they could not be allowed to shape the education and environment of higher ones. Both the labor organizations and the Immigration Restriction League that Commons advised thought that these arguments provided ample ammunition against older liberal traditions of equal rights and open immigration.[17]

The great shift that had occurred in U.S. thought from the Radical Republicans to the Progressive Era was even more visible in a lecture by Charles Francis Adams, Jr., to distinguished Virginians assembled at the Richmond Academy of Music in 1908. First Adams reminded all of who he was: great-grandson of John Adams, who had signed the Declaration of Independence; grandson of John Quincy Adams, who had defeated the gag rule; son of the ambassador who had kept Britain from siding with the Confederacy; an "old anti-slavery man" himself who had fought "four long years" as a Union officer and who had then pioneered railroad reform. He also told his listeners, inaccurately but in line with Northern mythology, that the American System was "founded on the assumed basis of a common humanity," so that persons "of all races were welcome" to become first denizens and then "natives."

But, Adams announced, the nation's "archaic" political theory premised on "the equality of men" had "broken down." A modern "scientific" understanding of blacks had displaced "scriptural" accounts of human brotherhood. Reconstruction now seemed "absurd," "worse than a crime," a "political blunder, as ungenerous as it was gross." Adams did not know how the South should deal with its African-American population, but he believed that the region could resolve the problem by itself. Blacks "must not ask to be held up, or protected from outside," any longer. The message was clear: if white Southerners thought that blacks had to be segregated and relegated to inferior status, at least for a long period of "tutelage," liberal Northern whites and the federal government should not stop them. That policy was, after all, what modern science dictated, and what Northerners were proposing for peoples of color around the globe.[18]

Though many African-Americans condemned such acquiescence as bitter betrayal, whites attended more to the reassuring messages of Booker T. Washington, trained in industrial education at General Armstrong's Hampton Institute. Washington's famous Atlanta Exposition address in 1895 called for blacks to turn away from seeking political office and social equality to "cast down your bucket where you are." They should develop skills for "common labour" and the "common occupations of life." His rationale, too, echoed the Spencerian evolutionist reasoning of the day: blacks must obtain progress via "severe and constant struggle" rather than "artificial forcing." Only as African-Americans strengthened themselves and proved their fitness through competition in "the markets of the world" would they be turned into "useful and intelligent" citizens. In the meantime, Washington implicitly conceded, segregation and disfranchisement should be expected.[19]

Washington and men like Adams, Commons, and Croly could all support racial hierarchies at home and abroad while believing that they were sincerely attached to democratic republicanism and to individual rights—if those doctrines were properly understood in light of evolutionary theory and scientific evidence of racial capacities. Hence their various fusions of ongoing liberal democratic idealism with ascriptive Americanism promised to satisfy middle-class white Protestants' desires for social control and continued cultural hegemony. The revised intellectual outlooks of the day argued that the best in traditional American ideals had been race-specific all along. That is why many passages by these writers appear to exhibit allegiance to Myrdal's American Creed of equal rights and justice for all races. But to read these statements as implying that all races should have equal rights at present, as Reconstruction radicals had held, is to reject their self-understandings without warrant.

The manner in which these themes in progressive thought could produce juxtapositions that seem startlingly contradictory today is well shown in a neglected tract by S. J. Duncan-Clark, *The Progressive Movement: Its Principles and Its Programme.* Published in 1913 with a ringing introduction by Theodore Roosevelt, the book was a manifesto for his Progressive Bull Moose party. It is rich with Crolyesque motifs, including claims that progressivism combines the best of Jeffersonian democracy and Lincoln Republicanism, that it recognizes that the nation's "governmental clothes" must be "enlarged" to meet the needs of a growing "social organism," that "men at the top" must inspire a "social consciousness" more integrating than "class consciousness" which will enable the nation to turn the "Big Corporation" to the national good.[20] Duncan-Clark also called for more direct democracy, criticized the "plutocracy" and the judiciary for placing "property rights" over "human rights," and called for the "interdependent" nation's "organic welfare"—indeed, evolution itself—to be directed by "the reasoning power of man." This democratic, national regulatory vision promised to create forms of civic life that realized the "highest ideal of citizenship, which is politics in its true significance." That civic ideal was, as both social gospel reformers and civic republicans had urged, community "service."[21]

Amid these standard tropes, Duncan-Clark also promised that the Progressive party would not repeat the Republican error of "attempting to force the political recognition of an inferior race upon an unwilling and superior people."

Instead, it would let "justice for the negro and the white" be achieved by "voluntary" efforts, with the party displaying "the spirit of mutual forbearance and far-sighted patriotism." As with Adams's speech, forbearance meant accepting segregation. Then Duncan-Clark unashamedly cited the soaringly fatuous endorsement of "equal rights as a fact of life instead of a catch-word of politics" delivered by Indiana Senator Albert Beveridge, the chair of the 1912 Progressive party convention and a man made famous by his stunningly racist championing of American imperialism. For these centrist progressives, values of science, economic growth, equal rights, and democracy were part of a well-ordered modern society; but so were systems subordinating "inferior" races to "advanced" ones.

Similarly, Duncan-Clark promised that progressives would not "recognize sex distinctions in the rights of citizenship," and he firmly endorsed female suffrage. But here, too, his egalitarianism was sharply qualified. Progressives of his stripe, at least, continued to believe that "woman's happiest and most useful sphere is the home," and that the franchise should be extended to her "in order that she may be fitter equipped to defend her home domain." Duncan-Clark was especially concerned that women were being driven by economic forces to take outside jobs, thereby causing the "family circle" to break into "fragments," at a high cost to effective child rearing. The ultimate aim of the progressive laws that female suffrage would support was to enable "woman to return to her home, to regain her queenly place at the hearthstone, to be once more, in the sweetest and fullest meaning of the words, the wife and mother." Motherhood was, after all, "the highest and noblest function of woman." For these beliefs, too, progressives could cite leading intellectuals like the psychologist Stanley Hall. Again, the new sciences served to justify ascriptive, hierarchical elements in the nationalized democratic citizenship high-minded centrist progressives wished to create.[22]

Left Progressivism: Dewey and Democratic Cultural Pluralism. In contrast, many left progressives rejected doctrines of racial and gender inferiority and their associated policies of imperialism, immigration restriction, and involuntary segregation. The alternative, more tolerant, inclusive, and pluralistic conceptions of civic identity these writers defended have since become so familiar that progressivism now often first conjures up images of left progressives like John Dewey and Jane Addams. But up to 1912, even these figures produced few statements attacking the reigning hierarchical conceptions of Americanism. The most important (and contrasting) writings on American identity by Dewey, Kallen, and Bourne came first with the military preparedness campaign prior to World War I, and then in agitations over immigration restriction during the 1920s. Though culturally pluralist and cosmopolitan sensibilities are detectable in their earlier writings, during the Progressive Era these civic visions were still struggling to be born.

John Dewey agreed with Croly that American identity should center on realizing democracy, which would promote both individual development and social flourishing. But, shaped by his work with Jane Addams's Hull House program for immigrants, Dewey was wary of Rooseveltian New Nationalism and efforts to herd people into big, efficient organizations scientifically managed by strong leaders. Like Woodrow Wilson's rhetoric if not his practice, Dewey tilted instead toward Jeffersonian traditions of local, participatory democracy and openness to immigrants, reformulated on pragmatist premises and purged as far as possible of racism.

Dewey also agreed with Croly that man was a "social animal in the make-up of his ideas, sentiments, and deliberate behavior" shaped by the "social medium" in which he was raised, and that a person therefore learned to "be human" via developing into "an individually distinctive member of a community." But Dewey differed from Croly on two basic points. First, he contended that people are products of a great "pluralism" of groups—towns and neighborhoods, churches, families, ethnic groups, professions—and that no particular group identity could be treated as primary. Certainly Croly's "nation" could not; it was "infinitely many things," "many associations not a single organization." Fulfillment through group life therefore meant pursuing multiple memberships that could promote "all-around growth."

Second, Dewey insisted more strongly than Croly that persons could realize their best potential only by exercising "a responsible share . . . in proportion to capacity, in shaping the aims and policies of the social groups" to which they belonged.[23] Dewey also knew that it was impractical for most persons to exercise any meaningful role in directing the life of a community so large as a modern nation-state, and that its impact on their lives tended to be more remote and indirect. He therefore argued that smaller groups were "primary" in human life, the "real social units" where community in "its deepest and richest sense" would be found.[24]

The national society and government thus should not be, Dewey said, a "supreme end in itself." The national state was a "secondary and provisional," albeit crucial, "instrumentality" for "promoting and protecting other and more voluntary forms of association." In an image borrowed from Horace Kallen, Dewey likened the national state to "the conductor of an orchestra," who "harmonizes the activities" of those who actually produce sound. Yet no state did all the conducting: many communities, including families, cultural associations, and religions, crossed national boundaries. Still, nation-states were the primary harmonizers. Hence national governments should take democratically authorized measures to promote the prosperity of all groups and to prevent "negative struggle and needless conflict" so that all groups would "interact flexibly and fully." And because groups contributed to their members' realization only insofar as they were truly voluntary, Dewey thought that a democratic national state also should promote "desirable" democratic associations and restrain or even reconstruct "injurious" groups that denied their members "liberty and security."[25]

These precepts displayed internal tensions that would eventually plague policymakers. Dewey's ideas deprecated national civic identity on behalf of smaller but often transnational groups; yet they simultaneously urged the national state to intervene to render all groups internally democratic and voluntaristic. Indeed, Dewey finally had to repudiate Kallen's orchestra metaphor for the state. It denied what he saw as the prevailing reality, that large nation-states must exist, have purposes of their own, and have power sufficient for those purposes, which ought to be democratic. But Dewey was always opposed in principle to all forms of ascriptive Americanism, as well as to the deference to organizational "leaders" and "experts" that introduced new hierarchies into so much progressive thinking. He regularly called for democracy to embrace diversity and "develop the capacities of human individuals without respect to race, sex, class or economic status." He decried all narrow forms of "nationalism," including the "melting pot" ideal of Americanization, which he saw as a means to promote "Anglo-saxondom," not "genuine assimilation to one another" on a basis of equal respect. Dewey advocated "internationalism and interracialism" and warned against reproducing old inequalities via differentiated educational opportunities. Those concerns generated a civic vision that stressed democratic participation more sweepingly than in classical republican thought and universal opportunities for self-development even more than in earlier liberal thought. It also depicted national political structures as ultimately transitory devices, not objects of reverence; and it denied any principled place to traditional Americanist ascriptive hierarchies.

Yet Dewey not only admitted that modern technological and economic systems favored the existence of large states; he acquiesced at times in nationalistic foreign policies, immigration restriction, and restricted vocational education for American blacks. His erstwhile admirer, the brilliant young critic Randolph Bourne, bitterly criticized Dewey for failing to oppose World War I, which Bourne thought had been sold to Americans via a militaristic patriotism of "mystic blood." In wartime essays Bourne developed an ideal of a "new spiritual citizenship" that was even more explicitly "trans-national" than Dewey's. Bourne called for the United States to become the first "international nation," devoted to a "nationalism of internationalism" that would permit, even encourage Americans to have two or more national citizenships in order to replace jingoism with "sympathy" and cooperation across artificial political boundaries. Such a nation could, Bourne thought, be "integrated and disciplined," but it would be united around goals that were "democratic and pacific" as well as "socialized and international," fostered by a system of national service. Dewey thought that some of Bourne's ideas went too far, but he recognized in them the sort of new, cosmopolitan conception of American civic identity that he himself had already sketched.[26]

Indeed, even Dewey's view rejected all forms of ascriptivism too sweepingly for Horace Kallen, whose formulation of democratic cultural pluralism proved far more influential than Bourne's radical "trans-national Americanism" or even Dewey's cosmopolitan democratic creed. Kallen—a pragmatic philosopher trained by William James and a colleague of Dewey's at Columbia, but also a Jew who was proud of his ethnicity—was appalled by the assimilationist "Americanization" efforts and vilification of foreigners that accompanied mobilization for World War I. He agreed with Dewey that the American national state should be a democratic instrument aiding the life of "primary groupings." But for Kallen, by far the most important of these groups were ethnocultural communities, which played the role in his thought that racial or national identity did in the writings of evolutionary and historicist ascriptive Americanists. The traits of their cultural groups shaped people so much that cultural "acquisitions" became a "second nature" that people could not and should not ever discard. Hence, full realization of one's social identity could be found only within such cultural communities, not the broader polity.[27]

In Kallen's view, America should be a democracy, but a "democracy of nationalities, cooperating voluntarily and autonomously through common institutions in the enterprise of self-realization through perfection of men according to their kind." So should all other nations. To Kallen, American citizenship represented nothing special, "no more than citizenship in any land with free institutions." And because the "national cultures" making up the American "federation or commonwealth" were rarely confined within the borders of the U.S., Kallen agreed with Dewey and Bourne that Americans should see themselves as "trans-national" citizens or "citizens of the world." Every American cultural group, moreover, should display respect in public life toward "spiritual expressions having a different base." But Kallen's vision was not truly cosmopolitan. He stressed that it was within their cultural groups that persons found their own true "home."

Unlike Dewey's and Bourne's positions, Kallen's view was thus able to capture a crucial aspect of ascriptive Americanism's appeal: it assured everyone of their organic and unalterable membership in an inherently meaningful community, instead of seeing all group affiliations as voluntary. But by the same token, it seemed to preach public acquiescence to the traditional internal lives of different communities, no matter how undemocratic they might be, and it strongly suggested that people belonged to ineradicably different cultural "kinds." They might associate tolerantly, democratically, and productively, but they ultimately lived in unalterable separation. Dewey wrote Kallen that though they agreed on much, he feared that Kallen verged on endorsing "segregation," a charge that Kallen did not deny.[28]

But Kallen was responding to what he felt to be true of himself, to what many members of ethnic, racial, and religious groups in America also found true for themselves, and to what most intellectuals still taught. The view that one's culture constituted a "second nature" was starting to be challenged in its most literal form by geneticists like August Weismann, who waged a successful campaign to discredit the neo-Lamarckian notion that acquired characteristics could be inherited. Hence specific cultures were probably too short-lived to have any significant effect on biological evolution. The anthropologist Franz Boas was also disputing claims that northern European cultures represented later, unqualifiedly superior stages of human progress. Most scholars, however, remained unconvinced. Whatever their connections to human biology, cultural differences were real, deep, and virtually unalterable, and American Christian, Anglo-Saxon culture was best.

These views were so prevalent that during these years, even a radical African-American intellectual like W. E. B. Du Bois still argued in terms of Gilded Age evolutionary racial premises. In an 1897 essay, "The Conservation of the Races," Du Bois accepted that variations in historically shaped cultural identity did indeed make races, not individuals, the basic units of humanity, the "central thought of all history." In a manner reminiscent of historicist advocates of immigration restriction like Lodge, Du Bois defined a race as a "family of human beings, generally of common blood and language, always of common history, traditions and impulses, who are both voluntarily and involuntarily striving together for the accomplishment of certain more or less vividly conceived ideals of life." He also agreed that the "deeper differences" of the races were not "physical" but "spiritual, psychical differences—undoubtedly based on the physical, but infinitely transcending them." As the races had developed, physical differences had lessened, but "spiritual and mental differences" had increased. Du Bois thought that every race had some "spiritual message" to give to all humanity. To do so, however, each race must be developed "not as individuals," but as a "distinct" people.

Du Bois envisioned this "distinct" development of different races as ultimately only transitory, however. It was to culminate in a "human brotherhood," a realization of all races' shared humanity, once each race had accomplished its "mission" of making a special contribution to civilization. Thus he offered a sense of

American citizenship that was, for the present, something like Kallen's. The U.S. should be a country in which "men of different races" could strive for "their race ideals" while being united by other factors—"political ideals . . . language," even religion. The shared political ideals included an insistence that no races or individuals face "inequality in their opportunities of development" of the sort Du Bois saw Booker T. Washington as wrongfully accepting. But because beyond that "our Americanism does not go," Du Bois, like Washington, called not for "social equality" between the races but rather a "social equilibrium." It would include equal opportunities for all, but with each race living largely in distinct "race organizations" of education, communication, business, and culture. With elitist progressives like Lippmann, Du Bois was also skeptical of the current abilities of the masses, so he called for black progress to be led by a "talented tenth" of elites like himself. In the early 1890s he was even prepared to accept disfranchisement for the black masses, though he soon became a more militant opponent of all denials of equal opportunity on the basis of race.[29]

Du Bois's example underscores how heightened economic, racial, and ethnic tensions, a broader sense of turbulent change and disorder in American life, and intellectual developments appearing to cement the reality of racial differences, all converged during these years to strengthen the appeal of evolution-based ascriptive views across the spectrum of American civic thought. As Americans confronted these new circumstances and beliefs, republicanism was reconceived as more direct democracy, either national or local. Liberalism was recast as expert-guided social engineering. Yet ascriptive Americanism, recast as racial destiny, now seemed the most scientific and politically necessary tradition of all. For many it had become the master category defining access to citizenship and full rights within it.

Atop Ascription: Progressivism, Capitalism, and Democratic Citizenship

Even so, conventional accounts are right to stress that in many respects this was an era of democratization. Though few favored unbridled direct democracy, progressives worked for a wide range of institutional reforms aimed at increasing popular control over representatives. They favored a number of means to limit the power of party "machines": nominations via direct primaries instead of conventions; direct election of Senators and the President; popular recall of elected officials and of Supreme Court rulings on constitutionality; and secret ballots, short ballots, and nonpartisan, at-large local elections. Many came to support female suffrage, along with some direct popular decisionmaking via initiative and referendum. They supported regulations to improve the workplace and home conditions of both men and women and to direct the great corporate generators of wealth to the public good, if they were not to be broken up.[30]

This advocacy of laws that challenged laissez-faire principles and many corporate interests reflected both progressives' concern for consumers' well-being and their desires to make democratic citizens, not businesses, politically primary. Corporate lawyers, Spencerian economic ideologues, and some old Democratic opponents of governmental aid to any special interest joined in denouncing such measures, and they gained many allies on the federal bench. As Eldon Eisenach has argued, the courts and constitutional litigation thus formed the one arena where centrist progressive conceptions had limited success. The Progressive Era is instead also the start of the period that constitutional historians have long termed the *Lochner* era, after the 1905 case of *Lochner v. New York*. There the Supreme Court invalidated a law passed *unanimously* by the New York legislature which put an end to the sweatshop conditions recent immigrant workers suffered under in myriad small bakeries in New York City. The Court thought that the measure violated the economic liberties to contract and work as they wished for both bakery owners and employees, liberties it now believed to be implicit in the due process clause of the Fourteenth Amendment, contrary to the views of the *Slaughter-House* majority. Justice Rufus Peckham, a Grover Cleveland Democrat from New York, wrote for the Court and characterized the law in old Jacksonian terms as conferring a kind of unnecessary privilege on bakery employees, who were not wards of the state and needed no legislative aid to get fair contracts. In a remark suggestive of the alarm that many federal judges felt about the rising tide of progressive regulation, Peckham grumbled that such "interference on the part of the legislatures of the several States with the ordinary trades and occupations of the people seems to be on the increase." Four justices dissented, with the Massachusetts Republican Oliver Wendell Holmes, Jr., expressing the progressive view that "the majority" had the right to "embody their opinions in law" on economic issues without judicial interference: "The Fourteenth Amendment does not enact Mr. Herbert Spencer's *Social Statics*."[31]

As Holmes thus indicated, constitutional doctrines of robust individual economic liberties were defended not just by selfish businessmen or old-line believers in Jacksonian laissez-faire but also by followers of Spencer and Sumner, who believed that science showed how regulation impeded rather than furthered social progress. Thus the Progressive years were a time in which not only was much constitutional law recast in more firmly pro-business modes, but also certain strands of progressivism contributed to that pattern. Nonetheless, even centrist progressives like Croly who openly favored American support for large corporations were critical of the power of corporate lawyers and the restrictive interpretations of the Constitution they won from courts.[32] In general, the centrists' most striking departures from their commitments to democracy came not in their limited support for corporate legal privileges and class inequalities but in their open endorsements of renewed ascriptive hierarchies. That, at least, is the pattern visible in American citizenship laws.

Rights of National Citizenship: Article III Jurisdiction. This pattern is apparent if we compare how Progressive Era legislators and jurists treated corporate "citizens" with how they regarded citizens and would-be citizens who were not native-born white men. Corporations were not exceptionally favored, but ethnocultural outsiders were consistently placed at a disadvantage.

Access to federal courts under diversity of citizenship jurisdiction remained a central arena of conflict over corporate privileges during the Progressive Era. But even in these *Lochner* years, the Court rejected many corporate efforts to shift their disputes to federal courts whenever they so desired.[33] The justices faced dockets burgeoning at daunting rates, professional criticisms of the inefficiency of frequent removals of corporate cases to federal courts, and attacks by progressive leaders and the popular press on pro-corporate decisions. The justices seemed to save the political capital they wished to spend on corporate protection for their more substantive constitutional rulings.[34] In any case, they generally presented themselves not as championing corporate capitalism so much as steadfastly sustaining governmental neutrality toward the struggles of different economic actors. In so doing they were rejecting Croly's calls to abandon the ideal of economic neutrality and to side with the large-scale economic actors, corporate and union, that could build a better civic future.[35] They instead struck down laws they saw as conferring special favors, while sustaining some progressive state laws that they deemed valid exercises of state police powers.

The dominant rhetoric of the federal benches was well expressed in *United States v. Milwaukee Refrigerator Transit Co.*, a lower court case decided the same year as *Lochner*, 1905. District judge Sanborn wrote that there was

> no doubt some tendency in these days to accept general and vague charges of wrongdoing on the part of the corporations at a premium. Much has happened to arouse public feeling on this sensitive subject. For many years transportation development was encouraged in every possible way. The municipal aid craze was an early form of such stimulation. Praise for those who were seeking command of the trade of the world was unstinted and without dissent, and criticism forgotten. But now that we are beginning to feel the tyranny of arbitrary and overwhelming industrial and commercial power, the tendency is

to go to the other extreme, and it becomes easy to excite prejudice leading to injustice. The courts will no doubt be somewhat influenced by such tendency; but so far as possible it is for them to keep fundamental rules steadily in view, and with discrimination and careful reflection see to it that injustice is prevented.

Sanborn clearly wanted the judiciary to protect corporations, and he did so in the case, but not from unqualified admiration. Rather he criticized both undue governmental favoritism and hostility, a policy previously violated in favor of corporations.[36]

The path of diversity litigation gave some credibility to the insistence of many federal judges that they were seeking regulatory even-handedness, not pro-corporate rules. To be sure, the diversity citizenship of corporations remained unimpaired. Federal courts also still followed the *Railway Co. v. James* rule confining corporate citizenship to the state of first incorporation, a doctrine that maintained broad corporate access to federal courts.[37] But on many other points vital to corporations' forum-shopping capacities, the Supreme Court ruled against them.[38] Most striking was a decision written in 1906 by the author of *Lochner*, Justice Peckham. *Security Mutual Life Insurance Co. v. Prewitt* returned the Court to the thorny issue of state efforts to discourage corporate removals to federal courts. Astonishingly, Peckham sustained Kentucky's revocation of corporate licenses if companies exercised their acknowledged right to seek such removals.[39] He reasoned that because a state could exclude any out-of-state corporation it wished, it could constitutionally revoke its earlier permission to do business on this or any other ground. Although a corporation could not legally be compelled to renounce its removal rights, then, it could be denied the chance to do business in the state if it exercised them. Such state laws left businesses the "option" of either not using their removal rights or going elsewhere.[40]

To dissenting justices Day and Harlan, this ruling preserved only formal rights of removal while permitting states to negate them in practice. Four years later, Day managed to ignore the *Security Mutual* decision while ruling the opposite way for the Court, leaving the law unsettled on this point until the corporations prevailed in 1922.[41] Thus *Security Mutual* did not represent a major blow to corporate interests. Even so, it confirms that *Lochner* jurisprudence drew not just on social Darwinist laissez-faire and pro-capitalist views but also on traditional Democratic notions hostile to special privileges and accepting of state regulations truly aimed at the public good as the judges defined it.[42] Those outlooks still rejected corporate citizenship for anything other than diversity purposes and limited the pro-corporate cast even of diversity cases.[43] The Progressive years, then, were on balance an era of contraction, not growth, for the "citizenship" of corporations.

Privileges and Immunities. The Fuller Court's aid to corporations continued instead via clauses like the due process and equal protection guarantees, which referred to persons, not citizens. To read rights of citizenship expansively would have conflicted with the many forms of second-class political membership that centrist progressive lawmakers and judges generally accepted. Unsurprisingly, then, the Fuller Court eschewed many opportunities to give more expansive readings to the Constitution's two civic privileges and immunities clauses. There were exceptions, but they were few.[44] Exploited workers, abused African-Americans, and accused persons suffering under arbitrary state criminal procedures all tried to persuade the Court that they had privileges and immunities of U.S. citizenship under the Fourteenth Amendment that the states were violating.[45] Until his long service on the bench came to an end in 1911, Justice Harlan valiantly insisted that the clause deserved to be given some such broader reading, but to no avail.[46] His repeated failures did not, moreover, spark many public protests. With the federal courts striking down regulations in the name of non-explicit liberties, the day when progressives would see the judiciary as a vehicle for protecting the rights of disadvantaged citizens was far in the future.

The Guarantee Clause. The Supreme Court's new willingness to use the due process clause and other provisions to intervene more frequently against state governments did prompt more questions about the meaning of the Article IV guarantee of a "republican government" in each state. Remembering Reconstruction, some Republicans thought that the Court might be persuaded to use the clause to combat the ongoing efforts of Democrats to lock white and black Republicans out of the "redeemed" Southern governments. Conservatives thought that they might instead use it to challenge the efforts of Progressive reformers to introduce new democratic devices, like initiative and referendum, at the state level. But here, too, the Court resisted any departure from its passive guarantee clause precedents. Enforcement of the clause, it still held, was strictly a matter for Congress and the President. Despite an occasional Harlan dissent, the judges were neither partisan enough in regard to Republican voter exclusions nor conservative enough in response to Progressive reforms to overturn the mass of earlier deferential decisions.[47]

Voting Rights. Correspondingly, the retreat from federal judicial protection of voting rights that began during the late Gilded Age became virtually complete during the Progressive Era. Acquiescence in black disfranchisement, discussed below, drove all vote-related doctrines. Hence, across the board in voting cases, the Court either deferred to the states outright or encouraged the use of technicalities to void voting rights claims.[48] Such decisions plainly signaled that the Court would no longer respond to any but the most blatantly unconstitutional state denials of voting rights in federal elections, and that it would do even less in regard to state elections.[49]

The near-total failure of federal courts and Congress to expand either the content of national citizenship rights or the range of those entitled to claim them during the Progressive Era is significant. It indicates that, contrary to Hartzian expectations, the civic vision of the centrist progressives never defined national identity chiefly in terms of personal liberties. Instead, centrists sought to build both order and national loyalty through civic measures designed to bolster what they took to be traditional national traits, including the organic racial and ethnic character, of the U.S. citizenry. Doing so, they promised, would usher in a new era of national glory.

Ascriptive Progressive Citizenship: The New American Empire

That glory was to begin with the United States's emergence as a global imperial power. The debates among U.S. elites about what to do with the various islands obtained as a result of the Spanish-American War in 1898 (the Philippines, Guam, and Puerto Rico, accompanied by the final annexation of Hawaii) display familiar liberal and republican elements, but evolutionary racial ideologies are especially abundant. All three ideological strands were invoked and blended even by sharply opposed political actors. Imperialists deployed liberalism, republicanism, and racism to contend that America's lucky new subjects should be tutored in enlightened civilization and self-governance. Anti-imperialists used them to argue that a liberal constitutional republic should have no subjects, certainly not any drawn from the dregs of humanity's lower races. The first group prevailed.

The collisions and coalitions among American ideologies and interests produced a four-part hierarchical structure of citizenship laws that characterized Progressive Era civic orderings generally. This structure included: first, the excluded status of people denied entry to and subject to expulsion from the U.S., generally owing to their ethnic or ideological traits; second, colonial subjectship, reserved chiefly for territorial inhabitants declared racially ineligible for citizenship; third, second-class citizenship, usually understood as required by improvident grants of formal citizenship to races not capable of exercising it, and as the proper status for women; and fourth, full citizenship, including voting rights. Congress decided that Filipinos, somewhat like Chinese laborers, were in the first category. They were considered too racially distinct, inferior, and troublesome to possess any form of U.S. citizenship or nationality. Their acquisition had been imprudent. They should be tutored as subjects for a time, then gradually expelled from formal affiliation with the U.S. via independence (which came, finally, in 1946). The U.S. should, however, maintain a guiding role. The more compliant yet also racially inferior native residents of Guam seemed fit to be permanent colonial subjects, the second category. They did not obtain any measure of U.S. citizenship until 1950. Puerto Ricans were in the third category. They were thought suitable for citizenship, but only for something like the second-class citizenship of blacks and Native Americans, as well as women. Finally, there were enough nonaboriginal people in Hawaii and Alaska so that most of their residents could safely be treated as full citizens residing in a U.S. territory on its way to statehood, like the old Northwest.[50]

How did the U.S. come by possessions that prompted such complex civic structures? Many scholars concur that the Spanish-American War did not arise from any immediate economic or strategic necessity. It rather reflected quasi-Darwinian beliefs that American flourishing, especially in relation to the expansionist European powers, called for a war and a larger empire. Those beliefs were vigorously propagated by, among others, Assistant Secretary of the Navy Theodore Roosevelt, who argued to an enthusiastic Naval War College in 1897 that "All the great masterful races have been fighting races. . . . No triumph of peace is quite so great as the triumphs of war." Flamboyant publisher William Randolph Hearst thought that the war could both fulfill the nation's destiny and help sell newspapers. On the strength of such assertive sentiments and the mysterious explosion on the U.S.S. *Maine,* America attacked Spanish possessions in the Caribbean and the Pacific in 1898.[51]

After the fighting ceased, the issue remained whether, in José Cabranes's words, "racially and culturally distinct peoples brought under American sovereignty without the promise of citizenship or statehood could be held indefinitely without doing violence to American values—that is, whether certain peoples could be permanently excluded from the American political community and deprived of equal rights."[52] Imperialists unabashedly answered yes. It was the "manifest destiny" of Americans to spread white civilization and governance to more barbaric races around the globe by ruling them as subjects in tutelage, not citizens. None spoke more grandiloquently than the young Republican Senator from Indiana, Albert Beveridge, whose maiden speech caused a sensation in the national press. He insisted that the colonial question was "deeper than any question of party politics," or even national "policy" or "constitutional power"; it was "racial." In words chillingly like later Nazi claims, Beveridge announced:

> God has not been preparing the English-speaking and Teutonic peoples for a thousand years for nothing but vain and

idle self-contemplation and self-admiration. No! He has made us the master organizers of the world to establish system where chaos reigns. He has given us the spirit of progress to overwhelm the forces of reaction throughout the earth. He has made us adepts in government that we may administer government among savage and senile peoples. . . . And of all our race He has marked the American people as His chosen nation to finally lead in the regeneration of the world. This is the divine mission of America, and it holds all the profit, all the glory, all the happiness possible to man. We are trustees of the world's progress, guardians of its righteous peace. The judgment of the Master is upon us: "Ye have been faithful over a few things; I will make you ruler over many things."[53]

Though his senior colleagues thought Beveridge presumptuously outspoken, he was placed on the committee for the Philippines and Puerto Rico chaired by immigration restrictionist Henry Cabot Lodge, who soon made clear that he fully agreed with Beveridge's "manifest destiny" views.[54] Lodge and others argued that it was nothing new for the U.S. to govern colonies held in long-term pupilage, much like Britain, France, and other European powers. The U.S. had been ruling the native tribes as colonies ever since it first claimed sovereignty over them. And just as most Indians were under U.S. jurisdiction as wards, not citizens, so the members of the nation's new colonies need not receive equal civic status. By conquest and the 1898 Treaty of Paris they had been made American nationals, but not citizens. Full rights and republican self-governance might come in time if they proved able.[55]

Anti-imperialists replied, in more emphatically liberal and republican terms, that the Declaration of Independence demanded that government be only by the consent of the governed, and that a republic could have only citizens, not subjects.[56] Some, indeed, contended that cession had made Puerto Ricans U.S citizens already, though they avoided making that claim about Filipinos.[57] Many added, less high-mindedly, that the nation could not afford the problems for "free constitutional government" created by adding "mongrels of the East," marked by "ignorance and inferiority" as well as "pestilence . . . leprosy . . . [and] idolatry."[58] The imperialists answered in the manner of Southern whites. They insisted that the Declaration only applied to those "capable of self-government," noting that its authors denied the franchise to "four-fifths" of the population.[59] And though they agreed that the new colonial inhabitants were generally unfit for self-governance now and might always be, they believed that these lower races could, in the long run, be improved by American rule.[60]

The imperialists were more troubled by two other problems. They wished to define some special status for these islands that justified governing them without the constitutional restraints ordinarily applicable in U.S. territories. They also wanted to distinguish the legal status of Puerto Ricans, who had welcomed American rule and seemed much more assimilable, from Filipinos, who had launched an intense if unsuccessful war of independence against just such rule. The Philippines seemed culturally as well as geographically far more removed from the United States.

Senator Jonathan Ross, among others, argued that in the nation's previous acquisitions of land by treaty, the ceding powers had inserted provisions indicating that all inhabitants "except uncivilized tribes" should receive U.S. citizenship. In all cases except Alaska there had also been a clear indication that statehood would eventually follow. The Treaty of Paris ending the Spanish-American War gave no such guarantees. Instead, it explicitly left the "civil rights and political status" of these territories' inhabitants to be "determined by Congress." Thus, although there might be certain basic liberties that the U.S. government had to honor for all persons everywhere, the full range of constitutional guarantees applicable to citizens in territories destined for statehood was not compulsory or advisable.[61] Filipinos, moreover, resembled "uncivilized tribes" more than did Puerto Ricans. What was done in the latter case therefore had no bearing on the former.[62]

The McKinley administration and allied congressional leaders soon abandoned their initial leanings toward free trade and U.S. citizenship for Puerto Ricans, however, fearing that otherwise it might be difficult not to follow suit in the Philippines. The citizenship contemplated for Puerto Ricans had, in any case, been decidedly second-class. Senator Joseph Foraker explained that his bill granting them that status would not confer "any rights that the American people do not want them to have." As the Court had affirmed in *Minor v. Happersett*, citizenship, like common-law subjectship, required allegiance in return for protection, nothing more. In the end the Organic Act for Puerto Rico, or Foraker Act, merely labeled Puerto Ricans "citizens of Porto Rico," entitled to the protection of the United States, but not full members of it. Puerto Rico was given a civil government, subordinate to Congress, and funded by a special tariff imposed on goods going to and from the island.[63]

The Philippines, in contrast, were governed by a presidential commission, first headed by William Howard Taft. Taft had little respect for his "little brown brothers," but he warmed to the task of "civilizing" them. Through 1912 the U.S. colonial regime sought to impose an American mold on Filipinos via industrial education, modeled on Booker T. Washington's vocational training for blacks. Few thought these efforts successful, however, and in 1916 the U.S. agreed to point the

Philippines toward independence, so long as American economic and strategic interests were protected.[64]

Puerto Rico remained a different story. To many American leaders throughout the Progressive years, the island seemed much more valuable as an American possession, economically and strategically. It looked like a good permanent base from which to protect the Panama Canal. Yet despite support from Presidents Roosevelt, Taft, and Wilson, proposals to give many or all of its residents U.S. citizenship repeatedly failed. The Foraker Act had exempted Puerto Rico from federal taxes. To many in Congress, that abstention, along with America's protection and tutelage, seemed compensation enough for its colonial status. Views began to change only during World War I, when a disgruntled Caribbean colony seemed a dangerous liability. Consequently, in 1917 Congress grudgingly granted Puerto Ricans U.S. citizenship and a slightly greater measure of self-governance, despite fears that they were unready and would contribute to the "mongrelization" of America.[65]

Congress defined those changes in a way that led many Puerto Ricans to object to their new citizenship. Everyone understood that Puerto Ricans were not being granted civic equality. They still had no right to vote for the federal office-holders who wielded veto powers over all their legislation. They also did not have the full protection of the Bill of Rights and other constitutional guarantees. Those denials were authoritatively upheld by a highly race-conscious Supreme Court.[66]

Judicial Rulings. From 1900 on, the Court had to try to resolve many legal controversies over the political status of the residents of the Philippines and Puerto Rico, and also Hawaii and Alaska. In 1899, a set of articles in the *Harvard Law Review* on the status of the new possessions gained after the Spanish-American War provided most of the arguments that the justices would deploy. The most copied one was by Harvard professor of government (and later the university's president) A. Lawrence Lowell, who had written more generally on American colonial expansion in the *Atlantic Monthly* earlier that year. Scholars have focused on the legal doctrines that Lowell proposed in the law review article, but his *Atlantic* piece reveals their broader rationales. It shows that the doctrines the Court would embrace were self-consciously part of the retreat from racial egalitarianism that dominated this era.

In the *Atlantic,* Lowell contended that America's history of westward expansion had long made it "one of the greatest and most successful colonizing powers the world has ever known." He recognized that the nation was entering a new era with the end of its contiguous western frontier, and that it faced a choice whether to expand overseas next. But because "the Anglo-Saxon race is expansive," the question was not whether America would acquire new possessions, but whether America's acquisitions would be governed according to the "theory that all men are equal politically." Lowell noted that the nation had never fully followed that theory. The U.S. had instead claimed in regard to Native Americans and blacks that "they are not men." That claim was, Lowell remarked, "one of many illustrations of the political good sense and bad logic of the English-speaking race."[67]

The U.S. government's embrace of the "theory of political equality" had reached its high point with the Fifteenth Amendment. But, Lowell observed, this egalitarian tide then "began to ebb." He confessed that he had initially been "shocked" when this trend led to exclusion of Chinese immigrants. Like Charles Francis Adams, however, Lowell indicated that he had changed his mind. The decision that the Chinese were unassimilable was "sound." Political egalitarianism should be applied "rigorously only to our own race, and to those people whom we can assimilate rapidly." The Fifteenth Amendment should not be "carried out strictly"; hence the disfranchisement of African-Americans was also wise. Public affairs could not be entrusted to "people who were not accustomed to self-government" (like the "Spanish race," whose prevalence in the New Mexico Territory barred statehood). Only the "Anglo-Saxon race" had been readied for self-rule by "centuries of discipline." The U.S. must do "justice to all the races"; but it would be "sheer cruelty" to let Filipinos rule themselves, and Puerto Rico's acquisition of such powers must be "gradual and tentative." Like most Progressives, Lowell recommended that, instead, "experts, with a highly specialized training" play the leading role in colonial rule.[68]

With those imperatives in mind, in his *Harvard Law Review* article Lowell steered between those who said that the Constitution applied only to the states, a view that would make it inapplicable to western territories destined for statehood and to the District of Columbia, and those who said it "followed the flag" in full force. Reviewing the history of American territories since the Confederation, Lowell elaborated what he admitted to be a neglected if not novel distinction, in a way that was widely followed. The Constitution, he argued, applied fully only to U.S. citizens and, except for judicial organization, to territories "incorporated" into the Union. Apart from a few basic limits on Congress, it was irrelevant to "unincorporated" possessions. Congress had in all previous treaties and annexations explicitly "incorporated" civilized territorial inhabitants into the Union, or made them citizens, or (as in the case of Hawaii) extended the territorial limits of the U.S. But those actions had been choices of the political branches, and they had chosen in the Treaty of Paris not to do any such things. Hence Congress could act as prudence required, differentiating between Puerto Rico and the Philippines as it wished. This was just the conclusion imperialists sought, and it was, Lowell had previously argued, what a proper appreciation of racial capacities dictated.[69]

Although repeatedly echoed without acknowledgment in the Foraker Act debates, Lowell's reasoning became authoritative only when it was embraced by lower courts, then by a plurality, and at last by the Supreme Court. The issues came to court via challenges to congressional regulations on trade to and from Puerto Rico (*Goetze v. United States*). Because the "Duties, Imposts and Excises" imposed on Puerto Rico in lieu of taxes were not "uniform throughout the United States," they clearly violated Article I, section 8 of the Constitution, *if* Puerto Rico was a conventional part of the U.S. In June 1900, a New York district judge held instead that Puerto Rico had been "acquired, but not incorporated" via the Treaty of Paris, and remained "foreign." Against the argument that republics should not hold persons in colonial subjectship, Judge Townsend contended that the framers meant to make the U.S. "an unfettered sovereign in foreign affairs," not "a cripple among nations." And because it might "be best for us not to make its citizens fully our citizens," Congress could exercise its sovereignty without incorporating Puerto Rico or its people fully into the American republic.[70]

The following year in the *Insular Cases*, this ruling was overturned; but the opinions paved the way for the eventual triumph of a view close to Townsend's.[71] In *De Lima v. Bidwell*, Justice Brown wrote for a thin five-man majority that after the Treaty of Paris, Puerto Rico had become a territory of the United States, "although not an organized territory in the technical sense." He denied that a territory can be "at the same time both foreign and domestic," so he held that tariff laws applicable to foreign countries could not still be enforced against Puerto Rican goods. The four dissenters thought that some positive act by Congress was necessary to bring previously foreign territories under U.S. law. With that view rejected, the Court then overturned *Goetze*, along with a case involving goods from Hawaii.[72]

The Court then shattered into fragments in *Downes v. Bidwell*. There it considered challenges to the special duties on goods from Puerto Rico imposed by the Foraker Act in 1900 in order to finance the new U.S.-constructed Puerto Rican government. Lacking a majority, Justice Brown announced a judgment arising from the concurrences. Unlike tariffs imposed on goods from particular states, he indicated, these duties were valid. Via a long historical review, Brown argued that the Constitution had usually not been treated as applying to territories "acquired by purchase or conquest" any further than "Congress shall so direct." The author of *Plessy* said plainly that he was drawn to this conclusion because of fear that, otherwise, children born of all residents of American territories, "whether savage or civilized," would be full U.S. citizens, an "extremely serious" consequence. As for worries that, free of constitutional restraints, the U.S. might govern its territories despotically, Brown promised that, even if not written in "constitutions or statutes," the "principles of natural justice inherent in the Anglo-Saxon character" would prevent unfair laws. True, governance of "alien races" that fell under the "American Empire" might require some modifications of "Anglo-Saxon principles"; but that was "a political question."[73]

Though he invoked prevalent concerns about the racial character of the U.S. citizenry, Brown's refusal to apply the Constitution to any territory went too far for his brethren. Justice White's opinion tracked Lowell's distinction between "incorporated" and "unincorporated" territories more precisely, though it did not cite him, and it has since been treated as controlling. Like Judge Townsend, White invoked the law of nations and claimed that the U.S. had the same sovereign powers to acquire and govern territories as any other nation, its republican character notwithstanding. And the Louisianan justice dwelt even more on the specter that lack of congressional discretion over territorial inhabitants would result in "the immediate bestowal of citizenship" on uncivilized races "absolutely unfit" for it. That event would threaten "the whole structure of the government" and "the whole body of American citizenship." The answer was to recognize that the U.S. could "acquire and hold territory without immediately incorporating it." As the Treaty of Paris left the status of Puerto Rico and its residents to Congress, Congress could treat them as outside the (incorporated) United States and impose duties that would otherwise violate Article I, section 8.[74]

Chief Justice Fuller and the three other dissenters in the case denied that the U.S. could, like a monarchy, claim sovereign powers not derived from the Constitution. They stressed that the act organizing the government of Puerto Rico surely performed the "occult" act of incorporation, if the Treaty of Paris had not. And Harlan derided Brown's call for trust in "Anglo-Saxon character," noting that the Revolution had been waged against tyrannical Anglo-Saxons. He thought that the issue of whether a race would assimilate was "a matter to be thought of when it is proposed to acquire their territory by treaty."[75] Once the land was acquired, the residents' children, at least, must become American citizens.

The defeat of these views meant that the Court once again endorsed two highly illiberal doctrines. It embraced notions of unbridled sovereignty that suited a world of monarchical nation-states, not constitutionally limited liberal republics. It also gave great weight to concerns for a racially "fit" citizenry, instead of insisting that fitness be determined on an individual basis. The final *Insular Case, Huus v. New York & Puerto Rico Steamship Co.*, showed that when extensions of citizenship and constitutional requirements were not at stake, the justices were willing to treat Puerto Rico as much like other parts of the U.S. There, Brown held for a unanimous bench that the coasting trade between Puerto Rico and the mainland U.S. now formed part of the "domestic trade" of the nation. Hence New York pilotage laws applicable only to foreign vessels could not be applied to Puerto Rican ships.[76] Like Native Americans, Asian-Americans, African-

Americans, and women, Puerto Ricans fully belonged to the "American empire" in virtually all ways that carried no implication of political equality; but they could not have equal citizenship.

The next year the Court ruled that, after the Treaty of Paris, the Philippines, too, became sufficiently part of the U.S. to be no longer subject to tariff laws applied to foreign nations.[77] It did so despite recognizing that Congress did not wish the Philippines to have the same status as Puerto Rico. Hence earlier fears that justices might treat Puerto Rico as a constraining precedent for the Philippines proved to have some substance. But the Court generally continued to find ways to avoid taking constitutional guarantees too literally in relation to the nation's new possessions.

That fact was underlined by *Hawaii v. Mankichi* in 1903, a case arising from the U.S. acquisition of Hawaii in 1898.[78] Though titularly achieved by consensual treaty, this addition also resulted from American coercion, in this case initiated chiefly by American sugar planters. The Hawaiian monarchy fell in 1893 in a bloodless coup staged by the planters and aided by a show of force from Marines aboard the U.S.S. *Boston*, acting under orders from President Harrison's Minister to Hawaii, John L. Stevens. Sanford Dole, a missionary's son who was a justice of the Hawaiian Supreme Court, then became president of the "Republic of Hawaii" and sought its annexation by the U.S., with Harrison's approval. But Congress had still not acted when Grover Cleveland resumed the presidency in February 1893. He felt "ashamed of the whole affair," but he could not win congressional support for restoration of the old Hawaiian regime. Then under President McKinley, after the Spanish-American War whipped up enthusiasm for a Pacific American empire, Congress approved annexation. The U.S. thereby took title to the lands of the Hawaiian monarchy, amounting to nearly half the islands' total.[79]

The Newlands Resolution approving the annexation of Hawaii left in force all Hawaiian laws not contrary to the resolution, U.S. treaties, or the Constitution.[80] They were displaced only when Congress organized a new territorial government in 1900. In the interim, Mankichi was convicted of manslaughter via procedures standard in Hawaii, but inconsistent with the Fifth and Sixth Amendments. He appealed to the Supreme Court, insisting that from annexation the Constitution applied to Hawaii in full force. The four *Downes* dissenters agreed. Justice Brown's opinion for the Court did not, but the case caused him difficulty, perhaps because he saw Hawaiians as "civilized," populated by "large numbers of people from Europe and America" who had brought their "political ideas and traditions." Brown thus found it hard to deny them constitutional rights, and he conceded that, read literally, the resolution and the Constitution had been violated. The justice also thought "most, if not all, the privileges and immunities" in the Constitution did apply to Hawaii "from the moment of annexation," unlike the Treaty of Paris acquisitions. But he still decided that these procedural rights were "not fundamental" enough to be required prior to the establishment of territorial government.[81] As Hawaii soon received one, the decision was minor; but it confirmed the Court's reluctance to extend rights to those who were not "civilized" people "from Europe and America."

In *Gonzales v. Williams* (1904), Isabella Gonzales, a native-born, lifelong Puerto Rican resident, sought to enter New York without being subjected to checks imposed on "alien immigrants." A unanimous Court upheld her claim. It ruled that, just as Puerto Rico was no longer a "foreign country," Puerto Ricans were no longer "aliens" for purposes of immigration. The opinion did not comment, however, on whether they had become U.S. citizens.[82] The justices were apparently willing for Puerto Ricans, like other peoples of color, to be designated "American" so long as what that meant in terms of citizenship status remained unclear. Subsequent cases also showed that the Court was happy to enforce Bill of Rights guarantees in the new territories if Congress had explicitly extended them to the locales in question; but otherwise it refused to do so.[83] The Court also began treating the "incorporated territories" doctrine as authoritatively established. Its leading judicial advocate, Justice White, wrote for a dissent-free Court in *Rassmussen v. United States* (1905), holding that Alaska was an incorporated territory, so the Constitution applied in full force. White faced the difficulty that the Alaskan treaty did not contain the word *incorporated*, whereas the Hawaiian treaty, which was held not to incorporate Hawaii, did. White said that the Alaskan proviso that all but the uncivilized tribes should enjoy "all the rights, advantages and immunities" of U.S. citizenship was sufficient to bestow "incorporation."[84] That claim was not implausible; but the justices seemed far more ready to view extensions of citizenship status as full, and incorporation as achieved, in cases involving whites.[85]

Eventually, Congress did make Puerto Ricans U.S. citizens via the Jones Act of 1917, and, well after the end of the Progressive Era, in 1922 a Supreme Court led by former Philippines governor Taft decided what this change meant for Puerto Rico's incorporated status. Despite the ruling in *Rassmussen*, a Court that now included Louis Brandeis as well as Holmes held without dissent in *Balzac v. Porto Rico* that the island was still an unincorporated territory, and that constitutional rights to jury trials still did not apply there. Taft treated the "incorporated territories" doctrine as firmly established, and he dismissed Alaska as "a very different case," because it had been thinly populated, ripe for settlement by Americans. Puerto Rico, like the Philippines, was instead filled with people unfamiliar with Anglo-Saxon jury trials (though such trials had in fact been common in Puerto Rico since 1900). The Court also remained reluctant to infer any intention to incorporate "these distant ocean communities of different origin and language."[86] Incorporation of such people had to be very explicit. Thus the decision firmly enshrined the "unincorporation territory" doctrine concocted to achieve results dictated by racial theories. *Balzac* did not result in explicitly racial citizenship statuses, because Puerto Ricans who came to the mainland now had full citizenship rights, whereas all citizens who moved to Puerto Rico lost the benefit of the Bill of Rights and the franchise in federal elections. But if most Puerto Ricans had northern European ancestry, there can be little doubt that Congress and the Court would have found the parallel to Alaska more decisive. The status they assigned instead reiterated the power of concerns for the racial character of American citizenship.

Race and Birthright Citizenship

Yet even as the nation acquired the new possessions whose members would have their rights defined so heavily in racial terms, the Supreme Court reaffirmed one longstanding route to American citizenship without regard to race. In *United States v. Wong Kim Ark* (1898), a solid majority ruled that birth on U.S. soil sufficed to make citizens even of persons of Chinese descent. Though widely expected, the decision was momentous and not simple. Without discussion, Justice Gray conceded for the Court that if the laborer Wong Kim Ark, a native-born, lifelong resident of California, was a U.S. citizen, that status trumped the nation's exclusionary policy toward laborers "of the Chinese race." Gray then argued that the Fourteenth Amendment guarantee of birthright citizenship must be interpreted in light of English common law, going back to *Culvin's Case*. He thoroughly canvassed the cases and authorities and ruled correctly that, on common law premises, Wong Kim Ark must be a citizen. But Gray was too cursory in dismissing the relevance of the denial of birthright citizenship to members of native tribes in *Elk v. Wilkins*. Gray simply asserted that *Elk* was confined to the tribes and "had no tendency to deny" citizenship to children of other parents. The justice was clearly concerned about the implications of any further exceptions to birthright citizenship: he contended that ruling against Wong Kim Ark would "deny citizenship to thousands of persons of English, Scotch, Irish, German or other European parentage" born on U.S. soil.[87]

Although Gray's pro-immigrant ruling won votes from two recently appointed Cleveland Democrats, Edward White and Rufus Peckham, the dissent was written by Cleveland's Chief Justice Fuller, who had opposed the harsh *Fong Yue Ting* ruling on liberal grounds of procedural rights. He was joined, perhaps more surprisingly, by Harlan, the Court's only champion of black rights and a dissenter in *Elk v. Wilkins*. Fuller argued that American law embodied several modifications of common-law subjectship, making citizenship more a matter of mutual choice by individuals and the existing citizenry of nations. The "most vital constituent" of the common-law rule made allegiance at birth "permanent and indissoluble," but American law recognized broad expatriation rights. Coke's rule also made children born abroad subjects of foreign sovereigns, whereas U.S. statutes proclaimed children of U.S. citizens born abroad still to be Americans. And, of course, Indians born to tribes subject to U.S. jurisdiction were not citizens.

In line with the reasoning of *Elk v. Wilkins,* Fuller contended that citizenship and nationality should be construed according to principles of international law. He endorsed Vattel's argument about the premises of the hypothetical "social contract": societies should presume "as a matter of course, that each citizen, on entering into society, reserves to his children the right of becoming members of it," so that they eventually "become true citizens merely by their tacit consent," if they do not renounce membership at the age of discretion. The Fourteenth Amendment indicated, however, that for a child to have this right of membership in America, his parent must be "completely subject" to U.S. jurisdiction, owing America "direct and immediate allegiance," and being "in no respect or degree subject" to another government's jurisdiction. Chinese immigrants retained allegiance to China and were ineligible under treaties and U.S. naturalization laws to become "completely subject" by acquiring American citizenship. Fuller thought that, in addition to children of citizens, only children of permanent resident aliens who were eligible for citizenship were sufficiently embraced by U.S. jurisdiction to claim birthright citizenship under the Fourteenth Amendment.[88]

As the evidence of earlier history has indicated, Gray's common-law position reflected the bulk of American legal opinion, although Fuller was invoking contrary consensual traditions that also had much authority in American political and legal discourse. The predominance of the common-law view probably played an important role in producing the result, because Gray had previously been quite exclusionist in his treatment of the Chinese, as was the lower court judge in *Wong Kim Ark,* William Morrow.[89] Although the framers of the Fourteenth Amendment citizenship clause professed liberal, inclusive motives, these judges did not. The decision, moreover, accomplished something they had long opposed. Because many Chinese were already in the U.S. and fearful of leaving, *Wong Kim Ark* meant that a Chinese-free U.S. citizenry could no longer be achieved, though it might still be approximated. The ruling also gave Chinese litigants a powerful legal claim to advance, and in ensuing years many surely did profess falsely to be native-born citizens. No doubt Gray and his majority were heavily influenced by their worries about denying citizenship to children of northern Europeans. But Fuller's position allowed them to avoid that, as many such immigrants were both permanent residents and eligible for naturalization.

Wong Kim Ark thus may well be evidence of the capacity of legal precedents and traditions to prompt decisions contrary to judges' expressed policy preferences and to the broader climate of their times. But that second point should not be overstated: it is also likely that the compatibility of the birthright citizenship rule with broad interpretations of American sovereignty and natural authority over those born within the nation's bounds added to the rule's appeal. Concededly, Gray relied on seventeenth-century notions of sovereign power and nationality rather than late nineteenth-century ideas of racial evolution or historicist notions of peoples and nations, and in doing so he worked against racial homogeneity. But birthright citizenship nonetheless fit the ascriptive, nationalistic, and often mystical spirit of those doctrines better than the rationalistic, consensual account of citizenship that Fuller presented. *Wong Kim Ark* did win support from justices like David Brewer, who were more favorable to Chinese immigrants, and along with *Yick Wo v. Hopkins,* it exerted some restraining influence on anti-Chinese inclinations in later cases. Hence its results genuinely served liberal, inclusive positions, even if it was born more of the era's movements toward ascriptive naturalism.

Immigration and the Progressive Era

Despite the restrictive laws of the 1880s and 1890s, immigration continued to be central to American civic life during the Progressive years. From 1901 to 1910 the rate of immigration relative to the national population was the highest in U.S. history, more than ten per thousand. The nation's lawmakers continued to try to staunch the flow, particularly in regard to Asian immigrants. When the U.S. annexed Hawaii, Congress extended the Chinese exclusion laws to it, and in 1900 it imposed a registration system for Chinese laborers. In 1901, ongoing dissatisfactions with judicial decisions in Chinese immigration cases led Congress to authorize new U.S. Commissioners to hold such hearings, subject to extremely limited judicial review. In 1902, Congress again renewed Chinese exclusion, and failing a new treaty with China in 1904, it extended the policy indefinitely. It also expanded exclusion and registration beyond Hawaii to all U.S. insular territories and prohibited Chinese laborers currently living in such territories from coming to the mainland. These steps were chiefly aimed at the Chinese in the recently conquered Philippines. Japan wished to avoid the humiliation of a similar exclusion law, so it accepted President Roosevelt's Gentleman's Agreement in 1907. The Japanese promised not to issue passports to laborers seeking to come to the U.S. unless they were resuming a former residence or joining resident relatives. These efforts worked. After 1882 Chinese emigration always exceeded new immigration. Thus the numbers of the Chinese in the U.S., which had grown from some 63,199 to 105,465 between 1870 and 1880, declined from a high of 107,488 in 1890 (due to natural increase) to 71,531 by 1910. At the same time, though the number of Japanese in the U.S. grew steadily, no massive influx of Japanese laborers occurred.

The bitter opposition not only to Asian immigrants, but to immigration from everywhere except northern Europe, that Lodge and others continued to stir also had legislative consequences. In 1903, after President McKinley had been assassinated by a demented native-born man with a foreign-sounding name (Leon Czolgolz) and a history of attending anarchist lectures, Congress banned the immigration of those who were "opposed to all organized government" or who taught the "propriety of the unlawful assault or killing" of U.S. officials. It also made many illegal entrants deportable for up to two years and raised the immigrant head tax to two dollars. In 1906, Lodge joined in unnatural alliance with the AFL-CIO's Samuel Gompers to push Congress to reconsider the literacy test. Opposition from immigrant groups and from corporate interests like the National Association of Manufacturers, for whom uneducated immigrants represented cheap labor, prevented passage. Pro-immigrant interests did accept another increase in the head tax, to four dollars, in the 1907 Immigration Act; and Congress created the U.S. Immigration (Dillingham) Commission to investigate the evils of immigration. In 1910, Congress made immigrant prostitutes subject to deportation without time limit. These anti-immigrant efforts reflected not shared economic interests so much as profound anxieties about, in John Higham's words, "the accustomed dominance of a white Protestant people of northern European descent." Those fears were abundantly reflected in the forty-two-volume report of the Dillingham Commission in 1911. Its members managed to interpret huge mounds of contrary data as indicating that Lodge's 1896 views were essentially correct.

As a result, Congress passed a different version of the literacy test in early 1913, though this time Taft vetoed it on his way out of office. Despite his disdain for "lower races," he argued in terms of his pro-market economic convictions that the southern Europeans formed a useful labor pool who could be taught the relatively low levels of literacy their jobs required. Woodrow Wilson then vetoed new literacy test laws in 1915 and 1917, invoking the more left progressive cosmopolitan ideals of U.S. citizenship that appealed to white immigrant Democrats, even though he firmly supported both Jim Crow and Asian exclusion. The test was finally enacted over his veto in 1917 amid the anti-foreigner "100-percent Americanism" fervor stirring by the coming of World War I. That law also defined an "Asiatic barred zone" that encompassed virtually all Asian homelands except China, from which immigration was already banned, and Japan, with whom the Gentleman's Agreement prevailed. It further barred entry to foreign radicals and provided for the deportation of any aliens who engaged in radical agitation. Both racial and ideological barriers thus were strengthened. Congress did not yet enact a further proposal that had been put forth by the architects of the 1913 bill. They wished to make eligibility for naturalization a condition for admission as an immigrant, thus making all racial and ideological bars on naturalization also automatic bars on immigration. That massively racist and ideologically repressive restriction became law as part of the National Origins Quota system in 1924, the measure that at last provided the full ethnic and racial controls on immigration long favored by most centrist progressives.[90]

Judicial Actions. The *Wong Kim Ark* decision did not prevent immigration laws from casting an oppressive shadow on the lives of Chinese-Americans, legal Chinese residents, and other immigrants during the Progressive years.[91] With few exceptions, the Court repeatedly upheld broad federal authority over immigration, including expansive administrative powers to exclude Chinese who advanced citizenship claims, and also wives and children of legal residents. When its infrequent moderate decisions fueled lower court leniency toward immigrants, moreover, criticisms mounted, and the Court generally swung back the other way. That swing became more pronounced, not less, after some progressive Republicans joined the bench.

From 1901 through 1903, Fuller authored chiefly restrictive opinions. Dissents came only in votes by Brewer and Peckham, and not in cases involving citizenship.[92] Some lower courts still tried to stand against these exclusionist winds, but rarely.[93] And speaking through recently appointed Justice Holmes, the Supreme Court repeatedly refused to review decisions of immigration officials in cases involving assertions of U.S. citizenship until administrative appeals were completed.[94] Whether Holmes was expressing his progressive belief in deference to elected officials or his bleak Darwinian outlook is unclear, but his rulings underlined progressive support for immigration restriction. Brewer took issue with Holmes in these cases, and he now stressed how the Court was making racial distinctions in the rights of U.S. citizens. Brewer wrote in *United States v. Sing Tuck* that the Court's refusal to permit immediate appeal to the courts for determination of citizenship claims imposed a barrier that would never be enforced "against an American citizen of Anglo-Saxon descent."[95]

But in a major nonracial immigration decision, Brewer joined his brethren in upholding ideological limits on access to membership. In *Turner v. Williams* (1904), the Court sustained the 1903 Alien Immigration Act, including its provisions for excluding anarchists. Renowned attorneys Clarence Darrow and Edgar Lee Masters cited the leading nineteenth-century defenders of individual liberty, John Stuart Mill and Herbert Spencer, to claim that the act violated First

Amendment guarantees. They added Madison, Montesquieu, and Locke on behalf of the claim that quasi-judicial hearings by administrative boards violated the separation of powers. But Fuller gave these canonical liberal authorities short shrift, reiterating Congress's powers to exclude whom it wished, on grounds of sovereignty or the commerce clause, and to assign such hearings to executive officials. Fuller had no trouble finding that John Turner, an English labor activist who had declared his intent to become a citizen, had been rightly designated as the first person to be deported because of beliefs hostile to the survival of the U.S. government.[96] Thus Congress's sharpening of the heretofore diffuse boundaries to the leftist political beliefs that persons wishing to become American could hold continued to raise no constitutional problems.

In the shocking decisions of *United States v. Ju Toy* (1905), Holmes and the Court went further, ruling that so long as executive officials had not committed any abuse of discretion, judicial review of their denials of claims to citizenship, including examination of new evidence, was forbidden by the 1894 immigration statute and not required by due process. The district court in the case had undertaken such a review and found that Ju Toy actually was a citizen entitled to reenter the U.S. The Court overturned that result. Holmes held that even U.S. citizens wrongfully judged deportable by immigration officials had no due process rights to judicial trials. With icy bitterness Brewer and Peckham dissented. Brewer termed the decision an "appalling" proof that deportation was punishment, which the Court was allowing to be imposed by an executive "star chamber."[97] It was undeniable that, in terms of their basic rights to reenter or remain within the U.S., Holmes's approach treated Chinese-Americans as second-class citizens.

Subsequently, Holmes and his brethren backed off slightly. In *Chin Yow v. United States* (1908), a unanimous bench ordered a judicial trial to determine if Chin Yow was a native-born citizen. Holmes argued that immigration officials had to give such claims "a hearing in good faith, however summary in form," and Chin Yow alleged he had not received even that. Holmes's decision to order a trial, rather than a new and fair administrative hearing, might be seen as restoring some modest role for courts on immigration and citizenship claims. Yet Holmes stressed that the judge's primary task was to evaluate the previous administrative hearing, not to reach the merits, and that even a showing that Chin Yow's claim had been decided wrongly would not prove that he had been denied a fair hearing. The decision thus did not go far toward placing Chinese-American citizens on an equal footing with others.[98] With such minor ameliorations of its most exclusionary decisions, the Court then largely withdrew from cases involving immigration and citizenship until 1912.[99] In the interim the lower courts built up another mixed collection of more and less restrictive immigration rulings. In many cases involving Chinese claims to citizenship, courts upheld exclusions, usually citing *Ju Toy;* but more often than executive officials wished, some courts around the country still found grounds for reversals, often citing *Chin Yow.*[100]

When the Supreme Court moved to settle many of the issues in dispute, Brewer and Peckham, along with Fuller, Harlan, and Moody, had left the bench, and Edward White had become Chief Justice. The six Taft appointees who replaced them unanimously put the Court firmly on the side of extensive administrative exclusionary powers. In *Tang Tun v. Edsell* (1912), Justice Charles Evan Hughes wrote for the Court in an opinion resembling those of his fellow progressive Republican, Holmes. A Washington district court had concluded that immigration officials wrongly denied Tang Tun's claim to U.S. citizenship, only to be reversed by the Ninth Circuit Court of Appeals. Hughes sided with the Circuit Court and ordered deference to the administrative judgment. His opinion reviewed the record carefully to show why he thought that the executive officers had acted properly; but the message of deference to administrative exclusions came through.[101] For those who still missed it, the Court went on to uphold two deportations of women deemed alien prostitutes, each time stressing its limited power to review administrative immigration decisions. Most striking was *Low Wah Suey v. Backus* (1912), involving a Chinese woman married to a Chinese-American U.S. citizen. She was still judged to be an alien and a prostitute. The Court recognized that "the present is a hard application of the rule of the statute," but insisted that only Congress could provide relief. *Low Wah Suey* and similar rulings were quickly cited by lower courts refusing to look closely at exclusionary orders.[102]

In sum, the immigration decisions of the federal courts provided some mild drags on the rush toward exclusion and expulsion, most frequently in the name of rights and fair procedures guaranteed to persons, as sanctified in liberal traditions. It was the common law, however, that provided citizenship to native-born Chinese-Americans, an instance of how ascription can be humanely inclusive as well as exclusive. The judges were undoubtedly also concerned in part to preserve their own power. Yet, on the whole, neither liberal nor ascriptive premises nor judicial ambition prompted much resistance to anti-immigrant measures. The Supreme Court, and especially its newer progressive Republican members, successfully compelled a sometimes recalcitrant lower judiciary to accept that the government could exclude people on racial grounds and impose on Chinese-American citizens special burdens of proof. The desires of Congress and executive officials to make immigration decisions largely immune from judicial review generally were honored. Judicial fluctuations would continue up through the massive immigration restrictions of the 1920s, but this pattern would not change. Conflicts between liberal principles of procedural and substantive fairness and the new restrictive Americanism would remain an ongoing civic drama in which for decades restriction would triumph.[103]

Naturalization. As the Progressive Era dawned, the signals Congress gave on questions of race, ethnicity, and access to citizenship were confusing, even if their exclusionary thrust was clear. All Hawaiians gained U.S. citizenship in 1900, but Congress refused to naturalize Filipinos or Puerto Ricans.[104] As the federal government became more concerned to keep more classes of immigrants out, worries grew about fraudulent naturalizations, undertaken not only by ineligible aliens who perjured themselves but also by corrupt officials seeking either to register voters or simply to sell access to citizenship. Allegations of massive naturalization frauds prior to a St. Louis election spurred Congress in 1906 to adopt a major Naturalization Act that restricted the courts empowered to naturalize, established standardized procedures, and imposed new penalties for many varieties of fraud and corruption. The 1906 law also provided for denaturalization for the first time, in the form of declaring void those naturalizations obtained by fraudulent means. Enforcement of this law meant increased federal supervision of the operations and decisions of naturalizing state courts via a new Division of Naturalization, thereby once more enhancing federal power over naturalization at the expense of the states.[105] In 1907, Congress added another law clarifying procedures for expatriation and requiring children born outside the U.S. who were statutory citizens to declare their intent to become resident citizens and swear oaths of allegiance at age eighteen.[106] Even though the formalization of expatriation procedures made consensually based citizenship a bit more real, the main concern in all these changes was to give the federal government more control over who was and was not a citizen.

The use of that control to police racial boundaries during a period of highly diverse immigration meant that the federal courts found themselves inundated by still more cases turning on who was "white." Toward eastern Asians, their responses remained consistently severe. Not even honorable service in U.S. armed forces won access for persons who were even of only half-Asian ancestry, despite an 1894 statute offering special naturalizations for aliens who served in the navy or marines.[107] The courts were, however, more solicitous toward people from the Middle East and the Indian subcontinent. In 1909 Circuit Judge Lacombe indicated his attraction to Roger Taney's view that naturalization should extend to "only white persons belonging to those races whose emigrants had contributed to the building up on this continent of the community of people which declared itself a new nation."[108] But despite his fear that the category of "Caucasian" might let in undesirable "Afghans, Hindoos, Arabs, and Berbers," he decided to admit a "Parsee" of "the purest Aryan type." The Second Circuit Court of Appeals affirmed, noting that to confine the meaning of "white" to nationalities present in the U.S. in 1790 would produce "absurd" exclusions of "Russians, Poles, Italians, Greeks, and others." They thought it safer to define "white" as the "Caucasian race." Congress could always add more exclusions.[109]

Many other judges similarly saw the Caucasian category as a tempting way to resolve the meaning of "white." A Georgia district judge, for example, stated bluntly that the term white "refers to race, rather than to color." He admitted a Syrian to citizenship (while comforting readers that not only was color irrelevant, but also the applicant was "not particularly dark").[110] U.S. executive officials, in contrast, resisted the Caucasian standard as too inclusive. They urged the courts to define "white" more culturally than biologically. At the instigation of the U.S. Bureau of Naturalization, district attorneys in various immigration centers adopted the position that "white persons" meant "persons of European descent"; and not all Europeans, but only those who shared "the prevailing ideals, standards and aspirations of the people of Europe."[111] Such persons would "from tradition, teaching, and environment" be "predisposed toward our form of government."[112]

In one way this position made the racial restriction in the law more palatable from liberal republican perspectives. It focused on the compatibility of applicants' beliefs with American principles, rather than on their skin color. But if this recasting of the meaning of "white" helped achieve some surface harmony in American civic ideologies, it did not further inclusiveness or democracy. The definition still retained an ascriptive element, "European descent." The emphasis on "ideals" worked merely as an additional restriction, to rule out some who were European but radical.

Courts found this too convoluted a message to attribute to the term *white;* but their efforts to find a clearer one showed increasing exasperation. After reviewing the government's claims in light of history, legal doctrines, and ethnological treatises, even a Boston Brahmin, Massachusetts Circuit Judge Francis Cabot Lowell, concluded in 1909, "There is no European or white race, as the United States contends, and no Asiatic or yellow race which includes substantially all the people of Asia." Deciding to rely on common usages of the term *white,* and to err on the side of past inclusive practices, he admitted an Armenian to citizenship. The next year Lowell was more plaintive as he naturalized a Syrian. He wrote that no theory of race had won general acceptance and that hardly "any one classifies any human race as white," so "classification by ethnological race is almost or quite impossible." He begged for an "amendment of the statutes" in order to "make quite clear the meaning of the word 'white.'"[113]

Partly because "common understandings" displayed no consensus, either, Congress was not about to settle that question. Eventually the Supreme Court had to confront these issues in the 1920s. It then replayed the vicissitudes of the lower courts, appealing to notions of who the framers would have thought "white" in 1790, to the ethnological category of Caucasian, and to popular usage. Like the lower court judges, the justices finally relied on what they held to be common, traditional views of who was white. But even more than the lower courts, the Supreme Court defined these views restrictively. In keeping with the pattern of the anti-immigrant 1920s, the justices denied naturalization not only to Japanese but to Indian Hindus as well.[114]

These naturalization decisions confirm that Progressive Era elites maintained high hopes that new scientific and cultural accounts of race would resolve problems of who should be eligible for full civic membership. Those hopes were not fulfilled. Their disappointment did not, however, prevent the courts from opening wide legal vents in naturalization laws for the racially exclusionary attitudes that had come to dominate the politics of citizenship.

In other regards the courts had less difficulty enforcing Congress's naturalization mandates, even though its laws gave judges broad discretion. The long-standing demand that applicants be of "good moral character," for example, now generated a fair amount of legal deliberation over what sorts of past misdeeds might be overlooked: perjury for which a pardon was received, or arising from a misunderstanding? Drunkenness? Saloon-keeping? Presumably homosexuality and other forms of unconventional sexuality were also deemed immoral, but still, no recorded federal litigation explicitly addressed those issues. In general the courts read the requirements of "good moral character" fairly stringently (although saloon-keeping was judged to be no great sin, especially in Milwaukee).[115]

The final major set of naturalization case law developments to be considered here stemmed from the 1907 Expatriation Act. It chiefly aimed at immigration restriction, to be furthered by clarifying that U.S. women who married foreigners did not create automatic entitlements to citizenship for their husbands or children. Instead they sacrificed their own citizenship. As such, the law primarily represented a deepening of the second-class citizenship of women, so it is discussed in relation to female citizenship below.

Blacks

Perhaps the most far-reaching consequence of the government's embrace of racial rationales for imperial rule and immigration and naturalization restrictions was the manner in which they strengthened political coalitions and ideological defenses supporting segregation. With this backing, once Jim Crow survived judicial scrutiny in *Plessy,* all Southern and some border and western states and towns legally codified many other forms of segregation in factories, hospitals, asylums, prisons, parks, circuses, movie houses, theaters, sports arenas, and other locales during the Progressive Era. Many of these institutions had long been segregated in practice, and many Jim Crow practices were never legally enshrined; but the extensive new codes, often warmly anointed by federal judges, conferred the dignifying "majesty of law" on all segregation. The fact that most Northern states did not pass Jim Crow laws did not make them just a regional phenomenon. Throughout these years the states which passed them included about one-third of the U.S. population and the vast majority of blacks; the laws had to be obeyed by all U.S. citizens whenever they passed through these states; and the U.S. government declared these laws valid and itself mandated extensive segregation in the nation's capital.[116]

School Segregation. Progressive Era courts continued to find the now longstanding official racial segregation of schools unproblematic.[117] The Supreme Court did not itself deal extensively with school segregation, but its interventions only reinforced the system's inequities. Even Justice Harlan, the sole champion of racial equality on the high court, proved tolerant of them in *Cumming v. Richmond County Board of Education* (1899). The school board of Georgia's Richmond County had decided to close down its one black high school, serving sixty students, to convert it into an elementary school for three hundred black children. It told black high schoolers that until more funds became available, they could attend any church-affiliated school for the same fee they had paid to their public one. At the same time the board maintained a public high school for white girls and provided funds to a Baptist high school for white boys. Attorneys for black families complained that their tax dollars were being used to support greater educational services for whites than for blacks and asked that the tax system be enjoined. Harlan ruled that this "remedy" would harm whites without helping blacks. He affirmed the state court's denial of an injunction. Harlan noted that an appropriate remedy might involve spending existing funds on a black high school, but he raised no objection to segregated schools per se. Indeed, he stated that great deference should be shown to the state's judgment on how scarce funds might best be allocated, so long as there was no clear racist intent.[118]

Nearly a decade later, the Court upheld an even more invidious state segregation of education in *Berea College v. Kentucky* (1908). A 1904 Kentucky law prevented racially integrated classes in all colleges and schools, public and private, operating in the state. Only Berea College, a private Christian institution incorporated by the state, then had such classes. It was the law's target. The state defended its ban via a thorough compilation of the scientific racism of the day, including cranial studies, arguments from evolutionary theory, and genetics—all said to prove the dangers of "amalgamation." Writing for the Court, Justice Brewer did not comment on these authorities. He found the state's powers over corporations that it had chartered sufficient to justify the application of the law to Berea College, and he did not think it necessary to decide whether it could be applied to schools or teachers not so incorporated.

Harlan dissented, but he chose not to challenge public school segregation or even to rely on the equal protection clause. Instead, he argued that the law violated "rights of liberty and property guaranteed" by the Fourteenth Amendment. It deprived private citizens of both economic liberties and freedoms of voluntary association, deprivations that might be expected to horrify the *Lochner* Court. But though he used that rubric, Harlan's true target was not economic paternalism. In his finest spirit of moral outrage he stormed, "Have we become so inoculated with prejudice of race that an American government, professedly based on the principles of freedom . . . can make distinctions between . . . citizens in the matter of their voluntary meeting for innocent purposes simply because of their respective races?"[119] The answer was yes. Although Brewer's opinion spoke only of incorporated institutions, after *Berea College* few believed that there were any limits on state powers to mandate segregation in any sphere of life.

Transportation. After *Plessy,* for many years the federal courts also brooked no challenges to the notion that equal but separate local transport services satisfied the Fourteenth Amendment.[120] And though officially the Supreme Court continued to hedge on the unsettled issue of whether states could force interstate railroads to segregate their interstate passengers, it gave such measures an effective green light in two cases involving the Chesapeake and Ohio Railway. In *Chesapeake and Ohio Railway Co. v. Kentucky* (1908), Justice Brown construed a state rail segregation statute as applying only to trips originating and ending within that state, even though the Chesapeake was an interstate line.[121] The Court then dropped the other shoe two years later in *Chiles v. Chesapeake and Ohio Railway Co.*[122] Alexander Chiles was a black man traveling first-class from Washington, D.C., to Lexington, Kentucky, initially in an integrated coach. When he changed trains at Ashland, Kentucky, however, he was required to ride in the coach for colored persons mandated by state law. The Supreme Court accepted that the colored coach to which he was assigned was reasonably equal to the white one.

The crucial element of Justice McKenna's opinion, however, was his decision to disregard the Kentucky statute and treat the segregation as strictly a practice that the *railroad* happened to require in that state. The Chesapeake and Ohio had so presented the facts in their defense. Yet this same company had challenged the same Kentucky law before the Supreme Court just two years before, only to have the law upheld. The company also did not require segregation in areas lacking

Jim Crow statutes, and the record showed that the railroad's conductor claimed that he was forcing Chiles to change coaches because of Kentucky's segregation law.[123] Hence it was, at best, implausible to treat the company's policy as unrelated to the Kentucky law. But by ignoring the state's role in the proceedings, the Court made the case easy. As it was well-established that, absent congressional action, common-law rules applied to interstate commerce, and that the common law permitted separate but equal accommodations, the Court had no trouble upholding the railroad's view.

The Chesapeake and Ohio Railway might have claimed that its policy was indeed the result of state law, making the case harder for the Supreme Court. But even if the statute had been invalidated in its application to interstate traffic, the railroad would still have been compelled to segregate its intrastate passengers. It probably concluded that the Court's stance made it less costly to go ahead and segregate entirely. After these rulings, blacks largely stopped litigating against transport segregation, aiming with limited success only at gaining truly equal accommodations.[124] Thus the *Chiles* decision meant that states could indeed compel the segregation of interstate passengers traveling within their borders. Given that these decisions ran roughshod over the economic freedoms of an important railroad and many of its customers, and, at a minimum, cut some large chips in Congress's exclusive power over interstate commerce, the rulings present striking evidence of the power of the forces working to rebuild America's racial caste system.[125]

Disfranchisement and Jury Exclusion. In regard to juries, little new occurred during the Progressive Era: courts continued to void overt exclusions of blacks and their evidence, but they still ignored the massive practices of covert exclusion.[126] Voting rights remained the area that prompted the most egregious Court refusals to protect African-Americans. In 1898, for example, the Court held that even if Mississippi's registration requirements were, as the state supreme court indicated, aimed at exploiting various "weaknesses" of blacks, they were constitutional because "on their face," at least, they applied to "weak and vicious white men as well."[127] In 1900, a Kentucky district judge with a genuine passion for justice upheld one surviving provision of the 1870 Enforcement Act protecting voting rights, even when applied to private individuals acting to affect a purely state election. To do so, Judge Evans relied on *Ex parte Yarbrough* as well as the passages in Bradley's *Cruikshank* opinion stating that congressional enforcement power was not confined to state infringements.[128] But the Sixth Circuit Court of Appeals overturned Evans's ruling, arguing that this part of the 1870 Act, like those invalidated in *United States v. Reese,* banned exclusions of black voters for reasons other than race. Thus it went beyond Congress's Fifteenth Amendment powers.[129]

The Supreme Court then completed its dismantling of the 1870 Enforcement Act in 1903 by holding that the Fifteenth Amendment did not give Congress power to punish private individuals who used bribery to prevent blacks from voting.[130] Justice Brewer noted that the amendment referred to action "by the United States or by any State." Bradley had nonetheless interpreted it more broadly in parts of his *Cruikshank* opinion. Brewer ignored that fact, citing only the Court's discussion of the Fourteenth Amendment state action limitation in the case. He also thought that the Enforcement Act exceeded Congress's Article I, section 4, authority because it extended to state elections. Harlan and Brown silently dissented.[131]

That same year, in Montgomery, Alabama, blacks tried to circumvent the Court's restrictive rulings by suing to secure, not just voting rights in a particular election, but rights for all elections after 1902. Justice Holmes responded with a pathetically contrived rationale for judicial inaction.[132] Assuming for purposes of argument in *Giles v. Harris* that the "whole registration scheme of the Alabama constitution" might well be, as the black residents of Montgomery contended, "a fraud upon the Constitution," Holmes said that the Court could not become "a party to the unlawful scheme" by "adding another voter" to the state's "fraudulent lists." If the registration system was really massively unconstitutional, then, the Court had to allow it to stand. Holmes also argued, less sophistically but none too boldly, that the court had "little practical power" to remedy the wrongs unless it was "prepared to supervise the voting in that State by officers of the court." Holmes suggested that only the legislative and executive branches could provide that level of relief. Modern experience under the 1965 Civil Rights Act suggests that Holmes was absolutely right about what a remedy required. But by acquiescing in the state registration system and refusing to call for such a remedy, however impotently, he and the majority of the Court signaled that black disfranchisement would continue to go unquestioned.[133]

The next year that shameful signal became blinding in a follow-up case, *Giles v. Teasley*.[134] Reasoning like Holmes, the Alabama Supreme Court had held that if the state's registration scheme violated the Fifteenth Amendment, then there was no federal right to be registered under this unconstitutional system, and Montgomery's blacks could not seek federal judicial relief. If, on the other hand, the registration system did not violate the Fifteenth, they were also clearly not entitled to any such relief. The Supreme Court agreed with this ludicrous Catch-22, while reiterating the practical difficulties of providing judicial remedies when an entire state system violated the Constitution. These and similar decisions amounted not so much to constitutional interpretations as abject confessions of the Court's utter unwillingness to risk confronting massive and popular state violations of the Fifteenth Amendment.[135] Covering their ears and eyes, the majority huddled together and proclaimed that they could neither see nor hear any evil.[136]

Private Discrimination and Peonage. Many other federal court decisions confirmed that a judiciary willing to uphold such thinly masked state violations of black rights would rarely pay heed even to the most brutal oppressions of blacks by white private actors. Progressive Era judges continued to treat as void the remaining laws that sought to punish private individuals who conspired to keep blacks from contracting for their labor freely or who carried out a racially motivated physical assault.[137] Most important, in *Hodges v. United States* (1905), Justice Brewer dismissed the convictions of whites who had driven black laborers off the job at a lumber mill where they were employed. He focused on the Thirteenth Amendment and found that this coercion did not amount to a "badge or incident of servitude," as such tactics might well be employed against those who were not ex-slaves. Blacks must in any case take "their chances with other citizens," without any special protections.[138] Harlan argued at length that invasions of rights of free labor, motivated by racism, were precisely the sorts of incidents of slavery that Congress could address under the Thirteenth; but to no avail. Lower court judges who had maintained hardy hopes, as well as logical arguments, for congressional power to act against private violence now largely abandoned both.[139]

Still, counterarguments inherited from Reconstruction occasionally won lower court victories.[140] Federal judges held that private violence and the many new state laws aimed at preventing blacks from leasing lands, or seeking employment as laborers for hire, effectively imposed involuntary servitude. So did assignments of blacks to chain gangs on convictions for trivial or nonexistent offenses.[141] Here the Supreme Court eventually agreed; but its decisions in the *Peonage Cases* did little to secure equal black citizenship.[142] The Court professed to be concerned only with the forced service involved, not its racial character. In any case, the Thirteenth Amendment protected rights of persons, not citizens.[143] Thus overturning these forms of peonage did not require any insistence on full black civic equality. In practice, moreover, the decisions were not even very effective in combating the spread of peonage laws and practices.[144]

Women

In contrast, the civic prospects of women slowly began to brighten during the Progressive years. A variety of organizations mobilized more women than ever to act publicly on behalf of "maternal" social concerns. Upper- and middle-class reformers like Josephine Shaw Lowell, Florence Kelley, Mary Putnam Jacobi, Sophonisba Breckinridge, and Jane Addams began to attend to the problems of working women more than their predecessors. They formed not only Addams's famed settlement houses, which helped women cope with a wide variety of urban and industrial ills, but also the National Consumers League, started in 1898, and the Women's Trade Union League (WTUL), begun in 1903. Those groups focused on the brutal hours, wages, and working conditions many women felt compelled to accept. Their leaders favored but usually did not stress obtaining the suffrage. But in 1907 Elizabeth Stanton's daughter, Harriet Stanton Blatch, a member of the WTUL executive council, helped persuade that organization to endorse the vote for women even as she formed the Equality League of Self-Supporting Women to link working women with the suffrage cause. That effort, and the example of militant British "suffragettes," helped stir the flagging American suffrage movement. With the efforts of Blatch, Carrie Chapman Catt's Woman Suffrage Party, and new successes in western states in 1909 and 1910, the National American Woman's Suffrage Association attracted a larger and broader membership and the suffrage cause regained momentum.[145]

Gender and Ideology. These Progressive Era women activists varied significantly on whether female citizenship should be rendered identical to that of men, or whether women should still play some special civic role that required special protections. Hence, many scholars view women activists as on a "see-saw," in Nancy Cott's term, between a liberal rhetoric of equal rights and calls for protective laws that would enable women to realize their special virtues. Many women combined both arguments, but the see-saw still tilted toward an emphasis on gender differences. Some progressives, like Jane Addams, were directly influenced in this path by Frances Willard's "civic maternalism." For them, the progressive emphasis on the ways in which people were creatures of their cultures made traditional gender roles central to American womanhood. And as a tactical matter, emphasizing women's distinctive needs still proved most effective in getting laws passed to assist working women.

The progressives who advocated economic regulations thus spoke of gender differences in very conventional terms, while embracing forms of socialism that conservatives feared and loathed. For these reformers, transformations in the organization of labor at home and in industry seemed more essential to women's progress than the vote. The best example was the preeminent feminist book during the first half of the twentieth century, Charlotte Perkins Gilman's *Women and Economics* (1898), a work which helped persuade many middle-class women that their circumstances and interests were linked to those of working women.[146]

Gilman was a remarkable autodidact and prolific writer. Related to the famed Beechers, she nonetheless received relatively little formal education owing to the fact that her father, Frederick Beecher Perkins, left her mother soon after her birth. From the first sentence to the last, *Women and Economics* reveals her indebtedness to her own readings of late nineteenth-century evolutionary sociology, especially the works of Lester Ward and Herbert Spencer. But with bold originality, Gilman insisted that the human species had for too long made women economically dependent on men, to the point of rendering many women effectively enslaved, a relationship that deformed both sexes. Women were crafted to be part ornaments, part drudges. Men were equipped to do all kinds of necessary and creative work; but even men were diminished by relationships with women that encouraged selfishness and vice and denied true human companionship, and by a heredity and rearing conducted by ill-raised mothers.

Gilman thought that those conditions were changing, that the "mother of the race" was moving toward freedom in a "better world," via the "calm, slow, friendly forces of social evolution," including technological, educational, and economic progress. But with reform Darwinists like Ward, she thought that humans could assist these forces instead of ignoring or resisting them. To that end, she mapped out a world in which all work, including much traditionally domestic labor such as cooking, cleaning, and child-rearing, would be done voluntarily, equitably, and usually by professionals of both sexes. That agenda for social transformation remains radical today.[147]

Gilman often wrote of evolution as shaping the entire human race, but she also accepted that humanity had evolved into distinct "peoples" or "races," some more accomplished than others. She contrasted the "retarding effect" of female confinement on the "Oriental nations" to the "tall, strong, and brave" traits transmitted by the "comparatively free" women of the "early Germanic tribes." Gilman also indicated that it would be better for a child to be raised "without mother or family of any sort, in the city of Boston" than by "a large and affectionate family" in "Darkest Africa." And she cited Tennyson on behalf of the proposition that the "Anglo-Saxon blood" was "the most powerful expression" of "fresh racial life," built out of "those sturdy races where the women were more like men, and the men no less manly because of it." Among other feats, those traits had spawned the "strong, fresh spirit of religious revolt" that protested against repressive Catholicism. Eventually populating the U.S. with souls "strengthened, freed, emboldened" by the "Federal Democracy in its organic union," the American bearers of Anglo-Saxon blood were, quite naturally, continuing to pioneer new births of freedom.[148]

Gilman recognized, however, that "nervous strain" accompanied the transformation of traditional forms, including gender roles, family structures, and work. She saw such strain as so characteristic of American life that she labeled it "Americanitis." Much of her book tried to reassure Americans that these changes were natural—indeed, developments for which Americans were particularly well suited—and that they promised a fuller realization of their humanity and a strengthening of the race, not any significant losses. In part, then, Gilman was clearly drawing on themes of Anglo-Saxon superiority and America's special destiny to make change more palatable. But in so doing, she typified the turn in progressive reform thought to evolutionary based Americanist doctrines that provided support for some hierarchies and exclusions in American citizenship laws even as they criticized others. Not only white Southern women in the NAWSA, but also progressive supporters of women's suffrage made the nativist potential of these arguments explicit during the years leading up to the passage of the Nineteenth Amendment.[149]

Unsurprisingly, Americanist arguments were even more useful to those who opposed women's suffrage, including many women. Upper-class women, in particular, joined in several organizations, eventually merged into the National Association Opposed to Woman Suffrage in 1911, that contended that traditional homes and families were threatened by the spread of the franchise. Southern white women, like Southern white men, also feared that female enfranchisement would compound the difficulties of preventing blacks from voting. The South's congressional delegations thus formed the largest obstacle to passage of a national amendment. It would, indeed, win out only over the dissents of nine Southern states, plus Delaware.

But in the nation as a whole, perhaps the most potent opposition came from economic interests who feared how women might vote. The old opponents of the WCTU, the liquor interests, were most active. Because so many advocates of female suffrage were also progressives or socialists who supported extensive economic regulations, many other businesses also worked to defeat suffrage referenda. Regardless of their motives, however, virtually all those opposing female enfranchisement used ascriptive arguments about woman's proper sphere, and about the dangers of giving political power to lower races and foreigners. Most antisuffrage speakers were careful to claim equality—indeed, moral superiority—for white women at least; but they enthusiastically grafted arguments of evolutionary biology onto older religious doctrines to insist that the preservation of separate spheres was essential to the good of children, men, women, the nation, the races, and the fulfillment of God's will.[150]

Legislative Developments. The major Progressive Era federal law affecting women's citizenship was the 1907 Expatriation Act. It settled the main ambiguity left by the 1855 Naturalization Act, with which the courts had wrestled indecisively: Did an American woman lose her citizenship by marrying a foreigner? Many commentators thought that they should, deriding in particular wealthy women who tried to "play at being" aristocrats by marrying (allegedly) titled foreigners instead of "men of their own race." The result, critics claimed, was that conniving alien men married American women simply to get a foothold in the United States. Congress agreed that such practices had to be stopped, so it rejected some contrary Justice Department opinions and designated these marriages as acts of voluntary expatriation by American women. The 1907 law was therefore sometimes termed the Gigolo Act. Because the law rejected common-law traditions that had based female citizenship on birthplace, not marital status, it actually embraced coverture more fully than many early judicial decisions had done. Even so, the measure passed with little debate or fanfare.[151]

At the state level, there were more egalitarian developments. California gave women the vote in 1911. Native-born women wed to aliens then protested their disfranchisement by the 1907 act. California Representative William Kent introduced a repeal provision in 1912, but it did not get out of committee. Congressmen argued that it would be "abnormal" for a wife to vote when her foreign husband could not, and that, as Representative Kendall explained, "we do not want our girls to marry foreigners." The foreigners in question were usually Englishmen, Germans, and Scandinavians, because under California law white women could not marry "Malay," "Mongolians," or blacks.[152]

But new activists also won a state referendum in Washington in 1910; and after their ensuing California success many felt new hope for the suffrage campaign. These victories also, however, aroused opponents of women's suffrage, who won or stole victory in bitter referenda battles in Michigan, Ohio, and Wisconsin in 1912. Despite wins in Arizona, Kansas, Oregon, and the Alaska territory, many activists decided to return to the national amendment route. That course finally prevailed in 1920.[153]

Judicial Actions. Whether they considered old or new laws, federal judges during the Progressive years generally still took a protectionist stance toward women that often underlined the subordination of women to their husbands, fathers, and male legislators.[154] The basic rule, to which courts adhered unless new laws explicitly forbade them to do so, was that fathers and husbands had "property rights" to the "services" of their daughters and wives, including rights against those who led their women into "dishonor."[155] In 1904, for example, the Supreme Court specified that husbands had "certain personal and exclusive" property rights to sexual intercourse with their wives, rights upon which the Court thought "the whole social order rests." Wives could not affect those rights by "giving any consent" to sex with another (though, Peckham none too chivalrously asserted, such consent was "almost universally the case").[156] Wives could also still not sue abusive husbands for assault and battery. In so ruling, the Supreme Court construed narrowly a District of Columbia law that gave married women more rights to sue in tort. Though assault was a tort, Justice Day contended that such a "radical and far-reaching" change as granting a wife power to sue her husband must be specified in the law, not found by implication. The "atrocious wrongs" of battery could, he asserted, be addressed under the "statutes of divorce and alimony," should wives live long enough to employ them.[157] Similarly, wives still could acquire separate state citizenships from their husbands only when courts thought this necessary for their protection.[158]

And as many lower courts had already been ruling that a wife's national citizenship always followed her husband's, making expatriation the price of marrying a foreigner, they readily upheld the 1907 "Gigolo Act."[159] In MacKenzie v. Hare (1915), the Supreme Court also did so, holding that the law expatriated and disfranchised an American-born California woman who would have been able to vote in the state after 1911 had she not married a British singer. Justice Joseph McKenna wrote that the "identity of husband and wife," with "dominance" given to the husband, worked "in many instances for her protection." While expressing "sympathy" with Mrs. MacKenzie, a long-time suffrage activist, McKenna maintained that her expatriation and disfranchisement were "voluntary," as she had married with knowledge of the consequences for her citizenship. He also thought that the rule might somehow help the nation avoid unspecified diplomatic "embarrassments" and "controversies."[160]

Throughout these years, federal judges also remained wholly unsympathetic to the desires of alien women to obtain American citizenship for themselves when their alien spouses did not desire it. Even Henrietta Cohen, who had resided in the U.S. for thirty years, could not overcome the handicap of a foreign husband.[161] Anti-immigrant as well as patriarchal sentiments were also manifested in grudging judicial rulings on just when marriage to an American gave foreign women citizenship, and on how far such citizenship exempted women from normal restrictions on immigrants. A Rhode Island district court judge insisted in 1908 that a foreign woman must be present in the U.S. to be naturalized along with her husband. She could not claim automatic naturalization abroad as a means to ease entry into the U.S. Similarly, the Supreme Court ruled that marriage to an American offered no relief to an alien woman (one racially ineligible for naturalization) who was subject to deportation for prostitution.[162] Yet hostile as these decisions may seem, the "protective" elements in these judicial views of gender provided fertile grounds for some progressive reform legislation, as many scholars have noted. Economic regulations designed to shield women from the ravages of the marketplace received favorable treatment even from justices who regarded such laws as anathema when they applied to male workers.[163]

The landmark in this regard is *Muller v. Oregon.*[164] There Florence Kelley and other leaders of the National Consumers League, along with their attorney, Louis Brandeis, used massive statistical evidence to gain the first major constitutional victory for progressive economic regulation. Curt Muller, a laundry owner, challenged an Oregon law limiting the hours that women could work at certain jobs on the ground that women "equally with men" were "endowed with the fundamental and inalienable rights of liberty and property." States violated these equal rights when they stopped women from contracting for employment on any terms they wished. Justice Brewer disagreed, finding that the famous Brandeis brief in the case showed that women's "special physical organization" made long hours dangerous to them. Such work thus threatened their "maternal functions," including the "rearing and education of the children" and "the maintenance of the home," on which the "well-being of the race" rested. As to why women could not obtain contractual terms consistent with their performance of any maternal functions they should undertake, Brewer explained that a typical woman's "disposition and habits" would "operate against a full assertion" of her rights due to insufficient "self-reliance." No matter how equal her legal status, woman was destined to be "dependent upon man," and so laws "designed for her protection may be sustained, even when like legislation is not necessary for men, and could not be sustained."[165]

In so writing, Brewer transformed the discussion of women's physical capabilities in the brief into a much more complete endorsement of permanent female dependency than it had done. He also repudiated the possibility that men might also require protective legislation, which the brief had left open. As Judith Baer has noted, the case thus had limited value as a precedent for progressive economic regulation in general, and it seems to have stimulated laws premised on women's inherent dependency. Some of these laws valiantly combatted brutal conditions that women lacked the economic leverage to alter and real burdens that only they faced. Others constrained rather than enhanced women's employment opportunities. They all, moreover, reinforced beliefs that men could properly decide what women could do, in the name of protecting women, children, and the race.[166]

Native Americans. On its surface, the story of Native Americans during the Progressive Era departs even more sharply from the dominant pattern of renewed racial and ethnic civic stratifications than in the Gilded Age. Progressive Era officials redoubled efforts to make citizens of all Native Americans. Congress eventually did so by passing the Indian Citizenship Act in 1924, the very year in which it put its racist national origins quota system on a permanent footing. Hence the question arises: If doctrines of racial hierarchy were so prominent in centrist Progressivism, why did the civic status of these nonwhite peoples apparently improve?

Leading historians give different answers. Frederick Hoxie argues that any anomaly is confined to the religious reformers' efforts in the Gilded Age. After 1900, he contends, progressive legislators, bureaucrats, and courts made many Native Americans citizens, but they legally defined the status as a tutelary, second-class membership like that imposed on other Americans of color. Francis Paul Prucha believes instead that humanitarian impulses, however misguided, continued to shape federal treatment of Native Americans in the Progressive years, rather than any new racism.[167]

On balance, the developments of these years support Hoxie's interpretation. Even as federal officials continued to break up the tribes and promise Native Americans a citizenship status that few desired, legislators and judges also specified that after naturalization, the former tribesmen would still not be equal citizens.[168] Even so, Prucha is right that these inegalitarian positions reflected a deeper continuity. Most Gilded Age reformers had always been "intent on forcing" their own standards on their "wards."[169] The Progressive Era rulings defining second-class Native American citizenship stemmed from official recognition that many Native Americans were resisting being hammered into the centrist progressives' Americanist mold. As Hoxie notes, during a period when "growing social diversity and shrinking social space" threatened many Americans' "sense of national identity," they regarded such contestation over "the meaning of national citizenship" as unacceptable. The members of the "white Protestant majority culture" therefore structured the rights of Native American citizens to reaffirm their own "dominance."[170]

The failure of late nineteenth-century efforts to create self-supporting, "civilized," Christian Native Americans via forced division of tribal lands into individual allotments, and the ongoing admission of western states to the Union, led to a decline in the influence of religious reform groups and an increase in the power of western elected representatives and economic developers during the Progressive Era. These groups were hostile to the assimilationist goals of the Dawes Act. They wanted to limit federal assistance to Native Americans, and they opposed giving Native Americans equal rights. Many westerners thought that permitting Native Americans to sell their allotments and claim equal citizenship produced large numbers of drunken, aimless, dangerous former tribesmen. These anti-Indian whites formed an odd alliance with bureaucrats in the Indian Office, who feared that assimilationist policies were costing them many of their functions, including the protective regulation of former tribesmen that many believed to be still necessary.

Hence support grew not only for cutbacks in education and annuity programs, but also for the 1906 Burke Act.[171] It delayed citizenship for Native Americans until the end of the period during which they held their allotments in trust,

before they were able to claim full ownership. The time when they would get title to the land and be naturalized was now to be decided on by the Secretary of
the Interior. The act thus gave legal force to beliefs that Native Americans were a
near-savage race who could not be quickly improved and must still be firmly controlled. Critics protested that the new law created "an aristocracy of citizenship"
among those allotment recipients whom the Secretary permitted to become citizens, but the complaints had little impact.[172] Instead, in the prevailing spirit of
disdain for Native American abilities, in 1907 Congress gave Indian Commissioner Francis Leupp the power to sell the allotments of Native Americans judged
"noncompetent" to work them. Leupp used this power liberally, feeling that
whites should not be denied resources that Native Americans were not ready to
use properly.

Criticisms of these measures came from religious reformers and from a few
western whites who were suspicious of what they saw as a self-serving Washington bureaucracy. They correctly anticipated that the discretion the Burke Act gave
to federal bureaucrats would mean further rapid alienation of the dwindling
quantity of allotment lands, as officials complied with ongoing pressures from
whites to approve leases or sales.[173] The officials claimed, and no doubt many believed, that they were getting better deals for improvident former tribesmen, incapable of farming, who would otherwise be cheated out of their last assets. Even
so, that paternalism confirmed that Native Americans were not being treated as
civic equals. Their new status was instead akin to that of native-born African
Americans and Chinese-Americans: in different ways, all were being made second-class citizens. Here, too, the courts proved compliant.

The Courts and Native American Rights. For some time, however, judges continued to struggle with whether special limits on "emancipated" Native Americans,
and on lands to which Native American titles had been extinguished, were
valid.[174] Most ruled that racial identity mattered more than titular membership
in a tribe or in the U.S. citizenry, but what that fact implied for those who were
officially U.S. citizens was contested.[175] At times judges reached contradictory
conclusions.[176] The Supreme Court never went far toward respecting Native
Americans as equals: in *Lone Wolf v. Hitchcock* (1903), the Court unanimously
sustained congressional power to allot tribal lands as it wished, unconstrained by
prior treaties or a tribe's own wishes.[177] Shortly thereafter it ruled in *United States
v. Rickert* that so long as the government still held title in trust to their allotments,
Native Americans were "yet wards of the Nation," in a condition of pupilage or
dependency.[178]

But in *Matter of Heff* (1905), Justice Brewer observed that Congress had recently undertaken "a new policy" of freeing Native Americans from guardianship

and assigning them "all the rights and obligations of citizens." Even though their lands might not be alienable and the U.S. might still hold ultimate title, allotment recipients were thus both U.S. and state citizens, and therefore subject to state, not federal, liquor regulation.[179] Acknowledging that "the recognized relation between the Government and the Indians is that of a superior and an inferior," Brewer asked rhetorically whether the fact that "one has Indian, and only Indian blood in his veins" meant that a person was "to be forever one of a special class over whom the General Government may in its discretion assume the rights of guardianship which it has once abandoned," regardless of whether "the individual himself consents." He concluded to the contrary that once guardianship had ended, a Native American was a citizen like any other.[180]

The passage of the Burke Act the next year succeeded in limiting the impact of the *Heff* decision, but for a time some federal courts echoed Brewer's bold affirmation of equal citizenship for assimilated Native Americans.[181] Soon, however, other courts, and an increasingly divided Supreme Court, began to circumscribe the *Heff* ruling. Special rules for Native Americans living outside their former tribes and in them were often appropriate after all.[182] Some judges tried to reconcile these conflicting results by suggesting that, notwithstanding citizenship, federal guardianship over lands to which it still held ultimate title remained in effect. The personal conduct of citizen allottees, in contrast, was now subject to state regulatory authority, voiding, for example, federal liquor laws.[183] Other judges complained that the logic of that distinction led to virtual denials of Native American citizenship.[184]

By 1909, Brewer and a unanimous Court accepted that citizenship for allottees did not need to be taken seriously. Federal guardianship over their personal conduct, not just their lands, could be retained. In *United States v. Celestine*, the Court sustained federal jurisdiction over a murder committed on the Tulalip reservation in the state of Washington by one former Tulalip against another. Both were now citizen allottees.[185] Brewer lamely tried to distinguish the *Heff* case on the ground that it dealt with allottees under the Dawes Act, and those in *Celestine* had been made under a different treaty. But his conclusion admitted the influence of the 1906 Burke Act, which he said indicated that Congress "believed that it had been hasty" in "granting full rights of citizenship to Indians." He also echoed resurgent beliefs in racial inferiority. Brewer observed that notwithstanding "the gift of citizenship, both the defendant and the murdered woman remained Indians by race," and that Congress should not be thought to have surrendered jurisdiction over any "Indian within the limits of a reservation" unless it did so quite specifically.[186]

The retreat from full and equal citizenship for Native Americans was virtually complete.[187] In keeping with its developing jurisprudence of strong property rights, the Court paused only at recognizing congressional power to abrogate property titles acquired by Native Americans under previous statutes or agreements, finding that the Fifth Amendment prevented such takings without compensation.[188] But as Woodrow Wilson's first term ended in 1916, the Court formally overruled the *Heff* decision in *United States v. Nice*, confirming that Native Americans were second-class citizens as long as Congress wanted them to be.[189] Justice Van Devanter wrote that citizenship was "not incompatible with tribal existence or continued guardianship, and so may be conferred without completely emancipating the Indians or placing them beyond the reach of congressional regulations adopted for their protection."[190]

Civic Education. The topic of civic education aptly concludes discussion of the views of American citizenship expressed in the laws of the Progressive Era. Here, even more than in policies of exclusion and internal hierarchies, was where Americans tried to shape who and what future American citizens would be. In this regard, the failure of more nationalistic progressives to carry the day fully is immediately apparent: the story of civic education during the Progressive Era remained one of very little national legislative activity, and there are few federal judicial rulings.[191] Yet these were extraordinarily important years in the history of American civic education. Nothing was a more central concern for many progressives, so much so that "progressive education" became a catch phrase in twentieth-century American life.

But in education, too, the conflicting meanings of Progressivism were visible. For a few right progressives, progressivism meant hard-nosed recognition that education could do little more than prepare people for the economic roles that suited their abilities, as Spencer had preached. For most centrists, it could be an efficient means through which scientifically trained educational experts could endow people with not only the economic but also the cognitive, cultural, and moral traits needed for them to be better American citizens. And for the small number of left progressives, education was at the core of a vision of a democratic society in which expertise and technical efficiency would be subordinated to popular participation, a society in which, moreover, cultural pluralism would be celebrated, not decried.

These different perspectives converged on some points, particularly the value of vocational education, still the only type that Congress was willing to support for all Americans during this era.[192] But the various forms of Progressivism were in other ways opposed; and though no single outlook prevailed across the board, centrist progressive forms of ascriptivism again won the most victories. Emblematic in this regard was the one other major federal involvement in education, the programs run by the Bureau of Indian Affairs, which remained efforts to impose Anglo-Saxon Protestant values and practices upon a resistant population. Though some other ethnic and cultural groups gained schools more to their liking, by and large reformers consciously structured the fast-growing systems of American public education to prepare minorities and women for the ultimately subordinate vocations and civic statuses most of the nation's leadership thought proper for them.[193]

The Varieties of Progressive Education. William Torrey Harris's Hegelianism, Spencer's laissez-faire evolutionary theories, and Ward's reform Darwinism all served as philosophic precursors to the rise of the pragmatist educational outlooks of the early twentieth century, now most identified with John Dewey. Dewey in his younger years had in fact been a Hegelian who published his first essay in Harris's journal, and he had also been an ardent critical consumer of Spencer. Although Dewey came to reject the grand formal comprehensive systems that characterized the work of Spencer, Hegel, and, to a lesser degree, Ward, he derived from them and others certain points embraced by all advocates of progressive education. These included an acceptance of human social evolution and the institutionally and socially shaped character of human beings; an esteem for rational scientific progress; and a definition of knowledge in terms of what worked to solve human problems, an emphasis that Dewey took far beyond his predecessors. But progressives divided on other educational issues.[194]

Following David Tyack, many scholars refer to centrist progressive educational reformers as "administrative progressives," in contrast especially to more radically democratic left progressives like Dewey.[195] Although the centrists shared more of Spencer's vocational educational concerns than the left did, adherents of both viewpoints continued the American tradition of espousing public education as primarily an instrument of good citizenship, not economic welfare. Both also thought that public schools needed to be formalized and made compulsory, scientific, efficient, professional, and nonpartisan, while also being made more responsive to differing student needs, and more democratically legitimate. Only such schools could prepare students for "the complex nature of citizenship in a technological, urban society."[196]

Beyond these agreements, two key contrasts marked educational reformers as "administrative" rather than "democratic" progressives. The first was the degree to which they favored empowering expert specialists ensconced in new bureaucracies to govern school systems, as opposed to parents, local community representatives, or even teachers and students. Centrist proponents of giving power to nonpartisan bureaucratic experts conceived of good citizenship as conduct that expressed sensible support for modern specialists. Thus Harvard president and educational reform leader Charles Eliot advised in 1898 that confidence in "experts, and willingness to employ them and abide by their decisions, are among the best signs" of an educated community and thriving democracy. Left advocates of more direct popular control of schools instead thought of citizenship in terms of democratic participation, which education should equip all to do, and which should be embodied in the structure of the classroom and school supervision, as well as in the curriculum and in elective school boards.[197]

The second contrast was the degree to which educators thought that science dictated both the necessity of assimilating all citizens into progressive versions of Anglo-Saxon Protestant cultural values, and the propriety of providing different, lesser educations to most nonwhite, nonmale students. Many of the centrist "administrative" progressives, like Stanford's Ellwood Cubberley, believed that the new immigrants from southern and eastern Europe could not be equipped for either citizenship or the franchise until and unless they had mastered an Americanizing civic education in "Anglo-Saxon conceptions of righteousness, liberty, law, order, public decency, and government." And many thought that the members of the lower classes generally would remain fit only for vocational education, and that even with such education, the "lower races" should be viewed as in "pupilage." Women, too, should receive distinct educations appropriate to their distinct stations. These conclusions were thought to be supported by the most advanced scientific research, including intelligence testing. Left progressives instead carried forth the more egalitarian traditions of the Radical Republicans and their Gilded Age admirers. They accepted the propriety of allowing different religious and ethnic groups considerable, though not total, freedom to structure education for their members as they wished, and they also thought that the public schools should provide equal opportunities for all citizens without regard to their gender, race, religion, or ethnicity.[198]

Though scholars debate many aspects of the history of this period, few dispute that it was the camp favoring unelected expert control of schools and the propagation of considerable cultural homogeneity, combined with public education differentiated according to the perceived abilities and needs of different groups, that by and large prevailed.[199] Paul Peterson stresses that not just upperclass WASPs but Catholics, Lutherans, and white immigrants of all classes and national origins generally received good schooling from public or private institutions as a result of the contested politics of these years. Yet even he accepts that the professional educators had considerable success in shaping public schools in accordance with their administrative progressive vision, and their cultural standards affected notions of proper education in private Jewish, Catholic, and Lutheran schools as well as public ones. And however one assesses how far Americanization amounted to repressive forms of socialization of white immigrants, Peterson and most other scholars agree that the burgeoning American education systems of these years were firmly "caste-like" in their treatment of blacks, Native Americans, and Asian-Americans. They also used "ascriptive criteria" to justify more limited educational opportunities for women. The centrality of such inegalitarian ascriptive Americanism to administrative progressive school reformers has been affirmed in a comparative analysis by British scholar Andy Green. He concluded that, while "in Europe schooling was most coercive in relation to class formation, in America it showed its most authoritarian face in relation to the subordination of ethnic minorities, in the marginalization and segregation of blacks and in the coercive assimilation of immigrant cultures," as well as in "the construction of different gender roles for men and women."[200]

After its founding in 1909, the National Association for the Advancement of Colored People fought against these segregated schools and for the improvement of black colleges. John Dewey and Jane Addams also sought to create schools in which all had meaningful roles and experts were not privileged; and they, Catholic and Jewish groups, immigrant organizations, and others provided political support to combat the most repressive forms of Americanizing education for immigrants. Even so, the celebrations of diversity proposed by left progressives had little impact on the culturally Americanist public school paideia. Dewey, like William Torrey Harris, in fact endorsed programs stressing vocational training for blacks. Many of his most influential followers supported hierarchical educational systems much more wholeheartedly than he did. Hence the various culturally pluralist, radically democratic visions of the left progressives all had but minor impact on how the fast-growing American schools were run.[201]

Instead, the inegalitarian educational structures built up during the Gilded Age by and large only became more entrenched during the Progressive years. To be sure, public schooling as a whole continued to grow, to 17.8 million students in 1910, 16.9 million of them in kindergarten through eighth grade, versus only 1.5 million in private schools. A total of 355,000 students were enrolled in higher education. But schooling for Asian-Americans and African-Americans remained largely segregated, and for blacks education was confined largely to the primary level. By 1910, less than 3 percent of blacks aged fifteen to nineteen attended high school in the Southern states (where most blacks still lived), versus more than 10 percent for whites. Black migration to Northern cities meant that more black children lived in urban school districts with higher attendance. Some Southern states responded by accepting improved black schooling to discourage migration. Private philanthropic efforts and black self-help also increased; but, on the whole, black education remained separate and highly unequal. Girls continued to outnumber boys in high schools, but they were still tracked for a variety of women's vocations, which did not include professions requiring graduate education or political life.[202]

A few social scientists, led by anthropologist Franz Boas, began to criticize conceptions of different races in favor of different cultures, and to dispute denigrations of non-Christian, noncapitalist cultures. Other factors, however, played more of a role in combating harshly assimilationist schooling, especially in regard to Native Americans. The failures of the Dawes Act dampened enthusiasm for Indian education programs, though federal support continued. Government ethnologists like John Wesley Powell's assistant, W. J. McGee, and Powell's successor as head of the Bureau of Ethnology, W. H. Holmes, argued once more that Native Americans were "fading out to total oblivion" in the "final battle of the races." Hence educational efforts seemed wasted on them.[203] In 1900 Congress made the most emphatic of several proclamations that the declining dollars still supplied to Catholic contract schools for Native Americans would end that year. Catholics nonetheless still managed to gain some funds thereafter. Precisely because President Theodore Roosevelt and Indian Commissioner Leupp had little real faith in Indian education, even vocational education, they were willing to leave it to others. Protestant Indian reformers then mounted an unsuccessful judicial challenge to the propriety of Catholic missions receiving funds; but victory at the Supreme Court did not stop the waning of missionary schooling.[204]

At this point Leupp and many educators began to stress vocational education for Native Americans more heavily, a fact which has sparked some debate among scholars. Some like Prucha see the government as continuing the goal of promoting full assimilation of Indians on ultimately equal terms, whereas Hoxie sees this development as a product of the newly influential theories of racial inferiority and as amounting to acceptance that Indians would always remain a subordinate group. The egalitarian case is buttressed by the fact that many progressives stressed more practical, vocational education for all groups, including native whites. But in light of the fact that more affluent white men, at least, had opportunities for broad-ranging higher education that others usually did not, and in light of the reliance on racial theories to defend much of this vocational orientation, Hoxie's arguments seem stronger. In any case, the education provided Native Americans remained heavily assimilative, a policy continually justified in terms of preparing them for full American citizenship. At the same time, the largely vocational and religious training imposed on often unwilling students gave them little chance to advance much above the lower ranks of American society.[205]

Overall, the designs visible in education for citizenship during the Progressive Era etched in miniature the broader patterns of U.S. citizenship laws for these years. Most policymakers believed that, in order for American civilization to be preserved and advanced, the highest stations of U.S. intellectual, economic, social, and political life must, for the foreseeable future, be largely occupied by middle- and upper-class men of northern European descent. Most blacks, Native Americans, Latinos, Asian-Americans, immigrant working-class whites, and women were expected to be unfit for full and equal citizenship for generations to come, at best. Hence they normally received tutelary, vocational education, often in segregated environments, and afterward entered political and economic systems in which by law they could rarely hope to buy, sell, or rent property, borrow money, vote, hold office, or serve on juries on an equal footing with white men. Immigration and naturalization policies were equally hostile to all Asians and increasingly so to poor whites, as well as to women who married most men of color. Ironically, Reconstruction's legal legacies did leave Africans officially eligible to come to the U.S. and gain citizenship. But in other respects, myriad laws and customs pinned African-Americans to the bottom rung of the nation's racial and class hierarchies. They remained the "race" against which all others favorably contrasted themselves. By and large, all these groups achieved levels of success consonant with the very different opportunities that these systems afforded them.

These patterns suggest that, although intellectual, economic, demographic, and social conditions had wrought extraordinary changes in the nation's political culture, at the deepest level some basic imperatives of civic life still operated during the Progressive years. That fact was true even though Progressive Era thinkers and politicians recrafted the nation's political traditions in ways that brought them much closer to their modern form, and in ways that produced major liberalizing and democratizing changes. American leaders now expressly built their civic principles more on recognition of the evolving, complexly interconnected character of social life than on doctrines of unchanging, divinely endowed individual rights; most took pragmatic scientific competence and democratic will, along with mainstream religious views, as appropriate guides for political means and ends. Those innovations altered traditional liberal doctrines of economic and personal freedoms in ways that often permitted more regulation in the name of the common good, in the manner of many liberals today, and they transformed older doctrines of republican self-governance in ways that expanded many citizens' opportunities for direct participation in democratic governance, thereby pioneering much current democratic thought. The changes were also calculated to win the support of the great masses of Americans who felt threatened by the economic and social conditions and mounting inequalities of the turn-of-the-century United States. Many of those voters wished government to help them surmount those challenges, but desired assurances that they could shape how government did so.

Yet progressive notions of scientifically designed and democratically authorized reforms were far from universally popular. Many in the nation's more affluent and educated classes still harbored doubts about the competence of much of the rest of the citizenry, even as many of the masses, and indeed Americans of all classes, were not so sure that they would be well governed by the new scientific professionals who claimed to know how to achieve their good. Nothing in the new pragmatic liberalism or the new notions of more direct democracy suggested, moreover, what made the rapidly changing, increasingly polyglot U.S. population into one people, to which its members should feel loyal. The widespread preoccupation with conflicting notions of Americanism during the Progressive decades shows how important that political imperative of nation-building remained.

In response to it, amid a climate of racial Darwinism and European imperialism as well as rising economic inequalities, the nation's dominant groups found that they could best entrench and expand their support by portraying Americans as the world's greatest master race, as Theodore Roosevelt's centrist Progressivism did most resoundingly. The notion that their nation had a special mission to perfect and extend modern civilization at home and around the globe inspired patriotic allegiance in millions of voters, as similar claims had in turbulent times going back to the Revolution. And because most voters were still middle-class white men, most found reassuring the fact that this mission justified keeping the poorer classes, the nonwhite races, and women in subordinate places for the foreseeable future, even if it promised more freedom and equality eventually to those who proved worthy.

Thus inegalitarian ascriptive doctrines of racial, gender, and cultural superiority, reformulated like the nation's liberal and republican traditions in light of contemporary knowledge and conditions, continued to provide potent, perhaps irreplaceable narratives of distinctive national worth in the most politically successful conceptions of civic identity that Americans articulated as the nation moved into the twentieth century. Indeed, the question of whether the United States could sustain itself without maintaining such ascriptive myth and systems of inequality in one form or another would not be seriously addressed until our own time. And it is likely that for a long time to come, the answers will remain far from clear.

Epilogue

The Party of America

L
ike a far greater political analyst in an even more divided time, I am "loath to close" on the somber note with which the preceding chapter ends.[1] Many readers will wonder what this history suggests about the moral status of American civic identity today. Though no definitive answers can be offered, I think some lessons can be drawn from the story of U.S. citizenship laws as Americans have written it up through the early years of the twentieth century. If these conclusions are less than comforting, they still suggest that Americans have grounds to hope that they can make their civic lives significantly better than they are.

I believe there are two central types of lessons: the first, descriptive and explanatory, the second, normative or moral. My descriptive and explanatory claims have been the main focus of the preceding chapters. The yet more speculative normative lessons will be the main focus of this chapter. The implications I draw are, however, based on the historical political realities just reviewed, as I believe moral theorizing generally should be. It is of course questionable whether such theorizing ever has much effect on politics. But the course of U.S. history, including recent history, suggests that the elites who do so much to shape civic identities are likely to draw on political theories that promise to have broad appeal, so long as they do not unduly threaten the elites' own interests. Thus there is reason to hope that, if Americans can learn from historical experience which elements a political ideology must contain if it is to speak to popular and elite aspirations in the United States, they may be better able to craft a civic vision that is both morally defensible and politically feasible.

The basic descriptive and explanatory lessons of this study are first, that U.S. citizenship laws have always expressed illiberal, undemocratic ascriptive myths of U.S. civic identity, along with various types of liberal and republican ones, in logically inconsistent but politically effective combinations; and second, that we should expect this to be the case. The founders of the United States did indeed define and construct their new nation in accord with Enlightenment doctrines of individual liberties and republican self-governance more than any regime before and most since, as so many analysts have insisted. And the principles and institutions that those early elites adopted have contributed in many ways to movements that eventually achieved greater liberalization and democratization of the U.S. than the founders ever anticipated. But from Thomas Paine's identification of European-descended American men as the new chosen people of the Protestant God, to the Federalists' and the Whigs' Anglophilic nativism, to the Jeffersonian and Jacksonian doctrines of scientific racism, to the stark evolutionary theories of racial and gender hierarchies during the Gilded Age and the Progressive Era, U.S. leaders always fostered senses of what made Americans a distinct "people" that relied in part on inegalitarian ascriptive themes. The history of U.S. citizenship policies demonstrates incontrovertibly that the legal prerogatives of the majority of the domestic population through most of the nation's past have officially been defined in conformity with those ascriptive doctrines, at least as much as purely liberal and republican ones. And many examples, like the reductions in the rights of African-Americans from the Revolution to the 1850s, and from Reconstruction to the Progressive years, as well as the new restrictions imposed on married women in 1855, Asian-Americans in the late nineteenth century, and homosexuals in the twentieth, all indicate that neither the possession nor the fresh achievement of greater equality can guarantee against later losses of status due to renewed support for various types of ascriptive hierarchy.

In the foregoing chapters, the persistent attractions of such ascriptive views, and their periodic resurgence in popularity, have seemed traceable to three main factors. The respectability that intellectuals have bestowed on such views out of honest belief in their truth cannot be discounted, even if the political motivations of men like Jefferson, Morse, Nott, Lodge, and Commons have often been clear. The two prime causes, however, appear to be unequivocally political. The most obvious source is the threat posed by many liberalizing and democratic reforms to institutionalized systems of status and meaning in which a large number of Americans have been deeply invested, prompting many to hunt for rationales to preserve or even extend their traditional political, economic, and social places and privileges. The further source of ascriptivism's appeal stressed here is the inability of egalitarian liberal republican views to provide an understanding of why Americans should see themselves as loyal members of this society in preference to all others, a task that ascriptive myths perform well. To be sure, the very real material and moral attractions of liberal democratic ideals and institutions have often checked the sway of ascriptive doctrines. Furthermore, the reforms of the second half of the twentieth century have been momentous enough to support beliefs that, in the long run, Tocqueville's view of history's democratic trajectory may prove right. There is, however, little reason to think that the traditional limitations of liberal democratic doctrines in meeting the imperatives of nation-building, or the distinct advantages of various ascriptive doctrines for meeting those imperatives, are as yet things of the past.

If these arguments are right, it is likely that they apply not just to the United States but more generally. In most if not all societies, we should expect citizenship or nationality laws to be products of ongoing contestation and compromise that display significant internal tensions. They will generally be webs that are politically woven out of competing civic myths, with ascriptive elements visible everywhere, though far more predominant in some periods, some political visions, and some regimes than others. And they are likely to have most appeal just when prevailing senses of political identity have been severely shaken, creating voids that they are well equipped to fill.

Today, the prestige of doctrines of democracy and human rights has never been greater around the globe, and politicians have strong incentives to cast civic ideologies in these terms. Many can also be counted on to try to build political communities that are as extensive as possible, so it is not surprising that some leaders support institutions that transcend existing national boundaries. It is also evident, however, that momentous changes in the former Soviet bloc, the European Community, the Middle East, and many other parts of the world continue to provide fertile soil for ethnic and religious nationalisms and other ascriptive doctrines of political identity. It remains true as well that champions of new, more cosmopolitan political orders still seem utopian in comparison with politicians who offer to lead and to serve smaller, more cohesive populations. Such politicians and their citizenries remain likely to be drawn to accounts of just why they rightly form a separate people that contain compelling, confirming ascriptive myths.

These lessons may seem obvious, or they may seem wrong. But in any case, they have not been absorbed by most leading twentieth-century normative thinkers who have tried to define political principles, for the U.S. and other modern societies, free of the invidious ascriptive inequalities that have so pervaded the histories of many nations. This highly regrettable state of affairs weakens the philosophic case and political cause of liberal democracy, a cause that I share. In the remainder of this chapter, I will show how many leading versions of modern liberal democratic theory falter because they remain oblivious to the political imperatives that have structured U.S. civic identity and nation-building more broadly. Then I will suggest how those who favor liberal democratic ideals over ascriptive ones might better define and advance their principles.

The Costs of Neglecting Nation-Building

Although left progressives like John Dewey, W. E. B. Du Bois, Charlotte Perkins Gilman, Randolph Bourne, and Horace Kallen had limited impact on the civic policies of the U.S. during the first half of the twentieth century, versions of their different visions have been visible in the later politics of the modern civil rights era, and they have had even more influence on modern normative theorizing. Leading contemporary liberal and radical democratic theorists offer views that carry forward the various brands of democratic cultural pluralism that their progressive predecessors put forth. In contrast to the traditional ascriptive doctrines that they have opposed, the lines of modern democratic theory that run from John Dewey to John Rawls and from Horace Kallen to Iris Marion Young are in many ways normatively commendable. The reform movements that these theorists have striven to defend and assist have also accomplished much that seems worthwhile.[2] Yet current theorists have done more to replay than to remedy the shortcomings of left progressive thought in regard to nation-building.

For present purposes, the multiple variants of democratic cultural pluralist civic visions can be placed under two headings, which might be termed *universalist integrationists* and *separatist pluralists*.[3] For as Charles Taylor has noted, modern political philosophies emphasizing equal respect for all instead of traditional ascriptive inequalities have proven capable of elaboration in two rather different directions.[4] The concern to make public institutions available to all, ending all forms of second-class citizenship, points to a politics that promotes greater inclusiveness in public life. That spirit characterized the writings of Dewey, Bourne, and Du Bois during his middle years, especially. It was also visible in the early civil rights movement and Great Society laws, which opposed segregated schools, discrimination in hiring and in places of public accommodation, and disfranchisement. It was thus the civic ideology most clearly expressed in the landmark laws, such as the 1964 Civil Rights Act, the 1965 Immigration Act, and the 1965 Voting Rights Act, that did the most to end the reign of ascriptive centrist progressive civic views. The same outlook infuses the work of the leading modern left liberal political philosopher, John Rawls.

Equal respect can, however, also be understood as an imperative to recognize and preserve group differences, in ways that can reassert support for certain sorts of separate institutions. That was the consistent message of Kallen and at times the message of Du Bois. And in part due to disenchantment with the fruits of inclusion, demands for group recognition that were at least partly separatist also became prominent among modern African-American leaders and other racial and ethnic minorities, as well as women, from the late 1960s onward. The black nationalism of Malcolm X and later Louis Farrakhan, along with some strains in radical feminism and Latino activism, have all articulated such anti-integra-tionist visions. A focus on the "politics of difference" and multiculturalism sim-ilarly characterizes much recent work in political theory, by revisionist liberals like Will Kymlicka and contemporary advocates of a radically democratic cul-tural pluralism like Iris Marion Young.[5]

But in both their more universalist integrative and their more separatist plu-ralist versions, modern democratic theories give little explicit attention, much less due weight, to the fundamental political imperatives shaping citizenship laws that have framed the analysis in this book. In reaction to the harsh nationalism of the Progressive Era Americanizers, and then the vastly more virulent racist na-tionalisms of mid-century, they have refused to recognize the pressures that lead-ers of any enduring political community recurringly face to foster a sense in all or most of its members that they are indeed a properly separate "people," and a people properly governed by those leaders, institutions, and laws. The dangers that these theorists have wished to avoid are very real. But political leaders have rarely felt able to heed their admonitions entirely, lest they be displaced as lead-ers by rivals offering more potent civic visions, or face the disintegration of their community, as almost happened even in the U.S. after more than seven decades of national existence. Hence if proponents of a political outlook do not consider how it is likely to fare in competition with other perspectives as a basis for defin-ing a compelling sense of membership and civic identity, they neglect politically inescapable necessities and risk utopian irrelevancy.[6] I have argued throughout that the weaknesses of America's egalitarian liberal republican traditions as civic ideologies have recurringly permitted and indeed fostered conditions in which illiberal, inegalitarian ascriptive policies and outlooks have flourished. The clear lesson is that failure to take the political requirements of nation-building seri-ously may produce morally culpable complicity in malevolent forms of national community.[7]

These failures to attend sufficiently to the tasks of forming and sustaining a sense of common political identity, of Benedict Anderson's "imagined commu-nity" or nationhood, are, moreover, not simply analytical and tactical shortcom-ings.[8] Because the imperative to constitute a people that feels itself to be a peo-ple is politically necessary, it is also a weighty though certainly not absolute *moral* imperative. It is, after all, undeniable that the interests of all people in belonging to viable and valued political communities are enormous. Even though virtually every human need and aspiration might be met within a variety of different types of political societies, so that no sets of community boundaries or institutions are natural or mandatory, few if any people can hope to pursue their needs and as-pirations successfully in the absence of such bounded political communities. And most people cannot be fully happy unless they live in a political society that they regard as in some sense worthy in itself, as well as supportive of their identities and interests as they understand them.[9] The things that are necessary for such communities to exist thus necessarily have some significant moral weight, if we value any of the interests, needs, and aspirations of human beings.

That is not to say that we can ever safely afford to be blind to the fact, abundantly clear in U.S. history, that all political communities are human creations extensively crafted by elites past and present in ways that advance the interests and values of some people far more than others. It only means that no public philosophy can persuasively claim to serve most peoples' interests if it fails to suggest how they can properly regard their political community as both intrinsically worthy and especially appropriate to them. These points can be made more specific by considering the strengths and weaknesses of both progressive and modern versions of democratic cultural pluralism from the standpoint of these nation-building imperatives.

Civic Strengths and Weaknesses of Democratic Cultural Pluralism. Although I am focusing on the political and normative shortcomings of left progressive and modern democratic political theories, I do not wish to minimize their attractions on both counts. Not only were they always more morally compelling than centrist progressive views; under certain circumstances they were able to take competitive advantage of the liabilities of those positions. The centrists' imperialist and domestic racist policies severely harmed the image of the United States in the view of many other nations and, as the new century developed, appeared increasingly destructive of international peace. These considerations gained ever greater force as the U.S. assumed an ever larger world leadership role during World War II and the ensuing Cold War. At home, efforts to exclude immigrants or compel their massive assimilation inevitably generated political conflicts with aspiring and recent immigrants themselves, their affiliates already within the U.S., and often their home countries. Many employers also regarded exclusionary measures as economically costly, though they favored assimilation. In extreme form, both sorts of policies ran contrary to powerful liberal democratic civic myths of the U.S. as a welcoming asylum nation with equal citizenship available to all those who shared American political ideals. In the 1950s and 1960s these factors helped to build support for domestic citizenship policies providing more equal respect and opportunities for African-Americans, Chinese-Americans, women, and other traditionally subordinated groups. All the subordinations had to be sustained at times by costly coercion; all cut off workers from some would-be employers even as they assisted others; all limited the economic and social contributions that people with a wide range of talents could make.

By arguing against restrictive immigration policies and for more equal opportunities for most or all persons and groups within America, democratic cultural pluralist positions like those first formulated by Dewey and Kallen offered to reduce these harms and to retain much of what had been attractive in traditional liberal and republican conceptions of American civic identity. Democratic pluralist proposals also carried further the longstanding liberal promise that American citizenship would provide extensive individual economic and political rights in systems conducive to peace and prosperity for all, and they offered more widely the democratic republican sense of the dignity and benefits of participating in collective self-governance. Whatever the other deficiencies of liberal democratic views, these benefits have always been profoundly appealing, and democratic pluralists sought to extend them to more people than ever before.

At the same time, they also responded to the great historic weakness of these consensual civic ideologies. Cultural pluralism provided some of the ascriptive Americanist sense of belonging to a meaningful human community, even if these communities were understood as "primary group" or subgroup memberships, not the whole nation. The U.S. gained additional legitimacy from its contributions to the flourishing of such groups. The attractions of these views for coalition-building were such that even centrist progressives like Theodore Roosevelt and Woodrow Wilson often found it politically prudent to appeal to them, although at other times inegalitarian forms of ascriptive Americanism appeared more advantageous.

After World War II, the nation's altered circumstances permitted more left progressive views to gain considerable triumphs. To be sure, the great victories for more democratic and inclusive policies that came from the 1950s through the early 1970s had many sources. They included the end of colonialism internationally and the delegitimation of racist Nazism, pressures to reduce American inequalities coming from competition with communist nations, a larger black vote in the North, and a range of energetic new social movements that gave national elites very different strategic interests than in the days of Western European imperialism and the Solid South.[10] But even with all these external pressures, new policies could not have won out if democratic pluralist civic visions had not offered both instrumental and intrinsic attractions to elites and voters alike. Certainly the promise of building a society no longer anguished and impugned by its sharp racial divisions, poverty, and violence inspired many Americans during the Great Society years; and though both integrative and separatist versions of democratic cultural pluralist civic visions are controversial in the 1990s, quests to accommodate America's ever greater diversity harmoniously and equitably retain much support.

Yet the deficiencies and tensions that have always partnered the attractions of democratic pluralist visions have only grown more apparent since the mid-

1960s. From the standpoint of the imperative to foster a sustaining sense of American civic identity, the core problem from the outset has been that even the most ascriptive version of democratic cultural pluralism, that of Horace Kallen, provided no grounds for finding anything distinctive or special about American national identity. Concerned to combat the excesses of the "100 percent Americanism" movements of their era, most left progressives backed away from advancing any clear sense of Americanism at all. U.S. citizenship was for Kallen no more than "membership in any land with free institutions." For Dewey, American nationality was membership in a great democratic association, one among many to which people would and should belong. Primary allegiance for him went to democracy rather than to any particular community, certainly not the United States. Similarly, Bourne hoped that people would come to possess multiple national memberships and to view each nationality as only one among others, with every nationality evaluated by its contribution to more cosmopolitan human flourishing.[11] The two variants of modern political theory I have noted have not altered this pattern, as we shall see.

These minimizations of national identity have long left these democratic cultural pluralist positions both morally and politically ill-equipped to confront their characteristic problems. Internal to the thought of Dewey, Kallen, and Bourne, as well as evident in the differences between them, were four main types of difficulties, which were exacerbated by the absence of a strong sense of Americanism in their outlooks. All remain troubling in theory and practice today, for citizenship policies and a wide range of related issues. The controversies include: first, whether pluralist principles demand that groups be internally democratic or whether they can accept more hierarchical internal forms said to conform to distinctive group values; second, whether public institutions should promote equal access to both opportunities and resources for people on an individual or a group basis; third, whether equal access requires the pursuit of fully integrated political institutions or separate but equal group institutions (such as schools or local governments); and, finally, whether the national government, rather than various primary groupings, has final authority to resolve the first three difficulties and deserves citizens' ultimate allegiance in its efforts to do so.[12]

The first problem may be termed the conflict between democracy and subgroup "authenticity." It is the tension between, on the one hand, egalitarian liberal and republican beliefs that all group memberships should be viewed as voluntary and structured to preserve personal liberties to participate in shaping group life and to exit if members so choose, and, on the other hand, contrary claims that respect for the authentic way of life of different communities generally requires honoring ascriptive practices and beliefs that deny their members such liberties. Some modern political theorists have cast this issue as a controversy over how far people are "socially constituted," but the undeniable fact that they are is not really the key issue. Both Kallen and Dewey, after all, insisted strongly that people were "socially constituted" and rejected the possibility of radically individualistic "unencumbered selves," to use Michael Sandel's justly celebrated formulation. But Dewey, like modern liberals, contended that people were constituted by multiple groups and should be encouraged to develop their capacities to determine which aspects of their inherited and potential identities they would pursue, and to share in the direction of their preferred groups toward beneficial ends.[13] Kallen quietly rejected Dewey's call for all human communities to be rendered volitional, democratic associations. Because he instead viewed the community identities into which people were born as their "second nature," he thought that those communities should be accorded equal public respect, even if their traditions and norms were undemocratic.[14]

Public policies often must confront the contradictions between these perspectives: commitments to treat group memberships as legally voluntary, however they are regarded by their members, may require measures that override the claims of group leaders, as when the state recognizes secular marriages that particular religious groups do not. If government went further and required, as Dewey sometimes suggested, that every human association—including religions, ethnic groups, minority nations, businesses, and families—be run in ways that are defensibly democratic, the clash between this requirement and the values of many groups would be severe. In the absence of any compelling sense of identification with and loyalty to the national regime, it is not likely that efforts to transform groups in the ways Dewey envisioned could be politically sustainable.[15] Yet without such policies, many traditional forms of ascriptive subordination may go unchecked, leaving the commitment to democracy in democratic pluralism partial at best, easily subject to rejection by large groups with contrary values.

The second tension, individual versus group equality, is similar in one respect: efforts to ensure that all individuals have meaningful opportunities to participate in public institutions, such as higher education, employment, and civic offices, may require governmental intrusions into the education and health care of children, among other matters, in ways that violate the beliefs and practices of particular religious or ethnic groups. State efforts to require Amish children to attend public schools in their early teens and to give medical treatment to children of Christian Scientists are familiar examples. But this tension involves an additional dimension. Public institutions that provide reasonably equal opportunities for individuals to participate in public institutions and acquire resources may yet produce patterns in which certain groups are highly disadvantaged in comparison to others. Unalterably unequal starting points, intractable discriminatory practices, misfortune, and many other reasons make equal outcomes across groups wildly improbable. Efforts to advance even minimal equality among groups in terms of desirable positions and resources may impinge on individual opportunities, as measures including school integration, voting districts in which a "minority" is in the majority, and affirmative action in admissions and employment are widely thought to do.[16]

Michael Walzer has termed systems giving political recognition and economic assistance on a group basis forms of "corporatist" pluralism, and, as he notes, such measures have a further difficulty beyond potentially limiting individual options. They also may chiefly aid existing group elites in ways that undermine the capacity of new groups to form and many persons to flourish.[17] This issue is poignantly raised today by the U.S. Census requirement that citizens place themselves in one of five racial categories in order to clarify eligibility for race-targeted federal benefits; many people with multiracial backgrounds are thereby denied the means to say who they are. But if no attention is given to differing group circumstances, the formal guarantee of equal individual access to economic and political opportunities and resources may give unlimited reign to the inequalities generated by the operation of market forces. Such guarantees may also mask the effective continuation of old patterns of ascriptively rooted inequality. Here, too, a political community that lacks a strong sense of allegiance to its common government as opposed to its subgroups is not likely to be able to muster political support to prevent the latter outcome.

The third problem, whether government should pursue integrated or segregated equality, also involves some overlap with the preceding one, yet again it is distinct. The overlap is that efforts to provide equal opportunities for groups to participate in public institutions may require some measures, including affirmative action in educational admissions and employment and majority minority voting districts, that can make public schools, jobs, and legislatures more integrated, yet at the same time can reinforce senses of separate group identity. The latter result raises new and sharper problems, however, when it is taken a step further. Some types of democratic pluralist positions insist that real equal respect for groups requires public support for separate but equal institutions, such as all-black or all-Latino schools and businesses or self-governing neighborhoods or cities. Some groups with strong claims to recognition as minority nations seek significant political autonomy over regions, provinces, or islands, as in the cases of North American tribes, the native Hawaiians, and the Quebeçois. As Dewey worried, however, the versions of equal respect for groups that accord strong separatist rights may produce a society that does not really share many democratic institutions at all. It may only be a set of confederated and mutually suspicious separate communities.

All these conflicts both contribute to and are inflamed by the basic tension engendered by democratic cultural pluralist outlooks—the tension between the claims to allegiance made by national governments and those of the allegedly "primary groups that democratic pluralist perspectives defend. In the views of both Kallen and Dewey, as well as most recent cultural pluralist writers, whether integrationist or separatist, the national government still retains vital responsibilities to promote material welfare for all on a roughly equal basis, to enforce public tolerance and mutual respect among groups and individuals, and to protect and foster personal liberties that include some measure of individual control over one's group memberships. Those mandates mean that persons will often find themselves caught in conflicts among their more purely individual desires, their commitments to one or more primary groups, and their national allegiance.

And just as it is hard to see why national allegiances should often prevail, given democratic cultural pluralist views, it is also hard to see how these pluralist positions can be politically sustainable if national obligations are minimized. If citizens feel that their most profound commitments go to a racial, ethnic, religious, regional, national, or voluntary subgroup, then the broader society's leaders may find that their government lacks adequate popular support to perform some functions effectively. National elites are obviously not likely to be content to adhere to democratic pluralist civic visions in that case. They will probably find that many who are distressed by a sense of pervasive social division and fragmentation, as well as many members of less advantaged groups, will respond to more strongly nationalist appeals that promise to address their concerns. Thus a democratic cultural pluralist public philosophy may set the stage for a national politics that risks degenerating into either a public life of constant bickering among suspicious economic and ethnic groups, or it may come to be dominated by virulent nationalism, if it holds together at all.[18]

And because modern works carrying forward left progressive civic traditions have only begun to address the political imperative to foster a compelling sense of common civic identity, they have thus far made only limited headway in resolving any of these tensions. The works in political theory shaped by the context of the civil rights movement and the War on Poverty, such as those of Rawls and Bruce Ackerman, instead simply mandated fully integrated public institutions while focusing primarily on the task of justifying economic redistribution to disadvantaged classes of people. Some of these writers took loyalty to national political communities as currently defined as a given.[19] Most advanced democratic cultural pluralist civic visions like Dewey's, but stressed them less than the egalitarian implications of the requirements that justice imposed for providing opportunities more universally. These theorists also presented their views as applicable to any modern liberal democratic society. They deliberately abstracted from the particulars of specific national identities.

Writers like Kymlicka and Young have, like Kallen, been chiefly concerned to prevent various sorts of cultural minorities from being forcibly assimilated into, and thus culturally destroyed by, the white male northern European segments that still predominate in the populations of many modern Western societies like the U.S. and Canada. Laudable as these concerns are, they still have produced versions of democratic pluralist civic ideology that fail to respond well to the basic political imperatives driving citizenship laws and nation-building, and thus to their own most serious tensions. Though they recognize some pressures for shared political identity amid the diversity they applaud, their emphasis is on finding ways to grant increased recognition for certain subgroups, not on what sorts of national political identities can and should be advanced. A brief review of these leading positions can clarify these shortcomings.

Rawls's Evasive Nationalism. The evolution of Rawls's writing from his *Theory of Justice* (1971) to his *Political Liberalism* (1993) has made clear how much he shares the turn made by Dewey and other pragmatists away from higher law toward reliance on shared values, now defined as the "overlapping consensus" discoverable within modern societies shaped by the "tradition of democratic thought."[20] But despite this ultimate appeal to consensus, Rawls has always expected such societies to display a "plurality of conflicting, and indeed incommensurable, conceptions of the good." He also recognizes that it is hard to sustain social unity amid such diversity.[21] He has not, however, confronted the most basic political problems achieving such unity poses.

Instead, he has always made the task of social unity artificially easy by adopting some inexcusably evasive premises. He explicitly assumes that he is theorizing only for a "closed society" without relations to other ones, whose members "enter it only by birth and leave it only by death." Such a society would have to deny its members all expatriation rights and reject all immigrants and refugees, however needy they may be. Those policies are inherently illiberal and undemocratic, and in most modern societies they could be enforced only by harsh coercive measures. These premises allow Rawls to theorize largely without regard to the tasks of nation-building, and therefore his views are useless for considering how liberal democratic polities can properly deal with them.[22]

With that less than satisfying start, Rawls goes on to say little that is helpful concerning the central tensions of democratic pluralist civic visions. Like his progressive predecessors, Rawls is strongly tempted to respond to the diversity of modern societies by minimizing the national identity he has presumed and by urging significant limits on the role of national governments. Famously, the state in his "well-ordered society" is not to have any "dominant end" or "comprehensive ideal" that would serve as an authoritative public conception of the good.[23] Instead, the state exists to realize his principles of right, which constrain conceptions of the good somewhat and promote certain forms of equality, while still permitting great variety.[24] And like both Dewey and Kallen, Rawls has argued that needs for rich communal experiences should generally be met not at the national level, but within "the full and diverse internal life of the many free communities of interests that equal liberty allows."[25]

Yet as was true for the left progressives, Rawls's invocation of subgroups to solve the problem of finding community in modern societies is at war with other elements of his thought. Rawls says frustratingly little about the tension between national protection of individual rights and democratic values against claims of group authenticity. But, like Dewey more than Kallen, he clearly sides with individuals and with their protection by the larger society, in opposition to all illiberal, undemocratic subgroups.[26] Hence Rawls cannot rely on such groups to supply diverse forms of communal satisfactions.

Instead, he needs to provide a more compelling account of the claims to priority for the national political community and its values of justice over wayward subgroups, a point that Rawls partly concedes.[27] He accepts that his theory does, after all, have to supply liberal democratic societies with some unifying "shared final end" or "ends," though they must never advance any restrictive "dominant end."[28] Rawls's basic response is to say that a well-ordered society represents a cooperative effort to pursue the moral end of "supporting just institutions and of giving one another justice"—tasks he believes to be "good in themselves," if not the highest good.[29] Rawls expects people also to be motivated in these pursuits by their recognition that this course will give them desired opportunities and means to seek their own particular goods, so long as those are just.[30] Yet he does not want citizens to comply with his principles of justice only for instrumental reasons, because those may prove unreliable.[31] Thus Rawls also argues that just public institutions will provide social support for each person's sense of self worth. That shared moral aim is supposed to make the public life of the larger society an intrinsically worthy enterprise, not a mere negotiating arena for egoistic groups or a tool for their self-centered ends.[32]

But Rawls knows that this view of the state's moral status and aims is still flimsy. The government cannot, after all, assess the "relative value" of the disparate ways of life that citizens undertake; it can only affirm that all pursuits which are not unjust display desirable "moral" potentiality. That is an affirmation so vague that it will leave many persons "unsettled as to what to do" to lead a worthwhile life.[33]

Thus in the last part of the *Theory of Justice* and also late in *Political Liberal-*

ism, Rawls elaborates one final account of a national good his well-ordered society might achieve. Building on the romantic liberalism of Wilhelm von Humboldt (who advanced much the same themes as Dewey), Rawls argues that a large, pluralistic just society represents a "social union of social unions" that constitutes a "comprehensive good to which everyone can contribute and in which each can participate," if it is not indeed the "preeminent form of human flourishing." No human being can realize all his or her potentialities, Rawls notes. But as a member of a cooperative yet diverse society in which all just capacities can be realized by some, each person can "look to others to attain the excellences" he or she must "leave aside," just as members of an orchestra achieve "active cooperation" in realizing a range of individual and collaborative musical excellences none could do alone. When citizens recognize that others are assisting them in the "collective activity" of unfolding all possible human attainments, they will cease to feel like "mere fragments" and share a rich sense of meaningful civic membership. Rawls still insists, however, that the state must not officially take even this aim as a "comprehensive moral ideal" for the just society, as destructive conflicts might result. Hence his just government is to enact measures that permit, but do not deliberately promote, the achievement of such harmonious variegated excellences. In *Political Liberalism,* moreover, his concern to show that his principles are compatible with many reasonable "comprehensive views" leads Rawls to recast the place of this vision of the "social union of social unions" in his theory. He now indicates that it is only an "attempt" to show how persons "can" see the broader society as "enlarging" more personal goods, and he observes that he is still not satisfied with this part of his argument.[34]

But whatever weight Rawls may ultimately give to the notion of a "social union of social unions," this account still gives no clear basis for compelling senses of distinct national identity, for membership in one national "social union of social unions" rather than another. As Will Kymlicka argues, agreement on Rawls's principles is supposed to be possible in every liberal democratic society, and thus nothing in Rawls's view provides reasons why any particular person might rightly give greater loyalty to any particular society. Rawls still needs, as Kymlicka puts it, an account of "shared civic identity."[35]

Rawls's cautious evocation of a vision of multifaceted flourishing within the "social union of social unions" cannot, moreover, truly serve as the unifying social aim he needs. His struggles to locate this discussion properly in his theory arise from the fact that his view does not have any real place for it.[36] The vision is simply too particular a conception of the good either to serve as a basic motivation for Rawls's social members in their original position, or to be sanctioned subsequently by his liberal states as their explicit aim. If it is not to favor some just ways of life over others, Rawls's government can take no actions to prevent sheeplike mediocre conformity from prevailing instead of diverse excellences. Those resisting such interventions will be able to claim rightly that such actions violate the regime's professed principles. The realization of Humboldt's dream via Rawls's theory is thus at best a pious hope tacked on at the end, perhaps out of an uneasy awareness that the state of pure Rawlsian justice is indeed indistinguishable from an instrumental compact to assist egoistic ends. Attractive as his egalitarianism is and impressive as his achievement is in other regards, Rawls's work is thus flawed because it remains oblivious to some of the most basic political and moral imperatives that drive the political construction of, and contestation over, civic identities.[37]

These deficiencies have begun to be evident even to political theorists heavily influenced by Rawls. When his *Theory of Justice* first appeared and issues of egalitarian redistribution seemed most central, conservative academic critics like Robert Nozick tended to respond by defending libertarian economic positions in ways that had little initial impact on social policy. But already by the mid-1970s, other disagreements surfaced with both Great Society reforms and the sorts of egalitarian liberal theories that defended them. Integration of public institutions, especially by race-conscious measures, provoked resistance, and those efforts failed to produce dramatic, undeniable, and equitably distributed benefits for disadvantaged groups and citizens generally. At the same time, they did promote some enhanced group consciousness and organization in the form of heightened "movements of group specificity," as Iris Marion Young has delicately referred to black and Chicano nationalism, feminist separatism, white ethnic revivals, Native American reassertiveness, and related phenomena. Many political analysts who formerly esteemed the Great Society, especially white male liberals, were disturbed by the valorization of "primary" group identities that it seemed to foster. They feared that it was producing a divided and demoralized American polity. Many argued that the governing democratic cultural pluralist versions of American civic ideology needed to be modified or displaced by "a better theory," a "new public philosophy," a "unifying ideology" that could better support a sense of national community without suppressing legitimate variety.[38]

Few theorists, however, took up that challenge. More conservative philosophers, among them Alasdair MacIntyre, instead responded in the early 1980s by defending traditionalist and localistic visions of community. That position is ill-equipped to combat venerable ascriptive civic conceptions such as female subordination.[39] Heirs of left progressive traditions like Iris Marion Young and Will Kymlicka have since argued more broadly for recognition and embrace of diversity and difference, without sacrificing the main benefits of liberal democracy. But despite their contributions in other regards, these multicultural and "difference" theorists have only elaborated somewhat distinctive versions of democratic cultural pluralist ideals, leaving the difficulties of those ideals largely unameliorated. And, coincidentally or not, these left liberal to radical philosophic efforts have become increasingly removed from mainstream American political discourse. They have certainly not prevented modern liberalism from losing both some of its intellectual authority and much of its popular support in recent years.

Young's Radical Democratic Cultural Pluralism. For "difference" theorists such as Iris Marion Young, Rawlsian liberalism helped foster the new surge of identity politics through its failures. She argues that liberals like him did not acknowledge that they were effectively urging imposition of cultural assimilation on diverse disadvantaged groups in the name of "reasonable" standards of political justice, almost as much as centrist progressives did. Young urges modern progressives to turn instead to a "radically democratic cultural pluralism" that still insists on "mutual respect" among "socially and culturally differentiated groups." These groups should, however, "affirm one another in their differences," not simply practice toleration. As in earlier versions of democratic pluralism, the aim remains "social equality," defined primarily as the "full participation and inclusion of everyone in a society's major institutions, and the socially supported substantive opportunity for all to develop and exercise their capacities and realize their choices." But as barriers to such inclusion and opportunities often confront people because of their group identities, "group-conscious" measures to promote opportunity, like affirmative action and group representation, are appropriate. Young recognizes the worries that such policies lead to "conflict, divisiveness, factionalism, and ultimately disintegration." But she argues that efforts to create homogeneity are unrealistic and will generate disharmonies that group representation might mitigate.[40]

For that mitigation to occur, however, the social groups that Young envisions as represented in democratic institutions must feel themselves part of a "*public,* where participants discuss together the issues before them and come to a decision according to principles of justice." She acknowledges that she has no account of how people should feel to constitute such a "public" despite their differences, nor what to do about those who do not believe that justice requires participating in such processes of collective deliberation. She offers an attractive vision of "city life" in which, even without any "shared final ends" or strong "mutual identification," people feel themselves to be part of a political society that is stimulating, even erotic, precisely because it displays so much diversity. But Young, like Rawls, leaves questions about how to form such a "city life" regime, and why people might want to make one rather than another their home, unaddressed.[41]

Many of the most painful internal tensions of democratic cultural pluralist views also go untreated in Young's prescriptions. Like Dewey more than Kallen, she believes that social justice "entails democracy," so that "collective discussion and decisionmaking" should prevail not just in central governmental bodies but in a great variety of settings—"workplaces, schools, neighborhoods . . . universities, churches," and presumably social groups. She urges those seeking to "affirm a positive meaning of group specificity" to avoid trying to "enforce a strong sense of mutual identification," arguing that people should "recognize and affirm" both "the group and individual differences within the group." Her vision of political life as "city life" apotheosizes metropolitan regional governments, not small towns. But it is not clear how her regional government, or a national government with her radically democratic pluralist civic ideal, can respect group differences and simultaneously work to foster internal democracy and affirmation of individual differences within traditionally more authoritarian groups. Given her failure to address why they should embrace such broader political memberships at all, it is also not clear why the members of her groups would acquiesce in the decisions of such governments as in any way authoritative or morally binding over them.[42] Though Young's view comes down much more strongly in favor of group equality and a measure of segregated equality than other versions of democratic cultural pluralism, then, it does not do so unequivocally. Kallen's problems of justifying undue segregation, Dewey's problems of justifying efforts to democratize various groups, and the basic problem of fostering a sense of broader national identity capable of giving political support to such efforts, all emphatically remain.

Kymlicka and Multicultural Liberal Citizenship. Will Kymlicka's insightful writings probe all the difficulties discussed so far in the course of developing a revisionist liberal argument for granting special political rights ("differentiated citizenship") to minority cultural nations within multinational political societies, especially the aboriginal peoples of Canada as well as the Francophone residents of Quebec. Kymlicka's key contention is an argument that he rightly connects with Dewey, though it moves in the cultural group-centered direction of Kallen. Kymlicka maintains that the sort of deliberative self-direction that liberals value presumes a "context of choice," a cultural structure that endows persons with moral attachments, values, and commitments with which to deliberate. Because minority cultures are often in danger of eclipse by the dominant cultures in the societies they inhabit, their members have to confront erosion or destruction of key cultural constituents of their agency and freedom in ways that other citizens do not. A concern for liberal equality for all individuals can, therefore, justify special rights to protect minority cultures. In his 1995 book, Kymlicka has stressed that these rights include rights of group representation in governmental institutions and governmental support for national or ethnic group traditions, as well as some rights to relatively autonomous self-government. The first two sorts of rights, he contends, often work to integrate groups more fully into the shared endeavors of a political society, rather than producing balkanization and alienation. The last can promote separatism, but sometimes that outcome is desirable in light of liberal aims to expand and realize personal choices.[43]

But this liberal argument for protecting minority cultures has "built-in limits," according to Kymlicka. Because it derives from an argument for enhancing capacities of personal choice for all persons, his theory still supports "the rights of individuals within" minority cultures, including their rights of religious liberty, their rights to choose what parts of its traditions they will embrace and reject, and their rights to alter their memberships. Because such rights may "literally threaten the existence of the community," however, some "restrictions on the internal activities of minority members" in these regards might be "legitimate" in the case of national minorities. Because such minorities possess distinct cultures that empower many of their members, moreover, liberals in the broader political society should generally seek to alter illiberal minority practices through reason, example, and incentives, not coercion. But "gross and systematic" violations of human rights in minority nations do justify coercive interventions by the larger liberal society. The "exact point" when such an intervention is warranted is "unclear." Definitive general answers to such conflicts cannot be given, Kymlicka concludes. Resolutions will always require "reasonably detailed knowledge of particular instances" without a "simple formula."[44]

Kymlicka also recognizes that, especially when forms of "differentiated citizenship" are embraced, liberals need an account of the "ties that bind," a means of fostering "the sense of shared civic identity that holds a liberal society together." Doubting that "there are any obvious or easy answers" to this question, either, Kymlicka ultimately asserts that in any multinational state, the needed "sense of solidarity and common purpose" must involve accommodating national identities and valuing both diversity in general and the particular groups making up a country. But, as he concedes, "this sort of allegiance is the product of mutual solidarity, not the basis for it." Defining the sources of unity in a democratic cultural pluralist state is thus left by Kymlicka as an unmet "fundamental challenge facing liberal theorists."[45] Admirable as Kymlicka's efforts to grapple with cultural differences within a liberal frame are, then, he has by and large only underlined how intractable the difficulties are on the decisive problems of democratic pluralist civic views, including both the bases of shared civic identity and the resolution of conflicts between liberal democratic principles and the practices of subgroups.

The failure of modern theorists to improve on the left progressive responses to these difficulties has, I believe, left ample intellectual and political space for those who wish to attack many of the modern liberalizing and democratizing civic reforms that these writers have sought to justify. The measures to expand opportunities for minorities adopted during the 1960s and early 1970s, especially, have been assaulted by some as balkanizing and implicitly racist, and by others as misguided in light of fresh "scientific evidence" indicating that racial and ethnic minorities, as well as women, are in some respects inferior to white men after all. The result is that revived inegalitarian, ascriptive Americanist themes in the national intellectual and political culture are far more visible in the 1990s than seemed imaginable as late as 1975.[46] Racial tensions are vividly evident, with the Los Angeles race riot of 1992 rivaling the race-charged New York draft riots of 1863. Anti-immigrant sentiments have mounted, producing Proposition 187's restrictions on the rights of aliens in California and the 1996 welfare bill's denial of benefits to legal resident aliens generally. Efforts to restore religion in public life have also surged, sometimes including proclamations that the U.S. is after all a Christian nation. And best-selling books echo every theme of the Gilded Age and Progressive Era ascriptive ideologies.

In *The Bell Curve* (1994), Richard Herrnstein and Charles Murray have argued that intelligence tests show that blacks and Latinos are on average intellectually inferior to whites. One of their most frequently cited sources, J. Philippe Rushton, has contended in many essays, culminating in *Race, Evolution, and Behavior* (1995), that these disparities are rooted in different racial evolutionary paths and are associated with higher sexual drives, larger sexual organs, less capacities for self-control, and consequently higher crime rates among blacks than whites and "Orientals." Without relying on those claims, Peter Brimelow's *Alien Nation* (1995) contends that the need for cultural homogeneity and a high-quality citizenry justifies immigration curbs designed to keep America a nation with a "white" ethnic "core." Herrnstein and Murray also express alarm over the racial mix of current American immigration. Dinesh D'Souza's *End of Racism* has suggested that Jim Crow was in many ways beneficial to blacks, and even a scholar associated with the Democrats' Progressive Policy Institute, Joel Kotkin, has argued in *Tribes* (1993) that "race, religion, and identity" will properly play the most prominent roles in determining future economic and political winners and losers. These developments suggest that the old American pattern of liberalizing and democratizing changes generating conditions for the resurgence of ideologies of ascriptive ideology has, at a minimum, not been ended by the turns toward democratic cultural pluralism in the modern era.[47]

Toward Normatively Defensible Citizenship

It is possible at this point to conclude, as theorists like John Gray have done, that liberal democracy per se cannot work as a national civic ideology, and that turns toward more particularistic alternative political outlooks, including ascriptive ones, are not only inevitable but appropriate. I continue to think that such a conclusion is at best premature and in all likelihood deeply wrong.[48] To be sure, as I have argued previously, it does not appear possible to ground liberal democratic values on any unimpeachable evidence or reasoning from nature, divine will, or human history. This inability to appeal to unchanging, transcendental grounds places liberal democratic civic ideals at a great disadvantage in competition with many ascriptive ones.

I nonetheless believe that there are powerful if not self-evident reasons to decide in favor of what I take to be the basic commitment of liberal democratic thought: to protect and enhance all persons' capacities for personal and collective self-governance. That aim can reasonably be judged to be a necessary constitutive feature of any defensible view of human flourishing and any worthwhile political philosophy. With all their limitations, liberal democratic policies promoting personal and collective freedom still offer more potential than any alternative to provide paths to greater human material prosperity, personal security and happiness, domestic and international peace, and intellectual and spiritual progress.[49] And even if liberalism is not hegemonic in America, its finest commitments remain deeply enough embedded in the traditions and institutions of the U.S, as well as many other societies, to make feasible the project of crafting national identities in fuller accord with it.

Feasible, but not easy. Beyond the much discussed but still pressing tasks of providing philosophic grounds for accepting liberalism thus understood, the history explored in this book—and current American political realities—set an additional normative challenge. Those who favor liberal democratic conceptions of citizenship must reconceive them in ways that can retain the historic strengths of egalitarian liberalism and respond to its greatest weaknesses, especially its failure to define compelling senses of national identity that can build support for living in accordance with liberal democratic principles within specific political societies. In particular, Americans who espouse liberal democratic principles must consider how these ideals can be blended with arguments for the distinctive worth of U.S. citizenship, without justifying the subjugating forms of ascriptive inequality that have been so deeply rooted in their national life. That is my goal here.[50]

Political Communities as Political Parties. I suggested earlier that the imperatives of nation-building deserve to be given significant moral weight, because membership in particular communities promotes human flourishing in morally significant ways that cannot now plausibly be provided otherwise. If so, then egalitarian liberals must consider how people with their values could reasonably recognize their particular national identities as especially valuable and appropriate for them and also make those values attractive to their fellow citizens. The task is all the more difficult because in every society, liberal democratic values and others usually give people good grounds to be dissatisfied with all the actual communities available to them. We therefore need to maintain a critical stance toward the tendencies of nation-building elites to craft and sustain regimes through compelling but fictitious stories of divine ordination, organic identity, historical destiny, racial superiority, and apparently more liberal myths of fabulously wise founders and universal social contracts. All such accounts are not only deceptive in ways that violate values of informed self-governance; they are also all too often accompanied by vilification of many outside and inside the community thus defined. We need a way to think about political societies that recognizes their value—indeed, their necessity—and yet also calls attention to their limitations and dangers.

In an influential 1981 essay, Michael Walzer explored the moral significance of political communities by invoking three possible analogies: a nation-state might be seen as akin to a neighborhood, club, or family. He concluded it had elements of all three, though it was not identical to any.[51] Earlier, both Dewey and Kallen had depicted the nation as an orchestra, with the national government as conductor, and Rawls has also turned to that image (though Dewey later decided that the metaphor favored too passive a role for the central state).[52] Even liberal republican doctrines of a "social contract," "compact," or "covenant" can be seen as metaphors of this sort, as they foster images of political societies as something like consensually created businesses or religious bodies.

Precisely because political communities are at once so indispensable and yet such potent sources of exploitation and inhumanity, it is difficult to decide what moral status to assign them, and the quest for an analogy to focus moral thinking is a sensible one. The analogies just listed are highly undesirable, however, because they all distract attention away from the central fact that makes nation and states so morally ambiguous and complex. As U.S. history abundantly illustrates, nations are, above all, political. They are endlessly contested and contesting human creations that dramatically and often coercively affect how people live, the resources they possess, the powers and liberties they can claim, in ways that greatly benefit some and disadvantage others. Yet the standard analogies are all "de-politicizing" devices. They direct us to associations we do not ordinarily think of as chiefly political. The most extreme in this regard is the family analogy, which to many people suggests an association that is both benign and natural. It is no accident that this analogy has often appealed to defenders of racial ascriptive hierarchies, from Roger Taney in Dred Scott to Peter Brimelow in Alien Nation.[53] If we instead think of a political society as something like a neighborhood, a club, an orchestra, a team, a business, or a voluntary religious community, we do not naturalize it in the same way. We do, however, largely drain away images of harsh coercion and injustice toward outsiders. We are instead led to think of a nation as something basically benign, whose members mostly find it rewarding to belong, and whose existence may not benefit outsiders but poses no great threat to them. But although nations are always of value to at least some of their members and may wreak no great harms on many outsiders, most contain significant numbers of people who rightly feel more abused than advantaged, and most work for their own prosperity in ways that damage at least some beyond their borders.

Thus to think about the moral value of political societies in ways that keep both their potential benefits and their evils in view, it is best to compare them to undeniably political entities. I suggest that we think of political communities as, from a moral point of view, most akin to political parties, though far more valuable and dangerous. We must, however, bear in mind the wide range of forms that political parties have taken in world history, from umbrella coalitions such as American political parties are often said to be, to the nationalist, ethnic, and religious parties in many regimes, such as Jean-Marie Le Pen's explicitly racist National Front in France, to militantly coercive parties that reject conventional democratic practices, like the Soviet Communist, Chinese Kuomintang, and German Nazi parties. Thinking of nations as weightier members of the same moral species as parties, thus broadly conceived, can serve a number of purposes. I press the analogy here first to make three normative points about political communities, then to derive some lessons from the example of parties on the political feasibility of liberal democratic conceptions of U.S. civic identity.

The first normative lesson, already suggested, is that whatever may be true of families, orchestras, clubs, and churches, political societies, like political parties, are neither natural nor inherently benign. They are not in any morally important sense primordial or "pre-political." Instead, like parties, and contrary to many exaggerated nationalist pretensions and myths, all political communities are human artifices that were created to serve particular purposes of particular people and survive so long as they continue to do so (though their beneficiaries change over time). Hence, tendencies to narrow partisanship are inherent in their very existence, even and perhaps especially in nations that proclaim their world-historical significance. Recognition of these tendencies of nations is, I believe, morally imperative even if on balance we deeply value our national memberships.[54]

Second, the analogy is also helpful for the reverse reason. Though often decried, political parties seem indispensable. At the least, they are useful much of the time, both to their members and to some degree to all the members of their broader societies. As the early defenders of parties in the U.S. argued, not only are like-minded people more likely to prevail if they support a common party; all citizens benefit when competing parties expose the abuses of those in power, help mobilize citizens to seek change and govern themselves, and provide them with both policy alternatives and people organized to execute them.[55] Even though strong attachments to parties have declined in recent U.S. history, political parties still are the basic agents performing these functions, and most reformers seek to invigorate, not end them. To a far greater degree, political communities provide material, cultural, and psychological services to their members also, and many offer opportunities for self-governance. To some degree, they also serve as bases of criticism and viable alternatives to rival societies, thereby assisting the flourishing of humanity as whole. However attractive cosmopolitan perspectives may be, they cannot be morally persuasive, much less politically potent, until they offer plausible ways of doing all these things.

Third, if we think of political communities as being akin to political parties in that they are largely crafted by political elites for less than universal purposes, we may come to believe, appropriately in my view, that membership in them ought to be matters of choice. That claim is controversial among those who prefer to see national identities as so organic and deeply constitutive of our identities as to be virtually unalterable. But though the premise that we are profoundly shaped by the culture in which we are raised is true, the implication that we should not alter our national allegiance is one that more often serves rulers than free citizens.

One final advantage of the analogy blends normative elements with descriptive ones and is more speculative. Insofar as political societies are not just normatively but descriptively akin to political parties, we may be able to learn from the operations of parties something about how and how far people can hope to craft a sense of civic identity that is both morally defensible and politically sustainable. That possibility arises first from the fact that people tend to acquire a party identification in their youth and then hold to it rather tenaciously thereafter (even if the socialization is toward party independence), just as they tend to acquire national identities through youthful socialization.[56] That similarity is especially intriguing because people have remarkably enduring identifications, even with parties that have made no claim of any natural or divine authority. The fact that such parties can thrive, at least under some circumstances, is significant because of a second descriptive parallel. Leaders of political parties, like leaders of nations, are always to some degree in competition with other would-be leaders, inside and outside their boundaries. It is true that party leaders tend to vie most often and ardently with leaders of rival parties, whereas national leaders generally compete most directly with rivals from within their own nations; but party heads face internal opponents and national elites sometimes struggle to hold their citizens' allegiance against the claims of outsiders. Thus, if it is possible for parties to flourish without relying heavily on inegalitarian ascriptive ideologies of party identity, perhaps political communities can as well. By examining the dynamics of party allegiance and competition, then, we may be able to get some notion of how political leaders can successfully offer national identities that accomplish the good things that political communities can do, while avoiding the dangers of ascriptive nationalism. In the next section, I try to draw some such lessons. I believe that they confirm the political inadequacy of the democratic pluralist visions of civic identity favored by many contemporary theorists and point out more potentially fruitful paths.

The Dynamics of Party Allegiance. Few findings in political science are as heavily supported as the tenacity of party identification, and it is striking that most of the evidence comes from the modern U.S. For even if their parties still offer partly ascriptive visions of American identity, most people in the U.S. today do not see their *partisan* memberships as something natural or providentially ordained (though some do). Most do not see the members of the main rival party as intrinsically inferior, and most concede that their party benefits some members of the political community more than others, rather than being equally and universally beneficial. Yet, even so, most people remain more or less firmly attached to the partisan identity that they generally acquire from their parents. Although there is no definitive answer as to why this should be so, scholars usually trace this enduring partisanship to the "psychological difficulty in changing long-held and deeply felt attachments."[57]

The fact that even partisan allegiances possess such stability suggests that the senses of national identity into which people are socialized should be far more central to them than much traditional liberal theory has recognized.[58] That fact does not necessarily guarantee political stability, especially in multinational states. But if people feel deeply attached to the political party of their youth, they are likely always to feel at least some sense of constitutive identification with the political society in which they were raised. Indeed, given its greater importance in the lives of most people, their sense of identification with their political community should be far stronger. And the example of parties suggests that this identification can be profound even if that society does not claim to be naturally or divinely ordered. National attachments therefore pose barriers, but also opportunities, for efforts to forge a liberal sense of political identity, especially in a country with genuine if contested liberal traditions like the U.S. In short, the party analogy suggests that, although existing national ties cannot be ignored, they may be tapped to strengthen support for a more genuinely liberal democratic society without public endorsement of any inegalitarian ascriptive beliefs.

But despite the tenacity of partisan identifications, parties do have to compete to hold on to many of their members and to attract new ones, for that is how they win elections or attract sufficient support to enact and sustain coups or even revolutions. They can do so because there are always people whose mixed and varied or weak childhood socializations leave them without strong senses of party identification. Such people can often be mobilized by parties with which they have not previously identified, particularly when broader events lead them to be dissatisfied with the prevailing state of affairs in their own lives and in their country. Similarly, as I have argued throughout, because national identities are political creations of varying force in peoples' lives, they are subject to change through the efforts of political elites to persuade or coerce people (usually compatriots, sometimes outsiders) into accepting different conceptions of their identities as more valuable to them.[59]

How do competing elites win support, as leaders of parties or entire political societies? The ways are greatly varied. Since the pioneering work of Anthony Downs and Mancur Olson, many rational choice models of parties and groups have stressed that most human associations must often motivate members by offering them "selective incentives," particular individual benefits. At least, most scholars argue, parties must advance general policies that their adherents see as serving their personal material interests. Some analysts broaden the possibilities to include provision of benefits to groups with which individuals already identify.[60] This standard Downsian picture of parties as umbrella organizations providing diverse benefits to as varied a range of constituents as possible is strikingly similar to the somewhat deflated views of national governments favored by democratic cultural pluralists from Kallen to Rawls, in which a liberal democratic nation is no more than a federation of mutually respectful groups, joined for limited purposes, with no distinct identity of its own. If these pictures of parties and countries seem none too elevated, it nonetheless seems true that neither parties nor polities will long endure if they are not perceived as providing benefits to their members. Both are often coalitions of fairly disparate groups who can profit in some respects from collective efforts but whose interests and aims differ in many other ways that will lead to disunity if such benefits are not clear.

But there is more to the dynamics of gaining and sustaining allegiance, in parties and in political societies, than tenacious youthful identifications and plausible promises of material benefits. Parties rarely maintain adherents over time if they are seen as nothing but instrumentally useful compacts among a fairly random assortment of groups that have some overlapping interests—compacts subject to revision in both their membership and their policies strictly as political opportunities dictate. The much-discussed decline in party identification among the American electorate may reflect in part the growing prevalence of just such narrow views of parties and their leaders. At least some of the time, a party needs to be perceived as championing both a distinct array of constituents who in some important senses have shared identities, and a distinct set of values, programs, and purposes that makes its political vision preferable to its competitors.[61]

Thus parties face ongoing tasks of persuading people that they should think and feel themselves to be Republicans and not Democrats, Labour and not Tory, Socialist and not National Front. To do so they often appeal to various economic and ascriptive characteristics along with inherited affiliations (for example, Democrats are properly the party of labor, immigrants, and blacks), and they promise programs benefiting those groups. They often, however, also find it necessary to define an array of purposes and principles attractive to their present and potential constituents and different from those of their opponents. If they are successful, that normative vision also becomes part of the sense of identity of their allegiants. Republicans stand not just for certain economic and ethnic groups but for principles of reliance on private action and decentralized government, protection of rights through tough law enforcement and strong national defense, and so forth. Post–New Deal Democrats have instead generally defended a greater role for the national government, greater reliance on programs to combat social causes of crime rather than police and prisons, a greater emphasis on programs of domestic uplift rather than defense, and so forth. Both parties argue that their platforms articulate the most defensible understanding of American national identity, but both also accept that their opponents are advancing a different yet still historically "American" political vision. Indeed, in elections they often exaggerate those differences while seeking to remain close to, but on opposing sides of, the perceived political center.[62] At the same time, they generally recognize the legitimacy of their opponents' political outlooks, at least to the extent that they will obey the laws their rivals enact until they manage to gain power themselves and institute changes.

Hence, to a significant degree, even ardent party members within the same polity recognize their society's conflicting partisan visions as simultaneously distinct and broadly acceptable. The preceding chapters have shown that much of the time, major parties have blended American civic traditions in ways calculated to please their traditional adherents, distinguish themselves from their rivals, and yet spark allegiance in as many supporters as possible. Only rarely, however, have they refused allegiance when their government fell into their rivals' hands.

Again, the circumstances of national governments can be plausibly compared to parties in all these regards. It is true that because national governments claim to champion the good of the whole, they can more often claim rhetorically that they are not tied to any particular constituency and that they are simply trying to achieve basic goods for all and the common good generally, without favoring any particular view of the good life, as progressive democratic pluralists and modern liberal theorists like Rawls have urged. But this rhetorical claim is misleading and, if taken too seriously, highly problematic as a philosophy for actual governance. All governments do claim to represent one political community, one people, far more than the whole of humanity. Indeed, they often treat some of the groups within their putative borders as virtual outsiders. All governments also often have to defend the distinctive affiliations, institutions, and ways of life fostered by their governance as more desirable than the alternatives that are never absent. Like a political party, they can do so without necessarily judging other political outlooks prevailing among their internal opponents or in other political societies as utterly illegitimate and unacceptable.[63] The example of parties suggests that they are in fact more likely to do so if leaders and citizens alike routinely acknowledge the deflating reality that national political leaders are partisan leaders, both of their party within their country and of their country within the larger world.

Finally, the dynamics of party competition suggest that American liberal Democrats, in particular, ought to reject the longstanding democratic pluralist normative view that they should never seek to define any dominant national purposes. To be sure, it is imprudent to be ideological purists, insisting on adhering consistently to a particular civic vision when it drives off the support of many who could be brought into their fold with a few relatively minor compromises. Liberal democratic national elites, like politicians generally, often make such compromises, and properly so. But if any society's leaders consistently fail to express a compelling sense of national identity, principles, and purposes, they are not likely to be able to sustain acceptance of their legitimacy by rivals inside and outside their borders. They will have trouble generating political support for measures that involve the difficult tensions engendered by democratic pluralist policies.

Hence recognition of the ways political societies resemble political parties indicates that to gain and sustain support, liberal democratic leaders in the U.S. and other political communities must address the task that democratic cultural pluralist perspectives have eschewed, that of making their community's members feel like a "people." It also suggests that they must often do so by promising more than particularized benefits. As commentators on America's civic difficulties have increasingly argued since the 1970s, they must convey a sense of shared civic identity and purposes.

The Road Not Taken: Allegiance to the Party of America

How can these tasks be met in the United States? What can be the basis of a conception of *American* national identity as something distinctive and meaningful,

and what sense of shared principles and purposes is possible or desirable in today's complex, divided U.S.? Can the answers realize the best features of egalitarian liberal democracy and mitigate the worst?

I believe so. The basic answer I propose is twofold. First, Americans should
value their civic identity as something real with a rich and distinctive history, not
as something valorized in ascriptive myths of national superiority. Second,
Americans should recognize their civic history and destiny as their own collective enterprise. They should take responsibility for continuing their national
story, and hence the stories of their own lives, in ways that express what seem on
reflection to be their finest principles and purposes, not necessarily their historically most central ones.[64] To do so credibly, I think, they must embrace purposes
and institutions embodying the liberal democratic commitment to preserving
and expanding the practical enjoyment of freedom by all citizens, and insofar as
possible by others as well. If they do so, U.S. citizens will have good grounds to
see their civic identity as something that expresses their personal identities and
ideals, and as something that advances their own well-being, that of their fellow
citizens and society, and, to some degree, the well-being of humanity generally.
And even if American advocates of liberal democratic principles fail to persuade
their compatriots to pursue those ideals more fully at any particular time, they
will still have reason to help carry forward the shared national political endeavor
within which their partisan effort can best continue. Hence, except in the most
extreme circumstances, they can be counted on to give suitable support even to
elected leaders with very different views of American purposes.

Conceiving of American civic identity as a partisan, humanly created historical enterprise in these ways may seem intellectually persuasive but psychologically and politically unsatisfying. Every entity and endeavor that exists has a history; moral worth may seem to require a special place in a transcendent natural
or divine moral order. But even seen as simply a human political creation, American nationality can rightly fulfill human longings to belong to a meaningful
larger whole constitutive of and expressive of its members' individual identities
and aims. The life of that rather monumental historical entity, the United States
of America, is, after all, something that genuinely transcends any and all of the
individuals who ever have or ever will participate in it. Its history precedes them
in time and will extend in all likelihood far beyond their lifetimes, and it has an
almost incalculable role in shaping the personalities, values, and opportunities
of most of its citizenry.[65]

And disturbing as many of its past and present features are, the U.S. is undeniably a quite distinctive historical entity, very much part of the broader human
saga, but with a linked set of compelling stories that are very much its own. America's special role in human history includes standing as a "city on the hill" for

some, the land of opportunity and plenty for others, the "first new nation," the last great western slave nation, the country of frontier cowboys and pioneering industries and technologies, the incubator of capitalism and consumerism and also fervent religiosity and grand altruistic idealism, a homeland of rich resources, staggering physical beauty, incredible diversity, and horribly severe hardships, abuses and inequalities, along with much more. Today the U.S. is the world's sole yet troubled superpower, a startlingly complex, conflicted, still evolving, yet still specific set of territories, institutions, peoples, historical affiliations, and future possibilities.

All these elements provide almost overwhelming material for Americans to consider themselves part of a special historical collectivity of immense significance for themselves and humanity, even if they do not embrace myths of American identity as divinely or naturally favored, and even if they value different aspects of their common traditions than do some of their fellow citizens. Its history and contemporary circumstances thus present current and potential citizens with constraints and opportunities for how they can find and construct meaning in their lives that they would not find in identical form in any other nation. People can therefore deeply value universalistic principles of human rights and democratic governance and still feel that they have good reasons to belong to the "party of America," or some other distinctive national community, in preference to the other extant liberal democratic national regimes.

Liberal democrats can forcefully argue, moreover, that the credibility of such a sense of belonging would be enhanced, not diminished, if U.S. citizens constructed their national identity in line with their more consensual traditions and institutions. If political institutions made democratic self-governance as much a reality as possible, and citizenship laws made nationality as much a matter of choice as possible, then Americans could more genuinely regard their Americanism as something they could define as they saw fit. To be sure, making national policies responsive to individual citizens' concerns and making national memberships matters of relatively alterable choices are extraordinarily difficult tasks in such large, highly unequal, and complex societies as the U.S. and in an increasingly interconnected and interdependent world. But the very effort to discover and achieve what can be done in these regards can reasonably support beliefs that American national identity is simultaneously guided by liberal democratic principles and expressive of who U.S. citizens are and what they want to be. Being American might then be felt to be both a conscious political commitment and a shared identity, not an arms-length alliance in pursuit of a limited range of goods.[66]

A number of theorists have begun to explore this possibility, that a sense of shared identity, of "imagined community," can be based on a sense of shared history. Will Kymlicka is, however, skeptical about the adequacy of this option. His concern stems from his assumption that consciousness of a shared history can be a source of valued civic identity only if it is an "inspiring history," a history of great achievements and great people to be venerated. He worries that many societies lack such a history, and that, in any case, reliance on this device will produce senses of national pride and identity based on "deliberate misrepresentation" of ugly realities in "sanitized" historical accounts. If bleak truths about the construction of civic identities through power politics of the sort reviewed here were acknowledged, this argument suggests, few could feel loyal to their country. Elizabeth Kiss rightly points to the need for liberals who rely on a sense of shared historical national identity to "support those elements of a nation's historical self-definition that are more inclusive and tolerant," but this formula may seem to invite the kinds of "illegitimate" mythmaking that Kymlicka criticizes.[67]

I believe, however, that it is a major error to think that a sense of meaningful shared identity based on the history of one's political society requires regarding its history as uniformly or even predominantly glorious. A strong sense of partisan or familial allegiance, after all, need not express a sense that the political party or family has chiefly been populated by saintly figures. Precisely because psychological senses of identification from childhood affiliations are already so strong, most people need only see in their personal or group histories certain elements, strains, or possibilities that they believe are worth embracing and developing, and that they think they are positioned to help develop. They then are usually motivated to try to do so, even if those possibilities have been largely unrealized so far.

Indeed, I suspect that a national history is in many ways more able to supply a sense of broader meaning if it is understood to include serious struggles among people, movements, principles, and causes with different aims and interests—struggles in which the actors a particular citizen decides to regard as the "good guys" may not always, perhaps even not often, win.[68] That kind of account fosters awareness that there are prospects for accomplishing much that seems valuable in civic life, but that those prospects are not automatic. In short, conflict gives the national story a plot, and citizens can often be energized, not demoralized, by the sense that it is up to them to write a happy ending, or at least a better next chapter.

Hence, a powerful sense of meaningful historic civic identity can be achieved in ways supportive of liberal democratic aspirations if Americans see themselves as what I believe they truly are. The U.S. is not an inherently and automatically liberal democratic nation, as many glorifying histories would have it. Americans are, rather, a people with powerful liberal and democratic traditions and achievements of which they can justly be proud, but with many clashing traditions and institutions that many citizens still greatly value. American liberal democracy thus is not the "core" meaning, but rather an available meaning, that U.S. citizens can and, I believe, should give to their distinctive, highly contested historical collective creation. To do so they should strive not to find and follow a golden past full of mythic heroes. They should try to become architects of a better civic life today.

That claim leads to the second element Americans need to build a stronger sense of national civic identity that is more effectively liberal and democratic than in the past. The United States, like most political parties and political communities, needs a fairly robust sense of shared purposes and principles to give content to its collective life from time to time. It should not be conceived as simply a federation neutrally umpiring the pursuit of a limited range of collective goods and a variety of distinctive private goods by an instrumentally allied collection of subgroups.[69] To be sure, Rawls and others are transparently right to insist that any effort to define a single narrow national purpose and conform to it rigidly is politically unsustainable in large, diverse modern societies. My two claims in this regard are more modest.

First, leaders should be aware that, at times, forging unity around a sense of common purpose will be required for the nation to survive serious foreign and domestic crises and dilemmas. Second, in such times, American leaders should pursue realization of the consensual liberal democratic values that can be founded and extended in American life, rather than inegalitarian ascriptive ones. Before defending those claims, let me note that despite the considerable emphasis on neutrality toward a range of conceptions of the good life in all versions of democratic cultural pluralism from the progressives to the present, in fact, all these views do see larger political societies as aiming to provide a range of goods. In most accounts they are the goods that liberal societies have long promised, with great if not unqualified popular appeal: opportunities for material prosperity, civic peace, considerable freedom of conscience and expression, a share in the ongoing achievements of human inventiveness and artistic creativity, and a measure of political self-governance. The democratic pluralist emphasis on neutrality and the absence of any dominant national purpose has come out of awareness that often citizens are divided on many important questions of political ends in ways that are not likely to be resolved, and need not be for most of these sorts of goods to be obtained. But, given that aim, it is both intellectually incorrect and politically imprudent to allow this emphasis on neutrality to obscure the need for and propriety of governmental efforts to aid citizens' acquisition and enjoyment of these many other, less divisive goods. A state that is seen as helping people to gain and keep desirable goods is more likely to win the hearts of citizens than even the most just umpire, a fact that political candidates have long understood.

The value of such less controversial goods is so great that there will often be times in the governance of any political society when efforts to define more specific common purposes and principles should be avoided, and times when certain common projects that have become too controversial should be abandoned. Prohibition gave enriched moral meaning to American civic life for many millions of Americans, and it probably saved and extended millions of lives; but it also bred crime and frustrated millions of other citizens, in ways that finally made it a common cause not worth pursuing. Many think that desegregation and affirmative action have become so divisive today that they, too, should cease, though the danger of acquiescing in deeply entrenched patterns of racial inequality is great if that course is followed.

However one stands on that issue, my main contention here is that, although there are times when leaders of a political society would be ill-advised to define a very concrete common purpose, there are also times when they must do so. At certain points they are faced with unavoidable choices that will commit the nation to the view of its purposes supported by some citizens and not others. Then they must decide which way to go, as even inaction will represent a choice of some sort. Such a situation arose in the U.S. when the constitutional and political positions of Roger Taney and Stephen Douglas required American leaders to decide if their society would explicitly treat slavery as protected in perpetuity or if America would officially aim at the institution's eventual extinction, with liberty and justice for all. It came again during the Depression, when massive poverty compelled American leaders to choose between unbridled free market ideology and economically interventionist government. They had to decide whether they regarded all those who were failing in market systems as unfit weeds who should be left just as they were, or if they believed that government's task of preserving and promoting human freedom included duties to act to ensure that all possessed the material prerequisites of life and liberty, insofar as government could so act successfully. In such cases, leaders cannot escape defining a controversial sense of national purposes, and the choices they make inevitably affect the legitimacy of their own leadership and of the broader political society in the eyes of many of its members, and many outsiders as well.

And if American leaders are to sustain devotion to U.S. citizenship as a historically significant, collectively shaped entity, I believe that in such times they must take as their purposes the liberal democratic goals of protecting and expanding civic capacities for personal and collective self-governance. They must do so in order to sustain the allegiance of most citizens and perhaps their own sense of political identity and purpose as well, even though these purposes, like any purposes they might choose, will probably alienate other citizens permanently. In opposition to the Rawlsian emphasis on neutrality, a swelling chorus of contemporary liberal theorists has agreed instead that in modern liberal

democratic societies, the purposes that must never be abandoned, and sometimes must be taken as politically authoritative, are the preservation and promotion of autonomous human agency, which I have termed *rational* or *reflective
liberty*.[70] To those philosophic arguments I wish here to add the claim that during those periods when Americans have found it inescapably necessary to define
their shared purposes and principles more sharply, choices in favor of egalitarian liberal democratic values have consistently proved far more defensible than
the opposing directions.[71]

Though the critics of Reconstruction have been numerous in America, few
can seriously contend that the nation would have been better off if Lincoln had
agreed that slavery was a vital expression of an authoritative vision of America as
a white man's nation instead of insisting that it was hostile to American commitments to liberty. And though the opponents of centralized public assistance
are more legion at the moment than they have been in generations, even leading
conservative Republicans from Ronald Reagan through Newt Gingrich have at
times conceded that during the Depression, Franklin Roosevelt was broadly right
to accept national responsibility for finding effective strategies to provide an
emergency material "safety net" and more genuine long-run economic opportunities to all Americans in need. Along with these historical judgments, the argument here contends that if the purposes chosen in times of national crisis do
not plausibly represent liberal democratic efforts to secure basic political and
economic resources and liberties for all, American leaders will not be able to
claim that their society deserves the loyalty of its members because it is a collective enterprise that expresses the identities of all and aims to enable all to share
in its benefits.[72] Elites will have to rely on some other, more inegalitarian and
more fictitious national narrative, like the racial fables of the early twentieth century. I do not see how such courses can ever deserve to be deemed morally superior directions.

Thus there are times when, if they are not to be lost, liberal democratic traditions must serve as a national "fighting faith." Indeed, because the practical obstacles to citizens' choices to change their nationality, or the direction of American public policies, are so great, American leaders must recurringly seek new ways
to make personal decisions regarding nationality more effective and democratic
direction of public policies more real. The aim of making American political life
a more truly collective enterprise should itself be an ongoing collective enterprise. To be sure, relentless pursuit of liberalizing and democratizing reforms is
politically counterproductive, as this book has shown repeatedly. But if Americans are to have a sense of civic identity that they can both value as their own and
defend as morally right, they must recognize that the purpose of trying to live up

to their egalitarian liberal democratic civic ideals is one that they can never abandon and at times must labor to extend.

Such a sense of shared purpose does not by itself resolve any or all of the tensions evident in democratic cultural pluralist outlooks. It does tend to tilt the scales of decision toward national actions to expand practical liberties and opportunities for every individual whenever it is politically feasible to do so. Hence the thrust of this position is, like Dewey's, to support policies that enforce the volitional character of subgroups and that try to provide all citizens with the educational, economic, and legal prerequisites to be real decisionmakers in how they live personally, and in the governance of all the societies to which they belong, in cluding their political society.[73]

Nothing in this view takes away the power of contentions like those of Iris Young, that many cannot be brought to share equally in the practices and benefits of national self-governance without recognition of group disadvantages, like those historically inflicted on racial minorities and women. I believe that Americans should take their ultimate goal to be expansion of individual opportunities and integrated inclusiveness within a common political culture shaped by all its members on an egalitarian basis, not valorization of subgroup identities. But even in a society riddled with politically fostered inequalities such as the U.S., anti-individualistic measures like majority minority districts and affirmative action programs will often still be defensible means to that end. More broadly, *Americans in particular* are well advised in evaluating issues like immigration policies, bilingualism, economic development programs, housing and transportation plans, systems of political representation, and civic education to keep one general criterion in view. They should consider how they can adopt measures that will erode the invidious ascriptive hierarchies past policies and laws have built up throughout their history, instead of perpetuating or heightening them.

Even though this guideline would rule out many proposals currently being advanced, Kymlicka is right to suggest that these sorts of questions require particularized and detailed consideration, rather than being resolvable by any theoretical formula. Answers that work in one broadly liberal polity might not be right in another. The role of theory is inescapably limited once we recognize that membership in a particular historical political community is a valuable context for human flourishing. Then we must conclude that the distinctive histories and circumstances of nations may make quite different sorts of liberal democratic institutions appropriate in different countries. For example, the United Kingdom provides extensive religious liberty via policies of toleration while maintaining an established church; but the creation of a similar Church of the United States would rightly be seen as an illiberal measure, because of America's long and unprecedented history of providing religious freedom through separation of church and state.

Similarly, in complex multinational societies, the dissimilar situations of various subgroups may well require dissimilar treatment even by the same national government. If native tribes in America have strong claims to regain the political autonomy denied them by deception and force, and if African-Americans can instead claim special assistance to break down the severe burdens left by Jim Crow and ongoing discrimination, other groups may merit different treatment yet. The Old Order Amish, for example, might well be thought to have some claim to be a separate nationality involuntarily incorporated into the U.S., as Jeff Spinner suggests; but their case is less strong than that of Native American tribes coerced in violation of treaty guarantees. Chinese-Americans once suffered severely from segregation, but its impact may be judged to have been overcome (sometimes, sadly, by means of Chinese-American acquiescence in anti-black policies) to a far greater degree than that of Jim Crow.[74] Still other groups, such as immigrant communities who have experienced relatively little discrimination and segregation, may merit no special protection or assistance in relation to the broader culture; but massive forced assimilation would remain inappropriate. They should have as much right as any other citizens to determine the content of American political culture, rather than having to accept an Anglo mold.

Because adequate resolutions of such problems require more thorough consideration than I can now provide, these examples are meant only to be suggestive. Rather than laying out just how an egalitarian liberal vision of the "party of America" should respond to all the ongoing tensions in prevailing versions of democratic pluralist civic ideology, my goal, again, has been to improve on democratic cultural pluralism by offering a view of American citizenship that captures some of the appeal of ascriptive Americanism for a liberal democratic conception of U.S. citizenship. But fostering a morally appropriate and politically viable sense of U.S. civic identity, requires more than one book or author can provide. I conclude, then, by identifying a set of tasks that many Americans would have to pursue if they were to make this sense of their citizenship more a reality.

Conclusion: The Political Tasks of American Citizenship

The first task is to debunk both ascriptive and liberal myths about America's past and present when these support unjust inequalities or simply foster complacency in the face of them. Americans—especially teachers, scholars, and other opinion-shapers—should replace such accounts not with rival myths but, in so far as they can, with complex truths about the people, the struggles, and the causes that have collectively crafted American life. Then citizens can judge for themselves who have been the heroes and villains and how those struggles can best be resolved or, more likely, continued. That is what I have tried to do here in challenging standard accounts of American civic development with a narrative that I believe to be more truthful; and though I have thought truth better served by making my own heroes and villains clear, I hope that the evidence here is abundant enough to assist reflection from all points of view on the realities of American life, its potentials, and its limitations.

Second, American political leaders face tasks that are in many ways harder. They must decide how they can acquire and maintain power and foster a sense of common allegiance in ways that are consonant with liberal democratic values, without resorting to winning support via ascriptive mythologies that can easily become demonologies. Political elites must also make difficult judgments about when and how far to compromise between three camps—those comfortable under current arrangements, those seeking new but illiberal arrangements, and those committed to carrying forward the broader national endeavor of finding ways to protect and promote basic liberties and opportunities for all citizens, in ways respectful of, and if possible beneficial to, outsiders. Leaders must know when not to push too hard for reforms; but they must also recognize that hard choices in favor of liberal purposes must sometimes be made if they are not to give grimmer meaning to American national life. Those are political and policy challenges of major proportions. Yet accomplishments in these directions are possible, and such achievements can earn the respect, honor, and power that many political leaders seek.[75]

Third, the responsibilities of citizens according to this civic view are probably the most difficult of all. Though they are encouraged to live according to their own lights and need not be constant political participants, citizens are nonetheless called upon to be truer liberal democrats than most Americans have ever hoped to be. They must strive to be skeptical of flattering civic myths advanced by aspiring leaders. They must try to look unblinkingly at the realities of their history and their present, with all their deficiencies as well as their great achievements on view. And they must retain an awareness both that their regime may well merit their loyalty and sacrifices despite its flaws, and that, even if their nation is in many respects worthy of their loyalty, there may be times when its interests are not justified in light of their broader membership in the community of humanity. Their patriotism must thus be at once profound and qualified, recognized as something both necessary and dangerous, and thus as an allegiance that is deepest when it harbors searching doubts. They must recognize that their ties are both to all the real people that inhabit their country, to whom their obligations are deep, and to the ideals which their nation should advance, to which their obligations are also deep even when those ideals point beyond, and against, their country's narrower interests. Americans should in fact accept that a time may come when the United States itself, like preceding human political creations, is less rather than more useful as a way of constituting a political community that can engage people's loyalties and serve their finest aspirations. But they should give support and guidance to their country so long as it seems the best hope available to them for leading free and meaningful lives, and for allowing others to do so as well.

Whether Americans can realize such a demanding sort of citizenship is ultimately up to Americans themselves. This often iconoclastic study of U.S. civic ideals has been written out of a profound sense that the realities of American history need to be confronted more fully if we are to recognize the dangers of renewed inegalitarian and illiberal civic policies in the present. Doing so should not obscure, however, the fact that there is much in the historical values and accomplishments of Americans in which we can rightly take pride, and much on which we can build to craft a common civic life that benefits all Americans, that helps more than harms other peoples, and that serves as a source of well-founded self-respect for all U.S. citizens in ways that enhance human dignity more generally. But the U.S. will not be that nation, the America that "never has been yet, and yet must be," unless its people see themselves for who they really are and what they have been. Americans must then draw from their highly imperfect past the will to continue to strive to form a more perfect union, with each other and with their endlessly troubled and promising world.

Notes

Introduction

1. Among those tensions is the controversy over whether it is imperialistic to refer to United States nationals as "Americans," as the other inhabitants of North, Central, and South America are all undeniably "Americans" as well. I have not been able to identify a suitable substitute, however: "U.S.A. citizen" is cumbersome, and the abbreviation *U.S.* could equally stand for a number of other nations that also have the words *United States* in their official names. Hence I have reluctantly elected to follow conventional usages here.
2. Hartz, 1955; R. M. Smith, 1985.
3. Bailyn, 1967; G. S. Wood, 1969; Pocock, 1975; MacIntyre, 1981; Sandel, 1982, 1984. In *Democracy's Discontent* (1996), Sandel extends this argument to a critique of contemporary American public philosophy as embodied in statutes and court cases, particularly stressing a modern decline in attention to citizenship. He continues, however, to employ the conventional liberal/republican dichotomy and to pay relatively little attention to the ascriptive traditions in American life that, he admits, have often been bound up with the republicanism he admires (6).
4. During this early work, Peter Schuck of the Yale Law School and I discovered that we both regarded citizenship by birth as an ascriptive anomaly in America's titularly consensual laws of membership. We collaborated on *Citizenship Without Consent* (1985), exploring how Fourteenth Amendment birthright citizenship could be understood as more consistent with consensual premises. The book has since been cited in support of harsh antiimmigrant views that neither Schuck nor I favor, and I modify my endorsement of its argument here in chapter 9. The opposition to ascriptive membership expressed in that book continues, however, to animate this work.
5. R. M. Smith, 1988a; 1993a. Here as there I use the term *tradition* to refer to (1) a world view or ideology that defines basic political and economic institutions, the persons eligible to participate in them, and the roles or rights to which they are entitled, and (2) institutions and practices embodying and reproducing such precepts. Hence traditions are not *merely* sets of ideas. The use of the term *liberalism* to designate a specific set of political traditions is largely the invention of twentieth-century scholars, and we might reasonably choose to define this liberalism and its adherents in a number of ways. But with Hartz, I here take liberal traditions to stress government by consent, limited by the rule of law protecting individual rights, and a market economy, all officially open to all minimally rational adults (cf. also Greenstone, 1993, 35, 53, 61). With Pocock, I treat America's interlinked republican traditions as grounded on popular sovereignty exercised via institutions not just of formal consent but of mass self-governance.

They generally preach an ethos of civic virtue and economic regulation for the public good (Pocock, 1975, 507, 550–52). Adherents of what I term inegalitarian ascriptive Americanist traditions believe that "true" Americans are "chosen" by God, history, or nature to possess superior moral and intellectual traits associated with their race, ethnicity, religion, gender, and sexual orientation. Hence many ascriptive Americanists have believed that nonwhites, women, and various others should be governed as subjects or second-class citizens, not as equals, denied full individual rights, including many property rights, and sometimes excluded from the nation altogether. Because ascriptive positions stress the significance of involuntarily acquired traits that differentiate people, they always have the potential to support exclusionary and hierarchical citizenship policies. Nonetheless, ascriptive views can undergird universalistic, egalitarian civic positions, as when religious believers esteem the sacredness of all humanity, indeed all creation, on the ground that everything equally comes from God. Despite their ultimate theological moral ascriptiveness, the fact that such egalitarian views almost always urge civic inclusiveness and treat national citizenships as legitimately alterable political memberships makes them effectively liberal and consensual in regard to citizenship laws. Hence I subsume them under liberalism here. If ascriptive positions instead deny people the right to base their political memberships on consent, I do not see them as genuinely egalitarian, because some people will inevitably be wielding power to impose civic memberships on others.

These liberal, republican, and inegalitarian ascriptive traditions are analytically distinguishable and in some respects logically inconsistent, but, as I stress throughout, most American political actors have nonetheless advanced outlooks combining elements of all three.

6. Previously, some writers had suggested kindred "multiple traditions" views of American political culture. For example, as Jacqueline Stevens, 1995, has noted in a critique of Smith, 1993a, W. E. B. Du Bois published a bitingly satirical dialogue in 1940 in which a wealthy white discovered he operated under multiple contradictory "codes" (Christian, Gentleman, American, White Man) (Du Bois, 1968, 153–69). Other points of the analysis here have similar precursors, more than it would be merciful to detail. Nonetheless, I do claim significant value added for what follows. Though many particular points were anticipated by Du Bois and other scholars, no author has explicitly critiqued Tocquevillian accounts and then described the content and explained the appeal of ascriptive inegalitarian traditions in the ways I do here. For a more extensive reply to Stevens see Smith, 1995. Since my first citizenship articles appeared, Brimelow (1995) and Lind (1995) have advanced views of American civic identity that also give greater recognition to America's racial and nativist traditions than do Hartzian accounts. Their frameworks still differ from mine, however, particularly by paying less attention to gender, and they also draw very different normative lessons, as I will discuss.

7. Most of the citizenship topics are based on the references to and criteria for citizenship in the Constitution. To these I add public education, the main governmental effort to craft citizens, and classifications used to deny full citizenship. With the republican tradition dating back to Aristotle, I define "full" citizenship, or citizenship in the strict sense, as including voting rights, while recognizing that noncitizens sometimes have possessed U.S. voting rights. The categories thus include: (1) rules of naturalization; (2) expatriation; (3) immigration; (4) Art. IV privileges and immunities of citizenship; (5) Fourteenth Amendment privileges and immunities of citizenship; (6) Art. III "diversity of citizenship" jurisdiction; (7) voting rights in federal elections; (8) loyalty oaths; (9) the guarantee of republican government clause; (10) the federal citizenship status of women; (11) persons born within U.S. jurisdiction. of African descent; (12) persons of Native American descent; (13) residents in American colonies; (14) civic education.

I believe that this list encompasses all the important issues involved in access to U.S. citizenship and possession of basic rights of political participation during the years I have examined. An exact figure for the cases examined cannot be given, because so many irrelevant cases involve reference to "diversity of citizenship" jurisdiction that we did not record all that were scanned and discarded. But every case of potential substantive significance was not only read but "shepardized" to identify all later cases that cited it. This process was supplemented by keyword searches and examination of every pertinent case discussed in several hundred secondary sources. Hence I do not believe that any significant decisions have gone unexamined. The index of cases includes all cases referred to in the text and notes but not all scanned. Since the existence of these new technologies makes such an exhaustive study possible, it seemed inappropriate to do less.

Although this data base reveals clear patterns that I believe support my claims for the prevalence of "ascriptive Americanist" notions of American civic identity, I have not tried to strengthen the case through more sophisticated statistical testing of those patterns. Such investigations are in some ways more rigorous than the historical interpretive methods I employ here, but in some ways they are less so. They quantify the patterns discerned more precisely, but usually do so by adopting schemes of categorization that amount to cruder interpretations of the cases, statutes, and arguments than can be provided in a more discursive approach. Hence I feel more confident making arguments of the latter sort, though I concede that other scholars might do better using more quantitative methods.

8. See R. M. Smith, 1989a, 292–93; Herrnstein & Murray, 1994; Rushton, 1995; Brimelow, 1995.

9. I intend to carry the story forward in a successor volume to whatever constitutes the present when that volume is done.

10. See, for example, the contrasting opinions of Justices Anthony Kennedy and Clarence Thomas in *U.S. Term Limits v. Thornton*, 115 S. Ct. 1842 (1995), as well as the calls for decentralization in the 1994 Republican Contract with America.

11. I believe that similar patterns are visible in most other political communities, although I do not try to make that case here. This view of civic identities as products of political struggles over state-building that include certain ideological dynamics draws in part on older analyses of nationalism, state-building, and citizenship by political sociologists and intellectual historians such as Marshall (1950), Bendix (1964), Seton Watson (1977), Kedourie (1961), and Minogue ((1967), as well as more recent arguments by Gellner (1983), B. R. O. Anderson (1983), Hobsbawm (1990), and Balibar & Wallerstein (1991). But unlike these previous authors, my primary emphasis is on the legally embedded ideological structures that Americans have had available to them in forging their senses of their political values, their legal rules governing membership, and their very conceptions of their own political identities. This focus on institutionalized ideologies is shared with other political scientists and sociologists who have stressed, in Stephen Krasner's words, how a critical purpose of modern states is "to represent symbolically the existence and unity of the political community," achieved in part by embodying ideologies in citizenship laws that can serve as "a basic source of identity" (Krasner, 1984, 228, 233; 1988, 74–75). More than others, however, I stress how citizenship laws do more than foster loyalty and obedience to nation-state authorities ideologically. They also represent a concrete distribution of political powers that play a significant role in shaping the nation's development (cf. Boli, 1987, 132).

12. There are many "new institutionalisms" favored by quite varied political scientists, political sociologists, and practitioners of other disciplines (Hall & Taylor, 1994). The approach here derives from themes in historical sociology as well as political science. It involves several elements that distinguish it from other analytical approaches.

First, instead of taking groups, economic classes, or grand unitary social systems as the basic objects of analysis, a historical new institutionalist account is open to hypotheses stressing these or a wide range of other political entities (R. M. Smith, 1988b; 1992). Historical institutionalists begin by identifying some among many structures that are thought to shape the conduct of political actors; but different analyses will feature different structures. Choices must be made in each particular project, for a very broad range of structures are arguably important, including biological, physical, and psychological systems, economic and political arrangements, kinship and civil associations, and ongoing structures of ideas, including religious beliefs and political ideologies, held by identifiable political actors. None of those structures are necessarily wholly determined by or reducible to any others, and so they probably will not display concerted paths of development. Hence we must often analyze the interaction of various partly independent orders of economic organization, political parties, evolving belief systems, and so forth (Orren & Skowronek, 1994).

Such structures influence political action by endowing or constituting both the actors and their environments in ways that set imperatives and constraints for the actors; but they also give them identifiable capacities or powers to act in a range of ways. Hence explanations of political conduct can to some degree be provided by analyzing the structures that provide actors with their problems, opportunities, and repertoires of behaviors, including characteristic modes of reasoning and arguing. But such analysis may result only in showing the range of options an actor had and making comprehensible the positions the actor adopted, without rendering the choices fully predictable. The choices may then significantly alter some of the structures that comprise the actors' environment and own constitution. Thus this approach is open to the possibility that the decisions of political actors may be crucial independent variables, significant causes of human history.

13. The argument thus helps fill a gap noted by Martin Sklar. He observes that not only occupation but also "sex, race, nationality, religious denomination, or ethnicity" should "affect our understanding of periodization with corresponding dimensions of inquiry and meaning." But he argues that "so far none per se nor some combination of them constitutes or represents itself as an adequate periodization concept" (1991, 179n4).

In *The Next American Nation,* Michael Lind attempts such a periodization. He divides American civic history into three "racial, cultural, and political regimes," which he terms "Anglo-America" (1789–1861), "Euro-America" (1875–1957), and "Multicultural America" (1972 to the present). In between are periods of "cataclysmic and violent struggle" (Lind, 1995, 10). This framework is useful, but it risks minimizing the reality of admittedly short-lived but vital egalitarian reforms during the Confederation and Reconstruction eras. More important, it overstates the inclusiveness of the Gilded Age and the early twentieth century. In light of the biases against southern and eastern Europeans that culminated in the national origins quotas of the 1920s, Lind concedes that this era only enlarged the circle of full citizens "from Anglo-Saxon to Germano-Celtic," not such a revolutionary change (79). And, in fact, legally all Europeans were eligible for immigration and naturalization in Lind's "Anglo-American" era, while many faced closed doors in much of his "Euro-American" one. Lind's understatement of the exclusionary character of American civic policies during these "middle" years probably reflects the fact that he identifies with some of their architects, such as Theodore Roosevelt (285–86, 301–2).

14. The views of a chief sponsor of a congressional bill are, to be sure, generally good indicators of how the bill was understood by those who voted for it, although technically the only legally binding part of a judicial opinion is the *ratio decidendi,* the precise rule of decision, not all the reasoning justifying it. But exactly what constitutes the *ratio decidendi* is often

in dispute, so in practice the whole of a judicial opinion becomes something other officials must accord great respect.

15. Dahl, 1989, 207; Rawls, 1993a, 12.

Chapter 1. The Hidden Lessons of American Citizenship Laws

1. To be sure, many still think that man is by nature a political animal, as Aristotle persuasively contended (1968, 1253a, 5); but few concede that particular rulers hold their positions as result of divine or natural ordinances, as medieval kings claimed.

2. Aristotle, 1968, 1275a23, 93–94.

3. Gleason, 1982, 62–63. This section and the next draw extensively on R. M. Smith, 1993a.

4. Although this account of American identity became much more widely endorsed after World War II than before (Lind, 1995, 104–5), one can find quotations suggesting it in 1782. Hector St. John Crèvecoeur then insisted that Europeans, at least, became Americans simply by embracing "new principles," a "new government," and hence a new "mode of life" (Rischin, ed., 1976, 25–26). On the eve of the Civil War, the German-American Republican leader Carl Schurz defined "True Americanism" as simply belief in "liberty and equal rights" and the system of government that protected them (Fuchs, 1990, 29). As America's entry into the First World War approached, President Woodrow Wilson assured newly naturalized citizens in 1915 that they had just sworn allegiance "to no one," only to "a great ideal, a great body of principles" (R. M. Smith, 1988a, 225). During World War II, Franklin Roosevelt similarly contended that Americanism had always been a "matter of mind and heart." It "is not, and never was, a matter of race or ancestry" (Takaki, 1993, 374). But Roosevelt's claim was driven more by the war imperative of firing up support against a racist Nazism than by historical accuracy. The others cited here all also had recognizable political purposes, and they all nonetheless explicitly endorsed certain forms of ascriptive hierarchy, in passages less often quoted now but often more popular then.

5. The phrase is Karen Orren's. She has argued powerfully that even the relative equality often said to exist among white men in the U.S. has been exaggerated, because courts enforced essentially feudal structures of employer-employee rights up to the New Deal (Orren, 1991). Because all native white men were nonetheless granted formal citizenship relatively early on, the analysis here does not feature those important inequalities. But despite this and other real contributions, Orren's account is still too tied to Marx's view that relationships to the means of production (and the legal doctrines partly constituting them) are the key to political life. Its logic implies that the subordinate civic status for people of color, women, and others I will describe must all similarly be residual survivals of feudal labor structures, but that claim is untenable. Cf. Orren, 1996; R. M. Smith, 1996. Another discussion of inequalities among white men which still stresses their relative equality is G. S. Wood, 1991, 20–41, 112–23, 233–40.

6. The percentage varies with whether one dates the existence of the United States from 1776, the Declaration of Independence, or 1789, the ratified Constitution. State policies prior to 1790 on the whole made nonwhites and women ineligible for full citizenship. Women could always formally be U.S. citizens; but they had no constitutional protection against gender-based denials of the franchise until 1920, making them second-class citizens. Other overt legal discriminations on their political and economic rights continued through the 1960s. Naturalization was confined to whites from 1790 through 1870 and closed to most Asian nationals until 1952. By then the national origins quota system of immigration restrictions enacted in the 1920s prevented most Asians and many southern Europeans from coming to the U.S. and becoming permanent residents or citizens, explicitly because of

their original nationality or ethnicity. That system was not repealed until 1965. Despite formal constitutional guarantees enacted in the mid-1860s, blacks were also widely denied basic rights of citizenship until the 1964 Civil Rights Act and the 1965 Voting Rights Act (Higham, 1975, 29–66; Kettner, 1978, 287–333; R. M. Smith, 1989a). Thus, though the specifics changed, denials of access to full citizenship based explicitly on race, ethnicity, or gender always denied large majorities of the world's population opportunities for full U.S. citizenship up to 1965—about 83% of the nation's history since the Constitution, 88% since the Declaration. If one assumes that women became full citizens with the vote in 1920, then a majority of the domestic adult population became legally eligible for full citizenship then. Yet even by that measure, which seriously understates the racial and gender-based exclusionary aspects of American citizenship laws, a majority of domestic adults were legally ineligible for full citizenship on racial, ethnic, or gender grounds for about two-thirds of U.S. history (from either starting point).

These figures do not count young people under the age of majority as second-class citizens although they, too, have always been denied the franchise. I regard it as reasonable to attribute to them as a class a lack of political competence but do not think this has ever been true of adult women. Children, moreover, become eligible for adult civic privileges in due time, but until the twentieth century most American women were never eligible to vote. Disfranchisement of felons is a controversial policy, but I do not count it as an ascriptive bar on full citizenship, because criminals have forfeited their eligibility for voting through voluntary acts.

7. This book encompasses only the first two major eras of civic reforms, from 1776 through 1789 and 1860 through 1876. The dependency of racial progress in U.S. history on wars against antidemocratic opponents is elaborated in Klinkner with Smith, forthcoming.

8. For a more extensive critique of these works see Smith, 1993a, from which the arguments here are adapted.

9. Tocqueville, 1969, 9–12, 18.

10. Tocqueville, 1969, 33–36, 50–51, 280–81.

11. Myrdal, 1944, 3–4, 7–8, 25, 52.

12. Myrdal, 1944, lxxi–lxxiii, 6–9. For critiques on other grounds see Jackson, 1990, 199, and Southern, 1987, 295. As noted below, Myrdal's full story was more complex and belied these generalizations; but they accurately depict the way he portrayed his argument at the outset. That portrayal has greatly shaped interpretations of his work.

13. Hartz, 1955, 6–23, 35–36, 46, 51, 58, 62–63, 66, 284–309.

14. Hartz, 1955, 9, 14–22, 63, 75, 89, 91, 128–29, 140, 147. Greenstone thus errs when he says that Hartzian accounts are static, unable to explain change (1993, 41–44).

15. Tocqueville, 1969, 316. Tocqueville also saw the danger of an "aristocracy created by industry" in the U.S., but he thought that if this came, it would be an aristocracy "not at all like those that have preceded it" (557).

16. Tocqueville, 1969, 326, 342.

17. Tocqueville, 1969, 340, 356, 358.

18. Tocqueville, 1969, 600–601.

19. Tocqueville, 1969, 590–92, 601–2.

20. Indeed, it is a central argument of this book that Americans espousing liberal ideals have often failed to provide politically potent accounts of appropriate new social institutions, in this and many other regards.

21. Tocqueville, 1969, 601, 603. Tocqueville claimed that American women were thus so superior that they were the "chief cause of the extraordinary prosperity and growing power" of the U.S. (603). Mathie (1995) correctly argues that Tocqueville does not actually endorse

American men's views of the nature of the sexes, but he agrees that Tocqueville's arguments served to justify denying women equal participation in America's economic and political spheres (22–23, 30).

22. Myrdal, 1944, 1189n10.
23. Myrdal, 1944, 37–38, 91–92, 97, 99, 443, 529, 599, 1189, n12.
24. Myrdal, 1944, 89.
25. Myrdal, 1944, 97.
26. Fredrickson, 1971; Horsman, 1981.
27. Hartz, 1955, 58–172; cf. Fredrickson, 1971; Howe, 1979, 234–36; Beer, 1984 (on American romanticism); Ellis, 1991, 344–45, 350–51.
28. Hartz, 1955, 167–69, 291–92.
29. Hartz, 1964, 16–17, 49–50, 60–62, 102.
30. Hartz, 1964, 94–99. In these arguments Hartz actually overstated the egalitarianism of Lockean liberalism, which held that all humans possessed certain minimal rights but were not entitled to full *political* rights until and unless they had attained a properly socialized rationality, as discussed below. But he was right that many Americans believed that the Declaration of Independence asserted a fundamental moral equality of human beings that militated against second-class citizenship.
31. Some major works on American identity have employed frameworks closer to the one developed here. Hans Kohn's classic essay, *American Nationalism* (1957), analyzed American nationality in terms of "three foundations" similar to those I identify: the Enlightenment tradition of liberty, federal republicanism, and the interaction of the predominant Anglo-American cultural tradition with those of other national origins (9, 135, 165, 173, 252n45). But, writing before the "republican revival," Kohn treated republicanism as a structural determinant of American nationality, and saw its ideological content as derived from Enlightenment liberalism, in line with the standard narrative. And though Kohn recognized that the U.S. had often demanded assimilation into a "distinct national identity" built primarily on English roots, his focus on the English commitment to liberty led him to downplay how illiberally exclusivist this ethnocultural conception of national identity was (13, 21, 28, 165–69).

   Also in 1957, Mark Roelofs's *Tension of Citizenship* analyzed citizenship generally, and American citizenship incidentally, in terms of three patterns, one focused on "pride and participation" in the "communal life of the civic republic," one focused on "loyalty and service" to an "organic community," and one that was individualistic, universalistic, stressing defiance to claims of particular communities, and concerned to protect personal privacy. Though he labels these three "Greek," "Hebraic," and "Christian-Roman," respectively, they resemble the civic republican, ascriptive Americanist, and Enlightenment liberal elements that I see as the original ideological traditions shaping American citizenship. Roelofs, however, does not explore U.S. citizenship in depth, and again he conforms to orthodoxy in emphasizing the dominance of individualistic, rationalistic Enlightenment liberalism (Roelofs, 1957, 31, 37, 53, 76, 116–18, 125–31, 150–51, 159–65).

   In 1964, Yehoshua Arieli also chiefly identified American nationality with liberal republican political principles. But he discerned an "awareness of belonging to a national organic community whose values are to a certain degree not transferable." Thus he saw the tension created by these "two competing types of national consciousness" as perhaps the chief determinant of the "structure and course of American nationalism" (Arieli, 1964, 29–30). The present argument can be seen as a justification of that neglected insight.

   More recent writers have identified three strands in American nationality but placed a biblical or Christian tradition alongside civic republican and individualistic liberal ones

(Bellah et al., 1985; Kloppenberg, 1987). For some Americans, separating out and fore-grounding their religious traditions makes sense. It is vital to see, however, that religious elements partly undergird virtually every strain of public discourse in America, including liberalism and republicanism. When religious identities are taken as explicit grounds for granting or denying citizenship, as in American Protestant nativism, they are instead closest to my category of ascriptive Americanism. Religion is, however, not the only component of such Americanism, nor do I think that inegalitarian ascriptive Americanism has any claim to be the "authentic" expression of religious values in the U.S.

In 1985 Peter Schuck and I analyzed American citizenship dichotomously, in terms of whether membership rested on ascription or consent. From that standpoint differences between liberal and republican traditions are not decisive, for in principle they both stress a consensual basis for membership. Although here I maintain the normative opposition to ascriptive membership that animated that 1985 analysis, I elaborate more fully the contrary implications of liberal and republican strands in American civic thought in other regards and stress the frequent alliances between republican and ascriptive Americanist traditions.

Two more popular 1995 works discuss American identity in ways closer to my framework. Peter Brimelow's *Alien Nation* attacks the myth that U.S. nationality has been defined by ideas, not by race or blood, noting that the U.S. was long kept a hegemonically "white" nation by law and that many leading Americans endorsed this as a principled policy (10–18, 66–67, 122, 191–92, 206–11). In *The Next American Nation,* Michael Lind also denies that America has been an "Idea" nation instead of a "cultural" nation joined by a common language and folkways. He sees the latter reality as the source of a potent "nativist" American tradition of great "antiquity," in opposition to his own "liberal nationalism" and more radical "democratic universalist" and "multiculturalist" conceptions (1–11, 281, 286, 351–83). Neither writer pays much attention to the tensions between liberal and republican traditions, as I do, however. Brimelow's "nativism" is also narrower than my category of ascriptive Americanism because he focuses almost exclusively on race and ethnicity, omitting gender. And I describe as "egalitarian liberal democracy" what Lind labels "democratic universalism." Though I agree with him that the U.S. has a common culture with multiple elements within it, his concerns to protect that culture via immigration restrictions and requirements for linguistic and cultural assimilation make what he calls "liberal nationalism" a mild form of ascriptive Americanism in my terms. Normatively, I strongly reject Brimelow's nativism and also Lind's liberal nationalism, though the latter position does share some features with the "party of America" view of civic identity that I recommend in the epilogue.

32. Bloom, 1987. Other influential scholars on American political thought similarly influenced by Strauss include Harvey Mansfield (1991), Thomas Pangle (1988), and Harry Jaffa (1975). In comparison with the others, Jaffa and his students see more residuals of ancient aristocratic notions of virtue in revolutionary America; but they agree that these have since been submerged by excessively egalitarian versions of liberal democracy.

33. Huntington, 1981, 249. Other important Tocquevillian modern works that engage in contrasts with European politics to celebrate American exceptionalism include Daniel Boorstin's *Genius of American Politics* (1953) and S. M. Lipset's *First New Nation* (1963). Recent works by comparative sociologists have generally accepted and reinforced these claims for America's uniquely voluntarist civic identity. See, e.g., Brubaker, ed., 1989, 11–12; Greenfeld, 1992.

34. Kettner's enormously useful book tells the story of American civic development as a difficult but ultimately triumphant transition from feudal subject to "republican citizenship,"

resting on voluntary consent and equal rights for all adult citizens "without invidious gradations." He marks 1870 as the point where that triumph is reached, when Reconstruction achieves the overcoming of "deep-seated prejudices" against nonwhites, so that citizenship henceforth "would be determined by the authority of a sovereign people, a community of citizens, that formed a single and united nation." As is typical of more celebratory Tocquevillian accounts, however, the ultimate victory of liberal republican principles is proclaimed far too soon and too completely (Kettner, 1978, 3, 10, 345–51).

35. Walzer, 1990, 597–98, 610–11. Walzer echoes the concern of other scholars on the left that liberalism in America has buttressed unjust class inequalities, but he does not agree that it has been more the source than the solution for racial and ethnic hierarchies.

36. Karst at first indicates that the American Creed has contained internally contradictory values by including both universal human rights and white supremacy, a major advance on Myrdal's account. But he then persistently contends that when Americans have acted in accordance with inegalitarian values, they have been guilty of "hypocrisy" that generates "huge exceptions" to their defining national principles. He does not explain why compliance with inegalitarian precepts is simply inconsistent with American ideals, rather than a fulfillment of some American ideals at the expense of others. His labels have the effect of preserving Myrdal's contention that America's egalitarian traditions represent the central strain in the nation's culture (Karst, 1989, 30–32, 40, 47, 62, 172, 179, 181, 188, 210–11, 215, 228, 242). Huntington's Myrdalian notion of "Creedal Politics" also claims that U.S. history shows only clashes of egalitarian principles with practical expediency, not rival, inegalitarian principles.

37. Hartz, 1955, 125, 248–52; Katznelson, 1981, 14–16; Burnham, 1970, 176, 313; 1982, 15, 95, 127–28. Katznelson's recent writings are less vulnerable to this critique. In *The Democratic Wish*, James Morone employs a Hartzian frame, holding that liberalism "is dominant" in America but "repeatedly challenged by a recurring, subordinate ideology" of "direct, communal democracy." He then reaches conclusions that are partly celebratory, partly critical: the outcomes of these challenges are, he says, "fundamentally ambiguous" (Morone, 1990, 1–2, 18, 22–23).

38. Bercovitch, 1978, argues that the rhetoric of jeremiads reveals how Puritan traditions worked to reaffirm as well as criticize the liberal consensus dominating American life. Greenstone, 1986 and 1993, and in a different way Diggins, 1984, argue that the U.S. has been shaped by Protestant-inspired as well as secular rationalist versions of liberalism, with the first more concerned to foster virtuous human development rather than to satisfy existing preferences. Greenstone terms this Puritan-rooted liberalism "reform liberalism" (1993, 59), and though I think that American political culture is more complex, the normative view I will defend falls into this camp. For an overview of how most writers within the "republican revival" still see liberalism as ultimately triumphant, see Ackerman, 1991, 27–29, 327n45. Many historians and social scientists see the Progressive Era as a more decisive turning point than Hartz, at least, allowed; but they generally describe one form of liberalism replacing another. See, e.g., Hays, 1973; Wiebe, 1967; Galambos, 1970, 1983; Skowronek, 1982; Sklar, 1991; Lowi, 1979; Lustig, 1982; Kloppenberg, 1986; Ceaser, 1979; Tulis, 1987; Ackerman, 1991.

These works reinforce the pattern still visible in an impressively comprehensive 1990 study of America civic evolution by a Hartz student, Lawrence Fuchs. Though paying far more attention than Hartz to many of the forms of civic discrimination throughout U.S. history (while still ignoring the second-class citizenship of women), Fuchs casts these as the experiences of people "outside the civic culture," not subordinated within it. He also assures us that now, at long last, class barriers have indeed become the most important obstacles to social progress, as Hartzians have long believed (Fuchs, 1990, 4–6, 492–93). Thus, as much as Hartz, Fuchs's framework resists the notion that American political culture has had core conflicts over forms of ascriptive hierarchy that have not lost their appeal. Class inequalities remain the most important sources of conflict intrinsic to the American civic culture.

39. This tendency became more pronounced from the 1930s through the 1970s, an era when Communists supported civil rights efforts in the U.S. sometimes out of conviction, sometimes due to international rivalries. Those circumstances helped prompt many leading African-American intellectuals like W. E. B. Du Bois and, later, Angela Davis to identify themselves with Communism, which Du Bois did not do earlier in his career.

40. The Tocquevillian pattern appears in the seminal study of nativism in modern scholarship, John Higham's classic *Strangers in the Land* (1966, orig. pub. 1955). Higham correctly presented nativism as a species of "modern nationalism." He believed that it was built on "ethnocentric attitudes" that were virtually always present, but that during certain periods leaders elaborated those attitudes into full-fledged ideologies (Higham, 1966, 4). Higham thus found several nativisms, though all shared an "ideological core."

His distinction between an elaborated ideology and more inarticulate ethnocentric feelings has some force, though Higham has since acknowledged that it presents difficulties (1986, 223; 1988, 343–44). One consequence for most readers was that Higham's work did not compel reinterpretation of the ideological core of American identity. Nativist ideologies were occasional things. Liberal democratic ideology, on the other hand, could still be seen as a better articulated constant, as Myrdal argued.

That contrast is not defensible. As Myrdal admitted, sophisticated doctrines of racial inequality were dominant in American universities and public opinion through much of U.S. history. And, as Hartz recognized, Americans have not held liberal democratic values in the form of full-fledged ideologies any more than racial ones. These values have more often been unreflective, if not indeed subrational, sets of common beliefs, fully as deserving of the epithet "prejudices" as racial values. It is, then, not credible to distinguish Americanism from liberalism and republicanism on the ground that the Americanism has usually been a set of ethnocentric attitudes, whereas the latter outlooks have been constantly present as elaborate ideologies. Insofar as Higham's presentation of nativist ideology as a sometime thing has permitted many to believe that America has essentially been liberal democratic, it has been misleading.

41. Bell, 1992, 46–49, 60–61. The last formulation in the text may read more favorably to liberalism than Bell intends. In his view, a chief reason the white majority supports racial hierarchy is that it helps their position in the capitalist economy, an economy created in accordance with liberal principles. Hence the tension is really between white majorities with inegalitarian aims due in part to a liberal economy, versus liberal principles of individual rights.

42. Similarly, in 1994 Richard Delgado, like Bell a leading figure in the Critical Race Theory movement in contemporary legal studies, cited Tocqueville and Myrdal on behalf of the view that in America, the nation's "higher, official" values endorse racial equality, whereas racism is manifested in informal contexts. Then the protagonist of Delgado's dialogue advances the neo-Hartzian claim that Enlightenment values generate racism, so that "[l]iberal democracy and racial subordination go hand in hand, like the sun, moon, and stars." Delgado termed this claim "powerful" and "plausible" (Delgado, 1994, 726–30, 734, 737, 756). Again, racist ideologies are treated as epiphenomenal to a "higher, official" core liberalism.

43. A similar Gramscian neo-Marxian frame in which racial ideologies are treated as instruments of capitalist economic exploitation, rather than specifically racial exploitation, is

employed in Takaki, 1979. Takaki, 1993, takes no explicit stance on these issues but cites both Tocqueville and Myrdal without criticism. Like most of the literature critiqued here, Takaki's writings are nonetheless outstanding works from which I have greatly benefited.

44. Pateman, 1988, 38, 41, 54, 92–94; cf. Eisenstein, 1981, 3–5, 34–49; MacKinnon, 1987, 14–16, 164–65; Okin, 1979, 199; R. M. Smith, 1989a, 233–36. As argued in the latter essay, these points are not meant to deny that otherwise liberal writers did endorse patriarchy; that features of liberal thought—like distinctions between public and private realms and a minimization of the importance of political participation—were used to support patriarchy; and that liberal economic and political institutions were structured in practice on the assumption of female incapacities and patriarchal families. I regard these elements as features that made many earlier versions of liberalism empirically inaccurate and logically inconsistent with their own human rights arguments. If the assumptions and endorsements of patriarchy are eliminated, liberal theories lose nothing essential and instead become more internally coherent. And if consistency is sought instead by explicitly abandoning any commitment to universal rights for all minimally rationally individuals, then the result is a political doctrine few would label liberal. For a related critique of accounts of liberal exclusions in Pateman and C. B. Macpherson, see Mehta, 1990, 434–35.

45. This view is elaborated briefly in R. M. Smith, 1996.

46. See, e.g., Crenshaw, 1988, 1336; cf. Ansley, 1989, 998, 1023–49; P. J. Williams, 1991; C. I. Harris, 1993, 1715–45, 1791.

47. Mills, 1994, 863. Cf., e.g., Fredrickson, 1981; Saxton, 1990; Roediger, 1991, esp. 6–15.

48. Exemplary here is an influential article by Uday Mehta, who argues that despite the explicit "universality and politically inclusionary character" of Lockean liberalism, it has "spawned practices" involving "the political marginalization of various people." Mehta maintains rightly that, although Locke believed that all human beings had the potential for rationality, he also thought that realizing that potential required an education involving "a thick set of social inscriptions" limiting free conduct. Those inadequately or improperly "inscribed" were left too ignorant, too "inscrutable," or too "uncivilized" to be awarded equal political rights, though they retained minimal rights. Hence not just children and "naturally" less rational women but also adult workers and foreigners might be denied the franchise.

    Such liberal arguments have played important roles in America's history of hierarchical citizenship laws. But Mehta notes another source of exclusion in Anglo-American traditions: ideas of a "shared and exclusive inheritance" which explicitly favor the rights of some special groups over universal human rights. My evidence indicates that such ascriptive doctrines have played a larger role in spawning America's civic inequalities than Lockean concerns about inadequately socialized rationality. Mehta does not address that issue; but his focus on the grounds of exclusion within liberalism reinforces conventional views that the liberal sources matter far more (Mehta, 1990, 428–29, 430; 1992, 117, 127, 152–54).

49. Etienne Balibar's recent writings on race and national identity come close to the framework I am offering, but he has not to my knowledge written systematically on the United States. I also prefer to use "civic myths" for what Balibar terms "fictive ethnicities." By that term he means that national identities are politically constructed in part to valorize systems of power involving both exclusions and internal hierarchies. But these stories of common identity succeed, he contends, not merely by force but also because they "naturalize" a meaningful, indeed often transcendent "ideological world" for those they seek to unite as an "imagined community." At some point nationalists usually try to persuade people that they are not merely a community but a "chosen people." With all this I concur. I prefer the term *civic myths* to *fictive ethnicities*, however, because ethnicities, like nationalities, are always partly fictive—partly constituted by stories that create rather than merely express a

social and political identity (a point with which Balibar agrees) (Balibar & Wallerstein, 1991, 4, 10, 21–22, 37–38, 57–58, 62, 93–100).

50. Though politicians try every way possible to generate a loyal citizenry, they cannot provide what Mancur Olson (1965) calls "selective incentives" to all individuals to secure their participation (unless "selective incentives" are defined so expansively as to be meaningless). Hence they rely most heavily on the more general promised benefits that the text discusses.

51. As a result, citizenship laws are receiving much more scholarly attention than in the past. See, e.g., Brubaker, ed., 1989; Kymlicka & Norman, 1994.

52. As Edward Millican notes in discussing the *Federalist Papers,* it is "often-times the hardest task of the nation-builder to convince the members of the target group that they belong together" (Millican, 1990, 46).

53. My use of *myth* is broadly consistent with discussions of myths of political identity by other writers, e.g., Gellner, 1965; Slotkin, 1973, 23–24; Roelofs, 1992, 17–22; Lind, 1995, 350–52. The term is, of course, a controversial one, used differently in various disciplines. Writers like Slotkin and Wright stress more than I that myths respond to and express deep structural features of human psychology and the lives of particular cultures in ways that people may not fully recognize. Hence their content and their power are neither arbitrary nor infinitely manipulable, but rather profoundly expressive of lived realities. I do not dispute these accounts, but I agree with Slotkin that in modern cultures, myth-makers often have "a degree of critical distance" from their materials, so that they have greater awareness of their own constructive role (1973, 13). I therefore think that my emphasis on elite construction of myths for political purposes is appropriate, though I acknowledge that leaders often believe strongly in the moral truth of the civic myths they deploy.

54. Madison in Madison, Hamilton, & Jay, 1987, 314.

55. Anthony Smith is therefore probably correct to argue that all nations are defined in ways that combine "ethnic-genealogical" or ascriptive traits and "civic-territorial" features emphasizing shared political beliefs as well as land (A. D. Smith, 1991). The widespread pattern of classifying nation-states as belonging to one or the other of these models, as in, e.g., Brubaker, 1992, is misleading.

56. E. S. Morgan, 1988.

57. Jensen, ed., 1967, 402.

58. Shain, 1994, 198, 217n120, 224–25.

Chapter 2. Fierce New World

1. *Calvin's Case* was decided in the royal Court of Exchequer-Chamber, a composite body in which fourteen judges, drawn from the Exchequer, the King's Bench, and the Court of Common Pleas all participated, along with the Lord Chancellor. Coke was Chief Justice of Common Pleas. Harold Berman describes the courts of Exchequer, Common Pleas, and the Chancery as "pillars of the new English state," crucial to the centralizing state-building process (Kettner, 1978, 17; Berman, 1983, 444).

2. Kedourie, 1961, 9, 68, 72; Gellner, 1965, 150–51; Gellner, 1983, 1, 6–7, 49; Lipset, 1963; Rossiter, 1971; Minogue, 1967, 8, 11, 17–19, 25; Seton-Watson, 1977, 1, 5–7; B. R. O. Anderson, 1983, 12, 15, 104; Hobsbawm, 1990, 3–10.

3. Lyon, 1960, 75–91, 127–37; Berman, 1983, 297–300. In fact, in these largely subsistence agrarian societies ruled by martial and clerical aristocracies, economic, political, and religious responsibilities were so straightforward that rulers often did not need even to speak in the language of the ruled for most of their own activities. The elites' employment of "noble" and "sacred" languages—Latin in Christendom, classical Arabic or Mandarin else-

where—actually reinforced their claims to belong to, or at least be especially attuned to, a higher order of beings. These esoteric languages also enabled elites of varied backgrounds to communicate in administering extensive multilingual regions (Gellner, 1965, 155, 157; Gellner, 1983, 22–27; Seton-Watson, 1977, 7–9; B. R. O. Anderson, 1983, 20–21).

4. Bendix, 1977, 38–39; cf. Wallerstein, 1974, 67, 136, 145–47, 349.

5. Shakespeare, 1936, 651 (*Henry V*, Act IV, sc. III).

6. Baxter, ed., 1968, 103–4.

7. 7 Co. Rep. 1a (1697; orig. 1608); Kettner, 1978, 16.

8. Political offices would remain essentially confined to large landholders up to the Victorian era (Colley, 1992, 61).

9. Lyon, 1960, 457, 496–98; Kettner, 1978, 5–6.

10. 7 Co. Rep. 14a–14b, 25a–25b; Kettner, 1978, 7–8, 45; Colley, 1992, 11–12.

11. 7 Co. Rep. 4a, 15b.

12. 7 Co. Rep. 5b, 10a, 11b–12a.

13. 7 Co. Rep. 4a, 9b.

14. 7 Co. Rep. 6a–6b, 10a, 14a–14b, 18a–18b.

15. 7 Co. Rep. 3b–5b, 8a, 13b–14b, 25a.

16. Almost contemporaneously with *Calvin's Case,* Coke and "all the judges of England" sharply rebuked James I to his face when James claimed a right to decide cases himself. Coke insisted that the king was insufficiently "learned in the laws of his realm of England" for that task. James argued that it was treasonous to suggest that the king was under the law, but Coke insisted that he was under both "Deo et lege." Not long thereafter, Coke would pronounce the famous dictum in *Dr. Bonham's Case,* that the common law's embodiment of common right and reason could render contrary acts of parliament void, a passage that American jurists would seize on to defend judicial review (Corwin, 1955, 38–57; Pocock, 1967, 31, 36–37, 46).

17. 7 Co. Rep. 12b, 13a–13b. For related discussions of Christian Aristotelian conceptions of nature as great hierarchical "chain of being" see, e.g., Walzer, 1965, 152–60; Beer, 1993, 31–65. For these ideas in early America, see G. S. Wood, 1991, 19–42.

18. 7 Co. Rep. 13b–14a.

19. The political rights of naturalized subjects were later restricted in various ways in the eighteenth century (Kettner, 1978, 35).

20. Kettner, 1978, 29–34, 41.

21. 7 Co. Rep. 14b, 16b (for an alien "there must of necessity be several kings, and several ligeances"), 27b.

22. Locke, 1965b.

23. Pocock, 1967, 16–17, 124–25.

24. Milton, 1961, 45–46; cf. Summers, 1993, 101.

25. Pocock, 1967, 125–28, 135–36; Pocock, 1975, 412–17, 468–73; Pocock, 1985, 226–33; Beer, 1993, 128–31; G. S. Wood, 1991, 13–14.

26. Kettner, 1978, 44–61; G. S. Wood, 1991, 6, 11–12, 15–19; quotation is from Colley, 1992, 19; see also 5, 55, 367–69.

27. Bailyn, 1986, 94–97; Hobsbawm, 1990, 77–78; Colley, 1992, 134–36.

28. Kedourie, 1961, 95–96, 99, 101; Gellner, 1965, 151; Gellner, 1983, 18, 34–35, 49, 55–57, 110, 118–20; Lipset, 1967; Minogue, 1967, 20, 25–26, 32; Wallerstein, 1974, 336–39, 353; Seton-Watson, 1977, 7, 9, 113, 219, 470; B. R. O. Anderson, 1983, 20–23, 40–48, 50, 65, 70–73, 102–4. Ernest Gellner argues further that as industrialization spread during the nineteenth century, inhabitants had to become increasingly capable of a variety of specialized but changing and generically related economic and social tasks. That versatility is possible only

if they come to share a common language and education that enable them to function effectively as an adaptable, mobile work force. Those capacities, in turn, demand a relatively
complex and large-scale educational system, of a type not possible for small, traditional
political units, such as villages, tribes, and feudal estates. Hence Gellner believes that something like the nation-state was demanded by the spread of modern economic systems (Gellner, 1965, 152–53, 158–60; Gellner, 1983, 22–24, 26–29, 32–34, 63).

29. E. S. Morgan, 1956, 5–8, 101–4, 135–38; Merritt, 1966, 174–75, 180; Bailyn, 1967, 1–2, 19;
B. R. O. Anderson, 1983, 50, 65; Archdeacon, 1983, 22; Beer, 1984, 364, 366–67, 373; G. S.
Wood, 1991, 12.

30. Older studies estimated the New World population in 1492 at about 1 million, reduced to
500,000 when Virginia was settled. Revisionists put the population before Columbus between 7 and 18 million (out of a New World population estimated between 57 and 112 million). They believe that the tribes lost roughly 90% of their population to the plagues that
Europeans brought, a grim figure which brings their estimates for North America in 1607
closer to traditional accounts. Although the English colonists were not above deliberately
infecting tribes with smallpox, most of the devastation occurred before their arrival (Merrell, 1991, 122; Wright, 1992, 4, 13–14, 104, 123–24).

31. The Plymouth colony began in 1620, with Massachusetts Bay following in 1630, quickly
populated due to religious and civil strife at home, but soon ridden by conflict in turn, so
that dissenters established Connecticut and Rhode Island in 1662 and 1663. The proprie-
tary colonies of New Hampshire and the Catholic Lord Baltimore's Maryland were formed
during the 1630s; New Jersey and the Carolinas, in the 1660s; Pennsylvania, in 1682, and
Georgia, 1732. New York and Delaware were ceded by the Dutch in 1664.

32. P. Foner, 1975, 186–96, 256–57; Archdeacon, 1983, 1–26; Bailyn, 1986, 9–10, 60; Meinig,
1986, 24–55, 79–160, 216–17, 244–54; Franklin & Moss, 1988, 53–63; P. D. Morgan, 1991,
161–62; Roeber, 1991, 22; Wright, 1992, 115; Kivisto, 1995, 112–19, 136–38.

33. Though they were forced to give way to the English, the Dutch were for a long time more
enterprising than the French. Once they acquired independence from Spain in 1609, their
West India Company came to dominate shipping to the New World.

34. Nash, 1974, 34–35, 89; Archdeacon, 1983, 5; Meinig, 1986, 9–16, 25–28, 35–36, 58–60,
110–17, 191–203, 268; Wright, 1992, 126, 362n35.

35. Nash, 1974, 239–75; Prucha, 1984, 13; Bailyn, 1986, 120; Wright, 1992, 124–26.

36. Meinig, 1986, 267–70; Colley, 1992, 100.

37. Krout, 1966, 32–34, 37; Nash, 1974, 247–51, 275, 303–4; Jennings, 1976, 334–35; Prucha,
1984, 23–25; Meinig, 1986, 270–84; Wright, 1992, 104, 136; Colley, 1992, 135–37.

38. Wills, 1978, 376.

39. The British reestablished a parallel policy by creating the class of "British overseas citizens,"
former imperial subjects with special British passports that prohibit them from residing in
Britain itself, as a result of the British Nationality Act of 1981.

40. Heimert & Delbanco, eds., 1985, 91; Takaki, 1993, 31–32, 39–44. Colley notes that the
"Protestant worldview which allowed so many Britons to see themselves as a distinct and
chosen people" also characterized Americans before, and in a modified way after, independence (Colley, 1992, 368–69).

41. A liberalizing statute was passed in 1709 that permitted applicants to be naturalized simply by taking an oath of allegiance and disavowing transubstantiation in court. This benefited more than 13,500 Palatine refugees, who were naturalized as a group in New York.
After electoral victories in 1710, however, the Tories began a two-year struggle that ended
in repeal of the statute and restoration of the status quo ante. Kettner, 1978, 7, 65–73, 95–98;
Ueda, 1980, 734–35.

42. Hoyt, 1952, 248–50; Kettner, 1978, 79–88, 91.
43. In 1681, for example, Charles II encouraged the emigration of refugee French Huguenots to the colonies by promising them free denization and, later, naturalization (Kettner, 1978, 68–69).
44. Kettner, 1978, 81, 90, 94–99; Ueda, 1980, 735.
45. A 1747 amendment expanded the exemption from oath requirements to the Moravians (Kettner, 1978, 75).
46. The liberal 1740 act led to at least 6,911 naturalizations between 1740 and 1773, over 90% of them in Pennsylvania. Yet despite the greater convenience of naturalization via the act's provisions, some aliens continued to seek naturalization by special acts of colonial authorities, usually because they did not meet some of the act's requirements, such as seven years' residence. Those authorities often continued to comply; in New York and New Jersey, the rate of private act naturalizations actually increased. Hoyt, 1952, 251–55; Higham, 1975, 18–19; Kettner, 1978, 35, 69, 73–77, 103–5; Ueda, 1980, 734–35; Bailyn, 1986, 9–10, 73.
47. Hoyt, 1952, 256–57; Hyman, 1959, 19–30; Archdeacon, 1983, 21–22; Bailyn, 1986, 121. Colley notes that British support for Catholics in Canada also challenged "longstanding British mythologies" that Britain was "a pre-eminently Protestant nation" and the "land of liberty because founded on Protestantism and commerce" (1992, 368–69).
48. Wills, 1978, 378; Roeber, 1991, 221, 244; Kivisto, 1995, 113–14, 138. My thanks to Barry Shain for calling the reference to the "Scotch" to my attention.
49. C. Williamson, 1960, 25–28, 50–51; Porter, 1971, 3; Huntington, 1971, 30–31; Higham, 1975, 18–19; Rosberg, 1977, 1094; Kettner, 1978, 87–88, 101–14, 121–23; Archdeacon, 1983, 20.
50. The five were Massachusetts, Connecticut, Pennsylvania, Maryland, and Delaware.
51. C. Williamson, 1960, 19; Porter, 1971, 8–9, 14; Lutz, 1980, 101–3.
52. The limitations on alien land rights also reflected the desires of both crown and colonial officials to have any lands held by aliens revert at their deaths to the authorities instead of being passed on to the aliens' heirs.
53. The Carolinas were somewhat exceptional in promoting slavery for both groups. An Indian slave trade centered in Charleston began in the 1670s and continued in the first part of the eighteenth century, though Native American slaves proved hard to keep, as they had tribes to which they could escape.
54. Nash, 1974, 112–14, 174–82, 278–90; Archdeacon, 1983, 1–4; Prucha, 1984, 12; Bailyn & Morgan, 1991, 18.
55. Bailyn & Morgan, 1991, 26, describe British warfare against the tribes in virtually identical terms.
56. Nash, 1974, 67, 122, 125–28, 133; Archdeacon, 1983, 3–4; Prucha, 1984, 13; Merrell, 1991, 121, 144–47; Takaki, 1993, 35–36.
57. Washburn, 1971, 44; E. S. Morgan, 1975, 337; Kettner, 1978, 288–89.
58. E. S. Morgan, 1975, 233.
59. Washburn, 1971, 43, 49; Wise & Deloria, 1971, 117–18, 122; E. S. Morgan, 1975, 233, 330; Jennings, 1976, 331–32; Kettner, 1978, 288–90; Spicer, 1980, 115; Horsman, 1981, 103–4; Deloria & Lytle, 1983, 3–4; Merrell, 1991, 124; Takaki, 1993, 38–44.
60. Nash, 1974, 127–34; E. S. Morgan, 1975, 269; Archdeacon, 1983, 4; Takaki, 1993, 61–65. See below for the consequences of this rebellion for class and racial hierarchies.
61. Nash, 1974, 146–55; Archdeacon, 1983, 4.
62. Jennings, 1976, 338–39.
63. Merrell, 1991, 138; Wright, 1992, 94–95, 100, 116–17.

64. Nash, 1974, 262–75; E. S. Morgan, 1975, 250–70, 337; Prucha, 1984, 21–25.
65. For an argument as to why slavery proved economically and politically attractive in the southern colonies, see E. S. Morgan, 1975, 295–314. See also Bailyn & Morgan, 1991, 18; P. D. Morgan, 1991.
66. *Somerset v. Stewart*, Lofft 1, 98 Eng. Rep. 499 (K.B. 1772), reprinted at 10 *Howell's State Trials* 2; Davis, 1966, 1975; Zilversmit, 1967, 4; Berlin, 1974, 3–5; P. Foner, 1975, 111–12, 186–96, 256–57; Cover, 1975; Wiecek, 1977, 20–36; Fehrenbacher, 1981; Tushnet, 1981; Bailyn, 1986, 113–14; Tise, 1987, 21–24; Fields, 1990, 103–8; P. D. Morgan, 1991, 164–65. Thus although Gordon Wood may be right in arguing that many British Americans originally saw black chattel slavery as simply the "most severe sort of patriarchal authority," it quickly became more than that. Many justified it by denying that these slaves were human at all, and all had to concede that this level of subjugation went beyond any form of patriarchy in English law. Wood rightly stresses, however, that even white indentured servants were treated far worse in the colonies than in Britain (Wood, 1991, 51–55).
67. Although reliable figures are unavailable, there were undoubtedly few free blacks in the northern colonies and even fewer in the southern ones: in Maryland in 1755, for example, there were 1,800 free blacks, constituting 4% of the black population and 2% of the total population. Not surprisingly, the number of free blacks grew more rapidly in the North than in the South. The 1790 census discovered 59,000 free blacks in the U.S., with some 27,000 in the North and only 32,000 in the South, where almost 90% of American blacks lived (Berlin, 1974, 3; J. H. Franklin, 1980, 97, 158; Tise, 1987, 22–32).
68. Zilversmit, 1967, 56–108; P. Foner, 1975, 279–91; Berlin, 1976, 351, 354–56; Franklin, 1980, 62–62, 158.
69. Berlin, 1974, 7; P. D. Morgan, 1991, 186.
70. Jordan, 1968, 122–28; Berlin, 1974, 5–10; Nash, 1974, 166–67; P. Foner, 1975, 186–258; E. S. Morgan, 1975, 331–33, 337; Takaki, 1993, 79. Franklin was arguing against the slave trade by appealing to the idea of "excluding all Blacks and Tawnys" from America.
71. Nash, 1974, 167, 196–200; P. Foner, 1975, 259–78; Archdeacon, 1983, 19–20.
72. Jordan, 1968, 123–24; Nash, 1974, 166, 180; T. Morris, 1974, 2–3; Berlin, 1974, 4–5, 9–10; Wallerstein, 1974, 353; E. S. Morgan, 1975, 328, 344–45; Takaki, 1993, 65–68; P. D. Morgan, 1991, 198.
73. Zilversmit, 1967, 8–9; Nash, 1974, 201–5; P. Foner, 1975, 192–93, 252; E. S. Morgan, 1975, 331–33.
74. R. Morris, ed., 1970, 349–50; P. Foner, 1975, 283–91; Wills, 1978, 66–75.
75. Miller & Johnson, eds., 1939, 214; Heimert & Delbanco, eds., 1985, 156; Lauter et al., 1990, 259. The one massive exception to the patriarchalism of hereditary aristocracy and monarchy was that a woman might occupy the throne if her succession was the only way to fill it with a bearer of the proper blood line. In rebelling against such hereditary orders, the American revolutionaries would eliminate this exception and consign women to the "domestic sphere" more fully, as Eileen McDonagh has argued (1994).
76. J. H. Wilson, 1976, 393; Sachs & Wilson, 1978, 74; Degler, 1980, 8; Kerber, 1980, 15–16, 28, 119–21; Taub & Schneider, 1982, 118; Lebsock, 1984, 54–57; Salmon, 1986, xv–xvi, 14–30; Crane, 1987, 260–66; G. S. Wood, 1991, 44–49, 147–50, 184.
77. The linkage of female subordination to male concerns for racial purity is suggested in Balibar & Wallerstein, 1991, 100–103. Winthrop Jordan has also contended that linking the social treatment of blacks and women may be especially appropriate in the United States. Americans, he observes, have been unusual in refusing to make gradations among persons in each category, extending rights to them or not in all-or-nothing fashion. Jordan notes important differences between the circumstances of blacks and women as well (Jordan,

1987, 278–80). For other linkages of sexist, racist, and nativist hierarchies, see, e.g., Kraditor, 1965, 123–24; MacKinnon, 1979, 129–30; Sapiro, 1984, 3–4.

78. Flexner, 1975, 9; J. H. Wilson, 1976, 396, 414–15; Sachs & Wilson, 1978, 69–75; Harris, 1978, 3, 16; Degler, 1980, 5, 193–94; Elshtain, 1981, 56–61, 72–74; Taub & Schneider, 1982, 136; Crane, 1987, 258–62.

Chapter 3. Forging a Revolutionary People

1. Merritt, 1966, 174–75, 180; Bailyn, 1967, 1–2, 19–54; C. L. Black, 1970, 12–13, 44; Nagel, 1971, xii–xiii, 9, 17–21, 36, 47–50; E. S. Morgan, 1977, 5–8, 100–104, 134–39; Bender, 1978, 82–85; Wiebe, 1984, xi–xv, 3–5.

2. Thus Boston's James Otis in 1761, speaking of "the power of the British parliament": "'Tis from and under this very power and its acts, and from the common law, that the political and civil rights of the Colonists are derived: And upon those grand pillars of liberty shall my defence be rested." Rhode Island Governor Stephen Hopkins, in 1764, said that colonists were "subject to the King, and dependent on the kingdom of Great Britain," but, in return, they were entitled "to receive protection, and enjoy all the rights and privileges of free-born Englishmen." And Maryland's Daniel Dulany in 1765 noted, "We claim an exemption from all parliamentary impositions, that we may enjoy those securities of our rights and properties, which we are entitled to by the constitution" (Jensen, ed., 1967, 22, 43, 105).

3. On this process of radicalization in the colonists' political arguments, see, e.g., Arieli, 1964, 62–64; Bailyn, 1967, 184–89, 193–94; Gleason, 1982, 59–60; Appleby, 1984, 21–22; Murrin, 1987, 340, 342–43.

4. Bailyn, 1967, 20; Tuveson, 1968; Wood, 1969, 47–48; Gleason, 1982, 58; Morgan, 1977, 100–103; Murrin, 1987, 341, 344; Roeber, 1991, 221.

5. The Stamp Act was repealed in 1766 after colonial riots, and the Townshend Acts were repealed in 1770 (Jensen, 1950, xxvi, xi, 48–49, 71, 102–3, 142, 352; Morgan, 1977, 8–13, 18, 30–35).

6. Krout, 1966, 37–42; Jensen, 1950, 213–14; R. B. Morris, ed., 1970, 23–25, 134; E. S. Morgan, 1977, 14–60; Bailyn, 1986, 10.

7. G. S. Wood, 1969, 4–6, 45, 48, 75, 79–81; 1991, 181–83. Cf. Bailyn, 1967, 19, 184–88; Minogue, 1967, 29–30; Tuveson, 1968, 91–136; Nagel, 1971, 8; Seton-Watson, 1977, 9, 196–98; E. S. Morgan, 1977, 101; Pole, 1978, 41; Kelley, 1979, 39–40; B. R. O. Anderson, 1983, 50, 64–65.

8. Bland claimed even that "the British Government itself" implicitly recognized this fact, and he went on to complain of the colonists' lack of even virtual representation in Parliament (Jensen, ed., 1967, 114–15). Gordon Wood stresses the cosmopolitan character of the American revolutionaries. But much of his evidence shows that these appeals were blended with claims for a special American character and destiny (Wood, 1991, 191, 222).

9. Bailyn, 1967, 66; E. S. Morgan, 1977, 5–6; G. S. Wood, 1991, 12–14; Colley, 1992, 5, 19, 55, 103, 313, 368–69; Shain, 1994, 193–240.

10. Otis and Jefferson cited in Jensen, ed., 1967, 21, 258, 263, 272–76. See also Horsman, 1981, 18: "Josiah Quincy, Jr., wrote of the popular nature of the Anglo-Saxon militia; Sam Adams stressed the old English freedoms defended in the Magna Carta; Benjamin Franklin emphasized the freedom the Anglo-Saxons had enjoyed in emigrating to England; Charles Carroll depicted Saxon liberties torn away by William the Conqueror; and Richard Bland argued that the English Constitution and parliament stemmed from the Saxon period." Pennsylvania's Demophilus (probably radical Whig George Bryan) also rehearsed the An-

glo-Saxon myth in detail prior to endorsing the Declaration of Independence (Hyneman & Lutz, eds., 1983, 70–71, 340–63).

11. Otis's view was unusual but not unique: the radical Philadelphia Whig, Dr. Benjamin Rush, also spoke for black equality. But such radicalism was more common in England, where many fewer blacks resided, and those were free and often educated. Otis cited in Jensen, ed., 1967, 27–28; P. Foner, 1975, 295–96; Hyneman & Lutz, eds., 1983, 218–19; Wood, 1991, 221; Bailyn & Morgan, 1991, 18; P. D. Morgan, 1991, 159–60.

12. Wood, 1991, 110, 145–46. Boston preachers in Berens, 1978, 47–48. See also J. Adams, 1954, 8n7, 16; Kohn, 1957, 13, 21, 28; Tuveson, 1968, 21–25, 101–22, 142–44, 153–65; Horsman, 1981, 1–3, 9, 15, 81–82.

13. J. Adams, 1954, 18; Dickinson and Novanglus in Jensen, ed., 1967, 114, 160, 315–16, 328; and see Arieli, 1964, 64–69; Bailyn, 1967, 137–40; G. S. Wood, 1969, 98–102; Kelley, 1979, 46; Horsman, 1981, 3, 15, 18, 81–82. The ways these arguments intermingled with classical republicanism's "scenario of corruption" are noted below.

14. Higham, 1966, 9, 134, 137; Wise & Deloria, 1971, 93–94, 131–35.

15. Jensen, ed., 1967, 409–13, 423–24.

16. Crèvecoeur in Rischin, 1976, 25; Hopkins and Adams in Jensen, ed., 1967, 47, 240.

17. Crèvecoeur also expected that the different colonies would grow more distinct, not less, over time (in Rischin, ed., 1976, 31–33). See also Arieli, 1964, 65–68; Jensen, ed., 1967, 421–24, 431–36; J. Wilson, 1967, 580–81, 583; Jordan, 1968, 336–39; P. Foner, 1975, 186; Horsman, 1981, 18–24; Hyneman and Lutz, eds., 1983, 104; Wood, 1991, 221–22.

18. Jensen, ed., 1967, 402–4, 418–19, 421, 425–26, 431, 433–36.

19. Dolbeare, ed., 1981, 81–82; McDonald, 1985, 161. Even Abigail Adams presented women to men as "Beings placed by providence under your protection," urging men to use that power "only for our happiness." This argument tried to turn ascriptive and religious myths to the advantage of women without fully repudiating them.

20. Crèvecoeur in Rischin, ed., 1976, 26–27, 33.

21. Kohn, 1957, 13, 138; Gordon, 1964, 72–73, 89–91; Higham, 1966, 137; 1975, 20, 32; Rossiter, 1971, 116–18; cf. Arieli, 1964, 73–74.

22. Thus from the early 1760s on pamphlet authors such as James Otis and William Goddard appealed to the "laws of God" and "of nature" even as they stressed the guarantees of the British Constitution that they still professed to esteem above all others. And soon some writers were relying most heavily on the deistic and rationalistic Enlightenment rhetoric of natural law to assert that, regardless of the legal niceties, their natural rights were being violated. In 1766, after endorsing the tales of Saxon freedom, Richard Bland contended that the "civic Constitution of England" gave no clear "Directions" about the status of the colonies. Therefore, "to direct us in our inquiry, we must have Recourse to the Law of Nature, and those Rights of Mankind that flow from it." In 1768, Silas Downer argued that the Magna Carta and other bastions of English constitutional freedom were "only declaratory of our rights," which were founded in nature. Four years later, Samuel Adams also gave pride of place to the "Natural Rights of the Colonists as Men," and though he still defended their rights as "Subjects," he expounded those rights by relying less on law than on Locke's *Second Treatise of Government* (quoting paras. 134, 136, and 142). Adams's authorship of this pamphlet is uncertain (Jensen, ed., 1967, 22–24, 28, 36, 43, 89, 91, 116–18, 122, 236–39; B. Black, 1975–76; Kettner, 1978, 57–61; Colley, 1992, 135–36).

23. Jensen, ed., 1967, 272–76, 402, 418, 422; Bailyn, 1967, 185–89; Kettner, 1978, 170–72.

24. From the late 1960s through the early 1980s scholars debated intensely whether Lockean ideas played any significant part in the revolutionary era, much less the hegemonic role formerly assigned to them. For a time, the works of Bernard Bailyn, Gordon Wood, and

J. G. A. Pocock were treated as having proven a non-Lockean "republican" paradigm to be definitive of American revolutionary thought. Now, however, even the most ardent advocates of the importance of republicanism concede, as Lance Banning put it, that eighteenth-century opposition thought, and the thought of "America's Revolutionary generation," always presented a "complex blend" of "Lockean and liberal" notions and "classical republicanism"—and that recent republican scholarship "may have exaggerated the classical at the expense of the liberal dimensions." The massive influence on educated Americans of Locke's *Essay Concerning Human Understanding* and writings on religious toleration and education has, moreover, never been seriously disputed. Those works conveyed political themes consonant with his *Two Treatises on Government.* Steven Dworetz has documented convincingly the presence of Lockean ideas in the influential sermons of the revolutionary era (Dworetz, 1990; cf. Jensen, ed., 1967, 112, 235–36, 301; Bailyn, 1967, 30; Hyneman & Lutz, eds., 1983, 140–41, 163; Banning, 1986, 12–13).

25. Locke, 1975, 607, 646, 657; cf. Pocock, 1985, 226–33.
26. Locke, 1965a, 209–10; Locke, 1965b, 364–65. For the connections between Locke's revised view of the family and his rejection of natural political hierarchies, see Fliegelman, 1982, 4, 12–15, 98.
27. Locke, 1965a, 186, 209–10, 240–54; Locke, 1965b, 306–11, 391–92.
28. Locke, 1965b, 380–88, 392–94; Seliger, 1969, 20–21, 27; N. Wood, 1983, 5–7, 94–96, 137–40; Russell, 1986, 301–2; Resnick, 1987, 379; Millican, 1990, 51. Although Locke does not make the point explicitly, on his premises "tacit consent" must also include the consent of the existing members to recognize the inheritor as a fellow subject. As Locke says that no one has a natural political identity, all persons must gain membership via a consensual agreement. Locke's unpublished writings include a fragment on naturalization which confirms his belief that a community could legitimately decide how many aliens to accept for naturalization, though his economic views led him to argue for virtually unlimited immigration and naturalization. His brief discussion does not explore whether existing subjects might be deprived of their membership involuntarily via governmental denationalization. However, Locke's beliefs that governments always benefited economically from additional labor, and his general aim of defending individual liberties against traditional social restrictions, suggest that such powers should rarely be used even if they exist. As Peter Schuck and I have observed, Locke did at one point consider the possibility that a subject might be cut off from membership by "some public Act," but it is ambiguous whether he was referring to a broad governmental power to denationalize members, a form of punishment, or an improper sovereign violation of the social contract (Locke, 1965b, 339–40, 394; Schuck & Smith, 1985, 146n63; Resnick, 1987, 368–88).

   In the *Second Treatise,* Locke appears to assume that the community has a set policy of consenting to the membership of children born to parents who are already subjects. This implication arises because he argues that such children can gain membership by accepting their inheritance—and under English law, only the children of subjects could inherit. Hence Locke appears to take the law's permission for them to inherit as permission for them to assume subjectship (Locke, 1965b, 392–94; Kettner, 1978, 5–6; cf. Carens, 1987). If this inference is correct, Locke's position is consistent with the view of birthright citizenship as a condition of parental membership elaborated by later international law writers, notably Jean-Jacques Burlamaqui and Emmerich de Vattel, as discussed below.
29. In what appears to have been a rather inconsistent concession to concerns for political stability, Locke did say that those persons who had given their express consent to membership were bound perpetually, without a right of expatriation, as in Coke. That concession seems of limited importance, however, for on Locke's account most persons gained mem-

bership via revocable tacit consent. Locke, 1965b, 390–94; Schuck and Smith, 1985, 31–33; Russell, 1986, 302–3.

30. Burlamaqui, 1792, 267–68; Vattel, 1787, 170–73; Kettner, 1978, 44–61, 143–44, 165–66; Schuck & Smith, 1985, 45–47; Russell, 1986, 302–3.

31. Locke, 1965b, 311–17, 332–33, 395–99, 448, 460–62.

32. Blackstone, 1979, v. 1, 357; Kettner, 1978, 54–59, 139–41.

33. Locke, 1965b, 402, 459–60; Galloway in Jensen, ed., 1967, 354, 356, 362, 364, 368; Kettner, 1978, 142–46.

34. Locke, 1965b, 454–77, esp. 462–64; E. S. Morgan, 1975, 375; Kettner, 1978, 166, 169–71. Although Garry Wills has disputed the existence of any significant connection between the Declaration and Locke, a close comparison of its argument with Locke's discussion of valid rebellions, which Wills never undertakes, reveals that Jefferson's contentions met all of Locke's basic criteria and recurringly echoed his language, whatever the Virginian's conscious intentions may have been. See Wills, 1978, esp. 4–90. Note also that in 1774, Boston's pseudonymous author Monitor was already invoking Locke, as well as Vattel, to reject British sovereignty and hold that British actions had dissolved the bonds of government (Hyneman & Lutz, eds., 1983, 279–80).

35. G. S. Wood, 1991, 186–87, 235–36.

36. To summarize the leading ideological moves detailed in later chapters: eighteenth-century philosophes inspired Jefferson and others to suggest that racial differences might be biologically rooted, contrary to Locke's judgment. Jefferson also presumed, this time like Locke, that male supremacy was founded in nature. Furthermore, though cultural differences might not justify denials of anyone's natural rights to life and liberty, they suggested that some groups were as yet ineligible to claim property rights or political rights because their potential for rationality was insufficiently developed. The leading example of this type of argument among the colonists was their endless use of Locke's claim that property rights originated only in rational productive labor to deny land titles to "savage" Native Americans on the fictive ground that their ways of life did not include such labor. Locke's discussion of slavery imposed via just warfare was also sometimes invoked to defend the bondage of African-Americans, but much more rarely, as the conditions he laid out clearly were not met by the slave traders. The general Enlightenment calls for more limited government, more extensive personal freedoms, and more protection for market systems even if they generated economic inequalities would also all prove useful for arguing against government interventions against many systems of social inequality. Finally, though Locke himself had been so set against absolutism that he abandoned the notion of sovereignty altogether, the eighteenth-century international law theorists, particularly Vattel, revived it. They argued that in the anarchic international realm, the necessity for all sovereign peoples to decide for themselves what their self-preservation required meant that the rights of individuals against them were often "imperfect," morally valid but legally unenforceable. Hence, if a country mistreated its minorities, that was regrettable but incorrigible.

37. Vattel, 1787, 22, 175–76, 265, 279; Dunn, 1969, 175, 225, 240; Seliger, 1969, 29; Washburn, 1971, 38–41; Schochet, 1975, 268–71; Horsman, 1981, 46–48, 190–91; N. Wood, 1983, 32–33, 81–82, 121–29, 133; Schuck & Smith, 1985, 47–49; Farr, 1986, 274–78; Mehta, 1990, 1992; Antholis, 1993.

38. Hopkins in Jensen, ed., 1967, 43; Bailyn, 1967, 35–36; G. S. Wood, 1969, 11, 15–17, 200; 1991, 95–100; Pocock, 1975, 506–13; Banning, 1978, 25–62, 72–73; Horsman, 1981, 14–15, 18.

39. Examples of republican rhetoric are endless. Already in 1766, "The Tribune" asserted in the *Charleston (S.C.) Gazette* that "public virtue" was threatened by royal ministers who would

readily form a "conspiracy to betray and plunder" the people. Similarly, John Dickinson, wrapping himself in the agrarian virtue of a self-sufficient small farmer, presented Britain's policy as financial exploitation of a sadly "dependent state," enforced by a "STANDING army" and "dependent judges" enticed by a "sordid love of gain" to "turn their backs on virtue, and pay their homage where they ought not." Though he would eventually decide that his countrymen were going too far and oppose the revolution for a time, in 1768 Dickinson compared the deceptions and progressive "usurpations" of these British "artful rulers" to the processes by which "the Caesars ruined Roman liberty." Silas Downer also bemoaned the threat of a standing army in 1768, and the Declaration of Independence would include it among the colonists' complaints. John Adams's first letter written by Novanglus offered still another portrait of the colonists' declining circumstances, and Harrington and Alger-non Sydney, as well as Aristotle and Livy, were prominent among his authorities. Jensen, ed., 1967, 139, 144, 150, 153, 299–304; Bailyn, 1967, 94–143; G. S. Wood, 1969, 28–43, 49; Pocock, 1975, 506–9; Banning, 1978, 70–83; McDonald, 1985, 78; Hyneman & Lutz, eds., 1983, 92–96, 105–6.

40. Jensen, ed., 1967, 276, 404–7, 418, 434; G. S. Wood, 1969, 91–97; E. Foner, 1976, 198–99; E. S. Morgan, 1977, 90–91; Banning, 1978, 83–85.

41. Rush quoted in G. S. Wood, 1969, 427; see also 47–48, 58, 91–93. Preceptor in Hyneman & Lutz, eds., 1983, 177. See also Aristotle, 1968, 1274b.32–1275b.21; Bailyn, 1967, 142–43; Pocock, 1975, 4, 66–76, 515–16; Appleby, 1978b, 937; Banning, 1978, 82–84; Gleason, 1982, 60.

42. Preceptor in Hyneman & Lutz, eds., 1983, 177–78, 403; cf. Montesquieu, 1949, v. I, pp. 20–21, 37, 69, 96, 138; v. II, pp. 30–31, 52; Rousseau, 1979, 40, 358–63. In striving for in-ternational law doctrines that were not flagrantly illiberal but that upheld state sovereignty during the eighteenth century, Vattel confronted these tensions in ways the revolutionar-ies would sometimes follow, but his efforts were not successful philosophically. Stressing the community's consensual powers of self-determination, Vattel accepted that citizens who were viewed as harmful by a community might be expelled, and that polities could deny entry to outsiders. But he also contended that those who were driven from their home-lands by exile, banishment, hardship, or some other pressing cause had a natural right to seek residence elsewhere, and that concerns for human rights implied that other nations should usually accept them. Thus Vattel tried to balance these concerns by suggesting that persons had "imperfect"—unenforceable—moral rights to be admitted to other nations. He further maintained that an existing citizenry's property rights alone were never suffi-cient to justify denials of entry to those in need, and he urged nations to recognize their hu-manitarian duties not to forego "charity and commiseration" because of "groundless and frivolous fears." Vattel nonetheless concluded that if nations used their discretionary con-sensual powers over admissions in ways that he saw as improper, the only proper recourse was moral disapprobation. The rights being infringed upon were too "imperfect" to justify a resort to force. That seemed the most that early liberals could do to reconcile their de-fenses of the moral claims of all human beings with their recognition of particular com-munities' prerogatives to define memberships consensually but selfishly (Vattel, 1787, 176–77, 263, 265, 278–79, 284–85; Schuck & Smith, 1985, 48, 148n18).

43. Tuveson, 1968, 91–124; G. S. Wood, 1969, 114–18 (citing Adams at 118); Horsman, 1981, 14–18, 82–85; McDonald, 1985, 70, 76–77.

44. G. S. Wood, 1969, 60–61, 97–107, 120–22 (quoted passage is at 122); Petersen, ed., 1975, 124–25; R. B. Morris, ed., 1970, 338–40; McDonald, 1985, 50, 89–90; Jordan, 1968, 333, 350–53; P. Foner, 1975, 292–306; Pocock, 1975, 491–92; Pole, 1978, 25–26, 35; Storing, 1981, 16, 71.

45. Montesquieu, 1949, v. I, 126–28; Vattel, 1787, 18; Rossiter, ed., 1961, 73–76; Wood, 1969, 58, 356; Jennings, 1976, 322–324; Banning, 1978, 30–31, 107; Kelley, 1979, 88–89; McCoy, 1980, 86–90, 204–8.
46. Colley, 1992, 6.

Chapter 4. Citizens of Small Republics

1. Tocqueville, 1969, v. 1, pt. 1, ch. 8, described the Confederation years after the Revolution as a time when "the state seemed to dissolve all at once" (114). Hartz paid the Confederation no attention except to belittle the radicalism of Daniel Shays (1955, 74–78). Morone, 1990, 56–65, and other revisionist scholars he discusses there do more justice to the fidelity of the Articles to the democratic aspirations in the more radical strains of American revolutionary thought.
2. R. B. Morris, ed., 1970, 349–50, 352–54. Rhode Island's Slave Enlistment Act of Feb. 14, 1778, provided compensation to owners of "able-bodied negro, mulatto, or Indian man" slaves who gained emancipation by enlisting.
3. Ironically, the antislavery cause also flourished in Britain during these years, in part because the British wished to affirm to themselves that they were not the corrupt despots Americans had portrayed, but rather were more dedicated to freedom than their colonial critics (Colley, 1992, 354).
4. Krout, 1966, 45–46; E. S. Morgan, 1977, 77–79; Archdeacon, 1983, 22–23; Colley, 1992, 137–38.
5. New York continued to claim Vermont as part of its own lands until 1790, so that Vermont did not formally enter the union until 1791. The manner in which squabbles over land titles between New York and New Hampshire led the settlers of the disputed lands to set up Vermont as an independent state found parallels elsewhere. Western North Carolinians formed the state of Franklin from 1784 to 1787, and although North Carolina eventually regained control by force, the area was ceded to the U.S. in 1790 and became the state of Tennessee in 1796. In 1786 Virginia, which already had ceded claims to large amounts of western lands to the U.S., also permitted its remaining western settlers to form an independent state if they would then join the union. As a result, the state of Kentucky eventually formed in 1796 (G. S. Wood, 1969, 133; E. S. Morgan, 1977, 88–90, 115–16; Lutz, 1980, 44–45, 120).
6. The Declaration's origination with state representatives can be explained equally on Lockean grounds: all individual Americans were already members of political societies, the colonies, that were choosing to change their form of government but were not returning to an anarchic state of nature. Hence it was only natural for these individuals to exercise their political powers via the communities to which they already belonged. That choice did not alter the fact that sovereignty resided ultimately in the people as a whole, not in the states per se. Such Lockean arguments, however, became more salient in later debates over state and national authority. They had limited significance at the time. Some colonists, including the radical Berkshire Constitutionalists of Massachusetts, and the upstate New Yorkers who seceded to form Vermont, insisted that the Revolution *had* actually returned them to a "state of nature"; but this claim was widely opposed (G. S. Wood, 1969, 285–88; E. S. Morgan, 1977, 87; Kettner, 1978, 189–91; McDonald, 1985, 147).
7. Marylanders argued that the lands would be recovered from the British, if at all, by national action, so the Confederation should gain control over them. Otherwise, states with claims to extensive portions of those lands, particularly Virginia, might become spectacularly richer than their neighbors, endangering state equality within the Confederation. Land

speculators from outside Virginia had made private deals with various tribes, and they also lobbied for national control, believing that they would get a warmer reception for their claims in Congress.

8. Krout, 1966, 46–51; E. S. Morgan, 1977, 77–88, 101–2, 107–11; Carp, 1987, 22–25, 30–31.

9. Even then, these judges were to take an oath to be administered by judges of the state where the cause would be tried in order to decide the matter fairly, and in no case could a state be "deprived of territory for the benefit of the united states" (Art. IX).

10. Boorstin, 1967, 404–5; G. S. Wood, 1969, 354–57; E. S. Morgan, 1977, 106–7; Kramnick, 1987, 19–20.

11. 5 *Journals of the Continental Congress* 475 (1906), cited by the U.S. Supreme Court in *Cramer v. U.S.*, 325 U.S. 1, 9, 11 (1945).

12. Hyman, 1959, 74–87, 94–95, 108, 110–13; M. T. Bennett, 1963, 7; Kettner, 1978, 175–87, 219–20; Calhoon, 1987, 53–59.

13. C. Williamson, 1960, 117; Dixon, 1968, 60–78, 82; Onuf, 1987a.

14. G. S. Wood, 1969, 162–63; Lutz, 1980, 44–45, 115–18; Banning, 1987, 112–13; Kramnick, 1987, 17–18, 21–23.

15. G. S. Wood, 1969, 399–400; E. S. Morgan, 1977, 98; McDonald, 1985, 79; Friedman, 1985, 65–66; Carp, 1987, 28. Just how all "natural aristocrats" were to be tempted into their senatorial gilded cages was not well defined. Presumably the members of the lower house would know who they were. In practice, heightened property qualifications proved the leading means of differentiating the membership of the two houses.

16. G. S. Wood, 1969, 182, 206–14; E. Foner, 1976, 206–10; E. S. Morgan, 1977, 91–92; Hyneman & Lutz, eds., 1983, 402–9.

17. States with fully or partially established churches were New Hampshire, Massachusetts, Connecticut, South Carolina, and Maryland. Religious qualifications for office existed in Pennsylvania, Delaware, New Jersey, Georgia, and the Carolinas. Jensen, 1950, 132–34; Jefferson, 1955, 157–61, 223–25; G. S. Wood, 1969, 138–43, 156–61; Porter, 1971, 11; McDonald, 1985, 41–43; Carp, 1987, 31.

18. The requirement that applicants be of good moral character might well have been used to exclude not only persons with criminal records but those known to have committed homosexual acts. I am unaware of any systematic research on whether states denied citizenship on those grounds, however.

19. Jefferson, 1955, 84–85; Kettner, 1978, 214–19; Ueda, 1980, 736.

20. E. S. Morgan, 1977, 122–24; Rakove, 1987, 84–86.

21. Wiecek, 1972, 58.

22. Kettner, 1978, 221–24. For an example of such state court action, see *Camp v. Lockwood,* 1 Dall. 393 (Pa., 1788).

23. P. Foner, 1975, 375; Friedman, 1985, 110, 167–68; Onuf, 1987a, xiii–xiv, 45, 70–74, 111–16; Onuf, 1987b, 180–83, 191.

24. G. S. Wood, 1969, 272–76, 283; E. S. Morgan, 1977, 89; L. M. Smith, 1985, 72.

25. Jefferson, 1955, 146–49; Rossiter, ed., 1961, 81–82, 214–16, 342; G. S. Wood, 1969, 163–68; Pole, 1978, 30–31, 36–37, 50–51.

26. Not even most adult white males could meet the higher property qualifications for certain offices, such as senate seats, but in the history of republicanism such requirements were less controversial than total exclusions from any share in governance. C. Williamson, 1960, 136; G. S. Wood, 1969, 167–69; E. S. Morgan, 1975, 236–38, 345, 364–65; E. S. Morgan, 1977, 92–95; Pole, 1978, 44–45; McDonald, 1985, 161–62.

27. Such changes also helped promote a more democratic distribution of political privileges, reaching 70–90% of white adult men; turnout also increased (Kramnick, 1987, 23). But

Americans had broadened, not abandoned, their conceptions of the forms of property ownership suitable to citizenship.

28. C. Williamson, 1960, 135–37; Pole, 1966, 25; G. S. Wood, 1969, 171, 218; Porter, 1971, 11, 21; McCoy, 1980, 66–73, 130, 168–69; R. M. Smith, 1985, 44–45; Appleby, 1978b, 937–58.

29. Jensen, 1950; Jefferson, 1955, 120, 164–65, 175; G. S. Wood, 1969, 404, 409–13, 432–36, 446–63; Banning, 1978, 86–90.

30. G. S. Wood, 1969, 227.

31. 1 Dall. 53 (Pa., 1781) at 53, 58–59.

32. Cf. Jefferson, 1955, 155. The federal courts, in turn, subsequently endorsed these state actions. E.g., in *Hamilton v. Eaton*, 11 F. Cas. 336, 339 (1796), U.S. Chief Justice Oliver Ellsworth, sitting on circuit, applied North Carolina's 1777 legislation providing for such a right of election.

33. E. S. Morgan, 1975, 380–38; Tise, 1987, 22–23, 32–33. The emancipation movement appears to express liberal concerns more than republican ones because, as Larry Tise argues, it relied heavily on "natural rights theory," not doctrines of republican citizenship. The increased willingness to treat free blacks more or less equally with whites, on the other hand, possibly reflects the impact of republican notions of civic equality.

34. Zilversmit, 1967, 85–138; Berlin, 1974, 10–20; P. Foner, 1975, 292–344.

35. The extent to which the well-known *Quock Walker* cases in Massachusetts were responsible for ending slavery is in question, but they became at a minimum an important symbol of how the emancipation process was thought to express liberal egalitarian ideals. See Cover, 1975, 42–49.

36. Tise, 1987, 17–37. Cf. Zilversmit, 1967, 139–222; Berlin, 1974, 20–35; P. Foner, 1975, 345–87; Wiecek, 1977, 40–57; Frey, 1987, 238–45.

37. Jefferson, 1955, 87, 136–43, 155, 163. Lord Kames's *Sketches of the History of Man,* first published in 1774 but more available in the colonies in later editions, professed similar ambivalence but also leaned toward black "inferiority." He argued that whites and blacks did represent "different species of men." But Kames, too, criticized slavery, and though he initially regarded "negroes" as inferior in "understanding" to whites, he eventually conceded that this might be "occasioned by their condition." He still insisted, however, that other races in similar conditions proved more "industrious" than blacks (Kames, 1813, 12, 15, 20, 49–50).

38. S. S. Smith, 1965, 71–72, 93, 106, 109, 126, 149. In this edition, Smith's editor, Winthrop Jordan, exaggerated the degree to which Smith actually expected blacks to acquire white skin color (xliii–xliv).

39. P. Foner, 1975, 81, 508, 517–18.

40. Berlin, 1974, 58–66.

41. Wise & Deloria, 1971, 138; Washburn, 1975, 161–66; Horsman, 1981, 104; Merrell, 1987, 198–99.

42. Wise & Deloria, 1971, 125–28; Washburn, 1975, 146–48; Jennings, 1976, 341; Kettner, 1978, 292; Prucha, 1984, 36–37.

43. In 1839, the U.S. Supreme Court would refer to such land grants from "the Indian hunting grounds" as "one of the great resources that sustained the war" (*Clark v. Smith,* 13 Pet. 195, 201 [1839]).

44. New York authorities actually arrested some of the national government's agents who were attempting to negotiate with the Iroquois on its behalf (Gunther, 1958, 4; Washburn, 1971, 51–52; Wise & Deloria, 1971, 138, 141–42; Prucha, 1984, 38).

45. Jennings, 1976, 341–42; Cohen, 1982, 58–60; Merrell, 1987, 200.

46. Vattel, 1787, bk. I, ch. 1, 16–17; ch. 16, 155–59; ch. 19, 165–66; bk. III, ch. 13, 570–71, 576–77;

Gunther, 1958, 4; Locke, 1965b, 431–44; Ericson, 1970, 452–53; Washburn, 1975, 161–62; Jennings, 1976, 342–43; Cohen, 1982, 70–71; Prucha, 1984, 42–44; Merrell, 1987, 200–202.

47. On the other hand, the alleviation of legal disabilities for free blacks appears on paper to have aided fully assimilated individual Native Americans during these years, although how far past practices actually changed is unclear. Wise & Deloria, 1971, 136–38; Washburn, 1975, 158–62; Deloria & Lytle, 1983, 3–6; Prucha, 1984, 58.

48. A number of modern scholars write almost as if the doctrine of the tribes as dependent nations was the invention of the Supreme Court, especially John Marshall, in the 1820s and 1830s (see, e.g., Burke, 1969, 514–15, 522; Ericson, 1970, 449–52, 463–66; Satz, 1975, 45–46). The nation's seminal authority on Indian law, Felix S. Cohen, instead traced the roots of American legal thought on the status of Indians to the sixteenth-century Spanish theologian, Francisco de Vitoria; and the modern editors of Cohen's classic *Handbook of Federal Indian Law* similarly treat Vitoria as the philosophic source of American principles (Cohen, 1942; Cohen, 1982, 50–53).

But, as Cohen acknowledged, American legal authorities rarely cited Vitoria directly; the decisive opinions of the U.S. Supreme Court on Indian matters do not cite him at all. They rather "frequently refer to statements by Grotius and Vattel that are either copied or adapted from the words of Vitoria" (Cohen, 1942, 17). Cohen's modern editors instead acknowledge differences between Vitoria and Vattel (Cohen, 1982, 52n19). Although Vattel clearly was influenced by Vitoria, he connected those principles to Lockean foundations in a way that Americans found particularly congenial, and he was by far the writer most often cited by the Supreme Court in Native American cases. Consequently, here and in the ensuing chapters I will highlight the Vattelian conceptual framework that the courts stressed more than much current scholarship does. In addition to helping illuminate these cases, this emphasis will indicate the role liberal conceptions played in defining the status of Native Americans, and the ways that Native American problems in turn molded the specific forms that liberal principles were given in U.S. citizenship laws.

49. Washburn, 1975, 63; Wise & Deloria, 1971, 141–42; Merrell, 1987, 203–8; Wright, 1992, 224.

50. Washburn, 1971, 53; Wise & Deloria, 1971, 147–48; Prucha, 1984, 47.

51. Wise & Deloria, 1971, 138, 141; Washburn, 1975, 160–63; Deloria & Lytle, 1983, 5–6.

52. Jefferson, 1955, 43, 58–65, 93, 121, 133, 135–36

53. Kerber, 1980; Kerber, 1995, 24–25. Jefferson reported that the Virginia census defined "inhabitants" as "free males above 16 years of age, and slaves above that age of both sexes," omitting free women, whose numbers he had to estimate. Presumably Virginia did not regard such women as politically relevant "inhabitants." Jefferson, 1955, 82, 86–87; J. H. Wilson, 1976, 387, 414; DePauw, 1977, 109–10; Sachs & Wilson, 1978, 69; Crane, 1987, 254–58.

54. Massachusetts did treat wives' decisions to follow their spouses as treason, and it required women whose husbands were fighting for Britain to profess their own allegiance to the revolutionary cause in order to retain their property rights. But this attention to women's own choices was unusual (Kettner, 1978, 198; Kerber, 1980, 9, 123–36).

55. Turner, 1916; J. H. Wilson, 1976, 418; Sachs & Wilson, 1978, 74.

56. Locke, 1965a, sec. 47, 209–10; Locke, 1965b, sec. 82, 364; Axtell, 1968, 8, 364.

57. Okin, 1979, 199; Elshtain, 1981, 122; Eisenstein, 1981, 3–5, 34–49; Pateman, 1988, 38, 41, 54, 94.

58. Dunn, 1969, 236, 240, 250, 260; Schochet, 1975, 248–50; Harris, 1978, 78; Elshtain, 1981, 126–27; Kerber, 1980, 10–14; Eisenstein, 1981, 42–43; Hartog, 1988; Pangle, 1988, 172–76, 230–43.

59. Jefferson, 1955, 60; Gruber, 1968, 4; Kerber, 1980, 7–12, 21–22, 26–33, 102–6, 283–88; Kerber, 1985, 484; Kerber, 1995, 21, 24–26; McDonald, 1985, 70; Crane, 1987, 266–69.

60. Kames, 1813, 405–6, 413, 435, 453, 467, 474–475, 478–79; Montesquieu, 1949, v. I, bk. 6, 107–8; J. H. Wilson, 1976, 407, 426–27; Rousseau, 1979, 40, 358, 362–63; Kerber, 1980, 26–33; Crane, 1987, 255; Colley, 1992, 238.

61. J. H. Wilson, 1976, 419–21, 426–27; Kerber, 1980, 31, 35, 73–80, 87–95, 285–87; Kerber, 1995, 25; Crane, 1987, 256–58.

Chapter 5. The Constitution and the Quest for National Citizenship

1. Citizenship requirements for federal elective office are in Art. I, secs. 2, 3; for federal jurisdiction, Art. II, sec. 1. The naturalization power is in Art. I, sec. 8. The privileges and immunities clause is in Art. IV, sec. 2, which also contains provisions for returning fleeing traitors, criminals, and fugitive slaves from one state to another.

2. The "Indian" references are in Art. I, secs. 2, 8.

3. Art. III, sec. 3. Neither did the Articles of Confederation (Art. IV) or the Continental Congress's resolution (prepared by the Committee on Spies made up of John Adams, Thomas Jefferson, John Rutledge, James Wilson, and Robert Livingston), which explicitly made temporary visitors subject to treason laws, as noted in ch. 4.

4. Bickel, 1975, 33, 36; Kettner, 1978, 224, 230–32.

5. McDonald, 1965, 133–54; McDonald, 1985, 92–93, 143–44, 156–57, 177–79; Farrand, ed., 1966, I.18–19; G. S. Wood, 1969, 394–95, 404, 412–15; Lee & Passell, 1979, 41–45; Kramnick, 1987, 18–29.

6. Jillson, 1988, ix, 9–14, 131–32; D. F. Epstein, 1984, 85, 107–8, 163–65, 170, 192; Kramnick, 1987, 32–33; Millican, 1990, 45. Jillson also argues persuasively that, in addition to conflicts in their basic political visions, the regions clashed over narrower material interests and power structures. But he is less convincing in suggesting that disputes over commerce and slavery belong strictly on this "lower" level: those issues too turned on what the core civic values of the nation would be (14–17, 140–41).

7. McDonald, 1985, 167, 187. Cf. Kramnick, 1987, 68–70; Millican, 1990, 36–39; Elkins & McKitrick, 1993, 41, 100–101.

8. This figure includes disfranchised males who could not participate, but their exclusion, too, may well have aided the constitutional cause on balance. In any case, participation among those eligible appears not to have been high. McDonald, 1965, 196–99; G. S. Wood, 1969, 484, 486, 491; Wiebe, 1984, 26–27; Kramnick, 1987, 66–67.

9. Storing, 1981, 4–6, 8–11, 15–37; Kramnick, 1987, 36–54; Beer, 1993, 231–43.

10. Jillson, 1988, 32, 170–81, also stresses the compromises over the method of selecting an executive and the scope of executive powers. For arguments that the traditional focus on "compromises" underestimates principled defenses of federalism the framers embraced, see Zuckert, 1986; Beer, 1993, 289–301.

11. Farrand, ed., 1966, I.25, 245, 317, III.120; Kramnick, ed., 1987, #32, 221; #42, 277–78.

12. Farrand, ed., 1966, I.19; E. S. Morgan, 1977, 152–53; Lutz, 1980, 43, 237–38; D. F. Epstein, 1984, 121–24; McDonald, 1985, 288–89; Kramnick, ed., 1987, #84, 475.

13. The "necessary and proper" clause gives Congress power "To make all Laws which shall be necessary and proper for carrying into Execution the foregoing Powers, and all other Powers vested by this Constitution in the Government of the United States, or in any Department or Officer thereof." The "supremacy" clause declares that "This Constitution, and the Laws of the United States which shall be made in Pursuance thereof; and all Treaties made,

or which shall be made, under the Authority of the United States, shall be the supreme Law of the Land; and the Judges in every State shall be bound thereby, any Thing in the Constitution or Laws of any State to the Contrary notwithstanding." As Hamilton notes in *Federalist* #33, these two clauses were "the source of much virulent invective and petulant declamation against the proposed Constitution" (Kramnick, ed., 1987, 223). They would also be crucial to later constitutional disputes that established national powers to create a Bank of the United States and to override state interpretations of federal law. Those controversies were very much struggles over how local or national and how economically "republican" or "liberal" American identity would be. As they did not focus on citizenship they are not reviewed here.

Art. III, sec. 2, extends the federal judicial power "to all Cases, in Law and Equity, arising under this Constitution, the Laws of the United States, and Treaties made, or which shall be made, under their Authority;—to all Cases affecting Ambassadors, other public Ministers and Consuls;—to all Cases of admiralty and maritime Jurisdiction;—to Controversies to which the United States shall be a Party;—to Controversies between two or more States;—between a State and Citizens of another State;—between Citizens of different States;—between Citizens of the same State claiming Lands under Grants of different States, and between a State, or the Citizens thereof, and foreign States, Citizens or Subjects." Thus it gives the federal courts the decisive power to settle disputes between the United States and the states, and among the states (as well as disputes with foreigners). Combined with the supremacy clause's guarantee of primacy for federal laws, these provisions give the national government both textual authority and the institutional means to say just how far its powers prevail over the states.

14. Kramnick, ed., 1987, #9, 119; #10, 125–28; #39, 254–55; #51, 321. Cf. D. F. Epstein, 1984, 85–86, 107–8, 119–21, 163, 197. In #63, Madison finds "a most advantageous superiority" of the new Constitution over ancient republics to lie in the fact that it achieves "*the total exclusion of the people in their collective capacity, from any share*" in governing, as opposed to electing representatives (Kramnick, ed., 1987, 373). For Madison on filtration see Farrand, ed., 1966, I, 49–50

15. Kramnick, ed., 1987, #2, 91.

16. Farrand, ed., 1966, I.21, II.494, III.61; Millican, 1990, 65–66, 75.

17. Farrand, ed., 1966, II.370; Kramnick, ed., 1987, #14, 144; #37, 246; #63, 285.

18. For a review of the modern fate of Charles Beard's influential *Economic Interpretation of the Constitution* (1913), see Millican, 1990, 7–8, 34–36.

19. Farrand, ed., 1966, II.620, 651–63; Moore & Weckstein, 1964a, 3–4; Kramnick, ed., 1987, #70, 402; #78, 440.

20. Forrest McDonald speculates that Hamilton was the author of this contract clause, though no certain evidence is available (McDonald, 1985, 273).

21. Kramnick, ed., 1987, #63, 280.

22. Farrand, ed., 1966, I.227, II.154, 182–83, 651.

23. Farrand, ed., 1966, II.116, 660. No recorded discussion of the omission of a citizenship requirement for the judiciary exists. It is interesting that in *Federalist* #82, Hamilton remarks that the judiciary must look "beyond its own local or municipals" in some cases "to the laws of the most distant part of the globe. Those of Japan, not less than of New York, may furnish the objects of legal discussion to our courts." Hence perhaps those knowledgeable about foreign laws were more acceptable in the judiciary than in legislative offices (Kramnick, ed., 1987, #82, 459–60).

24. Luther Martin later stated this provision had been adopted "without much debate," though he said there were a few "*so unfashionable*" as to think that "some distinction between the

professors of Christianity and downright infidelity or paganism" was desirable to give "security for the good conduct of our rulers" (Farrand, ed., 1966, III.227).

25. Kramnick, ed., 1987, #80, 447; *Marshall v. Baltimore and Ohio Railroad Co.*, 16 How. 314, 326 (1853).

26. The diversity clause was a prime target of Anti-Federalists during the ratification debates, precisely because it appeared to significantly enhance national power at state expense. See Moore & Weckstein, 1964a, 3–8; Dry & Storing, eds., 1985, 52–54, 171–76, 236–38 (a sampling of Anti-Federalist attacks on federal diversity jurisdiction).

27. Farrand, ed., 1966, II.116–17, 121–24, 208.

28. Farrand, ed., 1966, I.80, 186, 266, 416.

29. The veterans never did more than grumble and point some guns at the state house where Congress was meeting, but the members felt sufficiently threatened to convene in Princeton for a time (C. M. Green, 1962, 10).

30. Tindall, 1916, 5; C. M. Green, 1962, 10-11; Best, 1984, 15, 20–22; Kramnick, ed., 1987, 279–80.

31. Earlier Hamilton had, however, submitted a "sketch" of government suggesting that the President "be now a Citizen of one of the States, or hereafter be born a Citizen of the United States" (Pryor, 1988, 889; Farrand, ed., 1966, III.617).

32. Farrand, ed., 1966, II.215–17, 228–29, 235–39, 243–44, 251, 268–72, 367, 574; Kettner, 1978, 225–30; Kramnick, ed., 1987, #52, 323, #62, 364, #54, 375; Jillson, 1988, 32, 122, 131–37.

33. Burlamaqui, 1792, II.213–14; Vattel, 1787, 166–67; Madison, 1979, 179. Because the approach of Burlamaqui and Vattel appeals to only hypothetical, not actual consent, it possesses all the problems of such arguments, although the parental desire they postulate is quite plausible. Their position also still involves an ascription of membership in practice, albeit an alterable one. For more discussion of these two conceptions of birthright citizenship, see Schuck & Smith, 1985, and ch. 10 below.

34. Madison, 1979, 179.

35. Masculine pronouns are used once in Art. I, sec. 2, twice in sec. 3, twice in sec. 6, eight times in sec. 7; six times in Art. II, sec. 1; four times in sec. 4, seven times in sec. 3. Three masculine pronouns appear in the Bill of Rights—one in the Fifth Amendment and two in the Sixth.

36. See, e.g., the speech of Senator Morgan, *Congressional Record*, 51st Cong., v. 21, pt. 7, 6581, 1890 (disputing the constitutionality of admitting Wyoming to statehood with female suffrage).

37. The terms *person* or *persons* are used, for example, 21 times, three times in Art. I, sec. 2, twice in sec. 3, once each in secs. 6 and 7, three times in sec. 9, seven times in Art. II, sec. 1, twice in Art. III, sec. 3, and twice in Art. IV, sec. 2. *Person* is also used twice in the Fifth Amendment. See also Kramnick, ed., 1987, #2, 91, #14, 144, #57, 345, #63, 463.

38. Some scholars assert that among the Constitution's silences in this area is an unspoken debt to Native American institutions. In striving to form significant unity while respecting the claims of the constituent states, the framers of both the Articles of Confederation and the Constitution were influenced in part by the example of the Iroquois confederation, the League of the Long House; at least, so Franklin and John Adams both suggested. Officials of the United States Confederation and the many states did have considerable experience in dealing with this confederated system. Jefferson referred to it knowledgeably in his *Notes*. Hence it probably did play some role in the framers' thinking. Jefferson, 1955, 93, 97; Wise & Deloria, 1971, 137, 149–50; Wright, 1992, 116, 360n3.

39. See, e.g., Farrand, ed., 1966, I.193, 201, 227, 229, 236, 316, 321, 330.

40. Kramnick, ed., 1987, #3, 96; #24, 191–92.
41. Farrand, ed., 1966, I.227, 243, 542, 561, 587, 592, 604–5; II.95, 220–22, 356, 370, 378, 415; III.210–11; Pole, 1966, 25, 354, 357–59, 364; P. Foner, 1975, 388, 390–91, 396; Fehrenbacher, 1978, 21–22, 27.
42. It is striking that Pinckney, the leading defender of slavery, also gave the most Tocquevillian account of America. He claimed that its "leading feature" was "equality," guaranteed by the large amounts of "unsettled" western lands and by the equality of rights and absence of extreme poverty in the U.S. In American exceptionalist fashion, he maintained that because the U.S. was "singularly situated, both as to fortune and to rights," it should not follow "the example of any of the European states or kingdoms," including Great Britain. He nonetheless used foreign examples to vindicate slavery. Clearly it was possible to make sweeping claims about the egalitarian character of America while fully expecting slavery and racial inequality to remain constitutive features of the regime forever. Farrand, ed., 1966, IV.31–35.
43. Farrand, ed., 1966, I.486–87; II.10, 364, 371, 374, 378, 449; III.333; Wiecek, 1977, 62–63.
44. Farrand, ed., 1966, III.160–61, 325; P. Foner, 1975, 405; Fehrenbacher, 1978, 24, 27, 602n41; Kramnick, ed., 1987, 332–35. Jillson, 1988, 140–50, provides an excellent discussion of the politics of compromise over slavery.
45. For a view of the Bill of Rights as a coherent set of guarantees of majoritarian local control over many governmental functions, see Amar, 1991.

Chapter 6. Attempting National Liberal Citizenship

1. *Chisholm v. Georgia*, 2 Dall. 419, 462, 465 (1793).
2. Elkins & McKitrick, 1993, esp. 591–92, 694.
3. Kettner, 1978, 248–49; E. S. Morgan, 1980, 21; Wiebe, 1984, 3; Elkins & McKitrick, 1993, 46–50, 456, 587–88.
4. Wiebe, 1984, 18–19; Elkins & McKitrick, 1993, 4, 21–24, 27, 78–79. Wiebe's argument, that this generation of Americans continued to display needs, born of their colonial origins, to prove their distinctiveness and their respectability to Europeans, accords with Benedict Anderson's account of the psychology of colonial nation-builders (1983).
5. Jefferson, 1955, 84–85.
6. Higham, 1966, 8, 19, 97, 210; Elkins & McKitrick, 1993, 694–95.
7. Rossiter, 1971, 201, 206–11; McDonald, 1982, 68–71; Wiebe, 1984, 49; Elkins & McKitrick, 1993, 103–18.
8. Hamilton, 1985, 283, 290–92; Elkins & McKitrick, 1993, 99, 114–20, 258–61. For Lind, 1995, 370–76, these features make Hamilton the founding figure in his "liberal nationalist" pantheon of American heroes. He correctly stresses that in contrast, Jefferson not only was a critic of cities and industry but also was far more racist, preaching Anglo-Saxon and white superiority and urging tougher laws against miscegenation.
9. They also continued the liberalizing trend toward converting real property qualifications to taxpayer requirements (Porter, 1971, 22–24; McDonald, 1979, 234–36; Wiebe, 1984, 46–47, 152–54).
10. *Annals of Cong.*, 3d Cong., 1st Sess., 64, 72, 455 (1793–95) (Gales & Seaton, 1849); 4th Cong., 1st Sess., 1171, 1349 (1796) (Gales & Seaton, 1849).
11. Berlin, 1974, 81; Cover, 1975, 62–82; Fehrenbacher, 1978, 44, 84; Kettner, 1978, 302–4, 315; Nash, 1990, 182–89; Elkins & McKitrick, 1993, 401–11, 434–35, 526–27.
12. *Annals of Cong.*, 1st Cong., 2d Sess., 1223–33, 1239–47, 1501–26 (Gales & Seaton, 1834); 5th Cong., 2d Sess., v. 1, 475, 1037 (1798) (Gales & Seaton, 1851); Elkins & McKitrick, 1993,

142–43, 151–52. In contrast to Smith, the black astronomer Benjamin Banneker wrote Jefferson to challenge his suggestions of black inferiority in his *Notes*. Jefferson conceded that apparent racial differences might be wholly traceable to the "degraded condition" of slaves after all, but he did not take up the causes of antislavery or improvement of the condition of free blacks in any serious way (Nash, 1990, 177–81).

13. St. Clair's actions perpetuating slavery helped win support for the establishment of thinly disguised "indentured" systems in Indiana in 1803 and Illinois in 1809. Thus these states were never fully "free."

14. Porter, 1971, 23–24, 26; P. Foner, 1975, 413, 462, 480; Wiecek, 1977, 102–3; Fehrenbacher, 1978, 37–38, 84–88.

15. *Annals of Cong.*, 2d Cong., 2d Sess., 861 (1793) (Gales & Seaton, 1855); Wiecek, 1977, 97–100; Fehrenbacher, 1978, 40–42.

16. Wise & Deloria, 1971, 173–80; Washburn, 1971, 54; Washburn, 1975, 162–63; Spicer, 1980, 115; Prucha, 1984, 60–66; Merrell, 1987, 206–8; Elkins & McKitrick, 1993, 250–55, 271–72, 436–37.

17. Washburn, 1971, 55; Prucha, 1984, 49–50; Merrell, 1987, 210; Elkins & McKitrick, 1993, 461–71.

18. Jefferson explained in his *Notes* how Virginia's laws claimed for the state "sole and exclusive power of taking conveyances of the Indian right of soil," including the provision that "an Indian conveyance alone could give no right . . . which the laws would acknowledge" (1955, 136). Federal policy followed similar lines.

19. Washburn, 1971, 55–57, 60; Washburn, 1975, 163; Wise & Deloria, 1971, 176; Spicer, 1980, 115; Horsman, 1981, 106–8.

20. Cohen, 1982, 7, 109–12; Prucha, 1984, 90–111.

21. Francis Paul Prucha contends that Knox's position rested on common decency, not "theoretical reasoning about the laws of nations." But in fact Knox's arguments—that Native Americans possessed natural rights, including land rights based on prior occupancy, that could not be qualified except "by their free consent, or by the right of conquest in case of a just war"—are fully consistent with Vattel's then-familiar views (Prucha, 1984, 59–60).

22. J. Wilson, 1967, 86, 102, 143, 217, 403–7, 579. Wilson's early advancement of the doctrine of two spheres as America's true legal philosophy is not mentioned by Taub & Schneider, 1982, 126, who find little evidence that legal thought "played an overt role in the initial articulation of separate-sphere ideology." I was pointed to Wilson by Conrad, 1984.

23. J. Wilson, 1967, 85–88.

24. J. Wilson, 1967, 599–603.

25. Wollstonecraft, 1967, 52–53, 57–59, 92, 128–48, 197, 223–24, 230–40, 278; Flexner, 1972, 162–66; Flexner, 1975, 15–17; Murray, 1973, 18; Sunstein, 1975, 214–15; Kerber, 1980, 224–25, 279; Sapiro, 1992, 92–93, 154–61, 182–85, 273–77. Wollstonecraft consciously focused on middle-class women and assumed that education would perpetuate class structures, but she also praised the virtues of hardworking "poor women" and expressed sympathy for the "African slaves" victimized by "prejudices that brutalize them" (1967, 33, 126, 218, 220, 251). She endorsed Samuel Stanhope Smith's environmentalist views of race (Sapiro, 1992, 45–46).

26. Higham, 1975, 31–32; Rischin, ed., 1976, 43–44; Hamilton, 1985, 291.

27. Locke, 1693; Locke, 1965b, 338–42; Schuck & Smith, 1985, 28, 30–31.

28. Elkins & McKitrick, 1993, count 48 Federalists and 4 Anti-Federalists in the first House, with an 18–2 margin in the first Senate; and they note that after some subsequent decline, Federalists resurged in the 1796 elections (33, 513). *Congressional Quarterly*, 1982, 897, counts only 38 "Administration" supporters, 26 "Oppositionists" in the first House, with a 17–9

margin in the Senate, but it also indicates that after Federalist declines in the 2d and 3d Congresses, with Democratic Republicans actually gaining control of the House in the 3d Congress, Federalists gained seats up to 1801 in the House and held steady in the Senate.

29. *Annals of Cong.*, 1st Cong., 1st Sess., v. 1, 812–13, 825–27, 836–44 (Gales & Seaton, 1834); Judiciary Act of 1789, ch. 20, Sec. 11, 1 Stat. 73, 78; Friendly, 1928, 500–501; Moore & Weckstein, 1964a, 1–6; Purcell, 1992, 14–15; Elkins & McKitrick, 1993, 62–64.

30. Jacobs, 1972, 27–40; Kramnick, ed., 1987, 455; Orth, 1987, 24–29.

31. 2 Dall. 419 (1793) at 434–35. At 433, Iredell argued that the Supreme Court did have the power to treat as "utterly void" any portion of the Judiciary Act "inconsistent with the Constitution," an early assertion of the power of judicial review established in *Marbury v. Madison.*

32. 2 Dall. 419 (1793) at 453, 455, 457, 460, 462. For transitions in the notion of sovereignty during this era, see Antholis, 1993.

33. 470–72, 476–77. Jay even remarked rather wistfully that if the "science of government" were sufficiently advanced, the United States might forego its sovereign right to immunity to suit from its citizens. But given the federal judiciary's inability to enforce any suit that the executive wished to ignore, he thought it futile to challenge the status quo in this regard (at 478).

34. *Annals of Cong.*, 3d Cong., 1st Sess., 30–31, 476–78 (1794) (Gales & Seaton, 1849). The Eleventh Amendment reads, "The Judicial power of the United States shall not be construed to extend to any suit in law or equity, commenced or prosecuted against one of the United States by Citizens of another State, or by Citizens or Subjects of any Foreign State." John Orth (1987, 18–21) has speculated that the delays in certifying ratification by both Federalist presidents may have reflected their interest in asserting a prerogative to approve congressionally initiated amendments, and their qualms about this one. See also Jacobs, 1972, 59, 65–72.

35. Indeed, much later the Court would all but disavow the decision in *Hans v. Louisiana*, 134 U.S. 1, 11–14 (1890), with only Justice John Marshall Harlan disputing the point. Jacobs, 1972, 72–74; Orth, 1987, 22–23.

36. In the oft-cited case of *Bingham v. Cabot*, 3 Dall. 382 (1798), the Court heard arguments that raised potentially far-reaching questions on the distinction between citizenship and mere long-term "inhabitancy," and on whether U.S. citizens were automatically citizens of the states in which they permanently resided. It decided, however, only that an averment of citizenship had to be clearly set forth in the record for the federal courts to have jurisdiction. If that decision had any deeper political roots, it probably displayed a post-*Chisholm* reluctance to claim jurisdiction too quickly. As a leading counsel argued in *Hope Insurance Co. v. Boardman*, 5 Cranch 57 (1809): "At the time the Court decided the case of *Bingham v. Cabot*, the jurisdiction of the courts of the United States was an object of jealousy, and there was probably a desire on the part of the court to remove all ground of suspicion, by deciding doubtful cases against the jurisdiction."

37. Unsurprisingly, *Bingham* produced a spate of decisions in the next two years in which jurisdiction was denied because citizenship had not been averred properly. See *Turner v. Enrille*, 4 Dall. 7 (1799); *Turner v. Bank of North America*, 4 Dall. 8 (1799); *Mossman v. Higginson*, 4 Dall. 12 (1800); *Course v. Stead*, 4 Dall. 22 (1800). In *Turner v. Bank of North America*, Oliver Ellsworth, now Chief Justice, indicated self-effacingly that in regard to federal circuit courts, created for limited purposes, the presumption was against asserting their jurisdiction (at 11). He also seemed to accept the legitimacy of a corporate litigant in this diversity of citizenship case, however, a point that would later become controversial; but that jurisdictional issue was not raised. Cf. Kettner, 1978, 261–64.

38. See in particular *Campbell v. Morris*, 3 Harris & McHenry's Repts. 535, 562 (Md. Gen. Ct., 1797, Ct. App., 1800). In the original case, Judge Chase contended that the clause's "privileges and immunities" (terms he viewed as virtually synonymous) were not to be given "full and comprehensive" reach, but rather "a particular and limited operation." They included not "the right of election, the right of holding offices, the right of being elected," but rather rights of "acquiring and holding real as well as personal property" (553–54). That definition favored a view of the provision as not a "comity clause," but rather a shield for certain limited substantive rights that inhere in American citizenship. And by describing these rights as economic, not political, Chase gave constitutional citizenship a more liberal, less republican cast. He found no violation of the clause in the case, even though it involved an economic claim (against a law that made it easier to attach the property of a citizen of another state than an absent Maryland citizen). He thought the right not so fundamental and substantially equal in any case. The Maryland Court of Appeals reversed Chase, however. It treated the clause more as an anti-discrimination, comity provision, holding unconstitutional the sort of "distinction between our citizens and others" involved in the statute (at 564–65). Thus the case displays different currents of thought on privileges and immunities, with the comity view ultimately prevailing.
39. *Van Horne's Lessee v. Dorrance*, 2 Dall. 304, 308–10 (U.S.C.C. Pa., 1795); Kettner, 1978, 257–58.
40. Elkins & McKitrick, 1993, 592, 694.
41. Ramsay, 1789.
42. *Annals of Cong.*, 1st Cong., 1st Sess., 413–24 (1789) (Gales & Seaton, 1834).
43. *Annals of Cong.*, 1st Cong., 1st Sess., 418 (1789) (Gales & Seaton, 1834).
44. *Annals of Cong.*, 3d Cong., 2d Sess., 1027–29 (1794) (Gales & Seaton, 1849); 5th Cong., 1st Sess., v. 1, 348–56 (1797) (Gales & Seaton, 1851). Sounding like a modern communitarian, Murray complained in 1794 that Virginia's permission for in-country expatriation permitted men to be stateless and thus to be "in the imaginary state of nature, which is, in reality, an unnatural state, for a being whose every faculty and quality constitutes him a moral agent, surrounded by essential relations, and of course, impel him to discharge duties of a social nature" (1029).
45. Tsiang, 1942, 25–27, 37–41, 50; F. G. Franklin, 1969, 71, 102–3; Kettner, 1978, 269–70, 281.
46. 11 F. 1099 (U.S.C.C. Pa., 1793).
47. 11 F. 1099 (1793) at 1100–1101, 1105–7, 1118, 1120, 1122–23.
48. 3 Dall. 133 (1795).
49. *Jansen v. The Christina Magdalena*, 13 F. Cas. 356, 360–61 (U.S.D.C. S. C., 1794).
50. 3 Dall. 133 (1795) at 139, 141, 150.
51. 3 Dall. at 152–53.
52. 3 Dall. at 162–65. Like Coke, Iredell recognized the "disagreeable dilemmas" dual citizenship could involve, but still thought his principles "warranted by law and reason," and he agreed with Paterson that such difficulties should be met by a federal law regulating expatriation.
53. 29 F. Cas. 1330 (U.S.C.C. Ct., 1799).
54. 29 F. Cas. 1330 (1799) at 1331. The hostility of Ellsworth and the Court to unpatriotic conduct was also visible the following year in *Cooper v. Telfair*, 4 U.S. 14 (1800). There the Justices unanimously upheld, against various state constitutional complaints, a 1782 Georgia law banishing all persons convicted of treason and one loyalist, Basil Cooper by name. Justice Chase suggested that the result might have been different if the federal constitution had then been in effect (18–19).

55. *Annals of Cong.,* 1st Cong., 1st Sess., v. 1, 1147–64 (1790) (Gales & Seaton, 1834); Act of March 26, 1790; Franklin, 1969, 38–39; Kettner, 1978, 238.

56. *Annals of Cong.,* 1st Cong., 1st Sess., v. 1, 1148–49, 1155–56 (1790) (Gales & Seaton, 1834); F. G. Franklin, 1969, 38.

57. *Annals of Cong.,* 1st Cong., 1st Sess., v. 1, 1156, 1159–60 (1790) (Gales & Seaton, 1834).

58. *Collet v. Collet,* 6 F. Cas. 105, 106–7 (U.S.C.C. Pa., 1792); see also *Portier v. Le Roy,* 1 Yeates 371 (Pa., 1794); F. G. Franklin, 1969, 38, 46–47; Kettner, 1978, 238–39.

59. *Annals of Cong.,* 3d Cong., 1st Sess., 47–53, 58 (1794) (Gales & Seaton, 1849); Kettner, 1978, 232–34.

60. *Annals of Cong.,* 3d Cong., 2d Sess., 1006–8, 1021–58 (1794) (Gales & Seaton, 1849).

61. The continuing belief that the Constitution did not by itself create exclusive federal naturalization powers was evident in *U.S. v. Villato,* 2 Dall. 370 (U.S.C.C. Pa., 1797). There, Attorney General Lee contended that the Constitution had granted the federal government concurrent, not exclusive, naturalization authority, and that the 1790 naturalization act had not altered that status, so that a 1793 naturalization by Pennsylvania was valid. Because that naturalization antedated the 1795 congressional statute, Lee did not have to address whether that law made federal power exclusive. The Circuit Court held that the 1793 state naturalization was in fact invalid under Pennsylvania's own recently adopted constitution. Justice Iredell indicated that he would have regarded federal naturalization powers as exclusive "if the question had not previously occurred" and been answered differently in *Collett* (373).

62. *Annals of Cong.,* 3d Cong., 2d Sess., 812–15 (1795) (Gales & Seaton, 1849); J. M. Smith, 1956, 22–23; F. G. Franklin, 1969, 51–57, 67–71; Kettner, 1978, 239–43; Ueda, 1980, 737.

63. Onuf, 1987a, 68–74.

64. This bill also explicitly concerned admission to citizenship "of the United States," although the debates still revealed much support for the view that the states could admit aliens to their own citizenship, if not federal citizenship. *Annals of Cong.,* 5th Cong., 2d Sess., 1554, 1567–82, 1776–84 (1798); Elkins & McKitrick, 1993, 694–95; Takaki, 1993, 29.

65. As opposition to the laws mounted, Jeffersonians then tried to compel reconsideration of the Sedition and Alien Friends laws late in the Congress, but failed. *Annals of Cong.,* 5th Cong., 2d Sess., v. 1, 554–55, 564–65, 589–90, 599, 609; v. 2, 1785–96, 1973–2028, 2049; v. 3, 2429–35, 2986–3016 (1798–99) (Gales & Seaton, 1851); J. M. Smith, 1956, 22–93; F. G. Franklin, 1969, 75–81, 92–93; Elkins & McKitrick, 1993, 590–92.

66. Grant & Davison, eds., 1928, 42, 46–51, 89–90; Arieli, 1964, 246–47, 249; Higham, 1966, 8, 19, 97, 210; Nagel, 1971, 21; G. Washington, 1973, 170, 173.

67. *Case of Fries,* 9 F. Cas. 826 (U.S.C.C. Pa., 1799) at 831, 834–39.

68. Elkins & McKitrick, 1993, 695–99, 741–43, gives some credence to the view that the Federalists were doomed to defeat regardless of these acts, the closeness of the 1800 electoral college results notwithstanding.

69. Bender, 1978, 83–86; Wiebe, 1984, 145; and, generally, Shain, 1994.

Chapter 7. Toward a Commercial Nation of White Yeoman Republics

1. Most notably, with the Federalists discredited after their near-treason during the War of 1812, but with its lessons of American weakness widely appreciated, Congress chartered a second Bank of the United States, adopted a mildly protective tariff, and flirted with a program of internal improvements in 1816. But the Republicans were always ambivalent about expanding national power, and such steps always encountered state opposition, so these

measures were not taken very far. The national leadership also remained concerned to assert America's independence and respectability vis-à-vis Europe, to the point of the second war with England. Nonetheless, the dominant policy was to turn away from Europe toward westward expansion (Dangerfield, 1965, 15; Kelley, 1979, 133, 136–37).

2. Though Jefferson thought Louisiana necessary for America's future, he was anxious about adding French Catholic citizens, so he unsuccessfully sought to transplant "30,000 volunteers, Americans by birth" into the new territory. Donald Meinig argues that the acquisition of Florida, completed under Monroe, was driven by "people who regarded free Blacks and Creoles and Seminoles," all groups thriving in Florida, "as anathema" (Meinig, 1993, 15–16, 24–31).

3. As many scholars have noted, the Jeffersonians benefited from an international context in which the European powers were too concerned with their own rivalries to place many obstacles in the way of American development. Those wars continued to provide Americans with foreign markets; they generally allowed the U.S. to pursue foreign trade and expansion without itself resorting to war; and they permitted it to survive even the embarrassing defeats of the War of 1812. The U.S. was also able to grow with largely state-led economic initiatives, as the Jeffersonians preferred, because national protection for American enterprises was rarely required. The characterizations of the Jeffersonians here and in the opening paragraphs derive from: Arieli, 1964, 67, 128, 154–60; Dangerfield, 1965, 1–32, 36–71, 80–90, 181–94; Rossiter, 1971, 202, 206–11, 271–72; M. L. Wilson, 1974, 63–70; Banning, 1978, 290; Kelley, 1979, 125–37, 141–46; McCoy, 1980, 104–8, 201–3; Remini, 1981, 39–42; Wiebe, 1984, 124–25, 152–56, 194–208, 221–29, 242–44; Tucker & Hendrickson, 1990, 3–47; Ben-Atar, 1993, 17–18, 23–29, 36–37, 169–72.

4. Hartz, 1955, 89, 119–24, 168–72; Rogin, 1975, 4–12; Appleby, 1984, 4, 22, 46–47.

5. Act of April 14, 1802. The most significant later laws included a mildly restrictive amendment passed in 1813, after the war with Britain, which required five years of continuous residence for naturalization, a provision repealed in 1848; amendments in 1824 and 1828 which accelerated naturalization in several ways, especially by permitting the declaration of intent to be made only two years prior to gaining citizenship, and to be omitted in the case of long-term residents and those who came to the U.S. as minors; and an 1855 act regulating the status of women and children and the 1870 law permitting naturalization of persons of African descent, both discussed in later chapters (F. G. Franklin, 1969, 108–10, 175–76; Kettner, 1978, 236n61, 245–46; Ueda, 1980, 737; Hutchinson, 1981, 17–20; Onuf, 1987a, 76–77).

6. Act of March 2, 1819; Hutchinson, 1981, 20–46. Recipient states continued to try, generally ineffectively, to protect themselves against the entry of paupers and convicts. Neuman, 1993, 1843, 1848–58.

7. P. Foner, 1975, 453, 475–78; Fehrenbacher, 1978, 100–101.

8. *Annals of Cong.*, 13th Cong., 1st Sess., 1094–99 (Robertson particularly criticized Oliver Ellsworth's revival of the common law in *Williams' Case*, and some Federalists rose to its defense); 15th Cong., 1st Sess., 449, 1056–1065, 1069–70, 1107. McLane, who soon played a key role in developing arguments against black citizenship during the Missouri Compromise debates, here sniffed that if the South American republicans "are capable of enjoying civil liberty and a free government," he hoped that their cause might prevail (1061). Cf. Tsiang, 1942, 45–61.

9. C. Williamson, 1960, 138–222; Porter, 1971, 36–76; Elliott, 1974, 34–39; Shade, 1981, 78.

10. Against the objections of the high Federalist Governor Arthur St. Clair, Congress first decided in 1798 to extend the franchise to Ohio residents who held town lots equivalent in value to fifty acres. Then in 1808, it similarly granted the vote to Indiana and Mississippi

residents who owned town lots worth $100, and in response to further complaints from Indiana inhabitants, it moved to a taxpaying, one-year residency requirement there in 1811. In 1812, it abolished real property requirements in Illinois, in 1814 it did so in Mississippi, and in 1817 it based the franchise in the latter state strictly on taxpaying (C. Williamson, 1960, 212–14, 218–19; Porter, 1971, 24). It also permitted all taxpayers to vote for representatives to the various territorial conventions that prepared for statehood until 1819, when in passing the Enabling Act for Alabama to draft a constitution it moved to universal white manhood suffrage. That pattern prevailed thereafter.

11. Ohio joined the union in 1803 with a state constitution that had no freehold requirements for voting, only taxpaying or, alternatively, work on a public highway. In 1812, Louisiana came in with a taxpaying qualification, and it also permitted white men to vote if they had purchased land from the U.S. within a certain period, in order to encourage homesteading. Like Maryland, Louisiana required voters to be U.S. citizens, a recognition of the importance of national political identity that few others states explicitly enacted. Indiana joined in 1816 with only a one-year residence requirement for the vote, Illinois in 1818 reduced that time to six months, and Missouri in 1820 asked only three months. In the states born of the western territories, with fewer entrenched hierarchies beyond race and gender, universal manhood suffrage normally seemed the way to structure citizenship (C. Williamson, 1960, 218–19; Porter, 1971, 24, 36–39, 48–49).

12. Subsequently, many Maryland Federalists and Republicans did try to win further changes, including repeal of religious and property qualifications for office. Not all their efforts succeeded, but they gained an additional amendment in 1810 that ended all property and tax qualifications for federal as well as state elections, granting the vote to all white males who were U.S. citizens and resident in the state for one year (C. Williamson, 1960, 146–51). A similar movement in South Carolina led to the adoption in 1810 of a bill extending the vote to all males who had been resident for two years in the state, six months in the election district (a reform supported by the young John C. Calhoun).

13. C. Williamson, 1960, 138–57; Porter, 1971, 39–40; Berlin, 1974, 91; Elliott, 1974, 42.

14. It provided military service and taxpaying alternatives to real property requirements, but it did not move directly to universal male suffrage. This modest success nonetheless satiated the reform movement (C. Williamson, 1960, 170–73, 182–90, 219–20; Porter, 1971, 53).

15. Porter, 1971, 51–53.

16. Litwack, 1961, 80–84; C. Williamson, 1960, 190–205; Porter, 1971, 54–72; P. Foner, 1975, 519–20.

17. Like most other states, Virginia did not alter the various special requirements, including property qualifications, that existed in its municipal elections. Even men of generally democratic views, such as Albert Gallatin, often favored real property standards for local governmental bodies that were almost exclusively concerned with land use issues, as opposed to the more general powers over persons of state and federal representatives. C. Williamson, 1960, 220–21, 225–34; Porter, 1971, 73–76; Elliott, 1974, 42.

18. In the 11th Congress, impassioned critics like Peter Early of Georgia sought repeal of federal governance, contending that it presented the "monstrous phenomenon of a country where the principles of freedom extend to the remotest extremity, whilst there is despotism at the heart." If the residents were "already so far degenerated as to attach no value to the blessings of self-government and prefer living destitute of political rights," he thundered, "they are already fit instruments for tyrants" who needed "a new lesson in the rights of man." Perhaps that message rang hollow from a Georgian. In any case, though district governance would be modified many times thereafter, D.C. residents continued to lack the full

federal voting rights of other U.S. citizens, an arrangement the federal courts upheld with little discussion. *Annals of Cong.,* 6th Cong. 869–73, 991–97 (1800–1801); 11th Cong., 2d. Sess., 881, 884, 889, 896 (1810c); Tindall, 1916, 5, 11, 17, 24–25; Green, 1962, 24–31; *U.S. v. Hammond,* 26 F. Cas. 96 (U.S.C.C. D.C., 1801).

19. S. S. Smith, 1965, 151–53, 166–68, 177, 187. Kames then elaborated his contrasting view in a much enlarged 1813 edition of his *Sketches* without addressing Smith's *Essay,* though he did qualify his earlier claim that black mental inferiority was not due to their "condition" (Kames, 1813, 49–50).

20. Fredrickson, 1971, 2, 12; Franklin & Moss, 1988, 155–57.

21. In 1818, an Indiana federal court upheld the constitutionality of the 1793 Fugitive Slave Law but also held that it superseded state laws regulating slave recaption, indicating that there could be no concurrent power for "the same end" (*In re Susan,* 23 F. Cas. 444–45, U.S.C.C. Ind., 1818). This brief decision does not, however, appear to have had much impact on state regulatory policies toward fugitive slaves.

22. Litwack, 1961, 31; P. Foner, 1975, 463–64, 510–11; Wiecek, 1977, 100–105.

23. *Annals of Cong.,* 16th Cong., 2d Sess., 1829–31, at 599; Litwack, 1961, 37–38; Kettner, 1978, 312–13; Schuck & Smith, 1985, 66–67. Hemphill later became a Jacksonian Democrat.

24. *Annals of Cong.,* ibid., at 555, 557, 615–22; Litwack, 1961, 35–36; Kettner, 1978, 313–14; Schuck & Smith, 1985, 67–68.

25. *Annals of Cong.,* ibid., at 1129, 1134; Litwack, 1961, 36–39; Dangerfield, 1965, 131–36; Wiecek, 1977, 123–24; Schuck & Smith, 1985, 68.

26. Opinion of Nov. 7, 1821, *Official Opinions of the Attorneys General of the U.S.,* v. 1, 507–8 (1852).

27. Litwack, 1961, 50.

28. *Elkison v. Deliesseline,* 8 F. Cas. 493, 496 (U.S.C.C. S.C., 1823).

29. *U.S. v. La Jeune Eugenie,* 26 F. Cas. 832, 840, 845–47 (U.S.C.C. Mass., 1822); *The Antelope,* 10 Wheat. 66–67, 85–86 (1825).

30. P. Foner, 1975, 442, 462, 474–75.

31. Berlin, 1974, 48–50, 90–99, 110, 115, 316–40; P. Foner, 1975, 453–55, 509–15; Fehrenbacher, 1978, 49–50; Neuman, 1993, 1868–75.

32. Litwack, 1961, 70–75, 80–83, 93, 113–15; P. Foner, 1975, 515, 523; P. Foner, 1983a, 193–95; Forten, 1990, 190–98.

33. *Rankin v. Lydia,* 2 A. K. Marsh. 467, 476 (Ky., 1820).

34. *Ely v. Thompson,* 3 A. K. Marsh. 70, 75 (Ky., 1820).

35. 1 Littell 326, 332–34 (1822); Kettner, 1978, 315–16, 321–22.

36. Cited in Wright, 1992, 206.

37. Horsman, 1981, 192, 300; Prucha, 1984, 114, 184, 234; Meinig, 1993, 78–86.

38. Beginning in 1796, and particularly from 1806 through 1822, the national Republican administrations continued to try to control trade with the tribes through a factory trading system administered by the War department, though eventually political pressures to permit private agents to carry on the trade proved too great. Subsequently, the Department attempted to enforce the intercourse acts through a Bureau (or "Office") of Indian Affairs created in 1824, but that office had to rely on local enforcement officials and was often ineffective. Indeed, this problem was chronic for federal efforts to implement Native American-related legislation (Washburn, 1971, 60, 65; Prucha, 1984, 115–34, 164–68).

39. Washburn, 1971, 60–64; Wise & Deloria, 1971, 181–85, 201–9; Rogin, 1975, 179–80; Cremin, 1980, 230–33; Horsman, 1981, 108–15; Prucha, 1984, 120, 139, 149–54.

40. Padover, 1953, 327–30; Wise & Deloria, 1971, 170, 191–92, 195–201; Washburn, 1971, 61; Rogin, 1975, 209–10; Prucha, 1984, 71–88.

41. *Fletcher v. Peck,* 6 Cranch 89. 122, 142–43, 146–47.

42. It did find some echo in three brief Supreme Court decisions that read several ambiguous North Carolina statutes as preventing whites from entering, surveying, or acquiring claims to Cherokee lands, but those decisions could be interpreted as recognizing a state sovereignty over tribal lands that might be used aggressively, not protectively. See *Preston v. Browder,* 1 Wheat. 115, 121, 124 (1816); *Danforth's Lessee v. Thomas,* 1 Wheat. 155, 157–58 (1816); *Danforth v. Wear,* 9 Wheat. 673, 677 (1824).

43. Ammon, 1971, 537; Washburn, 1971, 62–64; Rogin, 1975, 180–82; Kettner, 1978, 292–93.

44. *Jackson v. Goodell,* 20 Johns. Repts. 188, 191–93 (N.Y., 1822).

45. 20 Johns. Repts. 693, 711–12 (N.Y., 1823).

46. 8 Wheat., 543, 567–69. Locke, Vattel, Montesquieu, Adam Smith, and even Jefferson were all cited, rather misleadingly, to this effect. As noted above, Jefferson had argued for the more limited position of preemption; whatever the merits of Locke's views on property might be, the portrait of all Native Americans as purely nomadic was false.

47. Ibid., at 584–92. Marshall's approach was followed two years later by Smith Thompson sitting as Circuit Justice for New York in *Jackson v. Porter,* 13 F. Cas. 235 (U.S.C.C. N.Y., 1825). In the Cherokee cases of the 1830s, Thompson successfully pressured Marshall to give greater recognition to the partial sovereignty of the tribes, and his opinion here did give great weight to what a tribe had done via a formal treaty. But at a deeper level, it only made more explicit the very limited extent of the Indian rights Marshall had recognized. The case centered on whether an alleged 1763 grant by the Seneca Indians of lands near Niagara Falls to John Stedman was binding, despite the 1764 treaty between the Seneca Nation and Great Britain— which ceded those lands, among others, to the British crown. Thompson dismissed the claim derived from Stedman, arguing that although the Indians had a "right of occupancy" and discretionary use of the soil, by 1763 "ultimate dominion" had belonged to the first European "discoverer" of the land, Great Britain (who later gave it up to the United States). Great Britain's discovery was in itself held to have "necessarily diminished" Indian "rights to complete sovereignty as independent nations." The Indians thus were "incapable of transferring an absolute title to others" (240). Any grant from them was extinguishable either by themselves or the government of "ultimate dominion," Great Britain. And by formally granting Britain title to the lands, the 1764 treaty had extinguished any title Stedman may have had (242) Although those deriving their title from Stedman were most directly injured by this decision, it also indicated that any Indian land transferals not approved by the "ultimate" sovereign, now the United States, would be disregarded.

48. 5 Cranch 173, 177–78, 182–87. For a widely followed state decision that confined the membership claims of married women so greatly as to render them virtual "political aliens," see *Martin v. Commonwealth,* 1 Mass. 347 (1805). Cf. Kerber, 1980, 132–36, and Kerber, 1992, 351–53, 368–74, who rightly stresses that anti-Republican Federalist judges would not grant wives even the "freedom to be republican mothers." When unmarried women with property were not enfranchised by that state's new constitutional charter in 1820, some complained; but conservatives replied that unmarried women had "disobeyed God's injunction to multiply and subdue the earth" (C. Williamson, 1960, 194).

This era did see the bare beginnings of legal efforts to grant women more property, parental, and divorce rights, but largely as adaptations to family separations prompted by westward movement; most of the major changes in these directions came after 1830 (DuBois, 1978, 46; Leach, 1980, 178; Taub & Schneider, 1982, 119).

49. Blau, ed., 1954, xiii, xvii, 242–48, 376; Friedman, 1973, 205–11; Flexner, 1975, 24–29; Pocock, 1975, 529–42; Kerber, 1977, 120; Kerber, 1980, 154–231; DuBois, 1978, 41–42, 46;

Degler, 1980, 307–10, 332–33; Cremin, 1980, 143–45, 372; Speth, 1982, 66–91; Kaestle, 1983, 27–29.

50. *Livingston v. Van Ingen,* 9 Johns. Repts. 507 (N.Y., 1812).

51. In his seminal study of the law of citizenship, James Kettner argues that "most" judicial interpretations of the antebellum years did not treat the privileges and immunities clause in this way, as guaranteeing to out-of-state citizens the same basic "packages of rights" a state gave to its own citizens. Instead, he thinks state and federal courts generally held that there were substantive rights attached to national citizenship, by law or nature, that no state could violate. Most of the cases Kettner cites speak particularly of property rights. Many of the cases do not, however, explicitly refer to the privileges and immunities clause. The identification of the rights they protect with Article IV appears at times to be only Kettner's inference. He also cites cases defining a right of access to federal tribunals as a basic national right, but these generally rely on Article III's diversity of citizenship clause, not the privileges and immunities clause. Hence, though the more substantive view of the privileges and immunities clause Kettner describes was certainly present in the antebellum era (see, e.g., the 1856 argument of U.S. Attorney General Caleb Cushing, discussed in ch. 9), the "comity clause" interpretation was probably more powerful. See Kettner, 1978, 157–258; cf. Attorney General William Wirt's 1821 position, discussed below; *Van Horne's Lessee v. Dorrance,* 2 Dall. 304, 308–10 (U.S.C.C. Pa., 1795); *Terrett v. Taylor,* 9 Cranch 43, 50–51 (1815); *Wilkinson v. Leland.* 2 Pet. 627, 657–58 (1829); *Buckner v. Finley,* 2 Pet. 586, 590 (1829); *Catlett v. Pacific Ins. Co.,* 5 F. Cas. 291, 296–97 (1826) (but cf. *Campbell v. Morris,* 3 Harris & McHenry 553–56, 565 [Md., 1797, 1800]; *Douglass v. Stephens,* 1 Del. Ch. 465, 476–77, 1821).

52. 6 F. Cas. 612–14 (U.S.C.C. D.C., 1821); C. M. Green, 1967, 25–27; Chase et al., comps., 1976, 60.

53. 6 F. Cas. 546, 551–52 (U.S.C.C. N.J., 1823).

54. E.g., Kettner, 1978, 259–60. Cf. Wolfe, 1986, 128.

55. Whether or not Bushrod Washington was conscious of the implications of a privileges and immunities case like *Corfield* for Virginia's anti-black laws, there can be little doubt that he was unsympathetic toward the desires of free blacks for recognition as full and equal American citizens. He served as the first President of the American Colonization Society; he refused to free his uncle George's slaves after the latter's death, contrary to the President's will; and eventually he split up the slave families through sales (Witt, 1990, 809).

56. Cremin, 1980, 7, 125, 369.

57. Cremin, 1980, 18, 125–27, 495; Kaestle, 1983, x, 3–9; Tyack, James, & Benavot, 1987, 17–24.

58. Cremin, 1980, 104, 108, 113, 127, 158, 172–74, 215–16, 267–69, 335; Kaestle, 1983, 9–29.

59. Cremin, 1980, 166–67, 180–81, 228–29, 499, 507; Kaestle, 1983, 30–61.

60. 2 Wheat. 256, 264, 284 (1817). This claim was consistent with the view that the federal naturalization power was meant only to define a minimum of inclusiveness in naturalization policies, while permitting the states to be yet more inclusive. Earlier, however, Justice Bushrod Washington had suggested in passing in *Golden v. Prince,* 10 F. Cas. 542 (U.S.C.C. Pa., 1814) that congressional power over naturalization did indeed have to be viewed as exclusive, even if unexercised.

61. Kettner, 1978, 250, 326. *Chirac* was followed in, e.g., *Matthew v. Rae,* 16 F. Cas. 1112 (U.S.C.C. D.C., 1829). It was further defended by dicta in *Ogden v. Saunders,* 12 Wheat. 213, 277 (1827), where the Court distinguished the naturalization power from Congress's power over bankruptcy by insisting that permitting naturalization by the states would be incompatible with the national character of the general government. It was "peculiarly their province to determine who are entitled to the privileges of American citizens, and

the protection of the American government." (Justice Washington had used similar reasoning in *Golden v. Prince* to argue that national power over bankruptcy was equally exclusive.)

62. From purely liberal, Lockean premises, membership based on choice should have been the only legitimate form, as Locke rejected all claims of natural political membership. But, like most Americans, even the generally Lockean John Marshall was unwilling to dismiss claims of native identity completely. Thus, although he often insisted that naturalized citizens should be treated identically to native citizens in many respects, he acknowledged that important distinctions might exist. (See, e.g., *The Venus*, 8 Cranch 253, 317 [1814].) And as in *Prentiss v. Barton*, 19 F. Cas. 1276 (U.S.C.C. Va., 1819), he continued to accept that "Birth, alone, undoubtedly, gives a man permanent rights as a citizen," so that "in doubtful cases, birth will always have great influence" in deciding a person's true citizenship. Similarly, the Court relied on common-law doctrines emphasizing place of birth in inheritance cases such as *McCreery's Lessee v. Somerville*, 9 Wheat. 354, 355, 361 (1824).

63. Substantively, Marshall's position here was consistent with his general desire to foster a unified and highly valued national political identity expressive of liberal republican consensualism, largely purged of Cokean feudalism or nativism. In these regards he was closer to the Federalists of Washington's first years than Adams's last, and to the more consistent consensualism of Jeffersonian citizenship doctrines. The case, *Osborn v. Bank of U.S.*, 9 Wheat. 738, 827 (1824), was one where Marshall struggled with the civic status of the corporation, as described below.

64. See, e.g., *Desbois's Case*, 2 Martin 185 (La., 1812); *U.S. v. Laverty*, 26 F. Cas. 875–77 (U.S.D.C. La., 1812). The District Court held that when Congress permitted all inhabitants of a territory to join in forming a new state and then admitted that state to the Union, it tacitly naturalized all alien inhabitants who were qualified to vote under the territory's laws. Cf. Kettner, 1978, 251–52.

65. 1 Pet. 511, 542 (1828).

66. Locke, 1965b, 434–35, 439–40.

67. Such naturalizations via admission of territories to statehood, via conquest, and via treaty all were also arguably in violation of Congress's constitutional mandate to establish a "uniform" rule of naturalization. For example, these special naturalizations sometimes made citizens of Native American territorial and tribal inhabitants who were not eligible under the nation's racially restricted naturalization statutes. But because the context of these decisions permitted Jeffersonian commitments to westward growth to link arms with Marshall's Federalist nationalism, few raised that criticism. Thus the courts readily found ample constitutional authority for these mass naturalizations in the congressional and executive powers to declare and conduct war, to make and ratify treaties, and to admit new states, and ample precedents in the nation's past uses of these powers to create U.S. citizens.

68. *Murray v. McCarty*, 2 Munford 393, 396–97 (Va., 1811); *Ainslie v. Martin*, 9 Mass. 454, 460–61 (1812). For discussion of other state cases, see Tsiang, 1942, 61–66, 70; Kettner, 1978, 273–76.

69. *Read v. Read*, 5 Call 160, 199–202 (Va., 1804); Kettner, 1978, 191–93.

70. See, e.g., *Hollingsworth v. Duane*, 12 F. Cas. 356 (U.S.C.C. Pa., 1801), where the Court refused to decide if a man born in New York in 1760 but raised in Ireland had some sort of right of election in the revolutionary years, because he had never exercised it. The court did not regard such a right as a natural, universal one which he possessed regardless of the special circumstances of the revolution.

71. *Murray v. The Schooner Charming Betsy*, 2 Cranch 64–66, 120 (1804).

72. As such it appears to be an instance where Marshall's liberal concern for personal economic rights prevailed over his more nationalistic and partisan allegiances. It has long been noted that Marshall rarely had to confront conflicts between his broad assertions of national power and his commitments to vested property rights, because during his tenure Congress rarely used its economic powers, and it usually did so in ways that favored property holders (McCloskey, 1960, 57; Smith, 1985, 285n23). Hence this example of such conflict, and Marshall's liberal choice, are revealing; though as noted in the text, this was a milder revision in common-law views than a purely liberal outlook would have suggested.

73. See, e.g., *The Venus*, 8 Cranch 253 (1814); *The Frances*, 8 Cranch 335, 371 (1814); *The Mary and Susan*, 1 Wheat. 46, 54–55 (1816); *The Dos Hermanos*, 2 Wheat. 76, 96 (1817); *The Pizarro*, 2 Wheat. 227, 244 (1817); *The Friendschaft*, 3 Wheat. 14, 51–52 (1818).

74. Indeed, in *The Venus* (1814), Marshall's brethren refused to go along with his contention that a naturalized American citizen, returned to Britain, should be viewed as an American during a reasonable period of election after hostilities had broken out between the two nations. Justice Washington's opinion for the Court held instead that in the absence of an express election to the contrary, domicile in a foreign land made a person a subject of that land, at least in regard to property claims. Both Washington and Marshall cited Vattel, but Washington relied most heavily on English common-law doctrines in prize cases. Marshall instead quoted at length Vattel's doctrine that citizenship depends on birth to a father who is a citizen, and that domicile elsewhere makes a person only a "perpetual inhabitant," a "kind of citizen of an inferior order," who can alter that status by removal. And Marshall cited Burlamaqui's suggestion that in time of war, such persons should be given "a reasonable time to retire" to their original countries before being treated as aliens by those countries. Marshall's position would have extended the considerable weight given to personal choices, at least those of property holders, in the *Betsy* decision, thereby giving the law an even more consensualist cast. But here his brethren followed Washington's nationalistic insistence that those who did not join their country's cause immediately should be treated as siding with the enemy instead of their "deserted country" (280, 285). *The Venus*, 8 Cranch 253, 273, 283–86, 289–92, 298 (1814).

75. *U.S. v. Gillies*, 25 F. Cas. 1321, 1322 (U.S.C.C. Pa., 1815). Cf. also *Dawson's Lessee v. Godfrey*, 4 Cranch 321 (1808), where the justices followed *Calvin's Case* in determining whether a person had allegiance to the British crown for purposes of inheritance. But even while following Coke, they rejected his claim that this rule embodied requirements of nature. Rather, they said that this inheritance was a product of the "laws of society," instead of a "natural and perfect" right (at 323).

76. Though federal courts sustained state laws providing for a period of election, as discussed previously, in *McIlvaine v. Coxe's Lessee*, 4 Cranch 209, 213 (1808) the Supreme Court sustained several revolution-era New Jersey laws which indicated that persons leaving the state to aid the British cause were fugitives, not aliens. That holding sharply limited the scope of the revolutionary "right of election," much less any general expatriation right; but the Court did not discuss these broader issues.

77. *The Santissima Trinidad*, 7 Wheat. 283, 316, 347–48 (1822). The year before, Marshall had similarly refused to decide Chaytor's claim in related litigation that the Chief Justice considered while sitting on circuit in Virginia. Marshall did stress that Chaytor would lose all the rights of citizenship and become wholly an alien were he to be viewed as expatriated; his lands, for example, would be "escheatable" (*Chacon v. Eighty-Nine Bales of Cochineal*, 5 F. Cas. 390, 393 [U.S.C.C. Va., 1821]). That strong view of the effects of expatriation cut against highly naturalistic common-law views.

Sometimes federal courts went even further away from the common law. In *Juando v. Taylor*, 13 F. Cas. 1179, 1181–83 (U.S.D.C. N.Y., 1818), a federal district court upheld a claim similar to Chaytor's because the ship's captain in question had lived outside the United States for twelve years and had a certificate of naturalization obtained in Buenos Aires. That court indicated, too, that perpetual allegiance was a feudal notion that did not hold in the United States, where "expatriation is conceived to be a fundamental right."

78. See, e.g., Washington's opinions in *Cooper v. Galbraith*, 6 F. Cas. 472 (U.S.C.C. Pa., 1819); *Butler v. Farnsworth*, 4 F. Cas. 902–4 (U.S.C.C. Pa., 1821); and for other diversity cases, *Knox v. Greenleaf*, 4 Dall. 360–62 (U.S.C.C. Pa., 1802); *Wood v. Wagnon*, 2 Cranch 9 (1804); *Capron v. Van Noorden*, 2 Cranch 126 (1804); *Catlett v. Pacific Ins. Co.*, 5 F. Cas. 291, 296–97 (1826); *Blight's Lessee v. Rochester*, 7 Wheat. 535, 545 (1822); *Case v. Clarke*, 5 F. Cas. 254–55 (U.S.C.C. R.I., 1828); *Buckner v. Finley*, 2 Pet. 586 (1829).

79. Marshall also voiced doubts about the *Bingham v. Cabot* holding that citizenship must be explicitly averred on the record, a rule that limited the federal judicial role in deciding civic rights. *Abercrombie v. Dupuis*, 1 Cranch 343 (1803); *Sere v. Pitot*, 6 Cranch 332, 337–38 (1810); *Prentiss v. Barton*, 19 F. Cas. 1276 (U.S.C.C. Va., 1819).

80. Indeed, he accepted some formal bounds to federal jurisdiction by holding that inhabitants of the District of Columbia and the territories were not state citizens within the meaning of the diversity clause, though of course these areas were already under federal judicial authority. See *Reily v. Lamar*, 2 Cranch 344, 356–57 (1805); *Hepburn v. Ellzey*, 2 Cranch 445, 452–53 (1805); *Corporation of New Orleans v. Winter*, 1 Wheat. 91 (1816).

81. *Hope Ins. Co. v. Boardman*, 5 Cranch 57 (1809); *Bank of U.S. v. Deveaux*, 5 Cranch 61 (1809).

82. Dodd, 1954, 34–39; Barzelay & Smith, 1987, 94–95.

83. The precedent was *Strawbridge v. Curtiss*, 3 Cranch 267 (1806). The case does not indicate what sort of joint interest Curtiss and his associates were claiming. It only states that all but one of them were citizens of Massachusetts, as was Strawbridge.

84. *Bank of U.S. v. Deveaux*, 5 Cranch 61 (1809), at 86–88. Justice Story extended the *Deveaux* rule to foreign corporations, in this case, an English one, in *Society for the Propagation of the Gospel v. Wheeler*, 22 F. Cas. 756 (U.S.C.C. N.H., 1814).

85. It was augmented by the *Bingham* requirement that citizenship be explicitly averred, as lower court records were often incomplete. For corporate cases where jurisdiction was denied due to lack of proper averment, see, e.g., *Sullivan v. Fulton Steamboat Co.*, 6 Wheat. 540 (1821); *Breithaupt v. Bank of Georgia*, 1 Pet. 238 (1828).

86. Characteristically, Marshall did not let himself be too bound by *Deveaux* or, for that matter, the Eleventh Amendment. In *Bank of U.S. v. Planters' Bank of Georgia*, 22 U.S. 904 (1824), he gave the national bank access to the federal courts, where he could protect it, even when it was involved in a dispute with a state-chartered bank in which the state was itself corporate shareholder. Justice Johnson, in dissent, insisted that under the *Deveaux* doctrine, the state as "corporator" was a party to the case. Hence the Bank of the United States was being permitted to sue a state without its consent—in violation, Johnson thought, of the Eleventh Amendment (911–13). Marshall maintained that the state divested itself of its sovereign character, and its sovereign right to refuse to be sued, when it became a shareholder (907). He made it clear that he would resist any construction that "would defeat the power" of the national government to accomplish its ends by means of the nationally chartered bank (909).

87. It also helped make McLane a favorite of Jackson himself, who appointed him Envoy Extraordinary to England, Secretary of the Treasury, and finally Secretary of State (U.S. Government Printing Office, 1971, 1385–86).

Chapter 8. High Noon of the White Republic

1. If we count the Jacksonian era as extending through the 1850s, it is also central to seven of the ten chapters of J. David Greenstone's posthumous reformulation of Hartz, *The Lincoln Persuasion.* Greenstone analyzes that period and American political culture generally as dominated by the interactions of a "humanist liberalism" born of Enlightenment rationalism that stresses satisfaction of human preferences in this life, largely by passive governmental policies of "negative liberty," and a religiously rooted "reform liberalism" that has "positive liberty" notions of human perfection and inflexible moral duties, and so can accommodate a more active, reformist state. The Jacksonian Democrats, like the Jeffersonians, were "humanist liberals." Many Federalists, Whigs, and Republicans were "reform liberals." Though Greenstone's contrasts are real, and though he sees the presence of racism throughout U.S. history, it is not adequate to treat Jacksonian racism as a mere matter of value-neutral deference to preferences of the white majority, as Greenstone repeatedly does. Those racist preferences have to be explained as central parts of American political culture, particularly during these years. Many Jacksonians vigorously defended racial hierarchy as a principled position in ways that are not at all suggested by labeling them "humanist liberals" (Greenstone, 1993, 105–17, 124–27, 133–39, 148–53).

2. Blau, ed., 1954, 2–3, 10, 13.

3. Hartz, 1955, 92–98, 101, 111–13, 138–40, 206–7 ("stupidity" at 95, 101); Howe, 1979, 12–13; Huntington, 1981, 224; McDonagh, 1994, 62. Silbey, 1991, 153–54, notes that the Whigs led narrowly in overall popular voting in presidential elections from 1834 to 1853.

4. *Dred Scott v. Sandford,* 19 How. 393, 416 (1857).

5. Rogin, 1975, 275, 279. James Oakes agrees that some slaveholders defended the institution against rising criticism from religious abolitionists and free labor economic interests through modified versions of feudal paternalism, presenting slavery no longer as a necessary evil but, from the 1840s on, as a positive good. But most Southerners, Oakes contends, did not embrace some form of American feudalism. Instead, they espoused a distinctive brand of commercial "liberalism" which they wed to slavery by invoking the sanctity of their property rights in their slaves. Though this account outdoes Hartz by seeing even more liberal hegemony, Oakes acknowledges that the fit of slavery to liberalism's "philosophical boxes" was far from "perfectly comfortable." To win support from nonslaveholders, the institution's defenders had to rely "most heavily on racism," grounding these hierarchical relationships "in biology rather than culture or class" (Oakes, 1982; Oakes, 1985, 565–69; Oakes, 1990, 130–31).

6. E. Foner, 1970, 226–60; Walzer, 1990, 598–99. Cf. Anbinder, 1992, who recognizes that a revived "concept of republicanism formed an essential component" of Know-Nothing ideology while correctly insisting that at "the center" of Know-Nothing ideology was not republicanism so much as "an unswerving belief that Protestantism defined American nationality" (104, 118, 126). Whereas the "Rousseauian republicanism" of which Walzer writes would jettison Protestantism if it hampered republican goals, I agree with Anbinder that most of the Know-Nothings would instead have abandoned republicanism if they had thought their Protestant God so willed.

7. Oakes concedes that if liberalism is defined to include even the sort of formalistic moral egalitarianism that Hartzian scholars attribute to it, many racists rejected that liberalism, "belittling" Jefferson's Declaration. Rogin acknowledges that many Jacksonians rejected pursuing westward expansion via liberal political measures, i.e., consensual treaties and economic agreements with the tribes and the gradual elimination of slavery. Oakes, 1982, 196; Oakes, 1990, 74–75; Rogin, 1975, 190–93, 212. See also Remini, 1981, 265; Fredrickson, 1981, 45–46, 51–52; Saxton, 1990, 56; Takaki, 1993, 79–83.

8. Meyers, 1960, 11, 17, 31–32, 108–10; Rogin, 1975, 267, 272, 276–77, 289; Saxton, 1990, 142–45; Silbey, 1991, 72–89. The interregnum presidency of the short-lived Whig military hero, William Henry Harrison, and his renegade Vice President, John Tyler, had no impact on this pattern. The same was true of their counterparts of the early 1850s, General Zachary Taylor and his Vice President, Millard Fillmore, who held office when national politics were already too dominated by the slavery issue to make any major Whig innovations feasible.

9. Chambers & Davis, 1978, 174–75; Howe, 1979, 14; Wiebe, 1984, 293; Silbey, 1991, 144–51.

10. This is not to deny that, in spite of their leader's agrarian rhetoric, the Jeffersonians received significant support from urban mechanics. See, e.g., J. R. Nelson, 1987, 88–90, 97–99.

11. Meyers, 1960, vii, 20–21; Rossiter, 1971, 202, 206–7, 212; Rogin, 1975, 31–32, 46–49, 63, 277; Remini, 1984, 136–39.

12. Meyers, 1960, 57–100; Kelley, 1979, 153, 158, 160–84; Howe, 1979, 35; Daniels, 1990, 124–25; Saxton, 1990, 132–42; Le Beau, 1991, 103; Anbinder, 1992, 3; McCurry, 1992, 1259; Takaki, 1993, 139–55. Saxton notes that wealthy slaveholding planters leaned toward the Whigs until Northern Whig opposition to expanding slavery drove them to the Democrats in the late 1840s. Though Samuel Morse professed allegiance to the party of Jefferson and Van Buren in his nativist tracts, he was also the son of a fanatically Federalist minister, Rev. Jedidiah Morse, who denounced foreign conspiracies in the 1790s. Morse, 1969, 6, 14; Howe, 1979, 216; D. H. Bennett, 1988, 24, 40.

13. The nullification crisis generated one of the most comprehensive and fascinating state citizenship cases, *State ex rel. McReady v. Hunt*, 2 Hill 1 (S.C., Ct. App., 1834), although its national impact was too slight for detailed consideration here. South Carolina had required militia officers to take a test oath professing allegiance to the state, and mere "obedience" to any other authority to whom South Carolina might "delegate" control. Edward McReady was elected lieutenant of an infantry unit, refused the oath, and was denied his commission, for which he sued. The case required consideration of whether allegiance was owed primarily to the state or to the union, hence whether state or national citizenship was most fundamental. It was argued at length by very able attorneys, including the crusading reformer Thomas Smith Grimké, son of a prestigious judge and brother to the famed human rights lecturers Sarah and Angelina Grimké. The arguments and opinions occupy 282 pages of the state reports. They survey *Calvin's Case*, the international law writers, doctrines of sovereignty, the propriety of "allegiance" in a liege-less republic, American cases like *Talbot v. Janson*, the writings of John C. Calhoun, and many other topics.

In the end, the Court of Appeals invalidated the oath by a 2–1 vote. Judge John O'Neall stressed that the state and federal governments formed one larger government, to which Americans had given their allegiances, a fact that state legislatures could not modify (215, 225–26). Judge David Johnson also thought that the legislature lacked this power, and that the state Nullification Convention, which allegedly provided it, had exceeded its call (240–42). Chancellor William Harper in dissent derided the notion of dual sovereignty and insisted that allegiance was still owed ultimately to the state (269). The issues were then returned to other political arenas. For discussion see Freehling, 1966, 180–81, 309–23; Kettner, 1978, 265–67.

14. Meyers, 1960, 31–32; Freehling, 1966, 266–68, 297, 357–60; M. L. Wilson, 1974, 113; Rogin, 1975, 263–67; Kelley, 1979, 149–54.

15. M. L. Wilson, 1974, 120, 137–38; Chambers & Davis, 1978, 196; Ceaser, 1979, 123–69; Shade, 1981, 100–103; Skowronek, 1982, 22–23; Remini, 1984, xiv–xvi; Wiebe, 1984, 241–42, 248–52; Silbey, 1991, 18–19.

16. Rossiter, 1971, 142, 200, 202, 226–27, 234–36; Skowronek, 1982, 26–29; Wiebe, 1984, 242–43.

17. Fredrickson, 1971, 90–91; Rossiter, 1971, 122–23; Howe, 1979, 38–39; Wiebe, 1984, 255, 300, 321–50; Saxton, 1990; Takaki, 1993, 83, who writes similarly of a "need to reinforce interior borders."

18. See esp. Horsman, 1981, 1–2, 124, 157, 159, 189, 298–300; cf., e.g., Nagel, 1971, 63, 124–25; Rogin, 1975, 11–12, 46, 63–64; Kelley, 1979, 143–44; Wiebe, 1984, 337–47.

19. Nott & Gliddon, eds., 1855; Fredrickson, 1971, 73–82; Horsman, 1981, 115–36; Horsman, 1987, 170–200; Takaki, 1993, 108–9.

20. Nott & Gliddon, eds., 1855, 48–51, 67, 79, 86, 246.

21. Van Amringe, 1848, 360–421, 595–640; Van Evrie, 1853, 2, 9; Fredrickson, 1971, 71, 92–93; Horsman, 1981, 133–35, 139–49; P. Foner, 1983a, 374–75. For discussion of the use of widely recognized gender inequalities to buttress claims for racial inequality, see McCurry, 1992, 1251–53, 1257–58, who points out that the linkage was used to discredit and to advance both causes. In 1852, for example, a conservative South Carolina woman, Louisa Susannah Cheves McCord, contended that the "Enfranchisement of Women" was "but a piece with negro emancipation," favored only by "petticoated . . . would-be men" who were "moral monsters."

22. Like most Democrats, Pettit hastened to add that he did not believe that Jefferson had meant to include blacks in his Declaration. *Cong. Globe,* 33d Cong., 1st Sess., Appendix, 212–14, Feb. 20, 1854; 33d Cong., 2d Sess., Appendix, 234-37, Feb. 23, 1855. Quarrels over the Declaration of Independence as a symbol of liberal egalitarianism occurred often during these years, and many did not hesitate to reject the Declaration's apparent inclusive meaning. Ex-Governor James Hammond of South Carolina similarly wrote in the 1840s that the "much lauded but nowhere accredited dogma of Mr. Jefferson, that 'all men are born equal'" was "ridiculously absurd" (Horsman, 1981, 125, 250, 275, 298–99; see also Arieli, 1964, 254, 267; Fredrickson, 1971, 100–101, 125–27). Francis Paul Prucha has persistently argued against Reginald Horsman that the ideas of scientific racism were influential only with an idiosyncratic few and never affected American policy-making, especially in regard to Native Americans (see, e.g., Prucha, 1984, 336–38). He is surely right that the language of evangelical Protestantism was more dominant; but Horsman's evidence of the interest in American ethnology on the part of clergymen and in leading periodicals indicates that these ideas were often merged.

23. Genovese, 1971, 118–244; Fields, 1990, 116–17. Genovese presents Fitzhugh as the "logical outcome" of proslavery arguments that moved from "a focus on racial caste to a focus on social class." He insists repeatedly that "Negro slavery" was a genuinely "peripheral" concern to Fitzhugh, and claims that Fitzhugh "tacked an extreme racism" that "would have revolted him a few years earlier" onto his slavery defense only after the war (118, 196, 210, 235). In doing so, however, he ignores entirely the racist passages from Fitzhugh's first major work, discussed below, and he also has to dismiss Fitzhugh's call for European labor to support black slavery as self-contradictory.

24. Calhoun, 1953, 42–43; Fitzhugh, 1965, 83–84, 95, 262–67. Fitzhugh cited scriptural authority for slavery, and attacked the "infidel" and "arborescently fallacious" views of both Locke and Jefferson on equal rights, at length (109–17, 175–93). Calhoun attempted his own account of the physiological inferiority of blacks based on misreadings of inaccurate data in the 1840 census, producing arguments that were demolished by several scholars, including Dr. James McCune Smith, a black graduate of the medical school of the University of Glasgow (Delany, 1968, 110–11; Litwack, 1961, 40–46; Franklin & Moss, 1988, 152).

25. George Fredrickson has concurred that the "overwhelming majority of antebellum Southerners," who owned few if any slaves and hated aristocracy among whites, were not greatly attracted to "seigneurial" themes that could justify slavery for poor whites (even though

Fitzhugh reassured them that it was "very unwise and unscientific to govern white men as you would negroes"). Despite Fields's objections, it thus seems correct to call the "dominant political ideology" of the Jacksonians a "*Herrenvolk* egalitarianism" promising equality among whites and the dominance of whites over blacks and Native Americans, as Fredrickson argues. Some poorer whites doubtless perceived that, as Fields notes, Jacksonian leaders pursued racial domination far more ardently than full white equality; but many remained loyal because Jacksonians still championed white democracy more than most Whigs. Fitzhugh, 1965, 94; Fredrickson, 1971, 61–68; cf. Fields, 1990, 114n14, 116nn.43–45; Saxton, 1990, 148–50; McCurry, 1992, 1260–64.

26. Aristocratically inclined Southerners often preferred the term *Anglo-Norman*, connecting their origins to what they took to be a more noble line, and some of this group were wary about expansion, though the widely read Southern journalist William Gilmore Simms promoted it ferociously. Writers linked both "Anglo-Saxons" and "Anglo-Normans" to ancient Teutonic ancestors (Horsman, 1981, 27–29, 164–71, 182–84, 217, 289–97).

27. Van Evrie, 1853, 18. Against the Whigs, Van Evrie insisted that American superiority was "alone or mainly" racial in origin, rather than stemming from "Puritan sermons or Puritan morals." Cf. Tuveson, 1968, 125–27, 151–52; Howe, 1979, 140; Horsman, 1981, 208–9, 213–16, 235.

28. *Cong. Globe*, Appendix, 28th Cong., 1st Sess., 551 (May 20, 1844); Appendix, 28th Cong., 2d Sess., 97 (Jan. 14, 1845); Takaki, 1993, 173–76.

29. Rep. Washington Hunt of New York, *Cong. Globe*, 29th Cong., 2d. Sess., Appendix, 409 (Feb. 13, 1847). See also Sen. Berrien of Georgia in *Cong. Globe*, 29th Cong., 2d Sess., 329–31 (Feb. 5, 1847); Daniel Webster in *Cong. Globe*, 30th Cong., 1st Sess., 534–35 (March 23, 1848). Even the German-American political scientist Francis Lieber—who rejected Know-Nothingism, ardently supported the North in the Civil War, and was in many respects a voice for a historicized but recognizably humanitarian liberalism—still accepted innate racial differences and immigration restrictions that extended to exclusion of Asians. Curti, 1955, 129–30, 146; Fredrickson, 1971, 101; Howe, 1979, 38, 92–94, 140–41, 202–3; Horsman, 1981, 171–73, 182, 229–31.

30. The preceding three paragraphs draw on Arieli, 1964, 296; Nagel, 1971, 133–34, 141–42; Rossiter, 1971, 234–36; Howe, 1979, 5, 12–19, 37, 93–94, 134–38, 140–41, 200, 300; Kelley, 1979, 162–63, 182–92; E. Foner, 1980, 15–33, 43–53; Horsman, 1981, 87, 182; Wiebe, 1984, 358–65; Norton, 1986, 66; D. H. Bennett, 1988, 32–33; Saxton, 1990, 59–60, 64, 67, 103, 132–33, 143, 147; Silbey, 1991, 77–88; Anbinder, 1992, 14–19.

31. These were all points of difference between the Whigs and most of their Republican and abolitionist successors, who revived Locke, treated the Declaration as the nation's birth certificate, and accepted a somewhat more secular social vision. Lincoln, 1905–06, v. 2, 253, 274; Webster, 1923, 143–44, 148; E. Foner, 1970, 290; Fredrickson, 1971, 126–27; Howe, 1979, 69–70, 81–83, 211, 227–36, 291, 302; Norton, 1986, 87, 264, 268; Saxton, 1990, 68–69.

32. Fredrickson, 1971, 101; Howe, 1979, 38–39, 202; Horsman, 1981, 87–89, 172–73; Stephanson, 1995, 48–63.

33. Lincoln, 1905–06, v. 1, 154–55, 160; Webster, 1923, 142–44; Arieli, 1964, 246–47; E. Foner, 1970, 229; Howe, 1979, 19–21, 35, 69–70; Horsman, 1981, 5, 300–301; Wiebe, 1984, 321–22, 346–47; Norton, 1986, 29, 31.

34. *Romanticism* is an umbrella label for a complex, diverse set of intellectual movements that included persons of conservative, liberal, and radical political views. Some were intolerant nationalists; many others valued cultural diversity. But all who sympathized with the romantic revolt against the Enlightenment tended to reject its stress on a narrowly conceived reason and universalism in favor of intuition and particularism, and to focus politically on

distinct national cultures instead of the atomistic individuals commonly attributed to liberal thought.

35. The varying labels for Americans' cultural and racial heritage included Anglo-Saxon, Anglo-Norman, Teutonic, Scandinavian, and Nordic, but always with the understanding that the American branch was the vanguard of all the rest. Curti, 1955, 126–27; Arieli, 1964, 267; Fredrickson, 1971, 97–98; Tuveson, 1968, 143–49; Nagel, 1971, 88–90, 97; Howe, 1979, 164, 283–84, 295–96; Horsman, 1981, 27–28, 38–40, 65, 81, 97, 158–64.

36. This is not to deny that romantic notions conditioned Jacksonian as well as Whig thought. Democratic authors like historian George Bancroft, Walt Whitman, and Herman Melville, along with kindred transcendentalist New England intellectuals like the Whig-leaning Ralph Waldo Emerson, were heavily influenced by romantic outlooks. And though these figures often endorsed romanticism's esteem for true individuality and cultural diversity rather than legal systems of racial hierarchy, they still tended to reinforce beliefs in the superiority of white, Anglo-Saxon American "democratic" culture and its providential Manifest Destiny, by conquest if necessary. Few contemplated equal coexistence with either Native Americans or African-Americans. Hence the political ideology of Anglo-Saxonism that emerged in the 1840s and 1850s was woven from both biological and cultural strands articulated by both Democrats and Whigs. Even so, the Whigs remained the predominant spokesmen for highly nationalistic romantic conceptions of America. Arieli, 1964, 246–47; Tuveson, 1968, 129–31, 156–58; E. Foner, 1970, 229; Howe, 1979, 19–21, 35, 69–70, 221; Horsman, 1981, 5, 159–63, 177–78, 183, 255–56; Wiebe, 1984, 321–22, 346–47; Beer, 1984; Kateb, 1984; McLoughlin, 1986, xv–xvii; Norton, 1986, 29, 31; Saxton, 1990, 146–49.

37. As George Fredrickson points out, the romantic racialists' "mixture of cant, condescension and sentimentality" closely resembled the "popular nineteenth-century view of womanly virtue." The resemblance is unsurprising, as both were part of the romantic paternalist conceptions of American Anglo-Saxon male superiority that the Whigs especially elaborated. Clay, 1842, 379, 451–55; Lincoln, 1905–06, v. 1, 131; Tocqueville, 1969, 291, 590–93, 597–98, 600–603; E. Foner, 1970, 233–36, 259; Fredrickson, 1971, 2, 12–16, 61, 68, 100, 125–29, 135–37; Bender, 1978, 88; Howe, 1979, 35, 38–39, 202–3; Degler, 1980, 8–9, 26–29; Horsman, 1981, 250, 298–99, 300–301.

38. Howe, 1979, 224–25, 238, 246–49; D. H. Bennett, 1988, 87–88, 111–13; Anbinder, 1992, 15–16.

39. Beecher, 1835, 154; D. H. Bennett, 1988, 81, 103–29; Le Beau, 1991, 111–12; Anbinder, 1992, 103–18.

40. Morse, 1969, 7–9, 17–22, 28; Le Beau, 1991, 103–6. Morse did admit the possibility that a long-time naturalized citizen might "become an American in reality, and not merely by profession" (24). See also Morse, 1977, 22–32, 57–58, 148–50.

41. D. H. Bennett, 1988, 76–78, 130; Roediger, 1991, 136–37; Anbinder, 1992, 6–7, 45–46; Takaki, 1993, 149–54.

42. Beecher, 1835, 63–64, 69, 130–31, 155–59, 175–76; Monk, 1962; Stowe, 1965; Tuveson, 1968, 169–73; Mabee, 1969, 342–51; Daniels, 1990, 266–70; Le Beau, 1991, 108. Lyman Beecher was the father of Harriet Beecher Stowe as well as the educator Catharine Beecher and several abolitionist preachers, with Henry Ward Beecher the best known. Collectively they played remarkably influential and complex roles in American discussions of race, ethnicity, and gender during the nineteenth century.

43. Lincoln, 1905–06, v. 2, 246–47, 253; D. H. Bennett, 1988, 50–60, 110–16, 131; Anbinder, 1992, 10–17, 86–87. Bennett notes that proslavery "Silver Gray" Whigs provided nativist votes in New York in the 1850s and that nativists drew in the South on proslavery Whigs there, though elsewhere many Know-Nothings were antislavery. Anbinder stresses that the

New York pattern was unique in the North and that nativism was predominantly Northern, so that Know-Nothings should generally be viewed as drawing most heavily on antislavery "Conscience" Whigs. Both argue, however, that the most ardently antislavery Whigs like Seward and Lincoln were also antinativist (D. H. Bennett, 1988, 131).

44. Hutchinson, 1981, 622; D. H. Bennett, 1988, 110–16; Anbinder, 1992, 52–102, 106, 121–25, 140–41.
45. D. H. Bennett, 1988, 118–23, 152–54; Anbinder, 1992, 162–219.
46. Jaffa, 1982, 28–37; Nagel, 1971, 134, 141–42, 151; M. L. Wilson, 1974, 12–19, 115–16, 124–26, 205; Kelley, 1979, 178–82; E. Foner, 1980, 34–53; Wiebe, 1984, 357–75; Oakes, 1985, 569–71; Baker, 1984, 532–33.
47. Meyers, 1960, 254–58; Rossiter, 1971, 140, 154, 183, 200; Huntington, 1981, 224.
48. Wisconsin's initial 1848 constitution pioneered the inclusive new policy of granting the franchise to those who had become declarant aliens under the nation's naturalization laws, which required such a declaration of intent at least two years prior to admission to citizenship. By 1861 Indiana, Kansas, Louisiana, Minnesota, and Oregon had followed suit, adding residency qualifications of varying lengths, and similar measures had narrowly been defeated in Michigan and Illinois. Although voting by men who were as yet aliens ran contrary to the xenophobic strains in much classical republican thought, the concerns to attract population that had motivated the precedent of alien voting in many territories remained, reinforced by the Democrats' political reliance on immigrants. Thus the trend accelerated through these years, even though alien voting provided ammunition for the ascending nativist forces to the east. C. Williamson, 1960, 277; Porter, 1971, 119–34; Shade, 1981, 78–79.
49. Widows and *femes soles* subject to taxation for school purposes gained the vote in Kentucky in 1838, beginning a slow movement toward suffrage in school-related elections for women that really began to grow only in the 1870s. Woody, 1929, v. 2, 442; C. Williamson, 1960, 260; Porter, 1971, 78; Elliott, 1974, 35, 40, 43.
50. Ten states entered the Union between Jackson's election and the early years of the Civil War—in the 1830s, Arkansas and Michigan, in the 1840s, Iowa, Florida, Texas, and Wisconsin, in the 1850s, California, Minnesota, and Oregon, and in 1861, "Bleeding Kansas." None had property or taxpaying qualifications. During the same period, the four of the five existing states that still had property tests abandoned them, Tennessee in 1834, Rhode Island in 1843, New Jersey in 1844, and Virginia in 1855 (and as of 1856, North Carolina retained only a fifty-acre freehold requirement for state senate elections). Mississippi, Louisiana, Ohio, and Connecticut all dropped their taxpaying requirements during these years, leaving such regulations only in Massachusetts, Rhode Island, Pennsylvania, Delaware, and North Carolina, where they were not significant barriers to voting for many. Taxpaying qualifications lasted longest because they could be defended (usually by Whigs) with arguments that the Revolution's principles linked taxation and representation, in both directions—and that in any case the requirements were easily met. Their critics, usually Democrats, often blended republican contentions with more individualistic liberal rights arguments by holding that voting was a "natural right," at least of white male citizens. C. Williamson, 1960, 264–69; Krout, 1966, 173–74; Porter, 1971, 105–11; Elliott, 1974, 36, 39–43.
51. C. M. Green, 1962, 159, 162–63, 173–74.
52. Oligarchic Rhode Island thus became the only state to repeal a disfranchisement of blacks before the Civil War. Naturalized citizens were later made eligible but subjected to freehold requirements. Porter, 1971, 101–2; C. Williamson, 1960, 242–58; P. Foner, 1983a, 209, 343–46; Shade, 1981, 78.

53. The case involved Martin Luther, moderator at the Dorrites' "people's election," versus Luther Borden, who searched Luther's home on behalf of the existing regime and harassed his female relatives. Luther claimed that the established government giving Borden his orders was illegitimate because it was unrepublican, not truly chosen by the people. *Luther v. Borden* (7 How. 1, 1849); C. Williamson, 1960, 242–57; Porter, 1971, 94–97, 101; Wiecek, 1972, 86–123; Elliott, 1974, 47–53; Howe, 1979, 18. George Dennison has argued with some force that by permitting the other branches to recognize an oligarchic state regime operating under a charter that had no provisions for amendment, the Taney Court contributed to what he sees as a widespread *rejection* during these years of egalitarian versions of republicanism emphasizing popular sovereignty, "out of doors" if necessary. He thus believes that the decision strengthened more Whiggish views stressing respect for established legal institutions (Dennison, 1976). Though the strongest forms of populist republicanism were implicitly rejected, the controversy still led Rhode Island to establish a more egalitarian suffrage by the time of the Court's decision, and arguments for property qualifications were discredited throughout the land in its wake. Hence I believe that the Dorr War reinforced, not repudiated, less radical but still significantly democratic Jacksonian civic conceptions.

54. *Cong. Globe,* Appendix, 29th Cong., 1st Sess., 605, 619 (1845); C. Williamson, 1960, 295; F. G. Franklin, 1969, 247, 258–64, 278–300; Porter, 1971, 118–19; Elliott, 1974, 43–44; Anbinder, 1992, 138, 248, 254.

55. By 1861, twenty of the thirty-four states prevented servicemen from voting, generally by not counting their stationing as residence. Seven states similarly denied college students the vote. F. G. Franklin, 1969, 264; Porter, 1971, 146–49; Elliott, 1974, 40, 43–44; Anbinder, 1992, 107–9.

56. Philip Foner states that New York's $250 freehold requirement left 84 of New York City's 15,061 blacks eligible to vote in 1835. In 1855 the numbers were 100 of 11,840 blacks. P. Foner, 1983a, 173, 207–9, 337–46; see also Williamson, 1960, 235, 278; Porter, 1971, 80–90, 117, 123–127, 131, 148; Elliott, 1974, 40–44.

57. By 1860 it was 57.7 percent, and in 1870, 61.1 percent. After Massachusetts pioneered the first compulsory attendance law in 1852, other areas bolstered enrollments via such measures, though enforcement was lax. And because high schools were generally available only in urban areas and were everywhere poorly attended, the percentage of enrollment among those of elementary school age was undoubtedly higher. In the North and much of the midwest, enrollment was close to 50 percent even if nonwhites are included. Cremin, 1980, 156, 165, 178, 488; Kaestle, 1983, 106–7, 120–21; A. Green, 1990, 182–87.

58. C. M. Green, 1962, 161–62, 184–85, 214.

59. Cremin, 1980, 215, 300–302; Kaestle, 1983, 23–24; A. Green, 1990, 188–90.

60. Various scholars following Michael Katz have sparked lively debate by arguing that bourgeois or capitalist concerns to socialize, train, and control workers were most important in the public school movement. Carl Kaestle argues that reformers blended all these concerns into a relatively coherent "native Protestant ideology" that aimed at achieving competent, virtuous citizens and workers through ethnocultural assimilation—a formulation that tends to make Whiggish ascriptive Americanist goals appear decisive. Katz, 1968; Kaestle, 1983, x, 91–103.

61. The Boston system strove to lead "the human being . . . upward by gradations as simple and beautiful as its own growth," until it produced "an American citizen complete." Cremin, 1980, 498–99; Kaestle, 1983, 61, 97–98, 120; Battistoni, 1985, 62; Norton, 1986, 81–84.

62. Blau, ed., 1954, 150, 152, 337; Howe, 1979, 36; Kaestle, 1983, 138–41; A. Green, 1990, 191–93.

63. Blau, ed., 1954, xvii–xviii; Cremin, 1980, 157; Kaestle, 1983, 63, 97, 140–41, 146; Norton, 1986, 43; A. Green, 1990, 194–97.

64. Nagel, 1971, 60–71; Cremin, 1980, 383; Kaestle, 1983, 56–57, 90–93, 95, 97, 102–3; Wiebe, 1984, 331–32. Richard Battistoni has usefully contrasted "liberal" and "participatory republican" conceptions of democratic civic education. He identifies a focus on "moral education" as fundamentally liberal, leading citizens to be law-abiding but not politically active. As he points out, however, liberals like Locke thought that such moral education was best provided in the home, and they were suspicious of public schools. While nineteenth-century American middle-class reformers emphasized moral education, and did so more to promote self-control than political participation, they all urged such education via common schools. They also stressed its role in developing political values and cognitive skills needed for republican citizenship. Hence they appear at an intermediate point between Battistoni's "liberal" and "participatory republican" ideal types (Battistoni, 1985, 33–34). I suggest, however, that this intermediate placement is better understood by recognizing how their Americanist objectives of sustaining the primacy of middle-class Anglo-Saxon Protestant values provided much of the steam of the public school movement.

65. Cremin, 1980, 157–59, 177; Kaestle, 1983, 56–57, 111–14, 147–48, 153–56, 192–217; Norton, 1986, 27–28; D. H. Bennett, 1988, 56–57; A. Green, 1990, 190–92, 198–202; Le Beau, 1991, 108.

66. This development also led to school principals, who were originally men designated the "principal" teacher among largely female staffs. Cremin, 1980, 143–45, 166–71, 372; Kaestle, 1983, 84–87, 123–24, 161–70; A. Green, 1990, 203–7.

67. Du Bois, 1992, 638.

68. Litwack, 1961, 113–52. Northern ambivalence toward black education is well illustrated by *Crandall v. State of Connecticut*, 10 Conn. 339, 347–48, 366–68 (1834), noted in relation to black citizenship in ch. 9. Connecticut passed a law in 1833 preventing the establishment of schools for "coloured persons, who are not inhabitants of this state," with a view toward "preventing the increase of this population." The law was prompted by public furor over Prudence Crandall's school, founded with the aid of William Lloyd Garrison and other leading abolitionists. They protested that the act violated the privileges and immunities of out-of-state black citizens. The trial judge informed the jury that blacks were not citizens, and they found the act constitutional; but that verdict was overturned on appeal, because the state's Supreme Court of Errors interpreted the statute as applying only to unlicensed schools, and the record did not indicate whether Crandall had a license. The law could be more plausibly construed, however, as requiring not a general license but rather explicit consent by certain authorities to teaching out-of-state, blacks, which had clearly not been granted. Hence the state supreme court's ruling appears to exhibit more sympathy for black education than the state legislature had felt. Nonetheless, the opposition she encountered led Crandall to abandon her school (P. Foner, 1983a, 217–18).

69. Cremin, 1980, 228–45; Kaestle, 1983, 171–79, 196–97; P. Foner, 1983a, 177–79, 187, 217–33, 326–37; Prucha, 1984, 151–54, 222–26, 231–41, 272, 283–92, 317–23.

70. *Capitalism* captures at least an aspect of liberal ideology; *Protestantism,* when made definitive for civic education, forms part of an ascriptive conception of American citizenship; and Kaestle uses *republicanism* much as I have employed it. In a comparative study, British scholar Andy Green similarly concludes: "As in Europe, education in America played an important part in the formation of nationhood and state. . . . Schools functioned above all to legitimate the values of popular capitalism, to assimilate minorities into the ascendant Protestant culture, and to instruct men and women into their differentiated roles as citizens." He contends that in Europe coercion was harshest in regard to class hierarchies, in America in regard to racial and ethnic minorities (A. Green, 1990, 201).

71. See, e.g., *Delassus v. U.S.*, 9 Pet. 117, 133 (1835), where Marshall read a treaty's protection of "all the rights, advantages and immunities of citizens of the United States" as unquestionably including "the perfect inviolability and security of property."

72. In *Bonaparte v. Camden & Amboy R.R. Co.*, 3 F. Cas. 821 (U.S.C.C. N.J., 1830), Baldwin wrote that although the Fifth Amendment requirement of just compensation might not apply to the states "as a constitutional provision," nonetheless "it is the declaration of what in its nature is the power of all governments, and the right of its citizens; the one to take property, the other to compensation. The obligation attaches to the exercise of the power," regardless of whether it is explicitly imposed by state or national law (828).

73. *Barron v. Baltimore*, 7 Pet. 243, 250 (1833).

74. Michael Kent Curtis suggests that the result might also have reflected the Court's unwillingness to arouse Southern fears about federal intervention on behalf of the rights of slaves and abolitionists (Curtis, 1986, 23). The Taney Court later refused to apply the Bill of Rights against the states even when religious freedom, a pillar of Jacksonianism, was at stake. The Court held in *Permoli v. Municipality #1 of the City of New Orleans* that the Constitution "makes no provision for protecting the citizens of the respective states in their religious liberties" (3 How. 589, 609 [1845]).

75. For what they are worth, the Supreme Court's few pertinent comments appeared to point in the direction of treating the provision as a comity clause, not a guarantee of substantive rights of national citizenship. In *Bank of Augusta v. Earle*, 13 Pet. 519 (1839), Chief Justice Taney reasoned in comity fashion when he held that if out-of-state citizens could claim the privileges of in-state citizens, but not their duties, in-state citizens would be improperly disadvantaged (586–87). In *Connor v. Elliott*, 18 How. 591 (1856), the Court considered whether Louisiana had to extend the community property rules it imposed on all marriages occurring in the state to a native-born Louisiana woman who had married and resided in Mississippi. Mrs. Connor wished to claim property that her deceased husband had purchased in Louisiana. Justice Curtis wrote for the Court that Louisiana's laws should be viewed as making certain stipulations for Louisiana marital contracts, not as establishing rights of Louisianan citizenship. Hence he viewed the privileges and immunities clause as irrelevant (at 593–94). That ruling suggests that the question under the clause is whether a state has discriminated against out-of-staters in the rights of citizenship it has created, not whether it has violated some fixed rights of national citizenship (and it militates against finding at least one aspect of "freedom of contract" to be such a national right, as Louisiana's power to regulate marital property agreements was not questioned).

    Curtis also argued that it was "safer, and more in accordance with the duty of a judicial tribunal" to leave the meaning of Art. IV's "privileges" to be "determined, in each case, upon a view of the particular rights asserted and denied therein," because "any merely abstract definition could scarcely be correct" (at 593). Cf. *Smith v. Maryland*, 18 How. 71 (1855); Kettner, 1978, 257–65. For a typical lower court treatment, see *Bennett v. Boggs*, 3 F. Cas. 221, 226 (U.S.C.C.D. N.J., 1830).

76. During his last years, Marshall continued to strike an occasional blow for federal judicial authority and national citizenship. He held in 1832, for example, that a person who had been naturalized into U.S. citizenship did not need to engage in a formal process to acquire state citizenship; mere residency was enough. Any additional states' rights requirements would "narrow" federal jurisdiction unacceptably (*Gassies v. Gassies Ballon*, 6 Pet. 761–62 [1832]). As indicated in, e.g., *Prentiss v. Brennan*, 19 F. Cas. 1278–80 (U.S.C.C. N.Y., 1851), a fixed residence or domicile in a state was required for U.S. citizenship to include citizenship in that state, whereas territorial residents and District of Columbia inhabitants could be U.S. citizens only, as Marshall had earlier ruled.

77. Marshall continued to uphold the *Bingham v. Cabot* requirements for clear averment of diverse state citizenship, long stressed by Bushrod Washington. Subsequently the Taney Court was somewhat less stringent. See, e.g., *Brown v. Keene*, 8 Pet. 112 (1834); cf. *Evans v. Davenport*, 8 F. Cas. 845 (U.S.C.C. Mich., 1849) (expressing opposition to Washington's views). Cf. also *Bank of U.S. v. Martin*, 30 U.S. 479 (1831), in which Marshall refused to uphold a district court's jurisdiction in a case involving a branch Bank of the United States because Congress had given jurisdiction only to the circuit courts, with *Irvine ex rel. Lumberman's Bank v. Lowry*, 39 U.S. 293 (1840), in which the Taney Court strained to find jurisdiction in a case involving a bank with some stockholders having the same state citizenship as the plaintiff.

78. Sometimes, of course, the Court both claimed jurisdiction and overruled state officials. See, e.g., *McNutt v. Bland and Humphreys*, 43 U.S. 9 (1844), where a seven-man majority permitted New Yorkers to sue Mississippi sheriff Richard Bland under the name of Mississippi's governor for damages to be paid out of a bond that Bland had posted with the governor. The Court overlooked the technical designation of the case to recognize it as in reality a dispute between citizens of different states. States' rights champion Justice Daniel fumed in dissent. For the more general pattern, see, e.g., *Suydam v. Broadnax*, 14 Pet. 67, 74–75 (1840); *Burnham v. Rangeley*, 4 F. Cas. 773, 775 (U.S.C.C. Me., 1845); *Shelton v. Tiffin*, 6 How. 103, 188 (1848); *Evans v. Davenport*, 8 F. Cas. 845 (U.S.C.C. Mich., 1849); *Union Bank v. Jolly*, 18 How. 503, 506–7 (1855).

79. As such, these cases could be cited as evidence of the hegemony of liberal capitalist outlooks during this era, but Hartzians have generally missed that opportunity. I agree that they show the power of commitments to market capitalism shared by Jacksonians as well as Whigs; but they also reveal the intense continuing regional and ideological contestation over those commitments, especially within Democratic ranks.

80. Hurst, 1970, 25–34; Trachtenberg, 1982, 4–7; Friedman, 1985, 197; Barzelay & Smith, 1987, 90.

81. Blau, ed., 1954, 71–72, 163, 222, 233–34; Trachtenberg, 1982, 83–84; Barzelay & Smith, 1987, 91.

82. Friedman, 1985, 188–98; Barzelay & Smith, 1987, 94, 97–101.

83. The pattern developed slowly. In *Commercial and Rail Road Bank of Vicksburg v. Slocomb*, 39 U.S. 60 (1840), for example, the Taney Court looked carefully at the state citizenships of all corporate stockholders on both sides of the controversy, as the Marshall Court had done, and denied federal jurisdiction because there were Louisiana citizens on both sides. But subsequent developments were more influenced by the important case of *Bank of Augusta v. Earle*, 13 Pet. 519 (1839). There Taney ruled not on jurisdiction, but on whether a corporation chartered in one state could contract in another. He held that it could, consistent with any express restrictions in its charter or in the law of the state in which it contracted. To reach that conclusion, Taney contended that although a corporation was a "mere artificial being, invisible and intangible, yet it is a person, for certain purposes in contemplation of law" (587–88, 595–97). He did so chiefly to stress that a corporation's contracting powers were its own, not capacities of the natural persons who constituted it, and as such were limited by its chartered powers, not coextensive with the full rights of natural persons. Taney did not want corporations to be able to claim all the privileges and immunities of full citizens, yet he did wish them to be able to contract when the states had not legislated otherwise. The effect of his decision, however, was to advance corporate claims to full legal "personhood," if not citizenship (Dodd, 1954, 151–52; Barzelay & Smith, 1987, 97–100).

84. *Louisville, Cincinnati, and Charleston Railroad Co. v. Letson*, 43 U.S. 497 (1844).

85. *Letson* at 551–52, 555, 558. For criticism see McGovney, 1943a, 873–83.

86. The *Letson* rule was particularly important because it came two years after Justice Story's famed decision in *Swift v. Tyson*, 16 Pet. 1 (1842). That case allowed the federal courts to rely on "general principles and doctrines of commercial jurisprudence" (18–19), not simply the law of the states in which they sat, to decide commercial law subjects. It thereby enabled the federal courts to generate a uniform national body of commercial law, to which corporations could resort against hostile state rules once *Letson* guaranteed them access to federal courts. Like *Letson*, *Swift* was decided without dissent, but became controversial as its nationalistic and pro-corporate potentials became clear (McGovney, 1943a, 884–85; Hyman & Wiecek, 1982, 71–74).

87. *Rundle v. Delaware and Raritan Canal Co.*, 18 How. 80, 95, 98–99, 101 (1852). Daniel, an opponent of liberalizing changes and national power in many forms, was harshly consistent with this stance when he denied married women even "quasi" citizenship in *Barber v. Barber,* as noted below.

88. In *Northern Indiana Railroad Co. v. Michigan Central Railroad Co.*, 15 How. 233, 246, 248–49 (1853), the majority decided the case on grounds apart from corporate citizenship. But Catron returned to the issue, reiterating that while the "fugitive stockholders" of corporations should not be viewed as its "members" for jurisdictional purposes, jurisdiction must rest on the citizenship of its officers. Otherwise, he warned, owners whose corporations operated in another state could drag "their next neighbors" into federal court by suing them in the corporation's name. Thus corporations could augment their legal powers improperly while also fostering unwarranted intrusions by the national judiciary into the domestic disputes of state citizens.

89. For the Court, Justice Robert Grier of Pennsylvania defended the new presumption of common state citizenship for all of a corporation's members on a populist ground. To ensure "impartial justice" for people who dealt with "powerful corporations," he argued, they had to be able to sue those corporations in federal courts, not the courts of the state or city where a corporation might have great influence. *Marshall v. Baltimore and Ohio Railroad Co.,* 16 How. 314, 236–28, 339, 343, 345–47 (1853); McGovney, 1943a, 885–89.

90. *Dodge v. Woolsey,* 18 How. (59 U.S.) 331 (1855) at 341, 354. See also *Mechanics' and Traders' Bank v. Debolt,* 59 U.S. 380 (1855).

91. Campbell was joined by Catron and Daniels. He derided the Court's willingness to say both that it presumed all the bank's stockholders were citizens of Ohio, and that stockholder Woolsey nonetheless had standing to sue as a citizen of Connecticut. Campbell called this an "invented" and "very compendious method" of gratifying the "morbid appetite for jurisdiction" of those "artificial beings" whenever they thought federal courts "more favorable to their pretensions." Campbell also cited Bentham's utilitarian arguments against treating contracts as so sacrosanct that every "misdeed" should be protected against "the powers of the people." The consequence, Campbell thundered, was to "establish on the soil of every State a caste made up of combinations of men . . . who will habitually look beyond . . . the authorities of the State to the central government" for the protection of "their special privileges and exemptions." Those privileges would stir "alienation and discord between the different classes" that might end in violence. Corporations, after all, displayed "durable dispositions for evil," preferring their own interests to "moral or political principles or public duties" and to "individual freedom." Better to deny that a corporation could be a citizen of the United States in any constitutional sense. *Dodge v. Woolsey* at 365–66, 369, 371–72, 375; McGovney, 1943a, 889–98.

92. In subsequent cases during the decade, the Taney majority followed the Marshall pattern by repeatedly asserting that considering corporations to be citizens could "have no sensible meaning" and was "simply impossible," even as it constantly found even infelicitously

phrased averments sufficient to grant corporations standing to sue (*LaFayette Insurance Co. v. French*, 18 How. 404–9 (1855): *Covington Drawbridge Co. v. Shepherd*, 20 How. 227, 233–34 (1857); *Philadelphia, Wilmington, and Baltimore Railroad v. Quigley*, 21 How. 202, 214 (1858). Of the dissenters, Justice Daniel proved most unrelenting. In *Quigley* he expressed particular ire because a joint railroad company formed from companies chartered in three separate states was allowed to sue as if it were a resident citizen of one, a stretch he thought a complete surrender to corporate wishes. But the company was also held sufficiently similar to natural persons to be responsible for libel, confirming that corporate personality and citizenship involved bitter as well as sweet consequences (218, 220).

93. *Smith v. Turner* and *Norris v. City of Boston*, decided together as *The Passenger Cases* at 7 How. 283 (1849); Barth, 1964, 72.

94. Hutchinson, 1981, 24, 35–39. In *Spratt v. Spratt*, 4 Pet. 393 (1830), for example, Marshall held for the Court that when naturalization questions were involved only indirectly in a case, the admitting court's decision in regard to naturalization would be treated as final. Otherwise, Marshall indicated, property titles would be rendered too insecure (at 408). This concern not to let citizenship questions jeopardize liberal personal property rights was characteristic of Marshall. The Court also strove in other ways to achieve settled legal rules and thereby avoid complicated naturalization questions. See, e.g., its technical approach to inheritance questions involving naturalization in cases like *Lessee of Mordecai Levy v. M'Cartee*, 6 Pet. 102, 109 (1832). According to press reports, a federal district court in San Francisco refused to find a Chinese applicant eligible for naturalization in 1855 due to the "white" requirement. Officially reported cases on the issue do not arise until after the Civil War (Takaki, 1993, 207).

95. F. G. Franklin, 1969, 184–300; Swisher, 1969, 205–7; Perlmutter, 1977, 44; Hutchinson, 1981, 25–46, 397–407, 410–11; Archdeacon, 1983, 37–38, 45, 70–82, 148; Neuman, 1993, 1843–44, 1848–49, 1855–56; Takaki, 1993, 178–79, 194–96.

96. 11 Pet. 102 (1837); but see *Holmes v. Jennison*, 14 Pet. 540 (1840), discussed below.

97. *Smith v. Turner* and *Norris v. City of Boston*, decided as the *Passenger Cases* at 7 How. 283 (1849); F. G. Franklin, 1969, 260, 98; Hyman & Wiecek, 1982, 78–82; Neuman, 1993, 1850–51.

98. Justice Wayne later denied that Barbour's opinion should be deemed the opinion of the Court. See *Passenger Cases* at 428–33; Hyman & Wiecek, 1982, 78–80.

99. The aged Justice Story dissented fiercely. He argued that the regulations were indeed commercial and that authority over interstate commerce was exclusively confined to the federal government. His view would have also bolstered federal authority over citizenship questions and maintained open immigration, though preservation of national commercial authority was probably Story's chief concern. Justice Thompson took an intermediate position, holding that the state could enact these regulations, but only because Congress had not exercised its authority over commerce in preemptive ways.

100. Justice McLean viewed the laws as commercial regulations, and he (alone) held that Congress's power over commerce was wholly exclusive (*Passenger Cases* at 400). Justices Wayne, Catron, McKinley, and Grier believed that although states could sometimes act on commercial matters, various existing congressional policies preempted these measures (at 411, 452, 463).

101. *Passenger Cases* at 427–28. Wayne referred explicitly to the slave regulation powers dealt with in *Groves v. Slaughter* and *Prigg v. Commonwealth of Pennsylvania* (see chapter 9). All the justices involved in the case had been appointed by Democrats except for Samuel Nelson, a New York Democrat appointed by the pseudo-Whig John Tyler. Nelson voted in dissent to uphold his state's laws.

102. *Passenger Cases* at 440–42, 452–54.

103. The complexity of these citizenship issues is further indicated by the fact that Taney wrote for Story and two of his opponents here, McLean and Wayne, in an earlier case where the Court divided evenly, *Holmes v. Jennison* (14 Pet. 540, 1840). (Justice McKinley did not participate.) Holmes was a Canadian whom the state of Vermont arrested and turned over to Canadian authorities so that he could be tried for murder there. Taney viewed this not as an exercise of the police power but as an unconstitutional state intrusion on federal regulation of intercourse with foreign nations. Justice Thompson thought that federal habeas corpus relief was unavailable, and he, Barbour, and Catron thought that in the absence of a preemptive federal treaty this state action was legitimate. Justice Baldwin went further, arguing that the Congress could *compel* a state to surrender an alien but could not intrude on its sovereign police powers by *preventing* it from doing so. In the absence of a Supreme Court ruling, the state's expulsion stood, but the case set no clear precedent.

   Taney's vote is hard to explain. Apparently he viewed extradition of criminals to foreign nations as a matter well removed from state power over slaves and free blacks, so that he did not feel his usual need to assert states' rights.

104. Justice Nelson simply concurred with Taney, whereas Justices Daniel and Woodbury (of New Hampshire) added separate dissents elaborating on the limits of congressional power over migration and the state police powers, respectively.

105. Tsiang, 1942, 71–82.

106. *Inglis v. Trustees of Sailor's Snug Harbour,* 3 Pet. 99 (1830); *Shanks v. DuPont,* 3 Pet. 242 (1830).

107. Justice Story's concurrence in *Inglis* insisted with Coke and Blackstone that nothing was "better settled at the common law than the doctrine that the children even of aliens born in a country, while the parents are resident there under the protection of the government, and owing a temporary allegiance thereto, are subjects by birth." But like Justice Thompson's opinion for the Court, Story accepted that the 1783 settlement had properly treated Vattel's "natural" doctrines of consensual membership, not the temporarily suspended common law, as valid under the special circumstances of the war. Accordingly, Inglis had been bound in his minority by the choice of his loyalist father; and as he never indicated any other preference as an adult, he was a British subject. (*Inglis* at 123–25, 155–56, 159, 164). Writing for the Court in *Shanks,* Story reiterated that the "general doctrine is, that no persons can, by any act of their own, without the consent of the government, put off their allegiance and become aliens." But Shanks, too, had exercised her special elective right by moving to Britain.

108. *Shanks* at 258–62. In *Inglis* (135), Johnson argued that New York had kept the common law in force when it succeeded to the birthright allegiance that Inglis owed his sovereign, and that Inglis had no right to alter his nationality.

109. Guadalupe Hidalgo Treaty of Peace, Art. VIII (Tate, ed., 1969); *U.S. v. Ritchie,* 17 How. 525 (1854).

110. Specifically, circuit court judge Matthew McAllister held that Forbes, an English-born, naturalized Mexican citizen, could not have his allegiance automatically transferred to the U.S. even though he had failed to reject this transfer explicitly, as the treaty's Art. VIII seemed to require. Birth, McAllister argued, gives a man a "natural allegiance to his native soil, and such allegiance gives, by the principles of universal law, to the country in which he was born rights unknown" to the nation he had voluntarily elected to join. When Mexico relinquished its claims over Forbes, then, he reverted to his birthright British status under the "law of nature," and none of Mexico's stipulations about how his further choices were to be interpreted had any force. *Tobin v. Walkinshaw,* 23 F. Cas. 1346, 1348–49 (U.S.C.C. Cal., 1856).

111. In 1839 the Kentucky Court of Appeals accepted that the government could "regulate the mode of expatriation," but it insisted that despite the "doctrines of feudal governments or ages," the right of expatriation was "a practical and fundamental doctrine of America." American allegiance was "altogether conventional," and could "be repudiated by the native as well as adopted citizen with the presumed concurrence of the government without its formal or expressed sanction." The case's facts paralleled *Shanks:* Mrs. Alsberry had moved with her husband from Kentucky to Texas in 1824, when it was not yet part of the United States. Her husband died there soon after, but she remained until 1836, when on a temporary visit to Kentucky she claimed dower in land as a nonresident citizen. Even though no special "period of election" could be claimed, the court held that she had voluntarily expatriated herself (*Alsberry v. Hawkins,* 9 Dana [Ky.] 177–78 [1839]). In contrast, a New York court rejected claims based on Vattel's consensualist views in *Lynch v. Clarke* (1844). It held that Julia Lynch, the daughter of a temporarily resident Irishman, was an American citizen simply by fact of her birth on U.S. soil. Like Justice Johnson in *Shanks,* the presiding judge here, Assistant Vice Chancellor Lewis Sandford, criticized "the theory of the formation of states and governments, by voluntary compact of their inhabitants," with "unqualified" rights of "throwing off allegiance by birth," as a doctrine too dangerous to the state to be sustained. American law followed the common law in regard to the assignment of membership via place of birth. Sandford took no stand on whether the common law also defined American expatriation rights, seeing the courts as divided on that question. Without much explanation, he declared the issue separable (*Lynch v. Clarke,* 1 Sanford 583, 587–99, 673–74 [N.Y., 1844]). Neither the Court nor any of the attorneys involved could locate any prior American court ruling precisely on the point of whether children of temporarily resident aliens were birthright citizens (at 663). Hence the issue was argued at length, in a direct clash of voluntaristic versus common-law ascriptive conceptions of membership. See Schuck & Smith, 1985, 57–62.

112. The Kentucky decision used broad, Democratic-sounding expatriation doctrines to deny title to lands in the state to a woman who had moved away; but she had gone with her husband to Texas when it was still part of Mexico, a choice aiding westward expansion toward which Democratic Kentuckians were not likely to be punitive. The *Lynch* decision made property rights more secure and affirmed naturalistic membership doctrines in good Yankee Whig fashion, but it did so on behalf of the daughter of an Irish immigrant, hardly a favorite of northeastern conservatives.

113. Tsiang, 1942, 61–70; Kettner, 1978, 267–84.

114. Tsiang, 1942, 71–82; James, 1990, 862–63.

115. As discussed further below, Cushing argued in 1856 that Indians and in all likelihood blacks could not be U.S. citizens. When asked "whether the mere fact of a person being born in the United States, constitutes a citizen thereof," he answered, "Clearly not." *Official Opinions of the Attorneys General of the United States,* v. VII, 748–49.

116. Stanton, Anthony, & Gage, 1881, v. 1, 15–16; Litwack, 1961, 221–23; E. Foner, 1970, 2–5, 75–79; Flexner, 1975, 74–75; Cott, 1977, 198–206.

117. Grimké, 1838, 108, 114, 118; Stanton, Anthony, & Gage, 1881, v. 1, 32–40; Flexner, 1975, 45–48.

118. Stanton, Anthony, & Gage, 1881, v. 1, 70–71; Flexner, 1975, 72–74; DuBois, 1978, 22–23; DuBois, 1981, 2, 7–12; Degler, 1980, 303–6; P. Foner, 1983b, 402–3, 409, 442–43, 450–53, 468–72; Dolbeare, ed., 1984, 255–58; McCurry, 1992, 1254–57. It is because Ellen DuBois's otherwise excellent study, *Feminism and Suffrage,* neglected republicanism that she could call the "widespread belief in the importance of the ballot" a "somewhat elusive aspect of the American political tradition" (1978, 42).

119. Even the ardent abolitionist writer Lydia Maria Child, who later petitioned for women's suffrage, agreed with Beecher during the antebellum era that there was probably "no country in the world where women, as wives, sisters, and daughters, have more influence, or more freedom," than in America. Child, 1845, v. 2, 265; Beecher, 1851, 24, 33, 56, 226, 231; Flexner, 1975, 89, 156, 226; Cott, 1977, 5–8, 120–25; Sachs & Wilson, 1978, 81–82; DuBois, 1978, 40–42, 184; Harris, 1978, 78–81, 85; Leach, 1980, 8, 23, 146; Eisenstein, 1981, 162–63; McDonagh, 1994, 62–64.

120. Examples of state judicial resistance to Married Women's Property Acts include *White v. White*, 5 Barb. S.C. 474 (N.Y. Supreme Ct., 1849); *Rice v. Foster*, 4 Harr. 479 (Del., 1847). For discussion of these acts and their litigation, see, e.g., Hyman & Wiecek, 1982, 23, 52–53; Chused, 1983, 1384–1412; Lebsock, 1984, 84–86; Basch, 1986, 97.

121. See, e.g., *Bein v. Heath*, 6 How. 228, 247 (1848), a rare U.S. Supreme Court incursion into marital property law. The case did not involve a Married Women's Property Act, but it did consider a provision codified by Louisiana in 1825 which made a wife independent of the debts of her husband (even when she had professed to underwrite them). The Beins unsuccessfully tried to use this provision to void Mary Bein's obligations to Mary Heath for a loan Mrs. Bein had secured to assist her impecunious husband, Richard.

122. Flexner, 1975, 62–65; Kerber, 1977, 120; Kerber, 1980, 154–61; DuBois, 1978, 41–46; DuBois, 1981, 4–9; Sachs & Wilson, 1978, 78; Leach, 1980, 174, 178; Degler, 1980, 332–33; Taub & Schneider, 1982, 119; Speth, 1982, 66–91; Basch, 1986, 103–4; Friedman, 1985, 205–11, 251.

123. *Shanks v. DuPont*, 3 Pet. 242, 245–46, 248 (1830). Story similarly regarded a divorced couple as having diverse nationalities in *Ex parte Barry*, 2 How. 65 (1844). A New York court held that Congress had the power to naturalize married women, "even against the consent" of their husbands, in *Priest v. Cummings*, 16 Wendell's 617, 627 (N.Y., 1837).

124. *Barber v. Barber* 21 How. 582, 594 (1858).

125. *Barber* at 601–3.

126. It imitated an 1844 English statute, which superseded the parallel common law requirement there, and which rested on similar "domestic sphere" notions (F. G. Franklin, 1969, 275; Sapiro, 1984, 8).

127. F. G. Franklin, 1969, 272–77; Degler, 1980, 26–27, 73; Sapiro, 1984, 8–9.

128. Takaki, 1993, 86–88.

129. Satz, 1975, 112–15, 156–65; Howe, 1979, 40–42; Prucha, 1984, 154, 179–80, 191–99, 214, 242–48, 258–61, 283, 293–94; Wright, 1992, 218–21, 230; Takaki, 1993, 90–97. The Five Civilized Tribes were the Cherokees, Creeks, Choctaws, Chickasaws, and Seminoles; northern tribes included the Brothertons, Kaskaskias, Peorias, Shawnees, Ottawas, Wyandotts, Miamis, Potawatomis, Menominees, Delawares, Sacs and Foxes, Piankashaws, Weas, Kickapoos, Chippewa, Sioux, Stockbridge, and other New York Indians. The most violent conflict probably came during the Seminole War in Florida, augmented by Southern slaveholders' resentment at the better conditions Seminoles provided their slaves. Some of the most infamous horrors of migration came on the Cherokees' Trail of Tears to the southwest Indian Territory in Oklahoma. That removal was authorized by the fraudulently obtained Treaty of New Echota in 1835, denounced by John Quincy Adams as an "eternal disgrace upon the country." Overviews of the removal process are provided in Satz, 1975, 64–135; Prucha, 1984, chs. 7–9.

130. Washburn, 1971, 69–70; Washburn, 1975, 168–69; Satz, 1975, 128–34, 249–78; Prucha, 1984, 222–26, 231–41, 272, 283–92, 317–23.

131. The Stockbridge tribe provides a small but pertinent example. Originally located in Massachusetts, then resettled in New York, then moved to Wisconsin, the tribe responded

to proddings for further land cessions by splitting into two factions, a Citizens Party seeking full assimilation and an Indian Party wishing to maintain traditional tribal life. In 1843, Congress granted those who desired it citizenship, but the rival faction succeeded in gaining a repeal of that law in 1846. Two years later a compromise was reached, whereby the tribe ceded all its Wisconsin lands, those seeking to regain their brief citizenship acquired some portions of the cession in severalty, and the Indian Party was given land in a corner of Wisconsin's Menominee Reservation after refusing to go to Minnesota (Kettner, 1978, 293; Prucha, 1984, 265–66).

132. Washburn, 1975, 170–96; Satz, 1975, 292–94; Kettner, 1978, 292–93; Archdeacon, 1983, 88–89; Prucha, 1984, 273–77, 316–23, 340, 360–65, 381, 390–92, 401–3; McLoughlin, 1986, 272–73; Wright, 1992, 294–97; Takaki, 1993, 100–105.

133. Racially ascriptive prejudices were, of course, visible in judicial decisions of earlier years, including state decisions that held (by and large) that Native Americans were not citizens, as the Supreme Court consistently confirmed. Thus a New York court upheld a state law forbidding Indians from making contracts as a measure to prevent them from "falling victims to their own weakness" and the superior "intelligence" of whites (*Chandler v. Edson*, 9 Johns. Repts. 362, 365, N.Y. 1812); five years later, New York Justice Ambrose Spencer referred to Indians as "incapacitated, from their mental debasement," to engage in individual land sales (*Jackson v. Reynolds*, 14 Johns. Repts. 335, 337, N.Y. 1817). Chief Justice Isaac Parker of Massachusetts similarly expected that many tribal members would prove to be "unfortunate children . . . incapable of civilization" (*Andover v. Canton*, 13 Mass. 547, 1816). But their status was in some ways higher than that of blacks, at least in South Carolina, where a child of a white father and Indian mother was held to be a citizen, unlike children of white-black unions (*Davis v. Hall*, 1 Nott & McCord 292, 294, S.C. 1818).

134. Burke, 1969, 503; Satz, 1975, 1–6; Horsman, 1981, 196–97; Prucha, 1984, 185–86, 195.

135. For further review of the background of these cases, see, e.g., Burke, 1969, esp. 503–7; Satz, 1975, 9–56; Prucha, 1984, 195–213. Burke's properly influential discussion of the Cherokee cases pays little specific attention to the international law writers, especially Vattel, as a source of the arguments involved; and so it, like many other accounts, exaggerates the novelty of Marshall's evolving views.

136. William Wirt had similarly written to the Cherokees' principal leader, John Ross, that in his view the Cherokee Nation was sufficiently a foreign state for jurisdiction to be granted (Burke, 1969, 511–12). Thompson, a Monroe appointee, cited not only Vattel but Kent's reading of Vattel in *Goodell v. Jackson*. Story concurred with Thompson's position, which clearly expressed the sentiments of many, if not most, old Federalists and National Republicans.

137. *Cherokee Nation v. Georgia*, 5 Pet. 1, 16–17, 20, 52–53, 60–62, 67 (1831). Marshall did, however, encourage Thompson and Story to write their dissents, which had not been prepared when the decision was delivered. He seems to have been perturbed by the anti-Cherokee gloss given his ruling by the concurring opinions: though Justice Henry Baldwin, a Jacksonian appointee from Pennsylvania, and William Johnson, appointed by Jefferson from South Carolina, both concurred with the result, each indicated that they did not view the tribes as sovereign states at all (20–27, 42, 48; Burke, 1969, 515–16; Satz 1975, 45–47; Prucha, 1984, 210).

138. *Worcester v. Georgia*, 6 Pet. 515, 543–47, 549–52 (1832).

139. 6 Pet. at 544, 546, 552, 555, 561. McLean added a concurrence which stressed the propriety of eventual removal or full assimilation and saw some weight in Georgia's claims, but which similarly asserted the national government's authority to override them (594–96). Baldwin indicated that his views were the same as in the *Cherokee Nation* case, though he

relied only on a technical flaw in the record to dissent (596). Johnson was too ill to participate (Burke, 1969, 524).

140. Though some language in *Worcester* appears to deprecate national claims to dominion as much as the strong opinion Thompson wrote on behalf of partial Indian sovereignty in *Cherokee Nation v. Georgia*, that comparison cuts both ways. In *Jackson v. Porter*, Thompson had emphasized that the U.S. did possess "ultimate dominion," as Marshall had indicated in *Johnson v. McIntosh*. Both men had clearly moved toward more liberal positions since the 1820s, as evidenced by Thompson's support in *Worcester* of Marshall's dismissal of the doctrine of discovery, on which Thompson had earlier relied; but it is unclear how far toward challenging U.S. rights of dominion they wished to go. Burke (1969, 531) speculates that the Court might have pressed Jackson harder on the enforcement issue if the nullification crisis had not arisen, leading the nationalist judges to rally around the President. See also Deloria & Lytle, 1983, 30–33; Schuck & Smith, 1985, 65–66.

141. Because Georgia ignored Marshall's decision, instead of formally refusing to comply with it, and the Supreme Court adjourned before recording Georgia's failure to comply, some writers argue that Jackson had no legal enforcement procedures or grounds available (see, e.g., Burke, 1969, 525–28; Satz, 1975, 49–52; Prucha, 1984, 212). But Jackson's past conduct against Indians showed him to be more than willing to act with dubious legal authorization when it suited his purposes, so it is doubtful that he simply felt straitjacketed by legal technicalities. (In 1833, Georgia's Governor Lumpkin settled matters by offering a pardon which Worcester and Butler were persuaded to accept.)

142. *U.S. v. Bailey*, 24 F. Cas. 937, 939–40 (U.S.C.C. Tenn., 1834).

143. Cohen, 1982, 264–65, 265n46.

144. *U.S. v. Cisna*, 25 F. Cas. 422–25 (U.S.C.C. Oh., 1835). For an opposing interpretation see J. M. Smith, 1988–89, 546–51.

145. Calabresi, 1982.

146. One might wonder whether the reasoning of *Cisna* should suggest that the denial of birthright citizenship to tribal members, on the ground that they owed allegiance to a dependent but still separate nation, had also become obsolete; but the Court had no observations on that point.

Perhaps if Marshall had survived past 1835, these circuit court decisions would have been modified or reversed, for in his final year the Court did decide *Mitchel v. U.S.* in accordance with the general outlook of *Worcester* (although, perhaps because of the various challenges to its authority, the Court did not rely on that opinion). Colin Mitchel claimed certain Florida lands via purchases from Creek tribes that had been approved by the state's previous British and Spanish governors. The U.S. contended that Spain had acquired the lands by conquest, held absolute sovereignty over them, and had ceded that sovereignty to the United States. Justice Henry Baldwin wrote for the Court that both the British and the Spanish had chosen to honor the Creeks' rights of occupancy and alienation with the approval of their European governors, that those rights were left unaltered by the treaty of cession to the United States, and that they consequently remained "as sacred as the fee simple of the whites." While the United States had succeeded to Spain's ultimate fee in unalienated Indian lands, it had to uphold Mitchel's claims (*Mitchel v. U.S.*, 9 Pet. 711, 720–22, 725, 753–58, 761 [1835]). This contention that U.S. sovereignty did not extend to negation of Native American occupancy rights and previously approved tribal land sales is in accord with *Worcester*, even if the language stresses the federal ultimate fee somewhat more firmly. (No doubt it also reflected the strong concerns for contractual and vested property rights that Marshall had expressed long ago in the somewhat parallel case of *Fletcher v. Peck*, 6 Cranch 87 [1810].)

147. *Clark v. Smith,* 13 Pet. 195, 200–201 (1839). Catron noted that the states' promises of "lands within the Indian hunting grounds" to soldiers was "one of the great resources that sustained" the Revolutionary War, without mentioning the Continental Congress's highly questionable authority to make such promises.

148. *U.S. v. Rogers,* 4 How. 567, 571–73 (1846).

149. The following year, however, the Circuit Court for Arkansas read the racial aspect of Taney's opinion as liberally as possible in *U.S. v. Ragsdale,* 17 F. Cas. 684–86 (U.S.C.C. Ark., 1847). In 1835, Thomas Ragsdale, a native-born Cherokee, had allegedly murdered a white, Richard Newland, who had intermarried and joined the Cherokee tribe. The 1846 Treaty of Washington tried to settle ongoing disputes among the resettled Cherokee factions by pardoning all crimes committed by citizens of the Cherokee Nation against the Nation and its "individuals." As a recognized member of the tribe, Newland was held to be such an individual despite his race, and Ragsdale was covered by the pardon. The court gave great weight to the treaty's purpose of achieving "peace and harmony among the hostile parties of the Cherokee tribe."

150. *U.S. v. Ritchie,* 17 How. 525, 538–40 (1854). The Court did display more respect for Cherokee autonomy and humanity in *Mackey v. Coxe,* 18 How. 100, 102–3, 105 (1855). The case centered on whether an appointment of estate administrators under Cherokee law was legally binding in the District of Columbia's courts. Justice John McLean, one of the Court's most liberal members, held that it was. He praised the "surviving remnants" of the Cherokees for their turn to cultivating "the soil, exchanging their erratic habits for the blessings of civilization," and he ruled that the United States' 1835 treaty of removal with the Cherokees left the tribe significant powers of self-government. He viewed the Cherokee country, in fact, as a "domestic territory" comparable to those in "the second grade of government," just prior to statehood, under the Northwest Ordinance. An 1812 statute gave such territories power to sue in the District of Columbia. McLean's warm words suggested perhaps too high an estimate of the Indians' legal status, however, for Justices Nelson and Benjamin Curtis, who concurred on other grounds. At any rate, this limited legal recognition for Cherokee self-governance was not a major blow to the dominant thrust of the Jacksonians' jurisprudence concerning Native Americans.

151. E.g., in *Fellows v. Blacksmith,* 19 How. 366, 371–72 (1856), the Court held that individuals who had acquired title to Native American lands ceded by treaty could not expel the native inhabitants by "irregular force and violence." The government, having made the treaty, had to implement it in ways consistent with its guardian role.

152. *State of New York ex rel. Cutler v. Dibble,* 21 How. 366, 370–71 (1858).

Chapter 9. Dred Scott Unchained

1. Stowe, 1965; Delany, 1968; Douglass, 1972, 259–60. Delany's book was *The Condition, Elevation, Emigration, and Destiny of the Colored People of the United States, Politically Considered.*

2. Woodward, 1988, xix.

3. Phillips, ed., 1845, 101–4, 116–19; Delany, 1968, 16–23.

4. Douglass, 1950, v. II, 470, 476, 478–79; McFeely, 1991, 41, 84–85, 124, 127–30, 242–44.

5. Delany had abundant experience of white racism, including being compelled to leave Harvard Medical School in 1850 when classmates objected to his presence. Thus, even as he stressed his patriotism, he doubted whether whites would ever truly accept blacks as equals. Though he scorned the Colonization Society as racist, he suggested that blacks might indeed have to build their own homeland, preferably in North or South America,

perhaps somewhere in Africa other than Liberia. Hence Delany is often called the father of black nationalism (Delany, 1968, 169–74, 191, 203; Takaki, 1993, 126–31; E. Foner, 1988, 27, 288).

6. Delany, 1968, 14, 29, 48–51, 181. Delany's complex later career included serving as a major in the Union Army, working as a Republican party organizer and political candidate in South Carolina during Reconstruction, and eventually joining the Democrats out of the belief that propertied interests must ultimately rule and that it was best for Southern blacks to ally with them. He also eventually came to support emigration to Liberia as an alternative (E. Foner, 1988, 27, 288, 543, 546–47, 574; Takaki, 1993, 129–30).

7. E. Foner, 1970, 75–87, 124–26; Wiecek, 1977, 153–55, 160–62, 216–48, 264–65; Wiecek, 1978, 47.

8. Lincoln, 1905–06, v. 2, 209; Litwack, 1961, 214–46; E. Foner, 1970, 2–5, 139–40; Fredrickson, 1971, 6–42; Flexner, 1975, 74–75; E. Foner, 1980, 15–33; Jaffa, 1982, 30, 375; P. Foner, 1983a, 290–308, 377–87, 390–93, 398, 401–5, 449–78, 511–35; Jones, 1987, 8–9; McPherson, 1988, 60–62.

9. Delany, 1968, 10; Stowe, 1965, xxvi, 436–37, 449; McPherson, 1988, 88–91. McPherson indicates that, in relation to the population at time of publication, *Uncle Tom's Cabin* was the best-selling novel in American history.

10. Lincoln, 1905–06, v. 2, 190, 217, 270, 274 (holding in 1854 that slavery violates, not God's will, but the "love of justice" intrinsic in "human nature," and in 1856 that it is a "sin . . . against human liberty"). See also 299 (arguing in 1857 that a "black woman" is in "some respects . . . not my equal; but in her natural right to eat the bread she earns with her own hands, without asking leave of anyone else, she is my equal and the equal of all others"). Cf. Johannsen, ed., 1965, 33–35, 46–47, 51–55, 221; McPherson, 1988, 127–29.

Hartzian scholars have not captured the ideological conflicts of this era well. David Ericson's interpretation of the Lincoln-Douglas debates concludes correctly that Lincoln's position rested more on "liberalism," Douglas's on "racism." But this racism, admitted to be perhaps "illiberal," appears out of nowhere in Ericson's analysis to explain Douglas and then disappears again. He makes no mention of it in his chapter discussing the "categories of American political thought." Instead he begins and ends his study by affirming that "Hartz was right about the consensually liberal nature of American political thought" (Ericson, 1993, 1, 10–26, 132–35, 158–63, 179). Ericson's approach echoes his mentor David Greenstone's interpretation of Douglas and other Jacksonians as "humanist liberals" (Greenstone, 1993, 142, 150–53). Harry Jaffa's classic earlier study of the debates argues, in explicit refutation of Myrdal, that the conflict cannot be seen as one "between precept and practice" because Douglas also stood for a "precept"; but Jaffa presents that precept as majority rule, "the consent of the governed," not white supremacy. Thus Jaffa, too, gives racist doctrines minimal attention (Jaffa, 1982, 30–37, 374–75).

11. William Gienapp's exhaustive study of the origins of the Republican party acknowledges the liberal elements in its ideology. He emphasizes, however, the links between the Republicans' opposition to the "slave power" and the fears of tyrannical conspiracies long part of classical republicanism's scenario of corruption and decline. Consistent with the general framework used here, he also stresses an ascriptive element, the anti-Catholicism of Republican thought. But despite his stress on republicanism, Gienapp concedes that "Lockeian liberal" elements became more prominent in Republican thought after 1856. And even for the 1852–56 period he studied, in which republican and nativist strains in Republican ideology are undeniably visible, Gienapp understates the extent to which opposition to the "slave power" was a liberal as well as republican tenet. The "slave power" was on his account hated for the threats it posed to individual liberties, white as well as

black; and republicanism was just as often invoked on slavery's behalf (Gienapp, 1987, 353–73). For a critique of other discussions of how "republican" or "liberal" Lincoln was, see Ericson, 1993, 140–43.

12. E. Foner, 1970, 8–39; E. Foner, 1980, 48, 104–5. I term this free labor ideology only quasi-Lockean because Locke failed to carry the logic of his own principles to a truly emphatic denunciation of the slave trade of his time. Instead, he invested in it. See, e.g., Dunn, 1969, 175n4; Farber & Muench, 1984, 241–42.

13. Lincoln, 1905–06, v. 5, 168–69; Hartz, 1955, 198–99, 204.

14. Though Eric Foner sometimes refers to the free labor ideology as a "republican" one, in partial contrast to what he sees as a postwar "classical liberal" ideology, he also connects the free labor position to Lockean ideas, as do most other scholars. Gienapp, for example, argues that the "concept of free labor had its roots in one of the two main sources of American political thought: Lockeian liberalism" (Gienapp, 1987, 356). See generally E. Foner, 1970, 11–39, 281–300; E. Foner, 1980, 192–93; E. Foner, 1988, 488–99; Farber & Muench, 1984, 235, 242–43; Smith, 1989a, 257; Greenstone, 1993, 256–57, 276–79). Before Greenstone, Harry Jaffa also portrayed Lincoln as having less of a "negative liberty" view of government than Jefferson and instead as striving "to achieve justice in the positive sense" (Jaffa, 1982, 321–27). For other works elaborating free labor interpretations, see, e.g., Boritt, 1978; Forbath, 1985.

15. Elazar, in Gilchrist & Lewis, eds., 1965, 98–99; E. Foner, 1970, 261–317; Forbath, 1985; McPherson, 1988, 192–95, 450–52.

16. Due to the sorts of efforts to combat their growth described in the text, free blacks nonetheless declined as a percentage of the overall Southern black population, from about 8 to 6.2% (Takaki, 1993, 110).

17. *Fisher's Negroes v. Dabbs*, 14 Tenn., 6 Yerger 119 (1834); Du Bois, 1992, 26; Takaki, 1993, 113.

18. C. M. Green, 1962, 141–43; Genovese, 1972, 592–97; P. Foner, 1983a, 147–56, 164–65; Franklin & Moss, 1988, 134–35; Takaki, 1993, 110–18.

19. For example, in *State v. Atlas Jowers*, 11 Iredell 555 (N.C., 1850), Pearson held that insolent language from a free black to a white was equivalent to a physical blow, and so properly answerable by one (at 556).

20. Berlin, 1974, 211–12; J. Williamson, 1980; P. Foner, 1983a, 105–11, 164, 170–71; Franklin & Moss, 1988; 114–15, 124–25. Southern courts advocated or insisted on expulsion of freed slaves to Liberia in *Fisher's Negroes v. Dabbs*, 14 Tenn., 6 Yerger 119, 131 (1834), *Cox v. Williams*, 4 Iredell 15, 18 (N.C., 1847), and *Bryan v. Walton*, 14 Ga. 185, 206 (1853).

21. *Foremans v. Tamms*, 1 Grant's 23, 25 (Pa., 1853), Thus the "effect of this act of manumission is to give the colored man the right to acquire, possess and dispose of lands and goods, as fully as the white man enjoys these rights."

22. Berlin, 1974, 209, 225–29, 316–33, 360–64; P. Foner, 1983a, 170–77, 187–89; Franklin & Moss, 1988, 138–42. Southern courts often declared that free blacks were worse off than slaves. See, e.g., Catron in *Fisher's Negroes v. Dabbs*, 14 Tenn., 6 Yerger, 119, 130–31 (1834), echoed in *Bryan v. Walton*, 14 Ga. 185, 205–6 (1853).

23. Paulding, 1836, 62, 65; Litwack, 1961, 40, 70–75, 84–104, 153–55, 168–70, 194–96; P. Foner, 1983a, 191–209; Franklin & Moss, 1988, 103, 153–54; Du Bois, 1992, 18, 28; Takaki, 1993, 107–10.

24. The *Crandall* trial court's denial of black citizenship was cited in, for example, *Heirn v. Bridault*, 37 Miss. 224 (1859), and *Mitchell v. Wells*, 37 Miss. 260 (1859). See also Litwack, 1961, 126–31; Wiecek, 1977, 162–67.

25. *Crandall v. State of Connecticut*, 10 Conn. 339, 345–47.

26. After public opposition finally discouraged Crandall, she married and moved to Illinois, where she continued to teach black children. In 1886, Connecticut extended her an official apology and an indemnity for the harassment she had endured (Wiecek, 1977, 164).

27. *Crandall* at 348–52.

28. *Crandall* at 353–61.

29. In 1837, however, Pennsylvania's Chief Justice John B. Gibson endorsed the state's positions in *Crandall* in *Hobbs v. Fogg,* 6 Watts 533, 557–58, 560 (Pa., 1837). The Pennsylvania Supreme Court later did grant blacks certain rights as "freemen," but it still held that the founding "white population" could deny blacks political privileges. *Foremans v. Tamms,* 1 Grant 23 (Pa. 1853).

30. In 1839, Justice Church of the Connecticut Supreme Court of Errors did state in passing that a free black was "entitled to all the rights and privileges of other free citizens of the state," but he upheld only a "right of acquiring a new place of settlement," leaving other Connecticut restrictions on free blacks untouched. *Colchester v. Lyme,* 13 Conn. 274, 277 (1839).

31. *Roberts v. City of Boston,* 5 Cushing 198, 206 (Mass., 1849); Litwack, 1961, 148–49.

32. *State v. Edmund,* 4 Devereaux 340, 343 (N.C., 1833).

33. *Fisher's Negroes v. Dabbs,* 14 Tenn., 6 Yerger 119, 126, 129–31 (1834). James Kettner appears to misinterpret this case as an endorsement of full black citizenship (Kettner, 1978, 316–17). Four years later, after Tennessee had ended black suffrage, its attorney general attacked the notions that birth alone could confer citizenship and that blacks were anywhere citizens within the meaning of the privileges and immunities clause. He termed them mere "sojourners in the land." The state supreme court agreed, holding that free blacks had too few political privileges to be citizens "in the sense of the Constitution." *State v. Clairborne,* 10 Meigs 331, 334–36, 339–40 (Tenn., 1838).

34. Judge William Gaston of the North Carolina Supreme Court endorsed both birthright citizenship and the separability of political rights from the status in *State v. Manuel,* 4 Devereaux & Battle's Law 20, 24–26 (N.C., 1838).

35. *State v. Newsom,* 5 Iredell 250, 254 (N.C., 1844).

36. *State v. Jowers,* 11 Iredell 555 (N.C., 1850).

37. In *Ford v. Ford,* 26 Tenn., 7 Humphrey 95–96 (1846), Nathan Green still drew on the nation's religious and Enlightenment traditions to assert that a slave "is made after the image of the Creator. He has mental capacities, and an immortal principle in his nature, that constitute him equal to his owner, but for the accidental position in which fortune has placed him." The owner's merely "conventional rights" over the slave could not "extinguish his high born nature, nor deprive him of many rights which are inherent in man."

38. *Pendleton v. the State,* 6 Ark. 509, 511–12 (1846).

39. *Cooper & Worsham v. Mayor of Savannah,* 4 Ga. 72 (1848).

40. *Bryan v. Walton,* 14 Ga. 185, 198 (1853). Lumpkin confessed himself strongly inclined "to go beyond the normal bounds of an opinion" in arguing against black citizenship, and he cited biblical authority, Greek and Roman political and legal examples, Aristotle and Cicero, the argument that blacks were not parties to the Constitution, and many preceding state opinions to support his resounding conclusion that whites alone "can be *citizens* in this great and growing republic which extends already from the Atlantic to the Pacific, and from the St. Lawrence to the Rio Grande" (at 198–207). The argument that blacks were the cursed children of Ham is discussed in Fredrickson, 1971, 60–61, 87–89, 276–77.

41. See, e.g., *State v. Harrison,* 11 La. 722, 724–25 (1856); *Shaw v. Brown,* 35 Miss. 246, 315 (1858); *Hughes v. Jackson,* 12 Md. 450, 463–64 (1858); *African Methodist Episcopal Church v. New Orleans,* 15 La. Annual Repts. 441, 443 (1860). Southern judges did vary in their at-

titudes. Justice Alexander Handy of Mississippi fiercely contested his brethren's efforts to deny free blacks even the most minimal rights. See *Shaw v. Brown* and also *Heirn v. Bridault*, 37 Miss. 209 (1859); *Mitchell v. Wells*, 37 Miss. 235, 260, 263 (1859) (where Justice William Harris, in a spectacularly racist opinion, argued that Northern states violated the privileges and immunities clause's requirements of comity when they conferred citizenship on blacks ineligible for citizenship in Mississippi). Finkelman, 1981, 4–6, 232–34, 287–95, sees Handy as actually favoring the even more extreme solution of secession, despite his "enlightened rhetoric"; but he agrees that Handy was more willing to recognize rights for blacks than Harris was.

42. He contended that unlike an alien, a slave "is a part of the family" who, once free, acquires "all the *rights* which mere birth, under the *ligeance* of a country bestows"; and Legare thought that those included civil though not political rights, *Official Opinions*, v. IV, 1843, 148.

43. *Official Opinions*, v. VII, 751–53. Cushing's main concern, as noted below, was to deny citizenship to Indians; but he acknowledged that his stance was heavily influenced by the implications of that issue for the status of "the African race" (751). See also Litwack, 1961, 50–54.

44. The Secretary of State's office influenced the debate over free blacks in one other way: its 1840 census professed to reveal that insanity and idiocy were eleven times more prevalent among free negroes than among slaves, and that the proportion of mental defectives decreased steadily from north to south. Dr. Edward Jarvis, later a founder and long-time president of the American Statistical Association, thoroughly refuted these findings, showing that the census frequently reported a higher number of insane blacks in the North than it did black residents. But in 1844, Secretary of State John C. Calhoun staunchly defended the overall findings of the census, helping to inspire James McCune Smith's rebuking pamphlet, and the census was invoked by defenders of slavery for years thereafter (Litwack, 1961, 40–46, 54–55; P. Foner, 1983a, 170).

45. In a minor but like-minded decision, Chief Justice Taney ruled in 1837 that the 1808 ban on the slave trade applied only to foreign blacks, so that it did not prevent American slaveholders from bringing back their slaves after sojourning with them abroad (*U.S. v. The Ship Garonne*, 11 Pet. 73, 77 [1837]).

46. The instructions went on to say that the United States "are not prepared to sacrifice" to slave trade suppression "any of their rights as an independent nation; nor will the object in view justify the exposure of their own people to injurious and vexatious interruptions in the prosecution of their lawful pursuits" (Fehrenbacher, 1978, 4, 21).

47. P. Foner, 1983a, 37–38; Fehrenbacher, 1984, 17–21; Franklin & Moss, 1988, 110–11, 177. In 1841, the Supreme Court delivered what some saw as a blow against the international slave trade in *U.S. v. The Schooner Amistad* (15 Pet. 518, 1841). The *Amistad*, a Spanish vessel, was seized off Long Island and found to be controlled by 49 African slaves who had mutinied and were trying to go back to Africa. The Spanish government demanded the return of the Africans on behalf of their alleged owners, but the federal district court judge, Andrew Judson (the Connecticut colonizationist who had prosecuted Prudence Crandall) ruled that the Africans' enslavement was illegal under current Spanish law. Hence, there were no genuine Spanish property claims to honor. Justice Story, writing for the Supreme Court, agreed; but he held that if their enslavement had been valid under Spanish law, the slaves would have had to be returned, so in fact the decision did not represent a major antislavery step (at 587, 593). For a book-length discussion of the case, which varies in some respects from this conclusion, see Jones, 1987, 12–13, 31–40, 193–96, 217–19.

48. *Groves v. Slaughter,* 15 Pet. 449, 481–96, 500–503 (1841). For discussion see Wiecek, 1978, 50–52; 1988, 73–74; Finkelman, 1981, 266–71.
49. *Groves* at 506–8, 513–16. These positions prefigured the stances that many of these justices would take regarding state power over immigration in the *Passenger Cases* eight years later.
50. See, e.g., *LaGrange v. Chouteau,* 4 Pet. 287, 290–91 (1830); *Menard v. Aspasia,* 5 Pet. 505, 517 (1831).
51. *Rhodes v. Bell,* 2 How. 397, 404–6 (1844). The district was then divided into Washington and Alexandria counties, with the former laws of Maryland and Virginia largely still in force in each. They conflicted on manumission.

    Somewhat similarly, a Maine federal district court permitted Polydore, a Guadalupe slave, to sue a ship's captain who had beaten him on a trip to Portland because Polydore was free according to local law. This ruling was in tension, however, with the deference to foreign slavery laws expressed in the *Amistad* case, and it was generally not followed. See *Polydore v. Prince,* 19 F. Cas. 950 (U.S.D.C. Me., 1837); cf. *Daggs v. Frazer,* 6 F. Cas. 1112 (U.S.D.C. Ia., 1849); and for other lower federal court decisions, occasionally sustaining black freedom, see Finkelman, 1981, 244–65.
52. *Strader v. Graham,* 10 How. 82, 93 (1851). Taney also delivered several provocative proslavery dicta irrelevant to the decision (Wiecek, 1978, 53–54).
53. From 1836 to 1845, Congress also tacitly supported slavery by adopting the infamous "gag rule" (formally in the House, informally in the Senate), requiring antislavery petitions to be tabled without discussion. In 1839, Ohio Rep. Joshua Giddings nonetheless dared to introduce a set of resolutions arguing that the blacks who had revolted on the slave ship *Creole* had legitimately reverted to freedom when they left the waters of the slave states. He was censured by the House, whereupon he resigned. He was immediately returned by his constituents, only to be censured again in 1842 for presenting antislavery resolutions. John Quincy Adams, "Father Adams" to Giddings, then led the fight that won repeal of the gag rule in 1844, the capstone of his noble post-presidential House career (Cover, 1975, 111–16; Wiecek, 1977, 213–17; Fehrenbacher, 1978, 120–24; Howe, 1979, 65–66, 173).

    The *Creole* mutineers, who had acted while en route from Virginia to Louisiana, took the vessel to Nassau, where British authorities permitted them and all the slaves aboard to go free. An outraged President John Tyler laid various demands on the British which eventually resulted in compensation for the slaveholders (Fehrenbacher, 1984, 16–17).
54. For a list of personal liberty laws, see Morris, 1974, 219–22. Before the pivotal *Prigg* decision, related laws were passed in New York (1827, 1828), Indiana (1831), Ohio (1831), Illinois (1833), Massachusetts (1837), Maine (1838), and Connecticut (1838).
55. *Prigg v. Pennsylvania,* 16 Pet. 539, 622–23, 625 (1842). The decision concurred with the results in the terse 1818 lower court decision noted in chapter 8, *In re Susan.* That case had lacked sufficient authority to deter passage of somewhat different types of personal liberty laws.
56. *Prigg* at 625–26, 631, 636, 641–42, 652, 656. Northern justices added different glosses. Justice Thompson thought that Congress's power did not prevent the states from enacting regulations that did not conflict with existing federal laws, although he found such a conflict between the 1862 statute and the Fugitive Slave Act (at 633–35). McLean agreed that the federal power was exclusive, but believed that Congress could authorize state officials to aid in enforcement. His main concern, however, was to insist that some sort of judicial process had to be employed. A general right of recaption via self-help was too great a threat to the public peace to be sustained (661, 664–65).
57. In *Moore v. Illinois,* 14 How. 13 (1852), the Court confirmed that *Prigg* did not ban all state regulations pertinent to recovery of fugitive slaves when it upheld a state law against har-

boring such fugitives. Morris, 1974, 94–129; Cover, 1975, 166–68, 240–43; Wiecek, 1978, 43, 47; P. Foner, 1983a, 498–99, 506–9; P. Foner, 1983b, 5–6.

58. *Jones v. Van Zandt,* 13 F. Cas. 1047, 1048 (Case #7502) (U.S.C.C. Oh., 1848): *Jones v. Van Zandt,* 5 How. 215, 231 (1847). For discussion see E. Foner, 1970, 76–77, 82; Cover, 1975, 172–74; Wiecek, 1978, 47–49; Finkelman, 1981, 159, 246–48.

59. Fehrenbacher, 1978, 124–35; Howe, 1979, 93–94; P. Foner, 1983a, 540–45.

60. Lincoln, 1905–06, v. 2, 186; Fehrenbacher, 1978, 157–59; P. Foner, 1983a, 546–51. Two economic historians argue that even though without the Civil War the free states might never have attempted to abolish slavery in the existing slave states, the South could sensibly have feared the existence of an enduring congressional majority willing to take more minor actions hostile to slave interests. Such actions could have caused the value of slaves, crucial to the Southern economy, to fluctuate intolerably (Lee & Passell, 1979, 216–17).

61. Morris, 1974, 130–47; Fehrenbacher, 1978, 160–63; Howe, 1979, 147–48; P. Foner, 1983b, 4–5, 8–15.

62. See *In re Booth,* 3 Wis. 1, 7–49 (1854); *Ex parte Booth,* 3 Wis. 145 (1854); *In re Booth and Rycraft,* 3 Wis. 157 (1854); *U.S. v. Booth,* 18 How. 476 (1855); *Abelman v. Booth,* 21 How. 506, 509, 514–15, 522, 526 (1859). However, in the crisis year of 1860, Taney ruled that when the governor of Ohio refused to honor his duty under the act to return a slave, there was "no power delegated" to any department of the general government to use "coercive means to compel him" (*Commonwealth of Kentucky v. Dennison,* 24 How. 66, 109–10 [1860]). For overviews of these and other important disputes of the period, see T. D. Morris, 1974, 140–85; Cover, 1975, 175–91; P. Foner, 1983b, 16–108. Previous to the *Booth* controversy, McLean provided an important endorsement of the constitutionality of the 1850 Fugitive Slave law in *Miller v. McQuerry,* 17 F. Cas. 335 (U.S.C.C. Oh., 1853).

63. E. Foner, 1970, 93–96; Potter, 1976, 160–76, 199–224; Fehrenbacher, 1978, 180–92; P. Foner, 1983b, 189–92, 199–200.

64. The second fort, Fort Snelling, was located near what is now St. Paul, Minnesota; but at the time it was part of the Wisconsin Territory, and it was shifted to the Iowa Territory in 1838. The courts generally referred to it as located in the Wisconsin Territory, as I will do here. The definitive treatment of the decision is Fehrenbacher, 1978.

65. In a number of previous cases Missouri courts had held that a master voluntarily taking a slave for permanent residence in a free jurisdiction thereby emancipated him, beginning with *Winny v. Whitesides,* 1 Mo. 472, 475 (1824). In the most apposite case, *Rachel v. Walker,* 4 Mo. 350, 354 (1836), the Missouri Supreme Court had held that an army officer who took a slave for extended residence in the free Wisconsin territory had voluntarily emancipated her. Although the army required him to reside at its fort, nothing required him to take his slave there (Fehrenbacher, 1978, 240–53, 658n11; Hyman & Wiecek, 1982, 172–73).

66. *Scott v. Emerson,* 15 Mo. 576, 585–86 (1852); Fehrenbacher, 1978, 264–65.

67. *Dred Scott v. Sanford,* 13 American State Trials 242, 252 (1921).

68. Fehrenbacher, 1978, 278–79; Hyman & Wiecek, 1982, 176–77.

69. *Dred Scott v. Sandford,* 19 How. 393, 406 (1857).

70. The case only required assessing whether Dred Scott's experiences had made him free and a citizen. As one born into slavery, Scott had a weaker claim than free blacks who were native-born to states that regarded blacks as citizens. Moreover, an 1825 Missouri law prohibited free blacks from entering the state unless they were citizens of other states, with naturalization papers (Wiecek, 1977, 124). Because no state issued such papers, Scott could have been held to be either a slave in the eyes of Missouri, or present illegally, leaving him in any case ineligible to claim state citizenship. Admittedly, such laws were rarely enforced, and in the various cases prior to *Scott v. Emerson* where Missouri courts held

that residence in a free jurisdiction had freed a slave, the pertinence of this law does not appear to have been raised. See, e.g., *Milly v. Smith*, 2 Mo. 171, 173–75 (1829); *Julia v. McKinney*, 3 Mo. 270, 272–73 (1833); *Rachel v. Walker*, 4 Mo. 350, 354 (1836); *Wilson v. Melvin*, 4 Mo. 592 (1837).

Perhaps more important, the case also did not require deciding whether Scott could claim *all* the rights of citizenship. Only citizenship for diversity clause purposes was in question. The corporation cases had already indicated that a litigant might exercise rights of citizenship under the Art. III diversity clause without being able to claim citizenship in other contexts, such as Art. IV privileges and immunities controversies. Taney thus could have focused only on whether Scott could sustain his Art. III claim. It is true that corporations supposedly received diversity citizenship only as an extension of the citizenship of the natural persons who composed them, so even Art. III recognition might have implied that Scott had some sort of broader citizenship lurking in the background; but the Court had long since displayed a positive appetite for upholding inconsistent fictions in this area of law.

71. *Dred Scott v. Sandford*, 19 How. 403, 416–17, 421–23 (1857).

72. *Dred Scott* at 405, 416.

73. *Dred Scott* at 405–6, 417.

74. *Dred Scott* at 417–19. As discussed below, Justice Curtis's dissent surprisingly also accepted that Congress could naturalize only the foreign-born (578–79). Taney did not address the fact that some blacks already had been naturalized by treaties. In particular, the Treaty of Guadalupe Hidalgo naturalized all affected Mexican citizens without reference to race, and it is likely that some of those citizens were black, as Mexico extended its citizenship broadly. McLean assumes this was the case in dissent at 533; Curtis, at 586–87.

75. *U.S. v. Rogers*, 4 How. 567, 571–73 (1846).

76. *Dred Scott* at 403–4.

77. He probably knew, too, that his comments regarding the tribes would be viewed as dicta on a side issue, not nearly so authoritative as his other Native American decisions or his views of blacks here.

78. *Dred Scott* at 419–20.

79. *Dred Scott* at 406–11.

80. *Dred Scott* at 406, 412–16, 572–76.

81. *Dred Scott* at 531.

82. *Dred Scott* at 422.

83. Taney ignored, as most white Southerners steadfastly did, the fact that Lincoln and others drove home: there were nearly 350,000 mulattos in the slave states, showing that many free people of color and slaves were parented by white U.S. citizens, usually rapacious slavemasters, despite their alleged aversion to close contact with blacks (Lincoln, 1905–06, v. 2, 304).

84. *Dred Scott* at 412–13, 417.

85. *Dred Scott* at 430–53. The concurring opinions added little to Taney's discussion of citizenship. The most significant one, by Justice Nelson, defended the conflict-of-laws rationale for applying *Strader v. Graham* and the Missouri Supreme Court's judgment in *Scott v. Emerson* to the instant case. His argument had weaknesses, but they concern only his analysis of comity between slave and free states, not citizenship (Fehrenbacher, 1978, 390–94). The fiercely proslavery Justice Daniel provided an elaborate discussion of the legal roots of slavery and citizenship that endorsed Vattel's understanding of birthright citizenship according to descent, not place of birth, as Southern jurists had long done in this context (476–77). He also assumed that blacks had no citizens among their relevant an-

cestors. Daniel added the reasonable argument that even a legal emancipation could only make a slave free, not a citizen; otherwise masters could perform personal "naturalizations" at their own discretion (480–81). These points merely received extra emphasis, however, in an argument that generally conformed to Taney's.

86. *Dred Scott* at 533, 536–40, 547, 550, 552–57, 563. At 531, McLean did make one striking assertion that might have justified finding for Scott, but he left it undeveloped. McLean thought that citizenship attached automatically to any "freeman" born "under our Constitution and laws." This ambiguous statement seems to deny that native-born freemen can ever be refused citizenship under the Constitution, and to endorse birthright citizenship by place, or at least jurisdiction, of birth. That claim might not by itself have made Scott's case, since he was probably born a Virginian slave; but if it applied to native-born persons who later became free, it could have sufficed. Yet McLean's view then would have made many native-born free blacks, and slaves who were later emancipated, citizens of states that claimed not to recognize black citizenship at all. That contention needed defense against traditional state prerogatives to determine their own citizens, at least among the native-born. But McLean did not draw this implication overtly, much less defend it adequately.

87. *Dred Scott* at 572–76.

88. *Dred Scott* at 576–79, 582.

89. *Dred Scott* at 580–82.

90. *Dred Scott* at 586–87.

91. Curtis went on to maintain that Scott had acquired a permanent domicile in the Wisconsin Territory, that his marriage there proved that Scott was regarded even by Emerson as free, and that Congress had ample power under the territorial clause to ban slavery there. Like McLean, Curtis felt entitled to disregard *Scott v. Emerson* as inconsistent with settled Missouri law, especially since the Missouri court had not taken adequate account of Scott's marriage. *Dred Scott* at 588–92, 587, 599–604, 617, 623–24; Fehrenbacher, 1978, 407 8.

92. The manner in which *Dred Scott* reinforced state-centered views of citizenship even in the North is shown by an influential 1863 Wisconsin Supreme Court decision, *In re Wehlitz* (16 Wis. 443, 1863). There Byron Paine cited *Dred Scott* extensively to hold that in the nation's "complex" federal system a state could make a person a citizen of that state, exercising the right of suffrage in its elections, who was not "a citizen of the United States in the full sense of the term" (446–47). (To be sure, *Ableman v. Booth* proved that Wisconsin could champion states' rights without, and against, Taney's posture.)

93. Krout, 1966, 132–33; *Congressional Quarterly,* 1982, 897; McPherson, 1988, 221–32; Stewart & Weingast, 1992, 243, 246; Du Bois, 1992, 49–50.

94. South Carolina's grievances included charges that Northern states tolerated abolitionism, sheltered runaways, opposed territorial slaveholding, passed personal liberty laws, permitted black voting, and even denounced slavery as sin. With South Carolina, founding members of the Confederate States of America were Mississippi, Florida, Alabama, Georgia, Louisiana, and Texas. Virginia, North Carolina, Tennessee, and Arkansas joined after the firing on Fort Sumter and Lincoln's call for militia from the loyal states on April 15, 1861. M. Keller, 1977, 7; Hyman & Wiecek, 1982, 210–15; P. Foner, 1983b, 295–311; McPherson, 1988, 234–35, 239–44, 259. I term the Southerners' appeal to property rights, made deliberately reminiscent of the Declaration of Independence, only quasi-liberal because, as argued earlier, I do not believe that early liberal thought provided any plausible justification for recognizing the Southerners' property claims.

95. Lincoln, 1905–06, v. 5, 253–56, 264–65. The rump 36th Congress had voted in February 1860 to send to the states the proposed amendment Lincoln referred to, guaranteeing slavery in the states against federal interference. Chase's Ohio, Lincoln's Illinois, and the cap-

ital's neighbor, Maryland, endorsed it before war made it chimerical (Kelly, Harbison, & Belz, 1983, 293).

96. Lincoln, 1905–06, v. 5, 266. Many commentators have noted Lincoln's own increasing reliance on religious language from the mid-1850s on, especially during the war, though disagreements remain on how far Lincoln's views ultimately rested on religion. See, e.g., E. Wilson, 1962, 99–106; Jaffa, 1982, 229–32, 316; Diggins, 1984, 296–333; Greenstone, 1993, 276–83; Ericson, 1993, 156–57.

97. In February 1862, Lincoln transferred the security program to a new and more moderate War Secretary, Edwin Stanton, after Seward's actions had been widely criticized as tyrannical. Hyman, 1954, 33–34; Hyman, 1959, 140–55; Hyman & Wiecek, 1982, 233–56, 350; E. Foner, 1988, 32–33; McPherson, 1988, 436, 492–94, 544, 600–611; Du Bois, 1992, 102–105; Takaki, 1993, 152–53.

98. The most important relevant Supreme Court statement these events prompted came in the *Prize Cases,* 67 U.S. 635 (1863), in which the justices confronted a Hobson's choice. Lincoln's blockade seemed justified by international law only if the U.S. was at war with another sovereign nation, formed by the legitimate secession and reconfederation of states exercising their sovereign rights. If the Southern states were instead disobedient subordinates still in the Union, as the Republicans insisted, the naval action seemed illegitimate. The Supreme Court managed both to uphold the blockade and to indicate that the nation was engaged in a civil, not an international war. Yet Justice Grier's majority opinion admitted that citizens owed "a qualified allegiance" to their states; that the rebels had "acted as States claiming to be sovereign"; and he indicated that their "right to do so" was being decided "by wager of battle" (673). Hence the means to resolve the issue were political questions to be decided by the President and the Congress. That was hardly a resounding endorsement of national supremacy; and as the decision was only 5–4, it did little to settle the broader issues it touched. In other respects, Chief Justice Taney strove mightily to invalidate Lincoln's assertions of startlingly broad executive powers. See, e.g., *Ex parte Merryman,* 17 F. Cas. 144 (U.S.C.C. Md., 1861) (M. Keller, 1977, 18; Hyman & Wiecek, 1982, 235, 263–65; McPherson, 1988, 273–74).

99. The intensity of demands for allegiance during the war era is dramatized by the fact that loyalty oaths were even required to obtain marriage licenses in occupied areas. Hyman, 1954, 1–2, 17–47; 1959, 162–218; C. M. Green, 1962, 284–85; Porter, 1971, 155–61, 173, 184–90; Hyman & Wiecek, 1982, 248–49, 55–56, 61–71; McPherson, 1988, 493, 699–703.

100. Hyman & Wiecek, 1982, 234; McPherson, 1988, 202–4; Takaki, 1993, 125. Sanford Levinson argues that liberalism's advocacy of citizenship by consent makes loyalty oaths, especially, more natural governmental instruments for pure liberals than they are for republicans. He believes that republicanism advises such complete socialization into civic loyalty that disloyal choices should not be psychically possible for republican citizens. Placing such emphasis on a single oath seems to him inadequate for this goal. But civic republicanism bases citizenship on consent just as much as liberalism; and loyalty oaths testifying that one not only is loyal but has always been loyal demand evidence of precisely that unwavering commitment Levinson rightly sees republicanism as seeking (Levinson, 1988, 111–14).

101. Hyman, 1954, 3, 17; Lincoln, 1905–06, v. 7, 330–31.

102. Lower courts upheld the primacy of allegiance to the nation and found rebels guilty of treason, in accordance with national republicanism; claims in favor of state allegiance, based on the compact theory of the Constitution, were firmly repudiated (e.g., in *U.S. v. Cathcart,* 25 F. Cas. 344 [U.S.C.C. Oh., 1864]). But in cases like *U.S. v. Greiner,* 26 F. Cas. 36 (U.S.D.C. Pa., 1861), this nationalism was tempered by liberal commitments to pro-

Notes to pages 276–280

cedural rights. With Georgia in secession, Greiner could not be returned for a treason trial in the proper district, and District Judge Cadwalader refused to allow him to be kept in custody indefinitely awaiting such a trial.

103. *Cummings v. Missouri,* 4 Wall. 277 (1866); *Ex parte Garland,* 4 Wall. 333 (1866). See also *In re Shorter,* 22 F. Cas. 16, #12,811 (U.S.D.C. Ala., 1865), a prior invalidation of the oath requirement the Supreme Court struck down in *Garland; Ex parte Law,* 15 F. Cas. 3 (U.S.D.C. Ga., 1866); *Pierce et al. v. Carskadon,* 16 Wall. 234 (1873); Hyman, 1954, 107–20 (arguing the limited impact of these decisions); Hyman, 1959, 260–61; Hyman & Wiecek, 1982, 374–81.

104. Field's language foreshadowed his later dissent in the *Slaughter-House Cases:* "The theory upon which our political institutions rest is, that all men have certain inalienable rights— that among these are life, liberty, and the pursuit of happiness; and that in the pursuit of happiness all avocations, all honors, all positions, are alike open to everyone, and that in protection of these rights all are equal before the law" (*Cummings v. Missouri,* 321–22).

105. *Ex parte Garland* at 385–86, 395.

106. In a prior decision that term, *Ex parte Milligan,* 4 Wall. 2 (1866), the Court undercut another drastic Union war measure when it unanimously ruled that a prisoner tried in military court in Indiana should have had access to the federal courts under the 1863 Habeas Corpus Act. Justice Davis wrote for Field, Clifford, Grier, and Nelson in holding that martial law could not prevail unhindered in an area where the civilian courts were open. Chief Justice Chase wrote for Wayne, Miller, and Swayne arguing that Congress could authorize such a military process but had not done so here. Although the case hampered Reconstruction by appearing to limit military powers in the South, it nonetheless upheld the potency of the 1863 Habeas Corpus Act, so it cannot be termed a total rejection of nationalist initiatives. The Court's divisions appear to reflect differences over judicial versus legislative authority, allied to liberal versus national republican commitments, but those issues go beyond my concerns here. Skirmishing over the extent of Congress's power to control the Court's habeas jurisdiction continued in *Ex parte McCardle,* 7 Wall. 506 (1868) and *Ex parte Yerger,* 8 Wall. 506 (1869). See also Hyman, 1954.

107. Congress also tried to keep the channels of domestic trade flowing by opening the U.S. mails to merchandise. It instituted free mail carrier service in cities of 50,000 or more two years later, adding railway mail service in 1864.

108. Unger, 1964, 14–16; E. Foner, 1970, 183; E. Foner, 1988, 21–22; M. Keller, 1977, 23–25; Boritt, 1978, 215–17; McPherson, 1988, 443–53; Skocpol, 1992, 102–51.

109. Unger, 1964, 17–19; Elazar, in Gilchrist & Lewis, eds., 1965, 98–107; M. Keller, 1977, 133–35; Boritt, 1978, 199–203; E. Foner, 1988, 22–23; McPherson, 1988, 594.

110. M. Keller, 1977, 101–6; E. Foner, 1988, 23; McPherson, 1988, 443, 447–48; Wiecek, 1988, 87. After the war, Salmon Chase as Chief Justice actually declared unconstitutional the paper currency created while he was Lincoln's Secretary of the Treasury, though the Court quickly backed off that ruling (*Hepburn v. Griswold,* 8 Wall. 603 [1870]; *Legal Tender Cases,* 12 Wall. 457 [1871]).

111. With Charles Sumner's leadership, Congress also banned racial discrimination on streetcars and railroads in the District of Columbia on March 3, 1863, and discrimination in U.S. courts in June 1864. He did not succeed in getting the vote for blacks or a ban on segregated schools in the district. C. M. Green, 1962, 272–73; Belz, 1976, 4–14, 35–37; Belz, 1978, 38–46; Oubre, 1978, 1–5; Hyman & Wiecek, 1982, 215, 248–54; P. Foner, 1983b, 324–25, 332–65; McPherson, 1988, 339–47, 352–57, 498–500, 557–67; Franklin & Moss, 1988, 182, 188–91, 195–98; Du Bois, 1992, 59–67, 79–83, 112–13, 146–49, 191–92; Takaki, 1993, 120, 131–33.

112. Belz, 1976, 31, 35, 76; Oubre, 1978, 3–5; P. Foner, 1983b, 422–24; McPherson, 1988, 509.
113. *Opinions of the U.S. Attorney General*, v. 10, 1868 (issued Nov. 29, 1862), 382–89, 394–99, 406–9; Belz, 1976, 24–27, 30, 40.
114. Fredrickson, 1971, 167; Belz, 1976, 47–51; Du Bois, 1992, 101–2, 132.
115. Wiecek, 1972, 171–75, 184, 193–94; Belz, 1976, 35, 42–53, 58; Kelly, Harbison, & Belz, 1983, 329–31; E. Foner, 1988, 35–37, 45–50, 61–66, 73; McPherson, 1988, 698–713; Du Bois, 1992, 157–65.
116. *Cong. Globe*, 38th Cong., 1st Sess., at 1202, 1482, 1489–90, 2985–86; 2d Sess. 155–56 (1864–65); Belz, 1978, 110–15; Hyman & Wiecek, 1982, 305–6; McPherson, 1988, 840; Du Bois, 1992, 192, 207–8. I have benefited also from an unpublished essay by Michael P. Zuckert, "Completing the Constitution I: The Thirteenth Amendment."
117. The full text of the amendment reads: "Section 1. Neither slavery nor involuntary servitude, except as a punishment for crime whereof the party shall have been duly convicted, shall exist within the United States, or any place subject to their jurisdiction. Section 2. Congress shall have power to enforce this article by appropriate legislation." Section 1 was derived from language in the Northwest Ordinance: "There shall be neither slavery nor involuntary servitude in the said territory, otherwise than in the punishment of crimes, whereof the party shall have been duly convicted."
118. Ten Broek, 1965; Belz, 1976, 116–17, 125–27, 130–31; Hyman & Wiecek, 1982, 386–406; P. Foner, 1983b, 458–69; McPherson, 1988, 838–41; Du Bois, 1992, 208–9.
119. In 1865, Illinois repealed its laws banning blacks from entering the state, sitting on juries, or testifying in court; Ohio eliminated its vestigial "black laws"; Massachusetts passed the nation's first major public accommodations act; after black demonstrations, Pennsylvania officially banned racial discrimination; various cities desegregated their streetcars and began agitations that would result in school desegregation in a few years; and Missouri, alone among the border states, adopted a constitution providing for racial equality in property and juridical rights. In Minnesota, Connecticut, Wisconsin, the Colorado territory, and the District of Columbia, however, referenda to give blacks the vote were defeated. Twenty-five hundred D.C. blacks had petitioned for the franchise in 1864, prompting the referendum. Along with the Freedmen's Bureau programs, discussed in the next chapter, Congress promoted more equal black citizenship in various ways, such as granting permission for blacks to be witnesses in federal courts, to carry mail, and to integrate the streetcars in the District of Columbia. C. M. Green, 1962, 284; McPherson, 1964, 225–37, 1988, 840–41; Gillette, 1965, 25; Hyman & Wiecek, 1982, 320, 327, 330; E. Foner, 1988, 28, 40–42, 223.
120. In 1863, Congress also curtailed tribal rights to sue in federal courts over treaty provisions without special legislative assent. In any case, the federal courts showed little taste for activism on Native American issues during the war years. They were particularly unlikely to discern any restraints applicable to federal actions. Justice Miller, sitting on circuit in Kansas in 1863, decided *U.S. v. Ward*, 1 Woolworth 17, 20, 24–25 (U.S.C.C. Kan., 1863) in favor of that state's police power to punish a homicide committed on the Kansas Indians' reservation. Finding no express guarantee by the U.S. to the tribe that the federal government would never cede its jurisdiction over them to any state, Miller held that Congress's admission of Kansas to the Union as a state equal to all others must be construed as just such a federal cession. The opinion revealed the sympathy for the rights of states that Miller would long display, and it favorably cited one of the leading pro-state (and anti-*Worcester*) Jacksonian circuit court decisions, *U.S. v. Bailey*. Miller made it clear, however, that the federal government had the authority to claim and retain rights over tribes in former federal territories whenever it chose to do so explicitly. Similarly, he displayed no dif-

ficulty in finding in *U.S. v. Holliday,* 70 U.S 407, 416–18 (1865), that the federal commerce power permitted the United States to ban sales of liquor to any Indian under the authority of an Indian agent, even if the sale took place off the reservation. Wise & Deloria, 1971, 255–61, 276; Prucha, 1984, 416–36, 440–47, 457–67; Utley, 1984, xx; Wright, 1992, 298–99.

121. Stanton, Anthony, & Gage, eds., 1882, v. II, 14–17, 26–39, 58–89; Woody, 1929, v. II, 432–34; Sklar, 1973, 259; Flexner, 1975, 106–14, 134–35; Leach, 1980, 173; Degler, 1980, 303, 332–33; Speth, 1982, 82–85; Clinton, 1984, 81–92, 124; DuBois, 1988, 184–85.

Chapter 10. The America That "Never Was"

1. From 1864 to 1912, the remaining years covered in this book, roughly two-thirds of all justices were Republicans. *Congressional Quarterly,* 1982, 896–97; Nelson, ed., 1989, 1439–40; Gunther, 1991, B2–B5.

2. Hartz, 1955, 197–200; E. Foner, 1988, xxi, 67–70, 144, 277; Du Bois, 1992, 130, 182–83, 277, 352, 591–92, 595. Foner's view also draws on Montgomery, 1981. Leading scholars who endorse this basic "contradictions and limitations of liberalism" view include Fredrickson, 1971, 178–79; Belz, 1978, 54–58; Oubre, 1978, 196. See also Benedict, 1974, 246–48; Nieman, 1979, xiv–xv, 46, 105; Hyman & Wiecek, 1982, 315–17; McPherson, 1988, 710, 842.

3. Du Bois, 1992, 210, 377.

4. Kersh, 1996, forcefully stresses another factor: the genuine desire of many Americans North and South to see the Union restored in something like its old and cherished form, but without the divisive institution of slavery.

5. Du Bois, 1992, 674, 700–701.

6. See especially Valelly, 1995.

7. Van Evrie, 1868; Hunt, 1868.

8. Stocking, 1968, 74.

9. Darwin, 1936, 530–31, 539, 541, 543, 552n57, 556; Stocking, 1968, 74; Russett, 1989, 7, 40.

10. Darwin, 1936, 554–55; Gossett, 1963, 66–68, 144–50; Stocking, 1968, 48–51, 122, 238–40; Boller, 1969, 49–50, 183–86; Miller, 1964, 193–95; Haller, 1971, vii–x, 17; Russett, 1976, 1 11, 91–92; Russett, 1989, 6, 65, 195, 200–202; Bannister, 1979; Kaye, 1984; Degler, 1991, 11–16, 20–21.

11. Insofar as the traits of members of what the examiners took to be different racial groups varied with the conditions under which they were raised, monogenesist claims that different environments had variously shaped an originally unitary human race were strengthened. Darwin's account of how species originated also seemed most compatible with monogenesis, and hence at war with polygenesis presumptions of inescapably different racial "essences," because it suggested that no sets of physical characteristics were fixed in a species for all time. Thus these statistics, and evolutionary theories, gave some support to antiessentialist views with egalitarian potential. But as most evolutionists thought truly distinct races had emerged from common ancestors in the distant past, the studies still presupposed the existence of the sharp racial differences that the American school ethnologists had proclaimed; and their analysts struggled against interpreting the data as supportive of racial equality. Many polygenesists and monogenesists had in any case always agreed that the colored races were inferior, whatever their origins. Spencer 1874, 338; Darwin, 1936, 541; Stocking, 1968, 57; Haller, 1971, 7, 19–34, 44, 80; Bannister, 1979, 183–84. Stout's 1862 book was *Chinese Immigration and the Physiological Causes of the Decay of a Nation* (Miller, 1964, 157, 161–62).

12. Spencer, 1865, 55, 120, 173, 175, 191; Gossett, 1963, 73–80, 148; Haller, 1971, ix, 125–27; Degler, 1980, 311–12; Degler, 1991, 26–27; Clinton, 1984, 130–31; Kugler, 1987, 33; Russett, 1989, 7–12, 27–28, 36–40, 54–55, 74–75, 81, 101–2, 116, 119, 131, 150; Stepan, 1990, 40.

13. Haller, 1971, 40; Fredrickson, 1971, 187–89; Bannister, 1979, 180. As noted below, such positions also worked against concern for Native Americans; James Garfield wrote in 1872 that the nation should "let the Indian races sink as gently and easily as possible in oblivion, for there they will go in spite of all efforts" (quoted in M. Keller, 1977, 156).

14. Fredrickson, 1971, 171–74; Haller, 1971, 28, 130; Spencer, 1972, 256–57; Bannister, 1979, 189.

15. Hofstadter, 1955, 172–74; Gossett, 1963, 101–8, 151; Stocking, 1968, 51, 60, 65, 242, 252; Boller, 1969, 2–3; Maine, 1972; Bannister, 1979, 22, 30–31, 45–46, 191, 184–89; Russett, 1989, 65, 191, 205, 212n15; Degler, 1991, 15–16; Ross, 1991, 55, 58, 64–66, 76, 95. Maine's book was published in England in 1861, with Charles Scribner bringing out an American edition in 1871. It did not itself glorify the "Teutonic Codes" of "our Anglo-Saxon ancestors," but its praise of Tacitus encouraged those who did (Maine, 1972, 6–7, 71, 216–17).

16. Most pertinent is Benedict (1979, esp. 46–48, 53–56), who somewhat understates how contested state-centered republicanism had been by Whig nationalists. See also Benedict, 1981; Benedict, 1985; Gillman, 1993, 19–60. My stress on attachments to state-centered republicanism might be challenged by Hartzians, who could correctly contend that many antislavery ex-Jacksonians were at least equally attached to laissez-faire free labor views. But at this point, many more lawyers and judges were willing to contend that states' rights were constitutionally required than would make similar claims for laissez-faire; and the resulting opposition of the courts to many nationalistic Reconstruction measures was a vital element in its demise.

17. Sumner in *Cong. Globe*, 39th Cong., 1st Sess., pt. 1, 673–87 (Feb. 6, 1866).

18. Donald, 1970, 199–200, 226–27, 245–47; Wiecek, 1972, 183, 193–94, 208; McConnell, 1995, 987, 997–98. Sumner was inspired to rely on the republican guarantee clause in part by the writings of the Hegelian pro-Republican German emigré political scientist Francis Lieber.

19. Israel, ed., 1966, 1148–49, 1167 (quotations from Johnson's third and fourth annual messages to Congress).

20. *Texas v. White*, 7 Wall. 700 (1869) at 729–30.

21. Wiecek, 1972, 172, 182–86, 220–30.

22. Du Bois, 1992, 179–80, 187–88, 319–20, 596.

23. From the perspective of ascriptive Americanism, moreover, the punishment of denationalization was something of a fiction: one could be a traitorous American, but native-born Americans, at least, could never truly be non-Americans.

24. 13 Stat. L. 490, sec. 21; Tsiang, 1942, 84. The leading case sustaining the law but designating it "highly penal" is *Huber v. Reily*, 53 Pa. 112, 114–15 (1866), written by future Supreme Court Justice William Strong. Reily was followed in, e.g., *State v. Symonds*, 47 Me. 148 (1869), *Goetscheus v. Matthewson*, 6 N.Y. 420 (1875), and *Kurtz v. Moffitt*, 115 U.S. 487 (1885). The denationalization provision of the desertion was invalidated by the Warren Court as "cruel and unusual punishment" in *Trop v. Dulles*, 356 U.S. 86 (1958).

25. McPherson, 1988, 851–52. Lincoln had in fact long been willing to take some contextually radical stances when it did cost him popular support, as when he made himself a one-term congressman by vociferously opposing the Mexican-American War.

26. E. Foner, 1988, 60–62, 66, 189, 216; Du Bois, 1992, 151–52, 157, 190, 596.

27. Fredrickson, 1971, 179; Belz, 1978, 54–58; Oubre, 1978, 196; E. Foner, 1988, 144, 167, 277; Du Bois, 1992, 591, 595.

28. Du Bois, 1992, 368.
29. E. Foner, 1988, 68–69. McKaye also advocated an apprenticeship system that others thought smacked too much of servitude; Du Bois, 1992, 245.
30. McFeely, 1968, 47, 97; Oubre, 1978, 53–54; E. Foner, 1988, 70–71, 105–6, 290; Freedman quoted at 164.
31. McFeely, 1968, 68–71, 120; Nieman, 1979, xiv–xvii; Hyman & Wiecek, 1982, 314–16; Du Bois, 1992, 221–24.
32. Lee & Passell, 1979, 309–10, who argue that the costly railroad grants were often of "dubious value"; McFeely, 1968, 230; McPherson, 1988, 451–52; E. Foner, 1988, 158; Lanza, 1990, 15; Du Bois, 1992, 211–12.
33. Stampp, 1965, 50–53; Du Bois, 1992, 249–51, 258; E. Foner, 1988, 176–79.
34. Stampp, 1965, 62–65, McFeely, 1968, 56, 93–94, 98–105, 133–40, 146–48, 171–75, 227; Benedict, 1974, 248–49; Belz, 1976, 72–76, 86; M. Keller, 1977, 64–65; Oubre, 1978, 12, 53–54, 57; Nieman, 1979, 46–49; P. Foner, 1983b, 468–69; E. Foner, 1988, 68–71, 158–62, 181–92; Du Bois, 1992, 252, 254.
35. McFeely, 1968, 149–65; M. Keller, 1977, 229; Oubre, 1978, 189; Litwack, 1979, 262, 282–85, 366–71; Nieman, 1979, x, 24–25, 72–98; Hyman & Wiecek, 1982, 303, 314–15, 319–21; E. Foner, 1988, 199–210, 215–16, 425–44.
36. McFeely, 1968, 149–65; E. Foner, 1988, 165–67, 172–75, 215–16.
37. Israel, ed., 1966, 1150, 1152; Belz, 1976, 70, 77–78; Belz, 1978, 73; Hyman & Wiecek, 1982, 420; Kaczorowski, 1985, 27–32, 49–52; E. Foner, 1988, 342–43, 429; Du Bois, 1992, 341, 591–93, 673, 678. On Johnson's pivotal role, Michael Les Benedict, who has argued against the radical potential of much Reconstruction legislation, still concludes that, to "a large degree, the failure of Reconstruction could be blamed on Andrew Johnson's abuse of his presidential powers." On the broader role of racism, Fredrickson notes that even the report of the Freedmen's Inquiry Commission anticipated that blacks as a group would occupy a single social niche, predictably a subordinate one. Hence racially based doubts about programs aimed at genuine black equality were present even among architects of Reconstruction from the outset. If their programs had been supported, fully implemented, and successful, however, those doubts might have been refuted (Fredrickson, 1971, 173, 179–80; Benedict, 1974, 251).

    Eric Foner points out that the racist violence "crossed class lines," involving rich and poor whites alike, supporting the relative independence of racial motives from purely economic concerns (1988, 432). The violence was effective. As early as 1868, nine Louisiana parishes with 11,064 registered Republicans produced only nineteen votes for Grant; seven produced none (M. Keller, 1977, 225).
38. McFeely, 1968, 210–20, 230–38, 243–46; Oubre, 1978, 84–90, 95, 100, 104–7, 110–16, 129–38, 141–44; E. Foner, 1988, 87, 246, 404, 568; Lanza, 1990, 14–15, 22, 29, 53, 63, 66, 74, 80–81, 84–85, 97, 113. In ending military governance in the South, Johnson also relied on the Supreme Court's decision in *Ex parte Milligan,* 4 Wall. 2 (1866), which held that military courts could not displace civilian ones in Indiana, where the civilian government was still operating. The author of the opinion, Justice David Davis, privately denied that the decision undercut the authority of military tribunals in Southern states undergoing Reconstruction, but Johnson ordered these military courts to turn civilians over to local agencies. Benedict, 1974, 249–51; Belz, 1976, 46; Belz, 1978, 57; Oubre, 1978, 87–10, 138, 156–57, 186–87, 192–93; Nieman, 1979, 54–57; Litwack, 1979, 379–85, 403–8; Hyman & Wiecek, 1982, 421–22; Kaczorowski, 1985, 30–31; Wiecek, 1988, 90–91; E. Foner, 1988, 153, 157–67, 208–9, 246–51, 272.
39. Belz, 1976, 37–38; Nieman, 1979, ix; E. Foner, 1988, 155–56, 169–70, 215, 246.

40. In recent years, Robert Kaczorowski has forcefully advanced a version of the radical inter-
    pretations of the postwar amendments and the 1866 Civil Rights Act. He believes that the
    Thirteenth Amendment authorized, and the 1866 act and the Fourteenth Amendment rep-
    resented, federal efforts to regulate the entire range of human and civic rights "directly, ir-
    respective of the presence of discriminatory state action and regardless of the source of the
    violation," public or private. Other scholars, including Michael Les Benedict, Herman Belz,
    and (at the extreme) Raoul Berger, contend that the Thirteenth Amendment merely au-
    thorized regulating the end of chattel slavery, and the 1866 act, as well as the Fourteenth
    Amendment, were intended only to prevent the states from engaging in racial discrimina-
    tion with regard to a narrow range of civil rights. See Graham, 1968; ten Broek, 1965; Hy-
    man, 1973; Benedict, 1974; Belz, 1976; Belz, 1978; Berger, 1977; M. Keller, 1977, 66; Hyman
    & Wiecek, 1982, 416–19; Kaczorowski, 1985; Kaczorowski, 1987; Zuckert, 1986; Curtis,
    1986.
41. W. E. Nelson, 1988, esp. 123–47; McConnell, 1995, 1014–16, 1024–29.
42. *Cong. Globe,* 39th Cong., 1st Sess., 1866, at 430, 1291 (Bingham), 527, 1756–57 (Trumbull),
    570 (Morrill), 741 (Sen. Henry Lane, Ind.), 1115–17 (Wilson), 1152 (Rep. Russell Thayer,
    Pa.), 1262 (Rep. John Broomall, Pa.).
43. *Cong. Globe,* 39th Cong., 1st Sess., 1866, at 430 (Bingham), 476, 572, 606, 1757 (Trumbull),
    1116–17 (Wilson), 1151 (Thayer), and cf. 867 (Rep. William Newell, N.J.).
44. A draft proposal to ban state racial discrimination "in civil rights and immunities" gener-
    ally was rejected due to conservative objections. The complete language of section 1 of the
    act is: "*Be it enacted by the Senate and House of Representatives of the United States of Amer-
    ica in Congress assembled,* That all persons born in the United States and not subject to any
    foreign power, excluding Indians not taxed, are hereby declared to be citizens of the United
    States; and such citizens, of every race and color without regard to any previous condition
    of slavery or involuntary servitude, except as a punishment for crime whereof the party
    shall have been duly convicted, shall have the same right, in every State and Territory in the
    United States, to make and enforce contracts, to sue, be parties, and give evidence, to in-
    herit, purchase, lease, sell, hold, and convey real and personal property, and to full and equal
    benefit of all laws and proceedings for the security of persons and property, as is enjoyed
    by white citizens, and shall be subject to like punishment, pains, and penalties, and to none
    other, any law, statute, ordinance, regulation, or custom, to the contrary notwithstanding."
    See also Belz, 1976, 161–70; Belz, 1978, 116–17; Nieman, 1979, 111–15; Hyman & Wiecek,
    1982, 394–98, 416–17.
45. Civil Rights Act, April 9, 1866, secs. 2–5; Kutler, 1968, 147–52; Hyman & Wiecek, 1982, 415.
46. *Cong. Globe,* 39th Cong., 1st Sess., 1866, at 504, 507, 530, 1776 (Johnson), 523, 529–30, 575,
    577 (Davis), 526 (Guthrie), 1122, 1153 (Rogers).
47. *Cong. Globe,* 39th Cong., 1st Sess., 1866, at 475 (Trumbull), 1088 (Rep. Frederick Wood-
    bridge, Va.), 1117 (Wilson) 1124 (Rep. Burton Cook, Ill.), 1152 (Thayer), 1160, 1293
    (Shellabarger). See also Belz, 1976, 160, 165.
48. Section 1 reads as follows: "All persons born or naturalized in the United States, and sub-
    ject to the jurisdiction thereof, are citizens of the United States and of the State wherein
    they reside [the citizenship clause]. No State shall make or enforce any law which shall
    abridge the privileges or immunities of citizens of the United States [the privileges and im-
    munities clause]; nor shall any State deprive any person of life, liberty, or property, with-
    out due process of law [the due process clause]; nor deny to any person within its jurisdic-
    tion the equal protection of the laws [the equal protection clause]."
49. *Cong. Globe,* 39th Cong., 1st Sess., 1866, at 1034 (Bingham), 2464 (Thayer), 2498
    (Broomall); Belz, 1976, 171–72; Schuck & Smith, 1985, 74.

50. In *Lanz v. Randall,* 14 F. Cas. 1131 (U.S.C.C.D. Minn., 1876), Samuel Miller sitting as Circuit Justice indicated his belief that states could only bestow their own citizenship via implementation of federal naturalization laws creating U.S citizens, but he did not decide the case on that ground. Thus, as late as *McDonel v. State,* 90 Ind. 320 (1883), the Indiana state courts could still claim that states could confer their own citizenships. The precedent clearly repudiating any state power to create even state citizens would not come until *Minneapolis v. Reum,* 56 F. Rep. 576 (1893).

51. *Cong. Globe,* 39th Cong., 1st Sess., 1866, at 2893 (Trumbull) to 2895 (Howard); Schuck & Smith, 1985, 72–89.

52. That is why the amendment's framers did not use the term *allegiance.* Almost no one wished to concede that these "semi-sovereign" tribes did not ultimately owe some basic allegiance to the fully sovereign United States.

53. See Schuck & Smith, 1985, 79–83.

54. Schuck & Smith, 1985, 116–19, 129–36. The jurisdiction requirement is thus understood to signal that the Fourteenth Amendment citizenship clause encompasses all persons born in the geographic U.S. of parents who had been implicitly promised citizenship for their children in return for their own permanent allegiance, the version of birthright citizenship endorsed by Vattel and Burlamaqui. If, moreover, we adopt the more inclusive position suggested (though ambiguously) by Burlamaqui, these parents would include both citizens and legally admitted permanent resident aliens. Then the children of immigrant as well as native-born blacks, Chinese, and other ethnic derivations would be citizens by birth, as the Fourteenth Amendment framers clearly intended. Excluded would be children of parents belonging to Native Americans tribes, claimed to have chosen to preserve their own national identities despite their partial dependence, as well as those of temporary visitors, diplomats, members of occupying armies, and, today, illegal aliens. The Fourteenth Amendment's framers intended all these groups to be excluded from their guarantee of birthright citizenships except for illegal aliens—an empty or nearly empty set then, and so not a group they explicitly considered.

55. The best developed critiques are Martin (1985, and see reply in Schuck & Smith, 1986), Neuman (1987; 1996, 166–87), and Carens (1987).

56. Joseph Carens has argued forcefully that, whatever the merits of our interpretation from the standpoint of liberal republican theory taken abstractly, adoption of it in the U.S. now, when the citizenship clause has been read more inclusively historically, would symbolically convey support for illiberal exclusionary policies. If so, he may be right to argue that the reading we proposed should be resisted (Carens, 1987, 436–38). Carens acknowledges (at 439) that as a matter of pure theory his preferred communitarian approach to membership also points to exactly the results we favored: no constitutional birthright citizenship for children of illegal aliens, but no expulsion of children of illegals who have grown up in the American community (cf. Schuck & Smith, 1985, 39–40, 134). Hence his argument about the symbolic message sent by altering American practices now is vital to his critique.

57. From 1873 to 1875, that situation was altered, but only as a result of an oversight. The compilers of the long-awaited U.S. Revised Statutes in 1873 made a number of errors in their efforts to arrange the nation's laws in more orderly fashion. One mistake achieved what Sumner had so ardently and unsuccessfully sought: the sections on naturalization omitted the phrase "free white persons," which had been included in the general provisions governing naturalization since 1790. But early in 1875, Congress passed a statute "to correct errors and to supply omissions in the Revised Statutes" which restored the missing words and once again limited access to citizenship via naturalization to whites and persons of

African nativity or descent. The mishap is discussed in a number of later cases, such as *In re Halladjian,* 174 F. 834 (U.S.C.C.D. Mass., 1909).

58. Sumner, 1900, v. 11, 418; 41st Cong., 2d Sess., Act of July 14, 1870, ch. 254, sec. 7, 16 Stat. 256. In relation to the exclusion of Asians from naturalization, it is noteworthy that in the 1869 case of *U.S. v. Lucero,* 1 N.M. 422, the territorial supreme court specified that the Treaty of Guadalupe Hidalgo had collectively naturalized the Pueblo Indians, along with all other citizens of Mexico who did not elect to stay Mexican. But Chief Justice Watts stressed that the Pueblo Indians were "law-abiding, sober, and industrious," and so in a superior legal category to the "wild, wandering savages" of the more northern and eastern tribes. He categorized those "wicked and wild savages" as "like other animals" (441–43). Hence the era's perpetuation of some claims of racial hierarchy despite the reduction of restrictions on blacks was apparent here, too.

59. Naturalization records of the late 1860s and 1870s do not reveal any naturalizations of illegally imported former slaves, a fact which may suggest that most courts assumed implicitly that all emancipated slaves were in some way made both free and citizens by the Thirteenth Amendment, the Civil Rights Act, and the Fourteenth Amendment. (I am grateful to Hillary Greene for an exhaustive if ultimately inconclusive search of records pertaining to this question.) One route to that result is suggested by Shellabarger's defense of Congress's power to naturalize native-born blacks. He appealed to the "law of nations," which designated some persons as "subjects" who were "not citizens of a given country, and yet who are not foreigners," since they "owed no foreign allegiance." Into that class he placed all "slaves" (*Cong. Globe,* 39th Cong., 1st Sess., 1866, at 1160). That position implies that all whom the law had treated as American-owned slaves, whether illegally imported or not, were American "subjects," either by birth or by the brutal "naturalization" that enslavement worked upon them. Thus all former slaves, foreign- as well as native-born, were declared U.S. citizens by the Fourteenth Amendment, as their contemporaries all assumed.

Gerald Neuman has instead suggested that though all native-born children of blacks were made citizens by the Civil Rights Act and the Fourteenth Amendment, illegally imported slaves were not naturalized by these measures (Neuman, 1987, 498–500; see also Neuman, 1996, 178–79). He assumes (1987, 498–99) that the arguments of Schuck & Smith, 1985, also imply the same result; but we read the citizenship clause in light of the international law views that Shellabarger invoked. It is true that by international law, illegally imported slaves should not have been on U.S. soil; but they were nonetheless the forcibly "naturalized" property of Americans, recognized as persons after emancipation, and therefore citizens under the rule of the Fourteenth Amendment.

On those premises it was also plausible to suggest that the Thirteenth Amendment, by ending the slaves' "subjectship," had already made them all citizens, as so many Republicans contended (see, e.g., *U.S. v. Rhodes,* 27 F. Cas. 785, 790, U.S.C.C.D. Ky., 1866; cf. Hyman & Wiecek, 1982, 402). But officials might also have held, as they later would in regard to nonwhite territorial inhabitants, that they were American nationals only, not citizens.

60. That fact again counts against the view that postwar liberals saw property rights as too sacred to warrant interference.

61. *Cong. Globe,* 39th Cong., 1st Sess., 1866, at 1121, 2538 (Rogers), 1157 (Rep. Anthony Thornton, Ill.), 1296 (Rep. R. W. Latham, W. Va.), 1681 (Veto Message of Pres. Andrew Johnson), 1777–78 (R. Johnson), 1782 (Sen. Edgar Cowan, Pa.).

62. *Cong. Globe,* 39th Cong., 1st Sess., 1866, at 497–98 (Sen. Peter Van Winkle, W. Va., citing "divine institutions" of racial hierarchy), 523, 575–76 (Davis, citing "ethnologists"), 2538 (Rogers, citing "the edict of God Almighty" against social equality of the races), 2891 (Cowan), 2939 (Sen. Thomas Hendricks, Ind.), 3038 (Sen. James McDougall, Ca.; see also

his remarks in the *Globe*, 38th Cong., 1st Sess., 1864, at 1490, invoking "science" and the "law of nature" to support racial separation).

63. See, e.g., *Cong. Globe*, 39th Cong., 1st Sess., 1866, at 2765–66 (Howard), 2961–62 (Sen. Luke Poland, Vt.); W. E. Nelson, 1988, 114–16, 119, 123–24.

64. Belz, 1976, 173.

65. The full text of section 2 of the Fourteenth Amendment reads: "Representatives shall be apportioned among the several states according to their respective numbers, counting the whole number of persons in each State, excluding Indians not taxed. But when the right to vote at any election for the choice of electors for President and Vice President of the United States, Representatives in Congress, the Executive and Judicial officers of a State, or the members of the Legislature thereof, is denied to any of the male inhabitants of such State, being twenty-one years of age, and citizens of the United States, or in any way abridged, except for participation in rebellion, or other crime, the basis of representation therein shall be reduced in the proportion which the number of such male citizens shall bear to the whole number of male citizens twenty-one years of age in such State." See also Stanton, Anthony, & Gage, eds., 1882, v. II, 172–73, 229–65, 327–28, 378, 400, 427, 756; Flexner, 1975, 145–54; DuBois, 1978, 53–104.

66. Congress also passed a Habeas Corpus Act that further expanded citizens' legal rights to remove cases to federal courts. Certain portions were subsequently repealed in order to aid military prosecution of an anti-Reconstruction publisher, William McCardle; but extensive habeas jurisdiction nonetheless survived. See *Ex parte McCardle*, 7 Wall. 506 (1869); *Ex parte Yerger*, 8 Wall. 85 (1869); C. M. Green, 1962, 296–301; C. M. Green, 1967, 78–96; Gillette, 1965, 28–31; Porter, 1971, 173–81; Benedict, 1974, 210–43, 252–56; Belz, 1978, 102–3; Hyman & Wiecek, 1982, 441–45, 453–55; Wiecek, 1988, 87–90; E. Foner, 1988, 272–79.

67. Barth, 1964, 188–89; Miller, 1964, 173–74; Lyman, 1974, 59–65; Higham, 1975, 33; Perlmutter, 1977, 44; Chen, 1980, 45–46, 137–39; Hutchinson, 1981, 48–60; Archdeacon, 1983, 147–49; E. Foner, 1988, 21, 213–14, 380, 391, 419–20; Takaki, 1993, 195, 205–8.

68. *Cong. Globe*, 40th Cong., 2d Sess., ch. 249, 223–24; Tsiang, 1942, 84–88.

69. Tsiang, 1942, 88–100.

70. The Nebraska Territory had rejected black voting rights in 1866, Michigan and Missouri would do so in 1868, and New York followed suit in 1869. Furthermore, the successful Minnesota referendum was misleadingly presented, and though the Iowa vote was a clear victory for black suffrage, blacks were still ineligible for the state legislature. Gillette, 1965, 26–27; Benedict, 1974, 257, 272–74; Brock, 1975, 92–93; E. Foner, 1988, 314–15, 338.

71. McPherson, 1964, 424–28; Gillette, 1965, 43–47; Fredrickson, 1971, 183–86; Benedict, 1974, 322–36; Brock, 1975, 94–107; M. Keller, 1977, 68–70; Belz, 1978, 126–27; E. Foner, 1988, 343, 446.

72. On the ratification fight see Gillette, 1965, 79–165.

73. Stanton, Anthony, & Gage, eds., 1882, v. II, 172–73, 229–65, 327–28, 378, 400, 427, 756; Flexner, 1975, 155–56; DuBois, 1978, 172–74, 189–99; DuBois, 1988, 187; Clinton, 1984, 93–94; Kugler, 1987, 45, 55–78. Ironically, these divisions flared in the year John Stuart Mill and Harriet Mill published their classic essay, *The Subjection of Women*.

74. O'Neill, 1969, 18–23; DuBois, 1978, 200–201; Degler, 1980, 344; Clinton, 1984, 93–94; Kugler, 1987, 35, 76–79, 87. In 1870, more than 350,000 women worked as industrial laborers, mostly in clothing industries. Numerous works summarize the general history of women and labor during these years, and the failed efforts of Anthony and the NWSA to ally with William Sylvis's short lived National Labor Union and the two unions that admitted women—printers and cigarmakers—along with incipient female unionization

among typesetters and shoemakers. See, e.g., Flexner, 1975, 134–44; DuBois, 1978, 104–61; Degler, 1980, 395–401; Leach, 1980, 163–67; Clinton, 1984, 114–17; Kugler, 1987, 115–47.

75. DuBois, 1978, 178. For similar statements by Stanton and Anthony, see Degler, 1980, 330; DuBois, ed., 1981, 118–24; Kugler, 1987, 104.

76. O'Nell, 1969, 70–72; Leach, 1980, 33–34, 147, 153, 157, 205–6; DuBois, 1978, 174–75, 188–90; DuBois, 1988, 189–91; Clinton, 1984, 93, 141. In these years, Catharine Beecher co-authored a work with Harriet Beecher Stowe, *The American Woman's Home; or, Principles of Domestic Science* (1869), and, in 1872, *Woman's Profession as Mother and Educator, with Views in Opposition to Woman Suffrage* (Sklar, 1973, 263–67). Antoinette Brown Blackwell was married to Samuel Blackwell, brother of Lucy Stone's husband, Henry Blackwell (the brothers of Elizabeth). Stone and Henry Blackwell were moving forces, and Antoinette an active participant, in founding the AWSA (Flexner, 1975, 30, 117; DuBois, 1978, 27, 186, 195–200).

77. Kentucky had given school suffrage to widows and single women in 1838, and Kansas granted it to all women in 1859. During the 1870s there was a burst of such activity. Illinois made women eligible for school committees in 1872; Massachusetts did so in 1874, although women could not vote in such elections until 1879; Michigan gave them school board suffrage in 1875, Minnesota in 1876, Colorado in 1877, Oregon and New Hampshire in 1878; and similar measures proliferated thereafter. Referenda and other attempts to give women the vote more generally failed in Michigan (1874), New Jersey (1874), Colorado (1877), Rhode Island (1877), and Massachusetts (1878) (Woody, 1929, v. II, 441–42; Leach, 1980, 174). See also M. Keller, 1977, 159; Degler, 1980, 334–35; Clinton, 1984, 110; Kugler, 1987, 99–100.

78. Victoria Woodhull's paper accused the Rev. Henry Ward Beecher, first president of the AWSA and the nation's most renowned clergyman, of committing adultery with Elizabeth Tilton, the wife of his friend and parishioner, reform editor Theodore Tilton. The latter's suit against Beecher ended in a hung jury after sensational publicity (Flexner, 1975, 157; Degler, 1980, 329; Kugler, 1987, 90–91).

79. Democrats regarded these laws as unconstitutional, labeling them "Force Acts." Act of May 31, 1870, 41st Cong., 2d Sess., ch. 114, 140–46; Act of April 20, 1871, 42d Cong., 1st Sess., ch. 22, 13–15; Belz, 1978, 126–35; Hyman & Wiecek, 1982, 467, 470–72, 489–92, 507; E. Foner, 1988, 454–59, 528–29, 555–56.

80. An incredulous Charles Sumner responded to Stewart's switch by reading the Gospel story of Peter renouncing Christ from the Senate Bible and proclaiming, "Thrice has a Senator on this floor denied these great principles of the Declaration of Independence." *Cong. Globe,* July 4, 1869, rep. *Cong. Globe,* 41st Cong., 2d Sess., 5150 (1869–70); ibid., 5154–55, 5171; Takaki, 1993, 208; Tichenor, 1995, 3–6.

81. Ironically, the slaveowning members of the Civilized Tribes found their former servants possessed of greater civic status than they possessed themselves, even though they had to accept responsibility for some forms of freedmen's aid, such as schooling (Mardock, 1971, 36; Wise & Deloria, 1971, 263; Prucha, 1984, 431–34).

82. Mardock, 1971, 3–4; Trachtenberg, 1982, 28–32; R. Keller, 1983, 9, 12, 17–30, 150, 154; Prucha, 1984, 481–82, 501–2, 512, 524–25.

83. Mardock, 1971, 88–98; Washburn, 1975, 237; M. Keller, 1977, 155; Cohen, 1982, 105, 121; R. Keller, 1983, 17–18, 184, 205; Prucha, 1984, 463–64, 475, 481–83, 496–519.

84. Washburn, 1975, 209; Cohen, 1982, 106–7; Prucha, 1984, 439, 528–32; Wright, 1992, 301–3.

85. Wise & Deloria, 1971, 268; Washburn, 1975, 238; M. Keller, 1977, 175–76; Cohen, 1982, 107, 127; R. Keller, 1983, 76–89, 127–28, 150, 164, 185; Prucha, 1984, 520–33.

86. R. Keller, 1983, 206–7.

87. M. Keller, 1977, 131–33; Cremin, 1980, 149–50, 341, 406, 516; Hyman, 1986, 36.
88. Total school and college expenditures rose from $16,162,000 in 1850 to $94,402,726 in 1870, an increase of nearly 600% in current dollars and 400% in constant dollars, during a period when the school-age population increased 160%. Woody, 1929, v. I, 396–99; Cremin, 1980, 179–80, 400; Degler, 1980, 309.
89. C. M. Green, 1962, 304–9; C. M. Green, 1967, 87–89; McPherson, 1964, 158–72, 386–94, 406–7; M. Keller, 1977, 215–16, 234; Cremin, 1980, 515–19; R. C. Morris, 1981, 3; Richardson, 1986, 17–37, 75–84, 109–11, 123; E. Foner, 1988, 40–41, 97–100, 144–48, 207–8, 319–22, 364–68. In addition to its contributions to lower education, the AMA set up seven rather rudimentary black colleges (Berea College, Fisk University, Atlanta University, Hampton Institute, Talladega College, Tougaloo College, and Straight University) and aided in establishing Howard University.
90. Clinton, 1984, 123, 128–31.
91. High among women's tasks was teaching, the occupation of 90% of female professionals in 1870 and a vocation which women were coming to dominate at the elementary school level. They did so only in the face of criticisms about the dangers of feminizing education. By and large, teaching at higher levels, as well as supervisory posts, remained closed to them. Even at the elementary level, female teachers were paid only 60% what men earned, and their rise in the profession led to a decline in its level of compensation. As women began to assume a few administrative offices in the mid-1870s, criticisms mounted, aided by the general conservative resurgence of the later 1870s. During that decade women also received more formal training in their other major profession, nursing, and had some access to business, commercial, and medical schools, although still in very limited numbers. Woody, 1929, v. I, 396, 493, 545; v. II, 67–87, 225–29; Leach, 1980, 173–74; Degler, 1980, 309–12, 379–81.
92. Eaton, 1874.
93. The Morrill Act's comparative thriving is traceable to the ways its provisions shrewdly blended Whiggish national action to promote development with republican and Jacksonian concerns for local control and the interests of agrarian and mechanical producers. The land grant colleges were state-run; and although they could encompass all "scientific and classical studies," their chief aim was the "practical education of the industrial classes" in "agriculture and mechanic arts." Hence, though the act aroused fear and opposition, it never threatened the institutions of agrarian, state-centered republicanism too directly. Eaton, 1874; Woody, 1929, v. II, 182, 225–29; McPherson, 1964, 394–98, 401–3; M. Keller, 1977, 133–36; Cremin, 1980, 165, 177–80, 488–97, 510–12; Morris, 1981, 23–32, 94–95, 131–34, 177–87; Clinton, 1984, 124–25; Richardson, 1986, 28–31, 137, 166; E. Foner, 1988, 99–100, 145–46, 428, 471.
94. Green, 1962, 320–21; Green, 1967, 99–101; McPherson, 1964, 395–400; Vaughn, 1977, 119–40; E. Foner, 1988, 40, 145, 320–22, 366–68, 553–54.
95. Armstrong's protégé Booker T. Washington soon demonstrated that many blacks were willing to endorse this separationist and repressive credo. McPherson, 1964, 393; Spivey, 1978, 17–38; R. C. Morris, 1981, 151–67, 170; Richardson, 1986, 41, 185, 199, 249, 255; E. Foner, 1988, 146.
96. By 1873, 53% of black children and 44% of white children in D.C. attended public schools, with the whites primarily attending private schools. Few of the public school teachers had more than grammar school educations (C. M. Green, 1962, 319–20, 369–70, 387–88; C. M. Green, 1967, 110, 113–14.
97. Tindall, 1916, 17–18, 31–32; C. M. Green, 1962, 332–62, 373; C. M. Green, 1967, 103–17.
98. C. M. Green, 1962, 321–22; McConnell, 1995, 987–90, 1049–86.

99. The law further excluded aliens serving a sentence for nonpolitical crimes or released on condition of their emigration. Barth, 1964, 197–99, 210–11; Miller, 1964, 153–54, 159, 162, 173–77, 193–97; Higham, 1975, 36; Hutchinson, 1981, 65–66; Archdeacon, 1983, 144; Takaki, 1993, 148–49, 209–15.

100. Quotation is from Wiecek, 1988, 88. The 1875 Civil Rights Act, like other enforcement bills, also clarified removal procedures. The Court expanded federal judicial powers in other ways, too, indicating that it would not be bound by state court interpretations of state contractual agreements in *Gelpcke v. Dubuque,* 1 Wall. 175, 206 (1864) and subsequent cases. See also Frankfurter, 1928, 501, 508; Moore & Weckstein, 1964a, 6–9; Kutler, 1968, 149–60; Hyman & Wiecek, 1982, 260–62, 365–69, 415; Friedman, 1985, 386–87; Purcell, 1992, 15.

    In the wake of the laws expanding federal jurisdiction, many lower federal courts and the U.S. Supreme Court considered newly salient issues of restrictions on federal jurisdiction imposed by the Judiciary Act of 1789. In a pattern that would heighten after Reconstruction, the federal courts frequently abjured expansive readings of their new jurisdiction, though they upheld the statutes. See, e.g., *Mayor v. Cooper,* 73 U.S. 247 (1867); *Bushnell v. Kennedy,* 76 U.S. 387 (1869); *Justices v. Murray,* 76 U.S. 274 (1870); *Coal Co. v. Blatchford,* 78 U.S. 172 (1870); *Case of the Sewing Machine Companies,* 85 U.S. 553 (1873) (requiring complete diversity of citizenship between adverse parties before removals to federal courts could be made, a restrictive reading that prompted the conferral of federal question removal jurisdiction in the 1875 act); *Ober v. Gallagher,* 93 U.S. 199 (1876).

101. Lyman Trumbull, Carl Schurz, and Horace Greeley were among the most prominent of the Liberal Republicans who retreated from any further strong federal role. Their views, elitist and at times overtly racist, were recognizable versions of liberalism; but they cannot be cited as proof of liberalism's inherent racism and elitism, as their views then had minority status. It is nonetheless true that something like their form of liberalism dominated the Republican party later in the century. Ahern, 1979, 52–55, 61–65; Hyman & Wiecek, 1982, 472, 490; E. Foner, 1988, 453–56, 498–99, 503–4.

102. For the much more divided pattern of state judicial interpretations, see Hyman, 1973, 484–86; Kaczorowski, 1985, 4–10, 12; W. E. Nelson, 1988, 149–55.

103. Swayne also confirmed that Talbot was a citizen, though he accepted that congressional naturalization authority extended only to the foreign-born (and, remarkably, that the states could still naturalize any native-born noncitizens). Relying on Cokean premises, he held that once emancipation removed the incapacities of slavery, all native-born blacks acquired the citizenship that their birth would otherwise have previously bestowed. Thus he regarded the citizenship clause of the 1866 act as unnecessary and "inoperative," though prudently provided. In passing, Swayne emphasized heavily the common law's minimalist view of what citizenship entailed. The status, he said, "determines nothing" as to whether the citizen possesses "any" rights, "civil or political." By viewing virtually all rights as positively established, Swayne may have made the structuring of civic rights via the 1866 act seem more appropriate; but he did so at the cost of denying virtually all inherent prerogatives of citizenship or, for that matter, personhood.

104. *U.S. v. Rhodes,* 27 F. Cas. 785–87 (U.S.C.C.D. Ky., 1866). The defendants' counsel also argued that Bristow had failed to aver that white citizens enjoyed the right to testimony, but Swayne simply took judicial notice of the fact that the Kentucky Code of Civil Practice granted whites that right (786).

    Reading the case expansively, Robert Kaczorowski has argued that Kentucky's ban on black testimony could not have been the basis for federal jurisdiction, because then the court would merely have voided the discriminatory state law. He believes that jurisdiction stemmed from the *vigilantes'* violation of Talbot's rights of person and property, secured under section 1 of the 1866 act. Thus he sees Swayne as endorsing the view that the 1866 act gave the federal courts authority to deal directly with private violations of all national civil rights (Kaczorowski, 1985, 7–8). Though ingenious, this reading is strained. At 787, Swayne says that the case has been properly brought because whenever a black person is denied "the right to testify as if he were white," the act gives "the courts of the United States jurisdiction of all causes, civil and criminal, which concern" that person.

105. *Rhodes* at 789–94. At 788, Swayne says the Thirteenth Amendment "trenches directly upon the power of the states and of the people of the states." But he may only mean that the ultimate power of each state lies with its people, or that the Thirteenth merely authorizes the federal government to prevent private actors from imposing slavery.

106. Kaczorowski, 1985, 52.

107. Prior to their emancipation in 1864, Betsey Turner and her daughter, Elizabeth, were slaves of Philemon Hambleton. Hambleton then gained Betsey's consent for Elizabeth to be apprenticed to him under terms harsher than state law allowed for whites. He did not have to educate her and could transfer her to another at will. Chief Justice Chase held that these terms amounted to involuntary servitude, and that in light of the greater legal rights of whites, the agreement also violated Sec. 1 of the 1866 Act. He added that all colored persons were U.S. citizens "equally with white persons." The terse decision aided efforts by Freedmen's Bureau agents to combat such apprenticeship schemes. Over 2,000 black minors gained release in its aftermath. *In re Turner*, 24 F. Cas. 339 (U.S.C.C.D. Md., 1867); Belz, 1978, 144–45; Hyman & Wiecek, 1982, 320, 433–34.

   That same year, the Supreme Court upheld the Military Reconstruction Acts twice. In *Mississippi v. Johnson*, 4 Wall. 475 (1867), Chase refused Mississippi's request to enjoin President Johnson from enforcing the acts, holding that their implementation was within executive discretion as defined in *Marbury v. Madison* (488–99). Then the Court rejected Georgia's claim that enforcing the acts displaced the state's legitimate government. As in *Luther v. Borden,* Justice Nelson wrote that this was a "political question" beyond the Court's scope. *State of Georgia v. Stanton,* 6 Wall. 50, 77–78 (1867).

108. While holding that the reconstructed Texas government did not have to honor agreements made to further the state's illegal war efforts, Chase remarked that the Thirteenth Amendment had merely "confirmed" the freedom the Union army had brought to blacks, and that once freed they "necessarily became part of the people" of each state (*Texas v. White*, 7 Wall. 700, 728 [1869]). Chase cited *Luther* and deferred to Congress's powers to reconstruct the state to render it truly republican (730). He also upheld broad federal jurisdiction by holding that Texas could never have ceased to be in the Union and so was a "state" qualified to sue under the Court's original jurisdiction.

   Soon after, a district court judge, H. H. Leavitt, told a jury that the 1870 Enforcement Act authorized direct judicial action against private actors who obstructed voting rights. He stated that full citizenship for all "not disfranchised by crime" fulfilled the "great principles" of "free republican government," and he saw "good reasons" to hope that giving blacks equal rights would "result in their moral and intellectual elevation" (*U.S. v. Canter*, 25 F. Cas. 281, 282 [U.S.C.C.S.C. Oh., 1870]). As circuit judge William Giles said in *Cully v. Baltimore and Ohio Railway Co.,* 6 F. Cas. 946 (U.S.D.C.C. Md., 1876), he had ruled that refusals of railroads and streetcars to serve blacks discriminated against out-of-state black citizens, and that their citizenship gave blacks the right to vote, even before the Fifteenth Amendment. The cases he cites are listed but not otherwise officially reported, though they received press coverage (Lofgren, 1987, 123–24).

109. The circuit case is *Live-Stock Dealers' and Butchers' Association v. Crescent City Live-Stock Landing and Slaughter-House Co.*, 15 F. Cas. 649 (U.S.C.C.D. La., 1870). The Enforcement Act of 1870 had been passed by the time of this litigation, but it was a relatively unknown quantity and the judges did not discuss it (655).

110. Kaczorowski, 1985, 144–45.

111. *Live-Stock* at 651–55; Kaczorowski, 1985, 145–46. In passing, Bradley built a liberal component into his definition of republicanism, arguing that a "republican government is not merely a government of the people, but it is a free government." To be free, a government must honor liberal rights; it especially must not deprive "its citizens of the right to engage in any lawful pursuit, subject only to reasonable restrictions" (652). Bradley did not address the question of whether the federal government could move against private actors under the amendment or the act, though he did say that after the war began, "several amendments to the constitution have been adopted, intended to protect the citizens from oppression by means of state legislation" (652).

112. Woods, a rare Republican from Georgia, was appointed to the Supreme Court by Rutherford Hayes in 1880, serving until his death in 1887.

113. *U.S. v. Hall*, 26 F. Cas. 79–82 (U.S.C.C.D. Ala., 1871); Hyman & Wiecek, 1982, 435–36; Kaczorowski, 1985, 14–17. Woods also took a strongly nationalistic view of the changes in the basis of citizenship the amendment had wrought. He contended that, previously, U.S. citizenship had been "a consequence of citizenship in a state," but that now matters were fully "reversed." National citizenship was "independent of citizenship in a state, and citizenship in a state is a result of citizenship in the United States" (81), an inversion more complete than Swayne had contemplated in the *Rhodes* decision.

The *Hall* opinion is the clearest evidence for Kaczorowski's thesis that initially federal judges embraced sweeping views of congressional enforcement powers under the Fourteenth Amendment. Kaczorowski errs only in making these views seem less controversial than they were. For example, the *Hall* case is also reported as *U.S. v. Mall*, 26 F. Cas. 1147 (U.S.C.C.S.D. Ala., 1871). But this brief report comments that in the decision, the 1870 act's constitutionality is "affirmed by a somewhat obscure course of reasoning." As to whether the states could deny equal protection by inaction, the report describes this position as "doubtful, and often strenuously denied," even though it agrees that there is "something in it." See also W. E. Nelson, 1988, 241n35.

114. For narrower readings see, e.g., *In re Hobbs*, 12 F. Cas. 262 (U.S.C.C. N.D. Ga., 1871), where Judge Erskine of Georgia's North District sustained the state's antimiscegenation law against complaints that it violated the Art. 1, sec. 10, contract clause and the protection for contracts provided in the 1866 Civil Rights Act, reenacted in 1870. Erskine followed Bradley's opinion in the *Live-Stock* case and accepted that all "essential rights" under the Constitution were protected by the privileges and immunities clause. But he held that though marriage had contract-like qualities, it was "something more . . . an institution of public concernment, created and governed by the public will," traditionally in each state. He thought that the amendment restrained state power in this regard only by insisting on equal protection. Noting that Georgia legislatures made up of blacks as well as whites had not repealed the marriage law and had established segregated schools, Erskine held that the law affected both races identically and so did not violate equal protection.

In *U.S. v. Crosby*, 25 F. Cas. 701–4 (U.S.C.C.D. S.C., 1871), South Carolina circuit judge Hugh L. Bond seemed to agree that the 1870 Enforcement Act properly authorized punishing the "individual citizen who acted by virtue of a state law or upon his individual responsibility" to interfere with constitutionally derived rights. He also thought that the federal government had implied powers to protect qualified voters' participation in federal elections that predated the postwar amendments. But in considering a brutal Klan-inspired private conspiracy to prevent a black Republican from voting which had included an assault on his family in his home, Bond indicated that federal law did not provide a right to vote per se. It simply protected the rights of voters otherwise qualified under state law against certain limited forms of discrimination. Because the record did not show that the black citizen, Amzi Rainey, was by state law qualified to vote on all grounds except race, it was insufficient to justify indictment. Moreover, Bond denied that the Fourth Amendment right to security in one's home was a right "derived from the constitution." It stemmed from the common law. Therefore it could not be included among the Fourteenth Amendment's constitutionally derived immunities. Such reasoning had great potential to limit severely the rights that the federal government could protect. Bond did uphold two counts of the indictment, and Kaczorowski views him as a liberal-minded judge who wrote a hasty and uncharacteristically narrow opinion here (Kaczorowski, 1985, 127–29).

115. *Crandall v. Nevada,* 6 Wall. 35, 43–45 (1867). Miller's reasoning in favor of implicit rights of national citizenship here made the content that he later ascribed to the Fourteenth Amendment's privilege and immunities clause already present in the Constitution prior to that amendment. His opinion in *Loan Association v. Topeka,* 20 Wall. 655, 663 (1874), is another example of Miller's peculiar tendency to find rights implicit in the "essential nature" of the nation's governmental systems, even as he refused to find them protected by explicit constitutional language. Cf. Fairman, 1939, 15–16, 22–27, 63–67, 209–10, 248.

116. *Yates v. Milwaukee,* 77 U.S. 497, 504–7 (1870), cited in *The Stockton Laundry Case, In re Tie Loy,* 26 F. 611 (U.S.C.C. Ca., 1886); *In re Sam Kee,* 31 F. 680 (U.S.C.C. Ca., 1887). At *Yates,* 506–7, Miller explicitly refused to be bound by the Wisconsin Supreme Court's recent contrary construction of common law in regard to the same property (*Yates v. Judd,* 18 Wisc. 118 [1864]). I am indebted here to Kobach, 1995. See also Fairman, 1939, 218; Purcell, 1992, 59–64.

117. Miller's tendency to read many explicit grants of federal power narrowly is also illustrated by his opinion as circuit justice in *Wisconsin v. Duluth,* 30 F. Cas. 382 (U.S.C.C. Minn., 1872). There he read the Constitution's grant of original jurisdiction to the Supreme Court in cases to which a state was a party as prohibiting Wisconsin from suing Minnesota citizens in any lower federal court. Miller thus read federal jurisdiction restrictively, though he also limited each state's power to use federal courts against other states (385).

William E. Nelson explains the puzzling pattern of Miller's opinions by noting that Miller suggested that the Supreme Court could "take jurisdiction" of "general principles" of constitutional law when sitting in review of circuit court decisions, but not when sitting in review of state court judgments. In the latter cases it could apply only the Fourteenth Amendment limits on state action, which he consistently read narrowly. The inspiration for this distinction, Nelson believes, was the Court's decision in *Swift v. Tyson,* 16 Pet. 1 (1842) (overruled in *Erie R.R. v. Tompkins,* 304 U.S. 64 [1938]), holding that circuits courts could reconcile rules in the different states they presided over by applying national common-law standards. That analysis seems consistent with *Yates.* Nelson observes, however, that it is unclear whether most of the Court followed Miller's reasoning (Nelson, 1988, 170–71). And *Wisconsin v. Duluth* suggests that, when sitting as a circuit judge and construing general constitutional principles, Miller still often strove to preserve more Jacksonian views of federalism, retaining a national role in curbing state rivalries but limiting federal displacement of state decisionmaking on most issues. Miller's leading biographer, Charles Fairman, described Miller as a nationalist in many respects but as very wary of both the Reconstruction Congress and corporate efforts to expand and exploit federal jurisdiction (Fairman, 1939, 66–67, 124, 138–40, 183–95, 207–49, 421–24).

118. In *Ward v. Maryland,* 12 Wall. 418, 426–29, 432 (1870), Clifford wrote for the Court striking down a Maryland law that required nonresident traders to pay much more for a license to conduct business than Maryland citizens did. Although Clifford noted arguments based on the commerce clause and on Miller's *McCulloch*-like reasoning, he rested this decision solely on the Article IV privileges and immunities clause. Clifford read it as a comity clause that protected basic economic rights of out-of-state citizens against state protectionist actions. Here it was Bradley who objected to the Court's failure to rely solely on the commerce clause, out of his desire to promote economic development. He thought that the commerce clause invalidated such licensing fees even if they were imposed equally on all U.S. citizens. Clifford argued that the Art. IV clause "plainly and unmistakably secures and protects the right of a citizen of one State to pass into any other State of the Union for the purpose of engaging in lawful commerce, trade, or business without molestation; to acquire personal property; to take and hold real estate; to maintain actions in the courts of the State; and to be exempt from any higher taxes or excises than are imposed by the State upon its own citizens" (430).

119. *Railroad Co. v. Richmond,* 96 U.S. 521 (1877). For the Court, Waite wrote as if the "constitutional prohibition" against takings without compensation applied against the states but permitted "appropriate regulation" (529). He did not clarify whether he was applying the state or national constitution, though his opinion reads as if he is considering first the due process, then the equal protection clauses of the Fourteenth Amendment. Hence, even though it constitutes a retreat from national judicial activism, even more than *Yates* it foreshadows later extensions of the federal takings requirement to the states via the Fourteenth Amendment due process clause. Justice Strong dissented without opinion.

120. E.g., *Welton v. Missouri,* 91 U.S. 275 (1875), relies on the commerce clause, though it has since sometimes been cited as endorsing the Art. IV reasoning in *Ward.* In other cases the Court was reluctant to find either Article IV or commerce clause violations in state laws that unintentionally and incidentally imposed greater burdens on out-of-state businesses. See, e.g., *Woodruff v. Parham,* 75 U.S 123 (1868); *Hinson v. Lott,* 75 U.S. 148 (1868).

As Reconstruction declined, Waite also gave the Art. IV clause a narrow reading, but one consistent with *Corfield v. Coryell,* by ruling in 1876 that Virginia could prevent citizens of other states from planting oysters in a tide-water river even though state citizens could do so. The people of Virginia owned the soil in question in common, and its use was deemed a special privilege of the state's citizens, not a right fundamental to the citizens of all free governments. *McCready v. Virginia,* 94 U.S. 391, 395–96 (1876)

121. The Supreme Court evaded its first opportunity to address these questions, *U.S. v. Avery,* 13 Wall. 251 (1871), a case involving a Klan-inspired murder of a black voter. The Court refused jurisdiction on narrow procedural grounds, claiming that it was improperly asked to act on preliminary motions that could still be ruled upon by lower courts (Kaczorowski, 1985, 129–31).

The Court did read an 1863 law expansively, as banning not merely exclusion but segregation of blacks on railroads operating in the District of Columbia, in *Railroad Co. v. Brown,* 84 U.S. 445 (1873); but this was a narrow precedent (Lofgren, 1987, 124–27; cf. McConnell, 1995, 1117–19, who regards the case as "forgotten" but fails to cite Lofgren's discussion).

122. 85 U.S. 581 (1873). Although its citation is dated 1873, the case was argued in February 1871 and the opinion is reported as December 1871. Kaczorowski states that the ruling was not announced until April 1872 (Kaczorowski, 1985, 140).

123. *Blyew et al. v. U.S.,* 80 U.S. 581 at 591–94, 598–601 (1873). Bradley also stated that the law was a proper exercise of Congress's Thirteenth Amendment enforcement powers, holding that those powers had to go beyond the abolition of slavery, as "the amendment did that," to include powers "to do away with the incidents and consequences of slavery, and to instate the freedmen in the full enjoyment of that civil liberty and equality which the abolition of slavery meant" (601). See also Hyman & Wiecek, 1982, 434–35; Kaczorowski, 1985, 135–42.

In adopting his stance, Strong may have simply been going along with the Court's majority. Writing as circuit justice in *U.S. v. Given* in 1873, he took a much broader view of the 1870 Enforcement Act. Strong ruled that the enforcement provisions of the postwar amendments gave Congress authority to secure the rights that those amendments guaranteed "against any infringement from any quarter." He had no doubt that federal interventions against "private persons" who hindered the exercise of voting rights, and against officers whose failure to protect such rights went uncorrected by the state, were constitutional. *U.S. v. Given,* 25 F. Cas. 1324 (U.S.C.C.D. Del., 1873); Kaczorowski, 1985, 19, 201–3, 227n7.

In two other 1871 cases, Swayne wrote for the Court reiterating his earlier nationalistic claim that the rebel states had never been out of the Union; but he did so in the service of rulings holding that notes involved in slave transactions were protected by the contract clause against subsequent reconstruction legislation rendering them void (*White v. Hart,* 13 Wall. 646 [1871]; *Osborn v. Nicholson,* 13 Wall. 654 [1871]; followed in *Boyce v. Tabb,* 18 Wall. 546 [1873]). Those rulings might well be taken as evidence of liberal obsessions with property rights. But note also that Chase dissented in them, arguing that slave contracts were "against sound morals and natural justice" and sustained only by positive laws which had been constitutionally repealed, with a further ban in the Fourteenth Amendment on compensating slaveowners (663–64). However "liberal" one judges these decisions on economic issues, moreover, they plainly display little concern for blacks.

124. *Slaughter-House Cases,* 16 Wall. 36, 83 U.S. 394 (1873). This litigation was a peculiar forum for interpreting the scope of the postwar amendments restructuring the relations of blacks and whites, as no blacks were involved. Some commentators speculate that the justices thought that the issues would be more safely explored in this less inflammatory context (e.g., Kaczorowski, 1985, 143).

125. *Slaughter-House Cases* at 403–5, 412, 422, 425.

126. W. E. Nelson, 1988, 158–60.

127. The Thirteenth Amendment, Miller argued, was concerned only with chattel slavery and forms of apprenticeship, serfdom, or other types of servitude that were its equivalent. The burdens imposed by the Crescent City Company's charter fell far short of that. On this score the dissenters did not much challenge him, preferring to rely on the Fourteenth Amendment, though Field saw some force in the Thirteenth Amendment claim (413–14).

128. Though Miller's distinction had never been made in the amendment's framing and ratification debates, it had been advanced by some state court judges in the early 1870s (W. E. Nelson, 1988, 154–55, 162–63).

129. *Slaughter-House Cases* at 408.

130. *Slaughter-House Cases* at 415, 421, 422, 424–25. Miller acknowledged at 409 that he had himself identified a right to interstate travel as an implicit right of national citizenship in *Crandall v. Nevada,* but he did not address the issue of whether that ruling made the Fourteenth, as he interpreted it here, a needless redundancy.

131. *Slaughter-House Cases* at 409–10. After this case Miller would never again assert—indeed, he would actively deny—that the Fourteenth Amendment's protections should primarily be confined to blacks (Fairman, 1939, 186–88).

132. Kaczorowski, 1985, 158–65; E. Foner, 1988, 530.
133. Benedict, 1985, 305–31; E. Foner, 1988, 530; W. E. Nelson, 1988, 163; Wiecek, 1988, 114–16: Gillman, 1993, 64–67.
134. *Slaughter-House Cases* at 424–25.
135. *Slaughter-House Cases* at 419, 422. By deleting the reference to "avocations," William E. Nelson presents this passage as emphasizing the importance of equal rights generally, supporting an emphasis on equality over specific substantive liberties that I think is misleading (1988, viii, 157, 160). Field is emphasizing that *all* are entitled to *free labor* rights. Scholars like Michael Les Benedict (1985) and Howard Gillman (1993, 66–67) are right to argue, however, that Field's position was not radically laissez-faire. Rather, it was a version of the Jacksonian ideology that led him, like other former antislavery Democrats, to make common cause with free labor Republicans. Field could and sometimes did support economic regulations he thought to be genuinely in service of the common good; but he warily presumed that most economic regulation was special interest legislation. He was also especially vigilant about interferences with the economic liberties of white men.
136. *Slaughter-House Cases* at 422, 423, 425. Field and Bradley continued their dispute with Miller while concurring in *Bartemeyer v. Iowa,* 18 Wall. 129 (1873). There Miller wrote for the Court sustaining Iowa's temperance law, passed in 1851, against claims that it violated the Fourteenth Amendment's privileges and immunities and due process clauses. Miller did not believe that the right to sell whiskey, "so far as such a right exists," was a right of U.S. or state citizenship (133). Here Bradley and Field agreed, apparently deeming the liquor trade not an ordinary vocation like butchering, and noting that the Iowa law had only prevented future liquor sales and purchases. It had not required anyone to give up their existing property in liquor supplies, and it was a legitimate police regulation for the health and morals of the community (135–37). But Field reiterated that the Fourteenth had done more than make blacks citizens. It had made national citizenship "primary" and given the U.S. power to protect the "fundamental rights belonging to citizens of all free governments" (140).
137. Kaczorowski, 1985, 165–66, 174–75.
138. *U.S. v. Cruikshank,* 25 F. Cas. 707 (U.S.C.C.D. La., 1874). Ironically, at roughly the same time, as previously noted, Justice Miller wrote in *Loan Association v. Topeka* permitting a city government to refuse to pay off municipal bonds issued to aid a private corporation. Agreeing with Bradley and Field that "all free governments" accepted certain implied "reservations of individual rights," he thought that courts could invalidate state laws rearranging marital partners or homesteads, and that they could similarly regard as invalid a government's improper promise to give tax dollars for a private purpose, such as aiding a corporation (663–65). Though Miller would later emphasize that he thought the Court had more scope for review when considering a federal circuit court decision, as here, than when reviewing state courts, and though he did not rely on the Fourteenth Amendment here, nor did he invalidate the local government's current policy, his reasoning would nonetheless provide precedent for the later rise of economic substantive due process doctrines that did aid corporations (*Davidson v. New Orleans,* 96 U.S. 97, 104–5 [1878]; Fairman, 1939, 209–10; W. E. Nelson, 1988, 169–71).
139. Kaczorowski, 1985, 175–79; E. Foner, 1988, 437, 530–31.
140. *U.S. v. Cruikshank* at 712–13. Kaczorowski (1985, 180–81), relying on Bradley's language at 710, suggests that he viewed the Fourteenth Amendment as protecting *only* the latter sorts of rights, in deference to the *Slaughter-House* majority. Although in his explicit discussion of the Fourteenth Amendment (at 714) Bradley permits direct federal action to

protect any constitutionally derived privileges, in practice this category is so limited that Bradley's position largely comes to what Kaczorowski describes.

141. *U.S. v. Cruikshank* at 710, 714–16.

142. Bradley himself added a widely remarked supplement in June when he held in a circuit court decision that cases could not be removed to the federal courts merely on the allegation that community prejudices would prevent a black from getting a fair trial; active state discrimination by law or custom had to be shown (*Texas v. Gaines*, 23 F. Cas. 869 (U.S.C.C.W.D. Tx., 1874). Shortly after it was handed down, Bradley's *Cruikshank* opinion was cited by a district judge to reject claims that municipal judges in Petersburg, Virginia—who obstructed blacks from registering and voting in municipal elections—had violated any federal rights guaranteed by the 1870 Enforcement Act. Although Virginia law assigned the right to vote in such elections to U.S. citizens, that very fact indicated to Judge Hughes that the right was a state-defined right, and he read Bradley as arguing that under the Fourteenth Amendment Congress had no power to regulate such rights (514). Hughes also noted that section 2 of the amendment seemed explicitly to leave voting qualifications to the states. The Fifteenth Amendment did authorize some federal interventions, Hughes conceded, but only against racially motivated infringements of voting rights. The indictments had only indicated that blacks were prevented from voting, not that these acts were "on account of race, color, or previous condition of servitude" (514–15). Here circuit judge Hugh Bond disagreed, holding that the *Slaughter-House* decision still permitted federal efforts to protect rights "peculiar to citizenship" against all violators. He thought that Virginia's confinement of the vote to U.S. citizens made it such a right (509). Their division left further action to the Supreme Court, which adhered to Bradley's new approach. For one of the dwindling few cases going the other way, see the district judge's charge to the grand jury in *U.S. v. Blackburn*, 24 F. Cas. 1158 (U.S.D.C.W.D. Mo., 1874), holding that if private persons conspired to deprive blacks of access to public schools due to their color, or if a community and its officers failed to punish private criminal acts because of the victims' color, indictments could be sustained. Cf. also Justice Field's circuit court opinion holding that a California law restricting Chinese immigration violated the equal protection aims of the 1870 Enforcement Act (*In re Ah Fong*, 1 F. Cas. 213, 218 [U.S.C.C.D. Ca., 1874]).

143. Elliott, 1974, 64–65; Kaczorowski, 1985, 188–93.

144. In a brief opinion in *Walker v. Sauvinet*, 92 U.S. 90, 92 (1875), Waite also ruled that a New Orleans African-American who had been denied service in a state-licensed coffeehouse because of his color, in violation of the Reconstruction state constitution, had no federal complaint after he was then denied a jury trial under a state statute. Jury trials at the state level were, again, neither privileges and immunities exclusively deriving from U.S. citizenship nor the requirements of due process. Hence they were matters of state regulation. Field and Clifford dissented without opinions.

145. According to Waite, citizens were "the members of the political community" who "have established or submitted themselves to the dominion of a government for the promotion of their general welfare and the protection of their individual as well as their collective rights," and who owed allegiance to their government because they have "voluntarily submitted" themselves to it (*U.S. v. Cruikshank*, 92 U.S. 542, 549, 551, 555 [1876]).

146. *U.S. v. Cruikshank* at 551–59; Belz (1978, 132–33) and Kaczorowski (1985, 214–16) stress how Waite's neglect of the possibility of state inaction made his opinion an even fuller endorsement of state-centered federalism than Bradley's. Justice Clifford concurred that the judgment in the case should be arrested, but only because the indictments were excessively vague. He did not see any need to reach the other issues addressed by Waite

(559–69). Kaczorowski notes that the government itself abandoned any broad theory of federal enforcement power under the Thirteenth and Fourteenth Amendments when arguing the case, perhaps due to *Slaughter-House* and Bradley's *Cruikshank* opinion (1985, 206–8).

147. *U.S. v. Reese*, 92 U.S. 214, 218–21 (1876); Hyman & Wiecek, 1982, 488–92; Kaczorowski, 1985, 199–204, 213–18, 226–27. Clifford concurred with the result, but on the ground that Garner had not proven that he was "otherwise qualified" to vote by producing evidence that he had paid a required poll tax. His alleged offer to pay was insufficient (227, 235). Ward Hunt dissented. He thought that Congress's intent to punish all denials of the vote based on the Fifteenth Amendment's reasons, and only such denials, was "too plain to be discussed." Secs. 3 and 4 referred to those reasons when they used the phrase "as aforesaid" to describe the rights they were protecting. He also thought the record showed that Garner had offered to pay the poll tax and been denied the chance to do so, and he affirmed the validity of the act (241–42, 245, 249, 254).

148. *Bennett v. Bennett*, 3 F. Cas. 212, 214–15 (U.S.D.C. Or., 1867).

149. 9 Wall. 108, 124 (1869). The issue of what to do about divorces recognized in one state but not another would plague the Court until the New Deal, largely because of its reluctance to displace respect for varying state policies with a uniform national approach.

150. 74 U.S. 219, 227 (1868).

151. 13 Wall. 418 (1871).

152. 62 U.S. 582 (1858).

153. 74 U.S. 227 (1868).

154. 74 U.S. 496, 498 (1868).

155. Woodhull, editor with her sister, Tennessee Claflin, of the *Woodhull and Claflin Weekly*, would later become the first woman to run (and run) for President, among other much-remarked deeds. Stanton, Anthony, & Gage, 1882, v. II, 407–16, 442–58; Flexner, 1975, 156–57, 171–72; Clinton, 1984, 94–95; Kugler, 1987, 90–95; DuBois, 1988, 192–97.

156. Stanton, Anthony & Gage, 1882, v. II, 586–755, recounts incidents of women voting or trying to vote in New Hampshire in 1870 and 1871, Michigan in 1871, and the District of Columbia in 1871. The latter effort produced an opinion by District Chief Justice David Cartter indicating that governments could define the extent of the franchise among their constituents and that universal franchise would produce "profligacy and violence verging upon anarchy." Although they indicate that the Cartter ruling was affirmed by the U.S. Supreme Court, no such opinion is recorded.

157. 83 U.S. 130, 137–39 (1872), quoting 71 U.S. 277, 321 (1866). See also Stanton, Anthony, & Gage, 1882, v. II, 601–23; Flexner, 1975, 122–23; Hyman & Wiecek, 1982, 374–79; S. Goldman, 1982, 198; Clinton, 1984, 139; DuBois, 1988, 198–99.

158. 83 U.S. at 137.

159. Swayne joined Miller's dissents in the *Test Oath* cases.

160. 83 U.S. at 139–41. See also R. M. Smith, 1989a, 260–61.

161. A number of Rochester, New York, election inspectors were tried for permitting Anthony and other women to register and vote, but President Grant pardoned them. *U.S. v. Anthony*, 24 F. Cas. 829, 830, 833 (U.S.C.C.N.D. N.Y., 1873). See also Stanton, Anthony, & Gage, 1882, v. II, 627–714; Flexner, 1975, 168–71; DuBois, 1988, 199–200.

162. 88 U.S. 162, 165–66, 171, 174–75, 178 (1874); Stanton, Anthony, & Gage, 1882, v. II, 715–55; R. M. Smith, 1989a, 261–63.

163. It is noteworthy that as a state justice, Stephen Field occasionally dissented from such state rulings, foreshadowing his later support for anti-Chinese actions; but he increasingly accepted that immigration was a national matter. Thus in 1874, sitting as a circuit court jus-

tice, he invalidated a California statute that required shipowners to post a $500 bond if they attempted to land aliens meeting any of a long list of undesirable descriptions, including "lewd and debauched" women. While indicating his sympathy with the anti-immigrant feelings in California, Field found this law a violation of federal immigration powers and treaty obligations. *In re Ah Fong,* 1 F. Cas. 213 (U.S.C.C.D. Ca., 1874) at 217–18; Barth, 1964, 143, 194; Miller, 1964, 134–36; Swisher, 1969, 206–13; Lyman, 1974, 59–65; Perlmutter, 1977, 44; Chen, 1980, 45–46, 137–39; Archdeacon, 1983, 148.

164. *Henderson v. Mayor of New York,* 92 U.S. 259 (1876) at 268–70, 273–74; Archdeacon, 1983, 144.
165. *Chy Lung v. Freeman et al.,* 92 U.S. 275, 1876, at 280–81.
166. The *Letson* approach was upheld in, e.g., *Ohio and Mississippi Railroad Co. v. Wheeler,* 1 Black 286, 297 (1861); *Insurance Co. v. Ritchie,* 5 Wall. 541, 542 (1868); *Cowles v Mercer Co.,* 7 Wall. 118, 121 (1868); *Paul v. Virginia,* 8 Wall. 168, 178 (1869); *Express Co. v. Kountze Bros.,* 8 Wall. 342, 351 (1869); *Railroad Co. v. Harris,* 12 Wall. 65, 82 (1870); *Railway Co. v. Whitton,* 13 Wall. 270, 283; *Insurance Co. v. Morse,* 20 Wall. 445, 453–54 (1874); *Maltz v. American Express Co.,* 16 F. Cas. 566 (U.S.C.C. Mich., 1876) (ruling at 568 that whether a business was termed "a corporation, joint stock association or guild," *Letson* applied).
167. In *Ohio and Mississippi Railroad Co. v. Wheeler* (1861), the still-surviving Chief Justice Taney did rule against federal jurisdiction in a context that triggered his Jacksonian unwillingness to make the national courts available to corporations too readily. He denied access to a railway corporation that was chartered in both Ohio and Indiana and attempted to sue a citizen of Indiana in an Indiana district court. Taney held that the corporation's Indiana charter made this a suit between citizens of the same state. Taney refused to recognize the corporation's Ohio identity, maintaining that it had two separate legal existences which were inextricably joined in the suit; and its Indiana identity made diversity jurisdiction unavailable. *Ohio and Mississippi Railroad Co. v. Wheeler,* 1 Black 286, 297–98 (1861). The contrary spirit of the Reconstruction courts is visible in, e.g., *Davis v. Gray,* 83 U.S. 203, 221–22 (1872), where the Court applauded the "wise policy" of giving parties, including corporations, "a choice of tribunals" so that they might "escape the local influences which sometimes disturb the even flow of justice" and have access, ultimately, to the Supreme Court. After the Civil War, the Supreme Court indicated that legislatures could regulate an out-of-state corporation's activities in their jurisdictions, but they did not thereby make the corporations in-state citizens without access to the federal courts. A corporation that formally obtained charters in more than one state could, however, be treated by courts in each of those states as an in-state citizen, whatever the corporation's desires might be. It could not obtain the benefits of in-state corporation and evade the state's other laws and judicial system. Thus, in *Railroad Co. v. Harris* 12 Wall. 65, 82–83, 86 (1870), the Court upheld a congressional act giving the federal courts jurisdiction over a railroad company chartered in Maryland but operating in the District of Columbia while indicating that such regulatory legislation did not automatically make a corporation a citizen of the regulating district. Any contrary suggestion in *Wheeler* was disavowed. Cf. Purcell, 1992, 17–18.

In *Railway Co. v. Whitton,* 13 Wall. 270, 283–84 (1871), the Court refused to permit a railway that was chartered in both Wisconsin and Illinois, and being sued by a citizen of Illinois, to claim in a Wisconsin district court that it was an Illinois citizen and thus exempt from the court's jurisdiction. The Supreme Court confirmed that the Wisconsin court must determine the corporation's status according to the law of the state in which it sat, and Wisconsin did not recognize the corporation's Illinois citizenship. Thus the-

Court showed concern both to prevent states from preempting federal jurisdiction and to deny corporations unlimited powers of forum-shopping.

168. *Insurance Co. v. Morse,* 20 Wall. 445, 454–55 (1874). Chief Justice Waite and Justice Davis dissented, arguing that because the Court had previously recognized that states might exclude this sort of company altogether, Wisconsin could require such companies to, in effect, renounce their out-of-state citizenship.

169. *Doyle v. Continental Insurance Co.,* 94 U.S. 535 (1876). Miller's adoption of the more pro-corporate and nationalistic view in dissent is another somewhat surprising departure from his usual stances.

170. *Paul v. Virginia,* 8 Wall. 168, 177 (1869).

171. Although his main thrust was to stress comity requirements, Field's language did not exclude holding that the clause protected certain implicit rights of national citizenship, such as the right to interstate travel. He wrote that it was "undoubtedly the object of the clause in question to place the citizens of each State upon the same footing with citizens of other States, so far as the advantages resulting from citizenship in those States are concerned. It relieves them from the disabilities of alienage in other States; it inhibits discriminating legislation against them by other States; it gives them the right of free ingress into other States, and egress from them; it insures to them in other States the same freedom possessed by the citizens of those States in the acquisition and enjoyment of property and in the pursuit of happiness; and it secures to them in other States the equal protection of their laws" (180).

172. At 182–83. The *Paul* denial of constitutional privileges and immunities to corporations was reiterated by the Court in *Liverpool Insurance Co. v. Massachusetts,* 10 Wall. 566, 573 (1870) and *Ducat v. Chicago,* 10 Wall. 410, 415 (1870). In *Insurance Co. v. New Orleans,* 13 F. Cas. 67 (U.S.C.C. La., 1870), circuit judge Woods held not only that a corporation was not "a citizen of the United States as that term is used in the 14th amendment," a position to which federal courts have adhered, but even that a corporation was not a "person" within the meaning of the equal protection clause, a position that the Supreme Court later rejected (see *Santa Clara v. Southern Pacific R.R.,* 118 U.S. 394 [1886]).

173. Minor issues of the adequacy of averments continued to arise in diversity cases as well. See, e.g., *Express Co. v. Kountze Bros.,* 8 Wall. 342, 351 (1869); *Hornthall v. The Collector,* 76 U.S. 560 (1869); *Parker v. Overman,* 18 How. 137 (1870); *Insurance Co. v. Francis,* 78 U.S. 210 (1870); *Berlin v. Jones,* 3 F. Cas. 267 (U.S.C.C. Ala., 1871); *Morgan's Expressers v. Gay,* 19 Wall. 81 (1872); *Railway Co. v. Ramsey,* 22 Wall. 322, 329 (1874); *Muller v. Dows,* 94 U.S. 444, 446 (1876).

174. 70 U.S. (3 Wall.) 407, 416–18 (1865).

175. *The Kansas Indians,* 5 Wall. (72 U.S. 737, 755–57 [1866]); *The New York Indians,* 5 Wall. (72 U.S. 761, 769–72 [1866]).

176. *The Cherokee Tobacco,* 11 Wall. 616, 620–22 (1870), affirming *U.S. v. Tobacco Factory,* 28 F. Cas. 195 (U.S.D.C.W.D. Ark., 1870). Here Bradley, joined by Davis, dissented, arguing that the presumption should be that Congress was respecting tribal autonomy unless a statute clearly specified otherwise. In light of his later views, Bradley's position may have expressed aversion to governmental taxation as much as solicitude for Native American interests. In any case, the majority of those participating thought that the Constitution allowed Congress to violate treaties if it so chose, giving it great freedom in dealing with the tribes. Swayne was joined by Justices Miller, Clifford, and Strong, with three justices not participating.

177. In *U.S. v. Yellow Sun, alias Sa-coo-da-cot,* 1 Dill. 271, 273, 279–80 (1870), circuit judge Dillon refused jurisdiction of a case in which four Pawnee tribesmen were accused of leav-

ing their reservation and murdering a white man on Nebraskan soil. The Pawnees wanted federal access because they feared that "the tide of local prejudice against them and their nation" would prevent a fair trial in state courts. But, lacking evidence that Congress meant to prevent Nebraska from having criminal jurisdiction over Pawnees who left their reservations, Dillon concluded that the admission of Nebraska to statehood had given it that authority. Dillon did note his disagreement from McLean's radically state-centric view in *Bailey*—that Congress had no power to punish crimes committed on reservations within state limits—but he showed no desire to read his own jurisdiction expansively.

178. *Karrahoo v. Adams,* 1 Dill. 344, 346–48 (U.S.C.C. Kan., 1870).
179. *McKay v. Campbell,* 2 Saw. 118, 121–22, 124, 126–29, 132–35 (U.S.D.C. Or., 1871). The willingness of Deady and many other U.S. jurists and lawmakers to give primacy to "white" identity in the case of intermarriages with Native Americans, but not African-Americans, probably reflects the more favorable views of Native American capacities in much white discourse going back to Jefferson, and especially the greater needs and capacities of U.S. whites to keep blacks defined as an enduringly subordinate caste. Whites had long depended much more on African-Americans for labor than they did Native Americans, and African-Americans were also much more of a political threat should they be granted genuinely equal rights. They were far more numerous than tribesmembers, and vastly less likely to seek a geographically and politically separate existence. Consistent with this explanation, some Southern states treated mulattoes as an intermediate "third class" between black and whites until fears of black uprisings and abolitionism made equal repression of mulattoes seem desirable (J. Williamson, 1980). Such political calculations also meant, however, that many whites found policies that effectively aimed at genocide much more plausible in regard to Native Americans than African-Americans. The differences here should in any case not be exaggerated: e.g., Deady later denied "whiteness" to a "half-breed" with a Native American mother (*In re Camille* 6 F. 256 [U.S.C.C. Or., 1880]).
180. As examples, the Court so reasoned in *Holden v. Joy* (1872), fending off a challenge to the way the U.S. had passed certain lands back and forth with the Cherokees before disposing of them without ever making them available to settlers as public lands. There the tribes were again "for certain municipal purposes . . . States," indeed "distinct, independent communities" with "natural" possessory land rights (84 U.S. [17 Wall.] 211, 242–44 [1872]). Judge Dillon gave force to federal treaty recognition of Wyandot inheritance customs and Miami land alienation practices in several further Kansas circuit decisions. *Gray v. Coffman,* 3 Dill. 393, 400 (U.S.C.C. Kan., 1874); *Hicks v. Butrick,* 3 Dill. 413, 417 (U.S.C.C. Kan., 1875); *Mungosah v. Steinbrook,* 3 Dill. 418–19 (U.S.C.C. Kan., 1875). And by a narrow 5–4 majority, the Supreme Court reasoned similarly in *Leavenworth, Lawrence, and Galveston Railroad v. U.S.,* 92 U.S. 733, 747, 753 (1875), protecting Osage land rights against claims that the U.S. had ceded them to Kansas, which in turn had made them available to the railroads. (The dissenters were clearly annoyed by the fact that here, federal power was being used to frustrate rather than to advance railroad development.) The Court also continued to show great deference to pueblo Indian land titles recognized by the U.S. in the Treaty of Guadalupe Hidalgo, although Justice Miller, like earlier lower court judges, stressed the unusually "superior" and "virtuous" character of these Indians as well as the earlier Spanish and Mexican sources of their rights. *U.S. v. Joseph,* 94 U.S. 614, 616, 618 (1876). But in *U.S. v. Cook,* 19 Wall. 591–93 (1873), Native American possessory rights seemed narrow indeed in relation to the United States' ultimate dominion over tribal lands. The tribes were not allowed to sell timber from their lands without U.S. government permission because that was too close to selling the land itself.

181. *U.S. v. Forty-Three Gallons of Whiskey,* 93 U.S. 188, 189, 194, 197 (1876).
182. McPherson, 1964, 387, 403–5; Leidecker, 1946, 243, 266–67, 290–91; M. Keller, 1977, 234–35; Richardson, 1986, 254–55; E. Foner, 1988, 422–23, 588–601.
183. Bontemps, ed., 1963, 193.

Chapter 11. The Gilded Age of Ascriptive Americanism, 1876–1898

1. Hartz, 1955, 203–27; M. Keller, 1977, viii, 1, 598–99. Like most scholars, Keller also stresses the enormous significance of immigration and urbanization on postbellum America, and he notes a further much-discussed factor, the international context of rising European imperialism, spurred in part by competitive quests for new resources, labor, and markets. For leading political science accounts of the era see, e.g., Skowronek, 1982, esp. 4, 39–162; Bensel, 1984; Bensel, 1990; Sklar, 1988; Orren, 1991; Skocpol, 1992, esp. 76–176; Hattam, 1993, esp. 112–79, 204–15. No bright line divides the Gilded Age from the ensuing Progressive Era, and though I generally treat 1898, the year of the Spanish-American War, as the transition, I will occasionally discuss later laws and cases when they are integral parts of the civic developments considered here.
2. Writing in 1950, the great white historian Henry Steele Commager looked back on the transformations of this era and reportedly reassured Americans in Myrdalian terms that "if popular practice failed to live up to the principles of the American Creed, it never repudiated them—not even when the Negro was involved." Shortly thereafter, the great black historian Rayford Logan retorted that political leaders and commentators North and South had "frequently repudiated the application to the Negro" and other nonwhites of that American Creed during these years (Commager cited in Logan, 1965, 174–75). The thesis of this chapter is that Logan was right, because American leaders concluded that they could build a more stable nation in those changing times by stressing racial hierarchy and ethnocultural homogeneity rather than inclusiveness.
3. Alger, 1962, 122–23, 151–53. Nackenoff, 1994, confirms that almost all the heroes of Alger's novels are white, Anglo-Saxon, Protestant boys. She also argues that this Alger hero is "the adolescent Republic" itself, seeking not so much to glorify capitalism as to affirm the nation's "moral fiber," "identity," and "destiny" in an age of wrenching transitions (9, 11, 237–38).
4. Trachtenberg, 1982, 84, 99.
5. Strong, 1885, 1; M. Keller, 1977, 268–69.
6. William Wiecek has termed this era "a time of legal transition comparable only to the era of the American Revolution" (1988, 110).
7. For overviews of these developments see, e.g., Wiebe, 1967, 1–163; Logan, 1965; M. Keller, 1977; Takaki, 1979; Lee & Passell, 1979, 266–74, 308–25, 337–38; Painter, 1987, xv–xliv, 1–140; Silbey, 1991.
8. See, e.g., H. Adams, 1964, v. II, 71–187; Russett, 1976; Ross, 1991, 53–140.
9. See, e.g., M. Keller, 1977, 285–564; Skowronek, 1982, 53–75; Rodgers, 1987, 144–75; Silbey 1991.
10. See additionally Bellamy, 1967; George, 1956; Goodwyn, 1978; Thomas, 1983; Forbath, 1985; Hattam, 1993, 112–79.
11. Sumner, 1982, 8, 10, 17, 58, 98, 107, 116; Cremin, 1988, 391–93.
12. Sumner, 1982, 55, 83, 114, 126.
13. Sumner, 1982, 19, 24, 32–35, 88–90, 122–23; Ross, 1991, 56, 60.
14. Strong, 1885; Crunden, 1984, 3–15, 45; Cremin, 1988, 17–18, 70–71.

15. Strong, 1885, 4–5, 14–15, 36, 43–45, 51–54, 61–62.

16. Strong, 1885, 12, 14–15, 85, 94–99, 105; Goldman, 1953, 93–94; Cremin, 1988, 25, 71, 111, 393–95.

17. Though he acknowledged his debts to others, Strong wished to be recognized as a leader in nativist thought. In a footnote to his chapter entitled "The Anglo-Saxon and the World's Future," he said he felt it "only just" to mention that he had developed these ideas in a public lecture given three years before the historian John Fiske's similar, influential endorsement of American "Aryan" imperialism in an 1885 *Harper's Magazine* article, "Manifest Destiny." Fiske, a disciple of Herbert Spencer, soon became president of the Immigration Restriction League (Strong, 1885, 159; Haller, 1971, 121, 133). See also Gossett, 1963, 84–122; Stocking, 1968; Boller, 1969, 213–15, 239; Bannister, 1979, 180–200; Ross, 1991, 68–77.

18. Strong, 1885, 159–61, 165, 168, 170, 172–80, 218–19.

19. Walker, 1891, 13. Walker, a vice president of the Immigration Restriction League, remained an ardent supporter of that cause for many years, arguing that the nation was admitting "beaten races" that were "the worst failures in the struggle for existence," in contrast to "those who are descended from the tribes that met under the oak-trees of old Germany to make laws and choose chieftains" (1899, 477). He also predicted that the "natural aptitudes and instincts" of the "colored race" would confine them to the tropical climes around the Gulf of Mexico (1899, 130–33). See also S. Anderson, 1981, 56.

20. Brinton, 1895, 248–51.

21. Ahlstrom, 1972, 733–34, 743–46, 798–99, 849–51; Cremin, 1988, 29–39.

22. Ross, 1991, 62, 90–92, 219.

23. Hofstadter, 1955, 68–83; Cremin, 1988, 394–98; Ross, 1991, 89–96, 233–35, 249–50.

24. Archdeacon, 1983, 114; Daniels, 1990, 124–25. Measuring immigration differently, Archdeacon notes how large a percentage the total influx in each ten-year period was in relation to the national population at the beginning of each period. This indicator renders the 1850s a time of greater immigration (12.1%) than the two decades of next largest immigration, 1900–1909 (10.8%) and 1880–1889 (10.4%). In comparison, Canada's population in 1911 was 22% foreign-born; Argentina in 1914 was almost one-third (Higham, 1966, 110; 1975, 13; Archdeacon, 1983, 115).

25. Only the tiny Prohibition party favored continuing a "liberal policy to immigrants from all nations," despite stereotypes of immigrants as drunkards.

26. Hutchinson, 1981, 75–77.

27. Hutchinson, 1981, 67–82, 408, 582–83, 624–25; Archdeacon, 1983, 145–49; Daniels, 1990, 56–57; Tichenor, 1995, 7.

28. *Cong. Record*, v. 13, pt. 2, 47th Cong., 1st Sess., 1515–16, 1521–22. See also Salyer, 1989, 41–49.

29. *Cong. Record*, v. 13, pt. 2, 47th Cong., 1st Sess., 2035. For related liberal attacks on exclusion, see, e.g., 1636, 1643, 1673, 1705, 1709–10, 2036–38, 2041, 2130–31, 2177–78, 2182, 2185.

30. Ibid. at 1482–85, 1589, 2211; see also 1581, 1636–37, 1645, 2126, 2207, 3267. Miller, 1964, 163–64, makes it clear that the immoralities were indiscriminate sexual practices thought to be responsible for "Chinese syphilis."

31. *Cong. Record*, v. 13, pt. 2, 47th Cong., 1st Sess., at 1485–87, 1546, 1583, 1635–37, 1645, 1713, 1740, 1978, 2042, 2138, 2166, 3269.

32. Ibid. at 1548, 1583, 1636–37, 1713, 2029, 2138–39, 2164; Miller, 1964, 193.

33. *Cong. Record*, v. 13, pt. 2, 47th Cong., 1st Sess., 2205–6; Higham, 1966, 115; Takaki, 1979, 13, 84–99.

34. *Cong. Record,* v. 13, pt. 2, 47th Cong. 1st Sess., 1486–87, 1545, 1581, 1583–84, 1588, 1674, 1979, 2126, 2208 (1882).

35. Miller, 1964, notes that the heavy support for Chinese exclusion came from throughout the country, reflecting longstanding negative stereotypes about the Chinese in the U.S. It tended to be congressmen from regions not directly confronting competition from Chinese laborers, like Saulsbury of Delaware and Joseph Hawley of Connecticut, who downplayed economic concerns in favor of cultural and racial ones (159, 189, 192–93).

36. Whether homosexuals were effectively excluded by the bans on those guilty of crimes involving "moral turpitude" remains a matter that needs further investigation, as I have found no reports of such (likely) enforcement. Konvitz, 1946, 19; Higham, 1966, 45–67, 98–101, 112–13, 128–30; 1975, 36–52; M. Keller, 1977, 443–47; Hutchinson, 1981, 85–148, 408–59, 546–48, 583–84; Archdeacon, 1983, 144–46; Takaki, 1979, 110–12; Salyer, 1989, esp. 49–57, 68–77, 99–125, 146–47, 228–37, 280–93; Daniels, 1990, 240, 271–75; Foss, 1994, 445–47.

37. The test was first proposed in 1887 by the reform economist Edward W. Bemis, who intended it to achieve racial exclusion, as Lodge did (Higham, 1966, 101).

38. Lodge closed with an 1882 poem by Thomas Bailey Aldrich, "The Unguarded Gates," that urged the "white Goddess" Liberty to stand fast against corrupting elements. *Cong. Rec.,* v. 28, pt. 3, 54th Cong., 1st Sess., 2817–20. The committee reports on literacy test bills made many of the same points. Stocking, 1968, 252–53; Higham, 1966, 70–75, 95–96, 101–3, 141–42; Hutchinson, 1981, 465–66, 481–82; Daniels, 1990, 275–78.

39. *Cong. Rec.,* v. 28, pt. 3, 54th Cong., 1st Sess., pt. 6, 5218–19.

40. As discussed more fully in the next chapter, a major exception to these restrictive patterns was the judiciary's maintenance of birthright citizenship regardless of race. But that exception officially rested on ascriptive notions of civic membership, not consensual ones; and it did little to alter the increasingly exclusionary outlook of American lawmakers.

41. *In re Ah Sing,* 13 F. 286 (U.S.C.C. Ca., 1882); *In re Ah Tie,* 13 F. 291 (U.S.C.C. Ca., 1882); *In re Low Yam Chow,* 13 F. 605 (U.S.C.C. Ca., 1882); *In re George Moncan, alias Ah Wah,* 14 F. 44 (U.S.C.C. Or., 1882); *In re Ho King,* 14 F. 724 (U.S.D.C. Or., 1883); *In re Ah Lung,* 18 F. 28 (U.S.C.C. Ca., 1883); *In re Chin A On and others,* 18 F. 506 (U.S.D.C. Ca., 1883); *In re Pong Ah Chee,* 18 F. 527 (U.S.D.C. Col., 1883); *In re Tung Yeong,* 19 F. 184 (U.S.D.C. Ca., 1884); *In re Leong Yick Dew,* 19 F. 490 (U.S.C.C. Ca., 1884); *In re Chow Goo Pooi,* 25 F. 77 (U.S.C.C. Ca., 1884). The Supreme Court reaffirmed that all state efforts to tax immigration were unconstitutional in *People v. Compagnie Générale Transatlantique,* 107 U.S. 59 (1882).

42. *In re Ah Quan,* 21 F. 182 (U.S.C.C. Ca., 1884); *In re Shong Toon,* 21 F. 386 (U.S.D.C. Ca., 1884); *In re Chin Ah Sooey,* 21 F. 393 (U.S.D.C. Ca., 1884); *In re Ah Kee,* 21 F. 701 (U.S.C.C. Ca., 1884); *In re Ah Moy,* 21 F. 785 (U.S.C.C. Ca., 1884); *In re Kew Ock,* 21 F. 789 (U.S.C.C. Ca., 1884); *In re Cheen Heong,* 21 F. 791 (U.S.C.C. Ca., 1884).

43. *The Citizenship of a Person Born in the United States of Chinese Parents, In re Look Tin Sing,* 21 F. 905 (U.S.C.C. Ca., 1884), followed in *Ex parte Chin King,* 35 F. 354 (U.S.C.C. Or., 1888); *In re Yung Sing Hee,* 36 F. 437 (U.S.C.C. Or., 1888).

44. *Chew Heong v. U.S.,* 112 U.S. 536 (1884), at 554, 568, 577–78.

45. 112 U.S. 580, 591, 594 (1884). A Michigan circuit court upheld the 1885 contract labor law under the commerce power in *U.S. v. Craig,* 28 F. 795 (U.S.C.C. Mich., 1886). The Supreme Court followed suit in a number of later cases, e.g., *Lees v. U.S.,* 150 U.S. 476 (1893).

46. See *In re Ah Ping,* 23 F. 329 (U.S.C.C. Ca., 1885); *In re Jung Ah Lung,* 25 F. 141 (1885), sustained by a more divided Supreme Court, with Harlan and Lamar joining Field in dissent, in *U.S. v. Jung Ah Lung,* 124 U.S. 621 (1888).

47. *In re Chae Chan Ping*, 36 F. 431 (U.S.C.C. Ca., 1888); *The Chinese Exclusion Case, Chae Chan Ping v. U.S.*, 130 U.S. 581 (1889). While deciding the case on other grounds, Oregon circuit judge Matthew Deady in *In re Yung Sing Hee* castigated the 1888 law as "harsh and unjust," arising from the desires of the parties to "outbid" each other for the Pacific coast vote in the upcoming presidential election (36 F. 437, U.S.C.C. Or., 1888). See generally Mooney, 1984, 612–27; Fritz, 1988, 352–72; Smith, 1988a, 243–44; Salyer, 1989, 49–61.

48. 130 U.S. 582–88 (1889).

49. 594, 599, 603–9. Field did not say why the abrogation of these "personal" rights, even if unavoidable, did not warrant some sort of compensation.

50. The connection between racial exclusion and the "sovereignty" rationale for immigration powers was underlined when a lower court still relied exclusively on the commerce clause in a case involving a European, *In re Florio*, 45 F. 114 (U.S.C.C. N.Y., 1890). Stephen Legomsky argues forcefully that the new reliance on unenumerated "sovereign" powers was unnecessary and ill-founded, and that it abetted the Court's subsequent excessive deference to administrative immigration decisions (Legomsky, 1987, 177–222). Legomsky does not offer any hypothesis about why the sovereignty rationale came to the fore.

51. *In re Oteiza*, 136 U.S. 330 (1890); *Quock Ting v. U.S.*, 140 U.S. 417 (1891); *Nishimura Ekiu v. U.S.*, 142 U.S. 651 (1892); *Law Ow Bew v. U.S.*, 144 U.S. 47 (1892). Field for the Court approved retroactive applications of the 1888 rules in *Wan Shing v. U.S.*, 140 U.S. 424 (1891).

52. See *In re Tong Wah Sick*, 36 F. 440 (U.S.C.C. Ca., 1888); *In re Jack Sen*, 36 F. 441 (U.S.C.C. Ca., 1888); *In re Wy Shing*, 36 F. 553 (U.S.C.C. Ca., 1888); *In re Tom Mun*, 47 F. 722 (U.S.D.C. Ca., 1888); *In re Wo Tai Li*, 48 F. 668 (U.S.D.C. Ca., 1888); *In re Chung Toy Ho and Wong Choy Sin*, 42 F. 398 (U.S.D.C. Or., 1890); *In re Leo Hem Bow*, 47 F. 302 (U.S.D.C. Wash., 1891); *In re Mah Wong Gee*, 47 F. 433 (U.S.D.C. Vt., 1891); *U.S. v. Chung Sam*, 47 F. 878 (U.S.D.C. Mich., 1891); *U.S. v. Lee Hoy*, 48 F. 825 (U.S.D.C. Wash., 1891); *Gee Fook Sing v. U.S.*, 49 F. 146 (9th C. 1892); *Lem Hing Dun v. U.S.*, 49 F. 148 (9th C. 1892); *U.S. v. Gee Lee*, 50 F. 271 (9th C. 1892).

53. *U.S. v. Hing Quong Chow*, 53 F. 233 (U.S.C.C. La., 1892); *In re Sing Lee*, 54 F. 334 (U.S.D.C. Mich., 1893).

54. *Fong Yue Ting v. U.S.; Wong Quan v. U.S.; Lee Joe v. U.S.*, 149 U.S. 698, 704–11, 728–30 (1893); Fiss, 1993, 304–12.

55. 149 U.S. 736–39, 744, 754–56 (1893). The eligibility of the Chinese for equal protection under the Fourteenth Amendment was strongly supported by *Yick Wo v. Hopkins*, 118 U.S. 356, 1886, discussed below, which all the dissenters relied on, compelling Gray to distinguish it at 725. Scholars have suggested that Field's fluctuations between strongly anti-Chinese rulings and decisions expressing respect for their human rights reflected his shifting ambitions for the presidency. Others feel that he wrote this dissent under his nephew's influence; some believe that he was becoming increasingly senile and erratic (Swisher, 1969, 205–39, 442–44; Fritz, 1988, 363–66, 371–72). For present purposes what counts is that some of his most racist stances came as opinions of the Supreme Court.

56. The Court reinforced this stiff line in *Lem Moon Sing v. U.S.*, 158 U.S. 538 (1895) (Harlan writing for the Court, Brewer in dissent), again stressing sovereignty and deference to executive powers. Some lower courts followed suit. See, e.g., *U.S. v. Chew Cheong*, 61 F. 200 (U.S.D.C. Ca., 1894); *In re Quan Gin*, 61 F. 395 (U.S.D.C. Ca., 1894); *In re Yee Lung*, 61 F. 641 (U.S.D.C. Ca., 1894); *U.S. v. Wong Ah Hung*, 62 F. 1005 (U.S.D.C. Ca., 1894); *U.S. v. Chung Fung Sun*, 63 F. 261 (U.S.D.C. N.Y., 1894); *U.S. v. Loo Way*, 68 F. 475 (U.S.D.C. Ca., 1895); *In re Gee Hop*, 71 F. 274 (U.S.D.C. Ca., 1895); *In re Li Foon*, 80 F. 881 (U.S.C.C. N.Y., 1897); *U.S. v. Lau Sun Ho* (U.S.D.C. Ca., 1898); *U.S. v. Chung Ki Foon*, 83 F. 143 (U.S.D.C. Ca., 1897); *In re Lee Yee Sing*, 85 F. 635 (U.S.D.C. Wash., 1898); *In re Li Sing*, 86 F. 896 (2d

C. 1898); *U.S. v. Chu Chee,* 93 F. 797 (9th C. 1899); *In re Ota,* 96 F. 487 (U.S.D.C. Ca., 1899); *Mar Bing Guey v. U.S.,* 97 F. 576 (U.S.D.C. Tx., 1899); *Lee Sing Far v. U.S.,* 94 F. 834 (9th C. 1899). See also Schuck, 1984, 24–27.

57. *U.S. v. Wong Dep Ken,* 57 F. 206 (U.S.D.C. Ca., 1893); *In re Lintner,* 57 F. 587 (U.S.D.C. Ca., 1893); *Lee Kan v. U.S.,* 62 F. 914 (9th C. 1894); *In re Martorelli,* 63 F. 437 (U.S.C.C. N.Y., 1894); *In re Tom Yum,* 64 F. 485 (U.S.D.C. Ca., 1894); *U.S. v. Chung Shee,* 71 F. 277 (U.S.D.C. Ca., 1895); *U.S. v. Sing Lee,* 71 F. 680 (U.S.D.C. Or., 1896); *U.S. v. Gue Lim,* 83 F. 136 (U.S.D.C. Wash., 1897); *In re Monaco,* 86 F. 117 (U.S.C.C. N.Y., 1898); *U.S. v. Yee Mun Sang,* 93 F. 365 (U.S.D.C. Vt., 1899); *U.S. v. Pin Kwan,* 94 F. 824 (U.S.D.C. N.Y., 1899); *U.S. v. Mrs. Gue Lim,* 176 U.S. 459 (1900). The lower courts tended to be especially generous in cases involving non-Chinese immigrants. See, e.g., *In re Yamasaka,* 95 F. 652 (U.S.D.C. Wash., 1899); *U.S. ex rel. Andersen v. Burke,* 99 F. 895 (U.S.C.C. Ala., 1899).

58. *Wong Wing v. U.S.,* 163 U.S. 228 (1896), in which the fading Field added sentiments quite favorable to the Chinese, but mystifyingly labeled his opinion a "dissent" because he opposed points in the government's brief.

59. *In re Wong Kim Ark,* 71 F. 382 (U.S.D.C. Ca., 1896) (decided by Judge William Morrow, otherwise the most consistently anti-Chinese of the lower federal court judges); *U.S. v. Wong Kim Ark,* 169 U.S. 649 (1898).

60. As with any significant extension of federal power, many cases arose querying how far national executive officials and courts were now entitled to oversee and challenge the state courts engaged in naturalizing persons in accordance with federal statutes. On the whole, the courts firmly upheld federal prerogatives. As mentioned previously, in *City of Minneapolis v. Reum,* 56 F. 576 (8th C. 1893), a federal circuit court held that states not only had no power to bestow U.S. citizenship, they could not bestow any form of state citizenship that would be recognized as such by federal courts. Foreign subjects remained foreign subjects, whatever rights, including voting, a state might choose to extend to them. And in *Boyd v. Nebraska,* 143 U.S. 135 (1892), the U.S. Supreme Court upheld congressional powers to grant collective naturalizations to whomever it wished. Federal courts did uphold naturalizations that state courts had conferred erroneously, if the errors were not due to any misrepresentations by applicants; see, e.g., *U.S. v. Norsch,* 42 F. 417 (U.S.C.C. Mo., 1890); *U.S. v. Gleason,* 78 F. 396 (U.S.C.C. N.Y., 1897).

61. *In re Ah Yup,* 1 F. Cas. 223 (U.S.C.C. Ca., 1878). Oregon circuit judge Deady cited Sawyer's opinion in 1880 to rule that a man born of a white Canadian father and an Indian mother was not a naturalizable "white person." Deady stated that it might seem strange that the U.S. naturalized Africans but not "the intermediate and much-better-qualified red and yellow races." He argued, however, that Africans were "not likely to emigrate," so the vaunted 1870 provision for their naturalization was "merely a harmless piece of legislative buncombe." *In re Camille,* 6 F. 256 (U.S.C.C. Or., 1880).

62. Act of May 6, 1882. The law did not address Japanese naturalization; but in 1894, a Massachusetts circuit court decision followed Sawyer's logic and rejected a Japanese applicant. See *In re Saito,* 62 F. 126 (U.S.C.C. Mass., 1894).

63. *In re Rodriguez,* 81 F. 337 (U.S.D.C. Tx., 1897). Note that Maxey was the judge who upheld the practice of white election officials filling out ballots for blacks and Mexican-Americans in *U.S. v. Dwyer* four years earlier. His allegiance to civic "liberality" thus should not be exaggerated.

64. *Ex parte Sauer,* 81 F. 355 (U.S.D.C. Tx., 1891), reported with *In re Rodriguez,* 81 F. 337 (U.S.D.C. Tx., 1897), as arising in the District Court of Texas, Uvalde County, September 1891.

65. For a trenchant critique of the tendency of even conscientious legal scholars to stress the

small pebbles of decency instead of the sea of judicial injustices during these years, see Kennedy, 1986.

66. Hayes vetoed 8 bills designed to weaken protection of black rights and Harrison threatened to reinstate federal control of Southern elections in 1889; but Hayes took no protective actions, and Harrison relented to win passage of his economic program (Logan, 1965, 43–45, 65–75; Valelly, 1995, 197–209).

67. They did occur often enough to oppress blacks enormously. I agree with Richard Epstein that railroads and other corporations cannot plausibly be painted as the villains behind segregation laws, which they often opposed, and that those laws greatly facilitated the rebuilding of racial hierarchies. But it does not seem plausible to expect, as Epstein does, that Jim Crow would have soon vanished without state enforcement. Railroads often voluntarily segregated their cars; they simply wanted to have the flexibility not to do so when it did not suit them. It is revealing in this regard that Epstein ignores the *Civil Rights Cases*, considered below, which involved widespread discrimination by businesses the Court considered private, not state laws. See Epstein, 1992, 91–103; cf. sources in n2.

68. Grady, 1929; Logan, 1965, 140–41, 180–92; Woodward, 1966, 60–93; Kousser, 1974.

69. *Ex parte Kinney*, 14 F. Cas. 602, 603, 605–6 (U.S.C.C. Va., 1879). See also *Ex parte Francois*, 9 F. Cas. 699, 700 (U.S.C.C. Tx., 1879), upholding a Texas law that punished whites for interracial marriages as within the state's prerogatives, even though the statute was "unjust in its discrimination against the white race"; *State v. Tutty*, 41 F. 753 (U.S.C.C. Ga., 1890), citing a state opinion noting that the "amalgamation of the race is not only unnatural" but produces "sickly and effeminate" offspring instead of "elevating the inferior race"; and Hovenkamp, 1985, 656–57, 657n182.

70. *Pace v. Alabama*, 106 U.S. 583 (1882).

71. *Roberts v. City of Boston*, 5 Cush. 198 (Mass., 1849), and see Kousser, 1986, 1–4.

72. See, e.g., *Bertonneau v. Bd. of Directors of City Schools*, 3 F. Cas. 294 (U.S.C.C. La., 1878); *U.S. v. Buntin*, 10 F. 730 (U.S.C.C. Oh., 1882); *Claybrook v. City of Owensboro*, 16 F. 297 (U.S.D.C. Ky., 1883) (invalidating a Kentucky law that taxed whites and blacks for schools separately, resulting in highly unequal school facilities); *Davenport v. Cloverport*, 72 F. 689 (U.S.D.C. Ky., 1896) (invalidating a state law that taxed only whites to support only white schools, but denying the request of blacks that the money collected be spent on black schools, in favor of reimbursing taxpayers). For an overview see Kousser, 1986.

73. In 1887 a third legal strand was added: the Interstate Commerce Act included a provision forbidding interstate common carriers from treating customers with "unreasonable prejudice," but the ICC interpreted this rule as permitting separate but equal accommodations. Lofgren, 1987, 117, 141–44.

74. See, e.g., charges to juries by district judges in *U.S. v. Newcomer*, 27 F. Cas. 127 (U.S.D.C. Pa., 1876), construing the 1875 Civil Rights Act as constitutional, and interpreting it in light of common law standards; *U.S. v. Dodge*, 25 F. Cas. 882 (U.S.D.C. Tx., 1877); and generally Lofgren, 1987, 118–28.

75. 55 Pa. St. 209 (1867).

76. *Hall v. DeCuir*, 95 U.S. 485, 489, 503 (1877).

77. See, e.g., *Green v. City of Bridgeton*, 10 F. Cas. 109 (U.S.D.C. Ga., 1879) (separate facilities on steamboat substantively equal and permissible); *Gray v. Cincinnati Southern R. Co*, 11 F. 683 (U.S.C.C. Oh., 1882) (railroad cannot compel a black woman and her sick child to ride in smoking car rather than ladies' car reserved for whites); *Houck v. Southern Pac. Ry. Co.*, 38 F. 225 (U.S.C.C. Tx., 1888) (judge and jury agree an almost-white woman rushing to see her sick infant was wrongly placed in an inferior car, but judge still finds damages awarded excessive).

78. *Charge to Grand Jury—The Civil Rights Act*, 30 F. 999 (U.S.C.C. N.C., 1875); *Smoot v. Kentucky Central Ry. Co.*, 13 F. 337 (U.S.C.C. Ky., 1882); *U.S. v. Washington*, 20 F. 630 (U.S.C.C. Tx., 1883); but cf. *U.S. v. Newcomer*, 27 F. Cas. 127 (U.S.D.C. Pa., 1876), viewing act as constitutional.
79. *Civil Rights Cases; U.S. v. Stanley; U.S. v. Ryan; U.S. v. Nichols; U.S. v. Singleton; Robinson & Wife v. Memphis and Charleston Railroad Co.*, 109 U.S. 3 (1883).
80. Ibid. at 13.
81. Ibid. at 18–25.
82. Ibid. at 36, 46–47, 52, 57, 59, 61; Peterman & Wechsler, 1972, 269–72; McFeely, 1991, 317–18.
83. See, e.g., *Cooper v. New Haven Steam-Boat Co.*, 18 F. 588 (U.S.D.C. N.Y., 1883); *The Sue*, 22 F. 843 (U.S.D.C. Md., 1885); *Logwood and Wife v. Memphis & C. R. Co.*, 23 F. 318 (U.S.C.C. Tenn., 1885); *Murphy v. Western & Atlantic R.R.*, 23 F. 637 (U.S.C.C. Tenn., 1885); *McGuinn v. Forbes*, 37 F. 639 (U.S.D.C. Md., 1889).
84. *McGuinn v. Forbes* at 639; *Murphy v. Western and Atlantic R.R.* at 638.
85. *Louisville, New Orleans and Texas Rwy. Co. v. Mississippi*, 133 U.S. 587 (1890).
86. Ibid. at 589–90, 593.
87. Schmidt, 1982a, 464–65; Fiss, 1993, 355–56.
88. See, e.g., *Anderson v. Louisville & Nashville Railroad Co.*, 62 F. 46 (U.S.C.C. Ky., 1894).
89. *Plessy v. Ferguson*, 163 U.S. 537 (1896). Fiss, 1993, 359–60, notes that the Court also ignored a broad theory of national citizenship rights put forth by Plessy's attorney, Albion Tourgée.
90. Ibid. at 550.
91. Lofgren, 1987, 110–11, 174–75. C. Vann Woodward notes the reliance of turn-of-the-century racists on the antiregulatory arguments of William Graham Sumner, Herbert Spencer, and Spencer's American disciple Franklin Henry Giddings (Woodward, 1966, 102–4; Woodward, 1971, 228; Nieman, 1991, 111). Brown cites no writers of this sort, but his reasoning places him in the same camp.
92. Lofgren, 1987, 32. Jennifer Roback has argued that streetcar companies, too, "frequently resisted segregation, both as custom and law," lending support to Woodward's contention that "race relations responded mainly to political and sociological rather than economic determinants" (Roback, 1986, 894; Woodward, 1971, 254). John Cell has argued, as I do here, that the "ultimate cause" of segregation was "white racism," not economics; but that segregation represented an aspect of "progressive" efforts to preserve white supremacy while building a more urbanized and industrialized "modern" political order (Cell, 1982, 3, 17–20, 143, 232–34).
93. Cf. Ackerman, 1991, 146–47.
94. *Plessy* at 551–52.
95. *Plessy* at 553, 557, 560–63; Woodward, 1966, 102, 115–18; Barnes, 1983, 10–15.
96. *Ex parte Reynolds*, 20 F. Cas. 586 (U.S.C.C.W.D. Va., 1878) at 591–92.
97. *Strauder v. West Virginia*, 100 U.S. 303 (1879) at 304, 306, 309.
98. *Ex parte Virginia*, 100 U.S. 339 (1879).
99. Ibid. at 340, 345–48.
100. Ibid. at 353.
101. Ibid. at 358, 359, 363, 367–69. Scholars usually attribute Field's pro-racist course here, as in many of the Chinese exclusion cases, to his presidential ambitions, at their peak in 1879. See, e.g., Swisher, 1969, 285.
102. *Virginia v. Rives*, 100 U.S. 313, 324 (1879).
103. Strong held that the 1866 Civil Rights Act and related federal statutes permitted removal

of a case to the federal courts only before a state trial had commenced. The civil rights removal statutes were aimed chiefly at state constitutional provisions, statutes, and executive acts, not state judiciaries. *Rives* at 319–20.

104. Ibid. at 322–23. Even so, Field and Clifford felt that Strong had not sufficiently repudiated Rives's position. They wrote to underline that equal protection did not imply that all persons would "be allowed to participate in the administration of its laws, or to hold any of its offices, or to discharge any duties of a public trust." For them, explicit denials of jury service to all blacks were permissible.

105. *Neal v. Delaware,* 103 U.S. 370, 393, 397–408 (1880); Purcell, 1992, 142–47.

106. *Bush v. Kentucky,* 107 U.S. 110, 117, 120–23 (1882).

107. *In re Wood,* 140 U.S. 278 (1891) (Harlan for Court); *In re Shibuya Jugiro,* 140 U.S. 291 (1891) (Harlan for Court, in case involving a Japanese subject's challenge to an all-white jury); *Andrews v. Swartz,* 156 U.S. 272 (1895) (Harlan); *Gibson v. Mississippi,* 162 U.S. 565 (1896) (Harlan); *Charley Smith v. Mississippi,* 162 U.S. 592 (1896) (Harlan); *Murray v. Louisiana,* 163 U.S. 101 (1896) (Shiras).

108. See, e.g., *Le Grand v. U.S.,* 12 F. 577 (U.S.C.C. Tx., 1882); *U.S. v. Sanges,* 48 F. 78 (U.S.C.C. Ga., 1891);

109. Schmidt, 1983, 1406–7.

110. A good overview is Kousser, 1974, who shows that the disfranchisement laws, coming in waves between 1888 and 1893 and again 1898 to 1902, reduced black voting turnout by over 90% in Alabama, Louisiana, North Carolina, and Virginia during these years, by over two-thirds in Arkansas, Mississippi, and Tennessee, and lesser amounts in other states (241). Kousser argues forcefully that disfranchisement "was a typically Progressive reform" designed to "rationalize the economic and political system," in accordance with racially biased notions of rationality (260–61).

111. Logan, 1965, 66, 71–89, Kousser, 1974, 27–29, 241–42; Schmidt, 1982c, 841–47; Valelly, 1995, 203.

112. See, e.g., *U.S. v. Amsden,* 6 F. 819 (U.S.D.C. Ind., 1881).

113. *Ex parte Yarbrough,* 110 U.S. 651 (1884).

114. Ibid. at 658, 665–66.

115. See, e.g., *U.S. v. Belvin, U.S. v. Wardell, U.S. v. Dwyer,* and *McPherson v. Blacker,* discussed below.

116. *Mills v. Green,* 67 F. 818 (U.S.C.C. S.C., 1895).

117. *Green v. Mills,* 69 F. 852 (U.S.C.C.A., 4th C. 1895), grudgingly followed by Judge Goff in *Gowdy v. Green,* 69 F. 865 (U.S.C.C. S.C., 1895).

118. *Mills v. Green,* 159 U.S. 651 (1895).

119. *U.S. v. Harris,* 106 U.S. 629, 640, 643 (1882).

120. Flexner, 1975, 157, 183–86; Degler, 1980, 324–26; Bordin, 1981, 3–4, 60.

121. Degler, 1980, 286–87, 318–19, 342; Bordin, 1981, 8, 13–14, 46, 97–119; Marilley, 1993; DuBois, 1988, 201–2; Cott, 1989, 828–29; Skocpol, 1992, 326–27.

122. Because of Willard's heavy emphasis on protection against the multiple dangers of late nineteenth-century life, Suzanne Marilley has dubbed her view the "feminism of fear" (Marilley, 1993). See also B. L. Epstein, 1981, 99, 116–18, 121–25; Bordin, 1981, 5–7, 11–12, 56–61, 158; Skocpol, 1992, 318–19.

123. Marilley, 1993; Bordin, 1981, 78–87, 105, 120–22, 155; Flexner, 1975, 187–88; B. Harris, 1978, 129, 146n15; Painter, 1987, 232–34.

124. Flexner, 1975, 183–85, 190–96; Degler, 1980, 326; Bordin, 1981, 149–50; Painter, 1987, 234–35, 247–48; Cott, 1987, 23, 31–32; Skocpol, 1992, 328–37, 359–60, 396–401, 482–86. Jane Cunningham Croly, important in her own right, was the wife of Democratic jour-

nalist and miscegenation pamphleteer David Goodman Croly and the mother of Progressive philosopher Herbert Croly.

125. Flexner, 1975, 184, 198–205, 236; Degler, 1980, 337–38; B. L. Epstein, 1981, 116–25; Kessler-Harris, 1982, 84, 93–97, 153–59; Painter, 1987, 235.

126. On March 22, 1882, Congress had taken the vote away from all those who practiced polygamy, but that had not ended the practice. Sen. Edmunds therefore argued on behalf of his bill that granting the franchise to women in Utah only amplified criminal Mormon influences, including the virtual "serfdom" Mormon husbands imposed on many wives. Critics wondered why the criminal masters should retain the franchise but the abused serfs lose it (*Cong. Rec.*, 49th Cong., 1st Sess., v. 17, pt. 1, 406–7). See also *Cong. Rec.*, 49th Cong., 2d Sess., v. 18, pt. 1, 34–37 (Dec. 8, 1886); 980–83, 997–98 (Jan. 25, 1887).

127. Flexner, 1975, 176–78, 227–28; Harris, 1978, 86; Bordin, 1981, 96; DuBois, 1988, 201.

128. *Cong. Rec.*, 51st Cong., 1st Sess., v. 21, pt. 7, 6581–82, 6585 (June 17, 1890). See also *Bloomer v. Todd*, 3 Wash. Terr. Rep. 599 (1888), followed in *Isaacs v. McNeil*, 44 Fed. Rep. 32–33 (U.S.C.C. Wash., 1890).

129. Flexner, 1975, 228–31, 263–69.

130. See, e.g., *Bowman v. Bowman*, 30 F. 849 (U.S.C.C. Ill., 1887); *Cheely v. Clayton*, 110 U.S. 701 (1884); *Anderson v. Watt*, 138 U.S. 694 (1891).

131. *Ware v. Wisner*, 50 F. 310 (U.S.C.C. Ia., 1883); *Pequignot v. Detroit*, 16 F. 211 (U.S.C.C. Mich., 1883).

132. Deady was troubled by another, more technical point. He recognized that there might be doubt about whether at her marriage she had been in *every* way eligible for naturalization, as federal law seemed to require. But he argued that some of the requirements, such as evidence of good moral character and five years' residence, had not traditionally been imposed on women who gained American citizenship via marriage. He thought that they should not be, and that only racial restrictions should apply (*Leonard v. Grant*, 5 F. 11 [U.S.C.C. Or., 1880]). California circuit judge Morrow later held that the 1870 naturalization act had made the extension of U.S. citizenship to women marrying American citizens applicable to women of African descent as well as whites—again, whether the woman wished to be assigned U.S. citizenship or not (*Broadis v. Broadis*, 86 F. 951 [U.S.C.C. Ca., 1898]).

133. *Pequignot v. City of Detroit*, 16 F. 211 (U.S.C.C. Mich., 1883).

134. *Strauder v. West Virginia*, 100 U.S. 303 (1879).

135. *In re Lockwood*, 154 U.S. 116–17 (1894).

136. *France v. Connor*, 161 U.S. 65, 68 (1896).

137. Another expression of the federal judiciary's support for traditional gender roles and status, expansively defined, came in the treatment accorded common-law marriages and polygamy. The former were almost always upheld, as less conventional but still desirable forms of the marital relationship that the judges believed stood at the foundation of American society. See, e.g., *Meister v. Moore*, 96 U.S. 76 (1877); *Maryland v. Baldwin*, 112 U.S. 490 (1884); *Travers v. Reinhardt*, 205 U.S. 423 (1907). But even justices otherwise concerned to preserve contractual freedoms, like Field, eagerly sustained bans on polygamy, held to be a barbarism that endangered Christian civilization and the American way of life. See *Reynolds v. U.S.*, 98 U.S. 145 (1878) (decrying polygamy as "odious among the northern and western nations of Europe," favored only by "Asiatic and African people," at 164); *Murphy v. Ramsey*, 114 U.S. 15 (1885) (monogamy "the sure foundation of all that is stable and noble in our civilization"); *Cannon v. U.S*, 116 U.S. 55 (1885); *Davis v. Beason*, 133 U.S. 333 (1890) (polygamy is criminal in "all civilized and Christian countries," and to call it "a tenet of religion is to offend the common sense of mankind"); and *The*

Late Corporation of the Church of Jesus Christ of Latter-Day Saints (Mormon Church) v. U.S., 136 U.S. 1 (1890). See also R. M. Smith, 1989a, 268.

138. See, e.g., *Settlemier v. Sullivan,* 97 U.S. 444 (1878), where Field held that no "theoretical unity of husband and wife can make service upon one equivalent to service upon the other" (447), over dissents by Bradley, Waite, and Harlan; *Bank of America v. Banks,* 101 U.S. 240 (1879), upholding married women's *feme sole* trading rights under Mississippi law; *Fink v. Campbell,* 70 F. 664 (6th C. 1895), sustaining a married woman's right to sue with husband as only a nominal party; *Williams v. Paine,* 169 U.S. 55 (1897), reading an 1865 law as granting married women power of attorney in the District of Columbia.

139. Cases include *Vance v. Burbank,* 101 U.S. 514 (1879) (a married woman could not legally be the "settler" in Oregon; *Partee v. Thomas,* 11 F. 769 (U.S.C.C. Tenn., 1882) (a married woman can have no power of attorney to convey lands); *Bedford v. Burton,* 106 U.S. 338–39 (1882) (married woman can purchase lands only with her husband's consent); *Hopkins v. Grimshaw,* 165 U.S. 342 (1897) (a married woman cannot testify against her husband).

140. R. M. Smith, 1989a, 265–68, overstates how far greater attachments to individual economic rights produced real divisions on the Supreme Court in late nineteenth-century cases involving women; but they did lead Field, especially, to differ with some of his brethren in several cases, including *Settlemier v. Sullivan,* 97 U.S. 444 (1878), *Maynard v. Hill,* 125 U.S. 190 (1888), and *Mormon Church v. U.S.,* 136 U.S. 1 (1890). In these cases Field was most concerned to establish clear and robust economic rights, even at some cost to coverture and conventional marriages, whereas other justices stressed support for traditional monogamous families represented strictly by males.

141. Hoxie, 1984, 10–15, 41–44; Prucha, 1984, 621, 633–40.

142. Dippie, 1982, 98–106, 151–53, 164–71; Trachtenberg, 1982, 34–36; Hoxie, 1984, 17–29, 260–261n30; Degler, 1991, 13.

143. *U.S., ex rel. Standing Bear v. Crook,* 25 F. Cas. 695 (U.S.C.C. Neb., 1879). J. Dundy's opinion expresses sympathy for this "weak . . . and generally despised race" that has almost "*christian*" values (695, 699).

144. M. Smith, 1970, 28–29; Hoxie, 1984, 1–10; Prucha, 1984, 611–28.

145. See, e.g., Rep. Skinner, *Cong. Rec.,* 49th Cong., 2d Sess., v. 18, pt. 1, 190 (Dec. 15, 1886): "The effect of the tribal and reservation policy upon the Indian is to make him dependent, to pauperize him to a greater or less degree, to dwarf his mind, and to clog his energies."

146. M. Smith, 1970, 27–32; Dippie, 1982, 113–20; Trachtenberg, 1982, 30–33; Hoxie, 1984, 53–65; Prucha, 1984, 613, 660–79; Ragsdale, 1989, 409, 412–14. The Major Crimes Act was prompted by the Supreme Court's decision in *Ex parte Crow Dog,* 109 U.S. 556 (1883), and sustained in *U.S. v. Kagama,* 118 U.S. 375 (1886), discussed below. Advocates of citizenship for Native Americans sometimes invoked the egalitarian ideals of the Declaration of Independence, but arguments that citizenship was the best means for "cultivation" of a less advanced race were more frequent. See, e.g., remarks of Sen. Chace, *Cong. Rec.,* 49th Cong. 1st Sess., v. 17, pt. 2, 1633 (Feb. 19, 1886).

147. Dippie, 1982, 171–72; Hoxie, 1984, 44–51, 70–72; Prucha, 1984, 661, 664.

148. M. Smith, 1970, 30–32; Dippie, 1982, 172–77; Hoxie, 1984, 72; Prucha, 1984, 623–24, 665–69, 686; J. E. Martin, 1990, 82–83.

149. In 1890 Congress passed the Oklahoma Organic Act, organizing a territorial government for the Oklahoma District, which encouraged white settlement of the formerly protected Indian Territory. In 1893 Congress appointed a commission, headed by retired Sen. Henry

Dawes, to negotiate allotments in severalty with the Five Civilized Tribes (Dippie, 1982, 193, 246–47; Prucha, 1984, 746–57; 911–16).

150. The ever-dwindling tribal lands would total about 48 million acres in 1934, when federal policy changed. Dippie, 1982, 172–82, 190, 319–21; Prucha, 1984, 671–73; Ragsdale, 1989, 413–14.

151. 109 U.S. 556 (1883).

152. *Crow Dog* at 567, 571. Matthews was ambiguous on whether it was right to judge "the red man's revenge" by the "white man's" standards, though he was sure that tribal customs were "prejudices of their savage nature."

153. *U.S. v. Elm,* 25 F. Cas. 1006 (U.S.D.C. N.Y., 1877). See also *U.S. v. Osborn,* 2 F. 58, 61 (U.S.D.C. Or., 1880) ("an Indian can not make himself a citizen of the United States without the consent and co-operation of the government").

154. *Ex parte Reynolds,* 20 F. Cas. 582, 584–85 (U.S.C.C. Ark., 1879), citing the common law (inaccurately) and Vattel for the rule that, for free persons, children always follow the condition of their fathers. See also *U.S. v. Ward,* 42 F. 320 (U.S.C.C. Ca., 1890) (tribesman born of black father and Indian mother is black, not Indian). Issues of race, patriarchy, and citizenship remained confusing, however: *Lucas v. U.S.,* 163 U.S. 612 (1896), ruled an illegitimate child born to a Choctaw father and black slave mother a "colored citizen of the United States." Cf. also *Alberty v. U.S.,* 162 U.S. 499, 500 (1896) (a black former slave made a Cherokee citizen in 1866 is for jurisdictional purposes "a member of the Cherokee nation, but not an Indian"). *Raymond v. Raymond,* 83 F. 721 (8th C. 1897) confirmed that even when a white native-born American citizen took tribal membership, she did not thereby lose her U.S. citizenship; but she did lose access to federal courts for disputes with fellow tribespeople, even if she later left the tribe. See also *Roff v. Burney,* 168 U.S. 218 (1897).

155. 112 U.S. 94, 102–3, 106–7 (1884).

156. Ibid. at 121.

157. Schuck & Smith, 1985, 83–85.

158. Prucha, 1984, 678, 684; Hoxie, 1984, 74–75, 235; Ragsdale, 1989, 409; Martin, 1990, 82. And see, e.g., *Ex parte Kenyon,* 14 F. Cas. 353 (U.S.C.C. Ark., 1878), holding that when tribal members "scatter themselves among the citizens of the United States, and live among the people of the United States, they are merged in the mass of our people, owing complete allegiance to the government of the United States and of the state where they may reside." The opinion speaks of "citizens of the United States" as if they were distinct from such Native Americans, but treats their rights as identical (355).

159. Those commitments sometimes stemmed from genuine anger at state cruelty toward tribespeople. In *U.S. v. Barnhart,* 22 F. 285 (U.S.C.C. Or., 1884), Judge Deady bluntly stated that the region's Indian wars "have been the direct result of crimes committed by a few lawless and savage white men upon Indians, which the local authorities were powerless or indisposed to punish. . . . No white man was ever hung for killing an Indian, and no Indian tried for killing a white man ever escaped the gallows."

160. Native Americans still in tribal relations were fully subject to U.S. guardianship, but unless Congress so provided, tribal members had limited access to U.S. courts, and constitutional guarantees did not apply to tribal courts. See, e.g., *In re Mayfield,* 141 U.S. 107 (1891) (Congress has not given federal courts jurisdiction over adultery by a Cherokee within his nation); *Paul v. Chilsoquie,* 70 F. 401 (U.S.C.C. Ind., 1895) (without congressional authorization, danger of local bias not enough to warrant federal jurisdiction); and especially *Talton v. Mayes,* 163 U.S. 376 (1896) (Fifth Amendment does not apply to Cherokee courts; Harlan dissented without opinion).

161. 118 U.S. 375 (1886). The decision gave vital confirmation of judicial receptivity to the sort of direct federal regulation the Dawes Act would soon impose (M. Smith, 1970, 28). See also *Wau-Pe-Man-Qua, alias Mary Strack, v. Aldrich*, 28 F. 489 (U.S.C.C. Ind., 1886) (when titles are not fully extinguished and Congress has not explicitly relinquished control, states cannot tax Indian lands); *Kie v. U.S.*, 27 F. 351 (U.S.C.C. Or., 1886) (federal homicide laws apply to Alaskan natives because Alaska is not "Indian Country"); *U.S. v. Nelson*, 29 F. 202 (U.S.D.C. Alaska, 1886) (Congress can regulate liquor trade with Alaskan tribes); *In re Sah Quah*, 31 F. 327 (U.S.D.C. Alaska, 1886). (Congress can ban slavery among tribes—though Sah Quah denied he was a slave, and the case seemed set up to discredit tribal authority; see Harring, 1989, 310–14); *U.S. v. Clapox*, 35 F. 575 (U.S.D.C. Or., 1888); *U.S. v. Ewing*, 47 F. 809 (U.S.D.C. S.D., 1891); *U.S. v. Partello*, 48 F. 670 (U.S.C.C. Mont., 1891); *In re Blackbird*, 109 F. 139 (U.S.D.C. Wisc., 1901) (all following *Kagama* and upholding broad federal criminal jurisdiction); *Cherokee Nation v. Southern Kansas Railway*, 135 U.S. 641 (1890) (Congress can authorize a railroad through Indian Territory).
162. See, e.g., *Bates v. Clark*, 95 U.S. 204 (1877) (lands to which Indian titles have been extinguished are no longer Indian country unless Congress so specifies); *Pennock v. Commissioners*, 103 U.S. 44 (1880) (states can tax such lands); *Caldwell v. Robinson*, 59 F. 653 (U.S.C.C. Id., 1894); affirmed in *Robinson v. Caldwell*, 67 F. 391 (9th C. 1895) (an Indian agent cannot eject whites from reservation lands to which they had acquired title under prior federal laws).
163. *Ross v. Eells*, 56 F. 855 (U.S.C.C. Wash., 1893).
164. *Eells et al. v. Ross*, 64 F. 417 (9th C. 1894); appeal dismissed in *Ross v. Eells*, 163 U.S. 702 (1896). In *Draper v. U.S.*, 164 U.S. 240 (1896), the Supreme Court rather opaquely indicated that the U.S. did retain power to protect Indian lands versus state infringement even after allotment in severalty, but unless Congress specified otherwise, states could prosecute citizens for crimes committed on reservations within their borders (108–9). See also *U.S. v. McBratney*, 104 U.S. 621 (1881), critiqued in Cohen, 1982, 264–65; *Ex parte Kyle*, 67 F. 306 (U.S.D.C. Ark., 1895) (naturalization of a Cherokee does not enable him to escape jurisdiction of the Cherokee court for a murder offense, as he would otherwise escape punishment); *U.S. v. Mullin; In re Garrett*, 71 F. 682 (U.S.D.C. Neb., 1895) (acquisition of citizenship by allotment does not nullify U.S. right and duty to enforce treaty provisions protecting property rights); *U.S. v. Alaska Packers' Ass'n*, 79 F. 152 (U.S.C.C. Wash., 1897) (treaty does not protect allotment Indians from state-licensed white encroachments on their fishing operations); *Jones v. Meehan*, 175 U.S. 1 (1899) (title granted by treaty assumed to be alienable unless otherwise specified). Placed alongside the decisions holding that U.S. citizenship could never be relinquished for a tribal one (e.g., *Raymond v. Raymond*, 83 F. 721 (8th C. 1897), it is clear that the courts treated U.S. citizenship, however acquired, as primary; but they often embraced limitations on the U.S. citizenship of those who were born Native Americans or chose to become so. Hence there was really no point in the Gilded Age at which Native American citizens were judicially seen as fully equal to white citizens.

Hoxie (1984, 214) wrongly identifies *Mullin* as the first case to clarify that allotment citizenship did not end federal wardship. *Eells v. Ross* was prior, decided by a higher court, and more frequently cited; and the Supreme Court refused to overturn on appeal. *Mullin* was also preceded by *Beck v. Flournoy Live-stock and Real Estate Co.*, 65 F. 30, 34–35 (8th C. 1894), in which allotment recipients remain "wards of the nation" who need protection from the "greed and superior intelligence of the white man" so they will not "speedily waste" their allotments and become "paupers"; appeal dismissed in *Flournoy Livestock and Real Estate Co. v. Beck*, 163 U.S. 686 (1895).

165. Spencer, 1920, 13–17, 25–33, 55, 61, 106–9, 166–68; Cremin, 1988, 387–91.
166. Cremin, 1988, 8, 119; Kaminsky, 1993, xiii–xiv, 32–36.
167. Tyack, 1974, 66–67, 244; Cremin, 1988, 544–46, 551, 556.
168. Katz, 1971, 56–73; Tyack, 1974, 5–7, 25, 66–68; Peterson, 1985, 8–9, 73–75; Cremin, 1988, 13–14, 224–39.
169. Cremin, 1988, 19–29, 70–71, 111–12, 375, 393–99; Kaminsky, 1993, 5–9, 49–50.
170. Leidecker, 1946, viii, 243, 265–67, 286, 290–91, 308, 316; Holmes, 1956, 52–53, 62–66; Tyack, 1974, 29, 43, 71–73; Cremin, 1988, 157–64, 224; Spring, 1990, 164–68; Kaminsky, 1993, xvi, 31.
171. Richardson, 1986, 129–31, 255; J. D. Anderson, 1988, 79–109, 148–51, 154, 157–77, 189–95, 238–50; Cremin, 1988, 123, 213–21, 534.
172. Low, 1982, 55–65, 70–79, 92–107.
173. Prucha, 1984, 759–62; Hoxie, 1984, 68–69, 117–34, 198–99; Coleman, 1993, 43–47.
174. Woody, 1929, v. II, 57–64, 74–75, 182–90, 228–35, 248–54, 442–44; Tyack, 1974, 59–65, 258; Degler, 1980, 156–57, 309–15; Degler, 1991, 29–30; Clinton, 1984, 125–35; Cremin, 1988, 132, 278–82; Spring, 1990, 115–16, 128.
175. Like the Fourteenth Amendment, however, diversity jurisprudence contained a literally "nativist" ascriptive element of birthright citizenship within principles largely concerned to expand personal liberties. Diversity rulings treated "the domicile of origin or nativity" as more presumptively a citizen's "true" domicile, and as "more easily reacquired," than "a domicile of choice," which would not be recognized without proof of both the fact and intention of permanent removal. See *Marks v. Marks*, 75 F. 321 (U.S.C.C. Tenn., 1896).
176. As noted in previous chapters, the Habeas Corpus Act of 1863, subsequent Civil War removal acts, and, especially, the Jurisdiction and Removal Act of 1875, all dramatically expanded the powers of the federal courts. But the tide began to turn. In 1882, Congress prevented national banks from removing cases solely on the ground that they were incorporated under federal laws. In 1887 and 1888, under Cleveland, the first postwar Democratic President, Congress raised the amount required in diversity jurisdiction civil suits to $2,000, indicated that corporations were "inhabitants" only of their state of incorporation, required suits to be brought in districts where defendants were "inhabitants," and withdrew removal rights of plaintiffs and resident defendants, among other provisions. The statutes were badly drafted and sparked much litigation. In 1891, under a more nationalistic Republican President, Benjamin Harrison, Congress again strengthened the federal judiciary by creating courts of appeals for each circuit and adding an extra circuit judge, thus for practical purposes relieving Supreme Court justices of circuit duties in all cases but those they regarded as most important. But in 1894, under Cleveland again, Congress repealed the 1871 act permitting removal in prosecutions for electoral racial discrimination (Frankfurter, 1928, 507–12); Moore & Weckstein, 1964a, 6–9; Hyman & Wiecek, 1982, 282, 415, 454; Friedman, 1985, 386–87; Purcell, 1992, 15–17, 130–31).
177. As Felix Frankfurter wrote, corporate litigation had become "the key to diversity problems" (1928, 523).
178. In *Litigation and Inequality* (1992), Edward Purcell tries to sustain older, more Hartzian narratives of this era as essentially a period of pro-corporate rulings that, for a variety of reasons, conferred a "de facto subsidy on business enterprise" at the expense of other individuals. His evidence does not, however, support such a simple pattern. Purcell eventually defines three stages of corporate diversity litigation: 1870 to 1890, when the Court showed "suspicion of the growing power of the new national corporations" and a "desire to protect those who brought suit against them"; 1890 into the early 1900s, when the Court "enhanced the litigation position of corporate defendants"; and 1910 to the 1940s,

when litigation was "complex and varied" until the late nineteenth-century pro-corporate litigation system disintegrated. But Purcell also identifies a "striking series of decisions" through which the Court ruled against the "litigation interests of national corporations," often on "dubious legal grounds," beginning as early as 1900 (Purcell, 1992, 7–8,
128, 244–46, 262–91). Hence, though pro-corporate rulings can certainly be found before and after, especially in particular lower federal courts, Purcell's sharpest pro-corporate phase is actually confined to the 1890s. Even then he acknowledges some contrary
rulings and sees the Supreme Court as chiefly aiding corporations "obliquely," via "delay,
avoidance, and equivocation" (267). Thus, significant as the 1890s were, they represent
only a heavier pro-corporate tilt in a pattern that remained mixed. In addition to judicial
anxieties about radical labor and agrarian protest during the depression-burdened 1890s,
it is possible that the willingness of the Court under Cleveland Democrat Melville Fuller
to expand jurisdiction to aid corporations in those years increased once Republicans
ceased pushing for national judicial protection of black rights. Then the Court may have
backed off its strongest pro-corporate stances when middle-class progressive opposition
to such decisions began to be felt in the 1900s, as Purcell suggests (277–81). Cf. M. Keller,
1977, 174, 431.

179. E.g., in *Robertson v. Cease*, 97 U.S. 646 (1878), Harlan denied that the Fourteenth Amendment compelled any change in the longstanding presumption against federal jurisdiction
unless that jurisdiction had been affirmatively shown. He also held that even though the
amendment's citizenship clause made all persons born or naturalized in the United States
citizens of the U.S. and of the state in which they resided, averment of residence was still
not sufficient to justify an inference of state citizenship. Attorneys had argued quite logically that residents could now only be either citizens of the state in which they resided or
aliens, and that both statuses would justify federal jurisdiction. But Harlan refused to
open the federal courts based on logical inference alone, however inexorable. *Robertson*
was followed in, e.g., *Third Nat. Bank of Baltimore v. Teal*, 5 F. 503 (U.S.C.C. Md., 1881)
and later cases. In a similarly self-denying spirit, the Court ruled that the Eleventh Amendment prevented a citizen from suing his state government in federal court without its permission, even if a federal question were present (*Hans v. Louisiana*, 134 U.S. 1 [1890]).
Justice Bradley cheerfully volunteered that the nationalistic decision in *Chisholm v. Georgia* had probably been wrong, a view that prompted a protest from Harlan (at 20). But
Harlan joined the Court's refusal of expansive jurisdiction in *Chapman v. Barney*, 129 U.S.
677 (1889), which deemed partnerships ineligible for the diversity citizenship conferred
on corporations. Although that ruling might be seen as unfriendly to businesses broadly
conceived, it did also strengthen the advantages of the corporate form.

180. Harlan for the Court in *Barney v. Latham*, 13 Otto (103 U.S.) 205, 210, 211 (1880). Chief
Justice Waite and Justices Miller and Field dissented without opinion. The Court also read
the 1875 act as permitting corporate litigants to remove cases into federal court in every
state in which they transacted business in the landmark case of *Ex parte Schollenberger*,
96 U.S. 369 (1877), which reversed a number of contrary lower court rulings. This jurisdiction stirred largely anti-corporate opposition and was reduced somewhat by the restrictive Democratic laws of 1887 and 1888. And in the *Pacific Railroad Removal Cases*,
115 U.S. 1 (1885), Bradley ruled for the Court, over the dissents of Waite and Miller, that
all cases brought by or against a federally chartered corporation could reach the federal
courts, not under diversity jurisdiction, but as cases arising under the "laws of the United
States." The decision did not affect the denial of removal to national banks enacted by
Congress in 1882 and affirmed in *Leather Manufacturers' Bank v. Cooper*, 120 U.S. 778
(1887), and *Whittemore v. Amoskeag National Bank*, 134 U.S. 527 (1890). Congress even-

tually eliminated most of the jurisdiction defined in this case in 1915, and the rest in 1925 (Frankfurter, 1928, 509–11; McGovney, 1943b, 1121–24; Purcell, 1992, 18).

181. In *Bors v. Preston*, 111 U.S. 252 (1884), with Harlan writing, the Court also sustained Congress's addition to lower federal court jurisdiction of various matters constitutionally assigned to the Supreme Court's original jurisdiction, a ruling that helped the federal judiciary handle this expanded case load. Justices Gray and Miller concurred on other grounds, specifically reserving judgment on this issue; but Chief Justice Waite reached the same conclusion for a unanimous court later that year in *Ames v. Kansas ex rel. Johnston*, 111 U.S. 449 (1884), a case upholding a corporate removal into federal court on federal question, not citizenship grounds. These rulings are in some apparent tension with the famous argument of *Marbury v. Madison*—that the Constitution's grant of original jurisdiction to the Supreme Court is meant to be exhaustive, so that the Court cannot be given any extra original jurisdiction. One might deduce that the lower courts should not be given original jurisdiction of any matter that the Constitution assigns to the Supreme Court's original jurisdiction. Miller's opinion in *Wisconsin v. Duluth*, 30 F. Cas. 382 (U.S.C.C. Minn., 1872) had so reasoned. But that conclusion is not logically compelled, and, as Harlan and Waite noted, Congress gave the lower courts overlapping original jurisdiction early on, with judicial acquiescence.

182. Purcell, 1992, 16–147, is the best overview.

183. E.g., in *St. Louis National Bank v. Allen*, 5 F. 551 (U.S.C.C. Ia., 1881), an Iowa circuit judge accepted that banks organized under the 1864 National Banking Act could sue as "jurisdictional citizens" of states in which they were established or located, though it denied that they could sue in *any* U.S. circuit court, a ruling Congress affirmed the next year. In *Petri v. Commercial National Bank of Chicago*, 142 U.S. 644 (1892), the Court also stressed that the rights of such banks to sue citizens of other states in federal courts had survived the 1887–88 restrictions on removal. And in *U.S. and the Sioux Nation v. Northwestern Express*, 164 U.S. 686 (1897), followed in *Ramsey v. Tacoma Land Co.*, 196 U.S. 360 (1905), the Court interpreted the phrase "citizens of the United States" in a federal statute as including corporations (F. Green, 1946, 209–10; Purcell, 1992, 18–27, 48–58).

184. The Court generally continued to insist, for example, that diversity suits brought under the 1875 jurisdiction act had to involve complete diversity, not overlapping citizenships for any parties on opposite sides of a controversy. See, e.g., *The Removal Cases*, 100 U.S. 457 (1879), where Bradley issues a pro-corporate dissent; *Barney v. Latham*, 103 U.S. 205 (1880); *Blake v. McKim*, 13 Otto (103 U.S.) 336, 339 (1881), but cf. *Hamilton v. Savannah, Florida & Western Railway Co.*, 49 F. 412, 410–22 (U.S.C.C. Ga., 1892). See also Purcell, 1992, 106–8, 333–34n14, who notes that the courts failed to address why it was constitutional for the 1875 act to authorize full removal of cases in which only some of the issues involved parties with diverse citizenships. Purcell also stresses that the Court failed to clarify whether the 1867 removal act, most invoked by corporations, also required complete diversity of citizenship, permitting lower court rulings requiring only partial diversity to stand until the Progressive Era. Purcell stresses the Court's equivocal treatment of the issue in *Hanrick v. Hanrick*, 153 U.S. 192, 197 (1894) but without noting that the Court denied the requested removal (Purcell, 1992, 131–35).

185. *Hawes v. Oakland*, 14 Otto (104 U.S.) 450, 452; *Huntington v. Palmer*, 104 U.S. 482 (1881), and cf. *Greenwood v. Freight Co.*, 105 U.S. 13 (1881); *Detroit v. Dean*, 106 U.S. 537, 541 [1882]). Miller had long harbored worries about stockholder suits; see, e.g., *Samuel v. Holladay*, 21 F. Cas. 306 (U.S.C.C. Ky., 1869). The Court adopted Equity Rule 94 at 104 U.S. ix (1882) and reformulated it in 1891. The rule led to denials of jurisdiction in, e.g., *Quincy v. Steel*, 120 U.S. 241, 244–48 (1887); *Watson v. U.S. Sugar Refinery*, 68 F. 769 (U.S.C.C.A.

7th 1895); *Rogers v. Nashville, Chattanooga & St. Louis Ry. Co.,* 91 F. 299 (1898). Because Purcell, 1992, focuses on corporate efforts to get genuinely hostile plaintiffs into federal courts, he does not consider how the federal courts resisted these corporate efforts to evade state laws.

186. See, e.g., *Uphoff v. Chicago, St. Louis & New Orleans Railroad Co.,* 5 F. 545 (U.S.C.C. Ky., 1880), refusing to permit a Kentucky plaintiff to sue a corporation that claimed to be a citizen of both Louisiana and Kentucky because she had not affirmatively indicated she wished to sue the Louisiana corporate citizen; *Alabama v. Wolffe,* 18 F. 836 (U.S.C.C. Ala., 1883), indicating that a state did not count as a citizen for removal purposes; *Northern Pacific Railroad Co. v. Austin,* 135 U.S. 315 (1890), refusing a corporate removal request because the original damages sought were below the jurisdictional minimum, though the plaintiff later raised the amount; *In re Pennsylvania Co.,* 137 U.S. 451 (1890), confirming that monetary requirements for diversity jurisdiction applied in cases involving alleged local prejudice; *Fisk v. Henarie,* 142 U.S. 459 (1892), insisting that, like the 1875 jurisdiction act, the 1887–88 provisions required removals to be filed prior to or at the term in which a case could first be tried, not after (but cf. *Powers v. Chesapeake & Ohio Railway Co.,* 169 U.S. 92 [1898], construing the 1887–88 revisions in federal jurisdiction). The Supreme Court also refused to accept original jurisdiction to enforce a state fine imposed on an out-of-state corporate citizen for a minor violation of state criminal law, holding that it only possessed such original jurisdiction in civil suits (*Wisconsin v. Pelican Insurance Co.,* 127 U.S. 265 [1888]). See Henderson, 1918, 89–100; Purcell, 1992, 104–7, 131–34.

187. See, e.g., *Minot v. Philadelphia, Wilmington, and Baltimore Railroad Co.,* 17 F. Cas. 458 (1870), permitting a corporation to be recognized as a citizen of three different states in different litigation; *Muller v. Dows,* 94 U.S. 444 (1876), holding that a Missouri company consolidated with an Iowa one had only its Iowa identity in Iowa, so that it could be sued in an Iowa federal court by a Missouri citizen; *Memphis and Charleston Railroad Co. v. Alabama,* 107 U.S. 581 (1882), holding that a Tennessee corporation, reincorporated in Alabama to do business there, could not remove a suit against it by an Alabama citizen from the Alabama courts on diversity grounds, as its Tennessee existence had no force there; *Nashua & Lowell Railroad Co. v. Boston & Lowell Railroad Co.,* 136 U.S. 356 (1890), ruling that members of a company first incorporated in New Hampshire, then later incorporated in Massachusetts for the same ends, could claim still to be a New Hampshire corporation for diversity purposes. Note that though *Muller* and *Memphis Railroad* worked against the apparent forum preferences of the corporations involved, *Nashua and Lowell Railroad* permitted the corporation to choose its identity and forum. Hence it seemed to invite the circumstances in *Lehigh Manufacturing,* discussed in the text. These questions are now largely dealt with via the Diversity Act of 1958, creating 28 U.S.C. Sec. 1332c (Fink & Tushnet, 1987, 478).

188. *Lehigh Mining and Manufacturing v. Kelly,* 160 U.S. 327 (1895). Harlan wrote for the Court. Shiras, joined by Field and Brown, dissented.

189. *St. Louis and San Francisco Railway Co. v. James,* 161 U.S. 545, 563 (1896). Justice George Shiras dissented in *Lehigh,* believing corporations should be able to create offspring with different citizenships in other states, but he wrote for the Court in *James* that deeming the corporation to be both a Missouri and an Arkansas "citizen" carried the fiction of corporate citizenship too far. Harlan was now in dissent, arguing the separate incorporation indeed constituted a separate legal identity. Each time Shiras took the pro-corporate stance, Harlan the opposing view.

190. That circumstance gained added importance after New Jersey and Delaware passed laws making it attractive for out-of-state companies to incorporate there. Those businesses

then had diversity access for conflicts with most of their customers and neighbors (Purcell, 1992, 18–19, 245, 296n26). Purcell does not adequately acknowledge that, if corporations were able to designate which of multiple state citizenships applied in specific cases, the multiple corporate citizenships approach he favors would have given businesses even greater forum-shopping powers than the indulgent *James* rule. Cf. also Ely, 1995, 193.

191. Deady thought that only a more formal oath to that effect had been required, but the Supreme Court disagreed. See *Fisk v. Henarie*, 32 F. 417 (U.S.C.C. Or., 1887); *Fisk v. Henarie*, 35 F. 230 (U.S.C.C. Or., 1888); followed in *Cooper v. Richmond*, 42 F. 697 (U.S.C.C. Ga., 1890). The Court was closer to Bradley's view in *Short v. Chicago, Milwaukee and St. Paul Railway Co.*, 33 F. 114 (U.S.C.C. Minn., 1887), followed in, e.g., *Amy v. Manning*, 38 F. 536 (U.S.C.C. N.Y., 1889); *Collins v. Campbell*, 62 F. 850 (U.S.C.C. R.I., 1894).

192. *Fisk v. Henarie*, 142 U.S. 459 (1892). Harlan and Field dissented.

193. See e.g., *Whelan v. New York, Lake Erie & Western Railroad*, 35 F. 849 (U.S.C.C. Oh., 1888), corrected in *In re Pennsylvania Co.*, 137 U.S. 451 (1890); *In re Hohorst*, 150 U.S. 653 (1893), ruling that an 1888 provision banning civil suits brought in a district other than the one in which the defendant resided did not apply to alien or out-of-state corporations, as it might make them effectively immune from civil suits. Purcell, 1992, 128–37, 142–47.

194. See *Insurance Co. v. Morse*, 87 U.S. 445 (1874) and *Doyle v. Continental Insurance Co.*, 94 U.S. 535 (1876), discussed in ch. 10, as well as *Philadelphia Fire Association v. New York*, 119 U.S. 110 (1886).

195. *Barron v. Burnside*, 121 U.S. 86 (1887); M. Keller, 1977, 433–34. A unanimous Court upheld *Morse* and read *Doyle* so narrowly as to overrule it—or so it seemed. State measures hostile to removal were still popular, and because they were not definitively rejected, states kept passing them. *Barron*'s reasoning was followed in, e.g., *Southern Pacific Co. v. Denton*, 146 U.S. 202 (1892), *Martin v. Baltimore and Ohio Railroad*, 151 U.S. 673, 684 (1894), *Barrow Steamship Co. v. Kane*, 170 U.S. 100 (1898), and *Dayton Coal and Iron Co. v. Barton*, 183 U.S. 23 (1901), though *Doyle* was treated as good law in, e.g., *Manchester Fire Ins. Co. v. Herriott*, 91 F. 711 (U.S.C.C. Ia., 1899). See Henderson, 1918, 135–47; Purcell, 1992, 201–2.

196. Chief Justice Fuller read Art. IV, sec. 2, as providing no substantive rights per se, but rather assurance that a state could not refuse out-of-state citizens basic rights it granted its own, in *Cole v. Cunningham*, 133 U.S. 107, 113 (1890).

197. *Williams v. Bruffy*, 96 U.S. 176 (1877) at 183, 185. Field defended the Court's ruling by linking it with Vattel's views concerning when insurgent governments can claim full recognition.

198. See, e.g., *In re Watson*, 15 F. 511 (U.S.D.C. Vt., 1882); *Walling v. Michigan*, 116 U.S. 446 (1886); *Farmers' Loan & Trust Co. v. Chicago & Atlantic Railway Co.*, 27 F. 146 (U.S.C.C. Ind., 1886); *Martin v. Maysville St. Railroad & Transfer Co.*, 49 F. 436 (U.S.C.C. Ky., 1892); *Moredock v. Kirby*, 118 F. 180 (U.S.C.C. Ky., 1902).

199. Few lower courts strained to find Art. IV violations; e.g., in *Ex parte Thornton*, 12 F. 538 (U.S.C.C. Va., 1882), District Judge Hughes refused to find that a law which required licenses of some types of merchants and not others amounted to discrimination against out-of-state citizens.

200. Cases like *Brown v. Houston*, 114 U.S. 622 (1885) and *In re Barber*, 39 F. 641 (U.S.C.C. Minn., 1889) exemplify the tendency to focus on the commerce clause in most disputes about state laws affecting the economic activities of out-of-state citizens. Other cases later cited along with Art. IV, sec. 2 rulings in fact rely on the commerce clause: see, e.g., *County of Mobile v. Kimball*, 102 U.S. 691 (1880) and *Webber v. Virginia*, 103 U.S. 344 (1880).

201. The federal courts often let corporations benefit from statutes making public lands available to "citizens of the United States" or providing restitution for damages inflicted on

citizens. See, e.g., *McKinley v. Wheeler,* 130 U.S. 630 (1889); *U.S. and the Sioux Nation v. Northwestern Express Co.,* 164 U.S. 686 (1897).

202. Exemplary in this regard is Field's long opinion in *The Railroad Tax Cases; County of San Mateo v. Southern Pacific Railroad Co.,* 13 F. 722 (U.S.C.C. Ca., 1882). There he cites *Paul v. Virginia* to hold that corporations are not citizens under the privileges and immunities clauses, but he defends at length their status as persons entitled to Fourteenth Amendment due process and equal protection, and the judiciary's duty to protect them, especially in a hostile political climate. Field stresses his awareness of "the opinion prevailing throughout the community that the railroad corporations of the state by means of their great wealth and the numbers in their employ, have become so powerful as to be disturbing influences in the administration of the laws; an opinion which will be materially strengthened by a decision temporarily relieving any one of them from its just proportion of the public burdens." But Field insisted that the corporations he saw as so politically beleaguered were "entitled when they enter the tribunals of the nation to the same justice . . . which is meted out to the humblest citizen." Cf. Field's Court opinion in *Pembina Consolidated Silver Mining and Milling Co. v. Pennsylvania,* 125 U.S. 181, 187 (1888).

203. *The Stockton Laundry Case; In re Tie Loy,* 26 F. 611 (U.S.C.C. Ca., 1886). Circuit judge Sawyer chiefly relied on *Yates v. Milwaukee* (1870) which he interpreted as a Fourteenth Amendment privileges and immunities decision even though Miller had presented it as a federal common-law ruling, as noted previously. Sawyer knew full well the law was an extreme attempt to drive out the Chinese, and he was clearly reaching for a basis to void it. Subsequently he, like most federal judges, relied more on due process arguments. See, e.g., his decision in *In re Sam Kee,* 31 F. 680 (U.S.C.C. Ca., 1887), voiding another ordinance banning all laundries chiefly through reliance on a just compensation requirement implicit in due process, as well as, Sawyer added, the implicit liberty to select one's own occupation; privileges and immunities; and equal protection. The Supreme Court similarly treated the three clauses together, but stressed due process concerns, when upholding an 8-hour day law for miners in *Holden v. Hardy,* 169 U.S. 366, 382 (1898).

204. There are many such decisions. Strictly speaking, they did not make American *citizenship* policies more liberal, but they sustained important commitments to equal human rights in American public law. The most significant such case is *Yick Wo v. Hopkins,* 118 U.S. 356 (1886), where a unanimous Court voided a law requiring board approval of laundries in wooden buildings as a transparent device for discriminating against Chinese immigrants, in violation of the equal protection clause. Other examples include *Ho Ah Kow v. Nunan,* 12 F. Cas. 252 (U.S.C.C. Ca., 1879) (voiding an anti-queue ordinance on equal protection grounds); *Baker v. Portland,* 2 F. Cas. 472 (U.S.C.C. Or., 1879) (law banning Chinese labor in public works violates U.S. treaty obligations); *In re Tiburcio Parrott,* 1 F. 481 (U.S.C.C. Ca., 1880) (law preventing corporations from employing Chinese violates treaty guarantees of privileges and immunities and Fourteenth Amendment equal protection); *In re Ah Chong,* 2 F. 733 (U.S.C.C. Ca., 1880) (following *Parrott* in voiding a similar provision in new state constitution); *In re Wo Lee,* 26 F. 471 (U.S.C.C. Ca., 1886) (voiding a laundry licensing board as violating due process); *In re Baldwin,* 27 F. 187 (U.S.C.C. Ca., 1886) (provisionally holding civil rights laws based on the equal protection clause valid bases for prosecuting a conspiracy to expel Chinese); *In re Lee Sing,* 43 F. 359 (U.S.C.C. Ca., 1890) (voiding on equal protection grounds a San Francisco ordinance requiring Chinese citizens and aliens to reside in certain neighborhoods or be expelled). The pattern was, however, far from one way; and here as in the immigration area discussed below, the Supreme Court eventually proved more hostile to Chinese claims than many state judges. E.g., in *Baldwin v. Franks,* 120 U.S. 678 (1887), Chief Justice Waite wrote for

the Court reversing *In re Baldwin* and holding that the civil rights provisions in question were in part unconstitutionally overbroad, because they extended to private action against state as well as federal civic rights, and that the valid provisions protected only U.S. citizens. Harlan and Field dissented. Lower courts also sometimes denied due process and equal protection-based claims. See, e.g., *In re Ah Lee*, 5 F. 899 (U.S.D.C. Or., 1880), *California v. Chue Fan*, 42 F. 865 (U.S.C.C. Ca., 1890).

205. See, e.g., *Beer Co. v. Mass.*, 97 U.S. 25 (1877); *Foster v. Kansas*, 112 U.S. 201 (1884); *State of Kansas v. Bradley*, 26 F. 289 (U.S.C.C. Kan., 1885) (opinion by Circuit Justice David Brewer); *In re Hoover*, 30 F. 51 (U.S.D.C. Ga., 1887); *Mugler v. Kansas*, 123 U.S. 623 (1887); *Kidd v. Pearson*, 128 U.S. 1 (1888); *Eilenbecker v. District Court of Plymouth Co.*, 134 U.S. 31 (1890); *Crowley v. Christensen*, 137 U.S. 86 (1890). The litigation was fueled by the Court's willingness to hold in several cases following *Walling v. Michigan*, 116 U.S. 446 (1886), that state prohibition laws could violate comity clause and, especially, commerce clause guarantees against impeding out-of-state business. Notably, the Court held that Iowa prohibition laws violated the dormant commerce clause in *Bowman v. Chicago and Northwestern Railway Co.*, 125 U.S. 465 (1888), and *Leisy v. Hardin*, 135 U.S. 100 (1890). In *Bowman*, Field concurred with the Court; Waite, Harlan, and Gray dissented. In *Leisy*, new Chief Justice Fuller wrote for the Court with Gray, Harlan, and Brewer in dissent. Three months after *Leisy*, Congress passed a law affirming the rights of states to enact such regulations. Further litigation upheld the congressional act and state prohibition laws, especially *In re Rahrer*, 140 U.S. 545 (1891), where Fuller wrote for the Court and Harlan, Gray, and Brewer concurred on their previous grounds. After *Rahrer*, *Cantini v. Tillman*, 54 F. 969 (U.S.C.C. S.C., 1893), and *Giozza v. Tiernan*, 148 U.S. 657 (1893), challenges to such laws declined. But they did not disappear; see, e.g., *Cox v. Texas*, 202 U.S. 446 (1906), and cases cited therein.

Liquor laws prompted virtually the only expansion of Fourteenth Amendment privileges and immunities the federal courts sustained, on behalf of regulatory enforcers. A Tennessee circuit court ruled in 1893 that such privileges did not have to be possessed by all U.S. citizens. They could be prerogatives confined to civic subsets, such as federal officers. Thus the postwar enforcement statutes legitimately authorized punishing moonshiners who conspired to kill federal revenue agents. *U.S. v. Patrick*, 54 F. 338 (U.S.C.C. Tenn., 1893). It is notable that the circuit court was willing to read federal enforcement powers broadly in a context where offenses of liquor dealers were involved, not offenses against black citizens.

Subsequently, the Court stressed that these sorts of rights, like the right to interstate travel, were already implicit in the "creation and establishment by the Constitution itself of a national government." *In re Quarles and Butler; In re McEntire and Goble*, 158 U.S. 532 (1895). Fuller dissented. See also *Logan v. U.S.*, 144 U.S. 263, 293–94 (1892), holding, without reliance on the privileges and immunities clause, that U.S. citizens can be inferred to have a right to be protected by the government when in federal custody.

206. In 1890, for instance, Fuller held that the ban on cruel and unusual punishments was not a privilege protecting a murderer from electrocution. *In re Kemmler*, 136 U.S. 436 (1890). Similarly, in *Presser v. Illinois*, 116 U.S. 252, 265–66 (1886), Justice Woods ruled for the Court that, because the Second Amendment applied only against the federal government, there was no right of U.S. citizenship that prevented a state from banning the formation of private military companies. The right to practice law also remained a right of state citizenship, in line with *Bradwell v. Illinois*; see, e.g., *Philbrook v. Newman*, 85 F. 139 (U.S.C.C. Ca., 1898).

207. *Spies v. Illinois*, 123 U.S. 131 (1887) at 166, 181. "Spies" was the name of one of the peti-

tioners, not a designation of their occupations. For discussion see Goldstein, 1978, 37–42; Graber, 1991, 32.

208. In *O'Neil v. Vermont*, 144 U.S. 323, 335 (1892), the Court upheld Vermont's conviction of a New York liquor dealer for making deliveries to Vermont residents in violation of Vermont law, but Justice Field dissented. Along with commerce clause and other arguments, Field stated that he had come "after much reflection" to accept Tucker's view (much like his own *Slaughter-House* dissent) that all constitutional rights not specifically aimed at restricting the federal government were now privileges and immunities of U.S. citizenship enforceable against the states. Field believed this law amounted to "cruel and unusual" punishment (341, 361–62, 370). Harlan and Brewer concurred. Field did not discuss the 1890 congressional liquor act upheld in *In re Rahrer*.

209. Harlan's only real success in this line was in getting the Court to hold that the Fourteenth Amendment's due process clause, not the privileges and immunities clause, prevented states from taking property without just compensation (*Chicago, Burlington & Quincy Railroad Co. v. Chicago*, 166 U.S. 226 [1897]).

210. During these years the right to vote was often still discussed in the language of republicanism rather than ascriptive Americanism, with debates couched chiefly in terms of the importance of political participation for citizenship, on the one hand, and the necessity to enfranchise only a citizenry capable of self-governance, on the other. In regard to blacks and white women, however, the issue of capability was now argued chiefly in terms of new defenses of racial and gender hierarchies that were thought applicable in any regime and so not reducible to forms of republicanism.

211. *U.S. v. Goldman*, 25 F. Cas. 1350 (U.S.C.C. La., 1878).

212. *Ex parte Siebold*, 100 U.S. 371, 392–93, 395 (1879).

213. *Ex parte Clarke*, 100 U.S. 399 (1879) at 408, 414.

214. *Dubuclet v. Louisiana*, 103 U.S. 550 (1880); cf., e.g., *U.S. v. Munford*, 16 F. 223 (U.S.C.C. Va., 1883) (*Reese* does not restrict federal power re. congressional elections); *Weil v. Calhoun*, 25 F. 865 (U.S.C.C. Ga., 1885) (accepting jurisdiction for challenges to a referendum on prohibition, though finding the election reasonably conducted); *In re Coy*, 127 U.S. 731 (1888) (following *Clarke* and *Siebold* in regard to federal power over vote tampering in congressional elections; Field dissented); *Ex parte Morrill*, 35 F. 261 (U.S.C.C. Or., 1888) (sustaining 1870 and 1871 voting rights enforcement acts).

215. *In re Green*, 134 U.S. 377 (1890).

216. Ely, 1995, 4–24. Fuller displayed the Court's new attitude vividly in *McPherson v. Blacker*, 146 U.S. 1 (1892), another challenge to a state election of electoral college members. In 1891 Michigan had established a congressional district-based, as opposed to an at-large, system for selecting presidential electors. Fuller ruled that Art. II assigned the states plenary power over the manner in which their electoral college members were appointed. And citing *Slaughter-House, Minor v. Happersett*, and *Cruikshank*, he added that the Fourteenth and Fifteenth amendments placed only a few constraints on state regulation of voting rights, which remained largely a state-regulated privilege (at 24, 34, 37). Lower courts needed little such prompting. In *U.S. v. Belvin*, 46 F. 381 (U.S.C.C. Va., 1891) and *U.S. v. Wardell*, 49 F. 914 (U.S.C.C. N.Y., 1892) circuit courts ruled that even though Congress had power to prevent obstructions to voting in federal elections, *Cruikshank* showed that indictments had to be extraordinarily precise or they would be quashed, the course these judges took. Similarly, in *U.S. v. Dwyer*, 56 F. 464 (U.S.D.C. Tx., 1893), district judge Maxey ruled that nothing in federal law specifically prevented a local election officer from filling out ballots for black and Mexican voters by himself and returning them to those voters to be cast.

Chapter 12. Progressivism and the New American Empire, 1898–1912

1. In this chapter I capitalize *Progressive* only when referring to either the whole era or political parties bearing that name.
2. Wiebe, 1967, 214–23, 288–90; Crunden, 1984, 47, 109; Eisenach, 1994, 239–43.
3. Wiebe, 1967, 288–81; Eisenach, 1994, 67–73, 232–39, who especially stresses the "triumphalism" of progressivism.
4. On the manner in which the Wilson years saw more pervasive federal embrace of legal segregation than ever before, see, e.g., King, 1995, esp. 28–31. The generally excellent analysis of progressive thought in Eisenach, 1994, both identifies progressivism too completely with nationalism, so that he has trouble classifying Wilson as a progressive, and gives insufficient attention to the support for racial inequality and civic homogeneity, at home and abroad, that progressives provided.
5. The breadth of elite agreement can be seen in how the growing embrace of either secular or theologically liberal religious perspectives among elites eventually prompted withdrawal of Protestant fundamentalists from public life until the 1970s (Ahlstrom, 1972, 763–824, 915–17; Eisenach, 1994, 58–61).
6. Fittingly, Hoover would become a chief supporter of the presidential hopes of Taft's son, Senator Robert A. Taft (Pringell, 1964, 34; J. H. Wilson, 1975, 6, 33–40, 222–23; Eisenach, 1994, 124–26).
7. E. F. Goldman, 1952, 93–94, 105–10, 134–36; Quandt, 1970, 3–17, 26; Thelen, 1972, 81–83, 101; D. M. Kennedy, 1975, 454–55; Damico, 1978, 5, 124–26; McCormick, 1981, 248, 256, 271; Rodgers, 1982, 113, 126; Eisenach, 1994, 40–47.
8. E. F. Goldman, 1952, 77; Higham, 1966, 147, 174–75, 247–63; Wiebe, 1967, 113, 156–63, 176, 209–10, 217–18, 288; Rodgers, 1982; Eisenach, 1994, 124–25, 258–62; Bederman, 1995, 276n37, n40, 279n103 (discussing Roosevelt's views on the superiority of the "white American race").
9. Croly, 1963, 359, 387.
10. Croly, 1963, 196–97, 207–8; O'Leary, 1994, 542–49.
11. Croly, 1963, 196–97, 263, 406, 409, 414, 418.
12. Croly, 1914, 196–98; 1963, 263.
13. Croly, 1963, 441, 444, 448–51; Croly, 1914, 197–98.
14. Croly, 1963, 207–8; 1914, 144–45, 306–8, 406, 421–22.
15. Croly, 1963, 259–63, 268–70, 274. See Bederman, 1995, for a fine discussion of how many progressives understood "civilization" in terms of white male supremacy, strengthening the mutually reinforcing character of U.S. racial and gender hierarchies.
16. Croly, 1963, 139, 210–12, 229, 264, 267.
17. Commons in Rischin, ed., 1976, 279–84.
18. C. F. Adams, 1908, 4, 7, 16–19.
19. B. T. Washington, 1986, 219, 222–23.
20. Duncan-Clark, 1913, xiii–xiv, xvi–xvii, 13, 17, 20, 29.
21. Duncan-Clark, 1913, 15–16, 39, 115.
22. Duncan-Clark, 1913, 42, 90, 93–97, 103, 106, 123; Russett, 1989, 200–204; Bederman, 1995, 84–85, 95, 105–7, stresses how for Hall, the subordination of women was vital to maintaining the virility of white civilization.
23. These differences can be overstated: Croly also thought human development required participating in group self-governance and saw this as best realized in smaller groups, though he thought democratization of most groups was far in the future. Dewey's reference to governing power in proportion to "capacity" could conversely be taken to justify limited roles

for those now ill equipped to govern. He also conceded the necessity for membership in large-scale nations during his time. But in practice Dewey looked harder than Croly for ways to democratize life in smaller, more immediate communities.

24. Dewey, 1920, 186, 200–209; 1927, 12, 15, 25, 71–72, 147–48, 154, 211–13.

25. Dewey, 1920, 202–4; 1927, 12, 15, 71–74, 147; 1966, 97–99.

26. Dewey, 1920, 172–74, 209; 1927, 4, 114–16, 180–84, 201–7; 1966, 87, 97, 318–19; Bourne, 1964, 124–26, 129–31; 1977, 255–62; Eisele, 1975, 71, 75; Westbrook, 1991, 165–66, 180–82, 188–89, 195–212, 432–35.

27. Kallen, 1924, 60–61, 122, 184–85.

28. Kallen, 1924, 59, 64, 116, 123–24, 132; Westbrook, 1991, 214.

29. Du Bois, 1968, 817–25, 842, 847–48; Cremin, 1988, 120; Bederman, 1995, 28.

30. See, e.g., De Witt, 1968, 142–61; Higham, 1966, 158–93; Wiebe, 1967, 164–95, Buenker, 1988, 187

31. *Lochner v. New York,* 198 U.S. 45 (1905), reprinted and discussed in Kens, 1990, 57–59, 176–77, 183. See also Gillman, 1993; Eisenach, 1994, 3.

32. Croly, 1963, 136–37, 200.

33. In addition to the rulings discussed below, the Court continued to refuse to extend federal diversity jurisdiction to other associations resembling but not identical to corporations. See *Great Southern Fireproof Hotel v. Jones,* 177 U.S. 449 (1900) and *Thomas v. Bd. of Trustees of The Ohio State University,* 195 U.S. 207 (1904) (which refused to recognize a partnership and a university board as corporations or jurisdictional citizens without specific averments). These decisions suggest a reluctance to expand judicial power by adding further fictitious "citizens," though again that very denial made the privileges of corporations all the more advantageous. Understandably, progressive lawmakers whose acts were voided by courts were worried by the scope of federal judicial authority. Progressive politicians denounced judicial excesses and called for new forms of democratic control over the courts. In 1911 Congress raised the jurisdictional amount in diversity cases to $3,000 and, more important, abolished the circuit courts, transferring their trial jurisdiction to the district courts and leaving only the circuit courts of appeal, the basic system prevailing today (Frankfurter, 1928, 511–15; Moore & Weckstein, 1964a, 6–9; Hyman & Wiecek, 1982, 415, 454; Purcell, 1992, 26–27, 91–92, 97–100).

34. See, e.g., *Doctor v. Harrington,* 196 U.S. 579 (1905), an anti-corporate (though pro-federal jurisdiction) decision decided the same year as *Lochner v. New York.* Purcell, 1992, 272–91, offers the explanations noted in the text, though he also suggests that the Court's refusal to supervise many corporate disputes may have reflected a desire to let issues be settled by "private contract" (287). That effort to fit these rulings into the *Lochner* era seems strained, since they usually meant conflicts would be settled by state courts according to state law, instead of by either private or federal actors.

35. In *The Promise of American Life,* Croly also advised corporations to give up the notion that they could continue to be "efficiently protected in all their essential rights by the Federal courts" without "the efficient exercise of Federal regulative powers," because that situation would generate "a revival of anti-Federal feeling in its most dangerous form." Better for corporations and courts to accept federal policies that discriminated in favor of large corporations against small ones (Croly, 1963, 355–58).

36. *U.S. v. Milwaukee Refrigerator Transit Co.,* 142 F. 247 (U.S.C.C. Wisc., 1905). Sanborn's rhetoric is similar to that of Justice Field in the *Railroad Tax Cases,* noted in the last chapter. Field is commonly seen as a proto-Lochnerian.

37. *James* was followed in, e.g., *Hollingsworth v. Southern Ry. Co.,* 86 F. 353 (U.S.C.C. S.C., 1898); *Taylor v. Illinois Central R. Co.,* 89 F. 119 (U.S.C.C. Ky., 1898); *Louisville, New Albany, &*

Chicago Rwy. Co. v. Louisville Trust Co., 174 U.S. 552 (1899); *Smith v. New York, New Haven, and Hartford Railroad Co.,* 96 F. 504 (U.S.C.C. Mass., 1899); *Southern Railway v. Allison,* 190 U.S. 326 (1903); *Missouri Pacific Railway v. Castle,* 224 U.S. 541 (1912). In the circuit cases, corporations originally chartered elsewhere, but incorporated by state law also in the states where they were sued, successfully removed the suits to federal courts by contending that for diversity purposes they were citizens only of their original states. The Supreme Court was also now willing to rule that the same stockholders had created two corporations with the same officers and functions in two different states if their incorporation in both states was "substantially simultaneous and free." That ruling was less useful to corporate desires to forum-shop, however, for few new corporations could hope to incorporate simultaneously everywhere they might eventually do business. See *Patch v. Wabash Railroad,* 207 U.S. 277, 284 (1907); *Missouri Pacific Railway v. Castle;* Henderson, 1918, 74–76; Purcell, 1992, 406n89. For a good summary of the Court's mature rules governing change of state citizenship, see *Harding v. Standard Oil,* 182 F. 421 (U.S.C.C. Ill., 1910), sustained in *Ex parte Harding,* 219 U.S. 363 (1911).

38. E.g., the Court continued to uphold the 1895 *Lehigh Mining* ruling that a corporation could not gain federal jurisdiction by creating a new corporation elsewhere. See *Miller and Lux v. East Side Canal and Irrigation Co.,* 211 U.S. 293 (1908); *Green Co. v. Thomas's Executor,* 211 U.S. 598 (1909). For other anti-corporate rulings, see esp. *Chesapeake & Ohio Railway Co. v. Dixon,* 179 U.S. 131 (1900), refusing the out-of-state railway's request to separate its liability from that of two of its employees who shared the state citizenship of the original plaintiff, and thereby denying a diversity basis for removal; *Alabama Great Southern Railway Co. v. Thompson,* 200 U.S. 206 (1906), permitting a similarly situated railroad to be sued jointly with its employees even if only their negligence was alleged, thus also defeating removal; *Cincinnati, New Orleans, and Texas Pacific Railway Co. v. Bohon,* 200 U.S. 221 (1906), upholding a state denial of removal on state law grounds; but cf. *Wecker v. National Enameling and Stamping Co.,* 204 U.S. 176 (1907), upholding a removal against a disqualifying "joinder" of defendants viewed as a fraud to defeat federal jurisdiction. See Purcell, 1992, 114–26. In 1905, the Court almost off-handedly disposed of an ambiguity unresolved in the Gilded Age, confirming that the 1867 removal act and its successors, like other removal laws, required complete diversity of citizenship between the parties on each side of a case. *Cochran and the Fidelity and Deposit Co. v. Montgomery County,* 199 U.S. 260 (1905) (a unanimous decision); Purcell, 1992, 136–37.

39. 202 U.S. 246 (1906). The challenge this case poses to standard views of the *Lochner* era is exemplified by the way that Kathleen Sullivan correctly identifies rulings banning such state laws as leading early examples of the doctrine of "unconstitutional conditions." She describes that doctrine as originating in the *Lochner* era. But in fact the *Lochner* court upheld that kind of condition in face of the earlier *Morse* and *Burnside* precedents that had refused to do so (Sullivan, 1989, 1416). The invalidity of these laws was not firmly established until Chief Justice Taft overruled *Security Mutual* in *Terral v. Burke Construction Co.,* 257 U.S. 529 (1922), which remains good law.

40. *Security Mutual* at 257. Peckham had suggested these views in *Cable v. U.S. Life Insurance Co.,* 191 U.S. 288, 308–9 (1903), but there he had only indicated that such statutes were not themselves grounds for removal, not that they were constitutional.

41. In *Herndon and Swarger v. Chicago, Rock Island and Pacific Railway Co.,* 218 U.S. 135, 158 (1910), Day asserted with little discussion that recent decisions which had prevented states from infringing on out-of-state corporations' rights to engage in interstate commerce indicated that states also could not burden those corporations' rights of removal. He made no mention of *Security Mutual* or *Doyle.* Taft said little more when he recognized the conflict-

ing line of cases and overturned those two cases in the 1922 *Terral* decision. See Purcell, 1992, 201–7, 245, 281 (calling the *Security Mutual* decision "unexpected, surprising, and radical").

42. Peckham argued in Jacksonian fashion that the statute actually placed out-of-state insurance companies "upon a par with domestic ones doing business in Kentucky," whose powers of removal were similarly limited due to their *lack* of out-of-state citizenship (at 257). The contention shows great wariness of the ways guarantees against state discrimination can turn into special privileges for some, a wariness also visible in much modern opposition to federal civil rights laws.

43. See also *Ex parte Wisner*, 203 U.S. 449 (1906) (preventing removals of suits brought in districts whether neither the plaintiff or defendant resided, a ruling that litigants would use to prevent corporate removals); *In re Moore*, 209 U.S. 490 (1908) (clarifying that such venues could be used only if both parties waived their objections to them); Purcell, 1992, 182, 191–92, 204, 372–98.

44. In *Blake v. McClung*, 172 U.S. 239 (1898) at 253–54, Harlan's majority struck down a Tennessee law that required out-of-state corporations to pay off Tennessee creditors ahead of non-residents, even though the law explicitly disadvantaged out-of-state "residents," not citizens, and the Court had to infer the citizenship of the out-of-state creditors. The requirement clearly smacked of the sort of state protectionism that Article IV as well as the commerce power had been intended to curb. Harlan noted that he would probably not have been willing to infer the citizenship of the out-of-state creditors for purposes of Art. III diversity jurisdiction; but he was willing to be more expansive in an Art. IV context, especially since their citizenship had not been disputed in the state court (247). Brewer dissented, joined by Fuller, primarily on the ground that the state law discriminated against non-residents, not non-citizens (262–63). In *Belfast Savings Bank v. Stowe*, 92 F. 100 (1st C. 1899) the Circuit Court of Appeals found *Blake* "so far reaching in its character" and of such "sweeping effect" that it mandated the invalidation of a 71-year-old common law rule established by the Maine supreme court. Blake was also followed, though read a bit more narrowly, in *In re Standard Oak Veneer Co.* 173 F. 103 (U.S.D.C. Tn., 1903). In contrast, in *Chambers v. Baltimore and Ohio Railroad Co.*, 207 U.S. 142, 148–49, 151 (1907), the Court upheld an Ohio law that opened its courts to suits on behalf of Ohio citizens who had died in other states, but not to survivors of out-of-state citizens. Moody found the "right to sue and defend in the courts" to be "one of the highest and most essential privileges of citizenship," but he held it sufficient that Ohio permitted out-of-state citizens as well as Ohio citizens to sue on behalf of deceased Ohioans. Harlan dissented, with White and McKenna. The ineligibility of corporations to claim privileges and immunities clause protection, announced in *Paul v. Virginia*, was reiterated in, e.g., *Waters-Pierce Oil Co. v. Texas*, 177 U.S. 28, 45 (1900). Harlan dissented without opinion.

45. The right to organize laborers "for their own improvement and advancement" was deemed "a fundamental right of a citizen, protected in every free government worthy of the name," but not a right of U.S. citizenship in *U.S. v. Moore*, 129 F. 630 (U.S.C.C. Ala., 1904). In *Brawner v. Irvin*, 169 F. 964 (U.S.C.C. Ga., 1909) a black woman had been whipped by a local police chief in her yard during an arrest on a false charge. Despite the apparent brutal racial discrimination, she, too, was held not to have had any right of U.S. citizenship violated. See also the cases in the following note.

46. Harlan so argued in, e.g., *Maxwell v. Dow*, 176 U.S. 581, 605 (1900) (involving claimed rights to grand jury indictment and a 12-man jury); *Twining v. New Jersey*, 211 U.S. 78 (1908) (involving claimed rights against self-incrimination). In *Twining* the Court said the correctness of Harlan's privileges and immunities reading was "no longer open in this court" (98), and Harlan wearily averred his "sense of duty" required him to dissent (114).

47. In *Taylor and Marshall v. Beckham* (1900), the Court considered an appeal brought by two Republicans who had apparently been elected Governor and Lieutenant Governor of Kentucky, only to have their victory reversed when the predominantly Democratic General Assembly upheld a challenge by the Democratic candidates. The Democratic Chief Justice Fuller ruled that the Republicans had been deprived of no Fourteenth Amendment right, and that *Luther v. Borden* properly required the Court to stay out of guarantee clause disputes. Justices Brewer and Brown thought the Republicans did have a cognizable Fourteenth Amendment due process claim, but they thought due process standards had been met. With his customary vehemence, Harlan argued that his home state's action had indeed violated due process. The Assembly had decided in such "total disregard of the facts" that it had not even been able to announce a specific vote total (178 U.S. 548 [1900], at 577–78, 584–85, 607–9). Despite the ruling's seamless fit into a long line of guarantee clause decisions, in the Kentucky case the misconduct was remarkably flagrant, and the Court was then interpreting the Fourteenth Amendment expansively as a shield for economic liberties. Thus it is reasonable to ascribe the result not merely to the force of precedent and loyalty to state-centric republicanism, but also to the justices' eagerness to overlook the unsavory electoral practices of the increasingly Solid South. The Court subsequently adhered to the same course when challenges were made to the Oregon progressives' establishment of the initiative and referendum (*Pacific States Telephone and Telegraph Co. v. Oregon,* 223 U.S. 118 [1912]).

48. Thus in *Mason v. Missouri,* 179 U.S. 328 (1900), the Court sustained an 1899 Missouri law that ended state measures to aid voter registration in St. Louis while maintaining them elsewhere. The apparent denial of equal protection to St. Louis residents, where many left-leaning German immigrants, poor whites, and blacks lived, did not in the Court's eyes alter the fact that the voting rights affected were privileges to be regulated by the state at its discretion. Then in *Wiley v. Sinkler,* 179 U.S. 58, 67 (1900), the Court ruled that although the right to vote in congressional elections was constitutionally protected, a person whose vote was refused could not simply aver that he was a qualified voter. He had to aver that he was a registered voter, as required by state law. The well known fact that new registration systems were deliberately excluding many poor whites and virtually all blacks, who therefore could not make the necessary averment, went undiscussed. In *Swafford v. Templeton,* 185 U.S. 487 (1902), the Court overruled a lower court decision, *Swafford v. Templeton et al.,* 108 F. 309 (U.S.C.C. Tenn., 1901), which had wrongly held that the federal courts had no jurisdiction over a claim that a special registration system imposed on only certain Tennessee counties denied equal protection of voting rights in national elections. But the Supreme Court stressed that it was only holding the federal courts still had jurisdiction of such disputes, despite the weakness of this challenger's claim on the merits (492). *Pope v. Williams,* 193 U.S. 621 (1904), upheld a Maryland law that required recently arrived out-of-state citizens to declare their intent to become state residents and citizens a year prior to registering to vote. The challenger claimed the law denied equal protection to recent arrivals and infringed on their freedom to move from state to state, but the Court treated it as again within the range of the state's discretion. Similarly, in *Anthony v. Burrow,* 129 F. 783 (U.S.C.C. Kans., 1904), a district judge held that he lacked jurisdiction over a dispute between rival Republican factions as to whether fraud had occurred in the selection of the party's congressional candidate. The issue was deemed to involve a non-justiciable political right, not a cognizable civil or property right. Circuit judge Goff ruled similarly in *Brickhouse v. Brooks,* 165 F. 534 (U.S.C.C. Va., 1908), refusing to assess the constitutionality of Virginia's 1902 constitution, adopted to disfranchise blacks (and also left intact by the Supreme Court). But cf. the greater receptivity to a challenge to restrictions on voting rights imposed via constitutional amend-

ments in *Knight v. Shelton,* 134 F. 423 (U.S.C.C. Ark., 1905), and the continuing protection of rights to vote in federal elections in *Felix v. U.S.,* 186 F. 685 (5th C. 1911).

49. The pattern would begin to change near the end of the Progressive Era, when the Supreme Court reasserted more vigorous support for federal statutes protecting the right to vote for Congress in *U.S. v. Mosley,* 238 U.S. 383 (1915).

50. Aboriginal Alaskans were not made citizens, retaining a status like that of the other North American tribes. Native Hawaiians were not treated as a distinct group. Cabranes, 1979, 31, 95n460; Torruella, 1988, 3, 20, 66, 93n328: Karnow, 1989, 82–83.

51. Carr, 1984, 25–26; Roosevelt cited in Karnow, 1989, 85, and see also 10, 79–80, 119; Torruella, 1988, 11–24; Bederman, 1995, 184–96.

52. Cabranes, 1979, 4.

53. *Cong. Rec.,* 56th Cong., 1st Sess., v. 33, pt. 1, 711 (1900) (Sen. Beveridge). Regarded as a Progressive Roosevelt Republican, Beveridge would eventually be squeezed out of electoral office by the party's old guard. He then wrote his acclaimed *Life of John Marshall.* The legal hermeneutic he proposes in this speech is thus notable: "You cannot interpret a constitution without understanding the race that wrote it" (711).

54. Karnow, 1989, 11, 109, 137, 164, who also notes that Rudyard Kipling wrote his infamous poem, "The White Man's Burden," explicitly to persuade Americans to govern and "civilize" the Filipinos; *Cong. Rec.,* 56th Cong., 1st Sess., v. 33, pt. 3, 2621, 2629–30 (1900) (Lodge). See also pt. 2, 1866 (1900) (Stewart).

55. W. I. Williams, 1980, correctly stresses the heavy reliance by imperialists on the analogy of the new colonies to Native Americans, and he notes that votes on policies of tutelage for each correlate highly (810, 816–17, 823–24, 829). For congressional speeches invoking the "Indian analogy" see, e.g., *Cong. Rec.,* 56th Cong., 1st Sess., v. 33, pt. 1, 707 (1900) (Beveridge); pt. 3, 2618, 2620 (1900) Lodge; pt. 2, 1062 (1900) (Sen. Ross); pt. 3, 2097 (1900) (Rep. Moody). See also Thayer, 1899, 472; Torruella, 1988, 23–24, 29.

56. *Cong. Rec.,* 56th Cong., 1st Sess., v. 33, pt. 2, 1995–96 (1900) (Rep. Newlands); pt. 3, 2162 (Rep. Williams); pt. 4, 3610, 3612 (Sen. Bate). See also Cabranes, 1979, 27–29; Karnow, 1989, 82, 109–10.

57. *Cong. Rec.,* 56th Cong., 1st Sess., v. 33, pt. 3, 2064, 2066–67 (1900) (Rep. McClellan); pt. 4, 3610 (1900) (Sen. Bate).

58. *Cong. Rec.,* 56th Cong., 1st Sess., v. 33, pt. 2, 1996 (1900) (Newlands); pt. 4, 3610 (1900) (Sen. Bate); pt. 3, 2105 (1900) (Rep. Spight); 2162 (1900) (Rep. Williams). See also Cabranes, 1979, 39–41 (who goes too far when he asserts "racist overtones were most clearly discernible in the remarks of those who opposed American imperialism," a claim belied by the speeches of Beveridge, Lodge, and others; racism was pervasive); Torruella, 1988, 33–35; Karnow, 1989, 109–10, 137.

59. See, e.g., 707 (1900) (Beveridge); pt. 2, 1062 (1900) (Ross); pt. 2, 1866 (1900) (Stewart); pt. 3, 2618–19 (1900) (Lodge); cf. Thayer, 1899, 474–75; Lowell, 1899a, 150.

60. See, e.g., *Cong. Rec.,* 56th Cong., 1st Sess., v. 33, pt. 1, 709 (1900) (Beveridge); pt. 2, 1862 (1900) (Stewart); pt. 3, 2621–22 (1900) (Lodge).

61. *Cong. Rec.,* 56th Cong., 1st Sess., v. 33, pt. 1, 1057 (1900) (Ross); pt. 2, 2095 (1900) (Moody); pt. 3, 2874 (1900) (Teller); Torruella, 1988, 24.

62. *Cong. Rec.,* 56th Cong., 1st Sess., v. 33, pt. 3, 2696 (1900) (Sen. Lindsay).

63. *Cong. Rec.,* 56th Cong., 1st Sess., v. 33, pt. 3, 2473–74 (1900) (Sen. Foraker). The Foraker Act employed the misspelling "Porto Rico," following an error in the English version of the Treaty of Paris. Though "Porto" is an incongruous Portuguese, not Spanish, term, the U.S. government did not bother to correct the usage in official documents until 1932. Cabranes, 1979, 1, 6, 22–44; Carr, 1984, 35–38; Torruella, 1988, 32–39.

64. May, 1980, 9–10, 14, 89–93, 111–25; Karnow, 1989, 173–74, 242–56. Americans governed Guam, like other small Pacific island acquisitions to come, with very little congressional attention or debate (Cabranes, 1979, 95n460).

65. Cabranes, 1979, 51–79; *Cong. Rec.,* 64th Cong., 2d Sess., v. 54, pt. 3, 2250 (1917) (Sen. Vardaman); 3008–9 (1900) (Sen. Fall).

66. Cabranes, 1979, 80–101; Carr, 1984, 51–54; Torruella, 1988, 85–93.

67. Lowell, 1899a, 146–50. This comment makes clear that at least some American elites were aware that their laws combined different civic traditions in ways that sacrificed logical consistency to political expediency.

68. Lowell, 1899a, 149–54.

69. Lowell, 1899b, 156, 171, 176. See also Cabranes, 1979, 21; Torruella, 1988, 30; Cabranes, 1986, 453–58.

70. *Goetze v. U.S.,* 103 F. 72, 83, 85–86 (U.S.C.C. N.Y., 1900). Townsend did not cite Lowell, preferring to base the distinction between incorporated and unincorporated territories on Chief Justice Taney's opinion in *Fleming v. Page,* 50 U.S. 603 (1850). But since that case concerned goods imported from a Mexican port held by the U.S. military *prior to* the Treaty of Guadalupe Hidalgo, it did not answer the question of whether a treaty could give the U.S. title to territory without "incorporating" that territory. In *De Lima v. Bidwell,* 182 U.S. 1 (1901), five justices held that in any case *Fleming v. Page* had later been "practically overruled," though the dissenters disagreed (194, 204).

   In contrast to *Goetze,* a Minnesota district judge argued that the Constitution did apply to America's new possessions in *Ex parte Ortiz,* 100 F. 955 (U.S.C.C. Minn., 1900). But he concluded that, since hostilities were ongoing, the trial by a military tribunal challenged in the case was valid.

71. The *Insular Cases* were six decisions handed down consecutively in which the Court first ruled on the status of the territories the U.S. acquired via the Treaty of Paris: *De Lima v. Bidwell,* 182 U.S. 1 (1901); *Goetze v. U.S. (Crossman v. U.S.),* 182 U.S. 221 (1901); *Dooley v. U.S.,* 182 U.S. 222 (1901); *Armstrong v. U.S.,* 182 U.S. 243 (1901); *Downes v. Bidwell,* 182 U.S. 244 (1901); *Huus v. New York & Porto Rico Steamship Co.,* 182 U.S. 392 (1901). The decisions are, in effect, one great consecutive discussion, but as their length suggests, the *De Lima* and *Downes* cases were the most crucial.

72. In *Dooley v. U.S.* it sustained duties imposed prior to the Treaty's ratification. *Ibid.* at 182 U.S. 194, 199, 208–9, 222, 235.

73. *Ibid.* at 278–80, 282–83, 286–87.

74. *Ibid.* at 302–3, 306, 311–15, 336, 342.

75. *Ibid.* at 369, 373, 379–81, 384, 391; Fiss, 1993, 240–41, 254–56.

76. 182 U.S. 392 (1900); Torruella, 1988, 61. The Court fragmented again, however, along the lines of *Downes* the following year in *Dooley v. U.S.,* 183 U.S. 151 (1901) (*Dooley II*). There, Brown wrote for a 5–4 majority upholding the Foraker Act's requirement of duties on goods shipped from New York *into* Puerto Rico, despite Art. 1, Sec. 9's ban on taxes or duties on goods exported from any state. The ban had previously been held to apply only to goods exported to foreign countries, and here Brown again viewed Puerto Rico as part of the nation's domestic trade (154). Fuller again wrote for the dissenters, pointing out the obvious, that the Court was treating Puerto Rico as sufficiently domestic to be denied the benefit of the Art. 1, sec. 9 ban on export duties, but insufficiently domestic to be protected by Art. 1, sec. 8's requirement of uniform domestic duties (168–69). Neither side showed any inclination to go through the lengthy debates over Puerto Rico's status once more.

77. *Fourteen Diamond Rings, Emil J. Pepke, Claimant v. U.S.,* 183 U.S. 176 (1902). The four dis-

senters in De Lima dissented here, citing their earlier opinions. *Rings* was followed in *Lincoln v. U.S.; Warner, Barnes & Co. v. U.S.,* 197 U.S. 419 (1905).

78. *Hawaii v. Mankichi,* 190 U.S. 197 (1903).

79. Tabrah, 1980, 9, 99–116. One hundred years after the coup, Congress passed a resolution apologizing for the coercion leading to Hawaii's acquisition by the U.S. (Public Law 103–50, 1993). Congress later authorized a referendum among native Hawaiians, with consequences still pending at this writing, that might prompt recreation of some sort of native-governed Hawaii (Pertman, 1996, 1; Goldberg, 1996).

80. The Newlands resolution also banned all further immigration of Chinese into Hawaii, and all entry into the U.S. of Chinese currently in Hawaii.

81. 190 U.S., 210–11, 225, 212, 217–19, 225. Justice White concurred, finding Hawaii not "incorporated" until 1900. He ignored the fact, pressed by the dissenters, that the preamble of the 1897 Treaty preceding annexation had explicitly indicated that Hawaii was to be "incorporated into the United States" (224, 227; Torruella, 1988, 68; Fiss, 1993, 247–48). New appointees Justices Holmes and Day joined Brown's opinion.

82. *Gonzales v. Williams,* 192 U.S. 1, 12 (1904), overturning *In re Gonzales,* 118 F. 941 (U.S.C.C. N.Y., 1902). In 1912, a district court judge held that, from the Treaty of Paris until the 1906 Naturalization Act, neither citizens of the Philippines or Puerto Rico were eligible for naturalization, as they were not aliens. Since then they could be naturalized only if they were "free white persons or of African nativity or descent" (*In re Alverto,* 198 F. 688 [U.S.D.C. E.D. Pa., 1912]).

83. See *Kepner v. U.S.,* 195 U.S. 100 (1904) (Philippine Organic Act of 1902 extends the constitutional guarantee against double jeopardy to the Philippines; Holmes and Brown, dissenting) (followed in *Secundino Menodozana y Mendozana v. U.S.,* 195 U.S. 158 [1904]); *Dorr v. U.S.,* 195 U.S. 138 (1904) (constitutional right to jury trials do not apply to unincorporated territories in the absence of congressional action, as it is not fundamental in "territory peopled by savages" [148], Harlan dissenting).

84. *Rassmussen v. U.S.,* 197 U.S. 516 (1905) at 522, 528. Harlan concurred while disavowing the "incorporated territories" doctrine (530); Brown concurred while also objecting to "incorporation" reasoning, still finding it too restrictive of congressional power in the territories (532).

85. In *New York ex rel. Kopel v. Bingham,* 211 U.S. 468 (1909), for example, the Court held that Puerto Rico was a "completely organized territory" that was covered by extradition statutes applying to states and territories; but it was still not an "incorporated" territory (476). In *Martinez v. La Asociacion de Senoras Damas del Santo Asilo de Ponce,* 213 U.S. 20 (1909), the Court ruled that a charitable corporation in Puerto Rico originally organized under Spanish law was not a citizen of the United States for jurisdictional purposes, but rather, "if a citizen of any country, a citizen of Porto Rico" (25).

86. *Balzac v. Porto Rico,* 258 U.S. 298, 308–11 (1922); Torruella, 1988, 96–100.

87. *U.S. v. Wong Kim Ark,* 169 U.S. 649, 653–65, 673–81, 693, 704 (1898). See also Salyer, 1989, 80–81, 187–92, 212–19; Fiss, 1993, 313–15.

88. *Wong Kim Ark,* ibid., at 706–7, 711–14, 723–24, 729–30.

89. Unfortunately for the purposes of my argument, Harlan had at this point already become a rather strict Chinese exclusionist, and Fuller would be so hereafter. Hence their dissent does not necessarily show any commitment to consensualist doctrines of membership, as opposed to racial antagonisms.

90. Taft had tried to win the immigrant vote in 1912 by promising to veto the literacy test, but whether he would actually do so remained unclear until the last minute. He was influenced by his Secretary of Commerce and Labor Charles Nagel, a corporate lawyer and sec-

ond generation immigrant. The previous three paragraphs draw on Higham, 1966, 129–30, 163–68, 188–93, 310; 1975, 47–57; Hutchinson, 1981, 121, 136–58, 409, 466–67, 479–83; Archdeacon, 1983, 146, 162–67: Leibowitz, 1984, 35–37; Hong, 1990, 9–10, 19–20.

91. Seven months after the decision, a California district court ruled that courts could not only discount the testimony of Chinese witnesses in citizenship cases. They should also presume that Chinese persons arriving from that country but claiming to be returning U.S. citizens were aliens. In *re Jew Wong Loy*, 91 F. 240 (U.S.D.C. Ca., 1898). See also *Lee Sing Far v. U.S.*, 94 F. 834 (9th C. 1899); *U.S. v. Gin Fung*, 100 F. 389 (9th C. 1900); *In re Lee Lung*, 102 F. 132 (U.S.D.C. Or., 1900); *Woey Ho v. U.S.*, 109 F. 888 (9th C. 1901); *Fong Mey Yuk*, 113 F. 898 (9th C. 1902); *U.S. v. Lee Huen*, 118 F. 442 (U.S.D.C. N.Y., 1902) (where district judge Ray proclaims that "We are all brothers in the family of Adam" and that "ties of race" should not discredit Chinese witnesses, but then goes on to note that "it is common knowledge that enslaved peoples develop an inordinate propensity for lying, and this is characteristic of most oriental nations," so that Chinese testimony "may be regarded as more or less weak"). See Salyer, 1989, 218–24.

92. *Li Sing v. U.S.*, 180 U.S. 486 (1901); *U.S. v. Lee Yen Tai*, 185 U.S. 213 (1902); *Fok Yung Yo v. U.S.*, 185 U.S. 296 (1902); *Lee Gon Yung v. U.S.*, 185 U.S. 306 (1902); *Lee Lung v. Patterson*, 186 U.S. 168 (1902); *Chin Bak Kan v. U.S.; Ching Ying v. U.S.*, 185 U.S. 193 (1902); *The Japanese Immigrant Case, Yamatya v. Fisher*, 189 U.S. 86 (1903). Several commentators have stressed that *Yamatya* indicated in dictum that due process principles did apply to executive immigration officers, and subsequent more lenient cases did build on this point (Legomsky, 1987, p. 198).

93. See, e.g., *In re Chin Ark Wing*, 115 F. 412 (U.S.D.C. Mass., 1902); *Tsoi Sim v. U.S.*, 116 F. 920 (9th C. 1902); *Moffitt v. U.S.*, 128 F. 375 (9th C. 1904); *Sing Tuck v. U.S.*, 128 F. 592 (2d C. 1904); *Ark Foo v. U.S.*, 128 F. 697 (2d C. 1904). For restrictionist lower court rulings, including deference to administrative denials of citizenship claims, see, e.g., *In re Moy Quong Shing*, 125 F. 641 (U.S.D.C. Vt., 1903); *U.S. v. Sing Lee*, 125 F. 627 (U.S.D.C. N.Y., 1903); *In re Sing Tuck*, 126 F. 386 (U.S.C.C. N.Y., 1903). Owen Fiss (1993, 33) argues that Brewer and Peckham were the "intellectual leaders" of the Fuller Court, to whom the Chief Justice usually turned for major opinions. It is all the more noteworthy, then, that these very justices usually *failed* to sway their colleagues in the Chinese cases, even ones involving the economic rights the Fuller Court generally championed. Fiss, however, stresses the power of a liberal dissenting strain in these cases more than I do here (1993, 316–22). In 1904, the Supreme Court did show a bit of leniency, recognizing some procedural restraints on the discretion of immigration officials at the same time that it refused to permit Puerto Rican citizens to be treated as aliens. See *Tom Hong, alias Hom Poe, v. U.S.; Tom Dock, alias Hom Dock, v. U.S.; Lee Kit v. U.S.*, 193 U.S. 517 (1904); *Gonzales v. Williams*, 192 U.S. 1 (1904), discussed above. The Court also dismissed a challenge to federal court immigration jurisdiction in *U.S., Petitioner*, 194 U.S. 194 (1904). Lower court decisions limiting discretionary executive powers over immigration include *Hopkins v. Fachant*, 130 F. 839 (9th C. 1904); *U.S. v. Ah Sou*, 132 F. 878 (U.S.D.C. Wash., 1904), where a district judge refused to permit a woman to be returned to China on the unusual ground that she would be there kept in "perpetual slavery and degradation," coerced into prostitution, a "barbarous" consequence that Judge Hanford thought violated the "vital principle" of "liberty" enshrined in the Thirteenth Amendment. Though vulnerable in light of Supreme Court precedents, the opinion suggests the rulings that egalitarian interpretations of the postwar amendments could have made possible in these cases.

94. *Ah How alias Louie Ah How v. U.S.; Chu Do alias Chu Gee v. U.S.; Lew Guey v. U.S.; Yung*

Lee v. U.S., 193 U.S. 65 (1904); *U.S. v. Sing Tuck or King Do and Thirty-One Others*, 194 U.S. 161 (1904); *U.S. ex rel. John Turner v. Williams*, 194 U.S. 279 (1904). Lower court rulings deferential to broad exclusionary immigration powers include *U.S. v. Fah Chung*, 132 F. 109 (U.S.D.C. Ga., 1904); *U.S. v. Hung Chang*, 134 F. 19 (6th C. 1904), where the Circuit Court of Appeals overturned an Ohio district court judge's insistence that only "experts in the sciences of anthropology and ethnology" could determine who was a Chinaman. Circuit judge Richards thought their "racial characteristics are plain and apparent." See also Salyer, 1989, 240–50, 358–59.

95. 194 U.S. 178 (1904). Brewer concluded at 182 that "if the most populous nation on earth becomes the great antagonist of this republic," the U.S. would merely be reaping the Biblical "whirlwind" it had sown by its treatment of the Chinese over the last twenty years.

96. 194 U.S. 279 (1904) at 290, 293, 295, discussed in Hong, 1990, 10–18. Brewer's concurrence did, however, try to narrow the Court's ruling, to some avail. It was cited by district judge Holt in ordering the admission of two Chinese children of a resident merchant, *Ex parte Fong Yim*, 134 F. 938 (U.S.D.C. N.Y., 1905). Holt often looked for grounds to admit: see also *Ex parte Ng Quong Ming*, 135 F. 378 (U.S. D.C. N.Y., 1905).

97. *U.S. v. Ju Toy*, 198 U.S. 253, 260–62, 267–69, 279–89 (1905). Justice William Day also dissented, without opinion. The ardently exclusionist Judge Morrow worked with the U.S. Attorney General to present the Court with a case leading to this result (Salyer, 1989, 251–59). The ruling had immediate impact, foreclosing judicial review of many Chinese cases. See, e.g., *U.S. v. Yeung Chu Keng*, 140 F. 748 (U.S.D.C. Mont., 1905); *Wong Sang v. U.S.; Wong Den v. Same; Wong Chow v. Same; Goon Yin v. Same*, 144 F. 968 (1st C. 1906); *In re Tom Hon*, 149 F. 842 (U.S.D.C. Ca., 1906). But see also *Moy Suey v. U.S.*, 147 F. 697 (7th C. 1906), grudgingly conceding that citizens seeking to reenter the U.S. might be denied judicial trials, but insisting that residents cannot be.

98. *Chin Yow v. U.S.*, 208 U.S. 8, 10–12 (1908), Brewer concurring only in the result. But a unanimous Court also read the 1907 ban on women entering for "immoral purposes" broadly, as banning not only prostitutes but domestic "concubines," in *U.S. v. Bitty*, 208 U.S. 393 (1908); see Salyer, 1989, 260–62. Later the Court did add that the limited appeals to district courts permitted by the 1888 exclusion act had to be supplied by full hearings *de novo*, not cursory review of the actions of immigration officials [*Liu Hop Fong v. U.S.*, 209 U.S. 453 (1908)]. This ruling helped only the best legally supported Chinese. By statute, appeals had to be filed within *ten days* of the final adverse administrative decision. Many lower courts were displaying relatively moderate moods, preserving a judicial role to check abuses but in other ways supporting administrative decisionmaking, in, e.g., *Rodgers v. U.S. ex rel Buchsbaum*, 152 F. 346 (3d C. 1907); *Pang Sho Yin v. U.S.*, 154 F. 660 (6th C. 1907); *U.S. v. Hemet*, 156 F. 285 (U.S.D.C. Or., 1907); *U.S. v. Tom Wah*, 160 F. 207 (U.S.D.C. N.Y., 1908); *In re Tang Tun*, 161 F. 618 (U.S.D.C. Wash., 1908); *Ex parte Petterson*, 166 F. 536 (U.S.D.C. Minn., 1908); *In re Can Pon*, 168 F. 479 (9th C. 1909).

99. In 1909, Brewer at last wrote an immigration decision for the Court, albeit a tangential one, with Holmes in dissent, joined by Harlan and William Moody. The 1907 immigration act punished all those who assisted an alien to engage in prostitution within three years of the alien's entry. Brewer thought this went beyond sovereign exclusionary powers, amounting to an exercise of police powers, which he insisted the federal government did not possess. To that end he offered an increasingly anachronistic invocation of state-centered republican constitutional views, citing *Texas v. White*. Typically, Holmes saw no limit on national powers to punish those who helped someone continue in an "unlawful stay." *Keller v. U.S.*, 213 U.S. 138, 147, 151 (1909).

100. For exclusionary decisions see, e.g., *Looe Shee v. North*, 170 F. 566 (9th C. 1909) (where

Morrow relies on Holmes's *dissent* in *Keller*); *Ex parte Long Lock*, 173 F. 208 (U.S.D.C. N.Y., 1909); *Ex parte Chin Hen Lock*, 174 F. 282 (U.S.D.C. Vt., 1909); *Ex parte Li Dick*, 174 F. 674 (U.S.D.C. N.Y., 1909); *U.S. v. Sprung*, 187 F. 903 (4th C. 1910); *Mango v. Weis*, 181 F. 860 (U.S.D.C. Md., 1910); *Haw Moy v. North*, 183 F. 89 (9th C. 1910); *Hoo Choy v. North*, 183 F. 92 (9th C. 1910); *U.S. v. Yuen Pak Sune*, 183 F. 260 (U.S.D.C. N.Y., 1910); *U.S. v. Chin Ken*, 183 F. 332 (U.S.D.C. N.Y., 1910); *Dickman v. Williams*, 183 F. 904 (U.S.D.C. N.Y., 1910); *De Bruler v. Gallo*, 184 F. 566 (9th C. 1911); *Lew Quen Wo v. U.S.*, 184 F. 685 (9th C. 1911); *U.S. ex rel. De Rienzo v. Rodgers*, 185 F. 334 (3d C. 1911); *Sibray v. U.S. ex rel. Kupples*, 185 F. 401 (3d C. 1911); *Williams v. U.S. ex rel. Bougadis*, 186 F. 479 (2d C. 1911); *Yee Ging v. U.S.*, 190 F. 270 (U.S.D.C. Tx., 1911); *Ex parte Wing You*, 190 F. 294 (9th C. 1911); *Buccino v. Williams*, 190 F. 897 (U.S.C.C. N.Y., 1911); *Barlin v. Rodgers*, 191 F. 970 (3d C. 1911); *Frick v. Lewis*, 195 F. 693 (6th C. 1912); *Sinischalchi v. Thomas*, 195 F. 701 (6th C. 1912). For decisions emphasizing procedural protection for immigrant claims, including judicial review, see, e.g., *U.S. ex rel. D'Amato v. Williams*, 193 F. 228 (U.S.D.C. N.Y., 1909); *Botis v. Davies*, 173 F. 996 (U.S.D.C. Ill., 1909); *U.S. v. Jhu Why*, 175 F. 630 (U.S.D.C. Ga., 1910); *Davies v. Manolis*, 179 F. 818 (7th C. 1910); *U.S. v. Chu Hung*, 179 F. 564 (U.S.D.C. S.C., 1910); *Ex parte Saraceno*, 182 F. 955 (U.S.C.C. N.Y., 1910); *U.S. v. Louie Lee*, 184 F. 651 (U.S.D.C. Tenn., 1911); *Gee Cue Being v. U.S.*, 184 F. 383 (5th C. 1911); *Ex parte Chooey Dee Ying*, 214 F. 873 (U.S.D.C. Ca., 1911); *Lewis v. Frick*, 189 F. 146 (U.S.C.C. Mich., 1911); *U.S. v. Chin Tong*, 192 F. 485 (5th C. 1911); *Reinmann v. Martin*, 193 F. 795 (U.S.D.C. N.Y., 1912). Also Salyer, 1989, 373–78.

101. *Tang Tun v. Edsell*, 223 U.S. 673 (1912).

102. *Low Wah Suey v. Backus*, 225 U.S. 460, 476 (1912); *Zakonaite v. Wolf*, 226 U.S. 272 (1912); *Guan Lee v. U.S.*, 198 F. 596 (7th C. 1912); *Ex parte Cardonnel*, 197 F. 774 (U.S.D.C. Ca., 1912); *Ex parte Yabucanin*, 199 F. 365 (U.S.D.C. Mont., 1912); *Rosen v. Williams*, 200 F. 538 (2d C. 1912); but see also *U.S. v. Tsuji Suekichi*, 199 F. 750 (9th C. 1912). For the parallel developments in ensuing years, see Salyer, 1989, 391–403, 412–22.

103. Courts also became less receptive to equal protection claims on behalf of Chinese. They remained an important asset in, e.g., *Wong Wai v. Williamson*, 103 F. 1 (U.S.C.C. Ca., 1900) and *Jew Ho v. Williamson*, 103 F. 10 (U.S.C.C. Ca., 1900) (voiding the San Francisco measure requiring all Chinese residents, aliens and citizens, to receive a poisonous inoculation allegedly to ward off bubonic plague, without any evidence of the disease's presence). But in *Ah Sin v. Wittman*, 198 U.S. 500 (1905) the Supreme Court refused to find that a California anti-gambling law was enforced exclusively as an anti-Chinese law without proof positive that at least some non-Chinese also engaged in gambling. Peckham dissented without opinion.

104. Kansas, 1936, 30–2, 137–40.

105. Kansas, 1936, 33–34, discussing Naturalization Act of June 29, 1906; Higham, 1966, 118. After the 1906 law, first the lower federal courts and then the U.S. Supreme Court, upheld national powers to grant naturalization authority to state courts and to punish frauds committed in state-administered naturalization proceedings [see *U.S. v. Spohrer*, 175 F. 440 (U.S.C.C. N.J., 1910), and esp. *Holmgren v. U.S.*, 217 U.S. 509 (1910); *Johannessen v. U.S.*, 225 U.S. 227 (1912)]. The growth of a federal naturalization bureaucracy and its legitimation by the courts further cemented both the doctrinal and the practical supremacy of federal officials over access to citizenship.

106. The provision resolved some questions that had arisen in previous lower federal court decisions, some of which were inclined to grant citizenship liberally to minors whenever a parent was naturalized [cf. *U.S. v. Kellar*, 13 F. 82 (U.S.C.C. Il., 1882); *In re Di Simone*, 108 F. 942 (U.S.D.C. La., 1901); *U.S. ex. rel. Abdoo v. Williams*, 132 F. 894 (U.S.C.C. N.Y., 1904)].

In keeping with the policy thrust Congress affirmed in the 1907 act, the U.S. Supreme Court in *Zartarian v. Billings,* 204 U.S. 170 (1907) rejected such liberality in the case of minors residing overseas at the time of their fathers' naturalizations. But subsequently, some lower federal courts remained generous in construing how far parents' steps toward naturalization could confer "inchoate" citizenship on their resident minors, and how far minors could be permitted to take some necessary steps toward naturalization prior to reaching the age of consent. See, e.g., *In re Symanowski,* 168 F. 978 (U.S.C.C. Il., 1909); *In re Robertson,* 179 F. 131 (U.S.D.C. Pa., 1910).

107. *In re Buntaro Kumagai,* 163 F. 922 (U.S.D.C. Wash., 1908) (naturalization denied to an "educated Japanese gentleman" honorably discharged from the U.S. army); *In re Knight,* 171 F. 299 (U.S.D.C. N.Y., 1909) (naturalization denied to a decorated and honorably discharged veteran of the U.S. navy, born on a British schooner of an English father and a half-Chinese, half Japanese mother); *Bessho v. U.S.* 178 F. 245 (4th C. 1910) (Japanese subject not covered by 1894 act facilitating naturalization for aliens who have served in the navy or marines).

108. *In re Balsara,* 171 F. 294 (U.S.C.C. N.Y., 1909).

109. *U.S. v. Balsara,* 180 F. 694 (2d C. 1910).

110. *In re Najour,* 174 F. 735 (U.S.D.C. Ga., 1909).

111. *In re Halladjian,* 174 F. 834 (U.S.C.C. Mass., 1909).

112. *In re Ellis,* 179 F. 1002 (U.S.D.C. Or., 1910).

113. *In re Halladjian,* 174 F. 834 (U.S.C.C. Mass., 1909); *In re Mudarri,* 176 F. 465 (U.S.C.C. Mass., 1910). A Washington district judge similarly argued in an 1912 case that the term "white person" must "be given its common or popular meaning" rather than relying on how persons are "technically classified;" and the fact that the applicant was of half-Japanese ancestry was decisive, not his German citizenship. *In re Young,* 198 F. 715 (U.S.D.C. Wash., 1912). A year later, a South Carolina district judge wrote even more elaborately and despairingly of the inadequacy of the category "Caucasian" and the ambiguities of the naturalization statutes. Like most of his peers around the country, Judge Smith finally decided to rely on the common understanding of "free white persons" in 1790; but he thought Syrians must be denied citizenship by this standard. *Ex parte Shahid,* 205 F. 812 (U.S.D.C. S.C., 1913).

114. See *Ozawa v. U.S.,* 260 U.S. 178 (1922); *U.S. v. Bhagat Singh Thind,* 261 U.S. 204 (1923); *Toyota v. U.S.,* 268 U.S. 402 (1925), discussed in Konvitz, 1946, and Lesser, 1985–86. The *Thind* case overruled some more inclusive lower court decisions concerning Indians, such as the *Balsara* cases and *In re Akhay Kumar Mozumdar,* 207 F. 115 (U.S.D.C. Wash., 1913).

115. *In re Di Clerico,* 158 F. 905 (U.S.D.C. N.Y., 1908); cf. *In re Spenser,* 22 F. Cas. 921 (U.S.C.C. Or., 1878); *U.S. v. Dwyer,* 170 F. 686 (U.S.C.C. Mass., 1909); *In re Hopp,* 179 F. 561 (U.S.D.C. Wisc., 1910).

116. Woodward, 1966, 24, 97–108; Barnes, 1983, 4–5; Lofgren, 1987, 21–22; Nieman, 1991, 105–9. The longstanding controversy over how far practices of segregation preceded their codification in the 1890s seems to have issued in this conclusion, that there was much segregation and outright exclusion of blacks prior to Jim Crow laws, but these laws added further authority to segregation practices and in some instances expanded them. For discussions of the controversy see, e.g., Woodward, 1971, 234–60; Cell, 1982, 82–104; Hovenkamp, 1985, 637–41; Lofgren, 1987, 8–9.

117. E.g., *Wong Him v. Callahan,* 119 F. 381 (U.S.C.C. Ca., 1902) sustained a California law requiring children of Chinese descent who were citizens to attend "separate but equal" schools. The district judge adhered to precedents tracing back to Shaw's famous decision in *Roberts v. City of Boston.*

118. *Cumming v. Richmond Co. Bd. of Education,* 175 U.S. 528 (1899) at 543–45. For conflicting discussions see Schmidt, 1982a, 470–72; Kousser, 1986, 27–30; Fiss, 1993, 367–70.

119. *Berea College v. Commonwealth of Kentucky,* 211 U.S. 45 (1908) at 55–57, 66–69. See also Schmidt, 1982a, 446–50; Hovenkamp, 1985, 629–37; Fiss, 1993, 370–71, who believes Harlan was chiefly opposed to excessive state police powers.

120. See, e.g., *Billinger v. Clyde S.S. Co.; Fishburn v. Same,* 158 F. 511 (U.S.C.C. N.Y., 1908).

121. *Chesapeake and Ohio Railway Co. v. Kentucky,* 79 U.S. 388 (1900).

122. *Chiles v. Chesapeake and Ohio Railway Co.,* 218 U.S. 71 (1910).

123. Ibid. at 75–76.

124. Barnes, 1983, 12–17.

125. Legal disputes over segregation continued, of course, in a long line that leads through *Brown v. Board of Education* to depressingly extensive litigation today. In the last significant decision prior to 1912, *McCabe v. Atchison, Topeka, and Santa Fe Railway* 186 F. 966 (8th C. 1911), two circuit judges upheld an Oklahoma segregation statute against a number of challenges. Of particular interest is their ruling that for equal protection purposes it did not matter if the statute, as interpreted by the company, treated blacks unequally, denying them access to dining cars and sleeping cars, because the company was not a state actor subject to the Fourteenth Amendment. They also read the Supreme Court decisions just reviewed as indicating that all general state segregation laws should be construed as applying only to intrastate traffic unless the legislature should be so foolish as to indicate unequivocally otherwise. Circuit judge Sanborn dissented, arguing cogently if unsuccessfully that the company was treating blacks unequally under authority of the statute, and that it clearly did apply in terms and in effect to interstate travelers. On appeal, the Supreme Court also affirmed all of the act against Fourteenth Amendment and commerce clause challenges, except for its refusal to provide Pullman cars for blacks as well as whites. Even on that issue, the Court avoided overturning the Oklahoma law on procedural grounds; but Hughes's opinion contained language blacks could and did use to claim more equal services in later cases. *McCabe v. Atchison, Topeka, and Santa Fe Railroad Co.,* 235 U.S. 151 (1914).

126. See, e.g., *Carter v. Texas,* 177 U.S. 442 (1900) (sustaining an accused black because state court would not hear his witnesses); *Tarrance v. Florida,* 188 U.S. 519 (1903); *Brownfield v. South Carolina,* 189 U.S. 426 (1903); *Rogers v. Alabama,* 192 U.S. 226 (1904) (sustaining an accused black because a state court would not examine evidence that a ban on black voters had affected juror selection); *Martin v. Texas,* 200 U.S. 316 (1906); *Kentucky v. Powers,* 201 U.S. 1 (1906) (Harlan, invalidating the removal of a case of a Republican defendant accused of political assassination and tried by all-Democratic Kentucky juries); *Franklin v. South Carolina,* 218 U.S. 161 (1910) (Day).

127. *Williams v. Mississippi,* 170 U.S. 213, 222, 225 (1898).

128. *U.S. v. Lackey; Same v. Conners,* 99 F. 952 (U.S.D.C. Ky., 1900).

129. *Lackey v. U.S.,* 107 F. 114 (C.C.A. 6th C. 1901). Two years later, in *Karem v. U.S.,* 121 F. 250 (6th C.C.A. 1903), a member of that bench offered the incredible argument that individuals could never infringe upon the right to vote, because they did not confer the right; they could merely infringe upon the right's exercise by violence. The Fifteenth Amendment, according to circuit judge Lurton, only guaranteed the formal existence of voting rights. Violent infringements upon them were state concerns.

130. *James v. Bowman,* 190 U.S. 127 (1903).

131. Ibid. at 136, 142.

132. *Giles v. Harris,* 189 U.S. 475 (1903); Fiss, 1993, 374–79.

133. Ibid. at 485, 487–88. Justices Brewer, Brown, and Harlan dissented, with Brewer insisting

that a plaintiff should not be denied relief simply because many others were also denied their rights (491). Harlan agreed on that point, but unlike Brewer, he thought the Court did not have jurisdiction (503–4).

134. *Giles v. Teasley,* 193 U.S. 146 (1904).

135. Ibid. at 164, 166. The equally egregious *Jones v. Montague,* 194 U.S. 147 (1904), concerned a challenge to an election held under a 1902 Virginia constitution, adopted without popular ratification, which created a registration process that excluded African-Americans. Brewer wrote for the Court that since the election had been held and the resulting representatives admitted to the House, *Mills v. Green* controlled. It was too late to prevent the election, no relief was imaginable, and so the case was moot. The Circuit Court for Virginia later ruled the validity of the 1902 Constitution a political question, outside judicial cognizance, in *Brickhouse v. Brooks,* 165 F. 534 (U.S.C.C. Va., 1908).

136. Despite that example, some lower federal courts continued to take charges of black disfranchisement seriously. See, e.g., *Anderson v. Myers; Howard v. Same; Brown v. Same,* 182 F. 223 (U.S.C.C. Md., 1910); *U.S. v. Stone,* 188 F. 836 (U.S.D.C. Md., 1911); but cf. *McKenna v. U.S.,* 127 F. 88 (6th C.C.A. 1904). In the case of grandfather clauses, blatantly contrived to let illiterate poor whites vote while excluding blacks, the Supreme Court finally did support lower court rulings of unconstitutionality in *Guinn and Beal v. U.S.,* 238 U.S. 347 (1915), discussed in Elliott, 1974, 70–71, and Schmidt, 1982c, 851–81. That decision had little impact on voter registration, although, like *Yarbrough,* it would prove a useful precedent once the Court shifted its general posture on voting rights.

137. *U.S. v. Eberhart,* 127 F. 254 (U.S.C.C. Ga., 1899); cf. *In re Lewis,* 114 F. 963 (U.S.C.C. Fla., 1902); *Brawner v. Irvin,* 169 F. 964 (U.S.C.C. Ga., 1909).

138. *Hodges v. U.S.,* 203 U.S. 1, 18, 20 (1905); Fiss, 1993, 379–85.

139. See, c.g., *U.S. v. Powell,* 151 F. 648 (U.S.C.C. Ala., 1907) (where the author of *Ex parte Riggins,* Thomas Goode Jones, felt compelled to hold his earlier reasoning invalidated by the *Hodges* case).

140. See, e.g., *Ex parte Riggins,* 134 U.S. 404 (U.S.C.C. Ala., 1904) (finding congressional power under the Thirteenth and Fourteenth Amendments to reach private actors who harm black prisoners in state custody, interfering with state equal protection).

141. See, e.g., *Peonage Cases,* 123 F. 671 (U.S.D.C. Ala., 1903); *U.S. v. Morris,* 125 F. 322 (U.S.D.C. Ark., 1903); *U.S. v. McClellan,* 127 F. 971 (U.S.D.C. Ga., 1904), *Jamison v. Wimbish,* 130 F. 351 (U.S.D.C. Ga., 1904); *Ex parte Drayton et al.,* 153 F. 986 (U.S.D.C. S.C., 1907); *Smith et al. v. U.S.,* 157 F. 721 (8th C.C.A. 1907).

142. *Bailey v. Alabama,* 219 U.S. 219 (1911); *U.S. v. Reynolds,* 235 U.S. 33 (1914); cf. *Robertson v. Baldwin,* 165 U.S. 297 (1897); *Clyatt v. U.S.,* 197 U.S. 207 (1905); discussed in Schmidt, 1982b.

143. Justice Charles Evans Hughes wrote in *Bailey v. Alabama:* "We at once dismiss from consideration the fact that the plaintiff in error is a black man. . . . The statute, on its face, makes no racial discrimination, and the record fails to show its existence in fact" (219 U.S. 231).

144. Schmidt, 1982b, 646, 648, 663, 716–717.

145. Flexner, 1975, 209–21, 236–37, 262; Degler, 1980, 322–23, 347; Leach, 1980, 140; Painter, 1987, 243–52; Cott, 1987, 22–29; Skocpol, 1992, 319, 345–54, 382–96.

146. Kraditor, 1965, 15–19, 44–45, 52–53, 68, 97–101, 123–27; Gilman, 1966; Flexner, 1975, 208–10, 239–40, 261; Degler, 1980, 345, 351, 358; Leach, 1980, 8, 15, 23, 33–34; Kessler-Harris, 1982, 114–15; Painter, 1987, 246–47; Cott, 1987, 16–21, 41, 119; 1989, 818–20; Skocpol, 1992, 368–71, 407 12.

147. Gilman, 1966, 1, 66–67, 119–21, 169–72, 223, 330–40.

148. Gilman, 1966, 46, 147–48, 180. Bederman, 1995, 122–23, 145–47, stresses the white supremacist aspects of Gilman's thought.
149. Gilman, 1966, 52–57, 154–60. See also Kraditor, 1965, 46, 133, 139, 202; O'Neill, 1969, 70–76; Degler, 1980, 335; Baker, 1984, 642.
150. Flexner, 1975, 304–18; Degler, 1980, 339–41, 349–55.
151. Justice Department disagreements on the issue dated back to 1877, when Solicitor-General S. F. Phillips advised that a woman who had acquired U.S. citizenship via marriage did not lose it even if her husband died and she then married an alien (15 *Op. of U.S. Atty. Gen.* 599–600 [1877]). The 1907 act seemed plainly aimed at overturning such views; but in 1915, Attorney General T. W. Gregory advised the Secretary of Labor that a native-born American woman, married to an American who appeared to have expatriated himself, could not thereby have lost her own American citizenship (30 *Op. of U.S. Att. Gen.* 412–22 [1915]). For further discussion see Kansas, 1936, 74, 125–26; Cable, 1943, 2; Sapiro, 1984, 10; Bredbenner, 1990, 11–17, 61–72.
152. *Cong. Rec.,* 59th Cong., 2d Sess., 1463, 4116 (1907); Sapiro, 1984, 3, 8–11; *Committee on Foreign Affairs Hearings Relating to Expatriation, 61st Cong.,* 2d Sess., April 17, 1912, 3, 7, 9, 11; Bredbenner, 1990, 54–67.
153. Flexner, 1975, 228–31, 263–69.
154. Cases supporting female subordination are too numerous to canvass. For additional discussion, see Baer, 1978; R. M. Smith, 1989a. One question that raised difficulties for judicial protection of women was whether a state had to give "full faith and credit" to the marriage and divorce laws of other states. The justices sharply divided on this question after 1900. Although federalism and state's rights dominated the discussions, votes actually seemed often to turn on the merits of the claims of the husbands and wives involved. The Supreme Court generally held that earlier state marital proceedings must be honored. But Edward White, especially, sometimes led majorities that permitted states to override previous extra-state proceedings in order to treat women's claims more fully and fairly, and to ignore divorces granted elsewhere on more permissive or less protective grounds than the later state preferred. Although these decisions sometimes permitted women to establish domiciles independent of their husbands, they virtually always did so via an Americanist paternalistic rhetoric of protecting women, not on grounds of women's rights. See, e.g., *Atherton v. Atherton,* 181 U.S. 155 (1901) (Gray upholding, over dissents by Peckham and Fuller, a Kentucky divorce obtained by a husband whose cruelty had driven his wife away, instead of a later, more favorable New York divorce she had obtained); *Bell v. Bell,* 181 U.S. 175 (1901) (state not required to grant credit to a divorce obtained in a state where neither party was ever domiciled); *Streitwolf v. Streitwolf,* 181 U.S. 179 (1901) (state not required to credit a divorce obtained in a state where the wife never resided); *Lynde v. Lynde,* 181 U.S. 183 (1901) (state must credit an earlier alimony decree); *Andrews v. Andrews,* 188 U.S. 14 (1903) (White ruling, with Brewer, Shiras, and Peckham dissenting, that a state must be able to ignore out-of-state divorce decrees in order to preserve "rights of local self-government" [33]); *Harding v. Harding,* 198 U.S. 317 (1905) (White requiring a state to honor another state's award of support to a separated wife because the separation was not her fault); *Haddock v. Haddock,* 201 U.S. 562 (1906) (hotly contested ruling by White permitting New York to ignore a Connecticut divorce decree in favor of its own laws, a power White thought necessary to prevent states from being bound by most "lax" marital laws of other states, "thus causing marriage to be less protected than any other civil obligation" [574, 580]. Brown, Harlan, Brewer and Holmes dissented, pointing the New York award came to the woman 31 years after an unconsummated marriage in which the couple had never lived together); *Fall v. Eastin,* 215 U.S. 1 (1909) (state need

not recognize the property provisions of another state's divorce decree); *Sistare v. Sistare*, 218 U.S. 1 (1910) (White ruling that Connecticut can enforce New York alimony decree); *Olmsted v. Olmsted*, 216 U.S. 386 (1910) (state need not credit a divorce granted in another state to a bigamist without service on his first wife). The nationalistic New Deal Court settled these issues by overturning *Haddock* and holding that states must fully credit the prior marital proceedings of other states, however pernicious they might seem (*Williams v. North Carolina*, 317 U.S. 287 [1942]).

155. *In re Freche*, 109 F. 620 (U.S.D.C. N.J., 1901).

156. *Tinker v. Colwell*, 193 U.S. 473 (1904) at 481, 484. See also *In re Tinker*, 99 F. 79 (U.S.D.C. N.Y., 1900).

157. *Thompson v. Thompson*, 218 U.S. 611, 617 (1910). Harlan, Holmes, and Hughes dissented, with Harlan insisting that Congress had indeed explicitly made "a radical change in the relations of man and wife" (620).

158. See, e.g., *Nichols v. Nichols*, 92 F. 1 (U.S.C.C. Mo., 1899) (holding that a wife cannot acquire a separate domicile from her husband if she is apart from him "unjustifiably," a situation said to be unchanged by the citizenship clause of the Fourteenth Amendment); *Watertown v. Greaves*, 112 F. 183 (1st C. 1901); *Gordon v. Yost*, 140 F. 79 (U.S.C.C. W. Va., 1905) (affirming that husband's desertion or misconduct permits wife to establish own domicile and state citizenship); *Ruckgaber v. Moore*, 104 F. 947 (U.S.C.C. N.Y., 1900); *In re Rionda*, 164 F. 368 (U.S.D.C. N.Y., 1908); *U.S. ex rel. Nicola v. Williams; U.S. ex rel. Gendering v. Same*, 173 F. 626 (U.S.D.C. N.Y., 1909) (all affirming that women's citizenship is determined by their husband's, regardless of their own preferences).

159. See, e.g., *In re Martorana*, 159 F. 1010 (U.S.D.C. Pa., 1908); *U.S. v. Martorana*, 171 F. 397 (3d C. 1909).

160. *MacKenzie v. Hare*, 239 U.S. 299 (1915) at 308, 311.

161. *U.S. v. Cohen*, 179 F. 834 (2d C. 1910).

162. *In re Rustigan*, 165 F. 980 (U.S.C.C. R.I., 1908); *Loh Wah Suey v. Backus*, 225 U.S. 460 (1912). The judges of the Second Circuit did balk, however, at claims that women who were eligible for naturalization at the time of their marriage to U.S. citizens could be deported if, at later times, they developed contagious diseases or engaged in immoral activities. See *In re Nicola; Williams v. U.S. ex rel Gendering; Williams v. U.S. ex rel. Hohanessian*, 184 F. 322 (2d C. 1911).

163. Courts also continued their practice of upholding legislative efforts to expand the economic rights of wives. See, e.g., *Burns v. Cooper*, 140 F. 273 (8th C. 1905) (applying the 1871 Nebraska Married Women's Property Act).

164. 208 U.S. 412 (1908).

165. Muller at 414, 419–22.

166. Baer, 1978, 59–66; Sachs & Wilson, 1978, 111–18; Taub & Schneider, 1982, 128–30; Kessler-Harris, 1982, 185–87; R. M. Smith, 1989a, 271–72; Fiss, 1993, 176–79. This critique does not suggest that the law ought to have always insisted on "a fictitious equality where there is a real difference," an approach Oliver Wendell Holmes disavowed in *Quong Wing v. Kirkendall*, 223 U.S. 59, 63 (1912). But it matters greatly whether the law recognizes the distinct condition of women in order to empower them or in order to justify their constraint.

167. Hoxie, 1984, x, xii, 68–70, 242–43; Prucha, 1984, 759–61.

168. The last major group of Native Americans to have citizenship thrust upon them were the Southwest Indian Territory tribes. In 1898, the Curtis Act abolished tribal laws and courts and brought the entire Indian Territory under direct U.S. governance. The Supreme Court sustained these measures with cursory discussion in *Stephens v. Cherokee Nation;*

Choctaw Nation v. Robinson; Johnson v. Creek Nation; Chickasaw Nation v. Robinson, 174 U.S. 445 (1899). Then in 1901, Congress made all inhabitants of the Indian Territory U.S. citizens. Finally, in 1907 Oklahoma was admitted as a state that incorporated the former Indian Territory, despite efforts by the tribes to be admitted as a separate state. Members of the Five Civilized Tribes were outnumbered in the single new state 13–1 (Dippie, 1982, 193, 246–47; Prucha, 1984, 746–57, 911–16).

169. Prucha, 1984, 610.
170. Hoxie, 1984, 12–15; see also Martin, 1990, 85–86.
171. The act was passed partly to overturn the Supreme Court's decision in *Matter of Heff* (1905), discussed below, which denied the federal government continued power to control liquor purchases by naturalized Native Americans. See the remarks of the law's chief sponsor, Rep. Burke of South Dakota, *Cong. Rec.,* 59th Cong., 1st Sess., v. 40, pt. 4, 3599–3600 (March 9, 1906).
172. At the time of the Burke Act, about 166,000 Native Americans had become citizens since the Dawes Act, 65,000 via allotment and the rest as members of the Five Civilized Tribes. Dippie, 1982, 191–93; Hoxie, 1984, 108–12, 166; Prucha, 1984, 773–75, 784.
173. *Cong. Rec.,* 59th Cong., 1st Sess., v. 40, pt. 6, 5606 (April 20, 1906) (Sen. Heyburn); Prucha, 1984, 767, 772–73, 779–80, 875–77.
174. See, e.g., *U.S. v. Four Bottles Sour-Mash Whisky,* 90 F. 720 (U.S.D.C. Wash., 1898) (no federal right to enforce restraints on liquor trade on lands made available for mining); *In re Celestine,* 114 F. 551 (U.S.D.C. Wash., 1902) (allotment recipient is a citizen who must settle custody dispute in state, not federal court); *U.S. v. Kiya,* 126 F. 879 (U.S.D.C. N.D., 1903) (unless Congress specifies that allotment recipients are still wards, they are not); *U.S. v. Torrey Cedar Co.; U.S. v. Paine Lumber Co.,* 154 F. 263 (1904) (unless Congress specifies otherwise, allotment recipients may sell timber on their lands).
175. On the primacy of race, see, e.g., *U.S. v. Hadley,* 99 F. 437–38 (U.S.C.C. Wash., 1900) (son of white man living in tribe is a U.S. citizen by birth); *U.S. v. Higgins,* 103 F. 348 (U.S.C.C. Mont., 1900) (agreeing that "a white man, although adopted into an Indian tribe . . . cannot escape his responsibilities as a white man," but finding children may sometimes follow the race of their mothers, not their fathers); *U.S. v. Heyfron,* 138 F. 964 (U.S.C.C. Mont., 1905) (son of Spaniard formally adopted into his mother's tribe is a Flathead Indian); *Cherokee Intermarriage Cases,* 203 U.S. 76 (1906).
176. Cf. *U.S. v. Logan,* 105 F. 240 (U.S.C.C. Or., 1900) (holding that notwithstanding "the act of congress declaring them citizens," allottees "are still minors in the eyes of the law," incapable of disposing of lands or trading in liquor); *U.S. v. Kopp,* 110 F. 160 (U.S.D.C. Wash., 1901) (dismissing *Eells v. Ross* and holding that allotment recipients, as citizens, are no longer subject to Indian liquor laws); *Farrell v. U.S.,* 110 F. 942 (8th C. 1901) (following *Eells v. Ross* and holding that Congress could regulate liquor trade with allotment recipients because issuing land patents "did not change the appetites, passions, characters, habits, disposition, or capacity of these Indians").
177. 187 U.S. 553, 563 (1903).
178. 188 U.S. 432, 437 (1903).
179. 197 U.S. 488, 497–99, 509 (1905). In a kindred spirit, in *Goudy v. Meath,* 203 U.S. 146 (1906), the Supreme Court also affirmed that, if Congress had not specified an exemption or if it had expired, the land of allotment recipients could be taxed by the states. In *Francis v. Francis,* 203 U.S. 233 (1906) it ruled that the President could not unilaterally limit the alienability of lands patented to Native Americans. And in *U.S. v. Paine Lumber Co.,* 206 U.S. 467 (1907), it agreed with the lower courts that federal retention of ultimate title did not prevent allottees from selling the timber on their lands.

180. 197 U.S. 509 (1905).
181. See, e.g., *Ex parte Viles*, 139 F. 68 (U.S.D.C. Wash., 1905), following Heff and holding that "Congress has no power by special legislation to classify citizens, so as to create race or other distinctions, and subject one class or grade of citizens to police regulations not applicable to all citizens."
182. Hoxie, 1984, 220–21; Martin, 1990, 84. In *U.S. v. Winans*, 198 U.S. 371 (1905), the Court construed a treaty as preserving Yakima Indian rights to fish on lands for which the U.S. had given perfect title to whites; cf. *Winters v. U.S.*, 207 U.S. 564 (1908) (similarly affirming water rights). In *McKay v. Kalyton*, 204 U.S. 458, 465 (1907,) Edward White wrote for a 6–3 majority ruling that the federal government's continuing supervisory interest made it a party to all controversies over allotment titles and precluded state jurisdiction, *Heff* notwithstanding; Brewer (the author of *Heff*), Peckham, and Chief Justice Fuller dissented without opinion. In *Dick v. U.S.*, 208 U.S. 340 (1908), the Court claimed rather weakly that treaty agreements with the former tribes of allottees authorized the federal government to regulate their liquor purchases, despite *Heff*. The Court's unanimity shows that all the justices were now backing off the *Heff* decision.

   For lower court rulings see, e.g., *U.S. v. Thurston Co.*, 143 F. 287 (8th C. 1906) (states cannot tax allotment lands during trust period, as need to protect against "the unrestrained greed, rapacity, cunning, and perfidy of members of the superior race" remains); *Hollister v. U.S.*, 145 F. 773 (8th C. 1906) (sustaining federal criminal jurisdiction over reservation lands after allotment, as wardship has not yet ended); *Rainbow v. Young*, 161 F. 835 (8th C. 1908) (upholding Indian school superintendent who prevented bill collector from taking allottees' lease monies, as the allottees were "still in a state of dependency and tutelage").
183. See, e.g., the marvelous summary of anti-reservationist ideology in *U.S. v. Hall*, 171 F. 214 (U.S.D.C. Wisc., 1909) (observing that "finally the great truth was made manifest to the Indian Bureau that in civilization, as in education or religion, the individual is the unit, and that it is hopeless to undertake to civilize a tribe as such. . . . The reservation impaired the strength and vigor of the race, but did not weaken its instincts and prejudices." Hence eligible Native Americans had rightly been made citizens, whose personal habits and passions were properly restrained by the states' police powers; federal liquor laws no longer applied). Hall was written forcefully enough to be followed, with trepidation, in *U.S. ex rel. Friedman v. U.S. Express Co.*, 180 F. 1006 (U.S.D.C. Ark., 1910), decided when the Supreme Court was clearly going the other way.
184. See, e.g., *U.S. v. Allen*, 171 F. 907 (U.S.C.C. Okl., 1909), where district judge Campbell refused to let the U.S. sue on behalf of allotment recipients against persons claiming to have received lands from the allottees, insisting that "when Congress clothed the allottee with full citizenship" it did so because "his status as ward of the government was not in the nature of things compatible with full citizenship in the state and union." Hence "it was not intended by Congress that the guardianship should continue." Cf. also *Gearlds v. Johnson*, 183 F. 611 (U.S.C.C. Minn., 1911); *U.S. v. Shock*, 187 F. 862 (U.S.C.C. Okl., 1911); *Harris v. Gale*, 188 F. 712 (U.S.C.C. Okl., 1911). But higher courts soon disagreed: see *U.S. v. Allen*, 179 F. 13 (8th C. 1910); *Heckman v. U.S.*, 224 U.S. 413 (1912), discussed in Carter, 1976, 204–6.
185. 215 U.S. 278 (1909).
186. 215 U.S. 296 (1909). A week later the Court added that the federal government retained control over the liquor trade within the limits of reservations, even after allotment (*U.S. v. Sutton*, 215 U.S. 291 [1909]). The renewed climate of belief in the racial inadequacy of Native Americans is also visible in lower court opinions of these years, such as *La Clair v. U.S.*, 184 F. 128 (U.S.C.C. Wash., 1910). There district judge Whitson upheld allotments

to former Puyallup tribe members who had been adopted by the Yakima tribes. With genial arrogance, Whitson asked, "What could be more natural—more human—than for this primitive people—this dependent and fast decaying race—to take its last stand against encroachment that began upon the Atlantic and will finally end upon the Pacific with their extinction to retain as possible a community of their own, uncontaminated by association with the whites?" Whitson saw this motive evident in the "quaintly expressed" statement of one Yakima, "Yes; we get together some place, us Indians all the time." See also district judge Elliott's remark in *Sully v. U.S.,* 195 F. 113 (U.S.C.C. S.D., 1912), that the complainants in the case had "sufficient Indian blood to substantially handicap them in the struggle for existence."

187. In *Marchie Tiger v. Western Investment Co.,* 221 U.S. 286 (1911), the Court upheld a congressional extension of federal guardianship over allotment lands owned by a Creek who had become a citizen. Prior legislation had called for guardianship to terminate before the litigation arose. Day ruled that Brewer's opinion in *Celestine* settled the power of Congress "to determine for itself when the guardianship which has been maintained over the Indian shall cease," without any judicial interference (314). Then, in a brief opinion in *Hallowell v. U.S.,* 221 U.S. 317 (1911), Day sustained congressional power to regulate the liquor trade upon allotment lands to which the U.S. still held ultimate title. Hughes added his voice in support of congressional power over allotment recipients in *Heckman v. U.S.,* 224 U.S. 413 (1912). Lower courts increasingly followed suit: see, e.g., *U.S. v. Hemmer,* 195 F. 790 (U.S.D.C. S.D., 1912); *Mosier v. U.S.,* 198 F. 54 (8th C. 1912); *Truskett v. Closser,* 198 F. 835 (8th C. 1912). Perhaps the best statement of the new and clearly racist outlook is the circuit appeals court's opinion in *U.S. v. Allen* (1910), overturning the trial court's recognition of full Native American citizenship. The appeals court applauded the federal government for not hesitating to override tribes that had refused consent to allotment in severalty. It insisted federal guardianship should not be confined by "cramped" analogies to the private law of guardians and wards, and it stressed that clothing Native Americans with citizenship "did not change their character or invest them with industrial capacity." Hence continuing federal regulatory powers should not be denied "as a mere speculative inference from the definition of citizenship." A reduction in federal authority was a "radical change" that needed to be made unequivocally. Granting citizenship was not "express" enough; though an allottee might be a "citizen of the United States, he did not cease to be an Indian" (15, 20, 23).

188. *Choate v. Trapp,* 224 U.S. 665, 678 (1912).

189. *U.S. v. Nice,* 241 U.S. 591, 601 (1916).

190. 241 U.S. 598 (1916). Although the *Nice* case formally overruled *Heff,* the Court's renewed acceptance that race mattered more than citizenship was even more readily apparent in Van Devanter's opinion in *U.S. v. Sandoval,* 231 U.S. 28 (1913). There, the Justice wrote for a unanimous bench that whether or not the Pueblo Indians were citizens did not matter, "because citizenship is not in itself an obstacle to the exercise by Congress of its power to enact laws for the benefit and protection of tribal Indians as a dependent people" (48). It also did not matter that the pueblo peoples were highly advanced by white standards, "sedentary rather than nomadic in their inclinations, and disposed to peace and industry." They were "nevertheless Indians in race, customs, and domestic government" and "essentially a simple, uninformed and inferior people" (39).

191. Most education-related cases involved challenges to racial segregation and are treated here under the heading of the minority group involved.

192. Shortly after the years studied here, Congress passed the Smith-Lever Act of 1914, providing federal funding for agricultural extension projects teaching new methods to farmers

through the land-grant colleges. Three years later, Congress added the Smith-Hughes Act, providing federal funds for vocational education programs at the secondary school level (Cremin, 1988, 8, 228, 478–80; Kaminsky, 1993, 23–25, 36–44; Spring, 1990, 211–16).

193. Katz, 1971, 113–14; Tyack, 1974, 5–8; Bowles & Gintis, 1976, 181; Peterson, 1985, 5–9; J. D. Anderson, 1988, 81–82; Cremin, 1988, 154–55, 229–30; Spring, 1990, 153–62; cf. Kaminsky, 1993, 100–102.

194. Cremin, 1988, 164–68; Kaminsky, 1993, 16, 32, 36–40.

195. Much of the extensive scholarly debate over these reformers and their achievements centers on how far they should all be understood as essentially agents of a capitalist order, concerned to inculcate habits of obedience, orderliness, and loyalty as well as the vocational skills needed to forge a productive, compliant industrial work force out of a population of recalcitrant poor immigrants, blacks, Catholics, and other undesirable lower types. Their defenders insist the reformers had genuinely democratic aspirations and accomplishments. The "social control" critics of public education have significant differences among themselves (over, for example, whether service to capitalism, professional self-aggrandizement, or quests for cultural homogeneity drove reformers) and they have been criticized for minimizing the complexity of pluralist school politics in these years and the mixed results, with most white groups, at least, getting meaningful schooling in public or private institutions. Here I wish not to try to settle the thorny question of what ultimately drove the educational reforms of these years but instead to stress that, by and large, they resulted in an education still structured in terms of ascriptive Americanism, one which did provide opportunities for whites willing to embrace prevailing American values, but which severely constrained the mobility of populations deemed unfit for higher economic and political positions because of the lower levels of necessary cognitive skills allegedly associated with their race, ethnicity, class or gender. For the educational debates, see, e.g., Katz, 1971; Tyack, 1974; Ravitch, 1974 and 1978; Bowles & Gintis, 1976; Peterson, 1985; Katznelson & Weir, 1985; Spring, 1990.

196. Tyack, 1974, 7, 14, 25, 127–28; Katznelson & Weir, 1985, 24; Kaminsky, 1993, xv.

197. Katznelson & Weir, 1985, 87–89; Cremin, 1988, 7, 384; Spring, 1990, 175–79, 225–38, 262–63; Kaminsky, 1993, 40–44.

198. Tyack, 1974, 22, 45, 132, 232–46; Peterson, 1985, 5–8, 24; Cremin, 1988, 10–11, 119–20, 142–45, 220–21, 237–38, 246, 383–84, 395–98, 683; Spring, 1990, 154–56, 170–72, 189–91, 240–41.

199. Bowles & Gintis, 1976, 180–81; Katznelson & Weir, 1985, 61, 100; Cremin 1988, 180–87, 240–41, 522–23; Spring, 1990, 175, 270–71: Kaminsky, 1993, 100.

200. Tyack, 1974, 229–39; Peterson, 1985, 5–9, 73–75, 117; Carlson, 1987, 68–72; Cremin, 1988, 129–30, 139–45; Green, 1990, 201.

201. Tyack, 1974, 196–99, 217; Cremin, 1988, 162–63, 177–79, 196–97, 236–38, 242, 336, 383–84, 396–98, 436; Carlson, 1987, 60–72, 82–100; Spring, 1990, 175–78. Kaminsky, 1993, 12–16, 29–32.

202. Low, 1982, 55–65, 70–79, 92–107; Richardson, 1986, 129–31, 255; J. D. Anderson, 1988, 79–109, 148–51, 154, 157–77, 189–95, 238–50; Cremin, 1988, 213–21, 534–35, 545.

203. Hoxie, 1984, 122–23, 134–35.

204. Prucha, 1979, 1–40, 84–95, 128–69; Dippie, 1982, 181–85; Hoxie, 1984, 106–7, 198–210; Prucha, 1984, 819–20; *Quick Bear v. Leupp*, 210 U.S. 50 (1908): Coleman, 1993, 40–43. Roosevelt said that the "utterly undeveloped races" should not be expected to exercise the kinds of self-government "only the very highest races" could manage. It would "take generations" to prepare them.

205. Prucha, 1984, 759–62; Hoxie, 1984, 68–69, 117–34, 200–204; Coleman, 1993, 43–47.

Epilogue

1. Lincoln, 1905–06, v. 5, 266 (First Inaugural Address).
2. The task of tracing the connection between left progressive civic conceptions and modern American citizenship policies in detail must be left for another day, but for a similar identification of modern civil rights and multiculturalist policies with left progressive views, and a related critique of the difficulties of those positions, see Spinner, 1994, 60–72, 171–76. For characterizations of Great Society civic reforms that describe them in terms consonant with left progressivism, though without using that term, see, e.g., Black, 1970, 12–13, 31; Beer, 1978, 26–28, 31, 44. The contributions of liberal democratic traditions to modern reforms are stressed even by those who believe, like Young, 1990, 156–57, that Enlightenment republicanism sustained intolerable oppressions.
3. David Hollinger has plausibly distinguished between more cosmopolitan left progressive positions like Randolph Bourne's and more pluralist positions like Kallen's (Hollinger, 1995). I believe that Bourne's views were and are too cosmopolitan to have an extensive following in the U.S. The universalist integrationist view I describe shares his sense that all should have equal access to democratic public institutions without his strong emphasis on "trans-nationalism" and the desirability of dual citizenships.
4. Taylor, 1992, 37–44.
5. Between the Rawlsians and the "difference" theorists came the architects of the communitarian turn in American political theory. But insofar as those labeled "communitarian" offered positive visions of American civic identity, they tended to be either revivals of republicanism, as in the work of Michael Sandel and William Sullivan, or versions of democratic cultural pluralism, as in the work of Michael Walzer. See Walzer, 1983; Sandel, 1984; Sullivan, 1986.
6. In the final chapter of his fine 1995 book, Will Kymlicka raises the question of the "basis of unity in a multinational state," and though he acknowledges that he has no "clear answer" and that liberal theorists have neglected that question, he offers some insightful observations on which I build. Kymlicka does not, however, give sustained attention to how the quest for such unity forms part of the strategies of elites within the contested politics of nation-building (Kymlicka, 1995, 187–92).
7. In an insightful essay on nationalism, Elizabeth Kiss has argued similarly that neglect of the "aspirations and interests that fuel nationalist politics" can "backfire," leading people to "reject liberal democratic institutions and human rights" (Kiss, 1996, 314, 316, 321). Spinner also notes that if a liberal community is too hostile to "ethnic identity," it "may very well explode" (Spinner, 1994, 59).
8. B. R. O. Anderson, 1983.
9. The theorists particularly sympathetic to recognition of "difference," including some nationalist claims, all stress these points. See, e.g., Young, 1990, 43–45, 182–83; Tamir, 1993, 72–77; Kymlicka, 1995, 89–90; Kiss, 1996, 306–7.
10. These factors are explored in Klinkner & Smith, forthcoming.
11. Though neither Du Bois nor Gilman devoted extensive attention to how American nationality should be defined, Gilman all too zealously endorsed the Anglo-Saxon myth of white Americans' evolutionary shaped capacities for freedom, which most left progressives opposed. As noted in the previous chapter, in his early writings Du Bois was not free of a racial sense of "American" identity, and though he soon came to reject late nineteenth-century racial ideology, he was quite reasonably more concerned to reproach the failings of Americans than to define a more compelling alternate sense of American nationality.
12. Kymlicka has suggested some valuable further distinctions between groups that represent

longstanding national minorities within a polity, immigrant ethnic groups, and other groups characterized by commonalities of religion, gender, and physical disabilities, among other traits. Those distinctions are relevant in working out answers to the greatly varied specific manifestations of these tensions, which I will not try to do here; but to some degree these tensions apply to all, as Iris Young's discussions of oppressed "social groups" indicate (Young, 1990, 42–48; Kymlicka, 1995, 10–33).

13. Sandel, 1982; Sandel, 1990, 75–76. Many contemporary liberals have endorsed Deweyan sorts of reply to communitarian critics. See, e.g., R. M. Smith, 1985, 200–201; Kymlicka, 1989, 47–73; Tamir, 1993, 13–34.

14. Sandel, among others, has at times come close to endorsing this position (see, e.g., Sandel, 1990, 90–91), but like most American communitarians he does oppose certain illiberal forms of community.

15. Kymlicka has quite correctly discussed this tension as one between an individual's membership in a liberal democratic national political community and a less than fully democratic cultural subgroup (Kymlicka, 1989, 150–52).

16. This second tension is plainly also bound up with the much-discussed conflict between "equality of opportunity" and "equality of result," with measures designed to limit inequalities in wealth, particularly, seen as endangering individual freedoms to seek wealth, for these freedoms inevitably produce unequal results. But because meaningful opportunities and possession of resources are so tightly intertwined, the opportunities versus results problem haunts a wide range of political outlooks. I focus here on the more specific tension, most characteristic of democratic pluralist outlooks, of aiming at promoting both individual and group equality in these regards.

17. Walzer, 1980, 785–87.

18. Gordon, 1964, 238–39, 264; Kymlicka, 1995, 182–86; Kiss, 1996, 315–17.

19. Rawls, 1993a, 222, 277. Kymlicka argues that, in general, liberal theorists like Rawls, Ronald Dworkin, and others have long tacitly assumed largely homogeneous and cohesive nation-states in these ways, leaving many vital issues unaddressed (Kymlicka, 1989, 177–78; Kymlicka, 1995, 2, 77, 86–87, 93).

20. Rawls, 1985, 223, 225, 228, 233; 1993a, xv–xx, 36–40, 133–58.

21. Rawls, 1985, 225, 230; Rawls, 1993a, 36–43, 140–44, 277.

22. Rawls also assumes that the senses of cultural identity that people acquire through youthful socialization are profound and enduring, and that they will always be closely identified with the bounds of their "closed society," so that it can be expected to have a generally shared "public political culture." Those premises suggest that desires for expatriation are very unlikely, and that the range of internal differences will not be too great. But though his assumption of the large impact of youthful socialization is plausible, the notions that it will limit differences and desires for expatriation to this degree are not. See esp. Rawls, 1993a, 12, 14, 133–72, 222, 277; cf. Kymlicka, 1995, 88–91. Rawls's essay on the "law of peoples" gives no more attention to the politics of how peoples come to be or are kept "peoples." It is rather concerned with how existing peoples should relate to each other (Rawls, 1993b).

23. Rawls, 1971, 528; 1985, 245.

24. Rawls, 1971, 19, 100ff., 329, 505, 509; Rawls, 1975a, 94–99; Rawls, 1993a, 6–7, 174–76, 190–200.

25. Though he has since limited his reliance on this feature of his view, he has not abandoned it. Rawls, 1971, 441–42, 450, 536, 544; Rawls, 1975a, 95; Rawls, 1993a, 206–7.

26. Rawls gives priority to his principle guaranteeing basic liberties to all individuals, and he suggests that the national regime may have to compel all groups to provide their members with education and options of social mobility, although he has expressed "regret" about

the "unavoidable consequences" for some religious groups of doing so. As Will Kymlicka argues, Rawls's insistence on "the priority of the liberties of citizenship" in the broader society makes Rawls's view "incompatible with minority" groups claiming rights to deny their members such liberties. Rawls, 1971, 514–16; 1975b, 549; Rawls, 1993a, 199–200. Cf. Kymlicka, 1989, 162–66; Kymlicka, 1995, 160–63.

27. Sandel, 1982, 80, 145, 149; cf. Rawls, 1971, 222, 234, 388; Rawls, 1993a, 145–49.
28. Rawls, 1971, 396, 528; Rawls, 1993a, 201–6.
29. Rawls, 1971, 522–23; Rawls, 1985, 229; Rawls, 1993a, 202.
30. Rawls, 1971, 396; Rawls, 1993a, 187–200.
31. Rawls, 1985, 247; Rawls, 1993a, 147.
32. Rawls, 1971, 181–82, 442, 445, 505, 509, 529; Rawls, 1975a, 96; Rawls, 1980, 526–27; Rawls, 1985, 224n2, 250n33; Rawls, 1993a, 106, 180–81, 318–20.
33. Rawls, 1971, 442, 450, 505, 509.
34. Rawls, 1971, 523–25, 529; Rawls, 1975b, 547, 549, 554; Rawls, 1985, pp. 245, 248; Rawls, 1993a, 206–7, 320–24.
35. Kymlicka, 1995, 187–88.
36. Rawls, 1985, 250n33; Rawls, 1993a, 206–7.
37. The claim that these problems do in fact stem largely from Rawls's refusal to endorse any doctrines of special national identities and any determinate national ends is corroborated by Bruce Ackerman's *Social Justice in the Liberal State*. That work goes even further in resting liberalism on a commitment to public neutrality on questions of the good life, a position that denies a nation the possibility of valorizing a particular national way of life. And it clearly articulates the democratic cultural pluralist civic ideal. Ackerman also promises that in his liberal state, communal needs will be met by a "rich variety" of associations pursuing a "diversity of moral ideals" and "revealing the breadth and depth of human creativity in all its majesty" (Ackerman, 1980, 82–83, 191, 194–96, 375; Ackerman, 1983, 386). But precisely because he is even more insistent on the liberal state's purposive neutrality, Ackerman openly accepts, as Rawls does not, that allegiance to it may reflect no more than "minimally prudent" calculations of its instrumental value (Ackerman, 1980, 83). And he acknowledges, correspondingly, that his larger liberal society will provide at most the "thinnest form of community," the "community" of arms-length bargainers, not "fraternity in any meaningful sense of the word" (Ackerman, 1980, 347; Ackerman, 1983, 375). He also admits that its lack of a substantive moral vision may mean that this society will foster "much agony and self-doubt," with many following lives that seem "mean and narrow" even to them, "full of apathy, drift, and mediocrity" (Ackerman, 1980, 165, 375; Ackerman, 1983, 386). Consonant with his very thin sense of national community, Ackerman goes on to argue that a truly liberal society must be "internationalist" indeed. It can justify restraints on immigration only by a "very strong empirical claim" that it will either cease to be entirely, or cease to be liberal, unless such restraints are adopted (Ackerman, 1980, 93–95). Concerns simply to preserve feelings of social solidarity are impermissible.

Yet Ackerman's nation-state is far from an inert shell. He still finds grounds to justify extensive national intervention "on an ongoing basis" into the internal lives of primary groups in order to achieve equality among members of different groups, via affirmative action and similar measures (Ackerman, 1980, 237–42, 247–49). The tensions and controversies thus engendered are to be accepted as facts of life in a world full of struggle. Ackerman is surely to be commended for his honesty and boldness. But his example, too, makes it seem doubtful that an ardent pursuit of public neutrality concerning the good can forestall the alienation from the modern liberal nation-state and the resulting conflicts and fragmentation that many see as the fruits of democratic cultural pluralism.

38. Nozick, 1974; Higham, 1975, 246; Beer, 1978, 37, 44; Gordon, 1978, 89, 93; Lowi, 1979, 58–63, 207–36, 271–92; Gleason, 1982, 143; White, 1983, 429, 433; Archdeacon, 1983, 233–35; Young, 1990, 157–64; Kymlicka, 1995, 61–63, 176–86.

39. MacIntyre, 1981. For a feminist critique of MacIntyre and other communitarians, see Bresnahan, 1994.

40. Young, 1990, 101, 104, 157–58, 163, 168, 173, 178–80, 184, 189. Young has been criticized by Kymlicka (1995, 145) and others because her list of oppressed groups is so long, encompassing "everyone but relatively well-off, relatively young, able-bodied, heterosexual white males." Though the objection has force, it also reveals reluctance to acknowledge fully the reality evident in America's historical citizenship laws: the nation's institutions *did* in fact long systematically and explicitly favor propertied white males at the expense of virtually everyone else, creating patterns of highly unequal power and wealth that continue today. The list is long because most people were in fact second-class citizens. Recall that in the debates over the Spanish-American War colonies, imperialists contended that the Declaration of Independence had, quite properly, not applied to "four-fifths" of the population.

41. Young, 1990, 190, 227–28, 238–40.

42. Young, 1990, 191, 236.

43. Kymlicka, 1989, 165–76, 189–92, 207; Kymlicka, 1995, 26–33, 82–93, 176–86.

44. Kymlicka, 1989, 197–99; Kymlicka, 1995, 152–55, 163–70.

45. Kymlicka, 1995, 173–74, 187–92. Tamir (1993) argues eloquently that liberalism can and should endorse certain forms of nationalism, constrained to maintain their liberal character by, for example, eschewing nationality as a "criterion for participating in the political sphere" of a multinational society (10–11). She, too, however, does not address the question of whether the liberal nationalism she describes can compete politically with other versions of national civic identity. The fact that it disavows the central demand of many nationalists, to be governed chiefly by fellow nationals, makes its viability questionable (Yack, 1995, 173–74).

46. Kymlicka (1995, 179) concurs that it is "difficult to avoid the conclusion that much of the backlash against 'multiculturalism' arises from a racist or xenophobic fear" of new immigrant groups and others who are "non-white and non Christian." Devigne (1994) argues convincingly that the best modern American conservative intellectuals have urged that local communities be permitted to pursue diverse traditional values, including illiberal ones, and at the same time have espoused patriotic support for a strong national government in military and foreign affairs, a kind of "dual sovereignty" view (70–74, 196–200). As such, this type of conservatism represents a new version of democratic cultural pluralism that incorporates some traditional Americanist notions of national identity, a politically potent mix. This combination sacrifices too much of the traditional liberal democratic concern to continue to expand opportunities for all, however, for me to find it persuasive. I recognize that many conservatives genuinely believe that this formula, with its stress on less restrained market forces and considerable local autonomy, will in fact enhance personal opportunities more than any other; but I believe that the strategy involves too much acquiescence in economic and traditionalist inequalities.

47. Kotkin, 1993; Herrnstein & Murray, 1994, esp. 356–64, 549; Rushton, 1995; Brimelow, 1995, 10; D'Souza, 1995, 170, 177–79. Herrnstein, Murray, and Rushton lean to biological explanations of what they see as unequal racial and ethnic group abilities, like the nineteenth-century racial Darwinists. Kotkin and D'Souza favor cultural explanations, in the manner of many nineteenth-century romanticists and the "Teutonic" historical school. Like many late nineteenth-century intellectuals, Brimelow appears eager to entertain both, but he most stresses the currently more palatable cultural arguments.

48. Gray, 1992; Gray, 1994; cf. R. M. Smith, 1994.
49. I cannot argue these much-disputed claims here. I have tried elsewhere: R. M. Smith, 1985; R. M. Smith, 1989b, 106–18; R. M. Smith, 1994.
50. I undertake only to offer a politically viable conception of American nationality that features liberal democratic values. Although the strategies to do so pursued here may be suggestive for other national contexts, it is in the nature of the effort to define a distinctive sense of national identity that somewhat different arguments must be made in different locales.
51. Walzer, 1981, 5–26.
52. Rawls uses the orchestra analogy twice in *Political Liberalism*, where he also compares members of political societies to "players on a team, or even both teams in a game" (1993a, 204, 321).
53. *Dred Scott v. Sandford*, 19 How. 422 (1857); Brimelow, 1995, xix.
54. Kiss, 1996, rightly stresses that nationalist commitments must not take away the "power and meaning" of the "claims of our common humanity" (296).
55. James Ceaser (1979, 123–69) eloquently elaborates Martin Van Buren's defense of parties on both "partisan" and "constitutional" grounds, the latter appealing to arguments of the national common good.
56. The stability of party identification is one of the few relatively robust findings in American political science, and it appears true in many other western advanced industrial democracies. Even though some scholars think that young people are increasingly socialized not to identify strongly with a particular party, they continue to hold that "once a specific attitude towards a party has been formed during the first phase of political socialization, it will probably persist through time and change only very slowly" (Flanigan & Zingale, 1991, 25–26, 29; Biorcio & Mannheimer, 1995, 212–13, 221).
57. Flanigan & Zingale, 1991, 55, 59.
58. This point is stressed by Tamir, 1993, 148–50; Kymlicka, 1995, 184–85; Kiss, 1996, 301–9, 314.
59. Flanigan & Zingale, 1991, 33–40, 56–58; Tamir, 1993, 63–68; Kiss, 1996, 296, 302–4.
60. Downs, 1957; Olson, 1965.
61. Ceaser, 1979, 153–54; Flanigan & Zingale, 1991, 21–22, 169, 118–22. They suggest that the American decline in turnout may reflect absence of trust in national political institutions and leaders, a lack that is understandable if the relationship between those bodies and actors and the voters' interests is seen as so deeply contingent.
62. Flanigan & Zingale, 1991, 85–110, 122–33.
63. That conclusion is made all the easier in the international realm because ordinarily one society does not have to live under laws made by another (though national minorities like the Native American tribes are important exceptions).
64. I use the term *enterprise* to signal that, unlike Rawls and Michael Oakeshott, I believe that a liberal democratic state should be understood as a "purposive" or "enterprise association," though, as I stress below, it is often not sensible for national political leaders to insist on a narrow definition of shared national purposes. Cf. Rawls, 1993a, 41–42; Oakeshott, 1975, 111–22.
65. Spinner, 1994, 168–71, stresses how the American state shapes identities and provides citizens with "overlapping memories," even though most Americans also have strong subgroup and transnational group identifications.
66. I have previously referred to this sense of Americanism as "trans-American nationalism" (Smith, 1993c), and Michael Lind uses similar terminology to describe his "liberal nationalism." But Lind not only describes America as "concrete historical community" with a common civic identity, as I do. He insists that the U.S.A. is a nation that is "defined pri-

marily by a common language, common folkways, and a common vernacular culture," and
he says that once racial definitions of nationality are abandoned, "[l]iberal nationalism . . .
must put more emphasis, not less, on the common language and the common culture."
Thus the nation can legitimately restrict immigration and "require a high degree of accul-
turation as a condition of immigration," though Lind opposes "coercive and repressive
methods" of doing so (Lind, 1995, 5, 14–15, 285–86). I believe that a willingness to share
in a common history and join in the pursuit of American political purposes is sufficient to
foster an adequate sense of American civic identity, without requiring extensive assimilation to the "extrapolitical" cultural nation Lind perceives (5, 281). Lind self-consciously
identifies with centrist progressives like Croly and Theodore Roosevelt (301–2), and like
them his emphasis on shared culture can easily turn into the repressiveness he disavows.
His acknowledgment that his position is hostile to the claims of many immigrants, feminists, and domestic ethnic and racial minorities is not reassuring in this regard. Rather than
stressing collective endeavors to realize liberal aims more fully, Lind's "nationalism" is
chiefly an effort to add on to claims for liberal "rights" an emphasis on traditional "social
duties." He stresses, for example, the duties of children to parents (a position rejected by
Locke, whom Lind cites) (Lind, 1995, 281–83, 286–88, 319–22).

67. Kymlicka, 1995, 189, 238n14; Kiss, 1996, 319. Lind (1995, 351–52, 364–83) suggests that
there can be "believable myths" sustaining the liberal national republic he envisions, and
he holds up Frederick Douglass as "the central figure in the pantheon," a choice I applaud.
But Lind chooses Douglass, I believe, chiefly for his statements opposing special assistance
to blacks, which Lind views as manifestos against affirmative action and multiculturalism.
Lind fails to recognize that Douglass nonetheless supported many race-targeted Reconstruction efforts, such as the federally chartered Freedmen's Savings Bank he eventually
headed, because Douglass saw those efforts not as special favors but as steps that were necessary to counter ongoing discrimination, and as repayments to African-Americans of a
portion of the wealth they had built up for the nation (McFeely, 1991, 241–43, 284–86).

68. Spinner (1994, 170, 79–80) also endorses this sort of education, while noting that it may
not satisfy those who seek stronger curricular affirmation of their subgroups.

69. This argument is developed in somewhat different form in R. M. Smith, 1993b, 197–210.

70. Works arguing in this direction include Sen, 1985; Smith, 1985; Raz, 1986; Macedo, 1990;
Galston, 1991; Moon, 1993; Spinner, 1994; Kymlicka, 1995, 163.

71. For this reason my argument for liberal purposes has a distinctly more affirmative and
transformative spirit than that of William Galston, to whose work I am nonetheless indebted. Despite the title of his best-known book (Liberal Purposes), Galston's endorsement
of the pursuit of liberal goals is rather anxious and half-hearted. He stresses that the civil
rights movement broke down a "cultural consensus" on forms of "traditional morality"
that he concedes involved the marginalization and "thorough" subordination of many
racial, ethnic, and religious outsiders. He worries that the erosion of such traditions has
nonetheless produced many social ills, such as "crime, drugs, and teenage pregnancy."
Hence he calls for renewed accommodation of America's nonliberal traditions via a "functional traditionalism" that assists aspects of what I have termed "ascriptive Americanism"
when they appear to foster virtues needed to make a liberal society operate successfully
(Galston, 1991, 268–89).

I fear that this functionalist traditionalism is likely in practice to be a formula for acquiescence in the face of resurgent forms of ascriptive Americanism that will be excessively
illiberal and undemocratic, contrary to Galston's intentions. It is hard to believe that Galston's recommendations, which include making divorce more difficult and allowing moments for prayer in schools, will help solve the social pathologies that concern him. These

steps merely signal uneasiness about liberalizing changes. I think that both the extensive political appeal and the limited contributions to liberal virtues provided by ascriptive Americanism can instead be obtained by more unqualifiedly liberal democratic conceptions of civic identity of the sort I sketch here. The task of liberals should not be to accommodate illiberal traditions but to make full and honest cases for the contributions of past and present liberal democratizing reforms to better lives for a broader range of Americans, and to suggest how the deep problems that persist can be ameliorated in ways consonant with liberal purposes and values. Rather than sanction prayer publicly or pressure a man and woman to stay married when neither wants to, for example, it makes more sense to insist that education give greater recognition to the historical role of religion in American life, and to require parents to meet their child care responsibilities regardless of their marital status.

72. For a related argument that liberal aims of securing human agency require governmental efforts to promote economic welfare, see Moon, 1993, 121–45.

73. But insofar as those obligations are understood to flow from membership in a consensual national political endeavor, they require extensive respect for the rights of minority groups that are part of that broader nation only involuntarily, like many of the North American aboriginal peoples. Although there is a risk today that persons with relatively little connection to their ancestral communities will assert tribal identity to win legal benefits, many Native Americans can claim to be U.S. citizens more by coercion than consent. The arguments for unusual autonomy rights for these peoples advanced by revisionist liberals like Kymlicka and Spinner have great force. In *The Boundaries of Citizenship* Spinner argues in detail for greater autonomy rights for the Amish as well as Native Americans, and for majority minority districts and some other special empowering institutions for African-Americans, in pursuit of an ultimate goal not of cultural pluralism but "pluralistic integration" (Spinner, 1994, 73–108, 122–33, 200nn28–29). My argument here is in the same general spirit, though with some particular disagreements.

74. For a case study of how Chinese-Americans in Mississippi achieved acceptance by whites through endorsing segregation of blacks, see Rhee, 1994.

75. These first two points are also suggested briefly but deftly in Kiss, 1996, 320.

Bibliography

Ackerman, B. A. 1980. *Social Justice in the Liberal State.* New Haven: Yale University Press.

———. 1983. "What Is Neutral About Neutrality?" *Ethics* 93:372–90.

———. 1991. *We the People: Foundations.* Cambridge: Harvard University Press.

Adams, C. F. 1908. "'The Solid South' and the Afro American Race Problem." Boston.

Adams, H. 1964 (orig. 1918). *The Education of Henry Adams,* 2 vols. New York: Time, Incorporated.

Adams, J. 1954. *The Political Writings of John Adams.* Ed. G. A. Peek, Jr. Indianapolis: Bobbs-Merrill.

Ahern, W. H. 1979. "Laissez-Faire vs. Equal Rights: Liberal Republicans and Limits to Reconstruction." *Phylon* 10:52–65.

Ahlstrom, S. E. 1972. *A Religious History of the American People.* New Haven: Yale University Press.

Alger, H. 1962 (orig. 1867). *Ragged Dick and Mark, the Match Boy.* New York: Collier Books.

Amar, A. R. 1991. "The Bill of Rights as a Constitution." *Yale Law Journal* 100:1131–1210.

Ammon, H. 1971. *James Monroe: The Quest for National Identity.* New York: McGraw-Hill.

Anbinder, T. 1992. *Nativism and Slavery: The Northern Know-Nothings and the Politics of the 1850s.* New York: Oxford University Press.

Anderson, B. R. O. 1983. *Imagined Communities: Reflections on the Origin and Spread of Nationalism.* London: Verso.

Anderson, J. D. 1988. *The Education of Blacks in the South, 1860–1935.* Chapel Hill: University of North Carolina Press.

Anderson, S. 1981. *Race and Rapprochement: Anglo-Saxonism and Anglo-American Relations, 1895–1904.* Rutherford, N.J.: Fairleigh Dickinson University Press.

Ansley, F. L. 1989. "Stirring the Ashes: Race, Class, and the Future of Civil Rights Scholarship." *Cornell Law Review* 74:993–1077.

Antholis, W. J. K. 1993. "Liberal Democratic Theory and the Transformation of Sovereignty." Ph.D. dissertation, Yale University.

Appleby, J. O. 1978a. *Economic Thought and Ideology in Seventeenth-Century England.* Princeton: Princeton University Press.

———. 1978b. "The Social Origins of American Revolutionary Ideology." *Journal of American History* 64:935–58.

———. 1984. *Capitalism and a New Social Order: The Republican Vision of the 1790s.* New York: New York University Press.

Archdeacon, T. J. 1983. *Becoming American: An Ethnic History.* New York: Free Press.

Arieli, Y. 1964. *Individualism and Nationalism in American Ideology.* Cambridge: Harvard University Press.

Aristotle. 1968. *The Politics of Aristotle.* Ed. E. Barker. New York: Oxford University Press.

Axtell, J., ed. 1968. *The Educational Writings of John Locke.* Cambridge: Cambridge University Press.

Baer, J. A. 1978. *The Chains of Protection.* Westport, Conn.: Greenwood Press.

Bailyn, B. 1967. *The Ideological Origins of the American Revolution.* Cambridge: Belknap Press.

———. 1986. *The Peopling of British North America: An Introduction.* New York: Knopf.

Bailyn, B., and Morgan, P. D. 1991. Introduction. In *Strangers Within the Realm: Cultural Margins of the First British Empire.* Ed. B. Bailyn and P. D. Morgan. Chapel Hill: University of North Carolina Press.

Baker, P. 1984. "The Domestication of Politics: Women and American Political Society, 1780–1920." *American Historical Review* 89:620–47.

Balibar, E., and Wallerstein, I. 1991. *Race, Nation, Class: Ambiguous Identities.* New York: Verso.

Banning, L. 1978. *The Jeffersonian Persuasion: Evolution of a Party Ideology.* Ithaca: Cornell University Press.

———. 1986. "Jeffersonian Ideology Revisited: Liberal and Classical Ideas in the New American Republic." *William and Mary Quarterly* 63:3–34.

———. 1987. "The Problem of Power: Parties, Aristocracy, and Democracy in Revolutionary Thought." In *The American Revolution: Its Character and Limits.* Ed. J. P. Greene. New York: New York University Press.

Bannister, R. C. 1979. *Social Darwinism: Science and Myth in Anglo-American Social Thought.* Philadelphia: Temple University Press.

Barnes, C. A. 1983. *Journey from Jim Crow: The Desegregation of Southern Transit.* New York: Columbia University Press.

Barth, G. 1964. *Bitter Struggle: A History of the Chinese in the United States, 1850–1870.* Cambridge: Harvard University Press.

Barzelay, M., and Smith, R. M. 1987. "The One Best System? A Political Analysis of Neoclassical Institutionalist Perspectives on the Modern Corporation." In *Corporations and Society: Power and Responsibility.* Ed. W. J. Samuels and A. S. Miller. Westport, Conn.: Greenwood Press.

Basch, N. 1986. "The Emerging Legal History of Women in the United States: Property, Divorce, and the Constitution." *Signs* 12:97–117.

Battistoni, R. M. 1985. *Public Schooling and the Education of Democratic Citizens.* Jackson: University Press of Mississippi.

Baxter, S. B., ed. 1968. *Basic Documents of English History.* Boston: Houghton Mifflin.

Bederman, G. 1995. *Manliness and Civilization: A Cultural History of Gender and Race in the United States, 1880–1917.* Chicago: University of Chicago Press.

Beecher, C. E. 1851. *The True Remedy for the Wrongs of Women.* Boston: Phillips, Sampson and Company.

Beecher, L. 1835. *Plea for the West.* Cincinnati: Truman and Smith.

Beer, S. H. 1966. "Liberalism and the National Idea." *Public Interest* 5:70–82.

———. 1978. "In Search of a New Public Philosophy." In *The New American Political System.* Ed. A. King. Washington, D.C.: American Enterprise Institute.

———. 1984. "Liberty and Union: Walt Whitman's Idea of the Nation." *Political Theory* 12:361–86.

———. 1993. *To Make A Nation: The Rediscovery of American Federalism.* Cambridge: Belknap Press.

Bell, D. 1992. *Race, Racism, and American Law.* 3d ed. Boston: Little, Brown.

Bellah, R. N., Madsen, R., Sullivan, W. M., Swidler, A., and Tipton, S. M. 1985. *Habits of the Heart: Individualism and Commitment in Public Life.* Berkeley: University of California Press.

Bellamy, E. 1967 (orig. 1888). *Looking Backward 2000–1887.* Ed. J. L. Thomas. Cambridge: Harvard University Press.

Belz, H. 1976. *A New Birth of Freedom: The Republican Party and Freedmen's Rights, 1861 to 1866.* Westport, Conn.: Greenwood Press.

———. 1978. *Emancipation and Equal Rights: Politics and Constitutionalism in the Civil War Era.* New York: W. W. Norton.

Ben-Atar, D. S. 1993. *The Origins of Jeffersonian Commercial Policy and Diplomacy.* New York: St. Martin's Press.

Bender, T. 1978. *Community and Social Change in America.* New Brunswick, N.J.: Rutgers University Press.

Bendix, R. 1964. *Nation-Building and Citizenship: Studies of Our Changing Social Order.* New York: John Wiley and Sons.

Benedict, M. L. 1974. *A Compromise of Principle: Congressional Republicans and Reconstruction, 1863–1869.* New York: W. W. Norton.

———. 1979. "Preserving Federalism: Reconstruction and the Waite Court." *Supreme Court Review 1978.* Ed. P. B. Kurland and G. Casper. Chicago: University of Chicago Press.

———. 1981. "Free Labor Ideology and the Meaning of the Civil War and Reconstruction." *Reviews in American History* 9:179–85.

———. 1985. "Laissez-Faire and Liberty: A Re-evaluation of the Meaning and Origins of Laissez-Faire Constitutionalism." *Law and History Review* 3:293–331.

Bennett, D. H. 1988. *The Party of Fear: From Nativist Movements to the New Right in American History.* New York: Random House.

Bennett, M. T. 1963. *American Immigration Policies: A History.* Washington, D.C.: Public Affairs Press.

Bensel, R. F. 1984. *Sectionalism and American Political Development, 1880 1980.* Madison: University of Wisconsin Press.

———. 1990. *Yankee Leviathan: The Origins of Central State Authority in America, 1859–1877.* New York: Cambridge University Press.

Bercovitch, S. 1978. *The American Jeremiad.* Madison: Wisconsin University Press.

Berens, J. F. 1968. *Providence and Patriotism in Early America, 1640–1815.* Charlottesville: University Press of Virginia.

Berger, R. 1977. *Government by Judiciary: The Transformation of the Fourteenth Amendment.* Cambridge: Harvard University Press.

Berlin, I. 1974. *Slaves Without Masters: The Free Negro in the Antebellum South.* New York: Pantheon.

———. 1976. "The Revolution in Black Life." In *The American Revolution: Explorations in the History of American Radicalism.* Ed. A. F. Young. Dekalb: Northern Illinois University Press.

Berman, H. J. 1983. *Law and Revolution: The Formation of the Western Legal Tradition.* Cambridge: Harvard University Press.

Best, J. 1984. *National Representation for the District of Columbia.* Frederick, Md.: University Publications of America.

Bickel, A. M. 1975. *The Morality of Consent.* New Haven: Yale University Press.

Biorcio, R., and Mannheimer, R. 1995. "Relationships between Citizens and Political Parties." In *Citizens and the State.* Ed. H. Klingemann and D. Fuchs. New York: Oxford University Press.

Black, B. A. 1975–76. "The Constitution of Empire: The Case for the Colonists." *University of Pennsylvania Law Review* 124:1157–1211.

Black, C. L. 1970. "The Unfinished Business of the Warren Court." *Washington Law Review* 46:1–44.

Blackstone, W. 1979. *Commentaries on the Laws of England.* Chicago: University of Chicago Press.

Blau, J., ed. 1954. *Social Theories of Jacksonian Democracy.* Indianapolis: Bobbs-Merrill.

Bloom, A. 1987. *The Closing of the American Mind.* New York: Simon and Schuster.

Boli, J. 1987. "Human Rights or State Expansion? Cross-National Definitions of Constitutional Rights, 1879–1970." In *Institutional Structure: Constituting State, Society, an the Individual.* Ed. J. Meyer, J. Boli, and G. M. Thomas. Newbury Park, Calif.: Sage.

Boller, P. F., Jr. 1969. *American Thought in Transition: The Impact of Evolutionary Naturalism, 1865–1900.* Boston: Rand-McNally.

Bontemps, A. W., ed. 1963. *American Negro Poetry.* New York: Hill and Wang.

Boorstin, D. J. 1953. *The Genius of American Politics.* Chicago: University of Chicago Press.

———. 1967 (orig. 1965). *The Americans: The National Experience.* New York: Vintage Books.

Bordin, R. 1981. *Women and Temperance: The Quest for Power and Liberty, 1873–1900.* Philadelphia: Temple University Press.

Boritt, G. S. 1978. *Lincoln and the Economics of the American Dream.* Memphis: Memphis State University Press.

Bourne, R. 1964. *War and the Intellectuals.* Ed. C. Resek. New York: Harper & Row.

———. 1977. *The Radical Will: Selected Writings, 1911–1918.* Ed. O. Hansen. New York: Urizen Books.

Bowles, S., and Gintis, H. 1976. *Schooling in Capitalist America: Educational Reform and the Contradictions of Economic Life.* New York: Basic Books.

Bredbenner, C. D. 1990. "Toward Independent Citizenship: Married Women's Nationality Rights in the United States: 1855–1937." Ph.D. dissertation, University of Virginia. Ann Arbor: UMI.

Bresnahan, E., 1994. "Responding to Liberalism's 'Women's Problem': A Feminist Critique of Communitarianism." Ph.D. dissertation, Yale University.

Brimelow, P. 1995. *Alien Nation: Common Sense about America's Immigration Disaster.* New York: Random House.

Brinton, D. G. 1895. "The Aims of Anthropology." *Science* 2:241–52.

Brock, W. R. 1975. "Reconstruction and the American Party System." In *A Nation Divided: Problems and Issues of the Civil War and Reconstruction.* Ed. G. M. Fredrickson. Minneapolis: Burgess Publishing.

Brubaker, W. R., ed. 1989. *Immigration and the Politics of Citizenship in Europe and North America.* Lanham, Md.: University Press of America.

———. 1992. *Citizenship and Nationhood in France and Germany.* Cambridge: Harvard University Press.

Buenker, J. D. 1988. "Sovereign Individuals and Organic Networks: Political Cultures in Conflict During the Progressive Era." *American Quarterly* 40:187–204.

Burke, J. C. 1969. "The Cherokee Cases: A Study in Law, Politics, and Morality." *Stanford Law Review* 21:500–531.

Burlamaqui, J. J. 1792. *The Principles of Natural and Political Law.* Trans. T. Nugent. Boston: Joseph Blumsted.

Burnham, W. D. 1970. *Critical Elections and the Mainsprings of American Politics.* New York: W. W. Norton.

———. 1982. *The Current Crisis in American Politics.* New York: Oxford University Press.

Cable, J. L. 1943. *Loss of Citizenship; Denaturalization; The Alien in Wartime.* Washington, D.C.: National Law Book Company.

Cabranes, J. 1979. *Citizenship and the American Empire.* New Haven: Yale University Press.

———. 1986. "Book Review: Puerto Rico: Colonialism as Constitutional Doctrine." *Harvard Law Review* 100:450–64.

Calabresi, G. 1982. *A Common Law for the Age of Statutes.* Cambridge: Harvard University Press.

Calhoon, R. M. 1987. "The Reintegration of the Loyalists and the Disaffected." In *The American Revolution: Its Character and Limits.* Ed. J. P. Greene. New York: New York University Press.

Calhoun, J. 1953. *A Disquisition on Government.* Indianapolis: Bobbs-Merrill.

Carens, J. H. 1987. "Who Belongs? Theoretical and Legal Questions about Birthright Citizenship in the United States." *University of Toronto Law Journal* 37:413–43.

Carlson, R. A. 1987. *The Americanization Syndrome: A Quest for Conformity.* London: Croom Helm.

Carp, E. W. 1987. "The Problem of National Defense in the Early American Republic." In *The American Revolution: Its Character and Limits.* Ed. J. P. Greene. New York: New York University Press.

Carr, R. 1984. *Puerto Rico: A Colonial Experiment.* New York: New York University Press.

Carter, N. C. 1976. "Race and Power Politics as Aspects of Federal Guardianship over American Indians: Land-Related Cases, 1887–1924." *American Indian Law Journal* 4:197–248.

Ceaser, J. W. 1979. *Presidential Selection: Theory and Development.* Princeton: Princeton University Press.

Cell, J. W. 1982. *The Highest Stage of White Supremacy: The Origins of Segregation in South Africa and the American South.* New York: Cambridge University Press.

Chambers, W. N., and Davis, P. C. 1978. "Party, Competition, and Mass Participation: The Case of the Democratizing Party System, 1824–1852." In *The History of American Electoral Behavior.* Ed. J. H. Silbey, A. G. Bogue, and W. H. Flanigan. Princeton: Princeton University Press.

Chase, H., Krislov, S., Boyer, K. O., Clark, J. N., comps. 1976. *Biographical Dictionary of the Federal Judiciary.* Detroit: Gale Research.

Chen, J. 1980. *The Chinese of America.* San Francisco: Harper and Row.

Child, L. M. 1845. *Brief History of the Condition of Women, in Various Ages and Nations.* 5th ed. 2 vols. New York: C. S. Francis.

Chused, R. "Married Women's Property Law: 1800–1850." *Georgetown Law Journal* 71:1359–1425.

Clay, H. 1842. *Speeches of the Hon. Henry Clay of the Congress of the United States.* Ed. R. Chambers. Cincinnati: Shepard and Stearns.

Clinton, C. 1984. *The Other Civil War: American Women in the Nineteenth Century.* New York: Hill and Wang.

Cohen, F. S. 1942. *Handbook of Federal Indian Law.* Washington, D.C.: U.S. Government Printing Office.

———. 1982. *Felix Cohen's Handbook of Federal Indian Law.* Ed. R. Strickland et al. Charlottesville, Va.: Michie.

Coleman, M. C. 1993. *American Indian Children at School, 1850–1930.* Jackson: University Press of Mississippi.

Colley, L. 1992. *Britons: Forging the Nation, 1707–1837.* New Haven: Yale University Press.

Congressional Quarterly. 1982. *Congressional Quarterly's Guide to Congress.* 3d ed. Washington, D.C.: Congressional Quarterly Press.

Conrad, S. A. 1984. "Polite Foundation: Citizenship and Common Sense in James Wilson's Republican Theory." In P. Kurland, ed., *Supreme Court Review.* Chicago: University of Chicago Press.

Corwin, E. S. 1955 (orig. 1928–1929). *The "Higher Law" Background of American Constitutional Law*. Ithaca: Cornell University Press.

Cott, N. F. 1977. *The Bonds of Womanhood: "Women's Sphere" in New England, 1780–1835*. New Haven: Yale University Press.

———. 1987. *The Grounding of Modern Feminism*. New Haven: Yale University Press.

———. 1989. "What's in a Name? The Limits of 'Social Feminism'; or, Expanding the Vocabulary of Women's History." *Journal of American History* 76:809–29.

Cover, R. M. 1975. *Justice Accused: Antislavery and the Judicial Process*. New Haven: Yale University Press.

Crane, E. F. 1987. "Dependence in the Era of Independence: The Role of Women in a Republican Society." In *The American Revolution: Its Character and Limits*. Ed. J. P. Greene. New York: New York University Press.

Cremin, L. A. 1980. *American Education: The National Experience, 1783–1876*. New York: Harper and Row.

———. 1988. *American Education: The Metropolitan Experience, 1876–1980*. New York: Harper and Row.

Crenshaw, K. W. 1988. "Race, Reform, and Retrenchment: Transformation and Legitimation in Antidiscrimination Law." *Harvard Law Review* 101:1331–87.

Croly, H. 1914. *Progressive Democracy*. New York: Macmillan.

———. 1963 (orig. 1909). *The Promise of American Life*. New York: E. P. Dutton.

Crunden, R. M. 1984. *Ministers of Reform: The Progressives' Achievement in American Civilization, 1889–1920*. Urbana: University of Illinois Press.

Curti, M. E. 1955. *Probing Our Past*. New York: Harper.

Curtis, M. K. 1986. *No State Shall Abridge: The Fourteenth Amendment and the Bill of Rights*. Durham, N.C.: Duke University Press.

Dahl, R. A. 1989. *Democracy and Its Critics*. New Haven: Yale University Press.

Damico, A. J. 1978. *Individuality and Community: The Social and Political Thought of John Dewey*. Gainesville: University Presses of Florida.

Dangerfield, G. 1965. *The Awakening of American Nationalism, 1815–1828*. New York: Harper and Row.

Daniels, R. 1990. *Coming to America: A History of Immigration and Ethnicity in American Life*. New York: HarperCollins.

Darwin, C. 1936. *The Origin of Species and The Descent of Man*. New York: Modern Library.

Davis, D. B. 1966. *The Problem of Slavery in Western Culture*. Ithaca: Cornell University Press.

———. 1975. *The Problem of Slavery in the Age of Revolution, 1770–1823*. Ithaca: Cornell University Press.

Degler, C. 1980. *At Odds: Women and the Family in America from the Revolution to the Present*. Oxford: Oxford University Press.

———. 1991. *In Search of Human Nature: The Decline and Revival of Darwinism in American Social Thought*. New York: Oxford University Press.

Delany, M. R. 1968 (orig. 1852). *The Condition, Elevation, Emigration, and Destiny of the Colored People of the United States, Politically Considered*. New York: Arno Press and the New York Times.

Delgado, R. 1994. "Rodrigo's Seventh Chronicle: Race, Democracy and the State." *UCLA Law Review* 41:721–57.

Deloria, V., Jr., and Lytle, C. M. 1983. *American Indians, American Justice*. Austin: University of Texas Press.

Dennison, G. M. 1976. *The Dorr War: Republicanism on Trial, 1831–1861*. Lexington: University Press of Kentucky.

DePauw, L. G. 1977. "Women and the Law: The Colonial Period." *Human Rights* 6:107–13.

Devigne, R. 1994. *Recasting Conservatism: Oakeshott, Strauss, and the Response to Postmodernism.* New Haven: Yale University Press.

Dewey, J. 1920. *Reconstruction in Philosophy.* Boston: Beacon Press (enlarged ed., 1948).

———. 1927. *The Public and Its Problems.* New York: Henry Holt.

———. 1966 (orig. 1916). *Democracy and Education: An Introduction to the Philosophy of Education.* New York: The Free Press.

De Witt, B. P. 1968 (orig. 1915). *The Progressive Movement: A Non-partisan, Comprehensive Discussion of Current Tendencies in American Politics.* Seattle: University of Washington Press.

Diggins, J. P. 1984. *The Lost Soul of American Politics: Virtue, Self-Interest, and the Foundations of Liberalism.* New York: Basic Books.

Dippie, B. W. 1982. *The Vanishing American: White Attitudes and U.S. Indian Policy.* Middletown, Conn.: Wesleyan University Press.

Dixon, R. G., Jr. 1968. *Democratic Representation: Reapportionment in Law and Politics.* New York: Oxford University Press.

Dodd, E. M. 1954. *American Business Corporations until 1860, With Special Reference to Massachusetts.* Cambridge: Harvard University Press.

Dolbeare, K., ed. 1981. *American Political Thought.* Monterey, Calif.: Duxbury Press.

———. 1984. *American Political Thought.* Rev. ed. Chatham, N.J.: Chatham House.

Donald, D. 1970. *Charles Sumner and the Rights of Man.* New York: Knopf.

Douglass, F. 1950 (orig. 1860). "The Constitution of the United States: Is it Pro-Slavery or Anti-Slavery?" In *Life and Writings of Frederick Douglass,* Vol. 2 (of 5). Ed. P. Foner. New York: International Publishers.

———. 1972 (orig. 1852). "Fourth of July Oration." In *American Political Thought.* Ed. L. I. Peterman and L. F. Wechsler. New York: Appleton-Century-Crofts.

Downs, A. 1957. *An Economic Theory of Democracy.* New York: Harper and Row.

D'Souza, D. 1995. *The End of Racism: Principles for a Multiracial Society.* New York: Free Press.

Dry, M., and Storing, H., eds. 1985 (orig. 1981). *The Anti-Federalist: An Abridgment of the Complete Anti-Federalist.* Chicago: University of Chicago Press.

DuBois, E. C. 1978, *Feminism and Suffrage: The Emergence of an Independent Women's Movement in America, 1848–1864..* Ithaca: Cornell University Press.

———. 1981. *Elizabeth Cady Stanton, Susan B. Anthony: Correspondence, Writings, Speeches.* New York: Schocken Books.

———. 1988. "Outgrowing the Compact of the Fathers: Equal Rights, Woman Suffrage, and the United States Constitution, 1820–1878." In *The Constitution and American Life.* Ed. D. Thelen. Ithaca: Cornell University Press.

Du Bois, W. E. B. 1968 (orig. 1940). *Dusk of Dawn: An Essay Toward an Autobiography of a Race Concept.* New York: Schocken Books.

———. 1992 (orig. 1935). *Black Reconstruction in America.* New York: Atheneum.

Duncan-Clark, S. J. 1913. *The Progressive Movement: Its Principles and Its Programme.* Boston: Small, Maynard and Company.

Dunn, J. 1969. *The Political Thought of John Locke.* Cambridge: Cambridge University Press.

Dworetz, S. M. 1990. *The Unvarnished Doctrine: Locke, Liberalism, and the American Revolution.* Durham, N.C.: Duke University Press.

Eaton, J. 1874. *A Statement of the Theory of Education in the United States of America.* Washington, D.C.: U.S. Government Printing Office.

Eisele, J. C. 1975. "John Dewey and the Immigrants." *History of Education Quarterly* 15:67–86.

Eisenach, E. J. 1994. *The Lost Promise of Progressivism.* Lawrence: University Press of Kansas.

Eisenstein, Z. 1981. *The Radical Future of Liberal Feminism*. New York: Longman.

Elkins, S., and McKitrick, E. 1993. *The Age of Federalism*. New York: Oxford University Press.

Elliott, W. E. 1974. *The Rise of Guardian Democracy: The Supreme Court's Role in Voting Rights Disputes, 1845–1969*. Cambridge: Harvard University Press.

Ellis, R. J. 1991. "Legitimating Slavery in the Old South: The Effect of Political Institutions on Ideology." *Studies in American Political Development* 5:340–51.

Elshtain, J. B. 1981. *Public Man, Private Woman*. Princeton: Princeton University Press.

Ely, J. W., Jr. 1995. *The Chief Justiceship of Melville W. Fuller*. Columbia: University of South Carolina Press.

Epstein, B. L. 1981. *The Politics of Domesticity*. Middletown, Conn.: Wesleyan University Press.

Epstein, D. F. 1984. *The Political Theory of the Federalist*. Chicago: University of Chicago Press.

Epstein, R. A. 1992. *Forbidden Grounds: The Case Against Employment Discrimination Laws*. Cambridge: Harvard University Press.

Ericson, D. F. 1993. *The Shaping of American Liberalism: The Debates over Ratification, Nullification, and Slavery*. Chicago: University of Chicago Press.

Ericson, R. 1970. "The Indian Battle for Self-Determination." *California Law Review* 58:445–90.

Fairman, C. 1939. *Mr. Justice Miller and the Supreme Court, 1862–1890*. Cambridge: Harvard University Press.

Farber, D. A., and Muench, J. E. 1984. "The Ideological Origins of the Fourteenth Amendment." *Constitutional Commentary* 1:235–79.

Farr, J. 1986. "'So Vile and Miserable an Estate': The Problem of Slavery in Locke's Political Thought." *Political Theory* 14:263–89.

Farrand, M., ed. 1966. *The Records of the Federal Convention of 1787*. 4 vols. New Haven: Yale University Press.

Fehrenbacher, D. E. 1978. *The Dred Scott Case: Its Significance in American Law and Politics*. New York: Oxford University Press.

———. 1981. *Slavery, Law, and Politics: The Dred Scott Case in Historical Perspective*. New York: Oxford University Press.

———. 1984. "The Federal Government and Slavery." Claremont, Calif.: The Claremont Institute for the Study of Statesmanship and Political Philosophy, Bicentennial Essay 1.

Fields, B. J. 1990. "Slavery, Race and Ideology in the United States of America." *New Left Review* 181:95–118.

Fink, H. P., and Tushnet, M. V. 1987. *Federal Jurisdiction: Policy and Practice*. Charlottesville, Va.: Michie.

Finkelman, P. 1981. *An Imperfect Union: Slavery, Federalism, and Country*. Chapel Hill: University of North Carolina Press.

Fiss, O. M. 1993. *History of the Supreme Court of the United States*, vol. VIII, *Troubled Beginnings of the Modern State, 1888–1910*. New York: Macmillan.

Fitzhugh, G. 1965 (orig. 1854). *Sociology for the South, or the Failure of Free Society*. New York: Burt Franklin.

Flanigan, W. H., and Zingale, N. H. 1991. *Political Behavior of the American Electorate*. 7th ed. Washington, D.C.: Congressional Quarterly Press.

Flexner, E. 1972. *Mary Wollstonecraft: A Biography*. New York: Coward, McCann and Geoghegan.

———. 1975. *Century of Struggle: The Woman's Rights Movement in the United States*. Cambridge: Belknap Press.

Fliegelman, J. 1982. *Prodigals and Pilgrims: The American Revolution Against Patriarchal Authority, 1750–1800*. New York: Cambridge University Press.

Foner, E. 1970. *Free Soil, Free Labor, Free Men*. New York: Oxford University Press.

———. 1976. "Tom Paine's Republic: Radical Ideology and Social Change." In *The American Revolution: Explorations in the History of American Radicalism.* Ed. A. F. Young. Dekalb: Northern Illinois University Press.

———. 1980. *Politics and Ideology in the Age of the Civil War.* Oxford: Oxford University Press.

———. 1988. *Reconstruction: America's Unfinished Revolution, 1863–1877.* New York: Harper and Row.

Foner, P. 1975. *History of Black Americans: From Africa to the Emergence of the Cotton Kingdom.* Westport, Conn.: Greenwood Press.

———. 1983a. *History of Black Americans: From the Emergence of the Cotton Kingdom to the Eve of the Compromise of 1850.* Westport, Conn.: Greenwood Press.

———. 1983b. *History of Black Americans: From the Compromise of 1850 to the End of the Civil War.* Westport, Conn.: Greenwood Press.

Forbath, W. E. 1985. "The Ambiguities of Free Labor: Labor and the Law in the Gilded Age." *Wisconsin Law Review* 1985:767–817.

Forten, J. 1990 (orig. 1813). "Letters from a Man of Colour on a Late Bill Before the Senate of Pennsylvania." In *Race and Revolution,* G. Nash. Madison, Wisc.: Madison House.

Foss, R. J. 1994. "The Demise of the Homosexual Exclusion: New Possibilities for Gay and Lesbian Immigration." *Harvard Civil Rights-Civil Liberties Law Review* 29:439–75.

Frankfurter, F. 1928. "Distribution of Judicial Power Between United States and State Courts." *Cornell Law Quarterly* 13:499–530.

Franklin, F. G. 1969 (orig. 1906). *A Legislative History of Naturalization.* Chicago: University of Chicago Press.

Franklin, J. H. 1980. *From Slavery to Freedom: A History of Negro Americans.* 5th ed. New York: Knopf.

Franklin, J. H., and Moss, A. A., Jr. 1988. *From Slavery to Freedom: A History of Negro Americans.* 6th ed. New York: Knopf.

Fredrickson, G. M. 1971. *The Black Image in the White Mind: The Debate on Afro-American Character and Destiny, 1817–1914.* New York: Harper and Row.

———. 1981. *White Supremacy: A Comparative Study in American and South African History.* Oxford: Oxford University Press.

Frehling, W. W. 1966. *Prelude to Civil War. The Nullification Controversy in South Carolina, 1816–1836.* New York: Harper and Row.

Frey, S. R. 1987. "Liberty, Equality, and Slavery: The Paradox of the American Revolution." In *The American Revolution: Its Character and Limits.* Ed. J. P. Greene. New York: New York University Press.

Friedman, L. M. 1973. *A History of American Law.* New York: Simon and Schuster.

———. 1985. *A History of American Law.* 2d ed. New York: Simon and Schuster.

Friedman, L. M., and Scheiber, H. N., eds. 1988. *American Law and the Constitutional Order: Historical Perspectives.* Cambridge: Harvard University Press.

Friendly, H. J. 1928. "The Historic Basis of Diversity Jurisdiction." *Harvard Law Review* 41:483–510.

Fritz, C. G. 1988. "A Nineteenth-Century 'Habeas Corpus Mill': The Chinese Before the Federal Courts in California." *American Journal of Legal History* 32:347–72.

Fuchs, L. H. 1990. *The American Kaleidoscope: Race, Ethnicity, and the Civic Culture.* Hanover, N.H.: University Press of New England.

Galambos, L. 1970. "The Emerging Organizational Synthesis in Modern American History." *Business History Review* 44:279–90.

———. 1983. "Technology, Political Economy, and Professionalization: Central Themes of the Organizational Synthesis." *Business History Review* 57:471–93.

Galston, W. A. 1991. *Liberal Purposes: Goods, Virtues, and Duties in the Liberal State.* Cambridge: Cambridge University Press.

Gellner, E. 1965. *Thought and Change.* Chicago: University of Chicago Press.

———. 1983. *Nations and Nationalism.* Oxford: Basil Blackwell.

George, H. 1956 (orig. 1881). *Progress and Poverty.* New York: Robert Schalkenbach Foundation.

Genovese, E. D. 1971. *The World the Slaveholders Made: Two Essays in Interpretation.* New York: Vintage Books.

———. 1972. *Roll, Jordan, Roll: The World the Slaves Made.* New York: Vintage.

Gienapp, W. E. 1987. *The Origins of the Republican Party, 1852–1856.* Oxford: Oxford University Press.

Gilchrist, D. T., and Lewis, W. D., eds. 1965. *Economic Change in the Civil War Era.* Greenville, Del.: Eleutherian Mills-Hagley Foundation.

Gillette, W. 1965. *The Right to Vote: Politics and the Passage of the Fifteenth Amendment.* Baltimore: Johns Hopkins University Press.

Gilman, C. P. 1966 (orig. 1898). *Women and Economics: A Study of the Economic Relation Between Men and Women as a Factor in Social Evolution.* Ed. C. N. Degler. New York: Harper and Row.

Gillman, H. 1993. *The Constitution Besieged: The Rise and Demise of Lochner Era Police Powers Jurisprudence.* Durham, N.C.: Duke University Press.

Gleason, P. 1982 (orig. 1980). "American Identity and Americanization." In *Concepts of Ethnicity,* W. Petersen, M. Novak, and P. Gleason. Cambridge: Harvard University Press.

Goldberg, C. 1996. "Native Hawaiians Vote in Referendum Creating an Ethnic Government." *New York Times,* July 23, A10.

Goldman, E. F. 1952. *Rendezvous with Destiny.* New York: Knopf.

Goldman, S. 1982. *Constitutional Law and Supreme Court Decision-Making.* New York: Harper and Row.

Goldstein, R. J. 1978. *Political Repression in Modern America: From 1870 to the Present.* Cambridge: Schenkman Publishing.

Goodsell, W. 1923. *The Education of Women: Its Social Background and Its Problems.* New York: Macmillan.

Goodwyn, L. 1978. *The Populist Moment: A Short History of the Agrarian Revolt in America.* Oxford: Oxford University Press.

Gordon, M. 1964. *Assimilation in American Life.* New York: Oxford University Press.

———. 1978. *Human Nature, Class and Ethnicity.* New York: Oxford University Press.

———. 1981. "Models of Pluralism." *Annals of the American Academy of Political and Social Science* 454:178–88.

Gossett, T. F. 1963. *Race: The History of an Idea in America.* New York: Schocken Books.

Graber, M. A. 1991. *Transforming Free Speech: The Ambiguous Legacy of Civil Libertarianism.* Berkeley: University of California Press.

Grady, H. W. 1929 (orig. 1889). "The Race Problem." In *Famous Speeches by Eminent American Statesmen.* Ed. F. C. Hicks. St. Paul: West Publishing.

Graham, H. J. 1968. *Everyman's Constitution.* Madison: State Historical Society of Wisconsin.

Grant, M., and Davidson, C. S., eds. 1928. *The Founders of the Republic on Immigration, Naturalization and Aliens.* New York: Charles Scribner's Sons.

Gray, J. 1992. "Against the New Liberalism: Rawls, Dworkin, and the Emptying of Political Life." *Times Literary Supplement,* July 3, 13–15.

———. 1994. "After the New Liberalism." *Social Research* 61:719–35.

Green, A. 1990. *Education and State Formation: The Rise of Education Systems in England, France and the USA*. London: Macmillan.

Green, C. M. 1962. *Washington: Village and Capital, 1800–1878*. Princeton: Princeton University Press.

———. 1967. *The Secret City: A History of Race Relations in the Nation's Capital*. Princeton: Princeton University Press.

Green, F. 1946. "Corporations as Persons, Citizens, and Possessors of Liberty." *University of Pennsylvania Law Review* 94:202–37.

Greenfeld, L. 1992. *Nationalism: Five Roads to Modernity*. Cambridge: Harvard University Press.

Greenstone, J. D. 1986. "Political Culture and American Political Development: Liberty, Union, and the Liberal Bipolarity." *Studies in American Political Development* 1:1–49.

———. 1993. *The Lincoln Persuasion: Remaking American Liberalism*. Princeton: Princeton University Press.

Grimké, A. E. 1838. *Letters to Catharine E. Beecher*. Boston: Isaac Knapp.

Gruber, M. 1968. *Women in American Politics*. Oshkosh, Wisc.: Academic Press.

Gunther, G. 1958. "Governmental Power and New York Indians: A Reassessment of a Persistent Problem of Federal-State Relations." *Buffalo Law Review* 8:1–26.

———. 1991. *Constitutional Law*. 12th ed. Westbury, N.Y.: Foundation Press.

Hall, P., and Taylor, R. C. R. 1994. "Political Science and the Four New Institutionalisms." Paper presented at the Annual Meeting of the American Political Science Association, New York, September 1994.

Haller, J. S. 1971. *Outcasts from Evolution: Scientific Attitudes of Racial Inferiority, 1859–1900*. Urbana: University of Illinois Press.

Hamilton, A. 1985. *Selected Writings and Speeches of Alexander Hamilton*. Ed. M. J. Frisch. Washington, D.C.: American Enterprise Institute.

Harring, S. L. 1989. "The Incorporation of Alaskan Natives Under American Law: United States and Tlingit Sovereignty, 1867–1900." *Arizona Law Review* 31:279–327.

Harris, B. 1978. *Beyond Her Sphere: Women and the Professions*. Westport, Conn.: Greenwood Press.

Harris, C. I. 1993. "Whiteness as Property." *Harvard Law Review* 106:1710–91.

Hartog, H. 1988 (orig. 1987). "The Constitution of Aspiration and 'The Rights That Belong to Us All.'" In *The Constitution and American Life*. Ed. D. Thelen. Ithaca: Cornell University Press.

Hartz, L. 1955. *The Liberal Tradition in America*. New York: Harcourt Brace.

———. 1964. *The Founding of New Societies*. New York: Harcourt, Brace and World.

Hattam, V. 1993. *Labor Visions and State Power*. Princeton: Princeton University Press.

Hays, S. P. 1973 (orig. 1957). *The Response to Industrialism: 1885–1914*. Rept. Chicago: University of Chicago Press.

Heimert, A., and Delbanco, A., eds. 1985. *The Puritans in America: A Narrative Anthology*. Cambridge: Harvard University Press.

Henderson, G. C. 1918. *The Position of Foreign Corporations in American Constitutional Law: A Contribution to the History and Theory of Juristic Persons in Anglo-American Law*. Cambridge: Harvard University Press.

Henkin, L. 1986–87. "The Constitution and United States Sovereignty: A Century of Chinese Exclusion and Its Progeny." *Harvard Law Review* 100:853–86.

Herrnstein, R. J., and Murray, C. 1994. *The Bell Curve: Intelligence and Class Structure in American Life*. New York: The Free Press.

Higham, J. 1966 (orig. 1955). *Strangers in the Land: Patterns of American Nativism, 1860–1925.* New York: Atheneum Press.

———. 1974. "Hanging Together: Divergent Unities in American History. *Journal of American History* 61:5–28.

———. 1975. *Send These to Me.* New York: Atheneum Press.

———. 1986. "The Strange Career of *Strangers in the Land.*" *American Jewish History* 76:214–26.

———. 1988. "Afterword: Reflections on the Life of *Strangers in the Land.*" In *Strangers in the Land: Patterns of American Nativism, 1860–1925.* 2d ed. New Brunswick, N.J.: Rutgers University Press.

Hobsbawm, E. J. 1990. *Nations and Nationalism Since 1780: Programme, Myth, Reality.* Cambridge: Cambridge University Press.

Hofstadter, R. 1955. *Social Darwinism in American Thought.* Rev. ed. Boston: Beacon Press.

Hollinger, D. A. 1995. *Postethnic America: Beyond Multiculturalism.* New York: Basic Books.

Holmes, B. 1956. "Some Writings of William Torrey Harris." *British Journal of Educational Studies* 5:47–66.

Hong, N. 1990. "The Origin of American Legislation to Exclude and Deport Aliens for Their Political Beliefs, and Its Initial Review by the Courts." *Journal of Ethnic Studies* 18:2–36.

Horsman, R. 1981. *Race and Manifest Destiny.* Cambridge: Harvard University Press.

———. 1987. *Josiah Nott of Mobile: Southerner, Physician, and Racial Theorist.* Baton Rouge: Louisiana State University Press.

Hovenkamp, H. 1985. "Social Science and Segregation before *Brown.*" *Duke Law Journal* 1985:624–72.

Howe, D. W. 1979. *The Political Culture of American Whigs.* Chicago: University of Chicago Press.

Hoxie, F. E. 1984. *A Final Promise: The Campaign to Assimilate the Indians, 1880–1920.* Lincoln: University of Nebraska Press.

Hoyt, E. A. 1952. "Naturalization Under the American Colonies: Signs of a New Community." *Political Science Quarterly* 67:248–66.

Hunt, J. 1868. "The Negro's Place in Nature." New York: Van Evrie, Horton and Co.

Huntington, S. P. 1971. "Political Modernization: America vs. Europe." In *Nation and State Building in America: Comparative Historical Perspectives.* Ed. J. R. Hollingsworth. Boston: Little, Brown. (Orig. 1966. *World Politics* 18:378–414).

———. 1981. *American Politics: The Promise of Disharmony.* Cambridge: Harvard University Press.

Hurst, J. W. 1970. *The Legitimacy of the Business Corporation in the Law of the United States, 1780–1970.* Charlottesville: University Press of Virginia.

Hutchinson, E. P. 1981. *Legislative History of American Immigration Policy, 1798–1965.* Philadelphia: University of Pennsylvania Press.

Hyman, H. M. 1954. *Era of the Oath: National Loyalty Tests During the Civil War and Reconstruction.* Philadelphia: University of Pennsylvania Press.

———. 1959. *To Try Men's Souls: Loyalty Tests in American History.* Berkeley: University of California Press.

———. 1973. *A More Perfect Union: The Impact of the Civil War and Reconstruction on the Constitution.* New York: Knopf.

———. 1986. *American Singularity: The 1787 Northwest Ordinance, the 1862 Homestead and Morrill Acts, and the 1944 G.I. Bill.* Athens: University of Georgia Press.

Hyman, H. M., and Wiecek, W. M. 1982. *Equal Justice Under Law: Constitutional Development, 1835–1875.* New York: Harper and Row.

Hyneman, C. S., and Lutz, D. S., eds. 1983. *American Political Writings During the Founding Era, 1760–1805.* Indianapolis: Liberty Press.

Israel, F. L., ed. 1966. *State of the Union Messages of the Presidents,* vol. II. New York: Chelsea House.

Jackson, W. A. 1990. *Gunnar Myrdal and America's Conscience: Social Engineering and Racial Liberalism, 1938–1987.* Chapel Hill: University of North Carolina Press.

Jacobs, C. E. 1972. *The Eleventh Amendment and Sovereign Immunity.* Westport, Conn.: Greenwood Press.

Jaffa, H. V. 1975. *The Conditions of Freedom: Essays in Political Philosophy.* Baltimore: Johns Hopkins University Press.

———. 1982 (orig. 1959). *Crisis of the House Divided: An Interpretation of the Issues in the Lincoln-Douglas Debates.* Chicago: University of Chicago Press.

James, A. G. 1990. "Expatriation in the United States: Precept and Practice Today and Yesterday." *San Diego Law Review* 27:853–905.

Jefferson, T. 1955. *Notes on the State of Virginia.* Ed. W. Peden. Chapel Hill: University of North Carolina Press.

Jennings, F. 1976. "The Indians' Revolution." In *The American Revolution: Explorations in the History of American Radicalism.* Ed. A. F. Young. Dekalb: Northern Illinois University Press.

Jensen, M. 1950. *The New Nation: A History of the United States During the Confederation, 1781–1789.* (1st ed.) New York: Knopf.

Jensen, M., ed. 1967. *Tracts of the American Revolution, 1763–1776.* Indianapolis: Bobbs-Merrill.

Jillson, C. C. 1988. *Constitution Making: Conflict and Consensus in the Federal Convention of 1787.* New York: Agathon Press.

Johannsen, R. W., ed. 1965. *The Lincoln-Douglas Debates of 1858.* New York: Oxford University Press.

Jones, H. 1987. *Mutiny on the Amistad: The Saga of a Slave Revolt and Its Impact on American Abolition, Law, and Diplomacy.* New York: Oxford University Press.

Jordan, W. D. 1968. *White Over Black: American Attitudes Toward the Negro, 1550–1812.* Chapel Hill: University of North Carolina Press.

———. 1987. "On the Bracketing of Blacks and Women in the Same Agenda." In *The American Revolution: Its Character and Limits.* Ed. J. P. Greene. New York: New York University Press.

Kaczorowski, R. J. 1985. *The Politics of Judicial Interpretation: The Federal Courts, Department of Justice, and Civil Rights, 1866–1876.* Dobbs Ferry, N.Y.: Oceana Publications.

———. 1987. "To Begin the Nation Anew: Congress, Citizenship, and Civil Rights after the Civil War." *American Historical Review* 92:45–68.

Kaestle, C. F. 1983. *Pillars of the Republic: Common Schools and American Society, 1780–1880.* New York: Hill and Wang.

Kallen, H. 1924. *Culture and Democracy in the United States.* New York: Boni and Liveright.

Kames, Lord Henry Home. 1813. *Sketches of the History of Man,* vols. 1–3. Edinburgh: William Creech, and Bell and Bradfute.

Kaminsky, J. S. 1993. *A New History of Educational Philosophy.* Westport, Conn.: Greenwood Press.

Kansas, S. 1936. *Citizenship of the United States of America.* New York: Washington Publishing Co.

Karnow, S. 1989. *In Our Image: America's Empire in the Philippines.* New York: Random House.

Karst, K. L. 1989. *Belonging to America: Equal Citizenship and the Constitution.* New Haven: Yale University Press.

Kateb, G. 1984. "Democratic Individuality and the Claims of Politics." *Political Theory* 12:827–49.

Katz, M. B. 1968. *The Irony of Early School Reform: Education Innovation in Mid-Nineteenth Century Massachusetts.* Cambridge: Harvard University Press.

———. 1971. *Class, Bureaucracy, and Schools: The Illusion of Educational Change in America.* New York: Praeger.

Katznelson, I. 1981. *City Trenches.* Chicago: University of Chicago Press.

Katznelson, I., and Weir, M. 1985. *Schooling for All: Class, Race, and the Decline of the Democratic Ideal.* New York: Basic Books.

Kaye, H. L. 1984. *The Social Meaning of Modern Biology.* New Haven: Yale University Press.

Kedourie, E. 1961. *Nationalism.* Rev. ed. New York: Praeger.

Keller, M. 1977. *Affairs of State: Public Life in Late Nineteenth-Century America.* Cambridge: Harvard University Press.

Keller, R. H., Jr. 1983. *American Protestantism and United States Indian Policy, 1869–1882.* Lincoln: University of Nebraska Press.

Kelley, R. 1979. *The Cultural Pattern in American Politics: The First Century.* New York: Knopf.

Kelly, A. H., Harbison, W. A., and Belz, H. 1983. *The American Constitution: Its Origins and Development.* 6th ed. New York: W. W. Norton.

Kennedy, D. M. 1975. "Overview: The Progressive Era." *The Historian* 37:453–68.

Kennedy, R. 1986. "Race Relations Law and the Tradition of Celebration: The Case of Professor Schmidt." *Columbia Law Review* 86:1622–61.

Kens, P. 1990. *Judicial Power and Reform Politics: The Anatomy of Lochner v. New York.* Lawrence: University Press of Kansas.

Kerber, L. K. 1977. "From the Declaration of Independence to the Declaration of Sentiments: The Legal Status of Women in the Early Republic, 1776–1748." *Human Rights* 6:115–24.

———. 1980. *Women of the Republic.* Chapel Hill: University of North Carolina Press.

———. 1985. "The Republican Ideology of the Revolutionary Generation." *American Quarterly* 37:474–95.

———. 1992. "The Paradox of Women's Citizenship in the Early Republic: The Case of *Martin vs. Massachusetts,* 1805." *American Historical Review* 97:349–78.

———. 1995. "A Constitutional Right To Be Treated Like American Ladies: Women and the Obligations of Citizenship." In *U.S. History as Women's History: New Feminist Essays.* Ed. L. K. Kerber, A. Kessler-Harris, and K. K. Sklar. Chapel Hill: University of North Carolina Press.

Kersh, R. 1996. "Dreams of a 'More Perfect Union': A Central Dilemma of American Nation-Building, 1643–1898." Ph.D. dissertation, Yale University.

Kessler-Harris, A. 1982. *Out to Work: A History of Wage-Earning Women in the United States.* New York: Oxford University Press.

Kettner, J. 1978. *The Development of American Citizenship, 1608–1870.* Chapel Hill: University of North Carolina Press.

King, D. 1995. *Separate and Unequal: Black Americans and the U.S. Federal Government.* Oxford: Oxford University Press.

Kiss, E. 1996. "Five Theses on Nationalism." In *Nomos XXXVIII: Political Order.* Ed. I. Shapiro and R. Hardin. New York: New York University Press.

Kivisto, P. 1995. *Americans All: Race and Ethnic Relations in Historical, Structural, and Comparative Perspectives.* Belmont, Calif.: Wadsworth Publishing Company.

Klinkner, P. A., and Smith, R. M. (Forthcoming). *The Unsteady March: The Rise and Decline of U.S. Commitments to Racial Equality.* New York: Free Press.

Kloppenberg, J. T. 1986. *Uncertain Victory: Social Democracy and Progressivism in European and American Thought, 1870–1920.* Oxford: Oxford University Press.

———. 1987. "The Virtues of Liberalism: Christianity, Republicanism, and Ethics in Early American Political Discourse." *Journal of American History* 74:9–33.

Kobach, K. 1995. "The Origins of Regulatory Takings: Setting the Record Straight." Student essay, Yale Law School.

Kohn, H. 1957. *American Nationalism.* New York: Macmillan.

Konvitz, M. R. 1946. *The Alien and the Asiatic in American Law.* Ithaca: Cornell University Press.

Kotkin, J. 1993. *Tribes: How Race, Religion and Identity Determine Success in the New Global Economy.* New York: Random House.

Kousser, J. M. 1974. *The Shaping of Southern Politics: Suffrage Restriction and the Establishment of the One-Party South, 1880–1910.* New Haven: Yale University Press.

———. 1986. *Dead End: The Development of Nineteenth-Century Litigation on Racial Discrimination in Schools.* Oxford: Clarendon Press.

Kraditor, A. S. 1965. *The Ideas of the Woman Suffrage Movement, 1890–1920.* New York: Columbia University Press.

Kramnick, I., ed. 1987. *The Federalist Papers,* J. Madison, A. Hamilton, and J. Jay. New York: Viking Penguin.

Krasner, S. D. 1984. "Approaches to the State: Alternative Conceptions and Historical Dynamics." *Comparative Politics* 16:223–46.

———. 1988. "Sovereignty: An Institutional Perspective." *Comparative Political Studies* 21:66–94.

Krout, J. A. 1966. *United States to 1877.* 7th ed. New York: Barnes and Noble.

———. 1967. *United States Since 1865.* 16th ed. New York: Barnes and Noble.

Kugler, I. 1987. *From Ladies to Women: The Organized Struggle for Women's Rights in the Reconstruction Era.* Westport, Conn.: Greenwood Press.

Kutler, S. I. 1968. *Judicial Power and Reconstruction Politics.* Chicago: University of Chicago Press.

Kymlicka, W. 1989. *Liberalism, Community, and Culture.* New York: Oxford University Press.

———. 1995. *Multicultural Citizenship: A Liberal Theory of Minority Rights.* New York: Oxford University Press.

Kymlicka, W., and Norman, W. 1994. "Return of the Citizen: A Survey of Recent Work on Citizenship Theory." *Ethics* 104:352–81.

Lanza, M. L. 1990. *Agrarianism and Reconstruction Politics: The Southern Homestead Act.* Baton Rouge: Louisiana State University Press.

Lauter, P., et al. 1990. *The Heath Anthology of American Literature.* Lexington, Mass.: D. C. Heath.

Leach, W. 1980. *True Love and Perfect Union.* New York: Basic Books.

Le Beau, B. 1991. "'Saving the West from the Pope': Anti-Catholic Propaganda and the Settlement of the Mississippi River Valley." *American Studies* 32:101–14.

Lebsock, S. 1984. *The Free Women of Petersburg: Status and Culture in a Southern Town, 1784–1860.* New York: W. W. Norton.

Lee, S. P., and Passell, P. 1979. *A New Economic Vision of American History.* New York: W. W. Norton.

Legomsky, S. H. 1987. *Immigration and the Judiciary: Law and Politics in Britain and America.* New York: Oxford University Press.

Leibowitz, A. H. 1984. "The Official Character of Language in the United States: Literacy Requirements for Immigration, Citizenship, and Entrance Into American Life." *Aztlan* 15:25–70.

Leidecker, K. 1946. *Yankee Teacher: The Life of William Torrey Harris*. New York: Philosophical Library.

Lesser, J. H. 1985–86. "Always 'Outsiders': Asians, Naturalization, and the Supreme Court." *Amerasia* 12:83–100.

Levinson, S. 1988. *Constitutional Faith*. Princeton: Princeton University Press.

Lincoln, A. 1905–06. *The Writings of Abraham Lincoln*, 8 vols. Ed. A. B. Lapsley. New York: Lamb Publishing Co.

Lind, M. 1995. *The Next American Nation: The New Nationalism and the Fourth American Revolution*. New York: Free Press.

Lipset, S. M. 1963. *The First New Nation*. New York: Basic Books.

Litwack, L. F. 1961. *North of Slavery: The Negro in the Free States, 1790–1860*. Chicago: University of Chicago Press.

———. 1979. *Been in the Storm So Long: The Aftermath of Slavery*. New York: Knopf.

Locke, J. 1693. "For a General Naturalization." Unpublished ms., The Houghton Library, Harvard University.

———. 1965a. *Two Treatises of Government*. Book I. Ed. P. Laslett. New York: New American Library.

———. 1965b. *Two Treatises of Government*. Book II. Ed. P. Laslett. New York: New American Library.

———. 1975. *An Essay Concerning Human Understanding*. Ed. P. H. Nidditch. Oxford: Clarendon Press.

Lofgren, C. A. 1987. *The Plessy Case: A Legal-Historical Interpretation*. New York: Oxford University Press.

Logan, R. W. 1965. *The Betrayal of the Negro from Rutherford B. Hayes to Woodrow Wilson* (orig. *The Negro in American Life and Thought: The Nadir, 1877–1901*, 1954). New York: Collier Books.

Low, V. 1982. *The Unimpressible Race: A Century of Educational Struggle by the Chinese in San Francisco*. San Francisco: East/West Publishing.

Lowell, A. L. 1899a. "The Colonial Expansion of the United States." *Atlantic Monthly* 83:145–54.

———. 1899b. "The Status of Our New Possessions.—A Third View." *Harvard Law Review* 13:155–76.

Lowi, T. 1979. *The End of Liberalism: The Second Republic of the United States*. 2d ed. New York: W. W. Norton.

Lustig, R. J. 1982. *Corporate Liberalism: The Origins of Modern Political Theory, 1890–1920*. Berkeley: University of California Press.

Lutz, D. S. 1980. *Popular Consent and Popular Control: Whig Political Theory in the Early State Constitutions*. Baton Rouge: Louisiana State University Press.

Lyman, S. M. 1974. *Chinese Americans*. New York: Random House.

———. 1991. "The Race Question and Liberalism: Casuistries in American Constitutional Law." *International Journal of Politics, Culture, and Society* 5:183–247.

Lyon, B. D. 1960. *A Constitutional and Legal History of Medieval England*. New York: Harper.

Mabee, C. 1969 (orig. 1943). *The American Leonardo: A Life of Samuel F. B. Morse*. New York: Octagon Books.

Macedo, S. 1990. *Liberal Virtues: Citizenship, Virtue and Community*. New York: Oxford University Press.

MacIntyre, A. 1981. *After Virtue: A Study in Moral Theory*. Notre Dame: University of Notre Dame Press.

MacKinnon, C. A. 1979. *Sexual Harassment of Working Women*. New Haven: Yale University Press.

———. 1987. *Feminism Unmodified: Discourses on Life and Law.* Cambridge: Harvard University Press.

Madison, J. 1979. *The Papers of James Madison.* Vol. XII. Ed. C. F. Hobson, R. Rutland, W. M. E. Rachel, and J. K. Sisson. Charlottesville: University Press of Virginia.

Madison, J., Hamilton, A., and Jay, J. 1987. *The Federalist Papers.* Ed. I. Kramnick. New York: Viking Penguin.

Maine, Sir Henry. 1972. *Ancient Law.* New York: Dutton, Everyman's Library.

Mansfield, H. C., Jr. 1991. *America's Constitutional Soul.* Baltimore: Johns Hopkins University Press.

Mardock, R. W. 1971. *The Reformers and the American Indian.* Columbia, Mo.: University of Missouri Press.

Marilley, S. M. 1993. "Frances Willard and the Feminism of Fear." *Feminist Studies* 19:123–46.

Marshall, T. H. 1950. *Citizenship and Social Class and Other Essays.* Cambridge: Cambridge University Press.

Martin, D. A. 1985. "Membership and Consent: Abstract or Organic?" *Yale Journal of International Law* 11:278–96.

Martin, J. E. 1990. "'Neither Fish, Flesh, Fowl, nor Good Red Herring:' The Citizenship Status of American Indians, 1830–1924." *Journal of the West* 29:75–87.

Mathie, W. 1995. "God, Woman, and Morality: The Democratic Family in Tocqueville." *Review of Politics* 56:2–30.

May, G. A. 1980. *Social Engineering in the Philippines: The Aims, Execution, and Impact of American Colonial Policy, 1900–1913.* Westport, Conn.: Greenwood Press.

McCloskey, R. G. 1960. *The American Supreme Court.* Chicago: University of Chicago Press.

McConnell, M. W. 1995. "Originalism and the Desegregation Decisions." *Virginia Law Review* 81:947–1140.

McCormick, R. L. 1981. "The Discovery that Business Corrupts Politics: A Reappraisal of the Origins of Progressivism." *American Historical Review* 86:247–74.

McCoy, D. R. 1980. *The Elusive Republic: Political Economy in Jeffersonian America.* Chapel Hill: University of North Carolina Press.

McCurry, S. 1992. "The Two Faces of Republicanism: Gender and Proslavery Politics in Antebellum South Carolina." *Journal of American History* 78:1245–1264.

McDonagh, E. L. 1994. "Gender Politics and Political Change." In *New Perspectives on American Politics.* Ed. L. C. Dodd and C. Jillson. Washington, D.C.: Congressional Quarterly Press.

McDonald, F. 1965. *E Pluribus Unum: The Formation of the American Republic, 1776–1790.* Boston: Houghton Mifflin.

———. 1979. *Alexander Hamilton: A Biography.* New York: W. W. Norton.

———. 1982. *A Constitutional History of the United States.* New York: Franklin Watts.

———. 1985. *Novus Ordo Seclorum: The Intellectual Origins of the Constitution.* Lawrence: University Press of Kansas.

McFeely, W. S. 1968. *Yankee Stepfather: General O. O. Howard and the Freedmen.* New Haven: Yale University Press.

———. 1991. *Frederick Douglass.* New York: W. W. Norton.

McGovney, D. O. 1943a. "A Supreme Court Fiction: Corporations in the Diverse Citizenship Jurisdiction of the Federal Courts." *Harvard Law Review* 56:853–98.

———. 1943b. "A Supreme Court Fiction II: The Fiction at Work." *Harvard Law Review* 56:1090–1124.

McLoughlin, W. G. 1986. *Cherokee Renascence in the New Republic.* Princeton: Princeton University Press.

McPherson, J. M. 1964. *The Struggle for Equality: Abolitionists and the Negro in the Civil War and Reconstruction.* Princeton: Princeton University Press.

———. 1988. *Battle Cry of Freedom: The Civil War Era.* New York: Oxford University Press.

Mehta, U. S. 1990. "Liberal Strategies of Exclusion." *Politics and Society* 18:427–53.

———. 1992. *The Anxiety of Freedom: Imagination and Individuality in Locke's Political Thought.* Ithaca: Cornell University Press.

Meinig, D.W. 1986. *The Shaping of America: A Geographical Perspective on 500 Years of History.* Volume I: *Atlantic America, 1492–1800.* New Haven: Yale University Press.

———. 1993. *The Shaping of America: A Geographical Perspective on 500 Years of History.* Volume II: *Continental America, 1800–1867.* New Haven: Yale University Press.

Merrell, J. H. 1987. "Declarations of Independence: Indian-White Relations in the New Nation." In *The American Revolution: Its Character and Limits.* Ed. J. P. Greene. New York: New York University Press.

———. 1991. "'The Customes of our Country': Indians and Colonists in Early America." In *Strangers Within the Realm: Cultural Margins of the First British Empire.* Ed. B. Bailyn and P. D. Morgan. Chapel Hill: University of North Carolina Press.

Merritt, R. L. 1966. *Symbols of American Community, 1735–1775.* New Haven: Yale University Press.

Meyers, M. 1960. *The Jacksonian Persuasion: Politics and Belief.* Stanford: Stanford University Press.

Miller, P., and Johnson, T., eds. 1939. *The Puritans.* New York: American Book Company.

Miller, S. C. 1964. *The Unwelcome Immigrant: The American Image of the Chinese, 1785–1882.* Berkeley: University of California Press.

Millican, E. 1990. *One United People: The Federal Papers and the National Idea.* Lexington: University of Kentucky Press.

Mills, C. W. 1994. "Under Class Under Standings." *Ethics* 104:855–81.

Milton, J. 1961. *Areopagitica.* Ed. J. W. Hales. Oxford: Oxford University Press.

Minogue, K. R. 1967. *Nationalism.* London: Batsford.

Monk, M. 1962 (orig. 1836). *Awful Disclosures of the Hotel Dieu Nunnery.* Hamden, Conn.: Archon Books.

Montesquieu. 1949. *The Spirit of the Laws.* New York: Hafner Publishing Co.

Montgomery, D. 1981 (orig. 1967). *Beyond Equality: Labor and the Radical Republicans, 1862–1872.* Urbana: University of Illinois Press.

Moon, J. D. 1993. *Constructing Community: Moral Pluralism and Tragic Conflicts.* Princeton: Princeton University Press.

Mooney, R. J. 1984. "Matthew Deady and the Federal Judicial Response to Racism in the Early West." *Oregon Law Review* 63:561–644.

Moore, J. W., and Weckstein, D. T. 1964. "Diversity Jurisdiction: Past, Present, and Future." *Texas Law Review* 43:1–36.

Morgan, E. S. 1956. *The Birth of the Republic, 1763–1789.* Chicago: University of Chicago Press.

———. 1975. *American Slavery—American Freedom: The Ordeal of Colonial Virginia.* New York: W. W. Norton.

———. 1977. *The Birth of the Republic, 1763–1789.* Rev. ed. Chicago: University of Chicago Press.

———. 1980. *The Genius of George Washington.* New York: W. W. Norton.

———. 1988. *Inventing the People: The Rise of Popular Sovereignty in England and America.* New York: W. W. Norton.

Morgan, P. D. 1991. "British Encounters with Africans and African-Americans, circa 1600–1780." In *Strangers Within the Realm: Cultural Margins of the First British Empire.* Ed. B. Bailyn and P. D. Morgan. Chapel Hill: University of North Carolina Press.

Morone, J. A. 1990. *The Democratic Wish: Popular Participation and the Limits of American Government*. New York: Basic Books.

Morris, R. B. 1970. *The Emerging Nations and the American Revolution*. New York: Harper and Row.

Morris, R. B., ed. 1970. *The American Revolution, 1763–1783: A Bicentennial Collection*. Columbia: University of South Carolina Press.

Morris, R. C. 1981 (orig. 1976). *Reading, 'Riting, and Reconstruction: The Education of Freedmen in the South, 1861–1870*. Chicago: University of Chicago Press.

Morris, T. D. 1974. *Free Men All: The Personal Liberty Laws of the North*. Baltimore: Johns Hopkins University Press.

Morse, S. F. B. 1969 (orig. 1835). *Imminent Dangers to the Free Institutions of the United States Through Foreign Immigration*. New York: Arno Press and the New York Times.

———. 1977 (orig. 1835) *Foreign Conspiracy Against the Liberties of the United States*. New York: Arno Press.

Murray, J. S. 1973 (orig. 1790). "On the Equality of the Sexes." In *The Feminist Papers from Adams to De Beauvoir*. Ed. A. S. Rossi. New York: Bantam Books.

Murrin, J. M. 1987. "A Roof without Walls: The Dilemma of American National Identity." In *Beyond Confederation: Origins of the Constitution and American National Identity*. Ed. R. Beeman, S. Botein, and E. C. Carter II. Chapel Hill: University of North Carolina Press.

Myrdal, G. 1944. *An American Dilemma: The Negro Problem and American Democracy*. Rept. 20th Anniversary ed., 1962. New York: Harper and Row.

Nackenoff, C. 1994. *The Fictional Republic: Horatio Alger and American Political Discourse*. New York: Oxford University Press.

Nagel, P. C. 1971. *This Sacred Trust: American Nationality, 1798–1898*. New York: Oxford University Press.

Nash, G. B. 1974. *Red, White and Black: The Peoples of Early America*. Englewood Cliffs, N.J.: Prentice-Hall.

———. 1990. *Race and Revolution*. Madison, Wisc.: Madison House.

Nelson, J. R. 1987. *Liberty and Property: Political Economy and Policymaking in the New Nation, 1789–1912*. Baltimore: Johns Hopkins University Press.

Nelson, M., ed. 1989. *Congressional Quarterly's Guide to the Presidency*. Washington, D.C.: Congressional Quarterly, Inc.

Nelson, W. E. 1988 *The Fourteenth Amendment: From Political Principle to Judicial Doctrine*. Cambridge: Harvard University Press.

Neuman, G. L. 1987. "Back to *Dred Scott?*" *San Diego Law Review* 24:485–500.

———. 1993. "The Lost Century of American Immigration Law (1776–1875)." *Columbia Law Review* 93:1833–1901.

———. 1996. *Strangers to the Constitution: Immigrants, Borders, and Fundamental Law*. Princeton: Princeton University Press.

Nieman, D. G. 1979. *To Set the Law in Motion: The Freedmen's Bureau and the Legal Rights of Blacks, 1865–1868*. Millwood, N.Y.: KTO Press.

———. 1991. *Promises to Keep: African-Americans and the Constitutional Order, 1776 to the Present*. New York: Oxford University Press.

Norton, A. 1986. *Alternative Americas: A Reading of Antebellum Political Culture*. Chicago: University of Chicago Press.

Nott, J. C., and Gliddon, G. R. 1855. *Types of Mankind, or Ethnological Researches*. 7th ed. Philadelphia: Lippincott, Grambo.

Nozick, R. 1974. *Anarchy, State and Utopia*. New York: Basic Books.

Oakes, J. 1982. *The Ruling Race: A History of American Slaveholders*. New York: Random House.

————. 1985. "From Republicanism to Liberalism: Ideological Change and the Crisis of the Old South." *American Quarterly* 37:551–71.

————. 1990. *Slavery and Freedom: An Interpretation of the Old South.* New York: Knopf.

Oakeshott, M. 1975. *On Human Conduct.* Oxford: Clarendon Press.

Okin, S. M. 1979. *Women in Western Political Thought.* Princeton: Princeton University Press.

O'Leary, K. C. 1994. "Herbert Croly and Progressive Democracy." *Polity* 26:533–52.

Olson, M. 1965. *The Logic of Collective Action.* Cambridge: Harvard University Press.

O'Neill, W. 1969. *Everyone Was Brave: The Rise and Fall of Feminism in America.* Chicago: Quadrangle Books.

Onuf, P. S. 1987a. *Statehood and Union: A History of the Northwest Ordinance.* Bloomington: Indiana University Press.

————. 1987b. "Settlers, Settlements, and New States." In *The American Revolution: Its Character and Limits.* Ed. J. P. Greene. New York: New York University Press.

Orren, K. 1991. *Belated Feudalism: Labor, the Law, and Liberal Development in the United States.* New York: Cambridge University Press.

————. 1996. "Structure, Sequence, and Subordination in American Political Culte: What's Traditions Got to Do With It?" *Journal of Policy History* 8:470–77, 491–94.

Orren, K., and Skowronek, S. 1994. "Beyond the Iconography of Order: Notes for a 'New Institutionalism.'" In *The Dynamics of American Politics: Approaches and Interpretations.* Ed. L. C. Dodd and C. Jillson. Boulder, Colo.: Westview Press.

Orth, J. V. 1987. *The Judicial Power of the United States: The Eleventh Amendment in American History.* New York: Oxford University Press.

Oubre, C. F. 1978. *Forty Acres and a Mule: The Freedmen's Bureau and Black Land Ownership.* Baton Rouge: Louisiana State University Press.

Padover, S. K. 1953. *The Complete Madison.* New York: Harper and Row.

Painter, N. I. 1987. *Standing at Armageddon: The United States, 1817–1919.* New York: W. W. Norton.

Pangle, T. L. 1988. *The Spirit of Modern Republicanism: The Moral Vision of the American Founders and the Philosophy of Locke.* Chicago: University of Chicago Press.

Pateman, C. 1988. *The Sexual Contract.* Stanford: Stanford University Press.

Paulding, J. K. 1836. *Slavery in the United States.* New York: Harper and Bros.

Perlmutter, P. 1977. "The American Struggle with Ethnic Superiority." *Journal of Intergroup Relations* 6:31–56.

Pertman, A. 1996. "Native Hawaiians Seek Self-Rule." *Boston Globe,* March 20, p. 1.

Peterman, L. I., and Wechsler, L. 1972. *American Political Thought.* New York: Appleton-Century-Crofts.

Peterson, M. D., ed. 1975. *The Portable Thomas Jefferson.* New York: Viking Press.

Peterson, P. E. 1985. *The Politics of School Reform, 1870–1940.* Chicago: University of Chicago Press.

Phillips, W., ed. 1845. "The Constitution a Pro-Slavery Compact." 2d ed. New York: American Anti-Slavery Society.

Pocock, J. G. A. 1967 (orig. 1957). *The Ancient Constitution and the Feudal Law: A Study of English Historical Thought in the Seventeenth Century.* New York: W. W. Norton.

————. 1975. *The Machiavellian Moment: Florentine Political Thought and the Atlantic Republican Tradition.* Princeton: Princeton University Press.

————. 1985. *Virtue, Commerce, and History: Essays on Political Thought and History, Chiefly in the Eighteenth Century.* Cambridge: Cambridge University Press.

Polan, D. 1980. "Patriarchal Ideology in the Supreme Court." Unpublished typescript, Yale Law School.

Pole, J. R. 1966. *Political Representation in England and the Origins of the American Republic.* New York: St. Martin's Press.

———. 1978. *The Pursuit of Equality in American History.* Berkeley: University of California Press.

Porter, K. H. 1971 (orig. 1918). *A History of Suffrage in the United States.* New York: AMS Press.

Potter, D. M. 1976. *The Impending Crisis, 1848–1861.* Ed. D. E. Fehrenbacher. New York: Harper and Row.

Pringell, H. F. 1964 (orig. 1939). *The Life and Times of William Howard Taft.* Vol. I. Hamden, Conn.: Archon Books.

Prucha, F. P. 1979. *The Churches and the Indian Schools, 1888–1912.* Lincoln: University of Nebraska Press.

———. 1984. *The Great Father: The United States Government and the American Indians.* 2 vols. Lincoln: University of Nebraska Press.

Pryor, J. A. 1988. "The Natural-Born Citizen Clause and Presidential Eligibility: An Approach for Resolving Two Hundred Years of Uncertainty." *Yale Law Journal* 97:881–99.

Purcell, E. A. 1992. *Litigation and Inequality: Federal Diversity Jurisdiction in Industrial America, 1870–1958.* New York: Oxford University Press.

Quandt, J. B. 1970. *From the Small Town to the Great Community: The Social Thought of Progressive Intellectuals.* New Brunswick, N.J.: Rutgers University Press.

Ragsdale, J. W., Jr. 1989. "The Movement to Assimilate the American Indians: A Jurisprudential Study." *University of Missouri-Kansas Law Review* 57:399–436.

Rakove, J. N. 1987. "From One Agenda to Another: The Condition of American Federalism, 1783–87." In *The American Revolution: Its Character and Limits.* Ed. J. P. Greene. New York: New York University Press.

Ramsay, D. 1789. "A Dissertation on the Manner of Acquiring the Character and Privileges of a Citizen of the United States." N.p.

Ravitch, D. 1974. *The Great School Wars: New York City, 1805–1973: A History of the Public Schools as Battlefield of Social Change.* New York: Basic Books.

———. 1978. *The Revisionists Revised: A Critique of the Radical Attack on the Schools.* New York: Basic Books.

Rawls, J. 1971. *A Theory of Justice.* Oxford: Oxford University Press.

———. 1975a. "A Kantian Conception of Equality." *Cambridge Review* 76:94–99.

———. 1975b. "Fairness to Goodness." *Philosophical Review* 84:536–54.

———. 1980. "Kantian Constructivism in Moral Theory." *Journal of Philosophy* 77:515–72.

———. 1985. "Justice as Fairness: Political not Metaphysical." *Philosophy and Public Affairs* 14:223–51.

———. 1993a. *Political Liberalism.* New York: Columbia University Press.

———. 1993b. "The Law of Peoples." *Critical Inquiry* 20:36–68.

Raz, J. 1986. *The Morality of Freedom.* Oxford: Oxford University Press.

Remini, R. V. 1981. *Andrew Jackson and the Course of American Freedom, 1822–1832.* New York: Harper and Row.

———. 1984. *Andrew Jackson and the Course of American Democracy, 1833–1845.* New York: Harper and Row.

Resnick, D. 1987. "John Locke and the Problem of Naturalization." *Review of Politics* 49:368–88.

Rhee, J. S. 1994. "In Black and White: Chinese in the Mississippi Delta." *Journal of Supreme Court History* 1994:117–32.

Richardson, J. M. 1986. *Christian Reconstruction: The American Missionary Association and Southern Blacks, 1861–1890.* Athens: University of Georgia Press.

Rischin, M., ed. 1976. *Immigration and the American Tradition.* Indianapolis: Bobbs-Merrill.

Roback, J. 1986. "The Political Economy of Segregation: The Case of Segregated Streetcars." *Journal of Economic History* 46:893–917.

Rodgers, D. T. 1982. "In Search of Progressivism." *Reviews in American History* 10:113–32.

———. 1987. *Contested Truths: Keywords in American Politics Since Independence.* New York: Basic Books.

Roeber, A. G. 1991. "'The Origin of Whatever Is Not English Among Us': The Dutch-Speaking and the German-Speaking People of Colonial British America." In *Strangers Within the Realm: Cultural Margins of the First British Empire.* Ed. B. Bailyn and P. D. Morgan. Chapel Hill: University of North Carolina Press.

Roediger, D. R. 1991. *The Wages of Whiteness: Race and the Making of the American Working Class.* New York: Verso.

Roelofs, H. M. 1957. *The Tension of Citizenship: Private Men and Public Duty.* New York: Rinehart.

———. 1992. *The Poverty of American Politics: A Theoretical Interpretation.* Philadelphia: Temple University Press.

Rogin, M. P. 1975. *Fathers and Children: Andrew Jackson and the Subjugation of the American Indian.* New York: Vintage Books.

Rosberg, G. M. 1977. "Aliens and Equal Protection: Why Not the Right to Vote?" *Michigan Law Review* 45:1092–1134.

Ross, D. 1991. *The Origins of American Social Science.* New York: Cambridge University Press.

Rossiter, C. 1971. *The American Quest 1790–1860: An Emerging Nation in Search of Identity, Unity, and Modernity.* New York: Harcourt Brace Jovanovich.

Rossiter, C., ed. 1961. *The Federalist Papers.* New York: New American Library.

Rousseau, J.-J. 1973. *The Social Contract and the Discourses.* G. D. H. Cole, transl. New York: Dutton.

———. 1979. *Emile, or, On Education.* Allan Bloom, transl. New York: Basic Books.

Rushton, J. P. 1995. *Race, Evolution, and Behavior: A Life History Perspective.* New Brunswick, N.J.: Transaction.

Russell, P. 1986. "Locke on Express and Tacit Consent: Misinterpretations and Inconsistencies." *Political Theory* 14:291–306.

Russett, C. E. 1976. *Darwin in America: The Intellectual Response, 1865–1912.* San Francisco: W. H. Freeman.

———. 1989. *Sexual Science: The Victorian Construction of Womanhood.* Cambridge: Harvard University Press.

Sachs, A., and Wilson, J. H. 1978. *Sexism and the Law.* Oxford: Martin Robertson.

Salmon, M. 1986. *Women and the Law of Property in Early America.* Chapel Hill: University of North Carolina Press.

Salyer, L. E. 1989. "Guarding the 'White Man's Frontier': Courts, Politics, and the Regulation of Immigration, 1891–1924." Ann Arbor, Mich.: University Microfilm International Dissertation Information Service.

Sandel, M. J. 1982. *Liberalism and the Limits of Justice.* Cambridge: Cambridge University Press.

———. 1984. "The Procedural Republic and the Unencumbered Self." *Political Theory* 12:81–96.

———. 1990. "Freedom of Conscience or Freedom of Choice?" In *Articles of Faith, Articles of Peace.* Ed. J. D. Hunter and O. Guinness. Washington, D.C.: Brookings Institution, 74–92.

———. 1996. *Democracy's Discontent: America in Search of a Public Philosophy.* Cambridge: Harvard University Press.

Sapiro, V. 1984. "Women, Citizenship, and Nationality: Immigration and Naturalization Policies in the United States." *Politics and Society* 13:1–26.

———. 1992. *A Vindication of Political Virtue: The Political Theory of Mary Wollstonecraft.* Chicago: University of Chicago Press.

Satz, R. N. 1975. *American Indian Policy in the Jacksonian Era.* Lincoln: University of Nebraska Press.

Saxton, A. 1990. *The Rise and Fall of the White Republic: Class Politics and Mass Culture in Nineteenth-Century America.* New York: Verso.

Schmidt, B. C., Jr. 1982a. "Principle and Prejudice: The Supreme Court and Race in the Progressive Era. Part 1: The Heyday of Jim Crow." *Columbia Law Review* 82:444–524.

———. 1982b. "Principle and Prejudice: The Supreme Court and Race in the Progressive Era. Part 2: The Peonage Cases." *Columbia Law Review* 82:646–718.

———. 1982c. "Principle and Prejudice: The Supreme Court and Race in the Progressive Era. Part 3: Black Disfranchisement from the KKK to the Grandfather Clause." *Columbia Law Review* 82:835–905.

———. 1983. "Juries, Jurisdiction, and Race Discrimination: The Lost Promise of *Strauder* v. *West Virginia*." *Texas Law Review* 61:1401–1499.

Schochet, G. 1975. *Patriarchalism in Political Thought.* Oxford: Basil Blackwell.

Schuck, P. H. 1984. "The Transformation of Immigration Law." *Columbia Law Review* 84:1–90.

Schuck, P. H., and Smith, R. M. 1985. *Citizenship Without Consent: The Illegal Alien in the American Polity.* New Haven: Yale University Press.

———. 1986. "Membership and Consent: Actual or Mythic? A Reply to David A. Martin." *Yale Journal of International Law* 11:545–52.

Seliger, M. 1969. "Locke, Liberalism, and Nationalism." In *John Locke: Problems and Perspectives.* Ed. J. Yolton. Cambridge: Cambridge University Press.

Sen, A. K. 1985. "Well-Being, Agency, and Freedom: The Dewey Lectures, 1984." *Journal of Philosophy* 82:169–221.

Seton-Watson, H. 1977. *Nations and States.* Boulder, Colo.: Westview Press.

Shade, W. C. 1981. "Political Pluralism and Party Development: The Creation of a Modern Party System, 1815–1852. In *The Evolution of American Electoral Systems.* Ed. P. Kleppner et al. Westport, Conn.: Greenwood Press.

Shain, B. A. 1994. *The Myth of American Individualism: The Protestant Origins of American Political Thought.* Princeton: Princeton University Press.

Shakespeare, W. 1936. "The Life of King Henry the Fifth." In *The Complete Works of Shakespeare.* Ed. G. L. Kittredge. Boston: Ginn and Company.

Shklar, J. N. 1991. *American Citizenship: The Quest for Inclusion.* Cambridge: Harvard University Press.

Silbey, J. H. 1991. *The American Political Nation, 1838–1893.* Stanford: Stanford University Press.

Sklar, K. K. 1973. *Catharine Beecher: A Study in American Domesticity.* New Haven: Yale University Press.

Sklar, M. J. 1988. *The Corporate Reconstruction of American Capitalism, 1890–1916.* New York: Cambridge University Press.

———. 1991. "Periodization and Historiography: Studying American Political Development in the Progressive Era, 1890s-1916." *Studies in American Political Development* 5:173–213.

Skocpol, T. 1992. *Protecting Soldiers and Mothers: The Political Origins of Social Policy in the United States.* Cambridge: Harvard University Press.

Skowronek, S. 1982. *Building a New American State: The Expansion of National Administrative Capacities, 1870–1920.* New York: Cambridge University Press.

Slotkin, R. 1973. *Regeneration Through Violence: The Mythology of the American Frontier, 1600–1860.* Middletown, Conn.: Wesleyan University Press.

Smith, A. D. 1991. *National Identity*. London: Penguin Books.

Smith, J. M. 1956. *Freedom's Fetters: The Alien and Sedition Laws and American Civil Liberties*. Ithaca: Cornell University Press.

Smith, J. M. 1988–89. "Republicanism, Imperialism, and Sovereignty: A History of the Doctrine of Tribal Sovereignty." *Buffalo Law Review* 37:527–82.

Smith, M. T. 1970. "The History of Indian Citizenship." *Great Plains Journal* 10:25–35.

Smith, R. M. 1985. *Liberalism and American Constitutional Law*. Cambridge: Harvard University Press.

———. 1988a. "The 'American Creed' and American Identity: The Limits of Liberal Citizenship in the United States." *Western Political Quarterly* 41:225–51.

———. 1988b. "Political Jurisprudence, the 'New Institutionalism,' and the Future of Public Law." *American Political Science Review* 82:89–108.

———. 1989a. "'One United People': Second-Class Female Citizenship and the American Quest for Community." *Yale Journal of Law and the Humanities* 1:229–93.

———. 1989b. "After Criticism: An Analysis of the Critical Legal Studies Movement." In *Judging the Constitution: Critical Essays on Judicial Lawmaking*. Ed. M. W. McCann and G. L. Houseman. Glenview, Ill.: Scott, Foresman.

———. 1992. "If Politics Matters: Implications for a 'New Institutionalism.'" *Studies in American Political Development* 6:1–36.

———. 1993a. "Beyond Tocqueville, Myrdal, and Hartz: The Multiple Traditions in America." *American Political Science Review* 87:549–66.

———. 1993b. "Equal Protection Remedies: The Errors of Liberal Ways and Means." *Journal of Political Philosophy* 1:185–212.

———. 1993c. "American Conceptions of Citizenship and National Service." *The Responsive Community* 3:14–27.

———. 1994. "Unfinished Liberalism." *Social Research* 61:631–70.

———. 1995. "Response to Jacqueline Stevens." *American Political Science Review* 89:990–95.

———. 1996. "Response to Karen Orren." *Journal of Policy History*, 8:479–90.

Smith, S. S. 1965 (orig. 1810). *An Essay on the Causes of the Variety of Complexion and Figure in the Human Species*. Ed. W. D. Jordan. Cambridge: Harvard University Press.

Southern, D. W. 1987. *Gunnar Myrdal and Black-White Relations*. Baton Rouge: Louisiana State University Press.

Spencer, H. 1865. *Social Statics*. New York: D. Appleton and Co.

———. 1874. *The Study of Sociology*. New York: D. Appleton and Co.

———. 1920 (orig. 1860). *Education: Intellectual, Moral, and Physical*. New York: D. Appleton and Co.

———. 1972. *On Social Evolution: Selected Writings*. Chicago: J. D. Y. Peel.

Speth, L. E. 1982. "The Married Women's Property Acts, 1834–1865: Reform, Reaction, or Revolution?" In *Women and the Law, vol. II: Property, Family and the Legal Profession*. Ed. D. K. Weisberg. Cambridge: Schenckman Publishing.

Spicer, E. H. 1980. "American Indians, Federal Policy Towards." In *The Harvard Encyclopedia of American Ethnic Groups*. Ed. S. Thernstrom. Cambridge: Harvard University Press.

Spinner, J. 1994. *The Boundaries of Citizenship: Race, Ethnicity, and Nationality in the Liberal State*. Baltimore: Johns Hopkins University Press.

Spivey, D. 1978. *Schooling for the New Slavery: Black Industrial Education, 1868–1915*. Westport, Conn.: Greenwood Press.

Spring, J. H. 1990. *The American School, 1642–1990: Varieties of Historical Interpretation of the Foundation and Development of American Education*. 2d ed. New York: Longman.

Stampp, K. M. 1965. *The Era of Reconstruction, 1865–1877*. New York: Vintage Books.

Stanton, E. C., Anthony, S. B., and Gage, M. J., eds. 1881. *History of Woman Suffrage*, v. 1, *1848–1861*. New York: Fowler and Wells.

———. 1882. *History of Woman Suffrage*, v. 2, *1861–1876*. New York: Fowler and Wells.

Stepan, N. L. 1990. "Race and Gender: The Role of Analogy in Science." In *Anatomy of Racism*. Ed. D. T. Goldberg. Minneapolis: University of Minnesota Press.

Stevens, J. 1995. "Beyond Tocqueville, Please!" *American Political Science Review* 89:987–90.

Stewart, C., III, and Weingast, B. R. 1992. "Stacking the Senate, Changing the Nation: Republican Rotten Boroughs, Statehood Politics, and American Political Development." *Studies in American Political Development* 6:223–71.

Stocking, G. W., Jr. 1968. *Race, Culture, and Evolution: Essays in the History of Anthropology*. New York: Free Press.

Storing, H. J. 1981. *What the Anti-Federalists Were FOR* Chicago: University of Chicago Press.

Storing, H. J., and Dry, M., eds. 1985. *The Anti-Federalist*. Chicago: University of Chicago Press.

Stowe, H. B. 1965 (orig. 1852). *Uncle Tom's Cabin; or, Life Among the Lowly*. New York: Harper and Row.

Strong, J. 1885. *Our Country: Its Possible Future and Its Present Crisis*. New York: American Home Missionary Society.

Sullivan, K. M. 1989. "Unconstitutional Conditions." *Harvard Law Review* 102:1415–1506.

Sullivan, W. M. 1986. *Reconstructing Public Philosophy*. Berkeley and Los Angeles: University of California Press.

Summers, J. 1993. *Collected Essays on Renaissance Literature*. Fairfield, Conn: George Herbert Journal.

Sumner, C. 1900. *Complete Works of Charles Sumner*. Ed. G. F. Hoar. 20 vols. Boston: Lee and Shepard.

Sumner, W. G. 1982 (orig. 1883). *What the Social Classes Owe to Each Other*. Caldwell, Idaho: Caxton Printers.

Sunstein, E. W. 1975. *A Different Face: The Life of Mary Wollstonecraft*. New York: Harper and Row.

Swisher, C. B. 1969. *Stephen J. Field: Craftsman of the Law*. Chicago: University of Chicago Press.

Tabrah, R. 1980. *Hawaii: A Bicentennial History*. New York: W. W. Norton.

Takaki, R. 1979. *Iron Cages: Race and Culture in Nineteenth Century America*. New York: Oxford University Press.

———. 1993. *A Different Mirror: A History of Multicultural America*. Boston: Little, Brown.

Tamir, Y. 1993. *Liberal Nationalism*. Princeton: Princeton University Press.

Tate, B., ed. 1969. *Guadalupe Hidalgo Treaty of Peace 1848 and the Gadsden Treaty with Mexico 1853*. Truchas, N. Mex.: Tate Gallery.

Taub, N., and Schneider, E. 1982. "Perspective on Women's Subordination and the Role of Law." In *The Politics of Law*. Ed. D. Kairys. New York: Pantheon Books.

Taylor, C. 1992. "The Politics of Recognition." In *Multiculturalism and the "Politics of Recognition."* Ed. A. Gutmann. Princeton: Princeton University Press.

Ten Broek, J. 1965. *Equal Under Law*. London: Collier Books.

Thayer, J. B. 1899. "Our New Possessions." *Harvard Law Review* 13:464–85.

Thelen, D. P. 1972. *The New Citizenship: Origins of Progressivism in Wisconsin, 1885–1900*. Columbia: University of Missouri Press.

Thomas, J. L. 1983. *Alternative America: Henry George, Edward Bellamy, Henry Demarest Lloyd, and the Adversary Tradition*. Cambridge: Harvard University Press.

Tichenor, D. J. 1995. "The Liberal and Illiberal Traditions in America: The Case of Immigration Policymaking." Paper presented at the 1995 Annual Meeting of the American Political Science Association, Chicago, Aug. 31, 1995.

Tindall, W. 1916. *The Origin and Government of the District of Columbia.* Washington, D.C.: L. G. Kelly.

Tise, L. E. 1987. *Proslavery: A History of the Defense of Slavery in America, 1701–1840.* Athens: University of Georgia Press.

Tocqueville, A. de. 1969. *Democracy in America.* Ed. J. P. Mayer. Garden City, N.Y.: Anchor Books.

Torruella, J. R. 1988. *The Supreme Court and Puerto Rico: The Doctrine of Separate and Unequal.* Rio Piedras: University of Puerto Rico Press.

Trachtenberg, A. 1982. *The Incorporation of America: Culture and Society in the Gilded Age.* New York: Hill and Wang.

Tsiang, I. 1942. *The Question of Expatriation in America Prior to 1907.* Baltimore: Johns Hopkins University Press.

Tucker, R. W., and Hendrickson, D. C. 1990. *Empire of Liberty: The Statecraft of Thomas Jefferson.* New York: Oxford University Press.

Tulis, J. 1987. *The Rhetorical Presidency.* Princeton: Princeton University Press.

Turner, E. R. 1916. "Woman's Suffrage in New Jersey: 1790–1807." *Smith College Studies in History* 1:165–87.

Tushnet, M. V. 1981. *The American Law of Slavery, 1810–1860: Considerations of Humanity and Interest.* Princeton: Princeton University Press.

Tuveson, E. L. 1968. *Redeemer Nation: The Idea of America's Millennial Role.* Chicago: University of Chicago Press.

Tyack, D. 1974. *The One Best System: A History of American Urban Education.* Cambridge: Harvard University Press.

Tyack, D., James, T., and Benavot, A. 1987. *Law and the Shaping of Public Education, 1785–1954.* Madison: University of Wisconsin Press.

Ueda, R. 1980. "Naturalization and Citizenship." In *The Harvard Encyclopedia of American Ethnic Groups.* Ed. S. Thernstrom. Cambridge: Harvard University Press.

Unger, I. 1964. *The Greenback Era: A Social and Political History of American Finance, 1868–1879.* Princeton: Princeton University Press.

U.S. Government Printing Office, 1971. *Biographical Dictionary of the American Congress, 1774–1971.* Washington, D.C.: Senate Document 92–8c.

Utley, R. M. 1984. *The Indian Frontier and the American West, 1846–1890.* Albuquerque: University of New Mexico Press.

Valelly, R. M. 1995. "National Parties and Racial Disenfranchisement." In *Classifying by Race.* Ed. P. E. Peterson. Princeton: Princeton University Press.

Van Amringe, W. F. 1848. *An Investigation of the Theories of the Natural History of Man by Lawrence, Prichard, and Others founded upon Animal Analogies: and an Outline of a New Natural History of Man founded upon History, Anatomy, Physiology, and Human Analogies.* New York: Baker and Scribner.

Van Evrie, J. H. 1853. *Negroes and Negro "Slavery"; The First, an Inferior Race—the Latter, Its Normal Condition.* Baltimore: John D. Toy.

——. 1868. *White Supremacy and Negro Subordination,* 2d ed. New York: Van Evrie, Hart and Co.

Vattel, E. de. 1787. *The Law of Nations.* Dublin: L. White.

Vaughn, W. P. 1977. *Schools for All: The Blacks and Public Education in the South, 1865–1877.* Lexington: University Press of Kentucky.

Walker, F. A. 1891. "The Tide of Economic Thought: An Address to the Fourth Annual Meeting of the American Economic Association by the President, F. A. Walker, President of M.I.T., Washington, D.C., Dec. 26, 1890." Publisher unknown.

———. 1899. *Discussions in Economics and Statistics*, v. II. Ed. D. R. Dewey. New York: Henry Holt.

Wallerstein, I. 1974. *The Modern World-System*. New York: Academic Press.

Walzer, M. 1965. *The Revolution of the Saints: A Study in the Origins of Radical Politics*. Cambridge: Harvard University Press.

———. 1980. "Pluralism: A Political Perspective." In *Harvard Encyclopedia of American Ethnic Groups*. Ed. S. Thernstrom. Cambridge: Harvard University Press.

———. 1981. "The Distribution of Membership." In *Boundaries: National Autonomy and Its Limits*. Ed. P. G. Brown and H. Shue. Totowa, N.J.: Rowman and Littlefield.

———. 1983. *Spheres of Justice: A Defense of Pluralism and Equality*. New York: Basic Books.

———. 1990. "What Does It Mean to Be an 'American'?" *Social Research* 57:591–14.

Washburn, W. E. 1971. *Red Man's Land/White Man's Law*. New York: Charles Scribner's Sons.

———. 1975. *The Indian in America*. New York: Harper and Row.

Washington, B. T. 1986 (orig. 1901). *Up From Slavery*. New York: Penguin Books.

Washington, G. 1973 (orig. 1797). "Farewell Address." In *Documents of American History*, 9th ed. Ed. H. S. Commager. New York: Appleton-Century Crofts, Meredith Corporation.

Webster, D. 1923. *The Great Speeches and Orations of Daniel Webster*. Ed. Edwin P. Whipple. Boston: Little, Brown.

Westbrook, R. B. 1991. *John Dewey and American Democracy*. Ithaca: Cornell University Press.

White, T. H. 1983. *America in Search of Itself: The Making of the President, 1956–1980*. New York: Warner.

Wiebe, R. H. 1967. *The Search for Order, 1877–1922*. New York: Hill and Wang.

———. 1984. *The Opening of American Society: From the Adoption of the Constitution to the Eve of Disunion*. New York: Knopf.

Wiecek, W. M. 1972. *The Guarantee Clause of the U.S. Constitution*. Ithaca: Cornell University Press.

———. 1977. *The Sources of Antislavery Constitutionalism in America, 1760–1860*. Ithaca: Cornell University Press.

———. 1978. "Slavery and Abolition Before the United States Supreme Court, 1820–1860." *Journal of American History* 65:34–59.

———. 1988. *Liberty Under Law: The Supreme Court in American Life*. Baltimore: Johns Hopkins University Press.

Williams, P. J. 1991. *The Alchemy of Race and Rights*. Cambridge: Harvard University Press.

Williams, W. L. 1980. "United States Indian Policy and the Debate over Philippine Annexation: Implications for the Origins of American Imperialism." *Journal of American History* 66:810–31.

Williamson, C. 1960. *American Suffrage: From Property to Democracy, 1760–1860*. Princeton: Princeton University Press.

Williamson, J. 1980. *New People: Miscegenation and Mulattoes in the United States*. New York: Free Press.

Wills, G. 1978. *Inventing America*. New York: Vintage Books.

Wilson, E. 1962. *Patriotic Gore: Studies in the Literature of the American Civil War*. New York: Oxford University Press.

Wilson, J. 1967. *The Works of James Wilson*. Ed. R. G. McCloskey. Cambridge: Belknap Press.

Wilson, J. H. 1975. *Herbert Hoover: Forgotten Progressive*. Boston: Little, Brown.

———. 1976. "The Illusion of Change: Women and the American Revolution." In *The American Revolution: Explorations in the History of American Radicalism*. Ed. A. F. Young. DeKalb: Northern Illinois University Press.

Wilson, M. L. 1974. *Space, Time, and Freedom: The Quest for Nationality and the Irrepressible Conflict*. Westport, Conn.: Greenwood Press.

Wise, J. C., and Deloria, V., Jr. 1971. *The Red Man in the New World Drama: A Politico-Legal Study with a Pageantry of American Indian History.* New York: Macmillan.

Witt, E. 1990. *Congressional Quarterly's Guide to the U.S. Supreme Court,* 2d Ed. Washington, D.C.: Congressional Quarterly Press.

Wolfe, C. 1986. *The Rise of Modern Judicial Review: From Constitutional Interpretation to Judge-Made Law.* New York: Basic Books.

Wollstonecraft, M. 1967 (orig. 1792). *A Vindication of the Rights of Woman: With Strictures on Political and Moral Subjects.* Ed. C. W. Hagelman, Jr. New York: W. W. Norton.

Wood, G. S. 1969. *The Creation of the American Republic, 1776–1787.* Chapel Hill: University of North Carolina Press.

———. 1991. *The Radicalism of the American Revolution.* New York: Vintage Books.

Wood, N. 1983. *The Politics of Locke's Philosophy.* Berkeley: University of California Press.

Woodward, C. V. 1966. *The Strange Career of Jim Crow.* 2d rev. ed. New York: Oxford University Press.

———. 1971. *American Counterpoint: Slavery and Racism in the North-South Dialogue.* Boston: Little, Brown.

———. 1988. Editor's introduction. In *Battle Cry of Freedom: The Civil War Era,* by J. M. McPherson. New York: Oxford University Press.

Woody, T. 1929. *A History of Women's Education in the United States.* 2 vols. New York: The Science Press.

Wright, R. 1992. *Stolen Continents: The Americas Through Indian Eyes Since 1492.* Boston: Houghton Mifflin.

Yack, B. 1995. "Reconciling Liberalism and Nationalism." *Political Theory* 23:166–82.

Young, I. M. 1990. *Justice and the Politics of Difference.* Princeton: Princeton University Press.

Zilversmit, A. 1967. *The First Emancipation.* Chicago: University of Chicago Press.

Zuckert, M. P. 1986. "Congressional Power under the Fourteenth Amendment—The Original Understanding of Section Five." *Constitutional Commentary* 3:123–56.

———. 1987. "Completing the Constitution I: The Thirteenth Amendment." Paper presented to the Second Bicentennial Conference of the Claremont Institute, "Novo Ordo Seclorum," February 13, 1987, Claremont, Calif.

Index of Cases

Cases are listed alphabetically under the following headings: African-Americans; Civic Education; Colonies and Territories; Diversity of Citizenship Jurisdiction (Art. III); Expatriation; Guarantee of Republican Government and National Powers; Immigration; Loyalty Oaths; Native Americans; Naturalization and Birthright Citizenship; Privileges and Immunities of Citizenship (Art. IV); Privileges and Immunities of Citizenship (Fourteenth Amendment); Voting Rights; and Women. An asterisk indicates that a case appears under more than one heading.

Expatriation

Guarantee of Republican Government and National Powers

Immigration

Loyalty Oaths

Native Americans

Naturalization and Birthright Citizenship

Privileges and Immunities of Citizenship (Article IV)

Voting Rights

Women

Index

DATE DUE

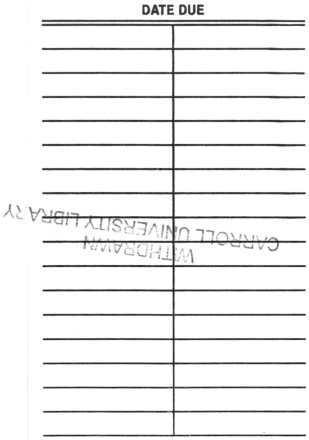

DEMCO, INC. 38-2931